Sharon Chester

The Arctic Guide
Wildlife of the Far North

Princeton University Press
Princeton and Oxford

For Jim Oetzel, my inspiration and guiding light

Copyright © 2016 by Princeton University Press

Published by Princeton University Press, 41 William Street, Princeton, New Jersey 08540

In the United Kingdom: Princeton University Press, 6 Oxford Street, Woodstock, Oxfordshire OX20 1TW

nathist.princeton.edu

ISBN 978-0-691-13974-6

ISBN (pbk.) 978-0-691-13975-3

Library of Congress Control Number: 2016931463

The publisher would like to acknowledge the author of this volume for providing the print-ready files from which this book was printed.

British Library Cataloging-in-Publication Data is available.

This book has been composed in Minion Pro and Myriad Pro.

Printed on acid-free paper.

Printed in China

10 9 8 7 6 5 4 3 2 1

Contents

ACKNOWLEDGMENTS

THE ARCTIC GUIDE IS THE PRODUCT OF MANY PEOPLE to whom I am greatly indebted. First, let me thank Robert Kirk and his staff at Princeton University Press for their patience, assistance, and unflagging support of this project from day one. Nigel Redman, former Head of Natural History at Bloomsbury Publishing, and George Armistead, from the Academy of Natural Sciences of Drexel University, Philadelphia, read the first draft and sharpened it considerably. Amy Hughes and Mary Bearden edited and proofed the book for PUP. Leslie Flis refined the cover. Ellen Foos and Steve Sears guided production.

The following specialists graciously contributed time, expertise, and a multitude of invaluable comments and corrections.

    Irwin Brodo, Museum of Nature, Ottawa
    James M. Graham, Department of Botany, University of Wisconsin Madison
    Matt Kirchhoff, Director of Bird Conservation, Audubon Alaska
    Gary Kofinas, Institute of Arctic Biology, University of Alaska Fairbanks
    Ken Muldrew, Department of Cell Biology, University of Calgary
    Don Russell, CircumArctic Rangifer Network, Yukon College, Whitehorse
    Bryant Tarr, Curator, International Crane Foundation, Baraboo, Wisconsin
    Skip Walker, Institute of Arctic Biology, University of Alaska Fairbanks

Special credit goes to Deborah Robbins, who read and re-read the text, all the while suggesting improvements to its content and clarity; to Wendy Lin, who color-corrected the range maps in the chapter on flora; and to Lee Zimmerman for her generous support.

To friends and family who provided encouragement and incisive commentary over the years, I thank you in alphabetical order: Lars Nørgaard Andersen, Stan Bousson, Judith Varney Burch, Page Burt, Michael Carson, Joseph and Lucia Chester, Justine Frederiksen, Kriss Ghafourpour, Jo Kelly, Jim Oetzel, Rick Rendon, Ed Seubert, Karl Stoltzfus, and Robert and Evelyn Vobernik.

I would also like to acknowledge the people of the Far North for their hospitality during my all-too-brief visits. Thanks to the Chukchi community at Uelen, the Yupik people of New Chapalino, the residents of Little Diomede Island, the Aleut community at Unalaska Island, the Narsaq Greenlanders, the residents of Pond Inlet, the Warner and Kapolak families at Bathurst Inlet, and the staff and researchers at the Arctic Institute at Devon Island.

And finally to you, the reader of this book: Have a wonderful journey through the wilds of the Arctic, whether you are traveling there in person or in your armchair.

Bon voyage, or as they say in Nunavut,

Naammaktsiarit

Sharon Chester

ABOUT THIS BOOK

THIS BOOK WAS DESIGNED to be used by travelers to the Far North, whether they are heading to places as far north as Svalbard and the Canadian Arctic Islands or as far south as Kamchatka, the Aleutians, or Hudson Bay. Thus, coverage was extended to plants and animals that occur from the High Arctic to the northern sectors of the boreal forests and taiga. Also included and illustrated are species that appear to be moving north into the higher latitudes in the wake of arctic warming.

TAXONOMIC ORDER
The species accounts are organized by order, family, genus, species, and subspecies. This grouping roughly reflects the evolutionary relationships among the taxa. The book attempts to employ the latest known taxonomic sequences, but taxonomy is a system in flux and what was current at the time of writing may be outdated by the time of printing.

ENGLISH AND SCIENTIFIC NAMES
Each account starts with the species' common English name, followed by the scientific name in italics. The scientific name consists of two words, or binomial, usually derived from Latin or Greek. The first word is the name of the genus; the second indicates the species within the genus. Common English names and scientific names were culled from sources that include the Integrated Taxonomic Information System (ITIS), the American Ornithologists' Union (AOU), Avibase, Fish Base, and the USDA Plants of N Amer.

ALTERNATE NAMES
Under ALSO the reader can find alternate English names as well as the German, French, Norwegian, Russian, Inuit, and Inupiaq names. Wikipedia was the main source for the European names. The Inuit and Inupiaq names were derived from old dictionaries and a random assortment of field notes, and the author wishes to apologize for any errors made in transcription. Meanings of the species' scientific name (SN) and common name (CN) are also given under this heading. In cases in which the common or scientific name refers to a person, a brief note about that individual is provided.

RANGE
Arctic and world distribution are detailed under RANGE. A range map accompanies most of the accounts. All range maps in this book are polar projection maps oriented in the same direction as the large map on pages 12–13; the North Pole

is in the center, Eurasia at the top, and North America at the bottom. Dark greenish gray identifies the breeding range of terrestrial animals and birds, and the general range of plant species. Blue indicates the oceanic range of marine mammals, seabirds, fishes, and marine algae, with darker blue used to show areas of unusual abundance. Pale yellow, not shown on the maps here, indicates the routes used by some migratory birds as they move between breeding and wintering grounds.

The PLATE CAPTIONS also provide the general range of mammals, fishes, insects, and plants, as well as the breeding range of birds.

ABBREVIATIONS used here and elsewhere in the book include Penin (Peninsula), Rvr (River), Mtn (Mountain), Is (Island), N Amer (North America), n (northern), s (southern), e (eastern), w (western), and c (central).

IDENTIFICATION
The identification section (ID) presents information about a plant or animal's approximate size, shape, color, and distinguishing marks, as well as vocalizations of birds and some mammals. Abbreviations and symbols used in this section include: L (length), H (height), SH (shoulder height), WT (weight), WS (wingspan), JUV or juv. (juvenile), AD or ad. (adult), ♂ (male), ♀ (female), LVS (leaves), FLS (flowers), FR (fruit), in (inch), cm (centimeter), ft (foot), m (meter), oz (ounce), g (gram), lb (pound), kg (kilogram).

HABITS
This section addresses habitat and food preferences, behavior, breeding, and rearing of the young.

STATUS
Endangered species and those with declining populations are noted under this heading.

GEOGRAPHIC COORDINATES

Below is a list of a few places mentioned in the text, along with their geographic coordinates, expressed in degrees (°) and minutes (') of latitude and longitude. The coordinates pinpoint where a place is located on the globe. LATITUDE is the angular distance of a place on the globe north or south of the equator. The latitude of the equator is 0°; that of the North Pole is 90°N, the South Pole 90°S, and the Arctic Circle 66°23' N. LONGITUDE is the angular distance east or west from the prime meridian at Greenwich, England, to any other meridian on the globe. A meridian is one of the lines of longitude that extends between the North Pole and the South Pole. Longitude is expressed in degrees from 0° to 180° east or west.

ALASKA AND ALEUTIANS

Anchorage	61° 13' N	149° 53' W
Attu Is	52° 55' N	173° 00' E
Barrow	71° 17' N	156° 45' W
Bering Strait	66° 00' N	169° 00' W
Bogoslof Is	53° 55' N	168° 02' W
Cape Prince of Wales	65° 36' N	168° 05' W
Fairbanks	64° 50' N	147° 43' W
Kodiak Is	57° 30' N	153° 30' W
Little Diomede Is	65° 45' N	168° 57' W
Nome	64° 50' N	165° 25' W
North Slope	68° 30' N	152° 00' W
Pribilof Is	57° 00' N	170° 00' W
Prudhoe Bay	70° 22' N	148° 22' W
Seward Peninsula	65° 00' N	164° 00' W
St Lawrence Is	63° 30' N	170° 30' W
Unaslaska Is	53° 45' N	166° 45' W
Yukon Rvr	62° 32' N	163° 54' W

CANADA

Baffin Is	68° 00' N	72° 00' W
Banks Is	73° 00' N	121° 00' W
Bathurst Inlet	75° 40' N	100° 00' W
Churchill	58° 46' N	94° 10' W
Davis Strait	65° 00' N	57° 30' W
Devon Is	75° 00' N	86° 00' W
Ellesmere Is	79° 30' N	81° 00' W
Frobisher (Iqaluit)	62° 40' N	66° 20' W
Great Bear Lake	66° 00' N	120° 00' W
Great Slave Lake	61° 30' N	114° 00' W
Hudson Bay	60° 00' N	85° 00' W
James Bay	53° 30' N	80° 30' W
Labrador	54° 00' N	62° 00' W
Lake Hazen	81° 48' N	71° 15' W
Lancaster Sound	74° 00' N	85° 00' W
Mackenzie Rvr	69° 20' N	134° 00' W
Newfoundland	52° 00' N	56° 00' W
Pond Inlet	72° 47' N	77° 00' W
Resolute	74° 41' N	94° 54' W
Thelon Rvr	64° 16' N	96° 05' W
Tuktoyaktuk	69° 27' N	133° 01' W
Yellowknife	62° 27' N	114° 21' W

GREENLAND

Ammassalik (Tasiilaq)	65° 36' N	37° 38' W
Baffin Bay	74° 00' N	67° 00' W
Davis Strait	65° 00' N	57° 30' W
Fredrikshåb	62° 00' N	49° 43' W
Godhavn (Qeqertarsuaq)	69° 15' N	53° 33' W
Godthåb (Nuuk)	64° 11' N	51° 45' W
Julianehåb (Qaqortoq)	60° 43' N	46° 02' W
Thule (Qaanaaq)	77° 29' N	69° 21' W

ICELAND

Grimsey Is	66° 34' N	18° 00' W
Reykjavik	64° 09' N	21° 51' W

NORWEGIAN ARCTIC

Bear Is (Bjørnøya)	74° 25' N	19° 00' E
Jan Mayen Is	71° 00' N	8° 20' W
North Cape (Nordkapp)	71° 11' N	25° 48' E
Svalbard Archipelago	78° 00' N	19° 00' E

RUSSIAN ARCTIC

Anadyr	64° 44' N	177° 31' E
Chukotka Okrug	66° 00' N	174° 00' W
Commander Is	55° 00' N	167° 00' E
Franz Josef Land	81° 00' N	55° 00' E
Kamchatka Penin	56° 00' N	159° 00' E
Kola Penin	67° 20' N	37° 00' E
Kolyma Rvr	62° 20' N	154° 50' E
Kuril Is	46° 00' N	150° 00' E
Magadan	59° 34' N	150° 48' E
Murmansk	68° 58' N	33° 05' E
New Siberian Is	75° 00' N	142° 00' E
Novaya Zemlya	74° 00' N	57° 00' E
Provideniya	64° 23' N	173° 18' W
Sakhalin Is	51° 00' N	143° 00' E
Sea of Okhotsk	53° 00' N	150° 00' E
Severnaya Zemlya	79° 30' N	98° 00' E
Taimyr Penin	76° 00' N	104° 00' E
Uelen	66° 10' N	169° 48' W
Wrangel Is	71° 00' N	179° 30' W
Yttygran Is	64° 37' N	172° 36' W

CONVERSION UNITS

Small Copper
Lycaena phlaeas
WS 1 in (2.5 cm)

LENGTH			WEIGHT			TEMPERATURE	
1 inch	=	2.54 centimeters	1 ounce	=	28 grams	−13°F	= −25°C
1 centimeter	=	0.39 inch	1 gram	=	0.035 ounce	+ 5°F	= −15°C
1 foot	=	0.3 meter	1 pound	=	0.45 kilogram	+32°F	= 0°C
1 meter	=	3.28 feet	1 kilogram	=	2.2 pounds	+50°F	= +10°C
1 mile	=	1.6 kilometers				+68°F	= +20°C
1 kilometer	=	0.62 mile				+86°F	= +30°C

0 cm	2	3	4	5	6	7	8	9	10
0 in	1		2		3		4		

achene. Small, dry, 1-seeded fruit that does not open to release the seed.

alga. Nonflowering plant that contains chlorophyll but lacks true stems, roots, leaves, and vascular tissue.

amphi-Beringian. Relating to flora and fauna that occur in both ne Siberia and nw N Amer.

amphi-Atlantic. Relating to flora and fauna that occur in both ne N Amer and nw Europe.

amphipod. Small marine crustacean.

anadromous. Of a fish, such as the Salmon, that migrates up rivers from the sea to spawn.

angiosperm. Plant that has flowers and produces seeds enclosed within a carpel, or ovary.

antler. Branched bony outgrowth on the head of adult (usually male) deer; antlers are grown and cast off annually. Contrast with HORN.

aquatic. Living or growing in or near water.

archipelago. A group of islands.

Arctic. The cold circumpolar regions of the N Hemisphere extending southward from 90°N (the North Pole) and bounded by an irregular line lying between 70°N and 55°N latitudes.

Arctic Basin. A deep submarine depression in the Arctic Ocean that is bounded by the continental shelves of Eurasia and N Amer.

Arctic Circle. A line drawn at 66°30′N latitude that marks the southern limit of the area within which, for one day or more each year, the sun does not set (around June 21) or rise (around December 21) above the horizon.

Arctic Ocean. A roughly circular body of salt water that surrounds the North Pole and lies within the Arctic Circle.

arthropod. An invertebrate animal of the phylum Arthropoda, such as an insect or crustacean.

axillaries. Feathers in a bird's axilla ("armpit").

benthic. Relating to the flora and fauna found on the bottom, or in the bottom sediments, of a sea, lake, or other body of water.

Bering Land Bridge. A strip of land that connected present-day Alaska and e Siberia during the last ice age, 18,000–12,000 years ago. Also called Beringia.

Bern Convention. The Bern Convention on the Conservation of European Wildlife and Natural Habitats of 1979 protects wild flora and fauna.

bioclimatic zone. A region of the earth's surface having characteristic climate, flora, and vegetation in common habitats.

biome. Large, naturally occurring community of flora and fauna occupying a major habitat, such as tundra.

bivalve. Aquatic mollusk with a compressed body enclosed within a hinged shell, such as oysters, clams, mussels, and scallops.

blowhole. A nostril on top of a cetacean's head that is used for breathing and for ejecting air and vapor in what is called a "blow."

boreal forest. Coniferous forest of high northern latitudes, especially those that lie between the tundra and unforested grasslands of Siberia and N Amer; English equivalent of TAIGA.

bract. A modified leaf or scale, typically small, with a flower or flower cluster in its axil.

bryophytes. Non-vascular land plants (liverworts, hornworts, mosses) having tissues and enclosed reproductive systems but lacking vascular tissue that circulates liquids. Bryophytes reproduce via spores.

calcareous. Chalky; soil rich in calcium carbonate.

calyx. Sepals of a flower, typically forming a whorl (usually green) enclosing the petals.

capitate. With knob-like head; of an inflorescence, with the flowers stemless and aggregated into a dense cluster.

capsule. A dry fruit formed from 2 or more united carpels and dehiscing when ripe, usually by splitting into pieces.

carbonate. Limestone or dolomite bedrock types that result in calcareous soils with high calcium content, high pH, and plant communities adapted to such conditions.

carnivorous. Feeding on other animals.

carpel. Female organ borne at the center of a flower, consisting of an ovary, style, and stigma.

caryopsis. A dry 1-seeded fruit in which the ovary wall is united with the seed coat; typical of grasses and cereals.

catkin. Reproductive spike of trees, typically downy, pendulous, composed of flowers of a single sex, and wind-pollinated.

cauline. Belonging to a plant stem, or caudex.

cere. Fleshy covering at the base of a bird's beak.

cetacean. A marine mammal of the order Cetacea; a whale, dolphin, or porpoise.

Chukchi. Member of an indigenous people of ne Siberia.

circumboreal. Of or pertaining to a region of abundant forest growth, particularly in Eurasia and N Amer.

circumpolar. Of or pertaining to a region surrounding the North or South Pole.

CITES. The Convention on International Trade in Endangered Species of Wild Fauna and Flora is an agreement between governments that regulates international trade in wild animals and plants. Species of concern are listed in 3 Appendixes.

compressed. Flattened lengthwise, either laterally (side to side) or dorsally (front to back).

cone. The dry fruit of a conifer, typically tapering to a rounded end and formed of a tight array of overlapping scales on a central axis that separate to release the seeds.

conspecific. Belonging to the same species.

continental shelf. Gently sloping, shallowly submerged portions of the continental margins.

coprophagy. A behavior in which one's feces are consumed and redigested.

cordate. Heart-shaped.

corymb. Flower cluster whose lower stalks are proportionally longer, so that the flowers form a flat or slightly convex head.

cotyledon. Primary leaf or leaves of an embryo, becoming the seed leaf or leaves.

coverts. Contour feathers that cover the bases of the flight feathers on a bird's wing and tail.

crenate. Having blunt-toothed or scalloped margins.

crustacean. Invertebrate animal of the mostly aquatic group Crustacea (e.g., crab, lobster, shrimp, barnacle).

cryoprotectant. Substance that prevents the freezing of tissues or damage to cells during freezing.

culm. Hollow stem of a grass or cereal plant, especially that bearing the flower.

culmen. The upper ridge of a bird's bill.

cuneate. Wedge-shaped.

cyme. Inflorescence in which the main axis and all lateral branches end in a flower.

cypsela. Dry, 1-seeded fruit formed from a double ovary.

deciduous. Of a tree or shrub that sheds its leaves annually. Opposite of EVERGREEN.

decumbent. A plant or part of a plant growing horizontally on the ground but turned up at the ends. Contrast with PROSTRATE.

deflexed. Bent or curving down or back.

dehiscent. Splitting or bursting open, as in a seedpod.

delayed implantation. A pause in mammalian embryonic development between fertilization and the time the fertilized egg attaches to the uterus.

demersal. Living close to the sea floor.

dental formula. A formula expressing the number and kinds of teeth possessed by a mammal.

dentate. Toothed, as in a leaf margin.

denticulate. Finely toothed, as in a leaf margin.

diapause. A period of suspended development in an insect, other invertebrate, or mammal embryo.

dicotyledon. A flowering plant with an embryo having 2 cotyledons, or seed leaves; most dicots have broad, stalked leaves with net-like veins. Compare MONOCOTYLEDON.

digitate. With segments spreading from a common center, like the fingers of a hand.

dioecious. Of a plant or invertebrate animal having both the male and female reproductive organs in separate individuals. Compare MONOECIOUS.

disjunct. Occurring in widely separated geographic areas; discontinuous distribution.

diurnal. Occurring or opening in the daytime.

division. A principal taxonomic category of botany that ranks above class and below kingdom; equivalent to PHYLUM in zoology.

DNA-hybridization. A technique of measuring degrees of genetic similarity or divergence between organisms by comparing molecules of DNA (deoxyribonucleic acid).

dorsal. Of, on, or relating to the upperside or back of an animal, plant, or organ. Compare VENTRAL.

drift ice. Ice that floats on the surface of the ocean and is moved by currents and winds.

drupe. A succulent fruit formed from 1 carpel; the single seed is enclosed by a stony layer of the fruit wall.

ecoregion. A major ecosystem defined by distinctive geography and receiving uniform solar radiation and moisture.

ecosystem. A biological community of interacting organisms and their physical environment.

endemic. A plant or animal restricted to a certain country or area. Contrast with NATIVE.

entire. Not divided; e.g., a leaf having a smooth margin, not lobed or toothed.

epiphyte. A plant that grows on another without taking nourishment from it. Compare PARASITE.

erect. Upright; perpendicular to the ground.

eudicots. Plants classified as "true dicotyledons" (i.e., those plants having 2 seed leaves).

eukaryote. Organism whose cells contain complex structures enclosed in membranes.

euphausiid. Krill; shrimp-like planktonic marine crustacean.

Eurasia. The combined continental landmass of Europe and Asia.

even-pinnate. Having an even number of leaflets in a compound leaf.

evergreen. Of a tree or shrub that has leaves year round. Opposite of DECIDUOUS.

falcate. Curved like the blade of a scythe.

family. Principal rank between order and genus.

fascicle. Cluster of leaves arising from the same node.

fast ice. Sea ice permanently attached to land.

fauna. Animals of a particular region or habitat.

fen. A low and marshy or frequently flooded area of land, with only slightly acidic, peaty soil.

Fennoscandia. Region comprising the Scandinavian Penin, Finland, Karelia, and the Kola Penin.

ferruginous. Rust-colored.

filamentous. Consisting of filaments; hair-like.

filiform. Thread-like, usually applied to leaf shape.

fledge. Of birds; develop wing feathers that are large enough for flight.

flight feathers. Large, stiff wing and tail feathers; remiges, rectrices.

flora. Plants of a particular region or habitat.

floret. A small flower, or individual true flowers clustered within an inflorescence, particularly in inflorescences of the daisy and grass families.

flower. Sexual reproductive structure of the angiosperms, with a gynoecium, androecium, perianth, and axis.

food chain. A hierarchical series of organisms each dependent on the next as a source of food. A system of interlocking and interdependent food chains is called a food web.

forage fish. Small fish that are preyed on by larger fish, seabirds, and marine mammals for food; bait fish.

forb. Any broadleaf herbaceous flowering plant, except graminoids (grasses).

forest. Vegetation dominated by trees with single trunks, including closely arranged trees with or without an understory of shrubs and herbs.

frazil ice. A slushy suspension of randomly oriented needle-shaped ice crystals in seawater.

fungus. Spore-producing organism that feeds on organic matter.

fusiform. Spindle-shaped.

gastropod. A mollusk with a large muscular foot and a single asymmetrical spiral shell.

genus. A principal taxonomic category that ranks above species and below family; genus is denoted by a capitalized Latin name that is written in italics.

geomorphology. The science concerned with understanding earth's surface and the processes that add material and those that remove it, both past and present.

glabrous. Smooth; without hairs, scales, or bristles.

glaucous. Dull grayish green or blue in color, or covered in a powdery bloom.

globose. Spherical.

graminoid. A grass-like herbaceous plant with leaves mostly very narrow or linear in outline; e.g., grasses, rushes, and sedges.

grease ice. A thin, soupy layer of frazil crystals on the sea surface that resembles an oil slick.

gregarious. Sociable; fond of the company of others; living in herds or flocks.

gymnosperm. A plant having seeds unprotected by an ovary or fruit; e.g., conifers and cycads.

gynoecium. Female parts of flower; collective term for the carpels of a flower.

habitat. The natural home or environment of an animal, plant, or other organism.

hair. Fine thread-like strands growing from the skin of humans, mammals, and some other animals; a fine thread-like strand growing from the epidermis of a plant.

haustorium. In parasitic plants, a structure developed for penetrating the host's tissues.

herb. A flowering plant with no significant woody tissue above ground; a plant that dies back to the ground at the end of the growing season.

herbaceous. Not woody; usually green and soft.

herbivore. An animal that feeds on green plants.

Herbst corpuscles. Tactile organs, or touch receptors, found in the dermis layer of the skin, beak, and legs of some birds, such as waterfowl and shorebirds, and in the tongues of other birds, such as woodpeckers.

herd. A group of animals of the same species that live together.

hibernation. The resting or dormant state in which some animals pass the winter.

High Arctic. A term applied to land at extremely high northern latitudes (e.g., Canadian Arctic and Svalbard archipelagos), where the mean July temperature is 32°–37°F (0°–3°C) and where vegetation is limited to sparse ground cover that has a low biological diversity.

hirsute. In botany, bearing coarse, longish hairs.

hoary. Covered with a gray to whitish layer of very short, closely interwoven hairs, giving a frosted appearance.

Holarctic. A zoogeographical region comprising the Nearctic (N Amer/Greenland) and Palearctic (Eurasia) regions combined.

horn. A hard, permanent bony outgrowth, often curved and pointed, found in pairs on the heads of cattle, sheep, and goats. Contrast with ANTLER.

hummock. A hump or ridge in an ice field, or a piece of forested ground rising above a marsh.

hybrid. The offspring of 2 plants or animals of different species or varieties.

hypopigmentation. The loss of skin color caused by a decrease in the amino acid tyrosine.

iceberg. Large pieces of ice that have calved (broken off) from an ice shelf or glacier.

ice shelf. A thick sheet of glacial ice that floats on the sea but is permanently attached to land.

immature. A young animal before it has acquired adult plumage or pelage and is able to reproduce.

incised. Cut deeply and usually unevenly.

indehiscent. A pod or fruit that does not split open to release the seeds when ripe.

indigenous. Native to the area, not introduced, and not necessarily confined to the region discussed or present throughout it.

indusium. Membrane covering the sporangia of ferns.

inflorescence. Complete flower head of a plant including stems, stalks, bracts, and flowers.

insectivorous. Of an animal or plant that feeds on insects.

instar. Phase between 2 periods of molting in the development of an insect, from larva to adult.

intertidal zone. The area of a seashore that is covered at high tide and uncovered at low tide.

Inuit. "The People"; members of an indigenous people of Alaska, n Canada, and Greenland; singular is Inuk.

Inuktitut. Language of the Inuit people.

inukshuk. A man-made stone cairn or landmark; when built into the shape of a human, it is called an inunnguaq.

Inupiaq. A member of a group of the Eskimo people inhabiting nw Alaska; also their language.

invertebrate. Animal lacking a backbone, such as an arthropod, mollusk, annelid, or coelenterate.

involucre. A whorl or rosette of bracts around a flower head or at the base of an umbel.

irrupt. Migrate into an area in unusual and abnormally large numbers.

isotherm. A line on a map connecting points having the same temperature at a given time or on average over a given period.

IUCN. World Conservation Union; an international organization that evaluates the status of world flora and fauna, and publishes findings in the *Red List of Threatened Species.* Assessment levels are Critically Endangered, Endangered, Vulnerable, Threatened, Near Threatened, or Least Concern.

juvenile. A young bird or other animal in its first year.

keel. Prominent longitudinal ridge.

krill. Shrimp-like planktonic crustaceans.

lamella. A thin membrane or plate-like tissue, especially in bone tissue, adapted for filter feeding or straining suspended matter and food particles from water.

lamina. Blade of a leaf, or the expanded upper part of a petal, sepal, or bract.

lanceolate. Shaped like a lance head.

land ice. Frozen fresh water or snow; glacial ice.

lanugo. The covering of fine fetal hair found in most mammals while still in the womb.

latex. A milky substance that exudes from plants.

leaflets. The segments of a compound leaf.

lenticel. Lens-shaped porous tissue in bark that allows direct exchange of gases between the internal tissues and atmosphere.

leucistic. Of an animal, having whitish fur, plumage, or skin due to a lack of pigment.

lichen. A composite plant-like organism consisting of a fungus containing photosynthetic algal cells.

ligneous. Woody.

Low Arctic. Term applied to tundra where the mean July temp is 45–54°F (7–12°C) and vegetation types include dwarf shrubs, low shrubs, sedges, forbs, bryophytes, and lichens.

margin. Edge, as in the outer edge of a leaf blade.

melanism. Dark coloration of the skin, hair, fur, or feathers because of a high concentration of melanin.

melon. A mass of adipose tissue found in the forehead of all toothed whales, which focuses and modulates the animal's vocalizations and acts as a sound lens.

meridian. An imaginary great circle of constant longitude on the earth's surface that passes through the north and south geographic poles.

molt, moult. A loss of plumage, skin, or hair, often as a regular cycle of an animal's life cycle.

monocotyledon. A flowering plant (e.g., grasses, lilies, palms) with an embryo that bears a single cotyledon, or seed leaf. Compare DICOTYLEDON.

monoecious. Of a plant or invertebrate animal having both the male and female reproductive organs in the same individual; hermaphrodite. Compare DIOECIOUS.

monotypic. A family with only one genus, or a genus that includes only a single species.

morph. A variant form of an animal or plant.

muskeg. A swamp or bog of N Amer, consisting of a mixture of water and partly dead vegetation, often covered by a layer of sphagnum or other mosses.

mycelium. The nonreproductive part of a fungus.

nares. The nostrils.

native. Indigenous to a place but not restricted to that place. Contrast with ENDEMIC.

Nearctic. Of or denoting a zoogeographical region comprising N Amer as far south as n Mexico, together with Greenland. Compare HOLARCTIC, PALEARCTIC.

nectary. A specialized gland that secretes nectar, a usually sweet fluid produced by flowers and collected by bees and other insects.

Nenets. A nomadic people of Siberia, whose traditional occupation is reindeer herding.

nilas. Layer of new sea ice up to 4 in (10 cm) thick.

nomenclature. The naming of things; often restricted to the correct use of scientific names in taxonomy.

Northern Hemisphere. The half of the world that lies between the equator and the North Pole.

North Magnetic Pole. The point on the surface of earth's N Hemisphere at which the planet's magnetic field points vertically downward.

North Pole. The point in the N Hemisphere where the earth's axis of rotation meets its surface.

noxious. Containing harmful or toxic qualities.

nut. Hard, dry, indehiscent fruit with only 1 seed.

oblanceolate. A lance-shaped leaf with the more pointed end at the base.

obovate. An oval-shaped leaf with the narrower end at the base.

odd-pinnate. Having an odd number of leaflets in a compound leaf.

Old World. The world known before the discovery of the Americas; essentially Europe and Asia.

opposite. Leaves or flowers borne at the same level but on opposite sides of a stem or axis.

order. A group of one or more families sharing common features, ancestry, or both.

orogeny. Process by which mountains form.

ovary. In botany, the hollow base of a flower's carpel that contains 1 or more ovules or seeds before fertilization.

pack ice. Pieces of floating sea ice driven together into a nearly continuous, large mass.

pagophilic. Ice-loving.

Palearctic. Denoting a zoogeographical region comprising Eurasia north of the Himalayas, together with N Africa and part of the Arabian Penin.

palmate. Of a leaf, with veins radiating out from a central point, resembling spread-out fingers pointing away from the palm.

pancake ice. Flat, floating plates of sea ice with upturned edges.

panicle. A loose, branching cluster of flowers

pappus. The tuft of hairs on each seed of thistles, dandelions, and similar plants that assists dispersal by the wind.

parasite. An organism that lives in or on another organism (its host) and benefits by deriving nutrients at the host's expense.

parasitoid. An insect whose larvae live as parasites that eventually kill their hosts.

parthenogenesis. Reproduction from an ovum without fertilization, especially as a normal process in some invertebrates, vertebrates, and lower plants.

pedicel. Small stalk bearing an individual flower.

peduncle. Stalk bearing a flower or fruit, or the main stalk of an inflorescence.

pelage. Fur, hair, or wool of a mammal.

pelagic. Of or relating to the open ocean (e.g., seabirds that come to land only to breed or fish that inhabit the open sea).

peltate. Shield-like.

perennial. Present at all seasons or having a lifespan that extends over several years.

perfect. Flower that bears both male and female reproductive organs (bisexual).

perianth. Outer part of a flower, consisting of the calyx (sepals) and corolla (petals).

permafrost. A thick subsurface layer of soil that remains frozen throughout the year.

petal. Each of the segments of the corolla of a flower, which are modified leaves and are typically colored.

photosynthesis. Process by which sugars are made from carbon dioxide and water in cells containing chlorophyll.

phylum. A principal taxonomic category that ranks above class and below kingdom.

physiognomy. General outward appearance of a plant community determined by life forms of dominant species (e.g., grassland or forest).

pinna. Primary segment of a compound leaf.

pinnate. Of a compound leaf having leaflets arranged on either side of the stem.

pinniped. Carnivorous aquatic animal (e.g., seal or walrus).

plankton. Small marine plants (phytoplankton) and animals (zooplankton) that form the base of the marine food chain.

plate tectonics. A theory of global-scale dynamics involving the movement of many rigid plates of the Earth's crust.

plumose. Having many fine filaments or branches that give a feathery appearance.

polymorphic. Occurring in different forms.

polar desert. Polar areas having an annual precipitation of less than 10 in (25 cm).

pollen. A fine powdery substance, typically yellow, consisting of microscopic grains discharged from the male part of a flower or from a male cone.

polyandry. A pattern of mating in which a female animal has more than one male mate.

polychaetes. Annelid worms, generally marine; each body segment has a pair of fleshy protrusions with bristles.

polygynandry. A pattern of mating in which both male and female animals have multiple mates.

polygyny. A pattern of mating in which a male animal has more than one female mate.

polynya. Any non-linear area of open water surrounded by sea ice; area of a polar sea that remains unfrozen for much of the year.

population. A group of individuals of a single biological species that occupy a defined area.

precocial. Of a young bird or other animal hatched or born in an advanced state and able to feed itself.

primary. One of the wing's outermost flight feathers.

proboscis. The nose of a mammal, especially when it is long and mobile; an elongated sucking mouthpart of an insect that is typically tubular and flexible.

procumbent. Of a plant spreading along the ground but not rooting at the nodes.

prostrate. Of a plant growing flat on the ground.

pubescent. Of a plant, covered in fine hairs or down. Contrast with HIRSUTE.

pyriform. Pear-shaped.

raceme. A flower cluster with the separate flowers attached by short equal stalks at equal distances along a central stem.

rectrices. A bird's tail feathers.

remiges. A bird's wing feathers.

reniform. Kidney-shaped.

rhizome. Perennial underground stem usually growing horizontally.

riparian. Of, relating to, or situated on riverbanks.

rush. Plant belonging to the family Juncaceae.

salverform. Flower composed of united petals forming a tube that spreads at the open end.

samara. Dry, indehiscent fruit with its wall expanded into a wing.

Sami. The Lapps of n Scandinavia.

scapular feather. Feather covering a bird's shoulder, growing above the area where the wing joins the body.

secondary. One of the wing's inner flight feathers.

sepal. In a flower, one of the segments of the outer whorl of non-fertile parts around the fertile organs; typically green and leaf-like.

serrate. Toothed, with asymmetrical teeth pointing forward, like the cutting edge of a saw.

sessile. Of a plant or animal, a structure attached directly by its base, without a stalk.

sexual dimorphism. Differences in form, size, or color that distinguish males and females of the same species.

shrub. A woody perennial plant without a single main trunk, branching freely, and smaller than a tree.

silique, silicule. A fruit (seedpod) of 2 fused carpels that separate when ripe, leaving a persistent partition, with the length being more than twice the width. Common in the mustard family, Brassicaceae.

sinuate. Having a wavy or sinuous margin; with alternate rounded notches and lobes.

sori. Spore-forming plant cells.

species. Group of living organisms consisting of similar individuals capable of exchanging genes or interbreeding. Species is the principal taxonomic unit, ranking below genus and denoted by a Latin binomial written in italics (e.g., *Ursos arctos*). The abbreviation "sp." (plural "spp.") indicates that the species is unknown or unidentified (e.g., *Viola* sp.)

spermatophyte. Plant that bears seeds.

spike. Unbranched, indeterminate inflorescence in which the flowers are without stalks.

sporangium. Structure in which spores are formed in non-flowering plants.

stellate. Star-shaped.

steppe. Large area of flat grassland, usually applied to the plains of Eurasia; called a savanna or plain in N Amer; its plant communities are composed of perennial herbs, grasses, and low, woody shrubs.

stolon. Creeping horizontal plant stem or runner that roots along its length to form new plants.

subarctic. Region in the N Hemisphere between 50°N and 70°N latitude; of or relating to the region immediately south of the Arctic Circle.

subspecies. Taxonomic category that ranks below species; usually a fairly permanent, geographically isolated race.

supercilium. A stripe or "eyebrow" that runs above a bird's eye toward the rear of the head.

syrinx. The lower larynx or voice organ in birds, situated at or near the junction of the trachea and bronchi and well developed in songbirds.

taiga. The coniferous forest of high northern latitudes; the Russian word for BOREAL FOREST.

taxonomy. Classification of organisms in an ordered system indicating natural relationships.

ternate. Arranged in threes, especially a compound leaf having three leaflets.

terrestrial. Relating to an animal or plant that lives or grows on land.

tertials. Innermost flight feathers of the wing.

thorn. A modified stem with a sharp, stiff point.

tomentose. Of a plant, having a dense covering of short, matted hairs.

tree. A woody plant, usually with a single distinct trunk and generally more than 15 ft (5 m) tall.

treeline. Latitudinal or elevational limit of tree growth. Synonymous with timberline.

torpor. A state of lowered bodily activity, as during hibernation, that is a response to an unfavorable environmental condition, as cold or drought.

tundra. A vast, flat, treeless region of arctic Eurasia and N Amer, in which the subsoil is permanently frozen; occurs at both high elevations (alpine tundra) and high latitudes (arctic tundra); from the Finnish word *tunturia*, meaning "treeless plain."

Tungus. Indigenous people of n Russia; Evenks.

tussock. Plant, usually a grass, with a tufted or bunch-forming growth form, usually well separated from neighboring tussocks.

type locality. Place where a specimen was first found.

umbel. A flower cluster in which stalks of nearly equal length spring from a common center and form a flat or curved surface.

US-ESA. United States Endangered Species Act of 1973, designed to protect critically imperiled species from extinction through conservation.

ventral. Of, on, or relating to the underside of an animal or plant. Compare DORSAL.

vertebrate. An animal distinguished by the possession of a backbone or spinal column, including mammals, birds, reptiles, amphibians, and fishes. Contrast with INVERTEBRATE.

vibrissae. Whiskers; the long stiff hairs growing around the mouth or elsewhere on the face of many mammals, used as organs of touch; or the coarse bristle-like feathers growing around the gape of certain insectivorous birds.

viviparous. Bringing forth live young that have developed inside the body of the parent.

wetland. Land consisting of marshes or swamps; saturated land.

woolly. Very densely covered with long, matted or intertwined hairs, resembling sheep's wool.

Yupik. Members of an Eskimo people of Siberia, the Aleutians, and sw Alaska; also their language.

ARKTOS

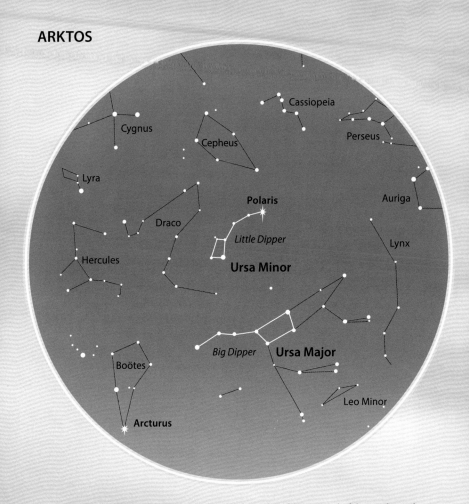

TO THE ANCIENT GREEKS, the Arctic was the realm of Boreas, god of the north wind, and the region where the celestial sphere of northernmost stars was always visible. They called this place Arktos, meaning "bear," alluding to the Great Bear and Little Bear constellations, Ursa Major and Ursa Minor.

There are many myths and legends about these groups of stars. Greek mythology relates that the bear constellations are the spirits of the nymph Callisto, the reluctant concubine of the god Zeus, and their son, Arcas. Zeus changed the pair into stars and placed them in the heavens, where they are tended by Arcturus, the bear guard, who faithfully follows them around the night sky.

The brightest stars of the bear constellations form the Big and Little Dippers, so named for their resemblance to ladles. At the end of the Little Dipper's handle is the bright triple star Alpha Ursae Minoris, known to us as Polaris, the North Star. Polaris marks the point of due north and has a seemingly fixed position in the arctic sky. The Inuit call it Nuuttuittuq, the star that never moves, and the Finns call it the North Nail.

DEFINING THE ARCTIC

THE ARCTIC is the region of land and ocean that centers roughly on the North Pole and extends southward to and beyond the Arctic Circle. It is a place of exaggerated seasonality with brief, cool summers and long, dark, icy winters. This vast wilderness, also known as the Far North, encompasses the Arctic Ocean, the world's largest island (Greenland), and parts of eight countries: the United States (Alaska), Canada, Denmark (Greenland), Iceland, Norway, Sweden, Finland, and Russia.

The Ancient Greek astronomers were the first to define the Arctic's boundaries. They based their conclusions on observations of the celestial sphere, an imaginary shell surrounding the earth. They believed that the stars and other celestial bodies were fixed on the inside surface of the sphere, as if it were the underside of a dome. It is easy to understand how the early astronomers came to this belief, for if one steps outside on a clear, starry night and looks up, the constellations appear to be set on a dome that surrounds the earthbound observer, who is standing in the middle of it. The stars seem to slowly rotate from east to west—an illusion caused by the earth's rotation.

Aristotle (384–322 BC) noted in his treatise *Meteorology* that some stars were always visible to an observer at a particular location and that these always-visible stars could be used to mark standard reference circles on the celestial sphere and earth. A short time later, in his essay *Phenomena*, Euclid hinted that astronomers had used Aristotle's hypothesis to approximate the position of the North Celestial Pole (the imaginary point where earth's axis of rotation meets the celestial sphere) as well as the celestial equator, tropics, and Arctic Circle.

In the first century BC, Greek Stoic philosopher Posidonius applied his observations of solar phenomena to define a precise boundary for earth's northernmost region. He proposed that the Arctic be delimited by a circle of fixed size, located 24° south of the North Celestial Pole. This put Posidonius's circle at 66°N latitude, a location nearly identical to the position of the present-day Arctic Circle at 66°33'N.

Today, the Arctic Circle is commonly used by political administrators, geographers, and cartographers to mark the Arctic's southern boundary and it also provides travelers a point to celebrate their entry into the Arctic.

More importantly, the Arctic Circle marks the northernmost point at which the sun is visible on the northern winter solstice, around December 21, and the southernmost point at which the midnight sun can be seen on the northern summer solstice, around June 21.

Scientists have many other words and ways to define the Arctic. Biologists often use the term Holarctic, which comprises the Palearctic (Old World) and Nearctic (New World) regions combined. The two regions have been linked intermittently by the Bering Land Bridge and their flora and fauna are closely related.

Climatologists and ecologists tend to use the Köppen climate classification system to delimit the arctic zone. The system, which is based on the concept that native vegetation is the best expression of climate, was first proposed in 1884 by Russian-German meteorologist, climatologist, and botanist Wladimir Köppen (1846–1940).

Köppen's system defines the arctic zone as the area enclosed by the 10°C July isotherm—a line connecting points where the average temperature for the warmest month of the year, usually July, does not exceed 10°C (50°F). The position of the 10°C July isotherm fluctuates between 62°N and 70°N latitudes and roughly parallels the boreal treeline, the northern limit of tree growth. The arctic tundra lies to the north of the 10°C July isotherm and the boreal forests and taiga lie to the south.

The map on pages 12–13 shows the approximate location of the 10°C July isotherm, the treeline, and the bioclimatic zones, including the Polar Desert, High Arctic, Low Arctic, Boreal Forest, and Taiga. Color-coded sidebars list some plant and animal species associated with each zone. Much of the information presented on the map was adapted from the *Circumpolar Arctic Vegetation Map* compiled by the Alaska Geobotany Center at the University of Alaska Fairbanks.

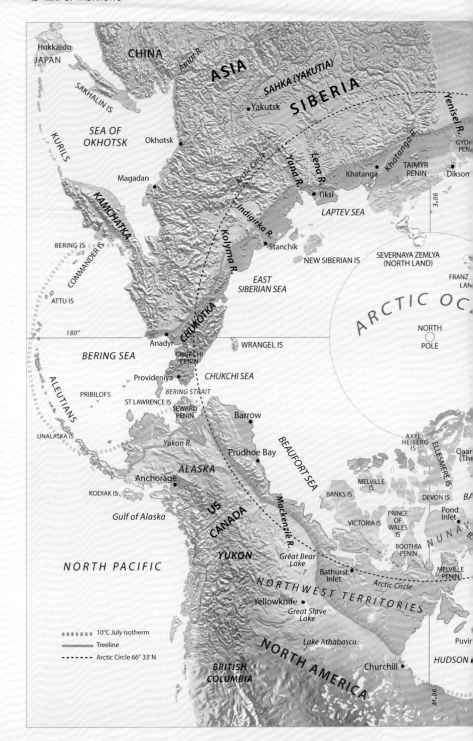

Hokkaido
JAPAN

CHINA

ASIA

SAHKA (YAKUTIA)

SIBERIA

Amur R.

SAKHALIN IS

Yakutsk

Yenisei R.

SEA OF
OKHOTSK

Okhotsk

Arctic Circle

Lena R.

Yana R.

Khatanga R.

GYDA
PEN.

Khatanga

TAIMYR
PENIN.

Dikson

90° E

Magadan

KURILS

KAMCHATKA

Indigirka R.

Tiksi

LAPTEV SEA

BERING IS

COMMANDER IS

Kolyma R.

Stanchik

NEW SIBERIAN IS

SEVERNAYA ZEMLYA
(NORTH LAND)

FRANZ
LAN

ATTU IS

EAST
SIBERIAN SEA

ARCTIC OC

180°

CHUKOTKA

Anadyr

WRANGEL IS

NORTH
POLE

BERING SEA

CHUKCHI
PENIN.

ALEUTIANS

Providentiya

CHUKCHI SEA

AXEL
HEIBERG
IS

ELLESMERE IS

Qaar
(Th

PRIBILOFS

BERING STRAIT

ST LAWRENCE IS

SEWARD
PENIN.

Barrow

BA

UNALASKA IS

Yukon R.

Prudhoe Bay

BEAUFORT SEA

MELVILLE
IS

DEVON IS

Pond
Inlet

ALASKA

Anchorage

BANKS IS

PRINCE
OF
WALES
IS

NUNAV

KODIAK IS

US

VICTORIA IS

Gulf of Alaska

CANADA

Mackenzie R.

BOOTHIA
PENIN.

MELVILLE
PENIN.

NORTH PACIFIC

YUKON

Great Bear
Lake

Bathurst
Inlet

Arctic Circle

NORTHWEST TERRITORIES

Yellowknife

Great Slave
Lake

Lake Athabasca

Puvir

┈┈┈┈┈ 10°C July isotherm

━━━━━ Treeline

╌╌╌╌╌ Arctic Circle 66° 33′N

BRITISH
COLUMBIA

NORTH AMERICA

Churchill

HUDSON

90° W

Polar Desert

Land is mostly barren and dry, with permanently frozen subsoil. Sites with more sun and moisture bear a thin cover of lichens, mosses, bryophytes, low grasses, and a few wildflowers such as saxifrages, poppies, and heaths.

Typical wildlife includes polar bears, arctic hares, lemmings, rock ptarmigans, snowy owls, and ivory gulls. Mean July temperature is 32°–37°F (0°–3°C).

High Arctic Tundra

Permafrost underlies the tundra, which bears a highly uneven cover of mosses, lichens, dwarf willows, scurvygrass, and wildflowers such as avens, saxifrage, and lousewort.

Typical wildlife includes muskoxen, arctic foxes, wolves, stoats, caribou, eiders, gyrfalcons, snow buntings, and red-throated loons. Mean July temperature is 37°–45°F (3°–7°C).

Low Arctic Tundra

Permafrost underlies the tundra, which bears a discontinuous cover of sedges, rushes, sphagnum moss, lichens, dwarf willow, dwarf birch, sorrel, crowberry, buttercups, and many other wildflowers.

Typical wildlife includes caribou, arctic ground squirrels, ravens, and a variety of nesting waders and waterfowl. Mean July temperature is 45°–54°F (7°–12°C).

Taiga/Boreal Forest

An irregular band of forest-tundra with groves of spruce, larch, pine, poplar, dwarf birch, willow, and tundra flowers occurs along the southern edge of the tundra. South of this is a parallel zone of sparse forest where tree crowns do not form a closed canopy; lichen mats and tundra vegetation make up most of the ground cover.

Farther south are closed-canopy coniferous and hardwood forests. The forests contain the greatest variety of fauna and flora, warmest soils, and longest growing season within the boreal zone.

Typical wildlife includes foxes, wolverines, lynx, moose, snowshoe hares, owls, goshawks, chickadees, tits, and woodpeckers. Mean July temperature is 54°–68°F (12°–20°C).

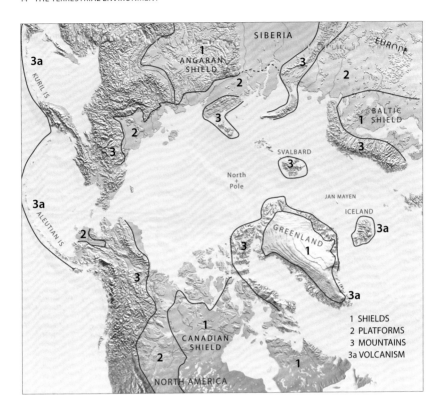

GEOMORPHIC PROVINCES

Shields, platforms, and mountains form the base of the arctic landscape. These natural features are known as geomorphic or physiomorphic provinces—large spatial entities that share common origins and geologic attributes.

Shields

Shields (1) are large, tectonically stable areas of very ancient rocks that have been exposed and leveled by erosion. The shields are composed mainly of Precambrian crystalline igneous and metamorphic rocks, which formed between 3 billion and 540 million years ago and which were largely unaffected by mountain-building episodes (orogenies).

The major shield areas of the Arctic occur in e Canada, Greenland, Scandinavia, and Siberia. The largest is the CANADIAN SHIELD, also known as the Laurentian Plateau or *Bouclier canadien*. It underlies 3,100,000 sq mi (8,000,000 sq km)

of N Amer, stretching from the Great Lakes to the Arctic Ocean, and covering over half of e Canada. The shield is an area of low relief, with most elevations below 2000 ft (610 m). Only a few isolated hills and low mountain ranges rise above this elevation. The Canadian Shield has been repeatedly uplifted and was the first part of N Amer to be permanently elevated above sea level. During the Pleistocene ice ages, glaciers depressed the land surface, scooped out thousands of lake basins, and carried away much of the region's soil. Baffin Bay separates the Canadian Shield from a similar shield area that underlies the Greenland ice sheet.

The BALTIC SHIELD occupies nw Russia and most of Scandinavia, except for the Norwegian coast. It is a very thick shield, extending 150–190 mi (250–300 km) deep into the earth. The shield contains the oldest rocks of the European continent, mostly Archean and Proterozoic gneisses and greenstones over 570 million years old, which have undergone numerous deformations due to tectonic activity. The Baltic Shield was also scoured by great continental ice sheets, which depressed the shield's surface, leaving a thin covering of glacial soils and a vast number of lakes and streams.

The exposed portion of Siberia's ANGARAN SHIELD is bounded by the Yenisei and Khatanga rivers on the west, the Lena Rvr on the east, the Arctic Ocean on the north, and Lake Baikal on the south. Its actual limits extend west to the Ural Mtns and south to the Himalayas, although this area is buried beneath sedimentary deposits.

Muskoxen on the Canadian Shield, Devon Is

Platforms: Plains and Steppes

Platforms (2) are areas where bedrock has been buried under deep glacial, alluvial, or marine deposits. They are more commonly known as plains and steppes, which occur as flat or gently rolling land in lowland areas and sometimes on high plateaus. Major platform regions include the Yukon–Kuskokwim river delta of Alaska, the plains of wc Canada, and the Siberian steppes.

Oxbow river on the plains near Alaska's Yukon Delta

Mountains

In some areas, thick sediments were uplifted and distorted by tectonic activity, producing folded mountains (3), many of which are eroded. The first orogeny occurred during the Paleozoic (570–245 mya). It produced the mountains of Canada's Queen Elizabeth islands and those of n Greenland, Svalbard, Novaya Zemlya, Severnaya Zemlya, the Taimyr Penin, and n Ural Mtns.

A second orogeny occurred later in the Mesozoic and Cenozoic. During these periods the mountains of the Russian Far East and those in Alaska's Brooks Range and the Seward Penin formed.

The Tertiary period (66–1.6 mya) was a time of igneous activity in the region. In the N Pacific, volcanic islands (3a) rose above sea level in the Aleutians and Kurils, and arc-shaped mountain belts formed in Kamchatka and parts of Alaska. Another area of igneous activity extended across the N Atlantic and produced the volcanic terrain that can be seen today in Iceland, Jan Mayen Is, and s Greenland.

Eroded folded mountains, Chukotka Penin

Volcanic bird cliffs, Bogoslof Is, Aleutians

Pond contained by permafrost, Ellesmere Is

Kettle ponds on the Canadian tundra

Trench outlining an ice-wedge polygon, Devon Is

Frost-heaved hummocks, Devon Is

PERMAFROST

Permafrost is a thick, subsurface layer of soil or sediment whose temperature has remained below 32°F (0°C) for two years or more. The term describes only the thermal condition of the ground, not its composition, which may include rock, clay, sand, silt, or ice.

Permafrost underlies about 82 percent of Alaska's land surface, 50 percent of Canada's, and much of n Siberia's. The layer ranges in depth from about 40 ft (12 m) at its southern limit to over 3300 ft (1000 m) in the higher latitudes.

Overlaying the permafrost is an *active layer* of soil about 2–13 ft (0.6–4 m) deep. The active layer freezes and thaws each year and because of this supports plant growth and other biological activities, which can take place only in soil that remains thawed for at least part of the year.

One of the main effects of permafrost is to prevent meltwater from draining away. This allows ponds and mires to form on the tundra in summer, thus providing breeding sites for migratory waterfowl and shorebirds.

The trapping of water in the soil's active layer also allows ground ice to form each winter. The annual melt-freeze cycle fosters the growth of ice lenses, which cause the ground to swell upward. Frost heaving can produce small raised earthen *hummocks* as well as large mounds of ice-cored earth, or *pingos*, which can be up to 230 ft (70 m) high and measure 2000 ft (600 m) in diameter.

Frost sorting occurs when larger rocks are heaved upward and outward, while smaller debris sinks and fills the interstices. This results in the formation of patterned ground—symmetrical geometric landforms such as stone circles, nets, stripes, and polygons.

Extensive patches of *ice-wedge polygons* are common on the tundra and are especially impressive when seen from the air. The polygons begin to take shape when the brittle, frozen soil of the active layer cracks into irregular plates resembling those of dried mud. In spring, any meltwater that trickles into the cracks is trapped by the underlying permafrost. When the water freezes in winter, the ice wedges enlarge the cracks and over time create deep, wide trenches around the polygonal plates.

GLACIAL ICE

Ice that forms from the recrystallization of fallen snow is known as *glacial ice* or *land ice.* Ice sheets, ice caps, glaciers, icebergs, and ice shelves, which develop from compacted snow, are the main examples of glacial ice.

Ice sheets cover extensive, continuous areas of land surfaces, with the ice spreading outward in many directions. The Greenland ice sheet, which covers 80 percent of the country, is the largest ice mass in the N Hemisphere. It has an average thickness of about 5000 ft (1524 m) and if melted would cause sea levels to rise more than 23 ft (7 m).

Glaciers flowing from the Ellesmere Is ice cap

Smaller, but still impressive, are the *ice caps,* domes of ice and snow that cover areas of less than 19,300 sq mi (50,000 sq km). They can be found on many mountain ranges, including those in Alaska, Canada, Norway, and Iceland.

Glaciers move ice and snow downhill from the ice caps and ice sheets. These masses of ice move under their own weight, always flowing toward the lowlands. They carry with them unsorted rock fragments called *till* or *drift,* which they deposit some distance down-ice in debris piles called *moraines.* Glaciers also move large boulders hundreds of miles from their original location. These are known as *erratic boulders,* from the Latin *errare,* "to stray."

Moraine at a retreating glacier's snout, Ellesmere is

Icebergs are large chucks of ice that break off, or calve, from glaciers that reach the sea. Icebergs are moved along the sea surface by winds and currents. One-fifth of their height and one-eighth of their volume float on the sea surface and the greater mass is submerged.

Lichen-covered erratic boulder, Devon Is

An *ice shelf* is a thick platform of ice that extends beyond the coast and floats on the sea surface. The Ward Hunt Ice Shelf on n Ellesmere Is, Canada, is the largest ice shelf in the Arctic, at 170 sq mi (440 sq km). Two huge, flat-topped *tabular bergs* broke off from the shelf in Jul–Aug 2008. One measured 1.2 × 2.5 mi (2 × 4 km), the other 4.3 × 1.2 mi (2 × 7 km). The shelf and Ward Hunt Is, which rises in the middle of the ice sheet, were named for George Ward Hunt (1825–1877), First Lord of the British Admiralty. The island is said to recall the silhouette of a recumbent Hunt, who tipped the scales at 300 lb (136 kg).

Icebergs calving from a Greenland glacier

NAME	LOCATION	AREA	MEAN DEPTH	DEEPEST POINT	NAMED AFTER
ARCTIC OCEAN	90°00′N, 0°00′E Around the North Pole Within the Arctic Circle	5,427,051 sq mi 14,056,000 sq km	3450 ft 1050 m	17,881 ft 5449 m	Arktos, the Bear constellations
BEAUFORT SEA	Arctic Ocean N of Alaska, Yukon, and the NWT	170,000 sq mi 450,000 sq km	3239 ft 1004 m	13,090 ft 3990 m	British captain Francis Beaufort (1774–1857), inventor of the Beaufort Scale for wind force
BERING SEA	N Pacific Ocean N of Aleutians E of Kamchatka W of Alaska	772,200 sq mi 2,000,000 sq km	5075 ft 1547 m	12,913 ft 3936 m	Vitus Bering (1681–1741), Danish navigator in the service of Russia
CHUKCHI SEA	Arctic Ocean N of Bering Strait E of Wrangel Is W of Pt Barrow, Alaska	230,000 sq mi 595,000 sq km	253 ft 77 m	475 ft 145 m	The Chukchi people of the Chukotka Penin, Russia
E SIBERIAN SEA	Arctic Ocean N of Siberia E of New Siberian Is W of Wrangel Is	361,000 sq mi 935,000 sq km	165 ft 50 m	510 ft 155 m	Nearest land
LAPTEV SEA	Arctic Ocean N of Siberia E of Taymir Penin W of Severnaya Zemlya	259,460 sq mi 672,000 sq km	165 ft 50 m	290 ft 88 m	Russian Arctic explorers Dmitry Laptev (1701–1771) and Khariton Laptev (1700–1763)
KARA SEA	Arctic Ocean N of Siberia E of Severnaya Zemlya W of Novaya Zemlya	340,000 sq mi 880,000 sq km	360 ft 110 m	1700 ft 519 m	Kara Rvr, a tributary river flowing from the Yamal Penin
BARENTS SEA	Arctic Ocean N of Norway and Russia SE of Svalbard SW of Franz Josef Land E of Novaya Zemlya	540,543 sq mi 1,400,000 sq km	760 ft 230 m	1480 ft 450 m	Dutch navigator Willem Barents (1550–1597)
WHITE SEA	Inlet of the Barents Sea N of nw Russia S of Kola Penin	34,750 sq mi 90,000 sq km	165 ft 50 m	1090 ft 332 m	English name may stem from 9-month ice cover
NORWEGIAN SEA	N Atlantic Ocean N of the North Sea S of Jan Mayen E of Iceland W of Norway	532,820 sq mi 1,380,000 sq km	5575 ft 1700 m	13,020 ft 3970 m	Nearest land
GREENLAND SEA	N Atlantic Ocean N of Denmark Strait SW of Svalbard E of Greenland	465,000 sq mi 1,205,000 sq km	4750 ft 1450 m	18,372 ft 5600 m	Nearest land
BAFFIN BAY	N of the N Atlantic S of the Arctic Ocean W of Greenland E of Baffin Is	30,888 sq mi 80,000 sq km	7000 ft 2100 m	7800 ft 2377 m	English navigator William Baffin (1584–1622)
LABRADOR SEA	N Atlantic Ocean S of Greenland E of Labrador	386 sq mi 1000 sq km	11,155 ft 3400 m	11,740 ft 3578 m	Nearest land
HUDSON BAY	S of the Arctic Ocean and Foxe Basin W of the N Atlantic and Hudson Strait	470,000 sq mi 1,230,000 sq km	330 ft 100 m	365 ft 111 m	English navigator Henry Hudson (1560–1611)

Sea of Okhotsk · KAMCHATKA · SIBERIA · TAYMIR PENINSULA · Kara Sea −68m · −60m · White Sea · KOLA PENINSULA · SCANDINAVIA · Laptev Sea −35m · Barents Sea −307m · EURASIAN BASIN · Nansen Basin · Gakkel Ridge · SVALBARD · Norwegian Sea −2953m · Norwegian Basin · North Sea · UK · East Siberian Sea · Siberian Shelf −53m · Amundsen Basin −4665m · −37m · Lomonosov Ridge · Makarov Basin · North Pole −4346m · −5449m Litke Deep · Greenland Sea · Bering Sea · CHUKOTKA −16m · Mendeleev Ridge · Alpha Ridge · Chukchi Sea · BERINGIA · Bering Strait −35 m · −51m · −3665m · AMERASIAN BASIN · Denmark Strait · −369m · ICELAND · ALEUTIAN ISLANDS · −3990m · Canada Basin · GREENLAND · Reykjanes Ridge · ALASKA · Beaufort Shelf · Beaufort Sea · CANADIAN ARCTIC ISLANDS · Baffin Bay −2377m · −3360m · −256m

SUBMARINE TOPOGRAPHY OF THE ARCTIC OCEAN

THE ARCTIC OCEAN

The Arctic Ocean is the body of salt water that surrounds the North Pole and lies within the Arctic Circle. It is set apart by several unique features, including a cover of perennial ice and nearly complete encirclement by the landmasses of N Amer, Eurasia, and Greenland.

The Arctic Ocean is the smallest of the world's five major oceanic divisions, covering only 2.6 percent of earth's water area. The combined area of the Arctic Ocean and its marginal seas—the Beaufort, Chukchi, East Siberian, Laptev, Kara, Barents, White, and Greenland—is about 5.4 million sq mi (14 million sq km).

The ocean's average depth is 3450 ft (1050 m), but many points on the seabed lie more than 13,000 ft (4000 m) below sea level. The deepest known point, 17,881 ft (5449 m) below sea level, is located at LITKE DEEP, an oceanic trench situated about 215 mi (350 km) north of Svalbard. Litke Deep was discovered in 1955 by the Russian icebreaker *Fyodor Litke*. The spot is named after Russian navigator, geographer, and explorer Fyodor Petrovich Litke (1797–1882), who designed the first tide gauges and had them installed on the shores of the Arctic Ocean in 1841.

UNDERSEA FEATURES

The central waters of the Arctic Ocean lie over a deep submarine depression known as the ARCTIC or NORTH POLAR BASIN. The basin is actually composed of two main basins and four smaller ones that are divided by three undersea ridges.

The LOMONOSOV RIDGE runs 1100 mi (1770 km) from the New Siberian Is to nw Greenland. It separates the two main basins, the Amerasian and Eurasian. Soviet polar expeditions discovered the ridge in 1948 and named it after Russian scientist and polymath Mikhail Vasilyevich Lomonosov (1711–1765), who was the first to explain how icebergs form.

Many of the other bottom features are named after persons having ties to arctic exploration or science. The MENDELEEV RIDGE is named for Russian chemist Dmitri Ivanovich Mendeleev (1834–1907), who formulated the periodic law, investigated the composition of petroleum, and helped to found the first oil refinery in Russia. He predicted that burning petroleum as a fuel "would be akin to firing up a kitchen stove with bank notes." GAKKEL RIDGE is named for Yakov Yakovlevich Gakkel (1901–1965), who created the first bathymetric map of the Arctic Basin.

The NANSEN (FRAM) BASIN is named after Norwegian explorer Fridtjof Nansen (1861–1930), who used a wooden-hulled ship, the *Fram*, in his 1893–1896 attempt to reach the North Pole by drifting in pack ice. AMUNDSEN BASIN honors Norwegian polar explorer Roald Amundsen (1872–1928), who was first to navigate the Northwest Passage. MAKAROV BASIN honors Russian Imperial Navy captain Stepan Makarov (1849–1904), designer and commander of the *Yermak*, the world's first icebreaker able to ride over and crash through thick sea ice.

The Arctic Basin is bordered by the CONTINENTAL SHELVES of Eurasia and N Amer. These shallowly submerged portions of the continental margins underlie nearly one-third of the Arctic Ocean's total area. The continental shelf measures less than 125 mi (200 km) wide off the coasts of N Amer and Greenland, but is 310–620 mi (500–1000 km) wide off Eurasia.

International interest in the Arctic's shelf area has steadily increased in recent decades, adding to our knowledge of the ocean floor aquatic resources, and the gas and petroleum reserves that lie beneath the continental shelves. Spurred by arctic warming and melting of the sea ice, the "Arctic Eight" (nations with land above the Arctic Circle) are investigating ways to tap into these vast reserves. The Beaufort Shelf is thought to contain at least 10 billion barrels of oil, the Chukchi Shelf 30 billion barrels, and the Siberian Shelf, the world's widest continental shelf, 80 billion barrels.

Of special note is the continental shelf area underlying the Bering and Chukchi seas. At the height of the Pleistocene ice age, about 18,000 years ago, much of the earth's water was locked in glaciers. Sea level was 100–300 ft (30–90 m) lower than it is today. Parts of the continental shelves became exposed and formed the BERING LAND BRIDGE, or BERINGIA, a name coined by the Swedish botanist Eric Hultén in 1937. The land bridge—in actuality a grassland steppe some 620 mi (1000 km) wide at its greatest extent—supported the migration of plants, animals, and humans between N Amer and Asia.

STRATIFICATION

Water stratification occurs when water masses with different salinities, temperatures, and densities form layers that act as barriers to water mixing. Water masses with the least density sit above the denser layers.

The Arctic Ocean has three strata of water. The SURFACE LAYER is about 500 ft (150 m) thick. Surface water temperature is 28.8°F (–1.8°C), which is also the freezing point of salt water. Due to freshwater inflow, this layer has a fairly low salinity of 32‰ (32 parts of salt per 1000 of water). Fresh water enters the Arctic Ocean from many sources, but Canada's Mackenzie Rvr and the Ob, Yenisei, and Lena rivers in Siberia are the main contributors.

An INTERMEDIATE LAYER of warmer (1–3°C) and saltier (34‰) water lies below the surface layer and extends down to 3000 ft (900 m). Finally, extending to the ocean floor, is a BOTTOM LAYER of very dense, cold (–0.5°C) water with a high salinity (35‰).

CIRCULATION AND CURRENTS

Arctic surface water circulates in large rotational patterns known as *gyres*, which occur as a result of directional winds and surface currents. In the N Amer sector, a strong surface current and the BEAUFORT GYRE drive the water and ice in a clockwise direction. In the Eurasian sector, the pack moves in a counterclockwise direction in response to currents and the BARENTS GYRE, which push the surface water eastward where it is expelled in the East Greenland Current.

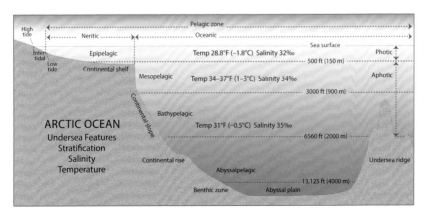

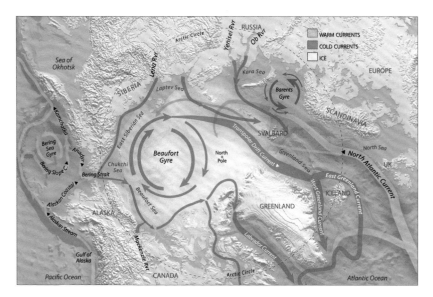

Warm water inflow to the Arctic Ocean comes mainly via the N ATLANTIC CURRENT, which carries warm water from the N Amer coast across the Atlantic and into the Arctic Ocean. When the flow reaches Svalbard, the saltier, heavier Atlantic waters dive down under the surface waters of the Arctic Basin. Waters cascade down the slope of the Eurasian Basin and mix with the colder waters until a succession of subsea basins gradually turns the waters toward the Norwegian Basin and Greenland Sea, where they are discharged back into the N Atlantic Ocean.

The Arctic Ocean also receives a lesser volume of warm water from the Bering Sea and Pacific Ocean via the Bering Strait. Waters passing through the strait are driven by the BERING SEA GYRE. The inflow of warm surface water is limited because it must flow over a sill only 130 ft (40 m) from the surface. The shallow sill also prohibits most outflow of water back into the Bering Sea and N Pacific Ocean.

POLAR MARINE HABITATS

Areas where waters of the Arctic Ocean mix with warmer waters of the N Pacific and N Atlantic are rich in marine organisms and support great numbers of marine mammals and seabirds. In the Atlantic sector, these areas of high marine productivity occur from Baffin Bay, Labrador,

and Newfoundland to the Kara Sea and Novaya Zemlya in Russia. In the Pacific sector, the area from Wrangel Is and the Chukotka Penin to the north coast of Alaska also has abundant marine fauna. The cover of sea ice is seasonal in this zone rather than permanent.

In contrast, a biological barrens with low species diversity occurs in waters that lie over the Arctic Basin and those that flow around e Greenland and the Canadian Arctic islands. The persistent cover of sea ice in this area inhibits the growth of plankton and other small marine organisms at the base of the food chain by filtering out sunlight needed for their growth.

However, even here, marine productivity can be found in places where the ice pack has broken up or fractured into *leads* and where large, fairly permanent areas of open water called *polynyas* exist. Polynyas (Russian for "ice holes") occur in places where warm-water upwellings keep the surface water temperature at or above the freezing point. Those such as the North Water Polynya between Canada and Greenland occur at the same time and place each year. They offer a winter refuge for marine mammals and seabirds, and in spring the broken ice cover allows light in, triggering the early blooming of phytoplankton and zooplankton, which are at the base of the marine food chain.

Grease ice with floating ice lumps called *shuga*

Plates of pancake ice formed by swell and wave action

Polar bear on a small ice floe near Wrangel Is, Russia

The *Fedor Matison* at a pressure ridge near Wrangel Is

SEA ICE

Sea ice is frozen ocean water. This is in contrast to icebergs and ice shelves, which float on the ocean but develop from fresh water or snow.

A more or less permanent cover of perennial, or *multi-year,* sea ice occurs on waters above 75°N latitude. Multi-year ice, which has survived at least one summer melting season, has a characteristic thickness of 12–30 ft (4–9 m) and has a much lower salinity than newly formed ice. This is because brine trapped between the ice crystals gradually leaches out through tunnels in the ice. These brine-filled channels serve as a home for microalgae, diatoms, ice worms, small crustaceans, and other zooplankton. As the ice melts in spring, these tiny organisms are released into the surrounding water, where they become food for fish and krill, which in turn feed seabirds and marine mammals.

The ice pack that occurs between 65° and 75°N is composed mostly of annual, or *first-year ice.* It is present only in winter and melts away in spring. First-year ice begins to appear almost as soon as the arctic summer is over. The ice forms outward from the land and by late fall it has expanded to cover almost the entire surface of the Arctic Ocean.

New sea ice begins to form when the ambient temperature drops to about 28.5°F (–1.9°C). A thick layer of free-floating ice crystals, or *frazil ice,* forms on the ocean surface. This congeals into a gelatinous slush called *grease ice,* which may contain frothy white ice clumps called *shuga.*

If waves are present when grease ice begins to solidify, ice crystals are pushed up onto the rims of nascent ice plates, resulting in the formation of *pancake ice*—flat plates of ice with upturned edges. In calm seas, grease ice solidifies into thin, unbroken sheets of ice, or *nilas,* that eventually form a solid layer of *new ice* up to 6 ft (2 m) thick.

Sea ice that is attached to the coastline or grounded icebergs is called *fast ice.* This is in contrast to *drift ice,* which occurs in areas of open water and which moves freely with the currents and wind. The two are known collectively as *pack ice* or the *ice pack.* Pack ice is a mixture of ice fragments of varying size and age that are squeezed together and cover the sea surface with little or no open water. The density of the pack ice is measured by using tenths to indicate ice density and the amount of visible open water. The scale ranges from open water with little pack ice (¹⁄₁₀ to ³⁄₁₀) to continuous pack ice (¹⁰⁄₁₀ or Pack 10).

Pack ice contains blocks of free-floating sea ice called *ice floes*. Floes can be quite small or extremely large, ranging from small floes that are 60 ft (18 m) across to giant floes called *ice fields*, which are more than 6 mi (10 km) wide. Arctic hunters often travel out onto the floe edge where the ice meets open water, as it is the best place for finding eider ducks, fish, seals, and narwhals. But this is also a dangerous place to be in spring, because the ice edge can suddenly fracture and set people adrift as the ice floe is carried out to sea.

Currents and strong winds can pile the floes into *pressure ridges* several feet in height. These are a formidable barrier to ships because, like icebergs, pressure ridges extend downward much farther than they rise above the sea surface. What appears to be a low ridge of ice is more likely to be an underwater wall that could stop even an icebreaker dead in the water.

The arctic sea ice typically reaches its maximum extent in March. The surface of the ice becomes covered with interlocking patterns of snow, ice, and turquoise blue meltwater pools. Soon after, long linear cracks, or *leads*, begin to open in the sea ice.

Both the thickness and extent of the Arctic's summer sea ice have shown a dramatic decline over the past 30 years. Multi-year ice is disappearing at a rate of 9 percent per decade, and researchers are seeing a greater proportion of thin, newly formed ice. The loss of arctic sea ice has myriad consequences, including threatening habitat for species like polar bears and undermining traditional hunting methods. But one of the most troubling effects involves the overall impact of this change on the arctic climate. If there is less arctic sea ice, then more dark ocean surface is exposed and less sunlight is reflected back into space. More sunlight is absorbed, which causes still more warming, more ice melting, and more exposed ocean.

Leads opening in sea ice near Resolute Bay, Canada

Patterns of ice and shallow meltwater in late spring

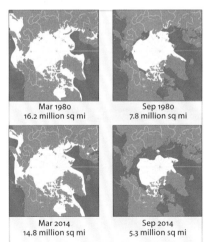

Mar 1980
16.2 million sq mi

Sep 1980
7.8 million sq mi

Mar 2014
14.8 million sq mi

Sep 2014
5.3 million sq mi

Maps redrawn from the US National Snow and Ice Data Center compare the extent of arctic sea ice in 1980 and 2014. They show a significant reduction in the summer ice cover over the 24-year period. Why is the ice melting? Sea ice has a bright surface and reflects 80 percent of the sunlight back into space. As sea ice melts in summer, it exposes the dark ocean surface. Instead of reflecting sunlight, the dark surface absorbs 90 percent of the sunlight, the ocean heats up, and arctic temperatures rise further.

SUNDOGS

Sundogs, also known as mock suns or *parhelia*, are brightly colored spots that appear on either side of the sun. They form when sunlight is refracted by hexagonal, plate-like ice crystals. Sundogs are visible when the sun lies 15–20° above the horizon and is on the same horizontal plane as the observer and the ice crystals. As sunlight passes through the ice crystals, it is bent by 22° before reaching our eyes, and this bending of light results in the formation of a sundog; the photo shown below was taken near Pond Inlet, Baffin Is, on a late afternoon in May.

AURORA BOREALIS

The *aurora borealis* (northern lights) is a show of curtains, arcs, rays, bands and fan-shaped coronas of light that appears in the northern night sky. It occurs most frequently in winter around 70°N latitude. In 1621 the French scientist Pierre Gassendi named the lights after the mythical dawn goddess Aurora. The aurora develops from light emitted from the upper atmosphere in a form similar to an electrical discharge. The green or reddish glow is caused

Aurora borealis over Devon Is

Sundog over Eclipse Sound, Baffin Is

when atoms in the thin upper atmosphere are bombarded by fast-moving electrons and protons. The magnetosphere—a cavity within the earth's magnetic field that contains Van Allen radiation belts—acts like a giant television tube, broadcasting the aurora image onto the "screen" of the upper atmosphere. A more poetic interpretation of the aurora comes from the Inuit, who say that the lights are *kikuyat*, the dance fires of ghosts.

FATA MORGANA (MIRAGE)

Fata Morgana was a fairy enchantress who sometimes made her undersea castle appear on a shoreline, luring seamen to what they thought was a safe harbor. Her name is given to an optical illusion, or mirage, that makes solid, well-defined coastal features appear where there are none. Distant objects are distorted and stretched vertically, or a flat shoreline may appear to have tall cliffs. A Fata Morgana occurs when alternating warm and cold layers of air near the ground or water surface cause light to be bent toward the colder, denser air above. The result can be a distorted light path and an image of a distant object that is, in fact, not there.

In 1818, on a voyage attempting to discover the Northwest Passage, British naval officer and Arctic explorer Sir John Ross (1777–1856), reached Lancaster Sound in Canada, where he encountered a Fata Morgana that showed mountains blocking his passage west. He wrote, "I distinctly saw the land, round the bottom of the bay, forming a connected chain of mountains with those which extended along the north and south sides." Ross named the illusory mountain range after Sir John Wilson Croker, First Secretary of the British Admiralty. He then turned his fleet of ships back to England despite the protests of William Edward Parry (1790–1855) and several other of his officers, who encouraged Ross to further explore the "Croker Mountains." The following year Parry was given command of an expedition on the *HMS Hecla*, on which he entered and successfully traversed Lancaster Sound, proving that the sound was indeed the long-sought-after eastern entry to the Northwest Passage.

ALL MAMMALS, from humans to lemmings to muskoxen to whales, share certain physical features. All mammals possess modified sweat glands called mammary glands, which in a female can produce milk. All have body hair, at least at the beginning of their lives, and all have a four-chambered heart, single-boned lower jaw, and a middle ear composed of three bones.

Arctic mammals are warm-blooded, or *endothermic*, creatures. They are able to maintain a constant body temperature despite changing climatic conditions. Their core body temperatures range from 97.7°F to 105°F (36.5°C–40.5°C), this despite the fact that marine species live in seawater of 28°F (−2°C) and land mammals experience winter temperatures averaging −33°F (−36°C).

Most of the northern mammals have developed well-insulated, compact bodies with short appendages, which minimize heat loss and conserve body heat. Mammals that spend most of their time in water usually have a thick layer of *blubber*—a subcutaneous sheet of fat, collagen, and elastin—that sheathes the vital organs, increases buoyancy, and acts as an energy reservoir during periods of fasting.

Terrestrial mammals typically have a dense coat of *fur*. Many have fur on both the upper and lower surfaces of the feet and have a double coat of fur that becomes heavier in winter. Air trapped between the dense inner coat and the outer layer of coarse, long guard hairs provides excellent insulation.

Some marine mammals also have fur for insulation. Sea otters have the greatest hair density of any mammal, ranging from 170,000 to more than 1 million hairs per sq in (26,000–165,000 hairs per sq cm). The highest hair density occurs on the forearms, sides, and rump, the lowest on the chest, legs, and feet. Polar bears have a double coat of fur, which is backed by a 4.5 in (11 cm) layer of fat.

Arctic mammals, particularly pinnipeds, have a complex circulatory system called *countercurrent heat exchange,* which minimizes heat loss to the surroundings and also prevents overheating. In this system, each artery carrying warm blood from the body core is surrounded by a network of veins. Warmth transferred from the arterial to the venous blood is carried back into the body rather than being dissipated into the air.

To prevent excessive heat loss from bare or lengthy body parts, pinnipeds, caribou, and beavers maintain two internal temperatures—a high body core temperature and a much cooler temperature in the flippers, legs, or tail, respectively. This is known as *regional heterothermy,* which is made possible through heat exchangers that shunt cooled blood to the extremities before returning it to be warmed in the countercurrent system.

Walruses have a similar heat-exchange mechanism that controls blood flow to the skin capillaries. When a walrus is warm, heat exchangers shunt blood to the skin, where it is air-cooled. The skin becomes flushed with blood, and the walrus acquires a rosy-red color. When a walrus is submerged in cold water, blood flow to the epidermis is reduced, the capillaries contract, the skin pales, and heat loss to the environment is minimized.

Mammals also alter their *behavior* in response to oncoming winter. Many marine mammals migrate south of the ice pack, some to subtropical waters, while others congregate around open areas in the sea ice (polynyas) where food is available. Caribou and sheep move to lower elevations, forested areas, or places with little snow cover in a response to food availability. Many of the smaller mammals such as lemmings and voles have adapted to living and sometimes breeding under the winter snow where they are sheltered from the cold and wind, and where food in the form of seeds and shoots can be found.

Surprisingly few of the arctic mammals hibernate—a condition characterized by low body temperature, slow breathing and heart rate, and low metabolic rate. The only arctic mammals to enter this form of deep winter sleep are arctic ground squirrels, marmots, chipmunks, American black bears, brown bears, and pregnant polar bears. Male and non-breeding female polar bears remain active in winter and "nap" now and then in shallow pits they dig into the snow.

Soricomorpha: Insectivores

Soricomorpha encompasses insect-eating mammals such as shrews, moles, and soledons. These small animals are the descendants of the first primitive placental mammals and are the predecessors of all other placental mammals. The earliest known fossils of shrews date back to 130 million years ago.

FAMILY SORICIDAE
SHREWS

These mouse-like insectivores originated in Europe and later spread throughout Africa, Asia, and the Americas.

The northern species are part of a group known as red-toothed shrews, owing to the presence of reddish-brown teeth. The color comes from iron pigments in the diet, which are deposited in the tooth enamel. Iron serves to harden the tips of the teeth, the parts most subject to wear. Unlike rodents, which have gnawing incisors that grow throughout life, the teeth of shrews are permanent and wear down throughout life. When the teeth are completely worn, a shrew starves to death—a factor contributing to shrews' lifespan of less than 2 years.

Shrews feed on insects, spiders, seeds, nuts, worms, and carrion, and will also attack and eat mice and frogs several times their own weight. Some species specialize in climbing trees, living underground, living under snow, or even hunting in water. Those that forage underground or in dark places rely on touch, smell, hearing, and echolocation to find their prey.

These insectivores have an extremely high metabolic rate and need to consume at least 90 percent of their body weight each day in order to survive. They have to eat every 2–3 hours, day and night, to achieve this goal. The digestive tract is short, and food passes through it without being completely processed. For this reason, shrews ingest their feces to recover nutrients.

Most shrews are active year round. They do not hibernate, but are capable of entering torpor in winter, during which time they can lose from 30 to 50 percent of their body weight, shrinking the size of bones, skull, and internal organs. These small animals are solitary in nature and very territorial. If a shrew enters the home range of another, one will kill and eat the other. They seem to tolerate another's presence only when breeding. Nests are usually made of finely shredded vegetation, and are set in a burrow or rotted log. Gestation lasts 2–3 weeks. The young are nursed for about 3 weeks. Litter size is 4–9 young, with up to 4 litters produced annually.

GENUS *SOREX*: The genus *Sorex* encompasses the long-tailed shrews, which inhabit the boreal forests and, more rarely, the arctic tundra. The genus contains some of the world's smallest mammals. Most species weigh less than 1 oz (28g) and measure less than 5 in (13 cm) from nose to tail tip. The skull is long, narrow, and extremely small, as can be seen here by the skull of a Dusky Shrew juxtaposed next to a US penny. The snout is long, pointed, and mobile. The small ears and beady eyes are almost hidden by facial fur. The feet are plantigrade (i.e., the full length of the foot is placed on the ground) and there are 5 toes on each foot.

Cinereus Shrew
Sorex cinereus

ALSO: American Masked Shrew, Amerikanische Maskenspitmaus, Musaraigne cendrée, Krattspissmus, Масковая бурозубка. Formerly conspecific with the ST LAWRENCE IS SHREW, *S. jacksoni,* and BARREN-GROUND SHREW, *S. ugyunak.* SN means "ashy gray shrew."

RANGE: Found from Alaska to Labrador and Newfoundland, and south to 45° N, in dense leaf litter and around fallen logs in moist deciduous and evergreen forests.

ID: L 3.5–5 in (9–13 cm). WT 0.1–0.25 oz (3–7 g). Dark brown to brownish gray on the back, with pale gray underparts. Bicolored tail.

HABITS: Active day and night, all year. Mostly terrestrial, but can swim well. Feeds on conifer

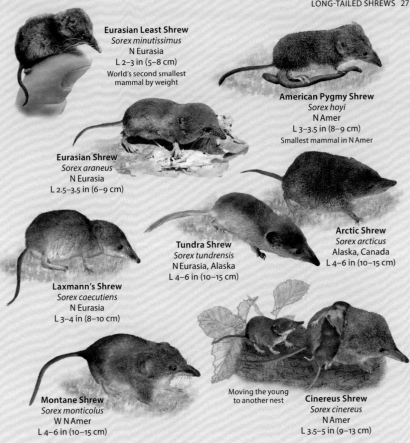

Eurasian Least Shrew
Sorex minutissimus
N Eurasia
L 2–3 in (5–8 cm)
World's second smallest
mammal by weight

American Pygmy Shrew
Sorex hoyi
N Amer
L 3–3.5 in (8–9 cm)
Smallest mammal in N Amer

Eurasian Shrew
Sorex araneus
N Eurasia
L 2.5–3.5 in (6–9 cm)

Arctic Shrew
Sorex arcticus
Alaska, Canada
L 4–6 in (10–15 cm)

Tundra Shrew
Sorex tundrensis
N Eurasia, Alaska
L 4–6 in (10–15 cm)

Laxmann's Shrew
Sorex caecutiens
N Eurasia
L 3–4 in (8–10 cm)

Montane Shrew
Sorex monticolus
W N Amer
L 4–6 in (10–15 cm)

Moving the young
to another nest

Cinereus Shrew
Sorex cinereus
N Amer
L 3.5–5 in (9–13 cm)

seeds, salamanders, mice, and invertebrates, including sawflies (*Pristiphora erichsonii*) whose larvae can defoliate a conifer. Builds a spherical nest of dry vegetation. The mother moves her young if the nest is disturbed. She carries one in her mouth, while others grasp her rump fur or tail, or the tail of the sibling in front of them.

American Pygmy Shrew
Sorex hoyi

ALSO: Zwergspitzmaus, Musaraigne pygmée, Бурозубка-крошк. Smallest mammal in N Amer and one of the smallest in the world by weight; adults weigh about the same as a US dime. SN means "Hoy's shrew," named after naturalist Philo Romayne Hoy (1816–1892), who aided Spencer Baird of the Smithsonian in investigating the fauna of Racine, Wisconsin.

RANGE: Occurs in Canada and Alaska, south to Appalachia and Rocky Mtns, in boreal forests, swamps, grassy clearings, bogs, and floodplains . **ID:** L 3–3.5 in (8–9 cm). WT 0.07–0.25 oz (2–7 g). Grayish brown above, pale gray below. Exudes a strong musky smell.
HABITS: Lives in areas of sphagnum moss, leaf litter, root systems, and stumps. Burrows and forages underground, often in mammal burrows. Very agile; can jump as high as 5 in (13 cm), almost twice its body length.

Montane Shrew
Sorex monticolus
ALSO: Dusky Shrew, Dunkle Rotzahn-spitzmaus, Musaraigne sombre, Горная бурозубка. SN means "mountain shrew."
RANGE: Occurs in Alaska and w Canada, and

south to w US in tundra, alpine meadows, forests, and prairies with dense ground cover.
ID: L 4–6 in (10–15 cm). WT 0.2–0.35 oz (5–10 g). Brown to reddish brown upperparts. Gray or silvery underparts. Tail indistinctly bicolored, dark above, paler below. Feet light brown.
HABITS: Forages in damp ground along streams and rivers. Nests in summer in stumps, under logs, and beneath forest litter.

Arctic Shrew

Sorex arcticus
ALSO: Saddleback Shrew, Musaraigne arctique, Арктическая бурозубка. SN means "Arctic-dwelling shrew."
RANGE: Occurs in Alaska and Canada, and south to nc US in grassy clearings in coniferous forests, at edges of tamarack and spruce bogs, and at edges of marshes in tangled vegetation.
ID: L 4–6 in (10–15 cm). WT 0.2–0.5 oz (5.5–14 g). Tricolored pelage; very dark brown to black above, lighter brown sides, and pale grayish brown underparts. Long, bicolored tail.
HABITS: Climbs trees. Clears its own runways and uses those of other small mammals. Forages in short bursts of activity, mainly at

night, followed by periods of rest. Feeds mainly on insects, including sawflies (*Pristiphora erichsonii*) whose larvae feed on and defoliate boreal conifers.

Tundra Shrew

Sorex tundrensis
ALSO: Tundra Rotzahn-spitzmaus, Тундровая бурозубка, *Sorex arcticus tundrensis*. SN means "tundra-dwelling shrew."
RANGE: Occurs from w Russia to Chukotka, south to Mongolia and ne China, and from Sakhalin Is east to the Aleutians, Alaskan mainland and Yukon, in riparian meadows with dense vegetation of willows, shrubs, and grasses, and in burned areas and overgrown thickets.
ID: L 4–6 in (10–15 cm). WT 0.2–0.4 oz (5–10 g). Tricolored (summer): dark brown upperparts,

grayish brown flanks, pale gray below. Bicolored (winter): dark brown above, pale gray below.
HABITS: Frequents hillsides with shrubs or grassy vegetation or dry ridges near marshes or bogs. Active day and night year round, burrowing through the snow in winter. Nests under a log or in a rock crevice. Feeds on beetles, earthworms, and flowers of low grasses.
SIMILAR SPECIES: PRIBILOF IS SHREW, *Sorex pribilofensis*, is found only on St Paul Is.

Eurasian Shrew

Sorex araneus
ALSO: Common Shrew, Waldspitzmaus, Musaraigne carrelet, Vanlig spissmus, Обыкновенная бурозубка. SN means "spider [-eating] shrew."
RANGE: Occurs from the UK and Scandinavia to the Kola Penin, White Sea, and Lake Baikal in Siberia in woodlands, grasslands, and hedges.
ID: L 2.5–3.5 in (6–9 cm). WT 0.2–0.4 oz (5–12 g). Grayish brown to velvety dark brown back; pale underparts.
HABITS: Feeds on insects, slugs, spiders, worms, and carrion. Agile climber. Extremely territorial and becomes aggressive when another shrew enters its home range. Builds its nest underground or under dense vegetation.

Eurasian Least Shrew

Sorex minutissimus
ALSO: Lesser Pygmy Shrew, Knirpsspitzmaus, Musara-igne naine, Knøttspissmus, Крошечная бурозубка. World's second smallest mammal by weight after the Etruscan Shrew, *Suncus etruscus*. SN means "smallest shrew."
RANGE: Occurs from n Europe across Siberia to Sakhalin, Kamchatka, and ne Asia, in forests, open fields, and edges of bogs.
ID: L 2–3 in (5–8 cm). WT 0.05–0.1 oz (1.5–3 g). Back chocolate brown (summer) to light brown (winter). Pale gray underside is separated by grayish brown flanks. Bicolored tail, dark above, paler below, with a dark brown tuft at the tip. Feet pale gray, with brown heels.
HABITS: Swims well. Excellent climber.

Laxmann's Shrew

Sorex caecutiens

ALSO: Masked Shrew, Lapplandspitmaus, Musaraigne masquée, Бурозубка Средняя. SN means "nearly blind shrew."

RANGE: Occurs across Eurasia in lowland and montane taiga, occasionally on tundra, in places with abundant berry bushes and small trees, and especially along the edges of swamps and streams.

ID: L 3–4 in (8–10 cm). WT 0.1–0.25 oz (3–7 g). Dark golden brown above, with contrasting silvery-white underparts. White feet with silvery hairs. Tail brown, with tufted tip.

HABITS: Feeds on beetles, spiders, millipedes, earthworms, and seeds of conifers.

Rodentia: Rodents

Rodents have 16 teeth, with a single pair of upper and lower incisors, and a *diastema* (a wide space without teeth) between the incisors and molars. The continuously growing incisor teeth must regularly be used for gnawing to keep them worn down and sharp. Many rodents are *fossorial* (burrowing) animals. Species that spend most of their lives underground tend to have small ears, small eyes, a short tail, and strong claws on the front feet. Those that live in burrows, and forage extensively on the surface, tend to have larger ears and longer tails. Some species are adapted to climbing trees and rocks; others are specialized for aquatic environments.

FAMILY SCIURIDAE
SQUIRRELS, MARMOTS, AND ALLIES

Sciuridae means "shadow-tail," referring to the bushy tail many members of this family possess. Sciurids occur on all continents except Australia and Antarctica. The family includes marmots, ground squirrels, tree squirrels, and flying squirrels. Most species have slender bodies and soft, silky fur. The hind limbs are generally longer than the forelimbs, and there are 4 or 5 toes on each foot. Sciurids have large eyes and excellent vision. They use their large incisors for gnawing on food items such as nuts, seeds, and occasionally insects and small vertebrates.

SUBFAMILY XERINAE: TRIBE MARMOTINI
GROUND SQUIRRELS

Xerinae is a subfamily of mostly terrestrial squirrels, which tend to live in colonies that have complex social structure. The largely Holarctic tribe Marmotini includes the marmots, ground squirrels, and chipmunks.

GENUS *MARMOTA*: Marmot and *Marmota* derive from the Latin *mures montani* and the Old French *marmontaine*, both meaning "mountain mouse."

Marmots are large, diurnal ground squirrels. They have a heavy body, short neck, bushy tail, and strong legs and feet. The thumbs of the forelimbs have a flattened nail instead of a claw. All the other digits have strong claws well suited to digging. The sharp, chisel-like incisors grow throughout life.

Marmots typically live in and hibernate in communal burrows. They dig summer burrows in rock fields lying adjacent to meadows where the marmots can forage for the flowers, leaves, and roots of forbs and grasses. These items are low in nutritional value, so marmots must consume large quantities in order to lay down enough body fat to sustain them for the long months of hibernation.

The rocks around the burrows protect them from wolverines, wolves, bears, and foxes, which find it difficult to dig in the stony soil. They also provide a spot where marmot sentries can watch for potential danger from eagles and other predators. Sentry duty rotates among individuals, assuring that each marmot will have equal time to forage. Sentries alert the colony by sounding a shrill whistle when they spot a potential predator. It has been observed that wolverines, wolves, bears, and eagles elicit an alarm call, while the sentries usually ignore the approach of caribou or sheep.

Alaska and black-capped marmots spend up to nine months in a special winter burrow called a *hibernaculum* that they dig into the permafrost soil of alpine terraces. Before hibernating, the marmot family piles earth on top of the burrow and plugs the entry hole and any cracks with an adobe-like mixture of soil and grass. This effectively closes off the chamber from the cold. The marmots huddle together for social thermoregulation as the heart and respiratory rates slow, metabolic activity declines, and the body temperature drops to below 45°F (7°C). The marmots have short periods of arousal, awakening for a few hours every 3–4 weeks to urinate, defecate, and allow the body to revitalize organs, tissues, and cells. During one of the spring arousals, the marmots mate, then fall back into a torpor until the young are born about 5 weeks later. The 3–11 pups are born naked, toothless, and with their eyes closed. By 6 weeks of age, they are independent enough to explore outside the den, at which point both sexes interact with the young.

Alaska Marmot
Marmota broweri
ALSO: Brooks Range Marmot, Arctic Marmot, Browers, Sikvikpuk,

Alaska-Murmeltier, Marmotte, Marmota, Murmeldyr, Сурки. Formerly considered a subspecies of the more southerly Hoary Marmot, *M. caligata*. SN means "Brower's marmot." Alaska celebrates Feb 2 as "Marmot Day," a substitute for Groundhog Day.
RANGE: Occurs from Brooks Range in n Alaska to the Alaska-Yukon border in boulder fields and rock slides; 3250–4000 ft (990–1220 m).
ID: L 21–27 in (54–67 cm). WT 5.5–8 lb (2.5–4 kg). Coarse, blackish fur covers the top of the head and the nose. Rest of fur is grizzled gray to brown, with a light-and-dark banding pattern on the dorsal guard hairs. Broad tail is brown with a black tip. Separated from the Hoary Marmot by its darker face and rump, and lack of a light patch on the snout.
HABITS: Lives in colonies of up to 50 animals in burrows dug in alpine boulder fields. Marmots are active until the first snowfalls in late Aug, when each family retires to its hibernaculum. Mating takes place in early spring within the hibernation burrow. Sexual activity is stimulated by odors from the anal scent glands of both sexes. Prior to giving birth, the female closes off her birthing den and gives birth alone.

USE: Early Native Americans hunted or caught marmots in rock fall traps. They were harvested for meat, and more often for their pelts, 20 of which would be sewn together to make a parka.

Black-capped Marmot
Marmota camtschatica
ALSO: Schwarzhut Murmeltier, Marmotte, Murmeldyr, Камчатский сурок. SN

means "Kamchatka marmot."
RANGE: Geographically isolated populations occur in Siberia, from Lake Baikal to Kamchatka, in alpine tundra, tundra-steppe, and open larch forest; 3550–6550 ft (1200–2000 m).
ID: L 21–29 in (54–73 cm). WT 9–17.5 lb (4–8 kg). Crown, nape, and upper face are black. Pale ring of fur around the large eyes. Rest of the coat is a grizzled mix of black, gray, ochre, and rusty tones. Outer layer of black-tipped guard hairs covers the dense undercoat.
HABITS: Forms family groups of 10–15 individuals containing one breeding pair, a few subordinate adults, yearlings, and young. Digs summer burrows in rock fields lying adjacent to meadows where the marmots can forage. Maze of tunnels, each of which has many entry holes, can reach a total length of 230 ft (70 m). The family enters a shallow hibernaculum dug into the permafrost as winter approaches. Hibernation lasts roughly Sep–May. Mating takes place in the burrow.
STATUS: Until the 1950s, when they became protected by law, marmots were hunted in Russia for their meat, fur, and fat. Lifespan is 5 years in the wild, 14 years in captivity.

GENUS *SPERMOPHILUS*
Arctic Ground Squirrel
Spermophilus parryii
ALSO: Parka Squirrel, Arktische Ziesel, Écureuil

terrestre arctique, Суслик арктический; local names Siksik and Souslik refer to the species' call, *tsik-tsik*. SN means "Parry's lover of seeds," a name bestowed by Scotch naturalist John Richardson (1787–1865) to honor Arctic explorer William Edward Parry (1790–1855).
RANGE: Occurs from ne Yakutia to Chukotka

Siberian Flying Squirrel
Pteromys volans
Eurasia
L 10–13 in (25–33 cm)

Northern Flying Squirrel
Glaucomys sabrinus
N N Amer
L 10–15 in (25–38 cm)

Siberian Chipmunk
Eutamias sibiricus
Eurasia
8–14 in (20–36 cm)

American Red Squirrel
Tamiasciurus hudsonicus
N Amer
L 11–13 in (28–33 cm)

Black
morph

Red squirrel
in summer

Silvery winter pelage
Note tufted ears

Eurasian Red Squirrel
Sciurus vulgaris
Eurasia
L 13–17 in (33–43 cm)

Arctic Ground Squirrel
Spermophilus parryii
NE Russia, Alaska, Canada
13–20 in (33–50 cm)

Black-capped Marmot
Marmota camtschatica
NE Russia
L 21–29 in (54–73 cm)

Alaska Marmot
Marmota broweri
N Alaska, Yukon
L 21–27 in (54–67 cm)

in Russia, and across Alaska and nw Canada on arctic tundra and subarctic meadows.

ID: L 13–20 in (33–50 cm). WT 25–28 oz (700–800 g). Elongated body, with a dark brushy tail, large eyes, small ears, cheek pouches, and strong claws suited for burrowing. Pale yellowish brown and tan coat, with diffuse white spots on the back and white markings around the eyes.

HABITS: Forms colonies of 5–50 individuals dominated by a male that marks his territory with scent from glands located on the cheeks and back. Digs communal burrows in dry, vegetated tundra where permafrost lies deep below the soil surface. A sentry will sound a chattering *tsik-tsik* or piercing whistle to alert the colony to danger. Either vocalization causes other siksiks to pop their heads out of the burrow entrances. After one or two "emergency drills" and no perceived imminent threat, the squirrels emerge from their burrows to go about their normal activities.

Feeds on the roots, stalks, leaves, flowers, and seeds of grasses, sedges, willows, forbs, and mushrooms. Also known to be cannibalistic. Forages at midday, and often stuffs the cheek pouches full of food to take back to the burrow for later consumption. With little cover in their habitat, arctic ground squirrels make themselves less obvious to predators by running with their bodies pressed close to the ground in the so-called "tundra glide."

Arctic ground squirrels retire to special hibernation burrows Sep–Apr. They are perhaps the only known warm-blooded animals to use supercooling of the body fluids to survive a freezing hibernation environment. The mechanism is not fully understood, but during hibernation these animals are able to keep their brain, thoracic, and abdominal cavities at temperatures slightly above freezing, while letting the peripheral and colonic areas fall to slightly below freezing—all without triggering an ice nucleator, which would induce crystal-lization and cause the squirrel to freeze solid.

Mating takes place in the hibernation burrow in mid-May. Gestation is about 25 days. Five to 10 blind, hairless pups are born in June. Pups are weaned in about 6 weeks.

GENUS *EUTAMIAS*
Siberian Chipmunk

Eutamias sibiricus

ALSO: Asiatisches Streifen-hörnchen, Tamia de Sibérie, Сибирский бурундук. SN means "Siberian treasurer," referring to the habit of caching food.

RANGE: Occurs mainly in understory of larch and Scots pine forests from n Europe to Sahkalin, Kamchatka, and Kurils, and south to nc Asia. Introduced or escaped from captivity and now feral in wooded town parks in Austria, Germany, France, Holland, and Italy. Only member of its genus found outside N Amer.

ID: L 8–14 in (20–36 cm). WT 2–3.5 oz (50–100 g). Bright russet to brownish ochre coat, with 4 light and 5 dark longitudinal stripes on the back. Light brown tail, with narrow white edges and broad black lines on the sides.

HABITS: Most active in the morning. Mainly terrestrial but is an agile climber. Vocalizations include an alarm call of repetitive *cheeps* reminiscent of a bird's call, and a soft, deep croaking sound related to courtship. Feeds on pine nuts, seeds, young plant shoots and leaves, cloudberry, mushrooms, grain crops, and occasionally insects and young birds. Stores food in late summer, carrying nuts and seeds in its cheek pouches and burying them about 2 in (5 cm) underground. Hibernates in winter in burrows dug near tree roots. Both sexes mature at about 1 year of age. Mates in late Apr, shortly after awakening from hibernation. Gestation is about 5 weeks. One to 2 litters of 4–6 young are born each year. Young are nursed for 40 days. Maximum lifespan is 10 years.

STATUS: Threatened (IUCN).

SUBFAMILY SCIURINAE: TRIBE SCIURINI
TREE SQUIRRELS

Tree squirrels spend little time on the ground, preferring to live in the tree canopy. Sharp, curved claws aid in tree climbing. Their strong hind legs enable them to leap between trees and also to swim well. These slender-bodied rodents have a long bushy tail that helps them to balance when running along branches and to steer when jumping from tree to tree. Tree squirrels wrap their tail around them to keep warm when sleeping, and also arc it over their back and head when feeding, sometimes using it as a foil to detract aerial predators.

GENUS *SCIURUS*
Eurasian Red Squirrel

Sciurus vulgaris
ALSO: Eichhörnchen, Écureuil roux d'Eurasie, Rødt ekorn, Обыкновенная белка. SN means "common shadow-tail."

RANGE: Occurs in coniferous forests and broadleaf woodlands in subarctic–temperate Eurasia from the UK east to Kamchatka and Sakhalin Is, and south to Mongolia and China.
ID: L 13–17 in (33–43 cm). WT 7–17 oz (200–480 g). Summer coat ranges from coppery red to silvery gray or black on the upperparts; winter coat is usually silvery. Chest and belly are always white or cream. In summer, the tail hairs are very long. Long ear tufts develop in winter.
HABITS: Solitary. Most active in the morning and late afternoon. Feeds mainly on conifer seeds, stripping the cones to get at the seeds. Also eats acorns, fungi, bird eggs, berries, and plant shoots, and strips tree bark to access the sap. Caches food in hollow trees (*larder hoards*) or buries it under surface litter (*scatter hoards*). Does not hibernate. Rests in its nest in midday. In inclement weather may remain in the nest for several days. Builds multiple domed nests (*dreys*) in forks of tree branches. The nest is about 12 in (30 cm) across, made out of twigs, and lined with moss, leaves, grass, and bark. Also nests in tree hollows and woodpecker holes. Breeding

occurs in Feb–Mar and in Jun–Jul. Males detect females in estrus by their scent. Several males chase the female prior to mating. Gestation is 38–39 days. Beginning at 2 years of age, a female can bear 1–2 litters of 3–4 young each year. Newborns are blind and deaf. Eyes and ears open at 21 days. Young are fully toothed at 42 days and weaned at 7–10 weeks. Lifespan is 3–7 years in the wild, 10 in captivity.
STATUS: Habitat destruction, road kills, and hunting are threats to survival. Populations are in decline in Great Britain due, in part, to the introduction of eastern gray squirrels from N Amer and fragmentation of native woodland. Protected in most of Europe; listed in Appendix III of the Bern Convention; Vulnerable (IUCN).

GENUS *TAMIASCIURUS*
American Red Squirrel

Tamiasciurus hudsonicus
ALSO: Pine Squirrel, Chickaree, Fairydiddle, Gemeines Rothörnchen, Écureuil roux américain, Красная белка. SN means "shadow-tailed nut hoarder of Hudson Bay."
RANGE: Occurs in coniferous and mixed forests across subarctic–temperate N Amer.
ID: L 11–13 in (28–34 cm). WT 7–9 oz (200–250 g). Soft, dense, glossy fur. Olive brown to reddish on the back; legs and back of ears are cinnamon; white to cream underparts. White eyering. Ears are tufted in winter.
HABITS: Diurnal. Solitary. Does not hibernate. Arboreal in summer; more terrestrial in winter, using a system of runways through the snow. Territorial; both sexes defend their home

In Norse mythology and Icelandic eddas, the red squirrel Ratatoskr runs up and down Yggdrasil, the world tree, carrying messages, slander, and gossip. Ratatoskr is notorius for ferrying insults between the eagle Veðrfölnir, who sits atop the world tree, and the dragon Níðhöggr, who lives under the tree's roots.

The 17th-century Icelandic illumination on the left depicts Ratatoskr as a green squirrel with long horns instead of tufted ears. The rascally squirrel is shown climbing up the world tree, undoubtedly with some delicious aspersion to deliver to Veðrfölnir.

The illumination is from a manuscript stored at the Árni Magnússon Institute in Reykjavik, Iceland.

range against their own and other squirrel species. Feeds mainly on the seeds of conifers, especially those of white spruce (*Picea glauca*). Harvests and caches cones in autumn. Fallen cone scales often collect in middens more than 3 ft (1 m) across. Also feeds on spruce buds and needles, willow leaves, poplar buds and catkins, flowers, berries, birds' eggs, and mice; gathers mushrooms, then places them in tree branches to dry in the sun. Sexually mature at about 1 year. Females produce 1 (rarely 2) litter of 2–7 young. Gestation is 35–40 days. Before weaning her young, the female moves them to a nest at the edge of her range where they eventually establish their own territory.

SUBFAMILY SCIURINAE: TRIBE PTEROMYINI
FLYING SQUIRRELS

These little nocturnal squirrels live in forests and wooded areas. They move long distances each night, gliding effortlessly from tree to tree. Glides of 150 ft (46 m) have been recorded. They extend their *patagium membrane* (the flap of skin between the wrists and ankles) to increase lift. They regulate direction and speed in midair by flexing the small cartilaginous wrist bones and changing the position of the arms and legs. The flattened tail acts as an in-flight stabilizer and adjunct airfoil, and also functions as an air brake when landing.

The diet includes seeds, tree buds, bark, leaves, lichens, fruit, nuts, tree sap, insects, and bird eggs and fledglings. Food is often cached in tree holes for later use. These squirrels forage for mushrooms in places where they previously found fungi; they locate mushrooms by smell.

Flying squirrels are active year round. They do not hibernate, but sleep in their nest for several days during bouts of severe weather. They nest in tree holes, abandoned woodpecker holes, birdhouses, and in leaf nests (*dreys*) built in crotches of high trees. The nest is usually lined with soft vegetation such as lichens. A female reaches sexual maturity at about 9 months of age and can bear 1–2 litters of 1–6 young annually. Gestation is 4–5 weeks. Lifespan is 4–5 years in the wild, 10 in captivity.

GENUS *PTEROMYS*
Siberian Flying Squirrel
Pteromys volans

ALSO: Europäisches Gleithörnchen, Polatouche de Sibérie, Обыкновенная летяга. SN means "winged mouse that flies."
RANGE: Found in Finland and Estonia, and east across Russia to Chukotka, Sakhalin, Kamchatka, and south to n Japan, n China, and Korea, in old-growth mixed forests, especially along rivers; sea level to 8200 ft (0–2500 m).
ID: L 10–13 in (25–33 cm). WT 4.5–5.3 oz (130–150 g). Soft, silky, dense coat is grayish to silvery overall, with the abdomen slightly paler than the back, and with a black stripe between the neck and forelimb. Back is tinged with olive brown in summer. Large, luminous black eyes.
HABITS: Nocturnal. Arboreal.
STATUS: Felling of old-growth forests in n Europe is a serious threat to this species' survival. Threatened (IUCN).

GENUS *GLAUCOMYS*
Northern Flying Squirrel
Glaucomys sabrinus

ALSO: Nördliche Gleithörnchen, Grand polatouche, Северная летяга. SN means "gray mouse-like river nymph," with river referring to the Severn Rvr in w Hudson Bay, Canada, where this species was first identified.
RANGE: Occurs in old-growth coniferous and mixed forests of Alaska and Canada.
ID: L 10–15 in (25–38 cm). WT 2.5–5 oz (71–142 g). Light brown or cinnamon back. Gray flanks. Dark brown stripe running along the sides. Underparts cream, with lead gray at the base of the individual hairs. Large dark eyes. Broad flattened tail is grayish above, paler below, and darker toward the tip.
HABITS: Nocturnal. Arboreal. Non-breeding squirrels move from nest to nest and, although generally solitary, will share a nest in winter, which is important in maintaining body temperature. A pile of seed hulls and fecal pellets at the tree base reveal the presence of a nest.

FAMILY ERETHIZONTIDAE
NEW WORLD PORCUPINES

Porcupines are large arboreal rodents that are covered with long hairs and spiny quills. Ancestors of the N Amer porcupines are thought to have moved north from S Amer about 3 million years ago as a land bridge formed between the continents.

GENUS *ERETHIZON*
North American Porcupine
Erethizon dorsatum
ALSO: Canadian Porcupine, Urson, Porc-épic d'Amérique, Kanadanpuupiikkisika, Поркупин. SN means "irritating back." CN derives from Middle French *porc d'épine*, meaning "spiny pig." A group of porcupines is aptly called a *prickle*.
RANGE: Occurs in boreal forests from Alaska, east across Canada to s Hudson Bay and Labrador, and south through the w US states to nw Mexico. Northernmost of the world's porcupines.
ID: L 25–31 in (73–78 cm). WT 10–25 lb (4.5–13 kg). Second largest N Amer rodent after the American Beaver, *Castor canadensis.* Stout and short-legged. The front feet have 4 toes, the hind feet have 5. Three layers of fur: thick, dark underfur; long, coarse guard hairs; and stiff, hollow quills all over the body, except for the belly. Tail is club-like;

upper surface is heavily covered with stiff quills that have microscopic barbs on the tips. Stiff bristles on the tail underside and long, curved front claws are used to support the animal when it is climbing trees.
HABITS: Mainly nocturnal but may be seen during the day curled into a ball in the crotch of a tree or lumbering with a clumsy gait through the forest. Frequently seen along roads at night in the glare of a car's lights; eyeshine from reflected headlights is dark red. Does not hibernate, but rests in caves, hollow logs, or dense vegetation during periods of cold or snowy winter weather. Has excellent senses of smell, hearing, and taste, but poor eyesight. Vocalizations include whimpers, hisses, and screams.

Feeds on buds, twigs, and inner bark of trees. In spring and summer, it eats the buds and young green leaves of birch, aspen, and willow. To replenish the sodium lacking in its vegetarian diet, it seeks out salt found in natural mineral licks and road salt deposits, and gnaws on shed antlers, bones, and ax handles and other wooden tools permeated with human perspiration.

The 6–10 in (15–25 cm) barbed quills on the lower back and tail are used for defense. As a first measure when threatened, the porcupine lays its quills flat against its body to expose contrasting bands of black and white quills. This serves as a visual warning by mimicking

Porcupines were once killed for their quills, which were sewn onto deerskin and used as trade wampum by Native American tribes. Today any quills used in handicraft work are obtained by cornering the porcupine and tapping its back with a styrofoam paddle, which retains the quills. The porcupine is then released unharmed.

the fur pattern of skunks. If this visual warning fails, the animal attempts to scare its assailant by loudly and rapidly chattering its teeth. It may then excrete a pungent odor from a gland located at the base of its tail. The hair and quills on the back normally lie flat and point backward, but when attacked, the porcupine contracts the skin on its back to erect the quills. It keeps its bristling back facing the attacker and shakes its tail back and forth to dislodge quills into the attacker's face and mouth. The quills rarely cause infection, as they are coated with a natural antibiotic (this is the only N Amer mammal that has antibiotics in its skin).

Predators such as fishers and wolverines have found ways to kill and eat porcupines without getting stung. They circle the porcupine until they can bite its nose and eyes, which renders the animal helpless and blind. Then they flip the body over to feed on the spineless belly.

Males reach sexual maturity at 2 years of age, females at 12 months. Breeding season is Sep–Nov. Females are in estrus for only a few hours and mate only once a year. Males fight for breeding rights using their incisor teeth and quills. Upon meeting a female, a courting male sprays her with urine. Females not in heat shake off the urine and walk away. A receptive female curls her tail over her back, covering most of her quills, and allows the male to mount her.

Gestation is about 7 months, an extremely long period for a rodent. A single young is born in Mar–May. It weighs about a pound (500 g), is about 10 in (25 cm) long, and has open eyes. Long, dark gray hairs and soft quills cover the body. The precocious newborn is able to follow its mother out of the den within a few hours. It is nursed for 3–4 months, during which time it stays close to its mother, learning about denning sites and food sources.

USE: Quills were formerly used for wampum (barter) and are still used in Native American clothing and jewelry. Porcupine hunting season is open all year, with no bag limit, but most northerners do not kill porcupines without cause, regarding them as a surplus food supply to be taken in times of need. Most people find porcupine meat too strong-flavored and fatty.

FAMILY CASTORIDAE
BEAVERS

Castoridae contains two living species of beaver and a single genus, *Castor*, which is indigenous to the rivers and lakes of the N Hemisphere. The earliest castorids date back 34–23 million years and giant beavers came into being about 15,000–12,000 years ago. *Castoroides ohioensis*, which lived in N Amer, measured 10 ft (3 m) long and weighed about 800 lb (360 kg). Its large incisors extended 4 in (10 cm) past the gum line.

Although much smaller than *Castoroides*, the extant species—the American Beaver, *Castor canadensis*, and Eurasian Beaver, *C. fiber*—are the largest rodents in the N Hemisphere and the world's second largest rodents after the Capybara (*Hydrochoerus hydrochaeris*) of S Amer.

The extant *Castor* species are very similar to each other, differing mainly in the shape of the nasal bones. The small, unwebbed forepaws have long, sharp claws suited to digging. The dexterous forefeet are used like hands, capable of holding and carrying building materials for dams and lodges, and performing a variety of complex construction tasks. The large, webbed hind feet have nails, and the second toe of each hind foot has a pincer-like double nail that is used to groom the coat.

Frequent grooming and application of castoreum oil from the anal glands ensure that the beaver's dense pelt is kept waterproof. The long, chisel-sharp, ever-growing incisors enable the beaver to gnaw and fell large trees. The front surface of the incisors is dark orange. The flat, muscular, paddle-shaped tail acts as a fat-storage organ and also as a rudder when the beaver is swimming.

Beavers can swim at speeds up to 4.5 mph (7 kmh), and remain underwater for 2–15 minutes. The ears, nostrils, and transparent eye membranes close when the beaver submerges. A thick layer of subcutaneous fat acts as insulation. The large, webbed hind feet propel the beaver through the water.

When alarmed, a beaver will slap the water with its tail, making a sound like a gunshot to warn other beavers of danger. On land, beavers use their tail as a prop when sitting or standing

Eurasian Beaver
Castor fiber
N Eurasia
31–46 in (79–117 cm)

Beaver tracks

American Beaver
Castor canadensis
N Amer
Introduced into Eurasia & S Amer
41–50 in (104–127 cm)

Should you ask me whence these stories,
Should you ask where Nawadaha
Found these songs, so wild and wayward,
Found these legends and traditions,
I should answer, I should tell you,
'In the birds' nests of the forest,
In the lodges of the beaver.'
— Henry Wadsworth Longfellow,
Hiawatha (1855)

upright, or when walking on the hind legs while carrying mud or branches to their lodge.

Beavers are adapted to an herbivorous diet, having large, chisel-like, orange-pigmented incisors suited for stripping tree bark and for gnawing tree branches and saplings. Their long appendix helps to digest the high-cellulose bark diet. Microorganisms in the gut break up the nutritional mush of bark that the beaver swallows and build up bacterial proteins that the beaver can digest. In spring and summer, the beaver feeds on grasses, herbs, leaves and twigs of woody plants, berries, and aquatic plants. In autumn, the beaver begins cutting down trees so it can set in its winter food supply of bark. It fells poplar, willow, birch, and aspen trees by gnawing at the trunk while standing upright, supported by the tail.

Beavers live in family groups of roughly 5–10 individuals, including a pair of breeding adults and their sexually immature offspring. Family members work together to gather and store food for winter, to dig deep canals for moving building materials, and to construct dams and lodges.

The family clears logging trails and digs canals so they can move heavy sticks more easily. Canals can measure 5 ft (1.5 m) wide by 3 ft (1 m) deep and extend for several hundred feet. The water level is maintained by diverting nearby streams into the canal or by damming.

To build a dam across a stream, the beavers first push sticks into the river bottom and then fill in the gaps with stones and sections of deciduous trees. Finally, they plaster the outside of the dam with mud carried in their forepaws or pushed up from the pond bottom. The result is a structure measuring 16–96 ft (5–29 m) in length that is able to withstand pressure and erosion by running water.

The deep pond created by a large dam allows year-round underwater access to the beaver's food cache and lodge. The lodge, which can measure 16.5 ft (5 m) across by 6.5 ft (2 m) high, is essentially a pile of sticks, mud, and stones built in the middle of the artificial pond that forms below the dam. It typically contains two interior living chambers, an air intake vent near the top, and 1–2 underwater entrances. The family's food cache is stored near the lodge entry and is held underwater by a thick layer of small, leafy branches. Snow falling on the branches creates an insulating cover, which prevents the food from freezing.

European beavers typically live in dens dug into riverbanks. The den interior resembles the American Beaver's lodge. It has a two-chambered burrow that opens into an underwater entry. If the riverbank is shallow, beavers will sometimes expand their den upward by piling up branches, twigs, and mud on top of the burrow.

GENUS *CASTOR*
American Beaver
Castor canadensis
ALSO: Canadian Beaver, Kanadischer Biber, Castor canadien, Amerikansk bever, Канадский бобр, Kigiaq. SN means "beaver of Canada." State animal of Oregon and New York. Appears on the Canadian 5-cent piece and on the first Canadian postage stamp, the Three Penny Beaver. The emblem for engineering schools such as California Institute of Technology

and Massachusetts Institute of Technology. Mascot for Oregon State University. Appears on the coats of arms of the University of Toronto and the London School of Economics.

RANGE: Widespread in rivers and lakes in Alaska and Canada north to the Arctic Circle, and south through most of the US states. Introduced into Eurasia (Finland, Poland, Austria, Germany, nw Russia, Kamchatka) and into S Amer (Tierra del Fuego).

ID: L 41–50 in (104–127 cm), including an 11–15 in (28–38 cm) tail. WT 33–77 lb (15–35 kg). Stocky body. Rounded head. Normal coat color is dark brown, but russet and blonde morphs are sometimes seen. The pelage consists of a dense undercoat of fine, short hairs, and an outer layer of guard hairs about 2.5 in (6.5 cm) long. Continual grooming and applications of oil from the anal glands keeps the fur waterproofed.

HABITS: Largely nocturnal. Does not hibernate. Vulnerable to predators on land, thus it tends to remain in the water as much as possible. Lives colonially in small family groups of 5–8 individuals, consisting of single pair of monogamous adults, yearlings, and newborns. Family members communicate by using scent, posture, tail slaps, and whistling and hissing calls. Marks its territory with urine mixed with castoreum from castor sacs near the anal glands. Deposits excretions on scent mounds built of mud and sticks.

Two to 5 kits are born Apr–Jul after a gestation of about 128 days. They are nursed in the den for about 1 month and weaned at 6–8 weeks. When offspring reach sexual maturity at 2 years of age, they leave parental territory and establish their own lodge.

Felted beaver fur was the material of choice for military hats and top hats for the gentry from 1550 to 1850. Beaver hat production became a major industry of the British economy. English hatters first imported beaver pelts from Russia and Scandinavia, but when European beaver populations dwindled there, they turned to fur traders in the American colonies for their raw materials.

At the peak of the fur-trade era in the 1800s, North American traders supplied some 200,000 beaver pelts a year to the European market. The largest American fur-trading empire was built by German-born John Jacob Astor. In 1808, he established the American Fur Company, which soon expanded into Canada. Trading in beaver pelts made Astor a fortune, which he later invested in New York real estate and the opium trade.

USE: Beavers were hunted historically for their meat and for their thick, water-repellent pelts. They were a popular totem animal of Native American tribes, and legends relate that beavers, often helped by muskrats or otters, created the first land by dredging up earth from the bottom of the sea—a parody of the beaver's lodge building techniques. Impressed by the size and complexity of the beaver lodges, early European explorers carried stories of a sophisticated beaver society back to Europe. It was rumored that beavers built with mortar, used their tails as trowels, and had a system of parliamentary law. In 1774, in his *History of Animated Nature*, the Anglo-Irish writer Oliver Goldsmith penned, "The beavers in those distant solitudes are known to build like architects and rule like citizens."

STATUS: European fur traders of the 18th century found there was great profit in beaver pelts and by 1800 the species was almost hunted out. The later use of steel traps eliminated the beaver from most of its original range by 1860.

Today beavers are considered pests because their dams can cause flooding. At times the only effective measure is to remove the beavers, but water levelers and other non-lethal methods of containing beaver-related floods have been developed. The current beaver population is estimated at 10–15 million, a 10th of the number existing in N Amer before the fur-trade era of the 1800s began.

Eurasian Beaver

Castor fiber

ALSO: European Beaver, Europäische Biber, Castor européen, Eurasisk bever, Евразийский бобр. SN means "beaver beaver."
RANGE: Occurs around rivers and lakes of Scandinavia and Russia. Reintroduced to many European countries where it had become extinct.
ID: L 31–46 in (79–117 cm). WT 29–70 lb (13–32 kg). Largest European rodent. Females are slightly larger than males. Pelage ranges from a rich glossy brown to yellowish brown on the upperparts, and from brown to tawny on the underparts. Separated from *C. canadensis* mainly by smaller size and paler pelage.

HABITS: Largely nocturnal. Does not hibernate. Typically lives in riverbank burrows in family groups of 5–8 animals. Feeds on tubers and rootstocks of aquatic plants, and on the buds, shoots and bark of trees such as aspen, black poplar, and hazel (*Corylus* sp.). Alder and oak are seldom eaten but are used as building materials.

Mating takes place in Jan–Feb. Females are in estrus for two weeks but are receptive to mating for only 12–24 hours. Average gestation is 105 days. One to 5 kits are born in Apr–Jun. They are nursed within the lodge for the first 2 weeks and weaned at 3 months. Newborns often have difficulty adjusting to the change from drinking mother's milk to eating bark, and many do not survive this period. Lifespan is 7–8 years in the wild, up to 35 years in captivity.

USE: Hunted historically for its soft, dense, waterproof pelt, and also harvested for *castoreum,* a yellowish exudate from the beaver's scent glands, or *castor sacs,* which are located at the base of the tail. Castoreum gives out a distinctive odor, and beavers use the castoreum exudate mixed with their urine to scent-mark their territory.

In ancient times, physicians and naturalists attributed curative and aphrodisiac properties to the oil. Today we use a natural component of castoreum, acetanisole, as a food additive and flavoring agent for nuts, spices, boiled sweets, and cigarette tobacco. Acetanisole has a sweet smell and tastes somewhat like cherry or vanilla. Castoreum extracted from the beaver's dried castor sacs is used in perfumes such as Shalimar, Emeraude, and Givenchy III, to add a leathery note to the fragrance.

STATUS: Currently protected in many countries. Attempts have been made to reintroduce the beaver to areas where it became extinct. The introduction of American beavers to areas where Eurasian populations are recovering poses a threat. Major threats to survival include reclamation of wetlands, the building of hydroelectric plants and dams on rivers, and the introduction of detergent pollutants that damage the water-repelling quality of the beaver's fur. Various populations in Eurasia are classed as Critically Endangered, Near Threatened, or Vulnerable (IUCN).

FAMILY CRICETIDAE
MUSKRATS, VOLES, LEMMINGS, AND NEW WORLD RATS AND MICE

Cricetidae is one of the largest families of mammals, containing 5 subfamilies, 130 genera, and 681 species. Cricetid rodents are Holarctic in distribution, with many species having expanded from Eurasia into the New World in prehistoric times via the Bering Land Bridge.

SUBFAMILY ARVICOLINAE
MUSKRATS, VOLES, LEMMINGS

The subfamily Arvicolinae includes a diverse group of herbivorous rodents. These rodents are active year round and do not hibernate. Muskrats den in lodges and are able to forage beneath the winter ice. Arctic voles and lemmings forage and live under the winter snow.

Arvicolines have hypsodont dentition, with 16 high-crowned, ever-growing teeth and enamel that extends beyond the gum line. In most species, the frontal surface of the incisors is pigmented yellowish orange. The molars have prismatic cusps consisting of alternating triangles. Shown here are the molars from a muskrat's upper jaw.

GENUS *ONDATRA*
Common Muskrat
Ondatra zibethicus
ALSO: Mudcat, Muskbeaver, Bisamratte, Rat musqué, Piisami, Ондатра, Kivgaluk, Avinngarjuaq. SN means "musky-smelling muskrat," referring to the scent of breeding males. Musquash (*mòskwas*) is the Abnaki (Algonquin) Indian name for the muskrat and the archaic British fur trader's term for a muskrat's pelt.
RANGE: Occurs around freshwater marshes, streams, and ponds throughout N Amer, except on the tundra. Introduced for fur farming into the Czech Republic in 1905 and later throughout Eurasia. Escapees have become naturalized across n Eurasia (pale green on map). Introduced into Tierra del Fuego in S Amer in 1948.
ID: L 18–25 in (46–64 cm). WT 2–4 lb (1–2 kg). World's largest murid. Waterproof undercoat of dense fur is overlaid with coarse, shiny guard hairs. Pelage is silvery brown to glossy dark brown, with chestnut or hazel flanks and pale gray underparts. Hairless, scaly, black, rat like tail is flattened from side to side—a feature that distinguishes it from the larger beaver. Nose and foot soles are black. Forefeet and hind feet have 5 finger-like toes; inner toe of the front foot is so small that it rarely shows in the tracks. Hind feet are fringed with bristles and partially webbed.
HABITS: Nocturnal and crepuscular. Chiefly aquatic, although some muskrats migrate short distances overland in fall. Feeds mainly on aquatic and wetland plants such as cattails, water lilies, sedges, and horsetails. Prefers roots, tubers, and basal stalks of plants, which are rich in carbohydrates and proteins. Occasionally eats fish, freshwater mollusks, crustaceans, frogs, small turtles, and young waterbirds.

Muskrats den in a wide variety of habitats, ranging from large lakes and rivers to small ponds and marshes. In autumn, in areas where the water surface freezes, muskrats construct denning mounds containing 2 or more living chambers, a food storage chamber, a chimney vent, and underwater entrances. The insulating piles of organic debris and vegetation, which may rise 2–3 ft (61–91 cm) above the water, prevent a thick ice cover from forming and enable the muskrat to keep its breathing holes open all winter. Muskrats also construct domes, called "pushups," over a hole in the ice where they can emerge to feed. This allows them to conserve body heat that would be lost from their naked feet and tail in the icy water. In warmer climates, where a solid riverbank is available, muskrats will dig and live in burrows. The burrow has underwater entries to a grass-lined nesting chamber located above the water level.

A single mated pair of muskrats and their adolescent young occupy their own mound or burrow. They signal to one another with sharp whistles, and mark their territory with piles of dark olive, pebble-like droppings. During the mating season, the male's anal glands enlarge and leak an oily, musky secretion. Males advertise their maturity by dragging their anal glands along the ground, thus depositing musk mixed with urine around their home territory.

Muskrat tracks are small, hand-like prints. The front print appears 4-toed, as the inner toe is extremely small, and may be obliterated by the rear footprint. Tail drag usually shows in the track.

Muskrat
Ondatra zibethicus
N Amer
Introduced into Eurasia & S Amer
18–25 in (46–64 cm)

Breeding season extends from Apr to Aug in the north, and may continue into winter in the south. Sexually mature females are particularly aggressive, and will fight other females for control of a denning site. Gestation is 25–30 days. Females usually bear 2 litters of 5–6 young each year. The young are born naked and blind, and are tended solely by the female. The male lives in a separate chamber on the den periphery when the female is nursing. Young are weaned at 21–28 days. They reach sexual maturity at 12 months, at which time they leave the parental lodge to establish their own territory. Lifespan is about 3 years in the wild, 10 years in captivity. **USE:** Muskrats are a valuable species in the N Amer fur trade. More importantly, they are appreciated for their positive impact on marshes. Their denning mounds, abandoned in summer, provide nesting sites for waterbirds. Muskrats also consume large tracts of marsh vegetation, creating open water areas attractive to waterfowl and vital to marsh plants that do not grow in thick stands of cattails and reeds.
STATUS: Populations fluctuate in a 6–10 year cycle. The American Mink, *Neovison vison*, is the most serious predator; its swimming ability and streamlined body allow it to take muskrats in the burrow. Foxes, coyotes, wolves, weasels, raccoons, black bears, lynx, bobcats, otters, owls, marsh hawks, and ravens also prey on muskrats, and pike and snapping turtles take the young.

GENUS *ARVICOLA*
Eurasian Water Vole

Arvicola amphibius
ALSO: Northern Water Vole, Water Rat, Ostscher maus, Vånd, Campagnol terrestre, Водяная полёвка, *Arvicola terrestris*. Also known as Ratty, the water vole character in Kenneth Grahame's 1908 children's tale, *The Wind in the Willows*. SN means "inhabitant of watery fields."
RANGE: Found from the UK and Europe east through Siberia to the Lena Rvr, and from the arctic coast south to Lake Baikal, China, and Mongolia. Inhabits banks of slow-flowing rivers, ditches, dikes, and lakes; in c Europe it occurs in woods, fields, and gardens.
ID: L 10–12 in (25–30 cm). WT 5–10 oz (150–300 g). Rat-like, with a long, laterally flattened tail. Partially webbed hind feet, fringed with bristles. Blunt muzzle. Small ears. Shaggy, dense dorsal pelage varies from brown to dark chestnut, with black guard hairs. Cheeks and body sides light brown. Underparts buffy. Dark brown tail covered in short, stiff hairs. Dark brown feet bear long claws. The 4-toed forefeet leave star-shaped tracks in the mud, while the 5-toed hind feet leave tracks showing the first and fifth toes at right angles to the 3 central toes.
HABITS: Most active at dusk and dawn. Expert swimmer. When disturbed, dives with a marked *plop*. Usually silent; alarm call is a rasping

crick-crick. Feeds on riverbank vegetation, grasses, sedges, roots, twigs, and agricultural root crops; also eats insects, mollusks, and small fish. Sits on haunches while eating, and leaves piles of chopped grass pith on the riverbank. Deposits shiny black droppings in latrines located at the edge of the home range. Males mark their territory with a secretion scraped from the flank glands.

Excavates complex, shallow burrows in steep, vegetated riverbanks. Burrows have entries above and below the water level, and have sleeping and nest chambers in the steepest parts of the bank. "Lawns" of closely cropped grass often surround the burrow entrances. Breeds in summer. A gravid female is very territorial and will attack any vole that invades her range. The female prepares the nesting chamber by lining it with grasses and rushes, and plugging the entry holes with grass and mud. If no suitable banks are available, the female will build a ball-shaped nest in a reed bed. Up to 5 annual litters are produced, each with 4–6 young. Gestation is 21 days. Newborns are blind and naked. The eyes open at 3 days of age. Young are weaned at 14 days, and are usually evicted by the mother at 22 days when she produces the next litter. Lifespan is about 5 months to a year in the wild. **STATUS:** Main predators are minks and stoats. Populations are stable, except in the UK where numbers declined from 2.3 million in 1990 to about 220,000 in 2004. Decline is attributed to predation by introduced American minks (*Neovison vison*) and to poor farming practices.

GENUS *MICROTUS*: The genus *Microtus* encompasses the meadow voles, which are small, mouselike or ratlike rodents. Meadow voles are distinguished by a stocky body, rounded muzzle, short tail and limbs, and small, fur covered ears. The forefeet have 4 toes, the hind feet 5 toes. The fur is typically colored grayish brown above and paler below. Most weigh about 1–3 oz (28–85 g).

Voles feed on grasses, sedges, grains, seeds, roots, bark, and occasionally insects, and cache food for winter in underground burrows. Most species dig short burrows with tunnels leading to nesting and food storage chambers. Both males and females mark their territory with secretions from preputial (genital) and hip glands, which are usually largest in old males.

These are some of the world's most prolific mammals, with both sexes reaching sexual maturity by 4–6 weeks of age. The northern species breed mainly in summer, but young can be born year round, even in nests under the snow. Gestation is 18–23 days. Up to 5 annual litters are produced, each with 2–12 young. Young are born in underground burrows and are tended mainly by the female. Newborns are naked and blind. Body hairs develop by day 6 and the eyes open by day 10. Once the young are weaned at 14 days, the female usually abandons the nest.

Populations fluctuate markedly in a 3–4 year cycle. Average lifespan is 5–8 months in the wild, 2–3 years in captivity.

Meadow Vole

Microtus pennsylvanicus
ALSO: Meadow Mouse, Field Mouse, Wiesenwühlmaus, Campagnol de Pennsylvania, Markmus, Пенсильванская полёвка. SN means "small-eared [vole] of Pennsylvania," the type locality.
RANGE: Found across N Amer, from c Alaska to Labrador, and south through c and e US into n Mexico. Inhabits forest clearings, open meadows, streambanks, lakeshores, swamps; also occurs in high, open grasslands, forests with little ground cover, and orchards with grassy undergrowth.
ID: L 4.5–7.5 in (11–19 cm). Small ears. Short tail. Long, soft pelage. Upperparts grayish brown to dark reddish brown. Silvery, buff, or dark gray underparts. Feet are dark gray. Tail may be uniformly dark gray or bicolored, with dark gray above and light gray below.
HABITS: Mostly nocturnal. Abundant in areas with dense plant cover where voles can escape from predators. Makes narrow runways through matted vegetation. Good swimmer. Nests in grass-lined underground burrows in summer and in tunnels under the snow in winter. Round openings on the snow surface reveal the presence of winter nests. Small piles of brown droppings

Lemming Mountain Vole
Alticola lemminus
NE Siberia
L 5.5–6 in (14–15 cm)

Northern Red-backed Vole
Myodes rutilus
Eurasia, nw N Amer
Forest and forest-tundra
L 4–6 in (10–15 cm)

Gray Red-backed Vole
Myodes rufocanus
Eurasian forests
L 5–6 in (13–15 cm)

Field Vole
Microtus agrestis
Eurasia
Wet meadows with vegetation
L 4–7 in (10–18 cm)

Meadow Vole
Microtus pennsylvanicus
N Amer
Damp forest meadows
L 4.5–7.5 in (11–19 cm)

Narrow-headed Vole
Microtus gregalis
Eurasia
Tundra and mountains
L 4.5–6.5 in (11–17 cm)

Tundra Vole
Microtus oeconemus
Eurasia, nw N Amer
Meadows in tundra and taiga
L 4–8 in (10–20 cm)

Singing Vole
Microtus miurus
Alaska–nw Canada
Tundra
L 4.5–6.5 in (11–17 cm)

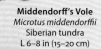

Middendorff's Vole
Microtus middendorffii
Siberian tundra
L 6–8 in (15–20 cm)

Taiga Vole
Microtus xanthognagus
Alaska, nw Canada
L 7–9 in (18–23 cm)

Eurasian Water Vole
Arvicola amphibius
Eurasia
L 10–12 in (25–30 cm)

and short pieces of grass stems along the runways indicate summer burrows. Breeds year round, with peak reproduction in midsummer.
USE: Serves as a food source for larger mammals and birds of prey, and as an agent of dispersal for mycorrhizal fungi and seeds in burned areas. Researchers in the US have used changes in meadow vole populations as a biological indicator of chemical leakage around Love Canal and radiation releases at the Three Mile Is nuclear plant.

Singing Vole

Microtus miurus
ALSO: Alaska Vole, Alaska-Wühlmaus, Campagnol chanteur. SN means "curtailed vole," referring to the very short tail. CN refers to the vole's habit of "singing"—emitting a high-pitched, trilling alarm call from the burrow entrance.
RANGE: Occurs from Alaska east to the c Yukon and w NWT, and south to nw Brit Columbia. Inhabits tundra regions above the treeline, on open, well-drained slopes and rocky flats with abundant shrubs, sedges, and dwarf willow.
ID: L 4.5–6.5 in (11–17 cm). TAIL 1–1.5 in (2.5–3.6 cm). WT 1–2 oz (28–57 g). Small. Very short, bristly tail. Small ears. Pale gray or pale brown upperparts. Gray underparts.
HABITS: Active day and night. Lives in small colonies. Feeds on lupines, arctic locoweeds (*Oxytropis*), knotweed, horsetails, sedges, and willow leaves and twigs. Sometimes climbs up into vegetation while foraging. Caches tubers underground for winter use. Cuts and stacks large piles of vegetation on the ground under low willow and birch boughs. Digs its own burrows, and also occupies those of ground squirrels. Nests Jun–Aug in underground burrows.
SIMILAR SPECIES: The INSULAR VOLE (*not illus.*), *Microtus abbreviatus*, is found on uninhabited St Matthew Is and Hall Is marine reserves in the Bering Sea region of Alaska. Occurs in moist lowland and ryegrass (*Elymus*) plant communities, along beach ridges, in piles of driftwood, and on well-drained slopes to about 800 ft (240 m) elevation.

Taiga Vole

Microtus xanthognathus
ALSO: Yellow-cheeked Vole, Chestnut-cheeked Vole, Gelbwangenwühlmaus, Желтощёкая полёвка. SN means "vole with a yellow jaw."
RANGE: Found from ec Alaska to w NWT and w Hudson Bay, and south to Alberta. Occurs in riparian habitats, especially in newly formed sphagnum bogs in lightly burned areas or in early successional stage forests containing Black Spruce (*Picea mariana*); also occurs along streams at forest edge.
ID: L 7–9 in (18–23 cm). WT 4–6 oz. (11–17 g). Large vole with a short tail. Dull brown dorsal pelage, with gray underparts and a rusty yellow patch on the cheeks.
HABITS: Largely active at dawn and dusk. Lives in small colonies. Gives a warning call ("sings") to alert other colony members of danger. Diet includes grasses, horsetails, lichens, and berries. Stores rhizomes and other plant matter in underground burrows for winter use. Digs burrows in areas with heavy moss cover, and creates runways through sphagnum. Burrows may have large mounds at the entries, some measuring 2–10 ft (0.6–3 m) across and 1–2 ft (0.3–0.6 m) high.

Tundra Vole

Microtus oeconomus
ALSO: Northern Root Vole, Sumpfmaus, Nordische Wühlmaus, Campagnol nordique, Fjellmarkmus, Полёвка экономка. SN means "economic vole," referring to its habit of storing seeds and rhizomes for winter use.
RANGE: Found in damp tundra, taiga, and moist grassy meadows, usually near water, from nc Europe east across Siberia to Kamchatka, Kurils, n China, and n Mongolia; and from Alaska to w Nunavut and nw Brit Columbia.
ID: L 4–8 in (10–20 cm). WT 1–2.25 oz (25–62 g). Grayish brown with buff flecking on the back; pale gray flanks; white to pale buff underparts. Tail grayish brown above, paler below.
HABITS: Nocturnal in summer; diurnal in

winter. Makes runways through surface growth in warm weather and tunnels through the snow in winter. Swims and dives well. Feeds on grasses, sedges, seeds, and shoots of rushes and other aquatic plants. Caches winter reserves of seeds and roots, especially licorice root (*Glycyrrhiza* sp.), in underground burrows. Territorial, especially during breeding season (May–Sep). Any vole intruding into another's home range is attacked and driven off. Builds a nest of moss, dry rushes, and grass, above ground in damp areas, otherwise in a shallow burrow. **STATUS:** European populations are in decline. Critically Endangered to Vulnerable (IUCN).

Field Vole

Microtus agrestis

ALSO: Short-tailed Vole, Erdmaus, Markmus, Campagnol agreste, Пашенная полевка. SN means "small-eared field vole."
RANGE: Found from the UK and n Europe, east through Siberia to the Lena Rvr basin, and south to nw China in moist, densely vegetated meadows, lakeshores, riverbanks, forestry plantations, mountain heath, open woods, and dunes.
ID: L 4–7 in (10–18 cm). WT 0.5–1.75 oz (14–50 g). Long shaggy fur. Dark brownish gray above. Buffy flanks. Gray neck, underparts, and feet. Black and piebald color morphs occur. Winter pelage is denser, brighter, more ochre. Short tail is bicolored, dark brown above, white below.
HABITS: Most active at dawn and dusk. Very vocal, with loud chattering and chirping sounds; emits a staccato *tuck-tuck-tuck tuck tuck* alarm call. Feeds on grass, roots, bulbs, and bark. Feeding sites are littered with broken grass blades. Runways show piles of oval, green droppings. Burrows under bushes, stumps, or piles of twigs.

Middendorff's Vole

Microtus middendorffii

ALSO: Peltomyyrät, Полевка Миддендорфа. SN means "Middendorff's vole," refer-
ring to the Baltic-German zoologist Alexander Theodor von Middendorff (1815–1894), who explored the Taimyr Penin for the St Petersburg

Academy of Sciences. He later published his findings on the effects of permafrost on the spread of animals and plants in *Travels in the Extreme North and East of Siberia*.
RANGE: Found in boggy tundra, sedge and sphagnum marshes, and waterlogged riverbanks from the Ural Mtns east to the Yenisey and Kolyma rivers, and in the Lena Rvr valley.
ID: L 6–8 in (15–20 cm). WT 2–3 oz (55–85 g). Grayish brown upperparts sometimes tinged with rufous. Silvery to pale buff underparts. Long tail is bicolored, with dark gray above and paler below.
HABITS: Active year round. Feeds on sedge leaves and stalks in summer, cached roots in winter. Digs shallow burrows and constructs runways between grass tussocks.

Narrow-headed Vole

Microtus gregalis

ALSO: Narrow-skulled Vole, Campagnol des hauteurs, Узкочерепная полёвка.
SN means "small-eared comrade." CN refers to the laterally compressed skull, an adaptation to living in narrow burrows and cracks in the permafrost soil.
RANGE: Disjunct populations occur from the White Sea east to the Ob Rvr; Taimyr Penin east to the Kolyma Rvr; in the Lena and Volga Rvr basins; and in steppes from the Altai Mtns into sw Siberia, Yakutia, n China, and n Mongolia. Inhabits tundra, plains, wet meadows, open grassy areas in forests and semi-deserts, and mountain steppes to 13,125 ft (4000 m).
ID: L 4.5–6.5 in (11–17 cm). WT 1.75–2.75 oz (50–80 g). Dorsal pelage pale ochre (summer) to reddish ochre (winter), with white-tipped hairs giving a silvery sheen to the pelt. Grayish buff underparts. Dark stripe runs from the back of the head to the upper back. Tufted tail may be entirely pale ochre, or bicolored with dark brown above and pale ochre below.
HABITS: Mostly nocturnal. Lives in colonies. Breeding begins in early spring; in tundra zones reproduction often starts under snow cover . Up to 5 annual litters are produced Feb–Mar, each with 2–12 young.

GENUS *MYODES*
RED-BACKED VOLES

These small rodents have reddish backs, gray or yellow flanks, gray to silvery underparts, and a bicolored tail. In summer, they move from place to place through runways trampled in the vegetation and via tunnels made under the snow in winter. These voles are sexually mature at 1–4 months of age. Males mark their territory with secretions from flank glands. Breeding season is Apr–Oct. Gestation is 17–20 days. Females bear 2–3 litters per year, each with 2–11 young.

Gray Red-backed Vole
Myodes rufocanus

ALSO: Gray-sided Vole, Graurötelmaus, Campagnol de Sundevall, Gråsidemus, Красно-серая полёвка. SN means "red and gray vole."
RANGE: Found from Scandinavia to Kamchatka and ne Asia in open coniferous or birch forests with dense undergrowth or fallen trees.
ID: L 5–6 in (13–15 cm). WT 0.5–1.75 oz (15–50 g). Rich reddish brown from crown to rump. Sides of face and flanks gray to buffy. Tail bicolored, blackish brown above, silvery below.
HABITS: Primarily nocturnal. Feeds on the shoots, buds, and fruit of bilberry (*Vaccinium*) and crowberry (*Empetrum*), and leaves and bark of dwarf birch (*Betula nana*) and low-growing shrubs. In summer, builds nests of grass, moss, lichens, and shredded leaves, which are hidden under roots, logs, or brush piles, or in holes and high branches of trees. Nests under the snow in winter, building round grass nests with snow tunnels radiating out from them. Vocalizations include a chirp-like bark when disturbed, and a gnashing or chattering of teeth.

Northern Red-backed Vole
Myodes rutilus

ALSO: Ruddy Vole, Tundra Redback Vole, Polarrötel- maus, Raudmus, Красная полёвка. SN means "red vole."
RANGE: Found from Scandinavia to Chukotka, China and Mongolia, and from Alaska east to

Hudson Bay in boreal forest and adjacent tundra, especially damp wooded habitats that have open stands of pine, birch, and willow.
ID: L 4–6 in (10–15 cm). WT 1 oz (30 g). Small, slender vole. Deep rust-colored dorsal stripe. Sides of face and flanks yellowish brown. Underparts light brown to silvery. Winter pelage is brighter and more yellow. Short, thick, well-furred, bicolored tail is reddish brown above, pale buff below, and has a brush of hairs at its tip.
HABITS: Active year round. Primarily nocturnal. Feeds on tender vegetation, nuts, seeds, berries, roots and fungi, and occasionally on small, dead rodents. Vocalizations include chattering of the teeth, squeaking, and a chirp-like bark. Uses runways created by other small rodents in the surface vegetation. Makes a nest of grass and moss in trees or on the ground under tree roots, stones, or shrubs.

GENUS *ALTICOLA*
Lemming Mountain Vole
Alticola lemminus

ALSO: Lemming-Wühlmaus, Лемминговая полёвка. SN means "lemming-like alpine vole."
RANGE: Occurs in n Siberia, from the Lena Rvr east to Chukotka, in river valleys and alpine boulder fields; sea level to 6500 ft (0–2000 m).
ID: L 5.5–6 in (14–15 cm). WT 1 oz (30 g). Grayish brown in summer; much paler in winter. Brown, brush-tipped tail.
HABITS: Mainly nocturnal. Lives and nests in rocks and boulder piles with adjacent grassy areas. Feeds on mosses and lichens.

GENUS *LEMMUS*
TRUE LEMMINGS

True lemmings resemble large, plump, large-headed mice. They measure 3–7 in (8–18 cm) in length and weigh 2.5–4 oz (70–115 g). They are gray or brown in color, and unlike the collared lemmings, their coats do not become white in winter. Their tails are extremely short. Their ears are hidden by fur. The foot soles and toes are covered with long stiff bristles, and the feet have strong claws for digging into permafrost.

These small herbivores live in colonies on the tundra or in alpine meadows. They are active year round. In summer, they live and nest in shallow burrows and create runways through tangled vegetation that lead to feeding areas. In winter, they live in tunnels beneath the snow.

True lemmings are sexually mature at 2–3 weeks of age, and even though they breed mostly during the warmer months, they are very prolific. In a single summer, a female can produce 2–6 litters, each with 2–11 young, at intervals of 3–4 weeks.

Lemming populations fluctuate widely in 3–4 year cycles. Population peaks called "lemming years" occur every 30 years or so. These years are characterized by exhaustion of the food supply, high mortality, and the mass migration of lemmings, which fan out across the countryside in search of new feeding grounds. If the lemmings reach a stream or pond, they are able to swim across it. However, if the lemmings reach the ocean and swim out from shore, they drown. This event led to the belief that lemmings commit mass suicide by jumping into the sea.

The myth was popularized in the 1958 Walt Disney film *White Wilderness*, which was filmed in Canada near the city of Calgary—a place far from the ocean and well outside the lemmings' range. The animals used in the film were trapped at sites along Hudson Bay and shipped to Calgary. The mass migration scene was feigned by running the rodents on a spinning, snow-covered turntable and filming it from several different angles. The lemmings were then herded off a raised bank overlooking a river to simulate the death-plunge sequence.

Norway Lemming

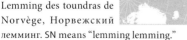

Lemmus lemmus
ALSO: Berglemming, Lemen, Lemming des toundras de Norvège, Норвежский лемминг. SN means "lemming lemming."
RANGE: Found in Fennoscandia on tundra and alpine moorlands north of the timberline, and occasionally in birch and pine woodlands.
ID: L 4–6.5 in (10–17 cm). Striking pelage, variably patterned in black, ochre, brown, and white.

HABITS: Feeds on sedges, grasses, dwarf shrubs, and mosses. Vocalizations include whistles and squeaks. Scent glands are used for marking territory and communication; males have preputial (genital) scent glands, and both sexes have scent glands on the lips, ears, foot soles, and rump. Droppings along runways also mark territory. In summer, the lemmings live and breed in lowland areas. In autumn, the lemmings return to sheltered higher elevations where there is enough snow cover to tunnel under.

Nearctic Brown Lemming

Lemmus trimucronatus
ALSO: Brun lämmel, Lemming commun, Brauner Lemming, Лемминг Avinngaq, Kajuqtaq. SN means "lemming with 3 sharp points."
RANGE: Found in tundra and alpine tundra above the treeline, mainly in damp meadows and near water bodies, from the Kolyma Rvr in ne Siberia to coastal Chukotka, on Bering Sea islands, and from w Alaska and c Brit Columbia across Canada to Baffin Is and Hudson Bay.
ID: L 5–7 in (13–18 cm). Back and rump rufous; head and shoulders gray; flanks brown.
HABITS: Main summer foods are tender shoots of grasses and sedges as well as heathers, cottongrass, seeds, green mosses, berries, and roots. In winter, feeds on the bark and twigs of willow and dwarf birch and browses on frozen, but still green plant material that lies beneath the snow. Territorial and aggressive toward other lemmings during the Jun–Aug mating season and when overpopulated. Constructs nests of balls of grass on the soil surface. Gestation is 16–23 days. Lifespan is less than 2 years.
USE: In years when this species is scarce, arctic foxes and jaegers may not breed.

Siberian Brown Lemming

Lemmus sibiricus
ALSO: Sibirischer Lemming, Sibirisk lemen, Lemming de Sibérie, Лемминг сибирский. SN means "lemming of Siberia."

RANGE: Occurs from the White Sea east to the Lena and Kolyma Rvr basins, and on Wrangel Is, Novaya Zemlya, and the New Siberian Islands, on tundra lowlands, foothills, and forest edge in areas with moss and sedge cover.
SUBSPECIES: SIBERIAN BROWN LEMMING, *L. s. sibiricus*; common in most of the distribution area. NOVOSIBIRSK BROWN LEMMING, *L. s. novosibiricus*; endemic to New Siberian Islands. WRANGEL IS BROWN LEMMING, *L. portenkoi*; endemic to Wrangel Is. A major food source for Wrangel Is snowy owls, whose breeding success is tied to this lemming population.
ID: L 5–6.5 in (13–17 cm). Lower back and flanks yellowish brown; head and neck gray; underparts pale gray. Faint dark stripe runs down the back.
HABITS: Feeds on sedges, cottongrass, green moss, and shrubs. Forms large colonies. Digs its own burrow, or occupies existing burrows of other animals. In winter, lives in tunnels under snow cover. Breeding peak is Jun–Aug. Builds large spherical nests. Females bear 4–5 litters, each with 5–6 young. Despite marked population oscillations every 3–4 years, migrations are less pronounced than those of other *Lemmus*.

GENUS *DICROSTONYX*
COLLARED LEMMINGS

These small lemmings of the arctic tundra have an adult total length of less than 7 in (18 cm). The foot soles are densely furred, and the ears are entirely concealed in fur. The summer coat is gray to reddish brown, with a conspicuous dark line running from the head down the back. *Dicrostonyx* is the only genus in Rodentia in which individuals have completely white coats in winter. These lemmings also develop enlarged claws on the third and fourth digits of the front feet for digging in frozen soil. Their generic name *Dicrostonyx*, Greek for "forked claw," refers to these appendages.

Collared lemmings live in colonies. They excavate communal underground burrows above the permafrost level, and also forage and live beneath the winter snowpack. They experience extreme fluctuations in population size, generally on a 3–4 year cycle. When populations peak, collared lemmings disperse from overcrowded areas. However, they move only a short distance from their original locations, and do not undertake long migrations such as those of the Norway Lemming.

Northern Collared Lemming

Dicrostonyx groenlandicus
ALSO: Nearctic, Green-
land, Peary Land, or Bering Collared Lemming, Nördlicher Halsbandlemming, Lemming à collerette, Лемминг, Avinnagaq. Qilangmiutaq, the Inuit name for the white winter phase, means "drops from the sky," referring to the sudden appearance of white lemmings in winter. SN means "fork-clawed [lemming] of Greenland."
RANGE: Occurs on the tundra from n Alaska east across n Canada and Canadian Arctic Is into n Greenland. Range extends farther north than that of any other rodent.
ID: L 4.5–7 in (11–18 cm). WT 1–4 oz (35–110 g). Short, stocky body. Small ears, short legs, and a very short tail. Summer pelage is gray, often with a buffy to rufous tone and pale brown chest band; dark line down the back and sometimes on the sides of the head; underparts light gray. In winter, coat is pure white.
HABITS: Active year round. Occupies high, dry, rocky areas in summer, lower elevation meadows in winter. Feeds on grasses, sedges, and other green vegetation in summer, and snow-covered twigs of willow, aspen, and birch in winter. Maintains runways beneath the snow and burrows down to permafrost level. Females become sexually mature by 40 days, males by 85 days. Males mate with multiple females and protect their nests. Females produce 2–3 annual litters, each with 4–8 young. Gestation is 19–21 days. Young are born in a nest located in an underground burrow or concealed in vegetation.
SIMILAR SPECIES (*not illus.*): RICHARDSON'S COLLARED LEMMING, *D. richardsoni*; open, dry tundra in nc Canada. UNALASKA COLLARED LEMMING, *D. unalascensis*; Umnak and Unalaska Is, Aleutians; fur does not turn white in winter, nor do the enlarged foreclaws develop. OGILVIE MTNS COLLARED LEMMING, *D. nunatakensis*;

Northern Bog Lemming
Synaptomys borealis
N Amer
4.5–6 in (11–15 cm)

Norway Lemming
Lemmus lemmus
Scandinavia, nw Russia
4–6.5 in (10–17 cm)

Siberian Brown Lemming
Lemmus sibiricus
N Siberia, Russian Arctic Is
5–6.5 in (13–17 cm)

Nearctic Brown Lemming
Lemmus trimucronatus
NE Siberia, nw N Amer
5–7 in (13–18 cm)

Palearctic Collared Lemming
Dicrostonyx torquatus
N Eurasia
5–7 in (13–18 cm)

Wood Lemming
Myopus schisticolor
N Eurasia
3–4.5 in (8–11 cm)

Northern Collared Lemming
Dicrostonyx groenlandicus
Arctic N Amer, Greenland
4.5–7 in (11–18 cm)

The collared lemmings' dark summer coat molts
to white in winter—these are the only rodents
known to undergo this transformation.

rocky alpine tundra in nc Yukon. NELSON'S COLLARED LEMMING, *D. nelsoni*; tundra; Seward Penin to Kuskokwin Bay, sc Alaska; synonymous with *D. exsul*, endemic to St Lawrence Is. UNGAVA COLLARED LEMMING, *D. hudsonius*; Ungava Penin and Belcher Is in ne Canada.

Palearctic Collared Lemming

Dicrostonyx torquatus
ALSO: Arctic Collared Lemming, Echter Halsband-lemming, Lemming arctique, Копытный лемминг. SN means "fork-clawed collared [lemming]."

RANGE: Occurs on tundra and forest-tundra, in areas with small willows, from the White Sea to Chukotka and Kamchatka, including Novaya Zemlya and the New Siberian Is.

ID: L 5–7 in (13–18 cm). WT 1.75–4 oz (50–110 g). In summer, back is reddish to grayish brown, spotted with buff or cream and with a wide, dark dorsal stripe and pale gray collar. Underparts are buffy to gray. Winter pelage is entirely white, and enlarged claws develop on third and fourth digits of the forepaws. Foot soles are densely furred. Ears are entirely concealed in fur. Tail is reddish brown at the base, whitish at the tip.
HABITS: Active year round. Feeds on willow and birch leaves and shoots, and the fruit of cloudberry (*Rubus*) and bilberry (*Vaccinium*) in summer. In winter, feeds on willow buds, leaves, twigs, and bark. Lives in colonies. Occupies high, dry, rocky areas in summer, where it shelters in shallow underground burrows or under rocks. Burrows have seed-storage and nesting chambers located near runways leading to food. In winter,

these lemmings often move to lower meadows where they can nest on the tundra surface under the protective blanket of snow. Females bear 2–3 litters annually, each with 5–6 young. Nesting chambers are lined with dry grasses, feathers, and often fur from muskoxen.

SIMILAR SPECIES: WRANGEL IS COLLARED LEMMING (*not illus.*), *D. vinogradovi*; endemic to Wrangel Is, Russia. Dorsal stripe is faint or absent.

GENUS *SYNAPTOMYS*
Northern Bog Lemming
Synaptomys borealis

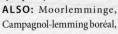

ALSO: Moorlemminge, Campagnol-lemming boréal, Северный мышевидный лемминг. SN means "boreal lemming."

RANGE: Found in Alaska and Canada, and south to n US, in sphagnum bogs, damp tundra, alpine meadows, and forest clearings.

ID: L 4.5–6 in (11–15 cm). Grayish brown above, pale gray below. Rust-colored fur at base of ears.

HABITAT: Lives in small colonies in wetlands, where sedges and grasses provide food and cover. Digs underground burrows in summer. Tunnels under the snow in winter. Makes runways through vegetation where it leaves piles of cuttings. Deposits droppings in special latrines. Breeds May–Aug. Gestation is about 21 days. Females produce 2–3 annual litters of 4–6 young in a burrow nest or one concealed in surface vegetation.

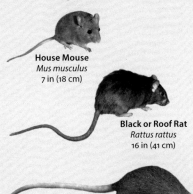

House Mouse
Mus musculus
7 in (18 cm)

Black or Roof Rat
Rattus rattus
16 in (41 cm)

Brown or Norway Rat
Rattus norvegicus
20 in (50 cm)

GENUS *MYOPUS*
Wood Lemming
Myopus schisticolor

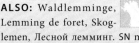

ALSO: Waldlemminge, Lemming de foret, Skoglemen, Лесной лемминг. SN means "particolored lemming."

RANGE: Found from Scandinavia across Siberia to Kamchatka, n China, and n Mongolia. Occurs in floodplain larch forest, pine bogs, old spruce forest marshes, mainly in areas with abundant mosses and fallen tree trunks.

ID: L 3–4.5 in (8–11 cm). WT 0.7–1.6 oz (20–45 g). Stout. Small ears. Silvery gray to slaty black, with a rufous saddle on the back and slightly paler underparts. Tail is heavily furred. Forefoot soles are naked. Hind feet are densely haired between the pads. Small forefoot "thumb" has a large, flattened nail with a grooming notch at the tip.

HABITS: Shy resident of forests with a dense moss-covered floor. Feeds almost exclusively on the tips of green mosses; also consumes grass, sedge, bilberries (*Vaccinium uliginosum*), and juniper bark. Gnaws tunnels through the moss substrate. Collects whole moss cushions for winter food, caching them under rocks and fallen logs where they are sheltered from the weather.

FAMILY MURIDAE
OLD WORLD MICE AND RATS

Muridae is the largest family of rodents, containing over 700 species that occur naturally in Eurasia, Africa, and Australia.

The Brown Rat, Black Rat, and House Mouse have been inadvertently introduced worldwide and now are resident pests in many arctic and subarctic towns, except in areas of extreme cold. The large BROWN or NORWAY RAT, *Rattus norvegicus*, lives communally with other rats in cellars, sewers, tunnels, and burrows. Its long-tailed relative, the BLACK or ROOF RAT, *Rattus rattus*, nests in attics, trees, and rubbish piles. The little HOUSE MOUSE, *Mus musculus,* is a highly successful colonist of homes and farms, where it feeds on grain, seeds, animal fodder, and human foods.

Northern Pika
Ochotona hyperborea
Siberia–e Asia
6–8 in (15–20 cm)

Collared Pika
Ochotona collaris
Alaska–nw Canada
7–8 in (17.5–20 cm)

Lagomorpha: Pikas, Hares, Rabbits

Members of this cosmopolitan order have big rounded ears, a short tail, and a unique dental formula. Most species have 28 teeth. The first incisors are enlarged while the second incisors are small, peg-like, and located immediately behind the first. Canine teeth are absent, and in the hares, a large gap (*diastema*) separates the incisors from the premolars and molars. The teeth are ever-growing and must be worn down by chewing on coarse plant material that forms the bulk of the diet. Lagomorphs produce hard, round, fecal pellets as well as soft, wet droppings. They re-ingest the wet droppings—a behavior called *coprophagy*—so their digestive system can reprocess the food for added nourishment.

FAMILY OCHOTONIDAE
PIKAS

Pikas are small, round-bodied herbivores. They have soft dense pelage, rounded ears, and appear to lack tails. There are 5 digits on the forefeet and 4 digits on the longer hind feet. Hearing and vision are excellent, and pikas climb with agility. As to habitat, they require a rocky area for cover and a nearby meadow or other vegetation where they can forage. Pikas are diurnal and do not hibernate. Young are born blind and nearly hairless following a gestation period of about 30 days.

GENUS *OCHOTONA*
Northern Pika

Ochotona hyperborea
ALSO: Nördlicher Pfeifhase, Pika du Nord, Sibirpipehare, Северная пищуха. SN means "pika of the Far North," the generic name coming from *ochodona*, the Mongolian name for pikas. CN derives from the Tungus (Siberian) word *piika*, or possibly from the Russian *pikat*, meaning "to squeak." Pika is also onomatopoeic for the species' loud, shrill alarm call, *peeka*.
RANGE: Occurs on talus slopes in mountains and rocky terrain at the edge of coniferous forests from the Ural Mtns across Siberia to Chukotka, Kamchatka, and e Asia.
ID: L 6–8 in (15–20 cm). WT 4.5–6.7 oz (122–190 g). Reddish brown in summer, grayish brown in winter; paler underparts. Some have dark patches on sides of the neck or lower back. Long whiskers.
HABITS: Gathers grass and dries it in "hay piles" near the burrow. Plant matter is stored and consumed in winter to supplement food they find under the snow. Colonial in some areas. In other locations, solitary pairs defend large territories. Vocalizations include the *peeka* alarm call and the chattering and whistling "song" that males emit in courtship. Two litters of 3–4 young are born in summer in burrows made under rocks, fallen logs, and tree stumps.

Collared Pika

Ochotona collaris

ALSO: Cony, Rock Rabbit, Mouse Hare, Whistling Hare, Little Chief Hare, Piping Hare, Alaska-Pfeifhase, Pika à collier, Alaskapipehare, Воротничковая пищуха. SN means "collared pika."

RANGE: Occurs in mountains on talus slopes and boulder fields, generally above the timberline, in Alaska from the Yukon-Tanana uplands and Chigmit Mtns to Skagway and possibly Brooks Range; and in Canada from the Richardson Mtns in n Yukon, south into nw Brit Columbia and east to the Mackenzie Rvr in NWT.

ID: L 7–8 in (17.5–20 cm). WT 4–5 oz (117–145 g). Dorsal pelage gray or blackish. Indistinct gray collar on nape and shoulders. Buff-colored on the side of the face and neck. Underparts creamy white without any buffy wash.

HABITS: Lives in loose groups, sharing its alpine habitat with marmots, arctic ground squirrels, northern red-backed voles, and ermines, which are the pika's main predator. Sounds a loud, sharp *peeka* when alarmed. In summer, accumulates and sun-dries "hay piles" of cut grass and other vegetation that will supplement food found under the winter snow. Peak of breeding season is May–Jun. Females give birth to 2–3 young in a nest within the rocks. The young remain in the nest for about 30 days before they are weaned and emerge above ground. Young disperse in a few days and leave to establish their own territories.

FAMILY LEPORIDAE
HARES AND RABBITS

Leporids have thick, soft fur. Arctic species undergo a seasonal molt, and the color of their coat changes from white in winter to brown in summer. The foot soles are covered with hair, which in the arctic species provides insulation and traction on the snow. The toes terminate in long, nearly straight claws. Hearing is acute. Many of these animals use their hind limbs to produce thumping beats that can be heard at a long distance. These serve to warn other members of their herd of potential danger and also play a role in courtship.

Hares and rabbits are similar in that they are herbivores that feed on a great variety of plant material and do not store food as pikas do. They also differ in many ways. Hares are generally larger than rabbits and have longer, black-tipped ears. They are long-legged, jumping mammals. Young hares, or *leverets*, are born above ground. Leverets are precocial, meaning that at birth they have a coat of fur and open eyes, and are able to walk and run. Rabbits, in contrast, are short-legged, running animals. The young are born naked and blind, and are nursed and reared in a burrow.

GENUS *LEPUS*
Arctic Hare

Lepus arcticus

ALSO: Polarhase, Lièvre arctique, Polarhare, Арктический заяц, Ukaliq, Ukaliarjuk. SN means "hare of the Arctic."

RANGE: Occurs on open dry tundra north of the treeline in Greenland and Canada, north through the Canadian High Arctic, and south along the arctic coasts of Nunavut and NWT to Hudson Bay. Isolated populations occur on tundra and barrenland mountains in n Quebec and Labrador, and the coast of Newfoundland.

ID: L 24–32 in (60–80 cm). WT 6–12 lb (2.7–5.4 kg). Ear length is 3–4 in (7.5–10.5 cm). AD WINTER: Pure white coat, with black-tipped ears. AD SUMMER: Coat color varies with latitude. Hares in the High Arctic are mostly white in summer, with a cinnamon or gray wash on the nose, forehead and ears, and occasionally on the back. At lower latitudes, the summer coat (worn for only a few weeks) is brown with bluish gray patches and a frosting of white, pink, or cinnamon. Tail, ears, and legs remain white. JUV: Leverets are born with grizzled grayish brown fur, which turns white and brown on the head as they age.

HABITS: Arctic hares live in groups called *herds*, which can contain a few scattered individuals or large assemblies of up to 100 hares. Diet includes low-growing tundra plants such as saxifrage, crowberry, the twigs and roots of arctic willows, seaweed, carrion, and food scraps scavenged from garbage dumps. In winter, hares forage in areas of shallow snow cover where plants are exposed by wind. Relying on their sense of smell to locate food buried beneath the snow, they dig into the snow with a rapid, sharp stamping of the clawed forefeet, or chew through the hard, icy crust with their teeth.

Arctic hares are active all winter because of the excellent insulation provided by the short, dense undercoat lying beneath a long, silky top coat. The black fur on the ear tips keeps the sensitive ear tips warm when the sun is shining. In addition, the typical crouched posture during periods of prolonged inactivity keeps the Arctic Hare warm.

After feeding, a hare will tightly tuck in its extremities, fold its tail down between the hind legs, tuck its forepaws into its chest, and lower its ears down into the fur on its back to conserve warmth. Only the thick, coarsely furred pads of the hind feet touch the ground. A solitary hare will sit like this for hours, back to the wind, often in the shelter of rocks, snow drifts, or buildings. For added protection, arctic hares dig dens up to 6 ft (1.9 m) long in snowdrifts and shelter in them during periods of extreme cold.

Breeding season is Apr–Sep. David Gray of the Canadian Museum of Nature in Ottawa has noted that at the start of the mating season, the male Arctic Hare becomes a "flasher" par excellence. When another hare is sighted, the male stands with legs tensed as it uncoils its long penis and repeatedly whips it along his belly. The function of this behavior is probably to visually stimulate females into breeding and receptivity, thus ensuring that the young are born in time to attain adequate food and growth to survive the coming winter.

Females bear 1–2 annual litters, each with 3–6 leverets. Gestation is about 50 days. The young are delivered in the open in a shallow depression on the tundra where their grayish brown fur blends into the surroundings. The mother remains close to her young for a few days after birth, but for most of the remaining summer, she visits the leverets at a specific nursing site only once every 18–19 hours. The leverets disperse from the nursing site after each visit and return there the next day about an hour before the mother is due to nurse them again. The young are weaned abruptly in late Aug, but remain together as a group for another few weeks.

USE: Northern cultures have long relied on arctic hares for food and pelts. Animal bones discovered in thousand-year-old middens indicate that arctic hares were the third most common animals used for food, after seals and caribou.

Hunters used pads of hare skins to keep their feet warm while they stood long hours at seal breathing holes. Seal hunters hid behind a white shield made of hare pelts to camouflage themselves against the snowy landscape. They preferred the hides of arctic hares because they are much whiter than those of arctic foxes or polar bears. Pelts were also made into children's clothing, socks, mittens, and sleeping bags, and the hare's pliable skin and subcutaneous membranes were used as bandages to help heal cuts and boils.

The people of the Far North also incorporated the Arctic Hare into their art and culture. Small ivory carvings of hares found in Dorset culture archaeological sites on Ellesmere Is date to 1000 years ago; they are thought to be offerings to the animal spirits to preserve good relations between hunters and their prey.

STATUS: Populations are stable over most of the range. It has been illegal to hunt arctic hares in Newfoundland since 1930 because of their low numbers and restricted range there.

Arctic hares are social animals and often gather in large groups known as herds. While some individuals rest and feed, others watch for predators. In winter, arctic hares huddle together to keep warm and in spring congregate to bask in the sun.

Alaskan Hare

Lepus othus

ALSO: Tundra Polar Hare, Ukalisukruk, Ushkanuk, Okhotsk, Ooskon, Alaskahase, Lièvre d'Alaska, Тундровый заяц.

RANGE: Occurs on windswept rocky slopes, coastal tundra, and alpine tundra to 2165 ft (660 m) in w Alaska, including the north slope of Brooks Range; also occurs in ne Chukotka, Russia (as *L. o. tschuktschorum*).

ID: L 22–30 in (56–75 cm). WT 8.5–16 lb (4–7.2 kg). AD SUMMER: Grayish brown with a white undercoat. AD WINTER: Entirely white, except for black ear tips.

HABITS: Solitary, except during mating season in Apr–May, when groups of 20 or more hares may congregate. Most active at dusk and dawn. Feeds on leaves, shoots, bark, and roots of arctic willows as well as grasses, berries, and flowers. Females bear a single litter of 4–8 leverets each year. Gestation is 63 days. Young are born in Jun–Jul in open nests, often in alder thickets. Both adults and young rely on hiding and protective coloration for defense. They do not dig burrows.

USE: The Alaskan Hare is an important food source for birds of prey, weasels, wolverines, foxes, and polar bears. It is seldom used for human food, but is trapped for fur, which is used to line shoes and clothing.

Snowshoe Hare

Lepus americanus

ALSO: Varying Hare, Schneeschuhhase, Lièvre d'Amérique, Snøskohare, Американский беляк. CN refers to the large, wide, furry hind feet that give a good footing on ice and soft snow. SN means "American hare."

RANGE: Occurs in Alaska and Canada, east to Hudson Bay and Newfoundland, and south into n US in the Sierra, Rocky, and Appalachian Mtns; introduced to Kodiak Is and other islands in the Aleutian chain. Found on tundra, in dense, brushy cover in open coniferous forest, in open fields, along fence rows, and in swamps, riverside thickets, and bogs.

ID: L 13–20 in (34–50 cm). WT 3–3.5 lb (1.4–1.5 kg).

Long, broad hind foot measures 5–6 in (12–15 cm); soles of the feet are densely furred, with stiff hairs on the hind feet forming the snowshoe. AD WINTER: Entirely white, except for black eyelids and black tips on ears. AD SUMMER: Grizzled rusty or grayish brown back with a blackish middorsal line; gray flanks; white underparts. Face and legs are cinnamon brown. Ears are brown, tipped with black, and edged with white or cream. Retains a brownish gray undercoat in all seasons—a feature absent in the Arctic Hare. Seasonal molts, which take about 72 days to complete, are probably regulated by day length.

HABITS: Solitary. Does not hibernate. Rests and hides in the cover of vegetation by day, and maintains trails and runways between open areas and cover. Takes dust baths, which help to remove parasites from the fur. Forages at dawn and dusk, at night, and on cloudy days. Summer diet includes green grasses, clovers, sedges, ferns, forbs, and new growth of aspens, birches, and willows. In winter, feeds on buds, twigs, bark, and evergreen leaves of woody plants; also takes frozen carrion and can be cannibalistic.

Usually silent, but squeals loudly when attacked, and hisses and snorts when fighting. Most communication involves thumping the large hind feet against the ground. Able to swim across small lakes and rivers, and also enters water to avoid predators. Escapes from predators by running away at speeds up to 27 mph (43 kmh), while frequently changing direction and executing vertical leaps.

Begins to breed at 1 year of age. Mating season is Mar–Aug. Several males will follow females in estrus. Female hares that are unreceptive to mating will box with males to repel their advances. Mating is polygynandrous, with males and females both having multiple mates. Gestation lasts 36–40 days. Females become highly aggressive and intolerant of males when about to give birth. They retire to a previously prepared birthing pad of packed-down grasses. Females bear up to 4 litters a year, each with 2–8 young. Parental care is by the female alone. Leverets hide in separate sheltered spots during the day, then return to a central location where the mother nurses them for 5–10 minutes before

Skull of a hare

Snowshoe Hare in winter pelage

Snowshoe Hare
Lepus americanus
N Amer
13–20 in (34–50 cm)

Snowshoe Hare in summer
Reddish brown tail

Hares boxing

Mountain Hare in molt

Mountain Hare in winter

Tail is white year-round

Mountain or Blue Hare
Lepus timidus
Eurasia
20–25 in (50–63 cm)

European Rabbit
Oryctolagus cuniculus
Europe
Introduced to Aleutians
13–18 in (34–45 cm)

Alaskan Hare in summer
White tail year-round

Alaskan Hare
Lepus othus
Chukotka, w Alaska
22–30 in (56–75 cm)

Arctic Hare crouching to conserve heat

The Arctic Hare turns brown in summer in the lower latitudes but stays white year-round in the High Arctic.

Arctic Hare
Lepus arcticus
N Canada, Greenland
24–32 in (60–80 cm)

they disperse again. Young are weaned at 4 weeks. Young hares freeze in their tracks when alarmed, and rely on cryptic coloration to escape notice. Mortality in the first year is about 85 percent. Lifespan is up to 5 years in the wild.

USE: Hunted for pelts and meat for human use. Rabbit-canning factories existed in the 1890s, and Newfoundland "bottled rabbit" is still available in season. Food source for lynx, foxes, coyotes, wolves, martens, minks, and birds of prey. Predator populations, especially those of lynx, are directly related to hare populations.

STATUS: Dramatic population fluctuations occur every 6–12 years, when numbers exceed the carrying capacity of the environment. Lack of food and overcrowding also lead to disease and lowered reproductive rates.

Mountain Hare

Lepus timidus

ALSO: Blue Hare, Variable Hare, Schneehase, Lièvre variable, Alminnelig hare, Nordhare, Заяц-беляк. SN means "timid hare."

RANGE: Occurs from Scandinavia and nc Europe, east to e Siberia and Chukotka, and south to Sakhalin and n Asia; isolated populations occur in the Alps, Scotland, Wales, and Ireland. Introduced into England, Scotland, and Faroes; introduced unsuccessfully into Svalbard. Found in pine, birch, and juniper forests, in grassy forest clearings, along rivers, in heather moorland, montane grassland, dry rocky hillsides, and woodland up to the snow line.

ID: L 20–25 in (50–63 cm). WT 4.5–6 lb (2–2.7 kg). Coarse fur. AD SUMMER: Brown to grayish black, with dusky blue underfur on flanks. AD WINTER: White, except for black-tipped ears. Tail remains white year round.

HABITS: Most active at dusk and at night, except during breeding season when it is more diurnal. Gregarious; groups of 20–100 may forage together, feeding on twigs, buds, and bark of birch, juniper, poplar, and willow as well as berries, grasses, clover, grain, and garden crops. Fights by boxing with forefeet and kicking with hind feet. Shelters in shallow depressions under vegetation and also digs burrows into hillsides

and under winter snow. Vocalizations include screams when alarmed and clicking sounds made with the teeth.

During the prolonged mating season (Feb–Aug), several males may pursue a single female, who "boxes" them away if she is unready to mate. Gestation is about 50 days. One to 4 litters of 3–6 leverets are born in a shallow den (a *couch* or *form*) under vegetation or a rocky outcrop. The mother remains with the young for a few days, after which she returns to suckle the leverets only once a day at a specific nursing site. Juvenile mortality is typically 80 percent in the first year. Maximum lifespan is 10 years.

STATUS: Large fluctuations in populations often occur, sometimes with a decline of 75 percent of adults in a single year.

GENUS *ORYCTOLAGUS*
European Rabbit

Oryctolagus cuniculus

ALSO: Coney, Wildkaninchen, Lapin européen, Kanin, Европейский кролик. Males are called *bucks;* females are *does;* young are *kits* or *bunnies.* SN means "burrow-digging rabbit."

RANGE: Introduced to Middleton Is in the Gulf of Alaska and to Umnak, Rabbit, and Hog islands in the Aleutians. Native to Europe.

ID: L 13–18 in (34–45 cm). WT 3–5 lb (1.3–2.2 kg). Grayish brown coat. Long ears, large hind legs, and short fluffy tail, which is dark on top and white underneath.

HABITS: Lives in small colonies called *warrens.* Digs burrows with separate living and birthing chambers; the female excavates the birthing chamber before giving birth. Sleeps in the burrow by day, and emerges to forage with other rabbits at night along established runways. Remains immobile when alarmed, then runs in a zigzag pattern to shelter in burrow. Hops using the long, powerful hind legs. Hind feet have a thick padding of fur to dampen shock of rapid impacts. Long toes are webbed, which keeps the toes from spreading apart when jumping. Dominant males are polygynous. Females produce 5–7 litters per year, each with 6–12 young. Both parents tend the offspring.

Perissodactyla: Odd-toed Ungulates

Odd-toed ungulates, or perissodactyls, are large hoofed animals. They first appeared about 60 million years ago on the open grasslands of N Amer. These animals support their body weight on the median third toe. The large foot bones absorb the stress of running, and the hooves ensure traction on almost any surface.

FAMILY EQUIDAE
HORSES

The horse (*Equus caballus*) is the only odd-toed ungulate found in the Arctic. Although the horse does not occur there in its feral state—the only remaining wild horse being Przewalski's Horse of Asia—it is represented by breeds developed in Siberia and Iceland.

Yakut Pony

The Yakut Pony is the world's northernmost horse breed. It ranges from the Siberian arctic coast south to Mongolia, with most living in the Republic of Sakha (Yakutia) in e Siberia. It can be white, russet, or dark brown in color, and stands about 5 ft (1.5 m) high at the withers.

The Yakut Pony lives outdoors year round, even in places where the winter temperature can plunge to −60°F (−50°C). Its compact body and short, heavy legs act to conserve heat. The thick, long mane and tail, dense winter coat, and subcutaneous reserves of stored fat insulate the body against the winter cold. The thick, sturdy hooves are used to dig out food plants from under the snow, and keen eyesight helps these ponies locate food on dark winter days. In addition, the Yakut Pony can alter its breathing pattern, lowering its average respiration rate from 20 breaths per minute in summer to 10 breaths per minute in winter, thus inhaling less cold air.

The Yakut Pony's reputation for strength and hardiness prompted explorers to employ it in attempts to reach the North and South Poles. About 130,000 Yakut ponies currently live in the Republic of Sakha. The ponies there are used as beasts of burden; the meat is used for human consumption, and the mares provide milk that can be fermented and made into the region's local drink, *kumiss*.

Icelandic Horse

The Icelandic Horse, or *Íslenski hesturinn*, is another pony-sized horse breed of the Far North. The Vikings introduced the ancestors of these horses to Iceland over a millennium ago. Norse settlers came by boat and, due to limited space, selected only the best and strongest horses from the British Isles and Norway to accompany them on their long sea voyage.

Old documents show that Icelandic horses were imported and exported freely until around 1100 AD, when fear of disease prompted Iceland to close its borders to livestock imports. The ban has never been lifted, and the Icelandic Horse has been bred for centuries without the addition of outside bloodstock. It is considered to be a perfectly preserved, pure breed of horse.

A typical specimen stands about 55 in (140 cm) at the withers and weighs up to 900 lb (410 kg). It can be white, beige, gold, tan, dark brown, or black and also occurs as a skewbald (white and another color) or piebald (black and white). In response to Iceland's harsh climate and limited food resources, the breed has become shorter and stockier, and has developed a thick double coat, long shaggy mane, dense bones, and a nasal chamber that warms the air before it is inhaled. The stomach is smaller by a third than other breeds, so less food is required. The gut is one third longer, which allows these horses to digest and retain nutrients more efficiently.

There are about 75,000 Icelandic horses in Iceland today. Some are used for rounding up sheep and cattle. Most are employed in leisure riding, sport racing, and gaited competition.

The Yakut Pony as pictured on an Azerbaijan stamp and the Republic of Sakha's coat of arms

Artiodactyla: Even-toed Ungulates

Artiodactyla, the order of even-toed ungulates, includes deer, moose, reindeer, sheep, camels, pigs and other ruminants (i.e., mammals that have a multi-chambered stomach and chew the cud regurgitated from the first stomach chamber, or rumen). The third and fourth digits of the feet terminate in hooves and bear most of the animal's weight.

FAMILY CERVIDAE
REINDEER, CARIBOU, MOOSE

The family Cervidae (Latin for "deer") includes grazing and browsing animals that grow bony structures called *antlers*. Antler formation is restricted to males, except in reindeer and caribou, in which females grow antlers as well as males. Antlers are shed in winter, regrow each spring, and reach their maximum size in adult males. The growing antlers are covered with a soft skin called *velvet,* which is lined with blood vessels that carry calcium and other nutrients to the developing bone. In late summer, prior to mating, the animals scrape off the velvet by rubbing their antlers against trees, woody shrubs, and posts. Rodents and other animals gnaw on the fallen antlers to assimilate the calcium.

GENUS *RANGIFER*
Caribou (N Amer) Reindeer (Eurasia)

Rangifer tarandus
ALSO: Ren, Renne, Rein, Северный олень, Карибу, Tuktuk, Tuttut. SN means "deer of the north." CN: Caribou derives from *qalipu*, a Mi'kmaq Indian word meaning "snow-shoveler" and referring to the habit of pawing the snow to uncover food. Reindeer derives from the Norse word *reinsdyr*.
RANGE: Circumpolar on tundra and in boreal forests. Introduced to the Pribilofs, St Matthew Is, Iceland, Scotland, Argentina, Chile, Island of South Georgia, and Kerguelen Is. High Arctic and forest herds are mostly sedentary. Tundra herds are typically migratory.
ID: L 71–95 in (180–240 cm). SH 32–59 in (82–150 cm). WT 130–330 lb (60–150 kg). Females (cows) are about 25 percent smaller than males (bulls). Both sexes develop forked antlers. Bulls' antlers begin to grow in spring and are shed in fall; cows shed their antlers in winter. Bulls have large antlers, with a prominent brow tine or *shovel;* antlers

can measure up to 51 in (130 cm) long, and can weigh up to 33 lb (15 kg). Females have smaller antlers measuring 10–20 in (25–50 cm) long. Winter coat is dense, with long whitish guard hairs and brownish undercoat. Outer coat is shed in spring, revealing the dark fur beneath.
SUBSPECIES: PEARY CARIBOU, *R. t. pearyi*, Canadian High Arctic. SH 37–39 in (94–99 cm). Compact body, short legs, and small, rounded head. Winter coat is whitish to cream, with a tan, brown, or gray saddle. Summer coat is slate gray, with white legs and underparts. Antler velvet is gray.

SVALBARD REINDEER, *R. t. platyrhynchus*, Norway's Svalbard Archipelago. SH 32–37 in (82–94 cm). Smallest subspecies. Compact, somewhat potbellied body. Short legs. Winter coat is pale gray to cream. Summer coat is buffy white, with a brown to gray saddle. Antler velvet is gray.

GRANT'S CARIBOU, *R. t. granti*, Alaska–Yukon tundra and Adak Is and Umnak Is (Aleutians). SH 47–59 in (120–150 cm). WT to 400 lb (182 kg). Long legs. Winter coat is brownish gray, with long, white-tipped guard hairs. Summer coat is dark grayish brown. Males have a white flank stripe and white "socks" above the hooves. Males develop conspicuous white manes prior to the rut. Largest antlers of any caribou in relation to body size. Antler velvet is dark brown.

BARREN-GROUND CARIBOU, *R. t. groenlandicus*, ne Canada–w Greenland, tundra. SH 42–50 in (107–127 cm). WT to 330 lb (150 kg). Long legs. Dark brown summer coat, with white underbelly and white "socks" above the hoofs. Males develop conspicuous white manes prior to the rut. Long whitish guard hairs cover the neck and back in winter. In all seasons, face is darker than the rest of the body and muzzle is white. Antler velvet is dark brown.

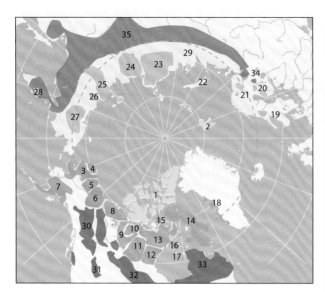

HIGH ARCTIC

1 Peary Caribou
2 Svalbard Reindeer

TUNDRA

Grant's Caribou

3 Western Arctic herd
4 Teshekpuk herd
5 Central Arctic herd
6 Porcupine herd
7 Alaska herd

Barren-ground Caribou

8 Bluenose herd
9 Bathurst herd
10 Ahiak herd
11 Beverly herd
12 Qamanirjuaq herd
13 NE Mainland herd
14 Baffin Is herd
15 Boothia Penin herd
16 Southampton Is herd
17 Coats Is herd
18 W Greenland herd

Reindeer

19 Norway herd
20 Finland herd
21 Kola Penin herd
22 Novaya Zemlya herd
23 Taimyr Penin herd
24 Lena-Olenek herd
25 Yana-Indigirka herd
26 Sundrunskaya herd
27 Chukotka herd
28 Kamchatka herd
29 Domesticated herds

FOREST (TAIGA)

Woodland Caribou

30 N Mountain herd
31 S Mountain herd
32 Boreal herd
33 George & Leaf Rvr herds

Forest Reindeer

34 Finnish Forest herd
35 Eurasian Forest herds

WOODLAND CARIBOU, *R. t. caribou*, lowland and alpine forests of n Canada. SH 39–55 in (100–140 cm). WT 240–600 lb (110–272 kg). Largest-bodied caribou. Summer coat is dark chocolate brown, with creamy white on underbelly, beneath the tail, and stockings. Males develop white manes prior to the rut. Winter coat is dark gray above, paler below. Antlers are thicker, wider, and more flattened than other subspecies. Up to half of the females lack antlers or have a single antler.

FOREST REINDEER, *R. t. fennicus*, *R. t. valentinae*, and *R. t. phylarchus*, Eurasian taiga from Finland to Kamchatka. SH 31–60 in (80–150 cm). WT 132–660 lb (60–300 kg). Gray winter coat. Brown summer coat, with a long whitish beard and pale flank stripe. Some animals have white markings around the eyes and muzzle. Narrow, upright, V-shaped antlers. Coat is darker, antlers larger, and legs longer than the domesticated reindeer's.

WILD AND DOMESTICATED REINDEER, *R. t. tarandus*, *R. t. sibiricus*, *R. t. angustirostris*, *R. t. pearsoni*, *R. t. setoni*, Eurasian tundra. SH 39–47 in (100–120 cm). WT 220–330 lb (100–150 kg). Light brown summer coat. Pale gray winter coat. Irregularly branched antlers. Domesticated reindeer are shorter-legged and stockier than their wild counterparts.

"Once upon a time there were no caribou on the earth. But then there was a man who wished for caribou, and he cut a great hole deep into the ground, and up through this hole came caribou, many caribou. The caribou came pouring out, till the earth was almost covered with them. And when the man thought there were caribou enough for mankind, he closed up the hole again. Thus the caribou came up on earth."

Told by Kibkarjuk and recorded by Knud Rasmussen
in *Report of the Fifth Thule Expedition, 1921–1924*

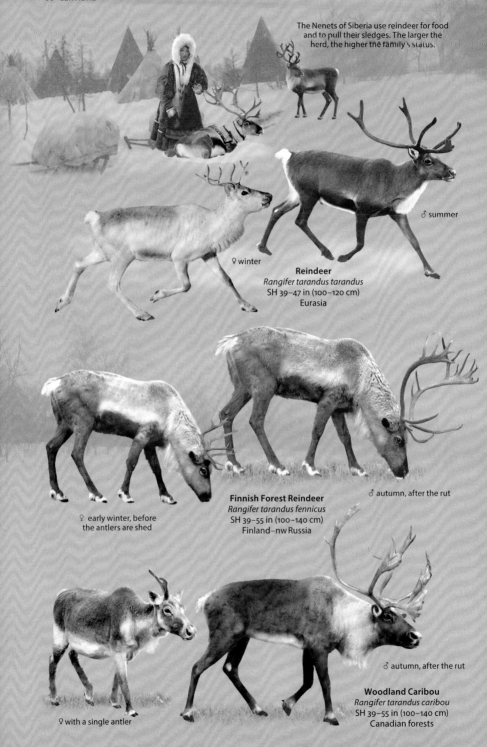

The Nenets of Siberia use reindeer for food and to pull their sledges. The larger the herd, the higher the family's status.

♂ summer

♀ winter

Reindeer
Rangifer tarandus tarandus
SH 39–47 in (100–120 cm)
Eurasia

♀ early winter, before the antlers are shed

Finnish Forest Reindeer
Rangifer tarandus fennicus
SH 39–55 in (100–140 cm)
Finland–nw Russia

♂ autumn, after the rut

♀ with a single antler

♂ autumn, after the rut

Woodland Caribou
Rangifer tarandus caribou
SH 39–55 in (100–140 cm)
Canadian forests

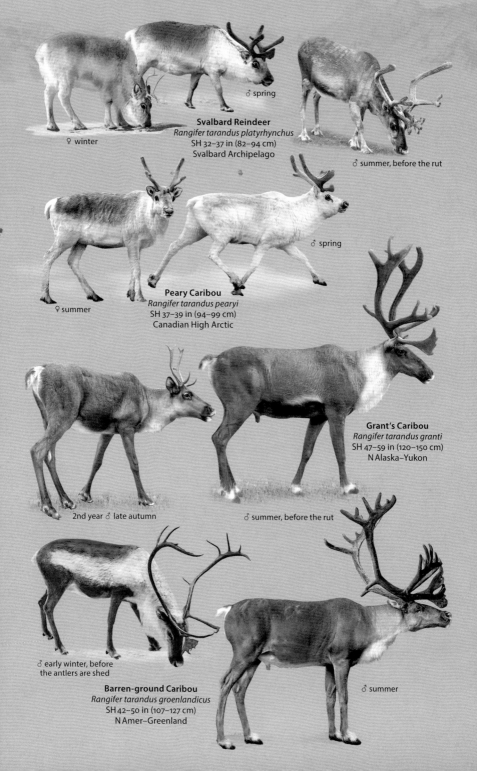

Svalbard Reindeer
Rangifer tarandus platyrhynchus
SH 32–37 in (82–94 cm)
Svalbard Archipelago

♀ winter

♂ spring

♂ summer, before the rut

Peary Caribou
Rangifer tarandus pearyi
SH 37–39 in (94–99 cm)
Canadian High Arctic

♀ summer

♂ spring

Grant's Caribou
Rangifer tarandus granti
SH 47–59 in (120–150 cm)
N Alaska–Yukon

2nd year ♂ late autumn

♂ summer, before the rut

Barren-ground Caribou
Rangifer tarandus groenlandicus
SH 42–50 in (107–127 cm)
N Amer–Greenland

♂ early winter, before
the antlers are shed

♂ summer

Widely splayed hooves and large dewclaws of caribou and reindeer reduce their sinking into snow or mud.

In spring the pads on the undersides of the hooves are plump and spongy, but they begin to dry as the animals travel over hard or rocky ground.

By winter, the hoof pads are reduced to hard, sharp shells. The underside becomes a scoop that is used to dig out lichens and other vegetation buried under the snow.

Native hunters hang dried caribou hooves on their belts. The hooves rattle together, imitating the clatter of caribou feet and masking the sound of the hunter's steps.

Caribou and reindeer have many adaptations for living in the cold. The large hooves and broad dewclaws splay widely and reduce sinking into soft snow or swampy soil. Compact, stocky bodies and short, heavily furred ears and tails conserve heat. Curled nasal passages increase the surface area of the mucous membranes, which warm and moisten the dry, cold inhalation before it enters the lungs. Facial hair extends down to and almost completely covers the lips, thus protecting the muzzle from frostbite. The dense, woolly undercoat of fine hairs and outer coat of long, hollow guard hairs provide insulation. The air-filled guard hairs make these animals so buoyant that when they are swimming across large lakes and rushing rivers, a third of the body remains above the water's surface.

HABITS: Peary caribou and Svalbard reindeer form small permanent herds. They are fairly sedentary, moving short distances only when hard icing conditions force them from their normal range. In summer, the High Arctic herds feed in fertile valleys and lowland plains. In winter, they paw vegetation from under the snow on ridges, mountain slopes, plateaus, and other areas having sparse snow cover.

The majority of woodland caribou and forest reindeer live in small bands in lichen-rich mature forests, open bogs, fens, and other low-lying wetlands, and generally occupy areas that have an annual snowfall of less than 10 ft (3 m). Most of these herds remain in the forest all year, moving only short distances with the changing seasons. Notable exceptions include the large George and Leaf Rvr herds of woodland caribou from Quebec and Labrador, which make annual migrations of 1250 mi (2000 km) between their winter range in the boreal forests and their calving grounds on the arctic tundra.

Barren-ground caribou, Grant's caribou, and some herds of wild reindeer also make long-distance migrations between inland wintering grounds and calving grounds on the coastal tundra. The Porcupine herd of Grant's caribou migrates over 1500 mi (2400 km) as it moves between its winter range in the interior and calving grounds on the Beaufort Sea. This is the longest migration of any of the world's land mammals.

Caribou and reindeer walk at about 4.5 mph (7 kmh), and on still days one can hear a clicking sound made by the tendons moving over the bones above the hooves. These animals can reach a running speed of 50 mph (80 kmh)—and they have great endurance. Only the wolf can overtake an adult caribou or reindeer in a long chase.

Both sexes mature at 2–3 years of age. Mature bulls are solitary or live in small bachelor herds that join the females during the mating season, or rut. A female usually bears a single calf (rarely twins) each year. Gestation is about 8 months. Females and young maintain a bond that lasts up to 1 full year. Average lifespan is 4.5 years; maximum lifespan is 9 years in males, 15 years in females.

Caribou and reindeer primarily eat lichens in winter and supplement their diet with lemmings, voles, birds, bird eggs, seaweed, and even their own calcium-rich fallen antlers. The winter diet of lichens, especially reindeer lichens, provides carbohydrates needed for energy. Small amounts

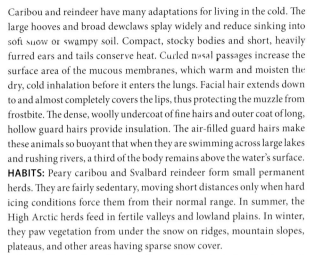

Reindeer lichens: *Cladina* (pale green), *Cetraria* (light brown)

of herbaceous plants, sedges, grasses, and mosses are also eaten. Because of their very good sense of smell, caribou and reindeer are able to sniff out these food plants even when they are buried up to 3 ft (1 m) beneath the snow.

In early spring, these animals seek out fresh, green vegetation that provides the proteins, vitamins, and minerals needed for antler growth and fat production. Cows that have just given birth are especially in need of protein to replenish their winter reserves and produce high-quality milk for their calves. In spring, caribou and reindeer feed mainly on newly unfurling leaves of willow and other deciduous shrubs. Flowers, plentiful on the tundra in summer, also attract attention. Mushrooms, especially large edible mushrooms of the genera *Boletus, Lactarius,* and *Russula,* provide a rich nitrogen source in the late summer and early autumn. These animals also feed on Fly Agaric (*Amanita muscaria*), a mushroom that induces a hallucinogenic "high" (*see p. 431*). Animals that eat these mushrooms, or drink the urine of another that has eaten one, often run about in a drunken state.

Reindeer and caribou are hosts to gut-dwelling parasites such as tapeworms (*Taenia* sp.) and hydatid worms (*Echinococcus granulosus*). Infection results from ingesting the eggs of the parasite from dirt or plants that are contaminated with feces of another infected animal.

In the summer months, the animals are harassed by mosquitoes, black flies, warble flies, and nose bot flies (*see p. 402*). The insect season is nearly intolerable for the tundra-dwelling herds, which can be seen violently shaking their heads, stamping their feet, and racing wildly over the terrain as they try to evade the swarms.

USE: Hunting of wild reindeer and herding of semi-domesticated reindeer for meat, hides, antlers, milk, and transportation are important to many people of the Far North.

The first attempt to domesticate reindeer is thought to have occurred about 3000 years ago by people living in the Altai Mtns on the Russian–Mongolian border. Over time, reindeer husbandry spread throughout the Eurasian north and today the industry represents the major land use of the tundra and, to lesser degree, of

the taiga. Between the North Sea and the Ural Mtns some 1 million reindeer are managed by the state and indigenous subsistence herders on an area of 290,000 sq mi (750,000 sq km). The general goal of the industry is meat and hide production, supplemented by the sale of antlers, antler velvet, blood, and endocrine glands to Asian markets. In addition, the Saami, Nenet, Tungus, Yakut, Chukchi, and Koriak peoples use their domesticated reindeer to pull sledges over the winter ice and snow.

Reindeer were introduced into Alaska in 1892 to provide meat for the coastal Inupiaq who had lost their traditional marine food sources to sealing and whaling. Seldon Jackson, a Presbyterian minister and Alaskan Commissioner of Education, hired one Captain Healy—an ex-slave from Georgia who became a merchant marine captain—to bring 171 reindeer from Siberia to Alaska and establish a domestic herd.

The reindeer industry boomed during the 1850s gold rush when gold miners used reindeer to pull sleds loaded with mining gear. Currently, there are about 20,000 free-ranging, semi-domesticated reindeer in Alaska. They are rounded up once a year and injected with Ivermectin to control parasites and warble and bot fly infestations. Some animals are harvested for meat and antlers.

STATUS: The world population of wild reindeer and caribou is about 4,215,000 animals: 3,000,000 in N Amer; 1,250,000 in Russia; 140,000 in Greenland; 25,500 in Norway; 2500 in Finland; 3500 in Iceland. The world population of domesticated reindeer is about 1,845,000 animals.

Populations of the N Amer herds experience natural cyclic fluctuations and many are currently in decline. WOODLAND CARIBOU have been affected mainly by loss of habitat and disturbance from human activities. Populations of the endangered PEARY CARIBOU have declined about 72 percent in the past 60 years. There were an estimated 10,000 individuals in 1994; present population is around 2000. About 2400 FINNISH FOREST REINDEER live in Salamajärvi Nature Park in sc Finland, another 5000 in Russian Karelia. The main threat to these populations is the increasing wolf population.

GENUS *ALCES*
Moose or Eurasian Elk
Alces alces

ALSO: Elch, Élan, Elg, Лось, Tuttuk, Tuktuvak. A mature male is referred to as a *bull*; a mature female is a *cow*; and a newborn of either sex is a *calf*. SN means "elk elk." CN "moose" derives from the Algonquin Indian word *moz*, meaning "twig-eater." State animal of Maine and Alaska. Largest living cervid and second largest land mammal in N Amer and Europe after the Bison, *Bison bison*.

RANGE: Sedentary near ponds, lakes, rivers, and swamps in coniferous and broadleaf forests, secondary growth in logged forest, tundra, farmland, open lowlands, and mountains to 5000 ft (1500 m). Occurs in Alaska and Canada, south through the Rocky Mtns, Great Lakes, and New England; occurs in Eurasia from n Europe east to Chukotka and Kamchatka, and south to n Mongolia and n China. Introduced to Newfoundland, Anticosti Is in the Gulf of St Lawrence, and Scottish highlands.

SUBSPECIES–ARCTIC: EURASIAN ELK (A), *A. a. alces*, n Europe–w Russia; differs from the other subspecies in the shape of the small cranial bones at the tip of the upper jaw, grayish brown pelage, and smaller size; considered a separate species by some authors. YAKUTIA MOOSE (Y), *A. a. pfizenmayeri*, e Siberia from the Yenisei Rvr to Yakutia; Mongolia; Manchuria. CHUKOTKA or EAST SIBERIAN MOOSE (C), *A. a. burulini*, ne Siberia from Yakutia east to Kamchatka. Largest Eurasian subspecies. EASTERN MOOSE (E), *A. a. americanus*, e Canada–ne US. WESTERN MOOSE (W), *A. a. andersoni*, nw Canada–nc US. ALASKAN MOOSE (G), *A. a. gigas*, Alaska–w Yukon; largest N Amer subspecies.

ID: SH 6–7 ft (1.8–2.1 m). WT 600–1598 lb (270–725 kg). Males are larger than females. Fur is brown to reddish brown (moose) or grayish brown with paler gray legs (Eurasian Elk). Undercoat is composed of dense brown hairs; outer coat has coarse, hollow, insulating guard hairs that grow to 8 in (20 cm) long on the mane. Coat is shed once a year, in spring. Well-developed shoulder muscles produce a humpbacked silhouette. Long, spindly legs. Short tail. Prominent dewlap, or *bell*, on the throat. Protruding muzzle with large nostrils. Long, pendulous upper lip.

Only males grow palmate antlers, which can measure 5 ft (1.5 m) across and weigh up to 77 lb (35 kg). Antlers begin to grow in spring, reach maximum spread in summer, and are shed in winter. They begin to grow at right angles to the skull and fork after a short distance. Lower fork has prongs, or *tines*, while upper forks develop a broad flat surface. Injury or poor nutrition can cause a bull to shed his antlers and grow a set of permanently deformed "devil's antlers."

HABITS: Solitary, except during autumn rut and during severe winters when a few animals may "yard" together where ample browse exists. Lacks sweat glands and can overheat when temperatures exceed 80°F (27°C). Runs at speeds up to 35 mph (56 kmh) and swims at speeds to 6 mph (9 kmh).

Has poor vision but exceptional hearing. Males are able to detect sounds that are more than 1 mi (1.6 km) away, thanks to their broad antlers. When sound waves hit and bounce off the antlers, the moose rotates its ears and "tunes in" to the amplified sound. Researchers George and Peter Bubenik demonstrated this cause and effect by using a set of trophy antlers, a remote speaker, and an artificial moose ear equipped with a microphone and sound meter. The sound meter recorded higher decibels when the artificial ear was turned toward the antlers than when it was turned toward the remote speaker.

Forages during the day, with peaks at dawn and dusk, eating up to 88 lb (40 kg) of plant material each day. In winter, feeds on shoots, twigs, and bark. In summer, consumes cereal crops and protein-rich forbs. To replace salt lacking in the winter diet, seeks out natural salt deposits and uses salt runoff from roads as an artificial lick. Eats sodium-rich aquatic plants, including water milfoil (*Myriophyllum*), pondweed (*Potamogeton*), and buckbean (*Menyanthes*). Forages for aquatic plants by putting its head underwater or completely submerging itself to a depth of 16 ft (5 m).

Both males and females are sexually mature at 2–3 years of age. Males are polygamous, mating

ad. ♂

ad. ♀

Moose or Eurasian Elk
Alces alces
Eurasia–N Amer
SH 6–7 ft (1.8–2.1 m)

calf

with more than one female. Bulls move to cows' territories during rutting season in Sep–Nov. They become very aggressive during this period. Bulls not only challenge one another with loud roars, bobbing antlers, and swaying gait, but will also charge at people and cars. The most consequential battles involve bulls butting their heads against one another, which can result in the antlers becoming locked and both animals dying of starvation.

Females are in estrus for 2–5 days at a time. If the female has not mated within the first cycle, she comes into season again about 3 weeks later. A female receptive to mating bellows to attract males to her. She will usually mate with the bull that has the largest antlers.

A single calf (rarely 2 or 3) is born in Apr–May after a gestation period of 226–264 days. Birth weight is 15–35 lb (7–16 kg). The calf can stand within a day and can swim within 2 weeks. It begins to eat green matter within a few days of birth, but is not weaned until about 6 months old. The calf retains a reddish brown natal coat for about 4 months, then acquires the dark brown coat of an adult. Calves remain with their mother for about a year until she delivers her new calf. The mother–calf bond is strong, and cows will often charge people who get too close to their offspring.

STATUS: Habitat alteration and, to a lesser degree, indiscriminate hunting, have caused Canadian moose populations to drop significantly in some areas. Moose were listed as Endangered in 2003 in Nova Scotia. The only Canadian populations that are currently increasing are those in the coastal rain forests of Brit Columbia. Clearing of the Canadian boreal forests poses a serious threat, as white-tailed deer have increased in the modified forests and with them has come the meningeal worm (*Paralaphostrongylus tenius*), which causes significant mortality in moose.

In Canada, the building of access roads produces an increase in highway collisions, which are frequent enough in some provinces that new highways are fenced off for their entire length. In Scandinavia, most mortalities are the result of elks being killed by autos and trains. The newspaper *Aftenposten* estimated that between 2000 and 2008, some 13,000 Eurasian elks died in collisions with Norwegian trains.

FAMILY BOVIDAE: SUBFAMILY CAPRINAE
MUSKOXEN, SHEEP, AND ALLIES

Bovids are cloven-hoofed, ruminant mammals. Both sexes typically have keratinous horns, which grow from the frontal bone. The horns are never branched or shed, and the horn's surface may be smooth or annulated (having raised rings).

GENUS *OVIBOS*
Muskox
Ovibos moschatus

ALSO: Moschusochse, Bœuf musqué, Moskus, Овцебык; Ummik and Oomingmak mean "animal with a skin like a beard." CN refers to the strong musky odor emitted by males during the seasonal rut. SN means "musky-smelling sheep-ox."

RANGE: Inhabits tundra, forest-tundra, and barrenlands of Greenland, Canadian High Arctic, and Canadian mainland east of the Mackenzie Rvr, south to ne Manitoba. Introduced to Quebec and n Yukon, Canada; Seward Penin and Nunivak Is, Alaska; Taimyr Penin and Wrangel Is, Russia; and Dovrefjell, Norway.

SUBSPECIES: BARREN-GROUND MUSKOX, *Ovibos moschatus moschatus*, n Canada. WHITE-FACED MUSKOX, *Ovibos moschatus wardi*, Greenland.

ID: L 6.9–8.1 ft (2.1–2.5 m). SH 4–5.25 ft (1.2–1.6 m). WT 400–880 lb (180–400 kg). Males are larger than females. Compact body; short, stocky legs; very large head; long, shaggy coat. Both sexes have long, pointed horns that curve downward and outward from the brow. On the males, the base of each horn extends across the forehead to meet as a solid "boss" of horn and bone up to 4 in (10 cm) thick. Females have a patch of fur on the forehead between the horns. Brown pelage, with a pale saddle on the back. Golden to pale gray stockings above the hooves. Undercoat is composed of long, extremely fine, grayish brown hairs called *qiviut;* outer coat of coarse, brown guard hairs hangs to the ground. Dense winter coat keeps the muskox warm to temperatures below −50°F (−45°C). Coat is shed in spring in straggly patches.

HABITS: Feeds on low tundra vegetation that is often covered with snow for most of the year. Uses its large rounded hooves to paw for food under light snow. If ice forms on top of the snow after a thaw-and-freeze cycle, the muskox strikes its head against the ice to break through the crust, then paws the broken chunks of hardened snow away to expose lichens, grasses, and other vegetation. In summer, herds move to river valleys or to forested areas where they feed on the protein-rich leaves of willows, dwarf birches, sedges, and other flowering herbs and low shrubs. The animals also seek out natural mineral licks to supplement the sodium lacking in the winter diet.

Muskox
Ovibos moschatus
N Amer–Greenland
SH 4–5.25 ft (1.2–1.6 m)

Typically lives in herds of 10–20 individuals, but if enough browse is present, up to 70 animals may congregate in winter. Basic social unit is a group of adult females, their young, and a male that leads the harem and remains with it for most of the winter. In spring, the bulls wander away from the herd to forage alone, then rejoin the females prior to the rut in late Jul–Aug. Males compete for dominance by charging and butting heads, reportedly running at each other at speeds of 25 mph (40 kmh). After several resounding crashes, one bull will declare dominance and drive away the other males. Non-breeding males form small bachelor herds or forage alone until the next breeding season.

Females reach sexual maturity at 2–4 years and usually bear a single calf (rarely twins) in the spring of every other year. Gestation is 8–9 months. Bonds between mother and calf are strong. A calf is able to feed on grasses within a week of birth, but needs its mother's milk to put on enough body fat to survive the next winter. A calf will lie next to its mother for warmth or stand under her "skirt" of hair.

The entire herd defends its young when wolves attack. If a lone wolf charges, adults form a line with the calves behind them and their heads and horns facing the attacker. An adult may charge out and try to head butt or hook the wolf with its horns. If a pack of wolves attacks, the herd forms a tight circle with horns pointed out and the calves in the center of the herd.

USE: Using dogs to keep muskoxen in a defense formation, Inuit hunters would single out an animal and kill it with bows and spears. They used the hides for making warm sleeping robes and the horns for weapons and implements. The meat was used for food except during the late summer rut, when a rotten taste permeates the flesh of the adult males. The Inuit also ate the raw, fermented, half-digested contents of the stomach or added it to soup made from meat or blood.

The fine, soft wool from the muskox's undercoat is called *qiviut* (pronounced *KIV-ee-ute*). Eight times warmer than sheep's wool and very lightweight, qiviut is one of the finest natural fibers known to man. It is often referred to as "cashmere of the north." It is also the world's most

expensive wool, with yarn currently selling for $40–$80 per ounce (28 g). Anthropologist John J. Teal began the industry of farming muskoxen for their fleece. In 1964, he took 33 calves from Nunivak Is, Alaska, and used a grant from the W. K. Kellogg Foundation to establish a herd at the Institute of Northern Agricultural Research (NARS) in Huntington, Vermont. Teal envisioned muskox farming as a cottage industry for native Alaskans and to that purpose established a herd at the University of Alaska–Fairbanks. Today the university and private companies such as Oomingmak, the native Alaskan Musk Ox Producers' Co-op, hand-comb qiviut from the shoulders and flanks of muskoxen living on their farms. Each animal yields 4–6 pounds of fleece, which is sold as raw fleece for spinning or as yarn for knitting hats, gloves, and scarves.

STATUS: European explorers and hunters armed with rifles gunned down entire herds as the animals formed a defensive phalanx around their calves, and by 1850 muskoxen had disappeared from Alaska's North Slope and many places in Canada. Today herds are protected in most of their range. In 1927 Canada established the Thelon Game Reserve for the muskox herds in NWT and w Nunavut.

Muskox cow and calf at Devon Is, Canada

GENUS *OVIS*
SHEEP

The genus *Ovis* includes wild sheep and their domestic counterparts. Male sheep are called *rams*, females are called *ewes*, and newborns are called *lambs*.

These animals are adapted for living in arid, marginal environments. They require very little drinking water and are able to digest rough plant materials with low nutritional value. Their dense coat, which insulates them from the cold, contains an outer layer of long hollow hairs called *kemps* and a short woolly undercoat called *fleece*.

In wild sheep, both sexes have horns with ribbed growth rings (*annuli*) that indicate the animal's age. The ewes have short spikes, while adult rams have massive spiraling horns. Both sexes have scent glands on the face and hind legs. The glands secrete a viscous substance that communicates information about territorial boundaries, status, and readiness to mate.

Rams and ewes live in different parts of the boreal mountains for most of the year. Ewes, lambs, and yearlings live in meadows with relatively poor fodder, as these areas attract fewer predators and offer greater security for the young. Rams over 5 years of age live in bachelor bands in meadows where nutritious grasses allow them to put on weight and develop horn mass. Social order in the bachelor herd is determined by the size of the horns. The ram with the largest horns is usually the alpha male, but if rams have similarly sized horns, rank is determined by butting heads. Thick skin and a dense layer of bone on the skull allow the males to absorb impacts suffered during head-butting battles.

As the fall rutting season approaches, the rams move to the ewes' meadows and begin to court and mate with the females. Mating system is polygynous; males mate with more than one ewe. Ewes usually select males with the largest horns and will thwart the advances of others. In spring, after a 6-month gestation, the ewe delivers a single lamb (rarely 2) on the most rugged cliffs within her territory. Mother and young remain on the lambing cliffs for several days before moving to adjacent meadows, where the lambs will graze until they are weaned.

Dall's Sheep
Ovis dalli

ALSO: Thinhorn Mountain Sheep, Alaska-Schneeschaf, Mouflon de Dall, Dalls snøsau, Баран Далля. SN means "Dall's sheep," referring to American naturalist William Healey Dall (1845–1927), who conducted the first US surveys of coastal Alaska and the Aleutians, explored the Kamchatka coast with whaler-naturalist Charles Scammon, and cataloged many of the Bering Sea marine mollusks.
RANGE: Inhabits steep mountain slopes with adjacent meadows for foraging. Disjunct populations occur in Alaska and w Canada.
SUBSPECIES: DALL'S SHEEP (D), *O. d. dalli*, Alaska, Yukon, nw Brit Columbia. STONE'S SHEEP (S), *O. d. stonei*, sc Yukon–nc Brit Columbia.
ID: L 39–59 in (100–150 cm). SH 30–41 in (75–105 cm). WT 100–200 lb (46–113 kg). Rams are typically about 40 percent heavier than ewes. Both sexes have amber-colored horns. Ram's horns spiral out and away from the head, and can measure up to 49 in (125 cm) long. Ewe's horns are recurved spikes less than 15 in (38 cm) long. VARIATIONS: *O. d. dalli* has a white or creamy coat and a white or black tail. *O. d. stonei* has a gray to brown pelage, with a pale facial blaze and white on the rump, belly, and backs of the legs. HYBRIDS (Fannin's Sheep) are gray, occasionally with a dark saddle, and with white on the belly, rump, and backs of the legs.
HABITS: Forages in alpine meadows and retreats to nearby steep cliffs to rest. Wintering flocks forage in areas of light snowfall where strong winds remove snow and expose alpine tundra vegetation. A ram courts a ewe in estrus by approaching in a low, stretched out posture as it flicks its tongue and smells her urine to make sure she is in season. The ram kicks the female with a foreleg to assess her willingness to mate. If receptive, she will butt and rub against the ram to elicit mating. Males guard the females they have mated with for 2–3 days, after which they wander off to look for additional mates.
STATUS: Lifespan is about 12 years. Populations increase steadily during long periods of mild weather and then suddenly decline as a result

juv.

♂

♀

♂

Dall's Sheep
Ovis dalli
Alaska–nw Canada
SH 30–41 in (75–105 cm)

♂

Stone's Sheep
Ovis dalli stonei

♂

juv.

Snow Sheep
Ovis nivicola
N Siberia–n Asia
SH 33–40 in (85–100 cm)

♂

♀

of unusually deep snow or other severe winter weather. Wolves, lynx, wolverines, mountain lions, and bears prey on adults; golden eagles have been observed seizing a lamb. Trophy hunting is limited to the taking of mature rams during Aug–Sep. Permitted subsistence hunting usually takes place in winter, when travel by snowmobile makes it easier to reach the sheep and retrieve the meat.

Snow Sheep

Ovis nivicola

ALSO: Siberian Bighorn Sheep, Schneeschaf, Mouflon des neiges, Snøsøau, Снежный баран. SN means "sheep that lives in snow." First described by Russian naturalist Johann Friedrich von Eschscholtz (1793–1831), who explored the Bering Strait region, Kamchatka, Aleutians, Chile, and California.

RANGE: Occurs in mountain forests, rocky meadows, and bare slopes to 6500 ft (2000 m) in Siberia and ne Asia, where open meadows for feeding lie adjacent to steep cliffs for resting. In years of heavy snow and ice, will migrate up to 75 mi (120 km) to find open ground for foraging.

SUBSPECIES: KAMCHATKA SNOW SHEEP (N), *O. n. nivicola*, Kamchatka. KORYAK SHEEP (K), *O. n. koriakorum*, Koryak Mtns. OKHOTSK SHEEP (A), *O. n. alleni*, Khabarovsk and Magadan; probably includes KOLYMA SHEEP of the Kolyma Mtns. YAKUT SHEEP (Y), *O. n. lydekkeri*, Verkhoyansk, Chersky, and Momsky Mtns of Yakutia, and n Kolyma Mtns in Anadyr. PUTORAN BIGHORN SHEEP (P), *O. n. borealis*, Putoran Mtns.

ID: L 55–63 (140–160 cm). TAIL 4 in (10 cm). SH 33–40 in (85–100 cm). WT 132–264 lb (60–120 kg). Males are larger than females. Rams have long spiraling horns that corkscrew back, down, and outward, forming a complete spiral. At maturity the horn base can be 15 in (38 cm) around and the rack may weigh up to 30 lb (13.5 kg). Ewes have fairly short, recurved spikes. VARIATIONS: *O. n. nivicola,* largest subspecies with the heaviest horns; grayish brown with a white rump and pale muzzle; the fronts of the legs are dark brown; rear of legs are lined with white. *O. n. alleni* has pale spots on the shoulder blades, and the tips

of its horns turn forward. *O. n. lydekkeri*, the smallest subspecies has white or creamy pelage and relatively small horns.

HABITS: Lives in groups of 7–20 individuals. Ewes and lambs, young males of 2–4 years of age, and adult rams over 4 years of age inhabit different parts of the mountains for most of the year. Rams move to the ewes' pastures for mating during the Dec–Jan rut.

STATUS: Largest numbers occur in Yakutia and Magadan. The 1992 Russian Red Data Book lists Kamchatka and Putoran Mtns populations as Endangered. Foxes, golden eagles, and white-tailed sea-eagles take lambs; wolves and wolverines take adults. Other mortality factors include falls from cliffs, perishing in avalanches, and loss of teeth, which may be completely worn by the age of 14. Maximum lifespan is 20 years, longer than any other wild sheep species.

Domesticated Icelandic Sheep

Ovis aries

ALSO: Íslenska sauðkindin. The breed descends from the *Spælsau*, a Norwegian short-tailed breed domesticated 8000 years ago. Viking ships that carried the first sheep to Iceland in the eighth century had sails woven from *Spælsau* fleece.

RANGE: Iceland. Introduced to Greenland.

ID: Face and short legs are bare. Usually horned, but some have no horns (*polled*), others have 4 horns. Famous for its double-layered fleece. The undercoat (*thel*) is down-like, springy, lustrous, and soft. The outer coat is similar to mohair, with long, coarse, wavy or corkscrewed hairs.

USE: The fleece of Icelandic sheep is sold through specialty markets to hand spinners, who weave it into sweaters and scarves.

Breeds of sheep, cows, and dogs native to Iceland

Eurasian Lynx
Lynx lynx
Eurasia
L 35–48 in (90–120 cm)

Canadian Lynx
Lynx canadensis
N Amer
L 26–42 in (67–107 cm)

Carnivora: Carnivores

Carnivores are meat-eaters that prey on other animals. They are distinguished from other mammals by the possession of 4 carnassial teeth (the fourth upper premolar and first lower molar on each side of the jaw), which cut against one another like scissors and act to shear flesh. They also have large canine teeth for seizing prey.

The order is divided into two suborders. FELIFORMIA contains the cat-like carnivores, which are distinguished by having double-chambered auditory bullae (bony capsules enclosing the middle and inner ear). The family Felidae represents the suborder in the Arctic. CANIFORMIA contains the dog-like carnivores. They are distinguished by having a single-chambered or partially divided auditory bullae. The families Canidae (wolves, dogs, coyotes, foxes), Mustelidae (mustelids, otters), Ursidae (bears), Otariidae (eared seals), Odobenidae (walruses), and Phocidae (true seals) represent the suborder in the Arctic.

FAMILY FELIDAE
CATS

Almost all cats are solitary, nocturnal hunters. They have a poor sense of smell, good hearing, and excellent vision, with eyes adapted for hunting in low light. Felids must eat meat to survive and require a much higher proportion of protein in their diet than most other mammals. They have 5 digits on the forepaws and 4 on the hind feet, and all have retractile or semi-retractile claws. The pupil of the eye contracts vertically.

GENUS *LYNX*
LYNX

Lynx are able to take prey several times their own weight. They stalk and ambush their quarry, then leap out on powerful hind limbs and seize the prey with their strong claws. They kill larger animals with a bite to the throat, then drag the carcass away to be eaten or cached in the snow. Sexually mature at about 12 months, lynx normally do not breed until they are 2–3 years old. The female dens in tree hollows, beneath overhanging rock ledges, or in thick brush. Gestation is 62–74 days, with 2–3 kits born in spring (May–Jun). Young are born blind; the eyes open at 10–16 days. The male leaves the den when the kits are born, but may provide food for the family for several weeks. Kits are weaned at 2–5 months. The mother and kits remain together through the winter. Lifespan is about 15 years in the wild, 20 years in captivity.

Eurasian Lynx

Lynx lynx

ALSO: Eurasischer Luchs, Lynx d'Eurasie, Eurasisk gaupe, Рысь. SN means "lynx lynx." In mythology, Lynx is an elusive, ghost-like animal that sees without being seen, and one who knows but does not readily reveal the forest's secrets. Lynx is also the name of a constellation lying between Ursa Major and Gemini.

RANGE: Occurs in dense forests of n Eurasia, and in c Asia in deciduous woodland and steep rocky terrain to 6500 ft (2000 m).

ID: L 35–48 in (90–120 cm). SH 24–30 in (60–75 cm). WT 22–44 lbs (10–20 kg). Heavy-bodied. Grizzled buffy brown fur, with indistinct or contrasting spots and rosettes on the legs and back. Prominent black ear tufts and a ruff of long fur around the face. Backs of ears have a central pale gray spot. Large golden yellow eyes. Short, black-tipped tail. Long legs, with hind limbs appearing longer than the forelimbs. The large, furred paws support the lynx on deep snow. The retractile claws do not show in the tracks.
HABITS: Solitary, except when breeding. Most active at dawn and dusk. Avoids water. Scarce in areas having large wolf populations. Climbs trees. Leaves scratch marks on bark. Feeds mainly on small deer and reindeer as well as hares, marmots, pikas, and ground birds such as grouse. Also actively seeks out and kills foxes. Breeds Jan–Mar.
STATUS: Lynx hunting is strictly regulated in most countries, and only Russia allows hunting for commercial purposes. Illegal trade in pelts, habitat loss, and prey base depletion are the main threats. Russian and c Asian populations are largely intact. European and sw Asian populations are small and fragmented; some isolated populations are Endangered (IUCN). CITES Appendix II. Bern Convention Appendix III.

Canadian Lynx
Lynx canadensis

ALSO: Kanadischer Luchs, Lynx du Canada, Kanadisk gaupe, Канадская рысь, Piqtuqsiraq. SN means "lynx of Canada."
RANGE: Occurs in dense forests from Alaska across Canada to Newfoundland and Labrador; small isolated populations exist in the n US and in Nova Scotia and New Brunswick. Generally found in lowland and montane forests with heavy stands of trees for cover. Non-breeders range widely, and may become nomadic when food is scarce. One Canadian Lynx was recorded traveling 620 mi (1000 km).
ID: L 26–42 in (67–107 cm). SH 20–26 in (50–65 cm). WT 18–37 lb (8–17 kg). Males are larger than females. Grayish buff fur is lightly flecked with brown. Large golden yellow eyes. Prominent

black ear tufts. Backs of ears have a central pale gray spot. Ruff of long fur around the face. Short, black-tipped tail. Large, furred paws with retractile claws.
HABITS: Solitary, except when breeding. Most active at dawn and dusk. Prefers shrubby areas for feeding but wanders onto open tundra in search of prey. Feeds mainly on snowshoe hares (*Lepus americanus*), taking an estimated 2 hares every 3 days. Also feeds on mice, voles, lemmings, squirrels, grouse, ptarmigans, carrion, and occasionally mammals as large as deer. Caches food for later use. Breeds Mar–Apr. Breeding success is tied to snowshoe hare populations, which increase and decline in a 6- to 12-year cycle. In years when hares are scarce, lynx females may not conceive, litter sizes may be smaller, or kittens may die from malnutrition.
STATUS: Limited hunting and trapping is permitted in the US and Canada. Nearly extirpated in the US, but recovering in some areas. Threats include habitat fragmentation due to forestry, agriculture, road building, and suppression of forest fires that reduce habitats that support snowshoe hares and other prey. CITES Appendix II. Threatened US-ESA.

FAMILY CANIDAE
WOLVES, DOGS, COYOTES, FOXES
Canids are the most social of all the Caniformia, with many living in packs. They feed mainly on animal flesh, but also consume plants. They have a relatively long rostrum, and the limbs are long and adapted for fast running.

Members of this family have 5 toes on each front foot; the inside toe (*pollux*) is high above the paw. There are 4 toes on each hind foot, and some domestic dogs have a fifth toe. Claws are non-retractile. Canids have a scent gland at the base of the tail. Arctic canids are divided into two tribes: Canini (wolves, dogs, coyotes) and Vulpini (foxes).

GENUS *CANIS*: In 2004, geneticists from the Wildlife Institute of India used DNA from wolf mitochondria to establish that the Asiatic wolf lineage originated about 800,000 years ago. Wolves may have migrated from Asia

Tundra Wolf

Arctic Wolf
White morph

Gray Wolf
Canis lupus
Circumpolar
L 52–85 in (133–215 cm)

Coyote
Canis latrans
N Amer
L 42–50 in (105–127 cm)

Timber Wolf
Dark morph

into N Amer as early as 400,000 years ago. However, the American lineage did not become widespread until about 12,000 years ago, when native American megafauna began to die out.

Gray Wolf

Canis lupus

ALSO: Loup gris, Ulv, Волк, Aligngix (Aleut), Kegluneq (Yupik), Amaguk (Labrador), Amaroq (Kalaallisut); Amaruq is a gigantic wolf in Inuit mythology that is said to track down and devour anyone foolish enough to hunt alone at night. SN means "dog wolf."

RANGE: Circumpolar. Occurs in tundra, forests, and mountains from the arctic coast south in N Amer to Mexico, and south in Eurasia to the Arabian Penin and Japan.

SUBSPECIES–ARCTIC: ARCTIC WOLF, *C. l. arctos*, Canadian High Arctic–Greenland. MACKENZIE VALLEY WOLF, *C. l. occidentalis*, Alaska–nw Canada. GREAT PLAINS WOLF, *C. l. nubilus*, s Alaska coast, ne Canada, n Great Lakes. EASTERN TIMBER WOLF, *C. l. lycaon*, forests in se Canada–ne US. EURASIAN TUNDRA WOLF,

C. l. albus, Eurasian tundra. EURASIAN WOLF, *C. l. lupus*, Siberian taiga. RUSSIAN WOLF, *C. l. communis*, Eurasian taiga.

ID: L 52–85 in (133–215 cm). SH 24–36 in (65–80 cm). WT 40–175 lb (18–79 kg). Largest canid. Fur color varies from pure white in the Arctic Wolf to shades of cream, brown, or black in tundra and timber wolves. The winter coat, which is shed in spring, is composed of long coarse guard hairs and short soft underfur. Northern wolves also grow stiff tufts of hair between the toe pads in winter to protect the bare sole from ice and snow. Eyes are deep yellowish orange; eyeshine from reflected light is greenish yellow.

HABITS: Typically lives in packs of 4–8 closely related animals in a well-developed hierarchy containing an alpha male and female, their pups, and subordinate aunts or uncles. The pack travels, hunts, and raises pups as a unit. Packs delineate their home territory by spraying urine on rocks, stumps, ice chunks, or other objects. Buffer zones separate the territories of different wolf packs, thus avoiding territorial disputes and offering a place for prey animals to feed and multiply. Wolves howl rather than bark, and the wild harmony of a pack's joint chorus is an unforgettable sound. Howling plays a role in letting other wolves know that a territory is already occupied. It may also be a wolf's way to tell pack members of its whereabouts. It is also possible that wolves simply derive pleasure from howling.

Females are sexually mature at 2 years of age, males at 3 years. Mating takes place in Feb–Mar. Gestation is about 63 days, with a litter of 3–7 young born Mar–May. Pups are born blind and hairless. Young remain with the pack for at least a year. Lifespan is about 10 years in the wild, up to 20 years in captivity.

Wolves feed on hares, foxes, rodents, birds, beavers, fish, eggs, and small amounts of plant matter, but the main prey of all wolves on all ranges is large game. Wolves as individuals are not physically formidable, nor are they capable of rapid, sustained pursuit of prey such as caribou and moose, which can easily outrun a wolf. Instead, wolves depend on hunting techniques that involve their pack and the use of sophisticated pursuit systems.

TUNDRA WOLVES feed mainly on caribou and reindeer. These cervids are long-distance migrants, and the wolves move with the herd. A wolf pack will often charge a group of caribou or reindeer, trying to separate a calf or an older, weak animal from the herd. They also pursue caribou and reindeer in relays. As one pursuing wolf tires, another takes over until the exhausted quarry can no longer keep ahead. The ambush method involves one wolf hiding behind a rock or in a gully, then charging out as the pack drives a lone animal past him.

TIMBER WOLVES, which live in boreal and mountain forests, take a variety of large game species, including prey as large as bison, moose, deer, wild boar, and wild sheep and goats.

ARCTIC WOLVES, which live in the Canadian High Arctic, hunt caribou and also attack muskoxen, which when attacked form a semicircle with the adults on the outside and the young bunched in the middle. The wolf pack circles the group attempting to break up the formation or scare out individual animals. If the muskox herd maintains its position with the massive

horns facing outward, the wolves eventually give up. If a calf or adult becomes separated from the herd, the wolves harass it until the animal becomes too weak to defend itself.

USE: Arctic people historically used wolf pelts for blankets and clothing. Later the wolf was personified in literature and music, and in myths about werewolves—men that change from human form to wolves when the moon is full. The wolf was the subject of the cleverly disguised social commentary *Little Red Riding Hood*, written by Charles Perrault and popularized as a fairy tale by the Brothers Grimm in 1812. As for music, in 1936 Sergei Prokofiev wrote of a Russian boy's encounter with a wolf in *Peter and the Wolf*, a piece spoken by a narrator accompanied by an orchestra.

STATUS: Once the world's most wide-ranging mammal, the wolf today inhabits a very small portion of its former range. This can be attributed to widespread destruction of its habitat and human encroachment. Baseless fear has led to the poisoning and persecution of the wolf, which has been extirpated from most of continental N Amer, Europe, se China, and Indochina. CITES Appendix I. Threatened–Endangered (IUCN).

Illustration by Gustave Doré (1832–1883)

Charles Perrault, the 17th-century author of *Little Red Riding Hood*, offered this advice to young ladies about the danger of consorting with wolves.

Little girls, this seems to say, never stop upon your way. Never trust a stranger-friend; no one knows how it will end. As you're pretty, so be wise; wolves may lurk in every guise. Handsome they may be, and kind. Gay or charming never mind!

Domesticated Dog

Canis lupus familiaris

The domesticated dog is descended from the Gray Wolf, with which it produces fertile hybrids. It is considered a wolf subspecies.

How closely are today's dogs related to their wolf-like predecessors? Studies involving the DNA components of domesticated dogs and wolves indicate that the two may have started to diverge genetically about 135,000 years ago. In 2008 archaeologists from the Royal Belgian Institute of Natural Sciences found fossilized skulls of the earliest known "true dogs" in Goyet Cave, Belgium. The skulls date to 31,700 years ago and show a close resemblance to the modern Siberian Husky breed.

In 2004 researchers also examined the genetic structure of 85 modern dog breeds and compared them to the DNA components of wolves. Breeds that had a genetic footprint very close to the wolf's were considered to be the most ancient breeds. Included in this category are the Siberian Husky, Alaskan Malamute, Canadian Inuit Dog, and Samoyed. These are Spitz-type dogs having a dense, double-coated pelage, small ears that help reduce the risk of frostbite, and thick pads and fur on the paws to protect the feet from sharp ice.

The story of these breeds goes far back to times when people used dogs for tasks vital to everyday survival. Dogs served as protectors, assisted in hunting and herding, and allowed people to travel across the ice by sled.

The GREENLAND DOG, or Grünlandshund, originated in coastal Siberia. Remains dating to 9000 years ago have been found in Russia's New Siberian Is, making this dog one of the world's oldest breeds. The breed reached Greenland 4000–5000 years ago with the Sarqaq people. This is a robust dog well suited to pulling a sled. The coat is coarse, straight, and dense, and comes in all colors and combinations except pure white. The tail curls over the back.

The SAMOYED breed derives its name from Samoyedic people of Siberia, who were nomadic hunters and fishermen that lived in family groups. Their dogs accompanied them everywhere. The Samoyed used these robust, white-furred dogs to herd reindeer and pull sledges loaded with goods. The first written comments about the breed appeared in 1696, when Adam Brand, who was traveling across Siberia with Russian envoys sent to China by Peter the Great, wrote of white dogs pulling sleds. He also noted that the dogs were shorn to the skin.

ALASKAN MALAMUTES are direct descendants of the wolf and are the largest and most imposing of the sled dog breeds. The coat of the Alaskan malamute is thick and fairly short-haired, with stiff guard hairs and a soft, woolly undercoat. The coat color varies from light gray to black, but the muzzle and legs are almost always white. The long-haired tail always curls over the back.

The Alaskan Malamute breed and name dates back 2000–3000 years to the nomadic Mahlemut people, who lived around Kotzubue Sound on the nw Alaskan coast. The Mahlemuts bred and used these big-boned and powerfully built animals as a freighting dogs capable of hauling heavily loaded sleds over considerable distances, for long periods at a time, in harsh and extreme conditions. Alaskan malamutes were employed during the gold rush of 1896 to carry supplies to villages and camps. Teams of 4 or more dogs were used to pull heavy loads. In 2009 the Alaskan Malamute was declared the official state dog of Alaska.

The CANADIAN INUIT DOG, also known as the Eskimo Dog or Qimmiq (Inuit for "dog"), is thought to have been present in the Arctic for at least 4000 years. These dogs were used as hunting companions and sled dogs by the Thule Inuit, who lived in the Canadian Arctic about 1000 years ago.

Inuit hunters armed only with spears or harpoons trained their dogs to harass polar bears until they could be killed. These sled dogs allowed families to take along their possessions and stores of food and fuel in the form of blubber when they moved from place to place. Their dog teams pulled immense loads of seals and other game back from trips to the ice edge. The Inuit way of harnessing dogs to a sled, or *komatik*, allowed them to fan out over the ice. This meant that even when crossing thin ice, there was less danger of breaking through.

Today the Canadian Inuit Dog is valued for its ability to pull heavy loads one and a half times its own weight over great distances. Like its ancestor the wolf, this breed does not bark, but howls plaintively. These dogs thrive on a high protein–high fat diet of fish and frozen meat. Their thick, double coat is completely weatherproof and is extremely dense on the belly. The coat may be colored white, gray, brown, or sable, or patterned in black and white, red and buff, or red and white. The Canadian Inuit Dog has been named the official animal of Nunavut.

The SIBERIAN HUSKY is another of the ancient breeds commonly employed as a sled dog. It is able to bear a lightly loaded sledge at a moderate speed over great distances. The coat can be patterned black and white, copper and white, gray and white, or be pure white. The feet, legs, facial markings, and tail tip are often white. The almond-shaped eyes can be dark blue, light blue, amber, or brown. Some huskies have one brown eye and one blue eye (*heterochromia*), and some individuals show eyes that are each half brown and half blue (*parti-colored*). The black nose may be streaked with pink or flesh (*hypo-pigmentation*), a condition known as "snow nose." The fox-brush tail is often held low, rather than curling over the back as in other Spitz types. This is another dog that howls like a wolf rather than barking like a dog.

Prehistoric seal hunters living in ne Siberia were the first to breed the Siberian Husky, calling it the Chukchi Dog. Teams of up to 20 dogs were required to pull a single sled loaded with seal meat and pelts, which they moved from the Bering Sea coast to camps situated inland on the Chukotka Penin. The Chukchi people and their dogs were nearly extirpated in the 18th century when Russia attempted to conquer Siberia and usurp the region's fur and mineral resources. However, the Chukchi used their sled dogs to race ahead of the advancing Cossack forces. They lured the Russian troops into mountain passes where, using only spears and sharpened rocks, they rousted the invaders.

In the early 1900s, Bolshevism cast its shadow over Siberia. The communists viewed the Chukchi dog breeders as wealthy and elite hindrances to collectivization. Many dog breeders were imprisoned or killed, and the Chukchi Dog all but disappeared from Siberia.

Fortunately, outsiders recognized the value of the breed. In 1908 dogs from the Anadyr area of Russia were imported into Alaska, where they were used to haul gear for Klondike gold rush miners. The Chukchi Dog became known as the Siberian Husky—"husky" being a contamination of "Eskie," the miner's name for Native Alaskans.

The breed attracted great interest when Admiral Robert Peary of the US Navy used Siberian huskies on his 1909 North Pole expeditions and when John "Iron Man" Johnson and his team of Siberian huskies won the 1910 All-Alaska Sweepstakes—a 408 mi (657 km) sled race from Nome to Candle and back. Johnson's huskies competed against larger, stronger Alaskan sled dogs and Johnson won the race in a record time of 74 hours, 14 minutes, and 37 seconds. His record stood unbeaten until 2008.

However, it was the Siberian Husky's role in the 1925 dog sled relay of diphtheria antitoxin from Nenana to Nome, Alaska—the "Great Race of Mercy"—that brought the breed to international attention. In Jan 1925 a diphtheria epidemic broke out among the children of Nome. Diphtheria is a highly contagious bacterial disease that causes inflammation of the mucous membranes. The hard membrane that forms in the throat slowly suffocates the victim, while the bacterial toxin in the blood causes heart and nerve damage.

The doctors in Nome had requested diphtheria antitoxin in anticipation of the epidemic, but supplies had been delayed because of weather. (At that time, the port of Nome was icebound in winter and was isolated from the rest of Alaska except for telephone links and an airways system that couldn't operate in icy weather.) It was decided to send the 300,00 units of serum stored in Anchorage to Nenana by train, and then relay it by dog sled to Nome.

Twenty mushers and approximately 150 sled dogs were organized along the route. Each was to carry the medicine for about 50 mi (80 km) before handing it off to the next musher. The relay was amazingly successful, with the teams covering

Greenland Dog
SH 24 in (60 cm)
WT 65 lb (30 kg)

Samoyed
SH 24 in (60 cm)
WT 65 lb (30 kg)

Canadian Inuit Dog
SH 20–28 in (50–71 cm)
WT 50–85 lb (22.5–38 kg)

Alaskan Malamute
SH 23–28 in (58–71 cm)
WT 85–125 lb (38–56 kg)

Some Siberian huskies
have one brown eye
and one blue eye.

Siberian Husky
SH 20–23 in (50–58 cm)
WT 45–60 lb (20–27 kg)

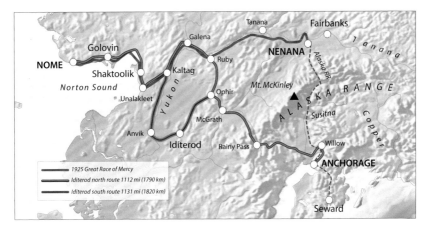

674 mi (1085 km) in a record-breaking 5.5 days. While all the teams were hailed as heroes, the highest praise went to Norwegian immigrant Leonhard "Sepp" Seppala (1877–1967), with his 12-year-old lead husky Togo, and Gunnar Kaasen (1882–1960), with another of Seppala's huskies, Balto.

Seppala and his Togo—fondly referred to as "50 pounds of muscle and fighting heart"—recorded the longest distance and fastest time of any of the teams, mushing a total of 261 mi (418 km) in 4 days. The team traveled from Nenana to Shaktoolik, where Seppala picked up the serum from Henry Ivanoff, then carried it to Charlie Olsen's team at Golovin, about 91 mi (146 km) to the north across Norton Sound and over Little McKinley Mtn. This was a remarkable test of endurance, as the route crossed treacherous sections of Alaska's wilderness that were plagued by blizzards, gale-force winds, and wind-chill temperatures estimated at −85°F (−65°C).

However, Seppala's heroic endeavor was upstaged by Gunnar Kaasen, who carried the antitoxin on the final 106 mi (170 km) run into Nome in whiteout conditions. Kaasen was not supposed to be the last man into Nome, but he bypassed the last relay station. Although Kaasen was suspected of grabbing glory, he and Balto became Nome's darlings of the day, capturing most of the media's attention. Kaasen was given a citation by the governor of the Alaska Territory and a $1000 reward from the H. K. Mulford Company. He was offered a movie role and went to Hollywood to film *Balto's Race to Nome*. In 1925, a bronze statue of Balto was erected in New York City's Central Park. Balto was present for the statue's unveiling and he appeared in Madison Square Garden before a crowd of 20,000 fans.

But fame was fleeting for Balto. Unfit for breeding because he had been neutered at a young age, Balto and the rest of Kaasen's dog team were sold to a vaudeville act. Two years later George Kimble, a former prizefighter turned businessman, found the dogs unhealthy and sadly neglected in Los Angeles. Kimble and the *Cleveland Plain Dealer* newspaper arranged to bring Balto and the rest of the team to Ohio, where they were welcomed in a triumphant parade. The dogs were placed at the Cleveland Brookside Zoo, where they lived out their lives in relative ease. After Balto's death in 1933, his remains were mounted and now are displayed in the Cleveland Museum of Natural History.

Leonhard Seppala with his lead husky Togo (left) and Gunnar Kaasen with Balto (right).

The reader may wonder what happened to Seppala and Togo. In 1926 Seppala and his dogs went on tour, drawing record crowds wherever they went. In New York City, Seppala drove his team from the steps of City Hall, up along Fifth Avenue, and through Central Park. During an appearance at Madison Square Garden, the Norwegian polar explorer Roald Amundsen awarded Togo a gold medal for bravery.

Togo was finally retired in Poland Spring, Maine, where he was euthanized in 1929 at the age of 16. His mounted skin is displayed at the Iditarod Trail Sled Dog Race Museum in Wasilla, Alaska. Yale's Peabody Museum of Natural History has Togo's skeleton. The rest of Seppala's dog team was sent to breeding kennels in Maine. Their pups formed the core of America's breeding stock, and as a result, most purebred huskies in N Amer are descended from a dog that ran in the 1925 Great Race of Mercy.

Alaska Purchase Centennial sponsor Dorothy G. Page organized the Iditarod Trail Seppala Memorial Race in 1967 as a tribute to Seppala's role in the 1925 diphtheria serum relay. The course, near Anchorage, ran 25 mi (40 km) along a trail created in 1910 that passes through the gold rush town of Iditarod. The purse of $25,000 attracted 58 mushers. In 1973, Joe Redington and friends organized the first Iditarod Trail Sled Dog Race. A purse of $51,000 attracted a field of 34 mushers. Twenty-two mushers completed the race, which was won by Dick Wilmarth.

The Iditarod is now one of Alaska's prestigious sporting events. The race starts in downtown Anchorage on the first Saturday in March. The mushers, each with a team of about 16 dogs, race 20 mi (32 km) to Eagle Rvr. From there, the teams are bussed 29 mi (47 km) to Willow in order to bypass a treacherous area of mud and ice. The race restarts near Willow and continues along the Iditarod Trail until Ophir, where the trail splits into two routes. In even-numbered years the teams run through Galena, in odd-numbered years through Iditerod.

The Nome finish line is marked by the "Red Fox" Olson Trail Monument, named for the gold miner and Iditerod musher who donated the spruce log forming the monument's original arch.

Hanging from the monument's arch is the Red Lantern, a lit kerosene "widow's lamp" awarded to the last musher to cross the finish line. In 1973 John Schultz won the Red Lantern by taking the longest time ever to finish the race—32 days, 15 hours, 9 minutes, and 1 second. In contrast, the fastest time to date is John Baker's 2011 record of 8 days, 18 hours, 46 minutes, and 39 seconds.

Coyote

Canis latrans

ALSO: Prairie Wolf, Kojote, Prærieulv, Койот. SN means "howling dog." CN derives from the Nahuatl (Mexican) word *cóyotl*.

RANGE: Occurs in open grasslands, plains, coniferous and mixed forests, woodlands, and agricultural areas in w and c N Amer and C Amer.

SUBSPECIES–ARCTIC: *C. l. incolatus* occurs in Alaska and w Canada, including the Yukon, NWT, n Brit Columbia, and n Alberta.

ID: L 42–50 in (105–127 cm). SH 23–26 in (58–66 cm). WT 15–46 lb (7–21 kg). Slender body. Long legs. Cinnamon-colored, with buff to whitish underparts. Dark-tipped guard hairs form a faint black dorsal stripe and dark cross on the shoulder area. Black-tipped tail. (*Illus p. 73*).

HABITS: Hunts in pairs or small family packs composed of closely related adults and young. Feeds on rodents, lagomorphs, carrion, birds, eggs, insects, reptiles, fish, acorns, fruit, and plant matter. Packs can bring down prey as large as adult elk, which can weigh 500 lb (225 kg) or more. Digs its own den or uses those of other mammals. Vocalizations, most often heard at dusk or night during the mating season, include a long rising and falling note (a howl), and a series of high-pitched, short notes (yips). Breeds Jan–Mar. Mated pair usually remain together for several years. Gestation is 60–63 days. Female can give birth to a litter of 1–19 pups. Lifespan is about 10 years in the wild, 18 years in captivity.

STATUS: With the gradual eradication of wolf populations, coyotes have expanded north and east from their origins in w N Amer.

GENUS *ALOPEX*
Arctic Fox
Alopex lagopus

ALSO: Polar Fox, Polarfuchs, Renard polaire, Fjellrev, Песец, *Vulpes lagopus*. SN means "hare-footed fox." CN: The word *fox* derives from the Proto-Germanic word *fukh* and the Sanskrit word *puccha*, meaning "tail." Male foxes are known as *dogs* or *reynards*, females as *vixens*, and young as *pups*, *cubs*, or *kits*.

RANGE: Circumpolar on arctic and alpine tundra, south to the treeline, with irruptions into the boreal forest when food is scarce in the north; also wanders onto polar sea ice. Some individuals are very nomadic, and one fox was recorded traveling 1250 mi (2000 km) across the tundra and sea ice.

ID: L 28–43 in (71–110 cm). SH 10–14 in (25–36 cm). WT 5.5–10 lb (2.5–4.5 kg). AD WINTER: Thick, white to ivory coat, with dense underfur and outer coat of long guard hairs. Feet are heavily furred. Five toes on forefeet, 4 on hind feet. Non-retractile claws. AD SUMMER: Most individuals have 2-toned pelage, with brown back, tail, legs, and head, and cream to buff sides and belly. Blue morphs are pearl gray, charcoal, or dark brown overall. VARIATIONS: Different color morphs can occur within the same litter. In Alaska and Canada, blue morphs occur in about 1–5 percent of individuals. Blue morphs predominate in the Aleutians and Pribilofs. In Greenland, the proportion of the white and blue morphs is equal. Arctic foxes in the Commander Is are grayish brown year round.

HABITS: Solitary, except when breeding and rearing pups. Lemmings and voles form the primary diet. During winter darkness, the Arctic Fox uses its acute sense of smell and hearing to locate rodents moving under the snow. It then pounces and digs down to the runway or nest of its quarry. In summer, it stalks rodents scurrying across the tundra, makes a dash after them, and quickly pounces on its prey. This species also feeds on ground squirrels, hares, birds, chicks, and eggs. It trails wolves and polar bears to obtain scraps from abandoned carcasses and scavenges food and garbage around human habitation. Occasionally kills Ringed Seal pups in their birthing dens. Caches excess food and buries it for later consumption.

Sexually mature at 10 months of age. Breeds in Feb–Jun. The female digs a birthing den in gently sloping, sandy sites near rivers or lakes, or on high ground that is free of permafrost. The dens have complex underground tunnels with numerous entrances and interconnecting tunnels. Gestation is about 51 days. Three to 10 pups are born blind, deaf, and toothless and have a soft, dark brown fur. The male guards the den and brings food for the mother and young. Pups emerge from the den at 3–4 weeks of age and are weaned at about 6 weeks. They are independent by mid-Aug, and are abandoned first by the male and then by the vixen. Average lifespan is 4 years in the wild.

USE: The white pelt of the Arctic Fox is valued both by international fur traders and native people of the Arctic whose economies are tied to the trapping industry. Trapping has declined in recent years due to a drop in the market value of pelts.

STATUS: Main predators are wolves and humans. Most mortalities are due to disease and reduced food resources. Fox populations closely follow the rise and fall of the lemming populations, which peak and crash in a 3- to 4-year cycle. Large numbers starve in winters following poor lemming years or do not breed the next spring.

GENUS *VULPES*
Red Fox
Vulpes vulpes

ALSO: Rotfuchs, Renard roux, Rødrev, Рыжая лисица. SN means "fox fox." Known in fables as Reynard, an anthropomorphic trickster who is wise, cunning, and resourceful.

RANGE: Found in almost every habitat in the N Hemisphere, including arctic and alpine tundra, forest clearings, coastal marshes, meadows, bushy fence lines, low shrub cover, farming areas, and around human habitation. Largest geographic range of any living carnivore. Range in N Amer has expanded since colonial times as their competitors, the wolves, were eliminated.

Arctic Fox
Blue morph

Red Fox
Black morph

Arctic Fox
summer

Red Fox
Cross morph

Arctic Fox
winter

Arctic Fox
Alopex lagopus
Circumpolar
L 28–43 in (71–110 cm)

Red Fox
Vulpes vulpes
Near circumpolar
L 30–57 in (76–145 cm)

ID: L 30–57 in (76–145 cm). SH 14–19 in (36–48 cm). WT 8–17 lb (3.5–7.65 kg). Largest of the vulpine foxes. Slender, with an elongated muzzle, large pointed ears, long slender legs, and a long white-tipped bushy tail. Amber-colored eyes with elliptical pupils. Forefoot and hindfoot have 5 and 4 toes, respectively. Each toe has a long, non-retractile claw.

Red, black or silver, and cross color morphs occur. All morphs interbreed, and offspring of different morphs can occur within a single litter. RED MORPH: Rusty red to deep golden, with a white underbelly. Black ear tips and legs. White-tipped dark tail. BLACK (SILVER) MORPH: Black, with a white tail tip and variable amounts of silver frosting; this phase comprises about 10 percent of the wild population. CROSS MORPH: Rust to dark gray markings on the face. A stripe runs across the shoulders and down the center of the back, forming a cross over the shoulders, which gives this morph its common name.

HABITS: Mostly nocturnal. High-strung animal with acute hearing and keen sense of smell. Runs with a quick, lively gait. When pursued, it breaks into a running trot and can maintain speeds of up to 30 mph (48 kmh) for short distances. Good swimmer and occasionally climbs trees. Feeds mainly on mice and other small rodents. Diet also includes muskrats, squirrels, hares, grouse, birds' eggs and chicks, beetles, grass, berries, garbage, and carrion.

Solitary or lives in pairs. Often mates for life, and pairs may use the same den year after year. Prior to breeding, the pair repairs an existing burrow or excavates a new den in sandy soils near water. Breeds Feb–Mar. Gestation is 51–53 days, and a litter of 5–7 pups is born Mar–May. The pups' eyes open at about 10 days. Both parents, and occasionally a female offspring from the previous year's litter, bring food to the pups. Pups are weaned after a month and disperse in Aug–Sep to establish their own territory. Average lifespan in the wild is 3–4 years, with a maximum of 9 years.

USE: Historically trapped for its pelt. Foxes are farmed in the Russian Far East.

STATUS: Predators include humans, wolves, dogs, lynx, bobcats, bears, wolverines, hawks, and owls. Other mortalities are attributed to rabies and parasitic diseases.

FAMILY MUSTELIDAE
WEASELS AND ALLIES

Members of the weasel family are called mustelids—a word that refers to the musky smell produced by the anal glands of these animals. The family includes many fur-bearing species, such as minks, ermines, sables, and otters. These animals have a long, slender body, a long neck, rounded ears, short legs, and feet with 5 digits and sharp non-retractile claws. The mustelid's body shape is a compromise between energy conservation and predation efficiency. Its shape is metabolically inefficient and loses substantial body heat, but it allows the animal to follow prey into narrow burrows and to escape into small crevices when pursued by larger predators.

SUBFAMILY MUSTELINAE
GENUS *MUSTELA*
Least Weasel
Mustela nivalis

ALSO: Short-tailed, Pygmy, or Mouse Weasel, Maus-wiesel, Belette, Snømus, Ласка, *Mustela vulgaris.* SN means "snowy weasel," referring to the white winter pelage. Collective nouns for weasels include *boogle, gang, pack,* and *confusion.*
RANGE: Occurs in arctic and temperate N Amer and Eurasia in meadows, marshes, farmlands, prairies, grassy fields, riparian woodlands, forest clearings, hedgerows, and coastal dunes.
ID: L 6.5–10 in (17–25 cm). TAIL 1–1.5 in (2.5–4 cm). WT 1–2 oz (30–55 g). Smallest carnivore. Flat, narrow skull. Large black eyes. Long whiskers. AD SUMMER: Rusty brown to chocolate above; white spotted with brown below. AD WINTER: Entirely white in northern populations; brown in southern range. Foot soles, except the pads, are furred. Separated from the Ermine by smaller size and lack of a black-tipped tail.
HABITS: Active day and night, year round. Solitary, except when breeding. Emits chirps, hisses, trills, and squeaks. Climbs trees after birds and squirrels. Slow but able swimmer. Territorial; females defend their ground against other females, males against other males. Individual territories are marked by anal gland secretions deposited with the feces. Lives in a den located

in a burrow or rock pile. Commandeers burrows of small mammals it has killed, then lines the den interior with grass or fur plucked from its prey. Feeds on small mammals, especially voles and lemmings. Searches for nesting rodents under the snow and in summer takes birds' eggs and nestlings; also takes young hares, shrews, squirrels, house mice, rats, beetles, reptiles, fish, worms, and carrion. Its extremely high metabolic rate—up to 400 percent higher than is usual for mammals of the same weight—means a Least Weasel must consume about half its body weight every day. Moves restlessly along its hunting routes, nervously exploring every hole and cranny. Stands upright on its hind legs looking and listening for prey and predators.

Breeds mainly in spring and late summer, but also breeds under the winter snow in the Arctic. Females are sexually mature at 4 months, males at 8 months. Fertilized embryos implant in the female's uterus after 10–12 days. Active gestation is about 25 days. Females produce 2 litters each year, each with about 4–5 young; Newborns are wrinkled, pink, naked, toothless, blind, and deaf. Teeth erupt in 11–18 days, ears open in 21–28 days, and eyes open in 20–26 days. Young are weaned at about 40 days. Lifespan is about 18 months.

Ermine or Stoat
Mustela erminea

ALSO: Short-tailed Weasel, Hermelin, Hermine, Røys-katt, Горностай, Tiriaq.
CN *stoat* refers to animals with a brown summer coat, *ermine* to animals with a white winter coat. SN means "weasel with white fur."
RANGE: Circumpolar. Occurs throughout N Amer, Europe, and Asia, from Greenland and the arctic islands of Canada and Siberia, south to about 35°N. Found in forests, alpine meadows, and tundra. Introduced to New Zealand in the 1880s.
ID: L 8.5–13 in (22–33 cm). TAIL 1.5–3.5 in (4–9 cm). WT 1–4 oz (30–116 g). Males are about 50 percent larger than females. Long, slender body. Short legs. Long neck. Flat, triangular head. Bright black eyes. Long whiskers. Foot soles are densely

Summer coat

Winter coat

Least Weasel
Mustela nivalis
Near circumpolar
L 6.5–10 in (17–25 cm)

Stoat summer coat

Ermine winter coat

Ermine or Stoat
Mustela erminea
Circumpolar
L 8.5–13 in (22–33 cm)

American Mink
Neovison vison
N Amer; introduced Eurasia
L 19–27.5 in (47–70 cm)

Sable
Martes zibellina
Eurasia
L 18–25 in (46–64 cm)

European Pine Marten
Martes martes
W Europe
L 18–21 in (46–54 cm)

Wolverine
Gulo gulo
Near circumpolar
L 30–42 in (76–107 cm)

American Marten
Martes americana
N Amer
L 18–26 in (46–65 cm)

furred; only the toe pads are bare and exposed. AD SUMMER: Reddish brown on the back; creamy white on the flanks, belly, feet, and front of the legs. Black-tipped tail. AD WINTER: Pure white, except for the black-tipped tail.

HABITS: Active day and night, year round. Territory is marked with scent from the anal glands. Individual ranges contain several dens in hollow trees, rock piles, or rodent burrows. Typically moves rapidly, looking for prey in every hole and crevice along its hunting route. Stops frequently and stands on its hind legs to watch for predators. Runs with the body held horizontal to the ground or, if alarmed, bounds along with the back highly arched. Swims well and can climb trees. Preys on small mammals up to the size of young rabbits or squirrels; also feeds on bird eggs and chicks, frogs, earthworms, and carrion. Hunts lemmings and other small rodents under the winter snow. Kills prey by biting the neck, then scratches prey with its hind claws so it can lick blood from the wounds. Caches surplus prey for later consumption.

The female delivers her pups in spring in a birthing den. A male enters the den and immediately mates with her. The same male will often mate with unweaned females in the nest. Implantation of the fertilized embryo is delayed almost a full year. Active gestation is about 25 days. A litter of 4–13 blind, naked young is delivered in Apr. A coat of fine white hair develops within a few days, and by week 3 a dense dark mane of fur appears on the neck. Milk teeth develop at week 3, eyes open at weeks

4–6, and the black tail tip appears at weeks 6–7. Young are weaned at 3 months of age. Females reach adult size at about 6 months; males are fully grown at 1 year. Lifespan is about 2 years.

STATUS: Locally threatened by unrestricted trapping, habitat loss due to timber harvest or natural disturbance, and scarcity of prey.

GENUS *NEOVISON*
American Mink
Neovison vison

ALSO: Amerikanischer nerz, Vison d'Amérique, Amerikansk mink, Американская норка. SN means "new weasel."

RANGE: Native to N Amer; introduced for fur farming and now feral in Iceland, UK, n Europe, and e Asia. Lives along streams and lakes, in swamps and marshes, and in second-growth woodland and brush at the edge of fields.

ID: L 19–27.5 in (47–70 cm). TAIL 5–8 in (13–20 cm). WT 1.5–5 lb (0.7–2.25 kg). Lustrous dark brown fur, which is nearly black at the tail tip. Distinctive white chin patch. Fur is water resistant due to the thick underfur and oily guard hairs. Feet are partially webbed and densely furred.

HABITS: Largely nocturnal. Semi-aquatic. Solitary, except when breeding. Marks its territory with strong-smelling excretions from anal scent glands. Patrols a hunting circuit within its territory, darting into crevices and burrows to prey on snakes, shrews, young rabbits, and even muskrats in their lodges; also hunts underwater, taking fish, crayfish, frogs, and waterbirds and their eggs. In coastal areas, feeds on marine invertebrates in intertidal zone.

Females are sexually mature at 12 months, males at 18 months. Breeding season is Feb–Apr. There is no courtship, but a violent, prolonged mating in which the male bites the female's neck during repeated copulations. Period of delayed implantation is about 20 days, followed by an active gestation of 31–32 days. A litter of 2–10 young (average 4) is produced Apr–Jun in birthing dens or burrows. Newborns are blind and are covered with short, fine, silvery white hairs. Eyes open at 25 days. Weaning occurs after 5 weeks. Young begin hunting at 8 weeks,

but remain with the mother until autumn. Lifespan is about 3 years in the wild. Humans are the primary predator.

USE: The mink is the most frequently farmed animal for its fur, exceeding the Silver Fox, Sable, and Marten in economic importance.

SIMILAR SPECIES: EUROPEAN MINK (*not illus.*), *Mustela lutreola*, inhabits wooded areas near ponds and streams in nc Europe and nw Russia. The European Mink has white fur on the lips and chin, in contrast to the introduced American Mink, which has white fur on the chin only.

GENUS *MARTES*
American Marten
Martes americana

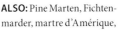

ALSO: Pine Marten, Fichtenmarder, martre d'Amérique, Amerikansk mård, Американский соболь. SN means "American marten."

RANGE: Occurs across Alaska and Canada, south to the Pacific NW, n New England, and Rocky Mtns and Sierra Nevada, in mature spruce forest, mixed beech-coniferous forest, and cedar swamps. Frequents camps, picnic sites, and garbage dumps.

ID: L 18–26 in (45–65 cm). TAIL 5–8 in (13–20 cm). WT 0.6–2.75 lb (0.3–1.25 kg). Long, bushy tail. Lustrous fur. Buff, russet, or blackish brown above. Pale brown below, with irregular cream to orange patches on breast. Head is paler than rest of body. Ears are edged with cream. One of the few mustelids with semi-retractile claws. Feet have dense, insulating fur between the toe pads; large foot pads act like snowshoes when walking on deep snow.

HABITS: Most active at dawn and dusk. Hunts on the ground but climbs well and will pursue its main prey, the American Red Squirrel (*Tamiasciurus hudsonicus*), up into trees. Also feeds on small rodents, birds, fruit, insects, carrion, amphibians, reptiles, fish, and shellfish. Solitary, except when breeding. Both sexes reach maturity at 12 months of age. Males are polygynous, mating with more than one female. Male establishes a territory and defends it against all other males. Females enter estrus and mate in Jul–Aug. Period of delayed implantation is

8–9 months. Active gestation is 42 days. Blind and naked kits are born in Mar–Apr in dens located in tree cavities, snags, stumps, fallen logs, brush piles, rock piles, and red squirrel nests. Females frequently move kits to new maternal dens once they are 7–13 weeks old. The female abandons the kits once they can feed themselves and mates again the next summer. Lifespan is 5–6 years in the wild, 15 years in captivity.

STATUS: Populations depleted by fur traders by the early 1900s have increased with protection, but localized declines occur due to illegal trapping and habitat loss from clear-cutting practices.

SIMILAR SPECIES: EUROPEAN PINE MARTEN, *Martes martes*, temperate forests of w Europe.

Sable

Martes zibellina
ALSO: Zobel, Zibeline, Sobel, Соболь. SN means "sable marten." CN "sable" is Slavic in origin and the name entered most European languages via the medieval fur trade.

RANGE: Occurs irregularly from the Ural Mtns across Siberia to Sakhalin, n Japan, Mongolia, and China in dense lowland and alpine forests dominated by spruce, pine, larch, cedar, and birch trees.

ID: L 18–25 in (46–64 cm). TAIL 5.5–7 in (14–18 cm). WT 2.2–4 lb (1–1.8 kg). Lustrous, soft, silky fur is brownish black to light brown, with gray, white, or yellowish throat bib. Black legs and feet.

HABITS: Largely nocturnal. Solitary, but not highly territorial. Able to climb up trees and steep embankments. Feeds mainly on hares and small vertebrates; also takes ermines, least weasels, birds, and fish, and in winter will eat berries hidden under the snow. Follows wolf and bear tracks, and feeds on remains of kills.

Digs denning burrows between tree roots along densely wooded riverbanks. Males mark territories by making shallow grooves in the snow, then urinating in them. Sexually mature at 2 years of age. Breeds Jun–Jul. When courting a female in estrus, males run, jump, and fight violently with each other. Delayed implantation of fertilized embryos is about 8 months. Active gestation is 25–30 days. Females give birth in Apr–May in tree hollows they have lined with moss, leaves, and dried grass. Single annual litter produces 1–7 young. Newborns are covered in a thin layer of hair. Their eyes, which are closed at birth, open after 30–36 days. Young are given regurgitated food and weaned at 7 weeks of age. Males sometimes assist females in providing food for the young.

USE: The richly tinted, luxuriously soft sable pelt has been highly valued in the fur trade since the early Middle Ages. Artists may note that sable-hair brushes used for watercolor or oil painting are not manufactured from sable hair, but from that of the SIBERIAN WEASEL, *Mustela sibirica* (*not illus.*), found in e Asia.

STATUS: Intensive hunting in European Russia nearly extirpated the Sable by the early 1900s. The collapse of the Soviet Union led to a recurrence of poaching, in part because wild-caught Russian furs demand higher prices than farmed pelts on the international market. Strict hunting regulations and re-introductions have allowed the species to recolonize much of its former range.

GENUS *GULO*
Wolverine

Gulo gulo
ALSO: Glutton, Skunkbear, Little Bear, Quickhatch, Vielfraß, Carajou, Glouton, Glotón, Jerv, Росомаха, Qavvik. SN means "glutton glutton."

RANGE: Near circumpolar. Found on arctic and alpine tundra, and in remote boreal forest wilderness areas.

ID: L 30–42 in (76–107 cm). TAIL 6.5–10 in (16.5–25 cm). SH 14–17 in (36–43 cm). WT 14.5–36 lb (6.5–16 kg). Largest terrestrial member of the family Mustelidae. Males are about 25 percent heavier than females. Sturdy, elongated, muscular body. Large head, with a broad forehead, short stout neck, short rounded ears, and small beady eyes. Legs are relatively short. Bushy tail, with long guard hairs. Head and tail are carried lower than the arched back. The heavily furred, snowshoe-like paws are suited to walking on deep snow and bear powerful semi-retractile claws. Pelage consists of dense, woolly underfur and an outer layer of long, coarse guard hairs.

Coat is medium brown to black, with a creamy yellow to pale brown stripe extending from the head and shoulders down to the tail base. Fur on the legs and feet is dark brown to black. Pale patches on the throat and chest are also common. Individuals with cream-colored coats and brown feet have been observed.

HABITS: Solitary, except when breeding. Far ranging, with territories of males extending across 38–230 sq mi (100–600 sq km). Even-tempered despite a fierce demeanor.

Feeds on carrion, small mammals, eggs of ground-nesting birds, roots, and berries. Can take down large vertebrates such as moose and caribou, especially if they are weakened or in deep snow. Kills large prey by biting the back of the neck, the spine, and the shoulders. Jaws and teeth are extremely strong and capable of crushing large bones. The rear molars are rotated inward, permitting the Wolverine to shear through frozen flesh. Huge claws and powerful forearms enable it to dig into frozen soil, tear apart rotting logs, and flip over large rocks. The sensitive nose allows the Wolverine to locate and scavenge carcasses that bears and wolves have cached in the snow.

Breeds May–Aug. Male remains with the female for a few days after mating, then leaves her. Implantation is delayed for several months, and the female delivers 2–5 kits in spring. A birthing den is dug into snow or set in a rocky crevice. The female assumes all parental care and feeding. She teaches the kits how to hunt, and lets them den with her for the first winter. By the next spring, the young are fully independent. Average lifespan is 4–6 years in the wild.

SUBFAMILY LUTRINAE
OTTERS

Otters are semi-aquatic to aquatic carnivores that feed mainly on fish and shellfish. Most have an elongated muscular body, with a broad flat head, short ears, long tapering tail, powerful legs, and fully webbed feet. An outer coat of coarse guard hairs protects the dense, oily, waterproof undercoat.

The word "otter" originally derives from the Sanskrit *udrah*, which gave rise to the English words *otor* and *water*. An otter's den is called a *holt* or *couch*. A male otter is called a *dog*, a female otter a *bitch*, and a young otter a *whelp, cub,* or *pup*. The collective name for a group of otters is a *bevy, family, lodge,* or *romp*. A group of otters in the water is called a *raft*.

GENUS *LONTRA*
North American River Otter

Lontra canadensis

ALSO: Waterdog, Nordamerikanischer Fischotter, Loutre de rivière, Nordlig elveoter, Канадская выдра, Pamiuqtuuq. SN means "Canadian otter."

RANGE: Found on wooded streambanks, marshes, inland waterways, tidal flats, estuaries, and marine coves throughout most of Alaska and Canada, south through the contiguous US.

ID: L 36–54 in (91–137 cm). WT 10–30 lb (4.5–14 kg). Fur is colored rich brown, with a silvery sheen on the head and throat.

HABITS: Largely nocturnal. Active year round. Gregarious, forming matriarchal family groups that hunt and travel together, groom each other, and use the same dens, resting sites, and latrines.

Has acute smell and hearing. Paws are dexterous and sensitive to touch. Can run, bound, slide, and walk for long distances overland, but is really in its element in the water. Swims by paddling with the legs and webbed feet, using the long, powerful tail for stability. Can swim at speeds up to 7 mph (11 kmh). Nostrils, ears, and eyes are exposed above water while swimming.

Feeds on fish, crayfish, crabs, waterbirds, and aquatic plants, which are taken in dives lasting up to 4 minutes to depths of 35 ft (10 m) or more. Small prey is eaten at the surface; large fish are taken and eaten on shore. Small rodents are captured with a quick lunge or, more rarely, after a prolonged chase overland.

Males and females mature at 2 years. Young males are usually rejected by females, and most males do not breed until their fifth year. Breeds Dec–Apr. Active gestation is 61–63 days after a delayed implantation of about 8 months. A litter of 1–5 fully furred, blind, and toothless pups is born Feb–Apr in a birthing den made in old muskrat or beaver lodges, hollow trees or logs, undercut banks, or rock cavities situated close to the water's edge. Female provides all parental care. Pups' eyes open by week 4. Young are weaned at week 12, but the mother continues to provide food for several months. Lifespan is 13 years in the wild, up to 20 years in captivity.

USE: Harvested for the fur trade.

STATUS: Historic range has been significantly reduced by habitat loss, unregulated trapping and harvesting of pelts, and environmental pollution. CITES Appendix II.

GENUS *LUTRA*
European Otter
Lutra lutra

ALSO: Old World Otter, Fischotter, Loutre d'Europe, Oter, Выдра. SN means "otter otter."

RANGE: Widespread in Eurasia in freshwater and marine habitats where ample cover is present on shore.

ID: L 36–54 in (91–137 cm). WT 10–30 lb (4.5–14 kg). Fur is rich brown, with a silvery sheen on the head and throat. Fur looks smooth upon emerging from the water, later appearing spiky as the guard hairs dry and clump together.

HABITS: Largely nocturnal, resting by day in subterranean dens (*holts*) or surface lairs (*hovers*). Marks territory with tarry, black, oily, somewhat sweet-smelling fecal deposits (*spraints*). Feeds mainly on fish taken in dives lasting 10–40 seconds. Also takes crayfish, crabs, worms, insects, small waterbirds, and rodents.

Sexually mature at 18 months. Breeding occurs throughout the year. Gestation is 61–63 days. In contrast to the N Amer River Otter, there is no delayed implantation. Females deliver an annual or biennial litter of 1–5 blind, toothless pups in a grass-lined den set in a tree hollow or hole in a riverbank, lakeshore, or rock cavity. The female provides all parental care. The pups' eyes open at about 30 days, and the young remain in the den for about 3 months. Weaning occurs at 4 months. The female takes her pups to the water and teaches them how to hunt. Pups usually remain with the mother for their first year. Lifespan is 3–4 years in the wild, up to 15 years in captivity.

STATUS: Mortalities are caused by food shortages, road kills, and drowning in lobster pots and eel nets. Dogs sometimes take cubs. A recent decline in numbers is attributed to pollution, habitat loss, human disturbance, and, in some cases, competition with the introduced American Mink, *Neovison vison*. Protected species in Britain. Vulnerable (IUCN).

European Otter
Lutra lutra
Eurasia
L 36–54 in (91–137 cm)

North American River Otter
Lontra canadensis
N Amer
L 36–54 in (91–137 cm)

Sea Otter
Enhydra lutris
N Pacific
L 55–58 in (140–148 cm)

GENUS *ENHYDRA*
Sea Otter
Enhydra lutris

ALSO: Seeotter, Kalan, Meerotter, Loutre de mer, Havoter, Sjøoter, Калан. SN means "otter that lives in water."

RANGE: Occurs in cold coastal waters of the N Pacific, especially areas with *Macrocystis* kelp beds, from Kamchatka and the Kurils, across the Aleutians to s Alaska, and south to c California. Sea ice limits the northern permanent range.

ID: L 55–58 in (140–148 cm). WT 72–100 lb (32.5–45 kg). Largest aquatic mustelid and smallest marine mammal. Brown body with a light brown head. Large blunt head, with a short thick neck and small ears that can be folded back and closed when diving. Large flipper-like hind legs are set far back on the body. Forepaws are mitten-like and have retractile claws.

HABITS: Largely aquatic, infrequently coming to land to rest. Locomotion on land is restricted to awkward bounds, in which the back is arched and the hind limbs are drawn toward the forelimbs. Lacks the dense layer of subcutaneous fat usually found in marine mammals, relying instead on a waterproof, double-coated pelage to keep warm. Vigorously grooms its fur to maintain its waterproof character.

Rafts of sea otters, normally segregated by sex, float near each other in the kelp beds. They rest on the sea surface by lying on the back, with front paws held together on the chest and the large hind flippers removed from the water to absorb the sun's warmth. Resting otters commonly anchor themselves and their pups by rolling kelp around their body.

Feeds on crabs, abalone, and other mollusks taken from or near the ocean bottom in dives lasting 1 minute or longer. The Sea Otter is also a major predator of sea urchins, which, if left unchecked, can devastate the kelp forests that lie at the very base of the coastal food web. Captures prey with the forepaws and transports it to the surface by tucking it into a loose flap of skin under each forearm. Floats on its back as it uses a favored "pet" rock as a hammer to pound open hard-shelled prey such as abalone and crab.

Breeding and pupping occur throughout the year. A mature female gives birth once a year or every 2 years. Copulation occurs in the water as the male clasps the female from behind and holds her nose or face in his jaws. The female abandons the male a few days after mating.

After delayed implantation of the fertilized embryo in the uterus, active gestation takes about 4 months. A single pup is delivered in the water. It is fully furred but nearly helpless, and is dependent on the mother for up to a year following birth. A small pup suckles while supported on its mother's chest as she grooms its fur. An older pup nurses while lying in the water next to its mother. When she dives, it floats on its back like a cork on the sea surface, often mewing loudly, until its mother resurfaces. She begins to share solid food with her offspring shortly after birth. The pup begins to dive and hunt with its mother by 8 weeks of age. Pup mortality is high, with only 25 percent surviving their first year. Maximum lifespan in the wild is about 23 years.

STATUS: In 1742 the survivors of the N Pacific expedition led by Vitus Bering returned to Russia with 900 sea otter pelts. Soon after, fur trappers began harvesting sea otters in the Aleutians and N Amer Pacific coast. Some 800,000 pelts were taken by trappers from various nations during the Russian occupation of Alaska alone. Sea otters were exploited for their fur until 1911, when fewer than 2000 individuals, living in 13 isolated colonies, remained in existence.

Subsequent international bans on hunting, conservation efforts, and reintroduction of sea otters into previously populated areas have caused numbers to increase steadily, and the species now occupies about two-thirds of its historic range. Populations in the Aleutians and California have recently declined or are at depressed levels. For these reasons, the Sea Otter remains classified as Endangered (IUCN). Threats include oil spills. Oil reduces the fur's insulting properties, and exposure causes the otter to die from cold in a few days. Some populations also face conflicts with fisheries that look upon the Sea Otter as a competitor for profitable seafood items such as abalone and crab.

FAMILY URSIDAE
BEARS

Bears are dog-like carnivores. They have a heavy boned body, stocky legs, a long snout, and short tail. They walk on the entire sole of the foot (*plantigrade*). There are 5 toes on the forefeet and hind feet, and each toe has a non-retractile claw. Except for male and non-breeding female polar bears, which are active in winter, all other N Hemisphere bears hibernate within a den in winter. The cubs are born and nursed within the den while the mother sleeps.

The diet of the northern species varies considerably. Polar bears feed mainly on seals; three-quarters of a black bear's diet comprises vegetable matter; and brown bears consume a variety of plant matter and fruit, carrion, fish, small rodents, and occasionally the young of larger mammals.

Genetic studies reveal that bear species of the N Hemisphere split from a common ancestor about 5 million years ago. Black bears are believed to have crossed from Asia into the New World about 3.5 million years ago, where they evolved into the American Black Bear.

Brown bears originated in China about 500,000 years ago. They reached Europe about 250,000 years ago, Alaska 100,000 years ago, and spread south through N Amer about 13,000 years ago.

Polar bears are thought to have diverged from brown bears some 600,000 years ago. Polar bears are closely related to the brown bears that live on the Admiralty, Baranof, and Chichagof islands off the coast of Alaska, and also show genetic similarities with the extinct Irish Brown Bear. Researchers from Trinity College Dublin, Oxford University, and Pennsylvania State University analyzed mitochondrial DNA from ancient Irish brown bear bones and found similarities in the genetic makeup of the two species. Their study published in *Current Biology* (July 2011) suggests that polar bears and Irish brown bears mated opportunistically just before or during the last ice age. The result of these chance breedings resulted in the DNA of Irish brown bears creeping into that of polar bears.

American Black Bear
Ursus americanus
N Amer
L 47–79 in (120–200 cm)

Brown Bear
Ursus arctos
Eurasia–nw N Amer
L 49–110 in (125–280 cm)

Polar Bear
Ursus maritimus
Circumpolar
L 79–120 in (200–305 cm)

GENUS *URSUS*
Polar Bear
Ursus maritimus

ALSO: Ice Bear, White Bear, Nanuk, Nanoq, Umka, Eisbär, Ours blanc, Oso polar, Isbjørn, Белый медведь. British Royal Navy captain Constantine John Phipps (1744–1792) recorded the first scientific description of the Polar Bear in *A Voyage towards the North Pole,* an account of his explorations in the Svalbard Archipelago in 1773. SN means "seafaring bear."

RANGE: Circumpolar on the Arctic Ocean sea ice and on adjacent landmasses. Six distinct population centers exist: w Alaska–Wrangel Is; n Alaska; the Canadian Arctic Islands; Greenland; Svalbard to Franz Josef Land; and nc Siberia. A separate southerly sub-population lives around w Hudson Bay in Canada. Most polar bears make extensive north-south migrations as they follow the seasonally changing ice edge. They have been recorded as far north as 88°N and as far south as St Matthew Is and the Pribilofs in the Bering Sea; James Bay, Newfoundland, and the Gulf of St Lawrence in Canada; and in Iceland.

ID: L 79–120 in (200–305 cm). WT 330–1325 lb (150–600 kg). World's largest land carnivore. Males are larger than females and have broader, more powerful necks. Females grow until they are about 4 years old and attain a maximum weight of 660 lb (300 kg). Males continue growing until 8 years of age, and can weigh 1325 lb (600 kg) or more. Long, narrow head is relatively small compared to the body. Small, heavily furred ears. Large oar-like forepaws, which aid in swimming, have strong, slightly curved, non-retractile claws, 2–3 in (5–7 cm) in length. Feet are insulated with dense fur between the pads. Fur can be white, yellow, gray, or light brown, depending on the season and light conditions. Coat consists of an outer layer of glossy guard hairs overlying thick undercoat, which in turn covers a heavy layer of subcutaneous fat. Mixed within the dense undercoat are hollow, translucent hairs that trap warm air. The nose and lips are black, as is the skin.

HABITS: Polar bears walk at speeds of about 3 mph (5 kmh). When pursued, they will break into a lumbering run that can carry them along at 20–25 mph (30–40 kmh) for short distances. They overheat and tire quickly as they clamber over hummocks of rough ice and dodge among jumbled ice floes, and at the first safe opportunity will lie down on the ice to cool off.

Adults are powerful swimmers, able to spend days at a time at sea and cover long distances. They swim at about 6 mph (10 kmh), dive to depths of several feet, and can remain submerged for up to 2 minutes. They keep their eyes open and nostrils closed when submerged, which allows them to catch seabirds by diving and swimming up beneath them. When entering the water from the edge of an ice floe, polar bears jump in like a dog or slide in backward. After emerging from a swim, they shake off any excess water to avoid chilling.

Seals, especially ringed seals and their young, are the main prey. A Polar Bear will wait for a seal to surface at a breathing hole, kill it with a rapid blow to the head, then yank it out of the water with the claws. They often eat only the skin and blubber of their kill, leaving a bonanza of leftovers for their entourage of scavenging gulls, ravens, and arctic foxes.

While ringed seals are the most common prey, the Polar Bear's diet extends to harp, hooded, and bearded seals, walruses, bodies of dead whales and caribou, nesting seabirds and their eggs, mussels, crabs, and small amounts of seaweed, lichens, mosses, sorrel, sedges, and grasses. Human encroachment into polar bear habitat has resulted in the bears' expanded taste for gourmet items such as bacon, cheese, fruit, trail mix, jerky, engine oil, rope, rubber boats, tents, and even snowmobile seats.

Largely solitary, except for females with cubs. Adult males and non-breeding females hunt alone and remain active year round, even in winter darkness. They do not den in winter, but instead dig snow beds and rest in them for 1–2 days at a time. In contrast, pregnant females hibernate in winter and deliver their cubs in birthing dens they excavate in deep snow.

Most polar bears spend the summer along the pack ice edge and around bays that retain shore-fast ice. Those that live around Churchill and sw Hudson Bay, however, escape the more intense summer heat by denning in caves or pits dug into the permafrost. The Churchill bears doze away the summer months lying on their ice beds, expending minimum energy. Some of the summer ice dens have reportedly been used and reused by generations of bears for hundreds of years. The largest known ice-denning area at Cape Henrietta Maria, about 40 mi (64 km) south of Churchill, has been designated as a provincial polar bear park.

Females reach sexual maturity at about 5 years of age, males at 8–10 years. During the spring breeding season, in Apr–May, males track the scent of females in estrus over long distances. A male may mate with several females in the same season, attending each for several days. Implantation of the fertilized embryo onto the wall of the female's uterus is delayed until late autumn. Pregnant females leave the drifting pack ice to find suitable areas for denning and dig out birthing dens in snowbanks.

The female sinks into a deep winter sleep for the next 4 months, during which time she lives on her stored fat. Her metabolic rate and body temperature drop to conserve energy. In early Jan, the sleeping female gives birth in the den. Litter size can range from 1–3 cubs, but twins are most common. Newborns weigh less than 16 oz (500 g). They are blind, deaf, and completely dependent on their mother. The first weeks after birth are spent in the security of the den as they suckle, sleep, and gain strength and weight. Polar bear milk is rich in fat, and by the time the young cubs leave their birthing den in Mar–Apr, they weigh about 22 lb (10 kg).

The mother, meanwhile, has fasted for 4–5 months, living only on her stored body fat. It is imperative that she find food. At this stage of their lives, the tiny cubs, which the Inuit call *ah-tik-tok* ("those that go down to the sea"), follow their mother as she leads the way onto the sea ice. Ringed seal pups are the favored prey at this time of the year. The mother bear digs down, pulls the seal pup out of its ice den, kills it, and feeds on the fat and skin stripped from the carcass. The cubs are nourished indirectly through her milk and acquire a taste for seal

blood and fat. By Aug the cubs weigh more than 100 lb (45 kg). They eat mainly fat and meat, but still nurse intermittently and will den with their mother again the next winter. Some follow their mother until they are almost 3 years old. Only 1 out of 3 cubs reaches maturity. Those that survive typically live to be 15–25 years old.

STATUS: For thousands of years, the Polar Bear has been a key figure in the material, spiritual, and cultural life of arctic indigenous people. Within the past decades, it has been threatened by pollution, oil spills, and shrinking of the coastal ice due to climate change. Early breakup of the sea ice means that seals are harder to find, resulting in a longer period of fasting for the bears, a decline in overall condition, and a higher mortality rate for cubs. Nations bordering the Arctic Ocean have committed to uphold the 1973 international agreement on the Conservation of Polar Bears, and in May 2008, the US Department of the Interior listed the Polar Bear as a threatened species under the Endangered Species Act.

Brown Bear

Ursus arctos
ALSO: Grizzly Bear, Old Ephraim, Moccasin Joe, Range Bear, Roach-back, Silvertip, Braunbär, Ours brun, Brunbjørn, Бурый медведь. SN means "bear of the Arctic."
RANGE: Occurs in Eurasia and nw N Amer in open tundra, high mountains, alpine meadows and forests, and coastal areas having ample cover.
SUBSPECIES–ARCTIC: EURASIAN BROWN BEAR (E), *U. a. arctos*, n Europe, Caucasus, w Siberia, Mongolia. E SIBERIAN BROWN BEAR (S), *U. a. collaris*, e Siberia; some bears in the upper Yenisei Rvr area have white markings on the neck. KAMCHATKA BROWN BEAR (B), *U. a. beringianus*, Kamchatka Penin and Paramushir Is, Russia. KODIAK BEAR (K), *U. a. middendorffii*, coasts of Kodiak, Afognak, and Shuyak islands, Alaska; largest member of the bear family and largest land-based predator. GRIZZLY BEAR (G), *U. a. horribilis*, interior of w Canada, Alaska, and nw US; variegated guard hairs give the coat a grizzled appearance, hence the name "grizzly."

ID: L 49–110 in (100–280 cm). SH 59 in (150 cm). WT 175–1325 lb (80–600 kg). Heavily built, with a prominent shoulder hump. Massive head with a broad face, prominent snout, rounded ears, small eyes. Short tail. Non-retractile claws on the forefeet are twice as long as those on the hind feet. Fur can be brown to near black, blond, gray, or cinnamon; head and shoulder fur is usually paler than the rest. Coat has an inner layer of dense fur and an outer layer of long guard hairs.
HABITS: Omnivorous, feeding on berries, grasses, succulent herbs, tender shoots, flowers, leaves, mosses, willows, bulbs, roots, insects, larvae, grubs, fungi, birds, eggs, acorns, cones, and nuts. Digs after small burrowing mammals and feeds on salmon returning to their spawning grounds. Can take down large hoofed mammals caught in deep snow or otherwise disabled, and can attack people without warning. E Siberian brown bears also prey on mountain hares, reindeer, and moose.

Brown bears have poor eyesight but have acute senses of hearing and smell. They are excellent swimmers. Adults seldom vocalize. Juveniles cry out when hungry, cold, hurt, or separated from their mother and siblings.

Brown bears dig their own den or utilize natural caves in areas far from human disturbance. Adult males forage and den alone. Females forage and den with their young, raising them alone. Adult males are dominant; females with cubs are dominant over juvenile males and females without cubs. Coastal bears maintain home ranges of about 10 sq mi (24 sq km), while the ranges of bears in the interior can exceed 350 sq mi (900 sq km). Home ranges can overlap without territorial defense, but bears leave visual and olfactory cues to their presence by rubbing, biting, clawing, and stripping tree bark. Frequently used trails are marked by rolling on the ground, urinating, and defecating.

Both sexes are sexually mature at 3–5 years of age. Mating season is May–Jul. Several males may follow a female in estrus and fight each other for breeding rights. Females experience delayed implantation. The fertilized embryos develop to the blastocyst stage, but do not implant in the uterus for about 5 months. The active gestation period of 6–8 weeks begins in late autumn as the female enters her den and covers the floor with mosses, grasses, and conifer boughs. One to 4 young are born in the den between Jan and Mar. They huddle next to the lactating female until she awakens in spring. Females and cubs emerge from the den in late spring. The mother continues to nurse her cubs for 1–2 years and leaves them only when she is ready to mate again. Some cubs remain with their mother for up to 4 years. Maximum lifespan is about 25 years in the wild.
STATUS: Humans are the species' only predator. N Amer brown bears are protected under CITES Appendix II. The Grizzly Bear, *U. a. horribilis*, is classified as Threatened under the US Endangered Species Act.

American Black Bear
Ursus americanus

ALSO: Amerikanischer Schwarzbär, Ours noir, Baribal, Amerikansk svartbjørn, Барибал. SN means "American bear."
RANGE: Occurs across most of Alaska and Canada, south through most of the US, and in the Sierra Madre Mtns of Mexico.
ID: L 47–79 in (120–200 cm). AVG WT 175–265 lb (80–120 kg); largest males can weigh up to 880 lb (400 kg), far outweighing the heaviest females. Stocky, with a short tail, small eyes, erect rounded ears, and non-retractile claws. Fur can be black (more common in the boreal forests), bluish gray, chocolate brown, cinnamon, or beige; a unique cream-colored morph occurs on the Kermode Is off the Brit Columbia coast. Muzzle color typically contrasts with the rest of the face. White chest markings occasionally occur. Distinguished from the Brown Bear by smaller size and lack of a shoulder hump.
HABITS: Found most frequently in areas of high fruit and berry production, and in hardwood forests that provide hard mast such as acorns and nuts. Feeds mainly on new plant growth and carrion in spring, and herbs and fruit in summer. In autumn, feeds mostly on berries, acorns, and nuts. Often congregates at garbage dumps or salmon streams where food is abundant.

Also able to kill moose cows and calves and fawns of white-tailed deer. Uses smell and sight for locating food items. Vocalizations include a threatening growl, or a bellow or bawl when in pain. Walks with a meandering shuffle, but can also sprint for short distances at speeds up to 35 mph (56 kmh).

Hibernates in winter throughout most of its range, denning in caves, tree cavities, brush piles, or underground burrows. Males den alone; females den with their cubs. Den chambers are lined with vegetation, and entrances are completely or partially plugged. For the 5–7 months of dormancy, the Black Bear does not eat, drink, urinate, or defecate, yet it maintains a near-normal body temperature without food or water and with no accumulation of toxic waste. It loses up to 30 percent of its body weight during winter sleep, and emerges from the den in Mar–May in a near anorexic condition.

Solitary, but home ranges of both sexes often overlap. A bear marks its territory by leaving scratches and bite marks on trees. Sexually mature at 2–8 years of age. Breeds in Jun–Jul. Males are promiscuous. More than one male may attend a female, but only the dominant male will actually mate with her. Delayed implantation of the fertilized embryos occurs around Nov–Dec; active gestation lasts 60–70 days. One to 4 cubs are born in the den around Jan–Feb. Newborns are blind, fully furred, toothless, and weigh about 7 oz (200 g). They huddle next to their sleeping mother for warmth, and nurse while she fasts. Cubs emerge from the den in spring and remain with their mother for about 16 months. Male yearlings leave the mother's territory, while 95 percent of the female offspring remain in the mother's home range. Lifespan is about 23 years in the wild.
STATUS: CITES Appendix II.

SUPERFAMILY PINNIPEDEA
PINNIPEDS

Pinnipeds (Latin for "fin-footed") are a widely distributed group of marine carnivores that developed from a bear-like ancestor about 23 million years ago. The superfamily includes the families Otariidae (fur seals and sea lions), Odobenidae (walruses), and Phocidae (true seals). The group is distinguished by wide, flat flippers that serve as paddles for swimming. They have a thick layer of blubber, which provides buoyancy and helps to conserve body heat while the animals are foraging in cold waters.

FAMILY OTARIIDAE
FUR SEALS AND SEA LIONS

The otariids, or eared seals, are so named for their characteristic external earflaps (*pinnae*). They are also distinguished by having hind flippers that can be rotated beneath the body, which allows them to move quickly on land. Otariids all exhibit sexual dimorphism, with adult males being significantly larger than adult females. The species commonly known as fur seals have a pelage composed of an undercoat of short, dense hairs and an outer coat of long, coarse guard hairs. Sea lions are named for the adult male's thick mane and lion-like roar.

These mammals spend much of the year at sea and return to land to mate and give birth to their young. Males arrive at the breeding beaches first, followed by the females, many of which are pregnant from the previous year. Females give birth to a single pup shortly after arrival and mate again within a few days of pupping. They stay with their pups for a few days after birth before alternating foraging trips at sea with nursing their pups on land. Males and females without pups abandon the colony first, leaving the pups and nursing females behind.

Steller sea lions on Bogoslof Is, Aleutians

GENUS *EUMETOPIAS*
Steller Sea Lion
Eumetopias jubatus

ALSO: Northern Sea Lion, Stellerscher Seelöwe, Lion de mer de Steller, Stellersjøløve, Сивуч. CN honors German naturalist Georg Wilhelm Steller, who first described the species in *De Bestiis Marinis*, which was written in 1741 while Steller was shipwrecked with Vitus Bering in Russia's Commander Is. SN means "maned seal with a broad forehead."

RANGE: Occurs in the N Pacific in the Bering Sea and Sea of Okhotsk, and coastal waters of n Japan, Kamchatka, Aleutians, Alaska, and south along the Pacific coast to California.

ID: L 9.5–11 ft (3–3.5 m). WT 770–2400 lb (350–1100 kg). Largest eared seal. AD: Blond to golden brown on the back, slightly darker below. Dark brown flippers. Broad front flippers; slim hind flippers. Short, straight snout. Males are much larger than females and have a heavy mane of long fur at the neck. JUV: Dark brown to black at birth, lightening to pale brown by 3 years.

HABITS: Forages in coastal waters, diving to average depths of 70 ft (21 m), with some dives recorded to 655 ft (200 m). Feeds mainly on pollock, mackerel, herring, Pacific cod, rockfish, and invertebrates such as squid and octopus. Occasionally enters freshwater river estuaries to feed on salmon moving upstream to spawn and young salmon migrating downstream to the sea. Hauls out on rocky reefs and cobble beaches, and occasionally on sea ice. Forms loose colonies on favored beaches in mating season. Adult males gather on the breeding beaches in early May and employ ritualized postures and vocalizations to establish territory. Females return to the colonies May–Jul, give birth to a single pup shortly after arrival, and mate 11–14 days after pupping. Females often continue to nurse their offspring for up to a year, weaning it when about to give birth again.

USE: Early Bering Sea cultures hunted these seals for food and clothing. When European and American sealers arrived in the 1800s, populations declined as thousands were culled each year for their blubber, which was rendered into lamp oil. During the last commercial hunts from 1959 to 1972, about 45,000 Steller sea lions, mainly pups, were harvested.

STATUS: Some 37,000 sea lions breed in the Gulf of Alaska, with one group ranging east of Cape Suckling (144° W) and another group to the west of that point. Western populations have declined by more than 64 percent in the past 30 years. Decline is attributed to reduced reproductive success, increased mortality of juvenile seals, incidental kills in trawl nets, and intensive fishing of sea lion prey species in the Bering Sea. Listed in 1991 as a threatened species under the US Endangered Species Act (US-ESA); w Alaskan population is Endangered (IUCN).

GENUS *CALLORHINUS*
Northern Fur Seal
Callorhinus ursinus

ALSO: Nördliche Seebär, Otarie à fourrure du Nord, Nordlig pelssel, Северный морской котик. SN means "beautiful-nosed [sea] bear."

RANGE: Occurs in the N Pacific, Bering Sea, and Sea of Okhotsk, with main breeding colonies on rocky beaches of the Pribilofs (US) and Commander Is (Russia). Males winter in coastal waters of the Aleutians; females migrate to the c Pacific or winter along the California coast.

ID: L 5–7 ft (1.5–2 m). WT 66–600 lb (30–275 kg). AD ♂: Dark brown. Much larger than female, with a massive chest, broad shoulders, and heavy mane. Head is relatively small, with a short snout and blunt nose. Very long hind flippers—the longest of any otariid. Broad front flippers, with the fur ending in a line across the wrist. AD ♀: Much smaller than male. Brown above, silvery gray below. JUV: Black at birth; brown at 1 year.

HABITS: Winters at sea, most frequently near the continental shelf edge within 100 mi (160 km) of shore. Feeds on pelagic fish and squid taken at depths of 50–165 ft (15–50 m). Rests in a "jug handle" position when at sea, with the flippers and head held above the surface to absorb heat from the sun and warm air.

Pup

♂

Northern Fur Seal
Callorhinus orsinus
N Pacific, Bering Sea, Sea of Okhotsk
L 5–7 ft (1.5–2 m)

♀

♂

♀

Pup

Steller Sea Lion
Eumetopias jubatus
N Pacific, Bering Sea, Sea of Okhotsk
L 9.5–11 ft (3–3.5 m)

♀

Pup

Walrus
Odobenus rosmarus
N Atlantic, Bering Sea, Arctic Ocean
L 10–12 ft (3–3.7 m)

Breeding is polygynous, with a single dominant male controlling a harem of 20-60 females. Males return to the breeding beaches in May to establish a territory. Females return from sea in May–Jun. Within 48 hours of arrival, females give birth to a single pup and mate again shortly after. Pups are weaned at about 4 months, and the colony is abandoned by late Oct.

USE: The Aleuts and other early fishing cultures harvested fur seals for food and clothing. They used harpoons with drag floats and seal-hide lines for taking seals at sea and employed decoys made of whole inflated sealskins when hunting seals on land.

In 1786, Gavril Loginovich Pribylov (Pribilof), captain of the Russian-American Company vessel *St George*, discovered breeding colonies in the islands that would later bear his name. Fur traders conscripted and moved Aleuts to uninhabited St Paul and St George islands to harvest fur seals. Millions of seals were killed. Populations became severely reduced, and in 1911 Japan, Canada, Russia, and the US signed an agreement that prohibited harvesting fur seals (mainly females) at sea, while permitting a managed harvest of subadult male fur seals in the Pribilofs. Commercial harvesting ended in 1985. A strictly controlled Native Alaskan subsistence hunt of the seals is allowed on St Paul Is.

STATUS: Beginning in the 1950s, for reasons that are unclear, populations began a slow decline, and since 1998, populations have declined at the rate of 6 percent a year. Vulnerable (IUCN).

FAMILY ODOBENIDAE
WALRUSES

Walruses are the sole surviving members of the formerly diverse family Odobenidae.

GENUS *ODOBENUS*
Walrus
Odobenus rosmarus
ALSO: Walross, Morse, Morsa, Hvalross, Морж, Aivik. SN means "tooth-walking sea whale," referring to a walrus using its tusks to haul out onto ice floes and beaches; *rosmarus* derives from *hvalrossen*, the Norse name for walruses.

RANGE: Disjunct circumpolar distribution in pack ice and coastal waters of Alaska, Canada, Greenland, Norway, and Russia.

SUBSPECIES: ATLANTIC WALRUS, *O. r. rosmarus*, e Canadian Arctic, Greenland, Svalbard, and Novaya Zemlya. PACIFIC WALRUS, *O. r. divergens*, Bering and Chukchi seas; largest subspecies. LAPTEV SEA WALRUS, *O. r. laptevi*, Russian arctic coast along the Laptev Sea.

ID: L 10–12 ft (3–3.7 m). WT 2600–4200 lb (1200–1900 kg). World's largest pinniped. Bulky body. Small head with small eyes, flat muzzle, and stiff vibrissae. Short, broad front flippers; long inner and outer digits on hind flippers. Pair of long, ever-growing tusks extend from the upper jaw of both sexes. Males have longer, heavier tusks than females; male's tusks can be 24 in (60 cm) long and can weigh more than 11 lb (5 kg). Sparse brownish body hair, which is gradually lost with age. Exposed skin appears grayish when animals become cold and blood vessels shrink to preserve heat; skin looks dark pinkish brown when walruses are hot and circulatory system shunts blood to the skin to be cooled.

HABITS: Forages on shallow sea banks at depths to 260 ft (80 m), feeding on mollusks, crustaceans, and small fish. Feeds by sculling along the sea bottom using highly sensitive whiskers to locate prey in murky light or even in complete darkness. Roots out mollusks using the hard ridge of skin on the top of the snout and also dislodges prey by jetting water from the mouth into the sediment. The high-vaulted palate and piston-like tongue create suction strong enough to pull clams and snails right out of their shells. Also scavenges dead whales, and some old rogue males attack and eat seals.

Gregarious. Hauls out in great numbers on beaches and ice floes around openings in the sea ice (*polynyas*). *Uglit*—Inuit for a walrus haul-out site—may derive from the loud grunting *oogh* walruses make when congregating. Other vocalizations include whistles, beeps, boings, rasps, drills, and knocks, all of which a courting male walrus can combine into a fugue-like love song.

Females mature sexually at 4–8 years of age, males at 6–10 years. Breeds in Apr–May. Males brandish their tusks in dominance displays—the larger the tusks, the higher the rank in the social hierarchy. Males attract receptive females to aquatic territories they establish in polynyas. Mating takes place in the water. After a gestation of about a year, the female delivers a single calf on the pack ice. They remain together on the drifting ice, which offers a resting platform for the calf and continually transports the pair to new feeding grounds. A calf is completely dependent on its mother's milk for the first year of life, and is not fully weaned until the end of the second year.

USE: Arctic cultures have historically hunted the Walrus for food and hides. The durable hide was used to make hulls of seagoing boats called *umiaks*. Inuits also used the male's penile bone, which can measure up to 26 in (65 cm) long, as a club, or *oosik*, for killing marine mammals. Intestines were inflated and made into fishing floats, windowpanes, or waterproof clothing. Walrus oil was used as fuel for lamps called *kooliks*. Bones were used to make spearheads and harpoon toggles, and tusk ivory was carved into necklaces or used in ceremonial masks.

In the 16th century, Europeans began to harvest walruses for oil. Hides were used to make ships' riggings, leather soles, and harnesses, and tusk ivory was turned into carvings. Commercial hunting ceased in 1928 in Canada and in the 1940s in the US. Subsistence hunting is still permitted. Russia allows hunting in the Bering and Chukchi seas, where walrus meat is used to feed farmed foxes, which are in turn harvested for fur. The US and other nations prohibit the import of walrus ivory and parts, except for fossilized materials.

STATUS: Melting of the arctic sea ice has greatly impacted walruses, which need the thick sea ice to support their weight. Unlike seals, they cannot swim indefinitely and must rest on a support between foraging dives. As the ice expanse diminishes, females and calves are pushed to join herds of males on coastal beaches, where calves are often trampled in stampedes triggered by approaching aircraft, boats, or predators. Nutritional stress can also occur when walruses are concentrated in small coastal feeding areas rather than spread out over the drifting pack ice.

A cross section of a fossilized walrus tusk reveals its layered structure consisting of an outer layer of cementum, or *bark*, several inner rings of lustrous dentine, and a core of crystalline dentine.

Inuit lore relates that the Walrus sprang from the severed hands of Sedna, or Taluliyuk, a child who was sacrificed at sea to calm a storm. Sedna became half woman and half fish, and controls all the beasts of the ocean.

Walruses hauling out on Arakamchechen Is, Russian Far East

FAMILY PHOCIDAE
TRUE OR EARLESS SEALS

True seals are descended from otter-like mammals of the Miocene. Unlike otariids, true seals lack external ears, and the hind limbs cannot be turned under the body. On land, phocids move by hunching their backs and wriggling from side to side. Females suckle their pups on extremely fat-rich milk for a short time before weaning and abandoning them.

Phocids found in arctic waters can be roughly divided into two groups—ice-loving (*pagophilic*) species commonly found on the sea ice and those species that occupy coastal habitats. Also included here is the Northern Elephant Seal, a temperate-water species whose foraging grounds extend to Alaskan and Aleutian waters.

GENUS *PUSA*
Ringed Seal
Pusa hispida

ALSO: Jar Seal, Ringelrobbe, Phoque marbré ou annelé, Ringsel, Кольчатая нерпа, Natiq, Pusa; Netsiak (whitecoat), Netsiavinerk (silver jar), Netsilak (adult), Tiggak (breeding male). CN refers to the circular body markings. SN means "seal with a bristly coat."

RANGE: Patchy distribution along leads, pressure ridges, polynyas, and offshore pack ice in the Arctic Ocean, Bering Sea, and Sea of Okhotsk, and in cold coastal waters off Baffin Is (Canada), Greenland, n Europe, and Russia.

SUBSPECIES: *P. h. hispida,* coasts of Alaska, Baffin Is, Greenland, Svalbard, n Europe, and Russia. *P. h. krascheninikovi,* Bering Sea. *P. h. ochotensis,* Kamchatka, Sea of Okhotsk, and south to 35°N along the coast of Japan. *P. h. botnica,* Baltic Sea, Gulf of Bothnia, and Gulf of Finland. *P. h. ladogensis,* Lake Ladoga, Russia. *P. h. saimensis,* Lake Saimaa, Finland; Critically Endangered; total population of 250 individuals.

ID: L 5.25 ft (1.6 m). WT 110–155 lb (50–70 kg). Small head with a narrow, short, cat-like snout. Small flippers; short claws on hind flippers; stout claws on front flippers. AD: Gray pelage marked with irregular white rings; belly is paler and bears indistinct white rings and a few dark spots.

JUV: White at birth. Molts to a gray, unspotted pelage at 6–8 weeks of age; at this point pups are known as "silver jars."

HABITS: Most common arctic seal, but difficult to approach, as the species is hunted by polar bears and native hunters. Feeds on a variety of fish including herring, smelt, whitefish, sculpin, perch, shrimp-like crustaceans, and planktonic krill. Fasting occurs during molting periods. In summer, often forages along the sea ice edge, where it mainly takes arctic cod. Vocalizations include whines, moans, and growls. Often seen basking on the ice near breathing holes that it keeps open by clawing the ice with the front flippers or by chewing away newly formed ice. Basks mostly on overcast days, as translucent hairs offer no protection against sunburn.

Sexually mature at 5–8 years of age. Breeds Aug–Sep. Males patrol the ice floes in search of a potential mate. Once a male finds a receptive female, the pair spends a few days together before mating, after which the male leaves to search for another mate. A delayed implantation period of 81 days is followed by a 9-month gestation. In Mar–May, the female excavates a birthing den in snow on the sea ice and gives birth to a single pup. She nurses the pup in the den, a behavior that provides some protection against predation by polar bears. Pup is weaned at 40 days, after which the female is receptive to mating again.

USE: Arctic people hunt these seals for meat and for pelts to make clothing. Ringed seals are a food source for orcas, wolves, and especially polar bears, which prey heavily on adult seals and take about 26 percent of pups in their dens.

STATUS: Due to the effects of global warming, the ice is breaking up earlier than in the past, which can destroy birthing lairs before seal pups are able to forage on their own.

GENUS *HISTRIOPHOCA*
Ribbon Seal
Histriophoca fasciata

ALSO: Bandrobbe, Phoque rubanné, Bandsäl, Тюлень полосатый. SN means "banded [harlequin] seal."

RANGE: Found mainly on pack ice in the N Pacific, including the Sea of Okhotsk, w Bering Sea, and s Chukchi Sea. Breeds and molts in spring on the sea ice; in summer and fall, forages in the open waters near the continental shelf edge.

ID: L 6.25 ft (1.9 m). WT 310 lb (140 kg). AD♂: Dark brown to black, with broad white bands around the neck, rump, and each of the front flippers. AD ♀: Resembles male but is paler and has less color contrast. JUV: Newborn pups have white natal hair, which molts to bluish gray on the back and silver beneath a few days after weaning. Attains adult pelage at about 4 years of age.

HABITS: Solitary. Rarely seen on land. Encountered infrequently on the sea ice in winter and spring, the season when these seals mate, give birth, and molt. Females reach sexual maturity at 2–5 years, males at 3–6 years. The male uses its large, inflatable, tracheal air sac to produce underwater whistles and puffing sounds to attract a mate. The female bears a single pup on the ice in Apr–May, nurses it for 3–4 weeks, then abruptly abandons it. The pup remains alone on the ice for a few weeks while it molts and loses enough weight to attain the negative buoyancy necessary for diving and foraging. In summer and autumn, most ribbon seals forage in the open ocean, moving with receding and advancing ice floes, and feeding on pelagic fish such as pollock and arctic cod, and squid and crustaceans taken in dives to depths of 650 ft (200 m).

USE: Between 1950 and 1980, Russia hunted these seals for their pelts, oil, and meat; this practice has been discontinued. About 100 ribbon seals are taken annually by Alaskan subsistence hunters, and there is a small bycatch in N Pacific trawl fisheries.

STATUS: Threatened by warming of the oceans, which decreases the amount of winter ice. Current population is 100,000–250,000 individuals.

GENUS *CYSTOPHORA*
Hooded Seal
Cystophora cristata

ALSO: Klappmütze, Phoque à capuchon, Klappmyss, Тюлень-хохлач, Akpak. SN means "bladder-crested seal," referring to the inflatable sac on top of the male's snout.

RANGE: Found at pack ice edge in the N Atlantic and Arctic oceans, from Nova Scotia, Newfoundland, and Baffin Is to Greenland, Iceland, and Svalbard. Major breeding areas are in the Gulf of St Lawrence, the "Front" east of Newfoundland, Davis Strait (between Greenland and n Canada), and the "West Ice" near Jan Mayen Is, Norway. Vagrant to the Yenisei Rvr (Siberia), Canary Is, and Guadeloupe (Caribbean).

ID: L 8–10 ft (2.5–3 m). WT 500–880 lb (230–400 kg). Bluish gray coat marked with irregular

Ringed seals use their canine teeth to abrade and maintain breathing holes in the sea ice.

A breathing hole is not only a place to catch a breath, but also serves as a portal between underwater foraging grounds and the seal's resting platform on the ice surface.

Emerging from the hole is an action that requires great caution on the part of the seal, as polar bears and native hunters attend breathing holes in hopes of taking an unwary seal.

black blotches. AD♂: Black, inflatable nasal hood extends from the forehead and along the top of the snout. Males fill the septal membrane between the nostrils with air, causing a large red balloon to pop out from the left nostril. Hood and septum are inflated mainly during aggressive interactions with other male hooded seals, but are also seen when humans approach males that are close to females on the ice. AD♀: Blackish face. Much smaller than male and lacks the inflatable hood. JUV: Newborns have a luxuriant "blueback" pelage—bluish gray on the back and silvery gray on the sides and belly—which is retained for the first year. Blueback pelts were once the most valuable hide in the sealing industry.

HABITS: Solitary. Breeds and molts on drifting pack ice; otherwise pelagic. Dives to depths of 975 ft (300 m). Feeds primarily on squid and fish such as Greenland halibut, redfish, and cod.

Female gives birth in Mar–Apr on the pack ice amid a loose aggregation of other hooded seals. Pup is born in an advanced stage of development, having undergone the first molt in the womb and amassed a layer of blubber. Female nurses her pup for only 4 days, during which time it doubles its birth weight of about 44 lb (22 kg), gaining more than 11 lb (5 kg) per day on a milk that is 50 percent fat. Pup remains on the ice after weaning, eventually entering the water alone and making its way north toward traditional feeding grounds.

Meanwhile, one or more males attend each mother and pup on the whelping ice, waiting for the opportunity to mate with the female once she weans her pup. Males compete with other males by inflating the hood, distending the red balloon-like septum, and making loud pinging noises. Males also bite and claw other males in their efforts to drive off competitors.

After the breeding season is over, hooded seals move to northern feeding grounds. They congregate on the arctic pack ice in Jun–Aug and molt there. In late summer and autumn they disperse again to forage at sea and by winter begin to head south toward the breeding grounds.

USE: Hooded seals have long been hunted for their oil, meat, and pelt. A period of intensive

hunting of "bluebacks" took place in the 1940s on the "Front" east of Newfoundland. In response to public pressure, the European Economic Community instituted an import ban on blueback pelts in 1983, and the commercial hunting of bluebacks was prohibited in Canada in 1987. Canada still permits an annual hunt of adult hooded seals in Newfoundland, and Norway and Russia allow a spring hunt on the "West Ice."

STATUS: World hooded seal population is currently estimated to be 650,000 individuals.

GENUS *PAGOPHILUS*
Harp Seal
Pagophilus groenlandicus

ALSO: Sattelrobbe, Phoque du Groenland, Grønlandssel, Grönlandssäl, Тюлень гренландский, Kairuli. CN refers to the harp-shaped pattern on the back and flanks of adult seals. SN means "ice-loving seal of Greenland."

RANGE: Occurs in the N Atlantic, Arctic Ocean, and coastal waters off Newfoundland (Canada), Greenland, Iceland, Svalbard, Norway, and Russia. Breeds in the Gulf of St Lawrence, Greenland Sea, and White Sea. Highly migratory, dispersing widely after molting in Apr–May. Seals that breed in the Gulf of St Lawrence travel to Baffin Is and sw Greenland in early summer. Most then move on to Ellesmere Is, with some reaching Hudson Bay by late summer. In late Sep they begin a southward migration back toward their breeding grounds.

ID: L 6 ft (1.8 m). WT 285 lb (130 kg). AD: Pale silver with a dark harp pattern on the back; pattern is more distinct on the bodies of adult males, which also have a darker head. JUV: White at birth. At 9–12 days of age, lanugo thins and gray undercoat begins to show through. White fur is completely shed by 3 weeks of age.

HABITS: Forages at depths of 330 ft (100 m), feeding on fish such as capelin, polar cod, herring, sculpin, Greenland halibut, and plaice, as well as amphipods, krill, and prawns. Reaches sexual maturity at 4–6 years. In the breeding and pupping season (Feb–Apr), gathers in large, gregarious groups on the ice floes. Male courting rituals include vocalizations, blowing bubbles,

Spotted Seal
Phoca largha
Bering Sea, Sea of Okhotsk
L 5.5 ft (1.7 m)

Ringed Seal
Pusa hispida
Arctic Ocean, Bering Sea, Sea of Okhotsk
L 5.25 ft (1.6 m)

Bearded Seal
Erignathus barbatus
Circumpolar Arctic Ocean
L 7–8 ft (2–2.5 m)

Harp Seal
Pagophilus groenlandicus
N Atlantic, Barents Sea
L 6 ft (1.8 m)

♂

♀

Ribbon Seal
Histriophoca fasciata
Bering Sea, Sea of Okhotsk
L 6.25 ft (1.9 m)

♂

♀

Hooded Seal
Cystophora cristata
N Atlantic, Arctic Ocean
L 8–10 ft (2.5–3 m)

Harp seal pups from 1–3 days old are stained yellow from amniotic fluid; at this stage they are called "yellowcoats."

"Whitecoats" are pups that have lost the yellow stain and have an all-white lanugo.

"Graycoats" are 9- to 12-day-old pups that begin to show their gray undercoat.

At about 2 weeks of age, pups begin to shed the white lanugo and are called "ragged-jackets."

When the white fur is completely shed at about 3 weeks of age, pups are called "beaters." They keep this name through the first year of life.

After molting the beater pelt and attaining a silver coat with dark spots, juveniles are called "bedlamers." This spotted coat pattern is kept until sexual maturity. Seals that never develop the harp pattern are known as "spotted harps."

and pawing. Females breed shortly after giving birth. Newborn pup weighs about 22 lb (10 kg); gains 65–100 lb (30–45 kg) on super-rich mother's milk before it is weaned at 12 days of age. Pup remains on the ice alone for about 4 weeks until it is able to swim and feed independently. It often simply drops into the water when the sea ice melts out from beneath it. Maximum lifespan is about 30–35 years.

USE: Hunted throughout its range for oil, meat, fur, and even its genitalia, which are powdered and sold as an aphrodisiac in Asia. An estimated 465,000 harp seals in the nw Atlantic are harvested each year.

The Canadian land hunt for whitecoat pups is probably the most controversial hunt of all time. In 1964, a film about the hunt showing images of bludgeoned, bloodied, and skinned whitecoat pups was broadcast on Canadian television. The film eventually aired around the world, and public outcry was so strong that in the 1980s the European Economic Community and the US prohibited the import of whitecoat products.

STATUS: In 1987, Canada banned the commercial hunting of pups under 25 days of age, but continues to permit an annual catch of pups over 25 days of age. The argument to revitalize the Canadian hunt continues. Fisheries in the nw Atlantic assert that increased harp seal numbers are responsible for declining stocks of cod and call for a massive cull of several million harp seals. This is despite analysis indicating that declining fish stocks are caused by overfishing and discarding juvenile cod as bycatch. Natural predators of harp seals include polar bears, orcas, sharks, and occasionally walruses. Threats include entanglement in gill nets and pollution. Early melting of the sea ice as a result of global warming has resulted in decreased birthing grounds on the sea ice and increased pup mortality due to drowning or being crushed by ice; mortality rate for first-year seals is 20–30 percent. Bern Convention Appendix III.

A "whitecoat" harp seal on the sea ice, Gulf of St Lawrence, Canada

GENUS *ERIGNATHUS*
Bearded Seal
Erignathus barbatus

ALSO: Bartrobbe, Phoque barbu, Storkobbe, Морской заяц, Ujuk, Oogruk, Mukluk (a word also applied to arctic boots). SN means "bearded jaw."
RANGE: Circumpolar. Found to 85°N on drifting sea ice in the Arctic Ocean and coastal waters of Alaska, Canada, Greenland, Iceland, Svalbard, Russia, and n Japan. Disjunct distribution, with main populations occurring in the Bering Sea, Chukchi Sea, Hudson Bay, and White Sea.
ID: L 7–8 ft (2–2.5 m). AVG WT 440–550 lb (200–250 kg); in winter and spring, bearded seals can weigh up to 750 lb (341 kg). Tawny brown to silvery gray or dark brown. Small head on a long, stocky body. Very long whiskers, rounded front flippers, relatively small eyes, and 4 mammary teats (rather than 2 as on other true seals).
HABITS: Solitary. Encountered most often on drifting pack ice or fast ice. Maintains breathing holes by chewing away the ice, causing the teeth to wear away in a few years; most bearded seals are nearly toothless by the age of 9 years. Forages on the seafloor in continental shelf waters, usually at depths less than 425 ft (130 m). Diet includes crabs, shrimp, clams, marine gastropods, and demersal fishes such as flounder, sculpin, and cod. Some feed on marine algae; seaweed found in the intestines of killed seals is considered a delicacy by some coastal villagers.

Female bears a single pup in Apr–May while on the pack ice and nurses it for 12–18 days. The mother's milk is extremely rich, allowing the pup to grow from its birth weight of about 75 lb (34 kg) to 190 lb (86 kg) at the time of weaning. Most females breed again within 2 weeks of weaning their pup. Implantation of fertilized embryos is delayed 45 days, followed by an active gestation of about 11 months.

Most populations move north with the receding ice after breeding. Seals in the Laptev Sea and Sea of Okhotsk sometimes remain in open, ice-free water or haul out on gravel beaches. Young bearded seals occasionally frequent ice-free bays and estuaries, and in Canada may be seen in rivers emptying into Hudson Bay.

USE: Coastal villagers, especially in the Bering Sea area, harvest bearded seals for meat and hides, which are used to make boat covers, rawhide line, and boot soles. Spring hunts in the Bering Strait are conducted in early Apr prior to the mating season using boats that drift through the loose pack ice. Hunters listen for the underwater "singing" of the adult male seals, which they call *au-uk-touk*. The "song" is a complex, frequency-modulated whistle, parts of which are audible to humans. Bearded seals are wary of boats in spring, and it is common to see a seal surface near a boat, immediately dive, and resurface far out of rifle range.

GENUS *PHOCA*
Spotted Seal
Phoca largha

ALSO: Largha-Robbe, Foca manchada, Largasäl, Ларга, Тюлень пятнистый. SN means "largha seal," *largha* being the name applied by the Tungus people from the Sea of Okhotsk area.
RANGE: Occurs mainly in the Chukchi and Bering seas, less so in the Beaufort Sea, Sea of Okhotsk, Yellow Sea, and Sea of Japan. Hauls out on pack ice, rarely on sandbars and beaches.
ID: L 5.5 ft (1.7 m). WT 290 lb (130 kg). Small seal, with a rounded head. Narrow, fairly long snout, with forward-facing nostrils. Flippers are short, narrow, and bear short claws. AD: Gray to grayish brown, with many small dark spots on the back and sides. JUV: White at birth, molting into an adult pelage at about 1 month of age.
HABITS: Seldom encountered, as this phocid spends most of the year foraging in the open ocean or hauled out on floes in impassable pack ice. Breeds Feb–Apr. Seals assemble on the ice in family groups consisting of a female, her single pup, and a male consort. Pup is weaned at 4 weeks of age, after which the female mates with the attending male and the family group disbands. Adults forage in the open ocean, feeding on schooling and bottom fish, crabs, and octopus taken in dives to depths of 1000 ft (300 m). Weaned pups are thought to feed on small crustaceans such as krill and amphipods.
STATUS: Beginning in the early 20th century, a

few hundred spotted seals were taken annually in seal hunts conducted by Russia and Japan. Quotas have been in force since the 1970s. A subsistence hunt is permitted in Alaska.

Harbor Seal

Phoca vitulina

ALSO: Common Seal, Seehund, Phoque commun, Stein-kobbe, Обыкновенный тюлень. SN means "sea-calf."

RANGE: Disjunct distribution in coastal and estuarine waters of the N Pacific, Bering Sea, Sea of Okhotsk, N Atlantic, Baltic Sea, and North Sea.

ID: L 5.5–6.25 ft (1.7–1.9 m). WT 290–370 lb (130–170 kg). Variably patterned with small dark spots or pale rings on a background color ranging from brownish black to tan or gray. Underparts paler than the back. Some individuals may show a green cast due to algal growth, or have rust-colored patches from iron oxide sediments. Short, spindle-shaped body, with a large, rounded head. Short front flippers bear large claws.

HABITS: Congregates in small numbers except when molting, when hundreds of animals may haul out on beaches, tidal flats, sandbars, or rocky reefs, and occasionally on glacial ice floes. Forages in coastal estuaries, fjords, along rough, rocky coasts, and sometimes in freshwater streams. Feeds on demersal and schooling fish, squid, shrimp, and octopus taken in short, fairly shallow dives to depths of 30–100 ft (10–150 m). Will approach human divers. Breeds Feb–Jul, varying with latitude, generally later in the north. Males display to attract females and ward off other males, typically slapping the water surface with the flippers or uttering loud grunts. Females mate shortly after delivering a single pup, which they nurse for about 1 month. Both sexes molt on shore after pups are weaned.

STATUS: Harbor seals escaped most commercial exploitation because of their small size, low oil yield, and scattered distribution. They are hunted in Norway, Canada, and the UK to protect fisheries and fish farms. World populations have declined, possibly due to increased trawl netting, viral infection, and pollution. Current estimated population is 500,000.

GENUS *HALICHOERUS*
Gray Seal

Halichoerus grypus

ALSO: Grey Seal, Horsehead Seal, Atlantic Seal, Kegelrobbe, Phoque gris, Havert, Длинно-мордый тюлень. SN means "hook-nosed sea pig."

RANGE: Disjunct distribution in the N Atlantic. Occurs on the Canadian coast off Newfoundland, Labrador, and Nova Scotia; off Iceland, Norway, and the UK; and in the Gulf of Finland.

ID: L 6.5–8.5 ft (2–2.6 m). WT 440–770 lb (200–350 kg). Males are much larger than females. AD ♂: Dark gray or brown with a few pale, irregular markings. Big "horsehead," with a long, broad snout and no obvious forehead. Large, wrinkled, often scarred neck and chest. AD ♀: Silvery gray with dark spots; much smaller than the male. JUV: Pale gray to tan at birth; gray upon weaning.

HABITS: Forages at depths of 65–130 ft (20–40 m), taking herring, other schooling, demersal, and benthic fish, and octopus and squid. Congregates in large groups on beaches, coasts, and ice floes when molting or breeding. Pupping season varies with locale: UK and Iceland, Sep–Nov; Finland, Nov–Dec; w Atlantic, Dec–Feb. Female delivers a single pup either on land or on the ice. Pup is weaned at 3–4 weeks, after which the female is ready to mate again. Breeding is polygynous, with one male mating with several females.

STATUS: Historically hunted for centuries with little impact on numbers until 18th-century sealers decimated local populations. Present-day threats include intentional kills, incidental kills in trawler nets, and disease caused by pollution. Baltic Sea population is Endangered (IUCN).

GENUS *MIROUNGA*
Northern Elephant Seal

Mirounga angustirostris

ALSO: Nördlicher See-Elefant, Éléphant de mer du nord, Nordleg sjøelefant, Северный морской слон. CN refers to the male's large nose, which resembles an elephant's trunk. SN means "narrow-nosed elephant seal"; generic name derives from the Australian aboriginal word for southern elephant seals.

Harbor seals exhibit varied color forms ranging from all tan to silver with dark spots.

Harbor Seal
Phoca vitulina
N Atlantic, N Pacific
L 5.5–6.25 ft (1.7–1.9 m)

Gray Seal
Halichoerus grypus
N Atlantic
L 6.5–8.5 ft (2–2.6 m)

Northern Elephant Seal
Mirounga angustirostris
N Pacific
L 11–14 ft (3–4.3 m)

RANGE: Breeds (Dec–Feb) mostly on offshore islands from Baja California to California. After breeding, males move to deep waters along the continental shelf north to Alaska and Aleutians; females migrate to the open ocean, north to Brit Columbia, Canada, and west to Hawaii.
ID: L♂ 14 ft (4.3 m); WT♂ 5000 lb (2300 kg). L♀ 11 ft (3 m); WT♀ 1400 lb (640 kg). Extreme sexual dimorphism, with males much longer and heavier than females. Tan to dark gray or brown fur. Light pink to tan neck and chest of adult males is hairless and rough, usually appearing cracked. Large black eyes aid capture of prey at depths where there is little light. Adult males in northern waters can be taken for walruses.

HABITS: Feeds on pelagic squid, Pacific hake, sharks, rays, and ratfish taken at depths of 1000–2600 ft (300–800 m). Males reach breeding islands first and establish territories and harems. Females deliver a single pup and mate shortly after pupping. Pup is nursed for 4 weeks on super-fatty milk, then is abandoned. Adults begin to molt, during which time they do not enter the water or feed, then depart the colony to feed at sea. Pups remain ashore for another 12 weeks. Once they lose enough body fat to attain negative buoyancy, they enter the sea unaided.
STATUS: Hunted almost to extinction by the end of the 19th century. With protection, populations now number about 100,000 individuals.

Cetacea: Whales, Dolphins, and Porpoises

Cetaceans are streamlined, nearly hairless, entirely aquatic mammals. The larger species are called whales; smaller cetaceans are called porpoises or dolphins. The forelimbs are modified to form paddle-like fins without visible digits. Hind limbs are absent. The pelvis is vestigial. The horizontal tail fin, or *fluke*, is used for propulsion. The skull has nasal openings called *blowholes* that are set far back on the dorsal surface. Cetacea is divided into two suborders: Mysticeti (baleen whales) and Odontoceti (toothed whales).

SUBORDER MYSTICETI
BALEEN WHALES

Mysticeti (Greek for "moustached sea animal") includes right, rorqual, and gray whales. These whales have two blowholes. Their upper jaw is lined with *baleen*—keratinous plates that hang like curtains from the roof of the mouth. The baleen's lower edge is a comb-like structure that filters small marine organisms from the water.

FAMILY BALAENIDAE
RIGHT WHALES AND BOWHEADS

Right whales and bowheads represent the Balaenidae in arctic waters. These are large, stocky whales characterized by a large head; a long, thin, arched rostrum; a bowed lower jaw; and very long, narrow baleen. They lack a dorsal fin and have no throat pleats. Balaenids are skim feeders—they swim and feed open-mouthed through masses of zooplankton, which are filtered out by the whale's baleen.

GENUS *EUBALAENA*
North Atlantic Right Whale

Eubalaena glacialis
ALSO: Black Right Whale, Biscayan Right Whale, Atlantischer Nordkaper, Baleine franche, Nordkaper, Гладкий кит. Whalers called these cetaceans "right whales" because they considered the balaenids the right whales to hunt they were relatively easy to approach, floated when harpooned, and yielded copious amounts of oil and blubber. SN means "right whale of the ice."
RANGE: Occurs in the N Atlantic along coasts and over continental shelf waters. Nearly extirpated in n Europe; rare offshore of Norway, Shetland Is, Faroes, and Iceland. In N Amer, occurs in the Bay of Fundy (Canada) in summer, and off

Cape Cod (US) in winter and spring; some winter calving grounds are in shallow coastal waters off Florida and Georgia (US). In 2007, scientists from Oregon State University and the National Oceanic and Atmospheric Administration (NOAA) used underwater hydrophones to record the presence of right whales off s Greenland, where they were thought to be extinct.
ID: L 45–55 ft (14–17 m); calves are about 15 ft (4.5 m) long at birth. WT 140,000 lb (63,500 kg). Females are larger than males. Black, with varying amounts of white on the belly. Broad, finless back. Paddle-shaped flippers. Strongly bowed jaws. Randomly scattered callosities (hard, rough patches of skin) on the lips and chin, above the eyes, and on the bonnet (the rostrum forward of the blowholes). Orange, white, yellow, or pink callosities, depending on whale lice species that live on them. Baleen is dark brown to gray, and is about 9.2 ft (2.8 m) long. Bushy, V-shaped blow.
HABITS: Raises flukes when diving. Breaches frequently, and also lobtails (slaps the water with its flukes). Feeds mainly from spring to fall on copepods and krill; may fast in winter. Largely solitary; said to form unstable courtship groups composed of a single female and several males. Females give birth to their first calf at 9–10 years of age. Gestation is about 1 year. Calves are weaned toward the end of their first year. Lifespan is at least 50 years, and possibly 100 years.
USE: Commercial whaling began in the 11th century with Basque whalers operating in the Bay of Biscay off the French coast. Whaling expanded to Labrador in 1530, to New England in the 1600s, and later to Norway and Russia. By the late 1800s, the species was nearly extirpated.
STATUS: Fully protected since 1935. About 300–400 individuals remain, mostly in e N Amer waters. CITES Appendix I. Endangered (IUCN).

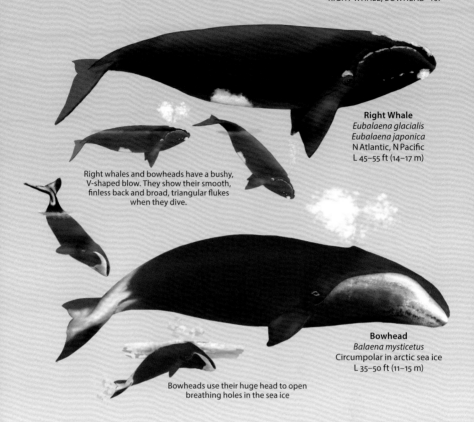

Right Whale
Eubalaena glacialis
Eubalaena japonica
N Atlantic, N Pacific
L 45–55 ft (14–17 m)

Right whales and bowheads have a bushy, V-shaped blow. They show their smooth, finless back and broad, triangular flukes when they dive.

Bowhead
Balaena mysticetus
Circumpolar in arctic sea ice
L 35–50 ft (11–15 m)

Bowheads use their huge head to open breathing holes in the sea ice

North Pacific Right Whale

Eubalaena japonica

ALSO: Pazifische Nordkaper, Baleine franche du Pacifique Nord, Pazifischer Nordkaper, Японский кит. SN means "right whale of Japan."

RANGE: Occurs in the N Pacific between 20°N and 60°N latitude; rare in the Gulf of Alaska, Bering Sea, Sea of Okhotsk, and off Kamchatka, the Kurils, and Commander Is. Since 1996 right whales have occasionally been seen in Bristol Bay (se Bering Sea) during the summer months. **ID:** L 45–55 ft (14–17 m). WT 140,000 lb (63,500 kg). Virtually identical in appearance and behavior to *E. glacialis*.

STATUS: Intense commercial whaling of the species began in the Gulf of Alaska in 1835, and by 1900 the species was rare. The species was afforded complete protection in 1935. However, between 1962 and 1968, illegal Soviet whaling killed several hundred right whales in the Bering Sea, Gulf of Alaska, and Sea of Okhotsk. Some 250–350 individuals are thought to remain, although no official estimates of current abundance have been published. A sub-population of about 200 right whales summers in the w Pacific off Japan. About 50 animals or less are estimated to live in the se Bering Sea and e N Pacific. In the past few years, small groups of right whales have been sighted in the Pacific zone, but calf sightings are extremely rare. One Pacific Right Whale was spotted off Brit Columbia in June 2013, which is remarkable, considering that the last previous sighting in the region was in 1951. In 1998 and 2004 an individual right whale was seen in the Gulf of Alaska, and in 2000 and 2013 scientists using underwater hydrophones recorded right whales' songs there. CITES Appendix I. Critically Endangered (IUCN).

GENUS *BALAENA*
Bowhead

Balaena mysticetus

ALSO: Greenland Whale, Steeple-top, Grönlandwal, Baleine boréale, Grønlandshval, Гренландский кит, Aquiq, Agvik, Arfivik. SN means "large moustached whale."

RANGE: Circumpolar in arctic pack ice and around polynyas. The only baleen whale to spend its entire life in arctic waters. Main populations in the e Canadian Arctic and Bering Sea. Small, highly endangered stocks occur around Svalbard and Sea of Okhotsk. Vagrant to Japan, Gulf of St Lawrence (Canada), and off Cape Cod (US).

ID: L 35–50 ft (11–15 m). WT 200,000 lb (90,000 kg). Dark gray to black, smooth skin, with a white patch on the lower jaw. White markings on the flukes and tail stock. Large and robust, with no dorsal fin. Massive bow-shaped skull is over 16.5 ft (5 m) long (almost one-third of the body length). Strongly arched mouth line. Narrow rostrum. Has the largest mouth of any animal. Dark baleen plates up to 14 ft (4.3 m) in length are the longest of any whale. Two distinctly separated blowholes located behind a peaked ridge, or crown, produce a wide, V-shaped blow. Broad, triangular flukes. Raises flukes on the last dive of a series.

HABITS: Uses its huge head to break open breathing holes in the sea ice. An 18 in (50 cm) thick layer of blubber insulates the body. Feeds by swimming open-mouthed through schools of copepods, krill, and other marine invertebrates, which are filtered through the baleen. Also forages near the seafloor in shallow areas, leaving a trail of mud in its wake. Known for far-reaching "songs," which can be heard for several miles underwater. Probably uses vocalizations to echolocate and steer around large obstacles such as icebergs. Male's low frequency grunts, pops, and moans coincide with the mating season, and may serve as sexual signals that attract females.

Sexually mature at about 20 years of age. Breeds in late winter to early spring. Females mate with more than one male and give birth to a single calf every 3–4 years. Gestation is about 13–14 months. Calves remain with their mother until they are weaned at 9–12 months of age.

Winters near the southern edge of the pack ice or in polynyas and moves north into high latitudes as the ice recedes in spring, migrating alone or in small groups. Bering Sea bowheads undertake an annual 3600 mi (5800 km) migration. They winter in the Bering Sea and begin to swim north in Mar–Apr. They move past St Lawrence Is and Diomede Is, and then pass through the Bering Strait as the pack ice retreats. Following leads in the Chukchi Sea ice, they migrate along the Alaska coast to Point Barrow. As the ice breaks up in May–Jun, they move offshore and summer in the Beaufort Sea. Some individuals follow leads to Banks Is and Prince Patrick Is, and then into Amundsen Gulf. In Sep–Oct the return migration takes them west along the continental shelf of the Beaufort Sea to Point Barrow, then into the Chukchi Sea. The bowheads move west toward Wrangel Is before returning south along the Russian coast in Nov and return back to the Bering Sea for winter.

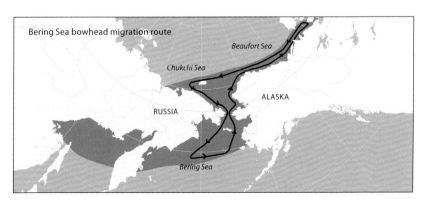

Bering Sea bowhead migration route

Beaufort Sea

Chukchi Sea

ALASKA

RUSSIA

Bering Sea

Ancient Bowhead jawbones at Whalebone Alley

USE: Bowheads were and are important subsistence animals for Bering Sea cultures. Hunts are conducted by native coastal whalers using handheld weapons. They paddle traditional umiaks when pursuing bowheads during the spring hunt, while motorized boats are used in the fall. Century-old slate, stone, and metal-tipped ivory harpoon tips have been found in whales killed in recent Alaskan subsistence hunts. Analysis of the tissues of the killed whales indicates that some were possibly 135 to 211 years old, which suggests that the Bowhead may be the world's longest-living mammal.

Little was known of the Bowhead's ritual significance until 1976, when Russian ethnographers discovered a 14th-century ceremonial site on Yttygran Is off the east coast of Chukotka. The monument, named Whalebone Alley (*Kitovaya alleya*), contains ancient Bowhead whale bones, stone structures, and places for caching whale meat. A row of Bowhead mandibles is fixed upright in the ground. Fifteen groups of skulls and vertebrae lie on the tundra, spaced 33 or 66 ft (10 or 20 m) apart—distances thought to represent the length and double length of the traditional umiak, while each group of skulls may represent a whaling crew.

STATUS: Bowhead whaling began in Norway's Svalbard Archipelago in the 17th century, and later extended to Greenland and Hudson Bay, Canada. Pacific bowheads were first hunted in the Sea of Okhotsk and Bering Sea in the mid-19th century. The bowhead whaling industry failed by the early 1900s, when plastics and spring steel replaced baleen, and petroleum products replaced whale oil. By then, eastern stocks were reduced from 30,000 to fewer than 1000 whales. Despite full protection since 1935, stocks have never recovered; the Svalbard population may be near extinction. The current population estimate for bowheads in the Bering Sea is about 8000 whales. CITES Appendix I. Endangered in the N Atlantic; Vulnerable–Endangered in the Bering Sea (IUCN).

FAMILY BALAENOPTERIDAE
RORQUAL WHALES
Rorqual whales have a streamlined body with a sickle-shaped (falcate) dorsal fin set behind the back's midpoint. The throat is wrinkled in deep longitudinal pleats. Rorqual whales are lunge feeders. They make a fast upward sloping swim while opening their jaws very wide and distending the throat. This allows them to ingest huge mouthfuls of water containing plankton, which is filtered out by the baleen. Most whales migrate to polar waters in summer to exploit seasonal abundance of food. They migrate back to warmer waters in winter and fast while they are there. Most rorqual species have a long lifespan. The age of large whales can be estimated by counting the layers present in the waxy ear plugs that form in the auditory canal.

GENUS *BALAENOPTERA*
Blue Whale
Balaenoptera musculus

ALSO: Sibald's Rorqual, Sulphurbottom, Blauwal, Rorqual bleu, Blåhval, Синий кит. SN: *Balaenoptera* means "winged whale"; *musculus* means "little mouse," but is perhaps better explained as a variant of *musculosus* (muscular).
RANGE: Found in oceans worldwide. N Atlantic stocks range from the subtropics to the Greenland

Sea; they are most frequently seen off e Canada and in the Gulf of St Lawrence, where they are present for most of the year. Greenland and Gulf of St Lawrence stocks also summer along the Canadian pack ice edge. Iceland, UK, and Norway stocks summer around Svalbard and the Russian coast near Murmansk. N Pacific stocks range from Kamchatka to s Japan and from the Gulf of Alaska and Aleutians south to Costa Rica.

ID: L to 110 ft (33 m). WT to 330,000 lb (150,000 kg). World's largest mammal. Bluish gray with pale mottling. Small triangular dorsal fin (visible when the whale dives). Broad, flat head. Black baleen. Slender conical blow to 30 ft (9 m) high.

HABITS: Solitary or forms small transitory pods. Occasionally raises flukes. Does not breach. Lunge feeder; feeds mostly on krill (euphausiids). Females choose mates based on size and possibly on vocalizations, which are the loudest of any whale. Most reproductive activity, including births and mating, takes place in winter. Females deliver a single calf after a 10- to 12-month gestation. Nursing calves gain 200 lb (90 kg) per day and are weaned at 6–8 months of age.

STATUS: There are presently about 25,000 blue whales, compared to 300,000 before intensive whaling began in 1900. Protected since 1965. CITES Appendix I. Endangered–Vulnerable (IUCN).

Fin Whale

Balaenoptera physalus
ALSO: Finback, Razorback, Common Rorqual, Finnwal, Rorqual commun, Finnhval, Финвал. SN means "winged whale with a [conspicuous] blow."

RANGE: Found in oceans worldwide. Separate N Pacific, N Atlantic, and Southern Ocean stocks. N Pacific whales summer in the Gulf of Alaska, Prince William Sound, Aleutians, Chukchi Sea, and Sea of Okhotsk. N Atlantic stocks summer in waters around the Canadian Arctic, Greenland, Iceland, Jan Mayen, Svalbard, and Barents Sea.
ID: L 75–80 ft (22–26 m). WT 80,000–160,000 lb (36,300–72,500 kg). Males are smaller than

females. Dark gray to brownish gray above, with some white on the belly and underside of flukes and tail. Right side of jaw, right lower lip, and right side of baleen is white; left jaw is black. Some show a whitish chevron behind head. Falcate dorsal fin. Ridged tail stock. Blow is an inverted cone to 19 ft (5.7 m) high.

HABITS: Solitary, or forms small unstable pods of 3–7 individuals, sometimes associating with blue whales. Seldom raises flukes when diving. Breaches occasionally. Can swim at speeds up to 29 mph (46 kmh). American naturalist Roy Chapman Andrews (1884–1960) said the fin whale "is built like a racing yacht and…can surpass the speed of the fastest ocean steamship." Feeds in deep, offshore ocean waters by lunging into schools of krill, squid, and small bait fish. Males are sexually mature at 6–10 years; females at 7–12 years. Male's mating song is a repetitive, low-frequency vocalization. Females give birth to a single calf in tropical waters in midwinter after 11–12 months of gestation. Calf is nursed for 6–8 months. Fin whales attain physical maturity at about 25 years of age and can live 80–90 years.

STATUS: Intensively hunted in the 20th century after the advent of explosive harpoons and steam-powered ships. N Pacific and N Atlantic populations are stable. Antarctic stocks are severely depleted and Endangered (IUCN). Protected species. CITES Appendix I.

Sei Whale

Balaenoptera borealis
ALSO: Coalfish Whale, Seiwal, Rorqual boréal, Seihval, Сейвал. SN means "winged whale of the north." CN "Sei" (pronounced "say" or "sigh") refers to the fact that these whales arrive off the Norwegian coast at the same time as schools of sei pollack (*seje*).

RANGE: Found in subtropical, temperate, and subpolar oceans worldwide, usually in deep waters over the continental shelf edge and slope. Separate stocks in the N Hemisphere and S Hemisphere. Both migrate to colder waters in summer and return to warmer waters in winter.
ID: L 40–60 ft (12–18 m). WT 100,000 lb (45,000 kg). Long, slim silhouette. Prominent falcate dorsal

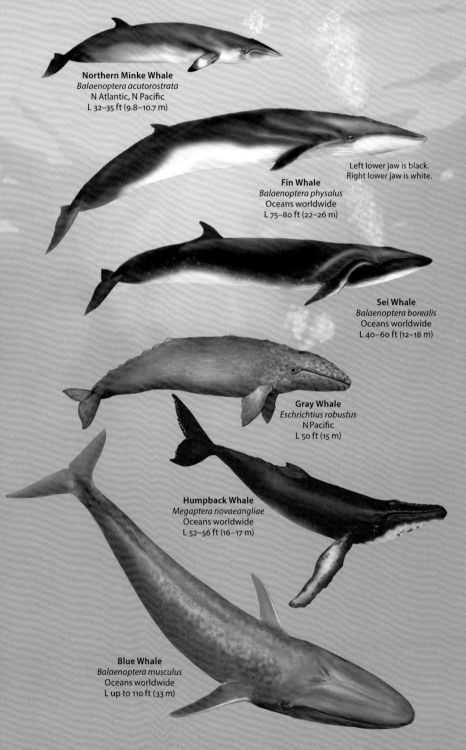

Northern Minke Whale
Balaenoptera acutorostrata
N Atlantic, N Pacific
L 32–35 ft (9.8–10.7 m)

Left lower jaw is black.
Right lower jaw is white.

Fin Whale
Balaenoptera physalus
Oceans worldwide
L 75–80 ft (22–26 m)

Sei Whale
Balaenoptera borealis
Oceans worldwide
L 40–60 ft (12–18 m)

Gray Whale
Eschrichtius robustus
N Pacific
L 50 ft (15 m)

Humpback Whale
Megaptera novaeangliae
Oceans worldwide
L 52–56 ft (16–17 m)

Blue Whale
Balaenoptera musculus
Oceans worldwide
L up to 110 ft (33 m)

fin. Dark steel gray, often marked with pale oval scars from bites of cookiecutter sharks (*Isictius*) and lampreys. Pale gray belly. Underside of flukes and flippers dark gray. Single longitudinal ridge on the rostrum. Baleen black, fringed with white. Columnar or bushy blow 10–13 ft (3–4 m) high. **HABITS:** Solitary or forms small pods of 2–5 individuals. Surfaces with dorsal fin and blowholes visible simultaneously. Seldom raises flukes when diving. Does not breach. Feeds on copepods, krill, small schooling fish, and squid by gulping or by skim feeding. Typically feeds at dawn. Sometimes leaves a line of bubble tracks on the sea surface when feeding. One of the fastest swimming whales, reaching speeds of 34 mph (55 kmh). Sexually mature at 6–12 years. Mates and gives birth during the winter while in lower latitudes. Females breed every 2–3 years. Gestation is 11–13 months. Females give birth to a single calf measuring about 15 ft (4.6 m) long and weighing 1500 lb (680 kg). Calf is weaned at 6–9 months. Can live 50–70 years. **STATUS:** Intensively hunted in the 20th century, mainly in the Antarctic, after the development of steam-powered ships. Northern stocks are of reasonable abundance. Southern Ocean stocks are Endangered (IUCN). CITES Appendix I.

Northern Minke Whale
Balaenoptera acutorostrata

ALSO: Piked Whale, Lesser Rorqual, Zwergwale, Baleine de Minke, Nordlig vågehval, Малый полосатик. SN means "sharp-nosed winged whale." CN is said to refer to an 18th-century Norwegian whaler named Minke, who harpooned so many whales that all rorquals were referred to as "Minke's whales."
RANGE: Found in the N Atlantic and N Pacific, from the arctic ice edge in summer to near the equator in winter. Minkes in Alaskan waters are migratory; Pacific NW stocks are resident and establish home ranges. Atlantic stocks migrate north in spring to Newfoundland, Greenland, Iceland, Norway, Svalbard, and the Barents Sea. **ID:** L 32–35 ft (9.8–10.7 m). WT 20,000 lb (9200 kg). Smallest arctic rorqual. Dark gray to black, with irregular gray chevrons across the back behind the head. White belly. White band across the flippers. Prominent falcate dorsal fin. White to gray baleen. Sharply pointed snout with sharp ridge on rostrum. Shallow, indistinct blow.
HABITS: Usually solitary or in small pods of 2–3 individuals. Often spy-hops, raising its head vertically out of the water with the eyes clear of the surface. Does not raise flukes when diving. Breaches. Feeds on small bait fish and krill. Sexually mature at 3–8 years. Females mate every other year. Mating and calving take place in winter. Gestation is 10–11 months. Female gives birth to a single calf, which is weaned at 4–6 months. Lifespan is about 50 years.
STATUS: Intensively whaled in the Arctic until the mid-1970s. Small numbers are still hunted by fisheries in Iceland, Greenland, Norway, Korea, and Japan. Fishermen from St Lawrence Is, Alaska, also harvest a few minkes. Natural predator is the Orca. CITES Appendix I & II.

GENUS *MEGAPTERA*
Humpback Whale
Megaptera novaeangliae

ALSO: Buckelwal, Baleine à bosse, Knølhval, Горбатый кит. SN means "big-winged New Englander," a reference to the humpback's flippers, which are the longest of any cetacean.
RANGE: Found in oceans worldwide in subpolar to equatorial waters. Separate N Pacific, N Atlantic, and Southern Ocean stocks. N Pacific stocks summer from s California and n Japan, north to the Bering and Chukchi seas; wintering grounds are off the coasts of Mexico and C Amer, Hawaii, Bonin and Ryuku islands, and n Philippines. N Atlantic stocks summer from the Gulf of Maine to Ireland and north to the ice edge in the Barents Sea, Greenland Sea, and Davis Strait; most winter in the West Indies.
ID: L 52–56 ft (16–17 m). WT 50,000–80,000 lb (22,000–36,000 kg). Females are larger than males. Dark gray to black above, with variable amounts of white on throat, flippers, and flukes. Distinctive small, humped dorsal fin. Long whitish flippers, with knobs on leading edge. Trailing edge of flukes is serrated; variable pattern on underside allows for identification

of individual whales. Broad rostrum covered with knobs. Low, rounded, bushy blow to about 9.5 ft (3 m) high.

HABITS: Forms pods of 12–15 individuals. Frequently raises flukes when diving. Slaps tail and flippers on the sea surface (lobtails) and sometimes lies on its side with a flipper in the air. Often breaches—a whaler's term

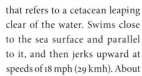

that refers to a cetacean leaping clear of the water. Swims close to the sea surface and parallel to it, and then jerks upward at speeds of 18 mph (29 kmh). About 90 percent of the body clears the water before the whale turns to land on its back or side. Humpbacks breach to stun fish prey or possibly to remove parasites from the skin.

Feeds on krill and bait fish. Often creates a bubble net around its prey. Feeds by lunging into schools of prey or swims underwater with its mouth slightly open, pumping the tongue against the palate to suck seawater into the mouth and then using pressure to force water out through the baleen. Fasts in winter while in tropical breeding and calving waters. Groups of males compete for a lone female, using lunges, tail slashes, and charges to attain dominance. Males also sing complex "love songs" that can last up to 20 minutes and be heard up to 20 mi (30 km) away. Females bear a single calf every 2–3 years and nurse it for about a year.

STATUS: A preference for coastal waters and slow swimming speed made the humpback an easy target for commercial whalers in the 20th century. Stocks were reduced to 10 percent of original numbers. Protected since 1964; numbers have increased to an estimated 12,000 animals in the N Pacific, 8000 in the N Atlantic. Subsistence hunts take a few whales each year. Main threat is entanglement in fishing gear. CITES Appendix I.

The distinctive dorsal fin of a Humpback Whale

FAMILY ESCHRICHTIIDAE
GRAY WHALE

The Gray Whale is traditionally placed in its own monotypic family and genus. The species once occurred in the N Atlantic, where it became extinct, possibly as late as 1700. It is now found only in the N Pacific, where two populations are recognized: the endangered nw Pacific or Asian stock and the ne Pacific or American stock.

GENUS *ESCHRICHTIUS*
Gray Whale
Eschrichtius robustus

ALSO: Devil Fish, Grauwal, Baleine grise, Gråhval, Серый кит. CN refers to English taxonomist John E. Gray (1800–1875). SN means "Eschricht's robust [whale]," honoring Danish zoologist Daniel Eschricht (1798–1863). California state marine mammal since 1975.

RANGE: Occurs in shallow coastal waters of the N Pacific. Two isolated geographic populations. Eastern N Pacific stock occurs along the west coast of N Amer; summers in the Bering, Chukchi, and Beaufort seas, and winters along Baja California and adjacent Mexican coast. The endangered w Pacific stock occurs along the e Asia coast from the Sea of Okhotsk to the E China Sea. Vagrant to the Mediterranean (1 record in 2010) and to coastal Namibia (1 record in 2013); these whales may have traveled via the increasingly ice-free Northwest Passage or around the southern tip of S Amer and across the Atlantic.

ID: L 50 ft (15 m). WT 80,000 lb (35,000 kg). Long, slim body. Narrow rostrum. Mottled gray. Skin is covered with barnacles (*Cryptolepas rhachianecti*) and whale lice (*Isocyamus* sp.), especially on the head. Inconspicuous dorsal hump, with a ridge of knobs called *knuckles* running along the top of the tail stock. Slightly arched mouth line. Short, cream to yellow baleen plates. Broad, mottled flukes. Low heart-shaped or columnar blow.

HABITS: Raises its flukes on long dives. Breaches, spy-hops, and often shows curiosity toward boats. Frequently found in shallow water near the shoreline where it often rolls in bottom gravel. Feeds in northern waters in summer, relying on extensive fat reserves to sustain it in migration and breeding. Feeds on benthic crustaceans such as amphipods, which it collects by turning on its side and scooping up sediments from the sea floor. The baleen sieves out any small invertebrates, which are ingested along with sand and water. Patches of muddy water and flocks of seabirds often mark the place where a Gray Whale is feeding.

The ne Pacific population undertakes one of the longest known mammal migrations—a round trip of 12,500 mi (20,150 km) between summer feeding grounds in the Bering, Chukchi, and Beaufort seas and breeding lagoons off Mexico's Baja Penin. The southward migration begins in late Oct with the population moving first along the Chukotka Penin and then down the California coast. The whales travel continuously, averaging 80 mi (120 km) each day, and reach the Baja lagoons by Dec. It is there that pregnant females deliver their young and mating occurs. In Mar the adults and calves begin to travel back up the Pacific coast, through Unimak Pass in the e Aleutians and past Nunivak Is into arctic waters, where they spend the summer feeding.

Acoustic studies made in 2003 along the coast of Barrow, Alaska, found that some gray whales remain in the Beaufort Sea ice in winter instead of migrating south. Increasing numbers and habitat change associated with sea ice reduction and warming in the Alaskan Arctic may be responsible for the extra-seasonal occurrence.

STATUS: E Pacific stocks of gray whales were nearly eradicated by whalers in the 1850s soon after New England whaler-naturalist Charles Melville Scammon (1825–1911) discovered their breeding grounds in San Ignacio Lagoon and Laguna Ojo de Liebre (formerly Scammon's

A Gray Whale covered with barnacles and whale lice

Lagoon) in Baja California, Mexico. Whalers would harpoon a calf to keep the mother nearby. The mother's fierce defense of her wounded calf earned the species the name "devil fish."

Protected since 1935, the e Pacific population has risen to around 26,000. W Pacific stocks were hunted until 1966 and are Critically Endangered (IUCN); about 130 individuals remain. There is evidence that the western and eastern stocks may occasionally intermingle; in Jan 2011, US and Russian researchers tracked a 13-year-old male western Gray Whale as it migrated across the Bering Sea and entered the continental shelf waters of Alaska north of the Aleutians.

Gray whales have also wandered into the Atlantic Ocean, where they have been absent since the 18th century. In 2010, a N Pacific Gray Whale made its way into the Mediterranean Sea. Scientists speculated it had come via the increasingly ice-free Northwest Passage. In 2013, researchers working off the Namibian coast confirmed a sighting of a N Pacific Gray Whale there, the first ever south of the equator.

SUBORDER ODONTOCETI
TOOTHED WHALES
Odontoceti is Greek for "toothed sea animal." These whales differ from the Mysticeti in that they have teeth instead of baleen and a single blowhole rather than two.

FAMILY PHOCOENIDAE
PORPOISES
"Porpoise" (Latin for "pig-fish") is often used to refer to any small dolphin, though porpoises and dolphins are quite different. Porpoises are shorter but stouter than dolphins and have a triangular dorsal fin rather than curved one. Porpoises also lack the conspicuous beak and bulbous head present on most dolphins, and have spade-shaped teeth rather than conical ones.

GENUS *PHOCOENOIDES*
Dall's Porpoise
Phocoenoides dalli
ALSO: White-flanked Porpoise, Spray Porpoise, True's Porpoise, Weißflankenschweinswal,

Marsouin de Dall, Stillehavsnise, Белокрылая морская свинья. SN means "Dall's porpoise," referring to William Healey Dall (1845–1927) American naturalist, malacologist, and one of the earliest scientific explorers of interior Alaska.

RANGE: Occurs over deep marine canyons and in cold inshore waters in the Bering Sea and Sea of Okhotsk, south to Japan and Baja California.

ID: L 7–8 ft (2–2.5 m). WT 400 lb (180 kg). Black, with contrasting white flanks; rare melanistic and leucistic forms also occur. Thick body. Small rounded head. Little or no beak. White-tipped, triangular dorsal fin. White-tipped flukes. Keel-like hump above the tail stock; males also have another hump at the tail base. Small, rounded flippers. Spade-shaped teeth, each separated by rigid "gum teeth," which aid in grasping slippery prey. Black to dark blue iris, with an iridescent dark bluish green pupil.

HABITS: Swims at the sea surface at speeds to 35 mph (55 kmh), creating a "rooster-tail" spray. Bow-rides. Forms small transitory pods of 2–20 individuals, but large numbers gather at feeding grounds, often in association with Pacific white-sided dolphins or long-finned pilot whales. Diet includes squid, crustaceans, and pelagic schooling fish, which are taken mainly at night at depths to 600 ft (180 m). In Jun–Aug, females give birth to a single calf, which is nursed for about 2 months.

STATUS: Natural predators include orcas and sharks. Japan harvests some 20,000 animals annually for meat for human consumption. Greatest threat is entanglement in nylon-filament drift nets. CITES Appendix II.

GENUS *PHOCOENA*
Harbor Porpoise
Phocoena phocoena

ALSO: Puffer, Gewöhnlicheschweinswal, Marsouin commun, Nise, Морская свинья; also called "puffing pig," a reference to sounds emitted from the blowhole. SN means "porpoise porpoise."

RANGE: Discontinuous distribution. Occurs in bays, estuaries, harbors, and fjords from the Chukchi and Beaufort seas south to Japan and c California; from w Greenland to the mid-Atlantic US coast; and from the Barents Sea to the UK and W Africa. Small numbers occur in the Mediterranean and Black seas.

ID: L 5–5.5 ft (1.5–1.7 m). WT 134–168 lb (61–76 kg). Dark gray, with lightly speckled, pale gray sides and white belly. Gray "chinstrap." Robust body, especially forward of the triangular dorsal fin. No distinguishable beak.

HABITS: Shy. Does not attend boats. Does not breach or splash when surfacing for air. Usually seen in groups of 2–5 animals. Feeds on demersal and benthic schooling fish such as herring, cod, hake, and capelin, as well as squid and shrimp. Makes clicking sounds (echolocates) in order to locate food. Females reach sexual maturity at 3–4 years. Gestation is 10–11 months. Mothers bring newborn calves to secluded coves to nurse them for 8 months. Lifespan is 10–12 years.

STATUS: Greenland harvests about 1000 porpoises each year in a direct hunt. Orcas and bottlenose dolphins are the primary predators. Main threat is incidental kills in gill nets and herring weirs. Vulnerable (IUCN).

FAMILY DELPHINIDAE
OCEANIC DOLPHINS
Oceanic dolphins have a single blowhole located on top of the head, slightly on the left. The dorsal fin is at mid-back. The tail bears a conspicuous notch. Most have a prominent bottlenose beak. Teeth are cone-shaped.

GENUS *LAGENORHYNCHUS*
Pacific White-sided Dolphin
Lagenorhynchus obliquidens

ALSO: Lag, Weißstreifendelfin, Lagénorhynque à flanc blanc du pacifique, Kortsnutedelfin, Тихоокеанский белобокий дельфин. SN means "bottlenose slanted-toothed [dolphin]," the latter a reference to its slightly angled teeth.

RANGE: Occurs in the N Pacific in open waters over the continental shelf from the Bering Sea and Sea of Okhotsk south to the S China Sea, Sea of Japan, and Baja California, Mexico.

ID: L 7.5–8.5 ft (2.3–2.6 m). WT 330–440 kg (150–200 kg). Dark gray back and flippers. Light gray patch on sides. Dark gray ring around the eyes. Creamy white chin, throat, and belly. Short dark beak. Black stripe runs from the mouth to the flippers, and then to the flank. Pale gray stripes (the "suspenders") run from above the eye to behind the strongly hooked, tall dorsal fin, which is dark in front and gray on the sides and back.

HABITS: Readily approaches boats. Bow-rides. Usually swims in pods of 10–100 individuals, but super-groups of more than 3000 have been recorded. Often feeds with other whales, seals, and seabirds. Feeds on hake, anchovies, squid, herring, salmon, and cod. Often works cooperatively to corral schools of prey fish. Sexually mature at 7 years. Gestation is 1 year. Can live up to 40 years of age.

STATUS: Most mortalities are caused by entanglement in drift nets. A few animals are killed each year in Japanese shore hunts. Total population is estimated at 1 million animals.

Atlantic White-sided Dolphin

Lagenorhynchus acutus
ALSO: Weißseitendephin, Dauphin à flancs blancs, Kvitskjeving, Атлантический белобокий дельфин. SN means "pointed bottlenose."

RANGE: Found from ne N Amer to Norway; highest populations occur between Cape Cod (US) and the Gulf of St Lawrence, and in waters between Greenland, Iceland, and the North Sea.
ID: L 8–9 ft (2.5–2.7 m). WT 400–570 lb (180–230 kg). Back, flippers, and dorsal fin dark gray to black. Chin, throat, and belly white. White to pale ochre patch on flank. Pale gray stripe runs from above the eye to the tail stock.
HABITS: Acrobatic. Approaches boats and bow-rides. Forms groups of up to 60 individuals, often in association with pilot whales and fin whales. Feeds on herring, mackerel, smelt, hake, squid, and shrimp. Reaches sexual maturity at 6–12 years. Gestation is 11 months. Females nurse calves for 12–18 months. Lifespan is 22–27 years.
STATUS: A few animals are taken each year in the Faroes, where meat and blubber are used for human food. Total world population is estimated at 200,000–300,000 animals. CITES Appendix II.

White-beaked Dolphin

Lagenorhynchus albirostris
ALSO: Weißschnauzen-delphin, Dauphin à bec blanc, Kvitnos, Беломордый дельфин. SN means "white-beaked bottlenose."
RANGE: Occurs in the N Atlantic from cold-temperate waters to the edge of the pack ice. Found off the N Amer coast from Labrador to Cape Cod; off sw Greenland; off the European coast from Norway and the Barents Sea south to the UK; small threatened populations exist in the sw Baltic and Black seas. Generally ranges north of the Atlantic White-sided Dolphin.
ID: L 9–10 ft (2.7–3 m). WT 680–770 lb (310–350 kg). Robust. Black back and sides, with a white saddle behind the dorsal fin and whitish to ashy gray bands on the flanks. Belly white to pale gray. Very short, thick beak is white (Europe) or gray (N Amer). Erect, strongly falcate dorsal fin located at mid-back.
HABITS: Gregarious. Acrobatic, especially when feeding. Breaches. Fast, powerful swimmer. Bow-rides in front of large, fast-moving vessels, but loses interest quickly. Forms groups of fewer than 50 individuals, sometimes in association with fin whales and orcas. Feeds on herring, cod, haddock, whiting, capelin, hake, cephalopods, and crustaceans. Females reach sexual maturity at 3–4 years of age and typically bear a single calf each year after that. Gestation is about 11 months. Calf is nursed for 8–12 months.
STATUS: Primary threat is entanglement in bottom-set gill nets. CITES Appendix II.

GENUS *GLOBICEPHALA*
Long-finned Pilot Whale

Globicephala melas
ALSO: Blackfish, Gewöhnli-cher Grindwal, Globicéphale noir, Grindhval, Обык-новенная гринда. SN means "black round-headed [whale]."

RANGE: Occurs in cold currents from the N Atlantic to the Southern Ocean. Northern stocks occur from w Greenland, east to Iceland, Faroes, and Norway, and south to the mid-Atlantic US coast and w Mediterranean.

Atlantic White-sided Dolphin
Lagenorhynchus acutus
N Atlantic
L 8–9 ft (2.5–2.7 m)

Harbor Porpoise
Phocoena phocoena
N Pacific, N Atlantic
L 5–5.5 ft (1.5–1.7 m)

White-beaked Dolphin
Lagenorhynchus albirostris
N Atlantic
L 9–10 ft (2.7–3 m)

Pacific White-sided Dolphin
Lagenorhynchus obliquidens
N Pacific
L 7.5–8.5 ft (2.3–2.6 m)

"Rooster-tail" spray of a
Dall's Porpoise

Dall's Porpoise
Phocoenoides dalli
N Pacific
L 7–8 ft (2–2.5 m)

Orcas swimming in formation

Orca or Killer Whale
Orcinus orca
Oceans worldwide
L 26–30 ft (8–9 m)

Bulbous head and prominent
dorsal fin are conspicuous
when pilot whales are at
the ocean surface.

Long-finned Pilot Whale
Globicephala melas
N Pacific
L 16–21 ft (5–6.4 m)

ID: L 16–21 ft (5–6.4 m). WT 2900–5000 lb (1300–2300 kg). Black to dark brown. Bulbous forehead, or melon ("pothead"). No distinguishable beak. Whitish blaze behind eye. Prominent, wide, falcate dorsal fin located forward on body. White to gray saddle on the back behind dorsal fin. Long, falcate, tapered flippers.

HABITS: Forms small, possibly familial groups of 10–20 animals; larger groups of 100 or more sometimes occur, sometimes with bottlenose dolphins. Groups congregate at the water's surface and remain motionless when resting. Forages at depths of 600–1650 ft (200–500 m). Feeds on squid, mackerel, and some shrimp. Spy-hops. Does not approach ships. Mating and calving take place May–Sep. Gestation is about 1 year. Female nurses her calf for 2 years.

STATUS: Pilot whale fisheries operate in the Faroes, Norway, and Greenland. Mass strandings are common. Main threats are entanglement in longlines, trawls, and gill nets. CITES Appendix II.

GENUS *ORCINUS*
Orca or Killer Whale
Orcinus orca

ALSO: Blackfish, Orque, Schwertwal, Spekkhogger, Косатка, Aaxlu, Mesungesak, Agliuk, Ardlursak. Called "wolves of the sea" because they hunt in packs. SN means "whale belonging to Orcus [Roman god of the underworld]."

RANGE: Most wide-ranging whale species, occurring in all of the world's oceans. Avoids pack ice, but frequents shallow bays and river mouths along arctic coastlines.

ID: L 26–30 ft (8–9 m). WT 8400–12,000 lb (3800–5600 kg). Stocky black body, with white patches on the flanks, lower jaw, and above the eyes; grayish saddle behind the dorsal fin. Males have an erect dorsal fin up to 6 ft (1.8 m) high; females and juveniles have a 3 ft (1 m) high falcate dorsal fin.

HABITS: Forms pods of up to 30 individuals. Highly vocal, producing a variety of clicks and whistles used for communication and echolocation. Each pod has its own vocal repertoire. Occasionally raises flukes when diving. Preys on other whales, seals, seabirds, turtles, and fish. Launches coordinated assaults on marine mammals as large as the blue whale. Males become sexually mature at 15 years but do not typically reproduce until age 21. Females become sexually mature at 15 years of age. Gestation is 15–18 months. Females deliver a single calf once every 5 years. Calves nurse for up to 2 years. All resident pod members, including males of all ages, participate in the socialization of the young. Females breed until the age of 40 and have a lifespan of about 50 years, with exceptional individuals living to 70–80 years. Males live about 30 years, with exceptions to 50–60 years.

STATUS: Never intensively hunted. A few animals are taken by Norwegian and Icelandic whalers in the N Atlantic and by Soviet ships in the S Hemisphere. Threats include pollution, depletion of prey species, conflicts with fishing vessels, and habitat loss. CITES Appendix II.

FAMILY PHYSETERIDAE
GENUS *PHYSETER*
Sperm Whale
Physeter macrocephalus

ALSO: Pottwal, Cachalot, Spermhval, Кашалот. CN derives from the Latin *spermaceti*, meaning "whale sperm," referring to the old belief that the waxy spermaceti in the head was whale spawn. SN means "large-headed blower." The huge, square head, which typically is one-third of the whale's length, contains the largest known brain of any living or extinct animal, weighing an average of 18 lb (8 kg). Whalers learned that sperm whales used their head like a battering ram to make a hole under the ship's waterline. In 1820 the American whaling ship *Essex* was sunk by a Sperm Whale, an incident inspiring Herman Melville's 1851 novel *Moby-Dick*.

In their spare time, whalers would etch designs onto sperm whale teeth, an art form known as *scrimshaw.*

Sperm Whale
Physeter macrocephalus
Ice-free oceans worldwide
L 40–55 ft (12–17 m)

The low, rounded blow projects forward and to the left.

In a typical dive the Sperm Whale arches its back, showing the hump, and then raises the tail flukes.

RANGE: Occurs in oceans worldwide. Found in ice-free waters of the Bering Sea north to St Lawrence Is; in Davis Strait between Greenland and Canada; in Denmark Strait; and off Norway. Highest densities occur over continental slopes, deep canyons, and edges of ocean banks.

ID: L 40–55 ft (12–17 m). WT 55,000–120,000 lb (24,000–57,000 kg). Males are 30–50 percent larger than females. The world's largest living toothed animal and largest living carnivore. Dark brownish gray in color; albinos are known. Massive, squared body with a blunt rostrum. Lower jaw is underslung and rod-like, and has 20–26 pairs of large, conical teeth that fit into sockets on the toothless upper jaw. The teeth measure 3–8 in (8–20 cm) long and can each weigh up to 0.5 lb (1 kg). Broad, triangular flukes. Small, thick, rounded dorsal fin. A series of bumps runs along a ridge on the lower back. The blowhole is set close to the left side and front of the head, giving rise to a shallow, rounded blow that projects forward and to the left.

HABITS: These whales feed on squid, giant squid, octopus, sharks, and rays taken on or near the sea bottom. Sperm whales use echolocation to find prey in the dark depths, emitting a wide-angle beam of high-frequency clicks generated in the bony nostrils and a structure called the *phonic lips*. Incoming echoes are received by the lower jaw, which transmits the pings to the inner ear via a fat-filled canal.

Sperm whales can dive to depths of 1300 ft (400 m) or more and remain submerged for 30–45 minutes. They can make these long dives because of the massive volume of oxygenated blood in their circulatory system. Buoyancy during the dive is controlled by the 500 gallons (1900 liters) of waxy, viscous spermaceti found in the *case*, an organ in the head cavity. As the whale dives, a specialized internal nostril carries cold water to the case. This causes the spermaceti to solidify and increase in specific density, generating a negative buoyancy that allows the whale to sink fairly effortlessly. When the whale pursues prey, its body temperature increases, causing the spermaceti to melt. The whale becomes more buoyant and rises to the surface with little physical exertion. After making a long dive, sperm whales will often bask at the sea surface for an hour or more.

Sperm whales live in pods segregated by age and sex. Females, calves, and non-breeding males form pods of up to 50 individuals. Mature bulls are normally solitary and move seasonally into much higher latitudes than females or young.

Females are sexually mature at 7–13 years of age and reproduce about every 4–5 years after that. Males reach puberty at 9–10 years of age but do not mate until they are 25–27 years old. Breeding takes place in tropical to subtropical waters in Jan–Aug in the N Hemisphere. During the breeding season several bulls may join a nursery school of females and calves and compete for breeding rights. Calves are born in temperate or tropical waters after a gestation period of about 15 months. Calves are nursed until they are 3 years of age or older. Calves will suckle from females other than their mother and continue to nurse for 13 years. Lifespan is 50–70 years.

USE: Sperm whales were harvested for their oil, spermaceti, and ambergris; their meat is not palatable. Sperm whale oil rendered from the blubber burned cleanly in oil lamps and made an excellent lubricant for delicate instruments.

The waxy *spermaceti* was used in making candles, ointments, and high-grade machinery and watch oil. Today it is used in automatic transmission fluid, as a lubricant for photographic lenses, and in cosmetics, detergents, and rust-proofing and pharmaceutical compounds.

Ambergris—a gray substance with an oddly sweet, earthy odor—is a biliary secretion of the Sperm Whale's lower intestine induced by sharp pieces of giant squid beak. Ambergris is valued as a perfume fixative.

STATUS: The only natural predator is the Orca, which takes sperm whale females with young. Sperm whales were hunted from 1700 to 1987. In 1960, the International Whaling Commission prohibited factory ships from taking this species. Nonetheless, in 1963 over 29,000 sperm whales were killed. CITES Appendix I. Vulnerable (IUCN). Endangered (US–ESA).

FAMILY ZIPHIIDAE
BEAKED WHALES

These cetaceans remain one of the ocean's mysteries due to their preference for deep water and avoidance of ships. Much of our knowledge of them comes from strandings and incidental whale catches. These whales all have a beak-like rostrum. They have 1–2 pairs of teeth, which erupt in the adult male's lower jaw. Placement, shape, and number of teeth are unique to each species. Beaked whales have a single, forward-facing, crescent-shaped blowhole and a pair of convergent grooves on the throat. Adult males often possess a dramatically bulging forehead. These cetaceans forage at depths exceeding 650 ft (200 m), feeding mainly on cephalopods, supplemented by fish. Most prey are thought to be taken by suction, as beaked whales have a mouth, tongue, and ventral throat grooves that help to create a vacuum within their mouths.

GENUS *BERARDIUS*
Baird's Beaked Whale
Berardius bairdii

ALSO: Giant Beaked Whale, Baird-Wal, Baleine à bec de Baird, Nordlig kjempenebbhval, Северный плавун. SN means "Bérard's Baird's [whale]," honoring American naturalist Spencer F. Baird (1823–1887) and French admiral Auguste Bérard (1796–1852), who brought a type specimen of the southern species, *Berardius arnouxii*, to France in 1846. *Berardius bairdii* was first described in 1883 by Norwegian-American Leonhard Stejneger (1851–1943) from a skull he found on Bering Is.

RANGE: Occurs in deep waters over submarine escarpments, seamounts, and steep continental slopes in the N Pacific, Bering Sea, Sea of Okhotsk, and Sea of Japan.

ID: L 39–42 ft (12–13 m). WT 20,000–24,000 lb (10,000–11,000 kg). Elongated, tubular body. Dark gray to brown, with a pale gray belly. Body is often scarred with pale lines, possibly from intraspecific fighting or Orca attacks. Bulbous melon forehead slopes steeply to a dolphin-like beak. A pair of triangular teeth erupts at the tip of the male's lower jaw; a smaller, secondary pair erupts behind these inside the closed mouth. Dorsal fin is set far back on body. Large, triangular flukes. Low, bushy blow.

HABITS: Forms fairly stable, possibly familial pods of 10–30 individuals. Wary of ships, and when startled, the entire group moves off as a unit, surfacing and diving in synchrony. Known to breach, spy-hop, and lobtail. Feeds on squid and benthic fishes taken at or near the sea bottom, usually at depths of more than 3300 ft (1000 m).

STATUS: Only Japan, where the meat is highly regarded as food, engages in a limited hunt on the Boso Penin. CITES Appendix I.

This skull of a Baird's Beaked Whale shows 2 large triangular teeth at the tip of the lower jaw and a pair of small peg-like teeth to their rear.

GENUS *ZIPHIUS*
Cuvier's Beaked Whale
Ziphius cavirostris

ALSO: Goose-beaked Whale, Cuvier-Schnabelwal, Baleine de Cuvier, Cuviernebbhval, Клюворыл. CN honors French anatomist Georges Cuvier (1769–1832), who first described the species. SN means "sword hollow rostrum," referring to the deep hollow in the skull forward of the blowhole.
RANGE: Occurs in most oceans, especially in deep waters above the continental slope.
ID: L 17–23 ft (5–7 m). WT 5700–6600 lb (2600–3000 kg). Robust body. Dark gray to pale rusty brown, with paler areas on the head and belly; head and upper back of adult males can be white. Back and sides can show scratches and circular marks. Small falcate dorsal fin is set about two-thirds of the way back from the beak tip. Sloping forehead. Short, poorly defined beak; mouth is upcurved at the rear. Lower jaw protrudes beyond the upper jaw, giving the appearance of a short goose-beak. Adult males (rarely females) have a single pair of forward-pointing conical teeth at the tip of the lower jaw; teeth erupt outside the closed mouth in large bulls. Low, diffuse blow.
HABITS: Forms groups of up to 7 individuals. Wary of ships. Dives to 3300 ft (1000 m) or more, with dives lasting 20–90 minutes. Feeds on deep-sea squid, octopus, fish, and crustaceans, which are sucked into the mouth. Sexually mature at 7–11 years of age. Females give birth to a single calf every 2–3 years. Gestation is about 12 months. Lifespan is up to 60 years.
STATUS: Threatened by entanglement in deep-water drift and gill nets. Mass strandings in the Mediterranean Sea and off the Bahamas indicate that the species is vulnerable to noise generated by strong underwater sonar transmissions linked to military exercises. CITES Appendix II.

GENUS *HYPEROODON*
Northern Bottlenose Whale
Hyperoodon ampullatus

ALSO: North Atlantic Bottlehead, Chaney John, Dögling, Nördlicher Entenwal, Hyperoodon boréal, Nebbhval, Высоколобый бутылконос. SN means "toothed bottlenose." First seen in 1717 when one stranded in Essex, England.
RANGE: Occurs in the N Atlantic in waters more than 6500 ft (2000 m) deep, especially around submarine canyons, seamounts, and continental slopes. Stocks concentrate around Sable Is, Nova Scotia; in Davis Strait; at the entry to Hudson Strait and Frobisher Bay; in seas between Iceland and Svalbard; and in waters north of the Faroes. Ranges south to Long Is Sound and Cape Verde Is. In Jan 2006 a vagrant entered the Rvr Thames and swam upriver to Albert Bridge in London. Rescuers moved it onto a barge, hoping to take it out to sea, but the whale had a convulsion and died. Its skeleton is now in the Natural History Museum in London.
ID: L 30–32 ft (9–10 m). WT 13,000–17,000 lb (5800–7500 kg). Long, rotund body. Chocolate brown to ochre; paler on the flanks and belly. Ochre color may be caused by a thin layer of phytoplankton and diatoms. Pointed, falcate dorsal fin about 12 in (30 cm) high and set far back on the body. Small flippers. Tail lacks central notch. Pronounced dolphin-like beak. AD ♂: White forehead and conspicuous melon. Males have 1 (occasionally 2) pair of 2 in (5 cm) long, conical teeth at tip of lower jaw. AD ♀/JUV: Brown, rounded forehead.
HABITS: Feeds on deep-sea squid, sea cucumbers, herring, cuttlefish, sea stars, and other benthic invertebrates. Dives to depths of 2625–4750 ft (800–1450 m). Surfaces to breathe for about 10 minutes, often in the same location where the dive began. Forms family groups of 4–10 individuals that may raft quietly for a few minutes and then erupt in frenzied swimming. Attracted by sounds of ships' generators. Breeds in spring and early summer. Gestation is about 1 year. Calves are born Apr–Jun and nurse for around 1 year. Lifespan is about 37 years.
STATUS: Hunted in the UK and Norway in 1885–1973. Subsistence hunt occurs in the Faroes in Sep. Disturbance caused by oil and gas explorations around the "Gully," a submarine canyon east of Nova Scotia, threatens a population of about 130 resident bottlenose whales. Estimated world population is 10,000. CITES Appendix I.

GENUS *MESOPLODON*
Sowerby's Beaked Whale

Mesoplodon bidens

ALSO: North Atlantic or North Sea Beaked Whale, Sowerby-Zweizahnwal, Mésoplodon de Sowerby, Sowerbys spisshval, Атлантический ремнезуб. CN honors natural history artist James Sowerby, who described and illustrated the species in his 1804 *British Miscellany*. SN means "middle weapon 2-toothed," denoting that the species is armed with a tooth on each side of the mid-lower jaw.

RANGE: Occurs in the N Atlantic, Norwegian Sea, Labrador Sea, Baltic Sea, and off Iceland, and south to Massachusetts, Madeira, and the Canaries. Mass strandings have been recorded along the n European coast, and in 2004 a stranding was recorded on the coast of Georgia (US). Most northerly beaked whale.

ID: L 17–18 ft (5–5.5 m). WT 2200–2900 lb (1000–1300 kg). Spindle-shaped, bluish to dark gray body, becoming progressively more scarred with scratches and white oval rings in maturity. Small dorsal fin located two-thirds of the way down the back. Rounded flippers, with a pointed tip. Small head, with a long, uniformly gray beak and a conspicuous bulge just in front of the blowhole. Lower jaw has white patches and slightly protrudes beyond the upper jaw. AD ♂: Pair of protruding teeth erupts 12 in (30 cm) back from the tip of the slightly arched lower jaw. Teeth are about 4 in (10 cm) high, and have a small, sharp point of dentine near the apex of each (often called a "tooth upon a tooth").

HABITS: Forms stable pods of 8–10 individuals. Uses suction to feed on squid and small fish taken in dives reaching depths of 4920 ft (1500 m) and lasting 10–28 minutes. Uses high-frequency sound for echolocation. Faint, inaudible blow. Brow and beak break the water first when surfacing. Sexually mature at around 7 years. Breeding season is thought to be from late winter to spring.

STATUS: Formerly hunted off Newfoundland, Iceland, and in the Barents Sea. Threats include deepwater trawling and noise pollution from offshore exploration and drilling along the w coast of Ireland. CITES Appendix II.

Stejneger's Beaked Whale

Mesoplodon stejnegeri

ALSO: Bering Sea Beaked Whale, Sabre-toothed Whale, Mésoplodon de Stejneger, Stejnegerspisshval, Stejneger-Zweizahnwal, Командорский ремнезуб, Kigan agaliusiak. SN means "Stejneger's middle weapon [whale]." CN honors Norwegian-American biologist Leonhard Hess Stejneger (1851–1943) of the US National Museum (now the Smithsonian). In 1883 Stejneger collected a worn skull lacking a lower jaw on Bering Is in the Commander Is group. Frederick William True (1858–1914), also of the US National Museum, examined the skull in 1885 and named the species after Stejneger. Because the lower jaw of the type specimen was missing, True was not able to fully describe the species until 1904 when one of these whales stranded on a beach near Newport, Oregon.

RANGE: Occurs in deep, offshore waters of the N Pacific, south to the c California coast, with an isolated population in the Sea of Japan.

ID: L 17–18 ft (5–5.5 m). WT to 2650 lb (1200 kg). Spindle-shaped body. Dark gray above, paler below. Flat or depressed melon. Upper surface of head is dark gray to black, forming a "cranial cap." Conspicuous arch on back half of mouth line. A pair of large tusk-like teeth erupts about 8 in (20 cm) back from the tip of the male's lower jaw; each tilts forward and inward. Teeth measure about 8 in (20 cm) high, 4 in (10 cm) wide, and 1 in (2.5 cm) thick. Body frequently bears oval scars from bites of cookiecutter sharks (*Isistius* sp.) or slashes from teeth of rival males. Underside of the flukes may have irregular white streaks.

HABITS: Most knowledge about this whale comes from multiple strandings in the Aleutians and Japan in the late 20th century. Data suggest that the species forages in deep water, feeding by suction on squid in the families Gonatidae and Cranchiidae. Thought to form groups of 3–15 individuals, which may be segregated by sex. May migrate south in winter.

STATUS: Mortalities occur in drift and gill nets set along the Pacific coast of N Amer. CITES Appendix II.

Males have large tusk-like teeth that erupt
from the mid-lower jaw.

Stejneger's Beaked Whale
Mesoplodon stejnegeri
N Pacific
L 17–18 ft (5–5.5 m)

Males have a pair of large teeth that erupt
from the mid-lower jaw.

Sowerby's Beaked Whale
Mesoplodon bidens
N Atlantic
L 17–18 ft (5–5.5 m)

Males, rarely females, have a pair of conical teeth
at the tip of the lower jaw.

Cuvier's Beaked Whale
Ziphius cavirostris
Oceans worldwide
L 17–23 ft (5–7 m)

Males have a pair of tiny teeth at the tip
of the lower jaw.

Northern Bottlenose Whale
Hyperoodon ampullatus
N Atlantic
L 30–32 ft (9–10 m)

Males have 2 large teeth and 2 peg-like teeth
at the tip of the lower jaw.

Baird's Beaked Whale
Berardius bairdii
N Pacific
L 39–42 ft (12–13 m)

FAMILY MONODONTIDAE
BELUGA AND NARWHAL

Monodontidae comprises the pure white Beluga and the tusk-toothed Narwhal. These are mid-sized whales, with a bulbous forehead, or *melon*, and a short or absent snout. A narrow dorsal ridge replaces the dorsal fin found on most whales—possibly an adaptation to living under the sea ice. The unfused cervical vertebrae allow their necks to bend and rotate unlike other cetaceans. Belugas have small peg-like teeth. Narwhals have 2 teeth, 1 of which erupts and grows into a long tusk in males. These whales communicate with a wide range of vocalizations and use echolocation to navigate. Their diet includes fish, cephalopods, mollusks, and small crustaceans. Both species reach sexual maturity at 5–8 years of age. Females bear a single calf after a gestation of 14–15 months. Young are weaned at about 2 years of age. Family groups travel together in large herds, or *pods*, which during migration may be composed of several hundred individuals.

GENUS *DELPHINAPTERUS*
Beluga

Delphinapterus leucas
ALSO: Belukha, White Whale, Weißwal, Béluga, Hvithval, Белуха. CN derives from the Russian word *bielo*, meaning "white." SN means "white wingless dolphin," with *-apterus* referring to the absence of a dorsal fin.
RANGE: Occurs between 50°N and 80°N, in estuaries, bays, inlets, and in some large rivers off Alaska, Canada, Greenland, and Russia. Isolated populations in the St Lawrence Rvr estuary and Saguenay Fjord in Quebec. Vagrant to Japan, France, and Massachusetts (US). In spring 2006, the carcass of a young Beluga was found in the Tanana Rvr near Fairbanks, Alaska—1100 mi (1700 km) from the ocean; it presumably had followed migrating salmon upstream.
ID: L 13–16 ft (4–5 m). WT 1500–3500 lb (700–1600 kg). Adults are entirely white; juveniles are gray, turning pure white at 7–9 years of age. Rotund body. Broad, short, spatulate flippers. Narrow dorsal ridge. Tail fin becomes ornately

curved and convex with age. Bulbous malleable melon changes shape as air moves around in the sinuses. Mouth lining is pink. Both sexes have 8–9 peg-like teeth in both the upper and lower jaws; teeth are often worn down to the gums in older animals. Thin blow to 3 ft (1 m) high.
HABITS: Forms small pods of up to 12 animals; during migrations herds of several hundred individuals are common. Vocalizations include whistles and bird-like twitters, hence the name "sea-canary." Sexually mature at 4–8 years of age. Mating occurs in winter or early spring. Females give birth to a single calf in spring after a gestation period of 15 months. Young are nursed for about 2 years.

In summer, belugas move to feed in shallow coastal bays, estuaries, and inlets. They molt their outer layer of skin and often rub against the coarse gravel bottom in the shallows to remove the old yellowed skin. When the shallows freeze over in fall, the pods move toward the advancing pack ice. Some pods winter in open water at the ice edge. Others move into the ice pack, surfacing and breathing in open leads and polynyas. In heavy pack ice, belugas use their remarkable echolocation abilities to locate open water or, if iced in, resort to breathing air trapped in pockets under the ice.

Belugas forage near the sea bottom at depths of about 1000 ft (305 m), feeding on fish such as capelin, char, sand lance, and cod, as well as squid, octopus, crabs, shrimp, marine worms, and zooplankton. Belugas sometimes spit or spray water at humans or other whales. Some speculate that this practice may be used to blow away sand from crustaceans at the sea bottom.
STATUS: High levels of mercury and PCBs periodically make beluga meat unfit for human consumption. Subsistence and commercial hunters harvest belugas for oil, hide, and meat, except in Canada, which banned the hunt in 1972. Whales killed with rifle shot often sink before they can be brought to shore. An increase in vessel traffic is a threat, especially in bays where belugas congregate in summer. Russia is considering starting a meat-for-export enterprise or a live-capture operation to supply foreign oceanaria. CITES Appendix II. Vulnerable (IUCN).

ad. ♂

juv.

Narwhal
Monodon monoceros
Arctic waters of e Canada,
Greenland, Svalbard, Russia
L 14–15.5 ft (4.2–4.7 m)

Beluga
Delphinapterus leucas
Circumpolar Arctic
L 13–16 ft (4–5 m)

GENUS *MONODON*
Narwhal

Monodon monoceros

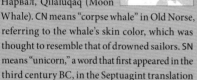

ALSO: Narval, Narhval, Нарвал, Qilaluqaq (Moon Whale). CN means "corpse whale" in Old Norse, referring to the whale's skin color, which was thought to resemble that of drowned sailors. SN means "unicorn," a word that first appeared in the third century BC, in the Septuagint translation of the Bible from Hebrew to Greek.

RANGE: Occurs in the N Atlantic and Arctic Ocean. Highest populations occur in Hudson Strait, Lancaster Sound, Davis Strait, Baffin Bay, and Foxe Basin. Small populations occur in the Greenland and Barents seas. Vagrant to the Beaufort, Chukchi, and Bering seas.

ID: L 14–15.5 ft (4.3–4.7 m). WT 2200–3500 lb (1000–1600 kg). Calves are gray when born, then darken in color and whiten from the belly up as they age. Adults are mottled and spotted with grayish green, black, and cream, and have white flanks. Old males can be almost completely white except for a narrow, dark-spotted band on the dorsal ridge. Short flippers have upturned tips. Tail fluke is strongly convex on the rear margin. Head is small and rounded in juveniles. Adults develop a melon head that is filled with waxy material thought to focus acoustic signals.

Two teeth are embedded in the gums of the upper jaw. In males (rarely females), the left tooth grows and protrudes through the upper jaw bone and skin of the rostrum. Occasionally males grow a second tusk. Tusks spiral to the left as they grow. Average tusk length is about 6.75 ft (2 m); the longest known tusk measured 8.75 ft (2.7 m) and weighed 22 lb (10 kg). Tusks tend to be covered in algae, except the tip.

Scientists formerly thought that the narwhal male used its tusk mostly for jousting battles in mating season. However, in 2005 Martin T. Nweeia of the Harvard School of Dental Medicine and scientists from the US National Institute of Standards and Technology tested the theory. They focused an electron microscope on a Narwhal tusk and found that some 10 million nerve endings stretch out from the tusk's core to its outer surface. This sensory system is thought to help detect changes in temperature, pressure, salinity, and other factors that contribute to the Narwhal's survival in the arctic environment.

HABITS: Closely associated with leads in the arctic ice pack. Moves toward coastal areas when the ice breaks up in spring, then moves back offshore when the sea ice freezes in fall. Usually swims in family pods of 2–10 individuals, but typically forms herds of hundreds of animals in summer. Herds are segregated by age and sex, with separate pods of mature females with calves, immature and bachelor males, and large mature males.

Forages over a wide range of depths, diving to at least 2600 ft (800 m), more than 15 times per day, with some dives reaching 4900 ft (1500 m).

Dives last about 25 minutes. Feeds on arctic cod, polar cod, Greenland halibut, cephalopods, squid, and shrimp. Feeds heavily during migrations, but very little when in open water in summer and early fall. Narwhals mate in Mar–May, when sea ice is still present. Gestation is about 15 months. A female nurses her calf for more than 12 months and typically gives birth every 3 years. **USE:** In medieval times, the Narwhal's tusk was thought to be the horn of a unicorn, a mythical horse with a single twisted horn projecting from its forehead. The myth was fostered by 12th-century Norse fishermen who discovered narwhals off the Greenland coast. They began to market the tusks, then called *alicorns*, often using Vikings and Arabs as brokers.

Alicorns were sold to wealthy kings, princes, physicians, cathedrals, and courts of Asia and Europe, often for many times their weight in gold. The crown jewels of Elizabeth I of England included an alicorn brought from Labrador in 1577 by Arctic explorer Martin Frobisher. It was valued at 10,000 English pounds—then the cost of an entire castle.

The alicorn's immense value was based on its supposed magical powers. It was thought to detect and neutralize poison, and in its powdered form was a powerful aphrodisiac. Mixed with amber, ivory, gold, coral, raisins, and cinnamon, it was said to remedy epilepsy. Miraculous cures were said to occur when churches displayed alicorns.

The Narwhal–alicorn myth persisted for more than 400 years, primarily because narwhals very rarely were seen south of the ice pack and also because the traders operated in utter secrecy. But by the 17th century, the deception began to falter. As New World exploration expanded, reports of bizarre whales that bore long tusks surfaced.

Ole Wurm, regius professor of Denmark and a zoologist of high attainment, investigated the matter and in 1638 exposed the alicorn's true origins in a public dissertation in Copenhagen. He declared that alicorns were the teeth of whales, citing as evidence the narwhal cranium and tusk that he had recently examined. The price of narwhal tusks fell off sharply soon after, not due as much to Wurm's revelations, but to a glut of narwhal tusks on the market.

The unicorn lives on in literary works such as Shakespeare's *The Tempest*, "Now I will believe that there are unicorns"; in Lewis Carroll's *Alice in Wonderland*, "Well, now that we have seen each other" said the Unicorn to Alice, "if you'll believe in me, I'll believe in you"; and in Tennessee Williams's *The Glass Menagerie*, when Jim asks, "What kind of thing is this one supposed to be?" and Laura answers, "Haven't you noticed the single horn on its forehead?" **STATUS:** The people of the Far North hunt the Narwhal for its meat, skin, and tusk. Natural predators include Greenland sharks, orcas, and polar bears. CITES Appendix II.

Narwhals and murres at the ice edge, Baffin Is

FEATHERS ARE THE DISTINGUISHING FEATURE OF BIRDS. Birds are also characterized by having a bony beak with no teeth, forelimbs modified into wings, a skeleton with hollow bones, and a four-chambered heart. They are warm-blooded (*ectothermic*) and have a high metabolic rate. They lay eggs (*oviparous*). Birds walk, hop, and run on two legs, and almost all species can fly.

Only a few bird species winter in the Arctic. These include gyrfalcons, ravens, snowy owls, rock and willow ptarmigans, redpolls, and a few gull and alcid species. These species have a number of physiological and behavioral adaptations for coping with the extreme winter climate.

Snowy owls, gyrfalcons, and ptarmigans are feathered right down to their legs and feet. Ptarmigans have learned to make snow burrows, where they can ride out the weather and hide from predators. Redpolls also shelter under the snow, often living in lemming runways, where they can find seeds to eat. Ravens scavenge food around human habitation and feed on carrion and the fresh kills of polar bears and other large predators. Marine birds such as ivory gulls, dovekies, thick-billed murres, and black guillemots move to polynyas and other open areas in the sea ice, where food is readily available throughout the winter.

The rest of the arctic bird species are migrants. Each spring, millions of birds come to the tundra, taiga, and bird cliffs where they fledge a new generation before heading south again in fall. The movements of the migratory species are of great import to the people of the Far North who have specific words to mark the birds' comings and goings. For example, in northern Alaska, April is known as *kilgich tatkiat* (hawks coming) and *tingmirat tatkiat* (geese coming), and the month of September is called *tingivik* (time when birds fly away).

Arctic migrants are adapted to the short period of time they have to establish territories, lay their eggs, and raise their brood. Adults typically arrive at their nesting grounds before all the snow has melted. Most have anticipated the lack of food available in early spring by fattening up at staging points on their northward migration. A migrant's timely arrival on the breeding grounds ensures that its chicks will be born at the peak abundance of food and its young will be strong enough for the southward migration.

The migration of birds has been a point of study since the time of the ancient Greek philosophers Aristotle and Herodotus. Yet even today the secrets of migration and birds' amazing navigational skills aren't fully understood.

Migrating birds can cover thousands of miles in their annual travels, often traveling the same course decade after decade with little deviation. It appears evident that their migration patterns are controlled at least partially by genetic makeup. This explains why first-year birds are able to make their initial migration on their own, find their winter home without ever having seen it before, and return the following spring to the same place where they were born.

Clearly, many birds have innate navigational tools they use to orient themselves on migration. These tools are thought to incorporate responses to geographic landmarks such as seacoasts, rivers, and mountains, and to prevailing winds, barometric pressure, the earth's magnetic field, the position of the sun, and, in the case of nocturnal migrants, the patterns of stars.

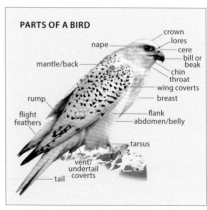

PARTS OF A BIRD

crown
lores
nape
cere
bill or beak
mantle/back
chin
throat
wing coverts
rump
breast
flight feathers
flank
abdomen/belly
tarsus
vent/ undertail coverts
tail

The Inuktitut word for "bird" is *tingmiaq*; the same word means "airplane."

Anseriformes: Waterfowl

The order Anseriformes comprises about 150 living species of birds, all of which are web-footed and highly adapted for an aquatic lifestyle.

FAMILY ANATIDAE
GEESE, SWANS, AND DUCKS

Anatidae is a large family of birds, with 14 species of geese, 4 species of swans, and 31 species of ducks occurring in the Arctic alone. These mid-sized to large birds are distinguished by long necks, narrow pointed wings, short legs, feet with webbing between the 3 front toes, and feathers that shed water easily due to oils stored in the preen glands. Geese, swans, and ducks occupy aquatic habitats such as lakes, ponds, streams, rivers, marshes, bays, estuaries, and seacoasts. They feed on a variety of foods, including plant matter, insects, aquatic invertebrates, mollusks, crustaceans, and fish.

SUBFAMILY ANSERINAE
GEESE

Geese are relatively large birds that are colored in browns, grays, blacks, and whites. They are mostly terrestrial in their feeding habits and have strong bills adapted for grazing on grasses and other plant matter.

Most geese breed first at 2–3 years of age and typically form lifelong, monogamous pair bonds, separating only on the death of a mate. However, about 6 percent of the breeding population will "divorce," this usually following several seasons of unsuccessful nesting. Most geese return to the area of their birth to mate and nest. The male (the *gander*) stands guard while the female (the *goose*) constructs the nest, piling up a mound of twigs, bark, and grasses, and lining the nest with soft feathers. The female alone incubates the clutch of 5–6 off-white, buff, or pale olive eggs for 28–30 days. Chicks are down covered at birth and can feed and swim a few hours after they hatch.

Both sexes remain with the brood until the young (the *goslings*) fledge at about 2 months of age. The maturing period of the young overlaps with the adult's 6-week molting period (*molting* is the term given to the period of flightlessness when the adults shed their outer wing feathers

and regrow new ones). During this time, adults and young gather on ponds or lakes, which provide a safe resting place and security from predators. Once the chicks can fly, the family migrates as a group and often remains together until the following spring. A flock of geese flying in a V formation is called a *wedge* or *skein*. A flock of geese on the ground is called a *gaggle*.

GENUS *ANSER*: This genus contains the gray geese, which all have grayish brown plumage, with a white undertail and white rump. The legs and bill are pink or orange.

Greylag Goose

Anser anser
ALSO: Graugans, Oie cendrée, Grågås, Серый гусь. CN refers to plumage color and habit of being one of the last species to migrate, "lagging" behind other geese. SN means "goose goose." Ancestor of the domesticated goose. Austrian ethologist Konrad Lorenz (1903–1989) used the Greylag in his study into the behavioral phenomenon of imprinting.
RANGE: Nests (Apr–Jun) in Iceland and across Eurasia, around reed beds, floodplains, marshes, estuaries, and lakes. Icelandic breeders winter in Scotland and Ireland; Eurasian birds winter south to nw Africa and s Asia. Birds escaped from captivity have established feral populations in N Amer.
ID: L 28–32 in (70–81 cm). Grayish brown overall. Rump and back feathers edged pale gray. White line along upper flanks. Undertail coverts white. Black splotches on belly. Dull pink bill and legs.
VOICE: Loud cackling or *honk*.
HABITS: Forages in waterside meadows and dry fields. Grazes on grass; occasionally feeds in the water on aquatic vegetation. Down-lined nest made of plant material is built on dry reeds or floating mats of sticks and aquatic plants.

Greater White-fronted Goose

Lesser White-fronted Goose

Greylag Goose

Pink-footed Goose

Bean-Goose

Greater White-fronted Goose
Anser albifrons
N Siberia, n N Amer, Greenland
L 26–28 in (65–70 cm)

Lesser White-fronted Goose
Anser erythropus
N Eurasia
L 20.5–23 in (52–60 cm)

Greylag Goose
Anser anser
Iceland, Eurasia
L 28–32 in (70–81 cm)

Greater White-fronted Goose

Greylag Goose

Pink-footed Goose
Anser brachyrhynchus
Greenland, Iceland, Svalbard
L 24–30 in (61–75 cm)

Pink-footed Goose

Bean-Goose

Tundra Bean-Goose
Anser serrirostris
Tundra of n Siberia
L 25.5–32 in (65–81 cm)

Taiga Bean-Goose
Anser fabalis
Taiga of n Eurasia
L 25.5–35 in (65–90 cm)

Taiga Bean-Goose

Anser fabalis

ALSO: Saatgans, Oie des moissons, Ánsar campestre, Sædgås, Гуменник. SN means "bean goose," referring to the species' habit of grazing in bean-field stubble.

RANGE: Nests (May–Jun) from Norway and Ural Mtns east to Lake Baikal, Russia, around forest bogs, marshes, and ponds. Winters in farmlands and river valleys in w Europe, Iran, China, Japan; uncommon winter migrant to the UK.

ID: L 25.5–35 in (65–90 cm). Grayish brown. Rump and vent white. Tail gray with a white tip. Wing coverts dark brown, edged with white. Bill black at base and tip, with a yellow orange band across the middle. Orange legs and feet. Longer-necked and longer-billed than *Anser serrirostris*. VOICE: A groaning *ung-ank*.

HABITS: Feeds on green plant matter, berries, and grain crops. Nests in the open or in bushes.

Tundra Bean-Goose

Anser serrirostris

ALSO: Östliche Saatgans, Oie de la toundra, Tundrasædgås, Восточный тундровый гусь. SN means "saw-billed goose."

RANGE: Nests (May–Jun) on the tundra of n Siberia. Winters in river valleys and around lakes in w Europe, China, and Japan. Uncommon migrant to the UK.

ID: L 25.5–32 in (65–81 cm). Dark gray, with contrasting pale breast. Pale-edged, dark brown tertials. Rump and vent white. Tail gray with a white tip. Bill black at base and tip, with a yellow orange band across the middle. Orange legs and feet. Smaller and shorter-necked than *A. fabalis*, with a shorter, deeper-based bill.

HABITS: Like those of *Anser fabalis*.

Pink-footed Goose

Anser brachyrhynchus

ALSO: Kurzschnabelgans, Oie à bec court, Kortnebbgås, Короткоклювый гуменник. SN means "short-billed goose."

RANGE: Nests (May–Jun) in Greenland, Iceland, and Svalbard on islets in tundra lakes and ponds, on cliffs and rock pinnacles near glaciers, on snow-free hummocks, and around bogs, streams, swamps, and wet meadows. Winters on mudflats and estuaries near fields with bean stubble and root crops. Greenland and Iceland breeders winter in the UK. Svalbard breeders winter mainly in Holland and w Denmark. Vagrant to Morocco, Canary Is, and ne N Amer.

ID: L 24–30 in (61–75 cm). Grayish brown overall. Head and neck dark brown. Upperwing coverts pale slate gray; primaries blackish. Rump and vent white; tail gray with a broad white tip. Pink legs and feet. Small, stubby bill is pink in the middle, with a black base and tip. VOICE: High-pitched, honking *ung-ung* or *wink-wink*.

HABITS: Feeds on aquatic and terrestrial plants, including oilseed rape, sugar beet, winter cereal crops, and grass. Breeds in close proximity to other geese. Nest is a low pile of plant material. Same nest sites are often used year after year.

Greater White-fronted Goose

Anser albifrons

ALSO: Speckled Brant, Specklebelly, Bar Belle, Laughing Goose, Gray Wavey, Bläßgans, Oie rieuse, Tundragås, Белолобый гусь. SN means "white-fronted goose."

RANGE: Nests (May–Jun) in n Siberia, n N Amer, and Greenland around lakes, ponds, and wet meadows on the tundra and in forest-tundra. Winters on farmlands, flooded fields, and freshwater marshes south to Mexico, Mediterranean, and s Asia. The w Greenland subspecies, *A. a. flavirostris*, flies 1900 mi (3000 km) over the Greenland ice cap and N Atlantic to winter in Ireland and w Scotland.

ID: L 26–28 in (65–70 cm). AD: Brownish gray, with black patches on belly. White vent. Dark tail, with a white terminal band. Bright white forehead and lores; white bill does not extend to crown as in *A. erythropus*. Bill pink. Legs orange. JUV: Bill is gray, streaked with purple. Lacks spots on belly. VOICE: High-pitched barking or yelping *kah-lah-aleuk* or *klew-yo-yo*.

HABITS: Feeds on grass, sedges, aquatic plants,

berries, seeds, grains; also takes some insects, insect larvae, and mollusks. Flies low in small flocks. Nest is a low mound of vegetation lined with dark feathers and built in tall grass or on hummocks near water.

STATUS: Declining numbers are attributed to intense hunting, flooded nesting sites, and disturbance from low-flying aircraft during molt.

Lesser White-fronted Goose

Anser erythropus
ALSO: Zwerggans, Oie naine, Fjällgås, Пискулька. SN means "red-footed goose."
RANGE: Nests (May) in

disjunct locations across n Eurasia on tundra, forest lakes and ponds, and forested alpine slopes to 2300 ft (700 m). Winters on open grasslands, coastal meadows, and around large lakes, rivers, and reed beds south to the Black and Caspian seas, Persian Gulf, e Asia, and (rarely) se Europe.
ID: L 20.5–23 in (52–60 cm). Grayish brown, with conspicuous black patches on belly. Broad bright white band extends from lores to forecrown. Pink bill. Yellow eyering. Orange legs and feet.
VOICE: High-pitched, yelping *dyee-yik*.
HABITS: Forages along lakeshores, rivers, and marshes, grazing on grasses and aquatic plants, and grain crops in winter. Often seen near the front of feeding flocks of other geese, especially *Anser albifrons*. Builds its nest on the ground in tall grass, low bushes, amid rocks, or in boggy hollows. Clutch is 4–7 white to ochre eggs.
STATUS: Intensely hunted on staging and wintering grounds. World population is 28,000–33,000 individuals. Vulnerable (IUCN).

GENUS *CHEN*: This genus contains the white geese, which have all-white or largely white plumage. The bill, legs, and feet are bright pink or red.

Snow Goose

Chen caerulescens
ALSO: Blue Goose, Wavy, Kanyuq, Kararjuk, Qaviq, Schneegans, Oie des neiges,

Snøgås, Белый гусь. SN means "bluish goose," referring to the blue morph.

RANGE: Nests (Apr–May) in scattered colonies on open tundra near ponds and streams from Wrangel Is, Russia, to n Alaska, Canada, and nw Greenland. Winters in marshes, wet grasslands, and flooded fields, south to California and Gulf and mid-Atlantic coasts. Vagrant to Europe, Japan, e China. Birds escaped from captivity have established feral populations in the UK.
ID: L 28–31 in (70–79 cm). Pink bill with a dark "grin" patch along side of bill. Pink legs and feet.
AD WHITE MORPH: White, with black primaries. Head is sometimes stained with rust from iron oxide in feeding ponds. JUV WHITE MORPH: Dirty white. Gray nape, back, and wing coverts; dark primaries. Dark gray legs, feet, and bill.
AD BLUE MORPH (BLUE GOOSE): Dark grayish brown body and lower neck; variable amount of white on head, neck, belly, vent. Upperwing coverts pale gray; scapulars dark-centered with white edges; primaries and secondaries dark gray; underwing coverts white. Tail gray, with white tip. JUV BLUE: Dark grayish brown overall. White and blue morphs interbreed. Color of offspring is controlled by a single gene; the dark gene is partially dominant over white. Offspring of a blue morph × white morph mating will be dark. A blue × blue mating produces dark offspring, with a few white young possible. VOICE: A barking *honk* or loud nasal *bow-whouk*. Foraging flocks make low grunting sounds.
HABITS: Migrates in large, noisy, high-flying flocks. Forages in shallow water and wet soil, feeding on plant matter and some aquatic invertebrates. Nest is a ground scrape lined with vegetation and down.

Ross's Goose

Chen rossii
ALSO: Zwergschneegans, Oie de Ross, Eskimogås, Гусь Росса. Samuel Hearne,

who discovered this bird in n Canada in 1770, named it the "Horned Wavy." Angus Gavin was first to find the species' nesting grounds near the Perry Rvr in c Canada in 1940. SN means "Ross's Goose," after Bernard Ross (1827–1874), a Hudson's Bay Company factor, who donated specimens of the species to the Smithsonian.

RANGE: Nests (May–Jun) on tundra and islands in shallow lakes in n Canada and Alaska; main population is in the Queen Maud Gulf Migratory Bird Sanctuary, n Canada. Winters in salt- and freshwater marshes, wetlands, and farm fields in c California, with fewer numbers in the sc US and n Mexico. Vagrant to w Europe and Hawaii.
ID: L 21–26 in (53–66 cm). AD WHITE MORPH: White, with black primaries and pink legs and feet. Small, triangular pink bill with a greenish gray base, often covered with warty growths; border at bill base is straight. JUV WHITE MORPH: Pale gray above, with a dusky cap. White below. Gray to dull pink legs, feet, and bill. AD DARK MORPH: Rare and considered to be a Ross's × Snow Goose hybrid by some. Dark body, with a whitish face and belly. Occasionally shows a small grin patch on bill edge. VOICE: High-pitched keek keek; also soft cackling and grunting notes.
HABITS: Feeds on grasses, sedges, legumes, grains, and some insects. Often forages with snow geese. Nest is a ground scrape lined with soft grasses, moss, and twigs. Female incubates the clutch of 2–6 white or rust-spotted eggs for 21–24 days, and covers the eggs with down when leaving the nest. Goslings escape from predators by running and crouching flat on ground or by diving underwater.
STATUS: Protected species; Ross's geese numbers have increased from a low of 2000 individuals in the early 1950s to an estimated world population of more than 1 million birds today.

Emperor Goose
Chen canagica
ALSO: Beach Goose, Kaisergans, Oie empereur, Keisergås, Белошей. SN

means "goose of Kanaga Is [w Aleutians]."
RANGE: Nests (May–Jun) in Chukotka and w Alaska, including St Lawrence Is and Nunivak Is, on riverbanks, elevated shorelines, marsh hummocks, grasslands, and islands on coastal tundra. Winters on beaches and rocky coasts in the Aleutians, with lesser numbers along the Alaska Penin coast and on Kodiak Is and Afognak Is; some stray down the Pacific coast to California.

ID: L 26–30 in (66–76 cm). AD: Dark silvery gray, with a white head and hindneck, often stained orange red from iron oxide found in feeding ponds. Tail white. Yellow-orange legs and feet. Small pink bill. JUV: Dark gray overall, with a white ring around the eye. VOICE: Loud, somewhat melodic kla-ga kla-ga.
HABITS: Feeds on seaweed, eelgrass, sea lettuce, beach rye, beach pea, sea-purslane, grasses, sedges, crowberries, clams, mussels, and crustaceans found in intertidal areas, salt marshes, and tundra meadows. A clutch of 3–8 cream colored eggs is laid in a ground nest lined with dead vegetation and down. Incubation is about 25 days. Young are led from the nest as soon as their gray down is dry. Alaskan breeding adults molt near nesting colonies; non-breeders move to St Lawrence Is to molt before migrating to wintering grounds.

GENUS BRANTA: This genus contains the black geese, which have prominent patches of dark plumage, black bills, and dark gray legs and feet. *Branta* means "burnt," referring to the large areas of dark feathering, which give the plumage a charred look.

Brant
Branta bernicla
ALSO: Brent Goose, Ringelgans, Bernache cravant,

Ringgås, Чёрная казарка, Niglignak, Nirlirmaarjuk. SN means "barnacle goose," referring to the Barnacle Goose, *B. leucopsis*, which was once considered conspecific.
RANGE: Circumpolar. Nests (May–Jun) on arctic coastal tundra. Winters on marshes, estuaries, and seacoasts of s Eurasia and N Amer.
SUBSPECIES: DARK-BELLIED BRANT (D), *B. b. bernicla*, breeds nc Siberia; winters in w Europe. LIGHT-BELLIED BRANT (L), *B. b. hrota*, breeds ne N Amer, Greenland, Svalbard, Franz Josef Land; winters N Atlantic coasts. BLACK BRANT (B), *B. b. nigricans*, breeds ne Siberia–w N Amer; Alaska birds migrate to Baja California, flying over 3000 mi (4800 km) nonstop in 60 hours.
ID: L 22–26 in (55–66 cm). Black head, neck, and upper breast, with a small white patch on

Rare dark morph
Ross's Goose

Ross's Goose

juv.

ad.

Ross's Goose
Chen rossii
N Amer
L 21–26 in (53–66 cm)

Snow Goose

Snow Goose
Blue morph

Emperor Goose

juv.

ad. Blue morph
(Blue Goose)

Ross's Goose

Snow Goose
White morph

ad.

Snow Goose
Chen caerulescens
N Amer
L 28–31 in (70–79 cm)

Snow Goose
Blue morph

Emperor Goose

juv.

ad.

Emperor Goose
Chen canagica
Bering Sea region
L 26–30 in (66–76 cm)

the sides of the neck. Pale gray to black belly.
VOICE: Low, hoarse *crr-ronk.*
HABITS: Feeds on Marine Eelgrass (*Zostera marina*); also grazes on terrestrial vegetation. Nest is a ground scrape lined with grass and down.

Red-breasted Goose

Branta ruficollis
ALSO: Bernache à cou roux, Rothalsgans, Raudhalsgås, Краснозобая казарка. SN means "red-necked goose."
RANGE: Nests (Jun) in Siberia, from the Yamal Penin east to the Taimyr Penin, on tundra and grassy banks of arctic rivers. Frequents marshes and flooded fields in migration. Winters in fields around the Black, Caspian, and Aral seas, UK (rarely), Finland, and w Europe. Widely kept in collections; vagrant birds are probably escapees.
ID: L 22–24 in (55–61 cm). Breast, throat, and cheeks deep reddish brown, edged with white. Nape and head black, with a white spot between the eyes and stubby, black beak. Back and belly black. Wings have 2 white stripes. Flanks and rear underparts white. Legs black. Iris reddish brown. VOICE: High-pitched *honk.*
HABITS: Grazes on grass, sedges, cottongrass shoots, grains, and seeds. Flies in dense flocks rather than in V formation like other geese. Breeds in loose colonies of 5–15 pairs. Often nests near aeries of birds of prey, which provide some protection from predators. Nest is a shallow ground scrape lined with grass, moss, and down.
STATUS: For unknown reasons, numbers have declined from about 50,000 individuals in the 1950s to 38,500 in 2005. Endangered (IUCN).

Barnacle Goose

Branta leucopsis
ALSO: Weißwangengans, Bernache nonnette, Barnacla carinegra, Kvitkinngås, Белощёкая казарка. SN means "white faced goose." CN derives from the medieval myth that these geese developed from goose barnacles (filter-feeding crustaceans that grow on floating driftwood). Clerics therefore put barnacle geese in the same category as fish, meaning that they could be eaten on Fridays and holy days when meat was strictly prohibited.
RANGE: Nests (May–Jun) in Greenland, Svalbard, Novaya Zemlya, and Baltic Sea area. Frequents brackish coastal waters in migration. Winters mainly around North Sea coasts. Vagrant to the Atlantic coast of N Amer.
ID: L 25.5–27 in (65–69 cm). AD: Black chest, neck and crown, with an ivory white face. Upper back black, fading to silvery gray toward the rump. Belly, undertail coverts and rump are white, contrasting with the black tail. Bill, legs and feet are black. Iris brown. JUV: Black plumage streaked with gray; brown marks on the back and wing tips. VOICE: Sounds like a barking dog.
HABITS: Forages for grasses and other plants in estuaries or tidal mudflats. Nests high on alpine cliffs. Parents brood the goslings for about 3 days, then fly to the cliff base. Their noisy calls encourage the goslings to jump down to the ground, which is often several hundred feet below them. Their small size, feathery down, and light weight helps to protect the goslings from serious injury when they hit the ground, but some die from the impact or are taken by arctic foxes attracted by the parents' strident calls. Foxes also stalk the goslings as the parents lead them to feeding areas in nearby wetlands.

Canada Goose

Branta canadensis
ALSO: Honker, Kanadagans, Bernache du Canada, Kanadagås, Канадская казарка, Nirliq, Ulluagullik. SN means "goose of Canada."
RANGE: Nests (Apr–Jun) on the N Amer tundra and also around marshes, meadows, lakes, and rivers southward in range. Frequents brackish coastal estuaries and bays in winter. Most wild populations are migratory. Introduced flocks are largely resident on golf courses and urban parks. Introduced to King James II's waterfowl collection in St James's Park, England, in the late 17th century. They have also reached Europe naturally and established feral populations.
SUBSPECIES–ARCTIC: ATLANTIC CANADA GOOSE (AT), *B. c. canadensis,* breeds in e Labrador,

Red-breasted Goose
Branta ruficollis
NW Russia
L 22–24 in (55–61 cm)

Dark-bellied Brant
B. b. bernicla

Black Brant
B. b. nigricans

Light-bellied Brant
B. b. hrota

Brant
Branta bernicla
Circumpolar
L 22–26 in (55–66 cm)

Marine Eelgrass
Zostera marina

Barnacle Goose
Branta leucopsis
Greenland, Svalbard, Russia
L 25.5–27 in (65–69 cm)

Canada Goose

Cackling Goose

Cackling Goose
Branta hutchinsii
N Amer, NE Asia
L 22–30 in (55–76 cm)

Canada Goose
Branta canadensis
N Amer
Introduced to Europe
L 36–45 in (90–114 cm)

Newfoundland, and Anticosti and Magdalen Is; winters on N Atlantic seaboard. HUDSON BAY CANADA GOOSE (H), *B. c. interior*, breeds at Hudson Bay and Quebec; winters on the Atlantic seaboard south to Texas. Resident in e US. DUSKY CANADA GOOSE (D), *B. c. occidentalis*, breeds from Glacier Bay and Copper Rvr delta, south to Vancouver Is; winters south to Oregon. VANCOUVER CANADA GOOSE (V), *B. c. fulva*, breeds in Copper Rvr delta and Prince William Sound, in old-growth spruce and hemlock forests. Winters on Oregon coast, where it feeds on marine algae, mollusks, fish eggs, and dead fish. LESSER CANADA GOOSE (L), *B. c. parvipes*, breeds in forest clearings from c Alaska to Hudson Bay; winters in Pacific NW. Smallest subspecies. **ID:** L 36–45 in (90–114 cm). Neck and head black, with white cheeks and chin. Back brown to grayish brown. Breast pale gray to brown. Undertail coverts white. Bill, legs, and feet black. VOICE: Loud honking; also cackles and barks. **HABITS:** Feeds on grasses, aquatic plants, and grains. Grabs grass blades with the bill and pulls them out with a head jerk. Also forages by upending in shallow water. Stretches out its neck and slides its bill across the bottom silt to take aquatic plants.

Forms lifelong pair bonds at 2 years of age. Nests on mounds of dry vegetation, often on islets or places surrounded by water. Clutch of 4–8 eggs is incubated for about 28 days. Adults lose their flight feathers at this time and cannot fly for several weeks. They defend the eggs and young by hissing and chasing after predators. Newborn goslings are led to water, with one parent at the front, the other at the back. Goslings fledge at 6–9 weeks of age and migrate with their parents, remaining with them until the next nesting season.

Cackling Goose

Branta hutchinsii
ALSO: Zwergkanadagans, Bernache de Hutchins. Polargås, Малая канадская

казарка. Formerly considered a *B. canadensis* subspecies. SN means "Hutchins's Goose," after British naturalist Thomas Hutchins (1730–1790),

who was employed as a surgeon by the Hudson's Bay Company in Canada.
RANGE: Nests (May–Jul) on the tundra in Kamchatka, Aleutians, n N Amer, and w Greenland. Winters in a variety of habitats, often with Canada Geese. Regular visitor to w Europe; usually seen with Barnacle Geese.
SUBSPECIES: TUNDRA CACKLING GOOSE (H), *B. h. hutchinsii*, breeds on Canadian arctic coast from Victoria Is to Baffin Is and w Greenland; winters from the Texas coast and panhandle to n Mexico. TAVERNER CACKLING GOOSE (T), *B. h. tavernari*, breeds on tundra from the Alaska Penin east to the Mackenzie Rvr and north to the Arctic Slope. Migrants stage at Izembek Lagoon near Cold Bay, Alaska, before flying along the Gulf of Alaska coast to winter in Washington, Oregon, and Texas panhandle. LESSER CACKLING GOOSE (C), *B. h. minima*, breeds on w Alaska coast. Migrates along the Pacific coast, wintering in Oregon and mainly in California's Central Valley. Smallest subspecies, weighing 3–5 lb (1.5–2.3 kg). ALEUTIAN CACKLING GOOSE (A), *B. h. leucopareia*, breeds in Aleutians, mainly at Buldir Is; winters south to California.
ID: L 22–30 in (55–76 cm). Black neck, with white chinstrap. Breast, abdomen, and flanks range from pale gray to dark chocolate brown, depending on subspecies. Back and scapulars are dark brown. Tail is blackish brown with U-shaped white band on blackish rump. Bill, legs, and feet are black. VOICE: Distinctive squeaky cackle; also loud honking and high-pitched yelp.
HABITS: Similar to *Branta canadensis*.
STATUS: Hunting and nest predation by foxes introduced by early fur traders nearly extirpated this species in the Bering Sea area. Cacklers have been restocked on fox-free islands in the Aleutians, boosting populations from 800 birds in 1967 to over 7000 in 1991.

In the 1980s Russian scientist Nikolai Nikolaevich Gerasimov, in association with the US Fish and Wildlife Service and Japanese Wild Bird Society, established a breeding facility for Aleutian cacklers in Kamchatka. The project has introduced more than 500 goslings into ne Asia, and sizable flocks now migrate between s Kamchatka and Japan.

SUBFAMILY CYGNINAE

SWANS

The name *swan* derives from the Indo-European root *swen*, meaning "sound" or "sing." A flock of swans is called a *ballet, bevy, drift, regatta,* or *school*. An adult male is a *cob* and an adult female is a *pen*. Young swans are called *cygnets*.

Swans are among the largest flying birds. The largest species can attain a length of more than 60 in (1.5 m), a weight of more than 33 lb (15 kg), and a wingspan of up to 10 ft (3 m). Like geese, they fly with their long neck outstretched and migrate in V formation. They land on the water with a slide, with feet held forward, and take off with running steps. Sexes are alike in plumage. Adults of the arctic species have all-white plumage, and juveniles are pale gray. Each species has a distinctively colored bill.

Cygnets dabble on aquatic vegetation stirred up by their parents and also eat aquatic insects and crustaceans. Adults feed on aquatic plants, supplemented by grasses, grain, and crop foods in winter. They use their strong webbed feet to expose roots, shoots, and tubers of aquatic plants, then upend to reach the food on the pond bottom. Their long necks allow them to reach submerged plants and snap off leaves and stems in waters that are up to 4 ft (1.2 m) deep.

Swans form lifelong pair bonds and breed at 4–5 years old. The typical clutch is 3–8 off-white eggs, which are incubated for 30–40 days. Cygnets can swim and feed within 48 hours of hatching. Nonetheless, the parents often carry their young on their backs when in the water. They aggressively defend their young. When the male drives off an intruder, the pair performs a "triumph ceremony," with mutual head waving and calling. Adults molt after breeding and are flightless for a time. Lifespan is 10–30 years.

GENUS *CYGNUS*

Whooper Swan

Cygnus cygnus

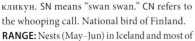

ALSO: Singschwan, Cygne chanteur, Sångsvan, Лебедь-кликун. SN means "swan swan." CN refers to the whooping call. National bird of Finland.

RANGE: Nests (May–Jun) in Iceland and most of Eurasia, around lakes, ponds, marshes, streams, and reed beds. Eurasian breeders winter south to the Black, Caspian, and North seas, N Africa, e Mediterranean, and se Asia. Iceland breeders winter along North Sea coasts.

ID: L 55–63 in (140–160 cm). AD: White overall. Bill black, with a large, wedge-shaped yellow patch at the base. Black legs. JUV: Brownish gray. Legs dull black. Bill dark gray, with a pinkish patch at the base. VOICE: A series of loud *whoops;* also a sharp, repetitive *heh-heh-whoo-oo.*

HABITS: Pairs are solitary nesters and drive other swans and waterfowl away from their territories. Nest is a large pile of reeds, aquatic plants, and moss built on the shore or in shallow water. The female incubates the clutch of 4–6 eggs for 35–40 days, while the male stands guard nearby.

Trumpeter Swan

Cygnus buccinator

ALSO: Trompeterschwan, Cygne trompette, Cisne trompetero, Лебедь-трубач.

CN *trumpeter* and SN *buccinator* refer to the trumpeting call; a buccinator was a member of the ancient Roman army who sounded a brass horn or *buccina* to announce the night watch.

RANGE: Nests (Apr–Jun) in w N Amer around marshes, ponds, lakes, and occasionally rivers, in boreal forests. Winters around springs, streams, rivers, ponds, lakes, reservoirs, and ice-free estuaries as far south as coastal California.

ID: L 60–72 in (150–180 cm). WS 72–96 in (180–240 cm). WT 20–24 lb (9–11 kg). Largest native N Amer waterfowl. AD: White overall; head and neck sometimes stained by rust from feeding ponds. Legs and feet black. Bill black, with a salmon red streak along the basal edge of the lower mandible and rarely with a small yellowish spot at base of upper mandible. JUV: Pale gray, with black bill and legs. VOICE: Deep resonant trumpeting and a tinhorn-like *toot-too-toot-too-oo.*

HABITS: Both sexes gather and deliver plant matter to the nesting site. The female arranges it into a mound and forms a nest bowl using her bill and body. Clutch is 6–10 creamy white eggs, which both sexes incubate. Hatchlings are brooded for up to 48 hours before the parents lead them to water.

STATUS: This species was exploited for its feathers during early European settlement. Only 69 individuals existed in 1935. Once protected, its population grew to 16,000 in 1990 and its numbers continue to increase.

RELATED SPECIES: MUTE SWAN, *Cygnus olor.* L 55–63 in (140–160 cm). Breeds in temperate zones of Eurasia. Often encountered in wildfowl collections or as an escapee. Adults can be immediately recognized by the knobbed, bright reddish orange and black bill.

Tundra (Whistling) Swan

Cygnus columbianus columbianus
ALSO: Qugjuk, Pfeifschwan, Cygne siffleur, Cisne de la tundra, Mindre sångsvan, Американский лебедь. CN: Whistling Swan, refers to the sound made by the beating of the wings in flight. SN means "swan of the Columbia," a river in the Pacific NW where this subspecies winters.
RANGE: Nests (Apr–Jun) around tundra ponds, lakes, streams, and bogs on St Lawrence Is and from Alaska east along the Canadian arctic coast to Hudson Bay and Baffin Is. Winters along the Pacific and Atlantic coasts on estuaries, lakes, rivers, and cultivated fields.
ID: L 47–58 in (120–147 cm). AD: Entirely white. Legs black. Holds its long neck straight up. Bill black, with a small patch of yellow near the lores. JUV: White mixed with dull gray feathering on the head and upper neck; attains adult plumage in second winter. Legs grayish pink. Bill black, with pinkish gray at the lores and along the ridge of the upper mandible. VOICE: High-pitched bark, *wow-wow-wow.* In flight, the leader swan gives a high-pitched, quavering call, *who-who who,* which is repeated by the following flock. This same call, reiterated by hundreds of swans, can also be heard just before dusk when migratory flocks begin to settle in for the night.
HABITS: Breeds in loose colonies. Nest is a large, open bowl of grasses, sedges, lichens, and moss, lined with down, and placed on a hummock or ridge on the tundra.

Tundra (Bewick's) Swan

Cygnus columbianus bewickii
ALSO: Zwergschwan, Cygne de Bewick, Dvergsvane, Тундровый лебедь. SN means "Bewick's swan," referring to English engraver Thomas Bewick (1753–1828), who specialized in illustrating birds and mammals.
RANGE: Northernmost breeding swan. Nests (May–Jun) on marshy tundra from Finland east to n Siberia and Chukotka, and north to Novaya Zemlya. Winters along seacoasts and large inland lakes in e Asia, Caspian Sea region, and nw Europe.
ID: L 45–50 in (115–127 cm). WT 11–14 lb (5–6.5 kg). AD: Entirely white. Legs black or (rarely) dark yellow. Bill black, with a yellow patch that is larger than that of *C. c. columbianus*, but smaller than that of *C. cygnus*. Bill pattern is unique to every individual Bewick's Swan. JUV: Pale grayish brown. Bill black, with pinkish gray to pale yellow at the base of the upper mandible. VOICE: Soft ringing bark, *bow-wow.* Very vocal during takeoff and landing. Excited, loud, high-pitched gobbling diminishes to collective murmuring as flocks settle in.

SUBFAMILY ANATINAE
DABBLING DUCKS

These gregarious birds, also known as "puddle ducks," live around freshwater lakes and ponds, and brackish estuaries. They feed mainly by *dabbling*—using the bill to skim plant matter from the water surface. A comb-like structure called a *pecten* on the side of the bill strains the water running out of the bill and traps food particles inside the mouth. These ducks also upend to reach aquatic vegetation on pond bottoms, and graze on grasses and grains in wetland fields.

As in other types of ducks, the male dabbling duck is called a *drake* and the female is called a *hen.* Drakes have bright nuptial plumage, which dulls in the post-breeding *eclipse plumage.* Females are typically a plain mottled brown year round. Both sexes show a band of color—a *speculum*—on the trailing edge of the wing.

Tundra (Bewick's) Swan
in flight

juv.

Tundra (Whistling) Swan
Cygnus columbianus columbianus
N Amer
L 47–58 in (120–147 cm)

ad.

Tundra (Whistling) Swan

Tundra (Bewick's) Swan

juv.

ad.

Whooper Swan

Tundra (Bewick's) Swan
Cygnus columbianus bewickii
Eurasia
L 45–50 in (115–127 cm)

Trumpeter Swan

juv.

juv.

ad.

ad.

Trumpeter Swan
Cygnus buccinator
N Amer
L 60–72 in (150–180 cm)

Whooper Swan
Cygnus cygnus
Iceland, Eurasia
L 55–63 in (140–160 cm)

Mute Swan

Tundra (Bewick's)
Swan

Trumpeter Swan

Whooper Swan

Tundra (Whistling) Swan

Dabbling ducks begin to breed at 1–2 years of age. Pairs form bonds that last for a single mating season. The female builds the nest, which is most often a ground scrape lined with soft plant matter and down. The female alone incubates the clutch of 3–14 off-white, buff, or pale olive eggs for 23–25 days. Males desert the nest before the eggs hatch and fly off to join other males on large lakes where they molt into eclipse plumage and undergo a period of flightlessness. The female leads the precocial chicks to water soon after hatching. She rears the chicks, then abandons them after about 6 weeks when she begins her post-breeding molt.

GENUS ANAS
American Wigeon

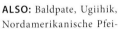

Anas americana
ALSO: Baldpate, Ugiihik, Nordamerikanische Pfeifente, Fuligule à tête rouge, Amerikablesand, Американская свиязь, *Mareca americana*. SN means "American duck."
RANGE: Nests (May–Jun) around tundra and forest marshes and lakes from c Alaska and nc Canada south to the contiguous US. Frequents streams, farmlands, and brackish marshes in migration. Winters from s Alaska and s Canada south along the Pacific and Atlantic coasts to C Amer, Bermuda, W Indies, Hawaii. Casual in Greenland, Iceland, UK, Azores, Japan, Commander Is, Caroline and Marshall islands, Venezuela, and Colombia.
ID: L 19–22 in (48–55 cm). AD ♂: Face speckled gray; creamy white crown; broad, dark greenish black stripe from the eye to the nape. Bill bluish gray, with a black tip. Breast and flanks warm brown. Large white patch on upper wing; speculum green. Tail black. In eclipse plumage, head is speckled gray. AD ♀: Head flecked gray, with a dark eye patch. Back mottled brown. Breast and flanks rufous brown. Speculum dark green bordered by white at front. VOICE: Male gives a clear whistling *whoee-whoe-whoe*. Female gives a low growling *qua-ack*.
HABITS: Forms large flocks, except when breeding. Nest is a ground scrape set on dry land, often far from water.

Eurasian Wigeon

Anas penelope
ALSO: Wigeon, Pfeifente, Canard siffleur, Brunnakke, Свиязь, *Mareca penelope*. SN means "Penelope's duck"; Linnaeus named this species after Penelope, the wife of Odysseus.
RANGE: Nests (May–Jun) in Iceland, UK, and Scandinavia, east across n Russia to Kamchatka, south to nc Europe and n China; breeds around ponds and marshes in forest-tundra and taiga, less frequently on open steppe. Frequents flooded fields and brackish marshes in migration. Winters along seacoasts, lakes, reservoirs, and swampy and cultivated fields south to ne Africa, s Asia, and Philippines. Regular visitor to Hawaii, Aleutians, and n coasts of N Amer.
ID: L 17–20 in (42–50 cm). AD ♂: Head reddish brown, with a golden yellow forehead. Bill bluish gray, with a black tip. Upper breast warm brown. Back and sides gray, with fine vermiculations. Belly white. Large white patch on upper wing; green speculum. Tail black. In eclipse plumage, head is entirely reddish brown. AD ♀: Warm brown, with dark mottling on head. Belly white. Legs lead gray. White on upper wing is reduced to a narrow band; dull, dark, grayish green speculum. VOICE: Male emits a clear, whistling *pjiew pjiew*. Female gives a growling *rerr*.
HABITS: Flies in small, fast moving flocks. Nests near water, with nest concealed in bushes or grass.

Baikal Teal

Anas formosa
ALSO: Bimaculate Duck, Squawk Duck, Gluckente, Sarcelle élégante, Gulkinnand, Клоктун, *Sibirionetta formosa*. SN means "beautiful duck." CN refers to Lake Baikal, Russia, the type locality.
RANGE: Nests (May–Jun) from nc Siberia east to Kamchatka, Sahkalin, and Sea of Okhotsk around shallow ponds, lakes, and rivers on tundra, forest-tundra, and taiga. Winters near large lakes and rice fields in e Asia.
ID: L 17–20 in (42–50 cm). AD ♂: Striking head plumage; iridescent green crescent from the eye to the nape encloses 2 golden facial patches,

Eurasian Wigeon
Anas penelope
Iceland, Eurasia
L 17–20 in (42–50 cm)

American Wigeon
Anas americana
N Amer
L 19–22 in (48–55 cm)

Baikal Teal
Anas formosa
Siberia, e Asia
L 17–20 in (42–50 cm)

Green-winged Teal
Anas crecca
Near circumpolar
L 13.5–16 in (34–43 cm)

Eurasian Wigeon ♂

Green-winged Teal ♂

American Wigeon ♂

Baikal Teal ♂

divided by a black stripe running from under the eye to the chin. White vertical line at side of breast and around black undertail coverts. Breast pinkish, with small dark spots. Sides gray. Back brown. Broad white trailing edge on upperwing; speculum green. AD ♀: Brown cap; gray cheeks; dark brown eye stripe; kidney-shaped dusky patch on cheek; round, pale spot on lores. Mottled brown back. Golden brown breast and flanks spotted dark brown. White belly and undertail coverts. Broad white trailing edge to the upperwing; speculum blackish, bordered with rufous in front. VOICE: Drake emits a soft *klo-klo-klo*; hen gives a wavering *quack*.

HABITS: Builds nest on dry tundra hummocks, in thickets of dry sedge or dwarf birch on lake islets, or under willow and juniper bushes beside small forest ponds.

STATUS: Hunted historically in Siberia and China for food and the drake's ornamental wing feathers. Formerly one of the most numerous ducks in e Asia. Most populations declined in the 1960s. However, wintering counts in S Korea have increased, ranging from 20,000 (1980) to a single flock numbering 265,000 birds (2001).

Green-winged Teal

Anas crecca

ALSO: Common Teal, Green-wing, Krickente, Sarcelle d'hiver, Krikkand, Чирок свистунок, Kainyik. SN means "duck [that calls] *krik-krik*," from the Swedish *krika*.

RANGE: Near circumpolar. Nests (May–Jul) around lakes, marshes, ponds, streams.

SUBSPECIES: EURASIAN TEAL (E), *A. c. crecca*, breeds in Iceland, UK, and n Europe east to Kamchatka and Commander and Kuril islands; winters south to s Europe and s Asia. N AMER TEAL (N), *A. c. carolinensis*, widespread breeder in N Amer; winters south to C Amer, W Indies, and (rarely) Hawaii. ALEUTIAN TEAL (A), *A. c. nimia*, resident in the Aleutians and Pribilofs.

ID: L 13.5–16 in (34–43 cm). Smallest dabbling duck. AD ♂: Head glossy cinnamon, with an iridescent green crescent running through the eye to a small crest at the nape. Breast pinkish with small black spots. Short, vertical, white stripe

along the side of the body, below the front of the folded wing (N Amer only). Sides gray, with fine vermiculations. Back gray. Yellow triangular patch along each side of black undertail coverts. Speculum green on inner wing, black toward outer wing, and edged with a tan stripe above, white stripe below. Resembles female in eclipse plumage. AD ♀: Mottled brown, with a dark bill, dark forewing, and white chin and belly. VOICE: Drake's display call is a whistled *krik-krik*.

HABITS: Feeds on seeds of grasses and rushes, stems and leafy parts of pondweed, and small invertebrates. Nest is a lined ground scrape concealed in dense vegetation.

Mallard

Anas platyrhynchos

ALSO: Greenhead, Stockente, Canard colvert, Stokkand, Кряква, Ivugasrugruk. CN stems from the Old French *malart*, meaning "wild drake." SN means "flat-billed duck." Ancestor of the domesticated duck.

RANGE: Circumpolar. Nests (Apr–Jun) in tundra, forest-tundra, and alpine areas around ponds, lakes, marshes, flooded fields, streams, and estuaries. Introduced into NZ, Australia, Hawaii. Casual in Svalbard, and the Marshall and Gilbert islands.

SUBSPECIES: COMMON MALLARD (C), *A. p. platyrhynchos*, breeds in N Amer, Iceland, and across Eurasia; winters south to the s US, Cuba, Mediterranean Sea, n Africa, Asia Minor, se Asia. GREENLAND MALLARD (G), *A. p. conboschas*, endemic resident in coastal w Greenland; breeds on small lakes; winters along coasts wherever open salt water exists.

ID: L 20–24 in (50–60 cm). AD ♂: Head and neck iridescent green; narrow white nuchal collar. Breast dark brown. Sides light gray. Back dark gray; rump and undertail coverts black. Wing speculum blue, with a band of black and white in front and behind. Dull yellow bill. Legs yellow orange. AD ♀: Mottled brown. Cap and eyeline dark brown. Bill orange, with some black along the sides. Blue speculum edged with a band of black and white in front and behind. VOICE: Quacks like a domestic duck.

Northern Shoveler
Anas clypeata
Near circumpolar
L 18–21 in (45–52 cm)

Mallard
Anas platyrhynchos
Circumpolar
L 20–24 in (50–60 cm)

Northern Pintail
Anas acuta
Circumpolar
L 22–27.5 in (55–70 cm)

HABITS: Dabbles on the water surface and also dives. Feeds on insects and insect larvae, snails, freshwater shrimp, and earthworms in summer, and on seeds, acorns, aquatic vegetation, and cereal crops in winter. Urban mallards often rely on human-provided food, such as bread or seeds. Migrates in small flocks. Flight fast and direct. Pairs form on wintering grounds and birds arrive in breeding areas as soon as open water exists. Nest is a low mound of vegetation concealed by dense grass, brush, or fallen logs; occasionally nests on floating vegetation or uses abandoned nests of herons and crows.

Northern Shoveler

Anas clypeata

ALSO: Spoonbill, Aluutak, Löffel-ente, Canard souchet, Skeiand, Широконоска, *Spatula clypeata*. SN means "duck with a shield-shaped bill." CN refers to the bill shape.
RANGE: Nests (May–Jun) around shallow lakes, marshes, wet meadows, reed beds, and streams in Iceland and Eurasia, and in N Amer from n Alaska east to Hudson Bay, south to the s US. Winters to n Africa, n Indonesia, Philippines, Micronesia, Hawaii, Mexico, W Indies, n S Amer.
ID: L 18–21 in (45–52 cm). Long, wide, flat, spoon-shaped bill is adapted for straining small aquatic invertebrates from the water surface. AD ♂: Head and neck iridescent dark green. Breast white. Belly and sides chestnut. Tail coverts black. Wings gray; broad white patch on leading edge of underwing; upper forewing bluish gray; dark green speculum bordered white at front. Iris yellow. Legs orange. AD ♀: Mottled brown. Brown belly contrasts with white underwing. Iris reddish brown. **VOICE:** Drake gives a soft, low *kvo-kvo-kvo*; hen emits a low *quack*.
HABITS: Occurs in pairs or small flocks. Feeds almost exclusively by dabbling. Male establishes nesting territory while female builds nest on the ground in dense vegetation or sometimes in open areas. Female incubates clutch of 6–12 eggs for 21–28 days, plucking down from her breast to insulate her eggs.

Northern Pintail

Anas acuta

ALSO: Arnaviaq, Ivugak, Qummuajuuq, Spießente, Canard pilet, Шилохвость, Stjertand. SN means "duck with pointed [tail]."
RANGE: Circumpolar. Nests (Apr–Jul) in wetlands on arctic and alpine tundra, barrens, steppe, and prairies in N Amer, w Greenland, Iceland, Faroes, Svalbard, UK, and Eurasia. Winters, often in large flocks, on open wetlands and flooded agricultural fields. Winters south to the s US, W Indies, C Amer, n S Amer, Hawaii, n Africa, Borneo, Philippines, and Micronesia. **ID:** L 22–27.5 in (55–70 cm). Long, thin neck. Long, pointed tail. AD ♂: Head brown, with an elegant, narrow crescent of white extending from the white breast and neck onto the nape. Back and sides gray, with fine vermiculations. Undertail black. Speculum violet green. Legs and bill dark gray. AD ♀: Mottled brown. Speculum dull bronze. **VOICE:** Drake gives a wheezy whistled *whee*, hens a hoarse *quack* or *kuk*.
HABITS: Feeds on aquatic invertebrates, crustaceans, and snails in summer, grains and seeds in fall and winter. Breeds shortly after the ice thaws in many arctic areas. Nest is a ground scrape often located far from water and concealed by loose vegetation and shrubs. Female incubates the clutch of 8–12 pale olive eggs. Males are promiscuous and abandon the nest shortly after incubation begins and seek out a second mate.

SUBFAMILY AYTHYINAE
DIVING OR BAY DUCKS

Aythyinae and *Aythya* derive from the Greek name for an unidentified waterfowl mentioned in the *Odyssey* and in Aristotle's *Natural History*.

These gregarious sea ducks occur on bays, brackish estuaries, and freshwater bodies where they dive and forage underwater, feeding on seeds, buds, leaves, rhizomes, tubers, and root stalks of aquatic plants as well as clams, snails, and aquatic insect larvae.

They have a compact build, large head, thick neck, and narrow flap of skin on the rear toe. Their legs are set far back on their bodies, a feature that reduces their walk to an awkward shuffle on land but aids in swimming. They have broad, blunt-tipped wings and fly with very rapid wingbeats. These ducks are sexually dimorphic. Females have a mix of brown and gray plumage year round. Males develop bright nuptial plumage in breeding season. Except for the scaups, they molt their bright plumage after mating and for a few weeks resemble females.

Pairs bond during spring migration or on breeding grounds. The female often selects the previous year's nesting site. She builds the nest on small floating mats of vegetation, in clumps of rushes or sedges, or on dry land that has ample vegetation for cover. The male usually abandons the hen early in the incubation period and joins other males to molt. The female alone incubates the 5–14 pale olive to buffy eggs for 23–25 days, broods the chicks, and leads them to water to forage. She remains with the young until she begins to molt her flight feathers, then leaves her brood. The abandoned ducklings often amalgamate into sizable crèches that forage together until they fledge at 40–50 days of age.

GENUS *AYTHYA*
Canvasback

Aythya valisineria

ALSO: Riesentafelente, Kanvasand, Fuligule à dos blanc, Длинноносый красноголовый нырок. CN refers to the canvas-colored feathering on the back. SN means "sea duck that eats *Vallisneria*," a freshwater eelgrass, whose buds and rhizomes are the duck's preferred food in winter; the genus was misspelled *valisneria* when the specific name was assigned.
RANGE: Nests (May–Jun) from nc Alaska and n Yukon south to the nw/nc US, around marshes, ponds, lakes, and rivers having emergent vegetation. Winters on seacoasts, estuaries, bays, and large lakes, south to Mexico and Florida, and (rarely) Hawaii.
ID: L 19–22 in (48–56 cm). Long black bill and sloping forehead. AD ♂: Deep reddish brown head and neck, darkening to brownish black on crown, forehead, and chin. Black upper back, breast, rump, undertail coverts, and tail. Canvas

Pochard ♂

Canvasback ♂

Redhead ♂

♀

Canvasback
Aythya valisineria
N Amer
L 19–22 in (48–56 cm) ♂

♀

Redhead
Aythya americana
N Amer
L 17–19 in (42–48 cm) ♂

♀

Common Pochard
Aythya ferina
Eurasia, Iceland
L 17–20 in (42–49 cm) ♂

♀

Trailing crest

♀

Tufted Duck
Aythya fuligula
Eurasia
L 16–19 in (40–47 cm) ♂

♂

♀

Brush-cut crest at back of head

♀

Ring-necked Duck
Aythya collaris
N Amer
L 20–22 in (50–56 cm) ♂

Angular head

♀

♂

Lesser Scaup
Aythya affinis
N Amer
L 15–17.5 in (38–45 cm)

♀

Rounded head

♀

♂

Greater Scaup
Aythya marila
Near circumpolar
L 17–20 in (42–50 cm)

white mantle, upperwing coverts, flanks, and underwing, with some fine dark vermiculations. Brownish gray primaries. Grayish blue legs and feet. Iris red. Resembles female when in eclipse plumage. AD ♀/JUV: Brown head, breast, and upper back. Pale grayish brown body. Iris reddish brown. VOICE: Soft *coo* or guttural *krrr*. **HABITS:** Nest is a large platform of coarsely interwoven reeds and grasses, lined with fine grasses and down, and built on water on emergent vegetation or occasionally on dry land. **RELATED SPECIES:** The REDHEAD, *Aythya americana*, of subarctic N Amer and COMMON POCHARD, *Aythya ferina*, of s Eurasia are shown for purposes of comparison with the Canvasback, which overlaps the Redhead's range in c Alaska and which occurs as a vagrant in Europe. Redhead drake has a red head; bluish gray, black-tipped bill; yellow iris; gray back and sides. Northern Pochard drake has a rounded, chestnut head; black bill, with a pale gray band across the upper mandible; red iris; pale gray back and sides.

Tufted Duck

Aythya fuligula

ALSO: Tufted Pochard, Fuligule morillon, Reiher-ente, Toppand, Хохлатая чернеть. CN refers to the long crown feathers. SN means "soot-colored duck." **RANGE:** Nests (May–Jun) near marshes, ponds, and lakes with emergent vegetation in Iceland, Faroes, UK, and from Scandinavia east across Russia to Kamchatka, Kuril and Commander islands, and south to s Europe and s Asia. Winters on rivers and brackish coastal waters south to n Africa and se Asia. Strays to the coasts of N Amer, Micronesia, and Hawaii. **ID:** L 16–19 in (40–47 cm). AD ♂: Black head with purplish gloss and a trailing crest. Black breast and black back. Sides and belly white. Iris yellow. Bill gray with a black tip. Legs gray. AD ♀: Brown with whitish belly. Narrow fringe of white feathers near the bill base. Short crest. **HABITS:** Dives to depths of 13 ft (4 m) as it probes for invertebrates and aquatic plants in bottom silt. Female builds a nest of plant matter on the ground in tall grass or under low shrubs.

Ring-necked Duck

Aythya collaris

ALSO: Ringschnabelente, Fuligule à collier, Morillon à bec cerclé, Ошейниковая чернеть, Ringand. SN means "ring-necked sea duck," a reference to the male's inconspicuous brown neck band.

RANGE: Nests (Apr–Jul) around sedge marshes, bogs, and rivers and lakes with dense emergent vegetation, from ec Alaska across nc Canada, and south to the contiguous US; pale green on map indicates extreme limits of breeding range. Winters south to the s US, W Indies, Panama, and (rarely) Hawaii. **ID:** L 20–22 in (50–56 cm). Distinctive bill markings. Brush-cut crest. Peaked, angular head profile. AD ♂: Black head, breast, and upperparts. Inconspicuous chestnut collar. Whitish to gray belly and flanks; triangular white wedge extends upward in the area in front of the folded wing. Bill slate, with white markings around base, nares, and dark tip. AD ♀: Grayish brown. Dark gray crown; pale gray on forehead, chin, and throat. White eyering; narrow pale line extends back from eye. Bill slate, with a faint white band near tip.

HABITS: Swims within the cover of emergent vegetation or floating aquatic plants. Dives to depths of about 5 ft (1.5 m) to feed. Female builds nest on small floating mats of vegetation, in clumps of rushes or *Carex* sedges, or on islands with ample vegetation for cover.

Greater Scaup

Aythya marila

ALSO: Bluebill, Bergente, Fuligule milouinan, Bergand, Морская чернеть, Kakluk-palik. CN may derive from the female's *scaup scaup* call or from "mussel-scaups," an old term for the shellfish beds where these ducks feed. SN means "sea duck with charcoal-colored [breast]. **RANGE:** Nests (May–Jul) near lakes and ponds on the tundra and in the forest-tundra in Iceland, the Faroes, n Eurasia, Aleutians and Bering Sea islands, and along the Pacific and Atlantic coasts of n N Amer. Winters on bays and deep lakes near marine coasts south to the Mediterranean, China, Philippines, s US, Baja California, and (rarely) Hawaii.

ID: L 17–20 in (42–50 cm). AD ♂: Head and neck black, with greenish gloss. Black rump. Back gray, with fine striations. Sides and belly white. White band on trailing edge of wing. Iris yellow. Blue gray bill and legs. AD ♀: Brown; white belly; white ring at bill base. White wing stripe.

HABITS: Forms large rafts in winter, often in the company of lesser scaups. Forages at depths of 5–25 ft (1.5–7.5 m). Feeds on amphipods and aquatic insect larvae in summer, mollusks and crustaceans in winter. Nest is built in dense grass, rock crevices, and under woody vegetation, sometimes amid gull and tern nesting colonies.

Lesser Scaup

Aythya affinis
ALSO: Little Bluebill, Petit fuligule, Veilchenente, Purpurhodeand, Малая морская чернеть. SN means "related to *Aythya*," an allusion to this species' close relationship with *Aythya marila*.

RANGE: Nests (May–Jul) around inland lakes and ponds with low islets, in sedge meadows, and in lightly wooded areas in nc Alaska and nc Canada, south to the nc US. Winters south to the s US, C Amer, and S Amer.

ID: L 15–17.5 in (38–45 cm). AD ♂: Slightly crested black head, glossed with purple, and often showing distinct bump at rear crown. Black neck, breast, and upper mantle. Back gray with coarse dark gray striations. Flanks and belly white. Vent and undertail coverts black. White wing stripe on trailing edge of wing. Slaty blue bill, with narrow black tip. Iris yellow. AD ♀: Chocolate brown overall. Wing coverts flecked with gray. Bill dark gray, with some white at bill base. Olive brown iris. White wing stripe.

VOICE: Soft *whee-oo* when courting.

HABITS: Forms large rafts in winter, often in the company of greater scaups. Forages to depths of 20 ft (6 m), feeding on amphipods and aquatic insect larvae in summer, and mollusks and small fishes in winter. Female builds the nest in tall grass or vegetation near water.

SUBFAMILY MERGINAE
SEA DUCKS

Sea ducks are species often associated with coastal waters of the northern oceans: eiders, scoters, goldeneyes, buffleheads, harlequin ducks, long-tailed ducks, and mergansers. These species have glands above the eye for excreting excess salt from their system. They have compact feathering with dense, insulating down. Most feed on mollusks and crustaceans taken in dives to the sea or lake bottom. A few species feed on fish. Breeding is seasonally monogamous. The female selects the breeding site, builds the nest, and incubates the 3–8 eggs for 22–30 days. The male abandons the nest before the eggs hatch and moves to areas where it molts with other males. The hen leads the chicks to water shortly after hatching and remains with them for several weeks, abandoning them when she begins to molt her flight feathers. The young join other broods, forming large rafts of ducklings that feed together until they fledge at 50–60 days.

GENERA *SOMATERIA* AND *POLYSTICTA*: These genera contain the eiders, a word that derives from *aethr*, the Icelandic name for these large arctic sea ducks. Males have elaborate, colorful plumage in breeding season, while females are mottled brown year round. The female builds the nest—a ground scrape surrounded by piles of loose vegetation and lined with down and lichens. The nest is usually located near the sea and is sometimes built in the middle of tern and gull colonies, possibly to deter predation by arctic foxes.

Common Eider

Somateria mollissima
ALSO: Eiderente, Eider à duvet, Обыкновенная rara, Ærfugl, Amauliqjuaq, Amauligruak, Mitiq, Arnaviaq. Known as Cuddy's ducks in the Farne Isles of England, where Saint Cuthbert established a sanctuary for the species in AD 676. SN means "sea duck with very soft feathers," a reference to the eider's down, which is harvested from abandoned nests and used as fill for bedding and outerwear.

RANGE: Circumpolar. Nests (May–Jul) in arctic N Amer, Greenland, Iceland, Faroes, Svalbard, Europe, and Bering Sea region on islands off rocky seacoasts, less frequently near freshwater ponds or rivers on the tundra. Winters along seacoasts, often as far north as open water permits. ID: L 24–28 in (60–70 cm). Largest diving duck. Diagnostic wedge-shaped bill, with large pointed or rounded extensions (*frontal processes*) from the middle of the upper mandible onto the forehead. AD ♂ OCT–JUN: White face; black crown; nape tinged with lime green. Bill horn-colored, with grayish green to golden frontal processes. Breast white to rosy buff. Back white. Sides, belly, rump, and undertail black, interrupted by rounded white flank patches, often partially covered by elongated, downward-curving tertial feathers. Wing primaries and part of greater wing coverts black; underwing pale gray to white. AD ♂ JUL–SEP: Dark brown to blackish, with a faint brown eye stripe. Breast flecked with white. Secondaries and wing coverts white. FIRST YEAR ♂: Brownish black head and upperparts; pale brown eye stripe. White at base of foreneck and breast. White flecking on dark wing coverts and scapulars. AD ♀: Reddish brown to grayish brown. Black-barred feathers on flanks. Dark speculum bordered by white. Bill greenish gray to olive green. VOICE: Courting male emits a hollow cooing *ah-OOOO-ooo*.
HABITS: Dives to depths of 33 ft (10 m) to forage for crustaceans and bivalve mollusks, especially mussels. Also probes with feet on muddy shores to uncover small clams or worms. Can fly at speeds up to 70 mph (113 kmh). Nests in large colonies. Pairs use nests from previous years, or seek out new sites under snow-free rocky overhangs, bushes, or driftwood.
STATUS: Commercial down hunters had nearly extirpated eiders on the N Amer eastern seaboard by the end of the 19th century. Protected since 1918, world population is now 1.5–2 million.

King Eider
Somateria spectabilis
ALSO: Prachteiderente, Eider à tête grise, Praktærfugl, Гага-гребенушка, Qingalik,

Mitiq, Qingalaaq, Arnaviaq, Kingalik. CN refers to the orange, crown-like knob on the drake's bill. SN means "remarkable downy sea duck."
RANGE: Circumpolar. Nests (Jun–Jul) on seaside tundra of the High Arctic, usually around ponds and lakes, occasionally in dry areas away from water. Winters on the open sea south of the ice edge, south to Iceland, UK, n Scandinavia, Kamchatka, Aleutians, and Newfoundland. Lives farther north than any other waterfowl, except for the Long-tailed Duck, *Clangula hyemalis*.
ID: L 22–25 in (55–63 cm). AD ♂ OCT–JUN: Head powder blue; cheeks pale green; bill reddish orange, with a large yellow-orange frontal lobe that is edged with black. Neck, breast, and upper back white, with a buffy wash on upper breast. Rest of body is black, with a white patch on side of rump and large white patch on upperwing coverts. Long black scapular feathers jut out from the wings, forming triangular "sails" on the back; inner secondaries are elongated and downcurved. AD ♂ JUL–SEP: Plumage fades to brown; dark wings bear a large white patch on forewing. Bill paler, with a small frontal lobe. FIRST WINTER ♂: Brown, with a white breast. Bill orange with a small frontal lobe. AD ♀: Reddish brown, with black and tan barring and scalloping on the underparts. Underwing linings and axillaries dull white. Bill olive or yellowish gray. VOICE: Courting male emits a dove-like, quavering *cooo-cooo-brOOO-broo*.
HABITS: Dives for benthic crustaceans, polychaete worms, and mollusks, especially mussels. Migrates in huge flocks. During spring migration, up to 100,000 birds move north along the Alaskan coast, flying high and attaining speeds up to 35 mph (60 kmh).

Spectacled Eider
Somateria fischeri
ALSO: Plüschkopfente, Eider à lunettes, Brilleærfugl, Очковая гага, Qavasuk,

Lampronetta fischeri. SN means "Fischer's downy duck," honoring German geologist-zoologist Johann Gotthelf Fischer von Waldheim (1771–1853), who founded the Natural History Society of Moscow. CN refers to the eyeglass-like

ad. ♀

ad. ♂ Oct–Jun

Steller's Eider
Polysticta stelleri
NE Siberia, Alaska
L 17–19 in (42–48 cm)

1st year ♂

ad. ♀

ad. ♂ Dec–Jun

Spectacled Eider
Somateria fischeri
Arctic Siberia, Alaska
L 20–23 in (51–58 cm)

1st winter ♂

ad. ♀

ad. ♂ Dec–Jun

King Eider
Somateria spectabilis
Circumpolar
L 22–25 in (55–63 cm)

ad. ♂ (Jul–Sep)

1st year ♂

ad. ♀

Common Eider
Somateria mollissima
Circumpolar
L 24–28 in (60–70 cm)

ad. ♂ Oct–Jun

pattern of feathers around the eye; adults, juveniles, and chicks all bear this field mark.
RANGE: Nests (May–Jun) on small coastal islands and marshy tundra in disjunct locations: the Yana, Indigirka, and Kolyma river deltas in Siberia, and along the nc Alaska coast and Yukon Rvr delta in N Amer. Molts offshore its breeding grounds at the Indigirka Rvr delta and Mechigmenski Bay in Siberia, and at Ledyard Bay and Norton Sound in Alaska (yellow on map). Wintering grounds were discovered in 1996 in dense pack ice halfway between St Lawrence Is and St Matthew Is in the Bering Sea. Vagrant to Vardø, Norway, and the Kola Penin, Russia.
ID: L 20–23 in (51–58 cm). AD ♂ DEC–JUN: Soft crest of pale green feathers on the sides and back of the head; velvet-like greenish plumage on the forehead and lores extends forward onto the bill. Circle of white feathers rimmed with black (the "spectacles") around the eyes. Throat, neck, back, wing coverts, and tertials creamy white. Underparts and hindquarters dark brown to blackish, except for white patches on the rump sides. Iris white, encircled with pale blue. Bill orange, with a paler tip. Legs and feet dull yellow to olive brown. AD ♂ JUL–NOV: Brownish gray, with pale area around the eye, gray back, and white patch on the forewing. FIRST WINTER ♂: Resembles breeding male, but with dark gray feathers on head and back. AD ♀: Barred brown and black. Best field mark is the circle of pale feathers around the eye. VOICE: Generally silent.
HABITS: Feeds on tundra ponds when nesting, taking insects, insect larvae, seeds, and plant material. In winter, feeds at sea on benthic clams and other mollusks. Flight is fast, buoyant, and low. Nest is a depression located in the open or under cover of tall grass and sedge.

Steller's Eider

Polysticta stelleri

ALSO: Ignikauktuk, Eider de Steller, Scheckente, Stellerand, Сибирская гага. SN means "Steller's many-spotted [eider]," referring to the drake's head spots and to German explorer Georg Wilhelm Steller (1709–1746), who discovered the species near Kamchatka.

RANGE: Nests (Jun–Jul) on coastal tundra around ponds and river deltas from the Khatanga Rvr to Chukotka in n Siberia and along the coastal plain near Barrow, Alaska. Molts in lagoons along the Murmansk, Finland, and Bering Sea coasts. Winters in shallow, inshore, often brackish waters, south to the Baltic Sea, Kamchatka, the Kuril, Commander, Pribilof, and Aleutian islands, and (rarely) Brit Columbia.
ID: L 17–19 in (42–48 cm). Smallest eider. Small, slightly drooping bill, with a thick base. Steep forehead and nape. Long, pointed tail carried above the water. Long tertials. Blue speculum edged with white. Bill and legs gray. AD ♂ OCT–JUN: White head, with a black spot around the eye, pale green spot on lores, and dark olive tuft on hind crown. Throat, nape, and middle of back glossy blue-black. Breast chestnut with a black spot in front of the wings. Dark chestnut belly. Prominent white shoulder patch. AD ♂ JUL–SEP: Resembles female, but head and barred chest retain some breeding plumage and white upperwing coverts. AD ♀: Head tinged with rust. Body purplish black. Elongated purple and black tertials, lightly edged with white. Blue speculum is edged with white (a very good field mark). VOICE: Generally silent; both sexes occasionally growl or bark.
HABITS: Feeds on amphipods and bivalve mollusks supplemented with insect larvae and some plant material such as pondweeds and crowberries in summer. In winter, feeds on amphipods and isopods, marine mollusks, and barnacles. The large flocks that form in winter and early spring exhibit massed synchronous diving behavior when foraging. Flies with rapid wingbeats, which produce a loud, ringing sound. The courting male performs a unique rearing display, rapidly raising the head and body out of the water to expose its chestnut underparts; rearing is often accompanied by rapid head waving as the male swims toward and then away from the female.
STATUS: Populations are in decline due to reduced breeding habitat and illegal harvesting of birds. Vulnerable (IUCN). Classed as Rare (Category 3) in the 1987 Red Book for the Yakutia Republic, Russia.

GENUS *BUCEPHALA*: Buffleheads and goldeneyes are less marine than other species of sea ducks and will often winter on fresh water. Males have white bodies, with black backs and distinctive head markings. Females are gray, with chestnut-colored heads.

Goldeneyes are seasonally monogamous, while buffleheads may keep the same mate for several years. These ducks typically nest in tree cavities. The female chooses a nesting hole near the spot where she was hatched. She lays her eggs on the bare surface of a natural tree cavity or old woodpecker hole, then adds down plucked from her breast as egg-laying and incubation progresses. The female alone incubates the eggs for 28–32 days. The down-covered hatchlings are precocial and leave the nest within a day of hatching. They jump down from the tree, and the female leads them to water. The ducklings are able to swim on their own. They feed on aquatic insects until they fledge at 55–65 days. Broods of different females often amalgamate, and a lone female that has not begun her post-breeding molt will sometimes adopt the mixed broods. In winter, most birds move to saltwater environments.

Bufflehead

Bucephala albeola
ALSO: Butterball, Büffelkopfente, Petit Garrot, Søkeresultater, Малый гоголь. CN derives from the French *buffle*, meaning "buffalo," a reference to this duck's large-headed appearance. SN means "large-headed sea duck with white [nape]."
RANGE: Nests (Apr–Jul) in woodpecker holes in woodlands and forests from c Alaska across nc Canada to Hudson Bay and Quebec, south to Brit Columbia and nw US; also accepts nest boxes. Winters in brackish coves, harbors, estuaries along the Pacific coast from the Aleutians to California and c Mexico, and along Gulf and Atlantic coasts from s Canada to Texas and Gtr Antilles; some birds winter on open lakes in the interior. Accidental to Kamchatka, Kurils, Japan, Greenland, Iceland, UK, and w Europe.
ID: L 13–16 in (33–40 cm). Smallest diving duck.

AD ♂ OCT–JUN: Head black, with green and purple iridescence; large white patch extends from behind the eye across the nape. Black back. White underparts. Wings black, with a broad white patch on secondaries and coverts. Short gray bill. Iris dark. AD ♂ JUL–SEP: Resembles female, but has larger white patches on wings and face. AD ♀: Dark brown head, back, and wings. Underparts pale grayish brown. White ear patch. White patch on secondaries.
HABITS: Feeds on aquatic insects, insect larvae, and invertebrates in summer; dives after mollusks, crustaceans, and some fish in winter. Migrates in flocks at night. Flies with rapid wingbeats at speeds of up to 40 mph (65 kmh). Monogamous, often keeping the same mate for several years. Nests near water in poplar or aspen trees, sometimes pine, mainly in holes excavated by northern flickers (*Colaptes auratus*).

Barrow's Goldeneye

Bucephala islandica
ALSO: Rocky Mountain Goldeneye, Spatelente, Garrot d'Islande, Islandsand, Исландский гоголь. CN refers to Sir John Barrow (1764–1848), Second Secretary of the British Admiralty, who advocated voyages to discover a northwest passage, and to this species' golden yellow iris. SN means "large-headed sea duck of Iceland," the type locality.
RANGE: Nests (Apr–Jul) in wooded areas near alpine lakes and ponds up to 10,000 ft (3000 m); breeds mainly in mountains of w N Amer with smaller breeding populations in the Laurentian highland forests of se Quebec, Iceland, and sw Greenland. Winters south of breeding areas on sheltered seacoasts, estuaries, bays, and coastal lakes.
ID: L 17–21 in (42–53 cm). Large rounded head. Short bill. Compact body. Short neck. Yellow legs. AD ♂ OCT–JUN: Head iridescent purplish black. White crescent between bill and eye. Black bill. Sides, breast, belly, and secondaries white. Back, wings, and tail black. Iris golden. Plumage dulls after breeding. AD ♀/JUV: Dark chocolate brown, rounded head. Slate gray back, wings, and tail. White flanks, belly, and

breast. Bill dark at base, yellowish toward tip. Iris golden; golden brown in juvenile. VOICE: Courting male gives a soft *ka-KAA*.

HABITS: Feeds mainly on aquatic insects when breeding and marine mollusks in winter. Flocks often dive in synchrony. Flies with deep, rapid wingbeats that produce a distinctive "whistle" in flight. Pair bonds can last for more than one season. Nests in a natural tree cavity, abandoned woodpecker hole, nest box, or rock crevice; sometimes lays eggs in the cavity nest of another goldeneye. Clutch is 6–12 bluish green eggs.

Common Goldeneye

Bucephala clangula
ALSO: Whistler, Schell-ente, Garrot à oeil d'or, Kvinand, Обыкновенный гоголь. SN means "noisy duck," referring to sounds made by the wings in flight.
RANGE: Nests (May–Jul) in Iceland, n Eurasia, and across n N Amer, mainly in forested areas near clear lakes, deep marshes, and slow-flowing rivers, less commonly along open seacoasts. Winters mainly in marine waters, particularly estuaries and bays; also found on inland lakes where there is enough forage south to the Mediterranean, Middle East, and SE Asia, and from the Aleutians and s Alaskan coast south to California, and from Newfoundland to Florida.
ID: L 16–20 in (40–50 cm). Compact body, with a short neck. Large, slightly angular head, with a sloping forehead. Iris golden; golden brown in juvenile. Legs and feet yellow. AD ♂ OCT–JUN: Head iridescent greenish black, with a white oval patch on feathers at the bill base. Sides, breast, belly, and secondaries white, contrasting with black back, wings, and tail. Plumage dulls after breeding. AD♀: Head dark chocolate brown. Slate gray back, wings, and tail. White flanks, belly, and breast. Dull yellow bill, with a blackish basal area and tip.
HABITS: Feeds mainly on aquatic insects in summer, and fish, crustaceans, and mollusks in winter. Nests in holes in broken branches and snags, in old woodpecker holes, and in nest boxes; frequently lays eggs in the nests of other goldeneyes.

GENUS *HISTRIONICUS*: Harlequin ducks are almost always seen in turbulent waters. They nest along fast-flowing mountain streams and winter along rugged seacoasts exposed to heavy surf.

Harlequin Duck

Histrionicus histrionicus
ALSO: Lords and Ladies, Kragenente, Arlequin plongeur, Harlekinand, Каменушки, Tulajunuk, Sagvak tingmiak; also known as Sea Mouse, referring to the squeaking display calls. SN means "actor," deriving from the Latin *histrio* and referring to Arlecchino (Harlequin), a colorfully dressed character in the 16th-century Italian theater, *Commedia dell'arte*.
RANGE: Nests (Apr–Jun) along cold fast-flowing streams and rivers from the Lena Rvr east to Kamchatka, the Kurils, and nw N Amer, and in Greenland, Iceland, and e N Amer, from Baffin Is to Newfoundland. Winters south of breeding areas along rocky seacoasts exposed to heavy surf.
ID: L 15–18 in (38–45 cm). AD ♂ OCT–JUN: Dark slaty blue head and neck. White crescent in front of the eye becomes chestnut as it extends to the nape. Round white spot behind the eye. White vertical slash on the nape. Nuchal collar white, edged with black. Back, breast, and underparts slaty blue, marked with bold stripes of white edged with black. Rump and pointed tail blackish. Flanks chestnut. Iridescent blue speculum; tertials white, edged with black. Iris brown. Bill bluish gray with pale yellow tip. AD ♂ JUL–SEP: Eclipse male resembles the hen, but retains vestiges of white markings. AD ♀: Olive brown. Broad white patch on the cheek below the eye; round white spots above and behind the eye. Iris dark brown. Bill and legs grayish blue.
HABITS: Lives along rugged seacoasts in winter, diving in intertidal and shallow subtidal waters to feed on fish roe, amphipods, snails, crabs, barnacles, and other invertebrates. Able to move swiftly and with agility in turbulent white water, diving to the bottom to pick larval insects from rocky substrates. Moves upriver in spring to traditional breeding streams in the interior. Pair bonds can last for more than one season.

Bufflehead
Bucephala albeola
N Amer
L 13–16 in (33–40 cm)

Common Goldeneye
Bucephala clangula
Near circumpolar
L 16–20 in (40–50 cm)

Barrow's Goldeneye
Bucephala islandica
N Amer, Greenland, Iceland
L 17–21 in (42–53 cm)

Harlequin Duck
Histrionicus histrionicus
NE Asia, N Amer,
Greenland, Iceland
L 15–18 in (38–45 cm)

Reunited pairs often reuse a nesting site from previous seasons. Female chooses a site near water and builds a well-concealed nest under vegetation, on small ledges, or in tree cavities or stumps. She lines the nest with conifer needles, moss, leaf litter, and small stones, and adds down once the clutch of 5–6 buff-colored eggs has been laid.

The female incubates the eggs and rears the brood. Male deserts the nest at the onset of incubation and flies or swims to the seacoast to molt. Chicks are able to swim and dive shortly after hatching, and soon can negotiate rapids with ease. Young fledge at 42–56 days and accompany the female as she swims or flies to wintering grounds on the seacoast.

GENUS *MELANITTA*: Scoters are dark-plumaged sea ducks with bills that are swollen at the base. They swim with the tail low in the water. Their wings produce a whistling noise in flight. Breeding is seasonally monogamous. Males abandon the nest at the onset of incubation and gather with other males to molt. The female alone incubates the 6–10 pale buff eggs for 25–30 days and leads the young to water where they feed on aquatic insects and insect larvae. Females often abandon their brood before the young fledge at 55–60 days. Scoters 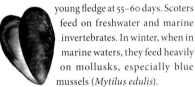 feed on freshwater and marine invertebrates. In winter, when in marine waters, they feed heavily on mollusks, especially blue mussels (*Mytilus edulis*).

Surf Scoter
Melanitta perspicillata

ALSO: Skunk-headed Coot, Brillenente, Macreuse à front blanc, Brilleand, Турпаны, Tuungaagruk. CN refers to the habit of swimming in the surf line. SN means "black duck with spectacles," referring to the male's facial markings.
RANGE: Nests (Jun–Jul) around small, shallow lakes in Alaska and n Canada, east to Labrador. Winters from Aleutians south to Baja California, the Great Lakes, and Florida. Vagrant in Chukotka and the Commander Is.

ID: L 22–26 in (56–66 cm). AD ♂: Velvety black, with white patch on forehead and nape. Feathering extends far onto the bill, which is patterned in white, red, and yellow, with a black circular knob on the side of the upper mandible. Iris white. Legs reddish orange. AD ♀: Dark to black brown above, paler brown below. White crescent on cheeks. White vertical mark at base of bill. Bill black, with a knob on side of upper mandible. **VOICE:** Courting male emits a liquid, gurgling call or a guttural, croaking *krrraak*.
HABITS: Feeds on aquatic invertebrates and occasionally herring spawn. Uses bill to tear mollusks off submerged rocks. Nest is a ground scrape, lined with vegetation and down, and concealed by overhanging vegetation or fallen tree branches. Female incubates the eggs and aggressively defends her young, attacking chicks of other hens and keeping her young away from common loons, which prey on young waterbirds.

Black Scoter
Melanitta americana

ALSO: Trauerente, Macreuse noire, Svartand, Синьга, Tuungaagrupiak, Uvinauyuk, *Oidemia nigra*. SN means "black duck of America."
RANGE: Nests (Jun–Jul) around shallow lakes and sloughs on the tundra, forest-tundra, and woodland in ne Siberia and Alaska, with a separate population in Quebec. Winters on seacoasts and large lakes south of breeding range.
ID: L 22–26 in (56–66 cm). AD ♂: Entirely dark black. Rounded head. Gray orbital ring. Yellow orange, swollen knob at base of upper mandible. AD ♀: Dark brown, with a dark cap and pale cheeks. **VOICE:** Melodious whistled *cour-cour-cour-loo-cour-lou* or *whe-oo-hoo*, and a reedy *tooo-oo-oo-it* call in flight.
HABITS: Forms small, monospecific foraging flocks in shallow coastal waters. When exercising the wings, throws its head downward in a distinctive motion.
RELATED SPECIES: COMMON SCOTER, *Melanitta nigra*, breeds in Iceland, Svalbard, and n Eurasia (paler green on map); yellow orbital ring; bill sides dark gray; black bulge and variable amount of yellow on upper mandible.

Surf Scoter

Surf Scoter
Melanitta perspicillata
N Amer
L 22–26 in (56–66 cm)

Siberian Scoter
Melanitta stejnegeri
NE Asia
L 20–23 in (50–58 cm)

White-winged
Scoter

Velvet Scoter
Melanitta fusca
N Eurasia, Iceland, Svalbard
L 20–23 in (50–58 cm)

White-winged Scoter
Melanitta deglandi
N Amer
L 20–23 in (50–58 cm)

Black Scoter

Common Scoter
Melanitta nigra
N Eurasia
L 22–26 in (56–66 cm)

Black Scoter
Melanitta americana
NE Asia, N Amer
L 22–26 in (56–66 cm)

White-winged Scoter
Melanitta deglandi

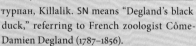

ALSO: Höckerschnabelente, Samtente, Sjøorre, Macreuse brune, Обыкновенный турпан, Killalik. SN means "Degland's black duck," referring to French zoologist Côme-Damien Degland (1787–1856).

RANGE: Nests (Jun–Jul) on tundra, forest-tundra, and in wooded areas in nw N Amer. Winters south of breeding range in bays, inlets, and lakes along the Pacific and Atlantic coasts of N Amer.

ID: L 20–23 in (50–58 cm). AD♂: Black overall. White "comma" under the eye. Prominent white speculum. Bill sides are pinkish yellow; cutting edge of bill is black; there is a square bulge on

upper mandible. Iris white. Legs reddish. AD♀: Brownish black, with a pale crescent on the cheek behind the eye and a pale buff oval patch over the bill. White speculum. **VOICE:** Courting male emits whistling notes.

HABITS: Nest is hidden in reeds or under dense, thorny vegetation and is often located far from water. Female incubates the eggs and rears the brood. Female aggressively defends her young and will pull predatory gulls out onto the water and attempt to drown them.

RELATED SPECIES: VELVET SCOTER, *Melanitta fusca*, breeds n Eurasia; reduced white eye patch; sides of bill yellow. Endangered. SIBERIAN SCOTER, *M. stejnegeri*, breeds ne Asia; sides of bill red, with yellow along the bill's cutting edge.

GENUS *CLANGULA*
Long-tailed Duck
Clangula hyemalis

ALSO: Oldsquaw, Eisente, Harelde kakawi, Cacaoui, Havelle, Морянка, Ahaalik, Aggiq, Aggiarjuk, Arnaviaq. SN means "noisy duck of winter," referring to the ducks' clamorous calls and Arctic breeding range.
RANGE: Circumpolar. Nests (Jun–Jul) on arctic tundra and forest-tundra to 80° N. Winters on cold water seacoasts and large lakes of Greenland, Eurasia, and N Amer, including the Great Lakes.
ID: L 16–19 in (40–47 cm), plus 4–6 in (10–15 cm) for the male's tail. AD ♂ MAY–AUG: Head, neck and breast blackish brown, with whitish eye patch. Scapulars russet with black centers. Pink band around dark bill. In Aug, the head, neck, and scapular feathers begin to turn white. AD ♂ NOV–APR: Head white, with grayish brown eye patch. Black ear patch extends down to the neck. Broad black band across the lower neck and breast. Back and rump black. White flanks and belly. Wings black, with long gray scapulars and dark chestnut secondaries. Tail black, with thin and elongated central rectrices, the outermost pair tinged with white. Pale pink band around the dark gray bill. AD ♀ MAY–AUG: Head dark brown, with small white patches around and behind eye. Faint white ring around neck. AD ♀ NOV–APR: Dark brown, with whitish face and neck. Dark brown ear patch extends down to the neck. Belly white. Flanks light gray. VOICE: Highly vocal, emitting nasal squawks, bays, and howls that can be heard from afar.
HABITS: Feeds on amphipods, aquatic insects, fish, fish eggs, and bivalves taken in dives to depths of 200 ft (60 m). Erratic, rapid flight. Nests in small colonies mainly on islets of freshwater ponds and sometimes on wet tundra or in willow or birch scrub. Nest is a ground scrape made under overhanging vegetation and lined with dry leaves and down. Female incubates the 3–10 pale olive eggs for 25 days and leads hatchlings to water. Broods frequently amalgamate, and 1–2 females often tend large rafts of ducklings until they fledge at 35–40 days. Some young fly to the seacoast before completing juvenal molt.

GENERA *MERGELLUS* AND *MERGUS*: These genera contain the so-called sawbill ducks. They have tooth-like lamellae along the cutting edge of the bill, which together with a small tooth, or *nail*, at the bill tip, help them grasp and hold fish, their main prey. These ducks are expert at diving and pursuing prey underwater. At times, they fish communally and dive in synchrony. They nest in tree cavities, except for the Red-breasted Merganser, which nests on the ground.

Smew
Mergellus albellus

ALSO: Weasel Coot, White Nun, Zwergsäger, Harle piette, Lappfiskand, Луток. CN derives from the Middle English *semawe*, or Sea Mew. SN means "white diver," referring to the male's white plumage and the Smew's habit of diving after prey. Fossils of Smew-like ducks found in England date back 1.5–2 million years to the early Pleistocene.
RANGE: Nests (May–Jun) in forest trees located near clear lakes and slow-flowing rivers across n Eurasia from Scandinavia to Chukotka. Winters on large lakes, quarry ponds, and reservoirs, and occasionally in estuaries and bays in disjunct locales from the s UK and n France east to the Black and Caspian seas, south to the Middle East and e Asia. Rare winter visitor to the Aleutians, Pribilofs, and the Great Lakes and Pacific and Atlantic coasts of N Amer.
ID: L 16–18 in (40–45 cm). Smallest merganser. AD ♂ NOV–JUN: Distinctive white and black plumage. Head and crest white (crest barely visible unless erect), with a black face and V-shaped black patch beneath the crest. Back and rump black. Flanks vermiculated white and black. Breast white, with 2 black stripes extending from the back onto the sides of the breast. Wings blackish gray, with white wing patches. Long, narrow, serrated, dark gray bill. Legs and feet gray. AD ♂ JUL–OCT: Closely resembles the female, but retains extensive white on wings. AD ♀: Gray body, with a chestnut head and white cheeks, chin, and throat. Wings dark gray, with white wing patches. VOICE: Courting male calls a soft, repetitive *kra-kra-kra-kra-kra*.

Smew
Mergellus albellus
Eurasia
L 16–18 in (40–45 cm)

Common Merganser
Mergus merganser
Near circumpolar
L 23–27 in (58–68 cm)

Red-breasted Merganser
Mergus serrator
Circumpolar
L 21–23 in (52–59 cm)

Long-tailed Duck
Clangula hyemalis
Circumpolar
L 16–19 in (40–47 cm)
plus ♂'s 4–6 in (10–15 cm) tail

ad. ♀ Nov–Apr

ad. ♀ May–Aug

ad. ♂ Nov–Apr

ad. ♂ May–Aug

HABITS: Solitary pairs when breeding. In migration, forms small flocks of 5–6 birds that fly in a straight line or in V formation. Flight is swift and direct, with rapid wingbeats. Feeds in shallow waters, often near reed beds, making short dives of 15–20 seconds for small fish, mollusks, crustaceans, aquatic insects, and insect larvae. Nests on wooded banks of rivers and lakes in the boreal forest and on wooded ridges. Uses tree cavities in burned trees and abandoned woodpecker nesting holes, especially those of black woodpeckers (*Dryocopus martius*); also accepts nest boxes. Clutch is 6–9 ivory-colored eggs. Nest is lined with white down. The female alone incubates the eggs for 28 days while the male departs to molt. Occasionally interbreeds with goldeneyes (*Bucephala* spp.)

Common Merganser

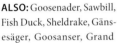

Mergus merganser
ALSO: Goosenader, Sawbill, Fish Duck, Sheldrake, Gänsesäger, Goosanser, Grand Harle, Laksand, Большой крохаль. SN means "diving merganser."
RANGE: Near circumpolar. Nests (May–Jul) in Iceland, Scotland, n Eurasia, Canada, Alaska, and w US around deep clearwater lakes and fast-flowing rivers in forests and mountains. Winters on large lakes, rivers, reservoirs, and marine coasts south to the Mediterranean, Black, and Caspian seas, India, China, and s US.
ID: L 23–27 in (58–68 cm). Elongated body. Rides low in water. Both sexes bear a crest at the back of the head, and have reddish bill and legs. AD ♂: Head black with a green iridescence. Back black. Neck, breast, and underparts white. Wing coverts and secondaries white; primaries blackish. In eclipse, resembles female, but retains extensive white on wings. AD ♀: Head and neck chestnut. Throat white. Back gray. White wing secondaries contrast with gray wing coverts and dark gray primaries.
HABITS: Solitary pairs when breeding. Forms very large flocks during late summer molt. Feeds almost exclusively on small fish. Nests in cavities in broken tree limbs, hollow treetops, and old woodpecker holes, especially those of

pileated woodpeckers (*Dryocopus pileatus*); also lays eggs in nests of other cavity-nesting ducks. Occasionally nests in rock crevices, under driftwood, in old sheds, chimneys, holes in riverbanks, and nest boxes. Female incubates clutch of 8–12 cream-colored eggs for 28–35 days and leads hatchlings to water. Chicks often form sizable rafts guarded by 1–2 hens.

Red-breasted Merganser

Mergus serrator
ALSO: Mittelsäger, Harle huppé, Длинноносый крохаль, Siland, Paiq, Nujaralik, Kajjiqtuq, Arnaviaq, Paisugruk. SN means "saw-billed merganser."
RANGE: Circumpolar. Nests (May–Jul) in tundra, forest-tundra, and mountains, north to 75°N in n N Amer, s Greenland, Iceland, UK, and across n Eurasia. Winters mainly in marine habitats south of breeding areas, frequenting shallow water along sheltered seacoasts.
ID: L 21–23 in (52–59 cm). Both sexes have a ragged crest at the back of the head, a red iris, red bill, and red legs. AD ♂: Head black with green iridescence. Back black. Neck, belly, and base of wings white. Upper breast reddish brown with dark mottling. Sides gray, with fine striations. White wing coverts and secondaries contrast with blackish primaries and upperwing coverts. AD ♀: Grayish brown. Head reddish brown, with a ragged, wispy crest. Breast whitish. White wing patch contrasts with dark wings.
HABITS: Feeds on small fish, crustaceans, worms, insects, and amphibians taken by diving after prey and skim-feeding at the water surface. Forages individually or through cooperative herding. Nests in loose colonies on forested riverbanks, marsh edges, lakeshores, rocky islets, coastal islands, sandy shores, and brackish bays and estuaries, usually concealing its nest in rock crevices, between boulders, or in reeds or tall grass. Nest is a ground scrape lined with leaf litter and down. Female incubates clutch of 5–24 eggs and leads hatchlings to water. She often abandons her young in a few days and flies off to molt. Broods amalgamate and swim behind any females that remain on the pond.

ad. Sep–Feb

juv.

Red-necked Grebe
Podiceps grisegena
N Amer, Europe, e Asia
L 17–22 in (43–56 cm)

ad. Mar–Aug

Pair-bonding display

Horned Grebe
Podiceps auritus
Near circumpolar
L 12–15 in (31–38 cm)

ad. Sep–Mar

ad. Apr–Aug
Presenting nesting material

Podicipediformes: Grebes

Podicipediformes is a widely distributed order of freshwater diving birds, some of which visit marine waters on migration and in winter.

FAMILY PODICIPEDIDAE
GREBES

Grebes are medium-sized, short-winged diving birds. The two Arctic-breeding species are dark brown to black above and paler below for most of the year. They develop russet or golden body feathers and facial plumes when breeding. Like many other waterbirds, grebes molt their flight feathers after breeding and are flightless for several weeks.

Grebes walk awkwardly on land because their legs are set far back on the body. This feature is reflected in the family name, which derives from the Latin *podiceps*, meaning "rump-footed." These birds are superb swimmers and divers, their agility and speed in the water aided by lobed toes. They feed on aquatic invertebrates, small fish, amphibians, and aquatic vegetation. They pursue fish and other swimming prey underwater, and seize it with quick snaps of the bill. Grebes also have the unique habit of eating their own belly and flank feathers and also feed feathers to their young. The feathers protect the stomach lining from being pierced by sharp fish bones and also serve as the base

material for pellets of undigested bones, which are regurgitated and cast out of the mouth.

Grebes form long-lasting pair bonds, some of them lifelong. Bonds are solidified during the performance of displays, which include presenting nesting materials and paddling side by side across the water with bodies erect. Most grebes nest in solitary pairs. Both sexes build a floating platform nest of decaying vegetation that is anchored to emergent aquatic plants. Both parents incubate the clutch of 2–7 off-white eggs for 20–30 days, and lead the chicks to water as soon as the last egg hatches. Although chicks can swim and dive from birth, the parents swim with the chicks on their backs for up to 10 days after hatching. They will even dive with the chicks in position to escape from predators.

GENUS *PODICEPS*
Horned Grebe
Podiceps auritus
ALSO: Slavonian Grebe, Suglik, Grèbe esclavon, Ohrentaucher, Horndykker, Красношейная поганка. CN refers to the erectable head feathers of the breeding bird. SN means "eared grebe."
RANGE: Nests (May–Jun) around marshes, ponds, lakes, and streams in forests and steppes in Alaska, Canada, Iceland, nw Scotland, and across n Eurasia; irregular in sw Greenland.

Winters on bays, seacoasts, large rivers, and lakes in N Amer and Eurasia. **ID:** L 12–15 in (31–38 cm). Long, slender neck. Straight, pointed bill with a pale tip. Short peak at back of flat crown. Iris red. AD APR–AUG: Crown and back black. Erectable golden "horns" behind eye; fan of black cheek feathers. Foreneck, lores, upper breast, and flanks chestnut. Belly white. AD SEP–MAR: Slaty gray crown. White cheeks and foreneck. Nape and hindneck black. White secondaries; small white patch on upper forewing. JUV: Gray, with black and white striping on head. VOICE: Tremulous trill or squeal made during courtship display.

Red-necked Grebe

Podiceps grisegena
ALSO: Holboell's Grebe, Gray-cheeked Grebe, Roth-alstaucher, Grèbe jougris,
Gråstrupedykker, Серощекая поганка, Suglitchaurak. SN means "gray-cheeked grebe."
RANGE: Separate populations nest (May–Jul) in Europe, ne Asia, and N Amer around small lakes in forest and steppe, north to the treeline. Winters on marine waters, less frequently on inland lakes, south to s Europe and China, and along the N Amer coasts south to California and Virginia. Rare in Greenland, Iceland, Hawaii. **ID:** L 17–22 in (43–56 cm). Long, heavy, pointed, dark bill, with a yellow base. Iris dark brown. AD MAR–AUG: Black cap, with a slight crest. Pale gray cheek patch edged with white. Foreneck and upper breast chestnut. Back brownish black. Underparts white to pale gray. Wings dark; white patches on secondaries and leading edge. AD SEP–FEB: Black cap. Gray ear coverts. White crescent from chin to behind ear coverts. White to light gray foreneck. Dark hindneck and back. JUV: Neck tinged with rusty red. Cheeks striped in black and white. VOICE: Loud whinnying brays during courtship display.
HABITS: Highly territorial; makes underwater attack dives against waterbirds that enter its breeding territory. Pair-bonding ceremonies involve both birds extending their neck and body straight up from the water as they swim rapidly across the lake.

Gaviiformes: Loons and Divers

This order contains five living species of aquatic birds that occur in N Amer and n Eurasia.

FAMILY GAVIIDAE
LOONS AND DIVERS

Birds in this family are called *loons* in N Amer and *divers* in Europe. These large waterbirds have torpedo-shaped bodies, dagger-shaped bills, short narrow wings, and large, 3-toed, webbed feet, which are used for underwater propulsion. Their short legs are set so far back on the body that locomotion on land is reduced to pushing along on the belly. This awkward movement is the likely source of the word "loon," which stems from the Old English *lumme* or the Scandinavian *lom*, both of which mean "lame." The European common name "diver" refers to their method of foraging, which is to make a surface dive and then pursue prey underwater.

Loons are monogamous and pair bonds are maintained for several breeding seasons. Males are very vocal on the breeding grounds. Their haunting tremulous yodel can be heard from afar. Pairs also make a cackling call, *ha-ha-hara'*, which recalls the Russian name for these birds, *gagara* (гагара).

Both sexes participate in building a nesting mound on the shoreline of an islet or on a mat of floating vegetation. Both parents share in incubating the 2 brown to olive, spotted eggs for 24–28 days. A day after hatching, they lead their chicks to water. The young are fed by the adults and will often ride on a parent's back to keep warm. Parents aggressively defend their young until they fledge at 8–12 weeks of age.

GENUS *GAVIA*
Red-throated Loon

Gavia stellata
ALSO: Red-throated Diver,
Qaqsuq, Sterntaucher, Plongeon catmarin, Smålom, Краснозобая гагара.
SN means "starry [-backed] loon," a reference to the faintly-spotted back of the winter plumage.
RANGE: Circumpolar. Nests (May–Jul) on ponds on the coastal tundra. Northernmost nesting loon. Winters mainly in marine waters

ad. Sep–Feb

ad. Mar–Aug

Pacific Loon
Gavia pacifica
NE Siberia, N Amer
L 25–29 in (63–74 cm)

ad. Sep–Feb

ad. Mar–Aug

Arctic Loon
Gavia arctica
Eurasia, w Alaska
L 26–30 in (67–76 cm)

ad. Sep–Feb

ad. Mar–Aug

Red-throated Loon
Gavia stellata
Circumpolar
L 22–26 in (55–67 cm)

ad. Oct–Feb

ad. Mar–Sep

Common Loon
Gavia immer
N Amer, Greenland, Iceland,
n Europe
L 29–32 in (74–81 cm)

ad. Oct–Feb

Yellow-billed Loon
Gavia adamsii
N Eurasia, nw N Amer
L 30–35 in (76–90 cm)

ad. Mar–Sep

in sheltered bays and estuaries, south to Baja California, Florida, the Mediterranean, Black Sea, Caspian Sea, and coastal e Asia.

ID: L 22–26 in (55–67 cm). Smallest loon. Thin, upward angled bill. AD MAR–AUG: Blackish brown back. Velvety gray head and neck. Deep red throat. Black and white wavy lines run from the hind crown to the sides of the neck and breast. Underparts white. Iris red. AD SEP–FEB: Gray back, speckled with white. Throat and face white, with the white extending above the eyes; dark gray crown. Iris brown. VOICE: Breeding pairs join in a unique duet of high-pitched wails, yodels, quacks, and a grating, discordant *gay-or-worrk*. **HABITS:** Feeds largely on fish. This is the only loon species that forages away from its breeding pond. Adults fly to large lakes, estuaries, or the seacoast to forage and carry fish back to their young. Also unlike other loons, *Gavia stellata*

can take off from land and take off from water without making a running start. Migrates singly or in small flocks, which fly along the coast about a mile offshore.

Common Loon
Gavia immer

ALSO: Great Northern Diver, Black-billed Loon, Tuullik, Tuulligjuaq, Taatchinyik, Eistaucher, Plongeon huard, Islom, Полярная rarapa. SN means "blackened loon," a reference to the dark breeding plumage.

RANGE: Nests (May–Jul) on tundra and in forest-tundra near deep lakes in N Amer, Greenland, and Iceland. Winters on bays, marine channels, and occasionally lakes in the Aleutians and along the coasts of N Amer, Europe, and nw Africa. One breeding record at Bear Is, Svalbard.

ID: L 29 _32 in (74–81 cm). AD MAR–SEP: Black head, with a white collar and breast. Back black with white checkering. Underparts white. AD OCT–FEB: Brownish gray above; throat, breast, and underparts whitish. Faint white eyering. **VOICE:** Male's territorial cry is a poignant, far-carrying, tremulous yodel, *whe-ooo-quee' hoo-lii'*. **HABITS:** Feeds mainly on small fish; also takes crustaceans, mollusks, aquatic insects, leeches, frogs, and aquatic plants. Prefers clear water, as this species often swims along the surface with head partly submerged before diving as it looks for prey. Runs up to 325 ft (100 m) before taking flight from water. Builds its nest mainly on islands, but has also been known to lay eggs on sedge mats, cranberry bogs, tops of muskrat lodges, logs, or artificial nest sites.

Yellow-billed Loon

Gavia adamsii
ALSO: White-billed Diver, Gelbschnabeltaucher, Gulnebblom, Plongeon à bec

blanc, Белоклювая гагара, Tuutlik. SN means "Adams's Loon," after English naval surgeon Edward Adams (1824–1855), who discovered this loon while taking part in Sir John Ross's search for the lost expedition of Sir John Franklin.
RANGE: Nests (May–Jun) around large lakes and slow-flowing rivers on lowland tundra along the arctic coast of Russia, n Alaska, and nw Canada. Winters on bays and marine inlets

along the n Eurasian coast and the Pacific coast of N Amer. Casual in the Aleutians and on man-made reservoirs in the N Amer interior.
ID: L 30–35 in (76–90 cm). Largest loon. AD MAR–SEP: Black head, with white collar and breast. Back black with white checkering. Underparts white. AD OCT–FEB: Brownish gray, with white throat, breast, and underparts, partial white collar, and white around the eyes. Pale yellow, uptilted bill. **VOICE:** Like that of *Gavia immer*, but lower in pitch and executed more slowly. **HABITS:** Forages for fish, crustaceans, mollusks, and other aquatic organisms at the ice edge, diving beneath the ice in pursuit of prey. Nests on shores of clearwater lakes having a sandy or stony bottom. Nest is a depression or mound of mud, loosely lined with grass and moss. Migrates along the coastline in pairs or in loose, low-flying flocks.

Pacific Loon

Gavia pacifica
ALSO: Weißnackentaucher, Plongeon du Pacifique, Ameri-kastorlom, Белошейная

rarapa, Kaglulik, Malgi. SN means "Pacific loon." **RANGE:** Nests (Apr–Jun) on freshwater ponds and deep lakes on the tundra and taiga. Breeds on the Siberian coast from Yakutia to Chukotka, and in N Amer from Alaska across most of arctic Canada. Winters far offshore on the open ocean off the Pacific coasts of e Asia and N Amer.

Red-throated Loon on its nest
Truelove Lowlands, Devon Is, Canada

ID: L 25–29 in (63–74 cm). Dagger-shaped bill is held horizontal. AD MAR–AUG: Pale gray crown and nape; dark gray face; throat black with a purple gloss. Fine black and white lines on sides of neck and breast. Wings and back black, with black bars and blocks of white feathers on upper back. Front of breast and underparts white. Distinguished from *G. arctica* by black flank patch. AD SEP–FEB: Forehead, crown, and hindneck dark gray edged with a dark line. Sides of face and throat white, with a dark necklace under the chin. Dull blackish brown back. Breast and underparts white. **HABITS:** Forms large migratory flocks in fall.

Arctic Loon

Gavia arctica

ALSO: Black-throated Diver, Prachttaucher, Plongeon arctique, Storlom, Чернозобая гагара. SN means "Arctic loon."

RANGE: Nests (Apr–Jun) from n Eurasia to w Alaska on islets in lakes in the tundra, taiga,

and taiga-steppe. Winters in marine waters and large bodies of fresh water.

SUBSPECIES: BLACK-THROATED DIVER (B), *G. a. arctica*, breeds in the UK, Scandinavia, and east to the Lena Rvr in Siberia; winters from sw Europe east to Aral Sea. GREEN-THROATED LOON (G), *G. a. viridigularis*, breeds from east of the Lena Rvr to w Alaska at Cape Prince of Wales; winters to the Kurils and e Asia.

ID: L 26–30 in (67–76 cm). Dagger-shaped bill held horizontal or slightly uptilted. Flat-topped head. Distinguished from *G. pacifica* by the arching white panel on flanks. AD MAR–AUG: Velvety, pale gray crown and hindneck; foreneck black; throat black with greenish gloss. Sweeping lines of black and white down sides of neck and breast. Wings and back black, with distinct squares of white feathers. AD SEP–FEB: Forehead, crown, and hindneck dark gray, edged with a dark line. Sides of face, chin, throat, and upper breast white. Back black. Underparts white. **VOICE:** Far-carrying *cloo-ee' co-cloo-ee'*; harsh croaking, and gull-like wail also given when breeding.

Suliformes: Gannets, Cormorants, and Allies

Suliformes is an order proposed by the International Ornithologists' Union to include the gannets, cormorants, frigatebirds, and anhingas.

FAMILY SULIDAE
GENUS *MORUS*
Northern Gannet

Morus bassanus

ALSO: Solan Goose, Basstölpel, Fou de Bassan, Havsule, Северная олуша. CN derives from the Old English *ganote*, meaning "goose-like sea fowl." SN means "foolish seabird of Bass Rocks," referring to the site of a large gannet colony in the Firth of Forth, Scotland.

RANGE: Nests (Apr–Jun) on sea cliffs or small rocky coastal islands in the UK, Iceland, Faroes, Norway, and Canadian Atlantic coast. About 70 percent of the world population breeds in the UK, but largest colony (60,000 breeding pairs) is on Bonaventure Is, Gulf of St Lawrence, Canada. Winters south to the Mediterranean, nw Africa, and Florida and Gulf coasts.

ID: L 34–38 in (85–97 cm). AD: White, with black wing tips and golden crown. Heavy,

wedge-shaped, pale gray bill contrasts with the black lores. Distensible throat pouch. Short legs and webbed feet black. Iris pale blue. JUV: Slaty brown above; white spotting on upperwings and back. Attains adult plumage at 3–4 years of age. **HABITS:** Feeds on fish by diving into the water, often from more than 100 ft (30 m) in the air. Pulls its wings back and strikes the surface like an arrowhead, then swims underwater after prey. Nests in large colonies on sea cliffs, making a ground scrape rimmed with guano, seaweed, and feathers. Parents incubate the single egg under their feet. Chick is fed by the parents for 3 months, at which point it can weigh 50 percent more than the adults. At fledging, the chick jumps and glides to the water on outstretched wings. Unable to fly up from the sea because of excess weight and incompletely developed wing muscles, the fledgling disperses by swimming south to the waters of the mid-Atlantic.

FAMILY PHALACROCORACIDAE
CORMORANTS

Phalacrocorax is Latinized Greek for "bald raven." *Cormorant* derives from the Latin *corvus marinus*, meaning "sea crow." Both names reflect the belief of early taxonomists that cormorants were related to ravens and crows, possibly because of their black plumage.

Cormorants occupy both fresh- and saltwater habitats. Arctic species are primarily marine and nest along rocky seacoasts. They eat fish and marine invertebrates and catch prey through underwater pursuit.

These birds have an elongated body and a long, stiff-feathered tail. The legs are short, the 4-toed feet are webbed, and the bill is long, thin, and hooked. The cormorant's bare throat, or *gular pouch*, is distensible (able to expand). Adults have black plumage, with some species having white or glossy, iridescent patches of feathers. In nuptial plumage, many species develop head or neck plumes and brightly colored facial skin. Cormorants lack oil glands for waterproofing feathers and must stand on exposed perches with their wings spread out to dry.

Cormorants nest colonially on remote islets, cliff ledges, dead trees in standing water, or in similar sites where they are protected from predators. Both sexes build the nest. The nest of cliff-nesting cormorants is a ground scrape rimmed with guano, seaweed, sticks, feathers, and flotsam. Tree-nesting birds build a platform nest of sticks. Both parents incubate the 1–7 (usually 3–4) pale blue or green eggs for 23–35 days, holding the eggs between the breast and tops of the feet. Chicks are born naked and grow a covering of down after 7 days. The young are fed via partial regurgitation. They access fluid and food carried in the parent's pharyngeal pouch by inserting their bill into the adult's throat.

GENUS *PHALACROCORAX*
Great Cormorant
Phalacrocorax carbo
ALSO: Cormorant, Kor-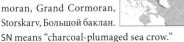
moran, Grand Cormoran,
Storskarv, Большой баклан.
SN means "charcoal-plumaged sea crow."

RANGE: Nests (Apr–May) along rocky seacoasts of e N Amer, Greenland, Iceland, and Europe, north to 74°N; winters to the US Gulf coast, and nw Africa. Other populations breed in se Asia, Australia, Tasmania, and New Zealand.
ID: L 30–37 in (77–94 cm). AD: Black with bluish iridescence. Wings have a greenish gloss; wing coverts and scapulars bronze with black margins. White thigh patch. Bill base and gular region yellow, with a posterior patch of white feathers. Short erectile crest on nape. Iris blue-green. Dark gray legs and feet. Breeding birds (Mar–Jun) develop orange facial skin above the gape and short white plumes on head and upper neck. JUV: Dark brown, with a white breast and belly.
HABITS: Surface dives and pursues prey underwater to depths of 65 ft (20 m). Normally feeds on small fish measuring under 10 in (25 cm), although *P. carbo* has been observed eating fish measuring 30 in (75 cm) long. Flies high, with slow wingbeats and kinked neck.
SIMILAR SPECIES: DOUBLE-CRESTED CORMO-RANT, *Phalacrocorax auritus*, overlaps the range of *P. carbo* on temperate Atlantic seacoasts; differentiated by smaller size and dark face.

European Shag
Phalacrocorax aristotelis
ALSO: Krähenscharbe,
Cormoran huppé, Toppskarv,
Хохлатый баклан. CN refers
to the bird's shaggy crest. SN means "Aristotle's sea crow," referring to the Greek philosopher.
RANGE: Nests (Mar–May) on rocky seacoasts in Iceland, UK, and n Scandinavia. Winters south to the Iberian Penin, Mediterranean, Morocco.
ID: L 27–31 in (68–78 cm). AD: Black, with green and purplish iridescence. Bare skin at base of bill bright yellow. Breeding birds develop a small crest of forward-curving feathers on the forecrown. JUV: Brown, with a mottled white neck and dark brown belly.
HABITS: Forages over sandy and rocky coastal seabeds, taking benthic, demersal, and schooling pelagic fish. Forms loose breeding colonies on sea cliffs, often with gulls, guillemots, and other cormorants. Nest is a mass of vegetation piled in a rock crevice, small cave, or next to a boulder.

Double-crested Cormorant
Phalacrocorax auritus
N Amer
L 33 in (84 cm)

juv.

ad.

ad.
Jul–Feb

Red-faced Cormorant
Phalacrocorax urile
N Pacific
L 29 in (74 cm)

Great Cormorant
Phalacrocorax carbo
N Atlantic
L 30–37 in (77–94 cm)

ad.
Mar–Jun

juv.

ad.

juv.

ad.
Feb–May

ad.
Feb–May

European Shag
Phalacrocorax aristotelis
Europe, Iceland
L 27–31 in (68–78 cm)

Pelagic Cormorant
Phalacrocorax pelagicus
N Pacific
L 25–29 in (64–74 cm)

juv.

subad.

ad.

Northern Gannet
Morus bassanus
Europe, Iceland, e N Amer
L 34–38 in (85–97 cm)

Diving for fish

Stretched-neck
sky-pointing
display

Pelagic Cormorant
Phalacrocorax pelagicus

ALSO: Baird's Cormorant, Cormoran pélagique, Meer-scharbe, Берингов баклан. SN means "marine sea crow."

RANGE: Nests (Mar–May) and largely resident on rocky seacoasts and islands from Alaska south to Baja California; in the Aleutian, Kuril, and Commander islands; on Wrangel Is; and along the Chukotka Penin south to Kamchatka, Sakhalin, and Taiwan.

ID: L 25–29 in (64–74 cm). Small head and very thin bill. AD: Black, with green and purple iridescence. Bare skin at base of bill is dull red. Breeding birds develop white patches on the flanks, double head crests, fine white neck plumes, and the red facial color intensifies. JUV: Dark brown overall.

HABITS: Forages on rocky substrates in sheltered and exposed inshore and intertidal waters. Feeds on fish, invertebrates, marine worms, and crustaceans taken from the seafloor. Nests on ledges of sea cliffs, in sea caves, and also on man-made structures.

SIMILAR SPECIES: RED-FACED CORMORANT, *P. urile*, is a non-arctic species that overlaps the range of *P. pelagicus* on cold to temperate Pacific seacoasts; distinguished by extensive red facial markings in breeding plumage.

Procellariiformes: Seabirds

This order includes the albatrosses, petrels, shearwaters, prions, storm petrels, and diving petrels. These birds are highly pelagic and come to land only to breed. They lay a single egg, experience a long period of immaturity, and have a long lifespan.

Procellariids are known as *tubenoses*, alluding to their external tubular nostrils. Albatrosses have a small tube on each side of the upper mandible, while petrels and others have united nasal tubes on top of the bill. The nostrils (*nares*) exude excess salt, which is removed from the body by a gland at the bill's base. Salty waste drips out of the nasal tubes, or is forcibly ejected in some species. The tubes open to an enlarged olfactory lobe of the brain, which suggests that smell plays an important role in the life of many seabird species. Most of the procellariids exude a musky odor derived from protein-rich oil they extract from marine prey and store in their stomach for later use. Recent studies indicate that most burrow-nesting species "sniff out" their nesting site and identify their mate by their distinctive smell.

FAMILY DIOMEDIDAE
ALBATROSSES

The family name Diomedidae refers to Diomedes, Greek warrior of myth whose companions were turned into seabirds. The name "albatross" can be traced from its Arabic origin *al-qudus* through the Spanish *arcaduz* and the Portuguese *alcatruz*, all meaning "bucket" and alluding to a waterbird, probably a pelican, which uses its expandable throat pouch as a sort of bucket. The word later was applied as a general name for large seafowl. In the narratives of his sea voyages, English buccaneer and navigator William Dampier (1651–1715) corrupted *alcatraz* into *algotross*. Later this was further distorted into *albatross*, perhaps through the influence of the Latin *alba*, meaning "white," which is the adult plumage color of most albatross species.

Albatrosses are the world's largest seabirds. They are distinguished by long narrow wings, a short tail, large webbed feet, and a strong, hooked bill with tubular nostrils on both sides of the upper mandible. Of the 21–24 recognized species, only 3 species, all in the genus *Phoebastria*, range into arctic waters. The Short-tailed, Laysan, and Black-footed albatrosses are restricted to the N Pacific, distanced from their southern relatives by the windless doldrums that encircle the equator. This geographic separation is an indication of the albatross's dependence on the wind for flight.

On calm days, albatrosses have to run across the water surface and flap their wings to become airborne. But on windy days, they simply open their wings and let the air currents lift them from the waves. They climb into the wind, stall out

ad.

Black-footed Albatross
Phoebastria nigripes
N Pacific
L 27–29 in (68–74 cm)

ad.

Laysan Albatross
Phoebastria immutabilis
N Pacific
L 31–32 in (79–81 cm)

subad.

juv.

ad.

Short-tailed Albatross
Phoebastria albatrus
N Pacific
L 33–37 in (84–94 cm)

Black-footed Albatross
Ad. and juv. plumages
similar

Short-tailed juv.

Short-tailed subad.

Laysan Albatross
Ad. and juv. plumages
similar

Short-tailed Albatross ad.

at an altitude where drag and body weight slow their ascent, then bank leeward and plummet down, gaining momentum. They glide across the ocean surface taking advantage of the uplift of individual waves before climbing into the wind again. This energy-efficient method of flight is called *dynamic soaring*.

With little perceptible movement of their wings, albatrosses can approach and easily round a ship making 14 knots. Effortless flight allows these birds to cover long distances when foraging for food, especially during breeding and adolescence, when the foraging range of most species covers thousands of miles of ocean. Albatrosses feed at night while swimming on the sea surface, where they prey on squid, fish, and krill. Some species follow ships for refuse and marine prey churned up in the wake. By day, they attend fishing trawlers and are attracted to the baited hooks of longlines, which results in the incidental hooking and drowning of thousands of albatrosses each year. Ingestion of floating plastic waste that clogs the digestion system of chicks and adults, predation by feral cats and rats, and the degradation of nesting habitat are other factors that threaten their survival.

Most albatrosses spend their adolescence exploring the vast open ocean. Young birds sometimes return to their natal colony, where they "practice" albatross courtship rituals and begin to select a mate. Once successful nesting is achieved, usually at 9–10 years of age, pairs form lifelong bonds and may continue to breed on the same site for several decades. Both sexes incubate the egg, and both brood and feed the chick. Because it takes many months to fledge a chick, most albatross species nest every other year.

GENUS *PHOFBASTRIA*
Laysan Albatross
Phoebastria immutabilis

ALSO: Gooney Bird, Laysan-albatros, Albatros de Laysan, Темноспинный альбатрос. SN means "unchanging prophetess," alluding to the similar juvenile and adult plumages. CN *Laysan* refers to a breeding colony in the nw Hawaiian Islands. *Gooney Bird* may derive from 19th-century

sailors' slang phrase "gooney fool," a reference to the birds' awkward landing methods. Military personnel on Midway Is during World War II probably popularized the name.

RANGE: Nests (Dec–Jun) on oceanic atolls and remote Pacific islands, mainly on Midway Atoll and Laysan Is in the Hawaiian chain; there are recently colonized breeding grounds in the main Hawaiian islands, Bonin islands, and on Guadalupe Is off Mexico. Post-breeders (Jul–Nov) migrate north through the Sea of Okhotsk and the Gulf of Alaska to concentrate north of 40°N in the Aleutians and Bering Sea (dark blue on map). Recorded at sea between 8°N–59°N and 132°E–105°W (pale blue on map). **ID:** L 31–32 in (79–81 cm). WS 77–80 in (195–203 cm). **AD:** Head, neck, and underparts white. Dark smudge in front of eye extends as a thin line behind the eye. Gray wash on cheeks. Bill pink, with gray hooked tip. Legs and feet flesh pink. Back and upperwing dark sooty brown. White vent; dark upper rump and dark tail band. Underwing has black leading edge and tip, and large black patches within the central white areas. **JUV:** Similar to adult, but lacks gray wash on cheeks and bill.

HABITS: Feeds mainly at night on squid taken by surface-seizing. Also forages by day, taking flying-fish eggs, fish, and crustaceans, and scavenging carrion and refuse from ships. Parents with nestlings tend to forage within 550 mi (900 km) of the breeding grounds. In later nesting stages, adults are known to forage as far as 1675 mi (2700 km) from the nest in trips lasting up to 17 days.

STATUS: Thousands of breeding Laysan albatrosses were lost in the 20th century to plume-hunters, and to military activity and airfield development on Midway Atoll in the Hawaiian chain. Vulnerable (IUCN).

Black-footed Albatross

Phoebastria nigripes
ALSO: Gooney Bird, Schwarz-fußalbatros, Albatros à pieds noirs, Svartfotalbatross, Черноногий альбатрос. SN means "black-footed prophetess."

RANGE: Nests (Dec–May) on oceanic Pacific islands, mainly on Midway Is and Laysan Is in the Hawaiian chain; small numbers nest in the main Hawaiian islands, and on Toroshima, Ogasawara, and Senkaku islands off Japan. Post-breeders (Jun–Aug) migrate into the N Pacific, moving to waters along the California coast. Some travel north into the Gulf of Alaska, Aleutians, and Bering Sea (dark blue on map), less frequently into the Sea of Okhotsk. Pelagic between 15°N–53°N latitude and 118°E–112°W longitude (pale blue on map).
ID: L 27–29 in (68–74 cm). WS 76–84 in (193–213 cm). AD: Dusky brown overall, with white rump and undertail coverts. Narrow white ring around the bill base and a white crescent under the eye. Bill dusky pink, with a dark gray base and tip. Legs and feet black. Iris blackish brown. JUV: Resembles adult, but has less white on the rump, undertail coverts, and around the bill base. Can be confused with first-year short-tailed albatrosses, which have large pink bills, pink legs, and pink feet.
HABITS: Feeds on squid, flying-fish eggs, and fish, taken by surface-seizing. Reported to snatch flying fish as they fly by and as they re-enter the water. Also scavenges ships' refuse, offal from fishing trawlers, and (rarely) floating carcasses of marine mammals. Makes epic journeys across the N Pacific. Satellite telemetry was used to track a Black-footed Albatross as it traveled a distance of 3150 mi (5067 km) in 35 days.

Short-tailed Albatross

Phoebastria albatrus
ALSO: Steller's Albatross, Golden Gooney, Kurz- schwanzalbatros, Albatros à queue courte, Gulhovudalbatross, Белоспинный альбатрос; the Japanese name, Ahodori, means "idiot bird," a reference to the ease with which plume-hunters could approach and kill nesting albatrosses. Described by German naturalist Peter Simon Pallas (1741–1811) from a specimen collected by Georg Wilhelm Steller (1709–1746). SN means "prophetess albatross."
RANGE: Nests (Oct–May) on Toroshima and Minami-kojima islands in s Japan, in open treeless areas with low or no vegetation. Nesting has also been reported on Bonin, Daito, and Ryukyu islands, Japan; Iwo Jima; and Agincourt Is, Taiwan. First successful nesting on Midway Is occurred in Nov 2010, with a single chick fledged in June 2011 despite being swept out of its nest by the tsunami that followed the Japanese earthquake of Mar 2011. Pelagic along the continental shelf margins of the Pacific Rim (darker blue), north to about 64°N, west to the Kurils, Sea of Okhotsk, and e China Sea, and south to about 20°N (pale blue on map). Breeding birds forage east of Honshu, Japan, mainly in places where the continental shelf ends and ocean depths increase markedly. Post-breeders disperse to waters off the Kurils and Kamchatka, later to upwellings along submarine canyons on the continental shelf edge of the Gulf of Alaska, Bering Sea, and Aleutians.
ID: L 33–37 in (84–94 cm). WS 84–90 in (213–229 cm). AD: Body white. Massive pink bill and pale legs. Head white, tinged with pale cinnamon and gold. Underwing white, with black leading and trailing edges. Upperwing coverts white; primaries, secondaries, and leading and trailing wing edges black. Tail white, with a terminal black band. JUV: First-year birds entirely dark brown. With age, plumage whitens on the belly and face; usually retains a dark brown collar. Underwing whitens and white patches appear on the upperwings, back, and tail. At sea, immature short-tailed albatrosses can be distinguished from juvenile black-footed albatrosses by their massive pink bill and pinkish legs.
HABITS: Feeds on squid, shrimp, and fish, taken by surface-seizing; also scavenges on offal and refuse from whaling and fishing vessels. Feeds mainly by day, either singly or in groups. Birds begin to breed at 5–6 years of age, after which most pairs breed annually. A single egg is laid in late Oct–Nov. Both sexes incubate the egg for 64–65 days. Chicks fledge about 5 months later.
STATUS: In 1933, fewer than 100 breeding pairs were known to exist on Toroshima due to activities of Japanese plume-hunters and continual volcanic eruptions at nesting colonies. Present population (2008) is about 2400 individuals, including approximately 500 breeding pairs.

FAMILY PROCELLARIIDAE
PETRELS AND SHEARWATERS

The family name derives from the Latin *procella*, meaning "gale," a fitting name as these birds are usually seen flying over rough waters of the open ocean.

These seabirds can easily be recognized by the pair of horny nasal tubes atop the bill. They feed on crustaceans, cephalopods, krill, and mollusks, taken at the surface or in shallow dives. The protein-rich stomach oil extracted from marine prey gives them a musky odor. Breeding is typically monogamous, with enduring pair bonds formed when birds are 5–6 years old. Both sexes build the nest, either on a bare cliff ledge or in a burrow. Females lay a single white egg once a year. Both sexes incubate the egg for about 7–8 weeks and both tend the young. Long-lived, with several species known to live over 30 years.

GENUS *FULMARUS*: This genus contains the fulmarine petrels, which have stout, deeply grooved, hooked, tubenose bills adapted for grasping and holding marine prey.

Northern Fulmar
Fulmarus glacialis

ALSO: Eissturmvogel, Fulmar boréal, Havhest, Глупыш. SN means "foul gull of the ice," referring to the species' musky odor and Arctic range.
RANGE: Nests (May–Sep) in burrows on sea cliffs of the northern oceans. Pelagic range extends between 40°N and 80°N; 1 record from Franz Josef Land (86°N). Irregular to Baja California.
SUBSPECIES: *F. g. glacialis* (G), breeds on Baffin Is, ne Greenland, Svalbard, Franz Josef Land; dark morph dominates. *F. g. auduboni* (A), breeds north to nw Greenland and Jan Mayen, south to UK and n Europe; pale morph dominates. *F. g. rodgersii* (R), breeds on coasts of e Siberia and Alaska Penin; dark morph dominates.
ID: L 17–20.5 in (43–52 cm). Heavy-bodied and bull necked. Stout stubby bill. Dark oval eye patch. Pale pink legs and feet. PALE MORPH: White head, neck, underparts, and tail. Mantle and upperwing pearl gray, with a flash of white on the primaries. DARK MORPH Dark gray overall, with a paler forehead and lores. Pale gray to whitish flash at base of primaries.
HABITS: Stiff flap-and-glide flight. Scavenges offal from fishing and whaling boats and also feeds on fish, squid, and plankton taken at the sea surface. Clutch is a single egg laid in a shallow scrape on inaccessible cliff faces, or occasionally in burrows dug into dunes or grassy slopes.

GENUS *PTERODROMA*: This genus contains the gadfly petrels, which are usually seen at a distance as they wheel over the open ocean in rapid, erratic flight.

Mottled Petrel

Pterodroma inexpectata
ALSO: Scaled Petrel, Regen- sturmvogel, Pétrel maculé, Søkeresultater, Тайфунник Пила. SN means "unexpected winged-runner," alluding to the swift, erratic fight. First described by German father and son Johann and Georg Forster, who served as naturalists on Captain James Cook's 1772–75 voyage to the S Pacific.
RANGE: Pacific transequatorial migrant. Nests (Oct–Apr) in New Zealand. Post-breeders disperse through the c Pacific to the Bering Sea, concentrating in the Gulf of Alaska and Aleutians (Apr–Aug) before returning south.
ID: L 13–14 in (33–36 cm). Upperparts mottled gray, with a dark M mark across wings and back. Face white, with dark eye patch and mottled gray cap. Dark gray belly. Dark diagonal slash across white underwing. Legs pink. VOICE: High pitched *te-te-te-te* sounded repeatedly in flight.
HABITS: Highly pelagic, rarely approaching land except to nest. Does not follow ships. Feeds mostly on small fish and squid.

GENUS *PUFFINUS*: This genus contains the shearwaters, which have long, slender, hooked bills with a low, united nasal tube atop the bill. These seabirds feed on small schooling fish, squid, krill, and offal taken by surface-seizing or by plunge diving from low heights, then pursuing prey underwater.

Mottled Petrel
Pterodroma inexpectata
Pacific transequatorial migrant
L 13–14 in (33–36 cm)

Dark morph

Pale morph

Northern Fulmar
Fulmarus glacialis
Northern oceans
L 17–20.5 in (43–52 cm)

Buller's Shearwater
Puffinus bulleri
Pacific transequatorial
migrant
L 16–17 in (41–43 cm)

Manx Shearwater
Puffinus puffinus
Atlantic transequatorial
migrant
L 12–15 in (30–38 cm)

Uniformly pale
underwing

Flash of silver
on underwing

Short-tailed Shearwater
Puffinus tenuirostris
Pacific transequatorial
migrant
L 16–17 in (41–43 cm)

Sooty Shearwater
Puffinus griseus
Pacific/Atlantic transequatorial
migrant
L 16–20 in (41–50 cm)

Manx Shearwater

Mottled Petrel

Short-tailed Shearwater

Northern Fulmar
Pale morph

Buller's Shearwater

Sooty Shearwater

Manx Shearwater

Puffinus puffinus
ALSO: Schwarzschnabel-Sturmtaucher, Puffin des Anglais, Havlire, менський буревісник. CN refers to a shearwater breeding colony on Skokholm Is near the Isle of Man in the Irish Sea. SN comes from the Middle English *pophyn*, a word denoting the cured carcasses of nestling shearwaters (not puffins). The genus was first applied by 17th-century English naturalists John Ray and Francis Willughby.
RANGE: Atlantic transequatorial migrant. Northernmost breeding shearwater. Nests (Feb–Aug) in burrows in Iceland, Faroes, UK, France, Azores, Madeira, and Newfoundland. Summer pelagic range extends to about 69°N; casual off s Greenland. Post-breeders migrate to winter in waters off Brazil, Argentina, Uruguay, and s Chile—a distance of 6200 mi (10,000 km) from their breeding grounds. Casual off S Africa.
ID: L 12–15 in (30–38 cm). Blackish upperparts. White underparts and white wing linings. Black cap extends to below the eye. Bill is long, slender, straight, hooked at tip, with a low nasal tube.
HABITS: Nests colonially. Parents incubate the single egg for 47–66 days. Six days after hatching, the parents leave the burrow, returning each night to feed the chick. The chick fledges at 69 days and makes its way independently to the sea.

Manx shearwaters were used in the first demonstration of long-range homing in birds. On June 2, 1952, two adult birds were taken from their nesting burrows on Skokholm Is. They were banded, taken by train to London, and flown to Boston's Logan Airport. One bird died in passage. The surviving shearwater was released at the end of the Logan Airport runway the next morning. It was found back in its burrow on Skokholm on June 16, after making a flight of 3200 mi (5150 km) in 12.5 days.

Sooty Shearwater

Puffinus griseus
ALSO: Titi, Muttonbird, Dunkler Sturmtaucher, Puffin fuligineux, Grålire, Сірий буревісник. SN means "gray shearwater."

RANGE: Pacific and Atlantic transequatorial migrant. Nests (Sep–May) in burrows in New Zealand, Australia, Tasmania, s Chile, s Argentina, and Falklands. PACIFIC: Post-breeders trace giant figure-8s around the Pacific, taking advantage of prevailing winds along the 39,000-mi (65,000-km) migration route. Birds fly northeast along the Pacific coast of S Amer, then fly northwest to Japan and Kamchatka Mar–May. They move east to the Aleutians and Alaska in Jun–Jul and south to the California coast in Aug, returning to breeding grounds via the c Pacific in Sep–Oct. ATLANTIC: Argentine and Falkland post-breeders make a circular migration around the Atlantic, flying up the e coast of N Amer in May and spending Aug–Oct in European waters. They then fly south along the w African coast, and turn southwest, reaching their S Atlantic nesting grounds by Nov.
ID: L 16–20 in (41–50 cm). Dark sooty to grayish brown. Median and greater underwing coverts silvery white; lesser coverts, primaries, and secondaries are dark, creating a dark border around the silvery underwing. Black bill. Legs and feet dark, with lilac webbing between the toes.
HABITS: Gregarious at sea, forming flocks of tens of thousands. Flies low over the water, with 3–7 quick, stiff-winged flaps followed by a glide of 3–5 seconds; glide is arcing and banked in strong winds. Feeds on fish, squid, and krill taken by surface-seizing or plunge diving to average depths of 46 ft (14 m). Does not follow ships. Marginally attracted to feeding flocks around boats throwing chum, but seldom joins the flock or dives for sinking scraps.
USE: Chicks are harvested from their NZ burrows and their meat sold fresh or pickled in brine.

Short-tailed Shearwater

Puffinus tenuirostris
ALSO: Slender-billed Shearwater, Yolla, Moonbird, Muttonbird, Kurzschwanz-Sturmtaucher, Puffin à bec grêle, Smalnebblire, Тонкоклювый буревестник. SN means "slender-billed shearwater."
RANGE: Pacific transequatorial migrant. Nests (Nov–Apr) in burrows in se Australia

and Tasmania. Post-breeders disperse north past Japan to the Aleutians (May–Jun); some move north into the Bering and Chukchi seas (Jul–Aug). Return migration along the N Amer Pacific coast (Sep–Oct) is followed by rapid flight to Australia via the c Pacific. Some juveniles stay on the Oregon–California coasts through winter. **ID:** L 16–17 in (41–43 cm). AD: Sooty brown to brownish gray overall. Gray underwing coverts. Indistinct dark cap. Whitish chin. Short, thin bill. JUV: Pale throat and breast. Contrasting dark helmet. Evenly pale underwings. **HABITS:** Attracted to boats throwing chum. Unlike *P. griseus,* dives for sinking scraps. Rapid and erratic flight, with little smooth gliding and arcing, and with frequent change of direction. Feet extend beyond the tail in flight. **USE:** Chicks (muttonbirds) are harvested from their burrows. Down and feathers are used to stuff pillows and bedding; the rich stomach oil is extracted and purified for pharmaceutical use; and the meat is sold fresh or pickled in brine.

Buller's Shearwater

Puffinus bulleri
ALSO: Gray-backed or New Zealand Shearwater, Graunacken-Sturmtaucher, Puffin de Buller, Grårygglire, Буллеров буревестник. SN means "Buller's shearwater," honoring New Zealand ornithologist Sir Walter Lawry Buller (1838–1906).
RANGE: Pacific transequatorial migrant. Nests (Oct–Apr) in burrows or rock crevices on forested slopes in the Poor Knights Is, New Zealand. Post-breeders disperse (May–Sep) across the Pacific Ocean, north to the Aleutians and Alaska, and south to c Chile before returning south.
ID: L 16–17 in (41–43 cm). Dark pattern across the mantle and upperwings appears as a broken black M with light gray interspersing bands. Dark gray cap extends to the eye and contrasts with the white cheeks. Underparts white. Tail wedge-shaped. Dark bill and iris.
HABITS: Feeds mainly on fish, squid, and krill, taken by surface-seizing. Occasionally follows fishing trawlers, joining a mixed-species feeding flock.

STATUS: Once used as a food source by the Maori. In recent times, colonies have suffered massive predation by feral pigs. By the 1930s, only 200 pairs were known to nest at the main colony on Aorangi Is, NZ. Conservation efforts have resulted in the population recovering to 200,000 pairs in the 1980s; estimated world population today is 2.5 million birds. Vulnerable (IUCN).

FAMILY HYDROBATIDAE
STORM PETRELS

The storm petrels' distinctive foraging posture is reflected in their family name Hydrobatidae, which means "water-walker." These birds peck at plankton, carrion, and bits of fat and oil floating on the sea surface while hovering or foot-pattering, with long legs extended and wings partly spread. George Edwards, an 18th-century English naturalist and artist, wrote: "They flutter so near the Surface of the Water that they seem to walk on it, for which Reason…they are called Peterils, because they imitate Peter's walking on the Sea."

Storm petrels are also called "sea swallows" because their shape and flight resemble those of true swallows.

Early mariners called these birds "stormy petrels," because they often appeared in advance of strong storms. Portuguese and Spanish fishermen caught in small boats during storms would invoke the help of the Virgin Mary by calling out *Mata Cara.* The phrase was corrupted into Mother Carey and storm petrels became Mother Carey's chickens. Mother Carey, by the way, was the fabled spouse of Davey Jones. Some say she held the key to his locker.

Storm petrels are the smallest seabird species, having an average weight of 1.5 oz (42.5 g). Their nostrils are united in a single tube on the bill. Drops of saline solution secreted by a gland at the bill base are ejected through the tubes as the bird faces into the wind. The nasal tube is attached to the olfactory lobe of the brain, thus enhancing the sense of smell. These birds are thought to locate their nesting burrow by its distinctive musky odor and may also use smell to locate food at sea.

Storm petrels are highly pelagic and are most often seen flying low over the open ocean far from land. They return to land only to breed in colonies located on remote islands and seacoasts. They nest in burrows or rock crevices. Breeding is monogamous. Pairs form enduring bonds and often use the same nest site for successive years. The female lays a single white egg that can weigh up to 30 percent of her weight. Both parents incubate the egg for 5–8 weeks and feed the chick in the burrow for 8–10 weeks or more. Adults typically abandon the chick before it fledges and return to the open ocean until the next breeding season. Fledglings make their way independently to the sea. Juvenile mortality rates are high, but adults can live for over 20 years.

SUBFAMILY HYDROBATINAE

Hydrobatinae contains the genera *Hydrobates* and *Oceanodroma*. Birds in this subfamily are found in the oceans of the N Hemisphere. They have forked or wedge-shaped tails, relatively long wings, and short legs.

GENUS *HYDROBATES*
European Storm Petrel

Hydrobates pelagicus
ALSO: Stormy Petrel, Sturm-schwalbe, Pétrel tempête, Havsvale, Британская качурка. SN means "ocean water-walker."
RANGE: Nests (May–Jul) in rock crevices and burrows on offshore islands and sea stacks in the Faroes, UK, Ireland, Iceland, Norway, and France. Winters at sea south to the African coast.
ID: L 6 in (15 cm). Blackish brown. Square white rump. Square tail. White stripe across underwing

coverts. Faint pale band on the upperwing coverts is visible only at close range.
HABITS: Fluttering, bat-like flight, with a series of fast, shallow wingbeats followed by short glides. Feeds on zooplankton, small fish, squid, jellyfish, and carrion. Sometimes follows ships.

GENUS *OCEANODROMA*
Fork-tailed Storm Petrel

Oceanodroma furcata
ALSO: Gabelschwanz-Wellenläufer, Océanite à queue fourchue, Gråstorm-svale, Серая вилохвостая качурка. SN means "forked-tailed ocean-walker."
RANGE: Nests colonially (Apr–Aug) in rock crevices or burrows along the n Pacific Rim, from the Kuril and Commander islands east across the Aleutians and south along the Pacific coast of N Amer to Oregon and n California. Widespread and abundant in winter on open oceans between 35°N and 55°N.
ID: L 9 in (22 cm). Bluish gray upperparts. Dark gray forehead; black ear patch. Pearl gray underparts contrast with blackish underwing coverts. Notched tail, often with a white outer margin and dark tip. Bill and legs black.
HABITS: Forages in small, same-species flocks at sea. Feeds on planktonic crustaceans, small fish, squid, and offal taken while foot-pattering. Sometimes ducks under the sea surface to capture prey. Low flight, with shallow, rowing wingbeats interspersed with short, stiff-winged glides. Follows ships and attends fishing vessels. Attracted by ships' lights at night; frequently lands on deck.

Leach's Storm Petrel

Oceanodroma leucorhoa
ALSO: Carrie Chicks, Wellenläufer, Océanite cul-blanc, Stormsvale, Северная качурка. SN means "white-rumped sea-walker." CN honors British zoologist and marine biologist William Elford Leach (1790–1836).
RANGE: Nests colonially (May–Sep) in burrows and rock crevices on remote islands in the N Pacific from Japan to the Aleutians and Alaska,

Leach's Storm Petrel
Oceanodroma leucorhoa
N Pacific and N Atlantic
L 8 in (20 cm)

Fork-tailed Storm Petrel
Oceanodroma furcata
N Pacific
L 9 in (22 cm)

Wilson's Storm Petrel
Oceanites oceanicus
Atlantic/Pacific transequatorial migrant
L 7 in (18 cm)

European Storm Petrel
Hydrobates pelagicus
NE Atlantic
L 6 in (15 cm)

and south to Mexico, and in the N Atlantic from e N Amer east to the Faroes, Scotland, and Norway. Baccalieu Is, off Newfoundland, Canada, has the largest colony with an estimated 3 million breeding pairs. Winters at sea near and south of the equator.

ID: L 8 in (20 cm). Dark brown. Pale gray band on upperwing. White rump, with a faint dark line bisecting it; some ne Pacific birds have dark rumps. Long, angled wings. Forked tail.

HABITS: Buoyant, bounding, erratic flight. Strictly nocturnal when breeding. Feeds mainly on zooplankton, also on bioluminescent lantern fish (myctophids) that rise to the sea surface at night in waters over the continental slope. Does not follow ships. Long-lived; average lifespan is 20 years with a maximum of 36 years.

SUBFAMILY OCEANITINAE

Storm petrels in the subfamily Oceanitinae have elongated skulls, short wings, long legs, and square tails. These storm petrels range in the southern oceans, the sole exception being Wilson's Storm Petrel, *Oceanites oceanicus*, which regularly migrates into the N Hemisphere.

GENUS *OCEANITES*
Wilson's Storm Petrel
Oceanites oceanicus

ALSO: Sturmschwalbe, Océanite tempête, Wilson-stormsvale, Прямохвостая качурка. SN means "son of the sea-god Oceanus." CN honors Scottish-American ornithologist and naturalist Alexander Wilson (1766–1813), who wrote and illustrated the 9-volume *American Ornithology*, which depicted 268 species of birds, 26 of which had not previously been described.

RANGE: Transequatorial migrant. Nests (Nov–May) in the Antarctic. Spends the rest of the year at sea, moving into the northern oceans (Jun–Oct) as far as 60°N latitude in the Atlantic and to about 24°N in the Pacific and Indian oceans.

ID: L 7 in (18 cm). Blackish brown. Pale bar on upperwing. White U-shaped rump extends to the lateral undertail coverts. Square tail. Long legs; feet extend beyond tail tip.

HABITS: Flies low over the water. Follows ships and fishing trawlers, tracing zigzag patterns across the vessel's wake.

Charadriiformes: Alcids, Shorebirds, Skuas, Gulls, and Terns

Charadriiformes comprises a diverse assortment of wading, swimming, and diving birds of worldwide distribution. Birds in this order live in a variety of habitats ranging from coastal waters and beaches to inland meadows and lakes. They are united mainly by anatomical similarities of the palate, voice organ (*syrinx*), and muscles. Sexes are alike. Plumages range from black and white to shades of brown. Many species have distinctive bright markings on the body or bill when breeding.

FAMILY ALCIDAE
AUKS, MURRES, GUILLEMOTS, PUFFINS

These seabirds, which are often collectively referred to as *alcids*, occur in temperate and polar oceans of the N Hemisphere. Many alcids bear scientific names derived from Scandinavian common names, this because the species were named by Carolus Linnaeus (1707–1778), the Swede who laid the foundation for the modern scheme of binomial nomenclature.

Alcids are pelagic in winter and go to land only to breed. Most species are monogamous, with strong mate and nest site fidelity. These birds have legs set well back on the body and stand with the lower portion of the leg resting flat on the ground. They feed on fish, crustaceans, and zooplankton taken in wing-propelled pursuit diving. All have physiological adaptations for deep diving, including tissues with enhanced oxygen-storing capacity and the ability to employ anaerobic respiration during long dives. Their stiff, short wings allow them to "fly" underwater—an adaptation that comes at the expense of easy flight through the air. They are unable to maintain loft at slow speeds, and thus must fly with continuous whirring wingbeats.

Perhaps the most famous alcid is the extinct Great Auk, *Pinguinus impennis,* which once bred on islands in the nw Atlantic. This large flightless seabird resembled the Razorbill, but stood about 32 in (81 cm) high and weighed around 11 lb (5 kg). For many early Arctic cultures, the meat of the Great Auk was an important food source, and the skins and bones were symbolic items in burial and religious ceremonies. High European demand for the Great Auk's eggs, meat, and down largely extirpated the species by the early 19th century. Museums and private collectors raced to acquire the skins and eggs of the increasingly rare bird, and the trend led to extinction of the species. The last known living pair of great auks

was killed by fishermen at Eldey Is off the coast of Iceland on July 3, 1844. While pursuing the adults, one of the men stepped on the egg the female had been incubating and crushed it with his boot, thus ending the line of great auks. There were rumored sightings of great auks for several years after, but a record of a bird spotted in 1852 in Newfoundland, Canada, is considered to be the last sighting of the species.

GENUS *ALLE*
Dovekie
Alle alle

ALSO: Little Auk, Krabbentaucher, Mergule nain, Alkekonge, Appaliarsuk, Люрик. CN is a Scots word for "little dove." SN is Swedish for "seabird."
RANGE: Nests (Jun–Aug) to 82°N in Greenland, Iceland, Jan Mayen, Novaya and Severnaya Zemlya, Bear Is, Svalbard, and Franz Josef Land; small colonies on e Baffin Is, Little Diomede and possibly other islands in the Bering Sea; major breeding concentrations in nw Greenland. Winters at sea around polynyas and at the edge of pack ice, and south to Long Is (US) and France.
ID: L 8–10 in (20–25 cm). Tiny, chunky, and short-necked. **AD APR–SEP:** Black head and upperparts. White streaks on the scapulars and tips of secondaries. Underparts white. Stubby black bill. **AD WINTER:** Black bib replaced by a wide white crescent from chin to behind the eye. **JUV:** Dark brown back, with pale chin and belly.
HABITS: Flocks forage mainly at the ice edge, taking planktonic crustaceans, small fish, and mollusks. Makes wing-propelled dives to depths of 65 ft (20 m). Nests colonially in burrows, rock crevices, or on open cliff ledges. Both parents incubate a single bluish white egg for 28–31 days. Parents feed the chick by regurgitating food

ad. winter

ad. summer

1st winter

Dovekie
Alle alle
Arctic Ocean, N Atlantic
L 8–10 in (20–25 cm)

ad. winter

ad. Apr–Sep

ad. winter

ad. summer

ad. winter

Bridled morph
ad. Apr–Aug

Common Murre
Uria aalge
Circumpolar
L 15–18 in (38–46 cm)

ad. winter

ad. winter

fledgling

ad. Apr–Sep

ad. summer

Thick-billed Murre
Uria lomvia
Circumpolar
L 16–18 in (41–46 cm)

ad. winter

1st winter

ad. winter

ad. summer

Razorbill
Alca torda
N Atlantic
L 15–17 in (38–43 cm)

ad. Apr–Aug

they carry in a specialized sublingual throat pouch. This is the only Atlantic alcid to use this method; all other Atlantic auks carry live food to their nestlings in their bill. Fledglings and adults abandon the colony in a synchronized departure in late Aug, leaving their burrows at night to avoid predation by gulls. The male parent continues to feed the fledgling at sea for a month or more until it can feed independently.

GENUS *ALCA*
Razorbill
Alca torda

ALSO: Tordalk, Petit Pingouin, Tordmule, Alke, Гагарка. SN derives from the Norwegian and Swedish names for this species. CN refers to the laterally compressed bill.
RANGE: Nests (May–Jul) on rocky islands and steep sea cliffs in ne N Amer, Greenland, Iceland (major breeding concentration), Faroes, Jan Mayen, UK, Norway, Baltic Sea, and nw Russia; small colonies in France and Germany. Winters in ice-free seas south to New York and Morocco.
ID: L 15–17 in (38–43 cm). Large head; short thick neck; long pointed tail. AD APR–AUG: Blackish head, neck, and back. White underparts. Large, laterally compressed, black bill; vertical white band near the tip and white stripe from base of upper beak to the eye. AD WINTER: Chin, throat, and ear coverts white. JUV: Bill lacks white bands.
HABITS: Feeds on schooling fish taken in wing-propelled dives to 325 ft (100 m) or more; also eats crustaceans and polychaete bristle worms. Breeds colonially on sea cliffs, nesting between boulders or in shallow caves or rock fissures; occasionally uses vacant puffin burrows. Single, 3 in (7.6 cm), off-white to greenish, darkly blotched egg is laid on bare ground or on a small pile of pebbles, vegetation, feathers, and flotsam. Both parents incubate the egg for 34–38 days, with egg tucked between wing and body. Parents carry several fish held crosswise in the bill and feed them one by one to the nestling. The half-grown chick fledges at 18–22 days and leaves the colony with the male parent, which feeds the young bird until it attains adult mass and has fully formed wing and tail feathers.

GENUS *URIA*: The mid-sized, slender, long-necked auks contained in this genus are known as *murres* in N Amer and *guillemots* in Europe (not to be confused with the guillemots in the genus *Cepphus*).

These seabirds nest in large colonies on bare cliff ledges, often using the same nesting ledge as other auk and seabird species. The clutch is a single, large, 3.25 in (8 cm) long, pear-shaped egg, which is pointed at one end and rounded at the other. An egg of this shape rotates in a tight circle rather than rolling off the nesting ledge. The shape also permits maximum exposure to the parent's brood patch (an area of bare skin on the belly). The murre incubates its egg while standing semi-upright. Parents use color and markings to identify their egg. Eggs show remarkable variation, ranging from dark green or turquoise with black spots and streaks to solid buff or cream. Both parents share in incubating the egg for 26–39 days. As the chick begins to pip, parents and chick call to one another—the initiation of vocal recognition, which enables the parents and chick to locate each other in the colony and later at sea. Both parents feed the nestling a single fish at a time, carrying it lengthwise and tail first in the bill. For a few days before the chicks fledge, adults congregate at the base of the cliffs and call to their young. The fledgling flutters or jumps down to the cliff base and enters the water, joining the male parent, which nurtures it for a month or two at sea until the young bird can feed independently.

Common Murre
Uria aalge

ALSO: Guillemot, Akpak, Trottellumme, Guillemot marmette, Тонкоклювая кайра, Lomvi. SN derives from the Greek word for "waterbird" and the Danish word for "auk."
RANGE: Nests (May–Aug) on coasts and islands along the Pacific Rim from the Sea of Okhotsk and Bering Sea to Alaska and Brit Columbia, and in the N Atlantic from ne N Amer, Greenland, Iceland, and Faroes to n Europe, Novaya Zemlya, and Svalbard. Winters at sea over continental shelf waters, south to Japan, California, and Spain.

ID: L 15–18 in (38–46 cm). Slender and long-necked. Long straight bill. AD APR–AUG: Blackish brown upperparts and head. Head and foreneck meet the white upper breast in shallow, inverted "U." Underparts white; brown striations on flanks. Bill and legs black. Atlantic bridled morph has a white eyering and white post-ocular line. AD WINTER: Throat, chin, and sides of face white, with a black post-ocular line.

HABITS: Forages in mixed species flocks, diving to depths of 325 ft (100 m) in search of fish, euphausiids, copepods, and squid. Flies low over the water, with rapid wingbeats and with neck extended. Nest is a bare ground scrape or a small pile of pebbles and sticks.

Thick-billed Murre
Uria lomvia

ALSO: Brünnich's Guillemot, Akpa, Dickschnabellumme, Guillemot de Brünnich, Polarlomvi, Толстоклювая кайра. SN means "diving bird" in Swedish. Alternate CN honors Danish zoologist Morten Thrane Brünnich (1737–1827), author of *Ornithologia Borealis*.

RANGE: Nests (Jun–Aug) on seacoasts; in the N Pacific from Kamchatka, Chukotka, and Aleutians to Alaska and Brit Columbia; in the N Atlantic from e Canada, Greenland, and Iceland to Norway; and in the Arctic Ocean at Svalbard, Novaya Zemlya, Taimyr Penin, New Siberian Is, and Wrangel Is. Winters at sea south of breeding areas.

Digges Is, located in Hudson Bay, has one of the largest thick-billed murre colonies in the Canadian Arctic. Henry Hudson provisioned his ship *Discovery* here in 1610 and feasted on the murres. After spending a cold winter at James Bay, Hudson's disgruntled crew mutinied and cast Hudson, his son John, and 7 loyalists adrift in an open boat. They were never seen again. The crew sailed to Digges Is to feed on murres once more, but encountered an Inuit hunting party that killed several of the sailors. The surviving men made a safe return to England but were arrested there and hanged as mutineers.

ID: L 16–18 in (41–46 cm). Large, stocky auk. Thick black bill, with a diagnostic white line on cutting edge of upper beak. AD APR–AUG: Dark above, white below. Upperparts deeply black (Pacific) or brownish to dark gray (N Atlantic and Siberia). Dark neck meets the white breast in an inverted V. AD WINTER: Dark cheeks and hindneck contrast with white chin, throat, and foreneck. Flanks and underparts white.

HABITS: Dives to average depths of 30 ft (10 m) in pursuit of schooling, bottom, and deepwater fish; also feeds on amphipods, euphausiids, squid, and annelid worms. Forages as far as 100 mi (170 km) from the breeding colony.

GENUS *CEPPHUS*: This genus contains the guillemots, black-and-white-plumaged seabirds that fly low over the water with rapid wingbeats. They feed primarily on bottom-dwelling fish and small invertebrates.

Guillemots breed in solitary pairs or in small colonies on rocky seacoasts and coastal islands in the northern oceans, nesting in rock cavities, vacant puffin or rabbit burrows, among boulders, under driftwood, or in similar sites that offer protection from predators. Unlike most of the other alcids, guillemots have a clutch of 2 eggs instead of one. Both parents incubate the eggs for 28–30 days. The parents brood the hatchlings for about a week, then fly out to sea to feed at night. They return to the nest each morning with fish held crosswise in the bill. Chicks fledge at about 42 days, and flutter or tumble down to the sea, where they disperse independently.

Black Guillemot
Cepphus grylle

ALSO: Sea Pigeon, Tystie, Greenland Dove, Gryllteiste, Guillemot à miroir, Teist, Pittiulaaq, Чистик, Inyagik. SN derives from the Greek *kepphos*, meaning "seabird," and *gryssla*, the Swedish name for this species.

RANGE: Nests (May–Jul) along rocky coasts and offshore islands in ne Canada, s Greenland, Iceland, Faroes, Jan Mayen, Svalbard, UK, Scandinavia, Baltic Sea, arctic Russia, and from Chukotka and Bering Strait islands to n Alaska and Yukon. Winters in shallow coastal waters, around polynyas, ice edge, and leads in pack ice.

ID: L 13–15 in (32–38 cm). AD MAR–AUG: Sooty black, with a solid white patch on the upper wing. White underwing linings. Slender black bill; vermilion mouth lining. Bright red legs. AD WINTER: Head and underparts mostly white. Crown, lores, and back are mottled dark gray and white. ARCTIC MORPH WINTER: Pure white, with dark flight feathers.

HABITS: Forages in shallow inshore waters for benthic fish such as sculpins and blennies; takes polar cod and krill in drift ice. Clutch is 2 pale bluish green, spotted eggs.

Pigeon Guillemot

Cepphus columba
ALSO: Taubenteiste, Bering-
teiste, Guillemot colombin,
Тихоокеанский чистик.
SN means "dove-like seabird."

RANGE: Nests (May–Jul) on rocky seacoasts in Chukotka, Kamchatka, Kuril and Commander islands, Aleutians, and from Alaska south to California. Winters mainly in sheltered inshore waters near breeding colonies; sea ice forces northernmost populations south in winter.
ID: L 13–14 in (33–36 cm). AD APR–AUG: Sooty black. White upperwing patch broken by a black triangular band. Dusky underwing linings. Slender black bill, with red mouth lining. Legs coral red. AD WINTER: Head and neck white, with variable dusky markings on crown and nape. Upperparts mottled gray and white.
HABITS: Feeds on bottom-dwelling fish, crabs, shrimp, and occasionally gastropods and mollusks. Dives to depths of 150 ft (45 m). Probes for prey in recesses and vegetation in rocky areas on the ocean floor. Clutch is 2 off-white eggs.

Spectacled Guillemot

Cepphus carbo
ALSO: Sooty Guillemot,
Ring-eyed Scoot, Bridled
Guillemot, Brillenteiste,

Guillemot à lunettes, Brilleteist, Очковый
чистик. SN means "sooty guillemot."
RANGE: Nests (May–Jun) on the rocky coasts along the Sea of Okhotsk, Sakhalin, Kurils, and n Japan. Winters mainly in coastal waters

near breeding grounds, with some southward dispersal into the Sea of Japan.
ID: L 15–16 in (38–40 cm). AD MAR–AUG: Sooty black. Conspicuous white spectacles, short post-ocular stripe, and white feathering around the bill base. Legs and mouth lining coral red. AD WINTER: Upperparts uniformly sooty black. Chin, throat, sides of neck and underparts white. Retains white spectacles. VOICE: Shrill *fi-fi-fee-fee* in breeding season.
HABITS: Dives to depths of 165 ft (50 m). Feeds on or near sandy sea bottoms, taking fish such as sand lances, sculpins, and tidepool gunnels, and small octopus and crabs. Nests in holes and crevices on sheer sea cliffs and steep rocky slopes.

GENUS *BRACHYRAMPHUS*: The genus contains the murrelets—small, stocky auks endemic to the N Pacific. These seabirds feed on small and larval fish, krill, and other marine invertebrates. Their short, stiff wings are better adapted for "flying" underwater than flying through the air. In order to remain aloft, murrelets must fly fast, often at 40 mph (64 kmh) or more, with rapid whirring wingbeats. Murrelets are unable to take off from the ground and have difficulty taking off from the water. As a result, most birds choose to dive underwater rather than fly away from an approaching boat.

Marbled Murrelet

Brachyramphus marmoratus
ALSO: Fogbird, Foglark,
Marmelalk, Guillemot
marbré, Marmordvergteist,

Длинноклювый пыжик. Also known as the "enigma of the Pacific" because of its secretive and elusive nesting habits; the first verified ground and tree nests in N Amer were reported from Big Basin Redwoods State Park, CA, in 1974, and from E Amatuli Is, Alaska, in 1978. SN means "short-beaked marbled [murrelet]."
RANGE: Nests (Apr–Aug) on forested and rocky islands and mainland coasts in the Aleutians, Alaska, and w Canada, south to Santa Cruz, California; rare in summer in ne Siberia. Winters in marine waters close to breeding areas, south to extreme nw Baja California.

ad. winter

ad. summer

ad. summer

Pigeon Guillemot
Cepphus columba
N Pacific
L 13–14 in (33–36 cm)

ad. winter

ad. winter

juv.

fledgling

ad. Apr–Aug

ad. winter

ad. summer

Adult feeding
a Butterfish,
Pholis gunnellus,
to its chicks

Black Guillemot
Cepphus grylle
Circumpolar
L 13–15 in (32–38 cm)

Arctic morph
ad. winter

Typical
ad. winter

juv.

ad. Mar–Aug

ad. winter

ad. summer

ad. winter

ad. Mar–Aug

Spectacled Guillemot
Cepphus carbo
NW Pacific
L 15–16 in (38–40 cm)

ID: L 9.5-10 in (24–25 cm). Small and chunky. AD APR–AUG: Cryptic brown plumage, mottled with white, gray, or russet. AD WINTER: Sooty-gray above. Black cap extends well below eye. White on face nearly encircles the neck, leaving only a thin dark line down the nape and making a large white patch behind the eye. Chin, throat, breast, and belly white. White scapular stripe. JUV: Like winter adult, but with brownish gray marbling on underparts and scapulars. VOICE: Vocal in flight and nesting sites, repeatedly calling *kleeer-kleeer-kleer* or high-pitched *quip*. **HABITS:** Forages in offshore waters in areas of upwellings as well as in protected bays and fjords. Feeds on sand lances, herring, capelin, and shiner perch (*Cymatogaster aggregata*) taken in wing-propelled pursuit to depths of 95 ft (30 m).

Breeds in solitary pairs in trees in old-growth coniferous forests up to 30 mi (50 km) inland and (rarely) in a scrape on rocky scree slopes, cliffs, and boulder fields near the sea. Forest-nesting murrelets make a nest of lichen or moss located either on a high branch or in undergrowth at the tree base. Both parents incubate the single greenish egg for 30 days, changing over in 24-hour shifts and relieving each other during periods of low light to avoid predation. Hatchling is brooded for up to 5 days, then both parents leave to forage at sea, returning to the nest each day with a fish held crosswise in the bill. Chick fledges at 28–40 days and makes its way unaccompanied to the sea, either by flying or by floating down a stream to the seacoast. **STATUS:** Habitat loss from the logging of old-growth forests has caused a decline in numbers. Threatened (US-ESA). Endangered (IUCN).

Long-billed Murrelet

Brachyramphus perdix
ALSO: Partridge Murrelet, Kamtschatkamarmelalk, Langschnabelalk, Guillemot à long bec, Langnebbdvergteist, Длин-ноклювый пыжик. SN means "short-beaked partridge," alluding to the bird's shape and cryptic plumage. Split from *B. marmoratus* in 1998.
RANGE: Nests (Jun) in trees in old-growth, coastal coniferous forests around the Sea of Okhotsk from Kamchatka, the Kuril and Commander Is, and Primorsky Krai (se Russia) south to Hokkaido, Japan. Winters in sheltered coastal waters from Sakhalin Is and Primorsky Krai south to Korea and n China. Very rare along Pacific coast of N Amer.
ID: L 10–10.5 in (25–27 cm). AD APR–AUG: Dark brown, lightly marbled, with a pale chin and cheek. AD WINTER: Sooty gray above, with a dark gray nape. Black cap extends to just under the eye. Prominent white arcs above and below eyes. White chin, throat, and underparts. White scapulars. Adults are distinguished from *B. marmoratus* by larger size, longer bill, prominent white eye arcs, and uniformly dark crown, nape, and cheek in winter plumage. JUV: Similar to winter adult, but with dark marbling on breast and flanks.
HABITS: Similar to those of *B. marmoratus*. The first verified nest in Asia was found in 1961.

Kittlitz's Murrelet

Brachyramphus brevirostris
ALSO: Glacier Murrelet, Kurzschnabelalk, Guillemot de Kittlitz, Kortnebbdvergteist, Короткоклювый пыжик. SN means "short-beaked short-billed [murrelet]." CN honors German zoologist Heinrich von Kittlitz (1799–1874), who first collected this species.
RANGE: Nests (May–Jul) on talus slopes and cliffs near mountain glaciers and formerly glaciated areas along most coasts of se–w Alaska, especially along Glacier Bay and Alaska Penin, with small colonies in the Russian Far East along the coasts of the Sea of Okhotsk and Chukchi Sea. Winters on open ocean.
ID: L 9–9.5 in (23–24 cm). AD APR–SEP: Cryptically marbled, with sandy brown upperparts. Belly and vent pale buff. White outer tail feathers visible when landing. AD WINTER: Dark sooty gray above; blackish cap, dark nape, and partial nuchal collar. White face, throat, and underparts. White scapular stripe.
HABITS: Forages singly or in small groups in milky waters near tidewater glaciers and outflows of glacial streams; large eyes probably aid in finding prey in cloudy water. Feeds on small fish,

The tree-nesting habit of the Marbled Murrelet was first observed in 1974, when a man climbing a Douglas-fir tree in California discovered a chick perched on a branch 145 ft (45 m) above the ground.

ad. winter

ad. summer

ad. winter

juv.

ad. Apr–Aug

Marbled Murrelet
Brachyramphus marmoratus
N Pacific
L 9.5–10 in (24–25 cm)

ad. winter

ad. winter

ad. summer

juv.

ad. Apr–Aug

Long-billed Murrelet
Brachyramphus perdix
NW Pacific
L 10–10.5 in (25–27 cm)

ad. winter

ad. winter

ad. summer

Kittlitz's Murrelet
Brachyramphus brevirostris
N Pacific
L 9–9.5 in (23–24 cm)

ad. Apr–Sep

Ancient Murrelet
Synthliboramphus antiquus
N Pacific
L 9.5–10.5 in (24–27 cm)

Two days after hatching, Ancient Murrelet chicks go to sea with their parents and complete their development on the open ocean.

juv.

ad. Feb–Sep

larval fish, krill, and other small zooplankton captured in wing-propelled underwater pursuit. The large fleshy tongue enclosed in a rigid horny shield is used to hold prey against toothed ridges on the upper palate.

Nests on the ground on barren scree and talus slopes, and occasionally on cliff faces of glaciated mountain peaks. This is the only alcid that nests on the ground at or near the tops of mountains. Clutch is a single, pale olive egg laid in a small scrape, usually on the downhill side of a large rock. Both parents incubate the egg for about 30 days. Hatchling is brooded for 1–2 days, after which the parents forage at sea and return 4–6 times per day with small fish for the nestling. Chick fledges at about 24 days and leaves the nest unaccompanied.

STATUS: Warmer summer temperatures have caused Alaska's coastal glaciers to retreat, reducing this species' foraging habitat. Alaska populations have declined by 80–90 percent since 1994. Critically Endangered (IUCN).

GENUS *SYNTHLIBORAMPHUS*
Ancient Murrelet

Synthliboramphus antiquus
ALSO: Silberalk, Alque à cou blanc, Nordstarik, Обыкновенный старик. SN means "ancient [bird with a] laterally compressed beak"; *antiquus* refers to the white-streaked collar and neck that resembles an elder's graying hair.
RANGE: Nests (May–Jun) on offshore islands of the N Pacific, at 52°N–60°N in the e Pacific and less commonly 35°N–62°N on the Asian coast. NE Pacific populations often disperse to Bering Strait waters post-breeding (Jul–Sep). Winters at sea near breeding areas, south to Japan, Korea, and California. One record from the UK.
ID: L 9.5–10.5 in (24–27 cm). AD FEB–SEP: Dark slaty gray above, white below. Head black, with black extending down to upper breast. White on sides of neck and lower face. Fine white breeding plumes from above the eye to nape. Short, pale pink bill, with dark base. Legs and feet dusky pink. AD WINTER: White breeding plumes reduced or absent. Black bib often speckled with white. JUV: Like winter adult, but with a white chin.

HABITS: Forages in areas of upwelling near the coast and also offshore along the continental shelf edge. Feeds on small fishes and zooplankton, especially euphausiids. Nests in burrows dug in soft soil, in cavities under tree roots, in shallow holes under grass tussocks, or less often in rock crevices. Pair bonds can last for several years, and pairs often reuse the nesting site from the previous year. Both parents incubate the 2 buff to brown eggs for about 32 days, alternating in 3-day shifts. Parents brood the hatchlings but do not feed them, and the young abandon the nest within 4 days of hatching. Departure begins when the off-duty adult returns to the burrow, usually 2–4 hours after sunset. Both adults repeatedly call *chirrup*, and chicks answer with a shrill *wee-wee*. After several minutes of calling back and forth, the adults fly off from the burrow and the chicks run and tumble down to the sea. Parents and chicks reunite in the waves through mutual recognition of calls, then swim out to sea where they remain together for at least a month while the chicks complete their development.

GENUS *AETHIA*: These small auklets of the N Pacific feed on small zooplankton taken in wing-propelled dives. They breed on rocky seacoasts and nest in rock crevices. Both parents share in incubating the single egg and brooding the hatchling. Parents visit the nest to feed the chick at night to avoid being taken by gulls or other predators. Food is carried to the chick in a specialized throat pouch that develops during the breeding season. The chick fledges at 4–5 weeks of age and makes its way to the sea without parental assistance.

Parakeet Auklet

Aethia psittacula
ALSO: Rotschnabelalk, Starique perroquet, Papegøyealke, Белобрюшка, *Cyclorrhynchus psittacula*. SN means "little parrot seabird," alluding to the head and bill shape.
RANGE: Nests (Jun–Aug) on rocky seacoasts of the Kuril and Commander islands, Sea of Okhotsk, Kamchatka, Chukotka, Bering Strait,

Aleutians, Bering Sea islands, and south to se Alaska. Winters in ice-free offshore waters, south to about 40°N.

ID: L 9–10 in (23–25 cm). AD APR–SEP: Dark sooty gray upperparts; mottled breast; white underparts. Thin white plume extends back and down from the white eye. Short, stubby, red bill is nearly circular; lower beak curves strongly upward. AD WINTER: Chin, throat, and foreneck white. Bill dull brownish red.

HABITS: Forages singly or in groups of 2–3 individuals. Feeds on small zooplankton such as copepods, krill, amphipods, jellyfish, comb jellies, and crustaceans that live among jellyfish tentacles. Bill is adapted for seizing gelatinous prey. Flight strong, direct, and fairly high, rolling from side to side.

Nests singly or in small colonies in rock crevices and rubble. Displaying male mounts a conspicuous perch when courting, stands with bill open and head inclined upward at 45° angle, and makes a whinnying call. Both parents share incubation of a single white to pale blue egg for 35–36 days, changing over in 24-hour shifts. After about a week, the chick is left by itself during the day, with both parents bringing food to the nest at night. Chick remains in burrow until fledged and leaves on its own.

Least Auklet

Aethia pusilla

ALSO: Zwergalk, Starique minuscule, Flekkdvergalke, Конюга-крошка, Chuuchii, Akmaaliighaq. SN means "little seabird."

RANGE: Nests (Jun–Jul) on rocky seacoasts in Chukotka, Kamchatka, Commander and Kuril islands, Aleutians, and isolated Bering Sea islands. Colonies of more than 1 million birds exist at Kiska Is and Gareloi Is in the Aleutians, at St Lawrence Is, and at Big Diomede Is in the Bering Strait. Winters offshore in the N Pacific as far north as open water permits.

ID: L 6–6.5 in (15–17 cm). Smallest alcid. Chubby and short-necked. White eye. Gray legs. AD APR–SEP: Dark gray above. Thread-like white feathers in front of and behind eye. White-tipped scapulars. White underparts, mottled with gray.

Short, swollen, red bill, with a small knob at base of upper beak. AD WINTER: Underparts white. Brownish red bill lacks knob.

HABITS: Feeds on small zooplankton such as copepods, larval shrimp, amphipods, and euphausiids, taken in wing-propelled dives. Nests in crevices in seaside talus slopes, cliffs, boulder fields, and porous lava flows. Forms enormous, twittering flocks that circle high in the air above the sea and nesting colonies. Clutch is a single white egg laid on bare floor of a crevice. Both parents incubate the egg for about 30 days and brood the chick for the first week, alternating in 24-hour shifts. Subsequently they return to the crevice only to feed the chick, staying with it for 5–10 minutes before returning to sea. Chick fledges at about 32 days and flies to sea unaccompanied.

Whiskered Auklet

Aethia pygmaea

ALSO: Bartalk, Starique pygmée, Praktdvergalke, Малая конюга. CN refers to the wispy head plumes. SN means "dwarf seabird."

RANGE: Nests (Apr–May) on volcanic islands of the Aleutian, Commander, and Kuril island chains. Winters in waters near breeding colonies.

ID: L 7.5–8 in (19–20 cm). AD MAR–SEP: Dark sooty gray plumage, with a pungent citrus scent. Single white facial plume springs from behind each eye, and another pair flares out from each side of the lores. Recurving plume of dark feathers extends from the forehead and hangs over the stubby red bill. Eyes white. Legs dark gray. AD WINTER: Facial plumes much reduced. Bill brownish red. JUV: Sooty gray, slightly paler below, with faint facial stripes and pale eye. VOICE: Highly vocal at nest, calling a short, plaintive *mew* or a loud, sharp, rapid *beedoo bedeer bidi bidi*.

HABITS: Feeds on zooplankton, taking mainly copepods in summer and euphausiids in winter. Typically forages within 10 mi (16 km) of land at convergent tidal fronts (sharp transition zones between 2 water masses of different density and current speeds). Flies low and fast, with deep whirring wingbeats. Nocturnal at breeding colonies. Nests in rock crevices on inaccessible sea cliff ledges and in cavities under beach boulders, often near nests of storm petrels and crested auklets. Both parents incubate the single white egg for about 30 days, alternating in 24-hour shifts. Both brood the chick for about a week, then return to the crevice each night to feed it. Chick fledges at 39–42 days and flies unaccompanied from burrow after dark.

Crested Auklet

Aethia cristatella
ALSO: Schopfalk, Starique cristatelle, Toppdvergalke, Большая конюга, Ciplagar, Cukilpag. SN means "crested seabird."
RANGE: Nests (Jun–Aug) on rocky seacoasts on the Chukotka Penin, Commander Is, Kurils, Aleutians, Pribilofs, and islands in the Bering Strait. Winters on the open ocean in ice-free waters, south to n Japan and Kodiak, Alaska. Accidental in Iceland and Brit Columbia, Canada.
ID: L 10–10.5 in (25–27 cm). AD APR–SEP: Dark sooty gray plumage, with a pungent citrus-like scent. Conspicuous crest curves over the stubby, swollen, orange-colored bill. Fine white plume extends from eye to ear coverts. White eyes. Legs gray. AD WINTER/JUV: Sooty brown. Bill pink and gray, smaller than in summer. Crest and facial plumes reduced. VOICE: Soft hoarse barks, trumpeting, cackling, hoots, and whines given at breeding colonies.
HABITS: Feeds on euphausiids, copepods, and some fish and squid, taken in wing-propelled dives. At breeding colonies, some with over 100,000 pairs, huge swarms of birds rise and circle above the colony and sea, then fly off to feeding areas on fast-whirring wings. Pairs engage in elaborate courtship behavior with bowing, billing, and neck-twisting displays. Both sexes compete for mates with large crests, as crest size correlates with dominance. Nests in rock crevices on cliffs, talus slopes, boulder fields, and lava flows. Both sexes incubate a single white egg for 33–35 days and brood the hatchling for 7–10 days. Subsequently the chick is left alone in the nest, with both parents returning several times a day to feed it. Chick remains in burrow until fledged and flies to sea unaccompanied.

GENUS *PTYCHORAMPHUS*
Cassin's Auklet

Ptychoramphus aleuticus
ALSO: Aleutian Auklet, Aleutenalk, Sotalke, Starique de Cassin, Алеутский пыжик. SN means "wrinkled-bill [auklet] of the Aleutians," referring to the small transverse ridges on the beak. CN honors Pennsylvania Quaker John Cassin (1813–1869), an illustrator, ornithologist, and taxonomist of the Philadelphia Academy of Natural Sciences.
RANGE: Nests (Mar–Jul) on islands and coasts along the Pacific coast of N Amer, from the e Aleutians, Alaska, Brit Columbia, and south to Baja California; rare breeder in the Kurils. Center of distribution is Brit Columbia with an estimated 2 million birds. Winters in waters off the continental shelf edge.
ID: L 8.5–9 in (22–23 cm). Small, stocky auklet with short, stubby wings. AD: Dark gray above; paler gray underparts fade to white on belly and vent. Pale eyes, with white crescents above and below eye. Dark bill, with pale yellow to cream patches at base. Bluish legs and feet. JUV: Paler than adult, with white chin and throat.
HABITS: Feeds singly or in flocks, taking krill, other small crustaceans, squid, and fish in wing-propelled dives to depths of 265 ft (80 m). Flies low, with rapidly whirring wings. Speed at full flight is estimated at 45 mph (73 kmh) with wings flapped in at least a 90° arc. Nests in shallow burrows dug into bare flat ground or heavily vegetated sea slopes; also nests in sea caves and rock crevices, and under trees or logs. Digs burrows using its sharp toenails. Clutch is a single creamy white to pale green egg, which both parents incubate for 37–42 days. Hatchling is born covered in dark down. It is brooded for 3–4 days, then left alone in the burrow by day and attended by both parents at night. Parents carry food for the nestling in a specialized throat pouch. Chick remains in burrow until fledged at about at 41–50 days and departs the burrow at night unaccompanied by the adults.
STATUS: Declining populations may be due to changes in ocean climate conditions, which affect the marine food web and prey of Cassin's auklets.

ad. winter

ad.
Apr–Sep

Least Auklet
Aethia pusilla
N Pacific
L 6–6.5 in (15–17 cm)

ad.
Apr–Sep

ad. winter

Parakeet Auklet
Aethia psittacula
N Pacific
L 9–10 in (23–25 cm)

ad. Mar–Sep

Whiskered Auklet
Aethia pygmaea
N Pacific
L 7.5–8 in (19–20 cm)

ad. winter

ad. winter

Crested Auklet
Aethia cristatella
N Pacific
L 10–10.5 in (25–27 cm)

ad. Apr–Sep

Rhinoceros Auklet
Cerorhinca monocerata
N Pacific
L 14–15.5 in (36–39 cm)

juv.

ad. winter

Cassin's Auklet
Ptychoramphus aleuticus
NE Pacific
L 8.5–9 in (22–23 cm)

ad.

ad. Apr–Sep

GENUS *CERORHINCA*
Rhinoceros Auklet
Cerorhinca monocerata

ALSO: Nashornalk, Macareux rhinocéros, Nashornlunde, Рогатый тупик. SN means "[auklet with] single horn on the bill."
RANGE: Nests (Apr–Jun) on forested and grassy islands. Breeds discontinuously from the s Kurils and Sakhalin Is south to Japan and Korea, and from the Aleutians and s Alaska south to California. Winters mainly on ice-free continental shelf waters and occasionally over deep inshore waters.
ID: L 14–15.5 in (36–39 cm). Largest auklet, weighing up to 1 lb (0.5 kg). **AD APR–SEP:** Upperparts black; breast brownish gray; belly and vent white. Two thin white plumes on each side of the face. Cream-colored "horn" at base of orange bill. Legs yellow. **AD WINTER:** White facial plumes reduced or absent. Bill faded orange, with horn reduced or absent. **JUV:** Darker than winter adult; lacks head plumes and has a smaller bill.
HABITS: Forceful, heavy flight powered by continuous, rapid flapping of wings. Forages singly or in small flocks. Feeds on small schooling fish (sand lance, anchovies, rockfish) and zooplankton taken in wing-propelled dives to depths of 100 ft (30 m). Seizes one fish while holding other fish at back of bill, thus able to carry several fish at once. Nocturnal at breeding colonies. Uses claws and bill to excavate a nesting chamber in a deep burrow, to 16 ft (5 m) long, in soft soil of wooded or grassy slopes. Both sexes incubate a single white egg for 42–49 days, alternating in 24–48 hour shifts. Both parents feed the chick nightly, presenting several fish held crosswise in the bill. Chick fledges at about 50 days of age and leaves the burrow on its own.

GENUS *FRATERCULA*: This genus contains the puffins. These stocky, short-winged, cavity-nesting alcids of the northern oceans were exploited in the past for meat, eggs, and feathers. Most present-day colonies are found in conservation areas where puffins' main predators are gulls, hawks, owls, and foxes.

During the breeding season, puffins sport a large, brightly colored, laterally compressed bill. In winter, they shed the bill plates and horny structure around the eye. Puffins are able to capture and hold a bill load of fish by clamping them against roof of mouth with the tongue, both of which have backward-pointing spines. Fish are carried with the heads and tails in alternate directions.

Puffins become sexually mature at 3–6 years of age and form monogamous pair bonds. Their breeding colonies are situated on steep, grassy slopes and sea cliffs on small offshore islands and mainland coasts. They nest mainly in earthen burrows excavated with their bill and strong clawed feet, but will also use rock crevices or natural cavities under boulders. Both sexes share in incubating the single white egg for 39–41 days, and both also brood the chick and feed it. One parent usually spends the night in the burrow until the chick fledges, at about 5 weeks of age. Fledglings typically leave the colony at night, and immediately go to sea unaccompanied by the parents.

Atlantic Puffin
Fratercula arctica

ALSO: Common Puffin, Papageitaucher, Macareux moine, Lundefugl, Lundi, Атлантический тупик. SN means "little brother of the Arctic," alluding to the puffin's black and white plumage that recalls a friar's robes.
RANGE: Nests (May–Aug) mainly on small offshore islands from Jones Sound in the Canadian High Arctic south to the Gulf of Maine, and in Greenland, Iceland, Faroes, UK, Norway, Jan Mayen, Svalbard, Novaya Zemlya, and Murmansk coast. Winters on open ice-free offshore waters of the N Atlantic between 45°N and 60°N. The majority of Atlantic Puffins breed in Iceland. The largest N Amer colony is at Witless Bay, Newfoundland.
ID: L 12–14 in (31–36 cm). **AD MAR–AUG:** Black above, white below. Large head, with colorful red, yellow, and bluish black bill. Face grayish white. Red eyering; dark, fleshy horn above the eye and a bluish black fleshy plate below the eye.

ad. summer

juv.

Tufted Puffin
Fratercula cirrhata
N Pacific
L 15–16 in (38–41 cm)

ad. winter

ad. Apr–Sep

juv.

ad. summer

ad. winter

Horned Puffin
Fratercula corniculata
N Pacific
L 15–16 in (38–41 cm)

ad. Mar–Aug

juv.

ad. summer

Atlantic Puffin
Fratercula arctica
N Atlantic
L 12–14 in (31–36 cm)

ad. winter

An Atlantic Puffin with a bill full of
sand lances (*Ammodytes* spp.)

ad. Mar–Aug

Crown, nape, and collar black. Underwing dark. AD WINTER: Sides of face dusky gray. Bill base black; bill plates fade and shrink. JUV: Dusky plumage; awl-shaped bill. VOICE: Low, droning moans or bellows sounded at the burrow. HABITS: Solitary when at sea in winter; forages in small groups in shallow waters near breeding colonies. Feeds on small schooling fish (sand lances, capelin, whiting, herring), taken in wing-propelled dives to depths of 80–150 ft (25–45 m). Flight is rapid, to 50 mph (80 kmh), with 300–400 wingbeats per minute. Flightless while molting (Jan–Mar). Excavates a burrow up to 6 ft (2 m) long in grassy seaside slopes or level tops of rocky coastal islets; also nests in rock crevices and under boulders where permafrost hinders digging. USE: Atlantic puffins are harvested for human food in Iceland and the Faroes.

Horned Puffin

Fratercula corniculata
ALSO: Hornlund, Macareux cornu, Тихоокеанский тупик, Qilangaq. *Corniculata* is Latin for "little brother with a horn [over each of the eyes]."

RANGE: Nests (Jun–Sep) on rocky seacoasts and offshore islands in the Chukchi, Beaufort, and Bering seas, Sea of Okhotsk, Gulf of Alaska (largest colonies), Kurils, and Aleutians. Winters in the N Pacific, generally over deep oceanic waters. ID: L 15–16 in (38–41 cm). AD MAR–AUG: Black crown, neck, back, and tail. Large head, with a brightly colored red and yellow bill. Red eyering and a fleshy horn over the eye. White face, breast and belly; flanks and underwing dusky. AD WINTER: Sides of face and base of bill dark, dusky gray. Rounded, shrunken bill, with a dark base and faded orange tip. JUV: Similar to winter adult, but with a smaller, less arched, pointed bill and a darker face. VOICE: Low groans or growls sounded at breeding colonies. HABITS: In winter, feeds mainly on deepwater lantern fish (myctophids) and squid. Forms feeding flocks with other alcids and gulls around breeding colonies, feeding on small schooling fish, squid, octopus, polychaete worms, and euphausiids. Breeds in colonies of tens to thousands of individuals. Nests in rock crevices, talus slopes, and among beach boulders, less frequently in earthen burrows.

Tufted Puffin

Fratercula cirrhata
ALSO: Sea Parrot, Gelb-schopflund, Macareux huppé, Topplunde, Топорик, Pugharuwuk, Och-chuh, Kilanyak, *Lunda cirrhata*. SN means "little brother with a curl of hair," referring to the flowing head plumes.

RANGE: Nests (Jun–Sep) on steep, rocky islands and mainland sea cliffs of the N Pacific, from the Chukchi and Bering seas south to se Alaska, Brit Columbia, Aleutians, Kamchatka, Kurils, and Sea of Okhotsk. Winters in the c N Pacific, generally over deep oceanic waters, south to the Sea of Japan and California. ID: L 15–16 in (38–41 cm). AD APR–SEP: Black, with white face mask and flowing yellow head plumes. Large reddish orange bill, with greenish base. Pale eye; bright red eyering. AD WINTER: Dark brownish black. Yellow tufts reduced or absent. Bill small and dull, with dusky base and orange tip. JUV: Bill dusky, smaller and more pointed than winter adult; pale gray underparts. HABITS: Forages offshore in continental shelf and slope waters in winter, feeding on squid, euphausiids, polychaetes, and pelagic fish taken in wing-propelled underwater pursuit. During breeding season, often forages with shearwaters, kittiwakes, and murres, feeding on invertebrates and small schooling fish (anchovies, capelin). Excavates long nesting burrows in deep turf on cliff tops or in steep talus slopes well above the shoreline. Where foxes are present, puffins will use inaccessible cliff crevices or sea caves. USE: Native Americans harvested these puffins for meat and skins, which were made into lightweight parkas. Puffin bills were strung together into ceremonial dance rattles by the Aleut, Aliituq, and Tlingit people. STATUS: Some N Amer populations are in decline due to decreasing numbers of fish, pollution, and predation by introduced foxes and rats.

**American Black
Oystercatcher**
Haematopus bachmani
w N Amer
L 17–18 in (43–46 cm)

Eurasian Oystercatcher
Haematopus ostralegus
Iceland, Europe, e Asia
L 15–17 in (38–43 cm)

FAMILY HAEMATOPODIDAE
OYSTERCATCHERS

These large, black or pied shorebirds use their long red bill for prying mollusks off rocks or for digging out crustaceans and worms from beaches and tidal flats.

GENUS *HAEMATOPUS*
Eurasian Oystercatcher
Haematopus ostralegus

ALSO: Austernfischer, Huîtrier pie, Tjeld, Кулик-сорока. SN means "blood-footed oyster-gatherer." CN: English naturalist Mark Catesby (1682–1749) coined the name "oystercatcher" and applied it to the American Oystercatcher (*Haematopus palliatus*), which had erroneously been described as feeding almost exclusively on oysters. Catesby is known for his *Natural History of Carolina, Florida and the Bahama Islands*, the first published account of the flora and fauna of the region.

RANGE: Nests (Apr–Jun) on sand or gravel beaches, occasionally in cultivated fields or on riverbanks. Winters on estuarine mudflats, salt marshes, and sandy and rocky seashores.

SUBSPECIES: *H. o. ostralegus* (O) breeds in coastal Europe and Iceland; winters south to the Mediterranean, Persian Gulf, and Africa. *H. o. longipes* (L) breeds in c Asia and wc Russia; moves to seacoasts in winter. *H. o. osculans* (A) breeds on seacoasts from Kamchatka to China; winters in se Asia.

ID: L 15–17 in (38–43 cm). Bill is 3–3.75 in (7–9 cm) long. Upperparts and head glossy black. Broad white wing bar. White lower back, rump, and uppertail coverts. Black terminal tail band. Lower breast and belly white. Long, straight, orange red bill, often paler and yellower at tip. Pink legs. Iris deep red; bright orange red eyering. VOICE: A loud, shrill, piping *kee-beep′ kee-beep′*, given in flight.

HABITS: Typically monogamous, with strong fidelity to mate and to breeding and wintering areas. Male performs aerial courtship displays punctuated by *tii-tiiip* notes and stiff, slow, deep wingbeats. Nest is a depression lined with seashells, pebbles, and flotsam in coastal sites, or with pebbles and small mammal droppings when inland. Both sexes incubate the 3–4 pale ochre, dark-spotted eggs for 24–35 days. Chicks leave the nest within 1 day of hatching, but are dependent on the parents for food until they fledge at 33 days. Young winter with the parents. Maximum recorded lifespan is 36 years (UK) and 43 years (Germany).

RELATED SPECIES: AMERICAN BLACK OYSTER-CATCHER, *Haematopus bachmani*, is resident on exposed rocky seacoasts from the w Aleutians and s Alaska south to California and Baja California. Head and neck black. Mantle and underparts brownish black. Long, straight bill bright scarlet, with yellow tip. Iris lemon yellow; eyering red. Forages in the intertidal zone for mussels and limpets. Typically nests on sand or gravel beaches, just above the high-tide line.

FAMILY CHARADRIIDAE
PLOVERS, DOTTERELS, LAPWINGS

Charadriidae is a family of small to mid-sized waders, which are distributed worldwide, mostly in open habitats near water. These shorebirds typically have a compact body and short, thick neck. Large eyes at the sides of the head provide a broad field of vision. The bill is short and swollen at the tip. The hind toe is lacking on all species except for the Black-bellied Plover.

Plovers and dotterels have long, pointed wings, a shape that enables sustained migratory flight at speeds of up to 60 mph (100 kmh). The epic migrations of many plovers span thousands of miles as the birds fly between boreal breeding grounds and wintering areas in the S Hemisphere. Lapwings, in contrast, have broad, rounded wings more suited to their sedentary lifestyle. These birds are resident on farmlands, pastures, grasslands, wetlands, and steppes, or at best are short-distance migrants.

Charadriids forage in small single-species parties when breeding and in larger mixed flocks of up to several hundred birds in winter. They feed mainly on invertebrates such as polychaete worms and small crustaceans, but their diet also extends to insect larvae, beetles, ants, flies, spiders, earthworms, mollusks, small fish, lizards, leeches, moths, seeds, and berries. These birds forage in a run-pause-snatch fashion. They race across the ground, come to an abrupt stop as they watch for prey, then pluck it from the sand or soil with the bill. Plovers also employ a foot-trembling technique in which they hold one foot forward and vibrate it against the soil or mud to attract prey or flush it out of hiding.

Most species are seasonally monogamous and nest in solitary pairs. Males have elaborate courtship displays, including the *butterfly display flight*, which plover males perform up to 300 ft (100 m) above the ground, as they fly with slow, measured wingbeats while repeatedly emitting melodious whistles. Charadriids nest in a shallow ground scrape made in a bed of low grass or lichens, which provide camouflage for the clutch of 2-4 mottled or scrawled eggs. The pointed ends of the pyriform eggs fit neatly into the center of the nest and allow maximum contact with the parents' brood pouch. Both parents incubate the eggs for 20-30 days. The cryptically colored, downy chicks leave the nest with a day of hatching, usually accompanied by one or both parents. Nesting birds are consummate performers of the *broken-wing display*, in which the adult feigns injury in its attempt to lure predators (and people) away from its nest and eggs. They flutter farther and farther away from the nest with one wing dragging on the ground. Once the parents sense they have led the predator far enough astray, they take off in full flight, leaving a perplexed pursuer behind.

GENUS *PLUVIALIS*: This genus contains the black-bellied and golden plovers. *Pluvialis* derives from the Latin *pluvia*, meaning "rain," alluding to folktales stating that the spring arrival of plovers signals the start of the rainy season.

Black-bellied Plover

Pluvialis squatarola
ALSO: Gray Plover, Kiebitzregenpfeifer, Pluvier argenté, Tundralo, Тулес, Tullikpak.
SN means "rain plover"; *squatarola* derives from *sgatarola,* the old Venetian word for "plover."
RANGE: Nests (May–Jul) on the arctic tundra of Siberia, Alaska, and Canadian Arctic. Winters on sandy beaches, estuaries, and mudflats along the coasts of the Americas, UK, Europe, s Asia, Africa, Australia, and NZ. Casual in Greenland, Iceland, Faroes, and Svalbard. Migration is primarily coastal, but scattered individuals often are seen inland, especially in the US Great Plains.
ID: L 10–12 in (25–30 cm). Largest plover. Diagnostic black axillaries, white rump, and strong white wing bar. AD APR–SEP: Back spangled silvery gray, with a few golden feathers. Crown, nape, sides of breast, and undertail white. Face, breast, belly, and flanks black. Heavy black bill. Legs blackish, with a vestigial hind toe. Female browner on underparts and shows some white feathering on face and breast. AD WINTER/JUV: Mottled gray or brownish gray overall. Throat, belly, and rump white. White wing band and black axillaries. Blackish bill and legs. Juvenile

White rump

Black axillaries

ad. summer

ad. winter

ad. winter

ad. Apr–Sep

Black-bellied Plover
Pluvialis squatarola
Eurasia, N Amer
L 10–12 in (25–30 cm)

ad. summer

White axillaries

ad. winter

ad. winter
Golden overall

ad. Mar–Oct

White flanks and undertail coverts

Greater Golden Plover
Pluvialis apricaria
Iceland, w Eurasia
L 10–11 in (25–28 cm)

ad. summer

Gray underwing

ad. winter

ad. winter
Dark ear spot

ad. Mar–Sep

White spotted flanks

Pacific Golden Plover
Pluvialis fulva
Siberia, w Alaska
L 9.5–10.5 in (24–27 cm)

ad. summer

Gray underwing

ad. winter

ad. winter
Grayish overall
Dark cap

ad. Apr–Sep

Solid black underparts

American Golden Plover
Pluvialis dominica
N Amer
L 10–11 in (25–28 cm)

has flanks and lower breast finely barred with dark gray. VOICE: Flight call is a high, clear, whining *plee'-ooee* or *pee-oo'-eee*. Plaintive, repetitive, ringing *plu'-ee-uu'* given in display.

Greater Golden Plover
Pluvialis apricaria

ALSO: Eurasian Golden Plover, Goldregenpfeifer, Pluvier doré, Золотистая ржанка, Heilo. SN means "sun-kissed plover," referring to the golden plumage.
RANGE: Nests (May–Aug) in Iceland and w Eurasia in damp tundra, swampy forest-tundra, and moorland bogs. Winters in large flocks in freshwater wetlands, salt marshes, grasslands, alpine steppe, seashores, and bays. Iceland breeders migrate to Scotland, Ireland, and w Iberia; Scandinavian birds to n France; Russian birds to Iberia and n Africa. Winter vagrant to ne N Amer.
ID: L 10–11 in (25–28 cm). Largest golden plover. Diagnostic white axillaries. Narrow white wing bar. Relatively small bill, short legs, and short wings. AD MAR–OCT: Black face and underparts are bordered by a white stripe that extends along the flanks and the undertail coverts. Upperparts show bright gold spangles. Black may be absent on the face and throat of breeding females. AD WINTER/JUV: Golden buff overall. Breast mottled golden brown; lower flanks and belly whitish, with fine dark barring. VOICE: Loud, whining whistle *tyou-you'-you*, or *pyou-peee'-oo*, and a repetitive, mournful, slightly downslurred *tyou-oo*.

American Golden Plover
Pluvialis dominica

ALSO: Amerikanischer Goldregenpfeifer, Pluvier bronzé, Американская ржанка, Kanadalo. SN means "plover of Santo Domingo," the type locality. Treated collectively with *P. fulva* as the Lesser Golden Plover.
RANGE: Nests (May–July) on the tundra from extreme ne Chukotka, east across arctic N Amer to Baffin Is. Fall migrants stage in e Canada before flying 2500 mi (4000 km) across the Atlantic to n S Amer; most continue to fly farther south for 4000 mi (6500 km) and winter in grasslands of c Argentina, Patagonia, and Tierra del Fuego; fewer numbers migrate south via the Great Plains and Pacific coast. In spring, birds migrate north via c S Amer and the US Great Plains. Rare in winter along the US Atlantic and Gulf coasts. Vagrant to coastal Europe.
ID: L 10–11 in (25–28 cm). AD APR–SEP: Gold-spangled upperparts. White neck stripe curves around the face and terminates abruptly at upper breast. Flanks and undertail coverts black. Pale gray underwing. Black bill. Dark gray legs. Breeding female is paler. AD WINTER/JUV: Grayer than other golden plovers in winter. Upperparts dull brownish gray, with a few flecks of pale yellow. Dark crown. Broad white supercilium. Faint dark spot on ear coverts. Dark rump and tail. Underparts gray, with fine lines of darker gray on breast and flanks. VOICE: Mournful *quee'-dle* or *tuu'-u-ee* given in flight. Displaying males give a whistled *chu-leek* in flight and *wit-weeyou-wit* upon landing.
STATUS: Populations are still recovering from excessive hunting in the 19th and early 20th centuries. Present threats include exposure to pesticides, habitat alteration, and collisions with wind farm towers on the Great Plains flyway.

Pacific Golden Plover
Pluvialis fulva

ALSO: Pazifischer Gold-regenpfeifer, Pluvier fauve, Азиатская бурокрылая ржанка, Sibirlo. SN means "tawny plover." Treated collectively with *P. dominica* as the Lesser Golden Plover.
RANGE: Nests (May–Jul) on the tundra in w Alaska and in Siberia from the Yamal Penin to Wrangel Is and Chukotka. Winters from Hawaii to Australia, and in se Asia, India, and ne Africa; rare to uncommon in winter from Brit Columbia to California. Bering Sea populations stage in the Aleutians and fly 35 hours nonstop to winter in Hawaii, a 2050 mi (3300 km) flight over the open Pacific. Vagrant to coastal Europe.
ID: L 9.5–10.5 in (24–27 cm). Smallest golden plover. AD MAR–SEP: Gold-spangled upperparts. White

neck stripe curves around the face and continues past the breast to sides, flanks, and undertail coverts. Brownish gray underwing. Black bill. Dark gray legs. In flight, toes project beyond tail tip. Female is paler and mottled with white on breast. AD WINTER/JUV: Head, neck, breast, and back mottled with bright yellowish buff. Pale yellowish eyeline. Flanks finely barred with brown. Belly whitish. VOICE: Plaintive *chu-it'* or *chu-wee'* or *pee-chew-ee* in flight.

GENUS *CHARADRIUS*: The genus contains the collared plovers. *Charadrius* alludes to a mythical waterbird able to cure jaundice that was mentioned around 347 BC by Aristotle and in AD 383 in the Vulgate Bible.

Ringed Plover

Charadrius hiaticula

ALSO: Greater Ringed Plover, Sandregenpfeifer, Grand gravelot, Sandlo, Галстучник. SN means "cleft-dwelling plover," referring to its nesting amid rocks and boulders. **RANGE:** Nests (Jun–Jul) on the arctic tundra in ne Canada, Greenland, Iceland, Svalbard, and n Eurasia east to Chukotka. Canada, Iceland, Greenland birds winter in s Europe and w Africa; other populations are sedentary or winter in s Europe, Africa, and sw Asia. Casual visitor to w Aleutians and St Lawrence Is, where it has bred. **ID:** L 7–8 in (17–20 cm). Only the 2 outer toes are webbed. AD MAR–SEP: Crown and back brown. Black patch from base of bill to cheeks; black bar above white forehead; white streak above eye. Underparts white, broken by a broad black breast band. White wing bar and white underwing. Very narrow orange eyering. Short, orange, black-tipped bill. Orange legs. AD WINTER/JUV: Black markings replaced by dusky brown. Back feathers brown with pale buffy fringes.

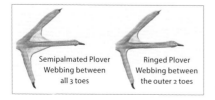

Semipalmated Plover
Webbing between
all 3 toes

Ringed Plover
Webbing between
the outer 2 toes

Breast band reduced, sometimes broken. Bill black. Legs dull yellow orange. Distinguished from *C. semipalmatus* by larger size, wider breast band, more white above and behind eye, webbing between only 2 toes, and call. VOICE: Melodic, whistled *kyou-ee'* or *too-li'*.

Semipalmated Plover

Charadrius semipalmatus

ALSO: Amerikanischer Sandregenpfeifer, Pluvier à collier, Amerikasandlo, Перепончатопалый галстучник. SN means "collared plover with partially webbed feet." **RANGE:** Nests (May–Jul) in N Amer in open areas near lakes, marshes, and rivers, and on sparsely vegetated sand, gravel, and tundra. Winters on beaches, mudflats, and shorelines along Pacific and Atlantic coasts of the Americas, south through S Amer to Patagonia. Vagrant to Greenland, Azores, UK (Isles of Scilly), e Siberia, and Johnston and Baker islands in the Pacific. **ID:** L 6–7 in (16–18 cm). Large head, large eyes, short bill, rounded body, and fairly short neck. All 3 toes are webbed. AD MAR–SEP: Crown and back brown. Black patch from base of bill to cheeks; black bar above white forehead. Underparts white, broken by a narrow black breast band. White wing bar and white underwing. Bill orange with a black tip. Orange yellow legs. Narrow yellow eyering. AD WINTER/JUV: Black head markings; breast band replaced by brown and often incomplete. Forehead and narrow supercilium whitish. Back brown. Abdomen white. Bill all black or with yellow at the base. Legs dull yellow orange. Distinguished from *C. hiaticula* by smaller size, narrower breast band, less white above and behind eye, slightly stubbier bill, webbing between all 3 toes, and call. VOICE: Soft, rising, hoarse whistle, *che-weee'*.

Lesser Sand Plover

Charadrius mongolus

ALSO: Mongolian Plover, Mongolenregenpfeifer, Pluvier de Mongolie, Mongollo, Монгольский зуек. SN means "collared plover of Mongolia," the type locality.

RANGE: Nests (Jun) on barren, high-alpine tundra in Chukotka, Kamchatka, Magadan, and Pamir and Tien-Shan Mtns of c Asia, and on sand dunes in the Commander Is. Winters on sandy beaches in e Africa, se Asia, and Australasia. ID: L 7–8.25 in (17–21 cm). AD APR–AUG: Back grayish brown; crown and nape brown tinged with chestnut. Black mask from base of bill to ear coverts; narrow black bar above white forehead; white supercilium. Underparts white, broken by a broad rufous breast band, edged at the top by a narrow black line. Upperwing grayish brown, with blackish primary coverts and flight feathers, and narrow white wing bar. Underwing white, with a narrow dusky trailing edge. Bill black. Legs and feet dark greenish gray. Breeding female has a dark grayish brown or rufous mask; chestnut markings are duller than male's. AD WINTER/JUV: Black or chestnut markings are replaced by grayish brown. Breast band is often incomplete or indistinct. VOICE: Short, soft, low-pitched *kruit-kruit*.

Eurasian Dotterel
Charadrius morinellus
ALSO: Mornellregenpfeifer, Pluvier guignard, Boltit, Хрустан. SN means "foolish

plover," alluding to the ease with which these birds were taken by fowlers hunting at night. RANGE: Nests (Jun–Jul) on high-altitude scree fields and dry rocky tundra from the UK and n Scandinavia to the Kola Penin and Novaya Zemlya, and in e Siberia from the Taimyr Penin to Chukotka. Winters in a narrow belt across n Africa, from Morocco east to the Arabian Penin and Iran. Rare winter visitor to Japan. Occurs on cultivated fields and salt flats in migration. ID: L 8–9.5 in (20–24 cm). AD APR–AUG: Mid-sized plover, with a broad white eyeline that meets in a V on the nape. Blackish cap. Back and wing coverts sandy brown, edged with cinnamon. No wing bar. Underwing coverts and axillaries dull white. Tail tip white, with dark subterminal bar. Upper breast gray, with a white line at lower edge. Upper belly chestnut (color brighter and more extensive in female); lower belly black; vent and undertail coverts

white. Black bill, sometimes tinged greenish at base of lower mandible. Legs dull yellow. AD WINTER: Drab and pale compared to spring. Bright chestnut color on breast fades to a warm buff. JUV: Back and wings dark brown with broad buffy fringes. Breast brownish buff, with faint, thin, white breast band; belly white. Forehead streaked. Broad white eyeline. VOICE: High, rapid, repetitive *pweet-pweet-pweet* whistle in flight; also sounds a harsh *keerr* when taking off.

Killdeer
Charadrius vociferus
ALSO: Keilschwanz-Regenpfeifer, Pluvier kildir, Tobeltelo, Крикливый зуёк.

SN means "noisy collared plover." RANGE: Wide-ranging in the Americas. The subspecies *C. v. vociferus* nests (Apr–Jun) on open and cultivated fields, golf courses, lakeshores, and disturbed sites in Alaska, c Canada, and the contiguous US south to Mexico. Winters south to the W Indies and C Amer. Rare but regular winter visitor to Britain and Ireland. ID: L 9–10 in (23–25 cm). AD: Brown crown and back. Distinctive tawny rump and white wing stripe seen in flight. White underparts broken by 2 black bands on breast. Black line from bill base to nape. Black bar across forehead bisects the white forehead and white eyeline. Black bill. Legs flesh colored. Red eyering in breeding plumage. JUV: Dark brown replaces most of the black markings of adult plumage. Area between bands on breast is brown rather than white. VOICE: Ringing alarm call, *kill-dee*, *kill-deer*, hence its CN.

GENUS VANELLUS
Northern Lapwing
Vanellus vanellus
ALSO: Peewit, Green Plover,

Kiebitz, Vanneau huppé, Vipe, Пигалица. CN derives from the Old English *hleapewince*, meaning "to wince or waver while leaping," a reference to the male's wild courtship flight. SN means "fanning [the air] with wings," a reference to the slow, flapping wingbeats. RANGE: Nests (Apr–Jun) on grasslands and

Killdeer
Charadrius vociferus
Americas
L 9–10 in (23–25 cm)

juv.

ad.
Mar–Aug

Semipalmated Plover
Charadrius semipalmatus
N Amer
L 6–7 in (16–18 cm)

ad.
Mar–Sep

ad. winter

Lesser Sand Plover
Charadrius mongolus
E Siberia
L 7–8.25 in (17–21 cm)

ad.
Apr–Aug

ad. winter

Ringed Plover
Charadrius hiaticula
Near circumpolar
L 7–8 in (17–20 cm)

ad.
Mar–Sep

ad. winter

Northern Lapwing
Vanellus vanellus
Eurasia
L 11–12 in (28–31 cm)

ad.

ad.♂
Apr–Aug

ad.♀
Apr–Aug

Eurasian Dotterel
Charadrius morinellus
Eurasia
L 8–9.5 in (20–24 cm)

juv.

farmlands in the UK, Faroes, Scandinavia, Russia (to 62°N), and Siberia (to 57°N), and south to s Europe and n China. Winters south to n Africa and s Asia, often migrating in huge flocks that feed in arable fields, meadows, and salt marshes. Vagrant in e N Amer from Baffin Is and Newfoundland to Barbados. **ID:** L 11–12 in (28–31 cm). Large, stocky plover. AD ♂: Long black crest. Upperparts blackish green with metallic gloss. Broad, rounded wings with white wing tips and white underwing coverts. Tail white with a broad black tip. Sides of face white, with a black line running under the eye. Black chin, neck, and breast; white belly; rufous vent. Reddish pink legs. Face is buffy in winter, with clear white chin and throat. AD ♀: White flecking on throat. Short crest. **VOICE:** Highly vocal. Plaintive *pee-wit'* sounded on the ground and in flight. Shrill whistled *chee-widdle-wip'*, *i-wip' i-wip'*, *peeo-wit'* given in display. **HABITS:** Forages on damp grasslands and marshes, taking insects, spiders, snails, earthworms, frogs, small fish, and some seeds. During aerial courtship dances, the male sweeps round in a wide circle before suddenly soaring upward, then rapidly tumbles earthward with wild twists and turns of its body and wings. Dramatic display is accompanied by the throb of wingbeats and whistled calls.

FAMILY SCOLOPACIDAE
SHOREBIRDS
The family Scolopacidae (Latin for "snipe-like") encompasses the godwits, curlews, dowitchers, sandpipers, turnstones, tattlers, phalaropes, snipe, and woodcocks. These birds have long slender bodies, long legs, and long narrow wings suited to long-range migratory flight. Most have cryptic plumage patterned in brown, gray, or black and white, although some display brighter colors during the breeding season. Sexes generally look alike.

These birds inhabit open areas, usually near water, where they feed on small invertebrates picked out of the mud or soil. Varying lengths and shapes of bills enable different species to feed in the same habitat without directly competing for food. Pressure-sensitive nerve endings called Herbst corpuscles located in pits at the bill tip allow these birds to "feel" for shellfish and other prey as they probe in the mud and sand.

The nest is typically a ground scrape made by the male and finished by the female. Pairs occasionally reuse nests, and some species use old tree nests of other birds. Both parents incubate the clutch of 2–4 (usually 4), pear-shaped or oval, mottled or spotted eggs for 17–32 days. The down-covered chicks are precocial and leave the nest within hours of hatching to forage with one of the parents, usually the male.

GENUS *LIMOSA*: The name *godwit* derives from the Old English *god wihte*, meaning "good creature," an allusion, perhaps, to the subtle flavor of roasted birds. *Limosa* is Latin for "mud," referring to the species' preferred foraging habitat on the mudflats.

Godwits are long-legged, long-billed wading birds that feed in small flocks on mudflats and along tidal shorelines. Females are typically larger than males and have longer bills. Godwits use their long bill to probe the mud for invertebrates such as annelid worms, mollusks, and crustaceans. Their diet also extends to beetles, mayflies, cranefly larvae, caterpillars, grasshoppers, dragonflies, earthworms, some aquatic plants and berries, and occasionally fish eggs, frog spawn, and tadpoles.

Breeding is largely monogamous, with pairs wintering separately and reuniting on the breeding grounds where they nest in small, loose colonies or in isolated pairs. Nest is a simple depression made in mossy or grassy tundra and set among grass tussocks or dwarf shrubs. Both parents incubate the 2–4 (usually 4) greenish, lightly spotted or blotched eggs for 20–25 days. Both sexes defend the nest by flying out with loud cries and circling over the intruder. Chicks are precocial and follow parents to feeding areas within a few hours of hatching.

Like many other shorebirds that breed in the Arctic, godwits are strongly migratory and fly great distances between their boreal nesting sites and wintering grounds in the southern latitudes.

Bar-tailed Godwit

Limosa lapponica
ALSO: Pacific Godwit, Pfuhlschnepfe, Barge rousse, Lappspove, Малый веретенник, Turraaturak. SN means "Lapland mud [-prober]."

RANGE: Nests (May–Jul) in loose colonies on open tundra and forest bogs along the n Eurasian coast, from Fennoscandia east to Chukotka, and in nw Alaska, from Cape Prince of Wales to Pt Barrow and south to the Yukon Delta. Winters on estuaries and coastal wetlands of Eurasia and the Philippines, south to S Africa, Australia, and NZ. Irregular to both coasts of N Amer.

In 2007, a female Bar-tailed Godwit, named E7 after the number on her leg band, completed an epic 18,000 mi (29,000 km) series of flights, which included the longest nonstop flight ever recorded for any land bird. Robert E. Gill of the US Geological Survey's Alaska Science Center along with colleagues in California and New Zealand tracked E7's odyssey. Flight details were recorded on a miniature battery-operated satellite tracking device inserted into the bird's gut.

On Mar 17, 2007, E7 left New Zealand's North Is and flew nonstop to Yalu Jiang, China, completing the 6300 mi (10,140 km) flight in about 8 days. She remained there for 5 weeks before departing for breeding grounds in Alaska. On May 1, E7 flew east out over the Sea of Japan and N Pacific, eventually turning northeast toward her nesting area on the Yukon-Kuskokwim Rvr delta in w Alaska. This second leg was also a nonstop flight, in which she flew 4500 mi (7242 km) in 5 days.

In late August, E7 was tracked to the Yukon Delta where she joined other bar-tailed godwits preparing for their return flight to New Zealand. On Aug 29, she flew out over the N Pacific, heading toward Hawaii. Less than a day's flight from Hawaii, E7 turned southwest over the open ocean and headed toward the islands of Fiji. Instead of landing in Fiji, she flew slightly west of the islands before continuing south again toward New Zealand.

On Sep 7, E7 passed just north of New Zealand, then turned back southeast, making landfall just

8 mi (13 km) east of where she had been banded 7 months earlier. She had completed the 7200 mi (11,587 km) transoceanic flight in just 8 days.

Professor Anders Hedenström of Sweden's Lund University has studied how bar-tailed godwits can fly so far without stopping and go without sleep or food for so many days. Hedenström found that in addition to their aerodynamic body shape that minimizes air resistance and their direct, rapid, and powerful flight, bar-tailed godwits consume very little energy in flight compared with other migrant species. He calculated that these birds consume less than 0.41 percent of their body mass during each hour of sustained flight.

In addition, bar-tailed godwits amass enough energy for long migratory flights by fattening up at staging grounds that are rich in mollusks, worms, and other invertebrates. Alaskan breeding bar-tailed godwits fatten up at staging grounds in the Yukon Delta. By the time they leave for New Zealand, these birds have increased their body weight by 50 percent, and most of that is composed of high-energy fat.

Bar-tailed godwits are truly remarkable birds that can live longer than 20 years. If one assumes that 22,000 mi (35,400 km) is an average annual flight distance for birds migrating between New Zealand and Alaska, then any one of these birds could conceivably fly 440,000 mi (708,000 km) or more in its lifetime.

ID: L 14–16 in (36–42 cm), incl 3–4 in (7–11 cm) bill. WT 9–20 oz (260–600 g), depending on season. Bill is long, slender, slightly upturned, pink at base, gray at tip. Tail barred brown and white. Whitish rump extends in a point up the back. Legs dark gray. AD APR–SEP: Back blackish brown, with russet flecks. Underwing and axillaries white, with faint brown streaking. Male's underparts are chestnut red; bill mostly dark. Female's underparts are pale pinky chestnut to gray, with breast often spotted with brown. AD WINTER: Upperparts pale grayish brown with darker shaft streaks. Underparts whitish; gray breast lightly barred with brown. JUV: Like winter adult, but with a strongly patterned back, and breast tinged with buff. VOICE: Nasal *kee-kee-ka* given in flight.

Hudsonian Godwit

Limosa haemastica

ALSO: Hudsonschnepfe, Barge hudsonienne, Svartvengspove, Канадский веретенник. SN means "blood red mud [-prober]," a reference to the breeding bird's rufous underparts. CN refers to Hudson Bay, Canada, a major nesting area.

RANGE: Nests (May–Jul) on wet tundra and sedgy marshland in disjunct locations in w/s Alaska, nw Canada, and along Hudson Bay. Most migrants stage at James Bay, Canada, and fly nonstop over the w Atlantic to S Amer, reaching inland and coastal wetland habitats in Chile, Argentina, and Falklands by late Sep. Rare visitor to Britain and Denmark.

ID: L 14–16 in (36–42 cm), including the 3–4 in (8–11 cm) long bill. Slightly upturned bill is dull pink to orange with a black tip. Black tail strongly contrasts with white rump. Black axillaries and underwing. Narrow white wing bar. Dark bluish gray legs. AD ♂ APR–SEP: Head and neck pale gray, with a dark eyeline and white supercilium. Upperparts dark reddish brown, spotted with buff. Deep chestnut below. AD ♀ APR–SEP: Female's underparts are considerably paler than male's and are spotted with buffy white. AD WINTER: Upperparts even mouse gray. Pale gray breast. White abdomen. JUV: Feathers of upperparts dark brown, edged with buff. Brownish buff wash to neck and breast. VOICE: High-pitched, slightly raspy *koe-wit' koe-wit' koe-wit'* or a repetitive *wit wit wit* sounded when displaying in flight or from treetop perches.

HABITS: Feeds around small ponds and wet meadows when breeding, taking insects, insect larvae, and small snails. In winter, forages for invertebrates on exposed tidal mudflats or in flooded areas. Probes the bill deeply into the mud or submerges entire head into water, sometimes feeding on submerged aquatic plant tubers. Regularly perches and displays on the tops of trees in breeding season.

STATUS: Highly vulnerable, with a population of only about 50,000 birds at fragmented breeding sites. Fully protected since 1927 in the US and Canada under the Migratory Bird Treaty Act.

Black-tailed Godwit

Limosa limosa

ALSO: Uferschnepfe, Barge à queue noire, Svarthalespove, Большой веретенник. SN means "mud [-prober]."

RANGE: Nests (May–Jun) in small colonies on wet meadows, grassy marshes, lakeshores, and boggy moorland in Iceland, Faroes, Shetlands, Lofoten Is, from wc Europe east to the Yenisei Rvr in Siberia, and in Mongolia and n China. Rare spring visitor to w Aleutians and Bering Sea islands. Winters in w Europe, w Africa, and Australia. Occupies estuaries, coastal mudflats, and inland freshwater marshes in migration.

ID: L 14–17 in (36–44 cm), incl 3–4 in (8–11 cm) long bill. AD APR–SEP: Bill is nearly straight, dark-tipped, with yellow at base. Upperparts grayish brown to blackish brown, with rufous edges. Underparts rufous with dark brown barring. White belly. Rump white. Tail black. Bold white wing bar. White underwing. Long, dark gray legs. Feet extend beyond tail tip in flight. Female's plumage duller in color. AD WINTER: Uniform gray breast and upperparts. Bill dull pink with a black tip. JUV: Paler than adult, with an orange wash to neck and breast. VOICE: Strident *weeka-weeka-weeka.*

GENUS *NUMENIUS*: This genus contains the curlews and whimbrels. *Numenius* means "new moon," alluding to similarity in shape between the curlew's bill and the crescent moon.

Curlews and whimbrels are large, long-legged, strongly migratory waders. Females are larger and longer-billed than males. These birds have mottled brown plumage and long, slender, downcurved bills, which they use to probe for worms, mollusks, and crustaceans living in mud or soft earth. Breeding is largely monogamous, with pairs wintering apart and reuniting on the breeding grounds. Curlews and whimbrels breed in small loose colonies. The nest is a depression made in tundra vegetation. Both sexes incubate a clutch of 3–6 (usually 4) eggs for 22–29 days. Chicks are precocial and within a day of hatching are led to feeding areas where they forage independently.

No wing bar
Streaked underwing

juv.

ad. winter

Barred tail
and rum

ad.
Apr–Sep

Bar-tailed Godwit
Limosa lapponica
Eurasia, Alaska
L 14–16 in (36–42 cm)

ad.♂
Apr–Sep

juv.

ad. winter

Bold white wing bar
White underwing
Black tail

ad.♂
Apr–Sep

Black-tailed Godwit
Limosa limosa
Iceland, Eurasia
L 14–17 in (36–44 cm)

ad.♂
Apr–Sep

Black
underwing

juv.

ad. winter

Breeding males
often display on
tops of trees

ad.♀
Apr–Sep

Hudsonian Godwit
Limosa haemastica
N Amer
L 14–16 in (36–42 cm)

The genus includes the Eskimo Curlew, *Numenius borealis,* which once was common on the plains of nw N Amer, but now may be extinct. The last recorded sighting was in 1987 in Nebraska, although there have been unconfirmed sight records in recent times. The species was last photographed in e Texas in 1962 and the last specimen taken in Barbados in 1963. The decline that began in the late 1800s has been attributed to excessive hunting, habitat conversion, and the extinction of a main prey item, the Rocky Mountain Grasshopper (*Melanoplus spretus*).

Bristle-thighed Curlew
Numenius tahitiensis

ALSO: Otaheite Curlew, Chiuit, Borstenbrachvogel, Courlis d'Alaska, Alaska-spove, Таитийский кроншнеп. CN refers to the elongated bare shafts of the thigh and flank feathers. SN means "new moon [bill] of Tahiti," referring to the first specimen collected in 1769 on Tahiti during Captain Cook's first voyage around the world. The species was assumed to spend its entire life on S Pacific islands until May 1869, when Ferdinand Bischoff collected the first N Amer specimen near Fort Kenai, Alaska. Seventy-nine years later, in 1948, David Allen and Henry Kyllingstad discovered the first nest, on a windy ridge about 20 mi (32 km) north of Mountain Village on the lower Yukon Rvr.
RANGE: Nests (May–Jun) on alpine tundra in two disjunct areas of w Alaska: in the Nulato Hills east of the Yukon Delta and on the Seward Penin. This is the only species of migratory shorebird to winter (Sep–Apr) exclusively on S Pacific atolls and islands, including those of Micronesia, French Polynesia, Pitcairn Is, Marquesas, Easter Is, and the Hawaiian chain. **ID:** L 15–17 in (40–44 cm), incl 3-4 in (8–10 cm) long decurved bill. Upperparts marked with tawny brown and buff. Rump and top of tail pale rufous. Neck and upper breast finely streaked buff and brown; flanks lightly barred brown; belly buff to near white. Bristles on thighs (visible at very close range). **VOICE:** Loud, clear, street-corner whistle, *pee-uu-weet'.*
HABITS: When breeding, feeds on insects, spiders, and large numbers of crowberries, blueberries, and flowers of berry-producing shrubs. Highly opportunistic on wintering grounds, feeding on intertidal and terrestrial invertebrates, seabird eggs and hatchlings, carrion, lizards, rodents, and fruit. Only known tool-using shorebird. Opens seabird eggs by tossing small pieces of coral or stones to break the eggs open, or else slams or drops eggs on a hard surface, then pecks them open. Uses the slamming technique to kill and dismember crabs, snails, mice, and Polynesian rats.

Forms long-term monogamous pairs, and is highly faithful to breeding and wintering sites. Both sexes perform soaring aerial displays and ground displays, accompanied by complex vocalizations. The nest is a shallow depression concealed by low vegetation in dwarf-shrub meadows. Both sexes incubate the clutch of 4 olive eggs spotted with brown for about 24 days. Hatchlings are able to feed themselves, but both parents tend the chicks until they can fly at about 21–24 days of age. Most adults abandon the breeding grounds and young in late July. They move to staging areas on the Yukon-Kuskokwim delta and the Alaska Penin,

The first nest of the Bristle-thighed Curlew was found in 1948 on the alpine tundra of w Alaska.

where they fatten up on berries and invertebrates that fuel their nonstop transoceanic migratory flights of 2500–3700 mi (4000–6000 km). The young move to staging grounds in late Aug and migrate independently. Subadults remain in Oceania for their first 3 years before returning to Alaska to breed. Lifespan is 15–23 years. **STATUS:** Rarest of the Nearctic curlews and godwits. Fewer than 3500 breeding pairs may exist and total population probably does not exceed 10,000 birds. The only shorebird known to become flightless when in molt. During their 2-week molt in the S Pacific, they lose all of their flight feathers, becoming open to predation by cats, dogs, and pigs. Vulnerable (IUCN).

Eurasian Curlew

Numenius arquata
ALSO: Western Curlew, Großer Brachvogel, Courlis cendré, Storspove, Большой кроншнеп. SN means "new moon bent [bill]."
RANGE: Nests (May–Jun) in forest bogs, grasslands, marshes, moors, and arable fields from the UK and Scandinavia east to ne China, e Siberia, and n Kazakhstan. Winters on wet meadows, tidal flats, and mudflats in Europe, Africa, and Asia. Occasional or accidental to Iceland, Bear Is (Norway), Jan Mayen, Azores, Madeira, and Cape Verde Is.
ID: L 19–23 in (48–57 cm), incl 4–6 in (9–15 cm) bill. Long, downcurved, dark horn-colored bill, with a pink or reddish base. Long legs and feet bluish gray to olive gray. AD: Head, neck, and upper mantle pale buffy brown, with dark streaks on the head and neck, and dark blotches and diffuse bars on the mantle. White lower back and rump. Tail barred pale and dark brown. Upperwings pale buffy brown with dark blotches; outer primaries blackish. Underwing white, variably streaked and spotted. Pale chin and upper throat. Upper breast whitish with dark streaks, grading to heavier streaking on lower breast, forming a bib; streaking continues onto the belly and vent. Drabber and duller-colored in winter, with whiter underparts that make the bib on the breast more obvious. JUV: Finely streaked rather than broadly barred on breast

and flanks. VOICE: A flute-like, mournful, far-carrying whistle, *cour-liii'* or *cue-cue-cew'*. **HABITS:** Forages by dipping bill deep into the water or silt. Feeds on insects, insect larvae, crabs, mollusks, and sometimes berries and small fish. Nest is a shallow depression set in mossy or grassy spots in damp lowlands, flooded meadows, or sometimes dry steppe. The male builds several nests, while the female chooses the one in which she will lay her eggs. Wary at nest. Will not approach intruder, but circles overhead and calls a plaintive *kooo-ee'*. Both sexes incubate the eggs and tend the young who can feed independently soon after hatching.

Far Eastern Curlew

Numenius madagascariensis
ALSO: Isabellbrachvogel, Courlis de Sibérie, Østspove, Дальневосточный крон-шнеп. SN means "new moon [bill] of Madagascar," the latter an erroneous toponym where *macassarensis* (after the Indonesian port of Makassar) was probably intended.
RANGE: Nests (Apr–May) in mossy bogs and swampy meadows from Kamchatka and ne Siberia south to n Mongolia and n Manchuria. Winters on mudflats, beaches, and marshes, south to Indonesia, Australia, and NZ.
ID: L 22–23 in (55–57 cm). Slightly longer-billed than *N. arquata,* but best separated by strongly barred underwing and barred rump, both conspicuous in flight.
STATUS: Vulnerable (IUCN).

Little Curlew

Numenius minutus
ALSO: Little Whimbrel, Pygmy Curlew, Zwerg-brachvogel, Courlis nain, Dvergspove, Кроншнеп-малютка. SN means "little new moon [bill]."
RANGE: Nests (May–Aug) on alpine tundra, open burned areas, and grassy clearings in larch or dwarf birch woodland in disjunct locations of Siberia, including the Verkhoyansk and Cherski Mtns, and possibly south to n Mongolia, Baikal, and Amurland. Migrates along the e Asia coast

and winters inland on meadows, fallow fields, near fresh water, on dry mudflats, or salt marshes from Indonesia south to Australia and NZ. **ID:** L 11–12 in (28–30 cm). Smallest curlew. Warm brown, strongly marked upperparts. Crown dark brown, with buff median stripe. Pale buff supercilium over large eyes. Long thin neck. Short, slender bill, downcurved at the tip, pink at base of lower mandible. Streaked buff breast. Pale belly. VOICE: Soft, rising whistle, *te-te-te';* also a melodic *quee-dlee* and a loud *tchew-tchew-tchew.* **HABITS:** Feeds on spiders, insects, insect larvae, seeds, and berries. Breeds in loose colonies of 3–30 pairs. Clutch of 4 greenish, brown-spotted eggs is laid in a shallow depression on open ground. Adult allows limited approach to the nest, then flushes and circles overhead or perches on a nearby shrub. When alarmed, stands tall and erect or crouches in the grass. Migrates in large, dense flocks that typically forage and roost in swampy meadows near lakes and rivers.

Whimbrel

Numenius phaeopus
ALSO: Hudsonian Curlew, Jack Curlew, Regenbrach-vogel, Courlis corlieu, Småspove, Средний кроншнеп, Siituvak. CN is possibly a derivation of *titterel*, a 16th-century English name imitative of the tittering call. SN means "new moon [bill] dusky-footed."
RANGE: Nests (May–Jul) on dry scrub heaths, moss and lichen tundra with stunted bushes, sedge meadows, wet moorland, mossy hummock bogs, and in birch forest-tundra in Alaska, nw Canada and Hudson Bay, Iceland, Faroes, Shetlands, Fennoscandia, and in scattered locations in arctic Siberia. Winters on coasts of S Amer, Africa, s Asia, and Australasia. Migration is primarily coastal and oceanic. Subadults remain in non-breeding areas for 1–3 years.
ID: L 15–18 in (40–45 cm), incl 2–4 in (6–9 cm) long, decurved bill. Gray legs. Upperparts brownish with a barred rump (N Amer) or grayish with a white rump (Eurasia). Crown dark brown with a pale median crown stripe. Dark eyeline. Buffy to whitish supercilium. Underparts and neck

buff, with heavy brown streaking and barring that extends along the flanks. Underwing is barred (N Amer) or white with barred axillaries (Eurasia). VOICE: Tittering *bibi-bibi-bibi-bi*; less frequently a whistled *cur-lew.*
HABITS: Walks and runs rapidly. Able to swim short distances. Sometimes perches in trees. On breeding grounds feeds on lichens, mosses, insects, and berries. Feeds on intertidal prey such as mollusks, small crabs, fish, and aquatic worms in winter. Prior to migrating, fattens up on berries, especially crowberries (*Empetrum*), which it pulls off the plant with the bill tip, then flips its head back to swallow the fruit. Nests in loose colonies. Males perform courtship display flights, steeply ascending to heights of 500–1000 ft (150–300 m), then circling and gliding down with stiff, downcurved wings. Both sexes display on the ground, with wing raising and fluttering and tail fanning.

GENUS *TRINGA*: *Tringa* refers to a thrush-sized shorebird mentioned by Aristotle but not further identified. The genus contains gray-plumaged, slender-bodied waders, including the shanks, tattlers, and yellowlegs. These shorebirds have long bills, long necks, and long legs, which are brightly colored in some species. Most are ground-nesters, except for solitary and green sandpipers, which nest in trees. The typical clutch is 4 buffy to greenish, darkly spotted eggs, which are incubated for 22–27 days. Both parents brood and feed the chicks for the first few days after hatching, after which a single parent, generally the male, tends the young.

Common Greenshank

Tringa nebularia
ALSO: Greater Greenshank, Grünschenkel, Chevalier aboyeur, Gluttsnipe, Большой улит. CN refers to the greenish legs. SN means "shorebird with cloudy gray [upperparts]."
RANGE: Nests on wet moorlands and in forests dotted with bogs, marshes, and small lakes in the n UK and across Eurasia from n Europe to Kamchatka. Winters on estuaries, creeks, and marshes in Africa, s Asia, Australasia. Vagrant

Eurasian Curlew
White rump
White underwing

juv.

Far Eastern Curlew
Barred rump
Barred underwing

ad.

Eurasian Curlew
Numenius arquata
Eurasia
L 19–23 in (48–57 cm)

Far Eastern Curlew
Numenius madagascariensis
NE Asia
L 22–23 in (55–57 cm)

Little Curlew
Numenius minutus
Siberia
L 11–12 in (28–30 cm)

Bristles on thighs
Rufous rump
Streaked breast ends
sharply at clean belly

Bristle-thighed Curlew
Numenius tahitiensis
Alaska
L 15–17 in (40–44 cm)

Eurasian subspecies
Grayish olive overall
White rump
Barred axillaries
White underwing

Whimbrel
Numenius phaeopus
Near circumpolar
L 15–18 in (40–45 cm)

N Amer subspecies
Brownish overall
Barred rump
Barred underwing

to the Pribilofs, w Aleutians, e Canada, Iceland, Faroes, Azores, and islands of the subantarctic. **ID:** L 12–14 in (30–36 cm). Long greenish legs. Long, slightly upturned bill. White rump and back. Upperparts grayish brown with white edging to feathers giving a scaled appearance. Belly white. Tail white with dark brown bars. Underwing barred. **VOICE:** Ringing *pill-e-wee, pill-e-wee, pill-e-wee* given in display; also loud, melodic whistles, *tew-tew-tew* or *too-hoo, too-hoo*. **HABITS:** Feeds on invertebrates located by sight; also takes small fish, insects, insect larvae, and occasionally small rodents. Chases after prey with neck outstretched and half-opened bill partly immersed in shallow water. Perches in low trees. Courtship flight involves turning and swerving at high speed, then circling higher and higher until out of sight, with only wild piping marking the bird's presence. Nest is a moss-lined depression near a stump or hummock.

SIMILAR SPECIES: SPOTTED or NORDMANN'S GREENSHANK, *Tringa guttifer*, breeds (Jun) on coasts of the Sea of Okhotsk and Sakhalin Is. Winters on se Asian coast. Gray above; whitish below with spotted breast. Greenish yellow legs. Dark-tipped yellow bill. Endangered; global population is fewer than 1000 individuals.

Spotted Redshank

Tringa erythropus
ALSO: Black Redshank, Dunkler Wasserläufer, Chevalier arlequin, Sotsnipe, Щеголь. SN means "red-footed shorebird."
RANGE: Nests (May–Jul) on boggy tundra and forest-tundra from Norway east across n Siberia. Winters near swamps, rivers, and lakes in n Africa, s Asia, and Mediterranean and Caspian sea areas. Vagrant to s Africa, e N Amer, w Aleutians, Pribilofs, Brit Columbia, Oregon, California. **ID:** L 12–13 in (30–33 cm). AD MAY–AUG: Sooty black, with white spotting on mantle and scapulars. White eyering. Bill black, with red at base of lower mandible. White patch on back (visible in flight). Tailed finely barred black and white. Legs blackish red. AD WINTER: Pale gray above; white below. Red legs. Bill black, with red at base of lower mandible. JUV: Grayish brown

back and chest, finely speckled with white. Boldly barred flanks. Light red legs. **VOICE:** Flight call *chu-eet, chu-eet*; alarm call *kyip, kyip, kyip*; display call *chu-vee-veeyou, tik-tik-tik, chu-vee-veeyou*. **HABITS:** Feeds on insects, insect larvae, crayfish, small fish, and mollusks, as it sweeps its bill from side to side. Wades and swims in deep water, sometimes upending like a dabbling duck. Male performs an aerial courtship dance at twilight, with rapid ascents and descents accompanied by wing rattling and excited calls. Nest is a scrape made in a raised area of a bog, often near a rock or stump that is used as a lookout perch.

Common Redshank

Tringa totanus
ALSO: Rotschenkel, Chevalier gambette, Rødstilk, Травник. SN derives from *totano*, the Italian name for a redshank.
RANGE: Nests (May–Jul) on wetlands in Iceland, UK, n Europe, and nc Siberia. Winters on tidal estuaries, mudflats, and some inland wetlands from Iceland and the UK south to n Africa, and from c Russia to s Asia. Vagrant to Greenland, Svalbard, Cape Verde Is, S Africa, Seychelles, Maldives, and n Australia. **ID:** L 10–11 in (25–27 cm). AD APR–AUG: Bright reddish orange legs. Bill is red at base, black at tip. Mottled brown and black back. Underparts whitish, heavily streaked with brown. White rump. Tail white with brown barring. Triangular white wing patch. AD WINTER: Upperparts plain grayish brown. Breast finely streaked and washed with grayish brown; streaks extend along flanks to undertail coverts. Bill and legs duller than in summer. Broken white eyering. JUV: Finely streaked underparts. Yellow-orange legs. **VOICE:** Musical, downslurred *tleu'-hu-hu*. Alarm call is *ti-yout, ti-yout, ti-yout*.
HABITS: Forages in shallow water or along the shoreline. Feeds by pecking rather than probing, taking small fish, mollusks, crustaceans, annelid worms, insects, and spiders. Wary and nervous "sentinal of the marsh," often the first wader to fly off with noisy calls. Nests in salt marshes and damp grasslands, often in high densities. Nest is a shallow depression set on a grass tussock.

Common Greenshank
Tringa nebularia
Eurasia
L 12–14 in (30–36 cm)

Barred underwing

ad. Apr–Aug
Drab green legs

ad. winter
Drab green legs

White underwing

ad. Apr–Aug
Greenish yellow legs

Spotted Greenshank
Tringa guttifer
Sea of Okhotsk
L 12 in (30 cm)
Endangered

ad. winter
Greenish yellow legs

ad. winter
Reddish legs

juv.
Light red legs

ad. May–Aug
Blackish red legs

Spotted Redshank
Tringa erythropus
Eurasia
L 12–13 in (30–33 cm)

ad. winter
Light red legs

juv.
Yellow orange legs

Common Redshank
Tringa totanus
Iceland, Eurasia
L 10–11 in (25–27 cm)

ad. Apr–Aug
Reddish orange legs

Lesser Yellowlegs

Tringa flavipes

ALSO: Kleiner Gelbschenkel, Petit Chevalier à pattes jaunes, Gulbeinsnipe, Желтоногий улит, Tinmiam kipmia. SN means "shorebird with golden yellow [legs]."

RANGE: Nests (May–Jul) around ponds and muskeg in burned and open woodland from Alaska to Quebec, Canada. Winters on marshes, estuaries, and other wetlands from S Carolina, c California, and Mexico south to Chile and Argentina. Vagrant to Europe (fall), Iceland, sw Africa, Japan, Australia, NZ, and Falklands. **ID:** L 9–11 in (23–28 cm). Long, bright yellow to yellow orange legs. Thin, straight, dark bill. White supercilium and eyering; dusky lores. Upperparts dark grayish brown, spotted with white. Uppertail coverts white; tail barred black and white. Head, neck, and chest finely streaked with gray. White belly. **VOICE:** Soft whistled *tew-tew*. Song is a repeated musical *pil-e-wee'*. **HABITS:** Forages in shallow water, sweeping the bill back and forth to stir up insects, spiders, small fish, worms, and crustaceans, which are then plucked from the surface. Rarely dashes after food. Bobs its head as it wades. Nests in loose colonies. Nest is a shallow depression lined with vegetation and set on a dry, mossy hummock, under cover of a fallen log or low shrub. Both sexes incubate the eggs. The female often leaves the breeding area before the chicks fledge, leaving the male to tend the brood. **SIMILAR SPECIES:** GREATER YELLOWLEGS, *Tringa melanoleuca*, breeds in marshes, estuaries, and wetlands in s Alaska and c Canada; winters south to Tierra del Fuego. Larger, heavier, longer-legged version of *T. flavipes*. Ringing call *pee-toy-toy*. Dashes about searching for prey in shallow water, a behavior that separates it from lesser yellowlegs feeding on the same pond.

Solitary Sandpiper

Tringa solitaria

ALSO: Einsamer Wasser-läufer, Chevalier solitaire, Eremittsnipe, Улит отшельник. SN means "solitary shorebird,"

alluding to the species habit of foraging alone. Although the species was described in 1813, the first nest wasn't found until 1903, when Evan Thomson discovered this species' eggs in an abandoned nest of an American Robin (*Turdus migratorius*) in Alberta, Canada. **RANGE:** Nests (May–Jun) in trees around muskeg ponds from Alaska to c Canada. Winters from s Texas and the Caribbean to S Amer. Vagrant to Bermuda, Greenland, Iceland, w Europe, Galapagos, Island of S Georgia, S Africa. **ID:** L 7.5–9 in (19–23 in). AD APR–AUG: Grayish brown head and neck. Bold white eyering. Dark brown back, finely spotted with white. Rump and center of tail dark, with black bars on white outer tail feathers. Dark underwing. White belly. Dull green legs. AD WINTER/JUV: Streaked with dark brown and white on head, neck, and chest. **VOICE:** Flight call is a clear whistle, *peet-weet-weet'* or *tou-tou-twit'*. **HABITS:** Solitary. Feeds mainly on insects and insect larvae found in flooded fields, quiet woodland pools, and ditches. Pecks food from the water surface. Wades in deep water, using its foot to stir up prey. Bobs when alarmed. Lays 3–5 pale green, red-spotted eggs in abandoned nests of arboreal songbirds. Downy young leave the nest soon after hatching, jumping as far as 40 ft (13 m) down to the ground.

Green Sandpiper

Tringa ochropus

ALSO: Waldwasserläufer, Chevalier cul-blanc, Skog-snipe, Черныш. SN means "shorebird with pale yellow feet."

RANGE: Nests (May–Jul) in trees in swampy wooded areas from Fennoscandia to Siberia, China, Mongolia, and n Manchuria. Winters around inland lakes and ponds from s Europe to tropical Africa. Frequents flooded fields during migration. Vagrant to w Aleutians (spring), Jan Mayen, Madeira, S Africa, n Australia. **ID:** L 8–10 in (20–24 cm). AD: Dark greenish brown upperparts; back variably spotted with white. Grayish head and breast. Short, blackish green bill. White supercilium in front of eye. Narrow white eyering. Bright white rump. Tail

Solitary Sandpiper
Tringa solitaria
N Amer
L 7.5–9 in (19–23 cm)

Wood Sandpiper
Tringa glareola
Eurasia
L 7–8.5 in (18–21 cm)

juv.

Green Sandpiper
Tringa ochropus
Eurasia
L 8–10 in (20–25 cm)

ad.
Apr–Aug

Lesser Yellowlegs
Tringa flavipes
N Amer
L 9–11 in (23–28 cm)

Greater Yellowlegs
Tringa melanoleuca
N Amer
L 13–15 in (33–38 cm)

ad.
Apr–Oct

ad. winter

Gray-tailed Tattler
Tringa brevipes
Siberia
L 9–10 in (23–25 cm)

ad. winter

Wandering Tattler
Tringa incana
Chukotka, nw N Amer
L 9–10 in (23–25 cm)

ad.
Apr–Oct

white, with 3–4 black bars. White belly. Blackish underwings. Dull green legs. JUV: Upperparts and breast browner and more evenly colored than adult's. VOICE: Loud, sharp, high-pitched whistle, *twit-wit-wit*.
HABITS: Nervous and wary. Usually seen singly in small pools and narrow freshwater watercourses, where it picks small invertebrates off the mud. Nests in trees in wooded areas that have numerous brooks, pools, marshes, and swamps. Uses abandoned or (rarely) active nests of thrushes, wood pigeons, or squirrels, or nests in a natural hollow amid tree roots. Both parents incubate the 2–4 eggs for about 22 days. Like *Tringa solitaria*, the young jump from nest height to the ground within hours of hatching.

Wood Sandpiper

Tringa glareola
ALSO: Bruchwasserläufer, Chevalier sylvain, Grønstilk, Фифи. SN means "shorebird of the gravel," from the conjectured habitat of the unrelated Collared Pratincole (*Glareola pratincola*).
RANGE: Nests (May–Jun) in swampy forests, mossy bogs, grassy meadows, and along forest rivers and lakes across n Eurasia and less commonly in the w Aleutians. Winters in the Mediterranean, Africa, s Asia, and Australia. Vagrant to Brit Columbia and ne N Amer. Forms small feeding flocks on shorelines in migration.
ID: L 7–8.5 in (18–21 cm). Slender-bodied, with a distinct white supercilium and capped appearance. Dark grayish brown above. Breast heavily marked with white spots. Rump white. Black and white barred tail. Underparts white. Underwing pale gray. Long, green to yellowish legs. Toes project beyond tail tip. VOICE: Loud, sharp series of high-pitched whistles, *chif-if-fifi*.
HABITS: Feeds in swamps, marshes, and flooded fields. Forages with a teetering gait as it searches for insects and other invertebrates. Pecks items from the water surface, sometimes submerging head as it attempts to seize underwater prey. Nests on the ground in dense marsh vegetation or damp open areas of boreal forests. Occasionally nests in trees in abandoned songbirds' nests.

Wandering Tattler

Tringa incana
ALSO: Wanderwasserläufer, Chevalier errant, Alaskavandresnipe, Американский пепельный улит, *Heteroscelus incanus*. CN possibly stems from the loud alarm calls that give away (tattle on) the bird's location. SN means "light gray shorebird." Adolph Murie (1899–1974), author of *A Naturalist in Alaska*, collected the first nest and eggs of this species in 1923.
RANGE: Nests (May–Jul) in remote mountains in Chukotka, Alaska, and nw Canada. Winters on rocky seacoasts from California to the Galapagos and Peru, and in Hawaii, sw Pacific islands, and ne Australia, the last more than 7500 mi (12,000 km) from breeding grounds.
ID: L 9–10 in (23–25 cm). Entirely plain gray upperparts in both breeding and non-breeding plumages. AD APR–OCT: Upperparts gray. Underparts barred with gray and white. Faint white supercilium. Short yellow legs. AD WINTER/JUV: Breast and flanks slate gray. Belly white. At very close range, a long nasal groove can be seen. VOICE: Rapid *lidididi* trill sounded in flight. Sharp *klee-ik* when alarmed. Ringing, whistled *deedle-deedle-deedle-dee* when displaying.
HABITS: Solitary. Probes and bobs as it forages for aquatic invertebrates, insects, and insect larvae. Nests on gravel bars of rivers and on streamside meadows in glaciated mountain areas. Nests among rocks in a shallow depression lined with intricately woven twigs, lichens, and leaves. Both sexes incubate the 4 pale greenish gray, brown-spotted eggs. Young leave nest with both parents within a few days of hatching. Juveniles migrate south after most adults and remain in non-breeding areas until about 2 years old.

Gray-tailed Tattler

Tringa brevipes
ALSO: Polynesian, Gray-rumped, or Siberian Tattler, Grauschwanz Wasserläufer, Chevalier de Sibérie, Sibirvandresnipe, Сибирский пепельный улит, *Heteroscelus brevipes*. SN means "short-legged shorebird."
RANGE: Nests (Jun–Jul) along stony riverbeds

in mountains of Siberia in disjunct locations including the Taimyr Penin, Yakutia, Chukotka, Koryak region, and Kamchatka. Migrates along the coast of e Asia and across the sw Pacific to winter on rocky coasts of Indonesia, Philippines, Polynesia, Australia. Rare but regular migrant to the Aleutians, Pribilofs, and St Lawrence Is. Casual on nw Alaska coast. Vagrant to Hawaii, Washington state, and s California. Single record at Burghead, Scotland, in Nov 1994; first reports of the sighting are said to have resulted in 90 arrests for speeding on the A9 roadway. **ID:** L 9–10 in (23–25 cm). AD APR–OCT: Upperparts evenly gray. White supercilium and dark lores. Underparts lightly streaked and barred with gray on the neck, breast, and flanks; belly white. Short yellow legs. At very close range, the overlapping horny tarsal scales (*scutellations*) may be visible. Breeding plumage underparts are not as strongly barred as Wandering Tattler's. AD WINTER: Breast evenly slate gray. Belly white. VOICE: Upslurred whistle, *tu-ueet'*. Sharp *klee-klee* when alarmed. **HABITS:** Solitary. Bobs and teeters as it moves about. Feeds by probing for worms, mollusks, crustaceans, insects, and some fish. Probes into burrows or submerges head to seize crabs, then throws the crab down repeatedly to break off the legs before washing and eating it. Nests on the ground along stony riverbeds and occasionally in trees in old thrush nests. Clutch is 4 light blue eggs speckled with black. First nest was discovered by a Russian geologist in 1959. **STATUS:** Near Threatened (IUCN).

GENUS ACTITIS: *Actitis* means "coastal dweller," a somewhat misleading name, as common and spotted sandpipers prefer inland freshwater habitats for breeding. These small waders are brown above and white below, and have short, yellowish legs. They fly on stiffly held, down-bowed wings, with quick, shallow wing strokes and frequent short glides.

Common Sandpiper
Actitis hypoleucos
ALSO: Flußuferläufer, Chevalier guignette, Strandsnipe, Drillsnäppa,

Перевозчик, *Tringa hypoleucos.* SN means "coastal dweller with white underparts." **RANGE:** Nests (Apr–Jul) near rivers and lakes in forested areas, less frequently along sheltered seacoasts, in the UK and across Eurasia. Migrates singly or in small flocks, roosting in wetland habitats. Winters to s Africa, c Asia, Philippines, Australia. Casual migrant in w Alaska. Vagrant to NZ, Hawaii, Amsterdam Is (Southern Ocean). **ID:** L 7–8.5 in (18–21 cm). AD APR–AUG: Upperparts greenish brown, faintly streaked and barred with darker brown. Tail brown; outer tail feathers barred black and white. White wing bar. Sides of breast washed with brown, forming a partial breast band. Underparts white. Underwing white, with 2 dark bars. Legs yellow. AD WINTER/JUV: Paler than breeding adult; juvenile's wing feathers edged with buff. VOICE: Flight call, often heard at night, is a rapid series of high-pitched whistles, *swee-swee-swee-swoooo*. Whistled *heeeep* alarm call. Rhythmic tittering *swidi-dii', dide, swidi-dii', dide* in display. **HABITS:** Feeds on insects and invertebrates. Forages with a slow, deliberate, bobbing motion. Perches on posts, trees, and moored boats. Nests in solitary pairs on the ground under waterside vegetation. Both sexes incubate the 4 pinkish, speckled eggs for 21–22 days and tend the precocial young.

Spotted Sandpiper
Actitis macularius
ALSO: Spotted Tattler, Iksriktaayuuk, Drosselu-feläufer, Chevalier grivelé,

Flekksnipe, Пятнистый перевозчик,*Tringa macularia.* SN means "spotted coastal dweller." **RANGE:** Nests (May–Jul) along rivers and lakes in Alaska and Canada, from the treeline south through the US. Winters on seacoasts and inland freshwater bodies from Brit Columbia south to the W Indies, Galapagos, n Chile, and Argentina. Recorded annually in small numbers in UK, w Europe, and Chukotka. Accidental in Iceland, Svalbard, Azores, Tristan de Cunha, and Canton and Marshall Is (c Pacific). **ID:** L 7–8 in (18–20 cm). AD APR–AUG: Bronzy olive above. White underparts dotted with black spots. White supercilium. Black eyeline. Bill yellow with dark tip. Legs yellow. **AD WINTER/JUV:** Upperparts grayish brown. Underparts white, with gray shading on upper breast. **VOICE:** Rolling clear whistle, *tototo-wee*, in display. **HABITS:** Feeds with its back parallel to ground, bobbing and nodding continually. Often forages on floating logs. Nest is a ground scrape lined with grass or moss and placed next to dense vegetation near water. Mainly the male incubates the 4 buffy, brown-spotted eggs for 20–22 days.

GENUS *XENUS*
Terek Sandpiper
Xenus cinereus

ALSO: Terekwasserläufer, Chevalier bargette, Tereksnipe, Мородунка. CN refers to a breeding site on the Terek Rvr, Russia. SN means "stranger with an ash-colored [back]," with *Xenus* (stranger) alluding to its seasonal appearance on breeding grounds. **RANGE:** Nests (May–Jun) on tundra and taiga-steppe from Finland across n Siberia. Winters on coasts of e Africa, India, NZ, Australasia. Casual in Alaska, Aleutians, Pribilofs, and c Pacific islands. Vagrant to Argentina. **ID:** L 9–10 in (23–25 cm). Long, slightly upcurved, black bill, with a yellowish base. Indistinct white supercilium. Back, face, and breast gray. Black patch at joint of folded wing. Broad white trailing edge to upperwing. Gray rump and tail. White belly. Legs yellow. **VOICE:** Sharp, flute-like *twit-wit-wit-wit* in flight. Song is a repeated 3-note whistle, *ka klee-rreee′*. **HABITS:** Feeds on insects, insect larvae, crustaceans, and mollusks, taken at water's edge or from the surface of shallow water. Dashes about when feeding, occasionally wagging tail and often running to water's edge to dunk prey. Nests in solitary pairs or small colonies along lakes, rivers, and streams; occasionally nests in harbors or on floating logs near sawmill factories. Nest is a ground scrape lined with grass, bark, and pine needles and set in a dry spot near water, usually under cover of bushes or tall grass. Clutch is 4 dove-gray eggs, speckled with dark brown.

GENUS *LIMNODROMUS*: Dowitchers are mid-sized, long billed waders. They resemble godwits, but are shorter-legged, and are more like the closely related snipes. *Dowitcher* is the Iroquois Indian name for these birds. *Limnodromus* means "marsh dweller."

Long-billed Dowitcher
Limnodromus scolopaceus

ALSO: Western Red-breasted Snipe, Greater Gray-backed Snipe, Long-beaked Snipe, Western Dowitcher, Großer Schlammläufer, Bécassin à long bec, Langnebbekkasinsnipe, Американский бекасовидный веретенни. SN means "snipe [-billed] marsh dweller." **RANGE:** Nests (May–Jul) on wet grassy tundra along the arctic coasts of ne Siberia, Alaska, and nw Canada. Winters along Pacific and Gulf coasts of N Amer. Rare winter visitor to the UK, Ireland, n Europe, Japan, Hawaii. **ID:** L 11–12.5 in (27–32 cm), incl 2–3 in (5.5–7.5 cm) bill. **AD MAY–JUL:** Upperparts dark brown, with feathers edged in buff and rufous. Rump white. Tail barred in black and white. Underparts rufous, with brown spotting and barring on foreneck, breast, and flanks. **AD WINTER:** Back dark gray. Head, breast, and flanks mottled gray. Belly white. **VOICE:** High, thin *keek-keek-keek* flight call. Song is a buzzy *pee-witch-er*, the basis of the common English name. **HABITS:** Feeds on insects, insect larvae, worms, small crustaceans, and marine invertebrates, probing in an up-and-down "sewing machine" motion. Several courting males will pursue a female while calling loudly. Nest is a deep depression or ground scrape lined with sedge, grasses, and small leaves. Both sexes incubate the clutch of 4 olive to greenish, brown-spotted eggs. The female deserts the hatchlings, leaving the male to rear the chicks until they fledge at about 30 days. **SIMILAR SPECIES:** SHORT-BILLED DOWITCHER, *Limnodromus griseus*, nests in the forests of s Alaska and c Canada; winters along both coasts of N Amer. Bill is shorter than that of the very similar Long-billed Dowitcher. Best separated by call, a whistled *tu-tu-tu*.

ad. winter

juv.

ad.
Apr–Aug

Common Sandpiper
Actitis hypoleucos
Eurasia
L 7–8.5 in (18–21 cm)

ad.
Apr–Aug

Spotted Sandpiper
Actitis macularius
N Amer
L 7–8 in (18–20 cm)

ad.
May–Jul

ad. winter

Terek Sandpiper
Xenus cinereus
Eurasia
L 9–10 in (23–25 cm)

Short-billed Dowitcher
Limnodromus griseus
N Amer
L 10–11 in (25–28 cm)

ad.
May–Jul

ad. winter

Long-billed Dowitcher
Limnodromus scolopaceus
Siberia, w N Amer
L 11–12.5 in (28–32 cm)

GENUS *CALIDRIS*: *Calidris* is a term Aristotle applied to small gray-and-white-plumaged sandpipers. Calidrids are called *stints* in Europe and known collectively as *peeps* in the Americas.

The calidrids are Arctic-breeding, strongly migratory wading birds that form large, mixed-species flocks on mudflats and estuaries in non-breeding season. In winter most feed on small crustaceans, mollusks, polychaete worms, and other invertebrates. When breeding, they feed on spiders, insects such as crane flies, midges, and mosquitoes, and also take some berries and seeds.

Breeding is monogamous, with one male mating with one female for a single season. Most species produce a single clutch of 4 relatively large, tan to olive green, spotted eggs, which one or both parents incubate for 19–27 days. Sanderlings, Temminck's stints, and little stints are exceptional in that the female usually lays 2 clutches of eggs—one for the male to incubate and rear, and another for herself. In most species, the young are brooded for a couple of days, after which the female abandons the nest and begins her southward migration, leaving the male to rear the brood.

Calidrids are notoriously hard to tell apart, especially in winter, when the plumage of most species is mouse gray above and white below. One must resort to careful observation of details such as bill length and shape, leg color, and differences in feeding behavior and habitat preference in order to secure identification. But there are times when even the most dedicated birder must give up and simply lower his or her binoculars to marvel at the spectacle of huge flocks scurrying about on the mudflats or banking and turning like a dense ball of schooling fish as they fly over the outgoing tide.

Spoon-billed Sandpiper
Calidris pygmea
ALSO: Löffelstrandläufer, Bécasseau spatule, Skeisnipe, Лопатень, *Eurynorhynchus pygmeus.* SN means "dwarf shorebird."

RANGE: Nests (Jun–Jul) on coastal tundra of Chukotka (ne Siberia), usually in grassy margins of freshwater ponds. Migrates 5000 mi (8000 km) along the e Asian flyway to winter on seacoasts of se Asia. Vagrant in Assam, Commander Is, w Aleutians, w Alaska, Brit Columbia.
ID: L 5.5–6.25 in (14–16 cm). Small wader with a unique spatulate bill. AD MAY–JUL: Head, neck, and back chestnut red, streaked with dark brown. Cap and scapulars blackish, edged with chestnut. Coverts grayish brown, some edged with white. Wing bar and sides of rump white. Underparts white. Legs black. AD WINTER: Silvery gray upperparts. White foreneck and underparts. White supercilium. VOICE: Cicada-like, buzzing trill, *preer-prr-prr,* in display flight.
HABITS: Feeds on insects and other small invertebrates taken by sweeping the bill side to side through shallow water or soft wet mud. Male's nuptial flight consists of dipping and circling high in the air while calling, then performing a sweeping dive to the ground. Nest is a depression on mossy tundra lined with a few dwarf willow leaves. Both parents incubate the 4 eggs for 21 days. Young can feed themselves a few hours after hatching, but return periodically to the nest for a day or two to be brooded. The female then leaves the breeding area and the male leads the young to the open tundra and remains with them until they fledge at about 20 days of age.
STATUS: Critically Endangered (IUCN); 120–200 breeding pairs remain. Decline is due to alteration of wetland habitat on the e Asian flyway and excess hunting on wintering areas. In 2011, the Wildfowl and Wetlands Trust (WWT) and Birds Russia began collecting the species' eggs in Chukotka, transporting them to the Moscow Zoo for hatching, and then transferring the chicks to the WWT at Slimbridge, England, for rearing.

Broad-billed Sandpiper
Calidris falcinellus
ALSO: Sumpfläufer, Bécasseau falcinelle, Fjellmyrløper, Грязовик, *Limicola falcinellus.* SN means "shorebird with a sickle-shaped [bill tip]."

RANGE: Nests (Jun–Jul) on wet upland tundra and forest-tundra bogs in disjunct sites in Scandinavia, Kola Penin, and n Siberia between the Yenisei and Kolyma rivers. Winters on coasts of Mediterranean, s Asia, Australia. Vagrant to w Aleutians, NZ, Iceland, Bear Is (Nor), e Africa. **ID:** L 6–7 in (15–18 cm). Fairly long, flattened, black bill with a decurved tip. AD MAY–AUG: Upperparts blackish, mottled with brown. Black and white striped crown. Split white supercilium. White rump; tail gray, with dark central feathers. Narrow white wing bar. White breast streaked with black. Belly white. Short legs. AD WINTER: Upperparts gray, with dark shaft streaks. Faint streaking on head and breast. Slightly smaller than the Dunlin, but with a longer, straighter bill and shorter legs. **VOICE:** Short *tirr-tirr-terek* in flight. Dunlin-like display trill, *jree-jree-jijrrr*. **HABITS:** Slow, methodical forager. Secretive and silent on the nest. Nest is a ground scrape lined with dwarf birch and willow leaves, and built on dry raised areas of bogs and sedge mires.

Red-necked Stint

Calidris ruficollis
ALSO: Rufous-necked Stint, Rotkehl-Strandläufer, Bécasseau à col roux, Raud-strupesnipe, Песочник-красношейка. SN means "red-necked shorebird."
RANGE: Nests (May–Jul) on low-lying tundra in the e Taimyr Penin, Lena Rvr delta, Chukotka, and Anadyr. Migrates up to 6900 mi (11,000 km) to winter in Australasia and NZ. Casual to n Europe and w Alaska. Vagrant to Pacific and Atlantic coasts of N Amer and Bermuda.
ID: L 5–6.25 in (13–16 cm). Short, straight, black bill. Dark legs. White wing bar. Dark rump. Central tail feathers dark; outer tail feathers white. AD MAY–AUG: Rusty red face, neck, and throat bordered by dark spots. Mantle feathers black, edged with bright rufous; faint white V on back. Scapulars and wing coverts mostly gray. Belly white. AD WINTER: Upperparts gray, with an incomplete grayish breast band. **VOICE:** High, scraping *quiit* sounded in flight. Prolonged series of *yek-yek-yek* notes during display.
HABITS: Forages with a hunched back; pecks rapidly and repeatedly before dashing to another spot. Nest is a shallow depression made on moss-lichen tundra or a scrape on rocky soil.

Little Stint

Calidris minuta
ALSO: Zwergstrandläufer, Bécasseau minute, Dverg-snipe, Кулик-воробей. SN means "tiny shorebird."
RANGE: Nests (Jun–Aug) on dry tundra from n Scandinavia and nw Russia east across Siberia to the Kolyma Rvr. Winters on mudflats and salt marshes in Africa, Arabian Penin, India. Vagrant to UK, n Europe, Iceland, Faroes, Svalbard, w Aleutians, Alaska, e N Amer, Japan, Australia.
ID: L 5–6 in (13–15 cm). Short, straight, black bill. Black legs. Strong white wing bar. Dark rump. Central tail feathers dark; outer tail feathers pale gray. AD MAY–AUG: Rusty orange head and upperparts; male deeper rufous than female. Breast washed orange with dark spots. Underparts white. AD WINTER: Upperparts gray, faintly mottled with black and rufous. Underparts white. JUV: Mantle and crown feathers black, edged with rufous and white. Split white supercilium. Two whitish stripes ("braces") down the back. **VOICE:** Sharp, high-pitched *stit* in flight.
HABITS: Forms mixed-flocks, often with dunlins (*C. alpina*), that roost together during high tide or at night. Forages on muddy pool edges and mudflats, pecking repeatedly, then darting to another spot. Nests on dry tundra among low willows and dwarf birch, or on moss-sedge tundra where crowberries are abundant. Nest is a depression lined with willow or birch leaves. Male and female incubate separate clutches.

Temminck's Stint

Calidris temminckii
ALSO: Temminckstrand-läufer, Bécasseau de Temminck, Temmincksnipe, Белохвостый песочник. SN/CN honors Dutch zoologist Coenraad Jacob Temminck (1778– 1858), author of *Manuel d'ornithologie*, the standard work on European birds for many years.
RANGE: Nests (Jun) around bogs, marshes, and river deltas on tundra and upland taiga, from n Scandinavia and Kola Penin east to Chukotka. Winters mainly on interior wetlands in Africa, the Mediterranean region, s Asia. Winter visitor to

Europe and UK. Vagrant to Aleutians, w Alaska, Brit Columbia, Azores, Canaries, Seychelles, Maldives, Philippines, Borneo. **ID:** L 5–6 in (13–15 cm). Thin, slightly decurved, dark bill. Yellow legs. Faint, narrow, white wing bar. Dark rump. Central tail feathers dark; outer tail feathers white. Tail projects beyond wing tips. AD MAY–AUG: Head, breast, and back mouse gray, with some black-centered, rufous-edged feathers on back. Underparts white. AD WINTER: Drab grayish brown on head, breast, and back. Underparts white. VOICE: Trilling *dirr-dirr-dirr* given in flight. Display song of melodic trills has been likened to tinkling bells. **HABITS:** Feeds in freshwater marshes and on sparsely vegetated edges of mudflats. Crouches with bent legs and belly near the ground as it feeds. When alarmed, flies off on an erratic course while giving trilling call. Nests in a scrape made in grassy or dwarf willow vegetation. Male and female incubate separate clutches.

Long-toed Stint

Calidris subminuta
ALSO: Middendorf's Stint, Langzehen Strandläufer, Bécasseau à longs doigts, Langtåsnipe, Длиннопалый песочник. SN means "very small shorebird."
RANGE: Nests (Jun) on alpine tundra and interior marshes in Magadan, Transbaikal, Verkoyanski Mtns, Koryak Plateau, Chukotka, Commander and Kuril islands (probable breeding range is pale gray on map). Winters near freshwater in se Asia, Philippines, Australia. Regular visitor to the Aleutians. Vagrant to w Alaska, Oregon, UK, Sweden, e Africa, Seychelles, Christmas Is. **ID:** L 5–6 in (13–15 cm). Short, slightly decurved, blackish bill; base of lower mandible tinged greenish yellow. Legs yellow. Long toes (visible at close range). AD MAY–JUL: Back feathers black edged with rufous. Rufous cap and dark forecrown contrast with white supercilium. Breast finely streaked and tinged with cream. Belly white. Faint white wing bar. White sides to the dark rump and dark central tail feathers; outer tail feathers gray. Underwing white, with dark flight feathers and conspicuous gray bands

across coverts. AD WINTER: Upperparts brownish gray, with dark-centered feathers. Breast finely streaked and washed with pale gray. VOICE: Soft, rippling *prrt* or a sharp *tik-tik-tik.* **HABITS:** Stands upright, appearing long-necked and long-legged. Forages for invertebrates on brackish and freshwater wetlands with bare muddy shores and floating mats of algae; long toes may aid in walking on floating vegetation. Nest is a depression on a sedge hummock.

Least Sandpiper

Calidris minutilla
ALSO: Lilivillilaurak, Wiesenstrandläufer, Bécasseau minuscule, Pygmésnipe, Песочник крошка. SN means "tiny shorebird."
RANGE: Nests (May–Jul) in bogs, muskeg, and sedge mires in Alaska and n Canada; flies up to 2500 mi (4000 km) nonstop across the N Atlantic between boreal staging grounds and S Amer. Large flocks winter along Pacific and Atlantic coasts of the Americas, south to Peru and n Brazil. Casual in ne Siberia, Pribilofs, Hawaii. Vagrant to Iceland, Azores, UK, n Europe, Baffin Is, and S Orkney Is (Antarctica). **ID:** L 5–6 in (13–15 cm). Short, slightly decurved, dark bill. Legs yellowish green. Short neck. Short wings. Narrow white wing bar. Dark rump. Central tail feathers dark; outer tail feathers gray. AD MAY–AUG: Back feathers black-centered, edged with rufous. Rufous face and cap. White supercilium. Breast finely streaked and tinged with cream. Belly white. AD WINTER: Gray above; white below, with brown streaks on the breast. VOICE: Shrill, rising *trre-eep* or purring *prrt.* **HABITS:** Forages at edge of mudflats or along dry margins of inland ponds. Crouches with bent legs and belly near the ground while pecking or probing for small invertebrates.

Western Sandpiper

Calidris mauri
ALSO: Bergstrandläufer, Bécasseau d'Alaska, Beringsnipe, Перепончатопалый песочник, *Ereunetes mauri.* SN honors Italian botanist Ernesto Mauri (1791–1836).

Temminck's Stint
Calidris temminckii
Eurasia
L 5–6 in (13–15 cm)

ad. winter

ad. May–Aug

Broad-billed Sandpiper
Calidris falcinellus
Eurasia
L 6–7 in (15–18 cm)

ad. May–Aug

ad. winter

Upright posture

ad. winter

Long-toed Stint
Calidris subminuta
Siberia
L 5–6 in (13–15 cm)

ad. May–Jul

Red-necked Stint
Calidris ruficollis
Siberia
L 5–6.25 in (13–16 cm)

ad. winter

ad. May–Aug

Least Sandpiper
Calidris minutilla
N Amer
L 5–6 in (13–15 cm)

ad. winter

ad. May–Aug

juv.
White "braces"
down back

ad. winter

ad. May–Aug

Little Stint
Calidris minuta
Eurasia
L 5–6 in (13–15 cm)

Male rears the chicks

ad. May–Jul

ad. winter

Spoon-billed Sandpiper
Calidris pygmea
NE Siberia
L 5.5–6.25 in (14–16 cm)

RANGE: Nests (May–Jul) on tundra in Chukotka and Alaska. Migrates in huge flocks along the Pacific coast between Alaska and San Francisco Bay; some birds migrate via N Amer interior. Winters along the coasts of se US, W Indies, C Amer, S Amer. Vagrant to Lake Baikal, Japan, Australia, Peru, UK, n Europe. **ID:** L 4.75–6 in (12–15 cm). Bill black, with slightly drooping tip. Black legs. White wing bar. White sides to dark rump; dark central tail feathers; outer tail feathers gray. AD MAY–JUL: Upperparts rich chestnut, spotted black. White throat and supercilium. Wing coverts grayish brown. Underparts white, with brown spots and streaks on breast and flanks. AD WINTER: Upperparts uniformly pale gray. White forehead and narrow white supercilium. Underparts white, with finely streaked, complete breast band washed with grayish brown at sides. VOICE: Thin, plaintive *chir-eep* or harsh *kreet.*
HABITS: In winter, forages for marine invertebrates in tidal areas, sand flats, and mudflats. Feeds on fly larvae, beetles, spiders, and freshwater invertebrates when breeding. Nest is a depression made under dwarf birch or grassy vegetation. Clutch is 4 cream-colored eggs, with elongated brown spots that spiral left to right on the larger two-thirds of the egg. Both sexes incubate the eggs and tend young after hatching.

Semipalmated Sandpiper

Calidris pusilla
ALSO: Sandstrandläufer, Bécasseau semipalmé, Sandsnipe, Малый песочник, Livilivillakpak, *Ereunetes*

pusillus. CN refers to the partial webbing between the toes. SN means "small shorebird."
RANGE: Nests (May–Jul) on coastal tundra of Alaska and Canada. Alaskan breeders migrate through the Great Plains; eastern populations undertake nonstop flights of some 2500 mi (4000 km) across the N Atlantic to winter in W Indies and S Amer. Spring and fall visitor to Pacific NW. Vagrant to Greenland, n Europe, UK, Chile, Argentina, Falklands.
ID: L 5–6 in (13–15 cm). Straight black bill, with a slightly enlarged tip. Black legs. Narrow white

wing bar. Dark rump. Central tail feathers dark; outer tail feathers gray. AD MAY–JUL: Upperparts blackish, feathers fringed dark gray, with pale rufous on some edges. Throat and supercilium white. Underparts white, with streaked breast. AD WINTER: Brownish gray above, whitish below, with diffuse streaking on sides of breast. VOICE: Thin, sharp *jeet.*
HABITS: Forages at low tide on mudflats in coastal areas and along marsh edges, lakeshores, and sewage ponds inland. Feeds on fresh- and saltwater invertebrates as well as insects and spiders, taken by pecking and probing. Males hollow out a nesting depression in areas near ponds or along small hummocks or ridges, usually in the cover of dwarf willows, dwarf birch, or sedge. Clutch is 4 tan eggs spotted with brown.

White-rumped Sandpiper

Calidris fuscicollis
ALSO: Weißbürzel Strandläufer, Bonapartesnipe, Bécasseau à croupion blanc, Бонапартов песочник. SN

means "dusky-necked shorebird."
RANGE: Nests (Jun–Aug) in Alaska and Canada on arctic tundra, usually on hummocks near marshy ponds. Migrates across the N Atlantic from N Amer to n S Amer—a 2500 mi (4000 km) nonstop flight of about 60 hours flown at speeds of up to 50 mph (80 kmh)—before moving on to winter in s S Amer. Vagrant to the Pacific NW, Galapagos, Iceland, UK, w Europe, Svalbard, Franz Josef Land, S Africa, Tristan de Cunha, Island of S Georgia, NZ, and Australia.
ID: L 6–7 in (15–18 cm). White rump. Bill blackish, with a slightly drooped tip and base of lower beak tinged olive brown. Legs greenish black. Wing tips project beyond tail, giving long-bodied outline. AD JUN–AUG: Back has black-centered feathers edged in chestnut, gray, and buff. Pale buff supercilium. Buffy tinge to cap and ear coverts. Underparts white, with breast and flanks streaked dark brown. AD WINTER: Mottled brownish gray upperparts. White supercilium. Underparts white, with breast washed and streaked with grayish brown. VOICE: Thin, high, metallic *prink-prink* or *tzeep.*

Semipalmated Sandpiper
Calidris pusilla
N Amer
L 5–6 in (13–15 cm)

ad. winter

ad.
May–Jul

Western Sandpiper
Calidris mauri
Chukotka, N Amer
L 4.75–6 in (12–15 cm)

ad. winter

ad.
May–Jul

Baird's Sandpiper
Calidris bairdii
Chukotka, N Amer
L 5.5–6.5 in (14–17 cm)

ad. winter

ad.
Jun–Jul

White-rumped Sandpiper
Calidris fuscicollis
N Amer
L 6–7 in (15–18 cm)

ad. winter

ad.
Jun–Aug

Sharp-tailed Sandpiper
Calidris acuminata
Siberia
L 6.5–8 in (17–20 cm)

ad. winter

ad.
Jun–Aug

ad. ♀
Jun–Aug

ad. ♂
Jun–Aug

Pectoral Sandpiper
Calidris melanotus
Siberia, N Amer
L 7.5–9 in (19–23 cm)

ad. winter

ad.
Jun–Jul

Stilt Sandpiper
Calidris himantopus
N Amer
L 7–9 in (18–23 cm)

HABITS: Feeds on insects, small mollusks, and aquatic worms by making a few quick probes into the substrate, then running a short distance before repeating. Forms small flocks that forage with other sandpipers wintering on estuaries, river deltas, and mudflats. Flies at speeds up to 50 mph (80 kmh); often flies in close-ranked flocks that bank and wheel as one body. Males are polygamous, mating with several females. Female prepares the nest—a depression lined with willow leaves, mosses, and lichens—incubates the 4 olive, red-spotted eggs, and rears the chicks.

Baird's Sandpiper

Calidris bairdii

ALSO: Bairdstrandläufer, Gulbrystsnipe, Bécasseau de Baird, Бэрдов песочник, Puviaktuuyaak. SN honors Spencer Fullerton Baird (1823–1887) of the Smithsonian Institution, who authored *Catalog of North American Birds*.
RANGE: Nests (Jun–Jul) in dry coastal and alpine tundra in Chukotka, Alaska, Canada, and Greenland. Siberian breeders join birds from N Amer and migrate up to 9300 mi (15,000 km) via the N Amer prairies and Andean wetlands to coastal mudflats of S Amer, south to Tierra del Fuego. Vagrant to Japan, Hawaii, Galapagos, Australia, NZ, Falklands, S Africa, nw Europe.
ID: L 5.5–6.5 in (14–17 cm). Back scaled, with whitish edges to dark-centered feathers. Crown brown, streaked with buff. Buff supercilium. Slightly drooping, black bill. Narrow white wing bar. Wings extend past tail tip of resting bird. Center of rump dark; sides white. Tail dark, with white at base. Throat, abdomen, and flanks white. Breast streaked buffy brown. Underwing coverts and axillaries white. Legs blackish green. VOICE: Low, trilling *preeet*.
HABITS: Forages mainly by pecking soft mud near the water's edge, taking insects and their larvae, amphipods, spiders, and some algae. Upon arriving on breeding grounds, with essentially no stored fat, the female Baird's lays a clutch of 4 eggs weighing some 80 percent of her body mass. Large eggs ensure large chicks able to weather their first few days on the open tundra. Both sexes rear the brood.

Stilt Sandpiper

Calidris himantopus

ALSO: Bindenstrandläufer, Bécasseau à échasses, Styltesnipe, Длинноногий песочник, *Tringa himantopus*. SN means "shorebird with stilt-like [legs]."
RANGE: Nests (May–Jul) on tundra in n Alaska and n Canada, east to Hudson Bay. Winters mainly in interior of c S Amer; small numbers winter in s California (Salton Sea), Gulf coast, and Florida. Vagrant to the UK.
ID: L 7–9 in (18–23 cm). Long greenish legs; partly webbed toes. Long, dark bill, with a slightly downcurved, broad tip. AD JUN–JUL: White supercilium contrasts with chestnut crown and ear coverts. Back feathers dark brown, edged with rufous and cream. White rump. Neck and upper breast heavily streaked; rest of underparts strongly barred. Underwing white. AD WINTER: Upperparts gray, with a few feathers edged in white. White supercilium and dark eye stripe. Underparts white, streaked with gray on neck and breast. VOICE: Low, soft *tu-tu* or *jeew*. Sounds nasal, dry, buzzy trills in display.
HABITS: Wades in grassy pools and shores of ponds and lakes, often with dowitchers and yellowlegs, moving about continually with nervous, jerky motions. Male makes initial nesting depression on sedge meadow; female enlarges and modifies the nest before mating. Both sexes incubate the 4 buff, brown-blotched eggs and brood the chicks. Females often desert the young after a few days, followed by the male. Chicks fledge independently.

Sharp-tailed Sandpiper

Calidris acuminata

ALSO: Spitzschwanz-Strandläufer, Bécasseau à queue pointue, Spisshale-snipe, Острохвостый песочник, *Philomachus acuminata*. SN means "gray shorebird with a pointed [tail]."
RANGE: Nests (Jun–Aug) on the Siberian tundra in n Yakutia between the Yana and Kolyma rivers. Winters on coastal and inland wetlands in New Guinea, Australia, NZ. Adults leave breeding

grounds and fly overland across Mongolia, China, and Manchuria to coastal Asia, then move south; juveniles fly east across the Bering Strait to coastal salt meadows in w Alaska and Aleutians before flying on to Australasia. Vagrant to India, Europe, w N Amer, Fiji.

ID: L 6.75–8 in (17–20 cm). Back feathers brown, broadly edged with rufous. Chestnut crown and nape. White supercilium. Straight black bill, with olive gray at base. Dark rump. Central tail feathers dark and pointed; outer tail feathers gray. Breast and flanks streaked and speckled with black, with a rufous tinge on the chest. Buffy underparts marked with bold dark streaks or chevrons. Yellow green legs. **VOICE:** Muffled trilling *pleep-pleep-trrt* or soft *weep*.

HABITS: Forages at water's edge, pecking prey from soil or mud surface. Feeds on mosquito larvae and some mollusks and crustaceans. Polygynous; male mates with several females. Nest is a shallow ground scrape lined with grass and leaves and hidden in vegetation. Female builds the nest, incubates the 4 olive to brown, blotched eggs, and rears the young.

Pectoral Sandpiper
Calidris melanotos

ALSO: Alaskasnipe, Bécasseau à poitrine cendrée, Graubrust Strandläufer, Дутыш, Puviaktuuk (Inupiaq for "inflates chest"). SN means "dark-backed gray shorebird."
RANGE: Nests (Jun–Jul) on marshy coastal tundra in Siberia and nw N Amer. Siberian breeders join birds from N Amer and migrate down the w Atlantic coast to s S Amer; lesser numbers winter in s Australia and NZ. Regular visitor to the UK and Europe. Vagrant to Svalbard, Africa, Hawaii, Falklands, Island of S Georgia.
ID: L 7.5–9 in (19–23 cm). AD JUN–AUG: Back feathers rufous with black centers; 2 white stripes run down the back. Center of rump and tail dark. Slightly downcurved dark bill. Yellow green legs. Underwing coverts white. Dark, densely streaked chest ends abruptly at white belly. Male develops an inflatable throat sac used in display. Female is much smaller, with duller plumage. AD WINTER: Plain brownish gray above, with dark feather

centers; streaked breast; white underparts. VOICE: Loud, harsh, reedy *trrit*. Male's throat sac expands and contracts rhythmically during display flights, producing a series of foghorn-like hollow hoots, *oo-ah' oo-ah' oo-ah'*.

HABITS: Probes for invertebrates in short grass or weedy vegetation at the edge of mudflats. Polygynous; male mates with several females. Female incubates the eggs and tends the brood. Clutch is 4 cream or pale green eggs, with large reddish brown spots. Nest is a depression lined with willow leaves set in long grass or low shrubs.

Curlew Sandpiper
Calidris ferruginea

ALSO: Sichelstrandläufer, Bécasseau cocorli, Tundrasnipe, Краснозобик. SN means "rust-colored gray shorebird," referring to breeding plumage. Hybridizes with sharp-tailed and pectoral sandpipers, producing the so-called Cooper's and Cox's sandpipers.
RANGE: Nests (Jun) on marshy or boggy tundra in arctic Siberia, mainly between the Yenisei and Kolyma rivers; rare breeder in n Alaska. Winters in Africa, Madagascar, s Asia, and Australia, infrequently in w Europe or Mediterranean. Rare visitor to the Pacific and Atlantic coasts of temperate N Amer.
ID: L 7.5–8.5 in (19–22 cm). Noticeably decurved long, black bill. Black legs and feet. AD MAY–JUL: Mottled rufous, white, and black upperparts. Head, neck, and breast rich cinnamon. White rump. Underwing, vent, and undertail coverts white. AD WINTER: Gray above, white below. JUV: Dark brown upperparts marked with buffy scaling. Buff patch on sides of breast. VOICE: Soft, musical *chirrup*. In aerial courtship display, male pursues the female with low aerial glides while calling a sharp *wheet-wheet*, followed by clear, rising *whaaay* notes.

HABITS: Pecks and probes continuously in an up-and-down stitching motion as it forages for aquatic insects, insect larvae, worms, mollusks, and crustaceans. Nest is a depression lined with lichens and willow leaves sited on elevated areas of rough grass next to bogs and pools. Polygynous; male mates with several females. Two to 6 females may build nests, incubate their eggs, and raise their broods close together, which allows them to cooperate in predator defense. During the hatchlings' first week of life, females lead the chicks from their nesting site to moist, grassy tundra where prey is more abundant.

Sanderling

Calidris alba

ALSO: Bécasseau sanderling, Sandløpar, Песчанка, Akpaksrukti. SN means "white shorebird."

RANGE: Nests (May–Jul) on rocky tundra in Canada, Greenland, Svalbard, and in Russia on the Taimyr Penin, Lena Rvr delta, Severnaya Zemlya, and New Siberian Is. Winters on coasts of the Americas, S Pacific islands, Australia, S Africa. **ID:** L 7–8 in (18–20 cm). Chunky, with a short, heavy, black bill. Black legs; no hind toe. AD MAY–JUL: Upperparts, head, and breast rusty, with black speckling; female paler. Belly white. Dark patch at bend of wing. White wing bar. AD WINTER: Upperparts ashy gray. Forehead, face, and underparts white. VOICE: Short, hard *kwit* or *veek-veek*. Display song is a mix of trills, churrs, and croaks.

HABITS: Feeds on mosquitoes and other insects, insect larvae, spiders, and plant buds while breeding. In winter, probes for marine invertebrates on beaches as it follows the ebb and flow of waves. Clutch of 4 olive, brown-spotted eggs is laid in a ground scrape lined with dead leaves and set under a willow bush. One parent usually deserts the nest at the onset of incubation; the remaining parent cares for young until fledged. Sometimes females lay 2 clutches, in which case the first is reared by the male, the second by the female.

Dunlin

Calidris alpina

ALSO: Red-backed Sandpiper, Alpenstrandläufer, Bécasseau variable, Myrsnipe, Чернозобик, Siyukpaligaurak. CN stems from the Anglo-Saxon *dunn* or *dunling*, meaning "little brown bird." SN means "alpine shorebird."

RANGE: Nests (May–Jul) on coastal and inland tundra in Alaska, Canada, e Greenland, Iceland, UK, Scandinavia, and east across n Siberia. Winters along the coasts of N Amer, s Europe, n Africa, and s Asia. **ID:** L 7–8 in (18–20 cm). Black bill is decurved at tip. Black legs. AD MAY–JUL: Upperparts rufous with black speckling. Underparts white, with conspicuous black belly patch. Fine black streaks on upper breast. White wing bar. White sides to dark rump. Dark central tail feathers; outer tail feathers pale gray. AD WINTER: Gray back. Faintly streaked gray wash on sides of breast. JUV: Sides of abdomen and lower breast spotted and streaked with blackish brown. Breast washed with buff and streaked with dark brown. VOICE: Flight call a distinctive buzzing, raspy *pjeev*. Display song is a series of rolling, harsh trills, *jree-jree-jrrrijijiji-jijrrr.*

HABITS: Forages with open bill and slightly hunchbacked posture while probing for freshwater and marine invertebrates. Flies in large, tight, synchronized flocks. Nests in a shallow scrape made in gravel. Clutch is 4 olive to blue-green eggs. Both parents incubate the eggs for 3 weeks. The female, followed by the male, deserts the brood a few days after the eggs hatch. Chicks fledge independently.

Rock Sandpiper

Calidris ptilocnemis

ALSO: Beringstrandläufer, Bécasseau des Aléoutiennes, Klippesnipe, Берингийский песочник. CN refers to the foraging habitat. SN means "feather-legged shorebird," referring to the upper leg, which is feathered to the knee.

RANGE: Nests (May–Jul) on low heath tundra and alpine tundra in Alaska, Aleutians, Chukotka, Kamchatka, and Commander Is. Winters in the Aleutians, Kamchatka, and Pacific coasts of N Amer south to n California. Winters farther north than any N Amer shorebird, with some birds regularly roosting on fast ice or large pieces of grounded or floating sea ice. **ID:** L 8–9 in (20–23 cm). Short-winged. Short-legged. Slightly drooping black bill, with varying amounts of yellow at base. Pribilof birds are

ad. winter

ad. winter

Rock Sandpiper
Calidris ptilocnemis
NE Siberia, Alaska
L 8–9 in (20–23 cm)

ad.
May–Jul

ad. winter

Dunlin
Calidris alpina
Circumpolar
L 7–8 in (18–20 cm)

ad.
May–Jul

ad. winter

ad. winter

Purple Sandpiper
Calidris maritima
Arctic Canada, Eurasia
L 8–8.5 in (20–22 cm)

ad.
May–Aug

Sanderling
Calidris alba
Canada, Greenland, Russia
L 7–8 in (18–20 cm)

ad.
May–Jul

juv.

ad. winter

ad.
May–Jul

Curlew Sandpiper
Calidris ferruginea
Siberia
L 7.5–8.5 in (19–22 cm)

ad. winter

ad. winter

Great Knot
Calidris tenuirostris
Siberia
L 10–11 in (26–28 cm)

ad.
May–Jun

Red Knot
Calidris canutus
Circumpolar
L 9–10 in (23–26 cm)

ad.
May–Jul

large and pale in all plumages; Aleutian birds are smaller and darker. AD MAY–JUL: Legs olive to dull grayish yellow. Back and crown blackish brown, edged in buff to cinnamon. White supercilium; dark triangle in front of eye; black patch on ear coverts. White chin; upper breast buffy and streaked with black; large blackish patch on lower breast; belly and flanks white. Upperwing dark, with white wing stripe. Underside of wing white. Rump and central tail feathers dark; outer tail feathers brownish gray with white fringe on outer web. AD WINTER: Legs yellow. Gray above. White below, with irregular dark gray marks on breast. VOICE: Brief, abrupt, grating or squeaking *chrreet* or *cheet*. Display song a series of complex trills.
HABITS: Forages on intertidal rocks in the surf zone and on gravel and sandy beaches. Feeds on marine mollusks, crustaceans, and larval flies in winter; on terrestrial invertebrates, especially beetles and spiders, when breeding. Both sexes incubate the clutch of 4 gray to olive eggs. One parent, usually male, remains with the chicks until they fledge.

Purple Sandpiper

Calidris maritima
ALSO: Meerstrandläufer, Bécasseau violet, Fjæreplytt, Морской песочник. CN

refers to the faint purple gloss on the feathers of the back. SN means "shorebird of the seacoast."
RANGE: Nests (Jun–Aug) on alpine and arctic tundra in Canada, Greenland, Iceland, Jan Mayen, Faroes, n UK, n Europe east to nc Siberia, Svalbard, and Russian High Arctic islands. Eurasian breeders winter on coasts of n Europe; e Greenland breeders winter in Iceland; Canadian breeders winter along the N Amer Atlantic seaboard.
ID: L 8–8.5 in (20–22 cm). Plump, fairly large sandpiper. Slightly drooping bill, with a yellowish base. Short legs. AD MAY–AUG: Legs olive. Bill base yellow. Dark-centered back feathers edged in white and chestnut. Whitish supercilium. White wing bar. Dark rump. Central tail feathers dark; outer tail fathers white. Underparts white; brownish black streaks on breast and flanks.

Pale gray axillaries and underwing coverts; dark primaries and primary coverts. AD WINTER: Legs yellowish. Head, back, and chest dark slaty gray. Underparts white; lower breast and flanks bear indistinct, grayish chevron markings. VOICE: Scratchy, low *keesh* or sharper *kwittit-kif.*
HABITS: Forages for mollusks and other marine invertebrates on intertidal rocks in winter, often in the surf zone, where it hops or flutters between rocks to dodge wave action. Feeds on insects and seeds when breeding. Male performs aerial courtship displays and makes the initial nesting depression, which the female amends. Both sexes incubate the 3–4 pale olive eggs. Distracts predators that approach the nest by performing a "rodent run," darting across the tundra with both wings lowered to the ground and back hunched so that it resembles a lemming. If a predator gives chase, the "lemming" launches into full flight, leaving a perplexed pursuer behind. Female leaves the area shortly after the eggs hatch, leaving the male to tend the young until they fledge at 5–6 weeks of age.

Red Knot

Calidris canutus
ALSO: Common or Lesser Knot, Eastern Knot, Knot-Snipe, Knutt, Bécasseau

maubèche, Polarsnipe, Исландский песочник. SN means "ash-colored shorebird."
RANGE: Nests (Jun–Jul) on High Arctic alpine tundra in N Amer and Eurasia. Winters on seacoasts. Greenland breeders migrate to w Europe via Iceland. Birds that nest in c Siberia migrate via e Europe to Africa; e Siberian birds migrate to Australasia. N Amer breeders winter along both coasts of the Americas.
ID: L 9–10 in (23–26 cm). Stout body. Relatively short, straight black bill. Short, greenish or dull yellow legs. AD MAY–JUL: Feathers on upperparts black, broadly edged with rufous and cream. Rump and tail pale gray. Underparts deep rufous to pale chestnut. Undertail coverts white. Underwing gray. AD WINTER: Upperparts plain gray, with larger feathers edged in white. Underparts white, lightly marked with gray scalloping. VOICE: Flight display song is a flute-like

poorr-mee, poorr-mee, poorr-mee, poorr-poorr.
Low *knut-knut* given in flight.

HABITS: Male prepares 3–5 lichen-lined nest scrapes on the barren tundra; the female chooses the one in which she will lay her eggs. Both sexes incubate the 4 olive, darkly spotted eggs. Female leaves the nest shortly after eggs hatch, leaving the male to rear the brood.

Forages on sand flats and beaches in winter and during migration, taking bivalves, small snails, crustaceans, and other marine prey. Pressure-sensitive nerve endings called Herbst corpuscles at the bill tip allow the knot to "feel" for prey buried in the sand. The bird inserts its bill into wet sand for a few seconds, creating a pressure wave that sends water flowing between individual sand grains, stones, and shells. It can distinguish between vibrations returned by sand grains or larger objects. However, it can't tell if the larger objects are stones or marine invertebrates, which may be why knots rarely forage on stony beaches.

Herbst corpuscles and other similar touch receptors are also present in the skin, legs, and beaks of waterfowl and many other shorebirds, and in the tongues of woodpeckers.

STATUS: Precipitous declines in some red knot populations have been observed in recent years, possibly due to the knot's reliance on eggs of horseshoe crabs (*Limulus polyphemus*), which fuel its northward migration along the US Atlantic seaboard. Horseshoe crab numbers are in decline. The clotting reaction of the crab's blood is used to detect bacterial endotoxins in pharmaceuticals and to test for several bacterial diseases. The crabs are bled, then released but, some 3 percent of them die during the process.

Great Knot
Calidris tenuirostris

ALSO: Japanese Knot, Slender-billed Knot, Striped-crowned Knot, Eastern Knot, Great Sandpiper, Great Dunlin, Großer Knutt, Bécasseau de l'Anadyr, Sibirsnipe, Большой песочник. SN means "slender-billed shorebird."
RANGE: Nests (May–Jun) in ne Siberia on alpine tundra between 1000 and 5250 ft (300–1600 m).

Winters in large flocks along the coasts of s Asia and n Australia.

ID: L 10–11 in (26–28 cm). Long, heavy, black bill. Legs greenish to dark olive. AD MAY–JUN: Upperparts mottled dark brown, with rufous scapular feathers. Breast heavily spotted with black (sometimes solid black in center). Belly white. Large black spots and chevrons on flanks. White wing bar. Underwing grayish white. Rump and tail white, lightly marked with dark gray. AD WINTER: Gray above; white below, with breast lightly spotted with gray. VOICE: Soft 2-note whistle, *nyut-nyut,* hence the name *knot.*

HABITS: Feeds on marine invertebrates in winter. When breeding, feeds on plants, including crowberries (*Empetrum*) and nuts of Siberian Dwarf Pine (*Pinus pumila*). Chicks feed on insects and insect larvae. Nests in solitary pairs on gravelly plateaus or gentle tundra slopes covered with lichens, herbs, and dwarf shrubs. Clutch of 4 grayish yellow, reddish-spotted eggs is laid in an open depression in reindeer lichen (*Cladonia*). Female leaves the nest shortly after laying, leaving incubation and chick rearing to the male. Capable of extremely fast, sustained flight between breeding and wintering grounds.

STATUS: Vulnerable (IUCN) due to reclamation of lands used as stopover points in migration.

GENUS *BARTRAMIA*
Upland Sandpiper
Bartramia longicauda

ALSO: Upland Plover, Prärieläufer, Maubèche des champs, Præriesnipe, Длиннохвостый песочник. SN means "Bartram's long-tailed [sandpiper]," honoring William Bartram (1739–1823), who failed miserably as a printer, engraver, and merchant, but who excelled as a botanist, birder, and illustrator. Bartram was the author of *Travels,* a book on the natural history of the s US.
RANGE: Small numbers nest (May–Jun) on remote grassy uplands and forest-tundra bogs in Alaska and NWT, Canada; most breed on the prairies of s Canada and c US. Migrates through the Great Plains and C Amer to winter in interior grasslands of S Amer, south to Argentina. Vagrant

to Europe, Guam, Australia, Tristan da Cunha, and Deception Is (Antarctica). **ID:** L 11.5–13 in (28–32 cm). Long, yellow legs. Long neck. Long, barred tail. Small head. Gray bill, slightly decurved at tip, with yellow at base of lower beak. Back brown; lower back blackish. White belly. Underwing barred black and white. VOICE: Loud, clear, liquid *whip-whee'-ee-you.* Display call *bububu-lee'-hlee'-yooooooooo* begins with notes that sound like water gurgling from a large bottle, followed by a long, mellow whistle.

HABITS: Forages in fields with low grass, feeding on grasshoppers, crickets, weevils, beetles, moths, ants, flies, centipedes, millipedes, spiders, snails, earthworms, and some grains and seeds. Males frequently perch and display on fence posts and telephone poles, with their wings raised, head held up, gular pouch puffed out, and tail cocked. In courtship flight, male and female rise in unison, crossing paths in a large aerial circle at heights of 100 ft (30 m) or more. When the circle tightens and they can almost touch wings, they make a rapid, nearly vertical descent to the ground, then sound the display call. Nests in solitary pairs or small loose colonies. Clutch of 4 large, buff-colored, brown-spotted eggs is laid in a ground scrape located in dense grass. Both sexes incubate the eggs. Hatchlings are led to open habitat where they feed independently. Chicks fledge at about 30 days of age.

GENUS *TRYNGITES*
Buff-breasted Sandpiper
Tryngites subruficollis
ALSO: Aklaktaq, Satka-
giilak, Gräsläufer, Bécas-
seau roussâtre, Rustsnipe,
Канадский песочник. SN
means "reddish-necked sandpiper."
RANGE: Nests (May–Jun) locally on the tundra in w Canada, n Alaska, and Wrangel Is (Russia). Migrates across c N Amer, east of the Rocky Mtns. Winters in c Argentina on short-grass prairies and grain stubble fields. Regular fall visitor to UK and Ireland. Vagrant to Svalbard, Azores, Africa, Kurils, Japan, Hawaii, c Pacific islands, Papua New Guinea, and Australia.
ID: L 7.5–9 in (18–23 cm). Dove-like head, with

short dark bill and steep forehead. Erect posture. Back scaled brown and buff. Sides of head and underparts clear buff; crown streaked dark brown and buff. Underwing white; feather edges strongly mottled with brownish black. Legs yellow. VOICE: Low *prrr-reet.* Makes *tic-tic-tic* sounds in display.

HABITS: Feeds mainly on insects, insect larvae and pupae, spiders, and plant seeds, taking some copepods, amphipods, and crane flies in fall. Forages in a plover-like manner—pauses to look for prey and then dashes after it.

Breeding males are promiscuous, gathering together on a tundra display ground, or *lek,* where they attempt to attract and mate with as many females as possible. Male display includes flashing wings, jumping, slow marching in place while voicing a rhythmic *tic-tic-tic,* and finally outstretching the wings while gazing fixedly skyward. Receptive females enter the arena and choose a mate—a choice seemingly based on a male's dance proficiency and brightness of the underwing plumage. At times the performance of a dominant male is sabotaged by a rogue male who flies in and chases females away from his rival, or sneaks in and mates with a female attracted to the dominant male.

By early July, shortly after mating, the male leaves the area and migrates, leaving the female to nest and rear the brood. Clutch of 3–5 buff-colored, heavily blotched eggs is laid in a ground scrape lined with lichens and leaves, set on a mossy hummock in a sedge meadow and often near nesting plovers, which cooperate in predator defense. Chicks are able to feed themselves within a day of hatching, but usually remain near the female for 2–3 weeks.

GENUS *PHILOMACHUS*
Ruff
Philomachus pugnax
ALSO: Kampfläufer,
Combattant varié, Brushane,
Турухтан. SN means "fond of fighting" and "pugnacious," referring to the aggressive behavior of males on the mating arenas. CN: Males are called *ruffs,* referring to the breeding male's ornamental neck feathers, which resemble the

ad. ♂
Display posture

Upland Sandpiper
Bartramia longicauda
N Amer
L 11.5–13 in (28–32 cm)

ad. ♂
Displaying at a lek

Buff-breasted Sandpiper
Tryngites subruficollis
N Amer
L 7.5–9 in (18–23 cm)

ad. Satellite ♂
May–Jul

ad. ♀
Reeve

ad. ♂
May–Jul

ad. ♂
May–Jul

ad. Faeder ♂
and non-breeding ♂

ad. ♂
May–Jul

Ruff
Philomachus pugnax
Eurasia
L ♂ 12–13 in (29–32 cm)
L ♀ 9–10.5 in (22–26 cm)

starched neck frill worn by Elizabethan and Jacobean courtiers. Females are known as *reeves*. Males with female-like plumage are called *faeders*, an Anglo-Saxon word for "father," alluding to their resemblance to primal males of the species.

RANGE: Nests (May–Jul) in n Eurasia in freshwater marshes and damp grasslands on arctic coastal tundra and forest-tundra. Winters, often in huge flocks, on wetlands in sw Europe, Africa, s Asia, and Australia. Most European breeders are short-distance migrants. Siberian breeders undertake a round trip of 18,500 mi (30,000 km) between the arctic coast and w Africa. Regular visitor to Alaska and coasts and lakes of the US and Canada. Vagrant to Bear Is (Norway), Iceland, Bermuda, Guatemala, Panama, Trinidad, Peru, Venezuela, Cape Verde, Madagascar, NZ.

ID: L ♂ 12–13 in (29–32 cm); ♀ 9–10.5 in (22–26 cm). Small-headed, long-necked, and potbellied, with long, yellow to reddish legs. Long-winged, with a narrow white wing bar. White ovals on sides of rump and tail. **AD ♂ MAY–JUL:** Extremely variable in plumage color and pattern. Dominant males have brightly colored ornamental head tufts and ruff when breeding, and bare facial skin, with golden, greenish, orange, or red facial warts and wattles around the bill. Satellite males have mottled grayish plumage, white heads, and white ruffs. About 1 percent of breeding males—the faeders—have plumage that mimics the female's. **AD ♂ WINTER:** Grayish brown upperparts, scaled with black or chestnut. White below, with dark mottling on the breast. **AD ♀:** Grayish brown upperparts with buff-fringed, dark-centered feathers. Breast and flanks are blotched with black. **JUV:** Resembles female, but with a yellow to buffy wash on underparts. **VOICE:** Generally silent.

HABITS: Forages in wet grassland. Probes in soft soil and mud or searches by sight for prey. Feeds mainly on insects and insect larvae in the breeding season; on small crustaceans, spiders, small mollusks, annelid worms, frogs, small fish, and grain crops in winter.

During breeding season, males gather on a mating arena, or *lek*, typically located on a dry mound or slope covered with low willow and dwarf birch. Each male's goal is to mate with as many females as possible. When females near the lek, the males display their elaborate neck and head feathers, flutter their wings, jump and crouch, and make aggressive pecks and leaps toward competing males.

Males of different plumage types employ different mating strategies. Dominant, brightly plumaged males, which represent 85 percent of males on a lek, are territorial; each defends his own spot on the mating arena. Drabber-plumaged satellite males do not establish a territory, but share the court with the dominant males, gaining acceptance by submissive behavior; satellite males help to attract females to the lek, but mate less often than the dominant males. Faeders, which have female-like plumage and testes 2.5 times the size of a dominant male's, behave as "sneakers." They arrive at the lek with the females, wait on the sidelines, and then furtively dash in to mate whenever an opportunity presents itself.

Females choose mates from displaying males. More than half the reeves mate with and have clutches fertilized by more than one male. Males migrate south soon after mating and the female alone establishes the nest and raises the brood in a sedge marsh where insect food is plentiful. The reeve makes a ground scrape in a place concealed by overhanging vegetation and usually chooses a site located near other nesting reeves. The clutch is 4 olive to greenish, brown-spotted eggs. Chicks are precocial and able to feed independently soon after hatching.

GENUS *PHALAROPUS*: *Phalaropus* is Greek for "feet like a coot's [*Fulica* spp.]," a reference to the coot-like lobed toes, which aid in swimming and walking on floating vegetation. Phalaropes bob and spin on the water surface, creating a vortex from which they pick out invertebrate prey. These ocean-going sandpipers have long, pointed wings and a long, straight bill. They exhibit reverse sexual dimorphism, the female being larger and more brightly plumaged than the male. The female is often polyandrous, mating with more than one male. She typically abandons the nest shortly after laying eggs. The male provides all parental care, including incubation and rearing of the young.

Snipes probe mud and wet soil in a jerky, up-and-down, stitching movement as they search for mollusks, crustaceans, insects, earthworms, and occasionally seeds and other plant matter.

These birds are known for their acrobatic courtship display flights. The male shoots upward into the evening sky, then plummets to earth with half-closed wings and fanned-out tail. The vibration of the outer tail feathers during descent produces eerie sounds known as *drumming* or *winnowing*. Differences in the number and shape of tail feathers produce drumming sounds unique to each species.

Common Snipe
Gallinago gallinago

ALSO: Old World Snipe, Bekassine-gallinago, Bécassine des marais, Enkeltbekkasin, Бекас, Flying Goat, Heaven's Ram, Heather-bleater. CN comes from *snut,* Middle German for "snout," a reference to the bird's long bill. SN derives from the Latin *gallina*, meaning "speckled hen," referring to the mottled plumage.
RANGE: Nests (Apr–Jun) in marshes, bogs, wet meadows, and tundra in Iceland, Faroes, UK, and across Eurasia to Kamchatka and w Aleutians (Attu Is). Winters in the UK, Ireland, Europe, Africa, Middle East, se Asia, and Philippines.
ID: L 10–10.5 in (25–27 cm), incl 2–2.75 in (5–7 cm) bill. Mottled brown above, with bold pale stripes down back. Crown dark; thin pale crown stripe; dark stripe through eye, with buffy stripes above and below it. Breast mottled in pale ochre and brown. Belly white. Long, straight bill is dull ochre at base and dark brown at tip. Legs yellowish green to greenish gray. Pointed wings; broad white trailing edge. Underwing gray, with white bars on underwing coverts. Seven pairs of outer tail feathers. VOICE: Harsh *scaape-scaape* when flushed. Repetitive *chip-per* call in display.
HABITS: Secretive and shy when not breeding, but perches on posts and grass tussocks during mating season. In courtship display, flies high in circles and then makes shallow dives, during which the outer tail feathers vibrate and produce a *bleating* sound likened to the wavering cry of a sheep or goat. Clutch of 4 dark olive, brown-spotted eggs is laid in a well-hidden ground scrape. Female alone incubates the eggs for 18–21 days; male feeds the female on nest. After hatching, the male and female each take 1–2 hatchlings to care for separately until the chicks fledge at about 20 days of age.

Wilson's Snipe
Gallinago delicata

ALSO: American Snipe, Amerikanische Bekassine, Bécassine de Wilson, Indianarbekkasin, Американский бекас, Kuukukiak. SN means "dainty snipe." CN honors Scottish-American ornithologist Alexander Wilson (1766–1813), who described the species.
RANGE: Nests (Apr–Jul) in bogs, marshes, swamps, edges of ponds, wet ditches, and slow-flowing rivers in the e Aleutians, Alaska, Canada, and south through many states in the US. Winters from the s US to n S Amer. Regular visitor to the Caribbean. Rare autumn and winter vagrant to Europe.
ID: L 10–10.5 in (25–27 cm), incl 2–2.75 in (5–7 cm) bill. Somewhat darker and drabber than *G. gallinago*. Dark brown back, with 4 bold white or buff stripes. Crown dark; thin pale crown stripe; dark stripe through eye, with buffy stripes above and below. Long, straight, dark bill, with a pale base. White below, with dark brown mottling on chest and flanks. Legs pale yellowish green. Rufous-tinged tail, with 8 pairs of outer tail feathers. Underwing dark gray. VOICE: Loud, sharp *tuk-tuk-tuk-tuk* in display.
HABITS: Behavior, nesting, and display like those of *G. gallinago*, except for drumming sound, a rapid hollow *hu-hu-hu-hu-hu-hu* resembling the call of the Boreal Owl, *Aegolius funereus*.

Pintail Snipe
Gallinago stenura

ALSO: Pin-tailed Snipe, Asiatic Snipe, Spießbekassine, Bécassine à queue pointue, Sibirbekkasin, Азиатский бекас. SN means "narrow-tailed snipe."
RANGE: Nests (May–Jul) in n Siberia from the Ob Rvr to Chukotka and the Sea of Okhotsk,

in wetlands up to 7550 ft (2300 m) elevation. Winters from Pakistan to se Asia on paddy fields, wet grasslands, marshes, and muddy shorelines. Rare vagrant to e Europe and Middle East.

ID: L 10–10.5 in (25–27 cm), incl 2–2.75 in (5–7 cm) bill. Mottled brown upperparts, with buff or sandy lines down the back. Broad supercilium bulges immediately before the eye, giving a wide-eyed expression. Long, straight, dark bill, with a pale base. Buffy to whitish underparts, mottled and barred with dark brown; belly white. Short tail, with 9 pairs of very narrow outer tail feathers. Legs yellowish green. No pale trailing edge on upperwing. Uniformly dark underwing. VOICE: Display call, *chivn-chivin-chivin,* has been likened to the quack of a Mallard duck.

HABITS: Occurs on damp meadows in river valleys, grassy and mossy swamps, swampy taiga forest, sphagnum bogs, and shrub tundra with patches of dwarf birch. In display, male makes repeated dives from great heights, accompanied by vocalizations and buzzing drumming sounds. Nests on hummocks in a well-hidden, shallow ground scrape lined with dry leaves, larch needles, and grass. Clutch is 4 olive brown eggs with reddish brown blotches. Incubation and chick rearing similar to hose of *G. gallinago.*

Great Snipe
Gallinago media

ALSO: Doppelschnepfe, Bécassine double, Dobbeltbekkasin, Дупель. SN means "intermediate snipe."

RANGE: Nests (May–Jul) on raised ground on marshes and wet meadows in forest and forest-steppe zones in ne Europe and nw Russia. Winters mainly in Africa, rarely in UK and s Scandinavia. Overflies Europe in migration, at speeds up to 60 mph (100 kmh); has been recorded flying 4200 mi (6760 km) nonstop in 48 hours. Vagrant to New Jersey (US), Svalbard, Capetown (S Africa), India, and se Asia.

ID: L 10–12 in (26–30 cm), incl 2–3 in (5–8 cm) bill. Upperparts dark brown with ochre and russet edging to feathers. Whitish stripes down back. Prominent white spots on wing coverts. Dark crown. Dark eyeline. Underparts whitish; dark

chevrons and bars on breast, flanks, and belly. Long, brown bill. Legs pinkish. White outer tail feathers. VOICE: A 3-part call of rising and falling twittering (*bibbling*), accelerated clicking, and wheezing in display.

HABITS: Known for elaborate lek displays. Up to 30 breeding males may congregate at leks at dusk. They stand tall, with chests puffed, wings raised, and tails fanned, sometimes jumping into the air, and all the while emitting a variety of rattles, buzzes, and bill clicks that can be heard from afar. Male is polygamous; female alone builds the nest and rears the brood. Nest is a well-hidden ground scrape lined with soft grass. Clutch is 3–4 drab yellow eggs spotted with brown. Takes off silently, with straight, low flight.

STATUS: European breeding populations are in steep decline. Near Threatened (IUCN).

GENUS *LYMNOCRYPTES*
Jack Snipe
Lymnocryptes minimus

ALSO: Zwergschnepfe, Bécassine sourde, Kvartbek-kasin, Гаршнеп. CN means "small snipe." SN means "little marsh-hider."

RANGE: Nests (May–Jun) on grassy marshes and peat bogs from Scandinavia to ne Siberia. Winters on wetlands from UK south to N Africa, Middle East, and se Asia.

ID: L 7–9 in (18–23 cm), incl 1.5 in (4 cm) bill. Blackish brown back, with a teal sheen and bold golden stripes. Breast gray with dark streaks. Dark crown (no pale median stripe); 2 pale buff stripes on each side of the crown are bisected by a dark line; another dark line runs from the bill through the eye. Long straight bill, pale at base, dark at tip. Short yellowish gray legs. VOICE: Silent in winter. During aerial display, male emits a hollow *tlok-tlok-tok', tlok-tlok-tok', tlok-tlok-tok',* likened to the sound of a galloping horse.

HABITS: Secretive and rarely seen until it flushes. Fluttering, butterfly-like flight. Forages mainly at night, probing in mud for insects, worms, and snails. Breeds in solitary pairs in grassy marshes, bogs, swampy coniferous forests, and alder woodlands in forest-tundra and taiga. In courtship displaying male sounds its "galloping

White bars on
underwing coverts

Common Snipe
Gallinago gallinago
Eurasia
L 10–10.5 in (25–27 cm)

Eurasian Woodcock
Scolopax rusticola
Eurasia
L 13–15 in (33–38 cm)

8–9 narrow outer
tail feathers

Underwing
gray

Pintail Snipe
Gallinago stenura
Siberia
L 10–10.5 in (25–27 cm)

Wilson's Snipe
Gallinago delicata
N Amer
L 10–10.5 in (25–27 cm)

Great Snipe
displaying at dusk

Jack Snipe
Lymnocryptes minimus
Eurasia
L 7–9 in (18–23 cm)

Great Snipe
Gallinago media
NE Europe–nw Russia
L 10–12 in (26–30 cm)

horse" call while in undulating flight 65–165 ft (20–50 m) above its territory, then drops steeply to the ground. Nest is a well-hidden scrape built on sphagnum moss hummocks, emergent grass tussocks on bogs, or on drier ground with dwarf birch and heather vegetation. Female incubates the 4 ochre, brown-blotched eggs; sits tight on nest unless flushed by chance. Post-breeding adults undergo a flightless molting period near the nesting grounds before migrating.

GENUS *SCOLOPAX*
Eurasian Woodcock
Scolopax rusticola
ALSO: Waldschnepfe, Bécasse des bois, Rugde, Вальдшнеп. SN means "woodcock of the countryside."

RANGE: Nests (Apr–Jun) in subarctic and temperate Eurasia in moist forests and woodland glades or clearings. Some 30 percent of the world's population breeds in Europe, the majority breeding in Russia and Scandinavia. Winters in breeding areas and south to Transcaucasia, c Asia, India, Mongolia, and Japan.
ID: L 13–15 in (33–38 cm), incl 2–3 in (6–8 cm) bill. Males are much larger than females. Stocky body, with rounded wings. Upperparts intricately patterned in reddish brown. Transverse black and buff bars on crown and nape. Large eyes located high on sides of the head provide near 360° vision. Bill long, straight, flesh-colored, darker on outer third; tip of upper mandible is flexible. Underparts buff, heavily barred with dark brown. Silvery tail tip; black subterminal bar. Legs gray to pinkish. VOICE: Male emits 3–4 deep croaks followed by an explosive, high pitched squeak *tsssee'* in display.
HABITS: Nocturnal; rarely seen by day unless flushed. Flushes straight up from the forest floor with a clatter of wings, then twists rapidly out of sight. Roosts by day in areas of dense shrub cover. Forages at night in soft soil in fields and forest clearings with dense shrub cover and a heavy concentration of earthworms, the main prey. Diet also includes insects and insect larvae, freshwater mollusks, and some plant seeds. Probes with a steady, rocking motion.

At dawn and dusk during breeding season, the male performs a courtship display flight known as *roding*, flying over the treetops with flickering wings and downward-pointing bill while vocalizing. Nest is a lined cup built under a bush or stump or on a hummock. The female alone incubates the 4 creamy, rusty-spotted eggs for 21–24 days. Chicks leave the nest with the female soon after hatching. When threatened, females have been observed flying off carrying the chicks between the legs or in the feet. Young fledge at 15–20 days.
USE: Bagged woodcocks are hung until "high" to maximize flavor. They are then skinned and cooked with head and inner organs intact. The pin feathers (covert feathers above the outer primary) are used as brushes to paint miniatures.

FAMILY LARIDAE
SKUAS, GULLS, AND TERNS
The family Laridae (Latin for "rapacious seabird") is divided into subfamilies—Stercorariinae (skuas), Larinae (gulls), and Sterninae (terns)—which are often considered separate families. These are mid-sized to large, web-footed birds that live around fresh- or saltwater bodies. A few species are strictly pelagic, living out their entire lives on the open ocean and coming to land only to nest. Like other charadriiform birds, the skuas, gulls, and terns can drink salt water. They have specialized internal salt glands located near the bill which expel sodium chloride through the nostrils, thus helping the kidneys maintain electrolyte balance.

SUBFAMILY STERCORARIINAE
SKUAS AND JAEGERS
The word *skua* derives from *skúgvur*, the Faroese name for the Great Skua, which has a large breeding colony on the island of Skúvoy. The smaller skua species are also known as *jaegers*, a German word for "hunter" and an allusion to the jaeger's predatory nature.

Skuas and jaegers are swift predatory seabirds that nest on the arctic tundra, but spend most of the year at sea. They typically have brown plumage, with conspicuous white patches on the underside of the wings. Their bills are strongly hooked and have a fleshy covering, or cere, at the base of the upper beak. Their feet are webbed and sharply clawed. Jaegers develop elongated tail feathers during the breeding season, the shape and length of which are unique to each species.

Skuas and jaegers are strong, acrobatic fliers. They commonly pursue gulls and terns, forcing them to disgorge their food, then snapping it up before it hits the water. This habit is called *kleptoparasitism*. These birds also feed on fish, insects, carrion, trawler discards, small mammals, and adult birds and their chicks and eggs.

Both sexes share in the nesting process, making a shallow scrape that may or may not be lined with tundra vegetation. Both sexes incubate the 2 olive, brown-speckled eggs for 22–29 days and feed the young until they fledge at 4–7 weeks of age.

Parent birds can be very aggressive toward people venturing onto their nesting territory. One can usually count on the adults flying and striking out with the feet, bill, or wings. Skuas usually target the area between a person's eyes for frontal attack, then wheel about and strike from the rear. A hat or other object held high above the head can divert the assault, but the wisest strategy is to make a hasty, albeit cowardly retreat.

GENUS *STERCORARIUS*
Great Skua
Stercorarius skua

ALSO: Bonxie, Große Raubmöwe, Grand Labbe, Storlabb, Большой поморник, *Catharacta skua*. SN means "dung [-eating] skua," alluding to the belief that seabirds ejected excrement rather than disgorging food when under attack by skuas.
RANGE: Nests (May–Aug) on rocky coasts and damp, elevated coastal moors in the n UK, Faroes, Iceland, Jan Mayen, Norway, and Svalbard, and recently east along the Barents Sea coast. Winters at sea off the coasts of nw Africa, Iberia, Bay of Biscay, w Ireland, and ne N Amer.
ID: L 20–23 in (50–58 cm). Largest of the northern skuas. Short, rounded tail. Barrel-shaped body. Very heavy, hooked, dark bill. Black legs. **AD:** Dark brown body, faintly mottled with ochre

or cream. Dark wings with large white patches at base of primaries. **JUV:** Uniformly cool dark brown on back. Underparts rufous brown. White wing patches smaller than adult's. **VOICE:** Silent away from nesting grounds. Loud *tek-tek* or a mewing *ji-ah, ji-ah* when breeding.
HABITS: Flight strong, purposeful, and high. Pirates food from other birds and feeds on fish, trawler discards, and carrion when at sea. Preys on other nesting seabirds and their chicks when nesting. Breeds in solitary pairs or loose colonies along the seacoast, usually in the vicinity of a seabird nesting cliff or gull colony. Exhibits mate and site fidelity year after year. Breeds for the first time when 4–9 years old, usually at a nest site near its birthplace. A long-lived species; oldest known individual was 34 years old.

Parasitic Jaeger
Stercorarius parasiticus

ALSO: Arctic Skua, Isunngarluk, Migiaksaayuk (Inupiaq for "likes vomit"), Schmarotzerraubmöwe, Labbe parasite, Kustlabb, Короткохвостый поморник. SN means "parasitic skua," referring to the kleptoparasitic habits.
RANGE: Circumpolar. Nests (May–Aug) on tundra, coastal moors, and barren islands. Pelagic in winter in the southern oceans. Migrates singly or in groups of 2–4 birds.
ID: L 15–17.5 in (37–44 cm); breeding adults develop 2–3.5 in (5–8.5 cm) long, pointed central tail feathers. Small head with a peaked crown. Slender, hooked bill is pale at the base and dark at the tip; cere is pale flesh. Shows 3–5 white primary shafts on upperwing. Distinct white patch at base of underwing primaries. **AD PALE MORPH:** Dark brown cap; grayish brown back. Pale yellow cheeks. White throat and underparts interrupted by a distinct to faint, brown breast band. **AD DARK MORPH:** Dark brown, with white wing patches. **AD INTERMEDIATE MORPH:** Dark brown, with white wing patches and faint yellowish tinge on cheeks. **JUV:** Short, pointed central tail feathers project only about 0.75 in (2 cm). Pale morph juvenile is warm brown; head and neck are barred; belly is mottled. Dark morph is chocolate brown, with a darker

head and neck. Juvenile Parasitic Jaeger differs from juvenile Pomarine by darker lines on head and neck; thinner bill; less barring on inside of wings; and darker tail coverts. VOICE: Wailing *feee-leerrr* or nasal *ke'-wet, ke'-wet*.

HABITS: Pirates food from other birds; also feeds on seabird eggs and chicks, and small rodents. Flight is light and twisting, especially when in pursuit of other birds. Nests on coastal tundra, typically near breeding colonies of arctic terns, kittiwakes, and auks. Breeds in single pairs and shows strong mate and nest site fidelity. Nest is a shallow depression lined with plant material and sited on raised dry ground in view of the sea.

Pomarine Jaeger

Stercorarius pomarinus
ALSO: Pomarine Skua, Isunnagluk, Spatelraubmöwe, Labbe pomarin, Polarjo, Bredstjärtad labb, Средний поморник. SN means "skua with a covered nose," referring to the saddle-like cere at the base of the upper beak.
RANGE: Nests (May–Aug) on low-lying arctic tundra in n Alaska, nw Canada, and Siberia, especially in areas with large lemming populations. Highly pelagic in winter, moving to tropical and subtropical oceans worldwide. Migrates singly or in small groups of 2–3 individuals.
ID: L 17–20 in (42–50 cm); adults develop 2–4 in (5–11 cm) long, club-shaped, twisted central tail feathers when breeding. Large, heavy skua, with broad wings and a broad, rounded head. Heavy, strongly hooked bill is pale at the base and dark at the tip. Shows 4–6 white primary shafts on upperwing. White bases of primaries on underwing appear as a small, pale crescent. AD PALE MORPH: Extensive blackish cap; dark brown back. Pale yellow cheeks. White underparts, with a darkly mottled breast band and flanks. Some adults lack the dark breast band and are completely white below. AD DARK MORPH (RARE): Dark brown, with white wing flashes. JUV: Dull brown, with sharply bicolored bill. Underparts may be dark or pale, but all show strong barring on underwings and tail coverts. VOICE: Harsh, gull-like *yowk, yowk, yowk* that can escalate into high-pitched screams. Sharp

which-yew, which-yew, week, week, week emitted by birds feeding at sea.
HABITS: Flight straight, with even wingbeats. Pirates food from other birds, feeds on fish and carrion, and follows fishing boats for scraps outside of breeding season. Lemmings and voles are the main foods on breeding grounds, and breeding success is tied to the abundance of rodent prey. Although wary, adults will not usually attack intruders on nesting territory. Both parents share in incubating the eggs and feeding the chicks, often continuing to feed the young after they fledge.

Long-tailed Jaeger

Stercorarius longicaudus
ALSO: Long-tailed Skua, Falkenraubmöwe, Labbe à longue queue, Fjelljo, Длиннохвостый поморник, Isunnyak. SN means "long-tailed skua."
RANGE: Circumpolar. Nests (May–Jun) on arctic tundra where large lemming populations occur; in Scandinavia, nests on alpine tundra above 2100 ft (650 m). Most widespread and numerous jaeger in the Arctic. Winters at sea, mostly off the Pacific and Atlantic coasts of S Amer and off S Africa.
ID: L 14–16.5 in (36–41 cm); adults develop 5–9.5 in (12–24 cm) central tail feathers in breeding season. Smallest jaeger. Small head, slender body, and long, narrow wings. Relatively short, fairly thick, 2-toned, hooked bill. Legs gray, with black feet. AD: Gray back and tail (lacks brown tones of other jaegers). Black cap. White underparts; no dark breast band. JUV: Variable plumage, with pale to dark underparts. Uppertail coverts and underwing finely barred. Central tail feathers protrude 0.5–1 in (1–3 cm) beyond other tail feathers. VOICE: High-pitched *kew-kew-kew* and a quarreling *kre-krep*.
HABITS: Graceful, agile flight, similar to a tern's. Hovers like a kestrel on breeding grounds. Piratical in winter, chasing other seabirds in twisting, acrobatic flight and forcing them to disgorge their food. Feeds almost exclusively on lemmings and other small rodents when breeding. In years when lemming and vole populations

juv.
Dark morph

juv.
Pale morph

ad. breeding

ad. Mar–Sep

Long-tailed Jaeger
Stercorarius longicaudus
Circumpolar
L 14–16.5 in (36–41 cm)

ad. breeding
Dark morph

ad. breeding
Pale morph

ad. Mar–Sep
Intermediate

ad. Mar–Sep
Dark morph

subad.
Pale morph

Parasitic Jaeger
Stercorarius parasiticus
Circumpolar
L 15–17.5 in (37–44 cm)

ad. Mar–Sep
Pale morph

juv.
Intermediate

ad. breeding
Pale morph

ad. breeding
Dark morph

ad. Apr–Oct
Pale morph
No breast band

juv.
Pale morph

ad. Apr–Oct
Dark morph

Pomarine Jaeger
Stercorarius pomarinus
Near circumpolar
L 17–20 in (42–50 cm)

ad. Apr–Oct
Pale morph

Great Skua
Stercorarius skua
N Atlantic
L 20–23 in (50–58 cm)

are low, does not breed and simply returns to sea. Arrives on breeding grounds when snow is still on the ground. Nests on small rises and gentle slopes that have low vegetation and clear views of surroundings. Both sexes incubate the eggs for 23–25 days and brood the chicks for 1–7 days. For the first week, the female remains near nest while the male forages and returns with insects, berries, and small prey for the female and chicks. The male regurgitates food in front of the female, who then feeds the chicks. Later, the male and female feed on the prey before they tear off small morsels for their young. Young can fly at about 30 days. Parents move to the coast with their offspring and continue to feed them at least until day 42. The familial bond may persist until migration, when the parent birds and young leave independently for the open sea.

SUBFAMILY LARINAE
GULLS

Gulls, also known as seagulls, have strong slender legs, with 3 fully webbed toes and a reduced hind toe. The leg and foot structure and leg placement toward the center of the body permit gulls to walk easily, while the webbed feet aid in swimming. The larger gull species have strong, slightly hooked bills, while the smaller species have thinner, more slender ones.

Distinguishing between various species is challenging since gulls take 2–4 years to attain full adult plumage and some pass through as many as 8 different plumage stages, or *cycles*, as they mature from juvenile to adult. Juvenile gulls have completely dark bills. The bill base pales as juveniles advance through their second and third years, and the dark tip is reduced to a dusky ring near the tip. Almost all first-year gulls have dark eyes, which typically begin to lighten in their second to third years. Breeding adults develop a brightly colored orbital ring. In addition, adults usually display different winter and summer plumages, and also display great individual variation. Clues to identification include size (useful when more than one species is present), eye color, bill color and shape, and the color and markings (if any) on the primary feathers, back, and head.

Gulls are opportunistic omnivores, feeding on almost anything. They take relatively large prey thanks to an expandable maw at the junction of the upper and lower mandibles. Foraging methods range from picking food from the ground or water surface, to plunge diving, aerial capture, and stealing food from other birds (*kleptoparasitism*). Many species attend fishing trawlers and frequent docks where they beg for food and scavenge on discards. The Ivory Gull, a High Arctic species, follows polar bears and Inuit hunters on the ice, and feeds on scraps from their kills.

Most gulls are colonial nesters. Most are monogamous and exhibit high mate and nesting site fidelity. Many have courtship rituals accompanied by noisy vocalizations that serve to cement pair bonds. Nests vary from simple ground scrapes to sizable mounds of mud, grass, seaweed, feathers, and flotsam piled on a cliff ledge. One species, the Bonaparte's Gull, builds a nest of twigs high in a tree. Pairs raise a single brood of about 2–3 young each year. Both sexes build the nest, incubate the eggs, brood and guard the hatchlings, and feed their young well beyond their time of fledging. Most of the northern species winter in coastal or nearshore waters. Others, like Sabine's Gull, are pelagic and winter far out at sea.

GENUS *LARUS*: *Larus* means "rapacious seabird," an apt name as gulls have a truculent nature and an insatiable appetite that extends to chicks and eggs of other seabirds.

Gulls in this genus are medium to large birds, usually grey or white, with white heads and pale gray to blackish backs in adult plumage. Adults of the larger species have a conspicuous angular bulge, or *gonys*, on the lower beak. A reddish spot develops forward of the gonys when the gulls are breeding. The spot triggers begging behavior in chicks, which peck at the spot, thus stimulating the parent to regurgitate food.

The gulls typically make a low mound of grass, moss, lichen, seaweed, feathers, and flotsam in which to nest. Both sexes incubate the 2–3 olive, gray, or brown, dark-spotted eggs for 24–32 days. Chicks fledge at 4–7 weeks of age, but in most cases they remain around the nesting area, and the parents continue to feed them for several weeks beyond fledging.

Gulls in this genus tend to hybridize where ranges of species overlap, and the hybrids show a confusing mixture of plumage traits. The eye color of adults—pale or dark—is a useful feature to note when identifying similar species or hybrids.

Great Black-backed Gull

Larus marinus
ALSO: Saddleback, Coffin-Bearer, Minister, Måantelmöwe, Goéland marin, Svartbak, Морская чайка. SN means "gull of the sea."

RANGE: Nests (May–Jul) on n Atlantic seacoasts and rocky islands in e Canada, s Greenland, Iceland, Svalbard, and Europe. Winters on the Atlantic coasts of Canada and the US and on coasts of w Europe south to Portugal.
ID: L 25–30 in (64–75 cm). One of the world's largest gulls, with a 57–65 in (144–166 cm) wingspan and a weight of up to 5 lb (2.3 kg). Large head. Massive bill. Dusky eye. Pale pink legs. Attains adult plumage at 4 years. AD MAY–JUL: Black mantle and back. White head, underparts, and tail. Upperwing dark slate gray; broad white trailing edge; large white spot on 2 outer primaries. Underwing white, with a band of gray at base of primaries. Dirty yellow eye; red orbital ring. Bill yellow; red spot on lower mandible. AD WINTER: Dark streaks on the crown. FIRST YEAR: Coarsely checkered, blackish brown upperparts. Head and underparts whitish, with fine dark streaks on crown and breast. Black bill. Dark eye. SECOND YEAR: Head white. Bill pinkish, with a black tip. Mantle mottled brown and gray. THIRD YEAR: Resembles winter adult. Bill yellowish, with a dark ring near tip. VOICE: Deep, hoarse growling *err'-ul* or laughing *kha-ga-ga* cry in display. Also sounds a loud *yeeah-yeeah-yeeah.*
HABITS: Forages on rocky or sandy coasts, estuaries, and marine waters. Omnivorous; also pirates food from other birds. Lumbering flight. Frequently glides or soars with outstretched wings. Nests singly or in small colonies on flat-topped stacks, sea cliffs, rocky coasts, beaches,

salt marshes, and abandoned piers. Sometimes nests inland on islets in large freshwater lakes and open moors.
STATUS: Nearly extirpated by 19th-century feather hunters and egg collectors, the species now exceeds its historical numbers as a result of protection and availability of plentiful food in the form of human garbage.

Lesser Black-backed Gull

Larus fuscus
ALSO: Heringsmöwe, Goéland brun, Silltrut, Sildemåke, Клуша. SN means "dusky gull."

RANGE: Nests (May–Jun) along seacoasts and lakes in Iceland, UK, w Europe, and nw Russia. Winters on coastal and offshore waters of the North, Mediterranean, Black, and Caspian seas, and seacoasts from n Africa to nw India. Winter visitor to N Amer, mostly to Atlantic and Gulf coasts, in lesser numbers to the continental interior and Pacific NW.
ID: L 19–22 in (48–56 cm). Large, dark-backed gull. Yellow legs. Pale eye. Attains adult plumage in 4 years. AD MAY–JUL: White head, tail, and underparts. Blackish back and wings; small white spot on outer primary. Clear yellow iris; red orbital ring. Bill yellow; red spot on lower beak. Legs yellow. Dense, dark streaking on head and around eye in winter. Shows almost no white spots on the wing tips at rest. FIRST YEAR: Dark dusky brown, with pale face and dark ear patch. Back dark and coarsely checkered. Wings neatly barred with dark and light. Rump pale. Broad dark band on tail tip. Two dark bars across back of spread wing; outer wing dark. Underparts variable, with dense dark streaks overall or with very little streaking on throat, breast, and belly. Legs chalky pink. Bill black. Dark eye. SECOND YEAR: Mantle slaty gray; wings still mottled. Tail white, with dark tail band. Head and underparts white; dark streaks on head and nape and around eye. Bill pale horn, with a black tip. Eye begins to pale. Legs may be tinged with yellow. THIRD YEAR: Resembles winter adult, but mantle lighter, legs paler yellow, bill yellow with dark ring at tip, and nape more heavily streaked. Faint tail

2nd year

3rd year

ad.

1st year

1st year

2nd year

3rd year

Slaty-backed Gull
Larus schistisagus
NW Pacific
L 22–27 in (56–69 cm)

ad. May–Aug
Pink legs
Pale eye

2nd year

ad.

1st year

3rd year

1st year
Pink legs

2nd year

ad. May–Jul
Yellow legs
Pale eye

Lesser Black-backed Gull
Larus fuscus
N Atlantic
L 19–22 in (48–56 cm)

3rd year

ad.

1st–2nd year

3rd year

1st year

2nd year

ad. May–Jul
Pale pink legs
Dusky eye

Great Black-backed Gull
Larus marinus
N Atlantic
L 25–30 in (64–75 cm)

1st year
L. argentatus

1st year
L. argentatus
Whitish tail base

2nd year

1st year
L. smithsonianus

2nd year

1st year
L. smithsonianus
Dark tail base

3rd year

ad.

ad. winter

Herring Gull
Larus argentatus Eurasia
Larus smithsonianus N Amer
L 22–24 in (56–60 cm)

ad. Mar–Sep
Pale eye

1st year

1st year
Pale morph

2nd year

2nd year

1st year
Dark morph

3rd year

3rd year

ad.

ad. winter

Thayer's Gull
Larus thayeri
N Amer, nw Greenland
L 21–23 in (53–58 cm)

ad. Apr–Sep
Dusky eye

band. VOICE: Loud, clear, bugling *kyau*. Long call given in display is a deep, laughing *aau kleee'a kay-a kay-a kay-a kyau*.

HABITS: Omnivorous. Forms small to large flocks that forage at sea, around garbage dumps, and in cultivated fields. Follows fishing fleets. Breeds, often with other gull species, in colonies of a few pairs to several hundred. Nests on coastal grassy slopes, dunes, cliffs, rocky offshore islands, around inland lakes and rivers, and occasionally on building rooftops. Prefers sites with short vegetation such as bracken or heather.

SIMILAR SPECIES: HEUGLIN'S GULL (*not illus.*), alternately known as *Larus heuglini, Larus fuscus heuglini,* and *Larus affinis,* breeds on n Russian tundra from the Kola to the Taimyr peninsulas. Distinguished from *L. fuscus* by darker streaking on head in winter and delayed molting period in Sep–Oct. Taimyr Penin gulls with pale mantles are sometimes considered a separate subspecies, the TAIMYR GULL, *L. h. taimyrensis.*

Slaty-backed Gull

Larus schistisagus
ALSO: Kamtschatkamöwe, Goéland à manteau ardoisé, Skifermåke, Тихоокеанская чайка. SN means "slaty-mantled gull."
RANGE: Nests (May–Aug) on rugged seacoasts and rocky islets in the nw Pacific from Cape Navarin, Siberia, south to Kamchatka, Commander Is, Kuril Is, and n Japan. Winters south to Taiwan and east to Alaska, where small numbers have bred in recent years. Rare in the Bering and Chukchi seas, Aleutians, Pribilofs, and the N Amer Pacific coast south to n California.
ID: L 22–27 in (56–69 cm). Very large, barrel-bodied gull, with a large head and relatively slender yellow bill. Attains adult plumage in 4 years. AD MAY–AUG: White head, belly, and tail. Deep slate gray mantle. Upperside of wings slaty gray, with a broad white trailing edge; black confined to webs of outer primaries. White underwing has a band of dark gray at base of primaries and outermost secondaries; a line of white subterminal spots—the diagnostic "string of pearls"— runs parallel to the white trailing edge. Lemon yellow eye; reddish orange orbital

ring. Yellow bill; orange red subterminal spot. Short, dark pink legs. AD WINTER: Grayish brown streaking on the nape. FIRST YEAR: Finely mottled brown plumage turns whitish by first summer, while outer primaries, secondaries, and tail remain mottled brown. Bill black. Dark eye. SECOND YEAR: Acquires a dark gray mantle that contrasts with mottled wings. Tail base white; broad black terminal tail band. Head white; brown streaks on crown, nape, and sides of breast. Bill yellow, with a black tip. Eye dirty yellow. THIRD YEAR: Resembles winter adult, but with heavy streaking on head and neck. Pale eye. Bill yellow, with a dark ring near tip.
HABITS: Feeds mainly on fish, marine inverte-brates, and garbage. Preys on eggs and chicks of other seabirds when nesting, and also eats fish and roe during salmon spawning, leftovers from bear kills, waste from fisheries, small rodents, berries, and insects. Breeds in small to large colonies on inaccessible cliffs on rugged seacoasts and rocky islets.

Herring Gull

Larus argentatus Eurasia
Larus smithsonianus N Amer
ALSO: Naujaq, Silbermöwe, Goéland argenté, Gråtrut, Серебристая чайка. SNs mean "silver gull" and "Smithsonian gull." In 1862 Elliott Coues described the N Amer Herring Gull, *L. smith-sonianus,* from specimens in the Smithsonian Institution (hence the specific name). The species was later classed as a subspecies of the Eurasian Herring Gull, *L. argentatus,* but once again is viewed as a separate species based on distinctive first-year plumage and slight genetic differences.
RANGE: Nests (Apr–Jul) in a variety of coastal and inland habitats of the Holarctic. EURASIAN HERRING GULL (E), *L. argentatus,* breeds and is resident in Iceland, n Europe, n Russia, and c Asia. N AMER HERRING GULL (S), *L. smithsonianus,* breeds in Alaska, Aleutians, and Canada, north to Davis Strait and Baffin Is, and south to the Great Lakes and US Atlantic coast; winters south to Mexico; casual or vagrant to Hawaii, W Indies, C Amer, n S Amer, UK, w Europe.
ID: L 22–24 in (56–60 cm). Large white-headed

gull, with a gray mantle, short pink legs, and strong bill. Attains adult plumage at 4 years. AD MAR–SEP: White head, tail, and underparts. Pale gray back and wings. Outer primaries black, with white spots at the tips of the outer 5. Pale yellow eye; orange to red orbital ring. Bill deep yellow; red spot on lower beak extends to cutting edge. AD WINTER: Head and neck show dark streaking and red spot on lower beak is replaced to some extent by black. FIRST YEAR: Dark eye. Dark bill. Brownish gray head. *L. argentatus:* Wing and back feathers chocolate brown, broadly edged with white or buff. Underparts streaked and mottled. Tail tip dark; tail base shows white barring. *L. smithsonianus:* Wings and back mottled brown and buff. Underparts uniformly brown. Rump and tail base densely barred with dark brown. Tail dark; little or no white at base. SECOND YEAR: Develops a pale eye, pale bill base, pale head, and gray mantle. THIRD YEAR: Resembles winter adult, but tail retains a black terminal band. Bill pale yellow, with dark tip. Eye appears pale, even at a distance. Some brown feathering remains on wings and body. VOICE: Laughing *ha-ga-ga* flight call. Loud, deep, laughing *aau kleee'a kay-a kay-a kay-a kyau* given in display. Strident *kyow* sounded in alarm.
HABITS: Gregarious occupant of beaches, lakes, rivers, coastal waters, mudflats, fields, docks, and garbage dumps. Omnivorous. Has been observed dropping shellfish onto hard surfaces to break open the shells. Nests, often in association with other gulls or alcids, in solitary pairs or in colonies on sea cliffs, sand spits, wet tundra hummocks, reed beds, islands in small lakes and rivers, and occasionally on roofs of urban buildings. Both sexes make several lined ground scrapes. The male and female display with breasts lowered to the ground and tails elevated, and emit a *huoh-huoh-huoh* choking call at the scrape chosen for egg laying.
SIMILAR SPECIES: VEGA GULL (*not illus.*) may be a full species, *Larus vegae*, or a subspecies of the N Amer Herring Gull, *L. smithsonianus,* or a subspecies of the Eurasian Herring Gull, *L. argentatus*. Breeds ne Siberia, winters e Asia; regular at St Lawrence Is, Gambell Is, and Nome,

Alaska. Has a darker gray mantle, darker pink legs and feet, and darker yellow eyes than other herring gulls. Pale forms that breed in nw Siberia are sometimes considered to be a separate subspecies, BIRULA'S GULL *L. vegae birulai.*

Thayer's Gull

Larus thayeri
ALSO: Thayermöwe, Goéland de Thayer, Eskimomåke, Чайка Тэйера. SN means "Thayer's gull," honoring American amateur ornithologist John Eliot Thayer (1862–1922), who sponsored the 1915 Alaska–Siberia expedition that discovered this gull. Thayer's Gull is alternatively considered to be a subspecies of the larger, pale-eyed N Amer Herring Gull, *L. smithsonianus,* or a dark-mantled subspecies of the Iceland Gull, *L. glaucoides*.
RANGE: Nests (May–Jul) in disjunct colonies on seacoasts and islands in the Canadian Arctic and nw Greenland. Winters around polynyas off Greenland and on the N Amer Pacific coast from s Alaska to the Gulf of California; small populations winter on the Great Lakes and upper Mississippi Rvr. Vagrant to Mexico, Japan, and w Europe.
ID: L 21–23 in (53–58 cm). Small rounded head, with peak just behind the eye. Dark eye. Slender bill. Deep pink legs. AD APR–SEP: Bright yellow bill, with red spot on lower beak; spot more oval in shape than Herring Gull's and does not reach the cutting edge. Eye dull yellow, with dark inclusions; eye usually much darker than adult Herring Gull's; purple red orbital ring. White head, tail, and underparts. Pale gray upperparts. Outer primaries black with white spotting; black generally confined to the outer web; large white half-oval spot on outer primary; white oval spot on inner web of ninth primary; white moon on inner web of eighth primary; primary tips appear gray from below. AD WINTER: Blurred brown streaking on head and nape. FIRST YEAR: Mottled brown overall. Pale brown flight feathers. Dark brown tail band. Black bill. Dark eye. Black legs turn pink. SECOND YEAR: Head, neck, upper breast, and belly white, with pale brown streaking. Dull

1st–2nd year
L. c. brachyrhynchus
L. c. kamtschatschensis

ad.
L. c. brachyrhynchus

ad.
L. c. canus

1st–2nd year
L. c. canus

1st year

ad. winter
L. c. brachyrhynchus
Dusky eye

2nd year

ad. winter
L. c. kamtschatschensis
Pale eye

ad. winter
L. c. canus
Dark eye

ad. Apr–Sep

Mew or Common Gull
Larus canus
Eurasia, w N Amer
L 16–18 in (40–46 cm)

1st year

1st year
Pale morph

2nd
year

1st year
Dark morph

2nd year

3rd year
Pale eye

ad. winter
L. g. glaucoides
Pale primaries

ad. Apr–Sep
L. g. kumlieni

ad. *L. g. kumlieni*
Outer primaries
dark gray

Iceland Gull
Larus glaucoides
N Canada, Greenland, Iceland
L 21–23 in (52–58 cm)

ad. Apr–Sep
L. g. glaucoides

2nd year

ad.

1st year

1st year

3rd year

ad. winter

2nd year

Glaucous-winged Gull
Larus glaucescens
N Pacific
L 24–26 in (61–66 cm)

ad. Feb–Sep
Gray and white
primaries
Dark eye

2nd year

ad.

1st year

3rd year

ad. winter

1st year
Some juveniles have
paler plumage

2nd year

Glaucous Gull
Larus hyperboreus
Circumpolar
L 25–27 in (63–68 cm)

ad. Mar–Sep
White primaries
Pale eye

brown upperwing coverts. Gray back. Tail base white; dark terminal tail band. Bill pinkish, with black tip. THIRD YEAR: Closely resembles winter adult. Often retains a partial tail band.

HABITS: Nests in colonies of 50–100 pairs on small rocky ledges of vertical sea cliffs, often in association with glaucous gulls, various seabirds, and occasionally ravens.

Iceland Gull
Larus glaucoides

ALSO: Kumlien's Iceland Gull, Polarmöwe, Goéland arctique, Grønlandsmåke, Полярная чайка. SN means "resembling a glaucous gull." CN refers to the type locality. *Kumlien* refers to Swedish-American ornithologist Thure Ludwig Theodor Kumlien (1819–1888). **RANGE:** Nests (Apr–Aug) on ledges of sea cliffs in n Canada, Greenland, and occasionally Iceland. Most adults winter around arctic polynyas (open water surrounded by sea ice). Juveniles disperse south of breeding areas. **SUBSPECIES:** ICELAND GULL (I), *L. g. glaucoides*;, breeds in Greenland. Has pale gray mantle, very pale gray wing tips, and little or no patterning on the wings. KUMLIEN'S GULL (K), *L. g. kumlieni*, breeds ne Canada. Has medium gray mantle and variable wing-tip pattern; most have slaty gray primaries similar to glaucous-winged gulls. **ID:** L 21–23 in (52–58 cm). Slender, yellowish green bill, with slightly angled gonys. Rounded head. Wing tips extend beyond tail at rest. Smaller than the Herring Gull (*L. argentatus*) and smaller and thinner-billed than the Glaucous Gull (*L. hyperboreus*). Attains adult plumage at 4 years. AD APR–SEP: White head, tail, and underparts. Pale gray to slaty gray wing tips. Pale eye; dark red orbital ring. Bill yellow, with grayish base, red spot on lower beak, and bright yellow on upper bill ridge (culmen). Pink legs. AD WINTER: Blurred brown streaks and spots on head and nape. FIRST YEAR: Black bill. Dark eye. Plumage ghostly white or buff, with pale brown edgings to feathers. White primaries and secondaries. White tail, speckled with gray or pale brown. SECOND YEAR: Bill pale pink at base, black at tip. Whitish head, tail, and underparts. Pale

gray back. THIRD YEAR: Resembles winter adult, but lacks adult bill pattern. VOICE: Laughing cry similar to a Herring Gull's, but higher pitched. **HABITS:** Omnivorous. Seizes food at or just below the water's surface when swimming or dipping. Breeds in colonies or solitary pairs on sea cliffs.

Glaucous-winged Gull
Larus glaucescens

ALSO: Beringmöwe, Goéland à ailes grises, Gråvengmåse, Серокрылая чайка. SN means "gray gull."

RANGE: Nests (May–Aug) on coastal islands and sea cliffs in Kamchatka, Commander Is, Aleutians, Pribilofs, St Matthew Is, and along the Pacific coast of Alaska and Canada. Winters on seacoasts south to California and Japan. **ID:** L 24–26 in (61–66 cm). Large, gray-backed gull, with a yellow bill, pink legs, and dark eye. Attains adult plumage at 4 years. AD FEB–SEP: White head, underparts, and tail. Wing tips patterned in gray and white. Dark brown to dusky yellow iris; pinkish orbital ring. Bill yellow, with red spot on lower beak. AD WINTER: Faintly barred on head and neck. FIRST YEAR: Mottled grayish brown. Dark bill. SECOND YEAR: Pale grayish brown to creamy white; some birds may show dark scapulars. Bill dark. THIRD YEAR: Resembles winter adult. White head, with light brown streaks. Dull yellow, dark-tipped bill. Some birds retain dark tail-feather tips. **HABITS:** Omnivorous. Breeds colonially or in solitary pairs on marine coasts. Nest is a mound of grass, moss, seaweed, and bones placed on low flat ground, less frequently on sea cliffs.

Glaucous Gull
Larus hyperboreus

ALSO: Eismöwe, Goéland bourgmestre, Polarmåke, Бургомистр, Naujaq, Nau-yavasrugruk. SN means "gull of the Far North." **RANGE:** Circumpolar. Nests (May–Aug) mainly north of the Arctic Circle. Winters along seacoasts from southern parts of breeding range south to California, Florida, France, China, and Japan. **ID:** L 25–27 in (63–68 cm). Large, powerful gull, very pale in all plumages, with no black in the wings or tail. Pink legs. Larger and thicker-billed than the similar Iceland Gull; head appears flatter, and wing tips barely project beyond tail. Attains adult plumage at 4 years. AD MAR–SEP: White, with a pale gray mantle. Thick yellow bill, with a red spot on the lower mandible. Clear yellow eye; bright yellow orbital ring. AD WINTER: Head and neck blotched with brown. FIRST YEAR: Mottled brown overall. Bill pink, with a black tip. Dark eye. SECOND YEAR: Creamy white overall, with scattered pale brown spots and streaks on body and wings. Black-tipped pink bill. Dusky eye. THIRD YEAR: Resembles winter adult. White head bears some brown streaking. Pale eye. Bill pale yellow, with dark ring near tip. VOICE: Similar to Herring Gull's, but harsher. HABITS: Feeds on fish, insects, mollusks, starfish, eggs and chicks of other birds, small mammals, carrion, trawler discards, seeds, and berries. Breeds colonially or singly on cliff ledges, grassy slopes above precipitous cliffs, coastal islands, and edges of ponds on open tundra.

Mew or Common Gull

Larus canus
ALSO: Sturmmöwe, Goéland cendré, Fiskemåke, Сизая чайка, Nauyatchiak. SN means "gray gull."
RANGE: Nests (Apr–Jul) on coasts and inland in nw N Amer, Iceland, Faroes, UK, and Eurasia.
SUBSPECIES: MEW OR SHORT-BILLED GULL (M), *L. c. brachyrhynchus*, breeds in Alaska and nw Canada. Winters on the Pacific coast south to California. Smallest race, with relatively slender bill. Olive brown eye. Often considered a separate species. COMMON GULL (C), *L. c. canus*, breeds in Iceland, UK, and east across n Russia. Winters from Europe to n Africa and Persian Gulf; rare in fall–winter along US Atlantic seaboard. Blackish brown eye. KAMCHATKA GULL (K), *L. c. kamtschatschensis*, breeds in ne Siberia, Sakhalin Is, Kamchatka, and Kurils. Winters in coastal e Asia. Rare in w Aleutians, St Lawrence Is, and Pribilofs. Largest race. Distinguished by pale yellow eye, longer and thicker bill, and longer legs.

ID: L 16–18 in (40–46 cm). Attains adult plumage in 2 years. AD APR–SEP: Head, tail, and underparts white. Back, scapulars, and wings medium gray. Primaries black with white tips and white mirrors on outer primaries. Bill yellow to greenish yellow. Legs yellow green to dull grayish green. AD WINTER: Heavy gray or brown mottling on head and nape; bill may have a dusky band near tip. FIRST YEAR: Plumage mottled grayish brown. Rump and uppertail coverts whitish; dark tail band (*canus*); rump and uppertail coverts buff, with heavy brown barring; dark brown tail band (*brachyrhynchus* and *kamtschatschensis*). Bill dark, with pale pink base. Legs and feet grayish pink. SECOND YEAR: Birds acquire a gray mantle and pale underparts. VOICE: High-pitched, laughing *ke ke ke kleee-a kay-a kay-a kay-a ke ke* or sharp, squeaky *keeya*. HABITS: Feeds on marine invertebrates, crustaceans, insects, worms, zooplankton, garbage, sewage, and carrion. Sometimes steals food and eggs from other gulls, shorebirds, and waterfowl. Attends fishing boats and trawlers. Forages by spinning and picking prey from water surface, or flutters wings and stoops with dangling legs to pick prey from surface. Breeds colonially or in single pairs on seacoasts, islands, marshes, and along rivers and lakes on tundra and steppe. Nest is a shallow cup of dry grass or reeds built on the ground or on boulders, pilings, roofs, or occasionally in low trees.

GENUS *XEMA*
Sabine's Gull

Xema sabini
ALSO: Schwalbenmöwe, Mouette de Sabine, Sabinemåke, Вилохвостая чайка, Iqiggagiarjuk, Akargiyiak. SN honors Irish naturalist Edward Sabine (1788–1883), who found the species at Melville Bay, Greenland; his brother Joseph Sabine (1770–1837) wrote the scientific description.
RANGE: Nests (Jun–Jul) on High Arctic tundra in Alaska, Canada, n Greenland, Svalbard, and Siberia, including New Siberian Is and Wrangel Is. Post-breeding, migrates in small flocks to feed on beaches, estuaries, and pack ice. Pelagic in winter, occupying upwelling zones off the Pacific

coast of S Amer and sw Africa. Accidental in Jan Mayen, Iceland, Faroes, Chukotka.
ID: L 12–14 in (30–36 cm). Striking upperwing pattern; large white triangle across inner primaries and secondaries contrasts sharply with black outer primaries and gray (adult) or brown (first year) mantle. Long, thin, pointed wings. Notched tail. AD APR–SEP: Dark gray hood, edged with a line of black feathers. Yellow-tipped black bill. Black legs. Gape, mouth lining, and eyering red. Dark gray mantle and upperwings. White underparts. AD WINTER: Black hood is reduced to a dark patch on the nape. JUV: Black bill and legs. Head and neck dusky brown. Back scaled in grayish brown. White tail, with a broad black terminal tail band. Dark gray of the adult is replaced by brown on the wings. Dark bill. Flight tern-like and buoyant, with steady wingbeats. VOICE: Tern-like chirping and rattling, or a chirring *krrrrree*.
HABITS: Feeds on zooplankton, crustaceans, fish, and fishing offal in winter. During breeding season, feeds on aquatic insects taken from ponds, lakes, rivers, meltwater pools, snowbanks, and pack ice. Breeds colonially on mossy edges of small ponds and on low-lying marshy tundra. Nest is an unlined depression pressed into vegetation or occasionally gravel. Clutch is 2–3 olive green eggs with darker, irregular blotches on the larger end. Incubation is 20–25 days. All adults in nesting colony cooperate in defending young by mobbing predators. Parents lead the chicks to feeding areas and remain with the young until they are fully independent.

GENUS *CHROICOCEPHALUS*
Black-headed Gull
Chroicocephalus ridibundus
ALSO: Lachmöwe, Mouette rieuse, Hettemåke, Озерная чайка, *Larus ridibundus*. SN
means "laughing [gull] with a colored head."
RANGE: Nests (Apr–May) in wetland habitats in interior Eurasia and in a few locations in coastal e Canada. Some populations are resident; others winter in s Eurasia and on coasts of nc Africa.
ID: L 14–16 in (36–40 cm). Attains adult plumage in 2 years. AD MAR–AUG: Chocolate brown

head (not black as the common name suggests). Broken white eyering. Red bill and legs. Pale gray upperparts. White underparts. Wings have white leading edge. Black tips to primaries. AD WINTER: Black-tipped red bill; the hood fades away, leaving a dark ear spot and dark vertical streak marking the hood edge. FIRST YEAR: Black-tipped red bill. Yellowish pink legs. Black terminal tail band. Dark areas on wings and mantle fade by winter, leaving dark wing stripe and dark trailing edge to wing. Hood begins to form at end of first winter. VOICE: Noisy species, with a familiar *kree-ar* call.
HABITS: Rarely seen far offshore. Feeds from the water surface while flying low or swimming, taking aquatic insects, fish, carrion, and scraps from fishing boats and docks. Forages on land, taking seeds, worms, rodents, and invertebrates in ploughed fields. Highly gregarious in winter; flocks feed and roost in inlets or estuaries with sandy or muddy beaches, ploughed fields, moist grasslands, urban parks, sewage ponds, garbage dumps, and reservoirs. Breeds in dense colonies of up to several thousand pairs, often with other gull or tern species. Prefers places with lush vegetation near water for nesting, including reed beds, marshes, riverbanks, islands in lakes, and flooded fields. Nest is a shallow scrape built up with vegetation and placed on a floating mat of vegetation, on broken reeds, on a hummock, or sometimes on dry, grassy or sandy ground. Clutch is 3 greenish brown or pale greenish blue, darkly spotted eggs. Long-lived species; one bird was recorded living 63 years in the wild.

Bonaparte's Gull
Chroicocephalus philadelphia
ALSO: Bonapartemöwe, Mouette de Bonaparte, Kana-
dahettemåke, Бонапартова чайка, *Larus philadelphia*. CN refers to Prince Charles Lucien Bonaparte (1803–1857), ornithologist and Napoleon's nephew. SN refers to Philadelphia, Pennsylvania, the US city where the type specimen was found.
RANGE: Nests (May–Jul) in trees in coniferous forests in Alaska and Canada. Migrates and winters in large flocks along Pacific and Atlantic

1st year

ad. winter

ad. breeding

ad. winter

Nests in trees

Bonaparte's Gull
Chroicocephalus philadelphia
N Amer
L 12–13.5 in (30–34 cm)

1st year
Black bill
Red legs

ad. Mar–Aug
Black bill
Reddish legs

1st
year

ad. winter

ad. breeding

1st year
Black bill
Black legs

ad. winter

Sabine's Gull
Xema sabini
Circumpolar
L 12–14 in (30–36 cm)

ad. Apr–Sep
Yellow-tipped black bill
Black legs

1st
year

ad. winter

ad. breeding

1st
year

ad. Mar–Aug
Dark brown hood
Red bill and legs

Black-headed Gull
Chroicocephalus ridibundus
Eurasia, e Canada
L 14–16 in (36–40 cm)

ad. winter
Black-tipped red bill
Reddish legs

coasts and inland, south to the Gulf coast and n Mexico. Occasional winter visitor to Hawaii. Casual in Azores, Europe, Japan. **ID:** L 12–13.5 in (30–34 cm). Black bill. Reddish legs. Attains adult plumage in 2 years. **AD MAR–AUG:** Black hood. Short, thin, blackish bill. Pale gray back. Tail white. Underparts white, often with a delicate pink flush on breast. Wings gray, with dark tips and white outer primaries; narrow triangle of white on outer primaries. Short reddish legs. **AD WINTER:** White head, with a black ear spot. **FIRST YEAR:** Mottled and scaled with brown on the back, neck, and crown. White underparts. Black ear patch. Black terminal tail band. By first winter, back fades to pale gray and wings show a dark, mottled wing stripe and black trailing edge. **VOICE:** Drawn out buzzy twang, *kaa-aa-aa-aa-aa*. Mews softly when roosting on water or when brooding chicks. **HABITS:** Graceful, buoyant, tern-like flight. Forages in flocks in winter in coastal and offshore marine habitats, taking insects, small invertebrates, and small fish from the water surface. Floats high in the water, spinning and picking prey from surface; rarely scavenges like other gulls. Feeds mainly on insects when breeding, sometimes hawking them in flight. Breeds in solitary pairs or loose colonies in remote forests around lakes, ponds, bogs, bays, and fjords. Nests in trees, especially in Black Spruce (*Picea mariana*) and Tamarack (*Larix laricina*); occasionally nests on the ground or in reed beds. Both sexes build a nest of twigs, small branches, and tree bark, lined with moss and lichens. Both parents incubate the 2–3 buffy or greenish, darkly blotched eggs for 23–24 days. Young jump down from the nest at 6–7 days of age and follow parents to feeding areas.

GENUS *PAGOPHILA*
Ivory Gull
Pagophila eburnea
ALSO: Naujavaaq, Elfen-beinmöwe, Mouette blanche,
Ismåke, Белая чайка. SN means "ice-loving ivory-colored [gull]." Described by English captain Constantine Phipps (1744–1792) from a specimen taken in Svalbard.

RANGE: Nests (Jun–Jul) on rocky coasts in the Canadian High Arctic islands, Greenland, Jan Mayen, Svalbard, and Russian arctic islands. Winters on the arctic pack ice, especially ice around polynyas (darker blue on map). Rare winter visitor to Iceland, Scandinavia, and UK. **ID:** L 16.5–18.5 in (41–47 cm). Attains adult plumage in 2 years. **AD:** Entirely ivory white. Bill bluish gray, with a yellow to orange tip. Dark eye, with a thin red eyering in breeding season. Very short, black legs. Wing tips extend beyond tail. **FIRST YEAR:** White, with dusky markings on face, mostly dark bill, and dark spotting on tips of flight feathers. Tail shows a narrow, dark terminal band. **VOICE:** High-pitched *kree-kree*. **HABITS:** Rapid, buoyant flight. Forages singly or in small groups. Takes fish and small invertebrates by dipping, surface plunging, wading in shallow water, and surface-seizing. Scavenges on carrion and offal. Follows polar bears and hunters and feeds on scraps from their kills. Congregates at hooded seal whelping sites to feed on discarded placentas. Breeds in small colonies on wide upper ledges of steep coastal or inland cliffs, broken ice fields, or barren rocky shorelines. Both sexes build a nest of mosses, lichens, and grasses on a snow-free area of rock, and incubate the clutch of 1–3 buff-colored, dark-spotted eggs for about 25 days. Chicks begin feeding themselves after just 3 weeks and fledge soon after this. **STATUS:** Rapid decline in parts of its range is attributed to climate change, pollution, and increasing human intrusion and hunting within breeding areas. Near Threatened (IUCN).

GENUS *RHODOSTETHIA*
Ross's Gull
Rhodostethia rosea
ALSO: Rosy Gull, Rosen-möwe, Mouette rosée,
Rosenmåke, Розовая чайка. SN means "rose-breasted rosy [gull]." CN honors British naval officer and explorer James Clark Ross (1800–1862), who discovered this species in 1823 on the Melville Penin, Canada. **RANGE:** Nests (Jun–Jul) on marshy tundra and boggy forest-tundra from the Taimyr Penin

1st year
Ross's Gull

ad. winter
Ross's Gull

ad. breeding
Ross's Gull

Ivory Gull
Pagophila eburnea
High Arctic
L 16.5–18.5 in (41–47 cm)

1st year
Ivory Gull

ad.
Ivory Gull

1st year

ad.

ad. winter

1st year

Ross's Gull
Rhodostethia rosea
Siberia, ne Canada, Greenland
L 11.5–12.5 in (29–32 cm)

ad. Apr–Aug

to the Kolyma Rvr in ne Siberia; locally in w Greenland; and in scattered, shifting colonies in arctic Canada (Churchill, Cheyne Is, Prince Charles Is, and Penny Strait). Migratory patterns poorly known, but known to move north from Point Barrow, Alaska, in fall. Winters on the open ocean or at the sea ice edge around large polynyas. Vagrant to nw Europe, Japan, and n US. **ID:** L 11.5–12.5 in (29–32 cm). Attains adult plumage in second year. AD APR–AUG: White head. Black neck ring. Black bill. Pale gray back and wings. White wedge-shaped tail. White below, with a variable amount of rose color on breast. Gray underwing; trailing edge white. Red legs. AD WINTER: Lacks rosy breast and neck ring, and has a very pale gray back. FIRST YEAR: Resembles winter adult, but shows a dark M mark across

back and wings. Black tip to white tail. Legs reddish pink. VOICE: High-pitched *miaw* or tern-like *kik-kik-kik-kik-kik*. Silent in winter. **HABITS:** Graceful, tern-like flight. Forages singly or in small flocks on the open sea or at pack ice edge in winter. Feeds on small fish, plankton, crustaceans, mollusks, and marine worms taken at the sea surface; also takes beetles and flies, and forages like a shorebird on mudflats. During breeding season, feeds extensively on crustaceans rich in red-pigmented carotenoids, especially astaxanthin, which produce the rosy flush on the breast feathers. Earlier it was thought that Ross's gulls painted the surface of their feathers with red-tinted oil from the preen gland, but now it has been confirmed that carotenoids from the food source pass internally into the feathers. Breeds in very small colonies. Pairs arrive on breeding grounds before snow completely melts and begin to court. Mates face each other, calling softly, and circle around each other. Nest is a ground scrape sited on a hummock surrounded by water or shallow pools of melted snow. Clutch is 2–3 olive green eggs with a ring of dark brown blotches at larger end. Both parents incubate the eggs and defend the nest, taking flight and diving at intruders while calling loudly.

GENUS *RISSA*: Kittiwakes are coastal breeding birds that form large, dense, noisy colonies during the summer reproductive period, often sharing nesting ledges on sea cliffs with murres. *Rissa* derives from *rita*, the Icelandic name for kittiwakes. *Kittiwake* is imitative of the Black-legged Kittiwake's call.

Black-legged Kittiwake

Rissa tridactyla
ALSO: Dreizehenmöwe, Mouette tridactyle, Krykkje, Обыкновенная моевка, Nauluktuapik. SN means "3-toed kittiwake," referring to the vestigial hind toe.
RANGE: Circumpolar. Nests (Apr–Jul) on sea cliffs in Alaska, Aleutians, Canadian High Arctic, Gulf of St Lawrence, Greenland, Iceland, Faroes, UK, w Europe, Scandinavia, Svalbard, Russian arctic islands, and from Chukotka south to Kamchatka and Kurils; birds in southern part of range often nest on window ledges of seaside buildings. Winters on the open ocean.
ID: L 14.5–16 in (37–42 cm). Black legs and feet; rarely orange-tinged. Tail slightly forked. Short legs. Appears large-headed, long-winged. Attains adult plumage in second year. AD: White head, tail, and underparts; head and nape smudged with gray in winter. Mantle pearl gray. Primaries pale gray; narrow white trailing edge; wing tips black, as if dipped in ink. Bill greenish yellow. Gape, mouth lining, and eyering red in breeding plumage. FIRST YEAR: White, with pale gray back. Blackish collar on hindneck; dark crescent on ear coverts. Dark M mark across back and wings. Tail white with black tip. Bill black, turning

yellow with age. VOICE: Plaintive *eea-eea-eea* and hollow, nasal *kitti-vey, kitti-vey.*
HABITS: Buoyant, tern-like flight. Forages at the sea surface, mostly by day, feeding on fish, squid, polychaete worms, euphausiids, and amphipods. Feeds in flocks, often with larger gulls, razorbills, puffins, murres, terns, and cormorants. Follows ships and scavenges at fishing trawlers. Breeds on steep sea cliffs with other seabirds in colonies containing a few to tens of thousands of kittiwakes. Mated pairs construct a nesting mound of mud, grass, seaweed, and feathers that they gather from the shore or pilfer from other kittiwakes' nests. Clutch of 2–3 brown, blue, gray, or olive, dark spotted eggs is laid over a period of 2–3 days. Both sexes incubate the eggs for about 27 days, brood the hatchlings, and feed the young. Chicks usually stand facing the cliff face, thus reducing the chance of falling off. The oldest, first-hatched chick sometimes attacks the younger sibling, killing it or forcing it to move to neighboring ledges, where is sometimes adopted by foster parents. Chicks fledge at 40–50 days when they are fully feathered. Fledglings often return to their nest to beg for food until the adults abandon the colony.

Red-legged Kittiwake

Rissa brevirostris
ALSO: Klippenmöwe, Mouette des brumes, Rosen-måke, Красноногая моевка.
SN means "short-billed kittiwake."
RANGE: Nests (May–Aug) on steep sea cliffs in the Commander Is, Pribilofs, and the Bogoslof and Buldir island groups in the Aleutians. Winters on the open ocean south of the Aleutians, along the ice edge in the Bering Sea, and in the n Gulf of Alaska.
ID: L 14–15 in (36–38 cm). Resembles the Black-legged Kittiwake but is slightly smaller, with a shorter bill, shorter, darker wings, slightly darker back, and bright red legs. Attains adult plumage in second year. AD: White head, neck, breast, belly, and tail. Mantle and upperwings dark gray. Wing tips black. Gray underwing. Legs bright red. Yellow, unmarked bill. Gape,

juv.
Red-legged

ad.
Red-legged

ad.
Black-legged

Red-legged Kittiwake
Rissa brevirostris
Bering Sea
L 14–15 in (36–38 cm)

juv.
Red-legged

ad.

juv.
Black-legged

ad.

Black-legged Kittiwake
Rissa tridactyla
Circumpolar
L 14.5–16 in (37–42 cm)

juv.
Black-legged

mouth lining, and eyering red when breeding.
FIRST YEAR: Dark nape, dark gray ear patch,
orange legs, and yellow, dark-tipped bill. Lacks
the dark wing stripe of the juvenile *R. tridactyla*.
Also lacks black, terminal tail band of other
juvenile gulls, making it the only N Amer gull
that has a completely white tail at all ages. VOICE:
Very high-pitched, repeated squeal *su-weeeer'*.
HABITS: Forages in flocks, taking small fish,
squid, and zooplankton at or near the surface
of the open sea. Typically forages over deep
water, feeding mostly during the day, but also
at night when deepwater prey migrates to the
ocean surface. Nests in mixed-seabird colonies,
often near *R. tridactyla*, on narrow ledges of
high, vertical sea cliffs. Pairs construct a shallow
cup nest of mud, grass, and kelp, and incubate a
single egg (rarely 2) for 23–32 days. Chicks are
fed by both parents until they fledge at 5 weeks.
STATUS: Vulnerable (IUCN).

SUBFAMILY STERNINAE
TERNS

The word *tern* derives from the Old English
stearn. The collective name for these birds is a
ternery, committee, or *U* of terns.

Terns are distinguished by having a forked tail,
long narrow wings, pointed bill, and black and
white plumage. They are smaller than gulls, most
weighing less than 5 oz (142 g). Terns feed singly

or in small flocks, taking
small fish, crustaceans,
and other invertebrates by
plunge diving, diving to
surface, or dipping. They
also hawk insects in flight
and pirate food from other
terns. Despite their proficiency in feeding on
aquatic prey, terns tend to avoid contact with
water, since they are poor swimmers- their
webbed feet are too small and weak to propel
them through the water. Terns remain airborne
when over open water, and if they must set
down, they find a piece of floating debris on
which to rest.

Terns are colonial nesters. Pairs aggressively defend their own nest against intruders,
and often the entire colony will rise in noisy
support—shrieking, dive-bombing, and
defecating on any interloper, be it fox, raccoon,
weasel, rat, gull, or birdwatcher. Other bird
species take advantage of this built-in alarm
system and often nest within the boundaries of
a tern breeding colony. Both sexes incubate the
1–2 (rarely 3), olive to buffy, streaked or spotted
eggs for 21–23 days. Hatchlings are brooded in
the nest for about a week, then are generally left
unattended in the colony except when being fed.
Young fledge at 22–30 days.

In the late 1800s, terns and other birds were
sought for use in the millinery trade. Their
feathers, wings, or entire stuffed birds were
mounted on women's hats. Opposition to the
slaughter resulted in the formation of Audubon
Societies and conservation initiatives such as
the 1916 Migratory Bird Treaty between the
US and Canada.

GENUS *STERNA*
Arctic Tern
Sterna paradisaea

ALSO: Sea Swallow,
Imiqqutailaq, Küsten-
seeschwalbe, Sterne arctique, Rødnebbterne,
Полярная крачка. SN means "paradise tern."
RANGE: Circumpolar. Northernmost nesting
tern. Nests (Jun–Jul) on rocky islands, beaches,
coastal tundra, and less frequently around
inland lakes, north to Svalbard and south to
about 50°N. Winters (Dec–Mar) on the ice
pack off Antarctica; also regular in winter in
small numbers in S Africa, Australia, and NZ.
ID: L 13–15.5 in (33–39 cm). Short-necked, dainty
tern, weighing about 4 oz (113 g). Extremely
short legs. Deeply forked white tail; outer tail
feathers extend beyond wing tips when bird
is at rest. AD MAR–OCT: Gray, with uniform
gray primaries. Bright white underwings, with
a narrow, sharply defined black trailing edge.
Black cap. Bill and legs bright red. AD WINTER:
Gray above, grayish white below. Forehead
and forecrown white. Hind crown and nape
black. Bill and legs dark red, nearly black. JUV:
Back and wings of fledglings gray, with a few
buffy brown feather fringes. Hind crown black.
Bill and legs pale reddish orange. Fall juvenile

retains some brown scalloping, and the bill rapidly darkens to black. Winter juvenile closely resembles winter adult. VOICE: Harsh, buzzy, upward-inflected *kree-errr.*
HABITS: Pelagic outside of breeding season. Forages in shallow nearshore waters when breeding, feeding on small fish such as polar cod, crustaceans, polychaete worms, and insects taken on or near the water surface. Hovers 30–40 ft (9–12 m) over the water and then dives in, seizing prey with its bill. Frequently rests on floating objects at sea and readily joins feeding flocks of terns and other seabirds.

Breeds in colonies. Sexually mature at 3–4 years of age. Pairs that have successfully raised a brood may mate for life. Pairs wait until the snow has melted before nesting. In years when thawing is late, they may not nest at all. Courting males perform a "fish flight" display, carrying a small fish in their bill and passing as low as they can over the female on the ground. If she joins him in flight, the pair mates. Nests on dry gravel or damp moss, and often lines the nest with grass, small stones, or shell bits.

In late Aug–Sep, the terns begin to migrate south to their wintering grounds off Antarctica. They spend a "second summer" there, making them the animal that sees the most sun. Until recently, the Arctic Tern's round-trip migration was thought to cover about 21,000 mi (33,800 km). But now, thanks to a 2009 study on Greenland nesting birds, we know that at least some arctic terns migrate more than twice that distance.

Scientists from Greenland, Denmark, US, UK, and Iceland conducted the study. Researchers trapped about 50 terns nesting on a sand island off e Greenland and attached geolocators weighing 0.05 oz (1.4 g) to the terns' legs. The tracking devices recorded the birds' daily geographical position from the time they left Greenland in fall to their arrival back in Greenland the next spring, when the geolocators were recovered.

The devices revealed that the terns did not fly straight for Antarctica, but instead stopped for 25 days in the N Atlantic to feed and acquire body mass. Then the terns flew south along the coast of w Europe and nw Africa until off the Cape Verde Is, where about half of the terns continued to fly along the African coast, while the other half swept west across the Atlantic and continued toward Antarctica along the Brazilian coast.

The arctic terns spent 4–5 months feeding in the Weddell Sea ice pack. In Apr, with the onset of austral winter, they began to trace a gigantic S-pattern northward up the mid-Atlantic. Utilizing beneficial prevailing winds, the terns reached their Greenland colony in May–Jun. The distance covered during the round-trip migration and flights in the Weddell Sea area totaled about 44,000 mi (70,900 km). Greenland researcher Carsten Egevang calculated that since arctic terns can live 30 years or more, any one of them may, over its lifetime, fly some 1.4 million mi (2.3 million km)—a distance equal to 3 round trips between earth and the moon.

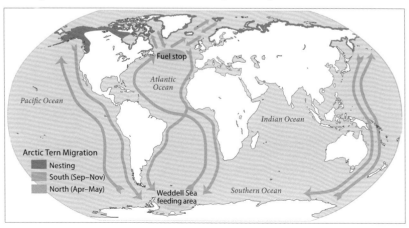

Record flights are not restricted to adult arctic terns. An Arctic Tern chick banded in the summer of 1982 on Farne Is in the UK reached Melbourne, Australia, 3 months later—a journey of more than 14,000 mi (22,000 km), in which the young bird flew more than 150 mi (240 km) per day.

Common Tern

Sterna hirundo
ALSO: Flußseeschwalbe, Sterne pierregarin, Makrellterne, Речная крачка. SN means "swallow-like tern."

RANGE: Nests (May–Jul) around lakes and seacoasts in subarctic and temperate N Amer and Eurasia, breeding north of the Arctic Circle only in Fennoscandia. Winters on seacoasts south to S Amer, Africa, n Indian Ocean, Australia. **ID:** L 13.5–14.5 in (34–37 cm). Tail and wing tips equal when bird is at rest. Has flatter crown, longer bill, and longer legs than the Arctic Tern. AD APR–NOV: Upperparts gray. Rump and forked tail white. Dark wedge on upperwing primaries. Black cap. Black-tipped red bill (mostly black in Siberian race). Underparts white. Red legs. AD WINTER: Bill blackish. Forehead and lores white. Dusky wing bar. JUV: Back and wings of fledglings gingery brown, sometimes flecked with dark brown. Conspicuous dark wedge on primaries. Underparts white. Hind crown black; forecrown pale ginger brown. Bill pale reddish orange at base, blackish at tip. Legs dull red. By Oct, juvenile closely resembles winter adult. VOICE: Rich, high, downward-inflected *keee-yurr.* HABITS: Buoyant flight, with body rising slightly with each downbeat of wings. Perches on and plunge dives from rocks, posts, boats, buoys, and floating kelp. Hawks insects in flight and picks small plankton from sea surface. Forms large flocks at sea over schools of predatory fish that drive bait fish to the surface. Breeds singly and in colonies on coastal islands, dune areas on barrier beaches, and islands in lakes and salt marshes. Nests on the ground in open areas with loose sand, gravel, or shell, and with scattered vegetation or other cover where chicks can shelter. Chicks are left alone in the colony except when being fed. They fledge at 22–29 days.

GENUS *ONYCHOPRION*
Aleutian Tern

Onychoprion aleuticus
ALSO: Kamchatka Tern, Aleutenseeschwalbe, Sterne

des Aléoutiennes, Beringterne, Алеутская крачка, *Sterna aleutica.* SN means "saw-nailed [tern] of the Aleutians." **RANGE:** Nests (May–Jun) in scattered colonies along coasts of Kamchatka, Sakhalin Is, Sea of Okhotsk, Aleutians, Alaska. Previously thought to winter in the N Pacific, but subadults collected in the Philippines in May 1984 and sightings of adults in Hong Kong in fall of 1992 support speculation that this species winters in the S Pacific near Australia and the Philippines. One record at Farne Is, UK, in May 1979. **ID:** L 12.5–15 in (32–38 cm). AD APR–SEP: White forehead and face; black cap and black bill connected by a black line through eye. Dark gray upperparts and underparts contrast with pure white rump and long, deeply forked white tail. Upperwing shows white leading edge and dark-tipped outer primaries. Dark secondary bar on pale underwing. Short black legs. AD WINTER: Black hind crown and nape; black line runs from nape to eye. Forecrown white. JUV: Rusty upperparts, with black-centered feathers on back and wings. Black hind crown. Bill tipped black, with red base to lower beak. Underparts white. Legs reddish. First-winter birds have a scaly brownish gray back and wings, and dark hind crown. Forehead, face, neck, and underparts white. VOICE: Thin, clear, whistled *whee-hee-hee.* HABITS: Largely pelagic. When breeding, forages over shallow ocean waters, estuaries, rivers, and ponds. Feeds by plunge diving for small fish, picking krill and isopods from the sea surface, and hawking insects in flight. Flight is direct, with deep wingbeats. Breeds in loose colonies, often with arctic terns in N Amer and common terns in Siberia. Nests near water on tundra, meadows, river deltas, and sandy spits. Clutch is 2 eggs laid in a depression in short, matted vegetation. Parents bring fish regularly for the chicks, but young are usually left unattended until they fledge at 25–31 days. Birds abandon colonies in Aug, and most fly straight out to sea.

juv.
1st summer

juv.
1st winter

ad. Apr–Sep
Black bill
Black legs
White forehead

ad. winter

Aleutian Tern
Onychoprion aleuticus
N Pacific
L 12.5–15 in (32–38 cm)

juv.
1st summer

juv.
1st winter

ad. winter

ad. Mar–Oct
Red bill
Red legs

Arctic Tern
Sterna paradisaea
Circumpolar
L 13–15.5 in (33–39 cm)

juv.
1st summer

juv.
1st winter
Dark carpel bar

Dark wedge
on primaries

ad. winter

Common Tern
Sterna hirundo
Temperate Eurasia, N Amer
L 13.5–14.5 in (34–37 cm)

ad. Apr–Nov
Black-tipped red bill
Red legs

Gruiformes: Cranes and Allies

Gruiformes (Latin for "crane-like") is an order containing a large number of loosely related, living and extinct, wading and terrestrial birds such as cranes, limpkins, trumpeters, rails, and other marsh-adapted birds. Only the cranes have representatives in the Arctic.

FAMILY GRUIDAE
CRANES

Cranes are heavy-bodied, long-necked, long-legged birds of open grasslands and freshwater marshes. Flocks fly in V formation, with necks outstretched. Their wingbeat is composed of a snapping upstroke and slower downstroke. Opportunistic feeders, cranes eat a variety of foods, including small rodents, fish, amphibians, insects, grain, berries, and other plant material.

Males are larger than females, but sexes are similar in plumage. Most of the face is covered with bare skin, sparsely covered with hair-like bristles. The bare, fleshy area can be expanded or varied in intensity of color to convey moods and motivation to neighboring cranes. The stout, heron-like bill has an opening in the upper beak where the internasal septum is perforated. The feet have 3 forward-facing toes and 1 elevated hind toe. Each wing has 10 primaries and 16 secondaries; the inner secondary coverts and tertials are elongated ornamental feathers that form a bustle over the relatively short tail.

Cranes are monogamous and typically mate for life. They are noted for their elaborate courtship dancing, which includes bowing, jumping, running, stick and grass tossing, and wing flapping. Mated pairs also perform electrifying vocal duets called *unison calls*, which can last from a few seconds to as long as 1 minute. The cranes stand with their heads thrown back and beaks skyward, then fling their heads up and down as they call. Their unique trachea, or windpipe, extends and coils into the sternum. This anatomical feature amplifies the call and alters the pitch of the voice, adding subtle harmonies to the vocalization.

Although a few species nest on dry ground, most cranes build a floating nest over water or nest on raised land surrounded by water. Both sexes participate in nest construction, collecting material from the immediate surroundings and tossing it onto the nest site until it eventually forms a large mound.

Both sexes incubate the clutch of 2 eggs for 27–31 days. Hatchlings are precocial and are able to walk and swim within 24 hours of emergence. The parents feed both chicks, but the more aggressive sibling usually gets the larger share. Thus, even though cranes lay 2 eggs, only one chick typically survives to fledge, at 65–70 days. Young remain with the adults until the following spring, then begin to flock with other juveniles and remain in a subadult group until sexually mature.

Crane populations worldwide are threatened by habitat loss caused by drainage of wetlands, dams, agricultural expansion, urbanization, and other development.

Lesser Sandhill Crane
Grus canadensis
NE Siberia, N Amer
L 31.5–37 in (80–95 cm)

juv.

When threatened, a crane may respond by dropping one wing and burying its bill in its back feathers.

A pair of Siberian cranes performs the unison call—a vocal duet of loud, flute-like notes accompanied by stylized postures and head tosses.

Siberian White Crane
Grus leucogeranus
Siberia
L 41–57 in (105–145 cm)
Critically Endangered

juv.

Courting cranes are noted for their balletic bows, leaps, and wing flapping.

Eurasian Crane
Grus grus
Eurasia
L 38–47 in (96–120 cm)

GENUS *GRUS*
Eurasian Crane
Grus grus

ALSO: Common Crane, Grauer Kranich, Grue cendrée, Trane, Серый журавль. SN derives from the Proto-Indo-European *gerh*, meaning "to cry hoarsely."

RANGE: Nests (May–Jul) near water in n Eurasia in forests, wooded swamps, bogs, steppes, and on treeless moors; 0–7200 ft (0–2200 m). Winters on shallow bays, wet meadows, and cultivated fields in n Africa, Middle East, India, and se Asia. Rare visitor to Japan and Korea. Vagrant to w N Amer where it associates with sandhill cranes.

ID: L 38–47 in (96–120 cm). WS 71–96 in (180–240 cm). WT 6.5–13 lb (3–6 kg). AD: Slate gray, but may appear brown as it often paints its feathers with mud. Forehead and lores black; bare red crown. White streak from behind eyes to upper back. Primaries, tips of secondaries, alula, tail tip, and edges of uppertail coverts are black; greater wing coverts droop over tail, forming a bustle of plumes. Red eye. Dark gray legs. JUV: Yellowish brown head. Gray body feathers tipped with buff. VOICE: Loud, piercing trumpeting.

HABITS: Probes and gleans for plant and animal foods on dry land, in wetlands, and in upland areas with short vegetation. Courtship involves a dancing display, in which the birds leap with wings uplifted. Post-breeding adults undergo a biennial molt and are flightless for 6 weeks.

Sandhill Crane
Grus canadensis

ALSO: Kanadakranich, Grue du Canada, Tattirgak, Kanadatrane, Канадский журавль. SN means "crane of Canada." One of the oldest living species of N Amer birds, with fossils dating to about 2.5 million years ago.

RANGE: The Arctic-breeding subspecies, the Lesser Sandhill Crane, *G. c. canadensis,* nests (May–Aug) on wet tundra, bogs, and sedge meadows in Siberia, Alaska, and n Canada, and migrates via Manitoba, the Dakotas, Kansas, Oklahoma, and Platte Rvr areas of Nebraska to winter in Texas, New Mexico, and n Mexico.

ID: L 31.5–37 in (80–95 cm). WS 79 in (200 cm). WT 6–10 lb (2.7–4.6 kg). AD: Gray plumage often appears brown due to the habit of painting the feathers with mud. Bare reddish skin, sparsely covered with black hair-like bristles on forehead, lores, and crown. White cheek. Golden eye. Bill dark horn. JUV: Cinnamon plumage, fading to gray by first winter. VOICE: Vocal repertoire includes trills and purrs (mainly chicks), rolling bugle or croak, and loud, resonant, rattling *kharrrr* (adults). In the unison call, the male emits a low-pitched, drawn-out rattle while the female gives a staccato *tucka, tucka, tucka.*

HABITS: Feeds on dry land or in shallow marshes with emergent vegetation. Forages for tubers and subsurface invertebrates by probing with bill; gleans seeds, grains, and berries. Nests on dry ground or builds a floating nest over shallow water.

Siberian White Crane
Grus leucogeranus

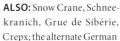

ALSO: Snow Crane, Schnee-kranich, Grue de Sibérie, Стерх; the alternate German name Nonnenkranich, meaning "nun crane," refers to the white feathers around the red face, which are reminiscent of the coif of a Roman Catholic nun. SN means "white crane." First illustrated by 17th-century Mongol artist Ustad Mansur; his painting hangs in the Hermitage Museum in St Petersburg, Russia.

RANGE: Nests (May–Jul) in shallow marshlands and bogs in lowland tundra and taiga in Siberia. Two widely disjunct populations. Most birds breed in Yakutia, ne Siberia, between the Kolyma and Yana rivers, and winter on the Yangtze Rvr and Lake Poyang in China. Remnant population breeds in w Russia along the Ob Rvr and winters in Fereydoon Kenar, Iran.

ID: L 41–57 in (105–145 cm). WS 83–91 in (210–230 cm). WT 11–19 lb (5–8.5 kg). AD: White overall, with black primaries. Dark red, naked forecrown and face; red fleshy area of the face extends onto the beak and past the nares. Yellow eyes. Dark bill. Pinkish legs. JUV: Dull brown to cinnamon plumage when at rest. In flight, when viewed from below, juveniles appear to be white with black primaries. Forecrown and face are feathered. Eyes are blue for first 6 months, then turn yellow. VOICE: Rolling *toyoya*. Unison call is a duetted *doodle-loo*. Male initiates call with rapid bows. Both sexes drop wings and begin calling a series of flute-like notes while flinging heads up and down. Their combined voices sound like a single bird rapidly repeating notes on 2 different pitches.

HABITS: Usually seen singly or in pairs. Omnivorous. Feeds on cranberries, rodents, worms, fish, insects, roots, and tubers. Serrated bill enables the bird to easily excavate underground roots from wet soil and hold onto slippery prey. May completely submerge head as it digs into wet soil or shallow water; raises head and swallows food with a backward head fling. Mated pairs return to same breeding site year after year. Pairs are highly territorial and use the unison call to cement pair bonds and delimit their territory. Both sexes construct a large platform nest of dry plant stalks at lake's edge or on a small island in the water. Long-lived in captivity; one individual survived for 62 years, another for 83 years.

STATUS: Hunting along migration routes and habitat degradation have contributed to a rapid decline of numbers, particularly in the western population, in which only 4–20 individuals may remain. In 2010 the eastern population was estimated to be 2900–3200 birds, almost all of which winter in the Lake Poyang basin, China—a habitat likely to be altered by the Three Gorges Dam. Critically Endangered (IUCN). Red Data Book of the Russian Federation (Category I). CITES Appendix I.

Captive breeding has been achieved in Siberia and at the International Crane Foundation at Baraboo, Wisconsin, through the use of artificial insemination, hatching of eggs by other crane species, and using floodlights to simulate the longer day lengths of the arctic summer.

In Sep 2012, Russian president Vladimir Putin was shown in a video flying a microlight aircraft leading young captive-bred Siberian cranes to wintering grounds in c Asia. Although it was generally regarded as a publicity stunt, Putin deserves a bit of credit for bringing world attention to a critically endangered species.

Galliformes: Gamefowl

Galliformes (Latin for "chicken-like") is an order of heavy-bodied, ground-feeding gamebirds such as grouse, ptarmigans, partridges, wild turkeys, and pheasants. These birds are hunted extensively by humans and are a food source for hawks, owls, and many mammals.

FAMILY TETRAONIDAE
CAPERCAILLIES, GROUSE, PTARMIGANS

These ground-nesting gamebirds are resident in the boreal forests and alpine slopes. They are typically seen walking or running on the ground. They fly infrequently, but when they do their flight is agile and strong, with several rapid wingbeats followed by a long glide.

Birds in this family are sexually dimorphic. Males are usually much larger than females and the females have cryptically patterned plumage, which camouflages them while on the nest. Both sexes have densely feathered bodies, legs, and feet. The feet have a single hind toe and 3 long forward-facing toes with stout claws that are used to scratch the ground for food and to dig out snow burrows that serve as shelters on cold winter nights.

These birds are primarily herbivorous and use the cutting edge of the bill to snip off twigs, leaves, berries, stems, seeds, catkins, buds, and conifer needles. They can extract energy and nutrients from coarse fibrous plant matter, and thus are able to exploit a vast source of accessible food that requires very little energy to harvest.

GENUS *TETRAO*: Capercaillies inhabit the forests of Eurasia. Males are known for their elaborate spring courtship displays performed on breeding arenas known as leks (Swedish for "play"). Females come to the lek only to copulate, then immediately leave the area to nest. The typical nest is a lined ground scrape made under cover of a bush, fallen log, or rock. The female incubates the clutch of 5–9 eggs for about 26 days and rears the brood. The chicks feed independently on insects and spiders, but are very sensitive to cold and require brooding until they are about 3 weeks old. They become independent at 10–14 weeks.

Western Capercaillie

Tetrao urogallus

ALSO: Eurasian Capercallie, Wood Grouse, Heather Cock, Auerhuhn, Grand tetrás, Storfugl, Глухарь. CN derives from the Gaelic *capull coille*, meaning "horse of the woods." SN means "gamebird with a cock's tail." Locally hybridizes with *T. urogalloides*; hybrids are called Dark Gray Capercaillie.

RANGE: Nests (Apr–Jun) in boggy pine, larch, and birch forests that have a fern and woody understory and abundant berry bushes. Occurs from n Europe east to the Lena Rvr in Siberia, and south to Mongolia, at elevations to 2625 ft (1800 m). Reintroduced into Scotland.

ID: L ♂ 29–35 in (74–90 cm); ♀ 21–25 in (54–63 cm). WT ♂ 9.5–14 lb (4.3–6.3 kg); ♀ 5–7 lb (2.2–3 kg). Large and robust. Bright red patch of naked skin above each eye is larger in males. Conspicuous rounded white patch at base of forewing. Rows of small elongated nails (courting tacks) on toes, which make clear tracks in winter snow. AD ♂: Grayish black, with dark brown wings, dark metallic green breast, white spots on belly, and white wing linings. Long, rounded tail is cocked and fanned in display. Cream-colored bill. AD ♀: Upperparts brown with black and silver barring. Lines of white spots ("braces") on scapulars. Throat and upper breast plain orange-brown. Rest of underparts barred and spotted in black, white, and rufous. VOICE: With head directed skyward and tail fanned out, the displaying male emits guttural clicks and pops, *urk-urk, click-click-click, pop-pop-pop.* Males at evening also give a bellowing *ko-krerk-korohr.* Female gives a slowly repeated *grak.*

HABITS: Arboreal in winter; rarely descends to walk on snow, instead feeds almost exclusively on conifer needles in crowns of trees. Terrestrial in snow-free months, feeding on the ground on leaves, buds, flowers, and fruits of plants such as bilberry, crowberry, horsetail, moss, and rushes. In autumn and winter, females and young males form small groups of 10–20 individuals. Starting in late winter, males display collectively on leks to attract females. Once a male has selected a lek site it will return to that site throughout its life.

Black-billed Capercaillie

Tetrao urogalloides

ALSO: Small-billed, Siberian, or Spotted Capercaillie, Felsenauerhuhn, Tétras à bec noir, Svartnebborrfugl, Каменный глухарь, *T. parvirostris.* SN means "gamebird resembling *T. urogallus.*"

RANGE: Nests (Apr–Jun) in larch forests bordering broad floodplain terraces and streams in e Siberia, from Lake Baikal to Kamchatka and south to n Mongolia and China. Not numerous, but locally common. Hybridizes with *T. urogallus* where ranges overlap.

ID: L ♂ 27–33 in (69–84 cm); ♀ 20–23 in (51–58 cm). AD ♂: Large white spots at tips of uppertail coverts and on wings. Blacker and smaller than *T. urogallus*, with a slightly longer tail and shorter black bill. AD ♀: Conspicuous white wing spots. Grayer above and more uniformly scaled below than female *T. urogallus*. VOICE: Displaying male emits a series of clicks, which accelerates into a short trill. Female gives a slow, cackling *grak.*

HABITS: Feeds on larch needles and buds as well as leaves, berries, and insects. Sits immobile on low tree branches in icy conditions when unable to dig snow burrows. Unlike *T. urogallus*, this species can walk on snow because it is lighter in weight and has densely feathered feet that act as snowshoes. Males form ill-defined leks for displaying; otherwise breeding and nesting similar to those of *T. urogallus.*

GENUS *LYRURUS*
Black Grouse

Lyrurus tetrix

ALSO: Black Cock, Gray Hen, Birkhuhn, Tétras lyre, Orrfugl, Тетерев-косач, *Tetrao tetrix.* SN means "lyre-tailed gamebird." Scottish pipers sometimes wear the male's lyre-shaped tail on their hats.

RANGE: Nests (Apr–Jun) at forest edge, on forest bogs, and on moors from n UK across nc Eurasia. Non-migratory, but nomadic in some locales.

ID: L ♂ 19–23 in (49–58 cm); WT to 3.2 lb (1.45 kg). L ♀ 16–18 in (40–45 cm). AD ♂: Glossy black plumage, with narrow white wing bars and pure white undertail coverts. Red comb above each

Rufous ♀

Gray ♀

♀

F. c. canadensis ♂
Tail tip bronze

Spruce Grouse
Falcipennis canadensis
N Amer
L 14–17 in (36–43 cm)

F. c. franklinii ♂
Tail tip dark

F. falcipennis ♂
Tail tip white

Siberian Spruce Grouse
Falcipennis falcipennis
E Siberia
L 14–17 in (36–43 cm)

♂

♀

Black Grouse
Lyrurus tetrix
Eurasia
L ♂ 19–23 in (49–58 cm)
♀ 16–18 in (40–45 cm)

♀

♂

Hazel Grouse
Tetrastes bonasia
Eurasia
L 14–15.5 in (36–39 cm)

♂
Tail cocked
and fanned
in display

♀

♂

♀

Western Capercaillie
Tetrao urogallus
Eurasia
L ♂ 29–35 in (74–90 cm)
♀ 21–25 in (54–63 cm)

Black-billed Capercaillie
Tetrao urogalloides
E Siberia, Kamchatka
L ♂ 27–33 in (69–84 cm)
♀ 20–23 in (51–58 cm)

eye. Lyre-shaped, 6 in (15 cm) long tail appears forked in flight. AD ♀: Rufous, with fine black and white barring overall. Narrow white wing bars. VOICE: Male sounds a loud, bubbling, dove-like *ko-ko-ko* that is repeated incessantly when displaying. Female cackles.

HABITS: Feeds on birch buds and catkins in winter, and leaves, berries, and insects in summer. Creates temporary winter snow burrows by diving from trees into snowdrifts, then digging under the surface. In early spring, 40–140 males may gather in the morning and perform mating displays on leks in fields, clearings, and mossy wetlands. The males call loudly and strut back and forth with combs flared and their lyre-like tail cocked to show off the pure white undertail feathers. After copulating, the females fly off and lay their eggs in a scrape made under cover of fallen branches or thick scrub. The female alone incubates the eggs and rears the brood.

GENUS *FALCIPENNIS*: Spruce grouse are resident in the boreal forest and taiga. On winter nights, these birds roost on the snow under low spruce boughs or, like other grouse, make a snow burrow where they are insulated from the cold and protected from predators. During winter, their staple food is conifer needles, snipped directly from the tree. Needles are stored for later digestion in the caecum (a pouch at the junction of the small and large intestines) or in the crop, which holds some 45 cc (about 9 teaspoons) of matter.

Spruce grouse are relatively quiet compared to other gamebirds. Their vocalizations are generally limited to a few clucks, hoots, or growls. Displaying males, however, produce non-vocal drumming sounds—muffled thumps produced by the bird's rapidly beating wings in flight. The male Franklin's Spruce Grouse (*Falcipennis canadensis franklinii*) also produces 2 loud, sharp wing claps at the end of its drumming flight, as it snaps its wings together over its back. The wing claps can be heard over a great distance and often are the only indication that this reclusive forest dweller is nearby. In spring, each male establishes a display territory where he struts, bows, fans out his tail, rustles his

feathers, stomps his feet, and emits a number of growls, booms, warbles, and clicks, all in hopes of attracting females to his court. A receptive female will squat with slightly extended wings and allow the male to mount her, after which she ruffles her feathers and flies away. She makes a nest in a leaf-lined scrape at the base of a spruce tree or log and independently rears the brood.

Spruce Grouse

Falcipennis canadensis
ALSO: Fool's Hen, Canada Grouse, Tannenhuhn, Tétras du Canada, Granjerpe, Канадская дикуша, Napaaktum akargik, *Dendragapus canadensis*. SN means "sickle-winged [grouse] of Canada."
RANGE: Nests (May–Jun) in coniferous forests of n Alaska and n Canada (*F. c. canadensis*) and in forested mountains from s Alaska to c Alberta, Canada (*F. c. franklinii*).
ID: L 14–17 in (36–43 cm). WT to 1.5 lb (0.65 kg). AD ♂: Slate gray, with bold white barring on lower breast and belly. Black throat edged with broken white line. Back gray, finely barred with black. Red combs above eyes; white arcs under eyes. Tail all dark (*F. c. franklinii*) or dark with golden bronze tips (*F. c. canadensis*). Undertail feathers black, with large white tips. AD ♀: Mottled brown or mottled gray, with dark and white bars on underparts. VOICE: Generally silent; occasionally emits a soft, hooted *whuh-whuh-whuh-whuh*.
HABITS: Largely solitary. Feeds on pine or spruce needles taken at mid-crown of trees. Also feeds on the ground, eating flowers, green leaves, fungi, insects, snails, and berries.

Siberian Spruce Grouse

Falcipennis falcipennis
ALSO: Sharp-winged Grouse, Sichelhuhn, Tétras de Sibérie, Amurjerpe, Дикуша. SN means "sickle-winged [grouse]."
RANGE: Nests (May–Jun) in upland coniferous forests of e Siberia from Yakutia to Sakhalin Is and the Primorsky region to the south. Prefers boggy areas with abundant berry bushes.
ID: L 14–17 in (36–43 cm). AD ♂: Brownish black

overall, with white spots on the back, black-and-white bands on the chest, and white tips to tail feathers and undertail coverts. Crimson eye combs. AD ♀: Brown, with ochre vermiculations above and heavy white spotting below. VOICE: Displaying males emit growls, clicks, and warbles. HABITS: Largely solitary. Seldom ventures into open areas. Feeds mainly on berries and conifer needles. Agile in flight, especially when pursuing rivals through dense forest. Spends the winter in mixed-sex flocks.

Male courtship displays include ground-to-ground flutter flights embellished by vocal clicks and (rarely) evening tree-to-tree drumming flights. A courting male stands upright at a female's approach, then slowly turns sideways and bows as he flicks his tail and vocalizes. He erects and spreads the tail, exposing the white tail tips; the stiff edges of the outer tail feathers produce rhythmical rustling sounds. In finale, the male fluffs his breast feathers and fares his neck feathers into a dark ruff. Copulation is brief and once complete, the female flies off to nest under the low branches of a conifer and rear the brood alone.

STATUS: Vulnerable (IUCN). Red Data Book of the Russian Federation, Category II. Declining numbers due to clearing of coniferous forests.

GENUS *TETRASTES*
Hazel Grouse
Tetrastes bonasia

ALSO: Northern Hazelhen, Haselhühner, Gélinotte des bois, Jerpe, Рябчик, *Bonasa bonasia*. SN means "hazel grouse"; *bonasia* is the Italian common name for the species.
RANGE: Nests (Apr–Jun) in Eurasia in damp lowland and alpine deciduous forests having dense underbrush and abundant fruit bushes.
ID: L 14–15.5 in (36–39 cm). AD ♂: Upperparts brownish gray, with fine dark barring on the crown, neck, mantle, and uppertail coverts. Underparts barred or spotted with dark gray and ochre. Chin and throat black, bordered with white. White lines below and behind the eyes and on sides of neck. Rounded, white fringed tail. Small erectile crest. Small red eye combs.

AD ♀: Resembles male, but has a shorter erectile crest; throat finely barred with gray and brown. VOICE: Male emits a thin, drawn-out, whistled *ti-ti-ti-ti-ti*; the female a liquid *teee-teeteervee*. HABITS: Lives mostly in pairs; rarely forms flocks. Prefers dense woodland with alder, birch, aspen, oak, or spruce trees. Feeds on buds, seeds, berries, leaves, alder and birch catkins, and insects. Tends to feed on the ground when nesting and raising young, but is primarily arboreal for the rest of the year. In midwinter, when the snow cover is deep and severe frost sets in, spends much of the day in snow burrows, flying out only briefly to nearby trees for feeding. When flying through dense forest, banks sharply so that its outstretched wings are on a vertical plane as it passes through the tangle of branches. When flushed, takes off with a rustle of wings and typically perches on the nearest tree, halfway up its height. In early spring, males call noisily to rival males and flutter from tree to tree. Once mated, pairs stay together for the season. Nests in a ground scrape concealed by undergrowth. Female incubates the 7–10 rufous, brown-speckled eggs.

GENUS *LAGOPUS*: In winter, ptarmigans have white plumage that blends into the snowy background of the northern forests. Their plump bodies are densely feathered from head to toe, the fully feathered feet acting as snowshoes. Feathers covering the nostrils serve to warm frosty air before it enters the respiratory tract. These birds keep warm at night by excavating and roosting in snow burrows. Come spring, ptarmigans molt into ever-changing cryptic plumages that camouflage them in the surrounding vegetation.

Willow Ptarmigan
Lagopus lagopus

ALSO: Willow Grouse, Red Grouse (*L. l. scoticus*), Moorschneehuhn, Lagopède des saules, Lirype, Белая куропатка, Aqalgiq, Akargik, Akalgik. SN means "hare-like feet," referring to the fully feathered feet and toes. CN derives from the Scottish Gaelic *tàrmachan*. State bird of Alaska.

RANGE: Circumpolar. Nests (May–Aug) in tall shrub zone on arctic and subalpine tundra; on damp, well-drained sites in willow or birch thickets; and on moors, heaths, grasslands, and bogs. Somewhat nomadic.
ID: L 14–17 in (36–43 cm). Largest ptarmigan. White wings and black outer tail feathers in all plumages. Legs and feet completely feathered year round. Both sexes have red supra-orbital combs; male's are larger. AD ♂ APR–JUL: Head and neck reddish brown. Tail feathers black. Rest of body white. By late summer, back and chest feathers are mottled and barred in brown and tan. AD ♀ APR–JUL: Body feathers dusky brown, barred with dark brown. White wings are largely concealed when at rest. AD WINTER: Snow white, except for black outer tail feathers. VOICE: Chicken-like *cluck*. Barking *kok-kok-kok*. Displaying males emit an accelerating *put-put-put-put-put, ko-dway'-oo, ko-dway'-oo,* also described as a harsh barking *ur-ur, to-bay'-go, to-bay'-go, to-bay'-go, ur.*
HABITS: Forages in willow and birch thickets, wet areas, grass and sedge meadows. Monogamous. Nest is a bowl-shaped ground scrape dug under overhanging vegetation and lined with feathers, grass, and moss. Clutch is 8–15 buff-colored eggs, heavily spotted and blotched with brown and black. Female incubates the eggs for 21–23 days, while male guards the nest. Both parents raise the chicks and remain together until Sep–Oct, when young are fully independent.

Rock Ptarmigan
Lagopus muta
ALSO: Alpenschneehuhn, Lagopède alpin, Fjellrype, Тундряная куропатка,

Niksaaqktuniq, Snow Chicken. SN means "silent [gamebird] with hare-like feet." Territorial bird of Nunavut, Newfoundland, and Labrador.
RANGE: Circumpolar. Nests (May–Jun) on rocky mountain slopes and tundra in Eurasia and N Amer, north to High Arctic islands of Canada, Svalbard, and Franz Josef Land.
ID: L 12–14 in (31–36 cm). White wings and black outer tail feathers in all plumages. Both sexes develop red supra-orbital combs in early spring.

AD ♂ MAY–JUL: Head and neck feathers brown, with a few blotches of white. Outer tail feathers black. Rest of body white. AD ♀ MAY–JUL: Body feathers dusky brown, barred with dark brown. White wings, largely concealed when at rest. In early spring females undergo a rapid molt from immaculate white to dark mottled brown, thus obtaining camouflage when on the nest. AD WINTER: White, with black outer tail feathers. Male has a black loral streak extending from bill base to behind the eye. Male retains its pure white plumage into breeding season. VOICE: Faint clucks and rattles. Male emits a rattling *ah-aah' ah-aaaaah'a-a-a-a* in display.
HABITS: Forms flocks in winter, pairs in breeding season. The male establishes a breeding territory where he displays. A series of rapid wingbeats sends the male high into the air, where he glides with wings bowed, tail fanned, and combs flared. He stalls and parachutes to the ground with head extended upward and open wings. On landing, he raises and fans his tail, droops his wings, and emits a rattling call.

The female nests in a ground scrape or natural depression sited near a boulder or bush and lines the nest with moss, lichens, and breast feathers. She incubates the 6–13 buffy, reddish-blotched eggs for 20–26 days. The chicks leave the nest within a day of hatching. They remain with the female until they are completely independent, at 10–12 weeks of age.

White-tailed Ptarmigan
Lagopus leucura
ALSO: Weißschwanz-Schneehuhn, Lagopède à queue blanche, Hvithalerype,

Белохвостая куропатка. SN means "hare-footed [gamebird] with a white tail."
RANGE: Nests (May–Aug) and is resident on high rocky mountain ridges in Alaska, w Canada, and the US Rocky Mtns.
ID: L 11–13 in (28–33 cm). Smallest ptarmigan. Wings and tail feathers white in all plumages. AD ♂ APR–JUL: Upperparts and bib dark brown, coarsely barred and spotted in white and black. Scarlet eye combs. Belly and wings white. Outer tail feathers white; central tail feathers

ad. ♂♀ winter
Tail all white

ad. ♂
Apr–Jul

ad.♀
Apr–Jul

ad. ♂♀ spring
White outer tail
feathers

White-tailed Ptarmigan
Lagopus leucura
N Amer mountains
L 11–13 in (28–33 cm)

Courting ♂
early spring

ad. ♀
May–Jul

ad. ♂
May–Jul

♂

Rock Ptarmigan
Lagopus muta
Circumpolar
L 12–14 in (31–36 cm)

♀

ad. ♂♀ winter
Black outer tail
feathers

ad. ♂♀ winter
Black outer tail
feathers

ad. ♂ autumn

Willow Ptarmigan
Lagopus lagopus
Circumpolar
L 14–17 in (36–43 cm)

ad. ♀
Apr–Jul

ad. ♂
Apr–Jul

dark. AD ♀ APR–JUL: Brown and black, with variable golden barring overall. Wings white. Small, salmon colored eye combs. AD WINTER: Snow white overall. Legs, feet, and toes heavily feathered. VOICE: Clucking *kuk-kuk-kuk*. Male emits a shrill scream, *kri-kriii-kriii*, in display. **HABITS:** Feeds mainly on buds and leaves of willows. Seasonally monogamous, but male sometimes mates with 2 females. A courting male approaches a female while bowing his head in a rhythmic pecking motion, then struts with eye combs flared, his fanned tail tilted toward the hen, and wing tips dragging on ground. If the female moves away, the male runs in pursuit while giving clucking and chattering calls. The female builds a nest among rocks and boulders. She scrapes out a depression with bill and feet, then pulls vegetation toward her to form a nest bowl, which she lines with vegetation and feathers. The female incubates the 3–9 pale cinnamon-colored, brown-spotted eggs for 22–25 days, leaving the nest once or twice a day to feed and defecate. The male feeds with the hen early in the incubation period, but deserts her before the eggs hatch. Female and chicks leave the nest within 12 hours of hatching. Chicks can feed independently, but the female remains with her young until fall.

Accipitriformes and Falconiformes: Raptors

Accipitriformes encompasses the osprey, eagles, hawks, harriers, and accipiters. Falconiformes includes the falcons. These birds are collectively known as *raptors* or *diurnal birds of prey*.

Raptors hunt for food by day, using their keen senses, especially vision, to capture vertebrate prey. Their vision is sharper than a human's due to the greater number of photoreceptors (light-sensitive cells in the retina), an exceptionally high number of nerves connecting photoreceptors to the brain, and an enhanced fovea (a small pit located near the retina's center) that magnifies the central portion of the visual field. The hooked beak is adapted for tearing flesh and has a fleshy *cere* covering the nostrils. The strong legs and feet have sharply hooked talons for grasping prey.

FAMILY PANDIONIDAE
OSPREY

The Osprey is one of the most widespread birds in the world, found on all continents except Antarctica. The species differs from other diurnal raptors in that its tarsi bear a net-like, reticulated pattern, its toes are of equal length, and its outer toe is opposable. The last feature allows the Osprey to grasp prey, almost exclusively fish, with 2 toes in front and 2 behind. Barb-like structures (*spicules*) on the foot soles help to hold the slippery prey, which is carried head forward to reduce drag. A long-lived species, the Osprey can survive up to 32 years in the wild.

GENUS *PANDION*
Osprey
Pandion haliaetus
ALSO: Sea or Fish Hawk, Fischadler, Balbuzard pêcheur, Fiskgjuse, Скопа, Kaluksiigayuk (Inupiaq for "hunts for fish"). CN derives from the Medieval Latin *avis prede,* meaning "bird of prey." SN means "Pandion's sea-eagle," alluding to the mythical Greek king Pandion, whose grandson Theseus was transformed into an eagle. **RANGE:** Nests (Apr–Jun in the north) on seacoasts, lakes, and rivers in N Amer, Eurasia, nw Africa. Winters to Cuba, Peru, Brazil, S Africa, India. **ID:** L 21–24 in (53–61 cm). WT 2.8–4.5 lb (1.25–2 kg). AD: Head, neck, breast, belly, and tarsi white. Dark lines on crown. Dark brown line from eye to neck. Back and upperside of wings blackish brown. Underwing white, with dark cross-barring on coverts, dark band at base of flight feathers, and black patch at carpal joint. Tail darkly barred, with darker trailing band. Yellow eye. JUV. Pale version of adult. Feathers of back and wings finely edged in cream. Barred tail lacks dark terminal band. Reddish orange eye. Fresh juveniles may show a buffy or golden wash on the throat and breast. VOICE: Short shrill whistles. Male also gives a screaming call in the "sky-dance" display, in which he flies in an undulating U-shaped pattern over the nest area, often carrying a fish in his talons.

Osprey
Pandion haliaetus
N Amer, Eurasia
L 21–24 in (53–61 cm)
WS 59–67 in (150–170 cm)

juv. ad. juv. ad.

HABITS: Hunts alone, sometimes from a perch, more often from flight above water. Hovers over prey, then dives into the water with talons extended and the legs and feet directed forward. Begins to breed at 3–4 years of age. Pair builds a large nest of twigs, usually situated at the top of a high pine, birch, or spruce tree; also uses power poles, rock ledges, or artificial nesting platforms. Nests are reused from year to year. Male supplies the bulk of nesting material, the female arranges it. Clutch of 2–3 (rarely 4) creamy white to pinkish, darkly spotted eggs is incubated, mostly by the female, for 38–41 days, while the male hunts for food and brings it to the nest. Chicks fledge at 50–60 days. First-year birds migrate south independent of the adults and remain in wintering grounds for up to 3 years.

FAMILY ACCIPITRIDAE
EAGLES, HAWKS, HARRIERS, ACCIPITERS

The Accipitridae is a family of small to large birds with large hooked bills, strong sharp talons, and rounded tails. The long, broad wings are carried flat or at a slight upward angle when soaring, and the flight feathers are fanned out like fingers at the wing tip. Juveniles show different plumages than adults. They pass through a series of molts and attain full adult plumage at 2–5 years of age, when they become sexually mature.

Accipiters typically mate for life, although most will take another mate if one of the original pair dies or if repeated breeding failures occur. Mates renew their bonds with aerial courtship

displays in which the pair locks talons and whirls and tumbles earthward, separating just before hitting the ground.

A few species nest on the ground, but most build a large nest of sticks set high in a tree or on a rock ledge. The nest is often reused for several years. The average clutch is 1–4 white eggs, from which only 1 or 2 of the older chicks survive. If none of the young survive, the adults abandon reproduction for that year. The female, which is typically larger than the male, does most of the incubation and brooding, while the male brings food for his mate and the nestlings. Young remain dependent on parents for food for several weeks after fledging. Birds in this family, especially the larger species can live 20–30 years or more.

GENUS *AQUILA*
Golden Eagle

Aquila chrysaetos

ALSO: Steinadler, Aigle royal, Kongeørn, Беркут, Tinmiakpak, Qupanuaqpaq, Nakturalik. SN means "golden eagle."

RANGE: Near circumpolar. Nests (Feb–Aug) in trees and on rock ledges in mountains and forests in N Amer, n UK, and Eurasia. Extirpated from Ireland, where a reintroduction program is under way. Adult birds mostly sedentary; juveniles often disperse widely.

ID: L 32–37 in (80–94 cm). WT ♂ 6.5–10 lb (3–4.6 kg); ♀ 8.4–15 lb (3.8–6.7 kg). Massive hooked beak for tearing flesh, and powerful talons for seizing prey. AD: Large dark brown eagle, with a golden buff crown and nape. Wings and undertail dark grayish brown. Faint, irregular white patches near wing joints and base of tail. Often shows pale rufous patches on the chest, leading wing edges, and belly. Yellow legs; upper legs feathered. Dark beak, with yellow cere. Golden eye. JUV: Dark brown overall, with distinct white patches on underwing at base of flight feathers. Tail white, with broad dark terminal band. Shows some rufous or golden color on nape and belly. Light brown eye. Attains full adult plumage at 4–5 years. VOICE: Weak, high yelping or a 2-syllable *kee-yep*.

HABITS: Feeds on marmots, hares, rabbits, foxes, young deer, lambs, grouse, seabirds, and carrion. Said to kill adult chamois (*Rupicapra rupicapra*) in Eurasia by pushing them off a cliff ledge. Wings are held in a slight V-shape when soaring. Pairs for life at 4–5 years of age. Pair builds several nests (*aeries*) of tree branches and uses them alternately for several years. Nest can measure 6.6 ft (2 m) across and 3.3 ft (1 m) high. Incubation is about 45 days. Young fledge at 68–77 days. Can live up to 38 years in the wild. **USE:** Used in falconry, especially in c Asia. Golden and bald eagle feathers are central to religious and spiritual rites of Native Americans in the US and First Nations tribes in Canada. US law stipulates that only individuals of Native American tribes are authorized to possess eagle feathers, and then only for use in ceremonies.

GENUS *HALIAEETUS*
Bald Eagle
Haliaeetus leucocephalus
ALSO: Weißkopf-Seeadler, Pygargue à tête blanche,
Hvithodet havørn, Белоголовый орлан, Tinmiakpak. SN means "white-headed sea-eagle." National emblem of the US.
RANGE: Nests (Mar–May) in tall trees near water, less frequently on rocky ledges, in Alaska, e Aleutians, and Canada; disjunct populations occur in lower US and n Mexico. Occasional in ne Siberia and Greenland.
ID: L 28–38 in (71–96 cm). WT 6.6–14 lb (3–6.3 kg).

females are larger than males. AD: Brown body; white head and tail. Bright yellow eye. Yellow legs and feet. JUV: Brown, with diffuse patches of white on the primaries and coverts. Tail feathers whitish, edged with dark brown. In years 2–3, tail and underwings show white feathering, but underwing pattern is never as clean-cut as the obvious white-and-dark pattern of juvenile golden eagles. Attains adult plumage at about 4 years. VOICE: Weak, flat, chirping whistle; also a shrill cry, punctuated by grunts.

HABITS: Feeds mainly on fish, swooping down over the water and snatching them with its talons. Occasionally feeds on carrion, small mammals, reptiles, and crustaceans. Sometimes pirates prey from other birds. Soars on thermals with wings held flat. Powerful flier, able to reach speeds of 35–44 mph (56–70 kmh); fairly stiff, shallow wingbeats. Builds a huge bulky nest of branches in tall trees near water; will nest on large boulders or cliffs in treeless areas. Nest is the largest of any N Amer bird, measuring up to 13 ft (4 m) deep by 8 ft (2.5 m) across, and weighing a ton or more. Incubation is about 35 days. Young fledge at 70–92 days.

STATUS: Nearly extirpated in the lower US in the late 20th century. With protection, populations have stabilized and the species was removed from the US list of endangered and threatened wildlife in 2007.

White-tailed Sea-Eagle
Haliaeetus albicilla
ALSO: White-tailed Eagle, Gray Sea-Eagle, Erne, Seeadler, Pygargue à queue
blanche, Havørn, Орлан-белохвост. SN means "white-tailed sea-eagle."
RANGE: Nests (Mar–Apr) locally on sea cliffs and in trees in forests near large rivers and lakes in sw Greenland, w Iceland, Eurasia, and (rarely) Attu Is in the w Aleutians. Reintroduced to Scotland after being extirpated in the early 1900s. Mostly sedentary; some northern populations migrate to s Europe, Egypt, and e Asia.
ID: L 30–37 in (77–95 cm). WT 9–15 lb (4.1–6.9 kg). Largest European eagle. Female larger than male. Large head, long neck, massive bill, and broad

Talons locked, a pair of eagles tumbles toward the ground in aerial courtship display.

White-tailed ad.

juv.

White-tailed Sea-Eagle
Haliaeetus albicilla
Greenland, Iceland, Eurasia
L 30–37 in (77–95 cm)
WS 100–120 in (250–300 cm)

ad.

Steller's ad.

juv.

Golden ad.

juv.

ad.

juv.

Steller's Sea-Eagle
Haliaeetus pelagicus
NE Siberia
L 34–42 in (85–105 cm)
WS 82–96 in (203–241 cm)

ad.

juv.

Golden Eagle
Aquila chrysaetos
Near circumpolar
L 32–37 in (81–94 cm)
WS 75–89 in (190–225 cm)

Bald Eagle
Haliaeetus leucocephalus
N Amer
L 28–38 in (71–96 cm)
WS 66–88 in (168–244 cm)

juv.

Bald ad.

juv.

ad.

wings. AD: Brown, with pale buff head and neck and black primaries. White, wedge-shaped tail. Yellow bill. Yellow legs. JUV: Brown, mottled with cream and buff. Lores whitish in first year. Bill dull yellow and gray, turning entirely yellow at 4–5 years. Dark tail becomes white with dark terminal band at 2–3 years and turns all white by 6–8 years of age. VOICE: Whistles and shrill, cackling yaps. Pairs duet a long repetitive *krick rick rick rick rick,* which increases in frequency and pitch. Alarm call is a barking *kli-kli-kli.* Generally silent except when breeding.
HABITAT: Feeds mainly on fish; also takes waterfowl, seabirds, small mammals, carrion, and occasionally food pirated from otters or seabirds. Seizes fish from the water surface with its talons. Flies with slow, stiff wingbeats and often soars. Builds huge, bulky nest of sticks lined with twigs, moss, grass, seaweeds, lichens, ferns, or wool. Nests are often reused, sometimes by successive generations of birds; one nest in Iceland has been in use for over 150 years. Incubation is about 38 days. Young fledge at 10–12 weeks. Can live 36 years in the wild.

Steller's Sea-Eagle

Haliaeetus pelagicus
ALSO: Kamchatka Sea-Eagle, White-shouldered Sea-Eagle, Riesenseeadler, Pygargue empereur, Kjempehavørn, Стелеров морски орел. CN honors German naturalist Georg Wilhelm Steller (1709–1746). SN means "sea-eagle of the open ocean."
RANGE: Nests (Apr–May) on seacoasts and near large interior rivers and lakes on the Kamchatka Penin, Amur Rvr basin, n Sakhalin Is, and Shantar Is, Russia. Winters in the Kurils and n Japan. Uncommon winter visitor to ne China and Korea. Vagrant to the Aleutians and Pribilofs.
ID: L 34–42 in (85–105 cm). WT 11–20 lb (5–9 kg). Female larger than male. AD: Large blackish brown body, with white shoulder patches, white leggings, white wedge-shaped tail; small patches of white feathers on forehead and crown. Massive, deep, arched yellow beak. Eyes, cere, and feet yellow. Feet have powerful, curved talons and rough pads for grasping slippery prey. JUV: Dark

brown, with paler feathers in areas where adults are white. Bill dark horn, with some yellow at base. Brown eyes. Attains adult plumage at 4–8 years. VOICE: Deep barking cry, *ra-ra-ra-raurau.*
HABITS: Inhabits coastal areas, islands, and forested valleys near lake and river estuaries. Feeds mainly on fish, including salmon and trout spawning near river mouths. Dives from a high perch and snatches fish from water surface or occasionally stands in the water and grabs passing fish. Also feeds on seabirds, gulls, waterfowl, small mammals, and carrion such as beached seal carcasses and deer carcasses left by hunters. Juveniles often pirate food from ospreys and other eagles. Builds several aeries high up on trees and rocky cliffs. Pairs add sticks to an existing nest, which may reach 5 ft (1.5 m) in height and 8 ft (2.5 m) across. Incubation is 38–45 days. Young fledge at about 10 weeks of age.
STATUS: Vulnerable (IUCN).

GENUS *BUTEO*: This genus contains the typical hawks. *Buteo* means "buzzard hawk" as applied by the ancient Greek naturalist Pliny the Elder. *Hawk* derives from the German *hab,* meaning "to seize or take hold." These birds are robust-bodied, broad-winged raptors. They are opportunistic hunters that prey on almost any type of small animal, especially on rodents.

Rough-legged Hawk

Buteo lagopus
ALSO: Rauhußbussard, Buse pattue, Fjellvåk, Зимняк, Qinnuajuaq, Kaajuuq, Kilgik. SN means "hare-footed buzzard-hawk," referring to the fully feathered leg, a feature that also gives us the CN "rough-legged."
RANGE: Near circumpolar. Nests (May–Jun) on cliffs and hillsides or in trees on tundra and alpine tundra throughout the Far North. Winters in open habitats and farmland from s Canada south through the US, and in the UK, c Europe, s Russia. Occasional in w Aleutians.
ID: L 19–23 in (49–59 cm). WT 1.3–3.7 lb (0.6–1.7 kg). TYPICAL AD: Brown above, paler below, with a solid (♀) or barred (♂), dark belly patch. Pale head and throat streaked with brown. Upperside of

juv.

ad. ♂

ad. ♀

Northern Harrier
Circus cyaneus
Near circumpolar
L 18–20 in (46–50 cm)

ad. ♂

ad. ♀

Common Buzzard
Buteo buteo
Temperate Eurasia
L 19–22 in (48–56 cm)

Dark morph
Red-tail

Light morph
Harlan's Red-tail

Dark
Harlan's Red-tail

Typical Red-tails

Dark morph
Harlan's Red-tail

Typical Red-tail

Red-tailed Hawk
Buteo jamaicensis
N Amer
L 18–26 in (45–65 cm)

ad.

juv.

ad.

ad.
Dark morph

juv.

Typical ad.

Rough-legged Hawk
Buteo lagopus
Near circumpolar
L 19–23 in (49–59 cm)

wings brown; white base to primaries. Underwing white, with dark patch at elbow and dark trailing edge. Tail white, with dark terminal band. Legs and feet fully feathered. Bill bluish black, with a yellow cere. Yellow eye. AD DARK MORPH: Dark brown overall, except for white underwing and dark-tipped white undertail. Dark eye. About 50 percent of e N Amer birds are dark morph. JUV: Dark streaks on pale head and breast. Belly patch solid black. Trailing edge of underwings, black elbow patch, and indistinct black tail band; forward underwing buffy. Yellow eye. VOICE: Drawn-out squeal, *keeeeer.*
HABITS: Feeds mainly on voles and lemmings when breeding, mice and shrews in winter. Pairs often do not breed in years when rodents are scarce. Hunts from a high perch or while soaring over open land, often hovering before swooping down on prey. Builds a nest of twigs, lined with moss, lichen, and dry grass on a cliff, boulder, steep slope, or occasionally at the top of a tall tree. Nest is used for several years. Female incubates the 2–6 greenish, brown-spotted eggs for about 31 days. Young fledge at 34–45 days, but are fed by parents for several more weeks.
RELATED SPECIES: COMMON BUZZARD, *Buteo buteo,* ranges in open woodland in temperate Eurasia. Birds are longer-winged and appear more eagle-like than *B. lagopus.*

sometimes considered a separate species; nests in Alaska and nw Canada. Polymorphic; dark morph predominates; pale morph rare. Tail feathers whitish or gray (rarely reddish brown), mottled or streaked longitudinally with black.
VOICE: Hoarse, screaming *kee-eeeee-arr,* given while soaring.
HABITS: Feeds on small and mid-sized mammals. Typically hunts from an elevated perch. Carries small prey to the perch before eating it; consumes large prey on the ground, then carries any remains to a perch. Builds large nest of twigs in trees in mature mixed forests adjacent to large open areas, grassland, or cultivated fields; uses cliffs, buildings, telephone poles, and transmission towers in treeless areas. Both sexes incubate the 2–3 white, dark-spotted eggs for about a month. Chicks are brooded mostly by the female, while the male hunts for food. Young fledge at about 45 days of age, but remain near the nest and are fed by parents for another 3 weeks.

GENUS *CIRCUS*: This genus contains the harriers, which are distinguished by their slender form and long wings and tail. They fly low over open country and glide with the wings raised in a shallow V. The name *harrier* stems from the phrase "to harry," the species' characteristic method of pursuing prey.

Red-tailed Hawk

Buteo jamaicensis
ALSO: Rotschwanzbussard, Rødhalevåk, Buse à queue rousse, Краснохвостый сарыч. SN refers to Jamaica, the type locality.
RANGE: Nests (Mar–Jul) in Alaska and Canada, south through the US to C Amer.
ID: L 18–26 in (45–65 cm). Females are much larger than males. Plumage extremely variable. TYPICAL RED-TAIL: Light, intermediate, and dark morphs. Upperparts pale auburn to dark brown. Underbelly usually pale, with a dark band across the abdomen. Adult tail brownish red (color more obvious on upperside), with a narrow black terminal band; juvenile tail barred in light and dark brownish gray. HARLAN'S RED-TAIL (*B. j. harlani):* Smallest subspecies,

Northern Harrier

Circus cyaneus
ALSO: Hen Harrier (Eur), Marsh Hawk (N Amer), Kornweihe, Busard Saint-Martin, Myrhauk, Полевой лунь, Papiktuuk (Inupiaq for "long parka tail"). SN means "hawk with bluish [male plumage]."
RANGE: Near circumpolar. Nests (May–Jul) on the ground on open taiga, moors, and marshes in much of the Holarctic. Winters south to s Europe, c Asia, C Amer, and S Amer. Most northerly breeding and most widespread harrier.
ID: L 18–20 in (46–50 cm). WT 0.7–1.6 lb (0.3–0.8 kg); females are about 50 percent heavier than males. Slim body, long wings, long tail, long yellow legs, and a distinctive white rump patch. Owl-like facial disc around eyes. AD ♂: Gray above, mostly

Sharp-shinned Hawk
Accipiter striatus
N Amer
L ♂ 9.5–10.5 in (24–27 cm)
L ♀ 11.5–13.5 in (29–34 cm)

Eurasian Sparrowhawk
Accipiter nisus
Eurasia
L ♂ 12–14 in (30–36 cm)
L ♀ 14–16 in (36–40 cm)

Northern Goshawk
Accipiter gentilis
Near circumpolar
L ♂ 20–22 in (50–56 cm)
L ♀ 23–26 in (58–65 cm)

white below, with black primaries and black tips to secondaries. Lemon yellow eyes. AD♀: Brown above. Buffy, with brown streaks below. Lemon yellow eyes. JUV: Resembles adult female, but darker chocolate brown above. Young birds show solid rufous underparts, which become streaked by winter. Juvenile ♂ has pale greenish yellow eyes; juvenile ♀ has dark chocolate brown eyes.

HABITS: Forages on the wing while flying low and buoyantly over the ground. Frequently relies on auditory cues to capture prey, adjusting the angle of the facial disc to sharply focus sounds. Prefers small rodents, but also takes birds and young rabbits, especially during breeding season. Often roosts on the ground. Nests on the ground amid low vegetation; occasionally nests in trees. Female incubates the clutch of 3–6 eggs for 29–31 days. She broods chicks while male provides food for nestlings. Young fledge at 31–38 days. The parents, especially the female, feed the young for 2–3 weeks after they fledge.

GENUS *ACCIPITER*: The genus *Accipiter* (Latin for "hawk") includes goshawks, sparrowhawks, sharp-shinned hawks, and other woodland raptors that ambush prey from a concealed perch. Accipiters have long legs with bare tarsi. Their long tails and relatively short, rounded wings allow them to maneuver through dense timber when chasing prey.

Northern Goshawk
Accipiter gentilis

ALSO: Habicht, Autour des palombes, Hønsehauk, Тетеревятник, Kirgavik. SN means "noble hawk." CN derives from the Old English *gōshafoc,* meaning "goose hawk," alluding to the belief that goshawks prey on geese.

RANGE: Near circumpolar. Nests (Apr–Jul) in fairly open forests, forest-steppe, and forest-tundra. Usually winters within breeding range; juveniles and northernmost breeders often

move south or to lower elevations. In N Amer, irruptions to the south occur at approximately 10-year intervals, which coincide with low populations of prey animals such as snowshoe hares and grouse.
ID: L ♂ 20–22 in (50–56 cm); ♀ 23–26 in (58–65 cm). AD: Gray to brownish gray upperparts. Head dark gray, with white eye stripe. Underparts very pale gray, with fine dark barring. Undertail coverts white. Tail gray, with 4–5 dark bars. Legs yellow. Eye yellow to reddish orange. Pale- or white-plumaged specimens are known from the Russian Far East. JUV: Upperparts brown. Underparts buff to pale cinnamon, with elongated dark spots. Yellow eye. VOICE: Ringing *kye-kye-kye* or gull-like *kree'-ah*.
HABITS: Hunts in forests, at forest edge, and along wooded riverbanks, flying suddenly out of cover and giving chase to prey with quick, agile movements through the trees. Powerful hunter, capable of killing large prey such as hares, tree squirrels, grouse, crows, and mid-sized raptors. Female gathers sticks from forest floor or breaks them from trees and builds a large nest high in a tree. Nests on or near the ground in treeless areas, and often builds on top of other birds' nests. Nests are reused for years and may reach 5 ft (1.6 m) across and more than 4 ft (1.3 m) deep. Female incubates the clutch of 3–4 bluish white eggs for 30–38 days, while male hunts for food. Young remain in the nest for about 35 days, then move to nearby branches to be fed, at which time they are called "branchers."

Eurasian Sparrowhawk

Accipiter nisus
ALSO: Sperber, Epervier d'Europe, Spurvehauk, Перепелятник. SN means "striving hawk." Preys on sparrows, hence the CN.
RANGE: Nests (Jun) at forest edge in open country with hedgerows and in urban woodland across most of Eurasia. Resident in temperate breeding areas, often moving to nearby villages and cities in winter; some northern populations migrate south to n Africa, c Eurasia, and s Asia.
ID: L ♂ 12–14 in (30–36 cm); ♀ 14–16 in (36–40 cm). AD ♂: Slate gray above, with finely russet-barred

underparts. Eyes orange. AD ♀: Dark brown to grayish brown upperparts. Underparts barred in gray or brown. Eyes yellow to orange. JUV: Warm brown above, with rusty fringes to the back feathers; throat has dark streaks. Coarsely barred or spotted brown below. Eyes pale yellow. VOICE: Loud *kik-kik-kik*.
HABITS: Feeds mainly on birds, often taking songbirds at winter bird feeders; occasionally preys on voles. Males take smaller prey than larger females, which can kill pigeons and young hazel grouse. Hunts by ambushing prey, using bushes, hedgerows, or buildings as cover. Builds a nest of sticks in trees in coniferous forests, woodlands, and urban parks and gardens. Clutch is 3–6 white eggs, spotted with bright reddish brown. Male chicks fledge at about 26 days, the larger female chicks at about 30 days.

Sharp-shinned Hawk

Accipiter striatus
ALSO: Sharpie, Eckschwanz-sperber, Épervier brun, Tverrhalehauk, Полосатый ястреб. SN means "streaked hawk." CN refers to the thin legs.
RANGE: Nests (Apr–Jun) in coniferous forest and deciduous woodland across most of the US and Canada. Resident in temperate breeding areas; northern populations migrate to s US, Mexico, Greater Antilles, and C Amer.
ID: L ♂ 9.5–10.5 in (24–27 cm); ♀ 11.5–13.5 in (29–34 cm). Smallest N Amer accipiter. AD: Upperparts bluish gray, often with a few random white spots on the back. Crown dark gray. Cheeks tinged rufous. Underparts barred white and rufous; breast may appear solid orange from a distance. White undertail coverts. Thighs rufous or barred white and rufous. Eyes dark orange to red. JUV: Dark brownish upperparts; back feathers edged rufous, giving a scaled appearance. Head brown, streaked with white. Underparts white, with extensive brown streaks and teardrop-shaped marks. Eyes yellow to pale orange.
HABITS: Feeds mostly on small songbirds. Ambushes prey from cover or pursues prey while flying through dense vegetation. Builds a stick nest in a large conifer or dense stand of deciduous

trees. Both sexes gather nesting material, but female does most or all construction. Secretive at nest in order to avoid attacks of larger raptors. Clutch is 4–5 bluish white eggs marked with splotches of brown, violet, or hazel. Incubation is about 30 days. Young fledge at about 30 days. **STATUS:** Populations declined in the 1960s and 1970s, probably due to the use of DDT and other pesticides. Numbers have rebounded as a result of the ban on DDT and proliferation of backyard bird feeders, which provide reliable, easy prey for these hunters.

FAMILY FALCONIDAE
FALCONS

Falcons are diurnal raptors that inhabit open countryside, fields, deserts, and tundra. They are characterized by a bullet-shaped body, thin pointed wings, and long tail. Most have gray to rufous plumage, with a pale underside that is often streaked or barred. The eye is dark, and the head is marked with a dark helmet or teardrop. Females are larger than males.

Most falcons feed on birds caught in flight. They spot their quarry from above and plummet downward, a movement called *stooping*. Projections in the nostrils help slow the flow of air as the falcon inhales, allowing it to breathe easily while in a rapid dive. The feet are used to snatch a bird or knock it out of the air. The prey is usually killed on impact, but if not, the falcon's bill is equipped with a *tomial tooth*—a jagged notch on the cutting edge of the upper beak—which can sever the prey's spinal cord.

Falcons form monogamous breeding pairs at 1–3 years of age. They do not build nests, but nest on bare cliff ledges, in tree cavities, and occasionally in other species' stick nests. It is typically the larger female that incubates the 2–5 cream-colored, brown-blotched eggs, while the male brings food. Incubation is 26–36 days in the northern species. The young remain near the nest after fledging, sometimes for over a month, relying on the parents to supply food.

Falcons can be trained to catch game, birds, and even large insects in the sport of falconry, a pastime once restricted to royalty. In early English falconry literature, the word *falcon* applied only to a female falcon. The male falcon was called a *tercel* or *tiercel*, meaning "third," as it is smaller than the female by roughly one third; *tercel* also reflects the old belief that only 1 in 3 eggs hatched a male bird. Crossword-puzzle fans may know that a falcon chick still in down is called an *eyas*. A group of falcons is known collectively as a *bazaar, eyrie, ringing up, stooping up,* or *tower.*

GENUS *FALCO*
Gyrfalcon
Falco rusticolus

ALSO: Gerfalke, Faucon gerfaut, Jaktfalk, Кречет, Qinnuajuaq, Kiggavik, Qakuqtaq. SN means "falcon of the countryside"; *Falco* derives from the Latin *falx*, meaning "sickle," a reference to the shape of the beak. CN derives from the Old High German *giri valke*, meaning "greedy falcon." Males are called *gyrkins*. National bird of Iceland. **RANGE:** Circumpolar. Nests (May–Jul) mainly on cliff ledges or man-made structures. Generally winters in breeding range; High Arctic breeders move south to avoid long hours of darkness and lack of prey; some winter on sea ice far from land, where they take small seabirds feeding in leads. Winter visitor to UK, Ireland, Denmark. Vagrant to Svalbard and the Faroes. **ID:** L ♂ 19–24 in (48–61 cm); ♀ 20–25 in (51–64 cm). WT 2.2–4.4 lb (1–2 kg). World's largest falcon. Legs and cere of adults are yellow, those of juveniles bluish gray. Plumage varies considerably. AD GRAY MORPH (common): Upperparts gray. Underparts whitish, with variable gray streaking. AD DARK MORPH (uncommon): Uniform dark gray to dark brown, with pale streaks on underparts. AD WHITE MORPH (Arctic): White overall, with variable dark spots and markings on wings, nape, and sides. VOICE: Shrill *kack-kack-kack.* **HABITS:** Feeds on ptarmigans, grouse, ground squirrels, hares, seabirds, waterfowl, voles, lemmings, and carrion. Pursues prey in fast, low flight, using terrain and vegetation to hide, then flies up and then dives straight down onto quarry. Kills prey on the ground or in flight. Usually nests on a rocky cliff ledge, taking over the stick nest of another species. Pairs will begin to nest when temperatures are still below freezing. Does not breed in years when food is scarce. Incubation is 34–36 days. Chicks fledge at 46–53 days.

Peregrine Falcon

Falco peregrinus

ALSO: Duck Hawk, Wander-falke-peregrinus, Faucon pèlerin, Vandrefalk, Сапсан, Kiggaviarjuk, Kakkajuuq, Kirgavik. SN means "falcon that wanders."

RANGE: Circumpolar. Nests (Apr–Jun) on bare rock ledges in open habitats. Most widely distributed raptor; occurs on every continent except Antarctica. Resident or highly migratory; some N Amer tundra breeders migrate to c Argentina and Chile.

ID: L ♂ 15–18 in (38–45 cm); ♀ 18–20.5 in (45–52 cm). WT 1.25–2.4 lb (0.6–1.1 kg). Variable plumage. Dark-plumaged birds are more common in coastal areas, pale-plumaged birds more common in cold, dry climates. AD: Bluish gray upperparts. Crown and nape black; thick black sideburns extend to below the eye, giving the impression of a helmet; cheek may be pale or dark. Underparts whitish, gray, or buffy, with variable amounts of black spots and bars. Underwing and undertail barred pale gray and black. Dark eye. JUV: Upperparts pale to slate gray or chocolate brown. Underparts buff, with heavy dark streaks. VOICE: Clear, raucous *cack*. Screams when performing courtship dives.

HABITS: Feeds on shorebirds, songbirds, waterfowl, and sometimes small mammals. Able to kill prey twice its own body weight. Hunts by stooping—flying high above its quarry, then plummeting downward with wings folded, using gravity to accelerate. Dives can reach speeds of 200 mph (320 kmh), making the Peregrine the world's fastest bird. Nests mainly on rock ledges, also on flat roofs and artificial nesting platforms. Site may be reused in successive years. Incubation is 33–35 days. Fledglings solicit food by flying after adults. Parents teach them to hunt by dropping dead and live birds from the air for the young to catch in flight.

STATUS: Numbers greatly reduced by pesticide poisoning. Extinct in some areas, but due to conservation programs, many formerly abandoned areas have been recolonized.

Merlin

Falco columbarius

ALSO: Pigeon Hawk, Zwerg-falke, Faucon émerillon, Dvergfalk, Tinmiagruum kirgavia, Дербник. SN means "pigeon falcon."

RANGE: Near circumpolar. Nests (May–Jun) in forests and on upland moors in N Amer, Iceland, UK, n Eurasia. Northern populations mostly migratory, wintering in open habitats and agricultural areas south of breeding areas.

ID: L ♂ 10–10.5 in (25–27 cm); ♀ 12–13 in (30–33 cm). Legs, cere, and orbital skin yellow. Dark eye. Blurred dark malar streak. Great individual variation in plumage. AD ♂: Upperparts dark to medium bluish gray. Pale supercilium and cheeks. White or tawny underparts streaked with brown. Lightly streaked, rufous leg feathers. Tail black, with 2–3 narrow bluish gray bands and a white terminal band. AD ♀: Upperparts brown. Underparts buff, with elongated, teardrop-shaped streaks. Uppertail shows 2–3 bands; fanned undertail shows 3–4 pale bands. VOICE: Shrill, halting *ki-ki-kee* or *kek-kek-kek*.

HABITS: Feeds mostly on songbirds and small shorebirds caught in low, fast flight; also preys on voles, lemmings, insects, bats, and reptiles. Nests on cliff ledges; sometimes uses old tree nests of other raptors or crows. Incubation is 26–32 days. Male brings food to a perch near the nest; female flies to the perch, then takes food back to feed chicks. Young fledge at 27–33 days. Parents provide food for another month.

Common Kestrel

Falco tinnunculus

ALSO: Eurasian Kestrel, Turmfalke, Faucon crécerelle, Tårnfalk, Обыкновенная пустельга. SN means "falcon with a shrill call."

RANGE: Nests (Apr–May) in the UK and Eurasia in open forests, grasslands, agricultural and urban areas, and mountains to 9350 ft (2850 m). Winters south to n Africa, Caucasus, Kazakhstan,

Gyrfalcon
Falco rusticolus
Circumpolar
L ♂ 19–24 in (48–61 cm)
L ♀ 20–25 (51–64 cm)

Gray ad.
Common
morph

Dark ad.

White ad.
High Arctic

ad. ♀
Rufous wings
Tail rufous with
back bars

♂

ad. ♂
Bluish wings
Tail rufous with black
subterminal band

American Kestrel
Falco sparverius
Americas
L 9–12 in (22–30 cm)

♀

♂

ad. ♀
Tail barred

ad. ♂
Bluish tail with
black terminal band

Common Kestrel
Falco tinnunculus
Eurasia
L 12–15 in (30–38 cm)

ad. ♀

Dark ad. ♂

Typical ad. ♂

Merlin
Falco columbarius
Near circumpolar
L ♂ 10–10.5 in (25–27 cm)
L ♀ 12–13 in (30–33 cm)

ad.

juv.

Rufous ad.

Pale ad.

juv.

Peregrine Falcon
Falco perigrinus
Circumpolar
L ♂ 15–18 in (38–45 cm)
L ♀ 18–20.5 in (45–52 cm)

c Asia. Casual visitor to w Aleutians and Bering Sea region. Accidental to both coasts of n N Amer. **ID:** L 12–15 in (30–38 cm). Legs, cere, and orbital skin yellow. Dark eye. Black malar stripe. AD ♂: Upperparts light chestnut brown, with round black spots. Bluish gray crown. Underparts buff, with narrow blackish streaks. Tail bluish gray, with black terminal band narrowly edged in white. Remiges blackish. AD ♀: More spotted and streaked than male, and crown is browner. Tail barred brown and black. VOICE: Shrill *kee-kee-kee*.

HABITS: Hunts from a perch or while hovering over open areas with low vegetation. Feeds mostly on small rodents (kestrels can detect ultraviolet light reflected from urine trails around rodent burrows); also takes large insects, earthworms, reptiles, and songbirds. Nests on bare cliff ledges, in holes in walls and attics of old buildings, in artificial nest boxes, and in old tree nests of other birds. Incubation is about 30 days.

American Kestrel

Falco sparverius

ALSO: Sparrow Hawk, Buntfalke, Crécerelle d'Amérique, Spurvefalk, Воробьиная пустельга. SN means "sparrowhawk." Smallest, most numerous, most widespread N Amer falcon.

RANGE: Nests (May–Jun in the north) throughout most of the Americas, from Alaska and Canada to s S Amer. Resident or migratory. Vagrant to UK, Denmark, Malta, Azores.

ID: L 9–12 in (22–30 cm). Large, dark eyes. Two parallel black stripes run down the face. Short black stripes at back of head look like eyes when viewed from behind. AD ♂: Crown bluish gray, with variable amounts of rufous. Back and rump rufous, with some black barring. Wings bluish gray, with black spotting. Tail rufous, with black subterminal band and whitish tip. Underparts cream to tawny, with a few dark streaks and spots. AD ♀: Wings rufous, barred with black. Tail barred in rufous and black. Underparts cream to buff, streaked with brown. VOICE: Rapid *klee-klee-klee-klee*.

HABITS: Hunts in open areas with low vegetation, including pastures and parks. Spots prey while hovering or when perched on a branch or utility wire. Seizes insects and small rodents on the ground; occasionally takes insects and small birds in flight. Nests in old woodpecker holes, tree snags, artificial nest boxes, and occasionally building niches. Female chooses the nesting cavity and makes a shallow scrape in loose material on the cavity floor. Female incubates the eggs for 27–30 days and helps young out of the shell, which she eats or tramples into the nest.

Strigiformes: Owls

Owls are among the oldest species of vertebrate animals in existence. Fossils dating back 60 million years show that these birds have changed very little over time.

FAMILY STRIGIDAE
TYPICAL OWLS

Over time, the owl has been portrayed in many roles—a witch's familiar, a bird of ill omen, a spiritual guide, and a sage (hence, the collective "a wisdom of owls"). Images of owls appear in prehistoric cave paintings. There is an outline of a long-eared owl on a wall of Chauvet Cave at the Ardèche gorge, France, and another of a snowy owl pair and their chicks etched onto the rock face of La Salle Monique at Grotte de la Vache, France. The snowy owl etching was made about 29,000 years ago, at a time the arctic climate extended farther south than it does today.

Owls can be found on all continents except Antarctica. About 10 species range into the arctic and subarctic regions. Most of these live in the boreal forests, and only one species, the Snowy Owl, nests exclusively on the tundra. Arctic owls are largely non-migratory, but periodically move south in winter. The magnitude and extent of the winter irruptions are thought be a result of high reproductive success followed by severe winter conditions and decreased food supplies.

The plumage color and pattern of individual species varies with habitat and serves to camouflage the owl at its daytime roost. White plumage provides a cloak of invisibility for the Snowy Owl in its arctic habitat and also provides excellent heat insulation. In contrast, the plumage of a forest-dwelling strigid is barred and streaked in shades of brown, black, gray, or buff. The cryptic plumage, plus the raised ear tufts of some species, masks the owl's silhouette when it is roosting in trees or in dappled shade.

Owls are adapted for locating and dispatching prey. All have a strong, hooked bill for tearing flesh. The feet have 2 toes facing forward and 2 toes facing aft, and the outer toe can be pivoted back and forth for efficient prey capture. The sharp talons are used to seize and kill prey.

These nocturnal hunters have large forward-facing eyes surrounded by a flat area of feathers called the facial disc. The forward-facing eyes provide binocular vision. An abundance of light-sensing cells (rods) in the eyes allow owls to see well in even the slightest illumination from the stars or moon. Although the eyes are large, the eyeballs are immobile. So instead of turning its eyes, an owl pivots its whole head to view its surroundings. An owl can turn its head more than 180° because of special adaptations to its neck vertebrae and blood vessels leading to its brain.

Most species of owls have skeletal ear asymmetry, with the ear opening on one side of the skull higher than on the other. This adaptation for directional hearing allows owls to locate sounds coming from above and below as well as from right and left.

Owls ambush prey from above. Most swoop down from a high perch to seize their prey, others hunt by flying low over the ground, scanning for moving prey, then pouncing. In either case, the frilled, soft edges of the flight feathers render their flight silent. Prey is swallowed whole whenever possible, and very large prey is eaten where it is killed. In the Far North, owls have been observed leaving uneaten food to freeze and later thawing it out using their own body heat. Pellets of bone and other indigestible matter from prey is regurgitated about 6–10 hours after eating. Often the ground around a perch is thickly covered in vegetation and lichens, due to the nutrients contained in the owl's droppings and pellets.

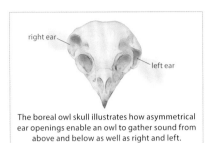

The boreal owl skull illustrates how asymmetrical ear openings enable an owl to gather sound from above and below as well as right and left.

As for breeding, most species are monogamous. Some pair for life, others change mates every year. Owls nest in tree holes or branches, or on the ground. They add little or no nesting material to the site. The female incubates the clutch of 2–8 white eggs for 21–35 days. The male brings food to the nest. The young leave the nest 12–36 days after hatching, often long before they can fly. The young remain near the nest and depend on their parents to provide food and protection for several weeks after they fledge.

GENUS *AEGOLIUS*
Boreal Owl
Aegolius funereus

ALSO: Tengmalm's Owl, Sparrow Owl, Partridge Hawk, Pearl Owl, Rauhfußkauz, Nyctale de Tengmalm, Pärluggla, Мохноногий сыч, Takpiilaagruk (Inupiaq for "blind one," because of its tameness in daylight). Alternate CN honors Swedish physician and owl enthusiast Peter Gustaf Tengmalm (1754–1803). SN means "bird of mournful bearing."

RANGE: Near circumpolar. Nests (Apr–May) in old woodpecker holes and tree cavities in forests of Alaska and Canada south to the n US, and from Scandinavia east across n Siberia; scattered populations occur in the Rocky Mtns.

ID: L 9–11 in (22–27 cm). Whitish facial disc, edged by a dark ring with tiny white spots. Small dark patches between the eyes and at bill base. Yellow eyes. Horn-colored bill. Upperparts rufous to gray, with bold white spotting. Short brown tail, with 4–5 white bars. Underparts off-white, with dark brown streaks on the breast. Legs and feet are fully feathered in white. VOICE: Male's song is a series of rapid fluted notes, *poo-poo-poo-poo-poo*, followed by a 3–4 second break, then another series.

HABITS: Nocturnal. Roosts close to the trunk in dense vegetation near the tree crown during the day. Hunts from a perch on a low tree branch. Scans the ground by moving its head slowly from side to side, listening for moving prey. Highly developed facial disc and pronounced skeletal ear asymmetry aid precise location of quarry. Feeds mainly on voles, lemmings, shrews, and mice; occasionally takes small birds, squirrels, bats, frogs, and beetles. Seasonally monogamous. Male sings from a potential nest site in an old woodpecker hole or other tree cavity. When a female approaches, male emits a string of rapid, stuttering *poo* notes. A receptive female will enter the hole and accept food from the male. Female incubates the 3–8 dull white eggs for 26–32 days. Young fledge at 28–36 days. They remain near the nest for 2 weeks or more, begging for food.

GENUS *ASIO*
Short-eared Owl
Asio flammeus
ALSO: Evening, Marsh, Swamp, Grass, Meadow, Owl,

Mouse-Hawk, Nipailuktak (Inupiaq for "flies silently"), Unnuaqsiuti, Sumpfohreule, Hibou des marais, Jordugle, Болотная сова. An Inuit legend relates how the Short-eared Owl became known as the Flat-faced Owl. A young girl was magically transformed into an owl with a long beak. She was so frightened that she flew into a wall face first, thus becoming the first owl to have a flat face. SN means "fire-eyed eared owl."
RANGE: Near circumpolar. Nests (Mar–Jun) on arctic and alpine tundra, and around salt marshes and estuaries in N Amer, Iceland, UK, n Eurasia, Kurils; also found in Hawaii, Galapagos, Caroline Is, Ponape, Azores, Philippines, Ryukyu, Borneo, Tierra del Fuego, and Falklands. One of the world's most widely distributed owls.
ID: L 13.5–16 in (33–40 cm). Buff-colored, with dark streaks on chest, belly, and back. Wings and tail strongly barred. Whitish or buffy facial disc rimmed with brown, and distinct white eyebrows above the yellow eyes. Black bill. Two small ear tufts. In flight, shows a dark "wrist" on the underwing. **VOICE:** Male's territorial song is a soft, pulsing *boo-boo-boo-boo-boo*.

HABITS: Active day and night. Sleeps and roosts on the ground, but will rest in trees in winter. Flies low over open country searching for voles and lemmings; also takes large insects, small birds, mice, ground squirrels, and small muskrats. Carries food in the talons to a feeding perch or boulder. Seasonally monogamous. Males perform aerial courtship displays, rising quickly with exaggerated wingbeats and wing claps, hovering, then gliding down and ascending again, sometimes to 1000 ft (300 m) in the air. Female makes a ground scrape or rarely a shallow burrow and lines it with grass, weeds, and feathers. Female alone incubates the 4–6 eggs for 24–28 days, while the male provides food. Young fledge at 31–36 days.

SIMILAR SPECIES: LONG-EARED OWL, *Asio otus*, occurs in temperate forests of N Amer and Eurasia. Nests (Mar–Jul) in trees, using old stick nests of crows, ravens, magpies, and hawks. Distinguished from the Short-eared Owl mainly by its golden-colored facial disc, orange (rather than yellow) eyes, and long blackish ear tufts, which may be held erect or folded down.

GENUS *BUBO*
Snowy Owl
Bubo scandiacus
ALSO: Arctic Owl, Ermine

Owl, Tundra Ghost, White Terror of the North, Scandinavian Nightbird, Highland Tundra Owl, Ookpik, Ukpik, Ukpigjuaq, Schnee-Eule, Harfang des neiges, Snøugle, Белая сова. SN means "owl of Scandinavia." Official bird of Quebec.

An Inuit tale tells of the day Snowy Owl and Raven made each other new clothes. Raven made Owl a pretty dress of white feathers dotted with black lamp oil. In return, Owl made Raven a lovely white dress. But when she asked Raven to try on the dress, Raven became so excited she couldn't hold still. She jumped around so much that Owl got mad and threw the pot of lamp oil at her. The black oil soaked into the white dress and Raven has been dressed in black ever since.
RANGE: Circumpolar. Nests (May–Jun) on

Northern Hawk Owl
Surnia ulula
Near circumpolar
L 14–17 in (36–43 cm)

ad. ♀

ad. ♂

Snowy Owl
Bubo scandiacus
Circumpolar
L 21–26 in (53–65 cm)

Boreal Owl
Aegolius funereus
Near circumpolar
L 9–11 in (22–27 cm)

Eurasian Pygmy Owl
Glaucidium passerinum
Eurasia
L 6–8 in (15–20 cm)

Ural Owl
Strix uralensis
Eurasia
L 20–24 in (50–61 cm)

Great Gray Owl
Strix nebulosa
Near circumpolar
L 24–33 in (61–84 cm)

Great Horned Owl
Bubo virginianus
Americas
L 17–25 in (43–64 cm)

Eurasian Eagle Owl
Bubo bubo
Eurasia
L 23–29 in (59–73 cm)

Long-eared Owl
Asio otus
Circumpolar
L 12–15.5 in (31–37 cm)

Short-eared Owl
Asio flammeus
Near circumpolar
L 13.5–16 in (33–40 cm)

open tundra, mountain slopes, and plateaus. Winters on windswept tundra with little snow accumulation and in forest-tundra; periodically irrupts south to c US, UK, n Europe, c Russia, n China, and Sakhalin Is. Accidental in Azores, Mediterranean region, Iran, n India, Japan.

ID: L 21–26 in (53–65 cm). WT 2.5–4.5 lb (1–2 kg). AD ♂: Entirely white or white with some pale gray to brownish bars on upperparts and breast. Golden eye. Strongly curved, sharply pointed, blackish bill. Legs and feet fully feathered to toes. AD ♀: White, with moderate to extensive dark barring on breast, wings, head, and tail. VOICE: High-pitched, drawn-out scream when defending territory. Female "barks" when alarmed. Male song is a deep, muffled *hrooo-hrooo*.

HABITS: Active from dawn to dusk in summer and throughout the winter darkness. Scans for prey while perched on a rise or while flying low in direct, unhurried flight. Main prey is lemmings, but when these are scarce, takes small mammals, birds, fish, and carrion. Nests on open tundra, making a shallow scrape on the ground or near a rise that the male uses as a look-out. Nesting success is dependent on lemming populations, as a family of nesting owls may eat 1500 lemmings before the young disperse. Average clutch is 4–7 eggs. In poor lemming years, however, the female may not lay at all, but when lemming populations explode she may produce up to 15 eggs. Parents aggressively defend their young, so much so that snow geese will nest near owls, relying on the owl's ability to chase off predators. Young leave the nest at about 25 days before they can fly, fledge at 50–60 days, and become independent at about 80 days.

Great Horned Owl
Bubo virginianus

ALSO: Tiger Owl, Hoot Owl, Nukisugaq, Virginia-Uhu, Grand-duc d'Amérique, Amerikahubro, Виргинский филин. SN means "owl of Virginia," the type locality.

RANGE: Nests (Feb–Apr in the north) in wooded areas near open fields from northern limit of the boreal forests to s S Amer.

ID: L 17–25 in (43–64 cm). WT 2–4 lb (0.9–1.8 kg).

Barrel-shaped build, with a large head, long ear tufts, and very large yellow eyes. Upperparts mottled brown, with a rufous, brown, or gray facial disc. White throat patch (male puffs this up when courting). Underparts light brown to buff, with some brown barring. Legs and feet fully feathered. VOICE: Loud, low-pitched *hoo-hoo-hoooo' hoo-hoo*. Males hoot year round, females during mating season. Courting male puffs up his throat and hoots; the female hoots back.

HABITS: Nocturnal. Solitary, except when nesting. Powerful enough to take prey 2–3 times heavier than itself. Hunts from a perch or by gliding above the ground; also wades into water to grab fish and frogs. Feeds mainly on hares and rabbits; also takes small rodents, squirrels, ducks, woodpeckers, pigeons, grouse, and smaller owls. Swoops down and pounces on prey, using its talons to sever the quarry's spinal column. Small prey is swallowed whole; larger prey is carried off and ripped apart at feeding perch or nest. Nests in old tree nests of hawks, crows, ravens, or squirrels, in caves, in abandoned buildings, and on artificial platforms.

Eurasian Eagle Owl
Bubo bubo

ALSO: Northern Eagle Owl, Uhu, Hibou grand-duc, Филин обыкновенный, Hubro. SN means "eagle owl."

RANGE: Nests (Apr) in forests, steppe, mountains, along seacoasts, and recently in European towns. Sedentary or nomadic.

ID: L 23–29 in (59–73 cm). WT ♂ 6.6 lb (3 kg); ♀ 9.3 lb (4.2 kg). Large, with a barrel-shaped build, long ear tufts (held erect or folded back), and yellow orange eyes. Plumage variable. Upperparts brownish black to tawny buff or pale creamy gray, with bold dark streaks and wavy lines. Facial disc gray to buff, with blackish brown along the outer edge and white around bill and eyes. Throat and center of upper breast white. Underparts tawny, with bold streaks and fine wavy barring. Fully feathered dark legs and feet. VOICE: Deep, loud, hooting *oo' hoo*; pairs duet when courting. Nasal barking *kwa* when alarmed.

HABITS: Nocturnal. Roosts during the day

in conifers in dense forest, in caves, or amid boulders. Slow, silent, low flight, with soft wingbeats interrupted by gliding. Seizes prey on the ground or in flight. Feeds on rodents, rabbits, hares, corvids, grouse, and ducks, but can take prey as large as foxes, marmots, and young deer. It also preys on young raccoons and is rumored to strike at anyone wearing a coonskin cap. Pairs for life. Reuses nesting site for years. Nests on cliff ledges, between boulders, in tree cavities in dense forests, under a fallen log, and occasionally in old magpie or hawk nests.

GENUS *GLAUCIDIUM*
Eurasian Pygmy Owl
Glaucidium passerinum

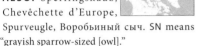

ALSO: Sperlingskauz, Chevêchette d'Europe, Spurveugle, Воробьиный сыч. SN means "grayish sparrow-sized [owl]."

RANGE: Nests (Apr–May) in old woodpecker holes in moist forests from nc Europe across c Siberia to Sakhalin. Generally resident; moves to lower altitudes and latitudes in severe winters. Irregular winter visitor to UK.

ID: L 6–8 in (15–19 cm). Dark rufous to grayish brown, with spotted sides. Tail dark brown, with 5 narrow whitish bars. Underparts white with brown speckles. Small, short head, with white to gray eyebrows and a white half-collar on back of neck. Yellow eyes. Dull yellow bill.

VOICE: Monotonous, high-pitched, clear fluted notes, *gewh, gewh, gewh,* spaced at about 2 second intervals. A 5–7 note rising-scale call is given at dusk or dawn, mostly before and post-breeding.

HABITS: Most active at dusk and dawn, but also hunts by day. Cocks and flicks tail from side to side when excited. Preys mainly on small birds and rodents; sometimes takes lizards, bats, fish, and insects. Hunts from a perch, swooping down to catch birds in flight. Can carry prey as big as itself, due to the disproportionately large feet. Caches food in tree cavities in winter.

Seasonally monogamous. Territorial; male may occupy the same territory in a stand of spruce, birch, or beech for its entire adult life. Courting male sings from a potential nest site in an old woodpecker hole. A receptive female will enter the hole at dusk and accept food from the male. Female incubates the 3–8 white eggs for 28–29 days, leaving the nest only to take food from the male at a nearby perch. She broods the hatchlings for 9–10 days, then vacates the hole, returning only to feed the chicks or remove waste. Young leave the nest at 30–34 days. Both parents, then the male alone, continue to provide food for another 4–6 weeks.

GENUS *SURNIA*
Northern Hawk Owl
Surnia ulula

ALSO: Sperbereule, Chouette épervière, Haukugle, Ястребиная сова, Niakuktuagruk. The origin of the SN is obscure, but may derive from the Greek words for screech owl. Built and flies like an accipiter, thus the CN "hawk owl."

RANGE: Near circumpolar. Nests (Apr–Jun) in open coniferous forests bordering boggy and burned areas from Alaska east to Labrador, and from Scandinavia east across Siberia to Kamchatka, Sakhalin, and n China. Nomadic, breeding where food is abundant. Juveniles periodically irrupt southward in autumn.

ID: L 14–17 in (36–43 cm). White facial disc, broadly rimmed with black. Black false eyespots on sides of nape. Crown densely spotted. Pale yellow eyes. Upperparts dark gray to dark grayish brown, spotted with white on mantle, back, and scapulars. Long, dark grayish brown tail, with several narrow whitish bars. Whitish underparts, barred with grayish brown. **VOICE:** Rapid, melodious, bubbling trill, *ululululululululul,* lasting up to 14 seconds. Alarm call is a piercing *kiiiiirrl* or kestrel-like *kwikiki-kikkik.*

HABITS: Diurnal. Flies low, with deep powerful wingbeats interspersed with glides. Agile in maneuvering around trees and shrubs. Hunts in semi-open country with scattered trees. Perches at the top of a tall tree, then swoops down on prey; also hovers and soars. Feeds largely on lemmings and voles; occasionally takes grouse, ptarmigans, hares, frogs, and fish. Lacks skeletal ear asymmetry but still can locate and capture prey concealed under deep snow cover . Flicks tail when excited. Seasonally monogamous.

Nests in dead tree snags, burned-out stumps, or woodpecker holes; occasionally uses abandoned stick nests. Female incubates the 3–13 (usually 7) white eggs for 25–30 days. Male feeds female away from the nest at a nearby perch. Young move out of the nest at 23–30 days, fledge at 5–6 weeks of age, and become independent by fall.

GENUS *STRIX*
Great Gray Owl
Strix nebulosa

ALSO: Phantom of the North, Cinereous Owl, Spectral Owl, Spruce Owl, Bearded Owl, Bartkauz, Chouette lapone, Lappugle, Бородатая неясыть, Naatak. SN means "owl with cloudy gray [plumage]."
RANGE: Near circumpolar. Nests (Mar–May) in mature forests adjacent to open meadows or bogs from Finland to the Sea of Okhotsk, and from Alaska and nc Canada, south through the Rockies to c California. Semi-nomadic.
ID: L 24–33 in (61–84 cm). WT 1.8–3.2 lb (0.8–1.5 kg). One of the world's largest owls. Appears bulky when at rest because of its dense fluffy plumage, long wings, relatively long tail, and large head. Dark gray, barred and flecked with light gray and white. Prominent white eyebrows and moustache. Black chin. Eyes and bill yellow. VOICE: Muffled, low-pitched, drawn-out *whooo-ooo-ooo-ooo*. Nesting adults growl, shriek, hoot, wail, and snap their bills when threatened.
HABITS: Hunts mostly at dawn and dusk. Feeds on small rodents, especially voles; also takes shrews, squirrels, rabbits, chipmunks, weasels, and occasionally grouse, reptiles, and insects. Seasonally monogamous. Nests in abandoned raptor nests, tree snags, natural tree cavities, or nest boxes. Lines nest with conifer needles, deer hair, moss, and shredded bark. Incubation is 28–36 days. Adults aggressively defend the nest, flying out against predators as large as bears.

Ural Owl
Strix uralensis

ALSO: Habichtskauz, Chouette de l'Oural, Slaguale, Длиннохвостая неясыть. SN means "owl of the Ural Mtns."

RANGE: Nests (Mar–Apr) in coniferous and deciduous forests near open meadows or bogs, from Scandinavia to Sakhalin Is, Japan, Korea. Relict population exists in mountains of c Europe.
ID: L 20–24 in (50–61 cm). Dark eyes. Yellow bill. Variable plumage. Pale to dark brown, with dark brown streaking on mantle, back of head, and underparts. Throat whitish. Uniform dirty white to beige facial disc is rimmed with small, dark and light, pearl-like spots. White patches on scapulars form a row across the shoulder. Flight feathers conspicuously barred. Dark brown tail, with 5–7 pale gray bars. VOICE: Male emits a deep *wuhu, huwuho-huwuho*, with a pause of 2–3 seconds after the first double note. Courting pairs duet; the female answers the male's hoot with a hoarse bark. Both sexes give a heron-like *kraoh* or yapping *wau-wau* when alarmed.
HABITS: Roosts during the day in dense foliage or next to a tree trunk. Active mainly at night, with peaks at dusk and just before dawn. Hunts from perches. Feeds largely on voles, shrews, mice, rats; also takes birds, frogs, insects, and mammals up to the size of small hares. Caches surplus food at or near the nest. High nesting site and mate fidelity. Nests in large holes in trees, snags, hollow trunks, fissures in cliffs, holes in buildings, and nest boxes; occasionally usurps tree nests of larger birds or squirrels.

Cuculiformes: Cuckoos and Allies
This order includes about 170 species of near-passerine, mostly subtropical to tropical birds, including cuckoos, coucals, roadrunners, turacos, and hoatzins.

FAMILY CUCULIDAE
CUCKOOS
Cuckoos have downward-curved bills, pointed wings, and long tails. They can be mistaken for small falcons in flight. Most species occur in woodland and forests. They forage in trees, bushes, and on the ground, taking insects, insect larvae, and sometimes small reptiles.

Some cuckoo species raise their own young, but most are *brood parasites*. In these species, the female lays her eggs one at a time in the nests of other birds, including small songbirds. The

Oriental Cuckoo
Cuculus optatus
Siberia, e Asia
L 12–12.5 in (30–32 cm)

juv.

ad. ♂

ad. ♀
Gray
morph

ad. ♀
Rufous
morph

ad. ♂

ad. ♀
Rufous
morph

Common Cuckoo
Cuculus canorus
Eurasia
L 12–13 in (30–33 cm)

female cuckoo removes one egg from the host's nest and replaces it with her own egg. Different females within a population parasitize different host species, and each female's eggs closely mimic those of its selected host. Hosts sometimes recognize the alien egg and abandon the nest, but many will incubate it to hatching. The cuckoo hatchling uses a scoop-like depression on its back to shove the host's eggs or young out of the nest. The host adults then face the monumental task of satisfying the cuckoo chick's gargantuan appetite, as it grows to 2–3 times the size of its foster parents before it fledges, at 17–19 days.

GENUS *CUCULUS*
Common Cuckoo
Cuculus canorus
ALSO: European Cuckoo, Kuckuck, Coucou gris, Gjøk, Обыкновенная кукушка. CN is onomatopoeic for the male's call, *cuck-coo*. SN means "melodious cuckoo."
RANGE: Breeds (May–Jun) in forests and woodland thickets in the UK and across most of Eurasia. Winters in Africa and s Asia.
ID: L 12–13 in (30–33 cm). AD ♂: Gray head and back. Underparts off-white with narrow dark bars; tail underside dark with white scallops. Iris yellow. Yellow orbital ring. Legs yellow orange.

AD ♀: Gray and rufous morphs; rufous morph occurs only occasionally in adult females but often in juveniles. GRAY ♀ is paler than male and has fine buff barring on the throat. RUFOUS ♀ is brownish red above, with barred back; no barring on rump. Underparts whitish with narrow dark barring. JUV: Dark grayish brown, barred with white. White nape patch. VOICE: Male emits a repetitive *cuck-coo,* given from an open perch as it raises tail and lowers wings. Female gives a loud bubbling trill, *klee-klee-klee.*
HABITS: Solitary. Obligate brood parasite; female lays her eggs in the nests of thrushes, robins, wagtails, pipits, and flycatchers.

Oriental Cuckoo
Cuculus optatus

ALSO: Horsfield's Cuckoo, Horsfieldkuckuck, Coucou oriental, Taigagjøk, Глухая кукушка. SN means "welcome cuckoo."
RANGE: Breeds (May–Jun) in damp coniferous and mixed forests from the Pechora Rvr, Siberia, east to Kamchatka and e Asia. Winters from Indonesia to Australia.
ID: L 12–12.5 in (30–32 cm). AD ♂: Gray head, neck, and back. Underparts off-white with bold dark barring; vent is often buff, with a few dark bars; tail underside pale gray. Iris brown.

Yellow orbital ring. Legs and feet orange yellow. AD ♀: Rufous and gray morph; rufous is more common. RUFOUS ♀ is reddish brown above, with strong dark barring. Whitish, densely barred underparts. GRAY ♀ resembles male but has a brownish wash on the breast. Both sexes are very similar to *C. canorus* but are more slender-bodied and often show a buffy

vent. VOICE: Male emits a series of low paired notes, *poo-poo, poo-poo, poo-poo, poo-poo,* with both notes stressed equally. Female gives a deep bubbling trill. Silent outside of breeding season. HABITS: Solitary and secretive, hiding in the crowns of tall trees in damp forests. Obligate brood parasite, laying its eggs mainly in the nests of pipits and *Phylloscopus* warblers.

Piciformes: Woodpeckers and Allies

The order Piciformes (Greek for "woodpecker-like birds") encompasses a diverse group of birds, including woodpeckers, flickers, sapsuckers, wrynecks, piculets, barbets, toucans, and honeyguides.

FAMILY PICIDAE
WOODPECKERS

Woodpeckers are arboreal specialists. One often sees them moving from tree to tree in undulating flight, folding the wings against the body after each series of flaps, or climbing and drilling into tree trunks to find food and excavate nesting holes.

Drumming—the noise made as a woodpecker beats its bill against a hard, hollow surface such as a stump, dead branch, or pole—serves to declare territory during spring mating season. Single *kick*-notes are used year round to contact a mate or alert a rival to its presence.

Stiff tail feathers support the bird on vertical surfaces. The strong, chisel-shaped bill is backed by an enlarged brain case with folded frontal bones and muscles that act as shock absorbers when the bird drills into hard wood. The long extensible tongue has a barbed and sticky tip, which helps capture insects living within bark crevices and tunnels in the wood.

Most woodpecker species have strong feet with 4 toes. Two toes face forward and 2 aft; the outer rear toe is mobile and can rotate to the side to provide a strong grip on irregular surfaces. Three-toed and black woodpeckers are exceptions. They have only 3 toes; the inner rear toe is lacking.

Woodpeckers are monogamous and usually form long-term pair bonds. Most begin to breed at 1 year of age. Pairs excavate a nesting cavity in a living or dead tree. They usually show preference to trees infected with fungal heart rot, as the heat produced by the decaying heartwood shortens

the time of incubation and chick development. A rounded or oval entry hole leads to a nesting chamber usually lined with wood chips from the excavation. Northern species produce an annual clutch of 3–12 (usually 4–6) white eggs. Both sexes incubate the eggs and tend the young, which fledge in 18–28 days.

GENUS *DENDROCOPOS*
Great Spotted Woodpecker

Dendrocopos major
ALSO: Buntspecht, Pic épeiche, Flaggspett, Большой пёстрый дятел. SN means "large tree-striker."

RANGE: Nests (Apr–Jun) and resident in forest, woodland, and parks in UK, Europe, and across c Siberia to Kamchatka and Mongolia.
ID: L 9–10.5 in (23–27 cm). AD: Black and white, with a prominent oval-shaped white patch on each wing, a red patch under the tail, and a red patch on the male's nape. Sides of the face and neck off-white; crown black; a black stripe extends from bill to nape and intersects with a black line from the shoulder halfway across the breast. Flight feathers barred black and white. Central tail feathers black; outer rectrices barred black and white. Slate-colored bill. Legs greenish gray. JUV: Like adult, but with a red forecrown, white shoulder patch lightly barred with black, and pale red undertail. VOICE: Sharp *kick*. Short, very fast, rattling drum; heard in spring.
HABITS: Feeds on insects, insect larvae, conifer seeds, acorns, nuts, and occasionally bird eggs and nestlings; also visits bird feeders for suet.

Extracts conifer seeds by wedging a cone in a special bark crevice, or "anvil," before picking out seeds and discarding the cone onto a pile at the tree base. Both sexes excavate a nesting hole on an aspen, oak, or other deciduous tree that has decaying heartwood. Round entry hole located high on the trunk leads to a lined chamber 6–12 in (15–30 cm) deep. Incubation is 16 days. Young fledge at 18–21 days.

Lesser Spotted Woodpecker

Dendrocopos minor

ALSO: Kleinspecht, Pic épeichette, Dvergspett, Малый дятел. SN means "small tree-striker."

RANGE: Nests (Apr–Jun) in open woodland, orchards, and parks in UK, Europe, and across c Siberia to Kamchatka. Generally sedentary, but may be irruptive in severe winters.

ID: L 5.5–7 in (14–17 cm). AD: Black above, with white bars across wings and back. Buffy face edged in black, with broad white crescent around ear coverts. Hind crown black. Male's forecrown is red, female's buffy. Central tail feathers black; outer rectrices white with black bars. Underparts white, with fine black streaks. JUV: Underparts streaked with brown. Some red on crown. VOICE: Short, sharp *kick*. Declares territory with weak, rattling drumming and 8–15 piping notes, *piit-piit-piit-piit-piit-piit-piit-piit*.
HABITS: Forages on underside of branches at the tops of tall trees. Feeds on larvae of wood-boring beetles, aphids, and other insects. Nesting cavity is high on trunk, often 30–40 ft (9–12 m) above the ground. Adults remove wood chips from the cavity excavation, leaving a pile of chips at the tree base. Clutch is 5–8 glossy white eggs.

GENUS *DRYOCOPUS*
Black Woodpecker

Dryocopus martius

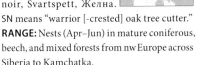

ALSO: Schwarzspecht, Pic noir, Svartspett, Желна. SN means "warrior [-crested] oak tree cutter."
RANGE: Nests (Apr–Jun) in mature coniferous, beech, and mixed forests from nw Europe across Siberia to Kamchatka.

ID: L 16–18 in (40–46 cm). Crow-sized, with a large chisel-shaped bill and powerful neck. AD: Black, with pale yellow eyes and dark-tipped pale bill. Male's slightly crested crown is crimson red; female has a black forehead and red hind crown. JUV: Dull black plumage. Crown pattern like adult of the same sex. White-tipped, pale yellow bill. Bluish gray eyes. VOICE: Loud *kakruk, kakruk, kree-kree-kree*. Nasal, shrill *klyoue* when alarmed. Very loud drum, sounding like machine-gun fire, is given mainly in spring.
HABITS: Feeds on wood-boring grubs and carpenter ants (*Camponotus* sp.) plucked out of stumps and lower trunks of living or diseased trees, especially pine and aspen. Pairs excavate a nesting cavity with an oval entry hole at a height of 16–30 ft (5–9 m) above the ground. Both sexes incubate the 2–8 white eggs for 12–14 days, and brood and feed the chicks. Young fledge at 24–28 days.

GENUS *PICOIDES*
Three-toed Woodpecker

Picoides tridactylus
Picoides dorsalis

ALSO: Dreizehenspecht, Fichtenspecht, Pic à dos rayé, Pic tridactyle, Tretåspett, Трёхпалый дятел. SN *P. tridactylus* means "three-toed woodpecker"; *P. dorsalis* means "woodpecker with [barred] back." The New and Old World populations were split in 2002. The Eurasian Three-toed Woodpecker (E) retained the name *Picoides tridactylus*, and the American Three-toed Woodpecker (A) became *P. dorsalis*. Nearly identical in appearance, the species differ in mitochondrial DNA sequences and voice. *Kick* call note of Eurasian birds is higher pitched and of shorter duration than that of N Amer birds.
RANGE: Near circumpolar. Nests (May–Jul) in spruce forest with abundant dead wood, often around swampy areas, from n Europe across Siberia to Kamchatka, and in N Amer in Alaska, w Canada, and nc US states. Locally abundant in burned or flooded forests heavily damaged by bark beetles. Generally sedentary, but northern birds may be nomadic or irruptive. Northernmost breeding woodpecker.

Back of Three-toed may be mostly white, or white with black laddering, or black with limited white markings.

ad. ♀
Three-toed

ad. ♂
Three-toed
Light back

Black Woodpecker
Dryocopus martius
Eurasia
L 16–18 in (40–46 cm)

ad. ♂

ad. ♀

ad. ♂
Three-toed
Dark back

Three-toed Woodpecker
Picoides tridactylus Eurasia
Picoides dorsalis N Amer
L 8.5–9.5 in (21–24 cm)

ad. ♀

ad. ♂

Lesser Spotted Woodpecker
Dendrocopos minor
Eurasia
L 5.5–7 in (14–17 cm)

ad. ♀

ad. ♂

Great Spotted Woodpecker
Dendrocopos major
Eurasia
L 9–10.5 in (23–27 cm)

ad. ♀

juv.

Solid black back separates
this species from dark-backed
three-toed woodpeckers.

ad. ♀
Black-
backed

ad. ♂
Black-
backed

Black-backed Woodpecker
Picoides arcticus
N Amer
L 8.5–10 in (21–25 cm)

ad. ♀

ad. ♂

Downy Woodpecker
Picoides pubescens
N Amer
L 5.5–7 in (14–18 cm)

ad. ♀

ad. ♂

Hairy Woodpecker
Picoides villosus
N Amer
L 8–10 in (20–25 cm)

ad. ♂
Yellow-shafted

ad. ♀
Yellow-shafted

ad. ♂
Red-shafted

Northern Flicker
Colaptes auratus
N Amer
L 11–12 in (28–31 cm)

ad. ♀
Red-shafted

ID: L 8.5–9.5 in (21–24 cm). Black and white woodpecker with 3 toes and a variably patterned back. Back can be white, ladder-backed, or almost completely black. In N Amer, dark-backed morph can be mistaken for the Black-backed Woodpecker, *P. arcticus*. Head black, with a narrow white supercilium, white malar stripe, and thin white line behind eye. Male's crown is yellow; female's white, with fine black streaks. Wings black, with white barring on flight feathers. Central tail feathers black; outer tail feathers white, with a few black bars. Back panel white or barred in black and white. Underparts white, with black streaks and barring on flanks. VOICE: Soft *kik* or *chik* given singly or in a loose series year round to maintain contact between a pair or family. Rattle call is a short, shrill *kli kli kli kli kli*. Drumming, which sounds like a hollow ball bouncing on wood, lasts 1–1.5 seconds, with about 8–14 strikes per second, slightly louder at the start and slightly faster toward the end. HABITS: Feeds on larvae of spruce bark beetles (Scolytidae) and other wood-boring beetle grubs; occasionally feeds on fruit and sap. Birds hammer and flake off bark in their search for food, often returning to the same tree until all the bark is stripped. Forms long-term pair bonds. Both sexes excavate a nesting cavity 5–50 ft (1.5–15 m) above the ground in a dead or dying tree. A 2 in (5 cm) round entry hole opens to a wood-chip-lined cavity 10–15 in (25–38 cm) deep. Both sexes incubate the clutch of 3–7 white eggs for about 2 weeks. Young fledge at 22–26 days.

Black-backed Woodpecker

Picoides arcticus
ALSO: Arctic Three-toed Woodpecker, Black-backed Woodie, Pic à dos noir, Schwarzrückenspecht, Svartryggspett, Североамериканский трёхпалый дятел. SN means "arctic woodpecker."
RANGE: Nests (May–Jul) in coniferous and mixed forests from c Alaska and n Canada south to California and New England. Irruptive species that forages opportunistically on outbreaks of wood-boring beetles in recently burned forests.
ID: L 8.5–10 in (21–25 cm). Black and white

woodpecker with 3 toes and a solid black back. Can be mistaken for a dark-backed Three-toed Woodpecker, *P. dorsalis*. AD: Upperparts black. Long white stripe below the eye, extending from bill to nape. Center of male's crown bright yellow; female's crown all black. Underparts white, heavily barred with black on sides and flanks. Primaries barred black and white. Outer tail feathers white. JUV: Crown dull black, with yellow crown patch reduced or absent. Underparts buffy. VOICE: Call note is a fast *click-click* that sounds like a sharp, single note in the field. Rattle call consists of 3 parts: an odd grating, a series of clicks, then a rasping snarl; rattle call often accompanies hunchbacked head-swinging, and wing-spreading displays used in territorial disputes. Drumming, given by both sexes and heard most frequently Apr–Jun, is longer than Three-toed's and distinctly accelerates.
HABITS: Feeds mostly on larvae of wood-boring longhorn beetles (Cerambycidae) and jewel beetles (Buprestidae) found in burned forests. Both sexes excavate nest in sapwood of dead or live trees and line the nest with wood chips. Both sexes incubate the 3–4 white eggs and brood the hatchlings. Young fledge at 22–25 days of age.

Downy Woodpecker

Picoides pubescens
ALSO: Dunenspecht, Pic mineur, Пушистый дятел, Tuuyuq. SN means "woodpecker with soft hairs," referring to the soft white feathers on the lower back.
RANGE: Nests (May–Jul) and resident in urban and wilderness woodlands and mixed forests from the treeline in Alaska and Canada south to Florida and s California.
ID: L 5.5–7 in (14–18 cm). Small, with a black-and-white-checkered plumage. At a distance can be mistaken for the bigger, larger-billed Hairy Woodpecker, *P. villosus*. AD: Upperparts mostly black, with white along center of back and white spots on wings; central tail feathers black; outer tail feathers white with a few black bars. Head black, with white stripes on head above and below black ear coverts. Male has a bright red spot at the back of the head. Small, pointed bill

has a tuft of bristles at base of upper mandible. Underparts white (pale buff in nw Pacific birds). JUV: Juvenile male has a dull red forecrown. VOICE: A soft *kik* or high-pitched *pik-pik-pik-pik-queek* when alarmed. Short, slow staccato drum is used to alert mate to a potential nest site.

HABITS: Actively forages on trees, shrubs, and tall weeds, often in mixed flocks with other small birds. Feeds on insects, fruit, seeds, and sap. Uses its small, chisel-shaped bill to pick tiny insect eggs from tree and leaf surfaces, and to probe for insects lying just under the bark. Sexes tend to forage separately, females on larger tree branches, males on small treetop limbs. When two birds meet on the same branch, they move to opposite sides and dance around the limb, keeping equidistant in the woodpecker version of peekaboo. Nests in trees in an advanced stage of fungal heart rot. Both sexes excavate a cavity on the underside of a dead branch, a process that can take over a week to complete. Round entry hole opens to a wood-chip-lined cavity. Both parents incubate the 3–8 glossy white eggs for 12 days. Young fledge at 18–22 days, but remain dependent on their parents for food for another 3 weeks.

Hairy Woodpecker
Picoides villosus

ALSO: Haarspecht, Hårspett, Tuuyuqpak, Pic chevelu, Волосатый дятел. SN means "shaggy-haired woodpecker," referring to the filamentous white back feathers.

RANGE: Nests (Apr–Jul) in mature forest and woodland from near the treeline in c Alaska and Canada south to Baja California, w Panama, and n Bahamas. Congregates in burned forests with bark beetle infestations.

ID: L 8–10 in (20–25 cm). Black and white, with a long, straight, chisel-like bill. Can be mistaken for a Downy Woodpecker, *P. pubescens,* a much smaller bird with a dainty bill. Upperparts mostly black, with a prominent white panel on the back. Wings black, with white coverts and white spots on the flight feathers. Central tail feathers black; outer tail feathers white in eastern birds, sometimes barred with black in the west and Newfoundland. Head black, with white stripes on head above and below black ear coverts. Bright red spot at back of male's head. Underparts white (buffy in nw Pacific and Rocky Mtns), with a comma-shaped black mark extending from the shoulder onto the breast. VOICE: Sharp, high-pitched *peek* or stuttered *peek-rr-krr* when alarmed. Rattle call is a rapid series of sharp, high-pitched notes. Loud, fast drum sounds like machine-gun fire; drums 4–9 times per minute, with a long pause after each drum.

HABITS: Forages on tree surfaces and under bark, pecking and probing for larvae of wood-boring beetles and bark beetles, ants, and moth pupae in their cocoons; also feeds on fruits and seeds. Both sexes establish and maintain territory by drumming, adding shrill cries, bill waving, and wing flicks to the display when rivals are nearby. Pairs excavate a nesting cavity on the trunk or underside of a bent tree limb of a living or dying tree or occasionally enlarge the abandoned nesting hole of a Downy Woodpecker. Oval entry hole leads to a wood-chip-lined cavity 8–12 in (20–30 cm) deep. The interior widens at the bottom to accommodate the 3–6 shiny white eggs and incubating parent. Incubation period is 11–15 days. Young fledge at 28–30 days.

GENUS *COLAPTES*
Northern Flicker
Colaptes auratus

ALSO: Goldspecht, Pic flamboyant, Guldspett, Золотой шилоклювый дятел, Tuuyusrugruk; Yellowhammer (as state bird of Alabama). SN means "gilded woodpecker."

RANGE: Nests (May–Jun) at forest edge from the treeline in Alaska and Canada south to Florida, Cuba, Grand Caymans, and C Amer. Winters from s Canada south. Ship-aided vagrant to Ireland, Scotland, Denmark.

SUBSPECIES: YELLOW-SHAFTED FLICKER (Y), *C. a. auratus*, breeds east of the Rocky Mtns from nc Alaska to Labrador and south to Texas and Gulf coast. RED-SHAFTED FLICKER (R), *C. a. cafer*, breeds in w N Amer from se Alaska and w Canada south to Mexico. HYBRIDS (H) occur in a narrow zone along the e Rocky Mtns from se Alaska to the Texas panhandle; hybrids show anomalies in moustache color, nuchal patch, and color of underwings and feather shafts.

ID: L 11–12 in (28–31 cm). Upperparts grayish brown, with irregular dark brown bars. White rump. Underparts off-white to buff, with small black spots and black crescent mark on upper breast. YELLOW-SHAFTED: Underside of wings and shafts of flight feathers yellow. Male has a black malar stripe. Male and female have a red nuchal patch. RED-SHAFTED: Underside of wings and shafts of flight feathers bright salmon. Male has a red malar stripe. Male and female lack nuchal patch. VOICE: Loud single-note *kyeer*. Sharp, rolling rattle of 7–8 seconds. Close contact call a quiet, rhythmic *wicka-wicka-wicka-wicka*. Loud, evenly spaced, rapid drumming is made by hammering against trees or metal objects such as poles and roof gutters.

HABITS: Forages on bare ground or in short grass near woodland edge. Probes and hammers in soil with its powerful bill, then uses its long sticky tongue to capture adult and larval ants and beetles. Feeds on berries and seeds in fall and winter. Diet furnishes yellow, orange, and red pigments (carotenoids) that color the feathers. During mating season, flickers flash their bright underwings at rivals or pair off on branches in mock fencing duels, using their bills as foils. The dance, often interrupted by long pauses and *wicka-wicka* calls, may last 30 minutes or more until one bird flies off in defeat. Pairs excavate a cavity in an aspen (*Populus tremuloides*) or other tree that has decaying heartwood. Both sexes incubate the 3–7 lustrous white eggs for 11–12 days. Young fledge at 24–27 days.

Coraciiformes: Kingfishers and Allies

Coraciiformes (Latin for "raven-like") contains a diverse group of near-passerine birds, including kingfishers, bee-eaters, rollers, and hornbills.

FAMILY CERYLIDAE
KINGFISHERS

The six species of American kingfishers are known as water or cerylid kingfishers. They are fish-eating birds that plunge dive into the water after prey, often after hovering. The outer and middle toes of the kingfisher's foot are partially joined. This anatomy makes for a foot more suited to perching than grasping prey.

GENUS *MEGACERYLE*
Belted Kingfisher
Megaceryle alcyon

ALSO: Halcyon, Gürtelfischer, Martin-pêcheur d'Amérique, Belteisfugl, опоясанный пегий зимородок, Nukuutchiqiq. SN means "large cerylid kingfisher."

RANGE: Nests (Apr–Jul) in Alaska, Canada, and nc US. Moves to ice-free areas in autumn, wintering in the Aleutians, Brit Columbia, and south to s US, W Indies, C Amer, and n S Amer. Vagrant to Greenland, Ireland, UK, Netherlands, Portugal, Azores, Galapagos, and Hawaii.

ID: L 11–14 in (28–36 cm). Stocky, with a large head and ragged, double-tufted crest. Back bluish gray, with a nearly complete white nuchal collar. Upperwing grayish blue, with a patch of white spots at base of primaries; underwing whitish. Tail finely barred. AD ♂: Underparts white, with a single bluish gray band across the breast. AD ♀: Underparts white, with a double band across breast; upper band bluish gray; lower

ad. ♀

ad. ♂

Belted Kingfisher
Megaceryle alcyon
N Amer
L 11–14 in (28–36 cm)

band rufous, with rufous color extending along the flanks. VOICE: Strident, mechanical rattle. **HABITS:** Feeds on small fish, mollusks, crustaceans, insects, amphibians, reptiles, young birds, small mammals, and berries. Perches on trees, low branches, or posts. Dives headfirst into clear, shallow water and grabs fish in its bill. Flies to a perch and pounds prey against the perch to stun it, then turns the fish and swallows it headfirst.

Nests in a horizontal tunnel up to 6.5 ft (2 m) long made in a bare riverbank or sandbank. Both sexes dig out the tunnel using the bill to loosen the soil and the feet to shovel the soil out of the hole. The tunnel ends in a unlined chamber where the female lays 5–8 pure white, glossy eggs. Both adults incubate the eggs for 22–24 days. The female broods the hatchlings for the first week. The male initially regurgitates partially digested fish for the nestlings. Later both parents bring whole fish to the burrow for the young.

Although the adults do not provide any nest sanitation, the burrow stays relatively clean. Chicks eject liquid excreta onto the chamber wall, then use the bill to hammer down some earth from above, thus burying the excreta while enlarging the nesting chamber and giving themselves room to grow. Fledglings leave the burrow at about 1 month of age. Adults continue to feed them for another 3 weeks, then the young disperse.

Apodiformes: Swifts and Allies

The order Apodiformes (Greek for "footless birds") contains the swifts, Asian treeswifts, and hummingbirds, which are alternatively placed in their own order, Trochiliformes.

FAMILY APODIDAE
SWIFTS

Swifts are black to dark brown aerial foragers, with torpedo-shaped bodies, long sickle-shaped wings, forked or rounded tails, and a small bill with a big gape. All 4 toes of the *Apus* species face forward. The feet are small, weak, and of limited function. Swifts are able to cling to vertical surfaces and nests, but are helpless on the ground; they cannot take off from a flat surface. Thus, these birds spend most of the day in the air, feeding on insects caught in flight. Flocks circle through the insect swarms on swept-back wings, looking much like high-altitude fighter jets. Swifts are among the fastest fliers in the animal kingdom. Some of the larger species can attain speeds of 100 mph (160 kmh) or more. Fast, effortless flight is indispensable to the highly migratory species, which may travel over 50,000 mi (85,000 km) each year as they forage and move between the hemispheres.

Most swift species nest in colonies, and pairs often breed together for many years. The far northern species build a nest of feathers and dry grass, cemented with saliva and attached to a wall or placed in a rock crevice or tree hole. Both adults incubate the clutch of 2–3 eggs for 17–20 days. Nestlings are fed small rounded boluses of insects, which the adults transport in the throat. During sustained periods of cold weather, when insects are scarce, the chicks may not be fed for days. Like the adults, they can slow their metabolism and survive on stored body fat.

GENUS *APUS*
Common Swift

Apus apus
ALSO: Northern Swift, Mauersegler, Martinet noir, Tårnseiler, Чёрный стриж. SN means "footless," referring to the small feet.

RANGE: Nests (May–Jul) in the UK and n Europe, east across subarctic Russia to China, and south to n Africa. Winters in Africa.

ID: L 6.75–7.25 in (17–19 cm). Blackish brown, except for a small whitish patch on the chin (visible on bird in hand). VOICE: Harsh, squealing scream, *vzz-vzz*, often heard on summer evenings when flocks of swifts gather in flight around their nesting area, calling out and being answered by other swifts on the nest.

HABITS: Forages in large flocks, taking small flying insects. Allegedly mates in flight and ascends to high altitudes to sleep on the wing. Returns to natal colony each year to mate. Nests in tree holes, rock crevices, or under house eaves. Both sexes incubate the clutch of 2–3 eggs for

19–20 days. Adults feed the nestlings for about 42 days, during which time adults have been recorded making foraging flights of up to 560 mi (900 km). Maximum known lifespan is 21 years.

Pacific Swift
Apus pacificus
ALSO: Fork-tailed or White-rumped Swift, Pazifiksegler, Martinet de Sibérie, Gaffelseiler, Белопоясный стриж. SN means "Pacific swift."
RANGE: Nests (Jun) in mountains and towns from c Siberia east to Sea of Okhotsk. Winters in Indonesia, Melanesia, Australia. Casual in the Pribilofs and Aleutians. Vagrant to Brunei, Maldives, NZ, and Macquarie Is (Australia).
ID: L 6.75–7 in (17–18 cm). Upper parts black, with a dark gray head, white rump, and deeply forked black tail. Underparts brownish black, scaled with white. Long, narrow, sickle-shaped wings are black above, brown below. VOICE: Shrill, high-pitched *spee-err* given in flight.
HABITS: Forages in flocks, feeding on insects caught in flight at heights up to 1000 ft (300 m); flies close to the ground only in poor weather. Nests in caves and rock crevices in mountains, or under roof eaves of city buildings. Both adults incubate the eggs for 17 days. The young fledge in 40–41 days.

Passeriformes: Perching Birds
Passeriformes (Latin for "sparrow-like birds") is one of the most diverse terrestrial vertebrate orders. It contains more than half of all bird species, with 5000 identified species in 110 families. This is roughly twice as many species as the largest of the mammal orders, the Rodentia. Birds in this order are known as passerines or perching birds, and some as songbirds.

FAMILY HIRUNDINIDAE
SWALLOWS AND MARTINS
Swallows and martins are often confused with swifts, which hunt in similar ways. Both are aerial foragers that feed on insects caught in flight. However, swifts spend most of the day in flight, while swallows perch and rest between short foraging flights. The main reason for this behavioral difference is due to dissimilarities in leg and foot structure. Swifts have small, weak feet and legs more suited to clinging to vertical surfaces than perching. The legs are so weak that swifts cannot push off from the ground, but must launch themselves into the air from an elevated surface. It is no wonder that these birds spend most of their time in flight and never voluntarily land on the ground. In contrast, the swallows' legs and feet are adapted to perching. Swallows are able to rest on utility lines, fence wires, and branches and often can be seen on the ground gathering mud for their nests.

Like the swifts, swallows and martins pursue and catch insects on the wing. They fly at speeds of 20–25 mph (30–40 kmh) when foraging and can attain speeds of up to 40 mph (65 kmh) when migrating. Their small, streamlined bodies and long, pointed wings allow great maneuverability and endurance, enabling them to twist, wheel, and dive after rapidly moving prey. Their small heads and short necks do not create drag, and their short, flat bills and wide mouths are ideal for snatching insects out of the air.

Swallows and martins nest in closed spaces such as tree cavities, holes in sandy banks, or in deeply cupped nests built from mud and other debris. Some species nest in colonies, others in isolated pairs. Northern species produce a single clutch of 4–6 white, beige, or speckled eggs, which are incubated for about 12–14 days. The young leave the nest at 16–24 days, but often assemble in nursery groups near their nest site and wait for their parents to feed them.

GENUS *HIRUNDO*
Barn Swallow
Hirundo rustica
ALSO: Rauchschwalbe, Låvesvale, Hirondelle rustique, Деревенская ласточка, Tulugagnasrugruk. SN means "rustic swallow." National bird of Austria and Estonia. Symbol of spring awakening and revival of life.

Common Swift
Apus apus
Eurasia
L 6.75–7.25 in (17–19 cm)

Pacific Swift
Apus pacificus
NE Asia
L 6.75–7 in (17–18 cm)

Apus apus

Apus pacificus

Barn Swallow
Hirundo rustica
Near circumpolar
L 5.5–6 in (14–15 cm)

Bank Swallow
Riparia riparia
Near circumpolar
L 4.75–5 in (12–13 cm)

Cliff Swallow
Petrochelidon pyrrhonota
N Amer
L 5–6 in (13–15 cm)

Violet-green Swallow
Tachycineta thalassina
N Amer
L 4.75–5 in (12–13 cm)

House Martin
Delichon urbicum
Eurasia
L 5–6 in (13–15 cm)

ad.

juv.

Tree Swallow
Tachycineta bicolor
N Amer
L 5.5–6 in (14–15 cm)

RANGE: Near circumpolar. Most widespread swallow species. Nests (May–Jul) throughout most of N Amer, Europe, and Asia. Winters south to S Amer, Africa, Middle East, India, Indochina, Malaysia, and Australia.
ID: L 5.5–6 in (14–15 cm), plus 1–2 in (3–5 cm) adult tail streamers. AD ♂: Steel blue upperparts. Rufous forehead, chin and throat, separated from buff to rufous underparts by a dark blue breast band. Deeply forked tail, with elongated outer tail feathers and a line of subterminal white spots. AD ♀: Short tail streamers; blue upperparts less glossy and underparts paler than male's. JUV: Browner than adult, with a pale rufous face and whitish underparts; lacks tail streamers. VOICE: Musical twittering interspersed by husky chatter; when excited, sounds a loud *splee-plink*.
HABITS: Forages and roosts in flocks. Sunbathes on the ground. Feeds on crane flies, horseflies, and robber flies caught in flight at heights up to 80 ft (25 m). Flies straight for some distance, then makes sharp dives and turns. Nests in colonies. Collects mud, grass, and feathers from puddles and streambanks, using materials to build a cup-shaped mud nest almost exclusively on man-made structures such as barn eaves and bridges.

GENUS *RIPARIA*
Bank Swallow
Riparia riparia
ALSO: Sand Martin, Ufer-

schwalbe, Hirondelle de rivage, Sandsvale, Береговая ласточка, Tulugabnaq. SN means "[swallow that nests on] streambanks."
RANGE: Near circumpolar. Nests (May–Jul) in N Amer and Eurasia. Winters in S Hemisphere.
ID: L 4.75–5 in (12–13 cm). Grayish brown upperparts and breast band. Flight feathers brownish black. Throat, breast, and belly white. Slightly notched tail. VOICE: Harsh twittering.
HABITS: Forages and roosts in flocks. Migrates in mixed-species flocks with cliff, tree, and barn swallows. Takes gnats and other small flying insects when in flight over water or open ground at heights up to 50 ft (15 m); also picks aquatic insects and larvae from water surface. Nests in

colonies. Excavates long tunnels in sand or gravel riverbanks and quarry walls. Male digs out the tunnel with bill, then kicks out loose material with the feet. Female lines nesting chamber with dry grass and feathers and incubates eggs for 13–16 days. Nestlings are fed an estimated 7000 insects before fledging at 18–22 days.

GENUS *DELICHON*
House Martin
Delichon urbicum
ALSO: Mehlschwalbe, Hiron-

delle de fenêtre, Taksvale, Воронок. CN honors the French saint Martin of Tours (316–397), whose feast day, Martinmas, is Nov 11, about the time these birds begin to migrate south. SN means "urban swallow."
RANGE: Nests (May–Jun) across Eurasia, east to Kamchatka, south to N Africa and temperate Asia. Winters in sub-Saharan Africa and tropical Asia.
ID: L 5–6 in (13–15 cm). AD: Steel blue head and back, with a conspicuous white rump and dark brown forked tail and upperwings. Underparts white, including underwings. Top of short legs feathered in white; feet and exposed parts of legs pink. JUV: Sooty black upperparts; wing coverts edged in white. VOICE: Soft twitter of melodious chirps. Alarm call is a ringing *teerch-teerch*.
HABITS: Feeds in flocks, taking insects in flight. Usually nests in colonies. Collects mud for nests at shallow ground pools. Builds a round mud nest with a side entrance under building eaves and on alpine cliffs to 7200 ft (2200 m).

GENUS *PETROCHELIDON*
Cliff Swallow
Petrochelidon pyrrhonota
ALSO: Fahlstirnschwalbe,

Hirondelle à front blanc, Mursvale, Белолобая горная ласточка, Tulugabnaq. SN means "rock swallow with a russet back."
RANGE: Nests (May–Jun) across most of Alaska and Canada, north to James Bay in the east, near the arctic coast in the west, and south throughout the contiguous US. Migrates in flocks of thousands along the C Amer isthmus, wintering south to s S Amer, east of the Andes.

ID: L 5–6 in (13–15 cm). AD: Back, wings, head, and square tail slaty black. Buffy rump. Throat and face rusty red, with a buffy or white forehead. Buffy to white underparts. JUV: Head and throat dark gray. VOICE: Thin, high-pitched rattle.

HABITS: Flocks feed on flying insects taken over fields, marshes, rivers, ponds, and towns at heights of 165 ft (50 m) or more. Nests in colonies. Collects mud for nests at shallow ground pools. Both sexes build nest, sticking up to 1000 small mud pellets together, forming a gourd-shaped structure on cliff faces, walls, building eaves, or bridges. Nest construction can take a week.

GENUS *TACHYCINETA*
Tree Swallow
Tachycineta bicolor

ALSO: White-Breasted Swallow, Sumpfschwalbe, Hirondelle bicolore, Tresvale, Древесная американская ласточка, Tulugagnaurak. SN means "fast-flying bicolored [swallow]."

RANGE: Nests (May–Jun) in nc Alaska and Canada, south to New England, Great Lakes, Rockies, Pacific coast. Winters in Florida, Caribbean, Mexico, n C Amer. Vagrant to w Europe.

ID: L 5.5–6 in (14–15 cm). AD: Iridescent bluish green above, white below, with a very slightly forked tail. JUV: Dull grayish brown above, white below, sometimes with a faint gray breast band. VOICE: Clear, sweet whistles, chirps, and twitters. **HABITS:** Isolated pairs nest near water in tree cavities lined with grass, twigs, and feathers, and also use abandoned sapsucker holes and nest boxes. Dive bombs intruders approaching the nest. Gregarious outside of breeding season, forming roosting flocks of several thousand birds.

Violet-green Swallow
Tachycineta thalassina

ALSO: Veilchenschwalbe, Hirondelle à face blanche, Talassinsvale, Фиолетово-зелёная американская ласточка. SN means "fast-flying sea-green [swallow]."

RANGE: Nests (May–Jul) in mountain forests of w N Amer, from c Alaska and w Canada south to Mexico. Winters in C Amer highlands.

ID: L 4.75–5 in (12–13 cm). AD: Emerald green to greenish bronze back, with some purplish violet on the nape and uppertail coverts. Ear coverts and underparts white. White patch on each side of rump, sometimes appears to form a continuous white band across the rump. JUV: Grayish above. White below. VOICE: Faint *chee-chee* sounded mainly at daybreak.

HABITS: Feeds on insects caught in flight, often at considerable heights. Nests in isolated pairs or small colonies in alpine forests, using abandoned woodpecker holes, rock crevices, nest boxes, or occasionally in a hole in a sandbank. Highly social outside of breeding season, forming flocks of several hundred birds.

FAMILY CORVIDAE
RAVENS, CROWS, MAGPIES, AND JAYS
Members of this family are large, bold, noisy, and aggressive, often mobbing cats, dogs, foxes, and birds of prey much bigger than themselves. Notable feats of problem solving, some rivaling those of primates, have been observed among these highly intelligent birds. Crows, for example, have been seen shaping and using tools to spear and lift food from otherwise inaccessible places.

Corvids are omnivorous, eating seeds, plants, insects, small mammals, the eggs and young of other birds, carrion, garbage, and scraps scavenged at campgrounds. Many species cache food for later use and months later are able to locate their hoards, even under deep snow.

Some species engage in a behavior called *anting*, in which they rub ants on their feathers. The ants secrete chemicals, such as formic acid, which act as an insecticide or fungicide and possibly supplement the bird's own preen oil. Anting birds assume unusual poses such as spreading their wings on the ground and fanning the tail while cricking the neck.

Most species begin to breed at 3–5 years of age. Breeding is monogamous, and pairs often mate for life. Corvids nest in trees or on rock ledges in an open or covered pile of sticks. Both sexes gather nesting material, but the female does most of the construction. The female incubates the 3–8 bluish green, spotted eggs for 17–20 days while the male brings food to the nest. Young fledge at 18–40 days. Parents continue to feed the young for several weeks after fledging and some remain as a family unit until the next breeding season.

GENUS *CORVUS*
Common Raven
Corvus corax

ALSO: Kolkrabe, Grand Corbeau, Ravn, Korp, Ворон, Tulugaq. SN means "raven raven." Official bird of Yukon Territory and city of Yellowknife, Canada. Revered as a spiritual figure or prophet in many indigenous cultures. Native American lore depicts the Raven as a key creation figure, a shaman, and a trickster.
RANGE: Circumpolar. Nests (Mar–Jun) and largely resident through most of the Holarctic. Most widely distributed of all the corvids.
ID: L 22–27 in (56–67 cm). Entirely black. Heavy, arched, dark bill. Shaggy "beard" (conspicuous when bird is calling). Wedge-shaped, tapered tail. **VOICE:** Resonant, far-carrying croak, *kro-kro,* given while soaring or perched; also calls *wonk-wonk* and emits repetitive *knocks* that sound like a woodpecker's drumming.
HABITS: Flies with fluid, even wingbeats. Soars on thermals and updrafts. Performs aerial acrobatics and sometimes hangs upside down from a perch, apparently in play. Feeds on carrion, eggs, insects, amphibians, small mammals, grains, and fruit; snatches groceries from truck beds and scraps from sealed garbage cans. In the Arctic, feeds on lemmings and accompanies wolves scavenging caribou carcasses in winter. Builds a moss-lined nest of sticks on cliff ledges or occasionally in tall trees.
SIMILAR SPECIES: AMERICAN CROW, *Corvus brachyrhynchos,* breeds across much of temperate N Amer. Distinguished from the raven by smaller size, smaller bill, and rounded tail.

Carrion Crow
Corvus corone

ALSO: Aaskrähe, Corneille noire, Svartkråke, Черная ворона. SN means "raven crow." Formerly conspecific with *C. cornix.*

RANGE: Nests (Mar–May) in open woodland, on moors, and around habitation. Separate populations exist in w Europe and in e Siberia; the two probably separated during the last ice age, after which the allied Hooded Crow, *C. cornix,* filled the gap between.
ID: L 17.5–20 in (44–51 cm). Plumage black with a green or purple sheen. Black bill, legs, and feet.
VOICE: Loud croaks and caws, *kraa kraa,* given 3–4 times in quick succession; calls from treetops.
HABITS: Flies with slow, deliberate wingbeats. Forms large, noisy communal roosts in winter. Displays anting behavior. Feeds on carrion, insects, earthworms, grain, small mammals, bird eggs, household scraps, and garbage. Harasses birds of prey and foxes for their kills. Builds a bulky stick nest in tall trees, on cliff ledges, and on old buildings. Incubation is 18–20 days. Young fledge at 29–30 days. Some remain with parents to the next spring and help raise the new brood.

Hooded Crow
Corvus cornix

ALSO: Scotch Crow, Danish Crow, Gray Crow, Corbie, Hoodie, Nebelkrähe, Corneille mantelée, Kråke, Серая ворона, *Corvus corone cornix.* SN means "raven crow."
RANGE: Nests (Mar–May) in open woodland, moors, farms, and towns in n UK, n Ireland, and n Europe east to w Siberia. Vagrant to Iceland.
ID: L 17.5–20 in (44–51 cm). Ashy gray body; black head, throat, wings, tail, and thighs. **VOICE:** Loud croaks and caws, *kraa kraa.*
HABITS: Omnivorous. Builds a nest of twigs, moss, and mud, lined with feathers and bark, in a tree at heights of 15–80 ft (5–25 m). Incubation is 17–21 days. Young fledge at 31–32 days.

GENUS *PICA*
Black-billed Magpie
Pica pica (Eurasia)
Pica hudsonia (N Amer)

ALSO: Eurasian Magpie, Elster, Pie bavarde, Skjære, Сорока; American Magpie, Hudsonelster, Pie d'Amérique, Svartnebbskjære, Американская сорока. SN *Pica* means "magpie"; *hudsonia* means "of Hudson

American Crow
Corvus brachyrhynchos
N Amer
L 16–21 in (40–53 cm)

Common Raven
Corvus corax
Circumpolar
L 22–27 in (56–67 cm)

Carrion Crow
Corvus corone
Siberia, Europe
L 17.5–20 in (44–51 cm)

American
Magpie

Eurasian
Magpie

Hooded Crow
Corvus cornix
Eurasia
L 17.5–20 in (44–51 cm)

Black-billed Magpie
Pica pica Eurasia
Pica hudsonia N Amer
L 16–20 in (40–51 cm)

Bay." CN is a combination of the 16th-century word *mag*, meaning "chatterer," and *pie*, meaning "pied [plumage]." Collectively called a *charm, gulp, mischief, tittering,* or *tribe* of magpies. Folklore links magpies with the devil and says one must always cross oneself upon seeing a magpie. Legend also relates that the magpie refused to enter Noah's ark and instead sat on the roof and swore for the duration of the flood. **RANGE:** Nests (Apr–Jul) around open woodland, brush-covered fields, and farms. *Pica pica* (E) is resident from the UK and Europe to Siberia and Kamchatka. *Pica hudsonia* (A) is resident from Alaska and Yukon south through w N Amer. **ID:** L 16–20 in (40–51 cm), including 8–12 in (20–30 cm) tail. AD: Pied plumage. Very long, graduated tail. Dark, stout bill. Head, neck, breast, back, and rump black. Green, blue, and violet iridescence on wings and tail. Wing coverts white. Primaries white with dark tips. White belly and flanks. Compared with the Eurasian

Magpie, *P. hudsonia* has a more slender build, longer tail and wings, thinner bill, and narrow whitish ring around the iris. JUV: Upperparts dull brown, belly cream. Milky gray iris. **VOICE:** Loud, harsh, repetitive chatter, *maag-maag-maag* or *shek-shek-shek.* Whining, rising *mea* or drawn-out, questioning *meeaaah.* Calls of *P. hudsonia* are much faster than those of *P. pica.* **HABITS:** Seen in pairs, family flocks of 6–10 birds, or large noisy flocks. Flies with shallow, steady wingbeats. Walks and hops while on the ground. Sunbathes and "ants" with head down, wings drooped, tail fanned, and back feathers erected. Feeds on carrion, insects, and ticks picked off deer and livestock. Caches excess food. Steals brightly colored objects. Male builds a bulky domed nest of twigs; female shapes and lines the mud eggcup at the nest bottom. Construction can take 5–7 weeks. Female incubates the 4–9 dull green, brown-speckled eggs for 18–25 days. Young fledge in 24–30 days.

GENUS *NUCIFRAGA*
Spotted Nutcracker
Nucifraga caryocatactes
ALSO: Eurasian Nutcracker, Casse-noix moucheté, Tannenhäher, Nøttekråke, Кедровка. SN means "nutcracker that shatters nuts."

RANGE: Nests (Mar–Apr) in spruce and pine forests from Fennoscandia to Kamchatka.
ID: L 12.5–14 in (32–36 cm). Chocolate brown; heavily spotted with white on face, neck, mantle, and underparts. Dark brown cap and nape. White loral spot and eyering. Broad wings. Dark tail, with white corners above, white terminal band below. White vent. Legs and feet black. Pointed black bill; Siberian birds typically have slender bills, while many European birds have thick bills with a special ridge on the inner edge—an adaptation for cracking hard-shelled hazelnuts.
VOICE: Drawn-out, harsh, rolling *krrrreh*.
HABITS: Flies with fluttering wingbeats. Winters in areas having nut-bearing hazel or pine trees. Caches nuts for winter consumption; also feeds on insects, small birds, bird eggs and nestlings, small rodents, and carrion. Picks grubs out of bee and wasp nests. Shy and wary when breeding. Builds a nest of twigs, decaying wood, juniper bark, and lichen, lined with dry grass. Both sexes incubate the 3–5 dark-spotted, greenish eggs for 18–19 days. Young fledge in 24–26 days, but stay with their parents for many months, learning nut-storage techniques essential for survival in their harsh environment.

GENUS *PERISOREUS*
Gray Jay
Perisoreus canadensis
ALSO: Whisky Jack, Camp Robber, Moose Bird, Caribou

Bird, Hudson Bay Bird, Canada Jay, Oregon Jay, Labrador Jay, Rocky Mtn Jay, Kiiriq, Meisenhäher, Mésangeai du Canada, Gråskrike, Канадская кукша. SN means "jay of Canada."
RANGE: Nests (Feb–Apr) in coniferous forests from Alaska and Labrador south to n California, Great Lakes, and through the Rocky Mtns to New Mexico. Generally sedentary.
ID: L 11–12 in (27–30 cm). Loose, fluffy, gray

plumage. Blackish crown, nape, and back; amount of black on head varies geographically. Forehead, neck, and upper breast whitish; rest of underparts gray. Nares covered by feathers; bill appears short. Primaries narrowly tipped with white. Bill, legs, and feet black. **VOICE:** Soft, whistled *weeoo* and *weef weef weef;* also a husky, dry *chef chef chef.*
HABITS: Tame and confiding. Flies with slow wingbeats interspersed with glides. Feeds on insects, berries, carrion, nestling birds, fungi, bird feeder offerings, and food scraps cadged from campers. Wades in shallow water to capture small amphibians. Hoards food under tree bark scales and lichens, using sticky saliva from its enlarged salivary glands. Nests early, often when temperatures are still below freezing. Builds a bulky nest of twigs in a conifer 13–85 ft (4–26 m) above the ground. Lines nest with bark, feathers, hair, and silky cocoons of forest tent moths (*Malacosoma disstria*) pried from under tree bark. Female incubates the 2–5 pale greenish gray, dark-spotted eggs for 18–19 days. Parents feed nestlings a dark brown, viscous paste composed of insects. Young fledge at 23 days and remain with the parents until early June. At that time, the dominant fledgling expels siblings from the territory. Evicted juveniles often join unrelated adults whose own nesting has failed.

Siberian Jay
Perisoreus infaustus
ALSO: Boreal Jay, Northern Jay, Red-tailed Jay, Unglückshäher, Mésangeai imitateur,

Lavskrike, Кукша. SN means "bird of ill omen," a misnomer, as this species is favorably regarded.
RANGE: Nests (Mar–Apr) in dense coniferous forests from n Europe across Siberia to Anadyr and Sea of Okhotsk. Non-migratory, but nomadic.
ID: L 10–12 in (26–30 cm). Grayish brown above; dark brown crown and wings; rufous wing patches; rufous tail with brown median stripe. Nares covered with buffy feathers. Throat and breast gray; flanks tinged with rufous. **VOICE:** Mewing *geeaih* and low, whistled *kook-kook.*
HABITS: Silent and shy when nesting, otherwise tame and confiding. Flies with tail fanned

Shown on
Siberian Dwarf Pine,
Pinus pumila

Spotted Nutcracker
Nucifraga caryocatactes
Eurasia
L 12.5–14 in (32–36 cm)

Eurasian Jay
Garrulus glandarius
Eurasia
L 12.5–14 in (32–36 cm)

Steller's Jay
Cyanocitta stelleri
N Amer
L 11–12 in (27–30 cm)

Siberian Jay
Perisoreus infaustus
Eurasia
L 10–12 in (26–30 cm)

Gray Jay
Perisoreus canadensis
N Amer
L 11–12 in (27–30 cm)

Great Gray Shrike
Lanius excubitor
Near circumpolar
L 9–10 in (22–26 cm)

Brown Shrike
Lanius cristatus
Siberia–e Asia
L 7–8 in (18–20 cm)

out. Feeds on insects, seeds, berries, bird eggs and chicks, carrion, scraps of food scavenged at campgrounds. Forages in trees and on the ground. Builds a feather-lined nest of spruce twigs and beard lichen in conifers at heights of 6-30 ft (2-10 m). Female incubates the 3-5 greenish gray, mottled eggs for 18-20 days. Young fledge at 18-23 days but are fed by the female for another 3 weeks before they disperse.

GENUS *GARRULUS*
Eurasian Jay
Garrulus glandarius

ALSO: Acorn Jay, Black-throated Jay, Eichelhäher, Geai des chênes, Nøtteskrike, Сойка. SN means "chattering acorn-gatherer."
RANGE: Nests (Apr–May) in wooded areas from the UK and Europe east across c Siberia to Sakhalin, s Kurils, and Japan.
ID: L 12.5–14 in (32–36 cm). Pinkish brown back and chest, black tail, and white rump. Bright blue and black barring, and white patches on wings. Black moustache. Black bill. Pale blue iris. Legs pale brown. VOICE: Loud, harsh screech, *chzhe-chzhe*; also a good mimic.
HABITS: Silent and wary when nesting, otherwise noisy and confiding. Omnivorous. Builds a loosely constructed nest of twigs lined with root fibers in a conifer at heights of 5–30 ft (1.5–9 m). Female incubates the 4–9 brown-spotted greenish eggs for 16–18 days. Young fledge at 19–22 days and remain with their parents for another 3 weeks.

GENUS *CYANOCITTA*
Steller's Jay
Cyanocitta stelleri

ALSO: Long-crested Jay, Mountain Jay, Pine Jay, Diademhäher, Geai de Steller, Furuskrike, Стеллерова черноголовая голубая сойка. SN means "Steller's dark blue jay," referring to German naturalist Georg Wilhelm Steller (1709–1746). Steller joined Vitus Bering's 1741 exploration of the seas east of Kamchatka, signing on as surgeon-naturalist aboard the *St Peter*. When the ship reached Kayak Is (near present-day Cordova, Alaska), Steller was allowed only a few hours ashore to collect specimens, one of which was a dark-crested jay unknown to Eurasian ornithology. Struck with the similarity to the painting of a Blue Jay, *Cyanocitta cristata,* he had seen in Mark Catesby's *Natural History of Carolina,* Steller was convinced that the expedition had reached the New World. Steller's specimens were lost when the *St Peter* was wrecked in the Commander Is, but his field notes made it back to St Petersburg, where in 1788 the German naturalist Johann Gmelin used them to formally describe Steller's Crow (now Steller's Jay).
RANGE: Nests (Apr–Jun) in coniferous and mixed forests and parkland of w N Amer from Alaska south to Nicaragua.
ID: L 11–12 in (27–30 cm). Vibrant dark blue, with a blackish head, crest, and upper breast, and small, light blue streaks on forehead. Wings deep blue. Tail blue; tail tip narrowly barred with black. Dark eyes, bill, and legs. VOICE: Loud, harsh squawks and growls, and low, warbling song. Mimics calls of mammals and birds, and sounds of sprinklers, telephones, and squeaky doors.
HABITS: Forms small, noisy groups. Feeds on nuts, seeds, acorns, berries, insects, eggs and young of small birds, bird feeder offerings, and scraps cadged from campers. Builds a bulky nest of plant fibers, dry leaves, moss, animal hair, sticks, and mud in bushes or in trees at heights of 10–100 ft (3–30 m). Female incubates the 4–5 bluish green, dark-spotted eggs for 16 days. Both parents feed young for about a month or more after they fledge at 16 days.

FAMILY LANIIDAE
SHRIKES

Shrikes are predatory birds that hunt for insects, reptiles, rodents, and birds in open country and along the forest edge. They perch on thorny bushes, trees, or fences when looking for prey, then swoop down and seize their quarry with their sharply clawed feet. They use their strong hooked bill to kill and dismember the prey. Shrikes often impale prey on a thorn, sharp twig, or barbed wire, or wedge it into forked twigs for later consumption—a habit that has earned these birds the name of "butcher-bird."

GENUS *LANIUS*
Brown Shrike

Lanius cristatus
ALSO: Red-tailed Shrike, Braunwürger, Pie-grièche brune, Brunvarsler, Сибирский жулан. SN means "crested butcher-bird."
RANGE: Nests (May–Jun) in forest and forest-steppe from w Siberia to e Asia. Winters in se Asia. Vagrant to Europe and N Amer.
ID: L 7–8 in (18–20 cm). Brown above, with a dark "bandit" mask, pale eyebrow, and white throat. Breast and flanks buff. Rump and graduated tail tinged with rufous; basal half of outer tail feathers white. Bill dark in summer, pale gray in winter. AD ♂ W SIBERIA: Crown and neck gray. Back chestnut. Mask black. AD ♂ E SIBERIA: Crown, back, wings, and tail clay brown. Mask brown. AD ♀: Finely scalloped underparts. VOICE: Harsh, chattering *chek-chek-chek-chek-chek*.
HABITS: Hunts from tops of thorny bushes around forest bogs and clearings. Builds a nest of dried grass on the ground or in willow, dwarf birch, or hawthorn scrub. Clutch is 4–7 pink or white, brown spotted eggs.

Great Gray Shrike

Lanius excubitor
ALSO: Northern Shrike, Siberian Red-tailed Shrike, Raubwürger, Pie-grièche grise, Varsler, Серый сорокопут, *Lanius borealis*. SN means "butcher-bird sentinel."
RANGE: Nests (Apr–Jun) in open spruce forest and in alder and willow scrub in forest-tundra in Eurasia and N Amer. Winters south to the n US, Africa, and s Asia.
ID: L 9–10 in (22–26 cm). Pearl gray above, with a black "bandit" mask. Underparts white. Wings black, with white patch at base of primaries. Tail feathers black with white tips. VOICE: Drawn-out, trilling *prrrih-prrriht*.
HABITS: Makes short running dashes or fluttering sorties from perch to flush prey. Builds a large, bulky open cup nest of twigs, root fibers, feathers, and hair. Female incubates 4–7 white or pale green, heavily blotched eggs for 15–18 days. Young fledge at 18–20 days.

FAMILY TYRANNIDAE
TYRANT FLYCATCHERS

Tyrannidae stems from the Latin for "tyrant" or "despot," which indicates the aggressive behavior of some family members. These birds inhabit American forests, woodlands, and wooded fields. They feed almost exclusively on insects they capture in midair or hover glean from foliage. They often can be spotted sitting motionless on a open perch, then sallying out to capture flies, gnats, and other prey with a snap of their broad, flattened bill. Tyrant flycatchers are usually difficult to tell apart, as size and color differences are subtle, and their distinctive songs are given only during the nesting season.

Tyrant flycatchers begin to breed at 1 year of age. Most are seasonally monogamous. The female builds the nest, most commonly an open cup nest placed anywhere from near the ground to 50 ft (15 m) up in a tree. The female typically incubates the 3–5 brown-spotted, white or cream-colored eggs for 12–17 days. Both sexes feed the young, which fledge at 12–20 days.

GENUS *EMPIDONAX*
Alder Flycatcher

Empidonax alnorum
ALSO: Alder Pewee, Erlen-schnäppertyrann, Mouche-rolle des aulnes, Oreempid, Мухоловка Элдера, *Empidonax traillii alnorum*. SN means "tyrant (literally, "gnat and mosquito king") of the alder trees." CN refers to the preferred habitat.
RANGE: Nests (Jun–Jul) in scrub, open woodland, and early successional forests in Canada, Alaska, and ne US. Winters to Colombia and Bolivia.
ID: L 5–6.5 in (13–17 cm). Greenish olive above; gray green on head. Narrow white eyering. White wing bars. White throat; cream to pale yellow belly with grayish breast band. VOICE: Harsh, raspy *fee-BEE-o;* sometimes a slurred *fee-beer*.
HABITS: Nests mainly in alder and willow thickets and stands of young deciduous trees, usually close to water. Builds a coarse, straggly nest of grasses in an upright crotch of a bush or tree 2–6 ft (0.6–2 m) above the ground. Both sexes incubate the 3–4 brown-spotted, cream-colored eggs for 12–14 days, and both tend the brood.

Hammond's Flycatcher

Empidonax hammondii
ALSO: Tannenschnäpper-
tyrann, Moucherolle de
Hammond, Granempid,
Мухоловка хаммонда. SN means "Hammond's
tyrant," honoring William Alexander Hammond
(1828–1900), surgeon general of the US Army,
who collected the type specimen.

RANGE: Nests (Jun–Jul) in coniferous and mixed
forests from lowlands to near the timberline in
c Alaska, w Canada, and w US. Winters in cool
forests south to Mexico and Nicaragua.

ID: L 5–6 in (13–15 cm). Compact, with a short
tail and small dark bill. Grayish olive above;
darker on wings and tail; grayish head. Distinct
white eyering. Narrow white wing bars (buffy in
fall adult and juvenile). Throat pale gray; breast
pale grayish olive; belly washed with yellow.
VOICE: Sharp *peek*. Song 3-phrased *see-WIT…
bzurrp-bzeep.*

HABITS: Nests in cool, shady, mature forests
containing clumps of tall conifers with well-
developed canopies. Builds a cup nest of bark,
plant fibers, pine needles, and twigs. Nest is set
in a tree fork or on a horizontal branch 6–60 ft
(2–20 m) above the ground.

Yellow-bellied Flycatcher

Empidonax flaviventris
ALSO: Birkenschnäp-
pertyrann, Moucherolle à
ventre jaune, Gulbukempid,
Желтобрюхая мухоловка.

SN means "yellow-bellied tyrant."
RANGE: Nests (Jun–Jul) in cool damp forests
from e Alaska across c Canada, south to Great
Lakes and ne US. Winters in C Amer.

ID: L 5–6 in (13–15 cm). Olive green above;
yellowish below, washed with grayish green on
the breast. Pale yellow eyering. Short, wide bill,
with dark upper mandible and yellowish lower
mandible. Mouth lining yellow orange (seen
when bird is singing). Buff or off-white wing bars.
Short tail. **VOICE:** Clear, rising whistled *tu-WEE.*
Song is an abrupt, hoarse *killink* or *che-bunk.*

HABITS: Elusive and easily overlooked in muskeg
forests. Nests on or near the ground in damp,

dark forests that have a dense understory of
mosses, herbs, ferns, bushes, and small trees.
Female alone constructs a cup nest of moss,
rootlets, and grasses on a mossy bank, among
tree roots, or at the base of ferns. Nest is usually
hidden from above by overhanging vegetation or
fallen branches. Female incubates 3–4 eggs for
15 days. Young leave the nest in 13–15 days, but
shelter as a group in dense vegetation where both
parents continue to feed them for several days.

GENUS *CONTOPUS*
Olive-sided Flycatcher

Contopus cooperi
ALSO: Boreal Pewee,
Moucherolle à côtés olive,

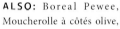

Olivflanken-Schnäppertyrann, Jakkepivi,
Оливковобокий мухолов. SN means "Cooper's
short-legged pewee," after American surgeon-
naturalist James Graham Cooper (1830–1902).
RANGE: Nests (Jun–Jul) in coniferous forests
to 11,000 ft (3350 m) across Alaska and Canada,
south to California and ne US. Winters in Panama
and Andes Mtns south to Bolivia.

ID: L 7–8 in (18–20 cm). Deep brownish olive
above, darkest on crown. Throat white; center
of breast and belly white to pale yellow; strongly
contrasting, often streaked, olive gray "vest."
Faint pale gray wing bars. Stout bill; upper
mandible black; lower mandible yellow, with
a dark tip. **VOICE:** Rapid *pip pip pip.* Song is a
loud, whistled *quick…THREE BEERS.*

HABITS: Perches at tops of tall trees and snags at
edges of forests and bogs. Female builds a loosely
formed nest of twigs, rootlets, lichens, grass, and
pine needles on conifer branches. Incubation is
15–18 days. Young fledge at 17–20 days. Parents
continue to feed young for a week or longer.

RELATED SPECIES: WESTERN WOOD PEWEE,
C. sordidulus, occurs at forest edge and in
riparian woodland to 10,000 ft (3000 m)
in se Alaska, w Canada, and w US south to
C Amer. This small, easily overlooked tyrant
has dull grayish olive upperparts, pale gray
underparts, 2 grayish wing bars, and a dark bill
with yellow at the base of the lower mandible.
Call is a loud buzzy *peeer.* Song is a descending
tsee-tsee-tsee-peeer.

Small, dark bill
Nests in mature coniferous
and mixed forest

Hammond's Flycatcher
Empidonax hammondii
W N Amer
L 5–6 in (13–15 cm)

Two-toned bill
Yellowish wing bars
Nests on the ground
in dense forest

Yellow-bellied Flycatcher
Empidonax flaviventris
N Amer
L 5–6 in (13–15 cm)

Sings and forages
in treetops

Olive-sided Flycatcher
Contopus cooperi
N Amer
L 7–8 in (18–20 cm)

Nests in alder and
willow thickets

Alder Flycatcher
Empidonax alnorum
N Amer
L 5–6.5 in (13–17 cm)

Gray Alder
Alnus incana

Grayish wing bars
Perches low
Hover gleans insects

Western Wood Pewee
Contopus sordidulus
W N Amer
L 6–6.5 in (15–17 cm)

Eastern Phoebe
Sayornis phoebe
N Amer
L 6–7 in (15–18 cm)

Perches low
Hover gleans insects
on the ground

Pumps tail
up and down

Eastern Kingbird
Tyrannus tyrannus
N Amer
L 8–9 in (20–23 cm)

Say's Phoebe
Sayornis saya
W N Amer
L 7–8 in (18–20 cm)

GENUS *SAYORNIS*
Say's Phoebe
Sayornis saya

ALSO: San Jose Phoebe, Yukon Phoebe, Zimtbauch-Phoebetyrann, Moucherolle à ventre roux, Brunfibi, Феб. SN means "Say's phoebe," after American entomologist Thomas Say (1787–1834), who first described the species.

RANGE: Nests (May–Jul) in open, dry country in n Alaska and nw Canada, south into the Great Plains and Mexico; avoids seacoasts and heavy forest. Northernmost breeding flycatcher, extending its breeding range farther north along the Alaska pipeline. Winters south to C Amer. **ID:** L 7–8 in (18–20 cm). Grayish brown above. Black tail. Buffy cinnamon below, becoming more orange at vent. **VOICE:** Slurred, whistled *phee-eur*. Song is a low, whistled *pit-tsee-eur, pit-tsee-eur*, followed by a burry upslurred *churr-eep*.

HABITS: Perches on bushes, fences, low rocks, and earthen mounds. Feeds on bees, wasps, flies, beetles, and grasshoppers taken from low vegetation. Nests in caves, abandoned mines, buildings, and bridges. Female builds an open cup nest of weed stems, grass, wood, moth cocoons, and spider webs, and lines it with hair, fibers, paper, and feathers. Female incubates 4–5 buffy eggs for 15 days. Young fledge at 17 days.

RELATED SPECIES: EASTERN PHOEBE, *S. phoebe*, nests in trees and on barn eaves, bridges, and buildings from c Canada south to the ne US; rare but regular north to Great Bear Lake and se Yukon. Brownish gray above, darker brown on head. Underparts white, sometimes washed with pale yellow on belly. Dips tail when perched. Call is a weak *chip*. Song is a clear, whistled *FEE-bee*, from which the species draws its name.

GENUS *TYRANNUS*
Eastern Kingbird
Tyrannus tyrannus

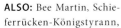
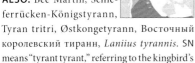

ALSO: Bee Martin, Schieferrücken-Königstyrann, Tyran tritri, Østkongetyrann, Восточный королевский тиранн, *Laniius tyrannus*. SN means "tyrant tyrant," referring to the kingbird's very pugnacious nature.

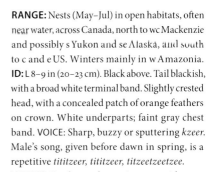

RANGE: Nests (May–Jul) in open habitats, often near water, across Canada, north to wc Mackenzie and possibly s Yukon and se Alaska, and south to c and e US. Winters mainly in w Amazonia. **ID:** L 8–9 in (20–23 cm). Black above. Tail blackish, with a broad white terminal band. Slightly crested head, with a concealed patch of orange feathers on crown. White underparts; faint gray chest band. **VOICE:** Sharp, buzzy or sputtering *kzeer*. Male's song, given before dawn in spring, is a repetitive *tititzeer, tititzeer, titzeetzeetzee*.

HABITS: Perches and nests in areas with trees, shrubs, or fence posts. Hawks insects from a perch 3–12 ft (1–4 m) above the ground. Female builds a bulky nest of twigs and grasses, lined with animal hair, rootlets, dry grasses, or willow catkins, 8–20 ft up in a tree or bush; occasionally nests on a fence post or tree stump.

FAMILY MUSCICAPIDAE
OLD WORLD FLYCATCHERS

Muscicapidae (Latin for "seizes flies") is a large family of small songbirds that breed in a variety of habitats ranging from dense forests to open scrub and savannahs in Europe, Africa, and Asia. These birds are mainly small arboreal insectivores that take insects on the wing. They hunt from prominent perches watching for prey, then sally out to snatch an insect before returning to the same or a new perch. Many northern populations are long-distance migrants that winter in the S Hemisphere.

SUBFAMILY MUSCICAPINAE
TYPICAL FLYCATCHERS

These flycatchers have small, thin bills fringed with bristles. Most have weak, buzzy songs and calls. The northern species nest in tree holes, niches in stone walls, and also accept nest boxes.

GENUS *MUSCICAPA*
Spotted Flycatcher
Muscicapa striata

ALSO: Grauschnäpper, Gobemouche gris, Gråfluesnapper, Серая мухоловка. SN means "flycatcher with streaked [breast]." CN refers to the spotted plumage of very young birds.

Tail pattern similar
in *F. parva* and
F. albicilla

ad. ♀

ad. ♂

ad. ♂

Red-breasted Flycatcher
Ficedula parva
Europe–w Siberia
L 4.5–5 in (11–12 cm)

juv.
F. parva
F. albicilla

Taiga Flycatcher
Ficedula albicilla
Siberia–ne Asia
L 4.5–5 in (11–12 cm)

ad. ♀

fledgling

ad. ♀

ad. ♂

Spotted Flycatcher
Muscicapa striata
Europe–c Asia
L 5.5–6 in (14–15 cm)

ad.

European Pied Flycatcher
Ficedula hypoleuca
Europe–wc Siberia
L 5–5.5 in (12–14 cm)

fledgling

ad.

ad. ♀

ad. ♂

European Robin
Erithacus rubecula
Europe–w Siberia
L 5–5.5 in (12–14 cm)

Red-flanked Bluetail
Tarsiger cyanurus
Eurasia
L 5–5.5 in (13–14 cm)

RANGE: Nests (May–Jun) in forests, woodland, gardens, and parks from Europe to c Siberia and c Asia. Winters in Africa.

ID: L 5.5–6 in (14–15 cm). AD: Grayish brown upperparts. Dark streaks on pale forecrown. White underparts, with dark streaking on breast. Short black legs. Dark, fairly long, thin bill. JUV: Fledglings have pale-spotted mantles. VOICE: Thin *see-tk-tk* or shrill *zree*.

HABITS: Forages in woodland clearings. Perches motionless in an exaggerated upright posture as it watches for prey, earning the local name "post bird." Pursues insects with agile, twisting flight. Nests in wall niches or nest boxes. Builds a cup nest from twigs, moss, and grass, lined with hair, wool, and feathers. Female incubates the 4–7 eggs for 12–14 days. Young fledge at 12–16 days.

GENUS *FICEDULA*
Taiga Flycatcher
Ficedula albicilla

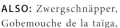

ALSO: Zwergschnäpper, Gobemouche de la taïga, Dvergfluesnapper, Малая мухоловка. Recently split from *F. parva*. SN means "small flycatcher with white [on] tail."

RANGE: Nests (May–Jun) in dense forests across Siberia to Kamchatka. Winters in Borneo. Vagrant to nw Europe, Aleutians, c California. ID: L 4.5–5 in (11–12 cm). Lead gray above, whitish below. Tail base white, with an inverted dark T formed by the black terminal band and dark central feathers. AD ♂: Orange throat surrounded by gray on head and breast. AD ♀: Whitish throat. Pale gray breast. VOICE: Fast sharp rattle, *trrrt*, or *chip-chip-chr-rrr*, likened to a tree branch creaking in the wind.

HABITS: Inhabits dense deciduous or mixed forest. Pumps tail when perched. Seizes insects in midair or on the ground. Nests in a tree hole. Clutch is 5–6 buffy, pink-spotted eggs. SIMILAR SPECIES: RED-BREASTED FLYCATCHER (pale gray on map), *F. parva,* nests in mature deciduous forests from n Europe to w Siberia where range abuts that of *F. albicilla*. Winters in s Asia. AD ♂: Orange throat bleeds into pale breast. AD ♀: Buffy throat and breast. VOICE: Slurred rattle, *serrrt*, or short, shrill *zree*.

European Pied Flycatcher
Ficedula hypoleuca
ALSO: Trauerschnäpper, Gobemouche noir, Svarthvit Flugesnapper, Мухоловка-пеструшка. SN means "small flycatcher with white underparts."

RANGE: Nests (May–Jun) in forests, open woodland, gardens, and parks in UK, Europe, and Siberia, east to Yenisei Rvr. Winters in Africa. ID: L 5–5.5 in (12–14 cm). AD ♂: Upperparts brownish black to deep glossy black. Bold white wing patch. Underparts white. Two white spots on forehead, just above beak; males with larger spots attract more females for breeding. AD ♀: Grayish brown upperparts, with a white patch on the folded wing. Throat and breast buff; rest of underparts white. VOICE: Loud *pik-peee*. Male's song is a complex of loud rhythmic trills, *peechee-peechee-kooleeleechi*, interspersed with a few melodious notes and sudden changes of pitch.

HABITS: Feeds on insects and insect larvae; also takes fruit and seeds in late summer. Lowers wings and pumps tail when perched. Monogamous or polygynous. Males with 2 mates usually maintain separate territories for each, but some females will nest close together or even use the same nest. Nests in tree holes and nest boxes. Female incubates 6–7 light blue eggs for 13–15 days. Young fledge at 16–17 days.

SUBFAMILY SAXICOLINAE
CHATS AND CHAT-THRUSHES

Saxicolinae contains flycatcher species formerly classified in the thrush family. These birds forage on or near the ground, where they feed on insects, insect larvae, spiders, and berries gleaned from the undergrowth. They hop along the ground, often flicking the tail, then pause as they watch for prey. Many have melodious, clear songs given at dawn and dusk.

GENUS *ERITHACUS*
European Robin
Erithacus rubecula
ALSO: Rotkehlchen, Rouge-gorge familier, Rødstrupe, Зарянка. SN means "red-breasted robin."

RANGE: Nests (May–Jul) in forests, woods, gardens, and parks, from the UK and Europe to wc Siberia. Winters in s Europe and n Africa. **ID:** L 5–5.5 in (12–14 cm). Stocky, with an upright posture. Short, frequently cocked tail. **AD:** Brown above, white below, with orange breast and orange face edged with gray. **JUV:** Brown above, buffy below, with a brown-spotted face, breast, and back. **VOICE:** Sharp, highly pitched, repetitive *twick*. Song is a melodic warbling. **HABITS:** Tame and confiding to humans, but very aggressive toward other robins. Hunts for insects, snails, and worms on the ground or from a low perch. Female builds a nest of leaves and grass on a densely vegetated bank or in a rotting stump, and incubates the 4–6 speckled eggs for 13–14 days.

GENUS *TARSIGER*
Red-flanked Bluetail

Tarsiger cyanurus
ALSO: Orange-flanked Bush Robin, Siberian Bluechat, Blauschwanz, Rossignol à flancs roux, Blåstjert, Синехвостка, *Luscinia cyanura*, *Erithacus cyanurus*. SN means "blue-tailed forest-robin."
RANGE: Nests (May–Jun) in coniferous and birch forests having dense undergrowth from Finland to Siberia, Kamchatka, and e Asia. Winters in s Asia. Vagrant to the UK and Aleutians.
ID: L 5–5.5 in (13–14 cm). AD ♂: Deep blue above. Azure blue eyebrow, wing coverts, and rump. Wings dull blue. White throat, grayish breast and belly, and orange flanks. Small, thin black bill. Slender black legs. AD ♀: Olive brown above, with a blue rump and tail. White throat, grayish underparts, and orange flanks. **VOICE:** Male's mating song, given from treetops at dawn, is a melancholic rolling *fyeet trr-tretritt*, followed by a rising *whew-wee-whew-wee*.
HABITS: Shy and secretive. Forages in trees and on the ground. Flicks wings, dips tail, and makes high, bouncy hops when foraging. Nest of twigs and moss, lined with feathers and grass, is built on or near the ground, often among roots or in a hole in a bank or tree stump. Female incubates 3–7 white, rusty-speckled eggs for about 15 days.

GENUS *LUSCINIA*
Rufous-tailed Robin

Luscinia sibilans
ALSO: Swinhoe's Nightingale, Red-tailed Robin, Schwirrnachtigall, Rossignol siffleur, Trillenattergal, Соловей-свистун, *Larvivora sibilans*. SN means "whistling nightingale."
RANGE: Nests (Jun–Jul) in damp forests from c Siberia to Sea of Okhotsk. Winters in se Asia. Vagrant to Attu Is, Pribilofs, St Lawrence Is, UK.
ID: L 5–5.5 in (13–14 cm). Stocky, with an upright posture. Warm brown above, becoming more rufous on tail. Underparts cream, with distinctive scaly brown and cream pattern on breast and sides. Whitish eyering. Long pink legs. **VOICE:** Insect-like *chirrrup* or soft whistle. Male's song is a long, loud, tremulous whistle given with its head raised.
HABITS: Secretive. Forages alone or in pairs on the ground in forest undergrowth and around fallen trees. Frequently flicks tail. Nests in a hole in a stump or fallen log.

Bluethroat

Luscinia svecica
ALSO: Blaukehlchen, Gorgebleue à miroir, Pechiazul, Blåstrupe, Варакушка. SN means "Swedish nightingale." English surgeon and naturalist Edward Adams (1824–1855) discovered this Eurasian species in nw Alaska in June 1851 while taking part in Sir John Ross's search for the lost expedition of Sir John Franklin. Bluethroats were first seen in Canada in 1974 and the first nest found there in 2003.
RANGE: Nests (May–Jul) in scrub and thickets from n Europe across Siberia to the Russian Far East; nests on the tundra in n Alaska and nw Yukon. Winters in n Africa, India, and s Asia. Regular visitor to Attu Is (w Aleutians).
ID: L 5–5.5 in (13–14 cm). Grayish brown above, whitish below. Tail base rufous, with a broad black terminal band. Broad white eyebrow. AD ♂: Bright blue chin and throat, with small rufous or white patch in center; throat patch edged below by narrow black and white bands and a wide rufous chest band. AD ♀: White throat edged

by pale blue band and necklace of dark streaks and spots. Dark lateral throat stripe. White moustache. JUV: Dark brown, with buff spots on back and scaled underparts. VOICE: Loud *chack-chack*. Male's mating song incorporates trills, whistles, and calls of other bird species. HABITS: Skulks in tangled thickets. Male often cocks tail and fans it open, flashing rufous tail base. Nests on or near the ground in grass tussocks or dense willow scrub. Female builds nest of sedges, twigs, and leaves, edged with bark strips, grass, and moss, and lined with hair. Female incubates 4–7 eggs for about 15 days.

Siberian Rubythroat

Luscinia calliope
ALSO: Kamchatka Nightingale, Rossignol calliope, Rubinkehlchen, Rubinstrupe, Соловей-красношейка. SN means "Calliope's nightingale," named after Calliope, sweet-voiced Muse and Greek goddess of poetry.
RANGE: Nests (May–Jun) in forests and woodlands with tangled undergrowth, from the w Urals across Siberia to Kamchatka and Kurils. Winters in se Asia. Rare visitor to w Aleutians, Pribilofs, St Lawrence Is, and w Europe.
ID: L 5.5–6 in (14–16 cm). Olive brown above. Grayish breast, buffy flanks, whitish belly. Bright red throat (diffuse or absent in AD ♀). Bold white eyebrow and malar stripe. VOICE: Harsh *chech* when alarmed. Male's song is a complex series of whistled *fee-you-eet, fee-you-eet*, clicks, and sometimes calls of other bird species.
HABITS: Forages for insects and berries on the ground, in low bushes, or in dense understory of forests, scrub, and flooded areas. Cocks and flicks tail. Nests on the ground in a spherical nest with a side entrance.

GENUS *PHOENICURUS*
Common Redstart

Phoenicurus phoenicurus
ALSO: Gartenrotschwanz, Rougequeue à front blanc, Rødstjert, Обыкновенная горихвостка. SN means "crimson-tailed." CN stems from the Old English *steort*, meaning "tail."

RANGE: Nests (May–Jul) in forests, oak woodland, gardens, and parks, from the UK and Europe east to Lake Baikal, Siberia. Winters in Africa and on the Arabian Penin.
ID: L 5–6 in (13–16 cm). AD ♂: Slate gray head and back. Sides of face and throat black. Forehead white. Rusty red rump. Outer tail feathers bright rusty red, central tail feathers brown. Breast, flanks, and underwing coverts rusty red. Belly white. Black legs and bill. AD ♀: Browner than male, with paler underparts and brownish face. VOICE: Loud *huit-tee-teek*. Male's song is a resonant trill, given from treetops and often accompanied by quivering and fanning of tail.
HABITS: Forages for insects in low trees and bushes, with short sorties to the ground in freshly mown meadows. Perches in an upright stance. Builds a loose cup nest of grass, roots, and moss, lined with hair and feathers, in a rotted stump, stone wall, low tree hole, or nest box. Clutch of 5–7 blue eggs is incubated for 12–14 days.

GENUS *SAXICOLA*: Stonechats and whinchats nest on or near the ground in dense vegetation or between rocks and boulders. These species are often parasitized by the Common Cuckoo, *Cuculus canorus*, and like other ground nesters, many lose their nests to weasels and other mammalian predators.

Stonechat

Saxicola spp.
ALSO: Common Bushchat, Schwarzkehlchen, Tarier pâtre, Черноголовый чекан, Svartstrupe. SN means "rock dweller."
RANGE: Nests (May–Jun) on moors, dry steppe, damp meadows, and grassy alpine slopes across Eurasia. Vagrant to w Europe and St Lawrence Is, Alaska. The following former subspecies of the African-breeding *S. torquatus* have been elevated to species status. EUROPEAN STONECHAT (E), *S. rubicola*, breeds in the UK, w Europe, n Africa; winters to the Middle East. SIBERIAN STONECHAT (M), *S. maurus*, breeds from Finland to c Asia; winters to Iran, Iraq, n India. STEJNEGER'S STONECHAT (S), *S. stejnegeri*, breeds from e Siberia to e Asia; winters to Indochina.

Whinchat
Saxicola rubetra
Eurasia
L 5–5.5 in (12–14 cm)

ad. ♀ ad. ♂

Stonechat
Saxicola spp.
Eurasia
L 4.5–5 in (11–13 cm)

ad. ♀ ad. ♂

Common Redstart
Phoenicurus phoenicurus
Europe–w Siberia
L 5–6 in (13–16 cm)

ad. ♀ ad. ♂

Northern Wheatear
Oenanthe oenanthe
Near circumpolar
L 5.5–6.5 in (14–17 cm)

ad. ♀ ad. ♂

Siberian Rubythroat
Luscinia calliope
Siberia–e Asia
L 5.5–6 in (14–16 cm)

ad. ♀ ad. ♂

ad. ♂

Bluethroat
Luscinia svecica
Eurasia, nw N Amer
L 5–5.5 in (13–14 cm)

ad. ♀

Rufous-tailed Robin
Luscinia sibilans
Siberia
L 5–5.5 in (13–14 cm)

ID: L 4.5–5 in (11–13 cm). AD ♂: Black head and chin (pales in fall). White patch on side of neck and on scapulars. Back black, mottled with chestnut. Rump plain white or white with dark spots. Tail black. Breast and most of underparts are rufous in European males. Siberian males have rufous only on breast; rest of underparts white. AD ♀: Head and throat dusky brown, with rest of plumage a faded version of male's. Siberian females have a plain, buffy rump. European females have a dark-spotted, buffy rump. **VOICE:** Male emits sharp, loud clicks that sound like 2 stones tapping together. Male gives twittering, trilling notes in display flight as he flashes his white wing patches and rump. **HABITS:** Feeds on insects hunted from an exposed perch on a low bush. Flies down to catch prey on the ground or pursues flying insects in fluttering flight. Flicks wings and tail when perched. Nest is a deep, loose cup of grass, leaves, rootlets, and stems, lined with hair, wool, and feathers, usually built on the ground at the base of a grass tussock or small bush; occasionally nests between boulders or in a hole in an earthen bank. Female incubates 5–8 greenish blue, red-spotted eggs for 13–14 days. Young fledge at 13–16 days.

Whinchat
Saxicola rubetra

ALSO: Marsh Bushchat, Braunkehlchen, Tarier des prés, Buskskvett, Луговой чекан. SN means "ruddy [-breasted] rock dweller." **RANGE:** Nests (May–Jun) on open grassland, meadows, and pastures in the UK, Europe, and east to wc Siberia. Winters south to Africa and the Middle East.
ID: L 5–5.5 in (12–14 cm). Brownish above, with chestnut mottling. Buffy throat and breast; pale buff to whitish belly. Tail blackish, with white at base of outer tail feathers. AD ♂: Blackish mask. White eyebrow. White malar stripe. Faded orange throat and breast. Small white patches on wing coverts. AD ♀: Duller than male, with browner face mask, pale buff breast, buff eyebrow and malar stripe, and smaller or no white wing patches. **VOICE:** Soft whistle followed by clicks, *whue tic-tic*. Male's nocturnal song is a mix of soft whistles, tics, and imitations of other birds' songs.
HABITS: Forages on the ground and in flight, taking insects, spiders, worms, snails, and some berries and seeds. Nests in dense low vegetation, usually on the ground. Clutch of 4–7 greenish blue, red-spotted eggs is incubated for 11–14 days. Precocial young leave the nest on foot 10–14 days after hatching; not yet unable to fly, they complete development away from the nest. Young fledge at 17–19 days, and adults continue to feed them for an additional 2 weeks.

GENUS *OENANTHE*
Northern Wheatear
Oenanthe oenanthe

ALSO: Iquligaq, Steinschmätzer, Traquet motteux, Steinskvett, Обыкновенная каменка. SN means "wheatear," as applied by Aristotle. CN is a corruption of the 16th-century name "white arse," referring to the white rump.
RANGE: Near circumpolar. Nests (May–Jun) on stony tundra, rocky slopes, alpine meadows, and open grasslands in Eurasia, n Africa, Asia Minor, and nw and ne N Amer. Winters in Africa and se Asia. Irregular breeder in Svalbard.
SUBSPECIES–ARCTIC: *O. o. oenanthe* (O) nests from UK and Eurasia to Alaska and nw Canada; w N Amer breeders migrate up to 9000 mi (14,500 km) as they fly southwest over Siberia and Arabia to winter in c Africa. *O. o. leucorhoa* (L) nests in ne Canada, Greenland, and Iceland; birds breeding in nw Canada migrate up to 2175 mi (3500 km) across the N Atlantic, set down in the UK, then fly over Europe, the Mediterranean, and Sahara Desert to winter in tropical w Africa.
ID: L 5.5–6.5 in (14–17 cm). AD ♂: Crown and back ashy gray. Wings blackish. Rump and tail base white, with a black inverted T pattern at tail tip. Black mask (faded in winter); white eyebrow; white malar stripe. AD ♀: Lacks male's facial markings. Upperparts dull brown. Underparts pale buff. **VOICE:** Sharp *chack-chack*. Male's song, given from an elevated perch or in display flight, is a melodious warble mixed with harsher notes and imitations of other birds' songs.

HABITS: Feeds on insects picked from the ground or snatched in flight from a low perch. Frequently flicks tail. Courting male displays in front of female, hopping and bowing, fanning his tail, and crouching with wings and tail spread. Male also performs an aerial display flight, rising high in the air and then descending with tail spread, singing all the while. Builds a nest of grass and moss, lined with hair, wool, and feathers in rock crevices, stone walls, and rodent burrows. Nest site may be reused the next spring after lining materials are replaced. Female incubates 5–7 pale blue eggs for 13–14 days. Young fledge at 15 days.

FAMILY TURDIDAE
THRUSHES

The family Turdidae encompasses woodland songbirds, many of which are known for their rich, melodious songs. The slender bill is adapted for feeding on soft foods such as insects, worms, and berries gleaned from the ground or plucked from vegetation. Thrushes tend to hop along the ground when foraging and often flick their tail and wings. Typically the female builds an open cup of grass, moss, and twigs, lined with clay or mud and fine grass in the fork of a tree, on the ground, or occasionally on a rocky ledge. Normally only the female incubates the 4–6 blue or buff, sometimes spotted eggs for 10–17 days. Both parents feed the young, which fledge 8–19 days after hatching.

GENUS *TURDUS*
Fieldfare

Turdus pilaris
ALSO: Wacholderdrossel, Grive litorne, Gråtrost, Рябинник. SN means "hairy thrush." CN derives from the Anglo-Saxon *feldefare*, a "traveler through the fields."
RANGE: Nests (Apr–Jul) in woodland and scrub across n Eurasia, from n Europe east to the Sea of Okhotsk, south to c Europe and s Siberia; rare breeder in Iceland and UK. Winters in the UK, s Europe, n Africa, and Middle East; some birds move just to south of the snow limit. Vagrant to Atlantic Canada, ne US, and Alaska.

ID: L 9–11 in (23–27 cm). Mantle and upperwing coverts reddish brown. Head, lower back, and rump gray. Tail black. Faint white eyebrow. Bill yellow orange with a dark tip. Throat buff, with dark streaks and chevron marks that continue onto ochre breast and buffy flanks. Belly white. Underwing coverts and axillaries white. Legs brown. **VOICE:** Chattering *schak-shak-shak*; male also gives this call in flight display.
HABITS: Forms noisy flocks that forage on the ground and in trees, taking insects, worms, snails, berries, and fallen fruit. Nests colonially in forest habitats, especially wooded areas around farmland, building a cup nest in trees or occasionally on a log pile or rocky ledge. Flocks communally defend the nesting area against corvids and other predators, flying after them and sometimes dropping excrement on them.

Redwing

Turdus iliacus
ALSO: Red-winged Thrush, Rotdrossel, Grive mauvis, Rødvingetrost, Белобровик, *Turdus musicus*. SN means "[red-] flanked thrush."
RANGE: Nests (May–Jun) in coniferous forests, birch woodland, and willow scrub in Iceland, Faroes, UK (rare), and across Eurasia, east to the Kolyma Rvr in ne Siberia, south to c Asia. Icelandic birds winter in nw Europe, others fly south to n Africa and the Middle East. Vagrant to e Canada and ne US; one record (2011) from Seward, Alaska.
ID: L 7.5–9 in (19–23 cm). Back and upperwings uniform brown. Underparts cream with blackish longitudinal streaks. Flanks and underwing coverts rusty red. Bold head pattern, with dark face edged by whitish eyebrow and whitish malar stripe. Bill dark brown; yellowish base to lower mandible. Legs pale brown. **VOICE:** Harsh, elongated *cheeh* given in flight. Male's song, given from treetops, is a series of 3–6 loud whistling phrases ending in faint twitters.
HABITS: Usually seen in flocks or breeding pairs that forage mainly on the ground. Nests in trees, stumps, bushes, or on the ground, building a cup-shaped nest of dry grass lined with clay. Both sexes incubate the eggs and feed young.

Mistle Thrush
Turdus viscivorus
Europe–c Siberia
L 10–11.5 in (25–29 cm)

European
Mistletoe
Viscum album

Fieldfare
Turdus pilaris
Eurasia, Iceland
L 9–11 in (23–27 cm)

Naumann's Thrush
Turdus naumanni
SE Siberia
L 8.5–9.5 in (22–24 cm)

Redwing
Turdus iliacus
Eurasia, Iceland
L 7.5–9 in (19–23 cm)

ad.♂

Dusky ad. ♀
Compare to
Redwing

Song Thrush
Turdus philomelos
Europe–c Siberia
L 8–9 in (20–23 cm)

ad.♂

Dusky Thrush
Turdus eunomus
Siberia–Kamchatka
L 8.5–9.5 in (22–24 cm)

juv.

juv.

ad.♂

ad.♂

Ring Ouzel
Turdus torquatus
Europe
L 9.5–10.5 in (24–27 cm)

Eurasian Blackbird
Turdus merula
Iceland, UK, Europe
L 9.5–11.5 in (24–29 cm)

Varied Thrush
Ixoreus naevius
W N Amer
L 8.5–9.5 in (22–24 cm)

ad. ♂

ad. ♀

Eyebrowed Thrush
Turdus obscurus
Siberia
L 8–9 in (20–23 cm)

juv.

1st winter

ad.

American Robin
Turdus migratorius
N Amer
L 8.5–10 in (22–25 cm)

ad. ♀
Pale morph

ad. ♂

juv.

Rufous tail

Hermit Thrush
Catharus guttatus
N Amer
L 6–7 in (15–17 cm)

Buffy
"spectacles"

Swainson's Thrush
Catharus ustulatus
N Amer
L 6.5–7.5 in (17–19 cm)

Plain
gray face

Gray-cheeked Thrush
Catharus minimus
NE Siberia–N Amer
L 7–7.5 in (18–19 cm)

Song Thrush

Turdus philomelos

ALSO: Throstle, Mavis, Sing-drossel, Grive musicienne, Måltrost, Певчий дрозд. SN means "Philomela's thrush," referring to a Greek myth in which Philomela, daughter of King Pandion, is changed into a nightingale.
RANGE: Nests (Apr–Jun) in woodlands and parks from the UK and w Europe to Lake Baikal in c Siberia. Northern populations migratory, wintering south to n Africa and Iran.
ID: L 8–9 in (20–23 cm). Upperparts uniform olive brown. Yellowish buff breast and flanks, and cream-colored belly densely marked with dark arrowhead marks. Underwing coverts rusty buff. Bill dark brown, with yellowish base to lower mandible. Legs pinkish. VOICE: Harsh *tik-tik-tik-tik*, like an electrical spark. Male's song, given while perched in a tree, is ringing, melodic, varied; repeats brief 1–4 note elements of songs 3–5 times, then moves on to new motif.
HABITS: Forages on the ground, taking worms, insects, and snails. Nests low in trees (especially spruce), hedges, and scrub. Builds a cup nest of grass, moss, and twigs lined with a sticky mixture of rotted wood splinters, clay, and bird saliva.

Mistle Thrush

Turdus viscivorus

ALSO: Misteldrossel, Grive draine, Duetrost, Деряба. SN means "mistletoe-eating thrush." CN refers to the species' appetite for the white gelatinous berries of semi-parasitic European Mistletoe, *Viscum album*.
RANGE: Nests (Apr–Jul) in conifer groves, open woodland, alpine meadows, and parkland from the UK and Europe to ec Siberia and c Asia. Nomadic. Winters south to n Africa and sw Asia.
ID: L 10–11.5 in (25–29 cm). Upperparts uniform grayish brown. Tail has white tips to outer tail feathers. Underparts white to cream, densely marked with dark round spots. Pale vertical cheek patch is edged with black. Pale underwings and axillaries. Pale yellowish brown legs. Dark gray bill, with a yellowish base to lower mandible. Can be mistaken for a large Song Thrush, but

presents a more upright posture. VOICE: Dry rattling *zrrrrr*. Song, given mainly in the morning, is a short series of loud, flute-like whistles with a few squeaky notes at the end of each phrase.
HABITS: Flight is a series of undulating bounds interspersed with glides. Pairs and flocks forage in open woods, parks, and cultivated fields, taking a wide variety of invertebrates as well as seeds and berries of mistletoe, holly, and yew. Nests in trees, usually high above the ground. Wary and shy except in mating season, when pairs fearlessly defend their nest against any intruder.

Eurasian Blackbird

Turdus merula

ALSO: Amsel, Merle noir, Svarttrost, Чёрный дрозд. SN means "blackbird thrush." CN "Eurasian" distinguishes it from unrelated N Amer blackbirds in the family Icteridae.
RANGE: Nests (Apr–Jul) in woodland, thickets, parks, and gardens in Iceland, Faroes, and from UK and Europe south to N Africa, southeast to China. Northern breeders migratory, wintering south to c Asia. Introduced to Australia and NZ.
ID: L 9.5–11.5 in (24–29 cm). AD ♂: Jet black. Bill bright yellow orange in summer; duller in winter. Dark brown legs. AD ♀: Dark brown, with paler throat and pale speckles on breast. JUV: Uneven mottled dark brown with a rusty tinge. Dark brown legs. VOICE: Rolling chirpy *srri*, more chattering when alarmed. Song clear, melodic, mellow fluting, given in spring mainly at dawn and dusk.
HABITS: Usually solitary or in breeding pairs, rarely in small flocks. Hops and flicks tail when foraging on the ground. Nests on the ground or low on a tree branch. Builds a nest of moss and dry grass, lined with clay.

Ring Ouzel

Turdus torquatus

ALSO: Ring Thrush, Ring-drossel, Merle à plastron, Ringtrost, Белозобый дрозд. SN means "collared thrush." CN derives from the Old English *ōsle*, meaning "blackbird."
RANGE: Nests (May–Jun) on rocky cliffs,

slopes, and gullies in the mountains of the UK, Scandinavia, c Europe. Winters in mountains along the Mediterranean, Caucasus, nw Africa. **ID:** L 9.5–10.5 in (24–27 cm). AD ♂: Black, with pale scaly patterning on underparts. Conspicuous white crescent-shaped patch on breast. Wing feathers are edged in white, making the wings appear pale in flight. Legs brown. Bill yellow, with a grayish tip. Resembles *T. merula,* but is more slender and has a longer neck and narrower wings. AD ♀: Dark brownish black, with a scaly patterning on underparts. Tan-colored crescent-shaped breast patch. JUV: Dark brown, with faint scaly pattern on body and barely visible paler brown breast patch. **VOICE:** Loud, clicking *trek jek jek.* Song includes 3 loud, melodic whistles followed by chirpy chatter. **HABITS:** Found in pairs in summer and flocks in migration. Nests on the ground near a boulder, or in a tree stump, bush, or hole in a wall.

Dusky Thrush
Turdus eunomus

ALSO: Brown Thrush, Rost-flügeldrossel, Grive à ailes rousses, Bruntrost, Бурый дрозд. SN means "orderly thrush," possibly alluding to the species' structured winter flocks. **RANGE:** Nests (May–Jun) in taiga, forest-tundra, wooded steppe, and riparian woodland having dense understory from w Siberia east to Chukotka and Kamchatka. Winters in s Japan, s China, Myanmar. Rare vagrant to Europe. Casual spring migrant in Alaska. Rare winter visitor to Aleutians and coastal Alaska and Brit Columbia. **ID:** L 8.5–9.5 in (22–24 cm). Brown upperparts, with rusty red wings. Head and face blackish, with a bold white eyebrow and malar stripe. Throat and partial collar white; densely scaled breast band. Rest of underparts white, with black scaling on flanks. Bill black, with yellow base to lower mandible. Legs and feet pinkish brown. **VOICE:** Clicking *shack-shack-shack* or squeaky *shreee.* Male sings his melodious whistled song while perched motionless in a tree. **HABITS:** Forages on the ground and in fruit-bearing shrubs and trees. Female builds the nest on a low tree branch, stump, or low rocky ledge.

RELATED SPECIES: NAUMANN'S THRUSH (N on map), *T. naumanni,* breeds in c Siberia, south to n Manchuria, Amurland, and Sakhalin Is; winters south to Korea. Brown above, with a rufous rump and tail. Eyebrow, throat, and partial collar rusty red. Rufous scaling on flanks. Belly white.

Eyebrowed Thrush
Turdus obscurus

ALSO: Gray-headed Thrush, Dark Thrush, White-browed Thrush, Weißbrauendrossel, Merle obscur, Gråstrupetrost, Оливковый дрозд. SN means "dusky thrush." Recently split from the e Asian-breeding Pale Thrush, *T. pallidus.* **RANGE:** Nests (May–Jun) near water in dense spruce, pine, and fir forests, and in sheltered valleys at larch forest edge from c Siberia to Kamchatka and Sakhalin. Winters in woodland and gardens in e Asia. Vagrant to w Europe and Australia. Casual to w Aleutians (Attu), where it can be mistaken for an American Robin; note the Eyebrowed's brown back that contrasts with gray head, gray throat, and the white belly that extends up into orange breast as an inverted V. **ID:** L 8–9 in (20–23 cm). AD ♂: Brown above, with a bluish gray head and throat. Blackish eyeline, bordered in white above and below. Breast and flanks orange buff. Belly white. Yellowish legs. AD ♀/JUV: Similar to the male but duller with a browner head and pale throat. **VOICE:** Loud *tsee* and a cracking *chuck-chuck* sound. Male's song is a monotonous whistle *tuvee-tulee, tulee-tuvee.* **HABITS:** Found in pairs when nesting, in small flocks in migration and winter. Builds a nest of rootlets, grass, sticks, and bark, lined with mud, on the ground or in a bush or low tree branch.

American Robin
Turdus migratorius

ALSO: Wanderdrossel, Merle d'Amérique, Vandringstrast, Странствующий дрозд. SN means "migratory thrush." CN taken from the European Robin, *Erithacus rubecula,* a flycatcher, because of the reddish orange breast. State bird of Connecticut, Michigan, and Wisconsin.

RANGE: Nests (Apr–Jul) in tundra, forests, and gardens from n Alaska and Canada south through the US. Winters to Mexico, Cuba, Guatemala. Vagrant to Greenland, Iceland, UK, Europe.
ID: L 8.5–10 in (22–25 cm). Largest N Amer thrush. AD ♂: Dark gray to dark brown back and tail, with white tips to outer tail feathers (Pacific robins are often paler than other populations). Blackish head, with white crescents above and below eye. Underparts rich rufous, except for white throat and white undertail coverts. Yellow bill. AD ♀: Paler than male, especially on the head. JUV: Similar to adult, but with black spotting on the underparts, entirely white throat, and often with a buffy eyebrow. VOICE: Song consists of a series of clear, melodic, whistled phrases, often transcribed as *cheerily, cheer up, cheer up, cheerily, cheer up.*
HABITS: Found in pairs during breeding season, in flocks during migration and winter. Takes worms and insects as it hops along the ground; also gleans fruit from trees and plucks caterpillars from foliage. Nests on the ground, in trees and bushes, on buildings, or on cliffs north of the treeline. Female incubates the eggs and both parents feed the nestlings, which fledge at about 12 days. Young remain in nesting territory for several months, flocking with the parents and later migrating with them to wintering grounds.

GENUS *IXOREUS*
Varied Thrush
Ixoreus naevius
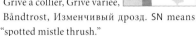
ALSO: Halsbanddrossel, Grive à collier, Grive variée, Båndtrost, Изменчивый дрозд. SN means "spotted mistle thrush."
RANGE: Nests (May–Jun) in dark, damp, mature forests from n Alaska and nw Canada south to the Pacific NW and California. Winters south to wc US and s California; periodically irrupts to c and e US and Canada.
ID: L 8.5–9.5 in (22–24 cm). AD ♂: Dark brown to dark gray above, with a bold orange and black wing pattern. Orange eyebrow. Throat and breast burnt orange, with a black to slate gray breast band. Bill black, with pale yellow at base of lower mandible. AD ♀: Duller than male.

Pale orange eyebrow. Throat and breast buffy orange. Grayish breastband. VOICE: Male's song, sounded from tops of conifers, is a single long monotone whistle followed by a short pause, then another long whistle on a different pitch.
HABITS: Forages on or near the ground, taking insects in summer, and fruits, berries, and acorns in fall and winter. Nest is a loosely woven cup of twigs and moss, lined with decaying wood, mud, fine grasses, leaves, and moss.

GENUS *CATHARUS*
Gray-cheeked Thrush
Catharus minimus

ALSO: Grauwangendrossel, Grive à joues grises, Gråkinnskogtrost, Серощёкий дрозд. SN means "pure-voiced small [thrush]."
RANGE: Nests (May–Jul) in forest and forest-tundra in ne Siberia, Alaska, n Canada. Winters to n S Amer. Vagrant to Greenland, UK, Europe.
ID: L 7–7.5 in (18–19 cm). Grayish brown above, with gray cheeks and face, and thin white partial eyering. Underparts cream, with dark spots on throat and breast; flanks gray. VOICE: High, nasal *jeeer*. Song is a descending series of rolling, flute-like notes that often ends in a short trill.
HABITS: Relatively shy. Forages for invertebrates on the forest floor or under dense shrubbery. Nests in willow-alder thickets and spruce forests having tangled understory. Nests on low branches of spruce trees, on willow or alder scrub, and sometimes on fallen trees or rotting stumps.

Swainson's Thrush
Catharus ustulatus

ALSO: Olive-backed Thrush, Russet-backed Thrush, Oregon Thrush, Zwergdrossel, Grive à dos olive, Brunkinnskogtrost, Дрозд Свэнсона. SN means "pure-voiced [thrush] with scorch marks on its plumage." CN refers to the English ornithologist William John Swainson (1789–1855).
RANGE: Nests (Jun–Jul) in spruce-fir forests and mixed woodland from nc Alaska south to w US states and east to e Canada. Winters south to US Gulf coast, Mexico, W Indies, n Argentina.

Bohemian Waxwing
Bombycilla garrulus
Eurasia, nw N Amer
L 7–8.5 in (18–21 cm)

ID: L 6.5–7.5 in (17–19 cm). Typically olive brown above; more russet in coastal Pacific birds. Distinct buffy eyering and lores. Underparts white, with dark spotting on throat and breast. **VOICE:** Flute-like, upwardly spiraling song described as *whip-poor-will-a-will-e-zee-zee-zee*. **HABITS:** Shy and secretive, especially when nesting. Forages near the forest floor, gleaning food from leaf litter and understory foliage; also captures insects in midair. Female builds nest low in thickets of deciduous shrubs or conifer saplings, or sometimes on a low tree branch.

Hermit Thrush
Catharus guttatus

ALSO: Einsiedlerdrossel, Grive solitaire, Eremittskog-trost, Дрозд-отшельник. SN means "pure-voiced spotted [thrush]." CN refers to the reclusive nesting habits of the species. **RANGE:** Nests (May–Jul) in coniferous and deciduous forests from coastal Alaska to e Canada and south to nw–nc US. Winters south to Mexico. Accidental in Greenland, Iceland, UK, Europe. **ID:** L 6–7 in (15–17 cm). AD: Head, mantle, and back brown, and a rufous rump and tail. Narrow but distinct buffy eyering; sometimes shows a pale area above the lores. Underparts creamy white, with buffy flanks and bold dark spots on breast. JUV: Similar to adult, but with buff-tipped upperwing coverts. VOICE: Melodious, ethereal, fluty warble, described as *oh, holy holy, ah, purity purity, ah, sweetly sweetly*.

HABITS: Forages on shady, leaf-littered forest floor, hopping along then pausing motionless as it watches for insects and other invertebrates. Typically perches in low branches of undergrowth, where it can be seen flicking its wings and quickly raising and slowly lowering its tail. Female builds a bulky cup nest on the ground, often in patches of clubmoss (*Lycopodium* sp.) and ferns, or low in densely branched bushes and trees.

FAMILY BOMBYCILLIDAE
WAXWINGS
Waxwings are soft, silky-plumaged songbirds. They have a few wing feather shafts that look as if they have been dipped in sealing wax, hence the common name "waxwing."

GENUS *BOMBYCILLA*
Bohemian Waxwing
Bombycilla garrulus

ALSO: Black-throated Waxwing, Suluktaatchialik, Seidenschwanz, Jaseur boréal, Sidensvans, Свиристель. SN means "chattering silktail." CN alludes to the nomadic habits and red-tipped wing feather shafts. **RANGE:** Nests (Jun–Aug) in damp forests of Eurasia and nw N Amer. Highly nomadic in winter, with flocks moving south to c Europe, s China and Japan, and n US. **ID:** L 7–8.5 in (18–21 cm). Brownish gray, with a rufous-tinged face, black mask, and black chin bisected by a thin white line. Pointed crest. Gray tail, with broad, dark subterminal band and lemon yellow tip. Reddish undertail coverts. Wings are dark gray, with yellow and white patches on edges of primaries, and white tips to secondary and primary wing coverts. VOICE: Soft, high-pitched, buzzing and trilling. HABITS: Stays in flocks for most of the year. Flocks in flight resemble dry leaves being blown by the wind. Feeds mainly on fruit plucked while perched or occasionally while hovering. Also feeds on insects, sap, buds, and flowers.

Nests late in summer, taking advantage of abundant supplies of ripe fruit such as hawthorn (*Crataegus*) and rowan (*Sorbus*) to feed its young. Nests in forest clearings, often near a lake or stream, swamp, beaver pond, or burned area. Birds with prominent red-tipped shafts appear to be more successful in mating. Courting pairs pass a small fruit back and forth before copulating. Female builds a loose, bulky nest of twigs, grass, and lichens, lined with moss, lichens, and soft grasses on a horizontal branch jutting out from tree trunk. Female incubates 4–6 pale blue or bluish gray, finely spotted eggs for 13–14 days. Both sexes feed nestlings, which fledge at about 18 days. Fledglings are barely able to fly when they leave the nest, and both parents continue to feed the young for 2 weeks or more after leaving the nest.

FAMILY CINCLIDAE
DIPPERS

The dipper's common name derives from its habit of frequently bobbing or "dipping" its entire body up and down.

These chunky, short-tailed birds are unique among passerines for their ability to forage underwater, where they feed on aquatic insects and small fish. These birds use their strongly muscled wings like oars when swimming and when submerged. Their sharply clawed feet help them hang onto rocks in swift-flowing streams. Enlarged sphincter muscles in the eyes are able to change the curvature of the lens, thus enhancing underwater vision. Dippers are also equipped with a large preen gland for waterproofing their dense plumage and have nasal flaps to prevent water from entering their nostrils. Finally, a

dipper's blood is rich in oxygen-storing red blood cells, which allows these birds to forage underwater for 15–30 seconds.

Dippers nest on ledges around fast-flowing water, sometimes building their nest behind a small waterfall or under a footbridge. The nest is a large sphere of grass, leaves, mosses, and lichens, with a large side entrance. Pairs usually mate for life. The female incubates a clutch of 3–5 white eggs for 14–17 days. Both sexes care for the young until they fledge at 18–26 days.

GENUS *CINCLUS*
American Dipper
Cinclus mexicanus

ALSO: American Water Ouzel, Grauwasseramsel, Cincle d'Amérique, Gråfossekall, Мексиканская оляпка. SN means "waterbird of Mexico," the type locality.
RANGE: Nests (Apr–Jul) and resident along mountain and coastal streams in the Aleutians (Unalaska Is), Alaska, w Canada, and w US south to Mexico, Guatemala, Costa Rica, w Panama.
ID: L 7–8 in (17–20 cm). Gray overall. Partial fringe of white feathers on eyelids is visible when the bird blinks. VOICE: Raspy *jik-jirac*. Sweet, varied, bell-like courtship song is piercing and loud enough to be heard over noise of a rushing stream. Both sexes sing.
HABITS: Jumps or dives headfirst into turbulent waters. Feeds on aquatic insects and insect larvae, and sometimes small fish, fish eggs, and flying insects taken from fast-flowing streams when breeding and from lakeshores, ponds, and estuaries in winter. Forages by flipping over small stones, probing into packs of leaf litter, gleaning rocks and cobbles. Seizes prey underwater, then eats it with the head out of the water.

White-throated Dipper
Cinclus cinclus

ALSO: Eurasian Dipper, Water Ouzel, Wasseramsel, Cincle plongeur, Fossekall, Оляпка. SN means "waterbird" as applied by Aristotle to an unidentified species. National bird of Norway.

RANGE: Nests (Apr–Jun) along alpine and urban streams in scattered locations in the UK, in Europe from Scandinavia to the Kola Penin and White Sea coast, in the Ural Mtns, and in c Asia and sw Siberia. Largely sedentary.

ID: L 7–8 in (17–20 cm). AD: Gray, with a brown head, conspicuous white bib, and chestnut breast. JUV: Grayish brown, with a whitish throat and upper breast crossed by wavy dark gray lines. VOICE: Short, sharp, piercing *dzeet-dzeet*. Song is a mix of harsh notes and far-carrying, ringing trills.

HABITS: Found singly and in pairs along banks of swift-flowing mountain streams having rocky bottoms, occasionally lives in lowland river valleys. Feeds on larvae of aquatic insects and occasionally on small fish. Monogamous. Both sexes defend their territory. Males without a mate will kill young of another pair in order to gain access to the other's mate. Female incubates the clutch of 4–5 white eggs for 15–16 days. Young fledge at 18–23 days, but are dependent on their parents while learning to forage. Young begin foraging in shallow waters and catch larvae instead of the larger invertebrates and fish their parents retrieve from deeper water. Young attain independence 9–15 days after fledging, depending on how quickly they learn to forage for themselves.

FAMILY PARIDAE
TITS AND CHICKADEES

Tits and chickadees are plump little birds whose bodies are covered in soft, fluffy plumage. They have short, thin bills, short wings, and fairly long, notched tails. Some call them *tits*, meaning "small," others *chickadees*—a name derived from the *chick-a-dee-dee* calls of some N Amer species.

These active, noisy, and social birds are territorial during the breeding season, but forage in mixed-species flocks for the rest of the year. They often join with other small birds in mobbing predators, driving them off amid a chorus of noisy calls.

Tits and chickadees feed on insects and spiders when breeding, and on seeds, nuts, and sunflower seeds taken at bird feeders in winter. In the UK, tits have been known to come to the doorsteps of homes and break open the foil seals of milk bottles to get at the cream. Parids are among the few passerine groups that can feed while hanging upside down. When tackling large seeds, they perch upright, holding the item with one foot and hammering it open with their bill. They also cache food for future use.

Pairs typically mate for life and remain together year round. All parids nest in cavities. They excavate a hole in a tree or stump with rotted wood or use an old woodpecker hole or a nest box. The female typically selects the nesting site and lines it with a felt-like mass of plant matter, moss, bark, and mammal hair. The female incubates the 2–19 (usually 5–10) white, often red-spotted eggs for 11–18 days. The male feeds the female and nestlings, and once the young fledge, both parents continue to feed the fledglings until they can hunt on their own.

juv.

ad.

ad.

White-throated Dipper
Cinclus cinclus
Europe–w Russia
L 7–8 in (17–20 cm)

American Dipper
Cinclus mexicanus
W N Amer
L 7–8 in (17–20 cm)

GENUS *PARUS*
Great Tit
Parus major

ALSO: Eurasian Great Tit, Kohlmeise, Mésange charbonnière, Kjøttmeis, Большая синица. SN means "large tit."

RANGE: Nests (Mar–Jun) in forests, woodlands, and gardens in the UK and Eurasia, east to Sakhalin Is, Japan, China, Mongolia, and south to nw Africa and Iran. Sedentary.

ID: L 5.5–6 in (14–15 cm). Back moss green. Wings gray, with a single white wing bar. Tail gray; outer tail feathers white. Head black, with a white face. Underparts yellow, with a black band extending from throat to undertail. **VOICE:** Harsh scolding *che-che-che-che-che*. Song is a thin, rather mechanical *tsee-tsee-tsee-pee*.

HABITS: Feeds on insects in summer, seeds in winter. In winter, forms roaming feeding flocks with other tits and small passerines.

GENUS *PERIPARUS*
Coal Tit
Periparus ater

ALSO: Coal Titmouse, Tannenmeise, Mésange noire, Svartmeis, Московка. SN means "dusky-colored *Parus*-like tit."

RANGE: Nests (Apr–Jun) in temperate forests, from e Asia and Siberia to Europe and the UK.

ID: L 4–4.5 in (10–11 cm). Lead gray above; dusky buff below. Two white wing bars. Head and throat black; face white; distinctive white nape spot; sometimes shows a tiny crest. **VOICE:** Rapid *tsee-pee, tsee-pee*, given from the treetops.

HABITS: Forages for seeds, insects, and spiders in the crown and high branches of trees, especially conifers. Nests in rotting tree stumps, rabbit burrows, rock crevices, and old nests of magpies.

GENUS *POECILE*
Boreal Chickadee
Poecile hudsonicus

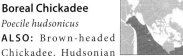

ALSO: Brown-headed Chickadee, Hudsonian Chickadee, Iknisailak, Hudsonmeise, Mésange à tête brune, Kanadameis, Лесная гаичка.

SN means "variegated [tit] of Hudson Bay [Canada]" the type locality.

RANGE: Nests (May–Jul) in coniferous forests at the northern tree limit in Canada, Alaska, south to the extreme n US. Generally sedentary within breeding range, with occasional irruptions into the south.

ID: L 5–6 in (12–15 cm). Grayish brown above. Crown and nape brown. Wings and tail dark slate, with pale edges. Cheeks white, merging into gray on ear coverts and sides of neck. Throat black. Underparts white, with cinnamon brown flanks. Separated from *P. cinctus* by its brown crown and cinnamon-colored flanks. **VOICE:** Distinctive wheezy *tsik-a-dee-dee*.

Siberian Tit
Poecile cinctus

ALSO: Gray-headed Chickadee, Alaskan Chickadee, Taiga Tit, Lapplandmeise, Mésange lapone, Lappmes, Сероголовая гаичка. SN means "variegated wreathed [tit]."

RANGE: Nests (May–Jun) in mature coniferous forests and upland birch forests from Scandinavia to Chukotka and Kamchatka, and in spruce and willow thickets in forest-tundra in n Alaska and nw Canada. The only parid known to breed in both the Old and New World. Sedentary.

ID: L 5–5.5 in (12–14 cm). Back warm brown to grayish brown; wings and tail gray; tertials broadly edged in white. Crown dull grayish brown. Black mask. Face, ear coverts, and sides of neck white. Black throat and bib. Underparts white, with pale brownish buff flanks. **VOICE:** Husky *dee-deer* or *chee-ee*.

HABITS: Forages in upper branches of trees. Hops along the ground and when moving from branch to branch.

Willow Tit
Poecile montanus

ALSO: Weidenmeise, Mésange boréale, Talltita, Буроголовая гаичка. SN means "variegated mountain [tit]."

RANGE: Nests (Apr–Jun) in montane coniferous forests, in deciduous forests at lower elevations,

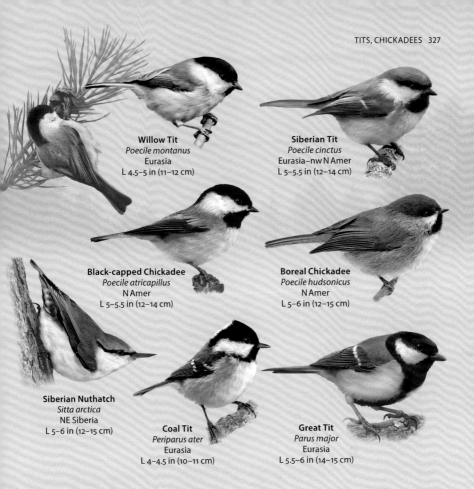

Willow Tit
Poecile montanus
Eurasia
L 4.5–5 in (11–12 cm)

Siberian Tit
Poecile cinctus
Eurasia–nw N Amer
L 5–5.5 in (12–14 cm)

Black-capped Chickadee
Poecile atricapillus
N Amer
L 5–5.5 in (12–14 cm)

Boreal Chickadee
Poecile hudsonicus
N Amer
L 5–6 in (12–15 cm)

Siberian Nuthatch
Sitta arctica
NE Siberia
L 5–6 in (12–15 cm)

Coal Tit
Periparus ater
Eurasia
L 4–4.5 in (10–11 cm)

Great Tit
Parus major
Eurasia
L 5.5–6 in (14–15 cm)

and in birch, alder, and willow thickets around bogs and gravel pits from the UK and Eurasia east to Kamchatka, Mongolia, China. Sedentary. **ID:** L 4.5–5 in (11–12 cm). Upperparts gray. Crown, nape, and throat black; large white patch on face. Underparts pale gray (buffy in UK birds). **VOICE:** Buzzing note followed by a cheery *dzee-dzee-dzee*. Song is *pee-oo pee-oo*. **HABITS:** Caches seeds and nuts in fall, and can be entirely dependent on this store in winter. Excavates its own nesting hole in a rotted stump or tree with decaying wood.

Black-capped Chickadee

Poecile atricapillus
ALSO: Schwarzkopfmeise, Mésange à tête noire, Ameri-kameis, Синица. SN means "variegated black-cap [tit]."

RANGE: Nests (Apr–Jun) in deciduous woodland, often around human habitation, from Alaska south through Canada and n US. **ID:** L 5–5.5 in (12–14 cm). Crown and nape black; back olive gray; wings and tail dark gray, edged with gray or white. Face and sides of neck white. Chin and throat black. Underparts white, with buffy flanks. **VOICE:** Clear, classic *chicka-dee-dee-dee* given throughout the year. Call sometimes serves to summon other birds to mob predators. Research indicates that the number of *dee* syllables at the end of the call increases with the level of perceived danger. **HABITS:** Forages in dry or wet woodlands, tall thickets, shrubbery and trees around homes, and occasionally in open, weedy fields. Frequent visitor to bird feeders, especially those filled with sunflower seeds. Both sexes excavate the nest, which is usually low, in a soft decaying stump.

FAMILY SITTIDAE
NUTHATCHES

These small woodland birds forage on tree trunks, using their strong legs and clawed feet to brace themselves as they move down a tree while searching for insects in bark crevices. Nuthatches also feed on nuts and seeds, which they wedge into a bark crevice, then use their bill to hack open the shell. This habit earns them the common name "nuthatch," a corruption of the Old English word *nuthack*.

GENUS *SITTA*
Siberian Nuthatch
Sitta arctica

ALSO: Kleiber-arctica, Sittelle de Sibérie, Spettmeis, Поползень. Considered a subspecies of the Eurasian Nuthatch, *S. europaea*, by some. SN means "woodpecker-like arctic bird."
RANGE: Nests (Apr–Jun) in ne Siberian taiga, from the Lena Rvr east to the Anadyr Rvr.
ID: L 5–6 in (12–15 cm). Stocky body, large head, thin straight bill, short tail, strong short legs, and feet with long, sharp hind claws. Upperparts bluish gray. Narrow black eye stripe, sometimes edged by a narrow white supercilium. White below, with chestnut on lower flanks. Tail dark, with a white patch at center of outer rectrices. Undertail coverts cinnamon, with faint white spots on tips. VOICE: Loud, whistled *wheet-wheet-wheet* or *tchoo-tchoo-tchoop*.
HABITS: Monogamous. Nests in cavities in tree stumps or uses old woodpecker holes. Smears clay on nest entrance to reduce size of entry. Clutch is 6–8 white, rufous-spotted eggs.

FAMILY TROGLODYTIDAE
WRENS

The tiny wrens of the boreal regions are similar in appearance, having reddish brown upperparts and rufous to buffy underparts that bear fine, dark vermiculations. They have short wings, thin, pointed bills, and all typically hold their tail cocked. They inhabit dense undergrowth and brush piles, which they investigate with great diligence, creeping mouse-like into dark crevices and tangles as they search for insects, spiders, and other small arthropods. Their flight is rapid and darting, with a whirring of wings.

Superb songsters, wrens readily reveal their location through their songs, which are performed with the entire body stretched upward, tail cocked, and head thrown back. Unaided, the human ear hears only a blur of high-pitched tinkles and buzzes, but if one records the song and plays it back at quarter speed, the rich aria of warbles and trills can be heard.

Most species are monogamous and territorial. The male builds a number of so-called "cock's nests" in rock crevices or cavities, constructing a domed nest of moss, cedar bark, twigs, rootlets, shreds of decayed wood, grass, feathers, and hair, with fine twigs at the side entry hole. The female chooses one in which to lay her eggs and lines it with feathers and occasionally deer, fox, or caribou fur. The female alone incubates the clutch of 3–10 cream to pink, often brown-spotted eggs for 12–15 days. Young fledge in 10–17 days and receive parental care for another 2 weeks, sometimes returning to the nest to roost.

Wrens in the *Troglodytes troglodytes* complex have recently been split into separate species based on differences in DNA sequences and vocalizations. The Eurasian Winter Wren retains the original scientific name, while the Pacific Wren becomes *Troglodytes pacificus* and the Winter Wren, *Troglodytes hiemalis*.

GENUS *TROGLODYTES*
Eurasian Wren
Troglodytes troglodytes

ALSO: Northern Wren, Winter Wren, Zaunkönig, Troglodyte mignon, Músarrindill, Gjerdesmett, Крапивник. SN means "cave-dweller," an allusion to the habit of roosting and foraging for insects in dark cavities and crevices. CN derives from the Old English *wrenna*.
RANGE: Nests (May–Jun) in coniferous forests and on moors in Iceland, Faroes, UK, and continental Europe, east across c Asia to Kamchatka and Kurils, and south to n Africa, Middle East, and e Asia. High-elevation breeders descend to lower elevations in winter; other populations are resident or short-distance migrants.

Pacific Wren
Troglodytes pacificus
W N Amer
L 3.5–4 in (9–11 cm)

Rusty Woodsia
Woodsia ilvensis

Eurasian Wren
Troglodytes troglodytes
Eurasia
L 3.5–4 in (9–11 cm)

Winter Wren
Troglodytes hiemalis
E N Amer
L 3.5–4 in (9–11 cm)

ID: L 3.5–4 in (9–11 cm). Small, round-bodied, with a short, cocked tail. Rufous above, grayer below; barred with darker brown, rufous, and gray on the wings, tail, and flanks. Dark brown bill. Pale brown legs. VOICE: Loud series of metallic, ringing notes and trills.

Pacific Wren

Troglodytes pacificus
ALSO: Aleutian Wren, Kiska Wren, Troglodyte de Baird. SN means "cave-dweller of the Pacific."

RANGE: Nests (Apr–Jun) from sea level to 10,425 ft (3178 m), in the Aleutians and s Alaska south to California and Utah. Most northern populations move to coastal areas in winter.
ID: L 3.5–4 in (9–10.5 cm). Size and color vary geographically; largest and palest birds are in the Aleutians; smaller, darker, and more richly colored birds inhabit the Pacific coast. Dark brown to rufous above, paler brown to rich rufous below; barred overall with dark brown. Pale eyebrow. Dark, thin, pointed bill. Pale brown legs. Short, cocked tail. VOICE: Sharp, husky *chek, chek-chek, chek-chek*. Song is a 5–10 second stream of rapid, high-pitched, melodious notes, trills, and chatters.
HABITS: In courtship, the male perches near the female, with wings half-opened and fluttering, tail moving from side to side, while he sings or

calls. Nests (Apr–Jun) in fallen logs, stumps, brush piles, and large trees in damp, old-growth forests and on cliff faces in the treeless Aleutians. Nest site is in any kind of natural cavity located close to the ground; this includes holes among upturned roots of downed trees, cavities in rotten stumps, old woodpecker holes, and rock crevices. Both sexes help build nest of grass, weeds, moss, rootlets, and line it with animal hair and feathers.

RELATED SPECIES: WINTER WREN, *T. hiemalis*, is a non-arctic species that breeds in e N Amer forests from s Canada to s Georgia. Paler overall than *T. pacificus*, with a distinct pale rufous eyebrow and a pale, often cream-colored throat and breast. Song is a rich, loud series of *churp-chick-crrrrip-chrrr* phrases, with each phrase rising at the end.

FAMILY VIREONIDAE
VIREOS

Vireo is Latin for "I am green," an apt name, as these New World woodland passerines are typically dull green above and white or greenish yellow below. The smaller vireos resemble wood warblers, but are larger-headed and have heavier, slightly hooked bills. They also move more deliberately than warblers, perching frequently between feeding forays. Vireos eat some fruit, but feed mainly on insects and other arboreal invertebrates gleaned from foliage.

Males of most species are enthusiastic and persistent singers in spring, although their songs are usually simple monotonic phrases. In the northern species, the female alone builds an intricately woven, open cup nest that is suspended from forks of horizontal twigs. The nest is typically made from dried leaves, bark strips, and coarse grass, and lined with fine grass and spider silk. The female incubates the clutch of 3–4 white, lightly spotted eggs for 12–16 days. Young fledge in 10–12 days but remain with parents and are fed by them for up to 40 days after leaving the nest.

GENUS *VIREO*
Red-eyed Vireo
Vireo olivaceus

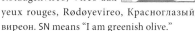

ALSO: Red-eyed Greenlet, Rotaugenvireo, Viréo aux yeux rouges, Rødøyevireo, Красноглазый виреон. SN means "I am greenish olive."

RANGE: Nests (May–Jul) in open woodland from se Alaska and Great Bear Lake, Canada, south to nw and e US. Winters to Cuba and Amazonia.
ID: L 6 in (15 cm). Upperparts olive green. Gray crown. Prominent white eyebrow, with a black line above and a dark line extending from lores to behind eye. Red iris (not always easy to see in the field). Underparts white, with pale yellow flanks and undertail coverts. Strong bluish gray legs. VOICE: Breeding male sings his monotonic song *cherr-o-wit, cheree, sissy-a-wit, tee-oo* incessantly from dawn to dusk, earning this species the nickname, "the Preacher."

Warbling Vireo
Vireo gilvus
ALSO: Sängervireo, Viréo mélodieux, Sangvireo, Поющий виреон. SN means "I am greenish yellow."

RANGE: Nests (May–Jul) in open deciduous and mixed woodland, often in aspen groves near water, from se Alaska, east across Canada, and south to Mexico and Florida. Winters to C Amer.
ID: L 5.5 in (13 cm). Plain; lacks distinctive markings. Upperparts grayish green. Whitish eyebrow and short dusky line through the eye.

Underparts whitish, washed with pale yellow on flanks and undertail coverts. VOICE: Males and sometimes females sing a rapid, husky warble, *vidervee, vidervee, vidervee, veet'*, often transcribed as *iggley, pigelly, wigelly, pig*. Calls include a nasal *eeah* and metallic *vit*.

FAMILY REGULIDAE
KINGLETS AND CRESTS
These tiny, lively songbirds breed in the northern coniferous forests. Their generic name *Regulus* means "little king" and, like *kinglet* and *crest*, alludes to the brightly colored crown.

Kinglets and crests feed largely on spiders, spider eggs, and insects, which they glean from the surface of leaves and branches, often while hovering over the foliage. The female alone builds a deep cup nest of moss, lichens, needles, and bark high in the treetops and incubates a clutch of 8–12 cream-colored eggs for 12–17 days. It is no small task for a tiny bird to keep a large clutch of eggs warm, and female goldcrests have learned to shift around in the nest so that their legs can warm those eggs not covered by her small brood pouch. The male's role is to feed his mate and nestlings and to join with the female in feeding the fledglings during the first days they are out of the nest.

GENUS *REGULUS*
Goldcrest
Regulus regulus

ALSO: Wintergoldhähnchen, Roitelet huppé, Fuglekonge, Желтоголовый королёк. SN means "little king." Smallest bird in Europe.
RANGE: Nests (May–Jun) in coniferous and mixed forests from the UK east across Eurasia to Kamchatka, s Kurils, and e Asia. Winters south to Mediterranean, Iran, China.
ID: L 3.5 in (9 cm). Upperparts olive gray, with 2 conspicuous white wing bars and a broken white eyering. Crown patch is golden orange in males, yellow in female; 2 parallel black stripes edge the crown. Underparts are yellowish olive. VOICE: Thin *tsee-tsee-tsee*. Song is a thin, high-pitched *pee-teet'-eeloo, pee-teet'-eeloo, pee-teet'-eeloo, zree-zree-o*.

ad. ♂ Ruby-crowned
with crest hidden

ad. ♂ Ruby-crowned
with crest raised

Kinglets and crests
often hover at branch
tips to glean insects

Ruby-crowned Kinglet
Regulus calendula
N Amer
L 4.25 in (11 cm)

ad. ♂

Golden-crowned Kinglet
Regulus satrapa
N Amer
L 4 in (10 cm)

Goldcrest
Regulus regulus
Eurasia
L 3.5 in (9 cm)

The beautiful
suspended nest of
the Warbling Vireo

Warbling Vireo
Vireo gilvus
N Amer
L 5.5 in (14 cm)

Red-eyed Vireo
Vireo olivaceus
N Amer
L 6 in (15 cm)

HABITS: Forms flocks except when nesting. Forages high in the treetops, restlessly moving and hovering among the leaves to glean insects. Nest is a domed cup built at the tip of a conifer branch. Clutch is 8–10 pinkish eggs speckled with reddish brown.

Ruby-crowned Kinglet

Regulus calendula

ALSO: Dusky Kinglet, Rubin-goldhähnchen, Roitelet à couronne rubis, Rubinfugle-konge, Рубиновоголовый королёк. SN means "little king with a glowing head dress."

RANGE: Nests (May–Jul) in alpine spruce-fir forests from Alaska south through Canada into ne US. Winters to s California, Guatemala, Cuba, Bahamas. Accidental to Greenland and Iceland, possibly ship-aided, as there are several records of birds landing on ships in the Atlantic, especially in the fall.

ID: L 4.25 in (11 cm). Upperparts grayish olive, with 2 conspicuous white wing bars and a broken white eyering. Underparts are buffy, with olive flanks. AD ♂: Scarlet crown patch, which is raised when agitated and otherwise concealed.
VOICE: Loud, lively song, beginning with high, clear *tzee* notes and ending with higher-pitched *tee-da-leet, tee-da-leet, tee-da-leet.*

HABITS: Moves through foliage and along branches with short hops, habitually flicking wings. Feeds on spiders, insects, and some seeds and fruit. Hovers as it gleans insects from the surfaces of leaves and branches; also pecks at fallen pine needles and flies out to hawk insects. Nests in conifers in dense foliage near the trunk and up to 100 ft (30 m) above the ground.

RELATED SPECIES: The more southerly GOLDEN-CROWNED KINGLFT, *R. satrapa*, breeds in coniferous forests from s Alaska and c Canada south through the contiguous US. The species is distinguished from *R. regulus* by the boldly patterned black and white face and golden crown patch of both sexes.

SYLVIIDAE & OLD WORLD WARBLERS

Sylviidae formerly encompassed more than 400 species of Old World warblers. The family has been reconstituted and most species placed in newly created families. Only the sylviid warblers, which are more closely related to Asian babblers than to other warblers, are now included in the family Sylviidae.

FAMILY SYLVIIDAE
SYLVIID WARBLERS

These Palearctic warblers inhabit thorny thickets in open woodland. Their plumage is muted brown to gray above, whitish to buff below. The stout bill has bristles at its base, and the wings have 10 primary feathers. Sylviid warblers glean insects from vegetation or capture them in flight. They also feed on berries and other soft fruits. Breeding is monogamous. Pairs build a cup-shaped nest near the ground in dense vegetation. Both sexes incubate 3–7 creamy white eggs with brown blotches for 11–12 days. The young fledge in about 10 days.

GENUS *SYLVIA*
Garden Warbler

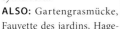

Sylvia borin
ALSO: Gartengrasmücke, Fauvette des jardins, Hage-sanger, Садовая славка. SN means "fig-eating woodland warbler."
RANGE: Nests (May–Jun) in open woodland with dense undergrowth from the UK and w Europe, east to c and sw Siberia. Winters to S Africa. Casual fall visitor to Iceland.
ID: L 5–6 in (13–15 cm). Olive brown above, off-white below. Fairly heavy, stubby bill. Gray legs. Shows slight crest when singing. VOICE: Clicking *chek, chek, chek*, given while hidden in vegetation. Thrush-like song of the male has been likened to the sound of a rippling brook.

Lesser Whitethroat

Sylvia curruca
ALSO: Klappergrasmücke, Fauvette babillarde, Møller, Славка-завирушка. SN means "woodland warbler," with *curruca* being

an unidentified warbler mentioned by the Roman satirist Juvenal (*c.* 60–140).
RANGE: Nests (May–Jun) in woodland thickets and edges of fields from UK and w Europe east to the Lena Rvr and south to c Asia. Winters in c Africa, Iran, India. Casual visitor to Iceland.
ID: L 4.5–5 in (11–13 cm). Back drab brown. Head lead gray, with dark ear coverts and sometimes pale spectacles. Throat and underparts off-white, with buffy flanks. Dark bill and legs. VOICE: Dry, clicking *tett* or chattering *che-che-che-che*. Song is a short, scratchy warble followed by a fast, rattling *tell-tell-tell*.

FAMILY PHYLLOSCOPIDAE
LEAF WARBLERS

Leaf warblers inhabit the Eurasian forests and woodlands. One species, the Arctic Warbler, occurs in w Alaska as well as Eurasia. Leaf warblers are small birds with slender bills and legs. The plumage is greenish gray above, white or yellowish below. Most have a pale eyebrow. Some show a single or double wing bar. These birds hover or flick their wings while gleaning insects from leaves at the tips of branches. Breeding is mostly monogamous. Pairs build a loosely woven, domed nest on or near the ground, or on a fallen log or stump. The female alone incubates 3–7 white or cream, rufous-spotted eggs for 10-12 days. Young sometimes roost with the female for 2–3 weeks after fledging.

GENUS *PHYLLOSCOPUS*
Arctic Warbler

Phylloscopus borealis
ALSO: Wanderlaubsänger, Pouillot boréal, Lappsanger, Пеночка-таловка, Sunyapaluktunyiq, *Seicercus borealis*. SN means "boreal leaf-watcher."
RANGE: Nests (Jun–Jul) in coniferous and mixed forests and thickets from Scandinavia east to Chukotka and w Alaska, and south to Mongolia, Manchuria, and N Korea. All populations winter to se China and Philippines. Alaskan breeders migrate (yellow lines on map) to the Asian coast via the Aleutian chain or Bering Strait before proceeding to the Philippines. The Arctic Warbler undertakes the longest migration of any Old

World insectivorous bird—no mere task for a bird that weighs only a third of an ounce (9 g). **ID:** L 4.5–5 in (11.5–13 cm). Upperparts grayish to brownish olive. Underparts paler olive, diffusely streaked on breast and with dusky flanks. Prominent, narrow, buffy eyebrow curves upward at rear of head and does not extend onto forehead. Bold black eye stripe. Pale crescent on lower half of eye. Single wing bar formed by pale tips of greater coverts and hint of second wing bar on median coverts. Dark bill, with yellow orange at base of lower mandible. Legs and feet pale yellow. **VOICE:** Soft *tzeet-tzeet*. Song is loud, vigorous, fast trill, *tzee-tzee-tzee*.

Willow Warbler

Phylloscopus trochilus
ALSO: European Leaf Warbler, Fitis, Pouillot

fitis, Løvsanger, Пеночка-весничка. SN means "small leaf-watcher."
RANGE: Nests (May–Jun) in forests, woodlands, reed beds, and tundra thickets of willow, alder, and birch from UK and w Europe to the Anadyr Rvr in Chukotka. Most populations winter in sub-Saharan Africa. Casual visitor to Iceland in summer.
ID: L 4.5–5 in (11–13 cm). Slim silhouette. Plain greenish brown upperparts with no wing bars. Underparts yellowish to off-white. Yellowish eyebrow and dark eyeline. **VOICE:** Rising whistled *fyoo-eet'*. Song is a repetitive descending whistle, often ending with a trill.

Common Chiffchaff

Phylloscopus collybita
ALSO: Brown Leaf Warbler, Zilpzalp, Pouillot véloce, Gransanger, Теньковка. SN

means "leaf-watching money changer," the latter referring to the species' *chiff-chaff* call, which sounds like coins clinking together.
RANGE: Nests (May–Jun) in forests and woods from the UK and Europe across Siberia to the Kolyma Rvr. Winters to Africa, w Asia, India.
ID: L 4–4.5 in (10–11 cm). Chunky silhouette. Brownish green above. Cream below, washed with yellow on the flanks. Short whitish eyebrow.

Habitually dips tail. **VOICE:** Cheerful, rising *hweet*. Song is a repetitive, jingling *chiff-chaff*.
SIMILAR SPECIES: SIBERIAN CHIFFCHAFF, *P. tristis*, which replaces the Common Chiffchaff in Siberia east to the Pechora Rvr, has a brownish gray rather than an olive crown and mantle; buffy flanks with no trace of yellow; buffy eyebrow; and densely black legs. Call is an evenly pitched, plaintive *eeep*.

Yellow-browed Warbler

Phylloscopus inornatus
ALSO: Gelbbrauen-Laubsänger, Pouillot à grands sourcils, Gulbrynsanger,

Зарничка. SN means "plain leaf-watcher."
RANGE: Nests (Jun) in lowland and montane forests and woodlands from the Ural Mtns to the Sea of Okhotsk, Mongolia, Manchuria, Korea. Winters in s Asia. Casual fall visitor to Iceland and coasts of w Europe. Accidental to St Lawrence Is, Alaska (1999) and Baja Calif (2007).
ID: L 3.75–4.25 in (9.5–11 cm). Moss green above, whitish below. Yellowish double wing bar. Long yellow eyebrow. Some individuals show a faint pale green central crown stripe. Dark legs. **VOICE:** Loud, piercing, often disyllabic *tseewees-tsweest*. Song is a short, high-pitched, whistled *veet-veet-tzhee*.

Dusky Warbler

Phylloscopus fuscatus
ALSO: Dusky Leaf-Warbler, Dunkellaubsänger, Pouillot brun, Brunsanger, Бурая

пеночка. SN means "dark leaf-watcher."
RANGE: Nests (May–Jun) in open forest, willow scrub along riverbanks, taiga bogs, wet meadows, and upland thickets of dwarf birch, from c Siberia east to Kamchatka and Sakhalin, south to Mongolia and w China. Winters in se Asia. Fall vagrant to w Europe. Irregular fall migrant to Shemya Is (c Aleutians), St Lawrence Is, w Alaska, and California.
ID: L 4–5 in (11–13 cm). Uniformly dark warm brown above, dusky buff below. Long, pale eyebrow is white and sharply defined in front of eye. Narrow, pointed, dark bill, with some

reddish brown at base of lower mandible. Flicks short, rounded wings while foraging. Thin reddish brown legs. VOICE: Sharp *chek-chek*, given as it forages for insects in thickets and low, rank vegetation. Song is a monotonic whistle.

FAMILY LOCUSTELLIDAE
GRASS WARBLERS

The mechanical, insect-like, chirring song of these warblers gives rise to the generic name, *Locustella*, the diminutive of the Latin *locusta*, a grasshopper. Grass warblers inhabit the open grasslands, scrub, and marshes of Eurasia. They skulk through heavy grass and low tangles in search of insects and nest on the ground or in grass tussocks in boggy areas.

GENUS *LOCUSTELLA*
Lanceolated Warbler

Locustella lanceolata
ALSO: Strichelschwirl, Locustelle lancéolée, Stripe-sanger, Пятнистый сверчок, Lanceolated Grasshopper Warbler. SN means "grasshopper warbler with spear-shaped [markings]."
RANGE: Nests (May–Jun) on the ground in wet open forests with rank undergrowth from Finland to Kamchatka, Sakhalin, n Japan. Winters to s Asia, Greater Sundas, and Philippines.
ID: L 4.5–5 in (11–13 cm). Upperparts olive brown, distinctly streaked with dark brown. Underparts rusty yellow buff to off-white, with small dark narrow streaks on breast, flanks, and undertail. VOICE: Call is a clicking *chick, chick*. Song is a locust-like chirring given while perched at the top of a reed or grass stalk.
RELATED SPECIES: PALLAS'S GRASSHOPPER WARBLER, *L. certhiola*, breeds from nc Siberia to Kamchatka. Separated from *L. lanceolata* by plain underparts, rufous rump, and rounded tail that is tipped in black and white.

FAMILY ACROCEPHALIDAE
REED WARBLERS

Acrocephalidae derives from the Greek *akeros*, pointed, and *kephale*, the head, referring to how some males slightly raise their crest when singing. Reed warblers are slim brown birds with long pointed bills and flattened foreheads. These birds inhabit marshes, reed beds, and grassy thickets of Eurasia, the Pacific, and Africa, and nest in grass tussocks and low bushes. They pluck insects from plant stalks or the water surface, or fly out to snatch prey from the air and typically forage at dusk and dawn when temperatures are lower and prey less mobile.

GENUS *ACROCEPHALUS*
Sedge Warbler

Acrocephalus schoenobaenus
ALSO: Schilfrohrsänger, Phragmite des joncs, Sivsanger, Барсучок. SN means "pointy-headed reed-walker."
RANGE: Nests (May–Jun) in reed beds, marshes, partially flooded ditches, grassy fields, and other wetland habitats in the UK and across Europe, east to the Yenesei Rvr in Siberia. Migrates across the Sahara to winter in sub-Saharan Africa.
ID: L 4.5–5 in (11–13 cm). AD: Upperparts brown, with diffuse streaks on back. Rump plain warm brown. Broad buffy eyebrow. Dark, diffuse streaking on crown and cheeks. Underparts cream, tinged with rufous on breast and flanks. Strong, pointed bill. Brownish pink legs. JUV: Resembles adult, but often with fine dark streaks on upper breast. VOICE: Soft *chrr-chrr-chrr* or *feweet-klee-klee*. Male's song, often heard at night, is composed of varied chattering phrases and chirrs and may include mimicry of other species; males with the greatest repertoire of songs mate with the largest number of females.

FAMILY PARULIDAE
NEW WORLD WARBLERS

Parulidae stems from the Latin word *parula*, a diminutive of *parus*, which means "little tit." Warbler derives from the Old French *werbler*, meaning "to sing with trills"; only male parulids sing, however.

The New World warblers are small passerines ranging in length from 4.25 to 6 in (11–15 cm). Most species are arboreal, except for the Palm Warbler, Northern Waterthrush, and Ovenbird, which largely feed on the ground. Breeding males typically have brightly colored plumage. Spring

Yellow-browed Warbler
Phylloscopus inornatus
Siberia
L 3.75–4.25 in (9.5–11 cm)

Arctic Warbler
Phylloscopus borealis
Eurasia, w Alaska
L 4.5–5 in (11–13 cm)

Dusky Warbler
Phylloscopus fuscatus
Siberia
L 4–5 in (10–13 cm)

Siberian Chiffchaff
Phylloscopus tristis
Siberia
L 4–4.5 in (10–11 cm)

Lesser Whitethroat
Sylvia curruca
Eurasia
L 4.5–5 in (11–13 cm)

Common Chiffchaff
Phylloscopus collybita
Eurasia
L 4–4.5 in (10–11 cm)

Garden Warbler
Sylvia borin
Europe–sw Siberia
L 5–6 in (13–15 cm)

Willow Warbler
Phylloscopus trochilus
Eurasia
L 4.5–5 in (11–13 cm)

Pallas's Grasshopper Warbler
Locustella certhiola
NC Siberia–Kamchatka
L 5–5.5 in (13–14 cm)

Sedge Warbler
Acrocephalus schoenbaenus
Europe–c Siberia
L 4.5–5 in (11–13 cm)

Lanceolated Warbler
Locustella lanceolata
E Europe–ne Asia
L 4.5–5 in (11–13 cm)

females, winter males, and juveniles display less colorful plumage.

Warblers are highly insectivorous when nesting, but add fruit and nectar to their diet on wintering grounds. Typical of birds that glean for small insects, warblers have small, slender bills. Some have rictal bristles—stiff hairs that surround the bill and increase the gape area of the mouth—a utilitarian feature for birds that dart out to snatch small flying insects midair.

Arctic-breeding warblers tend to lay fairly large clutches, typically 4–6 eggs, thus capitalizing on their one chance to breed during the short summer. The nesting cycle usually lasts fewer than 30 days, allowing the young to mature and become independent while it is still warm and abundant food is available. The female alone builds the nest and incubates a clutch of 3–5 buffy or cream, brown-spotted eggs for 10–14 days. The male often sings as he watches the nest from distant trees. Both sexes feed the nestlings, which fledge at 12–14 days.

Included in the species accounts and illustrations are warblers that breed just south of the range covered in this guide. These include the Black-and-white Warbler, Magnolia Warbler, Townsend's Warbler, Cape May Warbler, Bay-breasted Warbler, American Redstart, and Ovenbird, which are to be watched for in the Far North if the Arctic continues to warm.

GENUS *OREOTHLYPIS*
Orange-crowned Warbler
Oreothlypis celata
ALSO: Orangefleck-Waldsänger, Paruline verdâtre, Oransjekrone-parula, Рыжешапочная

древесница, *Vermivora celata*. SN means "mountain warbler with a hidden [crown]."
RANGE: Nests (Apr–Jun) in shrub thickets, open deciduous woods, and coniferous forest edges with low undergrowth from n Alaska and n Canada south through the w US. Winters south to the Bahamas and C Amer.
ID: L 4.75–5.25 in (12–13.5 cm). Plain, lacking distinctive markings; small, orange crown patch is usually concealed and is often absent

in female. Dull olive green above, with greenish yellow rump. Crown and nape gray. Yellow or white eyering, split by dark eyeline. Underparts greenish yellow, faintly streaked with gray or yellow. Undertail coverts yellow. VOICE: Call is a sharp *chip*. Song is a high-pitched, rising *chee chee chee chew chew*.
HABITS: Hover gleans insects from leaves, blossoms, and branch tips. Sometimes hawks for flying insects or searches through leaf litter on the ground. Builds a cup nest on the ground or low in bushes, ferns, and vines. Nest is usually sheltered by overhanging vegetation and often placed on shady slopes or steep banks.

Tennessee Warbler
Oreothlypis peregrina
ALSO: Brauenwaldsänger,

Paruline obscure, Møllparula, Теннесийская древесница, *Vermivora peregrina*. SN means "wandering [or migrant] mountain warbler." CN refers to the type specimen—a migrant bird collected by Alexander Wilson (1766–1813) on the banks of Tennessee's Cumberland Rvr.
RANGE: Nests (Jun–Aug) in clearings in spruce-fir forest, along margins of spruce-tamarack bogs, and in second-growth forests with balsam poplar in se Alaska and n Canada, south to n US. Migrates across the Gulf of Mexico to and from wintering grounds in C Amer and n S Amer.
ID: L 4.5–5 in (11–13 cm). Plain, lacking distinctive markings. Bright olive green above. Crown and nape gray, very rarely with a few rufous feathers on male's crown. Distinct dark eyeline. Narrow white eyebrow. Underparts white in adults (juveniles show some yellow on throat and breast). Distinguished from the Orange-crowned Warbler by white rather than yellow undertail coverts, brighter green on mantle, and lack of streaks on breast. VOICE: Call is a sharp, high *stik*. Song is a 3-parted, loud, staccato trill, *tip tip tip tip, teepit teepit teepit teepit, ti ti ti ti ti ti ti.*
HABITS: Gleans invertebrates, especially caterpillars, from the outer foliage of trees and shrubs. Builds a well-concealed ground nest, often in a bed of sphagnum moss at the base of a small shrub or tree, or in roots of a fallen tree.

GENUS *SETOPHAGA*
Blackpoll Warbler

Setophaga striata
ALSO: Streifenwaldsänger, Paruline rayée, Svarthette-parula, Пестрогрудый лесной певун, *Dendroica striata.* SN means "striped moth-eater." CN refers to the male's black cap, with *poll* deriving from the Middle English *polle*, meaning "hair at the top of the head."

RANGE: Nests (Jun–Jul) in alder thickets in forest-tundra and in subalpine and coastal spruce-fir forests in Alaska and Canada. Winters from Colombia to Peru and w Amazonia. Vagrant to Greenland, Iceland, UK, France.

Blackpolls undertake the longest migration of any N Amer songbird—a round-trip journey averaging 12,000 mi (19,300 km). In autumn, they stop to feed on the N Amer eastern seaboard before making a 40- to 60-hour, nonstop, trans-Atlantic flight of some 2000 mi (3220 km). They land in Venezuela or Guyana, and some remain there while others continue to Brazil, adding 1500 mi (2400 km) or more to their trip. The northbound migration takes them across the Gulf of Mexico or Caribbean Sea, then up the continental interior of N Amer to their northern breeding grounds.

ID: L 5–5.5 in (13–14 cm). AD ♂ APR–AUG: Top of head black; rest of head white, with black malar stripe. Back gray, streaked with black. Two white wing bars. Tail dark, with white spots on outer tail feathers. Underparts white, with black streaks on sides and flanks. Legs and feet yellow orange. AD ♀ APR–AUG: Olive gray above, with dark streaks on crown, nape, and mantle. Pale eyebrow. Dark streaking on malar area. Underparts whitish, narrowly streaked with black. Two white wing bars. AD WINTER: Olive gray above, variably streaked with black. Underparts whitish, sometimes washed with yellow and narrowly streaked with black on throat, breast, and flanks. Pale yellow eyebrow. Dark eyeline. VOICE: Call is a sharp *chip*. Male's song, given from treetops, is a high-pitched, staccato trill, *tsi-tsi-tsi-TSIT-TSIT-TSIT-tsi-tsi-tsi-tsi.* **HABITS:** Gleans insects from foliage and inner tree branches. Nests on the ground near a tree.

SIMILAR SPECIES: BLACK-AND-WHITE WARBLER, *Mniotilta varia*, nests in open woodland and mature mixed forest from c Canada south through the e US. Male is boldly streaked in black and

white and has 2 white wing bars. Female and juvenile are duller and less streaked. Song is a high *see wee-see wee-see wee-see wee-see wee-see.* Creeps like a nuthatch up and down tree trunks and along branches as it forages for insects and spiders in the bark. Nests on the ground against a shrub, tree, stump, rock, or fallen log.

American Yellow Warbler

Setophaga aestiva
ALSO: Goldwaldsänger, Paruline jaune, Gulparula, Жёлтый лесной певун, *Dendroica petechia.* SN

means "red-spotted moth-eater."
RANGE: Nests (May–Jul) in wet willow thickets and woodland edge from n Alaska and n Canada, south to Florida. Winters in C Amer and S Amer. **ID:** L 4.5–5 in (11–13 cm). AD ♂: Bright yellow overall, darkest on back. Two diffuse, pale wing bars. Breast and flanks marked with bold chestnut streaks. AD ♀: Uniformly yellow. VOICE: Call is a sharp *tchup*. Song is a whistling *swee'-swee'-swee'-swee-swit-su-su*, given from a snag or open perch.
HABITS: Builds a cup nest of twigs and bark in the upright fork of a bush, sapling, or tree.

Palm Warbler

Setophaga palmarum
ALSO: Yellow Redpoll Warbler, Palmenwaldsänger, Paruline à couronne rousse,

Myrparula, Пальмовая древесница, *Dendroica palmarum.* SN means "moth-eater of the palms."
RANGE: Nests (May–Jul) in bogs and fens in coniferous forests from c Alaska (rarely) and ne Yukon, east across Canada and south to n US. Winters along the US Atlantic, Pacific, and Gulf coasts, south to the W Indies and Nicaragua. **ID:** L 5–6 in (13–15 cm). AD APR–AUG: Grayish brown to olive brown above. Rufous crown.

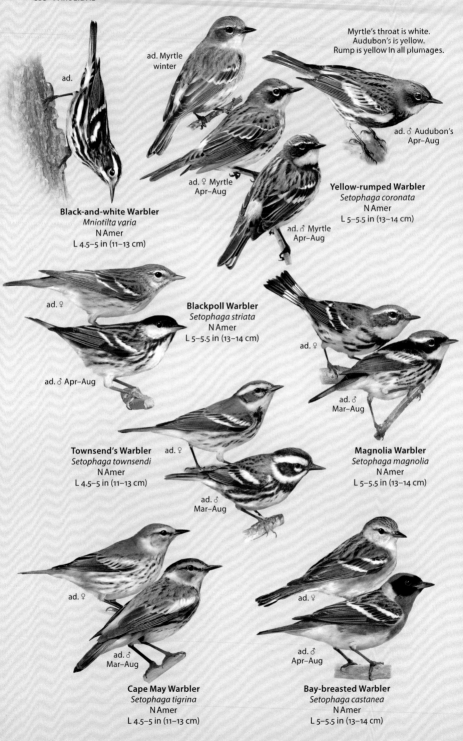

ad.

ad. Myrtle
winter

Myrtle's throat is white.
Audubon's is yellow.
Rump is yellow in all plumages.

ad. ♂ Audubon's
Apr–Aug

ad. ♀ Myrtle
Apr–Aug

ad. ♂ Myrtle
Apr–Aug

Black-and-white Warbler
Mniotilta varia
N Amer
L 4.5–5 in (11–13 cm)

Yellow-rumped Warbler
Setophaga coronata
N Amer
L 5–5.5 in (13–14 cm)

ad. ♀

ad. ♂ Apr–Aug

Blackpoll Warbler
Setophaga striata
N Amer
L 5–5.5 in (13–14 cm)

ad. ♀

ad. ♂
Mar–Aug

ad. ♀

Townsend's Warbler
Setophaga townsendi
N Amer
L 4.5–5 in (11–13 cm)

ad. ♂
Mar–Aug

Magnolia Warbler
Setophaga magnolia
N Amer
L 5–5.5 in (13–14 cm)

ad. ♀

ad. ♂
Mar–Aug

ad. ♀

ad. ♂
Apr–Aug

Cape May Warbler
Setophaga tigrina
N Amer
L 4.5–5 in (11–13 cm)

Bay-breasted Warbler
Setophaga castanea
N Amer
L 5–5.5 in (13–14 cm)

American Yellow Warbler
Setophaga aestiva
N Amer
L 4.5–5 in (11–13 cm)

ad. ♀

ad. ♂

American Redstart
Setophaga ruticilla
N Amer
L 5–5.5 in (13–14 cm)

ad. ♂

ad. ♀

Wilson's Warbler
Cardellina pusilla
N Amer
L 4.25–5 in (11–13 cm)

ad. ♀

ad. ♂

ad. ♀

Common Yellowthroat
Geothlypis trichas
N Amer
L 4.5–5.5 in (11–14 cm)

ad. ♂

ad.

Tennessee Warbler
Oreothlypis peregrina
N Amer
L 4.5–5 in (11–13 cm)

ad.

Orange-crowned Warbler
Oreothlypis celata
N Amer
L 4.75–5.25 in (12–14 cm)

ad.

Palm Warbler
Setophaga palmarum
N Amer
L 5–6 in (13–15 cm)

Wags and
pumps tail

ad.

Ovenbird
Seiurus aurocapilla
N Amer
L 5–6 in (13–15 cm)

ad.

Northern Waterthrush
Parkesia noveboracensis
N Amer
L 5–6 in (13–15 cm)

Yellow undertail coverts. Rest of underparts yellow to whitish, with brown or rufous streaks on breast and flanks. Indistinct buffy wing bars. AD WINTER: Brownish gray above, including crown, with a pale yellow eyebrow and dark eyeline. Undertail coverts yellow; rest of underparts dull yellow to brownish gray. VOICE: Call is a sharp, husky *chik*. Song is a continuous buzzy trill *zzizzizzizzizzizzi*.

HABITS: Feeds on the ground or in low shrubs and trees. Wags and pumps tail while foraging for insects. Builds a loose cup nest of twigs nestled in sphagnum on the ground near the base of a low conifer or shrub.

Yellow-rumped Warbler

Setophaga coronata
ALSO: Butterbutt, Kron-waldsänger, Paruline à croupion jaune, Myrtepa-rula, Миртовый певун,
Silaluksiiyaurak *Dendroica coronata*. SN means "crowned moth-eater."

RANGE: Nests (May–Jul) in forests and woods from Alaska and Canada south through the US. Winters in the W Indies and C Amer. Rare autumn vagrant to Iceland, Norway, UK.

SUBSPECIES: MYRTLE WARBLER, *S. c. coronata* (M), breeds in coniferous forests from n Alaska and n Canada to the n US. Winters along the Pacific, Atlantic, and Gulf coasts of the US, and south through C Amer. Winters as far north as Nova Scotia due to its unique ability to digest energy-rich waxes of bayberries, including those of wax-myrtle, *Myrica pensylvanica* (*illus. left*). AUDUBON'S WARBLER, *S. c. auduboni* (A), breeds in temperate woods and forests of sw Canada and w US. Winters in sw US and Mexico.

ID: L 5–5.5 in (13–14 cm). All plumages have a yellow rump. AD ♂ APR–AUG: Gray above, with black streaks on back. Yellow crown patch. Black cheeks. White spot on lores. White stripe above and behind eye. Throat white (Myrtle) or yellow (Audubon's). Breast black; yellow patches on sides; rest of underparts white. Wings blackish; 2 white wing bars. Tail black; white tail spots on

2–3 outer tail feathers. AD ♀ APR–AUG: Resembles male, but browner above and streaked below. Ear coverts brown or gray. AD WINTER: Brownish gray above and whitish below, with variable streaking. Lacks dark ear coverts. Distinguished from other yellow-rumped species by having mostly white and black underparts instead of yellow. VOICE: Call is *chep*. Song is a tinkling trill likened to the rattle of a small chain.

HABITS: Feeds on insects taken while hover gleaning, flycatching, climbing tree trunks, and hopping along the ground; includes fruit in winter diet. Female builds a cup nest of twigs and leaves on a conifer branch.

RELATED SUBARCTIC SPECIES: MAGNOLIA WARBLER, *S. magnolia*, nests in dense, new-growth coniferous forest in Canada and the ne US. AD MAR–AUG: Gray above, with a yellow rump. Dark tail, with conspicuous white patches on outer tail feathers. Head gray, with black mask and white eyebrow. Broad white wing patch. Breast and belly yellow, with necklace of thick black streaks running down flanks. Undertail coverts white. Song is a thin, weak *sweet, sweet, sweetest'*. Frequently fans tail, revealing wide white patches on each side of tail. Forages fairly low in dense foliage. Builds a cup nest near the base of a tree trunk or on a low conifer branch.

TOWNSEND'S WARBLER, *S. townsendi*, nests in coniferous forests of w N Amer. AD ♂: Back olive green, streaked or spotted with black. Crown black. Black cheek patch bordered by bright yellow stripes above and below. Black throat. Breast yellow; rest of underparts white; sides and flanks streaked black. Two white wing bars. Tail black; outer tail feathers white. Call is a soft *chip*. Song contains either clear whistled notes or buzzing notes, described as *weazy weazy weazy tweea* or *swee swee swee zee*. Gleans caterpillars, moths, winged insects, spiders, and honeydew of scale insects from clumps of coniferous foliage. Nests on conifer branches, mainly spruce or fir.

CAPE MAY WARBLER, *S. tigrina*, nests in spruce forests in Canada and ne US. All plumages show extensive narrow streaking on underparts; yellowish rump; yellowish patch on side of neck behind ear coverts; and thin, pointed, slightly downcurved bill. AD ♂ MAR–AUG: Olive above. Dark crown. Face yellow, with distinctive chestnut ear coverts. White patch on wing coverts. Rump yellow. Tail black, with white tail spots. Underparts yellow, with black streaks on throat, breast, and sides. AD WINTER: Olive gray above; yellowish white below, with narrow grayish stripes on breast. Song is high, thin, buzzy *seet seet seet seet*. Feeds on insects and insect larvae when breeding, including the spruce budworm (*Choristoneura fumiferana*), a pest that attacks conifers. Builds a bulky nest of twigs, moss, leaves, and bark near the top of a conifer.

BAY-BREASTED WARBLER, *S. castanea*, nests in spruce-fir forests in Canada and ne US. AD ♂ APR– AUG: Face black; crown, throat, breast, and flanks chestnut; pale yellow neck patch and belly; 2 white wing bars. AD ♀: Female has duller plumage than male; black and chestnut markings on face, cap, and throat reduced or absent. Song is a high, thin *teetee teetee teetee tee tee tee*. Feeds on insects and insect larvae when breeding, including spruce budworm. Nests on a low branch of a spruce or fir.

AMERICAN REDSTART, *S. ruticilla*, nests in alder and willow thickets, shrubby second-growth woodlands, and clearings in old-growth forests from s Alaska and c Canada south to s US. AD ♂: Glossy black, with bright salmon orange patches on sides of breast, base of flight feathers, and base of outer tail feathers. Belly, vent, and undertail coverts white. AD ♀: Gray to olive green upperparts, with pale gray head. Whitish below, with yellow patches on tail, wings, and sides. Song has varied, repeated, evenly spaced notes or phrases such as *see see see see* or *wee-see wee-see wee-see wee-see*. Forages from ground level to near top of canopy, taking leafhoppers, flies, wasps, beetles, moths, and caterpillars in aerial sorties and rapid hops through the trees. Often flashes color pattern as it spreads wings and tail to flush prey. Nest is a deep open cup attached to a 3-branched fork of a tree or shrub.

GENUS *GEOTHLYPIS*
Common Yellowthroat
Geothlypis trichas
ALSO: Weidengelbkehlchen, Paruline masquée, Nord- gulstrupe, Желтогорлый масковый певун. SN means "ground-warbler thrush."
RANGE: Nests (May–Jul) in marshes, thickets, and shrubby wetlands in se Alaska, across Canada, and throughout the lower US. Winters south to W Indies, C Amer, n S Amer. Vagrant to Greenland and UK.
ID: L 4.5–5.5 in (11–14 cm). AD ♂: Plain olive brown upperparts. Broad black mask edged by a narrow white line runs from forehead to sides of neck. Chin, throat, and breast bright yellow. Belly white; flanks dusky. Undertail coverts bright yellow. AD ♀: Plain brown to olive above, pale yellow below. JUV: Pale grayish brown overall, with some yellow on throat and undertail coverts. VOICE: Call is a soft *jip*. Song is *which-is-it, which-is-it, which-is-it*.
HABITS: Secretive resident of thick, tangled, damp vegetation. Feeds on insects and spiders taken on the ground or in low vegetation. Nests on the ground in a loose, bulky cup nest of grasses, sedges, reeds, and other marsh plants.

GENUS *CARDELLINA*
Wilson's Warbler
Cardellina pusilla
ALSO: Mönchswaldsänger, Paruline à calotte noire, Kalottparula, Малая вильсония, *Wilsonia pusilla*. SN means "tiny goldfinch." CN refers to Scottish-American naturalist Alexander Wilson (1766–1813), who first described the species.
RANGE: Nests (Jun–Jul) from sea level to alpine elevations along streams or in wet meadows with

extensive shrub thickets throughout Alaska and most of Canada, and south through the w US to s California and New Mexico. Winters to Costa Rica and w Panama.

ID: L 4.25–5 in (11–13 cm). AD ♂: Upperparts yellowish olive green. Forehead, eyebrow, lores, and entire underparts lemon yellow. Crown glossy black, forming a dapper cap on top of the head. Black eye is conspicuous against yellow face. AD ♀: Resembles male, but duller overall, with a variably colored crown that ranges from olive to olive mottled with black feathers. JUV: Similar to but duller than adults of their sex. VOICE: Call is a sharp, husky *jip*. Song is a rapid series of short chattering notes *chchchchchchchch*. **HABITS:** Habitually bobs tail. Flits through willow thickets and undergrowth as it searches for insects. Builds a cup nest of coarse plant material on or near the ground.

GENUS *PARKESIA*
Northern Waterthrush
Parkesia noveboracensis

ALSO: Drosselwald-sänger, Paruline des ruisseaux, Vannparula, Речной певун, *Seiurus noveboracensis*. SN means "Parkes's New York City [warbler]"; genus honors US avian taxonomist Kenneth C. Parkes (1922–2007). CN refers to the species' preference for watery habitats.
RANGE: Nests (Jun–Jul) in wooded swamps, marshes, and streamside willow thickets from Alaska and n Canada south to the n US. Winters to W Indies and n S Amer.
ID: L 5–6 in (13–15 cm). Dark brown above, with a white eyebrow, black eye stripe, and pointed, dark bill. Underparts white to yellowish, densely streaked in blackish brown on breast and flanks. Long, pinkish brown legs. VOICE: Call is a sharp, steely *chink*. Song is a loud, rapid *sweet sweet sweet swee wee wee chew chew chew chew*. Flight song, given at twilight on breeding grounds, begins with perched male sounding loud, sharp chips of increasing frequency. Male then flies up above the canopy, singing jumbled bits of primary song before descending to earth. **HABITS:** Forages unobtrusively in dense thickets and woodland understory, usually near water.

Feeds on larval and adult insects, spiders, and snails found in leaf litter. Walks with a swaying motion and frequently bobs tail. Builds a cup nest of leaves, bark, and rootlets in a stump or among tree roots. Furtive when nesting, female lures predators away from nest by creeping along the ground and flying out of distant vegetation with a loud *chink*.

SIMILAR SPECIES: OVENBIRD, *Seiurus auro-capilla*, nests in deciduous or mixed closed-canopy temperate forests in Canada and n US. Grayish olive above. Distinct white eyering.

Rufous crown edged with black stripes. White below, with prominent black streaks and spots on the breast and flanks. Song is a loud *teacher, teacher, teacher*. Forages on the ground, scratching up insects hidden in leaf litter. Builds a well-concealed dome-shaped nest of leaves on the ground.

FAMILY PRUNELLIDAE
ACCENTORS
The name accentor derives from the Latin *ad* and *cantor*, meaning "to sing," a reference to the male's trilled courtship song given from the treetops or while in lark-like flight. Prunellidae (Latin for "brown birds") includes small, drab-plumaged birds that can be mistaken for sparrows until one takes note of the thin, pointed bill. These reclusive birds feed in low undergrowth and nest low in trees. They walk along the ground when foraging, often while flicking their tail and wings, and using their bill to flip over leaf litter. They feed mainly on insects augmented by berries and seeds in winter. Typically the female builds the nest and incubates the 4–6 blue or green eggs for about 12 days. Both parents feed the young, which fledge at 12 days.

GENUS *PRUNELLA*
Hedge Accentor
Prunella modularis

ALSO: Dunnock, Hedge Sparrow, Heckenbraunelle, Accenteur mouchet, Jernspurv, Лесная завирушка; nicknamed "shuffle-wing" for male's habit of flicking his wings when courting. SN means "brown warbler." CN derives from the habit of nesting in garden hedges.

RANGE: Nests (May–Jun) in the UK, n Europe, and w Russia in undergrowth of forests, spruce plantations, woods, and parks. Winters in s Europe, Iraq, Iran.

ID: L 5–6 in (13–15 cm). Upperparts dark brown, with darker streaks on back. Head and breast lead gray; face streaked with brown. VOICE: Soft trilling *trrreee*. Male's song is monotonic trill.

HABITS: Shy and retiring, keeping in the cover of heavy undergrowth or thick hedges. Female alone builds a cup nest on a low tree branch and incubates the eggs. A female may breed with 2 or more males in the same season, resulting in a brood in which the chicks have different fathers. Broods may be raised by the female alone, by both parents, or with the assistance of auxiliary females and males.

Siberian Accentor

Prunella montanella
ALSO: Mountain Accentor, Bergbraunelle, Accenteur montanelle, Sibirjernspurv, Сибирская завирушка. SN means "brown mountain bird."

RANGE: Nests (Jun–Jul) in birch and willow thickets in forest-tundra and in stunted conifer forests from the Ural Mtns to ne Siberia and Sea of Okhotsk, south to the Altai Mtns and Lake Baikal. Winters in e China and Korea. Rare migrant to Alaska and w Aleutians. Vagrant to w Europe. Accidental in the states of Washington, Idaho, and Montana, US.

ID: L 5–6 in (13–15 cm). Back is warm brown with dark streaking; rump gray; wings and tail brown. Top of head and cheeks brownish black,

with an ochre eyebrow. Underparts ochre, with some streaking on flanks. VOICE: Thin *see-see-see*. Male's song is a loud trill.

RELATED SPECIES: The BLACK-THROATED ACCENTOR (B on map), *P. atrogularis*, breeds in the Altai Mtns, Tien-Shan, and in the Ural Mtns and lower Yenisei Rvr, where its range overlaps that of *P. montanella*.

FAMILY MOTACILLIDAE
WAGTAILS AND PIPITS

Motacillidae, meaning "family of little movers," derives from the Latin *motare*, to move about or shake, and *-cilla*, a diminutive suffix. The meaning of the word was corrupted when medieval writers mistakenly took *-cilla* to mean "tail," thus creating the word "wagtail." Indeed, many members of this family, and especially the wagtails, can be identified by their characteristic tail wagging performed at the end of a feeding run or when disturbed by intruders. It has been suggested that tail wagging flushes up prey and also may be a sign that a bird is alert to the presence of a possible predator.

Wagtails and pipits inhabit open habitats, where they feed on insects and insect larvae, spiders, worms, and small mollusks gleaned from the soil and edges of ponds and streams. They walk rapidly instead of hopping and have an undulating flight.

Hedge Accentor
Prunella modularis
UK, Europe–w Russia
L 5–6 in (13–15 cm)

ad.
May–Aug

ad, winter

Black-throated Accentor
Prunella atrogularis
w Siberia
L 5–6 in (13–15 cm)

Siberian Accentor
Prunella montanella
Siberia
L 5–6 in (13–15 cm)

Wagtails and pipits nest on the ground, usually placing their nest in a sheltered place, such as under the overhang of a grass tussock or among roots of shrubs. The northern species build a nest of grass, dead leaves, lichens, and moss, and line it with fine grasses; tundra-nesting species also line the nest with ptarmigan feathers and caribou or arctic fox fur. The clutch of 4–7 white, greenish, or dark buff, darkly spotted eggs is incubated for 11–15 days. The young fledge at 10–16 days and are fed by the parents for 14–18 days after leaving the nest.

Wagtails have bright yellow or contrasting pied plumage, while most pipits have drab brown, streaked plumage. The tail and often the wing feathers may be edged with white or yellow. One unusual feature of the wings is that the tertials—the innermost 3 secondary feathers—are very elongated and extend nearly to the tip of the folded wing. In the field, they almost entirely cover the primaries and secondaries, possibly protecting the important flight feathers from becoming faded and brittle from sun exposure.

GENUS _MOTACILLA_: This genus contains the wagtails. These birds inhabit open country, mostly in the Old World. Adults are sexually dimorphic; breeding males have brightly colored plumage, while the females (and juveniles) have more subdued plumage.

The taxonomic relationships of the _Motacilla flava_ and _M. alba_ complexes are unsettled. Some authors elevate certain subspecies to species level based on nuptial male plumages, while others recognize full species based on genetic data. The taxonomic order and scientific names shown here will undoubtedly be revised several times in the near future.

Western Yellow Wagtail
Motacilla flava

ALSO: Schafstelze, Bergeron-nette printanière, Gulerle, Жёлтая трясогузка. SN means "yellow wagtail."
RANGE: Nests (May–Jun) on wet meadows, bogs, and lakeshores from the UK and w Europe east across Siberia to the Kolyma River.

SUBSPECIES: BLUE HEADED WAGTAIL (F), _M. f. flava_, breeds in lowland wet meadows, forest bogs, and lakeshores from s Scandinavia to w Siberia; winters to Africa, India. SYKES'S WAGTAIL (S), _M. f. beema_, breeds in wet grasslands in w Siberia between the Volga and Yenesei rivers. GRAY-HEADED WAGTAIL (G), _M. f. thunbergi_, breeds in bogs from n Scandinavia to nw Siberia. NORTH SIBERIAN YELLOW WAGTAIL (P), _M. f. plexa_, breeds in floodplain meadows in Siberia between the Khatanga and Kolyma rivers.
ID: L 6–6.5 in (15–16 cm). Olive to greenish above, yellow below. Bluish gray to dark gray head. Most show a white or yellow eyeline. Dark tail, with white outer tail feathers. Black legs. Female, non-breeding male, and juvenile have paler and duller plumage compared to breeding male. VARIATIONS: _M. f. flava_: Male has a bluish gray head and mask, and white eyebrow and malar stripe. Female washed with buffy green. _M. f. beema_: Pale bluish gray crown and white patch under eye. _M. f. thunbergi_: Head dark gray, with blackish cheeks; no eyebrow. Female paler, washed with green, and with diffuse green eyebrow. _M. f. plexa_: Like _thunbergi_, but mask is darker and crown lighter; indistinct pale eyebrow.
VOICE: High-pitched _jeet_. Song consists of 2 or 3 scraping notes, _srrii-srriiht'_, given from a low bush, fence post, or wire.
HABITS: Runs and picks prey, hawks insects, and scratches through wet litter in search of insects. Perches on shrubs and tall grass.

Eastern Yellow Wagtail
Motacilla tschutschensis

ALSO: Alaskan Wagtail, Schafstelze-tschutschensis, Bergeronnette de Béringie, Østgulerle, Восточносибирская трясогузка, Iksriktaayuuk. SN means "wagtail of Chukotka."
RANGE: Nests (May–Jun) on tundra, wet meadows, bogs, and lakeshores across n Siberia to Chukotka, Kamchatka, and nw Alaska.
SUBSPECIES: EASTERN YELLOW WAGTAIL (E), _M. t. tschutschensis_, breeds in wet meadows and willow tundra in n Siberia, east to Chukotka and w Alaska; winters to s Asia. GREEN-CROWNED

YELLOW WAGTAIL (T), *M. t. taivana*, breeds from se Siberia to Sea of Okhotsk, Sakhalin, n Japan; winters to s Asia. KAMCHATKA YELLOW WAGTAIL (K), *M. t. simillima*, breeds in Kamchatka, Kurils, Commanders; winters in Australia; spring migrant to w Aleutians.
ID: L 6–6.5 in (15–17 cm). Olive to greenish above, yellow below. Bluish gray, brownish, or olive green head. White or yellow supercilium. Dark tail, with white outer tail feathers. Black legs. Female, non-breeding males, and juveniles are paler and have faded markings compared to breeding male. VARIATIONS: *M. t. tschutschensis*: Gray to grayish brown head and back. Dark cheeks. Narrow white eyebrow. White malar stripe. Pale yellow throat. Diagnostic broken pectoral band. *M. t. taivana*: Greenish olive head and back. Dark brown mask; yellow eyebrow. *M. t. simillima*: Bright olive back. Dark gray head and cheek. Broad white eyebrow. Breast sometime shows a faint pectoral band. VOICE: High-pitched *jeet*.

Gray Wagtail

Motacilla cinerea

ALSO: Gebirgsstelze, Bergeronnette des ruisseaux, Vintererle, Горная трясогузка. SN means "ash-colored wagtail."
RANGE: Nests (Apr–Jul) along fast-flowing rivers in the UK, Europe, and Asia. Resident or migratory south to n Africa, se Asia, New Guinea. Vagrant to the Aleutians and California.
ID: L 7–8 in (17–20 cm). Slate gray above, yellow below. Narrow white eyebrow; broken white eyering; white malar stripe. Throat and chin black in breeding male, white or mottled in all other plumages. Narrow white wing bar at base of secondaries. Yellow rump. Long, dark tail, with white outer tail feathers. Pale pink legs.
VOICE: Clear sharp *chichin chichin*, often given in song flight as male flies up into the air and descends slowly with fluttering flight.
HABITS: Forages in meadows and shallow water marshes. Feeds on aquatic invertebrates. Perches on partially submerged rocks and in trees. Nests between stones or tree roots on banks of fast-flowing rivers; also uses building ledges.

White Wagtail

Motacilla alba alba

ALSO: Bachstelze, Bergeronnette grise, Linerle, Maríuerla, Белая трясогузка. SN means "white wagtail."
RANGE: Nests (Apr–Jul) in open fields, wetlands, lakeshores, reservoirs, and around human habitation in se Greenland, Iceland, Faroes, and Europe, east to s Urals, south to Asia Minor. Winters in n Africa, Middle East, and s Asia.
ID: L 6.5–7.5 in (17–19 cm). AD MAR–JUL: Slate gray above, with a white face, black cap, and black bib that extends up to the bill base. White below. AD WINTER: Slate gray back and rump, white throat, and black crescent-shaped band across the chest. Crown gray, with a white forehead. White face; slightly mottled cheek. Greater coverts and tertials edged with gray. FIRST WINTER: Pale gray mantle, with a marked olive wash. Rump and uppertail coverts dark gray. Olive gray nape and crown. Ear coverts mottled olive to greenish white. Chin and throat white, washed with olive. Pale eyebrow. Thin, narrow black band on upper breast. Rest of chest, vent, and undertail coverts white. Pale gray flanks.
VOICE: Call is a 2–3 note chirring *tsli-vitt'* or *tsiti-tsuri'*. Song is a hesitant twittering.
HABITS: Forages for insects on lawns, golf courses, rooftops, roads, and lakeshores. Perches on rocks, occasionally in trees and bushes.

East Siberian Wagtail

Motacilla alba ocularis

ALSO: Bachstelze-ocularis, Bergeronnette de Sibérie, Linerle, Очковая трясогузка. SN means "white wagtail with an eyeline." Considered a full species by some.
RANGE: Nests (Apr–Jul) in n Siberia, from the Taimyr Penin east to Kamchatka, St Lawrence Is, and Seward Penin in nw Alaska. Common around Siberian settlements and seabird colonies. Winters south to ne India and Borneo.
ID: L 6.5–7.5 in (17–19 cm). Closely resembles *alba*, except for black eyeline. AD MAR–JUL: Slate gray back and rump. White face, with a narrow black eyeline and black cap. Wings dark, with coverts

and primaries narrowly edged white; in flight, white tends to be hidden and wing appears dark. White below, with a black bib that extends up to the chin. AD WINTER: Gray back, white throat, and black crescent-shaped band across the chest. Crown gray, with a white forehead. White face, with slightly mottled cheek. Greater coverts and tertials edged with gray.

Black-backed Wagtail
Motacilla alba lugens

ALSO: Bachstelze, Bergeronnette lugubre, Hvitvingeerle, Камчатская трясогузка. SN means "white wagtail with funereal plumage." Considered a full species by some.
RANGE: Nests (Apr–Jul) on coastal plains, fortified riverbanks, and fields in Kamchatka, Commanders, Kurils, Sakhalin, w Aleutians (Attu Is), south to Korea and Japan. Winters in se Asia. Vagrant to California and Alaska.
ID: L 6.5–7.5 in (17–19 cm). Appears shorter-legged and stouter-bodied than other *albas.* Distinguished from *ocularis,* which also has a black eyeline, by prominent white wing patch and white chin. AD ♂ MAR–JUL: Black back and rump. White face. Black eyeline. Solid white patch on wing appears as a large white window in flight. White below, with a black bib and diagnostic pure white chin; flanks often tinged gray. AD ♀ MAR–JUL: Back very dark gray, with black patches. Black cap extends down to nape and sometimes to mantle. AD WINTER: Back dark gray (darker than on *ocularis*) with black patches. Narrow black eyeline; white face. White throat and black crescent-shaped band across chest. FIRST YEAR: Gray head, back, and rump. Wings gray; wing coverts broadly edged in white. Narrow black eyeline on a white or yellowish face. Black, crescent-shaped bib. VOICE: *Tizs-it.*

Citrine Wagtail
Motacilla citreola

ALSO: Yellow-headed Wagtail, Zitronenstelze, Bergeronnette citrine, Sitronerle, Желтоголовая трясогузка. SN means "lemon-colored wagtail."

RANGE: Nests (May–Jul) in wet meadows, woodland bogs, and along riverbanks from the s Baltics to ne and c Siberian steppes, Mongolia, and Manchuria. Winters in s Asia.
ID: L 6–7 in (15–18 cm). AD ♂ APR–JUL: Head bright lemon yellow. Back dark gray, with black nape. Wings dark gray, with 2 prominent white wing bars and white edging to secondaries. Underparts yellow, with white vent. Tail black, with white outer tail feathers. AD ♀/WINTER ♂: Back, crown, and cheeks brownish gray. Yellowish eyebrow. Underparts pale yellow to white. JUV: Pale gray above, white below, with little trace of yellow. Conspicuous white wing bars. VOICE: Loud, clear *tsriit.* Song is a series of loud chirps.

GENUS ANTHUS: *Anthus* derives from *anthos,* a small grassland bird mentioned by Aristotle. The name *pipit* was applied by Welsh naturalist Thomas Pennant in 1768 and is imitative of the call note of several pipits, including the Pechora and American pipits, *A. gustavi* and *A. rubescens.*

Pipits are small, slender, short-necked birds. They have long, slender legs with elongated hind claws. They have drab brown, buff, and white, streaked plumage. The bill is fine and pointed and has a small hump over the nostrils. Pipits bob their tail and walk, rather than hop, along the ground. They feed on flies and their larvae, beetles, grasshoppers, crickets, true bugs, mantids, ants, aphids, and the larvae and adults of moths and butterflies. They also take spiders and seeds, and seaside species feed on marine crustaceans, mollusks, and small fish.

Olive-backed Pipit
Anthus hodgsoni

ALSO: Indian Tree-Pipit, Waldpieper, Pipit à dos olive, Sibirpiplerke, Пятнистый конек. SN means "Hodgson's pipit," referring to Brian Houghton Hodgson (1800–1894), English naturalist and diplomat to Nepal.
RANGE: Nests (Jun–Jul) on alpine tundra and near water in open woodland in Siberia, east to Kamchatka and Sakhalin, and south through the Himalayas to China and Japan. Winters in s Asia, India, Philippines, and Borneo. Rare

M. t. similima

M. f. thunbergi

M. f. plexa

M. t. taivana

M. f. beema

juv.

M. t. tschutschensis
ad. ♂ Mar–Jul

ad. ♀

M. f. flava
ad. ♂ Mar–Jul

Eastern Yellow Wagtail
Motacilla tschutschensis
N Siberia–w Alaska
L 6–6.5 in (15–17 cm)

Western Yellow Wagtail
Motacilla flava
Europe–w Siberia
L 6–6.5 in (15–17 cm)

juv.

ad. ♀

ad. ♂
Mar–Jul

ad. ♀

Citrine Wagtail
Motacilla citreola
NC Eurasia
L 6–7 in (15–18 cm)

ad. ♂ Apr–Jul

Gray Wagtail
Motacilla cinerea
Eurasia
L 7–8 in (18–20 cm)

M. a. ocularis
ad. ♂ Mar–Jul

M. a. lugens
ad. ♂ winter

M. a. alba
juv./ad. winter

M. a. lugens
ad. ♂ Mar–Jul

White Wagtail
Motacilla alba
Greenland–Eurasia–Alaska
L 6.5–7.5 in (17–19 cm)

M. a. alba
ad. ♂ Mar–Jul

annual migrant to w Europe. Vagrant to Bering Sea islands, Aleutians, and California. ID: L 5.5–6 in (14–15 cm). Back greenish olive with diffuse dark streaks. White eyebrow becomes buffy in front of eye. White spot and black patch at back of brown ear coverts. Bold dark streaks on buffy breast and flanks, rest of underparts white. Distinguished from *A. trivialis* by olive-toned, diffusely streaked back; buffy wing bars; and white supercilium. VOICE: Quiet *tsee* or loud sharp *speaze*, often given when flushed. Song is a series of loud trills and notes repeated in varied tempos. HABITS: Undulating, jerky flight. Often perches in bushes and trees when flushed.

Tree Pipit

Anthus trivialis

ALSO: Baumpieper, Pipit des arbres, Trepiplerke, Лесной конёк. SN means "common pipit."

RANGE: Nests (May–Jul) in open woodland, forest edge, and lightly wooded heath, from Europe east across c Siberia, south to Iran and China. Winters in sub-Saharan Africa and India. ID: L 5.5–6.5 in (14–16 cm). Upperparts olive gray, with fine streaks on head and mantle. Whitish eyebrow. White spot at back of gray ear coverts. Thin black malar stripe. Two whitish wing bars. Breast buffy, with bold streaks on breast and fine streaks on flanks; rest of underparts and throat white. Pale pink legs. Distinctive short, curved claw on hind toe. VOICE: Short, sharp *seep-seep*. Song is a loud *seep-seep-seep, tsia-tsia-tsia*, given from top of a tree or bush; often flies up while singing, then parachutes on stiff wings to land on its original perch in a tree or on the ground.

Pechora Pipit

Anthus gustavi

ALSO: Siberian Pipit, Pipit de la Petchora, Petschorapieper, Tundrapiplerke, Сибирский конёк. CN refers to the Pechora Rvr valley, Russia, where the species nests. SN means "Gustaaf's pipit," referring to Dutch ornithologist Gustaaf Schlegel (1819–1903).

RANGE: Nests (Jun–Jul) in damp tundra, bogs

in open coniferous forests, and willow thickets on sparsely wooded riverbanks across n Siberia, east to Chukotka, Kamchatka, Commander Is, south to ne China. Winters in e Asia, Philippines, Borneo. Vagrant to w Europe, w Aleutians (Attu Is), and St Lawrence Is, Alaska. ID: L 5.5–6 in (14–15 cm). Heavily streaked, dark brown upperparts. Distinctive whitish stripe runs down each side of back, forming a broken V. Breast, sides, and flanks washed yellow, with heavy black streaks; rest of underparts white. VOICE: Call is a harsh *pipit*, usually given 3 times, or *zip*, like an electrical spark. HABITS: Creeps mouse-like in long grass. Reluctant to fly when disturbed. Forages for insects and some seeds on the ground and in low trees and bushes.

Red-throated Pipit

Anthus cervinus

ALSO: Rotkehlpieper, Pipit à gorge rousse, Lappiplerke, Краснозобый конёк. SN means "pipit with a reddish brown [throat]."

RANGE: Nests (Jun–Jul) on grassy tundra, bare alpine tundra, grassy clearings in upland birch forests, and boggy willow thickets, from arctic Scandinavia east across Siberia to Chukotka, Kamchatka, St Lawrence Is, Little Diomede Is, and Seward Penin, Alaska; may also breed in arctic Yukon. Winters in sub-Saharan Africa and se Asia. Rare fall migrant to N Amer Pacific coast, where it often associates with American pipits. ID: L 5.5–6 in (14–15 cm). Brown above, buffy to whitish below, with heavily streaked sides, flanks, back, and uppertail coverts. Bold white mantle stripes. Faint to bold rosy pinkish wash on eyebrow, throat, and upper breast in breeding plumage. VOICE: Strident, single note, *speeeee*, given in flight and from the ground.

Meadow Pipit

Anthus pratensis

ALSO: Mippit, Mosscheeper, Titlark, Wiesenpieper, Pipit farlouse, Heipiplerke, Þúfu-tittlingur, Луговой конёк. SN means "pipit of the meadows."

Mantle brown with whitish streaks

ad. winter

ad. May–Jul

Red-throated Pipit
Anthus cervinus
N Eurasia, nw Alaska
L 5.5–6 in (14–15 cm)

Buffy underparts with diffuse dark streaks

American Pipit
Anthus rubescens
E Siberia, N Amer, Greenland
L 6–7 in (15–17 cm)

Drab plumage with diffuse streaks on breast

Eurasian Rock Pipit
Anthus petrosus
UK, Scandinavia, nw Russia
L 6–7 in (15–17 cm)

Bold white mantle stripes

Pechora Pipit
Anthus gustavi
Siberia
L 5.5–6 in (14–15 cm)

Mantle chestnut with bold dark streaks

Meadow Pipit
Anthus pratensis
Greenland, Iceland, Europe
L 5.5–6 in (14–15 cm)

Tree pipits' songs begin in the treetops and continue into flight.

Mantle olive with diffuse dark streaks

Olive-backed Pipit
Anthus hodgsoni
Siberia, e Asia
L 5.5–6 in (14–15 cm)

Tree Pipit
Anthus trivialis
Europe, c Siberia
L 5.5–6.5 in (14–16 cm)

Sky Lark
Alauda arvensis
Eurasia
L 6–7 in (15–18 cm)

Horned Lark
Eremophila alpestris
Near circumpolar
L 6–7.5 in (15–19 cm)

RANGE: Nests (Apr–Jul) in damp meadows, pastures, moors, grassy bogs, and mossy and rocky tundra in se Greenland (rare), Iceland, Faroes, UK, Europe, and nw Russia. Mostly resident; some northern populations winter south to n Africa and Iran.
ID: L 5.5–6 in (14–15 cm). Olive brown above and buff to gray below. Streaked with dark brown on most of its plumage and spotted on breast and flanks. Dark tail, with white outer tail feathers. Thin, pink to brown bill. Dull pink legs. Very long hind claw is longer than the hind toe itself. Shows a pinkish breast, gray head, and pale eyebrow in breeding plumage. VOICE: Weak *psweet-psweet*. Flight song is a series of shrill notes and trills, repeated in varied tempos.
HABITS: Feeds on the ground. Watches for prey from perches on bushes, fence lines, and utility wires. Undulating flight, alternating several rapid wingbeats with short glides. An important nest host of cuckoos and an important prey species for merlins and northern harriers.

Eurasian Rock Pipit
Anthus petrosus

ALSO: Strandpieper, Pipit maritime, Skjærpiplerke, Береговой конёк. SN means "pipit of the rocks." Split from the Water Pipit, *A. spinoletta*, which nests in mountains of s Europe and sc Asia.
RANGE: Nests (Apr–Jul) on rocky coasts of the Faroes, UK, nw France, Fennoscandia, and nw Russia. Winters south to s Europe and nw Africa.
ID: L 6–7 in (15–17 cm). Inconspicuous, with drab, faintly streaked plumage. Upperparts dark olive, with black streaks and pale brown edging to flight feathers. Narrow whitish eyering. Diffuse pale eyebrow. Tail dark, with dusky gray outer tail feathers. White throat, with narrow, dark malar stripe. Dark, fairly long bill. Brown to buff underparts, with heavy but diffuse dark streaks on breast. Breast of Nordic and Russian birds often tinged with pink in summer. Dark pinkish legs. VOICE: Call is a sharp, explosive *fiisst*. Song is a series of shrill, thin notes, *zru-zru-zru-zru-zru-zre-zre-zre-zre-zre-sui-sui-sui-sui-zre*, ending in a trill.

American Pipit
Anthus rubescens

ALSO: Buff-bellied Pipit, Red Lark, Titlark, Pazifikpieper, Pipit d'Amérique, Myrpiplerke, Американский конек, Kujamiqtaq, Siusiuk, Putukiiluk. SN means "reddish pipit." Split from the Water Pipit, *A. spinoletta*.
RANGE: Nests (Apr–Jul) on sloping rocky tundra and alpine meadows to 14,100 ft (4300 m) in e Siberia and across most of n N Amer to w Greenland. Winters south to s Asia and C Amer. Vagrant to Iceland, UK, Germany, Italy, and Hawaii.
ID: L 6–7 in (15–17 cm). Upperparts plain brown (paler in Siberia and e Asia, darker in N Amer). Pale eyebrow and malar stripe; brown ear coverts. White throat, with a large dark crescent on each side. Underparts varied (yellowish pink in Alaska, cinnamon pink in Siberia and n N Amer), with variable streaking and spotting on breast and flanks. Tail brown; white outer tail feathers. Legs dark pink; very elongated hind claw. VOICE: A sharp *chwee*. Flight call is a 2-noted *pipit*.

FAMILY ALAUDIDAE
LARKS
Larks inhabit open country and meadows in the Old World; only one species, the Horned Lark, breeds in N Amer. According to Pliny the Elder (AD 23–79), the family name Alaudidae is Celtic for "great songstress," a name that reflects the Sky Lark's elaborate calls and warbles, often given in song flight. During these displays, which advertise territory and attract mates, the male flies high into the sky and parachutes to the ground on opened wings, singing all the while.

Larks closely resemble pipits, but are stouter and larger and have thicker beaks. They have a long, nearly straight hind claw, and the hind toe is attached on the same level as the front toes. Most species have streaked brown or other cryptic plumage that camouflages them against the bare soil or grassy stubble where they search for seeds and insects. They walk or run in a scurrying, mouse-like fashion.

Most larks build their nest on the ground, next to a clump of grass or behind a rock. The female alone constructs an open cup nest of dead grass lined with softer grass and hair and incubates the clutch of 2–6 gray, greenish, or reddish, brown-spotted eggs for 11–16 days. Both sexes feed the nestlings, which often leave the nest before they fledge at 12–18 days.

GENUS *EREMOPHILA*
Horned Lark

Eremophila alpestris
ALSO: Shore Lark, Qupanu-arjuk, Ohrenlerche, Alouette hausse-col, Fjellerke, Рогатый жаворонок. SN means "solitude-loving lark of the mountains."
RANGE: Nests (Apr–Jul) on arctic tundra and in alpine meadows above the treeline. In N Amer, breeds from High Arctic islands south to Mexico; in Eurasia, breeds from Scandinavia, east across arctic Russia, and in mountains of the Middle East and c Asia. Northern populations are migratory.
ID: L 6–7.5 in (15–19 cm). AD: Upperparts brown to cinnamon, streaked with dusky brown. Tail brown, with black outer tail feathers edged in pale gray. Black mask; black occipital feather tufts (the "horns"), which can be raised or lowered but are usually erect in males; and white to yellow eyebrow, ear coverts, and chin. Black breast band. Underparts white, with some rufous on flanks. Dark bill. Reddish brown iris. Black legs. Plumage is darkest in arctic populations, palest in birds of sw N Amer, and redder in Pacific birds. Males are darker than females. JUV: Spangled in black and white on back and head. Whitish below, with buffy barring on flanks. Bill dull yellow. Legs pinkish gray. VOICE: Flight call is a soft, squeaky *su-weet*. Song is a high-pitched, tinkling trill, *reek trik treet tritilititi treet,* given from a perch or on the wing.

GENUS *ALAUDA*
Sky Lark

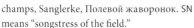

Alauda arvensis
ALSO: Eurasian Skylark, Feldlerche, Alouette des champs, Sanglerke, Полевой жаворонок. SN means "songstress of the field."
RANGE: Nests (Apr–Jun) in open cultivated fields, meadows, and heaths in the Faroes, UK, and most of Eurasia. Northern populations winter to n Africa, c Asia. Small breeding population in Pribilofs. Introduced and resident in Hawaii, Australia, NZ, and Vancouver, Canada. Vagrant to w N Amer and Bering Sea islands.
ID: L 6–7 in (15–18 cm). AD: Upperparts brown, with dark streaks. Breast buffy, with necklace of fine dark streaks; rest of underparts white. Plain face, with pale supercilium. Often raises short crest. Tail dark, with white outer tail feathers. White trailing edge on wings' inner primaries and secondaries. Legs brown. JUV: Resembles adult, but upperparts spotted and speckled. Fine white tips on crown feathers. VOICE: Call is a soft *chrr-ik*. Song is a variety of loud, rapid trills given from a perch or when on the wing.

FAMILY CALCARIIDAE
LONGSPURS AND SNOW BUNTINGS

Calcariidae is a small family of passerines that includes the longspurs and snow buntings. The generic names *Calcarius* and *Plectrophenax* as well as the common name "longspur" refer to the long claw on the hind toe of these birds. They forage in open areas, taking seeds and the occasional insect.

GENUS *CALCARIUS*
Lapland Longspur

Calcarius lapponicus
ALSO: Lapland Bunting, Spornammer, Bruant lapon, Lappsparv, Подорожник, Qirniqtaaq, Qupaluk, Putukiiluk. SN means "longspur of Lapland."
RANGE: Circumpolar. Nests (May–Jun) on tundra meadows in N Amer and Eurasia. Winters to c Europe, s Russia, e Asia, and s US.
ID: L 5.5–6 in (14–15 cm). AD ♂ MAR–AUG: Crown, face, and breast black, edged by a white to yellowish stripe that curves down to the wing coverts. Rufous nape. Back blackish streaked with buff. Two narrow white wing bars. Dark tail, with white at corners of outer tail feathers. Whitish below, with black streaks on flanks. Dark brown legs. Long claw on hind toe. Bill pink, with a dark tip. AD WINTER: Head and nape dull rufous, with a dark lateral crown stripe and

a pale, narrow median stripe; ear coverts warm brown, edged with a narrow black line and a buffy extended eyebrow. Chin and throat white, with a faint speckled breast. VOICE: Calls include a dry rattle, a sharp whistled *tew*, and a purring sound. Male's song, given in display flight, is a rapid series of loud, jingling notes, transcribed as *churtle churtle, seerilee-seerilee-serrilee, seetle-we-we-you*. HABITS: Crouches while foraging. Female builds a tightly woven cup nest of dead grass, leaves, and moss on the ground, in a hollow under a tussock or shrub, and lines it with ptarmigan, eider, or raven feathers; muskox, hare, lemming, or dog hair; or willow catkins. Female incubates the clutch of 4–6 greenish gray to brown, speckled and blotched eggs for 10–13 days.

Smith's Longspur

Calcarius pictus

ALSO: Painted Bunting, Goldbauch-Spornammer, Plectrophane de Smith, Tundraspurv, Разукрашенный подорожник, Putukiilukpak. CN refers to Gideon B. Smith (1793–1867), wealthy benefactor of John James Audubon. SN means "painted longspur."
RANGE: Nests (Jun–Jul) mainly on a narrow band of tundra extending from n Alaska east across the n Yukon mountains and Mackenzie delta to s Hudson Bay. Winter distribution restricted to a small area of short grasslands in sc US.
ID: L 6–6.5 in (15–17 cm). AD ♂ MAR–AUG: Breast, abdomen, chin, and nape rich caramel. Head black, with a broad white eyebrow, distinct white ear patch, and incomplete white eyering. Wings blackish brown; 2 white wing bars; diagnostic white shoulder epaulet is partly obscured while at rest. Central tail feathers dark, with 2 white outer tail feathers on each side. Legs dark brown. Bicolored bill is dark on top, pinkish below. AD ♀/ AD WINTER: Dull buff overall, with a streaked crown, breast, and sides. Resembles breeding male, but lacks white epaulets. Black elements of head pattern are replaced by streaked brown, white elements by buff. VOICE: Call is a dry staccato rattle. Male's song is a sweet whistling trill, *ta-ta-tee, twe-twe-twee, werr-tee, wee-chew*.

HABITS: The mating system of this species is polygynandrous each female mates with 2–3 males for a single clutch of eggs and each male mates with 2 or more females. Over a period of one week in spring, a female longspur may copulate over 350 times—one of the highest rates of copulation of any bird. At the same time the males compete for fertilizations by copulating frequently, thus diluting or displacing sperm from other males. Males can deliver such large numbers of ejaculates because of their large testes, which are about double the mass of those of other longspur species.

The female builds a nest of grass, lined with feathers, down, and fine grasses on a grassy or mossy hummock and incubates the 3–6 bluish green, dark-spotted eggs for 11–12 days. Most broods contain chicks of mixed paternity. At such nests, two or more males may assist a female in feeding nestlings. Observations of banded males suggest that the amount of assistance provided by any given male depends on the number of young he thinks he has sired within a nest.

GENUS *PLECTROPHENAX*
Snow Bunting

Plectrophenax nivalis

ALSO: Snowflake, Amauligjuaq, Qaulluqtaaq, Qupanuaq, Arnaviaq, Schneeammer, Plectrophane des neiges, Snøspurv, Пуночка. SN means "longspur of the snow."
RANGE: Circumpolar. Nests (Jun–Jul) between rocks and boulders on arctic and alpine tundra. Winters in open agricultural land and along shorelines south of breeding range to n US, Mediterranean, s Russia, c Asia, and Japan.
ID: L 6–7 in (15–18 cm). AD ♂ MAR–AUG: Pure white body contrasting with jet black on the back, primaries, and central tail feathers. Bill black. AD ♀ MAR–AUG: Back streaked with black. Nape and crown speckled with dark gray. White on underparts, primaries, and outer tail feathers. AD WINTER: White, with a streaked back and rust to pale brown markings on upperparts and flight feathers. Bill yellow, with a dark tip. VOICE: Short, musical *ti-ti-chu-ree* repeated numerous times on the ground or in flight.

ad. ♀
Mar–Aug

ad. winter

ad. ♂
Mar–Aug

McKay's Bunting
Plectrophenax hyperboreus
Bering Sea islands–Alaska
L 6–7 in (15–18 cm)

ad. ♀
Mar–Aug

ad. ♂
Mar–Aug

Snow Bunting
Plectrophenax nivalis
Circumpolar
L 6–7 in (15–18 cm)

ad. winter

ad. winter

ad. winter

ad. winter

ad. winter

Smith's Longspur
Calcarius pictus
N Amer
L 6–6.5 in (15–17 cm)

ad. ♂
Mar–Aug

ad. ♂
Mar–Aug

Lapland Longspur
Calcarius lapponicus
Circumpolar
L 5.5–6 in (14–15 cm)

HABITS: Prefers relatively barren, rocky areas. Feeds on insects when breeding and seeds and grains in winter. Forages while walking and running on the ground, picking up seeds from the ground or from plants. Feeds in flocks except when nesting. Nests in crevices in rock faces or boulder piles, in old lemming burrows, and sometimes on open tundra. Due to the cold, sunless nature of most nesting sites, the female cannot leave the eggs while she is incubating and is completely dependent on her mate to bring her food. Females that nest on open tundra can leave the nest for short periods to search for food. Nest is a sturdy cup of moss and grass, lined with fine grass, hair, and feathers, especially molted ptarmigan feathers. Clutch of 4–7 gray to bluish white, brown-speckled eggs is incubated for 12–13 days. Young fledge at 10–17 days.

McKay's Bunting

Plectrophenax hyperboreus
ALSO: Beringschnee-ammer, Plectrophane blanc, Hvitspurv, Белая пуночка.
Considered conspecific with *P. nivalis* by some. SN means "longspur of the Far North."
RANGE: Nests (Jun–Jul) in rock scree, holes in rock faces, shingle beaches, and hollow driftwood logs on 2 small, isolated islands in the Bering Sea region of Alaska: St Matthew Is (60°24′ N, 172°42′ W) and nearby Hall Is. May nest on St Lawrence Is, and on St George Is and St Paul Is in the Pribilofs, and may interbreed there with local snow buntings. Winters (blue on map) along the Bering Sea coast of Alaska from Kotzebue south to Cold Bay on the Alaska Penin.
ID: L 6–7 in (15–18 cm). AD ♂ MAR–AUG: White head, nape, breast, belly, rump, and back, with black on tips of primaries, scapulars, and central tail feathers. AD ♀ MAR–AUG: Resembles female Snow Bunting, except top of head and nape are usually mostly white, and back is only faintly streaked with gray. AD WINTER: White overall, with a few black feathers on wings and tail, and a rusty wash on crown. JUV: Grayish brown overall. VOICE: Like that of *P. nivalis*.
HABITS: Nesting behavior is not well known, but is probably similar to that of *P. nivalis*.

FAMILY EMBERIZIDAE
SEEDEATERS

Emberizidae is a large family of ground-dwelling seedeaters that includes the Old World buntings and New World sparrows, juncos, and towhees.

Emberizids are small passerines that have conical bills and 9 primary feathers. Breeding males are colored in shades of rich rufous, dark brown, black, and white or yellow. Females and juveniles have streaked brown plumage, which differs very little between the species. The diet consists mainly of seeds, supplemented with insects, especially when feeding the young. These birds make short, low flights, alternating rapid wingbeats with wings pulled in to sides.

With a few exceptions, emberizids nest on or near the ground in a site sheltered by a grass tussock, tree stump, or overhanging vegetation. The cup-shaped nest is made from grasses and other plant fibers and is lined with finer plant material and sometimes hair from mammals. The 4–6 cream to bluish green eggs, which are often marked with dark blotches or hair-like lines, are incubated for 11–14 days, mainly by the female. The young remain in the nest for 7–12 days and often leave the nest before they are fully fledged, at 11–13 days.

GENUS *EMBERIZA*
Yellowhammer

Emberiza citrinella
ALSO: Goldammer, Bruant jaune, Gulspurv, Обыкновенная овсянка; local names Scribbler and Writing Lark refer to the eggs, which bear dark wavy lines resembling handwriting scrawls. SN means "small yellow bunting."
RANGE: Nests (May–Jul) in thickets, forest clearings, coastal meadows, and farmlands from the UK and Europe east to c Siberia. Winters to n Africa, Iraq, and Mongolia. Introduced into NZ in 1862.
ID: L 6–6.5 in (15–17 cm). AD ♂: Bright yellow head and breast, rust-colored rump, and heavily streaked brown back. Long tail, with white outer tail feathers. Underparts yellow, with a diffuse breast band of olive to rufous flecks. Gray bill. Light brown legs. AD ♀/JUV: Plumage is duller

than male's, and yellow underparts are streaked in gray or black. VOICE: Call is a metallic *tsit* or a clicking *tit-tit-tit-tit*. Song is a rapidly repeated *zi-zi-zi-zi-zi-zi-zrii-zreeeee*, expressed as "little-bit-of-bread-and-no-cheese" in England and "may-the-Devil-take-you" in Scotland.

Reed Bunting

Emberiza schoeniclus

ALSO: Common or Northern Reed Bunting, Rohrammer, Bruant des roseaux, Sivspurv, Тростниковая овсянка. SN means "reed bunting."

RANGE: Nests (May–Jul) in reed beds, rushes, and waterside thickets from the UK across Eurasia to Kamchatka, Kurils, Sakhalin, n Japan. Winters to n Africa, Iran, and China in meadows and farmland. Spring vagrant to the Aleutians.

ID: L 5.5–6 in (14–16 cm). All plumages have rufous lesser wing coverts, finely streaked grayish brown rump, and white outer tail feathers. AD ♂: Back streaked in brown and black; gray rump. Head and throat black, with a broad, white nuchal collar and white malar stripe. Faintly streaked, white underparts. AD ♀/JUV: Head brown, with a buffy eyebrow and pale buff malar stripe. Whitish, darkly streaked underparts. VOICE: Call is a descending *seeoo* or *ching*. Song is a loud, staccato *shreep-shreep-teeree-tititick*.

HABITS: Eats seeds, but also takes insects and other invertebrates, especially in summer. Makes holes in bulrush stems to extract insect larvae.

Pallas's Reed Bunting

Emberiza pallasi

ALSO: Pallasammer, Bruant de Pallas, Krattspurv, Полярная овсянка. SN means "Pallas's bunting," honoring German naturalist-explorer Peter Simon Pallas (1741–1811).

RANGE: Nests (Jun–Jul) along tundra watercourses in willow and alder thickets, in grassy steppe, and in dwarf birch scrub on high plateaus in ne Siberia, n China, Tibet, and Mongolia. Winters south to c China and Korea. Vagrant to St Lawrence Is, Alaska.

ID: L 5–5.5 in (12–14 cm). All plumages have gray lesser wing coverts, pale plain rump, and

unmarked underparts. AD ♂: Upperparts boldly streaked in black and white; rump pale gray to white; white double wing bars; gray lesser wing coverts. Outer tail feathers white. Head and throat black, with a white malar stripe and broad white collar that is tinged with buff or yellow at nape. In winter, black head markings become grizzled brown, nape and breast infused with buff. AD ♀/JUV: Back boldly striped with buff and black; buff-colored double wing bars; dull gray lesser wing coverts. Head grayish brown, with buffy eyebrow and pale buff malar stripe. Lacks pale crown stripe of *E. schoeniclus*. VOICE: Call is a soft *tsee-see*. Song is a series of monotonic, rasping notes, *srih-srih-srih-srih*.

Little Bunting

Emberiza pusilla

ALSO: Zwergammer, Bruant nain, Dvergspurv, Овсянка-крошка. SN means "little bunting."

RANGE: Nests (Jun–Jul) in forest-tundra, open coniferous forest, and upland birch forest, mainly in birch and willow thickets, from Scandinavia east across n Siberia. Winters south to India, se Asia, Philippines. Fall vagrant to UK. Rare vagrant to California. Regular visitor to w Alaska.

ID: L 4.75–5.25 in (12–13 cm). Small. Back grayish brown, streaked with black. Rufous face and throat; rufous median crown stripe broadly edged with black; cheek patch edged with black; white malar stripe. Distinct pale eyering. Whitish wing bar. Outer tail feathers white. Underparts white, with dark narrow streaks. Sharply pointed gray bill, with paler lower mandible. VOICE: Sharp clicking *tsik-tsik*. Weak song with varied, high-pitched, rolling and rasping notes, often ending in a trill.

STATUS: Classed as Vulnerable in Finland.

Rustic Bunting

Emberiza rustica

ALSO: Waldammer, Bruant rustique, Vierspurv, Овсянка-ремез. SN means "bunting of the countryside."

RANGE: Nests (May–Jul) at edges of swampy

spruce or pine forests, in Labrador tea thickets in mossy swamps, and in riparian birch groves from Scandinavia to Kamchatka. Winters in e China and Japan. Vagrant to UK and Alaska. **ID:** L 5–5.75 in (13–15 cm). AD ♂ APR–JUL: Upperparts chestnut with dark streaking; rump plain rufous. Head black, with a white eyeline, white malar stripe, and distinct small white patch on cheek. Outer tail feathers white. Underparts white, with rufous breast band and bold rufous streaks on flanks. Sharply pointed bill, with pinkish lower mandible. Pink legs. AD ♀/JUV: Less brightly colored than male, with brown replacing black markings on head. VOICE: Call is a sharp *tslk*. Song is a rhythmic series of melancholic notes often transcribed as *duu'-dele-duu'do-deluu'-delu*.

Yellow-breasted Bunting

Emberiza aureola
ALSO: White-shouldered Bunting, Weidenammer, Bruant auréole, Sibirspurv, Дубровник. SN means "golden [-breasted] bunting."

RANGE: Nests (Jun–Jul) in riparian willow thickets, boggy fields with scrub, open burned forest, and mountain meadows with scrub and scattered trees from Finland east to Kamchatka, the Kuril Is and Commander Is, and south to Mongolia, Korea, and Japan. Winters south to Indochina. Summer visitor to UK and w Europe. Vagrant to St Lawrence Is, Alaska.
ID: L 5.5–6 in (14–15 cm). AD ♂ APR–JUL: Rich chestnut above. Bold white wing patch. Face and throat black. Outer tail feathers white. Underparts bright yellow, with a reddish brown breast band and streaked flanks. Pinkish bill. Pink legs. AD ♀/JUV: Heavily streaked, grayish brown back. Double white wing bar. Pale yellow to whitish face; crown and brownish cheek patch edged in black. Light yellow underparts, sometimes with a faint pectoral band. VOICE: Call is a sharp, clicking *tsick*. Song is a series of clear, loud, double notes, *filyou-filyou-filee'-filee'-tyou-tyou*.
STATUS/USE: Vulnerable (IUCN) due to pesticide poisoning and overhunting. Used in the Asian seasonal dish *he hua qiao*.

Pine Bunting

Emberiza leucocephalos
ALSO: White-crowned Bunting, Fichtenammer, Bruant à calotte blanche,

Hvithodespurv, Белошапочная овсянка. SN means "white-headed bunting."
RANGE: Nests (May–Jul) in thickets in open areas of coniferous and mixed forests from c Siberia to the Sea of Okhotsk, Sakhalin, and Kurils. Winters to Iraq and sc Asia. Vagrant to w Aleutians (Attu Is) and Pribilofs.
ID: L 6–7 in (16–18 cm). AD ♂: Heavily streaked brown back, with a rufous rump. Head bright chestnut, with white central crown and white cheeks edged with black lines; head markings duller in winter. Outer tail feathers white. Underparts white, with chestnut-spotted breast band and flanks. AD ♀: Plumage is drabber than male's, and white underparts are more streaked. VOICE: Call and song very similar to Yellowhammer's.

GENUS *SPIZELLA*
American Tree Sparrow

Spizella arborea
ALSO: Arctic Chipper, Canada Sparrow, Moun-

tain Sparrow, Tree Bunting, Winter Chippy, Baumammer, Bruant hudsonien, Bjørkespurv, Воробьиная овсянка, Pisikpisikpiisrak. SN means "little tree bunting." CN was given by early European settlers for superficial resemblance to the Eurasian Tree Sparrow, *Passer montanus*.
RANGE: Nests (Jun–Jul) across n N Amer in forests and tundra that has scattered small bushes or small trees. Winters south to the ec and sw US.
ID: L 5.5–6 in (14–15 cm). AD: Back streaked with black, buffy, and brown; 2 white wing bars. Rusty cap and rufous eyeline. Bill dark, with yellow lower mandible. Underparts grayish white, with a dark central breast spot. Pale brown legs; blackish feet. JUV: Resembles adult, but has a streaked brown cap and dusky streaks on breast and flanks. VOICE: Call is a soft, tinkling *teedle-doo*. Song is a sweet warbling *swee-swee-ti-sidi-see-zidi-zidi-zew*.

Yellow-breasted Bunting
Emberiza aureola
Finland–Sea of Okhotsk
L 5.5–6 in (14–15 cm)

ad. ♀

ad. ♂
Apr–Jul

ad. ♀

Yellowhammer
Emberiza citrinella
Europe–c Siberia
L 6–6.5 in (15–17 cm)

ad. ♀

ad. ♂

Pale crown stripe

ad. ♂ winter

Solid brown crown

ad. ♂ winter

ad. ♀

Reed Bunting
Emberiza schoeniclus
Europe–nc Siberia–Kamchatka
L 5.5–6 in (14–15 cm)

ad. ♀

ad. ♂
Apr–Jul

ad. ♀

ad. ♂
Apr–Jul

Pallas's Reed Bunting
Emberiza pallasi
NE Siberia–e Asia
L 5–5.5 in (13–14 cm)

Little Bunting
Emberiza pusilla
N Eurasia
L 4.75–5.25 in (12–13 cm)

juv.

Marsh Labrador Tea
Rhododendron tomentosum

ad. ♀

ad. ♀

ad. ♂
Apr–Jul

ad. ♂
Apr–Jul

Rustic Bunting
Emberiza rustica
N Eurasia
L 5–5.75 in (13–15 cm)

Pine Bunting
Emberiza leucocephalos
C Siberia–Sea of Okhotsk
L 6.25–7 in (16–18 cm)

HABITS: Sexes migrate and winter separately. Feeds mainly on seeds and catkins of alder, willow, and birch; also takes insects, especially mosquitoes.

Chipping Sparrow
Spizella passerina
ALSO: Chippy, Hair Bird, Social Sparrow, Schwir-rammer, Bruant familier,

Brunissespurv, Струйчатая овсянка. SN means "sparrow-like bunting."
RANGE: Nests (Apr–Jul) from ne Alaska and ne Canada south through most of the US. Winters to Mexico.
ID: L 5–6 in (13–15 cm). Mantle brown, with dark streaks. Gray rump. Crown rufous to chestnut; eyebrow white; lores and eyeline black. Plain gray breast and flanks; belly whitish. Black bill. **VOICE:** Call is a sharp *chip* (hence the CN). Male's song is a monotonous trill formed from a rapid series of *tssip* notes.
HABITS: Confiding. Forages on the ground or in low vegetation. Female alone builds a flimsy nest of plant material low in a conifer or shrub.
RELATED SPECIES: BREWER'S SPARROW,

S. breweri, breeds mainly in the US Great Basin region. Small numbers are resident in mountains from se Alaska to sw Yukon and sw Alberta. Drab plumage. Streaked grayish brown and black above. Dirty white below, with grayish, sometimes streaked flanks. Finely streaked brown crown; pale gray eyebrow; dark eyeline; white eyering; brown ear coverts.

GENUS *PASSERCULUS*
Savannah Sparrow
Passerculus sandwichensis
ALSO: Grasammer, Bruant des prés, Musespurv,

Саванная овсянка, Aanaruin suliuqpa, *Ammodramus sandwichensis*. SN means "little sparrow of Sandwich Bay [Labrador]." CN refers to Savannah, Georgia, the type locality.
RANGE: Nests (Jun–Jul) in grassy tundra, coastal plains, dunes, and marshes in the e Aleutians

and across most of N Amer. Winters to the s US and Mexico.
ID: L 5–6 in (13–15 cm). Upperparts brownish or grayish, with variable streaking. Crown shows a pale beige median stripe (lacking in salt marsh populations); eyebrow usually yellow, sometimes beige; thin, dark malar stripe. Short, notched, uniformly colored tail. Underparts whitish to pale beige; breast streaked with brown, and often with a small central spot. Pinkish legs. **VOICE:** Song is a very soft, barely audible, descending *tsip-tsip-tsip,* with a trill at the end.
HABITS: Low, undulating flight often ends with a sudden drop into the grass or low perch. Pairs often reoccupy the previous year's nesting site. Nests on the ground under overhanging vegetation, making a tunnel through the grass to a concealed entrance.

GENUS *MELOSPIZA*
Song Sparrow
Melospiza melodia
ALSO: Singammer, Bruant chanteur, Sangspurv,

Певчий воробей. SN means "melodious song finch." One of the most diverse and widespread songbirds in N Amer, with 52 named subspecies.
RANGE: Nests (May–Jun, in north) in thickets at woodland edge and brushy fields in N Amer south to Mexico. Winters to s US and n Mexico.
SUBSPECIES–ARCTIC: EASTERN SONG SPARROW, *M. m. melodia,* e N Amer. GIANT SONG SPARROW, *M. m. maxima,* w Aleutians. ALEUTIAN SONG SPARROW, *M. m. sanaka,* e Aleutians (Seguam Is to Unimak Is) and Alaska Penin. RUFOUS SONG SPARROW, *M. m. rufina,* outer islands of se Alaska and Brit Columbia.
ID: L 6.5–7.5 in (17–19 cm). Great geographical variation in plumage and body mass, with the largest and darkest subspecies occurring in the Aleutians. In general, mantle and breast are streaked in rufous, brown, gray, or black; streaking on breast typically converges into a dark central spot. Head has broad lateral median stripes bordering a paler central stripe; grayish eyebrow; pale malar stripe. Pale to white throat edged with a broad brown lateral throat stripe. **VARIATIONS:** *M. m. melodia:* Back brown with

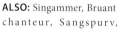

Savannah Sparrow
Passerculus sandwichensis
N Amer
L 5–6 in (13–15 cm)

American Tree Sparrow
Spizella arborea
N Amer
L 5.5–6.25 in (14–16 cm)

Swamp Sparrow
Mespiza georgiana
N Amer
L 5–6 in (13–15 cm)

Lincoln's Sparrow
Melospiza lincolnii
N Amer
L 5–6 in (13–15 cm)

Chipping Sparrow
Spizella passerina
N Amer
L 5–6 in (13–15 cm)

Eastern Song Sparrow
M. m. melodia
E N Amer

Aleutian Song Sparrow
M. m. sanaka
E Aleutians

Rufous Song Sparrow
M. m. rufina
SE Alaska

Giant Song Sparrow
M. m. maxima
W Aleutians

Song Sparrow
Melospiza melodia
N Amer
L 6.5–7.5 in (17–19 cm)

Sooty Fox Sparrow
P. i. unalaschensis
Aleutians–coastal Alaska

Red Fox Sparrow
P. i. iliaca
NW Alaska–se Canada

Fox Sparrow
Passerella iliaca
N Amer
L 6.5–7.5 in (17–19 cm)

rufous streaking and buffy gray fringes to feathers; underparts white with black streaks. *M. m. maxima*: About 25 percent larger than other subspecies; dark gray overall, with diffuse streaking; long slender bill. *M. m. sanaka*: Grayish overall; long, very slender bill. *M. m. rufina*: Streaked rufous overall. VOICE: Male's breeding song is a loud, clear *sweet-sweet-sweet*, followed by a trill. Call is a distinctive *chimp*. HABITS: Pumps tail in flight. Forages on ground with a cocked tail, scratching with both feet to expose food. Female alone builds a cup nest on the ground or low in grass and shrubs and incubates 3–5 bluish green, spotted eggs.

Lincoln's Sparrow
Melospiza lincolnii

ALSO: Lincolnammer, Bruant de Lincoln, Gråbryn-spurv, Воробей Линкольна. SN means "Lincoln's song finch," after US naturalist Thomas Lincoln (1812–1883), companion of John J. Audubon on an 1833 Labrador expedition. RANGE: Nests (Jun–Jul) in boggy sites having low willow cover and dense ground vegetation from nw Alaska to Canada and nw US. Winters to Mexico and Guatemala. Accidental in Greenland. ID: L 5–6 in (13–15 cm). Upperparts grayish brown, finely streaked with black. Wing and tail feathers edged in rufous. Crown often peaked, with brown lateral crown stripes and a narrow pale median stripe. Broad gray eyebrow; buffy eyering; buffy malar streak. Dark brown lateral throat stripes outline finely streaked white throat. Broad buffy breast band, with crisp black streaks continuing down the flanks and sometimes converging into a central chest spot. Belly white. Pinkish legs. Slender, bicolored bill, dark brown above, golden below. VOICE: Call is a sharp *chip*. Male's song is rich and warbling, with rapid wren-like chirping trills at varied pitches, as in *chur chur-chur-wee-wee-wee-wee-wah*. HABITS: Solitary and secretive. Gleans insects from the ground and low vegetation as well as from tree foliage and branch tips. Scratches ground litter with both feet to uncover prey. Also chases insects on foot and flies out after moths. Plucks wings from moths before eating them;

piles of moth wings can often be seen on the ground beneath favored perches. Female alone builds nest on the ground under low willows.

Swamp Sparrow
Melospiza georgiana

ALSO: Marsh Sparrow, Sumpfammer, Bruant des marais, Sumpspurv, Болотный воробей. SN means "song finch of [the state of] Georgia." RANGE: Nests (May–Jul) in forest bogs, fens, and marshes in Canada from c Mackenzie and NWT east to coastal Newfoundland, south to nc and ne US. Winters to s US and ne Mexico. ID: L 5–6 in (13–15 cm). Upperparts rusty brown, streaked with black. Dark rufous wings lack wing bars. Face and sides of neck gray; crown rusty brown to chestnut; gray eyebrow; dusky brown eyeline; buffy malar stripe. White throat. Pale gray below, with a broad gray breast band; rusty brown wash on flanks; pale gray belly. VOICE: Call is a sharp *chip*. Song is a slow, trilling *peat-peat-peat-peat-peat-peat-peat*, fading at end. HABITS: Forages at edge of open water, picking insects from mud, water surface, or overhanging vegetation. Also wades in shallow water, immersing head underwater to take aquatic insects from submerged leaves. Female alone makes a bulky cup nest from coarse dry grass and sedge, cattails, twigs, ferns, leaves, and rootlets, building it on the ground under dense vegetation or in a low bush near water.

GENUS *PASSERELLA*
Fox Sparrow
Passerella iliaca

ALSO: Fuchsammer, Bruant fauve, Revespurv, Пестрогрудая овсянка, Ikligvik. SN means "little sparrow with [streaked] flanks." RANGE: Nests (May–Jul) in e Aleutians, Alaska, and Canada, south to sw US. Winters to s US and Baja California. SUBSPECIES–ARCTIC: RED FOX SPARROW (I), *P. i. iliaca*, breeds in forests from nw Alaska to Labrador and se Canada; winters to se US. SOOTY FOX SPARROW (U), *P. i. unalaschensis*, breeds in

e Aleutians and coastal Alaska; winters along the Pacific coast to s California.
ID: L 6.5–7.5 in (17–19 cm). Overall plumage is rufous (*P. i. iliaca*) or sooty brown (*P. i. unalaschcensis*). Breast and flanks have well-defined spots and bold streaks, some of which form an irregular central breast spot. Bill dark above, yellow orange below. Legs pinkish brown. VOICE: Song of the rufous male is a melodic whistled warble *weet-weeto-teeoo-teeo-tze-tzer-zezer-reep*. Song of the sooty male is distinguished by a thinner, buzzing sequence of widely separated introductory notes. There is much individual variation in song.
HABITS: Forages for seeds and insects in leaf litter and on bare ground, scratching with both feet at once.

GENUS *ZONOTRICHIA*
White-crowned Sparrow
Zonotrichia leucophrys

ALSO: Gambel's Sparrow, Dachsammer, Bruant à couronne blanche, Hvit-kronespurv, Белобровая овсянка, Nunyaktuaguk. SN means "stripe-headed white-crowned [sparrow]."
RANGE: Nests (May–Jun in the north) in lightly wooded areas along streams or on tundra in dense shrubs and dwarf willows, from n Alaska and n Canada, south through mountains of sw Canada to sw US. Winters to Mexico. Accidental in Greenland, Iceland, UK, w Europe, and Japan.
ID: L 6–7 in (15–18 cm). AD: Striking head pattern. Top of head has 2 broad black stripes, separated by a broad white median stripe. White eyebrow and a narrow black line from eye to back of nape. Back light gray, streaked with brown; rump pale brown; tail dark brown; 2 white wing bars. Underparts gray, fading to white on throat and belly. Legs brown to fleshy pink. Bill orange (north), pinkish brown (mountains), or yellowish (Pacific). JUV: Resembles adult, but has brown lateral stripes rather than black and a buffy median stripe rather than white. VOICE: Song varies geographically, but in general consists of clear whistles followed by a series of buzzes or trills.

White-throated Sparrow
Zonotrichia albicollis

ALSO: Peabody Bird, Canada Sparrow, Weißkehlammer, Bruant à gorge blanche, Hvit-strupespurv, Белошейная зонотрихия. SN means "stripe-headed white-necked [sparrow]."
RANGE: Nests (Jun–Jul) at forest edge in n N Amer east of the Rocky Mtns. Winters to s US and n Mexico. Vagrant to UK and w Europe.
ID: L 6.5–7.5 in (17–19 cm). Striking head and throat pattern. Median crown stripe white, tan, or gray; eyebrow yellow in front of eye, and white, buff, or gray behind eye; lateral crown stripes dark brown to black. White throat patch edged with black, often with 2 black malar lines. Back chestnut, streaked with black, feathers edged with buff; 2 narrow white wing bars. Breast and lower throat gray, often streaked with brown; flanks light brown and streaked; belly white. Bill horn-colored. Pale brown legs. (Note: White-striped and tan-striped morphs occur in both sexes; different forms are maintained because each morph usually mates with its opposite.) VOICE: Song is a long, whistled note followed by higher-pitched notes, often interpreted as *Old Sam Peabody*.
HABITS: Nests in low shrubs or on the ground under overhanging vegetation.

Golden-crowned Sparrow
Zonotrichia atricapilla

ALSO: Kronenammer, Bruant à couronne dorée, Gulkro-nespurv, Чернобровая овсянка, Kianarutuuk. SN means "stripe-headed black-capped [sparrow]."
RANGE: Nests (Jun–Jul) in coastal scrub and in inland mountains to near the treeline in Alaska and w Canada. Winters along the Pacific coast south to Mexico. Vagrant to Wrangel Is, Chukotka, Japan.
ID: L 6–7 in (15–18 cm). AD APR–JUL: Striking head pattern. Crown and forehead black; broad median stripe with bright yellow on forecrown, light gray on rear crown. Back olive brown, boldly streaked with brownish black; rump

grayish brown; wings chestnut brown, with 2 thin, white wing bars. Throat and breast grayish; flanks washed with brownish buff. Bill blackish brown, with a paler lower mandible. AD WINTER: Head plumage dulls. Dark brown replaces black on crown, especially toward rear; median crown stripe dull yellow to gray. VOICE: Song is 3 clear, whistled, descending notes in a minor key, that sounds like *Oh, dear me* or *I'm so tired;* the latter prompted gold rush miners to call this species Weary Willie.
HABITS: Usually nests on ground, less frequently in stunted conifers or low shrubs.

Harris's Sparrow

Zonotrichia querula
ALSO: Harrisammer, Bruant à face noire, Granspurv, Воробей Гарриса. SN means "stripe-headed noisy [sparrow]." First collected in Missouri in 1834 by Thomas Nuttall. Later named by John J. Audubon for Edward Harris (1799–1863), who accompanied Audubon on an 1843 trip up the Missouri Rvr. First nest with eggs discovered at Churchill in 1931 by G. M. Sutton.
RANGE: Nests (Jun–Jul) amid dwarf trees and shrubs in dry heath tundra and forest-tundra from the Mackenzie Rvr delta to Churchill and sw Hudson Bay. Winters mainly in the Great Plains region, c US.
ID: L 6.5–7.5 in (16–19 cm). AD APR–JUL: Upperparts brown, with back and scapulars streaked with black. Underparts white. Black hood covers nape, crown, lores, throat, and center of upper breast; rest of face gray. Pink bill. AD WINTER: Golden brown replaces gray facial markings. JUV: Resembles winter adult, but has a mostly white throat and very little black on face or crown. VOICE: Call is loud *tchip* or distinctive *weenk*. Male's song consists of 1–3 plaintive whistles, all at the same pitch.
HABITS: Feeds on seeds, fruits, arthropods, buds, and young conifer needles. Forages on the ground; also foliage gleans and flies out after insects. Nests on the ground under a shrub or stunted tree located on a small hummock or under a rock overhang. Clutch is 3–5 pale greenish or grayish, rufous-spotted eggs.

GENUS *JUNCO*
Dark-eyed Junco

Junco hyemalis
ALSO: Snowbird, Junko, Junco ardoisé, Vinterjunko, Юнко, Kayuutaayuuk. SN means "winter junco."
RANGE: Nests (May–Jul) north to the treeline in Alaska and Canada, and south to the sw US and ne US. Winters south to Mexico.
SUBSPECIES–ARCTIC: SLATE-COLORED JUNCO (S), *J. h. hyemalis,* breeds in open and burned over areas of coniferous and mixed forest from n Alaska east to Newfoundland, south to ne Brit Columbia and ne US. Winters south of breeding range throughout the US. Casual to Alaska's arctic coast, Bering Sea islands, Aleutians (west to Shemya), ne Asia, w Greenland, w Europe. OREGON JUNCO (O), *J. h. oreganus,* breeds along the Pacific coast from se Alaska to California. Winters in w N Amer, west of the Rocky Mtns.
ID: L 5.5–6 in (14–15 cm). All races and stages have white outer tail feathers and a pink bill and legs. AD ♂: Slaty black overall, with dark breast sharply cut off from white belly (*hyemalis*); slaty black hood, rufous back and sides, and white belly (*oregonus*). AD ♀: Brownish gray to slate overall; gray flanks; white abdomen; rufous edges to wing feathers. VOICE: Short, musical trill.
HABITS: Forages in ground and leaf litter by hopping forward then kicking backward to uncover seeds and insects. Nests in a small hollow on sloping bank or rock face, among roots of fallen trees, bushes, and ferns, and under raised buildings; also relines and uses old robins' nests. Female alone builds nest and incubates the 3–5 bluish white, spotted eggs.

FAMILY PASSERIDAE
OLD WORLD SPARROWS
These stocky seedeaters have heavy conical bills.

GENUS *PASSER*
House Sparrow

Passer domesticus
ALSO: English Sparrow, Haussperling, Moineau domestique, Gråsparv, Домовой воробей. SN means "house sparrow."

juv.

ad.

Golden-crowned Sparrow
Zonotrichia atricapilla
W N Amer
L 6–7 in (15–18 cm)

juv.

White-crowned Sparrow
Zonotrichia leucophrys
N Amer
L 6–7 in (15–18 cm)

ad.

ad.
Tan eyebrow

ad.
White eyebrow

White-throated Sparrow
Zonotrichia albicollis
N Amer
L 6.5–7.5 in (16–19 cm)

juv.

Harris's Sparrow
Zonotrichia querula
N Amer
L 6.5–7.5 in (16–19 cm)

ad.
Apr–Aug

Eurasian Tree Sparrow
Passer montanus
Eurasia
L 5–5.5 in (13–14 cm)

ad.

ad. ♂
Oregon Junco
J. h. oregonus

ad. ♀
Slate-colored Junco
J. h. hyemalis

ad. ♀

ad. ♂

ad. ♂
Slate-colored Junco
J. h. hyemalis

Dark-eyed Junco
Junco hyemalis
N Amer
L 5.5–6 in (14–15 cm)

House Sparrow
Passer domesticus
Eurasia
Introduced into the Americas
L 5.5–6 in (14–15 cm)

RANGE: Nests (Apr–Jul) mainly around human habitation and grain storage facilities from the UK and Europe east across c Siberia and c Asia, and south to n Africa. Introduced to New York in 1850 and spread to California by 1910. Introduced to Argentina in 1872 and to Chile in 1904; now widespread throughout most of S Amer. Non-migratory.
ID: L 5.5–6 in (14–15 cm). AD ♂: Back chestnut brown with dark streaks. Gray crown and cheek bisected by a band of chestnut curving from the nape to the lores. Pale gray below, with a black chin and bib. Single white wing bar. AD ♀/JUV: Brownish gray overall, with paler underparts and faintly streaked back VOICE: Variety of chirps and chattering notes and a loud *zheev-zheev*.
HABITS: Seen in pairs and small flocks. Feeds on grains and some insects. Nests under house eaves, in holes in walls and rock faces, in nest boxes, and sometimes in openings in bulky corvid or raptor nests. Nest is a messy ball of twigs and vegetation. Clutch is 5–6 grayish blue, brown-spotted eggs.

Eurasian Tree Sparrow
Passer montanus

ALSO: Feldsperling, Moineau friquet, Pilfink, Полевой воробей. SN means "mountain sparrow."
RANGE: Nests (Apr–Jul) in open woodland near human habitation from the UK and Europe across c Siberia, east to Sakhalin Is, s Kurils, Japan, and China. Non-migratory. Introduced to N Amer in 1870; spread to various locations at first, but populations are now localized in e Missouri, wc Illinois, and se Iowa.
ID: L 5–5.5 in (13–14 cm). Back warm brown, with dark brown streaks. Bright chestnut crown. Side of head bright white (gray in juvenile), with a small black cheek patch. Underparts grayish, with a black chin and small black bib. Single white wing bar.
HABITS: Seen mostly in small flocks around human habitation and cultivated land. Nests in tree holes, crevices in walls, in nest boxes, and in the rim of bulky raptor nests. Clutch is 4–8 off white, dark-spotted eggs.

FAMILY FRINGILLIDAE
FINCHES

Finches are small arboreal passerines with short, conical bills. They forage in flocks, feeding on seeds, buds, and some insects. Sexes usually differ in appearance, with males more brightly colored. Flight is fast and undulating, with alternating bouts of flapping and gliding on closed wings. Most give complex songs in flight. Most species are monogamous. Typically the female alone builds a compact, open cup nest of twigs, grass, and moss in a variety of habitats, including trees, bushes, rock crevices, and grass tussocks. The female alone also incubates the clutch of 2–6 off-white to greenish, speckled eggs for 10–16 days, while the male brings food to her on the nest. The young fledge in 10–25 days and one or both parents provide food for an additional 15–30 days.

GENUS *FRINGILLA*
Brambling
Fringilla montifringilla

ALSO: Bergfink, Pinson du Nord, Bjørkefink, Вьюрок. SN means "mountain finch."
RANGE: Nests (May–Jun) in open birch-conifer forests and streamside willows from Scotland and Fennoscandia to Kamchatka. Winters in the UK and across sc Eurasia. Casual to coastal Alaska.
ID: L 5.5–6 in (14–15 cm). Diagnostic white rump. AD APR–JUL: Black head, back, tail, and wings; prominent white wing bar and shoulder patch, Rusty yellow breast; dark-spotted flanks; white belly. Bill black. AD WINTER: Plumage pales, and birds often look like chaffinches. Bill yellow with a black tip. VOICE: Harsh, nasal *yeck* given in flight. Song is a buzzing *chzhzhzh*, reminiscent of a distant cross-cut saw at work.
HABITS: Feeds on seeds, adding insects when breeding and beechnuts in winter. Nests in trees. Weaves bits of birch bark into outer wall of nest.

Chaffinch
Fringilla coelebs

ALSO: Buchfink, Pinson des arbres, Bokfink, Зяблик. SN means "bachelor finch,"

alluding to the habit of female chaffinches to winter in separate segregated flocks, leaving the males to lead a celibate life.

RANGE: Nests (May–Jun) in open woodland, farmland, parks, and gardens from the UK and continental Europe to sw Siberia and Asia Minor. Winters south to n Africa and s Asia. Introduced into S Africa and NZ.

ID: L 5.5–6 in (14–16 cm). Both sexes have white outer tail feathers (visible in flight) and a grayish green rump. AD♂ APR–JUL: Brick red breast and mantle (duller in winter). Grayish blue crown and nape. Black wings, with a prominent white wing bar and shoulder patch. Gray bill. AD ♀/JUV: Dull brownish gray, with similar wing markings as the male. VOICE: Both sexes give the familiar *chink chink* call. Male has a short, frequently repeated, rattling song.

HABITS: Nests in the fork of a tree. Camouflages nest by weaving lichens into outer rim.

GENUS *CARDUELIS*
European Greenfinch
Carduelis chloris
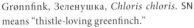
ALSO: Common Greenfinch, Grünling, Verdier d'Europe, Grønnfink, Зеленушка, *Chloris chloris*. SN means "thistle-loving greenfinch."
RANGE: Nests (May–Jun) in open woodland, forest-steppe, gardens, and parks in the UK, Europe, and sw Asia, reaching the Arctic Circle only in Norway. Nomadic. Winters south to n Africa, Iraq, Iran. Introduced into the Azores, Australia, NZ, Uruguay, Argentina.
ID: L 5.5–6 in (14–16 cm). Stout body, head, and bill. AD ♂: Greenish above, bright greenish yellow below; grayish head; yellow patches on wings and at tail base. Pale pink to ivory bill. AD ♀: Drabber than male with dirty white underparts (diffusely streaked in juveniles). VOICE: Bubbling trill, ending in a raspy *vzhzhzh*.

Twite
Carduelis flavirostris

ALSO: Eurasian Twite, Vinterhämpling, Linotte à bec jaune, *Acanthis flavirostris*.
SN means "thistle-loving golden-billed [finch]."

RANGE: Nests (Apr–Jun) in rocky steppe, alpine meadows, and bare coastal heaths in the UK and n Scandinavia, with disjunct populations in the mountains of Caucasus, c Asia, and Altai. Nomadic. Winters at lower elevations and south of breeding range, often foraging in large flocks at garbage tips and tilled fields.
ID: L 5–5.5 in (13–14 cm). Buffy brown, heavily streaked upperparts. Throat and upper breast buffy; rest of underparts off-white, with dark streaks on lower breast. White outer tail feathers. Bill brownish gray when breeding, golden yellow with a black tip in winter. Spring male has a pink rump. VOICE: Loud *pee-tee-tee* and drawn-out, rising bleat, *tveeiht* (hence the CN).

Eurasian Siskin
Carduelis spinus

ALSO: Spruce Siskin, Black-headed Goldfinch, Erlenzeisig, Tarin des aulnes, Grønnsisik, Чиж, *Spinus spinus*. SN means "thistle-loving siskin."
RANGE: Nests (Apr–Jun) in mixed and coniferous forest, especially spruce, with nearby birch and alder thickets from the UK and Fennoscandia across s Russia to Sakhalin, Kurils, and Japan. Winters to the Mediterranean, Middle East, China, and Ryukyu Is, Japan.
ID: L 4.5–5 in (11–13 cm). Small, with a sharply pointed bill. AD ♂: Greenish yellow, with black crown, chin, wings, and tail. Yellow patches on wings and sides of tail base. Eyebrow, breast, and rump plain greenish yellow. AD ♀/JUV: Resembles male, but with greenish gray upperparts and whitish, streaked underparts. VOICE: Rattling *tee-ee-tee-tee*. Song includes twitters and trills; often mimics calls of other species.
HABITS: Forages in birch and alder groves, often hanging upside down when feeding on alder cones. Nests in high branches of conifers.

Pine Siskin
Carduelis pinus

ALSO: Fichtenzeisig, Tarin des pins, Stripesisik, Сосновый щегол. SN means "thistle-loving [siskin] of the pines."

RANGE: Nests (Apr–Jun) in open coniferous and mixed forest from sc Alaska and c Canada south to sw and ne US and Mexico. Resident in southern sectors of breeding areas; infrequently winters to s Texas and Gulf coast of Florida.
ID: L 4.5–5.5 in (11–14 cm). Streaked brown above, paler below, with a short forked tail and yellow to off-white patches on wings and tail. Sharply pointed, conical bill.
HABITS: Forages in trees, shrubs, and weeds, taking thistle, red alder, birch, and spruce seeds, young buds of willows, elms, and maples, soft stems and leaves of weeds, and insects. Can store 10 percent of its body weight in seeds in the crop overnight, providing extra food that allows it to accelerate its metabolic rate and survive in temperatures below –50°F (–45°C). Eggs and nestlings are shielded from extreme cold by densely insulated nests and continual incubation by the female, which is fed by the male.

GENUS *ACANTHIS*: Redpolls are the only small passerines that overwinter in the Arctic. These birds lose body heat rapidly because of their small size. To minimize exposure, they pick up seeds and store them in a special sac in the esophagus, then move to a sheltered spot to digest their meal.

Common Redpoll
Acanthis flammea
ALSO: Mealy Redpoll, Saqquaruaq, Siqsigiaq, Sagsakiq, Birkenzeisig,

Sizerin flammé, Gråsisik, Чечётка, *Carduelis flammea*. SN means "finch with a flame-colored [crown]." CN refers to the reddish crown, or "poll."
RANGE: Circumpolar. Nests (May–Jun) in open birch woodland, scrub, willows, and tundra. Migratory and nomadic. Some birds winter on the arctic tundra; others winter south to the c US, n Mediterranean, and c Asia.
ID: L 4.5–5.5 in (11.5–14 cm). Barred brown upperparts, with white wing bars and a faintly streaked rump. Both sexes sport a red cap and small black chin patch. Underparts whitish, with streaked flanks; male has a reddish pink breast. **VOICE:** Loud *pee-you-ee* or a hard metallic

chett-chett-chett, often given in undulating song flight.
HABITS: Feeds on seeds, fruit, dwarf birch and willow catkins, and some insects. In winter, lives under the snow in lemming runways, where it is shielded from cold winds and can find seeds to eat. Nests in the fork of a shrub, sedge tussock, old lemming burrow, or rock crevice, often in close proximity to other nesting redpolls. Nest is made from twigs, grass, and moss, lined with soft plant matter, down, and hair.

Hoary Redpoll
Acanthis hornemanni
ALSO: Arctic Greenland Redpoll, Saqsakiq, Polar-Birkenzeisig, Sizerin

blanchâtre, Polarsisik, Пепельная чечётка. SN means "Hornemann's finch," honoring Danish botanist Jens Wilken Hornemann (1770–1841).
RANGE: Circumpolar. Nests (Jun–Jul) on rocky tundra, rock slides, and open birch forest in arctic N Amer, Greenland, and n Eurasia. Resident but nomadic throughout most of breeding range; some populations move south in winter to the ne US, s Canada, UK, c Europe, c Asia, and Japan.
ID: L 5–5.5 in (12–14 cm). Distinguished from the Common Redpoll by its whiter plumage, white unmarked rump, wash of pale pink on the breast, and smaller beak.
HABITS: Restless and nomadic. Feeds on seeds and insects. Burrows into snowdrifts in winter to avoid exposure to harsh winds and cold temperatures. Nests in bushes, rock crevices, and between rocks, often near other nesting redpolls. Nest is made from coarse grasses, cottongrass, willow down, alder and willow twigs and roots, caribou hair, vole fur, and ptarmigan feathers.

GENUS *PYRRHULA*
Eurasian Bullfinch
Pyrrhula pyrrhula
ALSO: Northern Bullfinch, Gimpel, Bouvreuil pivoine,

Domherre, Обыкновенный снегирь. SN means "flame-colored finch." CN refers to the species' bull-necked appearance.
RANGE: Nests (May–Jun) in coniferous forest,

Hoary Redpoll
Acanthis hornemanni
Circumpolar
L 5–5.5 in (12–14 cm)

ad.

Eurasian Siskin
Carduelis spinus
Eurasia
L 4.5–5 in (11–13 cm)

ad. ♂

Common Redpoll
Acanthis flammea
Circumpolar
L 4.5–5.5 in (11–14 cm)

ad. ♂

ad.

Pine Siskin
Carduelis pinus
N Amer
L 4.5–5.5 in (11–14 cm)

ad.

Twite
Carduelis flavirostris
Eurasia
L 5–5.5 in (13–14 cm)

ad.
winter

Brambling
Fringilla montifringilla
Eurasia
L 5.5–6 in (14–16 cm)

ad.
Apr–Jul

ad.

European Greenfinch
Carduelis chloris
Eurasia
L 5.5–6 in (14–16 cm)

ad. ♀

ad. ♀

Eurasian Bullfinch
Pyrrhula pyrrhula
Eurasia
L 6–7 in (16–18 cm)

Chaffinch
Fringilla coelebs
Eurasia
L 5.5–6 in (14–16 cm)

ad. ♂
Apr–Jul

ad. ♂

mixed woodland, parks, and gardens in the UK and Europe, east across Siberia to Kamchatka, Sakhalin, Kurils. Winters to the Mediterranean region, Iran, China, Manchuria, and Korea. **ID:** L 6–7 in (16–18 cm). Bulky, bull-headed finch. Gray above, with a white rump and a black cap and chin. Wings black, with bold white wing patch. Stout black bill. AD ♂: Salmon red face and underparts. AD ♀/JUV: Grayish buff face and underparts. **VOICE:** Fluted whistle, *phew-phew*. **HABITS:** Quiet and easily overlooked despite its striking plumage. Feeds on seeds, insects, and fruit tree buds, making it a pest in orchards. Builds its nest in a large bush or tall tree.

GENUS *LEUCOSTICTE*
Asian Rosy-Finch
Leucosticte arctoa

ALSO: Arctic Rosy Finch, Siberian Finch, Rosenbauch-Schneegimpel, Roselin brun, Koksfjellfink, Сибирский вьюрок. SN means "white-speckled arctic [mountain finch]."
RANGE: Nests (Jun–Jul) on barren mountain plateaus, alpine tundra, and till at edges of snowfields in Siberia, from the Lena Rvr east to the Sea of Okhotsk, Kamchatka, Kurils, and Commander Is. Moves to temperate grasslands in winter. Irregular migrant south to Japan.
ID: L 6–7 in (15–18 cm). Dark brown, washed with raspberry pink on wings, rump, and belly; Altai and Sayan Mtn races often have gray instead of pink on wings. Crown and face dark gray. Nape gray or buffy gray. **VOICE:** Soft chirps and twitters.
HABITS: Forages for seeds and insects on the ground. Nests in rock crevices.

Gray-crowned Rosy-Finch
Leucosticte tephrocotis

ALSO: Aleutian Rosy Finch, Gray-capped Finch, Graukopf-Schneegimpel, Roselin à tête grise, Grånakkefjellfink, Горный американский вьюрок. SN means "white-speckled ashy-eared [mountain finch]."
RANGE: Nests (May–Jul) on windswept scree slopes, rocky plateaus, around alpine glaciers, and occasionally on buildings in w Canada, n Alaska,

St Matthew Is, Nunivak Is, Pribilofs, Aleutians (Attu to Alaska Penin), and south through the Rockies and Sierra Nevada ranges. Most move to coastal areas or lower elevations in winter. **ID:** L 6–6.5 in (15–17 cm). Stout, with long wings and notched tail. Rich brown upperparts, breast, and flanks. Rosy pink on wings, belly, and rump. Black forecrown, with pale gray band from eye to nape; cheeks pale gray in some subspecies, brown in others. White nasal tufts. Bill yellow in winter, black in summer. **VOICE:** Buzzy *chew*. **HABITS:** Undulating flight. Forages on open ground, among rocks on talus slopes, and on snowfields and glaciers, picking insects and seeds off plants and snow. Female builds a coarse, bulky nest of grass, sedge, moss, lichens, hair, and feathers in a rocky crevice or on a small cliff ledge and incubates the 3–5 creamy white eggs for about 14 days. Both sexes feed young, which fledge at 15–22 days of age.

GENUS *CARPODACUS*
Common Rosefinch
Carpodacus erythrinus

ALSO: Scarlet Grosbeak, Karmingimpel, Roselin cramoisi, Rosenfink, Обыкновенная чечевица. SN means "red fruit-eater."
RANGE: Nests (May–Jul) in damp thickets, riparian woodland, mountains, parks, and farmland from Scandinavia east across Siberia to Kamchatka, Sakhalin, and south to Mongolia and China. Winters in se Asia, the Near East, and Egypt.
ID: L 5.5–6 in (14–15 cm). Dark, short, stout, conical bill. AD ♂: Back, tail, and wings brownish red. Head and breast bright red. Underparts pinkish. AD ♀/JUV: Brownish gray overall. **VOICE:** High-pitched whistle, *cheero-veecheeoo*, often given from an exposed perch.
HABITS: Feeds on berries, fruit, buds, seeds, and some insects. Nests low in a bush or sapling.

Pallas's Rosefinch
Carpodacus roseus

ALSO: Rosengimpel, Roselin rose, Karminfink, Сибирская чечевица. SN

Red Crossbill
Loxia curvirostra
Eurasia, N Amer
L 6–6.75 in (15–17 cm)

ad. ♂

ad. ♀

White-winged Crossbill
Loxia leucoptera
Eurasia, N Amer
L 5.5–6 in (14–15 cm)

ad. ♂

ad. ♀

Pine Grosbeak
Pinicola enucleator
Eurasia, N Amer
L 7.5–9 in (19–23 cm)

ad. ♀

ad. ♂

Parrot Crossbill
Loxia pytyopsittacus
Scandinavia–nw Russia
L 6.25–7 in (16–18 cm)

ad. ♂

ad. ♀

Gray-cheeked
morph

Gray-crowned Rosy-Finch
Leucosticte tephrocotis
W N Amer
L 6–6.5 in (15–17 cm)

Brown-cheeked
morph

ad. ♀

Pallas's Rosefinch
Carpodacus roseus
C Siberia–Sea of Okhotsk
L 5–5.5 in (12–14 cm)

ad. ♂

Asian Rosy-Finch
Leucosticte arctoa
E Siberia–Kamchatka
L 6–7 in (15–18 cm)

ad. ♀

Common Rosefinch
Carpodacus erythrinus
Eurasia
L 5.5–6 in (14–15 cm)

ad. ♂

means "rosy fruit-eater." CN honors Peter Simon Pallas (1741–1811), German naturalist who explored the Urals, Caspian Sea, China, and the Altai.

RANGE: Nests (Jun–Jul) in mountain forests in c Siberia, n Mongolia, and Sakhalin Is. Winters in flooded fields, aspen and birch groves, and parks south to Korea, n China, and n Japan. Nomadic. **ID:** L 5–5.5 in (12–14 cm). Smallest rosefinch. AD ♂: Raspberry pink, with a streaked brown back, white belly, and white wing bars. Head and throat spotted in silvery white. AD ♀/JUV: Streaked plumage, with whitish base color lightly washed with rose. VOICE: Soft whistle.

HABITS: Forages on the ground and in trees, taking berries, fruit, buds, and seeds. Secretive when breeding. Nesting habits poorly known.

GENUS *PINICOLA*
Pine Grosbeak
Pinicola enucleator

ALSO: Pine Rosefinch, Hakengimpel, Durbec des sapins, Tallbit, Щур, Kayuuttaak. SN means "pine-tree dweller that extracts pine nuts."
RANGE: Nests (Jun–Jul) mainly in mature coniferous forest having some alder, birch, and berry-bearing shrubs. In Eurasia, breeds in mixed woodland and Siberian pine forests from Scandinavia to Kamchatka and Kurils; in N Amer, breeds in coniferous forests from wc Alaska to Labrador and south to New England. Winters to the UK, c Europe, n China, and c US. **ID:** L 7.5–9 in (19–23 cm). Swollen black bill. AD ♂: Head, back, rump, and breast dull red to light poppy red. Grayish belly. Tail and wings black, with 2 white wing bars. AD ♀/JUV: Resembles male, but with a gray back and breast, and a yellowish olive to russet crown and rump. VOICE: Two to 3 high-pitched whistles on a descending scale.
HABITS: Builds a loosely woven cup of twigs, rootlets, grass, and moss, lined with fine rootlets, grasses, and hair on a conifer branch.

GENUS *LOXIA*: Crossbills are heavy-bodied finches with a crossed bill adapted for extracting seeds from the scales of open and closed conifer cones. Crossbills feed by inserting their bill between the cone's scales. They pry the scales

apart by opening the bill, then dislodge the seeds with the tongue. Birds sometimes snap off a cone, take it to a perch, and eat it while holding the cone in one foot. These birds are highly efficient at extracting conifer seeds and a single individual can eat up to 3000 seeds per day. Large flocks of crossbills congregate in areas where conifer cones are abundant and will leave the area when the food source is depleted. If crossbills are common in a spot one year, chances are they won't return there until years later when the local conifers produce another bumper crop.

All of the crossbill species nest in conifers. The female alone builds a nest from small twigs and lines it with lichens, needles, bark shreds, grasses, and hair. The female incubates the 3–4 pale bluish green, brown-spotted eggs for 11–16 days. Young fledge at 15–25 days. Fledglings have uncrossed bill tips; the tips cross over, either to the right or left, as the young mature.

Red Crossbill
Loxia curvirostra

ALSO: Common Crossbill, Fichtenkreuzschnabel, Bec-croisé des sapins, Grankorsnebb, Обыкновенный клест. SN means "crosswise curved bill."
RANGE: Nests (Mar–May in the north) in coniferous and mixed forests from s Alaska to Newfoundland, and south to Georgia, Arizona, California, n Mexico, and C Amer. In Eurasia, breeds from the UK and Europe across Siberia to Sakhalin, s Kurils, Japan; winters irregularly to the Near East, c Russia, c China, Vietnam. **ID:** L 6–6.75 in (15–17 cm). AD ♂: Deep brick red to reddish yellow, with uniformly dark blackish brown wings and tail. AD ♀: Uniformly olive to grayish olive, with a greenish breast and rump, and whitish throat. VOICE: High-pitched, metallic *chip-chip-chip*. Song is often transcribed as *pit-pit, tor-r-ree, tor-r-ree* or *whit-whit, zzzzt, zzzzt, zzzzt*. Both sexes sing, the female less frequently, when in flight or perched in the treetops.
HABITS: Feeds on cones of spruce (*Picea*), pine (*Pinus*), Douglas-fir (*Pseudotsuga*), and hemlock (*Tsuga*).

White-winged Crossbill

Loxia leucoptera
ALSO: Two-barred Crossbill,
Bindenkreuzschnabel, Bec-
croisé bifascié, Båndkorsnebb,
Белокрылый клест, Siyyuum Kipirnyaruk. SN
means "crossbill with white wings."
RANGE: Nests (Apr–Jun) in spruce and larch
forests from n Alaska to Newfoundland and
nc US states, and from Fennoscandia across
c Siberia to the Sea of Okhotsk. Nomadic in
winter, irrupting to c Europe, Japan, and c US.
ID: L 5.5–6 in (14–15 cm). AD ♂: Pink to reddish
head, rump, and underparts. Wings blackish,
with 2 bold white wing bars and white on tips of
tertials. Tail blackish. AD ♀: Resembles male, but
with yellowish olive head, rump, and underparts.
VOICE: Nasal, querulous *cheit-cheit-cheit* or
chut-chut-chut given in flight. Both sexes sing
while perched or in flight; the song is a series
of trills, chirps, and warbles.
HABITS: Feeds mainly on seeds of spruce (*Picea*),
larch (*Larix*), and hemlock (*Tsuga*). Also feeds
on buds, weed seeds, rowan berries (*Sorbus*),
and insects. Young are fed regurgitated seeds.

Parrot Crossbill

Loxia pytyopsittacus
ALSO: Kiefernkreuzschnabel,
Bec-croisé perroquet, Furu-
korsnebb, Клёст-сосновик.
SN means "parrot-billed crossbill of the pines."
RANGE: Nests (Jan–Apr) in pine forests from
Scandinavia east to the Kola Penin and Pechora
Rvr in Russia. Nomadic in winter, irrupting into
pine and spruce forests of n Europe.
ID: L 6.25–7 in (16–18 cm). Largest crossbill
species; heavier than other species, with a larger
head and bill, and thicker neck. Thick, crossed
bill, with a parrot-like, stout lower mandible
that bulges in the middle. AD: Brick red (male)
or olive green (female) overall, with plain dark
brown wings and tail. JUV: Brownish gray with
dark streaking overall. VOICE: Flight call is a
harsh *kip-kip-kip* or *choop-choop*.
HABITS: Feeds mainly on seeds of Scots Pine
(*Pinus sylvestris*) and some spruce (*Picea*). Nests
near the tops of pine trees.

FAMILY ICTERIDAE
BLACKBIRDS AND ALLIES
GENUS *AGELAIUS*
Red-winged Blackbird

Agelaius phoeniceus
ALSO: Rotflügelstärling,
Carouge à épaulettes,
Rødvingetrupial, Краснoплечий чёрный
трупиал. SN means "red [-winged] flocking bird."
RANGE: Nests (Apr–Jul) in marshes, roadside
ditches, rice paddies, fields, pastures, and urban
parks from se Alaska and n Canada to s US
states. Northern populations migrate to s US
and Mexico; other populations are sedentary.
ID: L 7.5–9 in (19–23 cm). Dark eye and a long,
wedge-shaped, pointed bill. AD♂: Glossy black,
with red scapulars (epaulets) edged with yellow.
Attains adult plumage in 3rd year. AD♀/JUV♂:
Mottled brown above; heavily streaked below;
pale eyebrow stripe. VOICE: Sharp *chek-chek-chek*.
Song is a trilled *oak-a-leeee*.
HABITS: Forms large flocks. Forages by forcibly
opening the bill against resistance to expose
insects in floating vegetation, under stones in
shallow streams, and under objects on the ground.
Also gleans insects from terrestrial vegetation
and picks seeds up from the ground. Female
builds nest by weaving thin strands of vegetation
around vertical supports, then packing mud and
wet vegetation into center, and finally lining the
nest with fine grass. Female incubates the 3–5
bluish green, dark-spotted and scrawled eggs
for 11–13 days. Fledglings migrate with adult
females, separate from adult males.

GENUS *EUPHAGUS*
Rusty Blackbird

Euphagus carolinus
ALSO: Thrush Blackbird,
Roststärling, Quiscale
rouilleux, Roststärling, Ржавчатый трупиал,
Tulukkam-ittuk. SN means "Carolina glutton."
RANGE: Nests (May–Jul) from n Alaska to
Newfoundland in damp woodlands, swamps,
and forest edge. Winters to the se US.
ID: L 8–10 in (20–25 cm). Pale yellow eye (brown
in juveniles). AD ♂ MAR–AUG: Black above with
a bluish green to greenish gloss. AD ♂ WINTER:

ad. ♂
winter

ad. ♂
Mar–Aug

ad. ♀
winter

Rusty Blackbird
Euphagus carolinus
N Amer
L 8–10 in (20–25 cm)

ad. ♀

ad. ♂

Red-winged Blackbird
Agelaius phoeniceus
N Amer
L 7.5–9 in (19–23 cm)

ad.
winter

ad.
Feb–Aug

European Starling
Sturnus vulgaris
Iceland, Eurasia
Introduced into N Amer
L 7.5–9 in (19–23 cm)

Black, with rust-edged feathers on wings, crown, nape, and back. Pale brown eyebrow, cheeks, throat, and breast. AD ♀ MAR–AUG: Slaty overall, with a bluish green gloss. AD ♀ WINTER: Rusty overall, with a conspicuous pale buff line above the eye and a dark eye patch. VOICE: Harsh *chek-chek*. Song sounds like a rusty hinge opening. HABITS: Feeds on aquatic insects, grasshoppers, and other invertebrates when breeding, adding acorns, pine nuts, and fruit in winter. Probes in mud and wetland vegetation. Nests near water in living and dead trees, in dense shrubbery, and on top of stumps. Female builds a bulky nest from twigs, grasses, and *Usnea* lichen, then presses rotting vegetation into the framework, and lines the interior with green and dried grass. Female incubates the 3–5 eggs for 10–13 days.

FAMILY STURNIDAE
STARLINGS AND ALLIES
GENUS *STURNUS*
European Starling
Sturnus vulgaris
ALSO: Northern Starling, Star, Étourneau sansonnet, Stær, Скворец. SN means "common starling." RANGE: Nests (Apr–Jul) in a variety of habitats in Iceland, Faroes, UK, Europe, and N Amer. Native to the Old World. Introduced to New York City's Central Park in 1890 by Eugene Schieffelin (1827–1906), who attempted to install all of the birds mentioned in Shakespeare's writings. ID: L 7.5–9 in (19–23 cm). Short, square tail, pointed wings, yellow orange legs, and long bill. AD FEB–AUG: Glossy black; purple and green iridescence on head, back, and breast. Yellow bill. AD WINTER: Whitish spots on dark head and body feathers. Blackish bill. JUV: Uniformly grayish brown. VOICE: Wheezing and sputtering notes, sometimes adding other birds' songs and sounds as unlikely as car alarms. HABITS: Feeds on insects, berries, seeds, grubs, snails, worms, orchard fruit, and suet at bird feeders. Forages in flocks, mostly on the ground in open areas, searching for prey. Nests in woodpecker holes, burrows, niches in walls, and nest boxes. Nest is a loose mass of twigs, weeds, grass, leaves, litter, and feathers. Both sexes incubate the 4–6 eggs for about 12 days.

FISHES

FISHES WERE THE FIRST VERTEBRATES TO EVOLVE, and from them most other forms of vertebrate life developed. There are about 32,000 fish species worldwide. Arctic waters are home to more than 250 species, the majority of which occupy salt water for all or most of their lives. Only a few of the major food and game fish, and those that have curiosity value, are described and illustrated here.

Fish are cold-blooded, or *ectothermic*, creatures whose body temperatures vary as ambient temperatures change. Their limbs, if present, are in the shape of *fins*. Fins are used for stability and to steer while traveling through the water. Fish actively use their pectoral and pelvic fins for maneuvering. The dorsal and anal fins contribute stability as the fish swims, propelled by the tail or caudal fin. The adipose fin, which has an uncertain function, is not present in all species.

Fish have no lungs, but instead take oxygen from the water directly into the bloodstream by means of *gills*. The gills consist of thread-like filaments, each of which contains a capillary network that provides a large surface area for exchanging oxygen and carbon dioxide. The gills are usually protected by a hard plate known as an *operculum*.

Nearly all fishes have an air bladder, which is used to regulate buoyancy. Scales are usually, but not always, present. In some cases, bony structures called *scutes* (closely packed folds of skin) protect the fish's exterior surface.

Most fishes have a well-developed sense of smell, and most have some sense of taste, sight, and hearing. Their sense of touch is generally poor, except those that have *barbels*, which help locate prey by touch. Most fishes have sensory pores along the *lateral line* that detect changes in pressure and temperature, and sense movement and vibration in the surrounding water.

Traditional taxonomy groups fishes into three extant classes. The largest class is Osteichthyes, which encompasses all fishes having a bony skeleton. Chondrichthyes contains fishes such as sharks and rays, which have a cartilaginous skeleton. Agnatha includes primitive jawless fishes, such as the lampreys and hagfish.

Fishes can also be classified on the basis of behavior and habits. This system notes such things as whether fishes spend their lives in fresh or salt water (or both); what level of the water column they frequent; whether their range is limited or if they swim freely across stretches of open ocean; and whether they are predator or prey.

Anadromous, or *searun,* fishes hatch in fresh water, mature in salt water, and migrate back to fresh water to spawn.

Freshwater fishes spend their entire lives in streams, rivers, or lakes.

Benthic and *demersal* fishes, also known as groundfishes, live on or near the sea bottom.

Pelagic fishes swim freely in the open ocean. Pelagic schooling species move in large groups. Mesopelagic species live in deep to mid-ocean waters; some make nightly migrations to the sea surface to feed. Nerito-pelagic fishes occupy shallow coastal or continental shelf waters.

Forage, or *bait,* fishes are small fishes that provide food for larger fishes, seabirds, and marine mammals.

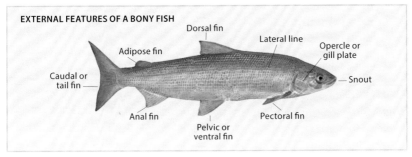

EXTERNAL FEATURES OF A BONY FISH

Dorsal fin · Adipose fin · Lateral line · Opercle or gill plate · Caudal or tail fin · Snout · Anal fin · Pelvic or ventral fin · Pectoral fin

AGNATHA: JAWLESS FISHES

The order Agnatha (Greek for "no jaws") includes primitive, jawless fishes such as lampreys and hagfish. Their fossil relatives lived during the late Devonian period, some 385 million years ago. The lampreys belong to the class Petromyzontida (Hyperoartia). They are distinguished by a round, toothed, funnel-like sucking mouth (illus. at right). The parasitic species clamp their mouth to a fish's body, then cut through skin with their sharp teeth until they can reach and consume the fish's flesh.

FAMILY PETROMYZONTIDAE
GENUS *LAMPETRA*
Arctic Lamprey

Lampetra camtschatica
ALSO: Arktische Lamprete, Lamproie arctique, Arktisk niøye, Minoga. SN means "Kamchatka stone licker," an allusion to the lamprey's habit of sucking algae off rocks.
RANGE: Occurs in salt and brackish water along the arctic coast of Siberia, east to Alaska and Amundsen Gulf, Canada, and south to the Aleutians, Japan, and Korea.
ID: L 12.5–40 in (32–100 cm). Brown, olive, or gray, eel-like body. Lacks scales. One nostril on the top of the head; 7 gill pores on side of the head.
HABITS: Parasitic. Feeds on blood and flesh of fishes, whales, and sharks. Mostly anadromous. Lives mainly in coastal and estuarine waters, but landlocked freshwater forms occur in Alaska. Spawns in fast-flowing rivers and streams. Large aggregations of adults migrate at night to spawning grounds. Both sexes dig a shallow nest, spawn, and then die. The blind larvae (*ammocoetes*) burrow into sand or clay sediments, where they feed on small aquatic invertebrates, algae, and organic matter contained in the detritus. The lampreys mature and move to coastal waters where they stay for about 3 years before returning to fresh water to spawn.

CHONDRICHTHYES: CARTILAGINOUS FISHES

Sharks, rays, and skates are jawed fishes that have paired fins, paired nostrils, scales, two-chambered hearts, and skeletons made of cartilage. Arctic representatives include the sleeper and dogfish sharks, which are members of the order Squaliformes. These sharks have 2 dorsal fins and 5 gill slits. They lack an anal fin. The order's name comes from squalamine, an aminosterol compound naturally derived from the livers of dogfish, sleeper sharks, and other shark species. The substance is presently used as a broad-spectrum antibiotic.

FAMILY SOMNIOSIDAE
SLEEPER SHARKS
GENUS *SOMNIOSUS*
Greenland Shark

Somniosus microcephalus
ALSO: Slurry Shark, Ground Shark, Gray Shark, Eishai, Laimargue du Groenland, Håkjerring, Гренландская полярная акула, Iqalugjuaq, Skalugsuaq. SN means "small headed sleeper." Northernmost shark. Largest arctic fish. Second largest carnivorous shark after the Great White Shark, *Carcharodon carcharias*.
   Inuit legend relates that this shark, which smells strongly of ammonia, sprang from a cloth used by an old woman who was washing her hair with urine. She dried her hair with the rag, and when a gust of wind blew the smelly cloth into the ocean, it turned into Skalugsuaq, the Greenland Shark.
RANGE: Occurs in deep, cold waters of the N Atlantic from the Gulf of St Lawrence north to Greenland, Baffin Is, Ellesmere Is, and south to the Gulf of Maine and (rarely) Gulf of Mexico. Also found in the White and North seas, and waters off Iceland, Svalbard, Norway.
ID: L 11–23 ft (3.5–7 m). WT 1540–2250 lb (700–1022 kg). Brown, black, or gray skin; sides may be tinged with purple or show dark bands or white spots. Rough skin bears small tooth-like projections (*denticles*), with curved, pointed cusps.

Small, spineless dorsal fin. Asymmetrical tail fin. In the Arctic, about 85 percent of Greenland sharks are partially blind due to a parasitic copepod, *Ommatokoita elongata*, which attaches itself to the cornea of the eye and feeds on the shark's corneal tissue.

HABITS: Solitary and sluggish. Prefers water temperatures of 28°F–45°F (−2°C to 7°C). Lives at depths greater than 600 ft (200 m) in summer; observed off the Georgia coast (US) at depths of 7200 ft (2200 m). Swims closer to the surface in winter, occupying the ice pack edge and bays and river mouths.

Hunts in near darkness in frigid waters beneath the winter ice. Feeds on fishes such as capelin, char, halibut, herring, lumpfish, and salmon. A lateral line running along each side detects motion of prey, while its keen chemical perception helps it "smell" its prey. The narrow, pointed upper teeth pin the prey into position. Meanwhile, as the shark swings its head in a circular motion, the broad, laterally curved bottom teeth cut a "cork" of flesh from its prey.

The Greenland Shark can be cannibalistic and is also known to take seals, sea lions, small cetaceans, and land mammals. Biologists in arctic Canada have observed these sharks ambushing and snatching caribou from the water's edge. An entire caribou, minus its antlers, was found in the stomach of one shark. The stomach contents of others have been found to contain body parts of polar bears, horses, and dogs.

The scars found on females' caudal fins suggest that the males bite the females until they submit to copulation. Eggs develop and hatch inside the female. She gives birth to about 10 pups, which are immediately independent of the mother. The pups measure 15 in (38 cm) long at birth and grow at a rate of about 0.5 in (1 cm) per year.

USE: The Inuit used shark teeth to cut hair and sharkskin to make boots. Greenland sharks are harvested commercially off Norway, Iceland, and w Greenland, chiefly for the liver oil. In Greenland, the dried meat is used as dog food.

Icelanders consider the Greenland shark's meat, *hákarl*, a delicacy. Eating it is said to promote hardiness and strength. The uncured meat contains a neurotoxin, trimethylamine oxide, which when ingested can induce a drunken state in humans. The flesh is edible only when it is dried, boiled in several changes of water, or "rotted" in frozen ground.

The traditional method of preparation is to bury large pieces of shark flesh in gravel for 6–12 weeks and let it undergo several cycles of freezing and thawing. The meat is then hung in a drying shack for 2–4 months, after which the flesh turns red or white in color; the red variety is said to be easier to digest. Cubes of hákarl are served as hors d'oeuvres and are usually chased with a shot of Icelandic schnapps, *Brennivín*. This strong liquor, also known as *Svarti Dauði* ("Black Death"), is made from fermented potato pulp flavored with caraway seeds.

Arctic Lamprey
Lampetra camtschatica
NE Asia–Alaska
L 12.5–40 in (32–100 cm)

Greenland Shark
Somniosus microcephalus
N Atlantic
L 11–23 ft (3.5–7 m)

The parasitic copepod
Ommatokoita elongata is shown
here attached to the shark's cornea.

OSTEICHTHYES: BONY FISHES

This extremely diverse and abundant group consists of over 25,000 species of fish with bony skeletons. It is the largest class of vertebrates in existence today. Most bony fishes belong to Actinopterygii, a subclass that comprises the ray-finned fishes. The fins of these fishes are composed of webs of skin supported by bony structures called fin rays, or *lepidotrichia*. A fin may contain only hard, spiny rays, only soft rays, or a combination of both.

Esociformes: Pikes
FAMILY ESOCIDAE
PIKE
GENUS *ESOX*
Northern Pike
Esox lucius

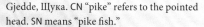

ALSO: Jackfish, Siilik, Eltin, Hecht, Grand brochet, Gjedde, Щука. CN "pike" refers to the pointed head. SN means "pike fish."

RANGE: Circumpolar. Occurs in clear cold-water lakes, weedy backwaters, and small to large rivers.

ID: L 16–60 in (40–150 cm). WT 2–20 lb (1–9 kg). Grayish green; mottled or spotted back and sides. Elongated body and head, with a large "duckbill" snout. Dorsal and anal fins set well back on the body. Jaws, roof of the mouth, tongue, and gill rakers armed with many sharp teeth that are constantly replaced.

HABITS: Freshwater resident. Solitary. Highly territorial. Feeds on fishes, frogs, crayfish, small birds, and invertebrates. Cannibalism is common. Ambush predator. Captures prey by darting out from pondweeds and impaling the prey on its sharp teeth. Then retreats to cover, turns its catch around, and swallows it headfirst. Spawns in spring. Lifespan is up to 30 years.

USE: Sport and food fish. White flesh is tasty but very bony. Thorough cooking is necessary, as pike can be infested with parasites, including broad tapeworms (*Diphyllobothrium* sp.).

Acipenseriformes: Sturgeons
FAMILY ACIPENSERIDAE
STURGEON

Sturgeons appeared in the fossil record about 200 million years ago. Their endoskeleton is largely cartilaginous, indicating their position as a very primitive form of bony fishes.

GENUS *ACIPENSER*
Siberian Sturgeon
Acipenser baerii

ALSO: Long-nosed Siberian Sturgeon, Sibirischer Stör, Esturgeon sibérien, Sibirsk stør, Сибирский осётр. SN means "Baer's sturgeon," honoring Estonian naturalist Karl von Baer (1792–1876).

RANGE: Found in Lake Baikal and rivers flowing into the Kara, Laptev, and e Siberian seas.

ID: L 39–79 in (100–200 cm). WT to 143 lb (65 kg); max 463 lb (210 kg). Back light gray to dark brown. Belly white to clear yellow. Partially covered with rows of bony plates called *scutes*. Long, flattened snout. Slit lower lip. Four barbels hang down like a moustache and act as tactile organs that aid in locating prey on silty substrates.

HABITS: Anadromous, but found most often in middle and lower reaches of rivers rather than at sea. Feeds on mollusks, crustaceans, and fishes. Matures at 9–28 years of age. Spawns in Jun–Jul in strong-current habitats in the mainstream of

Curly-leaf Pondweed
Pomatogeton crispus

Northern Pike
Esox lucius
Circumpolar (fresh water)
L 16–60 in (40–150 cm)

Siberian Sturgeon
Acipenser baerii
Siberia
L 39–79 in (100–200 cm)

large, deep rivers with stone or gravel bottoms. Lifespan is up to 60 years.

USE: Sport and food fish. Farmed both for meat and to produce caviar from its roe.

STATUS: Endangered (IUCN). Decline is attributed to overfishing, poaching, and damming of rivers.

Salmoniformes: Salmon-like Fishes
FAMILY SALMONIDAE
SALMON AND ALLIES

Salmonids are slender fish, with an elongated body, rounded scales, and forked tail. The pelvic fins are set far back behind the gills. The mouth contains a single row of sharp teeth. Most species are prized as game and food fish, and have been introduced to cold-water habitats throughout the world.

GENERA *SALMO* AND *ONCORHYNCHUS*: Salmon occupy cold and polar waters having temperatures below 62°F (16°C). Some species have non-migratory forms that spend their entire lives in fresh water. The more common searun, or *anadromous,* forms begin their life in fresh water, migrate to salt water to mature, then return to natal streams and lakes to spawn.

Prior to spawning, salmon stop feeding and use energy stored in body fat and muscle to fuel runs that take them many miles upstream past fast-flowing currents and rapids. The fish lose their silvery sheen and assume rich breeding colors. Males develop a hooked jaw (*kype*) and sharp teeth they use for fighting off rival males.

Each female excavates one or more nests (*redds*) in the gravel bottom by moving her body and tail back and forth. After a male deposits his sperm (*milt*) over the eggs and leaves to find other mates, the female covers the eggs with gravel and guards her nest for a few days.

All Pacific salmon (*Salmo*) die after spawning. A few Atlantic salmon (*Oncorhynchus*), usually females, make the journey back to the sea and sometimes return to fresh water to spawn again. Nevertheless, the stress of migration and spawning, during which time the fish do not feed, is so exacting that repeat spawners are the exception rather than the norm.

Salmon eggs hatch into *alevin* (young with yolk still attached), grow into *fry* (tiny fish that feed in spawning waters), and then become *parr* (young fish that feed more widely). Parr-stage fish are typically marked with dark horizontal bars (parr marks) on their silvery sides.

Parr develop into *smolt*, and those that are anadromous in nature begin their migration to the sea. During migration, the smolt's kidneys and gills gradually adapt to increasingly salty water. Research indicates that sea-bound smolt memorize the "smell" or chemical signature of their home river, a factor that may play an important role in adults being able to return to the exact stream or lake where they hatched.

Atlantic Salmon
Salmo salar

ALSO: Bay Salmon, Caplin-Scull Salmon, Outside Salmon, Sebago Salmon, Slink, Fiddler, Grilt, Atlantischer Lachs, Saumon atlantique, Atlanterhavslaks, Cëmra, Ouananiche. SN means "saltwater salmon."

RANGE: Occurs to 70°N in cold waters of the Arctic and N Atlantic oceans and tributary rivers. Introduced into the N Pacific and Great Lakes. **ID:** L 28–30 in (71–76 cm). WT 8–12 lb (3.6–5.4 kg); record 79 lb (35.9 kg) rod-caught in Norway. SEARUN: Back is brown, greenish, or bluish, with silvery sides. X-shaped black spots are scattered on the sides above the lateral line. Fins edged in black. SPAWNING: Bronzy overall, often with reddish spots on the head and sides. After spawning, the skin of some fish turns dark gray; this is the *kelt* or *black salmon* stage. FRESHWATER: Silvery blue, with black spots above the lateral line. Spawning males may be tinged with green or red.

HABITS: Smolt migrate to the ocean in Mar–Jun and move to feeding grounds off w Greenland, the Grand Bank, and Labrador Sea, where they feed on pelagic invertebrates and other fishes. Most spend 2 winters at sea before returning to rivers to spawn in Oct–Nov; those that return to spawn after only 1 year at sea are called *grilse*. **STATUS:** Endangered (IUCN). Decline is attributed to overfishing and damage to salmon spawning habitat.

Pink (Humpback) Salmon

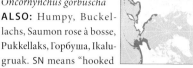

Oncorhynchus gorbuscha
ALSO: Humpy, Buckel-
lachs, Saumon rose à bosse,
Pukkellaks, Горбуша, Ikalu-
gruak. SN means "hooked
jaw *gorbuscha* [a Russian name]."
RANGE: Found in the N Pacific and Arctic
oceans and tributary rivers from the Lena Rvr
in Siberia south to Korea, east to Alaska and
the Mackenzie Rvr, and south to nc California.
Most abundant Pacific salmon. Accidentally
introduced to Lake Superior in 1956.
ID: L 16–30 in (40–76 cm). WT 3–5 lb (1.4–2.3 kg);
max 15 lb (6.8 kg). SEARUN: Greenish blue back,
with large black spots; silvery sides. Large oval
spots on both tail lobes. White mouth, with black
gum line. SPAWNING: Males have a warm brown
back, pink sides, and white belly, and develop
a large hump, a kype, and big teeth. Females
turn olive green, with lavender or gold on sides.
HABITS: Lives in genetically distinct, odd-year
and even-year populations. Completes entire
life cycle in 2 years. Eggs hatch in late winter or
early spring. Parr-stage juveniles migrate to deep
offshore waters where they feed on larval fish,
aquatic insects, and tiny marine crustaceans
that give the species its pink flesh. Matures at 18
months and returns to natal rivers or estuaries
to spawn in Jun–Oct. Except for Yukon Rvr
humpbacks, which spawn far upriver, these
salmon spawn less than 40 mi (65 km) inland.

Chum (Dog) Salmon

Oncorhynchus keta
ALSO: Calico Salmon, Silver-
brite, Ketalachs, Saumon
chien, Hundelaks, Кета.
CN *chum* comes from the Chinook term *tzum*,
meaning "spotted"; *dog* refers to the canine-like
teeth of the spawning male. SN means "hooked
jaw *keta* [a name used by the Evenks of e Siberia]."
RANGE: Occurs in ocean waters and coastal
rivers from the Lena Rvr in Siberia to Chukotka
and south to Japan, and from Alaska east to
the Mackenzie Rvr and south to n California.
ID: L 24–40 in (61–102 cm). WT 10–15 lb (4.5–6.8 kg);
max 31 lb (14 kg). SEARUN: Metallic bluish green

finely dotted with black above the lateral line;
silvery sides. Forked, unspotted tail, with silver
streaks along, but not between, fin rays. First gill
arch has 19–26 short gill rakers (distinguishes
this species from *O. nerka*). SPAWNING: Males
are olive to brown, with red to purplish, wavy,
vertical stripes, and develop a hooked jaw lined
with large, dog-like teeth. Females turn brown to
gray, with a broad dark bar along the lateral line.
HABITS: Strictly searun; no freshwater resident
populations. Spawns in summer and in fall in
lower reaches of rivers, except for Yukon Rvr
populations, which migrate far upstream. Eggs
hatch in 3–4 months and mature to smolt stage
in another 2–3 months. Smolt remain near shore
for several months, usually in shallow eelgrass
(*Zostera*) beds, where they feed on crustaceans,
insects, and small fishes. They move to the open
ocean for 3–4 years before returning to natal
streams to spawn.

Sockeye (Red) Salmon

Oncorhynchus nerka
ALSO: Blueback, Kokanee,
Rotlachs, Saumon rouge,
Нерка. CN *sockeye* derives
from the Fraser Rvr Indian name *sukkai*,
meaning "red fish." SN means "hooked jaw
nerka [a Russian name]."
RANGE: Occurs in the N Pacific from the Anadyr
Rvr south to n Japan, and from Alaska to the
Klamath Rvr, California. Small numbers reported
from the Mackenzie Rvr and Bathurst Inlet.
ID: L 18–30 in (46–76 cm). WT 4–15 lb (2–6 kg).
SEARUN: Back is dark steel blue to metallic
greenish blue; belly white or silvery. Small black
speckles on the back. Straight lateral line. Nearly
toothless mouth. First gill arch has 28–40 long,
slender, serrated gill rakers (distinguishes this
species from *O. keta*). Flesh ruby red to bright
orange. SPAWNING: Males develop a humpback
and whitish hooked jaws, and turn brilliant red,
with an olive green head, blackish snout, and
red adipose and anal fins.
HABITS: Searun and freshwater. Freshwater form
(Kokanee) does not migrate from its natal lake;
however, offspring occasionally are anadromous.
Searun fish may migrate up to 1000 mi (1600 km)

Kokanee
Freshwater Sockeye

Searun Sockeye
No dark spots

Steelhead

Sockeye (Red) Salmon
Oncorhynchus nerka
N Pacific
L 18–30 in (46–76 cm)

Spawning

Rainbow Trout

Rainbow or Steelhead Trout
Oncorhynchus mykiss
N Pacific
L 10–25 in (25–65 cm)

Searun Pink
Black spots on back
and both tail lobes

Spawning

Pink (Humpback) Salmon
Oncorhynchus gorbuscha
N Pacific
L 16–30 in (40–76 cm)

Searun Coho
Black spots on upper
part of tail fin

Spawning

Coho (Silver) Salmon
Oncorhynchus kisutch
N Pacific
L 24–38 in (61–97 cm)

Searun Chum
Silver tail streaks
Black spots on upper sides

Spawning

Chum (Dog) Salmon
Oncorhynchus keta
N Pacific
L 24–40 in (61–102 cm)

Searun Chinook
Black spots on upper
sides and tail fin

Spawning

Chinook (King) Salmon
Oncorhynchus tshawytscha
N Pacific
L 30–58 in (76–147 cm)

Spawning

Atlantic Salmon
Salmo salar
N Atlantic
L 28–30 in (71–76 cm)

Searun
Atlantic Salmon
X-shaped spots on
upper sides

Parr stage

upstream to spawn in Jul–Aug. Eggs hatch in 3–4 months, and parr spend 1–3 years in fresh water before going to sea. Smolt spend a few weeks inshore, feeding on minute crustaceans and insect larvae. They then move offshore, where they feed almost exclusively on zooplankton in the upper 65 ft (20 m) of the water column; their numerous gill rakers strain the plankton from the water. Juveniles spend from 1–4 years at sea, and are 2–8 years old when they return to rivers to spawn and die.

Coho (Silver) Salmon

Oncorhynchus kisutch
ALSO: Silberlachs, Saumon argenté, Кижуч. SN means "hooked jaw *kisutch* [a Russian name]."

RANGE: Occurs in coastal and inland waters from the Anadyr Rvr south to n Japan, and from Point Hope, Alaska, south to c California. **ID:** L 24–38 in (61–97 cm). WT 8–12 lb (3.5–5.5 kg); max 35 lb (16 kg). SEARUN: Dark metallic blue or green; sparsely spotted back; silvery sides; light belly. Black spots only on upper lobe of tail fin. SPAWNING: Reddish sides. Lower jaw gum line white. Males develop a kype and large teeth. **HABITS:** Mostly searun. Adults return to spawn at 3–5 years of age; precocious males called *jacks* return to spawn when 2 years old. Spawns in Jul–Nov in small streams with gravel bottom, then dies. Eggs hatch in May–Jun. Young spend 1–5 winters in streams or brackish estuaries before migrating to sea where they feed on fish.

Chinook (King) Salmon

Oncorhynchus tshawytscha
ALSO: Blackmouth, Quinnat Salmon, Spring Salmon, Tyee Salmon, Iqalugruaq, Königslachs, Saumon royal, Чавыча. SN means "hooked jaw *tshawytscha* [a Kamchatkan name]." CN refers to the Chinook Indians of Washington State, where this fish occurs. State fish of Alaska. **RANGE:** Occurs in coastal and inland waters, from the Anadyr Rvr south to n Japan, and from Alaska south to c California. **ID:** L 30–58 in (76–147 cm). WT 10–50 lb (4.5–23 kg);

sport-caught record 92 lb (42 kg); commercial record 126 lb (57 kg). Largest Pacific salmon species. SEARUN: Bluish green back; silvery sides; white belly. Black gums on lower jawline. Irregular black spots on the back and both lobes of the tail fin. SPAWNING: Bronze, coppery, or deep gray body, depending on location, age, and sex. Males develop a ridgeback and hooked jaw. **HABITS:** Mostly searun. Spawns in larger, deeper water bodies than other salmon species. Eggs hatch in 3–5 months. Parr remain in fresh water 12–18 months before migrating downstream to estuaries, where they remain for several months. Juveniles spend 1–8 years in the ocean before returning to home rivers in Sep–Dec to spawn and die. Precocious males known as *jacks* return to fresh water to spawn 1–2 years earlier than their counterparts; jacks are about half the size of mature chinooks.

Rainbow or Steelhead Trout

Oncorhynchus mykiss
ALSO: Salmon Trout, Regenbogenforelle, Stahlkopfforelle, Truite arc-en-ciel, Regnbueørret, Радужная форель, Микижа, *Salmo gairdneri*. SN means "hooked jaw *mykiss* [a Kamchatkan name]." This trout was a main food source for the Lewis and Clark expedition. In Mar 1806, Lewis wrote: "The Indians tell us that the Salmon begin to run early in the next month. It will be unfortunate for us if they do not, for they must form our principal dependence for food in ascending the Columbia above the Falls and its S. E. branch, Lewis's river [Snake Rvr] to the Mountains."

RANGE: Occurs in cold fresh and salt waters, from Kamchatka to Alaska and south to Mexico. **ID:** L 10–25 in (25–65 cm); record 45 in (114 cm); WT 2–8 lb (1–3.6 kg); record 51 lb (23 kg) for non-migratory fish, 35 lb (16 kg) for searun. Back bluish green to olive; faint pinkish band along silvery or brassy sides. Back, body, and fins heavily speckled in blackish brown. Steelheads turn silvery after a few weeks in the open ocean. SPAWNING: Conspicuous black spots and a pink to red band along the lateral line. Males develop a slightly hooked jaw and reddish gill plates.

HABITS: Searun (steelhead) and freshwater (rainbow trout) forms. Both forms spend the first 2–3 years of life in fresh water, feeding on plankton, insects, and small fishes. Trout remain in their natal lake or river for their entire life. Steelheads migrate to the sea at age 2 and spend another 2 years in salt water before returning to natal waters to spawn. Summer-run steelheads migrate upstream in May–Oct before their reproductive organs are fully developed and mature in fresh water before spawning the next spring. Winter-run steelheads fully mature at sea before migrating upriver to spawn in Nov–Apr. Unlike the other Pacific salmon species, these fish do not die after spawning, but can spawn several times during their lifetime of about 11 years.

GENUS *SALVELINUS*: Chars are distinguished from other salmonids by the presence of light spots on a dark body and by the lack of teeth on the vomer shaft (upper palate of the mouth). These fishes feed on planktonic crustaceans, amphipods, mollusks, insects, and smaller fishes. They do not feed while under the winter ice, but instead survive on fat reserves accumulated during the summer. Unlike the *Oncorhychus* species, chars do not die after spawning.

Arctic Char

Salvelinus alpinus
ALSO: Sea-run, Martson Trout, Quebec Red Trout, Blueback Trout, Ilkalupik,

Iqaluk, Tariungmiutaq , Nutiliarjuk, Seesaibling, Omble chevalier, Salvelino, Bleikja, Røye, Голец арктический. SN means "alpine char"; named in 1758 by Linnaeus who described the species from a specimen found in a mountain lake in Swedish Lapland. Northernmost freshwater fish. **RANGE:** Circumpolar. Freshwater forms live in rivers and lakes of N Amer, Greenland, Iceland, and n Eurasia. Searun forms occur on the arctic coasts of Canada, Greenland, Norway, and Russia. **ID:** L 18–42 in (46–107 cm). WT 2–20 lb (1–9 kg); max 33 lb (15 kg). Slim tail base and deeply forked tail. SEARUN: Silvery with a deep blue or greenish blue on the back and upper sides. FRESHWATER: Dark blue to olive green or brown. Both forms

are sparsely spotted with pink or reddish pink on the back and sides. Bright red to pale pink flesh. SPAWNING: Sides, underparts, and lower fins gold, orange, yellow, or rose. Male's kype is small or absent.

HABITS: Matures at 7–11 years, and typically spawns every 1–4 years after reaching that age. Spawns Sep–Oct. Female clears a nest with the tail in the gravel bottom of shallow rivers or lakes and deposits eggs. Male guards territories, which may include nests of several females. Smaller, faster males called *jacks* or *sneakers* sometimes charge in and fertilize eggs before a dominant male chases them away. Eggs develop over winter, and young emerge from the gravel in spring. Searun char remain in their natal river for 5–7 years, after which they make an annual spring migration to the sea and return to their river of origin each fall. Lifespan is 10–40 years. **USE:** Important food fish for Arctic peoples. Harvested and farmed commercially.

Dolly Varden

Salvelinus malma
ALSO: Calico Trout, Saibling, Truite Dolly Varden, Skrautbleikja, мальма. CN Dolly Varden is a character in Dickens's *Barnaby Rudge*. In the 1870s a California woman noted that her dotted, Dolly Varden–style dress resembled the color pattern of the Bull Trout (*S. confluentus*); the name was later applied to the arctic species. SN means "char *malma* [a Russian name]." **RANGE:** Occurs in coastal and inland waters of Chukotka and Kamchatka, e Aleutians, Alaska, and Canada, east to the Mackenzie Rvr. **ID:** L 10–40 in (25–100 cm). WT 5–20 lb (2–9 kg). Thick tail base and slightly forked tail. FRESHWATER: Orange to red spots on olive brown sides (when in clear streams) or pale silver gray sides (in glacial streams). Often dwarfed, maturing at 3–6 in (8–15 cm). SEARUN: Silvery, with a faint green sheen overlain with light orange spots; turns greenish brown with dark orange to red spots on entering fresh water. SPAWNING: Bellies and sides flushed with red; sides spotted bright orange to red; lower fins edged with bright white. Males develop a prominent, strongly hooked kype.

HABITS: Both searun and freshwater forms winter in small streams and rivers, then move to larger streams and rivers or coastal waters in spring. Spawns Aug–Sep in deep pools of cold rivers, lakes, reservoirs, or in streams with abundant cover and gravel bottom. During the month-long spawning season, feeds heavily on unhatched salmon eggs. Each Dolly Varden can eat a third to a half pound of salmon eggs every day. Afterward, their digestive tract shrinks to decrease energy requirements needed to sustain the fish through a long winter fast.

Young remain in their natal streams for about 3–4 years. Anadromous smolt migrate to brackish coastal waters, where they remain for 2–3 years. Some adults wander far afield, however. One tagged Dolly Varden was recorded swimming more than 1000 mi (1600 km) between N Amer and Russia.

Lake Trout

Salvelinus namaycush
ALSO: Laker, Mackinaw, Grey Trout, Lake Charr, Touladi, Togue, Siscowet, Paperbelly, Isuuraq, Amerikanische Seesaibling, Omble du Canada, Canadarøye. SN derives from *namegos,* an Algonquian name for the species. CN *trout* is a misnomer—this is a char. Alaska's largest freshwater fish.
RANGE: Found in cold lakes and streams in N Amer, south to the n US. Introduced into Europe, S Amer, and Asia.
ID: L 18–26 in (46–65 cm); record 49 in (125 cm). WT 2–6.5 lb (1–3 kg); record 102 lb (46 kg). Small, irregular, cream to yellow spots on a silvery to dark gray background. Deeply forked tail. Flesh varies from creamy white to deep orange.
SPAWNING MALE: Develops dark stripes on sides; lacks the red or orange of other chars. White leading edge on the pectoral, pelvic, and anal fins.
HABITS: Found only in large, deep lakes with water temperatures under 55°F (12°C). In summer, descends to depths of 200 ft (60 m) or more. Feeds on zooplankton, insect larvae, crustaceans, clams, snails, leeches, fishes, mice, shrews, and occasionally young birds. Matures at 7–8 years, after which it spawns every other year in Sep–Nov.

Large schools of fish spawn at night in shallow water over rocky lake bottoms. Eggs hatch the next spring. Lifespan is 20–60 years.
USE: Prized as sport and food fish. Fished commercially in the Great Lakes until lampreys, overharvest, and pollution reduced the stocks.

GENUS *THYMALLUS*
Arctic Grayling

Thymallus arcticus
ALSO: Bluefish, Sulukpaugaq, Sriijaa, Arktische Äsche, Ombre arctique, Сибирьысь кыны. SN means "arctic thyme-scented [fish]," referring to the smell of freshly caught graylings.
RANGE: Occurs in clear waters of cold rivers, lakes, and rocky creeks, from the Kara Rvr in Russia east to Alaska and Hudson Bay; remnant populations in Montana. Extinct in Michigan.
ID: L 6–30 in (15–75 cm). WT 2–6 lb (1–2.7 kg). Sail-like dorsal fin. Typically gray overall, but can flash a rainbow of colors. Dorsal fin is gray, spotted with red or green, with a wine-colored edge and often with a blue band below. Pelvic fins black, with wavy mauve or orange lines. Side scales are silvery gray, blue, or blue green outlined with yellow, with small dark spots.
HABITS: Fresh water only. Prefers cold lakes and swift-flowing rivers with sand or gravel bottom. Spawns upriver, depositing eggs between rocks or boulders. After spawning, adults move to traditional summer feeding grounds, where they fatten up on aquatic insects, small fish, fish eggs, zooplankton, and occasionally voles and shrews. In early fall, fish move downstream and winter there. Their tolerance of low dissolved oxygen levels allows them to survive long periods under the ice where other salmon would die. Matures at 4–6 years and may complete several spawning runs during its lifetime. Lifespan is up to 32 years.

GENUS *COREGONUS*
Arctic Cisco

Coregonus autumnalis
ALSO: Herring, Qaaqtaq, Treeluk, Pollen, Омуль.
Considered conspecific with *C. laurettae* (Bering Sea region) and *C. artedii* (n N Amer and Hudson

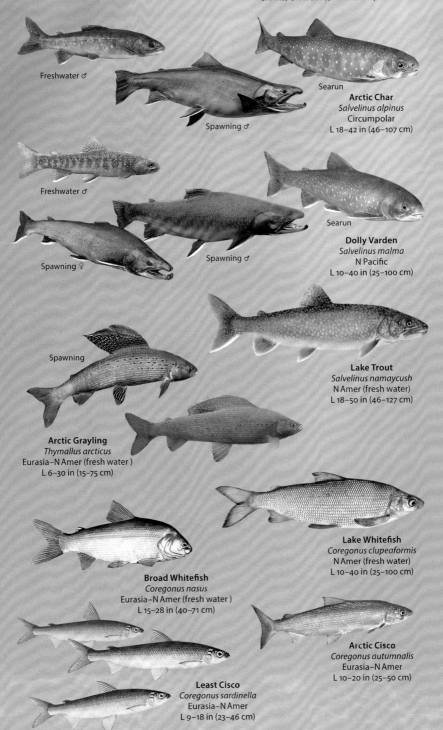

Freshwater ♂

Spawning ♂

Searun

Arctic Char
Salvelinus alpinus
Circumpolar
L 18–42 in (46–107 cm)

Freshwater ♂

Spawning ♀

Spawning ♂

Searun

Dolly Varden
Salvelinus malma
N Pacific
L 10–40 in (25–100 cm)

Spawning

Lake Trout
Salvelinus namaycush
N Amer (fresh water)
L 18–50 in (46–127 cm)

Arctic Grayling
Thymallus arcticus
Eurasia–N Amer (fresh water)
L 6–30 in (15–75 cm)

Lake Whitefish
Coregonus clupeaformis
N Amer (fresh water)
L 10–40 in (25–100 cm)

Broad Whitefish
Coregonus nasus
Eurasia–N Amer (fresh water)
L 15–28 in (40–71 cm)

Arctic Cisco
Coregonus autumnalis
Eurasia–N Amer
L 10–20 in (25–50 cm)

Least Cisco
Coregonus sardinella
Eurasia–N Amer
L 9–18 in (23–46 cm)

Bay). CN derives from the Canadian French *ciscoette* and from the Ojibwa *pemitewiskawet*, meaning "fish with oily flesh." SN means "autumn [-spawning] fish with angled eye pupils."

RANGE: Occurs in brackish estuaries and rivers in n Eurasia and nw N Amer; also occurs in Lake Baikal as *C. a. migratorius*.

ID: L 10–20 in (25–50 cm). WT 2 lb (1 kg). Elongate body, with a slightly falcate dorsal fin, forked tail, and mouth at terminus of snout. Dusky gray to greenish blue above, unspotted silvery on sides, and white belly. Pale or colorless pelvic fins.

HABITS: Searun only. Adults leave salt water in Jul–Aug and swim up to 950 mi (1500 km) upriver. Large aggregations spawn in Sep–Oct in shallow tributaries with gravel bottom and with water temperatures of about 40°F (4.5°C). Adults return to sea after spawning, where they feed on crustaceans, insects, small fishes, worms, and clams. Eggs hatch in 7 months. Smolt migrate downstream in May–Jun and spend 6–8 years in coastal waters before returning to natal rivers. Spawns 2–3 times in its lifetime of 10–20 years.

RELATED SPECIES: LEAST or SARDINE CISCO, *Coregonus sardinella*, occurs in lakes, rivers, and estuaries along the Arctic Ocean, from the Pechora Rvr in Siberia to Alaska and nw Canada. Searun only. Matures in brackish estuaries and lower river courses. Moves upriver at 3–4 years of age and spawns in Jun or Sep in deep pools with sand and gravel bottom.

Lake Whitefish

Coregonus clupeaformis
ALSO: Crookedback, Kavisilik, Kalupiat, Herings- maräne, Felchen, Corégon de lac, Sik. SN means "herring-like fish."

RANGE: Found in large rivers and deep, cold lakes in n N Amer. Introduced into Andean lakes.

ID: L 10–25 in (25–100 cm). WT 2–4 lb (1–2 kg); max 42 lb (19 kg). Small head; old fish develop a humped neck. Blunt snout overhangs the lower jaw. Back dark brown or pale olive; sides and belly silvery. Very large scales.

HABITS: Fresh water only. Forages on lake bottoms at depths of 60–165 ft (18–50 m), feeding on small crustaceans, insects, and small fishes. Spawns in cold lakes and tributary streams in late fall. Eggs are deposited freely in shallow water, settle to the gravel bottom, and hatch the next spring. Young move to deep water, where they feed on small crustaceans such as *Daphnia*. Lifespan is up to 50 years.

USE: Prized by sport fishermen and commercial fisheries. It has delicious flesh, and the liver and eggs are sometimes sold as caviar.

Broad Whitefish

Coregonus nasus
ALSO: Kavisilik, Anaakrik, Large Bottom Whitefish, Luk digaii, Sandfelchen, Grosse Bodenrenke, Poisson blanc, Чир. SN means "[blunt-] nosed fish."

RANGE: Occurs in arctic river drainage basins, brackish estuaries, and large lakes from the Pechora Rvr, Russia, to the Perry Rvr, Canada.

ID: L 15–28 in (40–71 cm). WT 3–6 lb (1.5–3 kg); max 35 lb (16 kg). Flattened sides and compressed body. Blunt snout; mouth points downward. Small pectoral fins below the gill opening. Large adipose fin. Deeply forked tail. Brown back, fading to yellow or silver on sides and belly. Dark gray fins. During fall spawning, white conical tubercles appear on the male's large scales. Migrating fish often bear scars from lamprey bites.

HABITS: Fresh water only. Bottom feeder, eating midges, mosquito larvae, snails, bivalves, and crustaceans. Matures at 4–9 years. Migrates upriver in Jul–Aug. Spawns Oct–Nov, often under ice, in areas with swift current and sand or gravel bottom. Spawning lasts 5–7 days. Adults leave the site soon after to winter in deep waters on lower stretches of rivers. Eggs hatch the next spring. Young drift downstream to feed in floodplain lakes and oxbows of rivers.

USE: Tasty flesh is sold fresh, smoked, or as *dryfish*, which are filets that are hung outside in the shade for a day and then lightly smoked. Taken with nets by locals who use the fish for food, to bait traps, and to feed dogs. Favored by brown bears.

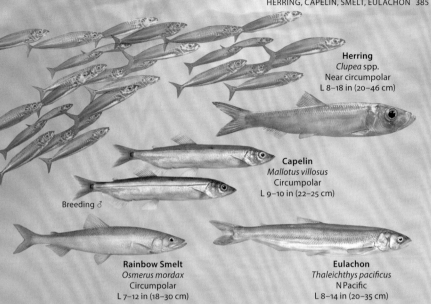

Herring
Clupea spp.
Near circumpolar
L 8–18 in (20–46 cm)

Capelin
Mallotus villosus
Circumpolar
L 9–10 in (22–25 cm)

Breeding ♂

Rainbow Smelt
Osmerus mordax
Circumpolar
L 7–12 in (18–30 cm)

Eulachon
Thaleichthys pacificus
N Pacific
L 8–14 in (20–35 cm)

Clupeiformes: Herring and Allies

FAMILY CLUPEIDAE
HERRING

Herring are pelagic schooling species that feed on small fishes, crustaceans, and plankton, which they filter from the water with their gill rakers. They have silvery, spindle-shaped bodies and lack scales on the head. Most species lack a lateral line, and the teeth are unusually small if present at all. Adults spawn huge numbers of eggs (up to 200,000 in some species) near the sea surface. These food fish are served salted, smoked, marinated, or creamed. Some are harvested for their oil or for use as bait. Atlantic and Pacific species are superficially indistinguishable and are illustrated simply as Herring, *Clupea* spp.

GENUS *CLUPEA*
Pacific Herring

Clupea pallasii
ALSO: Pazifischer Hering, Hareng du Pacifique, Sild, Kavisilâq, Pikoaktit, Сельдь тихоокеанская, Uksruktuuk. SN means "Pallas's sardine," after German naturalist Peter Simon Pallas (1741–1811).
RANGE: Occurs to depths of 1560 ft (475 m) from the Beaufort Sea south to Japan and Baja California, and from the White Sea to the Ob Rvr. N Amer stocks winter south of St Matthew Is.

ID: L 10–18 in (25–46 cm). WT 1 lb (0.45 kg). Dark blue to olive above, shading to silver below. No distinctive marks on body or fins.
HABITS: Adults migrate to estuaries to spawn in Apr–May. Largest breeding population in the e Pacific is in Bristol Bay, sw Alaska, where 200–300 million fish are known to spawn. Adults leave for sea in late summer. First-year young form schools near the surface of shallow bays and inlets; these schools disappear in the fall, and young mature over the next 2–3 years in deeper water.
USE: Food source for seabirds, marine mammals, and fishes. Harvested by subsistence and commercial fisheries. Fish are processed for Asian roe market. Divers harvest any eggs deposited on kelp. The eggs are salted and served as the Japanese delicacy *kazunoko-kombu*.
RELATED SPECIES: ATLANTIC HERRING, *Clupea harengus*, occurs in seawater to depths of 1200 ft (364 m) from e N Amer to Greenland, Iceland, n Europe, Novaya Zemlya, and Svalbard. Silvery, with bluish green back. Schools rise to the surface at night to feed mainly on copepods. Knocking and thumping sounds are produced as gas moves between the gut and air bladder, which acts as a resonating chamber.

Osmeriformes: Capelin and Smelt
FAMILY OSMERIDAE

These are small, herring-like fishes that form huge schools at or near the ocean surface. They feed on small marine organisms and in turn are prey for larger marine animals.

GENUS *OSMERUS*
Rainbow Smelt
Osmerus mordax

ALSO: Arctic Smelt, Frost-fish, American Smelt, Fresh-water Smelt, Ice Fish, Lee Fish, Qiqotiliqaoraq, Iłhuaġniq, Éperlan arc-en-ciel, Азиатская корюшка. SN means "pungent smell," alluding to the cucumber-like scent of freshly caught smelt.

RANGE: Occurs in nearshore and offshore waters of the N Pacific and N Atlantic; also occurs in the St Lawrence Seaway, west to Lake Superior.

ID: L 7–9 in (18–23 cm), rarely to 12 in (30 cm). WT 3 oz (85 g). Slender body. Long, pointed snout, protruding lower jaw, fang-like teeth, and deeply forked tail. Searun forms are silvery, with olive green back and flashes of pink, purple, and blue along the incomplete lateral line. Belly white. Freshwater forms are dark and almost black on the back. SPAWNING: Male's head, body and fins develop tiny tubercles (bumps).

HABITS: Searun and freshwater forms. Feeds on crustaceans, worms, squid, and small fishes. Searun forms occur from shallows to depths of 1400 ft (450 m) and typically migrate a short distance upstream to spawn. Freshwater forms spawn at night in lower reaches of streams shortly after the ice melts. Most adults die after spawning. Eggs are sticky and attach to substrates such as gravel, sand, mud, or submerged vegetation. Eggs are unattended and hatch in 1–4 weeks. Matures at 1–2 years of age. Lifespan is 6–7 years.

USE: Food fish, with an oily flesh. Key food for many large commercial fish species.

GENUS *MALLOTUS*
Capelin
Mallotus villosus

ALSO: Lodde, Capelan, Amagiak, Qoliiligaq, Мойва. CN is French for "codfish." SN means "woolly

haired," referring to the shape of the scales on the sides of breeding males.

RANGE: Occurs in cold-temperate to arctic waters of the N Pacific and N Atlantic.

ID: L 9–10 in (22–25 cm). Very elongated body. Pointed snout, with a projecting lower jaw. Small teeth on jaws and vomer bone on the upper palate. Dorsal fin is set far back. Back grayish green; skin of upper body and fins speckled. SPAWNING: Male's flanks show a broad silvery stripe with dark outline above; sides are sometimes flushed with pink or gold; small tubercules (bumps) on fins.

HABITS: Feeds on zooplankton. Forms shoals in offshore waters and on fishing banks to depths of 1000 ft (300 m). Matures in open ocean over the continental shelves. Spawns in summer. Lays sticky eggs in shallow water or on deep banks.

USE: Commercially important for use as fish meal and fish oil. Tastes a lot like herring. In Asia, the *masago* (roe) is mixed with *wasabi* (green horseradish) and sold as "wasabi caviar." Key food of the Atlantic Cod. Main forage species for large fishes, seabirds, and marine mammals.

Capelin are also known to be quick responders to sea temperature fluctuations, and some suggest they be regarded as "sea canaries" that give early warning of ocean warming and climate change.

GENUS *THALEICHTHYS*
Eulachon
Thaleichthys pacificus

ALSO: Hooligan, Oolichan, Ooligan, Candlefish, Pacific Smelt, Kerzenfisch, Poisson-chandelle. SN means "abundant fish of the Pacific." CN *Eulachon* is the Chinook Indian name for the species; *hooligan* is a corruption of the name. Early explorers called this species *candlefish* because it is so fatty during spawning that dried fish can be strung on a wick and burned as a candle.

RANGE: Occurs in nearshore ocean waters to depths of 1000 ft (300 m) from c Alaska west to Bowers Bank in the c Aleutians, and south to Monterey Bay, California.

ID: L 8–14 in (20–35 cm). Brown to bluish on back and top of head; sides silvery; belly white; some fine speckling on the back. Large canine teeth on the vomer bone (upper palate). Sickle-shaped adipose fin. Anal fin has 18–23 rays. SPAWNING: Male's fins lengthen and develop breeding tubercles (bumps). Males also develop a fleshy ridge along the length of the body.

HABITS: Feeds on plankton, fish eggs, insect larvae, and small crustaceans. Searun only. Adults migrate to natal streams and spawn from late winter to midspring. Males migrate first; females follow a few weeks later. Eggs are deposited on sand or coarse gravel in lower reaches of rivers fed by snowmelt. Most adults die after spawning. Eggs hatch in 20–40 days. Currents carry fry downstream and out to sea. Juveniles move to deeper ocean waters where they mature over 3–5 years.

USE: Eulachon serve as an important food source for marine predators and for people living near spawning streams. Fish are caught using traps, rakes, and nets. They are stored frozen and thawed as needed or are dried, smoked, or canned. Eulachon were formerly processed for their rich oil. The fish were allowed to decompose in a pit for a week or more, then they were boiled and the oil skimmed off. The oil, commonly known as *grease*, was traded into the interior over routes that became known as "grease trails."

Pleuronectiformes: Flatfishes
FAMILY PLEURONECTIDAE
RIGHTEYE FLOUNDERS

Pleuronectidae (Greek for "side swimming") includes bottom-feeding food fish such as halibut, flounders, soles, turbot, and plaice. These fishes are collectively known as *righteye flounders* because adults have both eyes on their right side. The fish are born with their eyes positioned on both sides of the head, but the left eye gradually migrates across the top of the head and settles on the right side.

Right-eye flounders lie on the sea bottom on their left sides, which blanch out as the fish ages. Meanwhile, the right side develops a dark, often mottled pattern that can change color to match the sand or gravel bottom and completely camouflage the fish.

Flatfish in this family make long-distance migrations between the shallow coastal waters

where they summer and the deep waters where they winter and spawn. Each female releases millions of eggs directly into the sea where they are fertilized by the males. The eggs drift in the ocean currents until the larvae develop and sink to the bottom, where they mature.

GENUS *HIPPOGLOSSUS*
Atlantic Halibut
Hippoglossus hippoglossus
ALSO: Nataarnaq, Heilbutt, Wei, Flétan atlantique,

Heilagfiski, Flisebrasme, Kveite, Paltus. CN stems from Middle English *halybutte*, meaning "holy flatfish," alluding to its being eaten on religious holidays. SN means "[shaped like a] horse tongue." Largest Atlantic flatfish.

RANGE: Occurs in cold N Atlantic and Arctic waters to 79°N, and south to the ne US seaboard and along the coast of Europe to the Bay of Biscay.
ID: L 45–125 in (122–318 cm). WT max published 705 lb (320 kg). Right side is dark brown or black; young have pale mottling or spots. Lateral line curves over pectoral fin. Both eyes on right side; eyes large, separated by a very broad flat area.
HABITS: Benthic. Occurs on the sea bottom at depths of 165–6550 ft (50–2000 m). Feeds on fishes such as cod, sandeels, herring, and capelin, but also takes cephalopods, large crustaceans, and other bottom invertebrates.
STATUS: Endangered (IUCN). Due to their slow growth rate and late onset of maturity, populations have been seriously affected by overfishing.
RELATED SPECIES: The PACIFIC HALIBUT, *Hippoglossus stenolepis*, occurs from the Chukchi Sea south to n Japan and Baja California. L 45–102 in (122–260 cm). Max published

WT 500 lb (227 kg). Right side dark brown; left side white. Elongated, diamond-shaped body. Crescent-shaped tail. Adults occupy shallow coastal waters in summer, then migrate to the edge of the continental shelf, where they winter and spawn at depths of 1200–1800 ft (365–550 m). Juveniles are highly migratory and move in a current-driven clockwise motion around the Bering Sea. Lifespan is up to 50 years.

GENUS *REINHARDTIUS*
Greenland Halibut

Reinhardtius hippoglossoides
ALSO: Flatty, Black Halibut, Greenland Turbot, Netarnârak, Qaleralik, Tikkalik, Schwarzer Heilbutt, Flétan du Groenland, Svartkveite, Палтус черный. SN means "Reinhardt's halibut," honoring Danish professor Johannes Reinhardt (1778–1845), who wrote *Ichthyological Contributions to the Fauna of Greenland.*
RANGE: Occurs in the N Pacific from the Chukchi Sea south to the Sea of Japan and s California; in the N Atlantic from arctic Canada, Greenland, Iceland, and Svalbard south to ne US and Ireland.
ID: L 22–59 in (56–150 cm). WT 60–155 lb (27–70 kg); max 400 lb (182 kg). Right side chestnut brown to blackish. Left side white. Left eye is positioned on the dorsal ridge, giving the fish the look of a cyclops when viewed from above.
HABITS: Summers in cold coastal waters; winters at depths of 3300–6550 ft (1000–2000 m). Feeds on crustaceans, fishes, and bottom invertebrates. Spawns Oct–Jan in southern range, May–Jul in the High Arctic. Lifespan is 30–40 years.

GENUS *PLATICHTHYS*
Starry Flounder

Platichthys stellatus
ALSO: Sternflunder, Flet étoilé, Nataaznak, Камбала зірчаста. SN means "starred flatfish." CN refers to star-shaped tubercles on the body.
RANGE: Found in inshore waters and estuaries along the Pacific Rim from s Japan to Alaska and nw Canada, south to s California.
ID: L 14–36 in (36–91 cm). Upperside brown to nearly black, with scattered star-shaped bony tubercles or pale blotches. Underside white to cream. Fins have 4–7 dark bars alternating with white or orange bars. Even though they are in the righteye flounder family, starry flounder often have their eyes on the left side.
HABITS: Benthic. Occurs in shallow inshore waters and estuaries, with young found as far as 75 mi (120 km) upriver; occasionally occurs down to 1230 ft (375 m). Feeds on crustaceans, worms, small mollusks, brittle stars, and small fishes.

GENUS *LIOPSETTA*
Arctic Flounder

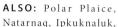

Liopsetta glacialis
ALSO: Polar Plaice, Natarnaq, Ipkuknaluk, Natagnak, Plie arctique, Полярная камбала. SN means "smooth flatfish of the ice."
RANGE: Occurs from ne Canada to Greenland and coastal Siberia, and from the Chukchi Sea south to s Alaska and Sea of Okhotsk.
ID: L 14–17 in (36–44 cm). Right side dark olive green to dark brown, occasionally with black spots or patches; left side white. Fins pale brown, sometimes with yellow or faint dark spots.
HABITS: Lives on mud bottoms of coastal waters to depths of 300 ft (90 m). Occurs offshore in the fall; moves inshore in spring on incoming evening tides. Spawns Dec–May under the ice.

GENUS *HIPPOGLOSSOIDES*
American Plaice

Hippoglossoides platessoides
ALSO: American or Canadian Plaice, Doggerscharbe, Plie canadienne, Gapeflyndre. SN means "resembles a halibut."
RANGE: Occurs in N Atlantic and Arctic waters from the ne US to Greenland, Iceland, the UK, and the Murmansk coast.
ID: L 14–33 in (36–83 cm). WT to 140 lb (64 kg). Brown to olive, spotted with chestnut. Dorsal fin starts above left eye. Lateral line straight.
HABITS: Benthic. Lives on soft bottoms at depths of 295–985 ft (90–300 m). Feeds on echinoderms, worms, mollusks, crustaceans, and fishes.

Gadiformes: Cods and Allies
FAMILY GADIDAE
CODS

Cods are demersal fishes that live near, but not on, the sea bottom. Most species have chin barbels (whisker-like appendages), 3 dorsal fins (instead of 1 or 2), and 2 anal fins (instead of 1). Lifespan is 12–20 years. Cod is a popular food fish with a mild flavor and dense, flaky white flesh. The liver is processed to make cod liver oil, which is a source of vitamin A, vitamin D, vitamin E, and omega-3 fatty acids.

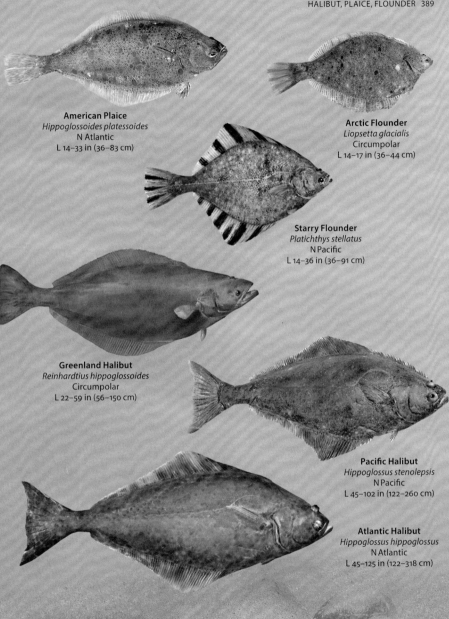

American Plaice
Hippoglossoides platessoides
N Atlantic
L 14–33 in (36–83 cm)

Arctic Flounder
Liopsetta glacialis
Circumpolar
L 14–17 in (36–44 cm)

Starry Flounder
Platichthys stellatus
N Pacific
L 14–36 in (36–91 cm)

Greenland Halibut
Reinhardtius hippoglossoides
Circumpolar
L 22–59 in (56–150 cm)

Pacific Halibut
Hippoglossus stenolepsis
N Pacific
L 45–102 in (122–260 cm)

Atlantic Halibut
Hippoglossus hippoglossus
N Atlantic
L 45–125 in (122–318 cm)

GENUS *BOREOGADUS*
Arctic Cod

Boreogadus saida
ALSO: Ogac, Uugavik, Polar
Cod, Ordlerit, Polardorsch,
Saïda franc, Polartorsk, Треска полярная. SN
means "blessed boreal cod."
RANGE: Occurs from just under the sea ice
down to 1300 ft (400 m). Frequents brackish
estuaries in the Beaufort Sea. Can tolerate
water temperatures down to 18°F (–8°C) owing
to antifreeze protein compounds in its blood.
ID: L 10–16 in (25–40 cm). Back brown to bluish,
with many fine dark marks; sides and belly
silvery; fins dusky, with pale margins. Tail fin
deeply concave. Chin barbel very small. Scales
small, embedded, and not overlapping.
HABITS: Forms large schools that attract predators such as seabirds, seals, and whales. Feeds on
small crustaceans, amphipods, copepods, fish
eggs, and fish fry. Spawns once in its lifetime,
always in winter. Each female can produce up
to 21,000 eggs.
USE: Pivotal component of the arctic marine
food chain. Harvested in Canada for fish meal
and fish oil. Russian, Norwegian, Danish, and
German trawlers fish for arctic cod in Jan–May;
the largest catches are taken in Feb.

GENUS *ARCTOGADUS*
Polar Cod

Arctogadus glacialis
ALSO: Istorsk, Morue
arctique, Saïda imberbe,
Треска ледовая. SN means "arctic ice fish."
RANGE: Occurs to 87°N in polar waters from
Ellesmere Is west to the Beaufort Sea and east to
Greenland, Svalbard, and Siberia, where it schools
with *A. borosovi*, a similar Eurasian species.
ID: L 13–19 in (33–48 cm). Brownish above the
lateral line; silvery belly. Dark, slightly forked
tail. Lower jaw projects slightly. Mouth has
numerous strong teeth. Lacks chin barbels.
HABITS: Lives at depths of 50–130 ft (15–40 m).
Occasionally descends to 3300 ft (1000 m). Enters
estuaries. Hides from predators and hunts for
fish and crustaceans under the pack ice. Main
prey is Arctic Cod (*Boreogadus saida*).

GENUS *GADUS*
Atlantic Cod

Gadus morhua
ALSO: Ogac, Scrod,
Saarullik, Dorsch, Morue
franche, Torsk, Треска. SN means "cod codfish."
RANGE: Lives in waters down to 2000 ft (600 m)
from the ne N Amer coast east to Greenland,
Iceland, and the Barents Sea.
ID: L 39–79 in (100–200 cm). WT 55–75 lb (25–34 kg).
Brown, greenish, or gray on back and sides; pale
and silvery on belly. Lateral line light, curving
upward to above the pectoral fin. An elongated
hair-like barbel hangs down from the chin
HABITS: Sexually mature at 2–4 years. Lifespan
is 20 or more years. Spawns in winter and early
spring in cold offshore waters at depths of
165–660 ft (50–200 m). Feeds at dawn or dusk on
invertebrates and bottom fish, including young
cod. The stomachs of adult cod have also yielded
unusual items such as oil cans, a rubber doll,
finger rings, clothing, and rare deep-sea shells
previously unknown to science.
STATUS: One of the most severely exploited food
fishes in the Western world. Vulnerable (IUCN).
RELATED SPECIES: GREENLAND COD, *Gadus
ogac*, closely related to or
conspecific with *G. morhua*.
Benthic. Occurs in inshore
and continental shelf waters
to 1300 ft (400 m) deep in the

Beaufort Sea, Hudson Bay, N Atlantic, Arctic
Ocean, and White Sea. White, flaky flesh.

PACIFIC COD, *Gadus macrocephalus*, pelagic
schooling fish taken by
fisheries in N Pacific continental shelf waters at depths
of 325–1300 ft (100–400 m).
Occurs from the Bering Sea

south to Korea and s California. Brownish gray
with dark golden spots or wavy lines on sides.
Dorsal, anal, and tail fins edged in white.

SAFFRON COD or UUQAQ, *Eleginus gracilis*,
occurs in shallow coastal
waters of the Bering Sea,
south to Korea and s Alaska.
Utilized as a food fish by
local fisheries.

Polar Cod
Arctogadus glacialis
Arctic
L 13–19 in (33–48 cm)

Arctic Cod
Boreogadus saida
Arctic
L 10–16 in (25–40 cm)

Alaska Pollock
Theragra chalcogramma
N Pacific
L 15–36 in (37–91 cm)

Saffron Cod
Eleginus gracilis
N Pacific
L 25 in (63 cm)

Greenland Cod
Gadus ogac
Arctic–N Atlantic
L 28–32 in (71–80 cm)

Pacific Cod
Gadus macrocephalus
N Pacific
L 24–47 in (60–120 cm)

Atlantic Cod
Gadus morhua
Arctic–N Atlantic
L 39–79 in (100–200 cm)

Walleye
Sander vitreus
N Amer (fresh water)
L 21–31 in (54–80 cm)

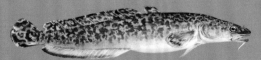

Burbot
Lota lota
Circumpolar (fresh water)
L 12–35 in (30–90 cm)

GENUS *THERAGRA*
Alaska Pollock
Theragra chalcogramma

ALSO: Walleye Pollock, Pazifischer Pollack, Colin d'Alaska, Alaskatheragra, Минтай. SN means "brass-marked good fish for hunting."

RANGE: Pelagic on the continental shelf and slope down to 1500 ft (500 m) from the Bering Sea south to the Sea of Japan and c California.

ID: L 15–36 in (37–91 cm). Olive green to brown back, with mottled brassy blotches on upper sides; silvery to white lower sides and belly.

HABITS: Forms dense schools, some hundreds of yards wide and miles long. Moves to deep waters in winter. Migrates to shallow inshore spawning waters in spring. Each female can produce up to a half million eggs.

USE: Larvae and juveniles are a food source for larger fishes, seabirds, seals, and cetaceans. Pollock supports one of the world's largest-volume fisheries. In Alaskan waters alone, the annual catch of nearly 2 million metric tons has a value of some 2 billion dollars. Used in the fast-food industry for fried fish sandwiches and imitation crabmeat. Salted or smoked pollock roe is popular in Japan and Russia.

FAMILY LOTIDAE
BURBOT AND ALLIES
GENUS *LOTA*
Burbot
Lota lota

ALSO: Mariah, The Lawyer, Loche, Chehluh, Tiktaalik, Nettârnak, Quappe, Lotte de rivière, Lake, Налим. SN derives from *lotte,* the Old French name for this fish. CN stems from the Latin *barba,* meaning "beard," referring to the single barbel. The only freshwater fish in this family.

RANGE: Circumpolar. Occurs in cold lakes and rivers in Europe, Siberia, and N Amer. Some populations range south to 40°N.

ID: L 12–35 in (30–90 cm). WT 2–20 lb (1–9 kg). Long body tapers to a rounded tail. Head is flattened, with a long snout and large mouth. Very long second dorsal fin. Single barbel on the chin; 2 short barbels forward of eyes. Back

and sides dark olive, yellow, or brown with dark mottling; belly whitish. Large fins mottled and dark-edged. Heavy covering of mucus gives the burbot a smooth, slippery feel when handled.

HABITS: Adults live on the bottom of cold-water lakes and rivers to depths of 690 ft (210 m). Voracious predator able to swallow fish nearly its own size; in a recent study, the stomach of one burbot contained 179 individual fish. Feeds at night on other fishes, fish eggs, and crayfish.

Spawns on midwinter nights under the ice in shallow water with sand or gravel bottom. The adults mass together in a squirming ball that moves over the bottom as the fish spew milt and tiny eggs. Eggs hatch after about 30 days. Young live in weedy areas along rocky shores, where they feed on aquatic insects. Lifespan is about 23 years.

USE: Tasty flesh is called "poor man's lobster." In Finland, roe is sold as caviar. The Gwich'in of NWT, Canada, catch burbot by cutting a hole in the ice and jiggling a baited hook near the bottom. They fish at night during a full moon when the burbot are active.

Perciformes: Perch-like Fishes
Perciformes are the largest order of vertebrates. The order contains about 155 families and over 7000 marine and freshwater species and contains about 41 percent of all bony fishes.

FAMILY PERCIDAE
PERCH
GENUS *SANDER*
Walleye
Sander vitreus

ALSO: Yellow Pike, Pickerel, Glasaugenbarsch, Doré jaune, Судак жовтий. CN refers to the fish's eyes, which point outward as if looking at the walls. SN means "glass-eyed [fish]."

RANGE: Occurs in e N Amer, from the NWT and Quebec south through Great Lakes and Mississippi Rvr basins to Alabama and Arkansas. Widely introduced in the US.

ID: L 21–31 in (54–80 cm); record 42 in (107 cm). WT to 20 lb (9 kg); record 25 lb (11.3 kg). Olive and gold in color. Elongated body. Mouth lined with narrow bands of numerous closely set teeth.

Eyes give off a whitish eyeshine in the dark. This is a result of a light-gathering layer in the eyes, the *tapetum lucidum*, which allows walleyes to see well in low light and turbid waters.

HABITS: Demersal in fresh, rarely brackish waters. Prefers large, shallow lakes with high turbidity; also occurs in pools, backwaters, and runs of rivers. Feeds at night on insects, fishes, crayfish, snails, frogs, and small mammals. Matures at 3–5 years. Adults migrate to tributary streams in late winter or early spring to spawn. A large female can lay up to 500,000 eggs, which hatch unguarded in 12–30 days.

FAMILY ANARHICHADIDAE
WOLFFISHES AND WOLF EELS

These fearsome-looking fishes with powerful eel-like bodies are native to cold continental shelf and slope waters of the northern oceans. They are most often seen at depths below 100 ft (30 m), lying with their large, rounded heads protruding from rocky crevices on the sea bottom. Those that live in near-freezing water have evolved with natural anti-freeze in their blood.

Wolffishes and wolf eels derive their common name from their formidable set of wolf-like canines and strong conical teeth, which are used for cracking the exoskeleton of hard-shelled invertebrates such as crabs and marine mollusks as well as sea urchins and starfish. The upper and lower jaws are armed with 2–3 rows of crushing molars and even the throat has serrated teeth guaranteed to dispose of any remnants of a meal.

Despite their fierce facade, wolffishes and wolf eels are known to be non-aggressive fish that form monogamous pairs and exhibit paternal care of young. Their breeding strategy has been studied at marine labs and aquariums.

Most species form pair bonds at 4–7 years of age. The pair seeks out a cave where the two can live for the rest of their life unless they are evicted by an octopus or other large cave-dwelling animal. Eggs are deposited on the sea bottom. When the female is ready to lay, the male coils around her until she releases her eggs (up to 10,000) and he releases sperm. The pair curls their bodies around the pile of large eggs. During the weeks it takes for the eggs to hatch,

the pair continues to guard the eggs and keep them oxygenated by circulating water around them. The parents take turns leaving the nest to feed to ensure the eggs are protected at all times. Once the eggs hatch, the young swim in the currents for 2 years, then begin to live in rocky crevices.

Wolf eels and wolffish species are harvested and marketed as fresh fish or frozen fillets. The skin is sometimes tanned and used as leather for making wallets and purses.

GENERA *ANARRHICHTHYS* AND *ANARHICHAS*
Wolf Eel

Anarrhichthys ocellatus
ALSO: Seewolf, Poisson loup à ocelles, Steinbiter, Угревидная зубатка. SN means "spotted wolffish." CN refers to this fish having the face of a wolf and the body of an eel.
RANGE: Occurs in the N Pacific in the Bering Sea and Sea of Okhotsk, and south to Baja California.
ID: L 80–98 in (200–250 cm). Eel-like body. Brown, olive, or bluish, with darker brown spots.
HABITS: Inhabits rocky reefs and pilings to depths of 740 ft (225 m).
RELATED SPECIES: The BERING WOLFFISH,

Anarhichas orientalis, occurs in the Sea of Okhotsk and Bering Sea. Brown to golden brown, with paler marbling. Occupies shallow inshore waters with rocky, weedy bottoms in summer. Moves offshore beyond the ice pack in winter.

The ATLANTIC WOLFFISH, *Anarhichas lupus*,

occurs from Greenland to Labrador and Cape Cod, and from Svalbard to the White Sea, Scandinavia, Iceland, and UK. Grayish blue to reddish brown, with 10–15 dark bars along the dorsal fin and sides. Inhabits rocky or sandy sea bottoms at depths of 250–400 ft (75–120 m).

The NORTHERN WOLFFISH

or BLUE SEA CAT, *Anarhichas denticulatus*, occurs from Greenland south to Nova Scotia, and from Svalbard and Barents Sea to the Faroes and Iceland. Deep brown, with faint spots on sides. Lives on rocky sea bottoms down to 2950 ft (900 m). Spawns at depths to 5575 ft (1700 m).

The SPOTTED WOLFFISH, *Anarhichas minor*, occurs from Greenland south to Maine, and from Svalbard to the White Sea, Norway, and Iceland. Grayish brown, pale olive, or chocolate- colored, with blackish brown, irregular spots on fins. Lives on muddy or rocky bottoms from shallows to depths of 1970 ft (600 m).

FAMILY ZOARCIDAE
EELPOUTS
GENUS *LYCODES*
Glacial Eelpout
Lycodes frigidus

ALSO: Lycode glaciale, Arktisk ålebrosme. SN means "glacial wolf eel."
RANGE: One of the dominant fishes and most abundant eelpouts in the Arctic Ocean basin.
ID: L 27 in (69 cm). Dark brownish gray or grayish violet, eel-like body. Large head. Anal fin and dorsal fin are connected at the end of the tail.
HABITS: Lives on mud bottoms at depths of 1550–9850 ft (475–3000 m). Moves along the seafloor, stirring up small bottom-dwelling fish, cephalopods, and mollusks.
RELATED SPECIES: POLAR EELPOUT, *Lycodes polaris*, circumpolar. Brown, eel-like body, with 9–11 broad, dark bands on the dorsal and anal fins. Lives on mud bottoms from the shallows down to 985 ft (300 m). Feeds on amphipods, crustaceans, worms, brittle stars, and fishes. Buries itself tail first into muddy bottom sediment. Spawns Nov–Jan.

FAMILY AMMODYTIDAE
SAND LANCES
GENUS *AMMODYTES*
Sand Lance
Ammodytes spp.

ALSO: Stout Sand Lance, Sand-eel, Sandaale, Lançon gourdeau, Tobisfisker. SN means "sand

burrower," referring to the fish's habit of burying itself in sand. CN refers to the lance-shaped body.
RANGE: PACIFIC SAND LANCE (P), *A. hexapterus*, Alaska to the Sea of Japan and s California, and from n Quebec to N Carolina. NORTHERN SAND LANCE (N), *A. dubius*, Greenland to the Atlantic coast of N Amer. LESSER SAND-EEL (L), *A. marinus*, Greenland, Iceland, and n Europe east to Bear Is, Jan Mayen, and Novaya Zemlya.
ID: L 5–15 in (12–37 cm). Silvery, elongated, very slender body. Underslung jaw. Sides of body have 125–130 fine lateral skin folds. Can move each eye independently as chameleons do.
HABITS: Lives on or near the sea bottom to depths of 325 ft (100 m). During the day, forms large schools that feed on zooplankton near the surface. At night and in winter, buries itself nose up in sand or gravel sediments to avoid predators and tidal currents, and to conserve energy. Sexually mature at 2 years. Spawning occurs Sep–Oct. Deposits eggs on coarse sand in the intertidal zone. Lifespan is about 7 years.
USE: Larval sand lances are a major food source for cod and salmon, and adult fish are major prey for puffins and auks. Harvested for fish meal.

FAMILY PHOLIDAE
ARCTIC BLENNIES AND GUNNELS
Blennies and gunnels are major food sources for seabirds, seabird chicks, and other fishes.

GENUS *PHOLIS*
Butterfish
Pholis gunnellus
ALSO: Rock Gunnel, Tansy, Nine-eyes, Crinkly Dick, Atlantischer Butterfisch, Sprettfiskur, Tangsprel, маслюк. CN refers to the mucus-coated skin that makes these fish as slippery as if coated in butter. SN means "spotted gunnel."
RANGE: Occurs off e N Amer and Iceland, and from Svalbard to the European coast.
ID: L 7–10 in (17–25 cm). Eel-like body. Golden brown with dark brown mottling. Row of 9–15 white-ringed, black eyespots under the dorsal fin. Dark bar from top of head to chin.
HABITS: Feeds on crustaceans, polychaete worms, mollusks, and fish eggs. Lives under

Northern Wolffish
Anarhichas denticulatus
Arctic–N Atlantic
L 28–71 in (70–180 cm)

Atlantic Wolffish
Anarhichas lupus
Arctic–N Atlantic
L 24–59 in (60–150 cm)

Spotted Wolffish
Anarhichas minor
Arctic–N Atlantic
L 31–71 in (80–180 cm)

Golden King Crab
Lithodes aequispina

Starfish
Hippasteria sp.

Sea Urchins
Diadema sp.

Bering Wolffish
Anarhichas orientalis
N Pacific
L 18–44 in (45–112 cm)

Wolf Eel
Anarrhichthys ocellatus
N Pacific
L 80–98 in (200–250 cm)

Wolf eels mate for life, and both sexes
guard the eggs until they hatch
some 4 months later.

algae-encrusted rocks and in tide pools; can breathe air when out of water at low tide. Spawns in deeper waters Nov–Jan. Female lays up to 200 eggs, curls her body around the eggs to form a clump, which she secures in rock crevices, empty bivalve shells, and kelp holdfasts. Female guards the eggs for about a month until they hatch.

RELATED SPECIES: BANDED GUNNEL, *Pholis fasciata*, occurs in the N Pacific and N Atlantic.

Reddish orange to greenish yellow, with narrow dark red bands across the belly. White blotches with black spots on back and dorsal fin. Olive and black stripe from head to eyes and cheeks.

FAMILY STICHAEIDAE
SHANNIES
GENUS *STICHAEUS*
Arctic Shanny

Stichaeus punctatus

ALSO: Prickleback, Stichée arctique, Akulliakitsok. SN means "row of dots."

RANGE: Occurs on rocky or sandy bottoms down to 325 ft (100 m) off Greenland, Siberia, Aleutians, and both coasts of N Amer.

ID: L 5–9 in (12–23 cm). Eel-like. Scarlet to brown, with a single row of 5–9 round black spots with pale margins on the long dorsal fin. Irregular dark bars on the cheeks and chin; belly is white. Anal fin dusky, edged with white; pectoral and tail fins crossed by pale bars; ventral fins yellow.

HABITS: Feeds on crustaceans and worms and is a food source for seabirds and their chicks.

Scorpaeniformes: Sculpins and Allies
FAMILY CYCLOPTERIDAE
LUMPFISHES AND LUMPSUCKERS

The pelvic fins of these fishes are modified into a ventral sucking disc that lets them adhere to rocks and bottom substrate.

GENUS *CYCLOPTERUS*
Lumpfish

Cyclopterus lumpus

ALSO: Hen-fish, Lump-sucker, Seehase, Grosse poule de mer, Lompe, Nipisa, Lepisuk, Qorkshuyoq,

Пинагор, Воробеи морской. SN means "round-finned lumpfish." CN refers to the fact that these fish look like a dark, bumpy lump.

RANGE: Occurs from Hudson Bay and Labrador south to New Jersey; off Greenland and Iceland; and from the Barents Sea south to Spain.

ID: L 16–24 in (40–61 cm). WT max 21 lb (9.5 kg). First dorsal fin is covered by thick layer of skin, forming a high ridge with embedded spines. Three rows of large, flattened, bony tubercles on sides of body. The male turns reddish when spawning; the female turns bluish green.

HABITS: Inhabits rocky bottoms down to 500 ft (150 m). Feeds on small crustaceans, jellyfish, polychaete worms, and fishes. Spawns Feb–May. Female deposits a dense yellow mass of eggs on stony bottom, often just below the low tide mark, then abandons the eggs. Male attaches himself to the nest with his ventral sucker and aggressively guards the eggs for up to 8 weeks.

USE: Lumpfish roe is processed and marketed as caviar. The roe comes in a rainbow of natural colors, but most of it that is sold commercially is dyed to be either red or black. Freshly cooked or smoked lumpfish is a popular menu item in the Nordic countries.

GENUS *EUMICROTREMUS*
Atlantic Spiny Lumpsucker

Eumicrotremus spinosus

ALSO: Petite poule de mer atlantique, Nipisarluk, Круглопер колючий. SN means "very large spines."

RANGE: Occurs in ne N Amer, Greenland, and Iceland, and from Franz Josef Land and Svalbard south to the Barents Sea.

ID: L 5.25 in (13 cm). Rounded body. Large head, with a rounded snout, small mouth, and thick lips. Cone-shaped tubercles on body.

HABITS: Lives on stony or mud bottoms at depths of 16–325 ft (5–100 m).

RELATED SPECIES: PACIFIC SPINY LUMPSUCKER, *Eumicrotremus orbis*, ranges in the N Pacific, north to the Chukchi Sea, south to Japan and the Pacific NW. Greenish above; light brown or plum ventrally; lips lavender. Male has orange body tubercles; female's are larger and pale green.

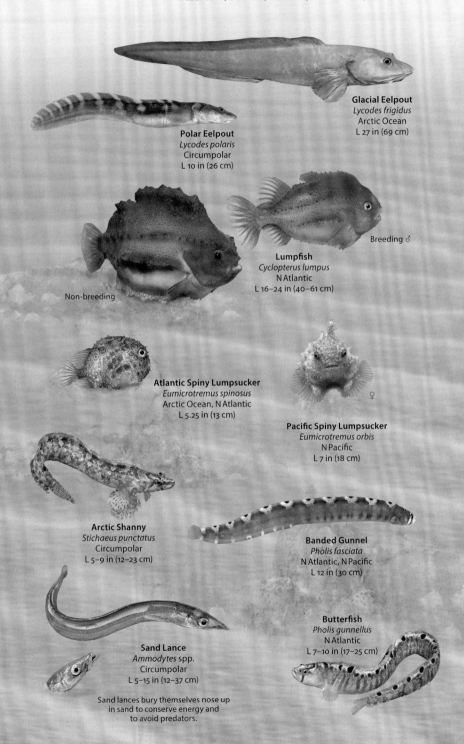

Glacial Eelpout
Lycodes frigidus
Arctic Ocean
L 27 in (69 cm)

Polar Eelpout
Lycodes polaris
Circumpolar
L 10 in (26 cm)

Breeding ♂

Non-breeding

Lumpfish
Cyclopterus lumpus
N Atlantic
L 16–24 in (40–61 cm)

Atlantic Spiny Lumpsucker
Eumicrotremus spinosus
Arctic Ocean, N Atlantic
L 5.25 in (13 cm)

♀

Pacific Spiny Lumpsucker
Eumicrotremus orbis
N Pacific
L 7 in (18 cm)

Arctic Shanny
Stichaeus punctatus
Circumpolar
L 5–9 in (12–23 cm)

Banded Gunnel
Pholis fasciata
N Atlantic, N Pacific
L 12 in (30 cm)

Butterfish
Pholis gunnellus
N Atlantic
L 7–10 in (17–25 cm)

Sand Lance
Ammodytes spp.
Circumpolar
L 5–15 in (12–37 cm)

Sand lances bury themselves nose up
in sand to conserve energy and
to avoid predators.

FAMILY SEBASTIDAE
ROCKFISHES AND REDFISHES

The family name Sebastidae derives from the Greek *sebastos*, meaning "respected because of wisdom or age." This may alude to the late maturation of most *Sebastes* species at 10–14 years of age or to their longevity, which can exceed 50 years. *Sebastes* species are unusual among the bony fishes in that fertilization and embryo development are internal, and female rockfish give birth to live larval young.

In March 2007, a vessel fishing off the Pribilofs caught a SHORTRAKER ROCKFISH (*S. borealis*) that measured more than 44 in (112 cm) long and weighed 59.5 lb (27 kg). Seattle's Alaska Fisheries Science Center examined the fish's ear bone (*otolith*), which contains growth rings similar to those in tree trunks, and estimated the fish's age to be about 90–115 years. Further examination revealed that the belly of the century-old female was full of developing embryos.

Most *Sebastes* species are excellent eating fish and are harvested commercially, sometimes from unsustainable fisheries. As a result, some of the more desirable species are classed as Threatened or Vulnerable (IUCN)

GENUS *SEBASTES*
Pacific Ocean Perch
Sebastes alutus

ALSO: Longjaw Rockfish, Pazifischer Rotbarsch, Sébaste du Pacifique, Тихоокеанский. SN means "venerable fish of the Aleutians."
RANGE: Widespread around the Pacific Rim from Japan to Alaska and s California.
ID: L 13–21 in (33–53 cm). Bright to light red, with dark markings on the back, sides, and tail base. Gill plates have spines. Continuous dorsal fin along the back, with a long spiny part toward the front and a softly rayed part at the back. Anal fin has 3 graduated spines and 7–8 longer rays.
HABITS: Pelagic schooling fish. Found on the outer continental shelf and upper continental slope at depths of 500–1375 ft (150–420 m).
SIMILAR SPECIES: GOLDEN REDFISH, *S. norvegicus*, are found in the N Atlantic from e N Amer to Svalbard at depths of 325–3300 ft (100–1000 m). Adults inhabit offshore waters; juveniles are found in fjords and bays.

DEEPWATER REDFISH, *S. mentella*, are found at depths of 985–3300 ft (300–1000 m) in the N Atlantic from e N Amer to Iceland and Svalbard. Red overall. Demersal and often pelagic. Maximum lifespan is 75 years.

Shortraker Rockfish
Sebastes borealis
Bering Sea
L 20–40 in (50–100 cm)

Gorgonia Sea Fan
Plumarella sp.

Golden Redfish
Sebastes norvegicus
Arctic–N Atlantic
L 18–39 in (45–100 cm)

Pacific Ocean Perch
Sebastes alutus
N Pacific
L 13–21 in (33–53 cm)

Deepwater Redfish
Sebastes mentella
Arctic–N Atlantic
L 12–28 in (30–70 cm)

ONLY ONE SPECIES OF LIZARD AND THREE SPECIES OF FROGS are known to occur in the arctic zone. These cold-blooded creatures must bask in the sun to warm to an optimal body temperature. They have adapted to the severe arctic climate by entering a state of winter dormancy—a period when growth, development, and physical activity are temporarily stopped in order to minimize metabolic activity and conserve energy.

Squamata: Scaled Reptiles

The order Squamata is the largest extant order of reptiles and the second largest order of vertebrates, after the perciform fishes. It contains all lizards and snakes, which are distinguished by skins that bear horny scales or shields.

FAMILY LACERTIDAE
TRUE LIZARDS
GENUS *ZOOTOCA*
Viviparous Lizard
Zootoca vivipara

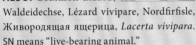

ALSO: Common Lizard, Waldeidechse, Lézard vivipare, Nordfirfisle, Живородящая ящерица, *Lacerta vivipara*. SN means "live-bearing animal."

RANGE: Eurasia, from the UK and n Europe to Japan, in a variety of habitats, including tundra and mountains. Northernmost reptile.

ID: L 5–6 in (13–15 cm). Variable in color. Brown, grayish green, or rufous, with dark lines on the back, often bordered with white or yellow; entirely black forms occur. Male has a conspicuous swelling at the tail base.

HABITS: Breeds Apr–May. Males hold females in their jaws before mating. If the female is unreceptive, she bites the male. Embryos develop for about 3 months inside the female (viviparous); some southern populations lay eggs (oviparous). In Jul, 3–10 young are born and disperse independently. In late fall, viviparous lizards enter a state of dormancy known as *brumation*. Groups crowd together in log piles or in burrows where they are shielded from the cold and predators. The body temperature drops, and they become immobile. The lizards can go for months without food but sometimes wake up to drink water before falling back to "sleep."

Anura: Frogs

The order Anura contains a diverse and largely carnivorous group of short-bodied, tailless amphibians that typically lay their eggs in water. The eggs hatch into aquatic larvae called tadpoles and metamorphose into semi-aquatic adults in a few weeks.

Frogs of the Far North have adapted to the arctic climate in a remarkable way—they freeze solid in winter and thaw out in spring. As winter approaches, each frog makes a shallow depression in leaf litter and places dead vegetation over the hollow for insulation. As soon as the frog's skin

Boreal Chorus Frog
Pseudacris maculata
N Amer
L 0.75–1.5 in (2–4 cm)

Wood Frog
Rana sylvatica
N Amer
L 2–2.75 in (5–7 cm)

♂ Breeding

Moor Frog
Rana arvalis
♀
Eurasia
L 2–2.75 in (5–7 cm)

Viviparous Lizard
Zootoca vivipara
Eurasia
L 5–6 in (13–15 cm)

touches an ice crystal, solid ice envelops the body cavity, bladder, and subcutaneous tissues. The frog stops breathing, its heart stops beating, its blood stops flowing, and it cannot move. Only the vital organs remain unfrozen, this due to high concentrations of glucose and urea that accumulate in its tissues in summer. Both act as cryoprotectants, which limit ice formation and reduce osmotic shrinkage of cells. When the soil warms in spring the frog's frozen parts thaw, its heart and lungs resume activity, and in a few hours, the frog can jump and mate.

FAMILY RANIDAE
TRUE FROGS
GENUS *RANA*
Wood Frog
Rana sylvatica

ALSO: Grenouille des bois, Waldfrosch, Amerikanske skogfrosk, Лесная лягушка, *Lithobates sylvaticus*. SN means "forest frog."

RANGE: N Amer, from Alaska to Labrador and south to the c US, in moist woodlands. Northernmost amphibian.

ID: L 2–2.75 in (5–7 cm). Females are larger than males. Brown, tan, or rufous, with a dark eye mask and prominent ridges along each side. VOICE: Breeding males emit a raspy *caw-aw-awk*, a sound often likened to the quack of a duck. As in other frogs, the sound is made by air passing over the vocal cords, with the male's distensible vocal sac acting as a resonating chamber.

HABITS: Lives in moist woodlands. Frequents roads on rainy summer nights. Breeds in large numbers in woodland pools for a few days beginning in Mar. Female deposits large globular egg masses on aquatic vegetation. Tadpoles metamorphose in about 8 weeks. Hibernates in moist soil under leaf litter, rocks, and logs.

Moor Frog
Rana arvalis

ALSO: Moorfrosch, Grenouille des champs, Spiss-nutefrosk, Остромордая лягушка. SN means "field frog."

RANGE: Eurasia, from Europe to Xinjiang

province, China, in damp meadows and bogs. **ID:** L 2–2.75 in (5–7 cm). Males are much smaller than females. Reddish brown, gray, or olive, with an unspotted whitish belly. A bandit-like dark stripe runs from nose to ears. A pale stripe often runs down the center of the back. Males develop bright blue coloration for a few days during the breeding season, possibly as a means of distinguishing themselves from their prospective mates, the brown females, during the frenzied mating bouts.

HABITS: Hibernates Sep–Jun in the Far North. Breeding takes place right after the frogs come out of hibernation. Females deposit 1–2 clusters of eggs, each containing up to 3000 eggs. VOICE: Hundreds of males can gather in a single large pond, forming breeding choruses that incessantly sing *waug...waug...waug*, a sound likened to the noise produced when you hold a bottle underwater and let the air escape.

FAMILY HYLIDAE
TREE AND CHORUS FROGS
GENUS *PSEUDACRIS*
Boreal Chorus Frog
Pseudacris maculata

ALSO: Rainette faux-grillon boréale, Квакши. SN means "spotted false locust," refer-ring to the frog's insect-like call.

RANGE: N Amer, from Great Bear Lake south to Arizona and Illinois (US), in marshes, ponds, small lakes in forests and pastures.

ID: L 0.75–1.5 in (2–4 cm). Green, brown, gray, or reddish, with 3–5 dark dorsal stripes and/or spots. Dark band runs from the snout, across the eye, and down the side. VOICE: Courting males make rasping *reeeek* calls, a sound likened to running a fingernail along the teeth of a pocket comb.

HABITS: Feeds on ants, spiders, flies, beetles, aphids, and other insects. Hibernates near breeding sites under logs, rocks, leaf litter, loose soil, or in burrows. Breeds Apr–Jul in the Far North. Males congregate around breeding ponds as soon as most of the snow has melted. Female deposits small clusters of 20–100 eggs on submerged vegetation. Eggs hatch in 10–14 days. Tadpoles metamorphose in about 2 months.

FLIES, BEES, AND BUTTERFLIES

INSECTS BELONG TO THE LARGE PHYLUM ARTHROPODA, which includes all jointed-legged invertebrates. With an estimated six to ten million living species, insects represent more than half of all known living organisms. They are the most numerous arctic animals, with some 2200 species occurring in the North American Arctic alone. These include insects as diverse as aphids, flies, bumblebees, beetles, and butterflies. Vital contributors to the arctic ecosystem, insects are in great part responsible for plant pollination, the breakdown of plant and animal remains, and aeration of the soil, and also are an important food source for many arctic birds and fishes.

What is most impressive about arctic insects is their capacity to remain alive in a very hostile environment. They survive despite strong winds that make flight nearly impossible, a short summer that gives little time for eggs to develop, and a long period of subzero temperatures in which earth and water are frozen solid.

Their ability to endure the arctic climate seems especially amazing when one realizes that insects are cold-blooded and cannot generate heat. (One of the few exceptions is the arctic bumblebee, which warms itself by "shivering" its flight muscles.) Thus, arctic insects seek out sites where the temperature is several degrees above the ambient. Insects of the tundra live mostly near the soil surface, where the air is warmer and the winds weaker. In summer, they bask on low plants with their wings or darkly haired bodies oriented so as to absorb maximum solar radiation. In winter, the eggs and larvae of most species lie hidden beneath an insulating blanket of snow.

Overwintering larvae exhibit extreme cold hardiness, and some survive temperatures as low as −58°F (−50°C). Many accomplish this feat by manufacturing cryoprotectants that prevent the freezing of tissues or prevent damage to cells during freezing. Biochemicals such as glycerol act as internal antifreeze and inhibit ice formation in the body tissues, allowing larvae to freeze solid and thaw without tissue damage.

In winter, many arctic insects also enter a state of suppressed development called *diapause*, which enhances cold resistance, conserves energy, and prevents premature emergence. Diapause allows the insect's life cycle to be in synchrony with the seasonal availability or lack of food, and ensures that growth and reproduction take place within the narrow window of summer.

The word "insect" derives from the Latin *insectum*, meaning "cut into sections," referring to the three body segments: head, thorax, and abdomen. All insects also have a chitinous exoskeleton, compound eyes, 6 jointed legs, and 2 antennae.

Insects undergo a physical transformation from one stage of their life cycle to another in a biological process called *metamorphosis*. Most species experience a complete metamorphosis in which each phase of the life cycle—egg, larva, pupa, and adult—is completely different from the others (*see p. 404*).

Diptera: Mosquitoes, Flies, and Allies

Dipterids, meaning "two-winged insects," are distinguished by having a single pair of functional wings. The vestigial hind wings, or *halteres*, consist of two knobbed filaments that are thought to stabilize the body during flight.

FAMILY CULICIDAE
MOSQUITOES

Mosquitoes (Spanish for "little fly") are small dipterids. Although viewed as blood-thirsty aerial predators by some, mosquitoes are an important food source for nesting shorebirds and fishes, and also serve as plant pollinators.

Mosquito larvae, or *wrigglers*, live near the water surface, where they feed on algae and microbes and take in air through external respiratory openings located on their abdomen. The larval stage is a short one. In only a few days the wrigglers become pupae, which hang motionless at the water surface until the adults emerge and enter the reproductive stage of the mosquitoes' life cycle.

Adult mosquito
L 0.25 in (0.6 cm)

Wriggler

Male mosquitoes usually live for only a few days. They spend most of their short life mating and sucking plant nectar, which provides enough energy to sustain flight. The females meanwhile have a more important task—taking protein-rich blood meals so they can produce eggs. They use their long, sharp proboscis to pierce the skin and suck the blood of mammals, birds, reptiles, amphibians, and even some species of fish. In the High Arctic, where blood hosts can be scarce, the females of some *Aedes* species have developed the ability to produce a small batch of eggs autogenously—that is, without partaking of a protein meal but instead using food reserves accumulated as a larva.

Once they mate, the females begin to lay their eggs. They dip their ovipositor into the banks of quiet ponds and once they have laid all of their eggs, most die. The eggs remain in the wet soil throughout autumn and later lie dormant under the winter snow. When the snowmelt raises the pond's water level the next spring, the eggs are submerged and hatch. Increasing sunlight warms the water, turning the pool into a nutrient-rich incubator for the wrigglers and pupae that signal the start of a new cycle of life.

Snow mosquitoes (*Aedes communis, Culiseta alaskaensis*) are exceptional in that the females can live for almost a year. The females of these species mate and engorge shortly after they hatch in summer, but do not deposit their eggs until the following spring. They overwinter under the snow and become active again in early spring when they lay their eggs in pools of melting snow. Females often live on into early summer when the new generation emerges.

FAMILY CHIRONOMIDAE
NON-BITING MIDGES

The most abundant arctic insects are non-biting midges, or *chironomids*. Chironomids are important food sources for migratory shorebirds and freshwater fish, especially arctic char (*Salvelinus alpinus*), which feed extensively on chironomids and would starve in spring were it not for midge larvae. The worm-like larvae may be gray or red in color; the latter are called bloodworms. They live in almost any aquatic habitat, where they feed on fine particulate matter and algae. Adult midges differ from mosquitoes in that they lack scales on the wing veins and rest with their front legs elevated (mosquitoes rest with their hind legs elevated). They lack the long proboscis of mosquitoes and do not bite. Adult midges emerge from pupae in spring and feed on flower nectar and pollen. The adults form dense mating swarms over the wetlands for a short time in spring and early summer, then die off.

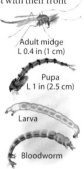

Adult midge
L 0.4 in (1 cm)

Pupa
L 1 in (2.5 cm)

Larva

Bloodworm

FAMILY OESTRIDAE
WARBLE AND BOT FLIES

Two circumpolar species—the Caribou Warble Fly (*Hypoderma tarandi*) and Nose Bot Fly (*Cephenemyia trompe*)—are parasites of caribou and reindeer. Their larvae live within the bodies of these mammals and feed on the host's flesh throughout the winter. The adult flies, which lack functional mouth parts, rely on food reserves accumulated and stored as larvae to sustain them through the summer breeding season.

WARBLE FLIES lay their eggs on the belly or leg hairs of caribou. The larvae that hatch from these eggs bore into the caribou's hide and migrate under the skin to the area along the spine. Each maggot carves a hole in the host's hide through which it extrudes its breathing apparatus. The

Adult warble fly

Warble fly larva

larvae live under the skin during the winter, feeding on the host's flesh. As many as 2000 larvae can live along the spine of a caribou, a condition that can weaken the animal and leave it susceptible to bacterial infections. In spring, the maggots emerge from the animal's hide, fall to the ground, pupate, and later emerge as adult flies.

NOSE BOT FLIES forcefully spray a single large drop of clear uterine fluid containing

Adult bot fly

first-stage larvae onto a caribou's nose. The larvae then crawl into the animal's mouth or nostrils and migrate to the nasal sinuses and throat where they overwinter. In heavy infections, there may be as many as 300 larvae occupying the nasal cavities. In an effort to rid themselves of the bot fly larvae, the caribou snort and sneeze, thus expelling the larvae from the nasal passage. The larvae fall to the ground, where they pupate and later emerge as adult flies.

FAMILY TIPULIDAE
CRANE FLIES

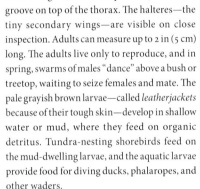

The large, grayish brown to golden crane flies live on muddy or mossy streambanks and lakeshores. They have long slender legs and a V-shaped groove on top of the thorax. The halteres—the tiny secondary wings—are visible on close inspection. Adults can measure up to 2 in (5 cm) long. The adults live only to reproduce, and in spring, swarms of males "dance" above a bush or treetop, waiting to seize females and mate. The pale grayish brown larvae—called *leatherjackets* because of their tough skin—develop in shallow water or mud, where they feed on organic detritus. Tundra-nesting shorebirds feed on the mud-dwelling larvae, and the aquatic larvae provide food for diving ducks, phalaropes, and other waders.

FAMILY SYRPHIDAE
HOVER FLIES

These important plant pollinators feed on nectar and pollen and are usually seen hovering over flowers, hence the common name. Hover flies have a characteristic fold on the wings, which is called the false vein (*vena spuria*). Hover fly larvae are slug-like. Some are scavengers or feed on decaying vegetation, but the larvae of most species are carnivorous and feed on aphids, those familiar garden pests that penetrate even onto the High Arctic barrens. Adults measure up to 0.75 in (2 cm) long, and their large eyes appear to cover the entire head. The

Bee-like hover fly
Arctophila superbiens

Wasp-like hover fly
Eupeodes americanus

body is typically patterned in black and yellow. Adults mimic the color and morphology of wasps and bees so well that one must draw close and check whether only 2 large wings are visible rather than the 4 of bees and wasps.

Hymenoptera: Bees and Allies

The large order Hymenoptera (Greek for "membrane-winged") includes 4-winged insects such as bees, parasitic wasps, ants, and sawflies. The hind wings are connected to the forewings by a series of hooked bristles called *hamuli*. Females typically have a special ovipositor that is modified for stinging or for inserting eggs into other insect hosts.

FAMILY APIDAE
ARCTIC BUMBLEBEES

Bumblebees are distinguished by their soft, fuzzy body hair, which typically is arranged in horizontal, black and yellow bands around the body. The hind legs of the adult females have a shiny concave surface that is surrounded by a fringe of hairs. These are the pollen baskets, or *corbiculae*, which are used to transport pollen. Females also have a barbless stinger that can be used more than once. Male bumblebees lack both the pollen baskets and the stinger.

Like their honeybee relatives, these social insects forage actively at flowers, feeding on protein-laden pollen and sugary nectar. Nectar is especially important as it provides energy for flight and for generating internal body heat. Bumblebees require a body temperature of 95°F (35°C) for sustained flight. They produce the needed heat by rapidly contracting, or *shivering*,

Bombus polaris

Bombus hyperboreus

the flight muscles in the thorax. By generating their own body heat, bumblebees can remain active in cool temperatures and later warm the eggs and larvae as they develop in the nest.

About 20 species of bumblebees have been recorded in the Arctic; *Bombus polaris* and *Bombus hyperboreus* are the best known. Both are widespread across the Holarctic. The species are difficult to tell apart unless seen together, when the smaller size, paler color, and narrower black tail band of *Bombus polaris* is apparent.

The life cycles of both species are similar in that the cycle lasts a single year and only the queens (fertile females) survive the winter. *Bombus polaris* queens mate in late summer and then hibernate in the frozen ground. Upon emerging from winter sleep, each queen collects pollen and nectar from flowers and searches for a suitable nest site, typically in an abandoned mammal burrow. Once the queen finds a site, she secretes a waxy substance that she makes into wax pots for storing nectar and pollen and wax cells in which to lay her eggs. The eggs of the first batch hatch into worker bees (sterile females), which assist the queen in tending and feeding a second batch of eggs. These develop into new queens and drones (fertile males) that mate in summer and produce the next generation.

In contrast, *Bombus hyperboreus* queens are "cuckoo bumblebees," so called because they make no nest of their own but instead take over the colonies of other bee species. *Bombus hyperboreus* queens emerge from the frozen ground each spring slightly later than the smaller *Bombus polaris*. The *hyperboreus* queen seeks out an established nest of *polaris*, invades it, attacks and kills the queen, then takes over the colony. She forces her victim's worker bees to tend her eggs, which ultimately hatch into fertile queens and drones. Thus, the *Bombus hyperboreus* queen avoids having to produce her own workers, but instead generates sexual forms that perpetuate her species. And so, the captured workers of the *Bombus polaris* queen spend their lives caring for the young of an entirely different species.

Lepidoptera: Butterflies, Skippers, and Moths

Lepidoptera, a word coined by Linnaeus in 1735, is Greek for "scale wing." The word refers to the flat, pigmented, powdery wing scales that distinguish the butterflies and moths from all other insects and give the adults their amazing range of wing colors and patterns.

Regarding the scientific names of butterflies, the reader may note that species described in the time of Linnaeus often bear fanciful names related to mythological figures of ancient Greece.

Like other insects, butterflies and moths develop in a biological process called *metamorphosis*. This involves an abrupt change in the insect's structure through cell growth and differentiation, which proceeds in distinct stages from egg to larva, pupa, and adult.

Butterfly and moth larvae, commonly called caterpillars, are distinguished by their cylindrical body, well-developed head, and eight pairs of fleshy abdominal limbs called *prolegs*. They have a pair of short antennae and a pair of simple, or more rarely compound eyes. Mouth parts include two segmented, sensory structures called *palpi*, and a pair of strong jaws. The lower lip, or *labium*, often has a *spinneret* adapted for spinning silk filaments. Most larvae are brightly colored and some are covered in bumps or knobs. To deter predators, Canadian swallowtail larvae inflate their heads so they look like snakes. Other larvae have stinging spines or hairs, and many species feed on plants containing alkaloids. They store

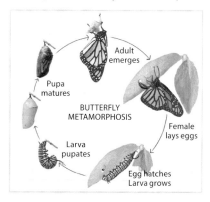

BUTTERFLY METAMORPHOSIS

Adult emerges

Pupa matures

Female lays eggs

Larva pupates

Egg hatches Larva grows

the toxins in their systems and pass them on to the adult stage. Adults of these species are distasteful and often advertise their toxicity with boldly colored markings. This is such an effective protection that some non-toxic species have transformed into mimics of noxious species.

After a caterpillar grows and molts its skin several times, it enters the pupal stage during which the larva transforms into an adult. Before its final molt, the butterfly larva spins a button of silk by which it attaches itself to a firm support such as a branch. As its skin molts and drops away, a tough, flexible casing forms around the naked pupa, or chrysalis. Moths have slightly different strategies. Most species of moths pupate in dead leaves or debris, or burrow into the ground and winter inside a hard casing they form around themselves.

Hormones trigger the pupa to excrete digestive juices that break down its own organs and tissues. A few cells are left intact and, in one of nature's little miracles, the remaining tissue cells and nutrients reorganize and grow into an adult butterfly or moth.

The adult emerges with limp, damp wings and rests immobile until its body fluids pulse into the wing veins, which expand and harden to provide a rigid support for the delicate wing membrane. The flight of most arctic butterflies occurs during a 2- to 6-week period during the summer months. Aided by volatile pheromones released by the female to attract a male, the sexes find each other, mate, and produce eggs.

The three primary body regions of butterflies and moths are the head, thorax, and abdomen. The head has a pair of large, rounded eyes and a pair of segmented antennae. The antennae of butterflies are usually thread-like and have a knobby antennal club at their tips; those of moths are feathery or branched. Butterflies and many moths have a coiled proboscis that unrolls into a long sucking tube used for feeding on nectar and other fluids. Adult lepidopterans have a pair of five-jointed legs on each of the three thorax segments and two pairs of membranous wings attached to the second and third thorax segments. Male and female sex organs are at the tip of the abdomen.

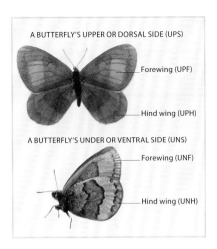

A BUTTERFLY'S UPPER OR DORSAL SIDE (UPS)

Forewing (UPF)

Hind wing (UPH)

A BUTTERFLY'S UNDER OR VENTRAL SIDE (UNS)

Forewing (UNF)

Hind wing (UNH)

FAMILY PAPILIONIDAE
SWALLOWTAIL BUTTERFLIES

Swallowtails differ from other butterflies in that the larvae have an *osmeterium*, a foul-smelling forked organ that can be extended out from the thorax to repel predators. The arctic swallowtails are large, brightly colored, and most have conspicuous swallow-like "tails" on the hind wing. These butterflies commonly indulge in "mud-puddling," i.e., siphoning mineral-rich moisture from mud.

GENUS *PAPILIO*
Old World Swallowtail
Papilio machaon

ALSO: Common Yellow Swallowtail, Schwalbenschwanz, Machaon, Grand Portequeue, Svalestjert, Махаон. SN means "Machaon's butterfly"; Linnaeus named this species after the physician Machaon, who clad himself in golden armor and led an army in the Trojan War on the side of the Greeks. *Papilio* (Latin for "butterfly") was originally the genus name for every known species of butterfly.
RANGE: Near circumpolar. Widespread throughout the Holarctic on open hilltops and alpine meadows to 9850 ft (3000 m).
ID: WS 2.5–3.5 in (7–9 cm). AD: Jun–Jul. Yellow, with 4 black tiger stripes on UPF. Wings edged with a long, narrow, diagonal black band bearing yellow, blue, and orange spots. Powerful gliding

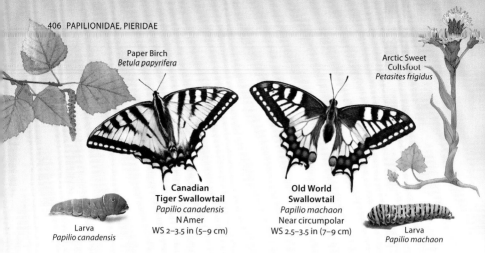

Paper Birch
Betula papyrifera

Arctic Sweet
Coltsfoot
Petasites frigidus

**Canadian
Tiger Swallowtail**
Papilio canadensis
N Amer
WS 2–3.5 in (5–9 cm)

**Old World
Swallowtail**
Papilio machaon
Near circumpolar
WS 2.5–3.5 in (7–9 cm)

Larva
Papilio canadensis

Larva
Papilio machaon

flight. Adults hover as they take nectar, mainly from pink or mauve flowers. Females mate on the morning of their emergence and the pair remains coupled for several hours. The females then fly low over vegetation searching for suitable plants on which to lay their eggs. LARVA: New larvae resemble bird droppings. Mature caterpillars are green, with black rings that are dotted with orange, yellow, or red. Host plants include wormwood (*Artemisia*), coltsfoot (*Petasites*), and umbellifers such as parsley (*Petroselinum*).

Canadian Tiger Swallowtail

Papilio canadensis
ALSO: Kanadischer Tiger-schwalbenschwanz, Papillon tigré du Canada. SN means "butterfly of Canada."

RANGE: Occurs in forests of Alaska and mainland Canada, north to the Arctic Circle in the Yukon, and south to the n US.
ID: WS 2–3.5 in (5–9 cm). AD: Jun–Jul. Yellow wings, with 4 wide black tiger stripes on UPF. UPH edged with a long, narrow, diagonal black band bearing rectangular to rounded yellow, blue, and orange spots. A rare black female form can occur. LARVA: New larvae resemble bird droppings. Caterpillars are green, with 2 yellow and black eyespots and a yellow and black stripe on the mid-thoracic segment. Birch trees (*Betula* spp.) are the larval host plants. Larvae fold the leaves, tie and line them with silk, and then feed within the webbed structure.

GENUS *PARNASSIUS*: *Parnassius* refers to Parnassus, the snow-capped mountain in Greece that was the home of the god Apollo—hence, the common collective name "snow apollos." These primitive swallowtails lack the "tail" on the hind wing. They are adapted to cold, windy, alpine climates. The dark body hairs help them to retain heat.

Adults rest on rocks with their wings spread flat to absorb the sun's heat and fly close to the ground to avoid the wind. The adult male has a special gland that produces a plug that seals the female oviduct after mating and prevents insemination by another male. Larvae feed mainly on poppies, sedums, and fumeworts and pupate inside a loose silken chrysalis.

Eversmann's Parnassius

Parnassius eversmanni
ALSO: Аполлон Эверсмана. SN means "Eversmann's snow apollo," honoring German

biologist and explorer Eduard Friedrich von Eversmann (1794–1860).
RANGE: Occurs in e Asia and nw NAmer in wet, open larch forests, along willow-lined streams, and on alpine scree to about 5000 ft (1500 m).
ID: WS 2.25 in (6 cm). AD: Yellowish wings. Black bar connects the tiny red central spot on UPH to inner wing margin. Flies low and fast over open ground and rocky slopes. LARVA: Mature larvae are covered with black hairs and have a row of yellow dots along the sides. Larval host plants are mainly fumeworts (*Corydalis* spp.).

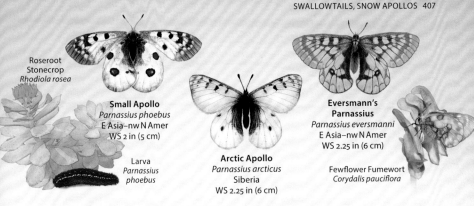

Roseroot
Stonecrop
Rhodiola rosea

Small Apollo
Parnassius phoebus
E Asia–nw N Amer
WS 2 in (5 cm)

Larva
*Parnassius
phoebus*

Arctic Apollo
Parnassius arcticus
Siberia
WS 2.25 in (6 cm)

**Eversmann's
Parnassius**
Parnassius eversmanni
E Asia–nw N Amer
WS 2.25 in (6 cm)

Fewflower Fumewort
Corydalis pauciflora

Arctic Apollo

Parnassius arcticus

ALSO: Аполлон аркти-
ческий, *P. ammosovi*. SN
means "arctic snow apollo."
RANGE: Occurs in Yakutia, Siberia, in mountains
to 5000 ft (1500 m). Northernmost swallowtail.
ID: WS 2.25 in (6 cm). AD: Jun–Jul. Grayish white
wings (darker in the female), with broken black
bands on UPF leading edge and blackish spots
on UPH. Black antennae. LARVA: Host plant is
typically a fumewort (*Corydalis*).

Small Apollo

Parnassius phoebus

ALSO: Hochalpen-Apollo,
Petit apollon, Apollosom-
merfugl, Фэбус. SN means
"radiant snow apollo." *Phoebus* is an epithet of
Apollo, a god of light and sun. Species was named
by Danish zoologist Johan Christian Fabricius
(1745–1808), a student of Carolus Linnaeus and
a distinguished entomologist who named more
than 9500 insect species and established the
basis for modern insect classification.
RANGE: Occurs in e Asia and nw N Amer on
moist alpine tundra and taiga to 6000 ft (1800 m).
ID: WS 2 in (5 cm). AD: Jun–Jul. Chalky white
above, with red and black spots. Males have a
solid band of pale gray on the outer margin of
UPF. Densely haired on body, head, and legs.
Banded antennae. Flies with powerful strokes
on large wings; sometimes seems to crash into
flowers to feed. LARVA: Black with yellow dots on
sides. Feeds mainly on sedums such as Roseroot
Stonecrop (*Rhodiola rosea*).

FAMILY PIERIDAE
WHITES, YELLOWS, AND SULPHURS

Pieridae contains about 1200 species of white,
yellow, green, or orange butterflies. Adults
have 6 fully developed, functional legs, with
strongly forked foot claws. Adults regularly visit
flowering plants for nectar. Tall, vase-shaped eggs
are laid singly on host plants such as legumes,
willows, and heaths. Larvae are
cylindrical and covered with
very short hairs. Larvae pupate
in an upright chrysalis, which
is attached to vegetation by a
hook-shaped protuberance—the
cremaster—at the bottom and a
silken girdle around the middle.

Pieridae
chrysalis

GENUS *PIERIS*: *Pieris* alludes to the Pierides, the
9 daughters of Pierus, who were defeated in a
singing contest by the Muses and turned into
magpies for their effrontery. Known collectively
as "whites," butterflies in this genus have white
wings with a few black markings. Newly emerged
adults have pale yellow, ventral hind wings.
Females lay white eggs on the leaves or flowers
of plants in the mustard family, Brassicaceae,
which also serve as host plants for the sparsely
haired larvae.

Cabbage White

Pieris rapae

ALSO: Kleiner Kohlweißling,
Petit blanc du chou, Liten
kålsommerfugl, Репница.
SN means "field mustard white," referring to
one of the larval host plants, *Brassica rapae*.

RANGE: Near circumpolar. Introduced in the 1860s from its native Europe into Quebec, Canada; now common across N Amer, north to the boreal treeline.
ID: WS 1–2 in (2.5–5 cm). AD: White wings, with black wing tips, 1 black UPF spot (2 in the female), and a black patch on UPH leading edge. UNH pale mustard yellow. LARVA: Bluish green, with yellow stripes on sides.

Arctic White
Pieris angelika

ALSO: SN means "Angelika's white," honoring Angelika Eitschberger, wife of German entomologist Ulf Eitschberger.
RANGE: Occurs in Alaska, Yukon, nw NWT, and nw Brit Columbia, in moist woodlands and adjacent open areas, and on alpine tundra above the treeline.
ID: WS 1.25–1.75 in (3–4.5 cm). AD♂: White above, with a thin black line on leading edge of UPF and with black shading on the veins. UNH and apex of UNF are pale yellow, with blackish green veins. AD♀: White or pale yellow overall.

GENUS *COLIAS*: Sulphurs are also known as clouded yellows because of the dark scaling on their yellow, orange, white, or green wings. The underwings are normally tinged with lime green, edged with a fine line of pink scales, and decorated with a small silver spot outlined with pink on the hind wing. Females have pale areas in the wing margin. Except for Labrador sulphurs, males show a solid black border. The antennae are often tinged with pink, and the eyes are leaf green.

Sulphurs rest with their wings closed over their backs, then orient their wings at a right angle to the sun to capture maximum warmth. Most species are avid mud-puddlers that collect around silty pools and probe the dirt with their tongues as they syphon up nutrients. Larval host plants include legumes (Fabaceae), heaths (Ericaceae), and willows (Salicaceae).

The genus name *Colias* alludes to the temple of the goddess Aphrodite at Cape Kolias in Attica (now Athens), Greece.

Hecla Sulphur
Colias hecla

ALSO: Northern Clouded Yellow, Greenland Sulphur, Ambré, Heklagulvinge, Желтушка Гекла. SN means "hecla sulphur"; *Hecla* is Old Icelandic for a fell or hill, a probable reference to the fell habitat in Greenland where the type specimen was found.
RANGE: Near circumpolar. Occurs on tundra meadows to 3000 ft (900 m) from n Scandinavia to the Kola and Yamal peninsulas, and across arctic N Amer and Greenland, north to 81°N.
ID: WS 1.25–1.75 in (3–4.5 cm). AD: Jun–Aug. Male dull orange above, with dark borders and dusky scaling near body. Female dull orange to yellowish above, with golden spots in the dark wing borders. Greenish yellow below, fringed with pink; pink-rimmed silver spot on UNH extends as a red streak toward the outer wing margin. Flies low and fast. LARVA: Green, with pale lateral stripes and tiny black points. *Astragalus alpinus* is a common host plant.
SIMILAR SPECIES: *Colias hyperborea* (*not illus.*), which ranges in ne Siberia (pale gray on map), is nearly identical in color and pattern to *C. hecla*.

Labrador Sulphur
Colias nastes

ALSO: Arctic Green Sulphur, Coliade verdâtre, Желтушка северная. SN is Greek for "resident sulphur." CN refers to the type locality.
RANGE: Near circumpolar. Occurs in n Scandinavia; from the Altai Mtns east to Chukotka; and in Alaska, n Canada, and Greenland. Found in tundra meadows on dry alpine ridges to 8800 ft (2700 m), and occasionally in open spruce-tamarack forests.
ID: WS 1–1.5 in (2.5–4 cm). AD: May–Aug. Dark grayish green above due to a heavy dusting of dark scales. Unlike other *Colias*, both sexes show pale markings in the dark wing margins. UNS has a silvery cell spot with a blurred red margin. The drab color and rapid, low flight across windswept, stony hilltops make these sulphurs difficult to follow. They are easiest to observe when taking nectar at flowers. LARVA:

Dwarf Fireweed
*Chamerion
latifolium*

♂
*Pieris
angelika*

♂
*Pieris
rapae*

Alpine Milk Vetch
Astragalus alpinus

♀

Arctic White
Pieris angelika
N Amer
WS 1.25–1.75 in (3–4.5 cm)

♂

Cabbage White
Pieris rapae
Near circumpolar
WS 1–2 in (2.5–5 cm)

♀

Hecla Sulphur
Colias hecla
Near circumpolar
WS 1.25–1.75 in (3–4.5 cm)

Field Locoweed
*Oxytropis
campestris*

White form ♀
Colias philodice

♂

♀

Red Clover
*Trifolium
pratense*

Labrador Sulphur
Colias nastes
Near circumpolar
WS 1–1.5 in (2.5–4 cm)

Giant Sulphur larva
on Woolly Willow
Salix lanata

Pale form ♂
Colias gigantea

♂

Clouded Sulphur
Colias philodice
N Amer
WS 1.25–2 in (3–5 cm)

Labrador
Lousewort
*Pedicularis
labradorica*

Giant Sulphur
Colias gigantea
N Amer
WS 2–2.75 in (5–7 cm)

♂

Palaeno Sulphur
Colias palaeno
Near circumpolar
WS 1.25–2 in (3–5 cm)

Narrowleaf
Arnica
Arnica angustifolia

Dark green, with 2 pink-edged stripes down each side. Host plants include locoweed (*Oxytropis*), milkvetch (*Astragalus*), sweet vetch (*Hedysarum*), and tufted saxifrage (*Saxifraga caespitosa*).

Clouded Sulphur
Colias philodice

ALSO: Coliade du trèfle. SN may refer to Philodice, daughter of the river-god Inachus and sister to Greek priestess Io, or may derive from the Greek words *philos* and *dice*, meaning "friend of the seasons."
RANGE: Occurs in fields and meadows from Alaska to NWT, Canada, north to the Arctic Ocean in the Yukon and south to the n US.
ID: WS 1.25–2 in (3–5 cm). AD: Male is clear yellow above, with solid dark edging and with a dark yellow spot in the central UPH. Female has 2 forms: yellow or greenish white, both with uneven black edging around yellow spots. UNS of both sexes has dark marginal spots and 2 silver spots edged in red. LARVA: Green with a dark stripe down the back and light stripes on the sides. Feeds mainly on clover and alfalfa.

Giant Sulphur
Colias gigantea

ALSO: Great Northern Sulphur. SN means "giant sulphur."
RANGE: Found in willow bogs from Alaska north to the Arctic Ocean in the Yukon, east along the boreal treeline to Hudson and James bays, and south in the mountains of w N Amer.
ID: WS 2–2.75 in (5–7 cm). AD: Jun–Jul. UPS of male lemon yellow, with black borders edged with a fringe of bright pink; yellow below, with almost no dark shading; silver, brown-rimmed spot on UNH. Female may be yellow or white. Both sexes may have a reduced black border or lack one. Flight is swift and strong along flyways created by creeks or roadbeds through the forest. These open paths provide a lush growth of willows suitable for egg-laying and dark red and yellow wildflowers for nectaring. LARVA: Green with a yellow stripe on the sides. Host plants are mainly willows (*Salix*).

Palaeno Sulphur
Colias palaeno

ALSO: Moorland or Pale Arctic Clouded Yellow, Hochmoorgelbling, Solitaire, Myrgulvinge, Желтушка торфяниковая, *Colias chippewa*. SN means "palaeno sulphur," possibly referring to Palaemon, epithet of Heracles, the Greek god who personifies masculinity. Colias Palaeno also is a character in the video game *Ace Attorney Investigations*. He is ambassador of Babahln, a country whose emblem is the butterfly.
RANGE: Near circumpolar. Occurs in woodland bogs and brushy areas where *Vaccinium* is present, and on alpine tundra above 1500 ft (500 m).
ID: WS 1.25–2 in (3–5 cm). AD: Jun–Aug. Male is pale sulphur yellow above; female is off-white. Solid black marginal band on UPF of both sexes shows through to the UNF when backlit by the sun. Adults commonly sip nectar on Narrowleaf Arnica (*Arnica angustifolia*). LARVA: Green with a yellow stripe on the sides. Host plants are mainly bilberries (*Vaccinium*).

FAMILY NYMPHALIDAE
BRUSH-FOOTED BUTTERFLIES

These butterflies have short, furry forelegs—hence the common name "brushfoot." They also have large prominent knobs at the tips of the antennae. The caterpillars are covered with hairs or spiky projections. Brushfoots hold their wings spread flat when resting on vegetation.

GENUS *BOLORIA*: *Boloria* derives from the Greek *bolos,* meaning "fishing net," a reference to the net-like (*reticulate*) underwing pattern. These butterflies are commonly referred to as *fritillaries*. Most species require 2 years to complete development from egg to adult. Newly hatched caterpillars hibernate the first winter, grow through two instar stages the next summer, and then hibernate in the second winter as fourth-stage instars. Larvae complete development in their second summer and emerge as adults. Adults rest with their wings spread open and pressed against the substrate, and orient their wings at 90 degrees to the sun's rays to gather warmth.

♀ *Boloria polaris*

♂ *Boloria polaris*

Polaris Fritillary
Boloria polaris
Circumpolar
WS 1.25–1.5 in (3–4 cm)

♀ *Boloria napaea
alaskensis*

♂ *Boloria napaea
alaskensis*

Mountain Fritillary
Boloria napaea
N Amer, Europe, Asia
WS 1.5–2 in (4–5 cm)

Bog Fritillary
Boloria eunomia
Circumpolar
WS 1.5 in (4 cm)

Alpine Bistort
*Bistorta
vivipara*

Boloria chariclea
Tundra form

Arctic Fritillary
Boloria chariclea
Circumpolar
WS 1.25–1.5 in (3–4 cm)

Freija's Fritillary
Boloria freija
Circumpolar
WS 1.5–2 in (4–5 cm)

Boloria frigga gibsoni

Frigga's Fritillary
Boloria frigga
N Amer, Europe, Asia
WS 1.5–2 in (4–5 cm)

Bog Rosemary
Andromeda polifolia

Larva
Boloria improba

♂ *Boloria improba*

Dingy Arctic Fritillary
Boloria improba
N Eurasia–nw N Amer
WS 1–1.5 in (2.5–4 cm)

Netleaf Willow
Salix reticulata

Bog Bilberry
*Vaccinium
uliginosum*

Polaris Fritillary

Boloria polaris

ALSO: Polarperlemorvinge, Перламутровка полярная, Nacré polaire, *Clossiana polaris*. CN derives from the Latin *fritillus*, meaning "dice box," referring to the upperwing's squared marks. SN means "northern fritillary." **RANGE:** Circumpolar. A High Arctic species, ranging to 81°N on tundra to 4500 ft (1400 m). **ID:** WS 1.25–1.5 in (3–4 cm). AD: Jun–Aug. Male reddish orange above, marked with black lines and spots; female cream to pale orange, with drab brown markings. UNF orange; UNH reddish brown, with 4 white dots at base, white streaks in middle portion, and white hourglass marks along margin. Produces one brood every other year. Flies in odd-numbered years in Alaska and even-numbered years in Canada. LARVA: Host plants include avens (*Dryas*) and bilberry (*Vaccinium*).

Arctic Fritillary

Boloria chariclea

ALSO: Purple Bog Fritillary, Dappled Fritillary, Arktisk perlemorvinge, Nacré lapon, Tundrapärlefjäril, Перламутровка хариклея, *Clossiana chariclea, C. titania*. SN means "fritillary of Chariclea," a nymph in Greek mythology. **RANGE:** Circumpolar. Occurs on windswept tundra and alpine meadows to 5900 ft (1800 m). **ID:** WS 1.25–1.5 in (3–4 cm). AD: Orange, with black spots, bars, and chevron-shaped markings. Tundra specimens have a silvery white band across the middle of the UNH and show faint black submarginal spots and chevron marks. Taiga specimens are more purplish and show a broken yellow to rust-colored band across the UNH, with white spots and black chevrons on the margins. LARVA: Gray, with black stripes and orange spines. Host plants include willow (*Salix*), violets (*Viola*), bistorts (*Bistorta, Polygonum*), and bilberries (*Vaccinium*). **SIMILAR SPECIES:** BOG FRITILLARY, *Boloria eunomia*, circumpolar; local in alpine bogs and marshes. Distinguished by the row of silvery submarginal spots on UNH.

Mountain Fritillary

Boloria napaea

ALSO: Alaskan Fritillary, Ähnliche Perlmutterfalter, Nacré des renouées, Fjellperlemorvinge, Болория аляскинская. SN means "fritillary of wooded vales." **RANGE:** Occurs in disjunct locations in N Amer, n Europe, and ne Asia in tundra and alpine meadows to 8200 ft (2500 m). **ID:** WS 1.5–2 in (4–5 cm). AD: Male bright orange above, with dark wing bases and delicate black markings; female cream, with drab brown markings. UNH delicately patterned in tan and rust. Outer margin of hind wing arched. Single brood Jun–Aug, every other year. LARVA: Host plants include bistorts (*Polygonum*) and violets (*Viola*).

Frigga's Fritillary

Boloria frigga

ALSO: Willow Bog Fritillary, Great Spangled Fritillary, Friggs perlemorvinge, Nacré boréal, Перламутровка фригга, *Clossiana frigga*. SN means "Frigga's fritillary," referring to Frigga, a goddess in Germanic mythology and the wife of Odin in Norse mythology. **RANGE:** Occurs in disjunct locations in N Amer, n Europe, and e Asia in willow thickets in wet tundra and in forest bogs. **ID:** WS 1.5–2 in (4–5 cm). AD: May–Jul. Orange, with black spots and marks; dark brown near the body, especially on hind wing. Outer half of UNH purplish, with distinct white spots in the middle and on the leading edge. LARVA: Host plants include bog rosemary (*Andromeda*), bilberries (*Vaccinium*), willows (*Salix*), dwarf birches (*Betula*), and cloudberries (*Rubus*).

Freija's Fritillary

Boloria freija

ALSO: Zigzag Fritillary, Frøyas perlemorvinge, *Clossiana freija*. SN means "Freija's fritillary," referring to Freija, the Norse goddess of fertility. **RANGE:** Near circumpolar. Occurs from

Scandinavia across Russia to e Siberia, and from Alaska across most of Canada, in pine, spruce, or larch forests, shrubby forest-tundra, and bogs to 5250 ft (1600 m). **ID:** WS 1.5–2 in (4–5 cm). AD: Very similar to, but paler-winged than *Boloria frigga*. Best distinguished by UNH, which has a distinct white zigzag distal line and "duck's head" marking mid-wing. Flight begins early in spring. Freija's fritillaries are often in flight by late April, well before any Frigga's fritillaries are on the wing.

Dingy Arctic Fritillary

Boloria improba
ALSO: Dusky-winged Fritillary, Uncompahgre Fritillary, Dvergperlemorvinge, Nacré nébuleux, Перламутровка арктическая, *Clossiana improba*. SN means "inferior fritillary," probably referring to the drab coloration. **RANGE:** Occurs n Eurasia–nw N Amer on wet tundra and grassy alpine slopes to 3250 ft (1000 m). **ID:** WS 1–1.5 in (2.5–4 cm). AD: Jun–Aug. Dull brown above, with indistinct orange markings and darker shading toward the wing base. UNH dark orange brown at base, paler and grayer at margin, with 2 ivory white chevron marks, one in the central area and another on the leading edge. Males patrol for females near the ground in the vicinity of host plants such as Alpine Bistort (*Bistorta vivipara)* and dwarf willows *(Salix arctica* and *S. reticulata).*

GENUS *EREBIA*: These northern butterflies are associated with mountain elevations, hence their common name *alpines*. They are known as *ringlets* in Europe, a reference to the eyespots *(ocelli)* on the wings. The genus name derives from the Greek *Erebus*, the dark abode of the dead, and alludes to the adult's somber colors. Most species have dark brown wings with reddish to orange wing patches or eyespots. Arctic species produce only 1 generation each year and the larvae take 2 years to mature. Larvae are sparsely haired and are yellow green with light and dark stripes running down the back and sides. Host plants are grasses (*Deschampsia)* and sedges (*Carex).*

White-spot Alpine

Erebia disa
ALSO: Arctic Ringlet, Disa Alpine, Taiga Alpine, Moiré boréal, Disas ringvinge. SN means "Disa's alpine," referring to the Norse goddess who used her net to capture evildoers. **RANGE:** Occurs on alpine tundra, forest-tundra, and spruce and sphagnum bogs from n Scandinavia to the Yamal Penin, in Yakutia, Chukotka, and on the arctic coast of w N Amer. **ID:** WS 1.25–1.75 in (3–4.5 cm). AD: UPH unmarked dark brown; UPF dark brown, with 3–5 orange-ringed black spots, which show through to underwing. UNH pale gray along margin, dark brown in the midsection, and paler gray near body, with 2 small whitish marks, one in the center and the other at the front edge of the wing. This alpine avoids bright sunlight. It flies in the morning and early evening, and rests during the day in foliage at the base of trees. Flight is slow, steady, and low.

Lapland Ringlet

Erebia embla
ALSO: Emblas ringvinge, Moiré lapon, Gulringad gräsfjäril, Эмбла. SN means "Embla's ringlet," referring to Embla, the first woman in Norse mythology. **RANGE:** Occurs in sunny spots in wet spruce and pine forests, in forest bogs, and on moors across n Eurasia, south to China. **ID:** WS 1.5–2 in (4–5 cm). AD: Dark brown above, with black spots encircled with yellowish orange; gray edging on UPH. UNF brown, with dark spots encircled with orange; UNH dark brown near body, with a wide band of gray along margin. Females are paler and have brighter spots. **LARVA:** Lettuce green.

Ross's Alpine

Erebia rossii
ALSO: Arctic Alpine, Alpin de Ross, Чернушка Росса. SN means "Ross's alpine," after Arctic explorer Sir John Ross (1777–1856). **RANGE:** Rare in the Sayan and Altai Mtns of

nc Siberia and uncommon in arctic Alaska and Canada on stony tundra to 9200 ft (2800 m). **ID:** WS 1.25–1.75 in (3–4.5 cm). AD: Blackish brown; 2 adjoining orange-ringed black eyespots with white pupils on UPF; UPH has no spots or an incomplete row of very small spots or flecks. UNF has a reddish orange central area with black eyespots; UNH shows a pale gray median band with jagged borders. Often basks on warm rocks.

Banded Alpine
Erebia fasciata
ALSO: Чернушка анаб-
арская. SN means "alpine
with banded [wings]."

RANGE: Occurs in moist tundra swales, wet tundra tussocks, and sedge mires on lee sides of ridges and gullies from Siberia to Alaska and Canada, east to Hudson Bay.
ID: WS 2 in (5 cm). AD: Late Jun. Wing color and pattern variable. Male black to dark brown above; female dark to light reddish brown above, with some dark banding near wing margins. UNS shows alternating bands of pale gray and brown.

Mountain Alpine
Erebia pawlowskii
ALSO: Theano Alpine,
Yellow-dotted Alpine,
Чернушка Павловского.

SN means "Pavlovskiy's alpine," after the 19th-century Russian insect collector M. Pavlovskiy.
RANGE: Occurs in grassy areas in wet tundra and bogs from Lake Baikal east across Siberia to Chukotka, Alaska south to Colorado, and Canada east to Hudson Bay.
ID: WS 1.25–1.5 in (3–4 cm). AD: Jul–Aug. Dark brown above, with a series of orange bars (or orange band in *E. p. canadensis*) along wing edges. UNF shows a reddish flush in the center; UPS markings appear as ivory spots on UNS. Regularly takes nectar at flowers. Slow, weak flight. Often drops to the ground when alarmed. Spends most of the day perched on long grass rather than expending energy in flight. LARVA: Hairy, light brown, with dark brown dorsal and lateral stripes. Host plants are grasses, sedges, and rushes.

Red-disked Alpine
Erebia discoidalis
ALSO: Alpin à disque rouge,
Чернушка мраморная. SN
means "[red-] disked alpine."

RANGE: Found in forests with wet meadows and grassy bogs from n Siberia to n N Amer.
ID: WS 1.75–2 in (4.5–5 cm). AD: May–Jun. Blackish brown above, with a diffuse rusty red patch covering much of the UPF center. No eyespots. Mottled brown and gray below, becoming frosty gray toward outer edge and with the reddish UPF patch repeated beneath.

GENUS *OENEIS*: Linnaeus named this genus after Oeneus, king of Calydon, an ancient city in w Greece. Oeneus is thought to be first person to cultivate grapes.

These butterflies, called *arctics*, are associated with high latitudes and alpine elevations, where they survive in incredibly harsh climatic conditions. They are difficult to spot. Their wings are translucent and are cryptically patterned on the underside, which makes them virtually invisible against the tundra vegetation. In addition, they rest flat on their side, which completely eliminates their shadow. Their flight is fast and erratic, and the adults often fly up into the wind where they are carried away. Arctics produce one generation every 2 years. Thus in some areas, adults may be seen only every second year or may show a considerable alternation in abundance. Early stage larvae overwinter and complete development the next spring. Host plants are mostly grasses and sedges.

Jutta Arctic
Oeneis jutta
ALSO: Baltic Grayling,
Forest Arctic, Chamoisé
lapon, Juttas ringvinge,

Бархатница ютта. SN means "giant arctic," alluding to Jotunn, a giant in Norse mythology.
RANGE: Near circumpolar. Occurs in wet tundra, sedge mires, open woodland near bogs, and pine forests with grass understory, from Scandinavia to Chukotka and from Canada south to the ne US.

♂ *Erebia embla*

Erebia embla

Erebia rossii

♀ *Erebia embla*

Lapland Ringlet
Erebia embla
Eurasia
WS 1.5–2 in (4–5 cm)

Ross's Alpine
Erebia rossii
N Amer, nc Siberia
WS 1.25–1.75 in (3–4.5 cm)

Erebia disa

Erebia disa

White-spot Alpine
Erebia disa
Europe, Asia, w N Amer
WS 1.25–1.75 in (3–4.5 cm)

♂ *Erebia fasciata*

Erebia discoidalis

Erebia discoidalis

Red-disked Alpine
Erebia discoidalis
N Siberia–n N Amer
WS 1.75–2 in (4.5–5 cm)

Erebia faciata

♀ *Erebia fasciata*

Mountain Alpine
Erebia pawlowskii
Siberia–w N Amer
WS 1.25–1.5 in (3–4 cm)

♂ *Erebia pawlowskii*

Banded Alpine
Erebia fasciata
N Siberia–nw N Amer
WS 2 in (5 cm)

♀ *Erebia pawlowskii*

ID: WS 1.75–2 in (4–5 cm). AD: Jul–Aug. Grayish to olive brown above, with paler veins; UPF and UPH are marked with several dark eyespots; the spots are either ringed with, or lie in a wide band of yellowish orange. Males have a region of dark scent scales (stigmas) on the UPF. UNF is grayish brown and marked with eyespots; UNH is mottled with gray, brown, and black, and may have an irregular, wide band of color across the center. Active in midday, flying about trees, then resting on tree trunks or grass tussocks. LARVA: Greenish body, with red hairs; striped in green, brown, and white; head reddish brown, or greenish dotted with brown.

Melissa Arctic

Oeneis melissa
ALSO: White Mountain Arctic, Mottled Arctic, Brown Mountain Butterfly, Nordique mélissa. SN means "honeybee arctic."
RANGE: Found on tundra, ridges, meadows, and talus slopes to 5000 ft (1525 m) from Urals to Chukotka south to Japan, and from Alaska to Labrador. Isolated populations in sw US and White Mtns, New Hampshire.
ID: WS 1.75–2 in (4.5–5 cm). Variable species with many subspecies. AD: Jun–Aug. Dull brownish gray above; wing fringes often checkered. UNH mottled with black and pale grey, with some black in the medial band. Males patrol rocky areas in search of mates. LARVA: Moss-green, with bluish green stripes, and a band of yellow spots on sides. Feeds at night. Pupates under mosses and rocks. Host plants are sedges.

Polixenes Arctic

Oeneis polixenes
ALSO: Nordique alpin. SN means "Polixenes's arctic," referring to Polixenes, the king of Bohemia in Shakespeare's play *The Winter's Tale*, written in 1610.
RANGE: Found on windswept summits and ridges to 4000 ft (1220 m) from the Urals to Chukotka, and in Alaska and arctic Canada, east to Hudson Bay. Isolated populations exist in sw US, Quebec, and Mount Katahdin, Maine.

ID: WS 1.5–2 in (4–5 cm). AD: Jun–Aug. Grayish brown overall, sparsely scaled with yellow; often virtually transparent and resembling lightly smoked glass. Male has no markings, female may have 2 small black eyespots. UNH mottled gray, brown, and black, with dark median band outlined in pale gray. Males patrol grassy swales to watch for females. LARVA: Grayish green dorsal stripe and tan, black, and gray lateral stripes; head greenish yellow, with 6 dark stripes. Host plants are grasses (Poaceae).

Norse Grayling

Oeneis norna
ALSO: Chamoisé fascié, Nornens ringvinge, Норна.
SN means "Nornes' Arctic," referring to the Nornes—Verdandi (Present), Urda (Past), and Skuld (Future)—the Norse goddesses of destiny, who were always present at the birth of a human and who weaved the thread of fate.
RANGE: Occurs in scattered locations from Scandinavia to Chukotka in bogs, damp grasslands, and mossy alpine forest clearings between 800 and 2625 ft (250–800 m).
ID: WS 1.5–2.25 in (4–5.5 cm). AD: Jun–Jul. Golden brown above, clearly marked with 1–3 black-edged white eyespots. Eyespots and dark transverse band on UNF. UNH has dark band broadly edged with pale gray.

White-veined Arctic

Oeneis bore
ALSO: Arctic Grayling, Chamoisé boréal, Tundra-ringvinge, *O. taygete*. SN means "boreal arctic," alluding to Boreas, Greek god of the north wind.
RANGE: Occurs on tundra, grassy alpine slopes, and bogs to 3250 ft (1000 m) in disjunct locations in n Scandinavia, Yakutia, and Magadan, and from Alaska to Labrador. Isolated populations in the Rocky Mtns and Mount Albert, Quebec.
ID: WS 1.5–2 in (4–5 cm). AD: Jul. Grayish brown above; no eyespots; dark scent stigma on the UPF of most males. Mottled gray and brown below, with conspicuous white veins; UNH has

Melissa Arctic
Oeneis melissa
NE Asia–N Amer
WS 1.75–2 in (4.5–5 cm)

Norse Grayling
Oeneis norna
Eurasia
WS 1.5–2.25 in (4–5.5 cm)

White-veined Arctic
Oeneis bore
Europe, Asia, N Amer
WS 1.5–2 in (4–5 cm)

Jutta Arctic
Oeneis jutta
Near circumpolar
WS 1.75–2 in (4.5–5 cm)

Polixenes Arctic
Oeneis polixenes
N Siberia–n N Amer
WS 1.5–2 in (4–5 cm)

Chryxus Arctic
Oeneis chryxus
N Amer
WS 1.5–2.25 in (4–5.5 cm)

Larva
Nymphalis antiopa

Mourning Cloak
Nymphalis antiopa
Near circumpolar
WS 2–2.75 in (5–7 cm)

Small Tortoiseshell
Nymphalis urticae
Eurasia
WS 2–2.5 in (5–6 cm)

Comma mark

Adult mourning cloaks and
hoary commas both feed
on tree sap.

Hoary Comma
Polygonia gracilis
N Amer
WS 1.5–2 in (4–5 cm)

dark median band outlined in white; UNF has dark transverse line mid-wing. Males patrol grassy hillsides for receptive females. LARVA: Pale brown, with a brown dorsal stripe, and lateral lines of white, reddish brown, and dark brown. Host plants are grasses (*Festuca*) and sedges (*Carex*).

Chryxus Arctic

Oeneis chryxus

ALSO: Brown Arctic, Nordique orangé, Ringvinge. SN means "golden arctic."

RANGE: Occurs on arctic and alpine tundra, dry grassy areas, open pine woods, and woodland edges in Alaska and Canada, south to mountains of New Mexico, with isolated populations in e Canada, Wisconsin, and Michigan.

ID: WS 1.5–2.25 in (4–5.5 cm). AD: May–Jun. Golden brown above, darker at margins and wing base, occasionally with a row of small diffuse orange spots or 2–4 small black eyespots on UPF. Large, dark gray scent stigma on male's UPF leading edge. Cryptically patterned in dark brown and pale gray below, with a well-defined dark medial band and a dark line across the UNF. Powerful flier, wary, and difficult to spot on lichen-covered rocks. LARVA: Reddish hairs; tan dorsal stripe; brown and white lateral stripes; head yellowish brown with brown vertical stripes.

GENUS *NYMPHALIS*: These butterflies, collectively known as *anglewings*, are distinguished by a jagged wing outline. The underwings are cryptically patterned, which provides camouflage when the butterfly is resting on bark or tundra vegetation with their wings folded. The adults undergo a period of dormancy in winter, when they shelter in log piles, crevices, hollows, and old buildings.

Mourning Cloak

Nymphalis antiopa

ALSO: Camberwell Beauty, Trauermantel, Sørgekåpe, Траурница. CN refers to the maroon wing color, the traditional hue of mourning garb in olden days. SN means

"Antiope's nymph," alluding to Antiope, wife of King Lycus of Thebes, and to the nymphs, the lesser deities of springs, groves, and mountains. RANGE: Widespread across temperate Eurasia and most of N Amer, ranging north to the tundra in Alaska and Canada, and south to c Mexico and n Venezuela. Found along streams, in forest borders, open woodland, parks, and gardens, from sea level to 6550 ft (0–2000 m). Northern populations migrate south shortly after breeding. ID: WS 2–2.75 in (5–7 cm). AD: Jun–Jul, in the north; southern populations produce a second brood in autumn. Rich maroon above, with a jagged yellow or cream margin edged with metallic blue spots. Brownish black below, with cream margins. Feeds on sap seeping from cracks in tree bark. Adults may live 10–11 months and overwinter in log piles and crevices. They can sometimes be seen flying over the snow in a characteristic flap-glide motion. LARVA: Spiny and black, with white specks and reddish orange spots on the back. Host plants include willows (*Salix*), elms (*Ulmus*), poplars (*Populus*), and hackberries (*Celtis*).

Small Tortoiseshell

Nymphalis urticae

ALSO: Kleiner fuchs, Neslesommerfugl, Крапивница, *Aglais urticae*. SN means "nettle-loving nymph," referring to the primary larval host plant. A very ancient species, virtually indistinguishable from fossils of *Aglais karaganica*, which are estimated to be 15 million years old.

RANGE: Occurs across Eurasia in fields, gardens, and alpine slopes to 9850 ft (3000 m). ID: WS 2–2.5 in (5–6 cm). AD: Mar–Oct. Orange, yellow, and black, with metallic blue spots along the jagged wing margin; UPF has alternating rectangular black and yellow patches on the leading edge; UPH has an irregular black patch near the body. Mottled brown below. Adults feed on flower nectar. Adults undergo a period of suspended development (diapause), overwintering alone or in small groups in crevices and litter, then emerging in early spring to mate and lay eggs. Males wait for receptive females in forest margins, hillsides, gullies, logs, or bushes. One to 3 broods per year. Females lay clusters of eggs on the underside of leaves of larval host plants, usually nettles. LARVA: Young larvae form colonies that feed together in a web. Older caterpillars feed alone and make silken cocoons of folded nettle leaves.

GENUS *POLYGONIA*
Hoary Comma
Polygonia gracilis

ALSO: Hoary Anglewing, Углокрыльница, Polygone gracile, *Nymphalis gracilis*. SN means "graceful anglewing." CN "hoary" refers to the silvery color on the wing underside; "comma" refers to the small, white curved mark on the underside of the hind wing.

RANGE: Occurs in forests, woodland clearings, along rivers, and on alpine ridges from c Alaska and Yukon east across n Canada, and south to the Great Lakes, New England, and w US.

ID: WS 1.5–2 in (4–5 cm). AD: Jagged wing edges. Orange and black above, with bright yellow spots in the dark wing margins; UPF has 2 irregular black bars on leading edge and 3–4 black spots mid-wing; UPH has 2 black patches near body. UNS dark brown near body, silvery gray toward margin; UNH has a tiny white comma mid-wing. Adults emerge in Jul–Aug, overwinter in diapause, and mate and lay eggs in spring. Feeds on tree sap and flower nectar. LARVA: Feeds on leaves of currants (*Ribes*), western azalea (*Rhododendron*), and mock azalea (*Menziesia*).

FAMILY LYCAENIDAE
GOSSAMER-WING BUTTERFLIES
These tiny and delicate butterflies are represented in the Arctic by about 18 species of coppers (Lycaeninae), hairstreaks (Thelinae), and blues (Polyommatinae). Only a few of the common species are described here. The wings of these butterflies are often brightly colored and irides-cent. The color and iridescence come from two different types of scales. The gray, brown, and orange scales contain pigments, while the blue, green, purple, and copper iridescence derives from light reflected off the scales. In most species,

the adult males have greatly reduced forelegs, while the females have 6 fully developed legs.

Lycaenid larvae are typically plump and shaped like a wood louse or pill bug. The larvae of many species feed exclusively on plant matter, but some are carnivorous and feed on aphids, scale insects, and ant larvae. About 75 percent of lycaenid species associate with ants in some way. Larvae are often attended by ants and some pupate within ants' nests. Meanwhile, the ants feed on a honey-like secretion produced from a gland on the larva's back.

GENUS *LYCAENA*: These butterflies are named for their copper-colored wings. Larval host plants of the arctic species are docks and sorrels (*Rumex*, *Oxyria*).

Small Copper
Lycaena phlaeas

ALSO: American Copper, Feilden's Copper, Kleiner Feuerfalter, Cuivré commun, Bronzé, Ildgullvinge, Червонец пятнистый. SN means "burning copper," referring to the bright copper-colored wings.

RANGE: Circumpolar. Common, but often local on tundra, rocky alpine sites, and sandy heath in Eurasia and N Amer. Ranges to 80°N at Lake Hazen, Ellesmere Is, Canada.

ID: WS 1 in (2.5 cm). AD: Jun–Jul in the north; May–Aug elsewhere. UPF bright orange, with a dark outside margin and with 8–9 black spots; UPH blackish, with an orange border; females of the subspecies *L. p. caeruleopunctata* also have a row of blue spots within the orange border. Black spots on UNF are outlined in white or yellow, and the dark coloring is replaced by a pale brownish gray; UNH brownish gray, with small black dots and narrow orange border. Fast flying. Rests with its wings half open as if ready for immediate takeoff. Males are very aggressive and drive away rivals as they wait for females on bare hilltops. Females lay white, dimpled eggs singly on the top side of host plant leaves. LARVA: Hairy and green, with varying amounts of pinkish purple down the back and on the sides. When viewed from above, the legs and head are hidden, so the larva looks like a part of the leaf. Feeds mainly on the underside of dock and sorrel leaves, creating translucent windows that can be seen on the upper leaf surface. Overwinters as a caterpillar. Pupates in leaf litter, where the pupa is often attended by ants.

Scarce Copper
Lycaena virgaureae

ALSO: Dukatenfalter, Cuivré de la verge d'or, Oransje gull-vinge, Червонец огненный, *Heodes virgaureae*. SN means "goldenrod copper," referring to *Solidago virgaurea*, a goldenrod often visited by these butterflies. CN "scarce" refers to the species being erroneously recorded as a great rarity.

RANGE: Occurs in the UK and across Eurasia in boggy woodland, dry grazing land, and flowered meadows at 2000–6500 ft (600–2000 m).
ID: WS 1.5 in (4 cm). AD: Jul–Sep. Males fiery golden red above, edged with black; females orange above, with a dark, patterned overlay of spots. UNH golden, with black dots; wing margin shows a band of white dots or streaks. Very active on sunny days and can be seen nectaring at flowers. Rests with wings held erect or at a 45 degree angle. Males wait for females at forest edge and aggressively chase off rival males. At dusk, several coppers often gather in sheltered spots and roost with heads facing down. Females lay white eggs on common and sheep's sorrel (*Rumex*). Overwinters as an egg. LARVA: Green and sparsely haired. Feeds at night.

GENUS *CALLOPHRYS*
Green Hairstreak
Callophrys rubi

ALSO: Grüner Zipfelfalter, Grønnvinge, Thècle de la ronce, Малинница. SN means "Rubus-loving butterfly with beautiful eyes," a reference to the exotic green eye color and to berry-bearing plants in the genus *Rubus,* which are common larval food plants. CN refers to the narrow white streaks on the green underwing.
RANGE: Widespread and common from n Africa and Asia Minor north to arctic Scandinavia and east to Chukotka on moors, spruce and mixed forest, dry heath, and south-facing hillsides to 7550 ft (2300 m) elevation.
ID: WS 1–1.25 in (2.5-3 cm). AD: Mar–Jul. Dull brown above; males have a small patch of pale scent scales on the UPF, which appear as a little raised pad on the UNF. Apple green, turquoise, or emerald below, with a line of thin white "streaks" across the wings. Green color is caused by light refracting and reflecting from a microscopic lattice within the wing scales; color varies with the direction of light and angle of view, providing camouflage when the butterfly closes its wings and perches on leafy vegetation. On cold days, tilts its closed wings to the side to catch the sun's maximum warmth; on warm days, the wings are held straight up to minimize heat absorption. Males wait for females in forest margins and clearings. They are territorial and engage in frenzied aerial battles with rival males. Females roam widely and lay their eggs singly on the leaves or buds of larval host plants such as blackberry (*Rubus*), bilberry (*Vaccinium*), currant (*Ribes*), and buckthorn (*Rhamnus*). LARVA: Green with white streaks on sides. Pupates under stones, leaves, or soil. Pupa moves around to produce a faint squeaking sound, once thought to be a defense mechanism for deterring predatory insects. However, researchers now believe that the sound may actually attract ants, which guard the pupa in their subterranean nests and in exchange drink the sugary substance the pupa secretes onto its skin.

GENERA *AGRIADES* AND *PLEBEJUS*: These tiny butterflies are collectively known as *blues*. Males are blue to bluish gray above, while females are mostly brown or gray and show only a bit of blue. Both sexes bear a cryptic underwing pattern of dark spots and bands against a grayish ground color. Blues are difficult to observe due to their small size and fast, erratic flight.

Arctic Blue
Agriades glandon

ALSO: Glandon Blue, Dunkler Alpenbläuling, Azuré des soldanelles,

Cranberry Blue
Plebejus optilete
Eurasia–w N Amer
WS 0.5–1 in (1.5–2.5 cm)

Broom
Genista pilosa

♀

Northern Blue
Plebejus idas
Near circumpolar
WS 0.5–1.25 in (1.5–3 cm)

♀

♂

Northern Cranberry
Vaccinium oxycoccos

♂

Purple Saxifrage
Saxifraga oppositifolia

Arctic Blue
Agriades glandon
Near circumpolar
WS 0.5–1 in (1.7–2.3 cm)

♀

♂

♀

Underwing
green

Northern
Red Currant
Ribes triste

Green Hairstreak
Callophrys rubi
Eurasia
WS 1–1.25 in (2.5–3 cm)

Small Copper
Lycaena phlaeas
Circumpolar
WS 1 in (2.5 cm)

Upperwing
brown

Branded Skipper
Hesperia comma
Near circumpolar
WS 1–1.25 in (2.5–3 cm)

Larva
*Lycaena
phlaeas*

Larva
Callophrys rubi

♂

Common Sorrel
Rumex acetosa

♂

Cloudberry
Rubus chamaemorus

♀

Grizzled Skipper
Pyrgus centaureae
Near circumpolar
WS 1–1.5 in (2.5–4 cm)

Scarce Copper
Lycaena virgaureae
Eurasia
WS 1.5 in (3.5 cm)

Larva
*Lycaena
virgaureae*

Larva
Pyrgus centaureae

Polarblåvinge, *Plebejus glandon.* SN means "Col du Glandon argus"; *Agriades* means "like Argus," a mythological giant who had 100 eyes, referring to the many eyespots on the underwing. Col du Glandon is a mountain pass in Savoie, France, where the species occurs.
RANGE: Near circumpolar. Found in arctic N Amer and Eurasia above 5900 ft (1800 m), on alpine tundra, fell fields, meadows, and ridges. **ID:** WS 0.5–1 in (1.5–2.5 cm). AD: May–Aug. Males can be dark grayish blue to steel blue above. Females are brown above, sometimes showing small black patches outlined in white. Both sexes are grayish brown below, with black spots ringed with white, and tiny white patches with or without black centers; females sometimes show a trace of orange and blue on the largest spot near the UNH margin. Female lays eggs singly under leaves or on flowers visited by nectaring adults. Adults also suck liquids and salt from moist sand, gravel, and soil. Overwinters as an egg or pupa. LARVA: Pale green, with reddish marks on the back; covered with long, fine hairs. Feeds on buds and flowers of vetches (*Astragalus*), rock-jasmine (*Androsace*), bilberries (*Vaccinium*), saxifrages (*Saxifraga*), and pincushion plants (*Diapensia lapponica*).

Northern Blue
Plebejus idas
ALSO: Idas Blue, Idas-Bläuling, Azuré du genêt, Idasblåvinge. SN means

"Idas's blue," referring to Idas, one of the Argonauts in Greek mythology.
RANGE: Near circumpolar. Occurs across n Eurasia and in western and eastern N Amer in meadows, bogs, and grassy woodland clearings to 6900 ft (2100 m).
ID: WS 0.5–1.25 in (1.5–3 cm). AD: May–Aug. Males are bright purplish blue above, with narrow black margins and with black submarginal spots on the UPH. Females may be dark purplish brown or deep blue above, with a broad edging of dark brownish gray and varying amounts of orange marginal spots. Both sexes are pale gray below, with central black spots; a marginal row of black spots have metallic blue centers, which

are capped with orange and black on UNH. Flies in early morning, even in dense fog. Single or double brooded depending on elevation and latitude. Overwinters as an egg. LARVA: Host plants include crowberry (*Empetrum*) and broom (*Genista* and *Cytisus*). Larvae are often attended by ants and pupate within ants' nests.

Cranberry Blue
Plebejus optilete
ALSO: Yukon Blue, Hochmoor-Bläuling, Azuré de la canneberge, Myrblåvinge, *Vacciniina optilete.*

RANGE: Occurs in alpine sites to 9200 (2800 m) from the Alps to arctic Scandinavia east to Siberia and n Asia, and in N Amer from c Alaska east to Hudson Bay. Found in moist scrub or damp forest clearings where cranberry (*Vaccinium*) is present. Males are often seen on muddy banks where they take salts.
ID: WS 0.5–1 in (1.5–2.5 cm). AD: Jun–Aug. Males are deep purplish blue above. Females are leaden gray above, with some traces of blue present. UNH distinctive; the 1–3 orange, crescent-shaped marks (*lunules*) toward the anal angle of the hind wing are enlarged, and the dark spots outside the swollen lunules have blue in them. Overwinters as an egg. LARVA: Host plants are Northern Cranberry (*Vaccinium oxycoccos*), Bog Bilberry (*V. uliginosum*), and Black Crowberry (*Empetrum nigrum*).

FAMILY HESPERIIDAE
SKIPPERS
Skippers got their common name from their characteristic rapid, darting flight. These small, mostly orange or brown butterflies have short fat bodies and angular wings. Skippers differ from other butterflies in that they have hooked antennae formed by a thin extension (*apiculus*) of the antennal club.

GENUS *HESPERIA*
Branded Skipper
Hesperia comma
ALSO: Holarctic Grass Skipper, Silver-spotted

Skipper, Kommafalter, Le Comma, Kommas-myger. SN means "Hesperides comma," an allusion to the Hesperides, the nymphs who guarded the apples of Hera. CN refers to the comma-shaped scent mark (stigma) of the male. Adults are known as grass skippers, referring to the larval host plants.
RANGE: Occurs in alpine zones of Eurasia and N Amer; rare in the chalk downs of s England. Found in forest edges, meadows, open slopes, and other open grassy sites, to 12,900 ft (3900 m). **ID:** WS 1–1.25 in (2.5–3 cm). **AD:** Jun–Sep. Yellowish orange above, with brown margins. Yellow below, with pale yellow to cream spots. The northern subspecies, *H. c. laurentina*, is dark above and below. Males have a black and silver scent stigma at the UPF medial cell. Adults feed on nectar from flowers such as asters (*Aster*), goldenrods (*Solidago*), and blazing star (*Liatris*). When these skippers alight, they either hold their wings closed, or hold the hind wings open and partially close the forewings so as to form a deltoid shape. Courting pairs perform aerial mating dances, repeatedly ascending rapidly to 30–40 ft (9–12 m), then descending to near ground level. **LARVA:** Larvae construct small tent-like structures from leaf blades and silk, and feed within the webbed structure. Larval host plants are grasses (*Poa, Festuca*).

GENUS *PYRGUS*
Grizzled Skipper
Pyrgus centaureae

ALSO: Alpine Checkered Skipper, Hespérie de la ronce, Moltesmyger. SN means "checkered centaury." *Pyrgus* means "fort's battlement," a reference to the checkered fringe on the wings. *Centaureae* refers to Common Centaury, *Centaurium erythraea*, a small plant with red flowers associated with Chiron, the centaur who, according to Pliny, discovered the plant's medicinal properties.
RANGE: Near circumpolar. Occurs on tundra and forest-tundra in marshes, bogs, damp heath, willow thickets, and mossy forests to 11,000 ft (3350 m); isolated populations occur in the Appalachian and Rocky Mtns.

ID: WS 1–1.5 in (2.5–3.5 cm). **AD:** May–Aug. Brownish black above, with bold white angular spots and checkered fringes on wing edges. White veins on underwings; UNH grayish brown, with angular whitish spots. Males patrol and occasionally perch all day waiting for receptive females. Flies low and fast over vegetation. Adults take nectar at flowers of low-growing plants. When skippers alight, they hold their wings spread open. Eggs are deposited singly on leaves of larval host plants, which include Wild Strawberry (*Fragaria virginiana*), Canadian Cinquefoil (*Potentilla canadensis*), Varileaf Cinquefoil (*P. diversifolia*), and Cloudberry (*Rubus chamaemorus*).

FAMILY LYMANTRIIDAE
TUSSOCK MOTHS
Tussock moth larvae have dense tufts of hairs along the back. The tufts slightly resemble grass tussocks, hence the common name.

GENUS *GYNAEPHORA*
Arctic Woollybear Moth
Gynaephora groenlandica

ALSO: SN means "Greenland fruitful female [moth]." CN: Woollybear refers to the larva's long, fur-like hairs.
RANGE: Occurs on the tundra in arctic Canada and Greenland.
ID: WS 1.25 in (3 cm). **AD:** Gray UPF; yellowish gray UPH. Antennae are feathered in males, long and thread-like in females. **LARVA:** Covered with dense tufts of long, dark brown to golden red hairs. The center of the back has 2 alternating black tufts and yellow tufts. There is a black tuft at the tail end.
HABITS: This moth is known for its 7-year larval development period. Larvae are active for about a month each summer and pass the other 11 months frozen solid in their cocoons.
The larval life cycle consists of 7 stages, or instars, each of which lasts a year. Larvae emerge from their cocoons in June, molt their outer skin, and remain active for about a month. Surprisingly, the caterpillars spend only 20 percent of the day feeding on host plants, such as *Salix arctica*, which are at a nutritional peak.

Arctic Woollybear Moth
Gynaephora groenlandica
Arctic Canada, Greenland
WS 1.25 in (3 cm)
♂

Larva
Arctic Woollybear

♂

Larva
Ross's Tussock Moth

Ross's Tussock Moth
Gynaephora rossii
NE Eurasia, N Amer
WS 1.25 in (3 cm)

Her brief life nearing the end, the female woollybear moth lays her eggs on the cocoon from which she emerged.

Most activity is directed to keeping warm. The larvae bask in the sun and orient their bodies to maximize the absorption of solar radiation.

By midsummer, the larvae stop feeding and begin to spin veil-like cocoons where they will spend the next 11 months. The cocoons, which are concealed in plant cushions and crevices, act as miniature greenhouses that keep the body temperature constant without expending energy. Cocoons also afford the larvae some protection from ichneumonid wasps (*Hyposoter pectinatus*) and tachinid bristle flies (*Exorista thula*), which lay their eggs on woollybear caterpillars. Once the eggs hatch, the wasp or fly larvae develop inside the caterpillar, using its body for food until they emerge as adults and the woollybear dies.

As temperatures drop to freezing, the larvae undergo biochemical changes that serve to conserve energy and prevent freezing. There is a slowing of the metabolic rate and deterioration of the mitochondria—the organelles in the cells that control respiration and energy production. In addition, the larvae's systems produce glycerol, which acts as internal antifreeze and allows them to survive temperatures as low as −76°F (−60°C). The following spring, when their body temperature warms naturally, the woollybear caterpillars thaw and once more become active for a month or so.

At the end of the 7-year larval cycle, the final instar pupates in a double-layered cocoon consisting of a dark inner layer and a pale translucent outer layer. The sun warms the pale outer layer of the cocoon, which accelerates pupal development. Once the adult moths

emerge, they have only a few days to reproduce before they die. Unlike the male, the female woollybear moth cannot fly. She rests atop the cocoon from which she emerged and relies on her pheromones to attract a passing male. If mating occurs, the female oviposits atop her cocoon and brushes scales from her abdomen onto the egg mass to provide insulation for the new generation of woollybears.

Ross's Tussock Moth

Gynaephora rossii

ALSO: SN means "Ross's fruitful female [moth]," referring to Scottish captain and Arctic explorer Sir John Ross (1777–1856).
RANGE: Occurs in open alpine sites and bogs from the Urals to Chukotka, and in arctic-alpine N Amer. Isolated populations in the Rocky Mtns and mountains of Maine and New Hampshire.
ID: WS 1.25 in (3 cm). AD: Grizzled gray UPF. UPH pale orange buff to grayish, with a wide black border. Body densely covered with woolly hairs. Males have feathered antennae, females have long, thread-like ones. Females can produce eggs without fertilization by a male (*parthenogenesis*).
LARVA: Covered in soft, gray tufts of hair; dorsal tufts black, fringed with yellow; lacks the black tail tuft of *G. groenlandica*.
HABITS: Like the arctic woollybears, larvae take multiple years to complete development. Final instar spins a single-layered, dark gray cocoon. Larval host plants include willow (*Salix*), saxifrage (*Saxifraga*), raspberry (*Rubus*), and cinquefoil (*Potentilla*).

FLORA

MORE THAN 2200 SPECIES OF VASCULAR PLANTS occur in the Arctic north of the treeline. Species diversity is generally low, and it decreases from the boreal forests to the polar deserts of the extreme north. Flowering plants constitute about 90 percent of the arctic flora, conifers less than 2 percent, and mosses, bryophytes, and algae the remaining 8 percent.

This chapter uses several terms employed by botanists to delineate the distribution of arctic plants. *Circumpolar* and *near circumpolar* indicate that a species ranges continuously around the north polar region or nearly so. *Circumboreal* indicates that a plant species is distributed around the world in the boreal forests, north to the treeline. *Amphi-Atlantic* means that a species occurs on both sides of the N Atlantic Ocean in e N Amer and w Europe, and often along the coasts of Iceland and Greenland. *Amphi-Beringian* means that a species occurs on both sides of the Bering Strait, mainly between the Lena Rvr in Siberia and the Mackenzie Rvr in Canada. Most species in this latter group are thought to have spread between the continents during the last ice ages via the Bering Land Bridge (*see pp. 19–20*).

Words used in this chapter to define zones of vegetation include *polar desert, High Arctic tundra, Low Arctic tundra, forest-tundra,* and *taiga,* a Russian word for *boreal forest.* The reader will find more information about these zones and typical plants found in each on the map and sidebars on pages 12–13.

Plants need warmth, sun, and rain to grow and reproduce—factors that are in short supply in the Arctic. Plant growth is curbed by winter temperatures that average −25.6°F (−32°C) at the treeline, an annual precipitation of less than 10 in (250 mm), strong desiccating winds, and a very short growing season.

In addition, the ground is often covered with snow until June, and below ground there is a thick layer of *permafrost*—subsoil whose temperature has been below freezing for several years. Permafrost blocks the growth of deep-rooted plants and keeps the meager summer rain and meltwater from draining off. Poor drainage creates acidic soils. Organic decay is very slow in acidic soils and because of their low content of soil bacteria, very little nitrogen is available, which plants need to flourish.

Arctic plants have adapted to these extreme conditions in a number of ways. Most tolerate very low temperatures. Species such as Mountain Sorrel (*Oxyria digyna*), Alpine Azalea (*Kalmia procumbens*), and Snow Buttercup (*Ranunculus nivalis*) continue to produce green foliage in temperatures of 23°F (−5°C), and lichens continue to grow, albeit extremely slowly, in temperatures as low as 14°F (−10°C).

Most arctic wildflowers survive the harsh climate by growing near the soil, often under snow cover, where they are protected from desiccating winds. These low, hardy perennials cluster on hummocks raised by frost heaving. The dark soil on the hummocks absorbs solar heat, and provides a warm microclimate for growth. Many plants maximize the absorption of solar radiation by angling their leaves toward the sun.

Some plants accumulate nutrients and carbohydrates for years before they produce flowers and seeds, while others reproduce vegetatively via layering or budding rather than bothering to set seed at all.

Rising temperatures brought on by global warming are altering the arctic landscape. Forest trees, for example, have been burning at an unprecedented rate in the past few decades due to increased temperatures and drier conditions in the region. Stored carbon freed from these ecosystems leads to more warming, and the soot emitted from the fires blackens the snow, which hastens melting. The Svalbard Global Seed Vault, located in a sandstone mountain on the Norwegian island of Spitsbergen, some 810 mi (1300 km) from the North Pole, was established in 2008. Its goal is to preserve a wide variety of plant seeds, which are duplicate samples of seeds held in the world's other 1750 gene banks. The Svalbard Global Seed Vault ensures against the loss of seeds from large-scale regional and worldwide catastrophes such as civil strife, flooding, fire, and global warming.

CYANOBACTERIA

Cyanobacteria, or blue-green algae, are microscopic, single-celled organisms in the kingdom Bacteria. They obtain their energy through photosynthesis. They are prokaryotes—organisms lacking a cell nucleus—and represent the earliest known form of life on earth. Calcareous mounds, or stromatolites, of fossilized oxygen-producing cyanobacteria have been found in Precambrian rocks dating to between 3.5 and 2.8 billion years ago. Cyanobacteria can be found in almost every conceivable environment from oceans to lakes, rain-moistened desert rocks, and damp soil. A few live as food-producing symbionts in the tissues of other organisms such as lichens. Some species produce extensive, occasionally toxic, blooms of blue-green scum on both fresh- and saltwater bodies.

Nostocales: Nostoc

Nostocales is an order of cyanobacteria containing most of this group's species.

FAMILY NOSTOCACEAE
GENUS *NOSTOC*
Nostoc
Nostoc spp.

RANGE: Circumpolar, mainly on moist tundra in the Arctic.
ID: These freshwater cyanobacteria form colonies composed of long chains of cells, which resemble a string of beads locked in a gelatinous sheath. When exposed to rain or snowmelt, *Nostoc* begins to reproduce. Thousands of individual chains bond together, rapidly forming gelatinous sheets that resemble rumpled mounds of greenish brown seaweed or crumpled plastic bags.

The mysterious and sudden appearance of *Nostoc* mounds led early observers to theorize that the organism fell to the earth during meteor showers or was "star jelly" from molecular clouds in space. The Flemish mystic and alchemist Jan Baptist van Helmont (1579–1644) suggested that *Nostoc* was the "nocturnal Pollution of some plethorical and wanton Star, or rather excrement blown from the nostrils of some rheumatic planet."

USE: *Nostoc* contains the bluish pigment phycocyanin, which enables the capture of light for photosynthesis. It also has specialized cells called heterocysts that are exclusive sites of nitrogen fixation—a process in which inorganic and organic sources of nitrogen are converted into natural fertilizers such as ammonia. Thus, *Nostoc* is an important contributor to the fertility of impoverished tundra soils. *Nostoc* is also edible, and some species are cultivated and consumed as a foodstuff, primarily in Asia.

MARINE ALGAE

Marine algae are also known as seaweeds and kelps. These organisms lack true leaves, stems, and roots. Instead, they have leaf-like *blades* or *fronds*, a stem-like *stipe*, and a *holdfast* that resembles an aerial root. They exhibit alternation of generations. The life cycle begins with a mature organism releasing its asexual spores, which germinate to become male or female gametophytes. These sexual cells unite, forming a zygote that grows into another adult.

For casual reference, marine algae can be grouped by color—brown, green, or red. Brown algae are in the phylum Phaeophyta (Greek for "brown plant"). Green algae are in the phylum Chlorophyta (meaning "green plant"), and the red algae are in the phylum Rhodophyta (meaning "red plant").

Laminariales, Fucales, Desmarestiales: Brown Algae

Most brown algae living in arctic waters are large kelp that attach themselves to the bottom of the ocean by holdfasts. The term *brown algae* is deceiving, as colors can range from olive green to gold or dark reddish brown. Color variations are due to the presence of brown and gold pigments, which can dominate the green-pigmented chloroplasts.

Brown algae are a source of alginate, a colloid with water-holding, gelling, emulsifying, and stabilizing properties. Alginate is used in food, pharmaceutical, cosmetic, and industrial preparations such as ice cream, shaving cream, medical dressings, and dental impression materials.

FAMILY LAMINARIACEAE
BROWN KELP

The family Laminariaceae includes the world's largest known seaweeds, Bull Kelp (*Nereocystis luetkeana*) and California Giant Kelp (*Macrocystis pyrifera*). These algae grow at an average rate of 1.5 ft (0.5 m) per day and can ultimately reach more than 100 ft (30 m) in height. They often form vast underwater "forests" that provide habitat and food for many invertebrates, fishes, seals, and sea otters.

Brown kelps thrive in nutrient-rich seawater having temperatures below 68°F (20°C). Because these organisms attach themselves to the sea bottom but need sunlight to photosynthesize, most live in the intertidal and shallow subtidal zones at maximum depths of about 50–60 ft (17–20 m). A long, tough stalk and air-filled bladders keep the fronds near the sea surface where photosynthesis occurs.

GENUS *NEREOCYSTIS*
Bull Kelp
Nereocystis luetkeana

ALSO: Bull Whip Kelp. SN means "Lütke's mermaid bladder," referring to Fjodor Petrowitsch Lütke, commander of the 1826–1829 Russian naval expedition to N Amer and to the air-filled bladders that keep the fronds near the surface.
RANGE: Subarctic to cold temperate waters of the N Pacific from c California to the Aleutian and Commander islands, on rocky sea bottom. Drifting kelp often reaches Japan. Dominant canopy-forming kelp in the Bering Sea region.
ID: H 100–165 ft (30–50 m). Annual, with some algae persisting over the winter. Large holdfast, to 16 in (40 cm) across, attaches to rocks. Hollow stipe topped with a bulbous pneumatocyst filled with carbon dioxide grows to more than 100 ft (30 m) long. The bulb and hollow stipe serve as floats to keep the algae vertical and floating near the sea surface, where more light is available for photosynthesis. Numerous blades branching off the pneumatocyst bear spore-forming cells (*sori*) arranged in patches. In autumn, the patches release from the blades and sink to the bottom where they develop into gametophytes.

Nereocystis is the only kelp to release spore packets directly onto its holdfast, thus promoting new growth in optimal locations.

GENUS *SACCHARINA*
Sea Belt
Saccharina latissima

ALSO: Sugar Wrack, Zucker-tang, *Laminaria saccharina*.
SN means "sugary broad [blade]."
RANGE: Near circumpolar, in the lower intertidal zone in arctic to temperate coastal waters.
ID: H 10 ft (3 m). Linear, golden brown to orange blade with sharply crinkled margins. Two rows of puckers (*bullations*) run lengthwise down the blade. Holdfast attaches to small rocks.
USE: Contains laminarin, a sugary polysaccharide carbohydrate that is harvested for use as a thickener in ice cream, toothpaste, and jelly.

GENUS *LAMINARIA*
Oarweed
Laminaria digitata
Laminaria hyperborea

ALSO: Tangle, Devil's Apron, Fingertang, Palmentang, Laminaire digitée, Tarer.
SNs mean "flattened blade with fingers" and "flattened blade of the Far North," respectively.
RANGE: Coastlines of the N Atlantic and Arctic oceans, on rocks in the lower intertidal and shallow subtidal zones.
ID: H 10 ft (3 m). Dark brown, with a claw-like holdfast and smooth, flexible stipe. Laminate blade, to 5 ft (1.5 m) long, split into strap-like segments. *L. digitata:* Stipe is oval in cross section and does not snap easily when bent. *L. hyperborea:* Stipe is longer than *digitata*'s, circular in cross section, stiff, and snaps easily when bent.
USE: Oarweed is harvested for manure or burned to produce a rich ash fertilizer.

Arctic Laminaria
Laminaria solidungula

RANGE: Circumpolar, on rocky sea bottoms in the subtidal zone.
ID: H 3 ft (1 m). Smooth, grayish brown blade, cinched toward the top, with wavy margins.

FAMILY ALARIACEAE
WINGED KELP
GENUS *ALARIA*
Ribbon Kelp
Alaria marginata

ALSO: California Nori, Short-stipe Ribbon Kelp. SN means "winged, with a distinct [blade] margin." CN *winged* refers to the small reproductive structures at the base of the blade.

RANGE: N Pacific, from the Commander and Aleutian islands, south to Japan, and Alaska south to California; grows in intertidal and shallow subtidal zones on rocky shores exposed to surf. A main canopy-forming kelp in the Bering Sea.
ID: H 10 ft (3 m). Small holdfast. Short cylindrical stipe, usually less than 1 ft (0.3 m) long. Lanceolate, olive green to brown blade, to 7 ft (2 m) long, with an undulating margin. Conspicuous gold-colored midrib runs along the entire length of the blade. The base of the mature blade has 2 opposite rows of small, spore-producing blades.

Dabberlocks
Alaria esculenta

ALSO: Badderlocks, Flügel-tang. SN means "edible winged kelp."
RANGE: Near circumpolar (absent Siberia), on exposed rocky seashores in subtidal zone.
ID: H 7–12 ft (2–4 m). Olive green to yellowish brown, tapering blade with a thin, wavy, often torn margin. Flexible stipe bears 2 rows of dark brown, club-shaped sporophylls, to 8 in (20 cm) long. Root-like holdfast.

FAMILY FUCACEAE
WRACK AND ROCKWEED
Swollen spore receptacles develop at the tips of the fronds of these algae.

GENUS *FUCUS*
Bladder Wrack
Fucus vesiculosus

ALSO: Black Tang, Sea Oak, Black Tany, Cut Weed, Rock Wrack, Blasentang, Fucus vésiculeux, Blæretang. SN means "seaweed with bladders."

RANGE: Arctic coasts of Alaska and N Atlantic, in the intertidal zone.
ID: H 2 ft (0.6 m). Branched, strap-like, olive green to brown blades. Spherical air bladders occur in pairs on either side of a distinct midrib.
USE: Iodine extracts from this seaweed have been used since 1811 to treat goiter, a swelling of the thyroid gland, and are also used in modern food supplements and additives.

Rockweed Algae
Fucus distichus

ALSO: Талломы фукоидов. SN means "seaweed with 2 lines," referring to plant parts that are arranged in 2 vertical rows.
RANGE: Near circumpolar (absent Siberia), in the lower intertidal zone in arctic waters.
ID: H 2 ft (0.6 m). Small, tufted, brown alga. Regularly and repeatedly branched from 2 in (5 cm) above the discoid holdfast, which attaches to rocks and driftwood. Blade is dark olive to yellowish green, erect, narrow, somewhat rigid and cartilaginous, and markedly flattened, with a thickened midrib.

FAMILY DESMARESTIACEAE
WITCH'S HAIR AND ACID KELP
These brown algae have cylindrical or flat, pinnately branched fronds and attach to the substrate by a discoid holdfast.

GENUS *DESMARESTIA*
Witch's Hair
Desmarestia aculeata

ALSO: Gruagach, Landlady's Wig, Mermaid's Hair, Oseille de mer, Urushi-gusa. SN means "Desmarest's stinging algae," referring to French zoologist Anselme-Gaétan Desmarest (1784–1838).
RANGE: Circumpolar, in arctic to temperate waters in the subtidal zone below the low-water level of spring tides. Also occurs off the Antarctic Penin and Island of South Georgia.
ID: H 4 ft (1.2 m). Dark reddish brown fronds are tufted, wiry, sharp-pointed, with alternate, compressed to flat, short branches. Discoid holdfast attaches to stones.

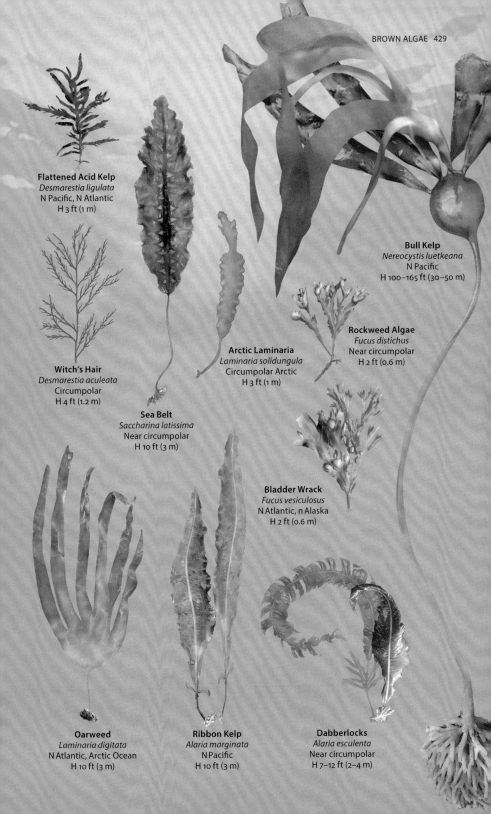

Flattened Acid Kelp
Desmarestia ligulata
N Pacific, N Atlantic
H 3 ft (1 m)

Bull Kelp
Nereocystis luetkeana
N Pacific
H 100–165 ft (30–50 m)

Witch's Hair
Desmarestia aculeata
Circumpolar
H 4 ft (1.2 m)

Arctic Laminaria
Laminaria solidungula
Circumpolar Arctic
H 3 ft (1 m)

Rockweed Algae
Fucus distichus
Near circumpolar
H 2 ft (0.6 m)

Sea Belt
Saccharina latissima
Near circumpolar
H 10 ft (3 m)

Bladder Wrack
Fucus vesiculosus
N Atlantic, n Alaska
H 2 ft (0.6 m)

Oarweed
Laminaria digitata
N Atlantic, Arctic Ocean
H 10 ft (3 m)

Ribbon Kelp
Alaria marginata
N Pacific
H 10 ft (3 m)

Dabberlocks
Alaria esculenta
Near circumpolar
H 7–12 ft (2–4 m)

Flattened Acid Kelp

Desmarestia ligulata

ALSO: SN means "Desmarest's strap-like kelp," referring to the flattened fronds.
RANGE: N Pacific and N Atlantic, in tide pools and in the intertidal zone; also occurs in Hawaii, Chile, NZ, Australia, and Antarctica.
ID: H 3 ft (1 m). Discoid holdfast. Frond has a flattened main axis and obvious midrib. Numerous thin, cylindrical to flat side branches.
USE: This algae produces and stores sulfuric acid. When stressed, it releases acid, causing its own tissues and the tissues of other nearby algae to break down. This is definitely one seaweed you don't want to eat.

Ceramiales: Marine Red Algae

The cells of marine red algae contain the photosynthetic pigments phycoerythrin (red), phycocyanin (blue), chlorophyll (green), and xanthophyll (yellow). Together these pigments combine to produce pink, dark red, black, violet, or golden algae. Red algae are usually found on rocky sea bottoms in deep water. Many are edible and are a source of agar and carrageenan, which are used to make biological culture media and thickening or emulsifying agents in food products.

FAMILY DELESSERIACEAE
MARINE RED ALGAE
GENUS *PHYCODRYS*
Batters or Sea Oak

Phycodrys rubens
ALSO: SN means "red algae."
RANGE: Near circumpolar (disjunct distribution), in tide pools and in the subtidal zone to depths of 100 ft (30 m).
ID: H 8 in (20 cm). Delicate, leaf-like, light crimson, branched blade, with serrated and lobed margins resembling an oak leaf's. Disc-like holdfast. Short, tough stipe attaches to rocks and stipes of *Laminaria* kelps. In winter the frond wears away, leaving just the mid-rib until the blade grows back in spring.

GENUS *PALMARIA*
Edible Dulce

Palmaria palmata
ALSO: Dilsk, Creathnach, Lappentang, Söl. SN means "palmate alga," referring to the fronds' shape.
RANGE: Near circumpolar (disjunct distribution), in the intertidal zone to depths of 65 ft (20 m).
ID: H 16 in (40 cm). Dark red to yellow orange. Leafy, leathery, palmately branched blade, with cuneate to lanceolate, spurred segments. Discoid holdfast attaches to rocks and to stipes of other algae.
USE: Dulce is dried and eaten as a snack food in Iceland. The monks of Saint Columba living on the island of Iona in Scotland harvested this algae for food 1400 years ago.

Ulvales: Marine Green Algae

Marine green algae grow in shallow coastal waters, estuaries, and brackish bays.

FAMILY ULVACEAE
ULVA
GENUS *ULVA*
Sea Lettuce

Ulva lactuca
ALSO: Green Laver, Meersalat, Laitue de mer, паренхиматозный. SN means "algae with milky juice."
RANGE: Occurs in cold to temperate coastal waters nearly worldwide.
ID: H 7 in (18 cm). Forms tufts to 12 in (30 cm) across. Green to dark green fronds are translucent (only 2 cells thick), broad, and crumpled, with a lettuce-like, ruffled margin. Small, thin, discoid holdfast attaches directly to rocks or seashells; there is no stipe. When washed up on beaches, it dries to a white or black color.
USE: *Ulva* can be eaten in salads and soups, and is used as a thickening agent in products such as ice cream. It is an important food source for marine herbivores, including shorebirds, waterfowl, fishes, and mollusks.

MUSHROOMS

Basidiomycota encompasses all mushrooms, from puffballs, stinkhorns, bracket fungi, chanterelles, earthstars, smuts, rusts, and mirror yeasts, to the human-pathogenic yeast *Cryptococcus*.

Agaricales: Amanitas and Puffballs

FAMILY AMANITACEAE: GENUS *AMANITA*

Fly Agaric

Amanita muscaria

ALSO: Fliegenpilz, Amanite tue-mouches, Fausse oronge, Rød fluesopp, Мухомор красный. SN means "fly-killer mushroom."

RANGE: Circumboreal, under pine and birch trees.

ID: H 3–8 in (8–20 cm). HALLUCINOGENIC and POISONOUS. White-spotted red cap. Develops within an egg-shaped structure called the universal veil. As it matures, the veil tears apart, leaving a ragged sheath (*volva*) at the stem base and a ring of tattered veil under the gills; veil remnants also appear as white spots on the red cap. Young amanitas can be mistaken for edible puffballs (*Lycoperdon* spp.). When cut in half, the puffball has undifferentiated white flesh within, while the immature amanita shows evidence of developing gills.

USE: Fly Agaric contains the toxins ibotenic acid and muscimol. Ingestion results in rapid heartbeat, dry mouth, and expanded perception—a condition that can manifest itself in visions and macropsia, where one perceives objects as enlarged. Muscimol is also believed to deactivate the amygdala, the part of the brain responsible for our perception of fear. The Vikings were probably aware of this effect, as they consumed Fly Agaric before staging a raid to enhance their sense of invincibility.

Some reindeer herding cultures feed Fly Agaric to their herds and reap the intoxicants passed through the animals' urinary tract. They collect and drink the reindeer urine to induce a "high" similar to that produced by LSD. During shamanist winter solstice rituals, people gather in their yurts and eat the fungus to induce out-of-body experiences. They are said to envision spirit-walkers on flying reindeer who enter the yurt through the smoke hole in the roof and distribute mushrooms as gifts. The amanita's white-spotted red cap, the flying reindeer and sleigh, and the gift-bearing shamans show striking parallels to the modern day imagery of Santa Claus, who, in his red coat with white trimmings, in his sleigh drawn by flying reindeer, comes down the chimney with presents for all.

Mature
Amanita

Young
Amanita

Fly Agaric
Amanita muscaria
Circumboreal
H 3–8 in (8–20 cm)
Poisonous

Puffball
Lycoperdon spp.
Circumboreal
H 3–6 in (8–15 cm)

Boletales: Boletes

FAMILY BOLETACEAE: GENUS *BOLETUS*

Edible Bolete

Boletus edulis

ALSO: Porcini, Gemeiner Steinpilz, Cèpe, Steinsopp, Белый гриб. SN means "edible mushroom."

RANGE: Circumboreal, in the forest understory.

ID: H 2–6 in (5–15 cm). Brown to pinkish in color. Thick, pestle-shaped stem, with a 4–6 in (10–15 cm) wide cap that resembles a hamburger bun. Cream-colored, spore-producing pores turn green at maturity.

Edible Bolete
Boletus edulis
Circumboreal
H 2–6 in (5–15 cm)

Lecanorales: Lichens

Lichens are composite organisms composed of a fungus and an alga. Because the fungus forms most of a lichen's structure, lichens are classed in the kingdom Fungi, the division Ascomycota (the *ascomycetes* or *sac fungi*), the class Lecanoromycetes, and the order Lecanorales.

Lichens are slow-growing, long-lived, and able to survive incredible extremes of climate. They grow on almost any surface, at any altitude, and in any terrestrial environment. They are pioneer species on bare rock, desert sand, cleared soil, dead wood, animal bones, rusty metal, and living tree bark. Able to shut down metabolically during long periods of unfavorable conditions, they can survive extremes of heat, cold, and drought. In addition, lichens produce more than 500 unique biochemical compounds that act to control light exposure, repel grazing animals, kill attacking microbes, and discourage competition from invasive plants.

Unable to make its own food, the fungal portion of the lichen cultivates partners that manufacture food through photosynthesis. The photosynthetic partners—also known as photosynthetic symbionts, or *photobionts*, for short—are usually green algae or less frequently cyanobacteria (blue-green algae). Lichen fungi and algae live together in what is called a symbiotic relationship. The fungus provides a solid framework or "house" for its symbiont, and the alga provides nutrients for itself and the fungus.

The algal partner is able to exist independently in nature, but not the fungus. When the two are grown separately in the lab, the fungus loses its form and inherent role. Yet if the two are recombined, the fungus reassumes its complex lichen structure and the alga or cyanobacterium returns to its role as photobiont within the fungal tissues. Fungi and algae are very selective in their choice of life partner. Only certain species combine to form a particular lichen. How the two organisms recognize their "perfect mate" is a puzzle still to be solved.

The fruiting, or spore-producing, bodies of most lichens are called *ascomata*. Disc- or cup-shaped ascomata are called *apothecia*; those that are flask-shaped and open by a pore at the summit are called *perithecia*. All ascomata have a layer or cluster of sac-like, spore-producing structures called *asci*—a word derived from the Greek *askos*, meaning "sac" or "wineskin."

Thallus refers to the vegetative framework, or body, of a lichen. For casual reference, lichens can be grouped according to the shape and structure of the thallus, which may be *crustose*, *foliose*, or *fruticose*, or occasionally be intermediate between the two growth forms.

Gray-green Reindeer Lichen
Cladonia rangiferina

Curled Snow Lichen
Flavocetraria cucullata

Crinkled Snow Lichen
Flavocetraria nivalis

Iceland Lichen
Cetraria islandica

Star-tipped Reindeer Lichen
Cladonia stellaris

FRUTICOSE LICHENS

Fruticose lichens are those whose thallus has no clearly differentiated upper and lower surfaces. They often resemble miniature shrubs, or hang down from branches in hair-like clumps.

FAMILY PARMELIACEAE
GENUS *CETRARIA*
Iceland Lichen
Cetraria islandica

ALSO: Isländisches Moos, Mousse d'Islande, Islandslav, Цетрария исландская.
RANGE: Circumpolar, on the ground in arctic and alpine tundra and forest understory, especially under stands of pine.
ID: H 4 in (10 cm). Pale to dark chestnut brown. Strap-like form, with channeled or tubular branches having fringed edges.
USE: Icelanders called this lichen "bread moss" (*brødmose*) because it could be ground and added to wheat flour to make bread. The lichen starch, lichenin, is still used as a starch substitute in some cocoa and porridge mixes. This lichen is fed to free-range reindeer in Lapland, and is used as livestock feed in Iceland and Scandinavia.

GENUS *FLAVOCETRARIA*
Snow Lichen
Flavocetraria spp.

RANGE: Near circumpolar, on mossy tundra, heath, and in open coniferous forest.
ID: H 2–3 in (5–8 cm). Pale greenish yellow. The CRINKLED SNOW LICHEN, or Nagjuujaq, *Flavocetraria nivalis*, forms tufts or cushions. Thallus lobes are erect or prostrate and do not curl inward; margins are deeply lobed

and ruffled. In the CURLED SNOW LICHEN, *F. cucullata*, the thallus lobes are erect, ruffled at the margins, and curl inward to form a tube-like structure.
USE: *F. nivalis* was used in Europe for a violet dye for wool, and in Bolivia it is made into a tea to counteract the effects of high-altitude sickness. Native Alaskans use *F. cucullata* as a condiment to accompany fish or duck soup.

GENUS *ARCTOPARMELIA*
Concentric Ring Lichen
Arctoparmelia centrifuga

RANGE: Near circumpolar. Grows on rocks.
ID: Prostrate. Concentric rings of radiating lobes form as the center of the thallus dies off. Dull greenish yellow on the upper thallus surface; the lower surface is white with dark rootlike filaments that attach the lichen to its substrate.
USE: In the Arctic, this lichen was boiled with wool to produce a reddish brown dye.

FAMILY CLADONIACEAE
GENUS *CLADONIA*
Reindeer Lichen
Cladonia rangiferina
Cladonia stellaris

ALSO: Caribou Moss, Nikaat, Echte Rentierflechte, Lichen des rennes, Grå reinlav, Кладония оленья.
RANGE: Circumpolar, on soil and rocks on the tundra and forest-tundra.
ID: H 4–8 in (10–20 cm). Forms pale gray to pale yellowish green, thick, foam-like cushions. An inner cartilaginous layer (the *stereome*) supports finely branched, hollow stalks (*podetia*).

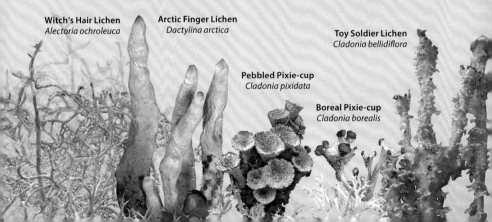

Witch's Hair Lichen
Alectoria ochroleuca

Arctic Finger Lichen
Dactylina arctica

Toy Soldier Lichen
Cladonia bellidiflora

Pebbled Pixie-cup
Cladonia pixidata

Boreal Pixie-cup
Cladonia borealis

USE: Reindeer lichens have many uses. They are the main winter browse for many wild arctic animals, and the Sami of Lapland and Nenets of Siberia feed Gray-Green Reindeer Lichen, *C. rangiferina*, to their herds. Star-tipped Reindeer Lichen, *C. stellaris*, is used ornamentally in wreaths, floral decorations, and trees for toy railroads. The European pharmaceutical industry extracts usnic acid from these lichens for use in anti-bacterial ointments.

Native Alaskans use partially digested lichens found in caribou stomachs to make a dish called "stomach ice cream." The lichen is removed from the stomach, mixed with raw mashed fish eggs, and then frozen. It may sound like a culinary disaster, but it's a favorite treat for the locals.

Lichens also have been used to make alcohol. As early as the mid-1700s, the monks at Ussolka Monastery in Siberia used lichens in place of hops to brew beer, and in the early 19th century the Frenchman Roy de Tonnerre developed a process to turn lichens into alcohol.

In 1867, after an abnormally cold, wet summer in Sweden, harvests failed and no potatoes or grain were available for making vodka. However, Sten Stenberg, professor of chemistry in Stockholm, discovered a way to brew vodka from lichens. He boiled clean, dry lichens with sulfuric or nitric acid for 4–5 hours, which turned most of the lichen bulk into glucose. He neutralized the acid broth with chalk, added a large helping of baker's yeast, distilled the mix, and bottled the brew. Stenberg established a large distillery, and by 1871 more than 250,000 lb (115,000 kg) of reindeer lichens had been brewed into 1500 gallons (5500 liters) of spirits. The industry was short-lived, however. By 1884, Swedish distilleries had exhausted the local lichen supply, and with improved grain harvests, brewers and consumers lost interest.

Pixie-cup Lichen
Cladonia pixidata
Cladonia borealis
RANGE: Near circumpolar, on soil or rocks in full sun.
ID: H 3 in (8 cm). Grayish green, with red or brown goblet-shaped "pixie-cups" (*apothecia*) borne at the tops of distinct stalks.

Toy Soldier Lichen
Cladonia bellidiflora
Cladonia cristatella
RANGE: Near circumpolar, on rotting wood, moss, or soil.
ID: H 3–4 in (8 cm). Yellow green to grayish green. Blunt stalk tip is crowned by a red apothecia.

GENUS *DACTYLINA*
Arctic Finger Lichen
Dactylina arctica
ALSO: Dead Man's Fingers.
RANGE: Near circumpolar, on mossy tundra in the arctic and alpine zones, especially around snowbeds that persist into spring.
ID: H 3–4 in (8–10 cm). Resembles ghostly human digits reaching out of the ground. Hollow stalk is pale greenish yellow tinged with brown. Brown, disc-shaped apothecia at the tips of side branches.

FAMILY ICMADOPHILACEAE
GENUS *THAMNOLIA*
White Worm Lichen
Thamnolia vermicularis
RANGE: Near circumpolar, on the tundra on gravelly soil and amid mosses.
ID: H 3 in (7 cm). Tufted, pure white, worm-like, with pointed, hollow stalks.
USE: The American Golden Plover, *Pluvialis dominica*, nests in patches of worm lichen, which provide camouflage for the eggs.

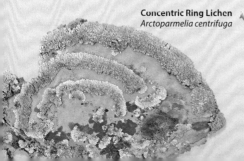

Concentric Ring Lichen
Arctoparmelia centrifuga

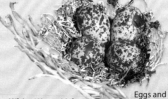

White Worm Lichen
Thamnolia vermicularis

Eggs and nest of the American Golden Plover

GENUS *ALECTORIA*
Witch's Hair Lichen
Alectoria ochroleuca
RANGE: Near circumpolar, on soil in the arctic and alpine zones.
ID: H 3–4 in (8–10 cm). Shrubby to pendent, pale greenish yellow lichens, with wiry, "bad hair day" branches.
USE: When beet sugar was scarce in Russia in the 1930s, this lichen was used to make molasses and syrup substitutes. The Inuit of Baffin Is, Canada, and Greenland use *Alectoria* as animal feed, and the North Slope Inuit of Alaska use the lichens as tinder. Witch's hair lichens are a favorite food of young caribou, and Inuit children sometimes use them to lure fawns in for taming.

CRUSTOSE LICHENS
The thallus of these lichens forms a crust so closely attached to the substratum that it is impossible to remove the lichen. The thallus can be colored white, gray, yellow, or orange, and can be smooth, cracked, or divided into tiny angular patches called *areoles*. Some crustose lichens have lobed edges and superficially resemble foliose lichens.

FAMILY RHIZOCARPACEAE
GENUS *RHIZOCARPON*
Yellow Map Lichen
Rhizocarpon geographicum
ALSO: Landkartenflechte, Lichen géographique, Kartlav, Ризокарпон.
RANGE: Circumpolar, on acidic rock such as granite or quartzite.
ID: Prostrate. Surface appears as a mosaic of flat, round to angular, yellow and black thallus patches, interspersed with black apothecia.
USE: Used to date glacial retreat due to its slow growth rate of 0.02 in (0.5 mm) per year.

FOLIOSE LICHENS
Foliose lichens typically have a prostrate, leaf-like thallus with distinct upper and lower surfaces. The thallus of many species is attached to a substrate by root-like threads called *rhizinae*. The entire lichen often forms a rosette, with the actively growing lobes at the margins.

FAMILY TELOSCHISTACEAE
GENUS *XANTHORIA*
Elegant Sunburst or Jewel Lichen
Xanthoria elegans
ALSO: Zierliche Gelbflechte, Ксантория.
RANGE: Circumpolar, on calcareous rocks such as limestone.
ID: Prostrate. Forms reddish orange rosettes and patches that are most strongly pigmented where fully exposed to the sun. This foliose, almost crustose, lichen is so firmly attached to the substrate that it cannot be removed without breaking it apart.
USE: Because it thrives on rocks fertilized with bird and mammal droppings, Inuit hunters use this lichen to locate prey.

FAMILY UMBILICARIACEAE
GENUS *UMBILICARIA*
Rock Tripe
Umbilicaria spp.
RANGE: Circumpolar, on siliceous rocks such as granite.
ID: Prostrate, to 1 in (2 cm) high. Dark brown to gray, dull or shiny, foliose lichens.
USE: European explorers and native people of the Arctic scraped these lichens off the rocks and ate them in times of need. Rock tripe were boiled in several changes of water to remove some of the bitter lichen compounds. *Umbilicaria* species are also used to produce a purple fermentation dye.

Yellow Map Lichen
Rhizocarpon geographicum

U. phaea

U. aprina

Rock Tripe
Umbilicaria spp.

Elegant Sunburst or Jewel Lichen
Xanthoria elegans

MOSSES

Mosses (division Bryophyta) are small, soft, non-vascular plants that require moisture to survive due to the thinness of their tissues, the lack of a waxy cuticle to prevent water loss, and the need for water to complete fertilization. Found chiefly in areas of dampness and low light, mosses are common in wooded areas, at edges of streams, and in bogs. A few are drought tolerant and occur on trunks of trees, in forest canopies, and on dry rock surfaces. Mosses do not produce flowers or seeds, but reproduce through spores held in beak-like capsules borne aloft on thin stalks.

Sphagnopsida: Sphagnum or Peat Mosses

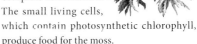

The class Sphagnopsida and order Sphagnales contains only the genus *Sphagnum*. There are about 150–350 sphagnum moss species, most of which occur in the N Hemisphere. The northernmost sphagnums are found in the Svalbard Archipelago, arctic Norway, at 81°N latitude.

Sphagnum and the peat that forms from it dominate wet tundra, muskeg, and the upper layer of bogs. Sphagnum does not decay readily in wet conditions because of the phenolic compounds embedded in its cell walls.

Sphagnum mosses have a distinctive spongy texture, are very light when dry, and are capable of holding 16–26 times as much water as their dry weight—the reason gardeners use it as a soil amendment. The water-holding capacity is due to translucent, non-living cells in the leaves that retain moisture for the moss so it can complete fertilization. The small living cells, which contain photosynthetic chlorophyll, produce food for the moss.

Sphagnum moss has a characteristic growth form, with the young leaves closely crowded at the top of a stem that becomes nearly defoliated toward its base. The sexual organs appear late in autumn or early spring. The branches of the *antheridium*, the male sex organ, are often conspicuously colored in bright red or yellow. The *spore capsules* are relatively short-stalked and nearly globular, opening by a lid at the top to disperse the spores. Sphagnum species also reproduce by fragmentation.

Arctic Peat Moss (*Sphagnum arcticum*) in a bed of reindeer lichens (*Cladonia rangiferina*), Churchill, Canada

Bryopsida: Higher Mosses

Bryopsida constitutes the largest class of mosses, containing 95 percent of all moss species. The class comprises 11–16 orders, 90–100 families, and about 11,500 species.

The most important characteristic of the Bryopsida is the architecture of the *peristome*, a ring of teeth encircling the spore capsule's mouth. All Bryopsida have what is called an *arthrodontous peristome*—a peristome in which the teeth are separated at the tip but joined at the base where they attach to the mouth opening. The teeth are exposed when the spore capsule's lid, or *operculum*, falls off so that the ripe spores can be released.

A good idea of the general structure of the higher mosses may be had from a study of almost any common species. One of the most conspicuous as well as widespread forms in the Arctic is the vividly colored Red Moss, *Bryum cryophyllum*. It grows in dense patches on the ground in damp crevices between rocks and boulders.

The plant has a short, thick stem, with oblong and pointed leaves. The base of the stem is attached to the ground by numerous fine brown root hairs. A careful examination of the lower stem will reveal a number of fine green filaments growing along the base. The mass of thread-like filaments (*protonemata*) typically looks like a thin mat of green felt. Tiny moss plants sprout up here and there from the mat and eventually a new clump of moss forms.

If the moss is fruiting, a close inspection with a hand lens should reveal the miniscule *spore capsules*, each borne on a long stalk that is more or less twisted and sensitive to changes in atmospheric moisture. The young spore capsules are covered by a pointed membranous cap that falls off when the spores are ripe and ready to be released.

Red Moss spore capsules

Red Moss (*Bryum cryophyllum*), Ellesmere Is, Canada

FERNS AND FERN ALLIES

The division Pteridophyta includes ferns, horsetails, clubmosses, and spikemosses. Unlike mosses, pteridophytes are vascular plants that contain xylem and phloem—tissues that transport water and nutrients throughout the plant. These plants reproduce asexually through spores.

Lycopodiales: Clubmosses

Lycopsids, or clubmosses, are structurally similar to the earliest vascular plants, having moss-like form, scale-like leaves, and *sporangia*—the receptacles in which asexual spores form. The sporangia are aggregated into a terminal cone-like structure called a *strobilus*.

FAMILY LYCOPODIACEAE
Stiff Clubmoss
Lycopodium annotinum

ALSO: Bristly Clubmoss, Stiff Groundpine, Sprossende Bärlapp, Lycopode innovant, Stri kråkefot, Плаун годичный, Siqpiijautit.

RANGE: Circumpolar, on dry heath, in damp coniferous forests, and in open grassy or rocky sites, from sea level to 6100 ft (0–1850 m).

ID: H 2–4 in (5–10 cm). Creeping forked stems, to 3 ft (1 m) long. Ascending clusters of long, curved branches increase in length and fork with age. Firm, stiff leaves, distinctly toothed, somewhat thin. Sporangia are borne in solitary strobili, sessile at the end of fertile branches.

USE: Lycopodium, a powder made of dried clubmoss spores, was used in Victorian plays as flash powder to produce flames that burned rapidly and brightly but with little heat.

FAMILY HUPERZIACEAE
Fir Clubmoss
Huperzia selago

ALSO: Northern Firmoss, Tannenbärlapp, Lycopode sélagine, Polarlusegress, Siqpiijautit, *H. arctica*. CN "fir" refers to the superficial resemblance to foliage of *Abies* firs.

RANGE: Circumpolar, on arctic and alpine tundra in wet, peaty soil.

ID: H 1–6 in (2.5–15 cm). Forms isolated tufts. Upright or ascending, stiff, greenish yellow stems. Leaves entire or with very tiny teeth; pointed leaf tip. Sporangia form between the leaves.

Selaginellales: Spikemosses

Spikemosses have scale-like leaves that have a minute flap, or *ligule*, at each leaf base. These delicate pteridophytes form the base of moist arctic and subarctic herb mats.

FAMILY SELAGINELLACEAE
Club Spikemoss
Selaginella selaginoides

ALSO: Northern Spikemoss, Prickly Mountain-moss, Dornige Moosfarn, Sélaginelle fausse-sélagine, Dvergjamne.

RANGE: Circumpolar, on mossy streambanks, lakeshores, wet talus slopes, and bogs from 2000 to 9500 ft (600–2900 m).

ID: H 1–4 in (2.5–10 cm). Forms loose or dense mats on rock or soil. Thread-like, creeping, branched stems at ground level; upright stems are stout and unbranched. Sporangia form in the axils of the tiny, lanceolate leaves.

SIMILAR SPECIES: SIBERIAN SPIKEMOSS (*not illus.*), *Selaginella sibirica*, ne Siberia to n Alaska (paler green on map).

Equisetales: Horsetails, Scouring-Rushes

Equisetales is an order of pteridophytes with only one living genus, *Equisetum*, which includes the horsetails and scouring-rushes. These plants were once much more extensive and diverse. They dominated the understory of the late Paleozoic forests and reached their maximum diversity in the early Carboniferous, about 350 million years ago. The extinct species *Calamites* closely resembled the living horsetails, except that it grew to 50 ft (15 m) high.

These spore-bearing plants have conspicuously jointed stems. Cone-like *strobili* containing the spores are borne at the tip of the stem. The stems of scouring-rushes are unbranched, while the horsetails have whorls of branches that can be mistaken for leaves. The true leaves are reduced to thin, fused *scales* that encircle each stem node.

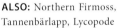

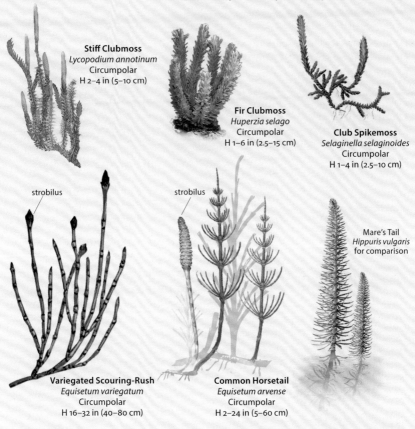

Stiff Clubmoss
Lycopodium annotinum
Circumpolar
H 2–4 in (5–10 cm)

Fir Clubmoss
Huperzia selago
Circumpolar
H 1–6 in (2.5–15 cm)

Club Spikemoss
Selaginella selaginoides
Circumpolar
H 1–4 in (2.5–10 cm)

strobilus

strobilus

Mare's Tail
Hippuris vulgaris
for comparison

Variegated Scouring-Rush
Equisetum variegatum
Circumpolar
H 16–32 in (40–80 cm)

Common Horsetail
Equisetum arvense
Circumpolar
H 2–24 in (5–60 cm)

FAMILY EQUISETACEAE
Common Horsetail
Equisetum arvense

ALSO: Giant Field Horsetail, Acker-Schachtelhalm, Prêle des champs, Åkersnelle, Хвощ полевой. SN means "field horsetail."

RANGE: Circumpolar. Grows on tundra, riverbanks, fields, marshes, and roadsides from sea level to 10,500 ft (0–3200 m).

ID: H 2–24 in (5–60 cm). Aerial, erect, hollow, jointed stems. Tall, bushy sterile stems resemble an inverted horse's tail. Fertile stems are shorter, with sporangia borne in terminal strobili. The tooth-like leaves lack chlorophyll; only the stem is photosynthetic. Can be mistaken for Mare's Tail, *Hippuris vulgaris* (see p. 512).

USE: Horsetails are rich in silicon, potassium, and calcium. Horsetail has been used medicinally to strengthen bones and counter gastroenteritis.

Variegated Scouring-Rush
Equisetum variegatum

ALSO: Bunter Schachtelhalm, Prêle panachée, Beitieski, Fjellsnelle, Хвощ пёстрый.

RANGE: Circumpolar. Grows in woodland, tundra, alpine scree slopes, lakeshores, and riverbanks from the High Arctic, south to Mongolia, Japan, and n US.

ID: H 16–32 in (40–80 cm). Rush-like, prostrate to erect stems, dark blue green, slender, rough to the touch, and usually unbranched. Sheath covering the stem nodes is marked with a black band. Stem is tipped with a small strobilus, usually green with a black tip.

USE: The abrasive silicates that coat the stems of scouring-rushes were used to polish pewter and scour tin. Hurdy-gurdy players used the silicate to dress their instruments' rosin wheels and also to remove rosin buildup from the drone strings.

Polypodiales: True Ferns

The order Polypodiales encompasses more than 80 percent of today's fern species. Polypod ferns are found in many parts of the world, including tropical, semi-tropical and temperate areas. Recent fossil evidence shows that some ferns now restricted to the tropics were present in the Arctic about 50 million years ago—a time when the arctic region was much warmer than it is today. In 2004, scientists from the University of Rhode Island drilled into the Lomonosov Ridge (*see p. 19*), a former continental fragment that presently lies more than 3000 ft (915 m) below the surface of the Arctic Ocean. Cores retrieved from the ridge contained reproductive spores of *Azolla*, a genus of now-subtropical aquatic ferns.

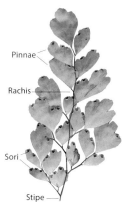

Pinnae

Rachis

Sori

Stipe

- True ferns have roots, stems, and leaves, like other vascular plants.
- A fern root is called a *rhizome*. It may creep along or under the ground, climb up other plants, or may grow erect into a trunk.
- A fern leaf is called a *frond,* which consists of a stalk, or *stipe*, and a broad green blade, or *lamina*.
- The midrib of the stalk is called the *rachis*. It may differ markedly from the stipe in both color and covering of hairs and scales.
- The blade may be undivided (simple), or divided into leaflets called *pinnae*; these may be arranged in opposite pairs or alternately along the midrib. The blade is termed *pinnate* if the leaflets themselves are undivided. It is termed *bipinnate* if the leaflets are divided into smaller secondary pinnae. If divided into yet smaller pinnae, the blade is termed *tripinnate*.
- Reproductive *spores* are produced in *sori*, which are clusters of receptacles, or *sporangia*, located on the underside of the vegetative fronds. Fern spores are usually partially enclosed by a small shield or hood called an *indusium*.

FAMILY DRYOPTERIDACEAE
WOOD FERNS

The fronds of wood ferns contain round sori on the underside of all of the pinnae. (This feature separates wood ferns from other spore-bearing ferns that produce spores only on specialized leaves.) Many of the sori have shield-shaped, or peltate, indusia. Most have prominent scales on the frond stipes. Many have stout, creeping rhizomes. Because of the short, dry arctic summers, severe winters, and limited soil cover, arctic wood ferns generally grow to only 8–10 in (20–25 cm) high.

GENUS *DRYOPTERIS*
Fragrant Shield Fern

Dryopteris fragrans
ALSO: Fragrant Buckler Fern, Duftender Wurmfarn, Dryoptère fragrante, Dufttelg, Щитовник пахучий.
RANGE: Near circumpolar (absent w Eurasia), on limestone cliffs and talus in the arctic and alpine zones, to 5900 ft (1800 m).
ID: H 2–10 in (6–25 cm), rarely 16 in (40 cm). Coarse, densely tufted fern, with nearly erect or erect stems. Fronds leathery, aromatic-glandular, rust-colored on the underside; dark green above, with green color persisting for several seasons. Rootstock is covered with shriveled curled old fronds that have a spicy fragrance.

**Fragrant
Shield Fern**
Dryopteris fragrans
Near circumpolar
H 2–10 in (6–25 cm)

GENUS *CYSTOPTERIS*
Fragile Bladderfern
Cystopteris fragilis

ALSO: Brittle Bladderfern, Fragile Fern, Zerbrechlicher Blasenfarn, Cystoptère fragile, Skjørlok, Пузырник ломкий. SN means "breakable bladder-fern," referring to the plant's brittle stipe and to the indusium's bladder-like shape.
RANGE: Circumpolar, in moist, shady sites such as rock crevices, damp slopes, and gravel scree in arctic and alpine zones, to 14,750 ft (4500 m).
ID: H 6–8 in (15–20 cm); rarely to 16 in (40 cm). Delicate fern with bright green, lanceolate, finely dissected fronds. Each blade is divided into many pairs of pinnae, each of which is in turn subdivided into lobed segments. Shiny, brittle stipes. Round, spiny sori with hooded, bladder-like indusia.

Fragile
Bladderfern
Cystopteris fragilis
Circumpolar
H 6–8 in (15–20 cm)

GENUS *WOODSIA*
Alpine Woodsia
Woodsia alpina

ALSO: Alpine Cliff Fern, Northern Woodsia, Alpenwinterfarn, Fjellodnebregne. SN means "Woods's alpine fern," referring to English botanist Joseph Woods (1776–1864).
RANGE: N Amer, Greenland, Iceland, nw Eurasia, in rock crevices, cliff ledges, and rocky slopes in the arctic and alpine zones, to 4900 ft (1500 m).
ID: H 4–6 in (10–15 cm). Bright green, narrowly lanceolate fronds, with 8–15 pairs of pinnae having saw-toothed or crenate margins; lower blade surface smooth or very sparsely haired. Stipe sparsely covered with pale russet or dark purple hairs. Indusium of narrow, hair-like segments.

Alpine
Woodsia
Woodsia alpina
N Amer–nw Eurasia
H 4–6 in (10–15 cm)

Smooth Cliff Fern
Woodsia glabella

ALSO: Dverglodnebregne, Woodsie glabre. SN means "Woods's fern with smooth fronds."
RANGE: Near circumpolar, in rock crevices, limestone cliff ledges, and talus slopes in arctic and alpine zones, to 4900 ft (1500 m).
ID: H 2–8 in (5–20 cm). Small, delicate fern. Forms small tufts, with slender rootstocks and completely smooth, yellowish green fronds. Green or straw-colored stipe. Round sori on the veins on the leaf underside.

Smooth
Cliff Fern
Woodsia glabella
Near circumpolar
H 2–8 in (5–20 cm)

Rusty Woodsia
Woodsia ilvensis

ALSO: Rusty Cliff Fern, Woodsie de l'île d'Elbe, Lodnebregne. CN refers to the rust-colored chaff on the frond's underside. SN means "Woods's fern of Elba."
RANGE: Near circumpolar, on dry sites, usually on Precambrian or acidic rocks and gravel, in arctic and alpine zones, to 4900 ft (1500 m).
ID: H 4–8 in (10–20 cm). Forms dense, firm, asymmetrical tufts, with persisting stipe bases. Young fronds have white hairs on leaf underside. Fronds curl up and turn rusty with age, but may turn green again after a rain. Hairy, scaly stipe is rust-colored at top, blackish at frond base.

Rusty
Woodsia
Woodsia ilvensis
Near circumpolar
H 4–8 in (10–20 cm)

SPERMATOPHYTA: SEED PLANTS

The division Spermatophyta encompasses the gymnosperms and angiosperms — vascular plants that reproduce through seeds. Each seed contains an embryo, or dormant plant, that germinates under favorable conditions.

GYMNOSPERMS: CONIFERS, CYCADS, AND GINKOS

These woody plants, commonly referred to as gymnosperms, have needle-like (*linear*) or scale-like (*imbricated*) leaves and bear naked seeds in reproductive structures called *cones*. Arctic representatives of the division Pinophyta, or Coniferae, are limited to the conifers.

Pinales: Pines and Allies

These hardy trees can be found growing to the boreal treeline—a wavering, shifting boundary at the southern fringes of the tundra. They have many adaptations to the harsh winter conditions of their Arctic environment. Many seasonally alter their biochemistry and harden off in fall, making them more resistant to freezing. The trees are often dwarfed in form, allowing them to shelter under the snow and avoid desiccating winds. The spire-like shape and downward-drooping limbs of tall specimens help them shed snow that might other break their branches.

FAMILY PINACEAE
PINES, SPRUCES, AND LARCHES

Trees in this family may be deciduous or evergreen. The leaves are resinous, linear, spirally arranged, and borne on subopposite or whorled branches. The Pinaceae are mostly monoecious, having both the male and female reproductive organs on the same tree. Male cones are small and fall soon after shedding their pollen to the wind. Female cones are persistent, large, and woody, with numerous spirally arranged scales, each of which bears 2 winged seeds.

GENUS *PINUS*: Pines have evergreen, linear needles in bundles of 2–6. The pendent cones mature in 2 seasons.

Siberian Dwarf Pine

Pinus pumila

ALSO: Japanese Stone Pine, Pin nain de Sibérie, Zwerg-Kiefer, Sibirsk dvergfuru, Кедровый стланик. SN means "dwarf pine."
RANGE: E Eurasia, from the Yenisei Rvr in Siberia east to Kamchatka, Kurils, and Sakhalin, and south to Manchuria, Korea, Mongolia, and China. Occurs mostly in pure stands between 3300 and 7550 ft (1000–2300 m), or sometimes mixed with alders or willows in lowland areas.
ID: H 3–10 ft (1–3 m), rarely 16 ft (5 m) at maturity. Evergreen shrub, spreading to 10 ft (3 m) wide. LVS: Grayish green, linear, 1.75–2.25 in (4–6 cm) long, in bundles of 5. CONES: Erect, conical-ovoid, 1–2 in (2.5–5 cm) long, maturing to pale purple or reddish brown. FR: Dark brown, edible pine nuts.

Scots Pine

Pinus sylvestris

ALSO: Waldkiefer, Pin sylvestre, Furu, Сосна обыкновенная. SN means "forest pine." National tree of Scotland. Lifespan is 150–300 years; the oldest recorded specimen, in Sweden, is about 700 years old.
RANGE: UK and w Eurasia, in a variety of habitats to 8200 ft (2600 m). Introduced to N Amer around 1600.
ID: H 30–80 ft (10–25 m), exceptionally to 145 ft (45 m). Evergreen. Tall, unbranched trunk topped by a rounded or flattened mass of foliage. BARK: Thick, scaly, dark grayish brown on lower trunk; thin, flaky, amber-colored on upper trunk and branches. Pale brown bark on new growth, with a spirally arranged scale-like pattern. LVS: Linear, to 2 in (5 cm) long, glaucous blue green, darker green in winter, in bundles of 2, with a persistent gray basal sheath. FEMALE CONES: Tiny, globose, red to pale brown in the first year; pointed, ovoid-conic, green to yellowish brown, to 3 in (8 cm) long when mature. MALE CONES: Yellow to pink, to about 0.5 in (1 cm) long.

GENUS *PICEA*: This genus contains the spruces, which have evergreen, squared or flat, stiff needles borne singly on peg-like projections. The pendent, papery cones mature in 1 season.

Black Spruce

Picea mariana

ALSO: Swamp Spruce, Bog Spruce, Schwarz-Fichte, Épinette noire, Svartgran, Ель чёрная. SN means "Mary's pine," possibly alluding to the bluish needles, a color associated with the Virgin Mary.

RANGE: N Amer, from w Alaska to n Labrador south into the n US, in muskegs, bogs, and peat mires, to 5000 ft (1500 m). Associates with *Picea glauca*, *Larix laricina*, and *Populus balsamifera* in the forest-tundra.

ID: H 15–65 ft (5–20 m); occurs in krummholz (dwarf) form in extreme environments near the treeline. Evergreen. Broadly conic to spired shape; northernmost trees often have a club-like top and nearly naked middle branches. BARK: Grayish brown to dark gray, broken into closely packed scales. Branchlets hirsute. LVS: Bluish green above, bluish white below, linear, plump, stiff, bluntly pointed, 4-sided, to 1 in (2.5 cm) long. CONES: Persistent, egg-shaped, pendent, dark purple, ripening to purplish brown, 0.5–1.5 in (1.5–4 cm) long.

White Spruce

Picea glauca

ALSO: Cat or Skunk Spruce, Weiß-Fichte, Épinette blanche, Kvitgran, Ялина канадська. SN means "spruce with a whitish bloom." State tree of South Dakota (US).

RANGE: N Amer, from Alaska east to Newfoundland, south to the n US, to 5000 ft (1520 m). Dominant tree in inland spruce-birch forests.

ID: H 30–80 ft (10–25 m); smaller at the treeline. Evergreen. Club-like crown and weathered branches midway up trunk. BARK: Pale grayish brown, thick, broken, plate-like scales. Branchlets smooth. LVS: Bluish green with white bands on both sides; linear, stiff, pointed, 4-sided, standing out in all directions, 0.5–1 in (1–2.5 cm) long.

Crushed needles have a pungent odor. CONES: Slender, elongated, cylindrical, 1–2.5 in (2.5–6.5 cm) long, nearly sessile with branch; light green, becoming reddish at maturity.

USE: Native Americans used powdered spruce wood in lieu of talcum powder for babies. Yellow dye was made from the wood. Roots were used for cordage and in basketry, bark for roofing and flooring. Wood was used to make canoe frames and paddles. Leading pulp producer of Canada. Used for reforestation and ornamental plantings.

GENUS *LARIX*: This genus contains the larches, which have deciduous, linear, flat needles borne in tufts. The upright cones mature in a single season and may persist for several years.

Tamarack

Larix laricina

ALSO: American Eastern Larch, Ostamerikanische Lärche, Mélèze laricin, Amerikansk lerk, Лиственница американская. SN means "larch larch." CN is an Algonquian word meaning "wood used for snowshoes." Territorial tree of Canada's NWT.

RANGE: N Amer, from c Alaska to Newfoundland, south to the ne US, in swamps and peat bogs.

ID: H 15–33 ft (5–10 m). Deciduous. Horizontal branches and thin crown. BARK: Scaly, reddish brown. LVS: Bluish green, linear, flattened, soft, to 1.5 in (3.5 cm) long, in dense bundles of 10–20 on short spur branches. Leaves turn yellow in autumn. CONES: Egg-shaped, brown, to 0.75 in (2 cm) long. Male cones yellow, drooping; female cones red, upright.

USE: Native Americans used the roots to stitch birch bark canoes together and the hard, durable wood to make snowshoes. Rapidly growing conifer, but not used for reforestation because larvae of Larch Sawfly, *Pristiphora erichsonii*, are serious pests that completely denude trees.

Dahurian Larch

Larix gmelinii

ALSO: Dahurische Lärche, Mélèze de Dahurie, Dahurialerk, Лист-венница

Гмелина, *Larix cajanderi, L. dahurica.* SN means "Gmelin's larch," honoring German botanist, geographer, and explorer of Siberia, Johann Georg Gmelin (1709–1755). Most cold-hardy tree, tolerating temperatures of –94°F (–70°C). Oldest known living tree is about 544 years old. **RANGE:** NE Asia, from the Taimyr Penin east to Kamchatka, Kurils, and Sakhalin, and south to China, Korea, and Mongolia, on rocky slopes, in peat bogs, swamps, lowland plains, and river basins, 1000–9200 ft (300–2800 m) elevation. Northernmost tree.

ID: H 33–100 ft (10–30 m); often dwarfed in polar or alpine climates. Deciduous. Variable shape; may show a broad conical crown, or a deformed crown and twisted trunk, or have a skeletal form in extreme conditions. BARK: Smooth, reddish brown on young trees; dark gray, scaly, and longitudinally fissured with age. LVS: Linear, flattened, to 1.25 in (3 cm) long, bright green in summer, yellow in autumn. CONES: Persistent, erect, ovoid, to 1 in (2.5 cm) long; 15–25 reflexed, velvety scales are green (rarely purple) when young, brown when mature.

USE: Timber is used for construction, poles, vehicles, bridges, and wood fiber. Wood is a source of resin, and bark yields tannins. Cultivated for afforestation and ornamental use.

Siberian Larch
Larix sibirica

ALSO: Russian Larch, Sibirische Lärche, Mélèze de Sibérie, Sibirlerk, Лиственница. SN means "larch of Siberia." Can live up to 100 years.

RANGE: C Siberia, from the Yenisei Rvr basin south to n China and n Mongolia, in alpine and foothill forests between 1650 and 11,500 ft (500–3500 m) elevation.

ID: H 65–130 ft (20–40 m). Deciduous. Large, pyramidal shape, with a conical to irregular crown; spreading, irregularly arranged, horizontal branches; and straight, tapering trunk, to 32 in (80 cm) diameter. BARK: Dark gray to dark brown, rough, longitudinally fissured on trunk. Bark on branchlets yellowish gray and densely haired. LVS: Linear, flattened, slender, flexible and soft to touch, spirally arranged, to 1.75 in (4 cm) long; light green in spring, dark green in summer, turning bright yellow before they drop in fall. FEMALE CONES: Persistent. Ovoid, to 2 in (5 cm) long, reddish brown, borne upright on the branch. Scales ovate, rusty brown, with a hairy lower surface. Light gray seeds.

USE: Because of its resistance to rot, the wood is used for posts, poles, railroad ties, mine props, and flooring in track cycling arenas.

FAMILY CUPRESSACEAE
CYPRESSES, CEDARS, AND JUNIPERS

GENUS *JUNIPERUS*
Dwarf Juniper
Juniperus communis nana

ALSO: Siberian or Mountain Juniper, Zwergwachholder, Einer, Genévrier commun, Kakillarnaq. SN means "dwarf common juniper."

RANGE: Circumboreal, in forests and on rocky tundra, to 5575 ft (1700 m).

ID: H 3–13 ft (1–4 m). Evergreen. Typically occurs in the Arctic in its dwarf form as a prostrate shrub, with multiple stems and spreading or ascending branches. BARK: Dark reddish brown, fibrous, exfoliating in thin, papery strips. LVS: Linear, to 0.5 in (1 cm) long, in whorls of 3; green or sometimes appearing silver, with a single white band on the inner surface; leaves are hard and sharp, making them prickly to the touch. This is the only N Amer juniper having linear, rather than imbricated leaves. MALE CONES: Tiny, yellow; fall in Mar–Apr after releasing pollen. FEMALE CONES: Mature over two seasons. Berry-like, spherical, to 0.25 in (0.65 cm) across; green when new, ripening in 18 months to purplish black with a blue waxy coating; cones usually have 3 fused scales, each containing a single seed.

USE: Since the early 17th century, juniper berries have been used to produce the volatile oil that is a prime ingredient in gin. Hungary is now the main producer of the oil. Juniper berries are also a key ingredient in *Sahti*, the traditional Finnish farmhouse ale, and *Borovička*, the tasty Slovak national alcoholic beverage.

Siberian Dwarf Pine
Pinus pumila
E Eurasia
H 3–10 ft (1–3 m)
Lvs 1.75–2.25 in (4–6 cm)

Scots Pine
Pinus sylvestris
UK, w Eurasia
Introduced into N Amer
H 30–80 ft (10–25 m)
Lvs 2 in (5 cm)

Mature cones

New cone

Dahurian Larch
Larix gmelinii
NE Asia
H 33–100 ft (10–30 m)
Lvs 1.25 in (3 cm)

Dwarf Juniper
Juniperus communis nana
Circumboreal
H 3–13 ft (1–4 m)
Lvs 0.5 in (1 cm)

Fall color

Larvae of the Larch Sawfly feed on Tamarack, often completely defoliating it.

Fall color

Tamarack
Larix laricina
N Amer
H 15–33 ft (5–10 m)
Lvs 1.5 in (3.5 cm)

Siberian Larch
Larix sibirica
C Siberia
H 65–130 ft (20–40 m)
Lvs 1.75 in (4 cm)

Fall color

Club-like top

Black Spruce
Picea mariana
N Amer
H 15–65 ft (5–20 m)
Lvs 1 in (2.5 cm)

White Spruce
Picea glauca
N Amer
H 30–80 ft (10–25 m)
Lvs 0.5–1 in (1–2.5 cm)

ANGIOSPERMS: FLOWERING PLANTS

The division Magnoliophyta, or Anthophyta, encompasses the vast world of the flowering plants, or *angiosperms*. These plants can be classed as either *monocotyledons*, which sprout with a single leaf attached to the seedling, or *dicotyledons*, which sprout with two leaves attached to the seedling. Both of these groups share certain common characteristics.

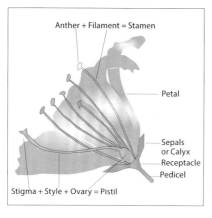

- All angiosperms are able to produce flowers, which are the plants' reproductive organs.
- The female reproductive parts are the *stigma*, *style*, and *ovary*, which make up the *carpel* or *pistil*.
- The male parts are the *anther* and *filament*, which make up the *stamen*.
- A *perfect* or *complete* flower has both the male and female parts in one flower.
- An *imperfect* or *incomplete* flower has only the male or the female parts, but not both.
- A *monoecious* ("one house") plant has both male and female flowers on the same plant.
- A *dioecious* ("two houses") plant has only the male or the female flowers on each plant.

DICOTYLEDONS

The seeds of dicotyledons, or dicots, sprout with a pair of leaves attached to the seedling. This large group of plants includes most of the world's trees, shrubs, vines, and herbaceous plants. Most dicots have stems with a central pith containing cylindrically arranged vascular tissues. The leaves of dicots are usually net-veined, with the central rib typically dividing or branching into a web-like pattern. Flower parts are most frequently in fours, fives, or multiples thereof.

Fagales: Beeches and Allies

This order contains catkin-bearing trees and shrubs. Catkins are long, slim, often without petals, and usually in unisexual flower clusters arranged closely along a central drooping stem.

FAMILY BETULACEAE
BIRCHES AND ALDERS

Birches and alders are deciduous trees. They drop their leaves in autumn and grow new ones in spring. The leaves have a toothed margin and small leaf-like appendages called *stipules* at the leafstalk base. Male and female catkins form on the same plant. The long male catkins drop off soon after shedding their pollen to the wind, while the shorter female catkins develop small, winged, seed-like nuts called *samaras* in fall. The soft female catkins of birches disintegrate to release the samaras. In contrast, the female catkins of alders develop into woody cones that shatter when they release the fruit.

GENUS *BETULA*
Arctic Dwarf Birch

Betula nana

ALSO: Swamp Birch, Zwerg-Birke, Bouleau nain, Dverg-bjørk, Берёза карликовая. SN means "dwarf birch." According to Pliny the Elder (AD 23–79), *Betula* derives from *betu,* the Gaulish word for bitumen—so named because the Gauls extracted tar from birches.

RANGE: Circumpolar, on tundra, rocky slopes, and in bogs; grows to 2000 ft (600 m) in e Canada, Greenland, and n Europe, to 7900 ft (2400 m) in Siberia and w N Amer.

ID: H 0.5–4 ft (0.2–1.2 m). Creeping to upright dwarf shrub. BARK: Smooth, gray to reddish brown. Young twigs of the amphi-Beringian subspecies *B. n. exilis* are smooth and covered with a thick resinous coating. Young twigs of the amphi-Atlantic subspecies *B. n. nana* are pubescent and lack a conspicuous resinous layer.

LVS: Dark green in summer; yellow, orange, or red in fall. Thick, 0.75 in (2 cm) across, slightly broader than long, with a crenate margin. FLS: Greenish brown catkins, to 0.5 in (1.5 cm) long.

Dwarf Resin Birch

Betula glandulosa
ALSO: Shrub Birch, American Dwarf Birch, Bog Birch, Ground Birch, Drüsige Birke, Bouleau glanduleux, Берёза Форреста; Avalaqiat, Napaaqturalaat are Inuit names meaning "little trees." SN means "glandular birch," referring to the resinous warts on the twigs and leaf veins.
RANGE: N Amer and Greenland, on tundra, forest-tundra, barrens, rocky slopes, muskegs, bogs, swamps, and along streams, to 11,150 ft (3400 m) elevation.
ID: H 1–10 ft (0.3–3 m). Dwarf, multi-stemmed, low, spreading shrub, or erect with a slender trunk. Forms dense thickets, often with spruce. BARK: Smooth, dark brown. Resinous glandular warts on young twigs and leaf veins. LVS: Green in summer; golden to red in fall. Thick, leathery, rounded to oval, 0.5–1 in (1–2.5 cm) long; bluntly toothed margin on blade sides. Unlike *B. nana*, leaf base is toothless. FLS: Erect, cylindrical catkins, to 1 in (2.5 cm) long; blooms in late spring. FR: Narrow-winged samara.
USE: This birch is a food source for moose, mountain goats, caribou, grizzly and black bears, beavers, snowshoe hares, meadow voles, northern red-backed voles, grouse, and ptarmigans. It even provides cover for grizzly bears, which are said to excavate their dens under resin birch cover more than any other arctic plant.

Downy Birch

Betula pubescens
ALSO: European White Birch, Woolly Birch, Arctic Downy Birch (*B. p. tortuosa*), Mountain Birch (*B. p. czerepanovii*), Moor-Birke, Bouleau pubescent, Vanlig bjørk, Берёза пушистая. SN means "downy birch," referring to the soft hairs on twigs and leaf underside.
RANGE: Greenland, Iceland, UK, and w Eurasia, in moist coniferous and mixed forests, spruce swamps, fens, ditches, lakeshores, damp fields, and roadsides, sea level to 1000 ft (0–305 m). Europe's northernmost broadleaf tree. Introduced into N Amer as an ornamental.
ID: H 6.5–20 ft (2–6 m) in the Arctic; 30–65 ft (10–20 m) in the south. Shrub with several main stems or a single-trunked tree; trunk slender and sinuous in *B. p. tortuosa*. BARK: Smooth, pale gray, finely marked with dark horizontal lenticels. Twigs grayish brown, smooth, finely pubescent. LVS: Green in summer; yellow to orange in fall; ovate, 1–2 in (2.5–5 cm) long, with finely serrated margin and pointed tip; often hairy on underside. FLS: Catkins to 1.75 in (4 cm) long, appear in early spring before the leaves.
USE: Birch wood is used for making furniture. Leaves are used for tea and in herbal medicines. The sap is drunk as a spring tonic.
RELATED SPECIES: SILVER or WEEPING BIRCH, *Betula pendula*. Grows to 80 ft (25 m) in Eurasian forests; 1000–7550 ft (300–2300 m). Distinguished from *B. pubescens* by drooping branch tips, dark and white fissured bark at the trunk base, doubly serrate to dissected leaf margins, and hairless young twigs covered with resinous warts. Sauna bath whisks (*vihtas*) are made from silver birch twigs. Finland's national tree.

Paper Birch

Betula papyrifera
ALSO: Canoe Birch, White Birch, Bouleau à papier, Papier-Birke, Papirbjørk, Берёза бумажная. SN means "paper-bearing birch," referring to the tree bark. State tree of New Hampshire (US).
RANGE: N Amer, subarctic to temperate zones, on rocky slopes of damp alpine forest and in swampy woodland, 1000–2950 ft (300–900 m).

ID: H 30–50 ft (9–15 m). Single or multiple trunks. Narrowly rounded crown at maturity. BARK: Smooth and reddish brown on young trees; becomes chalky white (cream to pale brown at the treeline) with age when it readily peels into paper-thin sheets. LVS: Dark green in summer;

yellow in fall. Ovate, rounded near the base, pointed at tip, 2–4 in (5–10 cm) long, with doubly serrate margin; smooth above, underside slightly hairy and covered with tiny resinous glands. FLS: Pendulous, cylindrical, spring-blooming catkins. Male catkins to 2 in (5 cm) long. Female catkins thick, short, greenish brown.
USE: Native Americans used the bark to make a waterproof skin for their birch-bark canoes. Soft, whitish wood is used to make baskets, clothespins, spools, ice cream sticks, toothpicks, and paper pulp. An important successional tree, growing readily after fires or logging.

GENUS *ALNUS*
Green Alder
Alnus viridis

ALSO: Sitka Alder (*A. v. sinuata*), Mountain Alder (*A. v. crispa*), Siberian Alder (*A. v. fruticosa*), Grün-Erle, Aulne vert, Grønnor, Ольха кустарниковая. SN means "green alder."
RANGE: Circumboreal, around streams, lakes, seacoasts, bogs, muskegs, sand flats, gravel slopes, and forest clearings, to 8200 ft (2500 m).
ID: H 3–10 ft (1–3 m). Spreading shrub in the Arctic; small tree elsewhere. BARK: Smooth, with small, scattered lenticels. LVS: Green, ovate-elliptical, to 3 in (8 cm) long, with serrate to coarsely doubly serrate margin, and acute to rounded apex. FLS: Male catkins pendulous, to 2.5 in (8 cm) long. Female catkins are enclosed in buds during winter and appear in late spring after the leaves emerge; the green catkins ripen into small, dry, woody, fruiting cones to 0.4 in (1 cm) long in late autumn.

Gray Alder
Alnus incana

ALSO: Thinleaf Alder (*A. i. tenuifolia*), Speckled Alder (*A. i. rugosa*), Kola Alder (*A. i. kolaensis*), Grau-Erle, Aulne blanc, Gråor, Вільха сіра. SN means "hoary white alder," referring to the whitish underside of the leaf.
RANGE: Near circumboreal (absent Greenland), on poor soils near streams, scree slopes, fields, and lakeshores, to 4900 ft (1500 m).

ID: H 16–65 ft (5–20 m). Tree or shrub. Shallow root system, with many root and stump suckers. BARK: Gray, reddish, or brown; smooth when the tree is young; bark forms irregular plates at maturity. LVS: Medium green above; whitish and often hairy on the underside; ovoid, 2–4 in (5–10 cm) long; leaf margins are wavy-lobed or saw-toothed. FLS: Catkins appear quite early in spring before the leaves emerge. Male catkins are pendulous, to 4 in (10 cm) long. Female catkins are cone-like, to 0.5 in (1.5 cm) long, and mature in fall. FR: Small brown samara, with a very narrow encircling wing.

Malpighiales: Willows and Allies
Malpighiales contains about 16,000 species of flowering plants, including plants as diverse as willows and violets. The order is named after Marcello Malpighi (1628–1694), an Italian physician and biologist regarded as the father of microscopical anatomy and histology, and author of *Anatomy of Plants*.

FAMILY SALICACEAE
WILLOWS, POPLARS, AND ASPENS
The leaves of willows, poplars, and aspens are deciduous, alternate, simple, and stipulate (bearing stipules). The flowers are catkins, with male and female catkins borne on separate plants. Individual flowers are supported by a scaly brown hairy *bract*, with 1–2 *nectar glands* at the base that attract pollinating insects. The fruit is a *capsule* containing many small seeds, each with a tuft of long silky down that aids in dispersal by wind and water.

GENUS *SALIX*: The genus *Salix* contains the willows, which occur as dwarf trees in the high latitudes and as mid-sized shrubs or trees farther south. The dwarf forms found in the Arctic are some of the world's smallest woody plants, with most measuring less than 10 in (25 cm) high. Their prostrate growth form capitalizes on warmer temperatures and lower wind velocities that occur near the ground surface. In addition, arctic willows have hairy or pubescent leaves, which trap warmth from the sun and insulate the leaves from extreme temperature oscillations.

Mature ♀ cones

♂ Catkins

♀ Cones in spring

Gray Alder
Alnus incana
Near circumboreal
H 16–65 ft (5–20 m)
Lvs 2–4 in (5–10 cm)

Underside of leaf is pale and downy

Downy Birch
Betula pubescens
Greenland, Iceland, UK, w Eurasia
H 6.5–65 ft (2–20 m)
Lvs 1–2 in (2.5–5 cm)

Sinuous growth form of the subspecies *B. p. tortuosa*

Mature ♀ cones

♂ Catkins

Green Alder
Alnus viridis
Circumboreal
H 3–10 ft (1–3 m)
Lvs 1–3 in (2.5–8 cm)

♀ Cones in spring

Conspicuous resinous glandular warts on the stem and leaf veins

Pendulous branches

Silver Birch
Betula pendula
Eurasia
H 25–80 ft (8–25 m)
Lvs 1–3 in (2.5–8 cm)

Dwarf Resin Birch
Betula glandulosa
N Amer, Greenland
H 1–10 ft (0.3–3 m)
Lvs 0.5–1 in (1–2.5 cm)

Fall color

Canadian Swallowtail, *Papilio canadensis*, laying eggs on Paper Birch

Spring foliage and catkins

Paper Birch
Betula papyrifera
N Amer
H 30–50 ft (9–15 m)
Lvs 2–4 in (5–10 cm)

Arctic Dwarf Birch
Betula nana
Circumpolar
H 0.5–4 ft (0.2–1.2 m)
Lvs 0.75 in (2 cm)

Many arctic mammals feed on the bark and twigs of willows, and willow buds are the main food source for ptarmigans. Willows are also food plants for larvae of many northern butterflies and moths. People of the north eat young willow leaves and buds, which contain vitamin C. The bark contains salicin, or salicylic acid, a bitter phenolic glucoside related to aspirin, which is used in home remedies to relieve pain.

Arctic Willow

Salix arctica

ALSO: Okpeet, Suputit, Uqaujait, Arktische Weide, Tundravier, Saule arctique, Ива арктическая. SN means "arctic willow." **RANGE:** Circumpolar, on moist tundra, alpine tundra, and rocky moorland. Found from the High Arctic south to the mountains of w N Amer and n China; occurs above 80°N latitude in the Canadian Arctic and at the northern limit of land in Greenland. **ID:** H 0.5–10 in (1–25 cm). Dwarf, creeping, decumbent shrub, with thick, smooth, trailing branches. Grows extremely slowly in the Arctic. Long-lived; one Greenland specimen is about 240 years old. LVS: Dull to shiny green in summer; yellow in fall. Elliptical or rounded, silky-haired below, to 2 in (5 cm) long, with entire margins. FLS: Male catkins yellow; female catkins red.

Polar Willow

Salix polaris

ALSO: Polar-Weide, Saule polaire, Polarvier, Ива полярная, *Salix pseudo-polaris*. SN means "Polaris willow," referring to the species' presence under the North Star. **RANGE:** Near circumpolar (absent e Canada, Greenland). Grows north to the limits of land on gravelly tundra and near alpine snowbeds, to 6550 ft (2000 m). **ID:** H 1–4 in (2.5–10 cm). Dwarf creeping shrub, with pale, thin, yellowish branches and roots that embed in soil, moss, or lichen layers. LVS: Dark green, rounded, to 0.5 in (1 cm) long, smooth on both sides, with entire margins. FLS: Small, few-flowered, reddish catkins.

Netleaf Willow

Salix reticulata

ALSO: Alagsaujut, Quarait, Netvein Willow, Netz-Weide, Saule réticulé, Rynkevier, Ива сетчатая. SN means "willow with small wrinkles," referring to the network of veins on the leaves. **RANGE:** Near circumpolar (absent Greenland), on moist tundra, gravel and sandy beaches, streambanks, edges of frost polygons, and near snowbeds, to about 6550 ft (2000 m). **ID:** H 1–6 in (3–15 cm). Dwarf, creeping shrub; forms extensive mats of trailing branches. LVS: Leathery, orbicular-elliptical, 0.5–2 in (1–5 cm) long; upper leaf surface glossy, dark green, wrinkled; undersurface strongly net-veined and hairy when young; leaf margins scalloped or entire and dotted with glandular hairs; petioles long. FLS: Reddish catkins to 2 in (5 cm) long appear with the leaves in spring.

Dwarf Willow

Salix herbacea

ALSO: Qupirrulik, Snowbed Willow, Kraut-Weide, Saule herbacé, Musøre, Ива травянистая. SN means "herb-like willow." **RANGE:** Amphi-Atlantic. Found in e Canada, Greenland, Iceland, Svalbard, n Europe, and nw Russia, in herb mats, usually near late snowbeds, to 4900 ft (1500 m). **ID:** H 0.5–2.25 in (1–6 cm). Dwarf, creeping shrub, with thin, slender branches often buried in moss. LVS: Smooth and dark green on both sides, rounded, to 1 in (2.5 cm) across, with finely scalloped margins and shallow, notched tip. FLS: Tiny catkins are hidden in the leaves.

Grayleaf Willow

Salix glauca

ALSO: Uquajaq, Glaucous Willow, White Willow, Arktische Grau-Weide, Saule gris, Saule à beaux fruits, Sølvvier, Ива сизая. SN means "willow with whitish bloom [on leaves]." **RANGE:** Circumpolar, in forest, tundra, and alpine habitats, on riverbanks, floodplains, old tundra terraces, and muskegs. Grows among

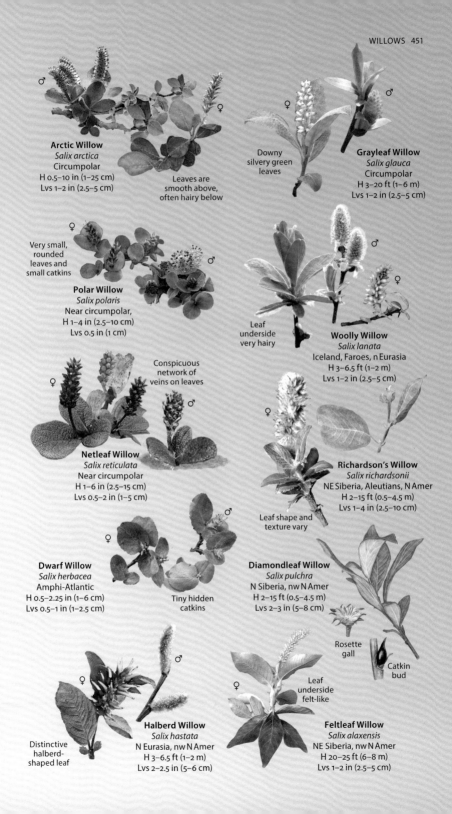

Arctic Willow
Salix arctica
Circumpolar
H 0.5–10 in (1–25 cm)
Lvs 1–2 in (2.5–5 cm)

Leaves are smooth above, often hairy below

Downy silvery green leaves

Grayleaf Willow
Salix glauca
Circumpolar
H 3–20 ft (1–6 m)
Lvs 1–2 in (2.5–5 cm)

Very small, rounded leaves and small catkins

Polar Willow
Salix polaris,
Near circumpolar,
H 1–4 in (2.5–10 cm)
Lvs 0.5 in (1 cm)

Leaf underside very hairy

Woolly Willow
Salix lanata
Iceland, Faroes, n Eurasia
H 3–6.5 ft (1–2 m)
Lvs 1–2 in (2.5–5 cm)

Conspicuous network of veins on leaves

Netleaf Willow
Salix reticulata
Near circumpolar
H 1–6 in (2.5–15 cm)
Lvs 0.5–2 in (1–5 cm)

Richardson's Willow
Salix richardsonii
NE Siberia, Aleutians, N Amer
H 2–15 ft (0.5–4.5 m)
Lvs 1–4 in (2.5–10 cm)

Leaf shape and texture vary

Dwarf Willow
Salix herbacea
Amphi-Atlantic
H 0.5–2.25 in (1–6 cm)
Lvs 0.5–1 in (1–2.5 cm)

Tiny hidden catkins

Diamondleaf Willow
Salix pulchra
N Siberia, nw N Amer
H 2–15 ft (0.5–4.5 m)
Lvs 2–3 in (5–8 cm)

Rosette gall

Catkin bud

Distinctive halberd-shaped leaf

Halberd Willow
Salix hastata
N Eurasia, nw N Amer
H 3–6.5 ft (1–2 m)
Lvs 2–2.5 in (5–6 cm)

Leaf underside felt-like

Feltleaf Willow
Salix alaxensis
NE Siberia, nw N Amer
H 20–25 ft (6–8 m)
Lvs 1–2 in (2.5–5 cm)

feltleaf and Richardson's willows and green alders in riparian habitats.

ID: H 3–20 ft (1–6 m). Semi-prostrate shrub on arctic tundra or a tall, spreading shrub on rich riparian sites to the south. BARK: Gray, smooth; often rough and furrowed with age. Twigs and winter buds are densely covered with gray, downy hairs. LVS: Grayish green, covered with grayish down on both sides. Elliptical, to 2 in (5 cm) long, mostly acute, with entire margin. FLS: Catkins, to 2 in (5 cm) long, persist over summer. FR: Tiny, twin-valved capsule releases small, lightweight seeds in fall. Seeds overwinter under the snow and germinate after the snow melts in spring.

Woolly Willow
Salix lanata
ALSO: Woll-Weide, Ullvier, Ива мохнатая. SN means "woolly willow," referring

to the densely pubescent leaves.
RANGE: Iceland, Faroes, and n Eurasia, on moist rock ledges, 1800–3300 ft (550–1000 m). Relic populations in Scotland.
ID: H 3–6.5 ft (1–2 m). Compact, rounded, bushy shrub. BARK: Young shoots covered with white woolly hairs. LVS: Silvery to dark dull green, oval, 1–2 in (2.5–5 cm) long, entire to wavy-margined, thickly coated with woolly hairs. FLS: Catkins golden to dull yellow, 2–3 in (5–8 cm) long.

Richardson's Willow
Salix richardsonii
ALSO: Uquajaq, Saule de Richardson. Considered a subspecies of *S. lanata*

by some. SN means "Richardson's willow," after Scottish naturalist Sir John Richardson (1787–1865) who traveled with John Franklin on the Coppermine Expedition of 1819–22 and wrote the sections on geology, botany, and ichthyology for the official account of the expedition.
RANGE: Amphi-Beringian (broadly); ne Siberia, Aleutians, and N Amer, on silty river beds, cliff ledges, and snowbeds, to 5600 ft (1700 m). Forms thickets with alders and birches in wet sites, and grows with spruces in lowland burned areas.

ID: H 2–15 ft (0.5–4.5 m). Erect, many-branched shrub. BARK: Young twigs densely haired; older branches smooth. LVS: Green in spring; reddish brown in fall. Thin or leathery; elliptical or obovate, 1–4 in (2.5–10 cm) long; underside with translucent to rust-colored down; upper surface smooth or pubescent. FLS: Catkins flower early in spring before leaf buds open.

Feltleaf Willow
Salix alaxensis
ALSO: Urpiq, Alaska Willow, Saule d'Alaska. SN means "Alaskan willow." CN refers

to the felt-like down on the leaf underside.
RANGE: Amphi-Beringian (broadly); grows from ne Siberia to nw N Amer, on riverbanks, wet sand, and scree slopes, to 5900 ft (1800 m).
ID: H 20–25 ft (6–8 m). Shrub or small tree. BARK: Young stems covered by white waxy powder or dense hairs. LVS: Glossy green above; felt-like white down on leaf underside; to 2 in (5 cm) long. A few reddish brown leaves persist to the next spring. FLS: Catkins. Buds develop in winter; bud scale detaches from the base, revealing the spring catkins, which are covered in silky down.
USE: The sweet inner bark, known as "fat of the willow," is a spring treat for northerners.

Diamondleaf Willow
Salix pulchra
ALSO: Tealeaf Willow, Sura. SN means "beautiful willow."
RANGE: Amphi-Beringian

(broadly); grows from n Siberia to nw N Amer, on riverbanks and in muskegs.
ID: H 2–15 ft (0.5–4.5 m). Low, erect or spreading, multi-stemmed shrub. BARK: Smooth or haired. Stipules persist on reddish twigs until following year. LVS: Grayish green in spring; reddish in fall. Elongated, diamond-shaped, 2–3 in (5–8 cm) long; margin entire. Shoots can be infected with small galls, each of which contains a pinkish larva that causes a chemical interaction and halts the lengthwise growth of the shoots. Leaves still develop but a brown rose-like gall forms at the tip of the affected branchlet. FLS: Spring catkins emerge from dark, shiny, long-beaked buds.

USE: Alaskan Inupiaq people pick and eat the young spring leaves (*sura*), which are rich in calcium and vitamins A and C. Dried leaves are used in tea and soup, or preserved in seal oil.

Halberd Willow

Salix hastata

ALSO: Spiessblättrige Weide, Saule hasté, Bleikvier, Ива копьевидная. SN means "willow with halberd-shaped leaves"; the shape of the leaf and stipules resembles the medieval halberd, a spear-and-battle-ax weapon still carried by the Vatican's Swiss Guards.

RANGE: Eurasia and nw N Amer, in woodland and coastal and alpine tundra; grows on streambanks, floodplains, moist slopes, and in alpine sedge bogs. A pioneer species on river sandbars and glacial moraines.

ID: H 3–6.5 ft (1–2 m). Slow-growing, thicket-forming, erect, multi-stemmed shrub, with dark purple brown shoots. LVS: Bright green, oval, entire to finely toothed, to 2.5 in (6 cm) long. FLS: Male catkins silvery gray, to 3 in (8 cm) long, appearing in early spring. Female catkins red, to 3.5 (9 cm) long, appearing May–Jun.

GENUS *POPULUS*: The genus *Populus* contains the poplars and aspens, which are the tallest deciduous trees found at the boreal treeline. In very cold locations they are usually stunted and dwarfed. Many species have leaves with long, laterally flattened petioles, which allow them to flutter in the breeze. The leaves are spirally arranged and are triangular to circular in shape. Leaf size is very variable, even on a single tree. The leaves turn bright gold to yellow before they fall in autumn. The foliage is bitter tasting, which makes it resistant to browsing by deer and other mammals.

Male and female catkins grow on separate plants. The drooping catkins appear in early spring before the leaves; they arise from buds formed in the axils of the previous year's leaves. Female catkins are wind-pollinated and lengthen considerably as they mature. The fruit is a green to reddish brown capsule with 2–4 valves that contain numerous, minute, light brown seeds.

Balsam Poplar

Populus balsamifera

ALSO: Tacamahac, Cotton-wood, Heartleaf Balsam Poplar, Balsam-Pappel, Peuplier baumier, Balsampoppel, Тополь бальзамический. SN means "poplar with a fragrant balsam," referring to the sticky, aromatic, yellow resin exuded from the spring buds, which protects the buds from insect damage.

RANGE: N Amer. Grows to 3950 ft (1200 m) in Alaska and Canada, at the timberline, in upland floodplains, river valleys, on gravel lakeshores, and along rivers that empty into the Beaufort Sea. Northernmost N Amer hardwood.

ID: H 50 ft (15 m); exceptionally to 100 ft (30 m). Broadly columnar tree. BARK: Gray and deeply furrowed. LVS: Glossy green and smooth above, pale and net-veined below. Broadly lanceolate to ovate, to 5 in (12.5 cm) long, with a pointed tip and finely toothed margin. FLS: Catkins appear in early spring. Female catkins can be 12 in (30 cm) long at maturity.

USE: A healing compound known as balm of Gilead is made from the tree's resinous gum; it is used to counteract eczema and dry skin.

Trembling Aspen

Populus tremula

ALSO: Eurasian or Swedish Aspen, Zitter-Pappel, Peuplier tremble, Osp, Осина. SN means "trembling poplar."

RANGE: Found from Iceland and the UK east across Eurasia to Kamchatka, in forest-tundra and on dry steppe.

ID: H 35–80 ft (10–25 m). Tree, with leaves that tremble in the wind. BARK: Young trees have smooth, pale greenish gray bark, with dark gray, diamond-shaped lenticels (raised stem pores). Bark becomes dark gray and fissured with age. LVS: Dark green in summer; yellow in fall. Leaves of mature trees are nearly round, to 3 in (8 cm) across, with a coarsely toothed margin; a laterally flattened petiole, to 3 in (8 cm) long, allows leaves to tremble even in slight breezes. Leaves of young trees are bronze in color, triangular to heart-shaped, 4–8 in (10–20 cm) long.

Balsam Poplar	**Trembling Aspen**	**Quaking Aspen**
Populus balsamifera	*Populus tremula*	*Populus tremuloides*
N Amer	Iceland, UK, Eurasia	N Amer
H 50–100 ft (15–30 m)	H 35–80 ft (10–25 m)	H 20–80 ft (6–25 m)
Lvs 4–5 in (10–13 cm)	Lvs 1–3 in (2.5–8 cm)	Lvs 1.5–3 in (4–8 cm)

FLS: Catkins appear in early spring before the new leaves open. Male catkins are green and brown, to 4 in (10 cm) long. Female catkins are green, to 2 in (5 cm) long. FR: Multiple capsules, each containing numerous tiny seeds embedded in downy fluff, which aid in wind dispersal when capsules split open. Also reproduces via root sprouts, which may sprout 130 ft (40 m) from the parent tree and form large clonal stands similar to the Quaking Aspen's.

Quaking Aspen

Populus tremuloides
ALSO: American Trembling Aspen, Mountain Aspen, Trembling Poplar, Quakies, Quakers, Popple, Amerikanische Zitterpappel, Peuplier faux-tremble, Тополь осинообразный. SN means "trembling poplar," referring to the movement of the leaves in the breeze.
RANGE: Grows to 12,000 ft (3700 m) elevation in forest-tundra and woodland from the southern slope of Alaska's Brooks Range and the boreal treeline south to Mexico.

Quaking Aspen and Black Spruce in autumn

ID: H 20–80 ft (6–25 m). A tree in favorable sites; dwarf shrub in marginal environments. BARK: Pale green to gray, smooth, with black horizontal scars where lower branches naturally self-prune. LVS: Glossy green above, dull beneath; brilliant golden to yellow in fall. Leaves of mature trees are 1.5–3 in (4–8 cm) across, nearly round, with small rounded teeth; laterally flattened petiole to 3 in (8 cm) long. Leaves of young trees triangular to heart-shaped, to 8 in (20 cm) long. FLS: Catkins, to 4 in (10 cm) long, appear in spring before the leaves. FR: Pendulous strings of capsules, with seeds embedded in cottony fluff.

Quaking aspens produce seeds but seldom grow from them. The seeds are viable for only a short time, as they lack a coating of stored nutrients. The trees propagate mainly via root sprouts, or layering, thus forming large clonal colonies composed of trees of the same sex.

A clonal colony can be considered a single organism since all the trees in the stand have identical genetic markers and share a single massive underground root system. This suggests that the world's oldest known living organism, dating to about 80,000 years of age, is the large clonal stand of male quaking aspens in the state of Utah (US). The colony is aptly named *Pando*, Latin for "I spread."

Pando may also vie for the title of world's heaviest organism, for if we consider the weight of the entire stand, the colony's more than 47,000 trunks and huge root systems collectively weigh 13.2 million lb (6 million kg).

Typical *Viola*
seed capsule

Aleutian Violet
Viola langsdorffii
Amphi-Beringian
H 3–6 in (8–15 cm)

Arctic Yellow Violet
Viola biflora
Eurasia, Aleutians, Alaska
H 3–6 in (8–15 cm)

Dwarf Marsh Violet
Viola epipsila
Near circumpolar
H 3–6 in (8–15 cm)

FAMILY VIOLACEAE
VIOLETS

These small perennial herbs have alternate, heart-shaped leaves with scalloped margins. The 5-parted, bisexual flowers bloom in May–Jul. Four side petals are fan-shaped and upswept, and a single broad lower petal points downward. The 3-valved fruit capsules split open in late summer to release the seeds.

GENUS *VIOLA*
Dwarf Marsh Violet

Viola epipsila
ALSO: Torfveilchen, Stor myrfiol, Фиалка лысая. SN means "partially naked violet," referring to the sparse foliage.
RANGE: Near circumpolar (absent ne Canada, Greenland), in wet meadows, streambanks, peat bogs, and boggy fir forests, to 5900 ft (1800 m).
ID: H 3–6 in (8–15 cm). LVS: Usually 2, in a basal rosette, widely cordate, stalked, stipulate, 1 stipule with a tapered tip; underside sparsely haired. FLS: Solitary, nodding. Petals 5, bluish violet; dark veins on lower petal.
USE: Flowers are edible; leaves are made into tea.

Arctic Yellow Violet

Viola biflora

ALSO: Yellow Wood Violet, Twoflower Violet, Pensée à deux fleurs, Zweiblütiges Veilchen, Fjellfiol, Фиалка остролистная.

SN means "2-flowered violet," referring to the blossoms, which occur in pairs.
RANGE: Eurasia, Aleutians, and Alaska; grows on damp soil in deciduous woodland, along streams and snowbeds, on scree slopes, and in alpine meadows, to 14,750 ft (4500 m).
ID: H 3–6 in (8–15 cm). LVS: Few, heart-shaped, about 1 in (2.5 cm) wide, with rounded-toothed margins; borne on long stems. Upper leaf surface smooth; downy below. FLS: About 0.5 in (1.5 cm) across, nodding; petals 5, yellow with brownish purple stripes. Green sepals form a short, flat spur at the back of the petals.

Aleutian Violet

Viola langsdorffii

ALSO: Alaskan Violet, Фиалка Лангсдорфа. SN means "Langsdorff's violet," after the Prussian naturalist Grigori Langsdorff (1774–1852), who explored Kamchatka, the Aleutians, Kodiak Is, and Sitka on the 1803–1805 Russian World Circumnavigation Expedition led by Ivan Fedorovich Kruzenshtern (1770–1846).
RANGE: Amphi-Beringian, in meadows, along streams, and near snowbeds. Grows from Kamchatka south to the Kurils and n Japan, and east across the Aleutians to s Alaska.
ID: H 3–6 in (8–15 cm). LVS: Heart-shaped, with scalloped leaf margins; basal leaves have petioles to 8 in (20 cm) long. FLS: Petals 5, lilac to violet, with dark veins; lower, lateral petals are white-bearded.

Ranunculales: Buttercups, Poppies, and Allies

Ranunculales is an order of mainly terrestrial, occasionally aquatic herbs that are widespread in temperate and boreal zones of the Nearctic and Palearctic. Well-known members of the order include the buttercups, poppies, delphiniums, clematis, and columbines.

FAMILY RANUNCULACEAE
BUTTERCUPS AND ALLIES

Most species in this family have 3- to 5-lobed leaves that are often cleft or toothed. Most of the arctic Ranunculaceae have 4- to 5-parted, bisexual flowers that are yellow in color, less commonly white, blue, or purple. Most have cup-shaped flowers, except those of *Delphinium* and *Aconitum*, which are asymmetrical. The flowers of *Ranunculus* and *Trollius* species have both petals and sepals. In *Caltha, Anemone,* and *Thalictrum*, only petal-like sepals are present.

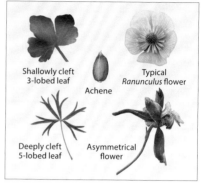

Shallowly cleft 3-lobed leaf

Achene

Typical *Ranunculus* flower

Deeply cleft 5-lobed leaf

Asymmetrical flower

The flower center of most species contains a domed seedhead, or *receptacle*, that supports the pistils and stamens and contains the developing nut-like seeds, or *achenes*, most of which are tipped with a small spine or hook called a *beak*.

The colorless, acrid sap of many Ranunculaceae species contains narcotic poisons and alkaloids. The sap of *Ranunculus, Anemone,* and *Caltha* contains protoanemonin, an acrid oil in fresh greens that can cause severe topical and gastrointestinal irritation or convulsions. *Trollius* contains a toxin that is poisonous to cattle and other livestock when eaten fresh. *Aconitum* and *Delphinium* contain poisonous alkaloids. A drink of *Aconitum* tea was the lethal drug used for applying the death penalty in ancient cultures.

GENUS *RANUNCULUS*: The genus name *Ranunculus*, transcribed here as "buttercup," actually means "little frog," referring to the amphibious nature of many of the species.

Lapland Buttercup
Ranunculus lapponicus
ALSO: Renoncule de Lapponie, Lappsoleie. SN means "Lapland buttercup."
RANGE: Circumpolar, in bogs, muskeg, spruce swamps, lakeshores, and along riverbanks on low-lying tundra and forests.
ID: H 4–8 in (10–20 cm). Elongated, creeping rhizome, with one erect stem per node, each with a single small flower. LVS: Basal, to 1.5 in (4 cm) long, long-stalked, reniform, deeply 3-lobed; margins crenate. FLS: Jun–Jul. Flowers to 0.5 in (1 cm) across. Petals 7+, yellow, linear; sepals 3, small. FR: Seedhead rounded; achene has a hooked tip. POISONOUS SAP.

Snow Buttercup
Ranunculus nivalis
ALSO: Iguttait, Renoncule des neiges, Snøsoleie, Fjäll-ranunkel, Лютик снежный. SN means "buttercup that grows near snow."
RANGE: Circumpolar, on tundra, wet meadows, in wet moss by brooks, and near snow patches, to 4250 ft (1300 m).
ID: H 3–8 in (8–20 cm). Tufted. Smooth or pubescent, erect stems. LVS: Basal, persistent or deciduous, smooth, reniform, cleft into 3–5 lobes, side segments again lobed or with toothed margins. Stem leaves 1–3, sessile. FLS: Jun-Aug. Yellow; 5 petals and 5 smaller sepals covered with brown downy hairs. FR: Seedhead cylindrical, smooth. Achene beak slender. POISONOUS SAP.
SIMILAR SPECIES: SULPHUR BUTTERCUP, *Ranunculus sulphureus*. Circumpolar, High Arctic; grows to 3600 ft (1100 m). Rounder, more shallowly lobed leaves than *R. nivalis*.

Pygmy Buttercup

Ranunculus pygmaeus
ALSO: Dwarf Buttercup, Zwerg-Hahnenfuß, Renoncule pygmée, Dvergsoleie. SN means "dwarf buttercup."

RANGE: Circumpolar, in wet meadows and around snow patches near scree slopes, animal burrows, and bird cliffs, to 6550 ft (2000 m).
ID: H 2–5 in (5–13 cm). Stems pubescent, ascending. LVS: Basal, persistent, reniform to elliptical, 3-lobed, with lateral segments again lobed; base truncate or nearly cordate. FLS: Jul–Sep. Yellow, solitary, with 5 tiny petals and 5 sparsely haired sepals. FR: Seedheads globose to cylindrical, smooth; beak of achenes straight or curved. POISONOUS SAP.

Birdfoot Buttercup

Ranunculus pedatifidus
ALSO: Northern Buttercup, Surefoot Buttercup. SN means "buttercup with a cleft foot," referring to the basal leaves.

RANGE: Near circumpolar (absent Europe), on gravelly or grassy slopes above 6250 ft (1900 m).
ID: H 4–12 in (10–30 cm). Erect, branching stems. LVS: Round or reniform, deeply cleft into 5–9 segments. Stem leaves sessile. FLS: Jun–Sep. To 1 in (2.5 cm) across. Petals 5, yellow; sepals 5, ovate, hairy. FR: Obovoid achene. POISONOUS SAP.

High Northern Buttercup

Ranunculus hyperboreus
ALSO: Floating Buttercup, Arctic Crowfoot, Renoncule hyperboréenne, Setersoleie, Iquttair. SN means "buttercup of the Far North."

RANGE: Circumpolar, in wet meadows, marshes, margins of streams and ponds, and on muddy seashores, to 11,000 ft (3350 m) elevation.
ID: H 2 in (5 cm). Semi-aquatic; floats in shallow water or creeps in mud. Can form large mats. LVS: Small, 3–5 lobed. FLS: Jun–Aug. To 0.5 in (1 cm) across. Petals 3–4, yellow. Sepals 3–4 small, smooth, with a short claw. FR: Achenes have a short hooked beak. POISONOUS SAP.

Pallas's Buttercup

Ranunculus pallasii
ALSO: Glossy Buttercup, Renoncule de Pallas, Glinsesoleie, Лютик Палласа,

Coptidium pallasii. SN means "Pallas's buttercup," honoring Peter Simon Pallas (1741–1811), German naturalist, botanist, and explorer of Russia.
RANGE: Near circumpolar (absent Greenland, w Europe), in estuaries and in shallow bogs and pools in muskeg and tundra, to 2300 ft (700 m).
ID: H 4–12 in (10–30 cm). Fleshy marsh plant, with decumbent or floating, freely branching stems, and creeping rhizomes. LVS: Basal, oblong, often 3-lobed. FLS: Jul–Aug. White or pink, strongly perfumed, to 1 in (2.5 cm) across; 6–11 petals; 6–10 spreading sepals. POISONOUS SAP.

Yellow Water Crowfoot

Ranunculus gmelinii
ALSO: Gmelin's Water Crowfoot, Renoncule de Gmelin, Лютик Гмелина.

SN means "Gmelin's buttercup," after Johann Georg Gmelin (1709–1755), German naturalist and author of *Flora Siberica.* CN refers to the deeply cleft "bird's foot" leaf.
RANGE: E Eurasia and N Amer, in shallow water or drying mud in wet meadows, swamps, marshes, ponds, and along shores of rivers, to 9200 ft (2800 m).
ID: Aquatic, with flowers rarely rising more than 3 in (7 cm) above the water surface. FLOATING LVS: Reniform, 3-lobed, with segments again dissected. SUBMERSED LVS: Dark green, finely dissected into thread-like segments, collapsing when withdrawn from water. FLS: May–Sep. Flowers small, solitary. Petals 5, yellow. Hairy, matted stems to 3 ft (1 m) long. POISONOUS SAP.

Creeping Spearwort

Ranunculus flammula
ALSO: Ufer-Hahnenfuß, Renoncule rampante, Grøftesoleie, Лютик жгучий, *R. f.*

var. *reptans.* SN means "little flame buttercup."
RANGE: Circumpolar, on muddy shores, riverbanks, and in water to depths of 6 ft (2 m).

ID: H 2–8 in (5–20 cm). Aquatic to semi-aquatic. Creeping. LVS: Basal, deltoid, with long petioles. Stem leaves reduced to bracts. FLS: Jun–Sep. Solitary, to 0.5 in (1.5 cm) across; borne on stem to 8 in (20 cm) long. Petals 5+, yellow; sepals 5, green, hairy. FR: Achenes smooth, compressed; beak strongly recurved. POISONOUS.

GENUS *ANEMONE*
Richardson's Anemone
Anemone richardsonii
ALSO: Yellow Anemone, Richardson-Anemone,

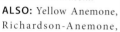

Anémone de Richardson. SN means "Richardson's anemone," honoring Arctic explorer Sir John Richardson (1787–1865), who found this plant on Melville Is, Canada.
RANGE: NE Asia, n N Amer, and w Greenland, in willow thickets, moist woods, meadows, slopes, and near snowbeds, to about 7200 ft (2200 m).
ID: H 2–8 in (5–20 cm). Slender, delicate, sparsely haired herb, with thread-like rhizomes. LVS: Basal, deeply 5-lobed, dark green. Whorls of 3-lobed, sessile stem leaves about halfway up the stem. FLS: May–Aug. Only arctic anemone with yellow flowers, to 1 in (2.5 cm) across; 5–6 bright yellow petaloid sepals. FR: Achene smooth, with a slender, hooked beak. POISONOUS.

Northern White Anemone
Anemone parviflora
ALSO: Windröschen, Ветреница мелкоцвет-ковая, Anémone à petites fleurs, Symrer. SN means "few-flowered anemone."

RANGE: Found on chalky soils near tundra ponds and snowbeds to 6500 ft (2000 m) in N Amer and isolated sites in Chukotka and Kamchatka.
ID: H 4–8 in (10–20 cm). LVS: Basal, dark green, glossy, with 3–5 bluntly toothed lobes. Whorl of sessile stem leaves below the flower. FLS: Single white flower, 1 in (2.5 cm) across; 4–7 petaloid sepals, white above, silky and tinged with lavender below. FR: Hairy achenes. POISONOUS.
RELATED SPECIES: NARCISSUS ANEMONE, *A. narcissiflora*, ne Asia–nw Alaska near snowbeds and on heaths; 5–9 white, pointed, petaloid sepals.

Pasque Flower
Anemone patens
ALSO: Cutleaf Anemone, Windflower, Prairie Crocus, Finger-Kuhschelle, Anémone

de prairie, Прострел раскрытый, *Pulsatilla patens*. CN *Pasque*, which means Easter, refers to the plant's flowering time. SN means "anemone of open [sites]." Floral emblem of Manitoba. State flower of South Dakota (US).
RANGE: Amphi-Beringian, in e Siberia, Alaska, and Yukon, on open plains and in foothills.
ID: H 3–8 in (8–20 cm). Tufted perennial. Stout, branched, vertical rootstock. LVS: Basal, long-petioled, in a rosette; leaflets pinnately divided into long, linear segments. Stem leaves sessile, deeply cleft into linear lobes. All leaves bear long, fine silky hairs. FLS: Early spring. Purple, pale blue, or white, solitary, 1–2 in (3–5 cm) across. Apetalous; 5–8 petaloid sepals. FR: Achenes in a spherical, plumed seedhead. POISONOUS.

GENUS *TROLLIUS*
Kamchatka Globeflower
Trollius riederianus
ALSO: Trollblumen, Troll, Smörskål, Купальница

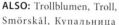

Ридера. SN means "rounded flower."
RANGE: Occurs in the Russian Far East, with isolated populations on Kiska Is (Aleutians) and Cold Bay (w Alaska), in lowland meadows that have heavy, wet, clay soils.
ID: H 3–8 in (8–20 cm). Tufted. Forms dense mounds, with thatch of leaf stems from previous years at plant base. LVS: Basal, bright green. Stem leaves 2–5, palmately divided into 5 toothed segments, with broad, clasping sheaths. FLS: Jun–Jul. Golden yellow, 1–2 in (3–6 cm) across; petals 5–7; sepals 5–7. POISONOUS SAP.

GENUS *CALTHA*
Marsh Marigold
Caltha palustris
ALSO: Cowslip, Kingcup, Sumpfdotterblume, Popu-

lage des marais, Bekkeblom, Калужница болотная. SN means "golden marsh flower."
RANGE: Near circumpolar (absent Greenland);

Sulphur Buttercup
Ranunculus sulphureus
Circumpolar
H 3–8 in (8–20 cm)
Poisonous

Snow Buttercup
Ranunculus nivalis
Circumpolar
H 3–8 in (8–20 cm)
Poisonous

*Anemone
narcissiflora*

Northern White Anemone
Anemone parviflora
N Amer, ne Asia
H 4–8 in (10–20 cm)
Poisonous

Richardson's Anemone
Anemone richardsonii
NE Asia, N Amer, Greenland
H 2–8 in (5–20 cm)
Poisonous

Pygmy Buttercup
Ranunculus pygmaeus
Circumpolar
H 2–5 in (5–13 cm)
Poisonous

Birdfoot Buttercup
Ranunculus pedatifidus
Near circumpolar
H 4–12 in (10–30 cm)
Poisonous

Kamchatka Globeflower
Trollius riederianus
NE Asia, Alaska
H 3–8 in (8–20 cm)
Poisonous

Lapland Buttercup
Ranunculus lapponicus
Circumpolar
H 4–8 in (10–20 cm)
Poisonous

Marsh Marigold
Caltha palustris
Near circumpolar
H 8–24 in (20–61 cm)
Poisonous

Creeping Spearwort
Ranunculus flammula
Circumpolar
H 2–8 in (5–20 cm)
Poisonous

Yellow Water Crowfoot
Ranunculus gmelinii
E Eurasia, N Amer
H 3 in (8 cm)
Poisonous

Pallas's Buttercup
Ranunculus pallasii
Near circumpolar
H 4–12 in (10–30 cm)
Poisonous

High Northern Buttercup
Ranunculus hyperboreus
Circumpolar
H 2 in (5 cm)
Poisonous

grows in Iceland, n Eurasia, and N Amer, in swamps, bogs, stream edges, and in shallow water. **ID:** H 8–24 in (20–61 cm). Semi-aquatic. LVS: Smooth, reniform or rounded, with crenate or entire margin, sometimes with sheath-like leaf base hugging stem. FLS: Apr–Jun. Yellow, 1–1.5 in (2.5–4 cm) across, 4–9 petaloid sepals. ALL PLANT PARTS ARE POISONOUS.

GENUS *THALICTRUM*
Alpine Meadow Rue
Thalictrum alpinum

ALSO: Alpen-Wiesenraute, Pigamon, Fjellfrøstjerne, Василистник альпийский. SN means "alpine medicinal plant"; named by the Greek physician Dioscorides (AD 40–90).

RANGE: Near circumpolar (absent nc Canada); grows to 6500 ft (2000 m) in alpine meadows on stony, south-facing hillsides.

ID: H 3–5 in (8–13 cm). LVS: Alternate, thin, and repeatedly divided in 3s; leaflets slender-stalked, round, with crenate margins. FLS: Jun–Jul. Small, grayish, apetalous, with numerous pendulous golden stamens. Grows in racemes.

GENUS *ACONITUM*
Larkspurleaf Monkshood
Aconitum delphinifolium

ALSO: Wolfbane, Devil's Helmet, Bluerocket, Eisenhut, Hjelmslekta, Аконит. CN *monkshood* refers to the hood-shaped sepal. SN means "poisonous delphinium-like leaves"; named by the Greek botanist Theophrastus (c. 371–287 BC).

RANGE: Amphi-Beringian; found from ne Siberia to w N Amer in meadows and on streambanks, to 5575 ft (1700 m).

ID: H 20–28 in (50–70 cm). Stem smooth, straight, thin. LVS: 5-lobed, divided again into many linear segments. FLS: Jun–Aug. Dark purple, rarely white, to 1 in (2 cm) across. Calyx hood (*galea*) covers the 2 upper petals, which have a hollow spur containing nectar; other petals small, scale-like. FR: Dry, single-chambered, many-seeded follicle bursts open along its ventral suture to release the seeds. POISONOUS ROOT.

GENUS *DELPHINIUM*
Northern Larkspur
Delphinium brachycentrum

ALSO: Rittersporne, Dauphinelle, Riddersporer, Живокость. CN refers to the spur's resemblance to a lark's hind claw. SN means "short-spurred dolphin's fin," alluding to the flower spur that somewhat resembles a dolphin's dorsal fin.

RANGE: Amphi-Beringian; found in disjunct sites in ne Asia and nw N Amer on tundra meadows and rocky slopes to 3950 ft (1200 m).

ID: H 12–24 in (30–60 cm). LVS: Rounded, cleft into 3 lobes almost to the center, then divided many times again. FLS: Jun–Jul. Blue to cream, asymmetrical, to 1 in (2.5 cm) long, borne in tall clusters on downy-haired stems. POISONOUS; all plant parts contain the alkaloid delphinine.

Glaucous Larkspur
Delphinium glaucum

ALSO: Mountain Larkspur, Hooker's Larkspur, Brown's Pale-flowered Larkspur, Duncecap Larkspur, Giant Larkspur, Tall Larkspur. SN means "dull blue-colored delphinium."

RANGE: Occurs in subarctic to cool temperate wet meadows and thickets of w N Amer.

ID: H 35–80 in (100–200 cm). Stems coarse, glabrous. LVS: Palmately lobed, with incised, toothed segments. FLS: Jun–Aug. Crowded racemes of violet purple, asymmetrical flowers, each with a long spur. Leaf-like lower bracts. ALL PLANT PARTS ARE POISONOUS.

FAMILY PAPAVERACEAE
POPPIES

These familiar herbaceous plants have ducts, or *laticifers,* that produce a milky white, yellow, or red latex sap, which can irritate the skin.

Leaves are lobed or much-divided, and lack stipules. The flowers are large, showy, perfect, 4-parted, terminal, and odorless. Poppy flowers follow the sun, and their petals are incurved to reflect the warm rays toward the reproductive parts. Insects often bask in this handy greenhouse and in turn pollinate the poppies. The fruit is a dry capsule, which splits open at maturity,

Arctic Poppy
Papaver radicatum
Circumpolar
H 5–10 in (12–25 cm)

Lapland Poppy
Papaver lapponicum
Circumpolar
H 8–10 in (20–25 cm)

Icelandic Poppy
Papaver nudicaule
Amphi-Beringian
H 8–24 in (20–60 cm)

Macoun's Poppy
Papaver macounii
Amphi-Beringian
H 10 in (25 cm)

Red Field Poppy
Papaver rhoeas
N Europe
H 10–35 in (25–90 cm)

Glaucous Larkspur
Delphinium glaucum
N Amer
H 35–80 in (100–200 cm)
Poisonous

Northern Larkspur
Delphinium brachycentrum
Amphi-Beringian
H 12–24 in (30–60 cm)
Poisonous

Alpine Meadow Rue
Thalictrum alpinum
Near circumpolar
H 3–5 in (8–13 cm)

Larkspurleaf Monkshood
Aconitum delphinifolium
Amphi-Beringian
H 20–28 in (50–70 cm)
Poisonous

Pasque Flower
Anemone patens
Amphi-Beringian
H 3–8 in (8–20 cm)
Poisonous

allowing the tiny seeds to escape through the capsule pores and be dispersed on the wind.

The most widespread poppies in the Arctic are *Papaver radicatum* and *P. lapponicum*. They were formerly considered conspecific. Both are variable in form, but Lapland poppies typically have taller, straighter flowering stems. The relationship of N Amer and Eurasian species is still debated. Nonetheless these plants, perhaps best identified simply as "arctic poppies," can be enjoyed for their ephemeral blossoms that enliven the barrenlands and polar desert throughout the summer months.

GENUS *PAPAVER*
Arctic Poppy
Papaver radicatum

ALSO: Arktischer Mohn, Pavot arctique, Melasól, Мак, Igutsat niqingit ("bumblebee food"). SN means "milky-sapped [poppy] with a large root."
RANGE: Circumpolar, to 7550 ft (2300 m) on barren, rocky tundra and clay soils in the High Arctic and on dry sandy soils, rocky tundra, and scree slopes in the subarctic.
ID: H 5–10 in (12–25 cm). LVS: Lanceolate, multi-lobed, 3–5 in (7–12 cm) long, with the petiole two-thirds the length of leaf; blade green on both surfaces. FLS: Jun–early Aug. Yellow or white, rarely tinged pink, to 2.5 in (6.5 cm) across. Flowering stems hirsute, erect or bowed and decumbent. FR: Seed capsules longer than broad.
SIMILAR SPECIES: MACOUN'S POPPY, *Papaver macounii*. H 10 in (25 cm); flowers yellow. Grows on rocky tundra to 6900 ft (2100 m) in the Russian Far East, Aleutians, Alaska, Yukon, and disjunct sites north to the Chukchi Sea.

Lapland Poppy
Papaver lapponicum

ALSO: Mohn, Pavot de Laponie, Kolavalmue, Мак лапландский, *Papaver radicatum lapponicum*. SN means "milky-sapped [poppy] of Lapland."
RANGE: Circumpolar; on dry tundra, sandy shorelines, and gravel on floodplain terraces to 3250 ft (1000 m).

ID: H 8–10 in (20–25 cm). Forms loose tufts or clumps. LVS: Green to grayish green; both surfaces densely haired. Lanceolate, multi-lobed, to 5 in (12 cm) long, with the petiole more than one-half the leaf length. FLS: Jun–Aug. To 1.5 in (3.5 cm) across, yellow, petal edges often tinged with pink. Flowering stems smooth or haired, erect, straight, usually longer than 8 in (20 cm), and generally taller than *Papaver radicatum*. FR: Seed capsules oblong, to 0.75 in (2 cm) long.

Icelandic Poppy
Papaver nudicaule

ALSO: Island-Mohn, Pavot d'Islande, Мак голостебельный. SN means "milky-sapped [poppy] with a naked stem."
RANGE: Amphi–Beringian; grows from Siberia to Alaska and Yukon on dry, exposed scree slopes and rocky wooded areas, between 1000 and 3250 ft (300–1000 m). Naturalized in Canada, sw Greenland, Iceland, and Europe.
ID: H 8–24 in (20–60 cm). Variable in form. LVS: Tufted, lobed, ovate to lanceolate, to 3 in (8 cm) long; blade covered with powdery bloom. FLS: Yellow or orange, rarely red, solitary, 4-petaled, to 2 in (6 cm) across. Buds ovoid, densely covered with brown hairs.
USE: Planted as an ornamental in temperate climates. Horticultural varieties are said to derive from wild species such as the Arctic Poppy, *P. radicatum*, and the Red Field Poppy, *P. rhoeas*, of n Europe.

Caryophyllales: Pinks and Allies
Caryophyllales (Greek for "pink stitchwort") includes a diverse assortment of flowering plants, many of which are succulents, having fleshy stems or leaves.

FAMILY CARYOPHYLLACEAE
PINKS
Arctic members of this large family include chickweeds (*Stellaria*), mouse-eared chickweeds, (*Cerastium*), sea-purslanes (*Honckenya*), pearlworts (*Sagina*), sandworts (*Minuartia*), campions (*Silene*) and bladder-campions (*Melandrium*). These plants have opposite, entire

leaves, and stems that are somewhat swollen at the nodes. Most arctic species form dense low tufts or cushions, which in the warmer months are covered with tiny flowers. The flowers are symmetrical, with or without petals, and 4- to 5-parted, or multiples thereof. Flowers of the various genera have distinctive shapes that are useful in identification.

CHICKWEEDS (*Stellaria* and *Cerastium*) have white, star-shaped flowers with 5 pointed or deeply cleft petals.

PEARLWORTS (*Sagina*) and sandworts (*Minuartia*) have small flowers with 5 rounded petals.

CAMPIONS (*Silene*) and bladder-campions (*Melandrium*) have a prominent tubular calyx and 5 pink, purple, or white petals.

GENUS *STELLARIA*
Chickweed

Stellaria spp.
ALSO: Starwort, Stitchwort, Star Chickweed, Stern-mieren, Stellaire, Звездчатка. SN means "star-like," referring to the flower. CN "chickweed" refers to *Stellaria media*, a weedy European species that chickens like to feed on; "stitchwort" refers to the plant's former use in a remedy for relieving "stitch" and other muscle pain.
RANGE: Circumpolar, in a wide variety of habitats, including tundra, shorelines, wet meadows, herb mats, rocky slopes, and barrens.
ID: H 6–8 in (15–20 cm). Perennial herb with creeping stems that have fine hairs in a line on one side of the stem. LVS: Sessile, opposite. FLS: White, star-shaped, to 0.25 in (1 cm) across, with 5 very deeply cleft, pointed petals. FR: Six-valved capsule. All arctic species reproduce through seeds and via axillary leaf buds, which persist through the winter and fall off the dried stems and root in spring. Two circumpolar species are distinctive enough to identify. SEASHORE CHICKWEED, *S. humifusa*, is a common seaside

species, with fleshy, matted, trailing stems and fleshy, wrinkled leaves that turn brown when dried. LONGSTALK CHICKWEED, *S. longipes*, typically has a solitary, white flower at the tip of a tall, erect stem.

GENUS *CERASTIUM*
Mouse-eared Chickweed

Cerastium spp.
ALSO: Hornkräuter, Céraiste, Arvsläktet, Ясколка. SN means "horned [capsule]."
RANGE: Circumpolar, in a

variety of habitats, including around bird cliffs and human habitation.
ID: H 6–8 in (15–20 cm). Tufted to matted herbs, with hairy or smooth stems. The stems of the amphi-Atlantic species, *C. alpinum* and *C. reglii*, feel clammy to the touch. Those of the amphi-Beringian species, *C. beeringianum*, feel dry. LVS: Small, oval to oblong, opposite. FLS: May–Aug. Petals 5, white, shallowly notched, "mouse-eared."

GENUS *MINUARTIA*
Boreal Sandwort

Minuartia rubella
ALSO: Reddish Sandwort, Boreal Stitchwort, Miere,

Minuartie rougeâtre, Минуарция красноватая. SN means "Minuart's reddish [sandwort]," after Spanish botanist Juan Minuart (1693–1768).
RANGE: Circumpolar, on tundra, heath, open woods, coastal barrens, rocky ridges, and gravelly slopes to 12,500 ft (3800 m).
ID: H 1–4 in (2.5–10 cm). Dwarf perennial. Forms tufts to 4 in (10 cm) across. LVS: Stiff, 3-veined, arranged in clusters that are evenly spaced on the reddish stems. FLS: May–Jul. Petals 5, white; flowers face upward at the end of stems.

GENUS *SAGINA*
Snow Pearlwort

Sagina nivalis
ALSO: Mastkraut, Sagine, Lindblom, Мшанка. SN means "snow pearlwort."
RANGE: Circumpolar. Occurs near snowbeds

and on wet sand or gravel, to 9200 ft (2800 m). ID: H 4–8 in (10–20 cm). Dwarf, cushion-forming herb. Many flowering stems, to 2 in (5 cm) long. LVS: Linear, in a basal rosette. FLS: Petals 4, white; sepals purple.

GENUS *HONCKENYA*
Sea-Purslane

Honckenya peploides
ALSO: Seabeach Sandwort, Seaside Sandplant, Sea Chickweed, Salzmiere, Pourpier de mer, Strandarve, Гонкения. SN means "Honckeny's spurge-like [plant]," honoring German botanist Gerhard Honckeny (1724–1805).
RANGE: Circumpolar, on sandy flats, dunes, and beaches above the high-tide line.
ID: H 4–8 in (10–20 cm). Prostrate to decumbent, with creeping, simple or branched, fleshy, edible stems. LVS: Small, succulent, elliptical to ovate, often with a pointed tip, arranged in boxy whorls along the stems. FLS: Jun–Jul. White to greenish yellow, strongly honey-scented, less than 0.5 in (1.5 cm) across, scattered in the axils.

GENUS *SILENE*
Moss-Campion

Silene acaulis
ALSO: Stengelloses Leim-kraut, Fjellsmelle, Silène acaule, Смолёвка бесстебельная, Airait, Anurisiutik. SN means "lacking an obvious stem."
RANGE: Near circumpolar (absent nc Siberia), on well-drained gravel barrens, cliffs, and rocky ledges to 13,775 ft (4200 m).
ID: H 4–8 in (10–20 cm). Dwarf perennial. Forms round or flat, firm, moss-like cushions to 24 in (60 cm) across. LVS: Linear, often edged with withered leaves from previous seasons. FLS: Petals 5, pink to lilac. Smooth, tubular calyx.

Arctic Campion

Silene involucrata
ALSO: Arctic Catchfly, Leimkräut, Silène involucré, Finnmarksjonsokblom, Смолёвка, Nakasuujait. SN means "[flower] surrounded by a ring of bracts."

RANGE: Circumpolar; widespread on tundra on stony, gravelly, sandy, or grassy sites, often near rodent burrows, to 6550 ft (2000 m).
ID: H 2–12 in (5–30 cm). LVS: Basal, densely tufted. FLS: Upright. Petals 5, milky white, occasionally pink. Calyx hairy, bell-shaped to ovoid.

GENUS *MELANDRIUM*
Purple Bladder-Campion

Melandrium apetalum
ALSO: Nodding Lychnis, Kronlose Nelke, Silène de l'Oural, *Silene uralensis*. SN means "dark without petals."
RANGE: Circumpolar; widespread on moist tundra, in damp or mossy meadows at edges of ponds and streams, on gravel barrens, and on rocky outcrops in mountains to 13,125 ft (4000 m).
ID: H 2–5 in (5–13 cm). Erect, slender, hairy, unbranched stems. LVS: Basal leaves linear, slightly hairy, to 1.5 in (4 cm) long; stem leaves small, few, opposite. FLS: Singular; nodding when young. Bladder-like calyx striped pink and purple; tiny purple petals. Translucent calyx acts as a greenhouse, concentrating heat and light on the reproductive organs.

FAMILY POLYGONACEAE
BUCKWHEATS, DOCKS, SORRELS

These plants have swollen stem joints. The leaves are alternate, simple, and a papery sheath encloses the base of the leaf stem. The small flowers are apetalous; the sepals are 3- to 6-parted and sometimes petaloid. Flowers are borne in spikes or racemes. Fruit is a 3-angled or lens-shaped nut called an *achene*.

GENUS *OXYRIA*
Mountain Sorrel

Oxyria digyna
ALSO: Wood Sorrel, Alpine Sorrel, Sweetleaf, Fjellsyre, Alpen-Säuerling, Кисличник двухстолбчатый, Qunullig, Heeknakotit. SN means "acidic [leaves] and 2 pistils." CN *sorrel* refers to the reddish brown color of the leaves and flowers.
RANGE: Circumpolar; widespread in cool, moist ravines where snowbeds persist into summer,

Snow Pearlwort
Sagina nivalis
Circumpolar
H 4–8 in (10–20 cm)

Mouse-eared Chickweed
Cerastium spp.
Circumpolar
H 6–8 in (15–20 cm)

Chickweed
Stellaria spp.
Circumpolar
H 6–8 in (15–20 cm)

Boreal Sandwort
Minuartia rubella
Circumpolar
H 1–4 in (2.5–10 cm)

Iceland Purslane
Koenigia islandica
Near circumpolar
H 2 in (5 cm)

Sea-Purslane
Honckenya peploides
Circumpolar
H 4–8 in (10–20 cm)

Roundleaf Sundew
Drosera rotundifolia
Circumpolar
H 2–10 in (5–25 cm)

Thrift
Armeria maritima
Circumpolar
H 2–12 in (5–30 cm)

Alpine Bistort
Bistorta vivipara
Circumpolar
H 6–12 in (15–30 cm)

Moss-Campion
Silene acaulis
Near circumpolar
H 4–8 in (10–20 cm)

Mountain Sorrel
Oxyria digyna
Circumpolar
H 1–12 in (2.5–30 cm)

Meadow Bistort
Polygonum bistorta
Eurasia, nw N Amer
H 20–36 in (50–90 cm)

Purple Bladder-Campion
Melandrium apetalum
Circumpolar
H 2–5 in (5–13 cm)

Arctic Campion
Silene involucrata
Circumpolar
H 2–12 in (5–30 cm)

Arctic Dock
Rumex arcticus
Amphi-Beringian
H 10–20 in (25–50 cm)

and especially in moist sites below bird cliffs and near human habitation.

ID: H 1–12 in (2.5–30 cm). LVS: Kidney-shaped, long-stemmed, somewhat succulent, fresh green to maroon. FLS: Small, reddish green or crimson, on slender pedicels; borne in racemes. FR: Lenticular, thin, flat achene, enclosed by a broad, translucent wing.

USE: The mildly acidic leaves and young stems are eaten raw in salads, preserved with seal oil, cooked as a green, or stewed with sugar. Due to a high vitamin C content and local abundance, sorrel is one of the most important edible plants for native people of the Arctic and also serves as a food source for caribou, muskoxen, geese, hares, and lemmings.

GENUS *RUMEX*
Arctic Dock
Rumex arcticus

ALSO: Ampfer, Oseille, Syrer, Щавель, Quagaq. SN means "arctic dock."

RANGE: Amphi-Beringian (broadly), on moist turf and in willow thickets by lakes and ponds.

ID: H 10–20 in (25–50 cm). LVS: Mostly basal, dark green, somewhat fleshy, oblong to narrowly lanceolate, 3–12 in (7–30 cm) long. FLS: Small, reddish, borne in spikes on ridged, erect, branching stems. In autumn, all plant parts turn red.

USE: Fresh green leaves are often cooked with water and sugar; they taste a little like spinach. Leaves can also be used to relieve nettle stings.

GENUS *BISTORTA*
Alpine Bistort
Bistorta vivipara

ALSO: Viviparous Knotweed, Knöllchen-Knöterich, Renouée vivipare, Harerug, Sapangaralannguat, Tursaq, *Polygonum viviparum*. SN means "twice twisted [root] plant produces bulblets."

RANGE: Circumpolar; widespread from the High Arctic south through the mountains of Eurasia and N Amer, in dry meadows and heaths, to 7200 ft (2200 m).

ID: H 6–12 in (15–30 cm). Short, thick, often contorted rhizome. LVS: Basal, slender, long-stemmed, oblong-lanceolate, dark green, somewhat shiny. Few short-petioled or sessile stem leaves. FLS: White or pink, 1–4 in (5–10 cm) long, in a terminal spike. FR: Rarely produces viable seeds. Instead the reddish bulblets on the lower portion grow into small plants that drop off and root; the bulblet plants take 3–4 years to reach maturity and flower.

USE: Spring rhizomes can be eaten raw; they taste like almonds. The starchy bulblets are a food source for ptarmigans and lemmings.

GENUS *POLYGONUM*
Meadow Bistort
Polygonum bistorta

ALSO: Pink Plumes, Dragonwort, Easter Giant, Patience Dock, Redlegs, Snakeweed, Sweet Dock, Ippik, *Persicaria bistorta*. SN means "many jointed [stems] and twisted [root]."

RANGE: Eurasia and nw N Amer, in alpine meadows and on tundra; grows in moist places with acidic or peaty soils, including wet meadows, grassy bogs, streambanks, ditches, shrub thickets, and damp forest edges and clearings.

ID: H 20–36 in (50–90 cm). Thick, knobby, S-shaped rhizome is black outside, red inside. LVS: Basal, long-petioled, lanceolate, square-based, green above, usually reddish below. Stem leaves few; no leaves on upper stem. FLS: May–Aug. Rose pink, in a club-like solitary spike, 2–4 in (5–10 cm) long. Becomes dormant in dry conditions, losing its foliage until enough moisture returns.

USE: Root and leaves are eaten raw or boiled.

GENUS *KOENIGIA*
Iceland Purslane
Koenigia islandica

ALSO: Koenigie d'islande, Кёнигия. SN means "König's Iceland purslane"; Linnaeus (1707–1778) named *Koenigia* after his pupil, the Baltic German botanist Johann Gerhard König (1728–1785).

RANGE: Near circumpolar. Isolated populations occur in the High Arctic, mountains of w China and in nw N Amer, Scotland, and s S Amer. Grows on stony slopes and mossy or sandy pond edge.

ID: H 2 in (5 cm). Dwarf annual. Red stems. LVS: Few, tiny, rounded, somewhat fleshy, reddish purple, sessile. FLS: Minute, apetalous; 3 greenish white sepals, with 3 red-anthered stamens, 3 yellow glands, and 2 styles; blossom encircled by a whorl of leaves.

FAMILY PLUMBAGINACEAE
LEADWORTS
GENUS *ARMERIA*
Thrift

Armeria maritima
ALSO: Sea Pink, Sea Cushion, Strand-Grasnelke, Armérie maritime, Strandnellik, Армерия. SN means "sea thrift." CN is thought to refer to the leaves, which are tightly packed together and conserve water in the salty air.

RANGE: Circumpolar, on gravelly tundra, floodplains, lakeshores, seacoasts, salt marshes and alpine meadows to 3900 ft (1200 m). Also occurs in S Amer. Distributed worldwide as a garden plant and cut flower.

ID: H 2–12 in (5–30 cm). Forms low, densely tufted clumps. LVS: Sage green, linear, fleshy, densely packed; leaves remain on plant after withering. FLS: Petals 5, rose pink. Long, funnel-shaped, dry, persistent calyx has pointed lobes. Borne in dense, hemispherical clusters at top of long stems.

FAMILY DROSERACEAE
SUNDEWS
Insects are attracted to the bright red color and glistening drops of sugary mucilage on the leaves of these carnivorous plants. Sundews use enzymes to dissolve insects that are stuck on the glandular leaf tentacles, and then extract nitrates and other nutrients from their bodies.

GENUS *DROSERA*
Roundleaf Sundew

Drosera rotundifolia
ALSO: Rundblättrige Sonnentau, Rundsoldogg, Drosera à feuilles rondes, Росянка круглолистная. SN means "dewy rounded leaves," referring to the foliage with its glistening glandular hairs.

RANGE: Circumpolar, in bogs, marshes, and in hollows of wet boulders.
ID: H 2–10 in (5–25 cm). LVS: Basal rosette of round leaves is densely covered with red, sticky tentacles. FLS: Petals 5, white or pink; flowers grow on one side of a slender stalk that rises from the leaf rosette center. In winter, buds form within tightly curled basal leaves, which protect the buds from freezing.

Brassicales: Mustards
A common characteristic of many Brassicales is the production of mustard oil (glucosinolate).

FAMILY BRASSICACEAE
MUSTARDS AND ALLIES
The distinguishing characteristic of this family is the 4 petals arranged in the shape of a cross, hence the old family name Cruciferae. The fruit is a seed pod called a *silique* or silicle, which is composed of 2 fused carpels that separate (dehisce) when ripe, leaving a persistent partition with seeds attached to the edges. The seedpod can be linear or rounded, smooth or covered with soft hairs. Juice from the plant's stem has a peppery, bitter, or acrid tang.

GENUS *COCHLEARIA*
Scurvygrass

Cochlearia officinalis
ALSO: Spoonwort, Echtes Löffelkraut, Cranson officinal, Skarfakál, Ложечница лекарственная, Qunguliit, Tipitsiarktut nunarait. SN means "[plant with] spoon-shaped leaves of use to man." CN refers to the leaves, which are high in vitamin C and therefore are a valuable anti-scorbutic.
RANGE: Circumpolar. Widespread on seacoasts, often near bird cliffs; found less frequently on inland tundra.
ID: H 2–12 in (5–30 cm). Erect (*C. o. groenlandica*) or sprawling (*C. o. arctica*) perennial. LVS: Fleshy,

long-petioled; heart-shaped, triangular, or kidney-shaped; in a basal rosette. Stems have a few arrow-shaped leaves. FLS: Petals 4, white or pink. Flowers borne in a terminal raceme. FR: Smooth, elliptical seedpod.

GENUS *CARDAMINE*
Cuckoo Flower
Cardamine pratensis

ALSO: Lady's Smock, Wiesen-Schaumkraut, Cardamine des prés, Engkarse, Polarkarse, Сердечник луговой, Turmaujuit, Niqingit. CN may refer to the plant's blooming in spring when the Common Cuckoo (*Cuculus canorus*) starts to call or to the extremely variable "crazy" or "cuckoo" shape of the basal leaves. SN means "cardamom-like meadow herb."
RANGE: Circumpolar. Grows along creeks, in swamps, damp thickets, woodlands, and fields to 1650 ft (500 m).
ID: H 6–20 in (15–50 cm). Slender, erect perennial. Unbranched, ascending stem from a short rootstock. LVS: Pinnately compound, to 5 in (12 cm) long. Leaflets on basal leaves large and elliptical; leaflets on upper stem linear. FLS: Apr–Jun. To 1 in (2.5 cm) across, showy, in a terminal spike. Petals 4, lavender to white, dark-veined. FR: Elongated, thin, linear seedpods, to 1.5 in (4 cm) long. Often reproduces by leaf buds.

Alpine Bittercress
Cardamine bellidifolia

ALSO: Høgfjellskarse, Cardamine à feuilles de pâquerette, Сердечник маргариколистный. SN means "cardamom-like herb with pretty leaves."
RANGE: Circumpolar. Grows in wet, mossy places by alpine brooks, in cold ravines, gravelly sites below melting snow, or on moss-covered rocks, to 6550 ft (2000 m).
ID: H 1–4 in (3–10 cm). Densely tufted dwarf perennial. Stems leafless. LVS: Oval, entire, slender-petioled, to 4 in (10 cm) long. FLS: In clusters of 2–5; petals 4, milky white; sepals 4, purple. FR: Linear, stiffly erect, short-stemmed seedpod, to 1 in (2.5 cm) long.

GENUS *PARRYA*
Arctic Wallflower
Parrya arctica

ALSO: SN means "Parry's arctic [flower]," honoring British Arctic explorer William Edward Parry (1790–1855), who collected this species on Melville Is, Canada, in 1820 while searching for the Northwest Passage.
RANGE: Canadian High Arctic and nw Greenland, on wet clay substrate, gravel barrens, wet meadows, hummocks, river terraces, slopes, and alpine ridges.
ID: H 2–4 in (5–10 cm), rarely to 8 in (20 cm) Tufted perennial. Thick, branching stems. LVS: Oblanceolate, acute, long-petioled, entire, to 1 in (3 cm) long. FLS: Jun–Aug. Large scentless flowers borne in clusters of 7–12. Petals 4, purple or creamy white. FR: Narrowly linear, straight, strongly keeled seedpods, to 1 in (2.5 cm) long.

Nakedstem Wallflower
Parrya nudicaulis

ALSO: SN means "Parry's naked stem [flower]."
RANGE: Found in Eurasia and nw N Amer, in river valleys, on tundra, sandy slopes, and alpine meadows, to 5900 ft (1800 m).
ID: H 8–12 in (20–30 cm); dwarf forms predominate in the High Arctic. Tufted perennial. Thick, branching stems. LVS: Long-petioled, 2–4 in (5–10 cm) long, narrowly oblanceolate, mostly smooth, somewhat fleshy, with entire or toothed margins. FLS: Jun–Aug. Showy, fragrant. Petals 4, prominently clawed, rose purple or white. FR: Linear, sinuate pods.

GENUS *ERYSIMUM*
Pallas's Wallflower
Erysimum pallasii

ALSO: Schöteriche, Vélar de Pallas, Желтушник, Nunaraapiit, Masu aigak. SN means "Pallas's helpful plant," referring to the edible root and plant's medicinal value, and honoring German naturalist Peter Simon Pallas (1741–1811).
RANGE: Found in the arctic zone in Siberia, N Amer, and Greenland, on tundra, stony or

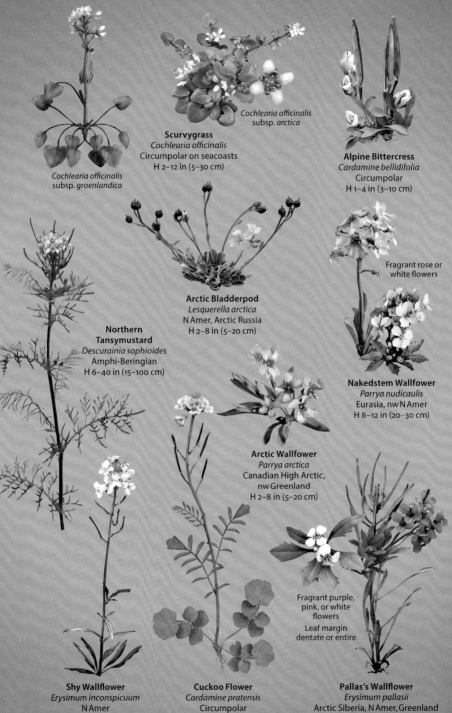

Cochlearia officinalis
subsp. *arctica*

Scurvygrass
Cochlearia officinalis
Circumpolar on seacoasts
H 2–12 in (5–30 cm)

Cochlearia officinalis
subsp. *groenlandica*

Alpine Bittercress
Cardamine bellidifolia
Circumpolar
H 1–4 in (3–10 cm)

Arctic Bladderpod
Lesquerella arctica
N Amer, Arctic Russia
H 2–8 in (5–20 cm)

Fragrant rose or
white flowers

**Northern
Tansymustard**
Descurainia sophioides
Amphi-Beringian
H 6–40 in (15–100 cm)

Nakedstem Wallfower
Parrya nudicaulis
Eurasia, nw N Amer
H 8–12 in (20–30 cm)

Arctic Wallfower
Parrya arctica
Canadian High Arctic,
nw Greenland
H 2–8 in (5–20 cm)

Fragrant purple,
pink, or white
flowers
Leaf margin
dentate or entire

Shy Wallflower
Erysimum inconspicuum
N Amer
H 12–32 in (30–80 cm)

Cuckoo Flower
Cardamine pratensis
Circumpolar
H 6–20 in (15–50 cm)

Pallas's Wallflower
Erysimum pallasii
Arctic Siberia, N Amer, Greenland
H 4–14 in (10–36 cm)

sandy substrates, clay banks, and sunny, grassy sites near animal burrows and human habitation, to 4265 ft (1300 m).
ID: H 4–14 in (10–36 cm). Biennial or short-lived perennial. Blooms in its second or third year, then dies. LVS: Linear-lanceolate, entire or dentate, to 3 in (7 cm) long, in a basal rosette; leaf underside has T-shaped hairs. FLS: Jun–Aug. Petals 4, white, rose, or purple. Showy, fragrant. Early blooming plants develop an elongated stem that holds the rounded raceme of flowers well above the leaves. Late blooms develop just above the basal leaves. FR: Linear, thin, somewhat curved pods.

Shy Wallflower

Erysimum inconspicuum
ALSO: Yellow Wallflower, Schöteriche, Vélar à petites fleurs. SN means "inconspicuous [small flowers]."
RANGE: Grows in n N Amer, in dry prairies and alpine woodland.
ID: H 12–32 in (30–80 cm). Short-lived, erect perennial, with unbranched, sparsely leaved stems. Blooms in the second year, then dies. LVS: Linear to oblong, mostly smooth, in a basal rosette. FLS: Small flowers, borne in a raceme. Petals 4, pale yellow. FR: Erect, long, thin, 4-angled seedpod.

GENUS *LESQUERELLA*
Arctic Bladderpod

Lesquerella arctica
ALSO: *Physaria arctica*. SN means "Lesquereux's arctic [bladderpod]," after Charles Léo Lesquereux (1805–1889), a Swiss bryologist and a pioneer of American paleobotany. His major work was a study of Carboniferous flora of Pennsylvania.
RANGE: Grows on cliffs and stony barrens in N Amer and isolated sites in arctic Russia.
ID: H 2–8 in (5–20 cm). Tufted. Erect or sprawling. LVS: In a basal rosette, silvery, covered with fine, star-shaped hairs. FLS: Borne on a long, stout stem in clusters of 2–8. Petals 4, pale yellow. FR: Small, round or pear-shaped seedpod, smooth or covered with small scales, borne at the top of a long fruiting stem.

GENUS *DESCURAINIA*
Northern Tansymustard

Descurainia sophioides
ALSO: Moutarde-tanaisie fausse-sagesse, Дескурайния гулявниковая. SN means "Descurain's flixweed-like tansymustard," honoring French botanist and pharmacist François Descurain (1658–1740).
RANGE: Amphi-Beringian; found on disturbed soils, wet meadows, slopes, ridges, gravel bars, and village refuse heaps.
ID: H 6–40 in (15–100 cm). Weedy biennial. Stems simple or branching, sparsely leaved. LVS: Feathery, bipinnate, greenish yellow. Leaves wither at the time of flowering. FLS: Small, borne in terminal racemes. Petals 4, yellow. FR: Many long, slender, slightly curved seedpods.

GENUS *DRABA*
DRABAS OR WHITLOWGRASSES

Draba derives from the Greek *drabe*, meaning "sharp, acrid, or burning," a reference to the peppery taste of the seeds and leaves. *Whitlowgrass* refers to the plant's use by herbalists to treat whitlow, a finger infection.

   In early summer these tufted perennial herbs bear yellow or white, 4-parted, cruciform flowers held in racemes at the top of erect, often hairy stems. The leaves, typically in basal rosettes, are fleshy, hairy, or smooth, with entire or dentate margins. The seedpods (*silicles*) persist for more than one season. Clues to draba identification include flower color (yellow or white); seedpod shape; leaf shape, color, and hairiness; presence or absence of stem leaves; and habitat and range.

Alpine Draba

Draba alpina
ALSO: Golden Draba, Alpine whitlowgrass, Drave alpine, Gulldraba, Крупка альпийская. SN means "mountain draba."
RANGE: Circumpolar, on tundra hummocks, along streams, on seepage slopes and other moist alpine sites.
ID: H 2–8 in (5–20 cm). Many erect, leafless stems. LVS: In a dense basal tuft; lanceolate, fleshy, to

0.75 in (2 cm) long, with a prominent midrib and long, stiff hairs on the margin. FLS: Borne in a corymb-like raceme of 4–10 blossoms. Petals 4, bright yellow, shallowly lobed; calyx green to purple, hairy. FR: Ovoid, flattened, purple or green seedpod, to 0.5 in (1 cm) long.

Golden Draba

Draba aurea
ALSO: Drave dorée. SN
means "golden draba."
RANGE: N Amer and Green-

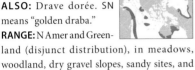

land (disjunct distribution), in meadows, woodland, dry gravel slopes, sandy sites, and around bird nesting colonies.
ID: H 4–8 in (10–20 cm). Tufted. LVS: Basal, petiolate or sessile, lanceolate, silvery green, with star-shaped hairs; margins dentate or entire. Stem leaves wedge-shaped, somewhat clasping, nearly vertical. FLS: Borne in racemes of 4–14 blossoms. Petals 4, yellow; calyx green, hairy. FR: Ovoid, flattened, often twisted, hairy pod.

Cushioned Whitlowgrass

Draba corymbosa
ALSO: Drave en corymbe,
Puterublom, *D. macrocarpa,*
D. bellii. SN means "draba
with flowers in a corymb."

RANGE: Circumpolar; found on wet gravel, sand, or clay, and on seepage slopes.
ID: H 2–4 in (5–10 cm). Forms compact cushions. LVS: Hairy, spatulate, with entire margins. FLS: Borne in a raceme of 4–10 blossoms. Petals 4, pale yellow, obovate, shallowly lobed; calyx green, hairy. FR: Yellow or purple, hairy, sessile, ovoid, flattened pod.

Snowbed Draba

Draba crassifolia
ALSO: Thickleaf Draba,
Drave à feuilles charnues,
Dvärgdraba. SN means

"thick-leaf draba," but leaves are fairly thin.
RANGE: Local in Chukotka, N Amer, Greenland, Norway, near snowbeds and partly drained areas.
ID: H 2–6 in (5–15 cm). Tufted. Stem erect, smooth or sparsely haired. LVS: Lanceolate, smooth, with

entire margins. FLS: Borne in racemes of 3–12 blossoms. Petals 4, yellow, fading to white; calyx green and purple, smooth. FR: Ovoid, flattened, smooth, purple or green pod.

Polar Whitlowgrass

Draba micropetala
ALSO: Polarrublom. SN
means "narrow-petaled
draba."

RANGE: Near circumpolar, but with disjunct distribution; found on High Arctic meadows, alpine ridges, and seepage slopes.
ID: H 2–4 in (5–10 cm). Densely tufted. LVS: In a basal rosette, fleshy, covered by coarse, simple hairs and longer, branched hairs. FLS: Borne on short, leafless flowering stems. Petals 4, pale yellow, narrow. FR: Thick, oval pod.

Grayleaf Whitlowgrass

Draba cinerea
ALSO: Grayleaf Draba,
Drave cendrée, *Draba*
arctica. SN means "ashy
gray draba."

RANGE: Circumpolar; found on river terraces, slopes, and poorly drained areas.
ID: H 5–10 in (12–25 cm). Densely tufted. Stem tall, hairy, with 2–3 leaves. LVS: Long, cuneate to spatulate, ashy gray, with dentate or entire margins edged with hairs. FLS: Small, borne in racemes of 6–12 blossoms. Petals 4, white. FR: Purple to green, hairy, ovoid, flattened seedpod.

Pale Whitlowgrass

Draba oxycarpa
ALSO: Bleikrublom, Fjal-
lavorblóm. SN means "draba
with pointed fruit."

RANGE: Amphi-Atlantic; grows in Greenland, Iceland, Svalbard, n Europe, and Novaya Zemlya on moist, stony sites.
ID: H 2–6 in (5–15 cm). Densely tufted. Erect, leafless stems. LVS: Lanceolate, to 0.75 in (1.8 cm) long, fleshy, covered with hairs. FLS: Petals 4, pale yellow, fading to cream. Flowers form and open in basal leaves. FR: Ovate, hairy, seedpods develop at tip of elongated flowering stem.

Smooth Whitlowgrass

Draba glabella

ALSO: Scree Whitlowgrass, Drave glabre, Skredrublom. SN means "smooth draba."

RANGE: Circumpolar. Widespread on dry, stony alpine sites, sand and gravel beaches and riverbanks, and below bird nesting cliffs.

ID: H 2–8 in (5–20 cm). Tufted or loosely matted. Stems covered with star-shaped hairs. LVS: Basal, coarse, oblong, with entire to dentate, haired margins. Stem leaves 1–7, with dentate margins. FLS: Petals 4, white; calyx green and purple, hairy. FR: Elliptical, purple to green pods, 0.5 in (1 cm) long.

White Arctic Whitlowgrass

Draba fladnizensis

ALSO: Austrian Draba, Fladnitzer Felsenblümchen, Drave de Fladniz, Alperublom. SN means "draba of Flattnitz," a mountain pass in Austria where the botanist–Jesuit priest Baron Franz Xavier von Wulfen (1728–1805) collected the species. Hybridizes with *Draba lactea*.

RANGE: Circumpolar; grows on rocky, open areas and alpine scree slopes.

ID: H 2–4 in (5–10 cm). Dwarf perennial. LVS: Narrowly lanceolate, to 1 in (2.5 cm) long, with entire margins, in a basal rosette. Leaves are covered with long, simple hairs, which separates this species from *D. lactea*. FLS: Borne in racemes of 3–12 blossoms. Petals 4, white to cream. FR: Smooth, flat, egg-shaped pod, to 0.5 in (9 cm) long, borne on erect or ascending stalks.

Milky Draba

Draba lactea

ALSO: Lapland Draba, Drave laiteuse, Lapprublom, Lappdraba, Крупкамолочно-белая. SN means "draba with milky white [flowers]." Hybridizes with *D. nivalis*.

RANGE: Circumpolar; grows on wet meadows and hummocks, around margins of ponds, streams, rivers, and lakes, and on alpine slopes, ridges, and cliffs.

ID: H 2–4 in (5–10 cm). Loosely matted. Stems tall, erect, smooth or sparsely haired. LVS: Lanceolate, with star-shaped hairs on the blade surface. FLS: Borne in racemes of 3–6 blossoms. Petals 4, pure white; calyx green and purple, smooth. FR: Ovoid, flattened, smooth, purple and green seedpod.

Snow Whitlowgrass

Draba nivalis

ALSO: Arctic Whitlowgrass, Drave des neiges, Snørublom, Isdraba. SN means "draba with snow white [flowers]."

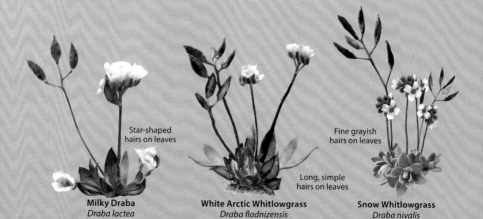

Star-shaped hairs on leaves

Milky Draba
Draba lactea
Circumpolar
H 2–4 in (5–10 cm)

Long, simple hairs on leaves

White Arctic Whitlowgrass
Draba fladnizensis
Circumpolar
H 2–4 in (5–10 cm)

Fine grayish hairs on leaves

Snow Whitlowgrass
Draba nivalis
Circumpolar
H 2–3 in (5–8 cm)

Hairy, oval
seedpods

Tiny
flowers

Previous year's
seedpods

Polar Whitlowgrass
Draba micropetala
Near circumpolar
H 2–4 in (5–10 cm)

Snowbed Draba
Draba crassifolia
Chukotka, N Amer, Greenland, Norway
H 2–6 in (5–15 cm)

Cushioned Whitlowgrass
Draba corymbosa
Circumpolar
H 2–4 in (5–10 cm)

Twisted
seedpods

Naked
stem

Clasping
stem leaves

Few stem
leaves

Pale Whitlowgrass
Draba oxycarpa
Amphi-Atlantic
H 2–6 in (5–15 cm)

Alpine Draba
Draba alpina
Circumpolar
H 2–8 in (5–20 cm)

Golden Draba
Draba aurea
N Amer, Greenland
H 4–8 in (10–20 cm)

Smooth Whitlowgrass
Draba glabella
Circumpolar
H 2–8 in (5–20 cm)

Few stem
leaves

Calyx
purple

Leaf base
covered with
withered
foliage

Smooth, oval
seedpods

Fine grayish
hairs on basal
leaves

Rock Whitlowgrass
Draba norvegica
Amphi-Atlantic
H 2–3 in (5–8 cm)

Hemispherical Whitlowgrass
Draba subcapitata
Near circumpolar
H 1–3.5 in (2–9 cm)

Grayleaf Whitlowgrass
Draba cinerea
Circumpolar
H 5–10 in (12–25 cm)

RANGE: Circumpolar. Grows in N Amer, Greenland, and Iceland, and in disjunct sites in arctic Eurasia on dry soils on river terraces, ridges, cliffs, and seepage slopes to 8500 ft (2600 m). ID: H 2–3 in (5–8 cm). Tufted. Erect, leafless stems. LVS: In a basal rosette, narrowly oblong, densely covered with fine grayish hairs. FLS: Petals 4, white; calyx green, densely haired. FR: Smooth, narrowly oval pod, to 0.5 in (9 cm) long, on ascending stalk.

Rock Whitlowgrass
Draba norvegica

ALSO: Norwegian Draba, Drave de Norvège, Bergrulom. SN means "draba from Norway," where this species is common. RANGE: Amphi-Atlantic; found in n Canada, Greenland, Iceland, n Europe, Svalbard, and Novaya Zemlya, on rocky and gravel substrates on river terraces, and alpine peaks and ledges. ID: H 2–3 in (5–8 cm). Loosely tufted. LVS: Basal, oblanceolate, hairy, with mostly entire margins. Single stem leaf near base. FLS: Borne in racemes of 4–7 blossoms. Petals 4, white; calyx purple, hairy. FR: Grayish green, ovoid, flattened, hairy pod, at tip of long stem.

Hemispherical Whitlowgrass
Draba subcapitata

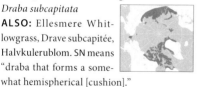

ALSO: Ellesmere Whitlowgrass, Drave subcapitée, Halvkulerublom. SN means "draba that forms a somewhat hemispherical [cushion]." RANGE: Near circumpolar; occurs in disjunct locations in the High Arctic of N Amer, Greenland, and Eurasia. Grows around snowbeds and on moist substrates on ridges and exposed gravel outcrops. ID: H 1–3.5 in (2–9 cm). Forms small, rounded cushions. Stems very short, erect, hairy. LVS: Oblanceolate, hairy; margins entire, with non-glandular hairs. Leaf base densely covered with withered foliage from previous seasons. FLS: Borne in racemes of 2–8 blossoms. Petals 4, white; calyx green, hairy. FR: Purple, oblong, smooth pod, on an ascending stalk.

Ericales: Heaths and Allies

Ericales is a large, diverse order of dicotyledons. It contains more than 8000 species and includes well-known plants such as blueberries, cranberries, wintergreens, heathers, azaleas, and primroses. Many species, especially those in the family Ericaceae, live in symbiosis with root fungi (*mycorrhiza*). The fungi grow in and around the roots and provide the plant with nutrients. Some members of this order have an exceptional ability to accumulate aluminum.

FAMILY ERICACEAE
HEATHS

The name Ericaceae derives from the Greek *ereiko*, meaning "to break," a reference to the brittle wood of most species. Members of this family are largely shrubs that grow in alpine sites or peat. The flowers can be tubular, funnel-form, or bell-shaped. Petals are often fused (*sympetalous*) and the corollas radially symmetrical (*actinomorphic*, like a daisy). Some species bear edible berries.

GENUS *EMPETRUM*
Black Crowberry
Empetrum nigrum

ALSO: Baongak, Paurngait, Schwarze Krähenbeere, Camarine noire, Krekling, Водяника чёрная; also known as Curlewberry because the fruit is an important food for curlews and whimbrels as they fatten up prior to fall migration. SN means "rock plant with black [fruit]." RANGE: Circumpolar; widespread in heaths, bogs, and sites with moist sandy, rocky, or acid soils; thrives in maritime climates. ID: H 2–4 in (5–10 cm). Procumbent, matted, evergreen shrub. LVS: Needle-like. FLS: Jul–Aug. Tiny, dark purple, solitary in leaf axils. Male and female flowers occur on separate plants, on the same plant, or flowers can be bisexual. FR: Round, watery, somewhat tasteless, purplish black berry with large, hard seeds. USE: Berries are juicy, crunchy, and very healthy to eat. They are used to make pies and jelly, and are delicious when mixed with caribou fat. The berries are gathered in the fall or plucked from under the winter snow.

GENUS *VACCINIUM*
Bog Bilberry
Vaccinium uliginosum

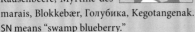

ALSO: Alpine Blueberry, Rauschbeere, Myrtille des marais, Blokkebær, Голубика, Kegotangenak. SN means "swamp blueberry."

RANGE: Circumpolar; widespread on wet, acidic soils on tundra, heaths, and in the forest understory. Grows mostly at sea level in the Arctic, and to 11,150 ft (3400 m) farther south.

ID: H 4–30 in (10–75 cm). Procumbent or erect, deciduous shrub. Stems angled in cross section. **LVS:** Oval, to 1 in (3 cm) long, with entire margin and rounded apex. Bluish green with pale net-like veins above, glaucous below. **FLS:** Pale pink, pendulous, urn-shaped, to 0.25 in (0.6 cm) long, produced in midspring in the leaf axils. **FR:** Dark bluish black berry, with white flesh; late summer berries are edible and sweet.

Lingonberry
Vaccinium vitis-idaea

ALSO: Cowberry, Lowbush Cranberry, Mountain Bilberry, Partridgeberry, Foxberry, Whortleberry, Kikminnaq, Kimmernaq, Preiselbeere, Airelle rouge, Tyttebær, Брусника. SN means "blueberry grapevine of Mount Idaea [Greece]." CN derives from *lingon*, the Swedish name for the species.

RANGE: Circumpolar; widespread on wet, acid soils in tundra, bogs, and the forest understory, to 3900 ft (1200 m).

ID: H 4–16 in (10–40 cm). Low, creeping, evergreen shrub. **LVS:** Lustrous, leathery, with reflexed margin and notched tip; underside glaucous, with dark glandular dots. **FLS:** Bell-shaped, white to pale pink, in nodding terminal clusters of 4–6. **FR:** Shiny, red berry ripens in late summer and remains on the plant through the winter.

USE: Lingonberries are rich in vitamin C (an anti-scorbutic), vitamin A (as beta-carotene), vitamin B, potassium, calcium, magnesium, and phosphorus. Seeds contain omega-3 fatty acids. The berries also contain phytochemicals useful in counteracting urinary tract infections. Fresh berries taste acidic and are usually eaten with

Black Crowberry
Empetrum nigrum
Circumpolar
H 2–4 in (5–10 cm)

Bog Billberry
Vaccinium uliginosum
Circumpolar
H 4–30 in (10–75 cm)

Lingonberry
Vaccinium vitis-idaea
Circumpolar
H 4–16 in (10–40 cm)

Spring flowers

Fall leaf and bearberry

Alpine Black Bearberry
Arctostaphylos alpina
Circumpolar
H 2–4 in (5–10 cm)

Berries and fall foliage persist into spring flowering

Red Bearberry
Arctostaphylos rubra
Amphi-Beringian
H 4–6 in (10–15 cm)

Kinnikinnick
Arctostaphylos uva-ursi
Circumpolar
H 4–8 in (10–20 cm)

sugar. With their high benzoic acid content, they can be preserved without boiling. Sugared berries can be stored at room temperature in unsealed containers, or hung in bags in ice cellars. In Scandinavia and Russia, lingonberry preserves and liqueurs are traditional companions to game meats and wildfowl. The berries are also relished by bears and foxes.

GENUS *ARCTOSTAPHYLOS*
Alpine Black Bearberry
Arctostaphylos alpina

ALSO: Alpen-Bärentraube, Raisin d'ours des Alpes, Rypebær, Толокнянка альпийская. SN means "mountain bear grape."

RANGE: Circumpolar, on acid soil on rocky and gravelly tundra and dry alpine heaths to 3300 ft (1000 m).

ID: H 2–4 in (5–10 cm). Matted, trailing, dwarf shrub. LVS: Oval, wrinkled, to 1.5 in (4 cm) long, with crenulate margin; dark green, shiny above; paler green and dotted with dark glands below. Leaves turn scarlet in autumn. FLS: Small, urn-shaped, ivory-colored, opening as new leaves unfold. FR: Watery, tasteless berry, purplish black in fall, green in spring. Foliage and berries persist under the snow.

SIMILAR SPECIES: KINNIKINNICK, *Arctostaphylos uva-ursi*, is a circumpolar subarctic species with dry, mealy, red berries. The common name *kinnikinnick* derives from a N Amer Indian tobacco mix, which contained leaves of this plant. RED BEARBERRY or KABLAK, *Arctostaphylos rubra*, is an amphi-Beringian species that produces tasteless, watery, scarlet berries in autumn. However, bears enjoy them.

GENUS *RHODODENDRON*
Bog Labrador Tea
Rhododendron groenlandicum

ALSO: Rusty Labrador Tea, Grönländischer Porst, Thé du Labrador, Grønlandspors, Рододендрон гренландский, Qijuktaaqpait, Qisiqtuti, *Ledum groenlandicum*. SN means "Greenland rosebay." Leaves are used to make tea and tonics in Labrador, Canada—hence the CN "Labrador tea."

RANGE: Alaska, Canada, and sw Greenland; found in bogs, wet coniferous forests, and dwarf shrub barrens.

ID: H 20–60 in (50–150 cm). Resinous evergreen shrub. Erect branches. Young stems bear orange, curly hairs; older stems are hairless. LVS: Leathery, dull green, alternate, lanceolate elliptical, to 2 in (5 cm) long, with inrolled margins and rust-colored woolly hairs below. FLS: May–Jun. Fragrant, borne in crowded corymbs at stem tips. Petals 5, white, sticky. FR: Oval, persistent capsule.

Marsh Labrador Tea
Rhododendron tomentosum

ALSO: Crystal Tea, Wild Rosemary, Porst, Lédon des marais, Finnmarkspors, Багульник болотный, *Ledum palustre*. SN means "woolly-haired rosebay."

RANGE: Eurasia, in peat bogs, swampy pine forests, moss-lichen heaths, rocky slopes, and cliffs ledges, to 5900 ft (1800 m).

ID: H 12–40 in (30–100 cm). Erect, resinous, evergreen shrub. LVS: Strap-like, leathery, thick, with inrolled margins; shiny and smooth above, with rusty brown woolly hairs below. FLS: Jun–Jul. White, borne at branch tips in erect umbels. FR: Pendulous capsule, covered with glandular hairs.

USE: POISONOUS. Plant contains ledol, a volatile narcotic oil whose smell can affect the nervous system and induce dizziness and paralysis. Despite its toxicity, in the Middle Ages the plant was used instead of, or in addition to, hops for flavoring beer. The aromatic oil also was used to deter clothing moths.

Lapland Rosebay
Rhododendron lapponicum

ALSO: Lapland Azalea, Lappland-Alpenrose, Rhododendron lapon, Lapprose, Рододендрон лапландский, *Azalea lapponica*. SN means "Lapland rosebay."

RANGE: E Asia, N Amer, and Greenland, with isolated populations in Scandinavia; occurs on tundra, forests, sandstone cliffs above rivers, and alpine meadows to 6250 ft (1900 m).

ID: H 4–12 in (10–30 cm); taller in protected sites.

Dwarf or low shrub, semi-prostrate, matted, with knotty branches. LVS: Thick, leathery, elliptical, to 0.5 in (1.5 cm) long; dark green, densely scaled on both sides with rust-colored resinous glands. FLS: Dark pink to purple, to 1 in (2.5 cm) across, bell- to funnel-shaped, with 5–10 protruding stamens; borne in an umbel-like cluster at top of stems. One of the first flowers to bloom in the arctic spring.

GENUS *KALMIA*
Alpine Azalea
Kalmia procumbens

ALSO: Creeping Azalea, Gämsheide, Azalée couchée, Greplyng, Кальмия лежачая, *Loiseleuria procumbens*. SN means "Kalm's creeping [azalea]," honoring Swedish-Finnish explorer Peter Kalm (1716–1779), an apostle of Carolus Linnaeus. **RANGE:** Near circumpolar, on acidic soil on dry heaths and scree slopes to 6550 ft (2000 m). **ID:** H 2–4 in (5–10 cm). Dwarf evergreen shrub. Forms mats that often clamber over rocks. LVS: Small, obovate to oblong, thick, leathery, with inrolled margins; dark green above; woolly white hairs below. FLS: Jun–Jul. Pink, bell-shaped, with reddish sepals, borne singly or in small terminal clusters. FR: Dehiscent, 4-chambered capsule.

GENUS *PHYLLODOCE*
Mountain Heather
Phyllodoce caerulea

ALSO: Blue Mountain Heather, Moosheide, Phyllodoce bleue, Blålyng, Филлодоце голубая. SN means "Phyllodoce's bluish [flowers]"; named after the sea nymph Phyllodoce. **RANGE:** Near circumpolar; disjunct distribution on alpine heaths, rocky sites where snow remains late into spring, and in birch and pine forests. **ID:** H 4–6 in (10–15 cm). Low evergreen shrub with densely branched stems. LVS: Small, linear, leathery, with margins so tightly inrolled that leaves resemble pine needles; shiny, smooth above, densely haired below. FLS: Jun–Aug. Reddish pink to bluish purple, long-stemmed, 5-parted, urn-shaped, in nodding terminal clusters. FR: Capsule covered with glandular hairs.

GENUS *CASSIOPE*
Arctic Bell Heather
Cassiope tetragona

ALSO: Arctic White Heather, Lappland Cassiope, Vierkantige Schuppenheide, Cassiope tétragone, Kantlyng, Кассиопея четырёхгранная, Iksulit. SN means "Cassiopeia's heather with 4-angled [stems]"; named after Cassiopeia, vain queen of Ethiopia, who continually boasted of her beauty. **RANGE:** Circumpolar, near late snowbeds on the tundra and scree slopes to 6500 ft (2000 m). **ID:** H 4–12 in (10–30 cm). Forms dense stands. Dwarf evergreen shrub. Erect, stiff, 4-angled stems. LVS: Small, scale-like, resinous, aromatic, closely pressed to the stem. FLS: Jul–Aug. White, bell-shaped, solitary, nodding, rising from leaf axils near the stem tips. FR: Round, ridged capsule. **USE:** Used as fuel for campfires; high resin content causes foliage to burn with a hot flame.

GENUS *ANDROMEDA*
Bog Rosemary
Andromeda polifolia

ALSO: Rosmarinheide, Polei-Gränke, Andromède, Kvitlyng, Подбел. SN means "Andromeda's plant with gray leaves"; named after Andromeda, daughter of Cassiopeia. Leaves resemble those of the garden herb Rosemary, *Rosmarinus officinalis*, hence the CN. **RANGE:** Circumpolar, in fens, mires, bogs, and on wet hummocks. **ID:** H 4–12 in (10–30 cm). Dwarf evergreen shrub. Creeping rootstock. LVS: To 0.75 in (2 cm) long, leathery, lanceolate, with inrolled margins; bluish green to purple above, whitish below. FLS: Jun. Pink, urn-shaped, 5-parted, in nodding, terminal clusters. FR: Round capsule, with 5 seed chambers (*loculi*). Contains andromedotoxin, which severely lowers blood pressure. POISONOUS.

GENUS *CHAMAEDAPHNE*
Cassandra
Chamaedaphne calyculata

ALSO: Liverleaf, Torfgränke, Vaivero, Хамедафне. CN refers to Cassandra, the Trojan princess to whom

Apollo gave the gift of prophecy but caused her prophecies to be disbelieved. SN means "creeping heath with a small calyx."

RANGE: Near circumpolar (absent Greenland); grows near peat bogs, mires, and swampy lakes. **ID:** H 8–12 in (20–30 cm); dwarf forms occur. Low-growing evergreen shrub with an underground stem to 5 ft (1.5 m) long. LVS: Aromatic, oval, stiff, held upright, about 1 in (3 cm) long; dark green above; brown scales below. FLS: May–Jun. White, nodding, bell-shaped, borne on a leafy, 1-sided raceme. FR: Round 5-chambered capsule.

FAMILY PRIMULACEAE
PRIMULAS
GENUS *PRIMULA*
Strict Primrose
Primula stricta

ALSO: Coastal Primrose, Primln, Primevère dressée, Smalnøkleblom, Первоцвет, Aupartuapinnik. SN means "straight [stem] primula." *Primula* is Latin for "first," referring to flowers that are among the first to open in spring.

RANGE: N Amer, Greenland, Iceland, and n Europe; found along seashores and in wet coastal meadows.

ID: H 2–12 in (5–30 cm). LVS: Oblanceolate to narrowly obovate, smooth, in a basal tuft. Stems leafless, slender, stiffly erect. FLS: Rosy purple with a yellow eye, small, 5-parted, in umbels of 3–8 blossoms.

SIMILAR SPECIES: CHUKCHI PRIMROSE, *Primula tschuktschorum*, is found mainly in the Bering Sea region, from Kamchatka and Chukotka across the Aleutians to Alaska. Grows on wet meadows and gravelly streambanks. Flowers are magenta-colored, with a white eye.

GENUS *ANDROSACE*
Pygmyflower Rock-Jasmine
Androsace septentrionalis

ALSO: Northern Fairy Candelabra, Nordischer Mannschild, Smånøkkel, Проломник. SN means "northern man shield," with *Androsace* referring to an unidentified plant of ancient Greece.

RANGE: Near circumpolar, often near villages and on dry, rocky, alpine sites to 6550 ft (2000 m). **ID:** H 2–12 in (5–30 cm). Annual. LVS: In a basal rosette, oblanceolate, sessile, entire or toothed. Stems erect, leafless, sparsely haired. FLS: May–Jun. Tiny, white to pink, 5-parted, borne in terminal umbels. Shortly after blooming, leaves and stems turn red.

SIMILAR SPECIES: ROCK-JASMINE, *Androsace chamaejasme*, Eurasia and w N Amer. Grows on rocky tundra slopes. Leaves and stems are hairy. Fragrant flowers are white, with a yellow eye.

GENUS *DODECATHEON*
Arctic Shooting Star
Dodecatheon frigidum

ALSO: Frigid or Alpine Shooting Star, Dodécathéon. SN means "plant of the cold that is protected by 12 gods [of ancient Greece]."

RANGE: Amphi-Beringian, in meadows and heaths to 5600 ft (1700 m); absent in lowlands. **ID:** H 4–12 in (10–30 cm). Tufted. LVS: Oval, with toothed margins. Naked stems. FLS: Nodding, terminal. Corolla tube maroon, yellow above, with 5 magenta to lavender reflexed petals creating the shooting star; black protruding stamens. The buzzing of bumblebees creates a sound wave that causes the anthers to vibrate and drop their pollen, thus fertilizing the flower.

FAMILY PYROLACEAE
WINTERGREENS
GENUS *PYROLA*
Arctic Wintergreen
Pyrola grandiflora

ALSO: Largeflowered Wintergreen, Wintergrün, Pyrole grandes fleurs, Грушанка крупноцветковая. CN *wintergreen* refers to the evergreen leaves. SN means "[plant with] pear-shaped [leaves] and large flowers."

RANGE: Circumpolar, in dry places on the tundra and in mountains to 6550 ft (2000 m). **ID:** H 4–10 in (10–25 cm). Tufted. LVS: Lustrous dark green, ovate-orbicular, leathery, with inrolled margins. FLS: Apr–Jun. Fragrant, creamy white to pink, saucer-shaped, with a long, protruding style.

Marsh Labrador Tea
Rhododendron tomentosum
Eurasia
H 12–40 in (30–100 cm)
Poisonous

Bog Labrador Tea
Rhododendron groenlandicum
N Amer, sw Greenland
H 20–60 in (50–150 cm)

Alpine Azalea
Kalmia procumbens
Near circumpolar
H 2–4 in (5–10 cm)

Lapland Rosebay
Rhododendron lapponicum
E Asia, N Amer, Greenland
H 4–12 in (10–30 cm)

Chukchi Primrose
Primula tschuktschorum
Amphi-Beringian
H 2–8 in (5–20 cm)

Arctic Shooting Star
Dodecatheon frigidum
Amphi-Beringian
H 4–12 in (10–30 cm)

Cassandra
Chamaedaphne calyculata
Near circumpolar
H 8–12 in (20–30 cm)

Strict Primrose
Primula stricta
N Amer, Greenland,
Iceland, n Europe
H 2–12 in (5–30 cm)

Arctic Wintergreen
Pyrola grandiflora
Circumpolar
H 4–10 in (10–25 cm)

Bog Rosemary
Andromeda polifolia
Near circumpolar
H 4–12 in (10–30 cm)
Poisonous

Mountain Heather
Phyllodoce caerulea
Near circumpolar
H 4–6 in (10–15 cm)

Nodding
flowers on
one side of
the stem

Arctic Bell Heather
Cassiope tetragona
Circumpolar
H 4–12 in (10–30 cm)

**Nodding
Wintergreen**
Orthilia secunda
Circumpolar
H 2–8 in (5–20 cm)

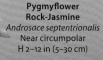

Rock-Jasmine
Androsace chamaejasme
Eurasia, w N Amer
H 1–6 in (2–15 cm)

**Pygmyflower
Rock-Jasmine**
Androsace septentrionalis
Near circumpolar
H 2–12 in (5–30 cm)

Pincushion Plant
Diapensia lapponica
Circumpolar
H 1–4 in (3–10 cm)

GENUS *ORTHILIA*
Nodding Wintergreen

Orthilia secunda

ALSO: Sidebells, One-sided Wintergreen, Birngrün, Pirole unilatérale, Nikkevintergrøn, Ортилия однобокая. SN means "1-sided flower spiral."

RANGE: Circumpolar. Widespread on mossy sites and in damp spruce forests.

ID: H 2–8 in (5–20 cm). LVS: In a basal rosette, fresh green, ovate, slightly leathery, with serrate margins and pointed tip. FLS: Jun–Jul. Tiny, bell-shaped, greenish white, in a nodding, 1-sided raceme.

FAMILY DIAPENSIACEAE
DIAPENSIAS

GENUS *DIAPENSIA*
Pincushion Plant

Diapensia lapponica

ALSO: Diapensie de Laponie, Fjellpryd, Uuvana, Диапенсия лапландская. SN means "Lapland diapensia."

RANGE: Circumpolar, on scree slopes and on exposed, windswept, snow-free rocky ledges.

ID: H 1–4 in (3–10 cm). Dwarf evergreen shrub. Forms wide, dense cushions that can persist for decades. LVS: Scale-like, curved, spatulate, yellowish green. FLS: Blooms for 10 days in Jun–Jul. Saucer-shaped, solitary. Petals 5, white, rounded; stamens bright yellow; calyx hairy.

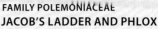

FAMILY POLEMONIACEAE
JACOB'S LADDER AND PHLOX

Arctic representatives of this family have 5-parted, blue to magenta flowers, and 3-valved, 3-chambered, few-seeded capsules. The family name Polemoniaceae has been attributed to several personages of ancient Greece, including King Polemon II of Pontus, the Athenian philosopher Polemon, and the herbalist and healer Polemos of Cappadocia.

GENUS *POLEMONIUM*
Tall Jacob's Ladder

Polemonium acutiflorum

ALSO: Blaue Himmelsleiter, Lappflokk, одолень-трава, *P. caeruleum*. CN alludes to the leaf arrangement, which resembles a ladder—figuratively Jacob's ladder to heaven as described in the Book of Genesis. SN means "phlox with pointed flower [petals]."

RANGE: Eurasia and w N Amer, in wet meadows, hedgerows, streambanks, roadsides, old logging sites, and around abandoned camp buildings, to 2600 ft (800 m).

ID: H 10–20 in (25–50 cm). LVS: Alternate, odd-pinnately compound, with lanceolate to elliptical, acute leaflets, with entire margins. Basal leaves large, with a long, angled stalk. Leafy flowering stem erect, unbranched; upper half hirsute. FLS: Jul–Aug. Blue to violet, rarely white, broadly bell-shaped, deeply 5-lobed, hairy-throated, somewhat nodding, to 1 in (2 cm) across; borne in a sparsely flowered raceme atop a tall stem. Petals fused. Sepals 5, united, sharp-pointed, densely glandular-hairy. FR: Round, yellow, 3-chambered seed capsule.

Tall Jacob's Ladder
Polemonium acutiflorum
Eurasia, w N Amer
H 10–20 in (25–50 cm)

Northern Jacob's Ladder
Polemonium boreale
Near circumpolar
H 4–6 in (10–15 cm)

Siberian Phlox
Phlox sibirica
N Siberia, nw N Amer
H 1–4 in (3–10 cm)

Northern Jacob's Ladder

Polemonium boreale
ALSO: Polarflokk, Polémoine
boréal, Синюха северная.
SN means "boreal phlox."
RANGE: Near circumpolar (absent e N Amer), in
meadows, dry sandy tundra, and gravel slopes,
and near animal burrows.
ID: H 4–6 in (10–15 cm). Low, loosely tufted,
hairy perennial with an unpleasant smell. LVS:
Basal, pinnately compound, with 8–12 pairs of
elliptical leaflets. FLS: Showy, with blue to purple,
dark-veined petals and deep yellow throat; borne
in clusters of 3–7 at top of stem.

GENUS *PHLOX*
Siberian Phlox

Phlox sibirica
ALSO: Boreal Phlox, Richardson's Phlox, Sibirischer
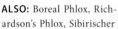
Phlox, Floks, Флокс сибирский, *P. richardsonii
alaskensis.* SN means "flame of Siberia."
RANGE: Disjunct locations in n Siberia and
nw N Amer, on barrens and dry, windswept
slopes to 6550 ft (2000 m).
ID: H 1–4 in (3–10 cm). Perennial herb. Grows in
clumps, forming small cushions or mats with
many-branched, woody stems. LVS: Opposite,
linear or scale-like, hairy, to 0.5 in (1 cm) long.
FLS: Showy, very fragrant. Magenta to pink
petals fade in color to blue or white with age.

Rosales: Roses and Allies

FAMILY ROSACEAE
ROSES, CINQUEFOILS, AND ALLIES

Most of these perennial trees,
shrubs, and herbaceous
plants have showy, radially
symmetrical, perfect flowers.
Most are 5-parted, and the
bases of the sepals, petals, and spirally arranged
stamens are fused together to form a cup-like
structure called a *hypanthium.* The flowers
may be arranged in racemes, spikes, or heads.
The leaves are generally arranged spirally, can
be simple or pinnately compound, and have
serrate margins.

GENUS *ROSA*
Arctic Rose

Rosa acicularis
ALSO: Prickly Wild Rose,
Rosier arctique, Nadel-Rose,
Finnros, Шиповник иглистый, Katitaġnaq. SN
means "rose with needle-like [thorns]." Provincial
flower of Alberta, Canada.
RANGE: Near circumpolar (absent Greenland,
w Europe) in woods, heaths, tundra bogs, thickets,
slopes, and along roads, to 1500 ft (1800 m).
ID: H 3–10 ft (1–3 m). Small shrub. Branches
reddish brown, straggling to erect, with thorny
branchlets. LVS: Deciduous. To 6 in (15 cm) long,
alternate, odd-pinnate, with 3–7 ovate leaflets
having toothed margins. FLS: Jun–Jul. To 2 in
(5 cm) across. Petals 5, pink, rarely white. FR:
Pear-shaped to ovoid, pome-like structure called
a *hip*; green at first, later ripening to orange and
deep rose red. Hips enclose hairy achenes that
contain a few seeds.

GENUS *RUBUS*
Arctic Raspberry

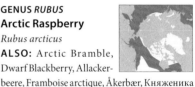

Rubus arcticus
ALSO: Arctic Bramble,
Dwarf Blackberry, Allacker-
beere, Framboise arctique, Åkerbær, Княженика
обыкновенная. SN means "arctic bramble."
RANGE: Near circumpolar (absent Greenland),
in bogs, woodland, tundra, and alpine meadows.
ID: H 1–6 in (2–15 cm). Long, woody, branching
rhizome. Stems softly haired. LVS: Trifoliate, with
entire stipules; 3 leaflets, ovate or obovate, to 1 in
(3 cm) long, with serrate margins. FLS: Terminal,
usually solitary. Petals 5–9; pink, crimson or
rose. Calyx finely haired, narrowly lanceolate,
reflexed. FR: Reddish purple aggregate drupe,
to 0.5 in (1 cm) across.
USE: Used to make jam and flavor liqueurs.

Cloudberry

Rubus chamaemorus
ALSO: Bakeapple, Knot-
berry, Aqpik, Naunraq,
Moltebeere, Plaquebière,
Molte, Морошка. SN means "low-growing
mulberry bramble."

RANGE: Circumpolar; grows to 78°N in peat bogs, marshes, wet meadows, and alpine sites. Tolerates temperatures of −40°F (−40°C). **ID:** H 4–10 in (10–25 cm). Low, creeping herb. **LVS:** Alternate, large, reniform, mostly 5-lobed, somewhat leathery, with toothed margins. **FLS:** Solitary, terminal on leafy stem. Petals 5, white. **FR:** Globose drupe, initially bright red and closely held in the calyx. Calyx lobes reflex (fold back) as the drupe ripens to amber. **USE:** Berries are a good source of vitamin C. Native Alaskans mix ripe berries with seal oil, whipped caribou fat, and sugar to make "Eskimo ice cream," or *agutak.* Cloudberries flavor liqueurs, including Finnish *Lakkalikööri,* Scandinavian *Aquavit,* and *Chicoutai,* which is made in Quebec, Canada. They have also been used to flavor beer, such as Arctic Cloudberry Imperial Wheat Beer, made by the Dogfish Head Brewery of Milton, Delaware (US).

Salmonberry
Rubus spectabilis

ALSO: Russian Berry, Pracht-Himbeere, Ronce remarquable, Alaskan-vatukka, Малина великолепная, Akpik. SN means "admirable bramble." CN stems from the practice of eating the berries with salmon roe. **RANGE:** Western N Amer, from the Aleutians and Alaska south to California, in thickets in moist alder woodland, swamps, and along streams. Introduced into nw Europe. **ID:** H 3–10 ft (1–3 m). Erect shrub, with arching branches, shredding brown bark, and bristly stems. **LVS:** Trifoliate, to 9 in (22 cm) long; leaflets ovate, doubly serrate, dark green; large terminal leaflet. **FLS:** May–Jul. To 1 in (3 cm) across. Petals 5, dark pink to purple. **FR:** Red to yellow orange, edible drupe.

GENUS *FRAGARIA*
Beach Strawberry
Fragaria chiloensis

ALSO: Coastal Strawberry, Chile-Erdbeere, Fraisier du Chili, Jordbær, Земляника чилийская, *Potentilla chiloensis.* SN means "Chilean strawberry."

RANGE: W N Amer, from the Aleutians, Alaska, and w Canada south to California, on beaches and sandy soils. Also grows in Hawaii, s Chile, and s Argentina. Introduced to Europe in 1716. **ID:** H 4–8 in (10–20 cm). Forms loose colonies. Spreads via thick, hairy, red stolons. **LVS:** Trifoliate; leaflets glossy green, leathery, obovate, to 2 in (5 cm) long, with coarsely crenate margins. **FLS:** Apr–Jun. Borne in an open cluster of 5–15 blossoms. Petals 5, white. **FR:** Jun–Aug. Edible berry is red on the outside, white inside. **USE:** Can be eaten fresh or made into jam.

GENUS *GEUM*
Glacier Avens
Geum glaciale

ALSO: Nelkenwurz, Benoîte, Humleblom, Гравилат, *Novosieversia glacialis, Sieversia glacialis.* SN means "ice avens."
RANGE: Amphi-Beringian (broadly), from Siberia to n Alaska, on stony slopes and heaths. **ID:** H 4–10 in (10–25 cm). Leaf base thick, woody, covered by withered foliage from previous seasons. **LVS:** Basal, in a spreading rosette; pinnate, with 11–15 toothed leaflets, densely covered below with soft, long, yellowish hairs. **FLS:** Early spring. To 1.5 in (3.5 cm) across. Petals 5–8, yellow, ovate, clawed. **FR:** Achene with short stiff hairs and 1 in (2.5 cm) feathery styles.

Alpine Avens
Geum rossii

ALSO: Nelkenwurz, Benoîte de Ross, Гравилат Росса, *Sieversia rossii.* SN means "Ross's avens," honoring British Arctic-Antarctic explorer, Sir James Clark Ross (1800–1862). **RANGE:** Amphi-Beringian; found in Chukotka, Kamchatka, the Aleutians, and nw N Amer, on alpine tundra, dry stony sites, and near snowbeds. **ID:** H 4–10 in (10–25 cm). **LVS:** 2–4 in (6–10 cm) long, pinnate, with 7 or more pairs of irregularly toothed leaflets that are downy above, smooth below. Leaf base thick, woody, purplish brown, covered with withered foliage. **FLS:** Jun–Jul. To 1 in (3 cm) across. Borne in clusters of 1–3 at tips of erect stems. Petals 5, yellow.

Largeleaf Avens
Geum macrophyllum
NE Asia, Aleutians, N Amer
H 6–12 in (15–30 cm)

Alpine Avens
Geum rossii
Amphi-Beringian
H 4–10 in (10–25 cm)

Arctic Rose
Rosa acicularis
Near circumpolar
H 3–10 ft (1–3 m)

Rose hip

Glacier Avens
Geum glaciale
Amphi-Beringian
H 4–10 in (10–25 cm)

Arctic Raspberry
Rubus arcticus
Near circumpolar
H 1–6 in (2–15 cm)

Salmonberry
Rubus spectabilis
W N Amer
Introduced to Europe
H 3–10 ft (1–3 m)

Cloudberry
Rubus chamaemorus
Circumpolar
H 4–10 in (10–25 cm)

Twisted
seedhead

Beach Strawberry
Fragaria chiloensis
Americas
Introduced to Europe
H 4–8 in (10–20 cm)

Leaf margins
deeply cleft

**Eight-petal Dryad or
Mountain Avens**
Dryas octopetala
Circumpolar
H 2–4 in (5–10 cm)

Leaf margins
entire

Arctic Dryad
Dryas integrifolia
Chukotka, N Amer, Greenland
H 2–6 in (5–15 cm)

Largeleaf Avens

Geum macrophyllum

ALSO: Nelkenwurz, Amerikahumleblom, Benoite, Гравилат крупнолистный. SN means "large-leaved avens."

RANGE: Kamchatka, Kurils, Aleutians, Alaska, and Canada, south to nw US, in thickets, meadows, and along roads.

ID: H 6–12 in (15–30 cm). LVS: Basal, large, rounded, pinnate, hirsute, with crenate margins. Stem leaves pinnate, trifoliate, deeply cleft, with toothed margins. FLS: Jun–Jul. Petals 5, yellow. Sepals 5, triangular, acute.

GENUS DRYAS: *Dryas* is Greek for "oak," referring to the oak-like leaves of some species. Adaptations to the polar environment include a waxy coating on the leaves' upper surface and woolly hairs on the underside. Both serve to conserve moisture in summer and shed ice in winter. The flowers are heliotropic and move with the sun. Their parabolic shape directs the sun's heat to the flower's reproductive organs. This encourages seed production and also attracts pollinating insects. The feathery plumes attached to each of the seeds aid in wind dispersal.

Eight-petal Dryad or Mountain Avens

Dryas octopetala

ALSO: White Dryas, Weiße Silberwurz, Dryade à huit pétales, Reinrose, Дриада. SN means "dryad with eight petals." Territorial flower of the Northwest Territories, Canada. National flower of Iceland.

RANGE: Circumpolar; forms large colonies on mountain slopes, limestone outcrops, gravel and rocky barrens, previously glaciated terrain, and sites where the snow melts early in spring. A pioneer species important in stabilizing thin soils on mountain slopes.

ID: H 2–4 in (5–10 cm). Dwarf prostrate shrub. Stems woody, twisted. LVS: Basal, oblong, deeply cleft, with crenate margins. Smooth and shiny above, with a dense layer of white woolly hairs below. FLS: Creamy white, anemone-like, to about 1 in (3 cm) across; petals 8–10, rarely 16.

FR: The persistent style holds reddish, feathery, twisted seedhead that expands into a whitish ball of seed-bearing plumes that are dispersed by wind.

Arctic Dryad

Dryas integrifolia

ALSO: Entireleaf Avens, White Mountain Avens, Silberwurz, Dryade à feuilles entières, Дриада. The Inuit name *Isurramuat* refers to the flowers following the daily path of the sun. *Isuqtannguat* refers to the plant's habit of leaning north in summer and south in fall. SN means "dryad with entire leaf margins."

RANGE: Chukotka, N Amer, and Greenland, on frost-heaved calcareous gravel on rocky barrens, tundra heath, and alpine sites to 4250 ft (1300 m). Often found on land recently exposed by receding glaciers.

ID: H 2–6 in (5–15 cm). LVS: Basal, flat, linear, leathery, to about 1 in (3 cm) long. Smooth and shiny above, with a dense layer of white woolly hairs below. Margins inrolled; entire or toothed only at base. FLS: Jun–Jul. Solitary, to about 1 in (3 cm) across; borne on leafless flowering stems. Petals 7–10, rarely 20, white; sepals in bud look black due to many coarse, glandular-tipped hairs. **FR:** Feathery styles, to 1 in (3 cm) long in fruit.

USE: The flowers and seedheads produce a green dye the Inuit call *piluit*. Pikas and ptarmigans feed on the seeds and buds.

GENUS POTENTILLA: Potentillas are commonly known as *cinquefoils*, meaning "five leaves." The leaves are compound, with 3–5, rarely 7, leaflets. Withered leaves from the previous season frequently persist at the plant base. Flowers are typically 5-parted. The fruits are small, dry, 1-seeded achenes, which develop on a rounded, usually hairy receptacle.

Arctic Cinquefoil

Potentilla hyparctica

ALSO: Polarfingerkraut, Potentille subartique, Mure, Лапчатка арктическая, *Potentilla emarginata*. SN means "northern

cinquefoil"; *Potentilla* means "potent," alluding to the medicinal properties of some species.
RANGE: Circumpolar, in meadows, rocky ravines, talus slopes, and around snowbeds.
ID: H 2–5 in (5–12 cm). LVS: Trifoliate, finely haired below; leaflet margins toothed, hirsute. FLS: Yellow, often with an orange base, 5-parted, to 0.75 in (2 cm) across; borne in groups of 1–3.

Snow Cinquefoil

Potentilla nivea
ALSO: Schnee Fingerkraut, Snømure, Potentille blanc de neige, Лапчатка снежная, *P. arenosa*. SN means "snow cinquefoil."
RANGE: Circumpolar in the arctic and alpine zones, on tundra and rocky, sunny sites, often near animal burrows and bird cliffs.
ID: H 6–10 in (15–25 cm). Erect, branching stems. LVS: Dark green and smooth above, woolly below. Compound, with woolly-haired petioles; leaflets 3-parted, with 4–6 teeth on each side. FLS: Petals 5, yellow; sepals 5, green.

Norwegian Cinquefoil

Potentilla norvegica
ALSO: Rough Cinquefoil, Strawberry-weed, Ternate-leaved Cinquefoil, Norwegisches Fingerkraut, Potentille de Norvège, Norsk mure, Лапчатка норвежская. SN means "cinquefoil of Norway."
RANGE: Near circumpolar, on wasteland and disturbed ground.
ID: H 12–36 in (30–100 cm). Tall, weedy. Stems leafy, stout, finely haired. LVS: Trifoliate; 3 oval leaflets, to 3 in (7 cm) long, with rounded teeth on margin. FLS: Jun–Aug. Yellow, 5-parted, to 0.5 in (1.5 cm) across, borne in a branched cyme.

Red-stemmed Cinquefoil

Potentilla rubricaulis
ALSO: Rocky Mountain Cinquefoil, *Potentilla pedersenii*. SN means "red-stemmed cinquefoil." Arctic explorer John Richardson (1787–1865) collected

the first specimen of this lovely plant in the 1820s in Canada's Great Bear Lake area, probably close to Fort Franklin.
RANGE: Greenland, Svalbard, and N Amer south through the Rocky Mtns, on dry tundra, barrens, slopes, river terraces, and margins of ponds; prefers well-drained calcareous substrate.
ID: H 4–12 in (10–30 cm). Forms large cushion-like mats. Stems erect or decumbent, stout, branched, reddish brown, with fine white hairs. LVS: Trifoliate; underside of leaflets woolly; shaggy tufts of hairs on leaf margins. FLS: To 1 in (2.5 cm) across, borne in cymes of 3–7 blossoms. Petals 5, pure yellow; sepals green, hairy.

Pretty Cinquefoil

Potentilla pulchella
ALSO: Tufted Cinquefoil, Potentille jolie, Tuemure, Лапчатка красивенькая. SN means "beautiful cinquefoil."
RANGE: Near circumpolar; found in N Amer, Greenland, Svalbard, and n Siberia (disjunct sites), on beaches, gravelly soil, and dry tundra.
ID: H 10–12 in (25–30 cm). Decumbent or tall arching stems. LVS: Pinnate, woolly-haired below; 3–5 deeply incised leaflets, with entire margins. FLS: To 0.4 in (1 cm) across, in clusters of 1–3 blossoms. Petals 5, pale yellow; sepals 5, bright green. Buds covered with long, silky hairs.

Vahl's Cinquefoil

Potentilla vahliana
ALSO: Cushion Cinquefoil, Potentille de Vahl. SN means "Vahl's cinquefoil," honoring Danish botanist Jens Laurentius Moestue Vahl (1796–1854), who described the flora of Greenland.
RANGE: Chukotka, n N Amer, and Greenland, on limestone barrens, dry meadows, and slopes.
ID: H 2–4 in (5–10 cm). Forms low cushions to 3 ft (1 m) across. Plant base densely covered with dark stipules from previous years. LVS: Densely covered with woolly or silky guard hairs. Basal leaves short-petioled; 3 deeply cleft leaflets, with toothed margins. FLS: Yellow with an orange base, 5-parted, solitary, to 1 in (2.5 cm) across.

Alpine Cinquefoil

Potentilla verna
ALSO: Potentille de Crantz,
Potentille de printemps,
Flekkmure, *Potentilla crantzii*. SN means "spring-flowering cinquefoil."
RANGE: Amphi-Atlantic; found in arctic and alpine zones in eN Amer, Greenland, Iceland, Svalbard, and nw Eurasia; grows in meadows, rock crevices, herb mats, and willow thickets.
ID: H 6–10 in (15–25 cm). Loosely tufted. Stems leafy, erect, and rising from sides of plant base. LVS: Smooth above, hairy below; 3–5 leaflets, with toothed margins. FLS: To 1 in (2 cm) across, borne at tips of stems. Petals 5, pale yellow, with a dark orange base; sepals 5, green.

GENUS *DASIPHORA*
Shrubby Cinquefoil

Dasiphora fruticosa
ALSO: Tundra Rose, Finger-strauch, Potentille ligneuse,
Potentille arbrisseau, Киргизский, *Potentilla fruticosa*. SN means "hirsute shrubby cinquefoil."
RANGE: E Asia, N Amer, and isolated sites in Siberia and n Europe; grows in forests, heaths, muskeg, and on scree slopes to 5000 ft (1500 m).
ID: H 12–60 in (30–150 cm). Spreading or erect, densely foliated branches that have shredded bark. LVS: Compound, covered with silvery, silky hairs; 5–7 linear to oblong leaflets, with entire margins. FLS: Yellow to orange, 5-parted, to 1 in (3 cm) across; borne on stem tips. FR: Hairy brown achenes.

GENUS *ARGENTINA*
Eged's Silverweed

Argentina egedii
ALSO: Seaside Cinquefoil, Potentille d'Egede, *Potentilla egedii*. SN means "Egede's little silver," referring to the silvery hairs on the leaflet underside and to Paul Egede (1708–1789), Danish-Norwegian missionary to Greenland, gentleman naturalist, and cataloger of the Greenlandic language.
RANGE: Disjunct coastal areas of ne Siberia, N Amer, Greenland, Iceland, and n Europe, in salt marshes and brackish wetlands.

ID: H 2–6 in (5–15 cm). Low, creeping perennial; spreads via cord-like, red runners (*stolons*), to 30 in (80 cm) long. LVS: Compound, 4–16 in (10–40 cm) long; 2–5 leaflets, with toothed margins; smooth above and with a few silky white hairs on the underside. FLS: Pale yellow, 5-parted, to 1.5 in (3.5 cm) across; solitary, at the tip of slender, naked stems.

GENUS *COMARUM*
Marsh Cinquefoil

Comarum palustre
ALSO: Purple Cinquefoil, Marsh Fivefinger, Sumpf-Blutauge, Potentille des marais, Myrhatt, Сабельник болотный. SN means "swamp strawberry-tree," referring to the red petals and seedheads that resemble the fruit of *Arbutus*.
RANGE: Circumpolar, on lakeshores, marshy riverbanks, and bogs.
ID: H 2–6 in (5–15 cm). Low, creeping perennial. Often grows partly submerged, with foliage floating on water surface. Reddish brown stems. LVS: Pinnately compound, with 3–7 serrate-margined leaflets. FLS: Jun–Aug. To 1 in (3 cm) across. Petals 5–6, reddish purple, with pointed tips; sepals 5–6, purple. Blossoms emit a fetid odor that attracts carrion-feeding insect pollinators. FR: Small, dry, hairless achene.

GENUS *SANGUISORBA*
Great Burnet

Sanguisorba officinalis
ALSO: Official or Salad Burnet, Großer Wieseknopf, Grande pimprenelle, Blóðkollur, Blodtopp, Кровохлёбка лекарст-венная. SN means "blood-clotting [plant] of use to humans," alluding to the plant's use as a coagulant.
RANGE: Iceland, Eurasia, nw N Amer, and in disjunct sites in ec N Amer; found on grassy slopes and in alpine meadows.
ID: H 25–40 in (65–100 cm). Stems tall, pubescent, with 1–2 reduced leaves. LVS: Mostly basal. Pinnate, 6–12 in (15–30 cm) long; 7–15 ovate to lanceolate leaflets with coarsely toothed margins. FLS: Jun–Jul. Reddish purple, to 1 in (2 cm) long; borne in cylindrical spikes.

Pretty Cinquefoil
Potentilla pulchella
Near circumpolar
H 10–12 in (25–30 cm)

Alpine Cinquefoil
Potentilla verna
Amphi-Atlantic
H 6–10 in (15–25 cm)

Snow Cinquefoil
Potentilla nivea
Circumpolar
H 6–10 in (15–25 cm)

Red-stemmed Cinquefoil
Potentilla rubricaulis
N Amer, Greenland, Svalbard
H 4–12 in (10–30 cm)

Eged's Silverweed
Argentina egedii
NE Asia, N Amer, Greenland,
Iceland, n Europe
H 2–6 in (5–15 cm)

Marsh Cinquefoil
Comarum palustre
Circumpolar
H 2–6 in (5–15 cm)

Shrubby Cinquefoil
Dasiphora fruticosa
E Asia, N Amer, Siberia
H 12–60 in (30–150 cm)

Norwegian Cinquefoil
Potentilla norvegica
Near circumpolar
H 12–36 in (30–100 cm)

Arctic Cinquefoil
Potentilla hyparctica
Circumpolar
H 2–5 in (5–12 cm)

Vahl's Cinquefoil
Potentilla vahliana
Chukotka, n N Amer, Greenland
H 2–4 in (5–10 cm)

USE: Root and leaves have astringent properties. Root is used in traditional Chinese medicine to stop bloody dysentery, nosebleeds, and is applied topically to treat burns and insect bites. Leaves taste like cucumbers and are used in salads.

Canadian Burnet
Sanguisorba canadensis
ALSO: White Burnet, American Burnet, Wiesenknopf, Sanguisorbe du Canada, Кровохлёбка, *S. stipulata*, *S. sitchensis*. SN means "blood-clotting [plant] of Canada."
RANGE: Grows in swamps, meadows, and along roads from Alaska south to Oregon; from Hudson Bay and Labrador south to Georgia; and in the Kurils, Korea, and Japan.
ID: H 40–60 in (100–150 cm). LVS: Alternate, odd-pinnately compound, with 7–15 oblong leaflets having serrated margins. Most leaves grow from lower half of stem. FLS: Jul–Sep. Creamy white, in terminal cylindrical spikes 2–8 in (5–20 cm) long. FR: A 4-winged capsule.

GENUS *SORBUS*
Rowan
Sorbus aucuparia
ALSO: Mountain Ash, Vogel- beere, Sorbier des oiseleurs, Rogn, Рябина обыкновенная. SN means "bird-attracting service-tree." CN derives from the German *raud-inan*, meaning "to turn red," referring to the berries.
RANGE: Found in Iceland and n Europe to 70°N, the northern limit of European trees. Naturalized in N Amer. Grows in coniferous forests, broadleaf woodland, wooded meadows, spruce swamps, and rocky slopes to 6550 ft (2000 m). Range of sister species *S. scopulina*, *S. sitchensis*, and *S. sambucifolia* is shown in pale green on map.
ID: H 25–33 ft (8–10 m), rarely 65 ft (20 m). Bark smooth, silvery gray on young trees; scaly, grayish brown at maturity. LVS: Deciduous. Pinnately compound, 4–11 in (10–22 cm) long; 9–19 somewhat hairy leaflets, with coarsely serrated margins; leaves turn red in autumn. FLS: Jun–Jul. Creamy white, 5-parted, to 0.5 in

(1 cm) across, borne in terminal corymbs to 6 in (15 cm) across. Purplish brown, hairy buds. FR: Aug–Sep. Clusters of small berries, 0.25 in (0.6 cm) across; green at first, ripening to bright red.
USE: Rowan fruit, seeds, foliage, and bark are important food sources for birds, deer, elk, and hares. Fresh berries are bitter to human taste, but can be made into tart-tasting jelly served as an accompaniment to game and venison. Widely planted as an ornamental tree. Its tough and flexible wood is used for woodworking.

FAMILY CRASSULACEAE
SEDUMS AMD STONECROPS
GENUS *RHODIOLA*
Roseroot Stonecrop
Rhodiola rosea

ALSO: Golden Root, Aaron's Rod, King's Crown, Rosenwurz, Orpin rose, Rosenrot, Родиола розовая, *Sedum rosea*. SN means "rose-like," alluding to the rootstock, which has a rose-like fragrance when cut and dried.
RANGE: Near circumpolar (absent c Canada), around villages and on rocky ledges, sea cliffs, bird cliffs, and scree slopes to 7200 ft (2200 m).
ID: H 2–14 in (5–36 cm). Succulent perennial herb. Thick, scaly rootstock. Dioecious. LVS: Fleshy, closely packed, waxy, pale grayish green to rose, spoon-shaped, to 1.75 in (4 cm) long, with entire or dentate margins. FLS: Bright yellow, sometimes rosy purple, 4-parted, small, star-shaped; borne in dense, flat-topped terminal clusters. FR: Plump, erect, red seed follicles.
USE: Young stems and leaves are bitter, but edible. Siberian Eskimos cook the plant with seal meat or reindeer fat. Plant extracts are used in Scandinavia and Siberia to alleviate depression, stress, and fatigue. This attractive succulent is also a food plant for *Parnassius* butterflies.

FAMILY ELAEAGNACEAE
OLEASTERS AND ALLIES
GENUS *SHEPHERDIA*
Canada Buffaloberry
Shepherdia canadensis
ALSO: Soapberry, Soopolallie, Kanadische

Büffelbeere, Шефердия канадская. SN means "Shepherd's [berry] of Canada," honoring John Shepherd (1764–1863), botanist and curator of the Liverpool Botanical Gardens. CN originates with the practice of cooking the dried berries with buffalo meat. The fruit contains saponin, which produces a soapy foam when mixed with water, hence "soapberry."

RANGE: N Amer; found in open woods, along streams, on beaches, dunes, gravel ridges, and around melting snowbeds, to 3950 ft (1200 m). **ID:** H 2–10 ft (0.5–3 m). Shrub, as wide as it is tall. Branchlets covered with brownish scale. Dioecious. **LVS:** Opposite, leathery, oval or ovate, 1–2 in (2–5 cm) long. Deep green above; leaf underside covered with small brown scales and downy hairs. **FLS:** Jun–Jul, just as the leaves emerge. Yellowish green, clustered in the leaf axils; 4 sepals, no petals. Male and female flowers borne on different plants. **FR:** Bitter but edible red (occasionally yellow) berry.

USE: The berries are rather bitter, so Canadian First Nations peoples whip them with some sugar into a frothy desert called "Indian ice cream," or *hooshum*.

Rowan
Sorbus aucuparia
N Europe, Iceland
Naturalized in N Amer
H 25–33 ft (8–10 m)

White flowers in spring

Fall color

Red rowan berries in late summer

Canada Buffaloberry
Shepherdia canadensis
N Amer
H 2–10 ft (0.5–3 m)

Great Burnet
Sanguisorba officinalis
Eurasia, N Amer, Iceland
H 25–40 in (65–100 cm)

Small Apollo
Parnassius phoebus
Siberia

Roseroot Stonecrop
Rhodiola rosea
Near circumpolar
H 2–14 in (5–36 cm)

Canadian Burnet
Sanguisorba canadensis
E Asia, N Amer
H 40–60 in (100–150 cm)

Saxifragales: Saxifrages

The flowers of these mostly perennial plants are typically 5-parted, bisexual, and star-shaped.

FAMILY SAXIFRAGACEAE
SAXIFRAGES

Saxifrage flowers are white, yellow, or purple, mostly 5-parted, and may be saucer-shaped, cup-shaped, or funnel-like. The word saxifrage derives from the Latin *saxum*, meaning "rock," and *frangere*, meaning "to break." The term may allude to the way the plant's roots burrow into rock and literally split it in two, or it may refer to the medicinal use of the plant for the treatment of kidney stones.

GENUS *SAXIFRAGA*
Spider Saxifrage
Saxifraga flagellaris

ALSO: Whiplash Saxifrage, Saxifrage des ruisseau, Камнеломка усатая, Kakillarnaliit, *S. platysepala*. SN means "saxifrage with whip-like stolons."
RANGE: Circumpolar, on scree slopes and along alpine streams, to 6500 ft (2000 m).
ID: H 1–6 in (3–15 cm). Slender, naked, red runners (*stolons*) radiate out from the mother plant and end in tiny, rooting rosettes. LVS: Entire, oblanceolate, acute, bristle-edged, in a basal rosette. FLS: Solitary; borne at tip of single, erect stem. Petals yellow; sepals purple, glandular. FR: Horned capsule.

Yellow Mountain Saxifrage
Saxifraga aizoides

ALSO: Fetthennen Stein-brech, Saxifrage faux Orpin, Gulsildre, Камнеломка жестколистная. SN means "evergreen saxifrage."
RANGE: N Amer, Greenland, Iceland, Svalbard, and Europe, on clay or gravel streambanks in the arctic and alpine zones.
ID: H 2–6 in (5–15 cm). Forms mats of trailing or decumbent stems. LVS: Linear, fleshy. FLS: Borne in racemes; 5-parted. Petals yellow with orange dots; sepals yellowish green.

Yellow Marsh Saxifrage
Saxifraga hirculus

ALSO: Bog Saxifrage, Moor-Steinbrech, Saxifrage oeil-de-bouc, Saxifrage affine. SN means "little goat [-eye] saxifrage."
RANGE: Circumpolar, on moist tundra, in bogs and meadows, and by brooks and lakes.
ID: H 2–10 in (5–25 cm). Tufted. LVS: Basal, strap-like, smooth, entire, to 1.75 in (4 cm) long. Erect stems bear 3–4 linear, sessile leaves. FLS: Small, cup-shaped, 5-parted, mostly solitary; nodding in bud. Petals pale yellow. Sepals bear rust-colored hairs. FR: Horned seed follicles.

Tufted Alpine Saxifrage
Saxifraga caespitosa

ALSO: Polstersteinbrech, Saxifrage cespiteuse, Tuvesildre, Камнеломка дернист. SN means "tuft-forming saxifrage."
RANGE: Circumpolar, on sandy tundra, rock ledges, and stony slopes to at least 7550 ft (2300 m).
ID: H 2–8 in (5–20 cm). Densely tufted, with numerous short, crowded, sterile branches. LVS: Basal, cuneate, 3-lobed, hairy, clammy to the touch. Withered leaves persist at plant base. FLS: Cream, with yellow centers; 5-parted. Flowering stems reddish, slender, erect, glandular, with a few reduced leaves and 1–2 terminal flowers.

Thymeleaf Saxifrage
Saxifraga serpyllifolia

ALSO: Yellow Alpine Saxi-frage. SN means "saxifrage with thyme-like leaves."
RANGE: Amphi-Beringian; grows on dry rocky sites and gravelly scree slopes to 6000 ft (1850 m).
ID: H 2–4 in (5–10 cm). Forms low, loose mats. LVS: Small, fleshy, resembling those of garden thyme. FLS: Five-parted. Petals yellow; sepals deep red. FR: Flask-shaped capsule.

Bulblet Saxifrage
Saxifraga cernua

ALSO: Nodding Saxifrage, Nickender Steinbrech, Saxi-frage penchée, Knoppsildre,

Thymeleaf Saxifrage
Saxifraga serpyllifolia
Amphi-Beringian
H 2–4 in (5–10 cm)

**Yellow Mountain
Saxifrage**
Saxifraga aizoides
N Amer, Greenland, Iceland,
Svalbard, n Europe
H 2–6 in (5–15 cm)

Spider Saxifrage
Saxifraga flagellaris
Circumpolar
H 1–6 in (3–15 cm)

Prickly Saxifrage
Saxifraga tricuspidata
N Amer, Greenland
H 2–6 in (5–15 cm)

Yellow Marsh Saxifrage
Saxifraga hirculus
Circumpolar
H 2–10 in (5–25 cm)

Brook Saxifrage
Saxifraga rivularis
Circumpolar
H 2–4 in (5–10 cm)

Foliolose Saxifrage
Saxifraga foliolosa
Circumpolar
H 2–10 in (5–25 cm)

Tufted Alpine Saxifrage
Saxifraga caespitosa
Circumpolar
H 2–8 in (5–20 cm)

Bulblet Saxifrage
Saxifraga cernua
Circumpolar
H 4–10 in (10–25 cm)

Камнеломка поникающая. SN means "saxifrage with nodding [bud]."
RANGE: Circumpolar, on moist ledges and gravelly substrates, around snowbeds, and in moss or wet sand on lakeshores.
ID: H 4–10 in (10–25 cm). LVS: Basal leaves lobed, kidney-shaped. Stem leaves bract-like, with clusters of bead-like, deep red, reproductive bulblets in leaf axils. FLS: White, 5-parted, solitary. Nodding in bud, upright when fully open.

Brook Saxifrage
Saxifraga rivularis

ALSO: Arctic or Pygmy Saxifrage, Bach-Steinbrech, Saxifrage hyperboréale, Bekkesildre, Камнеломка ручейная, *S. hyperborea*. SN means "streamside saxifrage."
RANGE: Circumpolar, on wet gravelly substrates and mossy sites along streams, near human habitation, and below bird cliffs.
ID: H 2–4 in (5–10 cm). Dwarf perennial. LVS: Basal, kidney-shaped, palmately 3- to 5-lobed, smooth, thin-stemmed. FLS: Borne singly or in inflorescences of 2–5 on hairy stems; 5-parted. Petals white or pale pink; sepals green.

Prickly Saxifrage
Saxifraga tricuspidata

ALSO: Three-toothed Saxifrage, Saxifrage à trois dents, Kakilahan. SN means "saxifrage with a 3-toothed [leaf margin]."
RANGE: N Amer and Greenland, on dry gravelly sites in the arctic and alpine zones.
ID: H 2–6 in (6–15 cm). LVS: Crowded in flat cushions; rigid, leathery, cuneate to spatulate, with 3 prickly, tooth-like lobes at apex. Green in summer, often red through winter. FLS: Nodding in bud; 5-parted. Petals cream, dotted with orange, brown or purple; sepals green.

Foliolose Saxifrage
Saxifraga foliolosa

ALSO: Grained Saxifrage, Stern-Steinbrech, Saxifrage à bulbilles, Stjernesildre, Mirquujaliit. SN means "few-leaved saxifrage."

RANGE: Circumpolar, on wet or mossy tundra and along streams, ponds, and snowbeds.
ID: H 2–10 in (5–25 cm). Tufted. Slender, erect, leafless, branched stem, with green bulblets at tips of side branches. LVS: Thin, cuneate-oblanceolate to spatulate, serrate or toothed, in a basal rosette. FLS: White, usually with 2 yellow spots near the base; 5-parted. Solitary at stem tip.

Purple Saxifrage
Saxifraga oppositifolia

ALSO: French Knot Moss, Gegenblättriger Steinbrech, Saxifrage à feuilles opposées, Rødsildre, Камнеломка супротивнолистная, Aupilaktunnguaq (something with bold spots and tasty petals). SN means "saxifrage with opposite leaves." Floral emblem of Nunavut, Londonderry, and Nordland.
RANGE: Circumpolar, on gravelly substrates and cliff ledges, to 3250 ft (1000 m); grows from 83°N latitude in Greenland, south to the Alps, Rocky Mtns, and mountains of n UK.
ID: H 2–3 in (5–8 cm). Low-growing, densely or loosely matted plant, with somewhat woody, creeping branches. LVS: Basal rosette of small, scale-like, opposite, linear, leathery, 4-ranked leaves, with bristle-edged margins. FLS: Purple to lilac, rarely white, elliptical to oval, to 0.5 in (1.5 cm) across; 5-parted. Begins to flower in early spring and continues to bloom for the entire summer in places where snow persists.

GENUS *MICRANTHES*
Stiffstem Saxifrage
Micranthes hieracifolia

ALSO: Hawkweed-leaved Saxifrage, Habichtskraut-Steinbrech, Камнеломка ястребинколистная, *Saxifraga hieracifolia*. SN means "saxifrage with hawkweed-like [*Hieracium*] leaves."
RANGE: Circumpolar, in damp mossy sites near streams and snowbeds.
ID: H 4–20 in (10–50 cm). LVS: Basal, smooth, oblong-lanceolate, short-stemmed, to 2.5 in (7 cm) long, with coarsely toothed margins. FLS: Borne in dense clusters near tip of a stout, glandular stem. Petals 5, green to purple; sepals 5, purple.

Purple Saxifrage
Saxifraga oppositifolia
Circumpolar
H 2–3 in (5–8 cm)

Heartleaf Saxifrage
Micranthes nelsoniana
Siberia, e Asia,
Aleutians, nw N Amer
H 12–20 in (30–50 cm)

Stiffstem Saxifrage
Micranthes hieracifolia
Circumpolar
H 4–20 in (10–50 cm)

Snow Saxifrage
Micranthes nivalis
Circumpolar
H 2–8 in (5–20 cm)

Northern Redcurrant
Ribes triste
NE Siberia, n N Amer
H 12–20 in (30–50 cm)

Kotzebue's Grass of Parnassus
Parnassia kotzebuei
NE Siberia, N Amer, Greenland
H 2–8 in (5–20 cm)

Northern Water Carpet
Chrysosplenium tetrandrum
Near circumpolar
H 1–4 in (3–10 cm)

Richardson's Brookfoam
Boykinia richardsonii
Alaska, nw Canada
H 6–25 in (15–65 cm)

Large Grass of Parnassus
Parnassia palustris
Circumpolar
H 4–16 in (10–40 cm)

Heartleaf Saxifrage

Micranthes nelsoniana
ALSO: Dotted Saxifrage, Brook Saxifrage. SN means "Nelson's saxifrage."
RANGE: E Eurasia, Aleutians, and nw N Amer, on alpine meadows, tundra hummocks, mossy hillsides, and around waterfalls.
ID: H 12–20 in (30–50 cm). LVS: Basal, hairy, heart-shaped, with deeply dentate margins. FLS: White, dotted with yellow or rose; 5-parted. Sepals purple. Reddish, hairy flowering stems.
USE: Inuit eat the leaves and stems in salads or ferment the plant and serve it with seal blubber and fish. Source of vitamin C and beta-carotene.

Snow Saxifrage

Micranthes nivalis
ALSO: Alpine Saxifrage, Schnee Steinbrech, Saxifrage des neiges, Snoesildre, Камнеломка снежная, *Saxifraga nivalis*. SN means "snow saxifrage."
RANGE: Circumpolar, on tundra, barrens, and dry rocky slopes to 5600 ft (1700 m); thrives on manured soil under bird cliffs.
ID: H 2–8 in (5–20 cm). LVS: Basal. Dark green above; reddish purple and fringed with hairs below; leathery, oval, coarsely toothed, to 2 in (5 cm) long; blade abruptly tapers into a broad petiole. FLS: Five-parted. Petals white; sepals purple. Borne in dense clusters on erect, slender, leafless, purple stems that are covered with sticky glands. FR: Long, plump seed follicles, with widely spread horns.

GENUS *CHRYSOSPLENIUM*
Northern Water Carpet

Chrysosplenium tetrandrum
ALSO: Northern Golden Saxifrage, Nördliches Milzkraut, Dorine à quatre étamines, Dvergmaigull, Селезёночник четырёхтычинковый. SN means "four golden anthers."
RANGE: Circumpolar, on moist tundra sites and often on nitrogenous soils near animal dens and old Inuit middens.

ID: H 1–4 in (3–10 cm). Small, creeping, perennial herb with erect, branched stems. LVS: Yellowish green, kidney-shaped, with 3–7 shallow lobes. FLS: Small, apetalous; sepals 4, bright yellow, set in the leaf axils; 4 golden anthers. FR: Tiny seeds form in the cup-like flowers and splash out when raindrops hit the cups.

GENUS *BOYKINIA*
Richardson's Brookfoam

Boykinia richardsonii
ALSO: Alaska Boykinia, Bear Flowers (any bear's favorite snack). SN means "Richardson's Boykinia," after Scottish naturalist Sir John Richardson (1787–1865) and Samuel Boykin (1786–1848), a plant collector from Milledgeville, Georgia.
RANGE: N Alaska to the coastal area between the Mackenzie and Coppermine rivers in nw Canada; grows at forest edge, in tundra meadows, and along streambanks and snowbeds, to 5900 ft (1800 m).
ID: H 6–25 in (15–65 cm). LVS: Basal leaves large, heart-shaped, dentate or shallowly lobed, smooth above, sparsely haired on the veins below. Stem leaves few, oval to lanceolate. FLS: White to pink, 5-parted; form in the leaf axils and also cluster at the stem tip.

FAMILY GROSSULARIACEAE
CURRANTS
GENUS *RIBES*
Northern Redcurrant

Ribes triste
ALSO: Swamp Redcurrant, Johannisbeeren, Gadelier rouge sauvage, Ripser, Смородина печальная, Nivingakutak. SN means "pendulous currant."
RANGE: NE Siberia and n N Amer, in meadows, swamps, spruce forests, and along streams.
ID: H 12–20 in (30–50 cm). Low shrub, with spreading or creeping branches. LVS: Alternate, palmately 5-lobed; to 4 in (10 cm) across. FLS: May–Jul. Pendulous raceme of 6–13 small purple flowers. FR: Jul–Aug. Edible, bright red berries.
USE: Berries are eaten fresh or made into jelly. The stem is made into a bitter tea.

Celastrales: Parnassia and Allies

FAMILY CELASTRACEAE

GRASSES OF PARNASSUS

These lovely wetland plants are wildflowers, not grasses, as the name implies. The inflorescence is a single, perfect, upward-facing, 5-parted flower. The method of fertilization is unique. As the flowers open, the male stamens elongate and one at a time bend inward and deposit pollen on the ovary. After about 24 hours, the spent stamen bends away from the ovary and another in turn leans over. The flower's center contains 5 sterile stamens (*staminodes*), each tipped with a golden false nectary, which exudes droplets of sweet liquid that attract insect pollinators.

GENUS *PARNASSIA*

Large Grass of Parnassus

Parnassia palustris

ALSO: Bog Star, Marsh Grass of Parnassus, Sumpf-Herzblatt, Parnassie des marais, Jåblom, Белозор болотный. SN means "parnassia of the marsh," referring to Mount Parnassus in Greece.
RANGE: Near circumpolar (absent Greenland); found from arctic N Amer and Eurasia south to the n US and China, on wet calcareous soils on grassy slopes, in damp meadows, and along streams, to 7200 ft (2200 m).
ID: H 4–16 in (10–40 cm). LVS: Heart-shaped, smooth-margined, in a basal rosette. Erect, unbranched stem, with a single clasping leaf at or below mid-stem. FLS: Jul–Aug. Solitary, terminal, 5-parted blossom, to 1.5 in (3.5 cm) across. Petals white with green veins; sepals green. Cream-colored stamens alternate with 5 filamentous staminodes, each tipped with a golden yellow nectary. FR: Small, oval, dry capsule with many small seeds.

Kotzebue's Grass of Parnassus

Parnassia kotzebuei

ALSO: Small Grass of Parnassus, Parnassie de Kotzebue, Белозор Коцебу. SN means "Kotzebue's parnassia," honoring Baltic German navigator, in Russian service, Otto von Kotzebue (1787–1846), who discovered and named Kotzebue Sound and Cape Krusenstern in the Chukchi Sea.
RANGE: NE Siberia, Aleutians, Alaska, Canada, and south to the n US, with isolated populations in Greenland; grows in moist tundra, subalpine meadows and thickets, bogs, wet sand around ponds, along creeks, and on rocky ledges to 6500 ft (2000 m).
ID: H 2–8 in (5–20 cm). LVS: Heart-shaped, smooth-margined, in a basal rosette. FLS: Jun–Sep. Solitary, 5-parted, to 0.75 in (2 cm) across, borne at top of leafless stems. Petals white, with a few pale green veins; sepals green. Stamens 5, cream-colored; 5 filamentous staminodes, each tipped with greenish yellow nectaries.

Fabales: Legumes

Fabales contains trees, shrubs, herbs, and vines whose root nodules harbor nitrogen-fixing bacteria. The order Fabales—as well as Asparagales, Arecales, Brassicales, Lamiales, and Magnoliales—was the creation of Irish mathematician and gentleman botanist, Edward Ffrench Bromhead (1789–1855).

FAMILY FABACEAE (LEGUMINOSAE)

LEGUMES

One of the major plant families, Fabaceae contains more than 500 genera and thousands of species. Most legumes have 5-parted flowers. Each has a single upright dorsal petal called a *standard*, *vexillum*, or *banner*; 2 lateral, horizontal petals called *wings*; and 2 lower petals that are more or less united into what is known as the *keel*. The flowers normally have 10 stamens, with the upper one free, the others united into a tube enclosing a long ovary. The fruit is a *pea pod*, or *legume*. Leaves are alternate and compound.

Most arctic legumes are edible, but a few are toxic. The root of Northern Sweet Vetch (*Hedysarum mackenzii*) is poisonous, and some of the locoweeds (*Astragalus*, *Oxytropis*) contain the indolizine alkaloid swainsonine, which is toxic to livestock.

GENUS *HEDYSARUM*
Liquorice-root

Hedysarum alpinum
ALSO: Alpine Sweetvetch, Bear Root, Eskimo Potato, Sainfoin alpin, Alpehanehode, Копеечник сибирский, Masru, *H. americanum*. SN means "pleasant tasting [plant] of mountain pastures."
RANGE: Amphi-Beringian (broadly), on riverbanks, lakeshores, and in alpine meadows.
ID: H 4–20 in (10–50 cm). LVS: Smooth, pinnately compound, with 9–13 dark-veined, lanceolate leaflets. Flowering stems erect, often Y-shaped. FLS: Pink or purple, 5-parted, unscented, borne in racemes. FR: Flat, net-veined pods, with 3–5 oval seed chambers.
USE: Liquorice-root is rich in vitamin C and helps to ward off scurvy. Inuit eat the root raw or cooked; it tastes like carrots. Siberians fry the root of the similar *H. hedysaroides* (pale green on map). Liquorice-root is also a favorite food of bears; patches of overturned earth and torn up plants signal their foraging activities.

Northern Sweet Vetch

Hedysarum mackenzii
ALSO: Wild Sweet Pea, Mackenzie's Sweet Vetch, Süßklee, Sainfoin de Mackenzie, Копеечник северный *H. boreale*. SN means "Mackenzie's sweet tasting [plant]," honoring the Scottish explorer of arctic Canada, Alexander Mackenzie (1764–1820).
RANGE: Amphi-Beringian (broadly), on tundra, slopes, and dry gravelly flats.
ID: H 6–16 in (15–40 cm). LVS: Silvery gray, pinnately compound, with 5–13 linear to lanceolate, pubescent leaflets. FLS: Magenta to deep purple, showy, sweet-scented; borne in a spike of 5–15 flowers. FR: Flat pods, with 3–6 oval or circular seed chambers. ROOT IS POISONOUS.

GENUS *ASTRAGALUS*
Alpine Milk Vetch

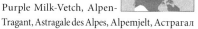

Astragalus alpinus
ALSO: Mountain Locoweed, Purple Milk-Vetch, Alpen-Tragant, Astragale des Alpes, Alpemjelt, Астрагал

альпийский. SN means "alpine [plant] with vertebrae-like knotted [roots]," as applied by Pliny the Elder (AD 23–79).
RANGE: Circumpolar, on stony margins of shallow ponds, grassy slopes, and scree slopes to 6500 ft (2000 m).
ID: H 2–10 in (5–25 cm). Low, matted, with spreading stems, to 30 in (76 cm) long, sprouting from vertebrae-like nodes of a branching underground rhizome. LVS: Pinnately compound, with 15–29 oblong to ovate, sparsely haired leaflets, 0.5 in (1.2 cm) long. FLS: May–Jul. Nodding pea flower, with a purple to blue keel and white wings. FR: Pendulous, densely pubescent pod, the lower side deeply marked with longitudinal grooves.

GENUS *LUPINUS*
Arctic Lupine

Lupinus arcticus
ALSO: Tundra Lupine. SN means "lupine of the north."
RANGE: Alaska and w Canada, in wet meadows, moist tundra, gravel bars, roadsides, grassy alpine slopes, heath, and woodland.
ID: H 4–20 in (10–50 cm). Tufted. Hollow, upright stems covered in long, silky white hairs. LVS: Palmately compound, long-petioled, bright green, with 6–8 pointed leaflets. FLS: Jun–Jul. Dark blue to purple lavender; borne in a raceme that blooms from the bottom up. FR: Yellow, hairy pods, to 1.5 in (4 cm) long, twisted after opening. SEEDS ARE POISONOUS if ingested in large quantities. In 1967, seeds of this plant were found in the Yukon in a burrow containing frozen lemming remains dating to at least 10,000 years ago. Seeds gathered at the site germinated in the laboratory within 48 hours, grew to maturity, and went on to produce healthy new plants.

Nootka Lupine

Lupinus nootkatensis
ALSO: Alaska-Lupine, Sand-lupin, Люпин. Species is named for its type locality near Nootka Sound, Vancouver Is, Canada.
RANGE: Aleutians, s Alaska, and w Canada, on dry slopes, gravel bars, sandy beaches, roadsides, and barren ground in disturbed areas, where

it is planted to enrich soil and control erosion. Introduced into Scandinavia in the late 1700s, to Iceland in 1885, and to Greenland and the Faroes around 1970.

ID: H 20–48 in (50–120 cm). Dies back annually to an underground rootstock. Plants increase in number of stems and size over a number of years; large plants may have over 100 stems and be about 10 years old. LVS: Palmately compound, with 5–7 oblong to oblanceolate, somewhat pubescent leaflets. Flowering stem covered with dense downy hairs. FLS: Blue, rarely white. FR: Pod. SEEDS ARE POISONOUS.

GENUS *LATHYRUS*
Beach Pea
Lathyrus japonicus

ALSO: Sea-pea, Strand-Platterbse, Pois-de-mer, Stranderteknapp, Чина японская, *L. maritimus.* SN means "pea of Japan."

RANGE: Seacoasts of N Amer, S Amer, and Eurasia; rare inland on sandy soil.

ID: H 4–6 in (10–15 cm). Downy-haired, trailing stems to 40 in (100 cm) long. LVS: Thick, fleshy, compound, with 6–12 oblong leaflets. FLS: Jun–Aug. Reddish banner; bluish violet keel and wings, to 1 in (2.5 cm) long. FR: Pod.

Beach Pea
Lathyrus japonicus
Seacoasts of Eurasia and
the Americas
H 4–6 in (10–15 cm)

Marsh Pea
Lathyrus palustris
Near circumpolar
H 12–30 in (30–120 cm)

Northern Sweet Vetch
Hedysarum mackenzii
Amphi-Beringian
H 6–16 in (15–40 cm)
Poisonous root

Alpine Milk Vetch
Astragalus alpinus
Circumpolar
H 2–10 in (5–25 cm)

Arctic Locoweed
Oxytropis arctica
Amphi-Beringian
H 2–8 in (5–20 cm)
Toxic to livestock

Nootka Lupine
Lupinus nootkatensis
Aleutians, s Alaska, w Canada
Introduced into Europe,
Iceland, Greenland, Faroes
H 20–48 in (50–120 cm)
Poisonous seeds

Field Locoweed
Oxytropis campestris
N Eurasia, n N Amer
H 8–20 in (20–50 cm)
Toxic to livestock

Liquorice-root
Hedysarum alpinum
Amphi-Beringian
H 4–20 in (10–50 cm)

Arctic Lupine
Lupinus arcticus
Alaska, w Canada
H 4–20 in (10–50 cm)
Poisonous seeds

Marsh Pea

Lathyrus palustris
ALSO: Marsh Vetchling,
Sumpf-Platterbse, Gesse des
marais, Myrflatbelg, Чина
болотная. SN means "pea of marshy ground."
RANGE: Near circumpolar, in subarctic to
temperate wet meadows, marshes, and swamps.
ID: H 12–30 in (30–120 cm). Climbing. Stems often
winged and with coiled tendrils. LVS: Pinnately
compound, with 2–4 pairs of leaflets. Asymmetrical, sharp-pointed, leaf-like appendages at
leaf base. FLS: Jun–Jul. Pinkish purple to white;
borne in clusters of 2–6 in a long-stalked raceme.

GENUS *OXYTROPIS*
Arctic Locoweed

Oxytropis arctica
ALSO: Spitzkiele, Mark-
mjeltslekten, Остролодочник.
SN means "arctic plant with a sharp-keeled [petal]."
RANGE: Amphi-Beringian (broadly), on arctic
tundra hummocks, river terraces, and ridges.
ID: H 2–8 in (5–20 cm). Densely tufted. Forms
soft cushions, to 12 in (30 cm) across. LVS:
Pinnately compound, with 9–13 oblong or
lanceolate leaflets, to 3 in (8 cm) long. FLS:
Jun–Jul. Fuchsia, fading to blue, rarely white;
contrasting color gradation from deep color
on tips to pale petal base; prominent veins on
banner. FR: Crescent-shaped, hairy pod, to 1 in
(2.5 cm) long. Toxic to livestock.

Field Locoweed

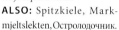

Oxytropis campestris
ALSO: Alpen-Spitzkiel,
Astragalus campestris. SN
means "field locoweed."
RANGE: N Eurasia and n N Amer; found in
woodland, meadows, prairies, and on gravelly
and rocky slopes.
ID: H 8 20 in (20–50 cm). LVS: Pinnately
compound, 3–16 in (8–40 cm) long, with 11–33
hairy, ovate leaflets, to 1 in (2.5 cm) long. FLS:
May–Jul. Cream or yellow; pointed keel blotched
with purple. Borne in a compact head or oblong
spike. FR: Oblong-ovate, mostly sessile, many-
seeded pod, to 1 in (2 cm) long. Toxic to livestock.

Myrtales: Myrtles and Allies
FAMILY ONAGRACEAE
FIREWEEDS AND WILLOWHERBS

These perennials have 4-parted flowers. The fruit
is a linear capsule that splits into 4 valves. The
numerous seeds have long, silky tufts of white
hairs at their apex to aid in wind dispersal. These
plants are of great value to Arctic residents. The
young leaves, roots, and shoots of the fireweeds
are rich in vitamins A and C. They can be used
as salad greens or cooked with seal or walrus
blubber. Leaves are steeped in water to make tea.
The pollen and nectar of late summer flowers
yield a rich, spicy honey that is used to sweeten
candy, jelly, and syrup.

GENUS *CHAMERION*
Dwarf Fireweed

Chamerion latifolium
ALSO: River Beauty,
Broad-leaved Willow Herb,
Arctic Fireweed, Arktisches Weiden-röschen,
Épilobe à feuilles larges, Kvitmjølke, Иван-чай
широколистный, Paunnat. National flower of
Greenland, where it is called *Niviarsiaq* ("little
girl"). SN means "low-growing with broad leaves."
RANGE: Near circumpolar; grows near melting
snowbeds, inundated gravel bars, floodplains,
river terraces, alpine talus slopes, and seashores.
ID: H 2–12 in (5–30 cm). Coarse, tufted perennial
herb. LVS: Alternate, lanceolate to oval, pointed
or rounded at the tips, to 4 in (10 cm) long. FLS:
Large, showy, 4-parted, often nodding. Petals
bright to deep pink, occasionally white. Sepals
dark pinkish purple, pointed. FR: Dry, elongated
capsule, to 4 in (10 cm) long, containing numerous
small seeds, each with a short tuft of yellow hairs.
USE: All plant parts can be eaten raw or cooked
with fat and oil. Cooked leaves taste somewhat
like spinach.

Fireweed

Chamerion angustifolium
ALSO: Rosebay Willowherb,
Yukon Fireweed, Tiirluk,
Naparutaujuq, Schmalblät-
triges Weidenröschen, Épilobe en épi, Laurier
de Saint-Antoine, Geitrams, Иван-чай

узколистный, *Epilobium angustifolium*. CN refers to the flowering plants, which look like banks of burning embers flickering across the hills. SN means "[plant] with narrow leaves." Yukon's territorial flower.

RANGE: Circumpolar, in forest clearings, willow thickets, along streambanks, near bird cliffs, and on burned sites and disturbed ground, to 13,000 ft (4000 m).

ID: H 6–32 in (15–80 cm). Coarse, tall perennial. Forms large colonies. Stems simple, erect. LVS: Alternate, lanceolate, 1–3 in (2.5–8 cm) long; veins pinnate. FLS: Jul–Sep. Showy, 4-parted, borne in an elongated, many-flowered raceme. Petals rose pink, rarely white; sepals purple, hairy to pubescent. FR: Pale yellow capsule, to 2 in (5 cm) long, containing up to 500 seeds.

USE: In Alaska young shoots are gathered and boiled, then cooked with sorrel (*Oxyria digyna*) and bacon.

GENUS *EPILOBIUM*
Marsh Willowherb
Epilobium palustre

ALSO: Épilobe des marais, Sumpf-Weidenröschen, Myrmjølke, Кипрей. SN means "marsh willowherb that has a flower located at the top of the ovary."

RANGE: Circumpolar, in wet meadows, and on streambanks and lakeshores.

ID: H 6–10 in (15–25 cm). LVS: Dark red to green, lanceolate, sessile; opposite at stem base, alternate at top. FLS: Small, with a long basal pedicel; nodding when young; solitary and terminal on an erect hairy stem. Petals 4, pink or white. FR: Elongated capsule that splits open when ripe.

Dahurian Willowherb
Epilobium davuricum

ALSO: Weidenröschen, Épilobe, Linmjølke, Кипрей. SN means "Dahurian willowherb," referring to Dahuria, the region east of Lake Baikal, Russia.

RANGE: Circumpolar, on tundra barrens, wet meadows, lakeshores, riverbanks, and around abandoned camps and mines.

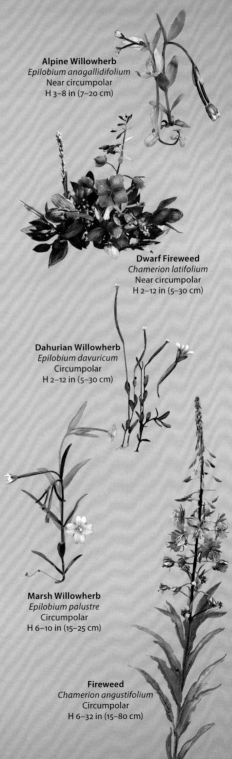

Alpine Willowherb
Epilobium anagallidifolium
Near circumpolar
H 3–8 in (7–20 cm)

Dwarf Fireweed
Chamerion latifolium
Near circumpolar
H 2–12 in (5–30 cm)

Dahurian Willowherb
Epilobium davuricum
Circumpolar
H 2–12 in (5–30 cm)

Marsh Willowherb
Epilobium palustre
Circumpolar
H 6–10 in (15–25 cm)

Fireweed
Chamerion angustifolium
Circumpolar
H 6–32 in (15–80 cm)

ID: H 2–12 in (5–30 cm). Delicate perennial herb. LVS: Stiffly erect, apex rounded, in a basal rosette. Dark green to purple stems. FLS: Few, small, with a long basal pedicel and swollen inferior ovary. Petals 4, white to pink. Sepals dark red.

Alpine Willowherb

Epilobium anagallidifolium
ALSO: Gauchheilblättriges Weidenröschen, Épilobe à feuilles de mouron, Dverg-mjølke, Pimpernel Willowherb. SN means "willowherb with unpretentious foliage."
RANGE: Near circumpolar, in wet meadows and on edges of ponds and streams.
ID: H 3–8 in (7–20 cm). Dwarf perennial with an unbranched, sinuous stem. Forms low clumps. LVS: Opposite, ovate, pale green, lanceolate, mostly entire. Basal leaves wide, rounded; narrow, hairy, stem leaves. FLS: Trumpet-shaped. Borne in pairs. Petals 4, pink to purple. Long, maroon, tubular calyx. FR: Nodding, dehiscent capsule.

Geraniales: Geraniums and Allies
FAMILY GERANIACEAE
CRANESBILLS OR GERANIUMS
Geraniaceae derives from the Greek word *geranos*, meaning "crane," referring to the fruit's long, narrow style beak, which resembles a crane's bill. When exposed to water, the fruit (*schizocarp*) splits apart with a sudden spring action, flinging the small, oval seeds in all directions. Plants in this family have lobed or otherwise divided leaves and symmetrical, bisexual, 5-parted flowers.

GENUS *GERANIUM*
Woolly Geranium

Geranium erianthum
ALSO: Woolly Cranesbill, Storknebb, Storch-schnäbel, Герань, *Geranium pratense*. SN means "hairy-leaved geranium."
RANGE: Amphi-Beringian; found from e Russia and Kamchatka to Alaska and nw Canada, in forests and meadows, to 3250 ft (1000 m).
ID: H 4–20 in (10–50 cm). Stem erect, solitary, with glandular hairs. FLS: Petals 5, rose to violet (rarely white); sepals 5, green, hairy; borne in

a cyme of 3–5 blossoms. LVS: Persistent basal rosette of 3- to 5-lobed, deeply cleft, cordate, hairy leaves, to 4 in (10 cm) across.
SIMILAR SPECIES: WOOD CRANESBILL, *G. sylvaticum*, grows in similar habitats in n Eurasia.

Herb Robert

Geranium robertianum
ALSO: Saint Robert's Wort, Stinky Bob, Red Robin, Géranium herbe-a-Robert, Stinkende storkenab, Stankstorkenebb, Герань Роберта. SN means "Saint Robert's geranium."
RANGE: N Europe; local in w/e N Amer; grows on lakeshores, streambanks, and in damp woods.
ID: H 6–8 in (15–20 cm). Stems reddish, branching. LVS: Edible but smell like burning rubber; 3–5 lobed, divided to the base. FLS: May–Oct. To 1 in (3 cm) across. Petals 5, pink to purple.
USE: Leaves can be used as mosquito repellent.

Gentianales: Gentians and Bedstraws
FAMILY GENTIANACEAE
GENTIANS

Gentians are herbs that have acrid watery sap, opposite leaves, regular 4- to 5-parted flowers, and 2-valved capsules that contain many small seeds.
Most gentians have tubular or salverform flowers of deep blue to azure. At times, blue-flowered plants may also bear white, yellow, or pink blossoms.

According to the Roman naturalist Pliny the Elder (AD 23–79), gentians are named for King Gentius (180–168 BC) of Illyria—now a part of Albania—who is said to have discovered the plants' healing properties and used them to treat his wounded soldiers.

GENUS *GENTIANA*
Pale Gentian

Gentiana glauca
ALSO: Glaucous Gentian, Inky Gentian, Smooth Alpine Gentian, Enziane, Storsøteslekta, Горечавка. SN means "pale gentian," referring to the rare yellow-flowered variety.

Herb Robert
Geranium robertianum
Europe, N Amer
H 6–8 in (15–20 cm)

♀ Cleobis Blue
Plebejus cleobis
NE Siberia

Woolly Geranium
Geranium erianthum
Amphi-Beringian
H 4–20 in (10–50 cm)

Geranium Argus
Aricia eumedon
N Eurasia

♂

♀

Wood Cranesbill
Geranium sylvaticum
Eurasia
H 4–14 in (10–36 cm)

Typical cranesbill
flower and fruit, with
the split schizocarp
on the right

Pygmy Gentian
Gentiana prostrata
Amphi-Beringian
H 1–3 in (3–7 cm)

Flowers
inky blue,
rarely yellow

Dane's Dwarf Gentian
Comastoma tenellum
Near circumpolar
H 2–6 in (5–15 cm)

Flowers pink
to purple

**Fourpart
Dwarf Gentian**
Gentianella propinqua
Chukotka–w N Amer
H 2–6 in (5–15 cm)

Pale Gentian
Gentiana glauca
Amphi-Beringian
H 2–6 in (5–15 cm)

Flowers lilac,
rarely white

Autumn Dwarf Gentian
Gentianella amarella
Near circumpolar
H 8–16 in (20–40 cm)

Northern Bedstraw
Galium boreale
Near circumpolar
H 10–16 in (25–40 cm)

RANGE: Amphi-Beringian. Grows from ne Asia to nw N Amer in moist alpine meadows to 4900 ft (1500 m); uncommon near the seacoast. ID: H 2–6 in (5–15 cm). Annual. LVS: In a basal rosette, smooth, obovate, yellowish green, somewhat succulent. Stem leaves elliptical, sessile, in 1–3 pairs. FLS: Deep greenish blue, rarely pale yellow, tubular, 5-lobed.

Pygmy Gentian
Gentiana prostrata
ALSO: Siberian Gentian, Moss Gentian, Niederlie-
gender Enzian, Storsøteslekta, Горечавка. SN means "low-growing gentian."
RANGE: Amphi-Beringian (disjunct sites in n Eurasia and w N Amer), in bogs and moist meadows, usually above 6550 ft (2000 m).
ID: H 1–3 in (3–7 cm). Annual. LVS: Spatulate to obovate, to 0.25 in (0.6 cm) long, green, sometimes edged with dull white. FLS: Solitary, tubular, about 0.5 in (1.5 cm) wide at the mouth. Petals blue or purple, greenish yellow at base. Sepals diamond-shaped, with deep blue to purple lobes. Flowers open only on bright, sunny days.

GENUS *COMASTOMA*
Dane's Dwarf Gentian
Comastoma tenellum
ALSO: Pribilof Dwarf Gentian, Lapland Gentian,
Slender Gentian, Zarter Enzian, Småsøte, Maríuvendlingur. SN means "soft reveller."
RANGE: Near circumpolar (disjunct distribution), in gravelly tundra meadows, subalpine forests, and alpine fell fields to 6550 ft (2000 m).
ID: H 2–6 in (5–15 cm). Dwarf, with several unbranched stems. LVS: Spatulate, in a basal rosette. FLS: Blue or white, tubular, with 4 fused petals and 4 sepals with fringed scales.

GENUS *GENTIANELLA*
Autumn Dwarf Gentian
Gentianella amarella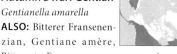
ALSO: Bitterer Fransenen-zian, Gentiane amère,
Bittersøte, Горечавка горьковатая, *Amarella plebeja*. SN means "little gentian with bitter [sap]."

RANGE: Near circumpolar (absent Greenland), in damp meadows and along streams.
ID: H 8–16 in (20–40 cm). Annual or biennial. Stems ascending or erect, simple or branched. LVS: Basal, spatulate; leaves wither and die early in summer. Stem leaves opposite, lanceolate to oval, to 2 in (5 cm) long. FLS: Jun–Sep. Violet, rarely white, tubular, 5-lobed, with lobes fringed in the throat. Borne in axillary or terminal clusters.
USE: Used to make bitters for alcoholic drinks.

Fourpart Dwarf Gentian
Gentianella propinqua
ALSO: Four-petaled Gentian,
Gentiane fausse-amarelle, Itsutiit, *Amarella propinqua*. SN means "little gentian closely related to *Gentiana*."
RANGE: Amphi-Beringian, with isolated sites around Hudson Bay; found on lakeshores, seashores, sandbars, in sedge mires, and on dry, sunny slopes above 2000 ft (600 m).
ID: H 2–6 in (5–15 cm). Annual. LVS: Oblong, in a basal rosette. Many, slender, leafy, branched stems. FLS: Jun–Aug. Pale bluish purple to pink, tubular; borne at stem tip and in leaf axils.

FAMILY RUBIACEAE
BEDSTRAWS AND ALLIES
GENUS *GALIUM*
Northern Bedstraw
Galium boreale
ALSO: Nordisches Labkraut, Gaillet boréal, Hvitmaure,
Подмаренник северный. SN means "northern milk [plant]," alluding to the use of *G. verum* to curdle milk for cheese-making. Bedstraws once were used for stuffing mattresses, thus the CN.
RANGE: Circumpolar, on stony slopes, dry meadows, forest edge, and roadsides.
ID: H 10–16 in (25–40 cm). Stem erect, 4-angled, stout; lower stem reddish. LVS: Three-veined, somewhat hairy, lanceolate, with blunt tip and entire, inrolled margins; arranged in whorls of 2 opposite leaves and 2 leaf-like stipules. FLS: Jul–Sep. Wheel-shaped, basally fused. Petals 4, white, broad, pointed; calyx absent. FR: Tiny, brown, 2-parted, dry, bristle-covered schizocarp.

Boraginales: Borage and Allies
FAMILY BORAGINACEAE
BLUEBELLS AND FORGET-ME-NOTS

These plants have bilaterally symmetrical flowers, with 5 petals fused into a tube. The leaves have coarse hairs containing silicon dioxide and calcium carbonate. Some species contain anthocyanins that cause flowers to change color from red to blue when aging—a possible signal to insect pollinators that flowers are spent and depleted of pollen and nectar.

GENUS *MERTENSIA*
Sea Bluebells
Mertensia maritima

ALSO: Oysterleaf Lungwort, Lungenkräut, Mertensie maritime, Østersurt, Мертензия приморская. SN means "Mertens's seaside [plant]," honoring German botanist Franz Carl Mertens (1764–1831). **RANGE:** Near circumpolar (large gap in Siberia), on sandy, gravelly, and shingle beaches. **ID:** H 4–6 in (10–15 cm). Spreading, decumbent perennial. LVS: Ovate or spatulate, fleshy, smooth, covered with grayish bloom. Leaves taste like oysters. FLS: Tubular. Pink at first, later blue, rarely white. Borne in a terminal cyme. FR: Nutlet with spongy outer coating that provides buoyancy and allows seeds to disperse on water currents.

Tall Bluebells
Mertensia paniculata

ALSO: Northern Lungwort, Languid Lady, Chiming Bells, Mertensie paniculée, Hestetunge, Мертензия. SN means "Merten's [plant] that bears flowers in a branched raceme."

RANGE: Grows in moist woodland and meadows from Alaska south to Oregon and the Great Lakes. **ID:** H 12–28 in (30–70 cm). Erect perennial. LVS: Hairy and rough to the touch. Basal leaves ovate, acute, with long petioles; stem leaves narrow. FLS: Pale blue; reddish in bud. Nodding, tubular. Grows from upper leaf axils in a branched raceme.

GENUS *MYOSOTIS*
Alpine Forget-me-not
Myosotis alpestris

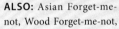

ALSO: Asian Forget-me-not, Wood Forget-me-not, Alpen Vergissmein-nicht, Myosotis des alpes, Незабудка альпийская. SN means "alpine mouse's ear," referring to the leaf shape. Alaska's state flower. County flower of Westmorland, England. German legend recounts that when God was naming all the plants, a tiny, unnamed blue flower cried out, "Forget me not, O Lord!" and God replied, "That shall be your name." **RANGE:** Eurasia and w N Amer; grows above 2000 ft (600 m) in rocky woodland and meadows. **ID:** H 4–15 in (10–38 cm). Perennial. Forms clumps. LVS: Lanceolate, pubescent, often withered, in a basal rosette. Stem leaves sessile, lanceolate. FLS: Jul–Sep. Salverform. Bright clear blue, with white inner ring and yellow eye. Very fragrant at night; little or no scent in the daytime.

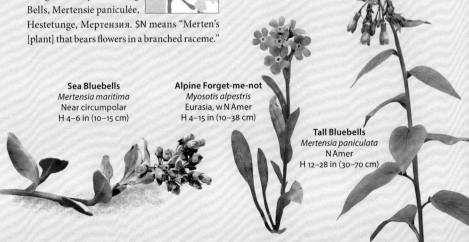

Sea Bluebells
Mertensia maritima
Near circumpolar
H 4–6 in (10–15 cm)

Alpine Forget-me-not
Myosotis alpestris
Eurasia, w N Amer
H 4–15 in (10–38 cm)

Tall Bluebells
Mertensia paniculata
N Amer
H 12–28 in (30–70 cm)

Lamiales: Mints and Allies

Most plants in this diverse order have bilaterally symmetrical flowers (irregularly shaped corollas with one plane of symmetry).

FAMILY OROBANCHACEAE
BROOMRAPES AND ALLIES

The arctic Orobanchaceae are perennial herbs. They are partly or fully parasitic on the roots of other plants. The *haustorium*, a slender projection from the root of the parasite, enables the plant to penetrate the tissues of its host and absorb nutrients from it. Holoparasitic species are represented by the groundcones (*Boschniakia*), which lack chlorophyll and therefore cannot perform photosynthesis; they are completely dependent on their host for nutrition. Hemiparasitic species include the louseworts (recently moved to this family from Scrophulariaceae), eyebrights, and Indian paintbrushes, all of which are capable of photosynthesis and thus are partially independent from their hosts.

GENUS *PEDICULARIS*: This genus contains the louseworts. The name derives from the Latin *pediculus*, meaning "little louse," which alludes to an old belief that these plants were responsible for lice infestations of livestock. Most louseworts have fern-like leaves with finely lobed, toothed margins. The irregular flowers have an upright helmet (*galea*) composed of 2 fused petals and a lower lip of 3 fused petals, somewhat resembling garden snapdragons. The fruit is a compressed capsule, containing a few large seeds. Arctic louseworts are early blooming, and by the end of July most have gone to seed.

Capitate Lousewort
Pedicularis capitata

ALSO: Pédicularie capiée, Мытник голо-вчатый. Kukiujait is Inuit for "bananas," referring to the flower's sweet, sugary taste. SN means "capitate lousewort."
RANGE: Disjunct sites in ne Asia and n N Amer; found on gravelly calcareous tundra, heath, and rocky slopes to 6550 ft (2000 m).

ID: H 2–6 in (5–15 cm). Dwarf perennial, Leafless, smooth or hairy, stem. LVS: Few, fern-like, in a basal tuft. FLS: Petals 5, fused, curving, creamy yellow, often with a reddish tinge; helmet is much longer than the lower petals. Borne in a terminal capitate head of 2–4, rarely 6, large, scentless blossoms.

Flame Lousewort
Pedicularis flammea

ALSO: Redrattle, Upright Lousewort, Pédiculaire flammée, Brannmyrklegg, Igutsait niqingit. SN means "lousewort with a flame colored helmet."
RANGE: Amphi–Atlantic; grows on moist calcareous tundra, snowbeds, and lakeshores.
ID: H 3–6 in (8–15 cm). A tiny gem of a plant, with seeds that rattle in the seed capsule. Stem reddish purple, smooth. LVS: Mostly basal, fern-like, deeply incised. FLS: Jun–Jul. Small, bright yellow, with a reddish purple helmet. Borne in a terminal spike-like raceme.

Oeder's Lousewort
Pedicularis oederi

ALSO: Crimson-tipped Lousewort, Buntes Läusekraut, Gullmyrklegg, Мытник Эдера. SN means "Oeder's lousewort," honoring German-Danish botanist Georg Christian Edler von Oldenburg Oeder (1728–1791), who initiated the work *Flora Danica*.
RANGE: Amphi-Beringian, in meadows, pastures, tundra, damp limestone ledges, and grassy alpine slopes to 4000 ft (1200 m).
ID: H 2–6 in (5–15 cm). Perennial. Stems usually woolly. LVS: Mostly basal, fern-like. Stem leaves few and small. FLS: Jun–Sep. To about 1 in (3 cm) long. Yellow corolla and purple-tipped helmet.

Elephant's Head
Pedicularis groenlandica

ALSO: Elephanthead Lousewort, Pédiculaire du Groenland. SN means "Greenland lousewort."
RANGE: Disjunct sites in w and e N Amer,

and a single locality in w Greenland; grows on calcareous soil in wet meadows, streambanks, and gullies in alpine and subarctic zones. **ID:** H 12–30 in (30–75 cm). Showy perennial. LVS: Sharply toothed, fern-like, evenly spaced along the erect, stout stem. FLS: Jul–Aug. Terminal spike of pink to purple flowers, each with a long, upward-curving beak that looks like a waving elephant's trunk and lateral petals that resemble an elephant's ears.

Hairy Lousewort
Pedicularis hirsuta

ALSO: Hairy Horsewort, Ugjunnait, Pédiculaire hirsute, Lodnemyrklegg, Мытник волосистый. SN means "hairy lousewort."
RANGE: Near circumpolar (absent nc N Amer), on moist, stony, and sandy soils on tundra, lakeshores, and riverbanks.
ID: H 2–8 in (5–20 cm). Slender, hairy stem. LVS: Hairy, fern-like, green to purple, with deep, irregular lobes and toothed margins. FLS: Pale pink; helmet is short, stubby, and lacks teeth. Flowers first appear in a capitate head, then elongate into a spike.

Woolly Lousewort
Pedicularis lanata
Pedicularis kanei
Pedicularis dasyantha

ALSO: Arctic Hairy Lousewort, Pédiculaire laineuse, Ullmyrklegg, Ugjungnaq, Umilik. CN refers to the dense covering of woolly hairs present on all of these closely related, very similar species.
RANGE: These very similar species grow on stony tundra to 5600 ft (1700 m). *P. lanata* occurs in N Amer. *P. kanei* is Amphi-Beringian. *P. dasyantha* is found in Svalbard, Novaya Zemlya, and Russia's Yamal Penin.
ID: H 4–6 in (10–15 cm). Thick, lemon yellow taproot. Short, densely white-woolly, ascending stem. LVS: Fern-like, pinnately divided into finely lobed segments. FLS: Deep pink, rarely white. Faintly scented, showy. Borne in a densely flowered, copiously white-woolly spike.

Labrador Lousewort
Pedicularis labradorica

ALSO: Pédiculaire du Labrador, Airaq, Мытник лабрадорский. SN means "Labrador lousewort."
RANGE: NE Eurasia, n N Amer, and w Greenland; grows on tundra hummocks, muskegs, and mossy heaths, to 6550 ft (2000 m).
ID: H 6–12 in (15–30 cm). Biennial, with a weak, spindly taproot. Stems leafy, simple or branched, smooth or downy. LVS: Fern-like. FLS: Yellowish, with a purple-tinged helmet that has 2 slender teeth near the tip. Inflorescence of 5–10 flowers is first borne in a head-like cluster that elongates into a spike.

Langsdorff's Lousewort
Pedicularis langsdorffii

ALSO: Arctic Lousewort, Arctic Fernweed, Мытник Лангсдорфа, *P. arctica*. SN means "Langsdorff's lousewort," honoring Prussian naturalist Georg Heinrich von Langsdorff (1774–1852), who sailed on Krusenstern's 1803–1805 Russian scientific expedition and explored Kamchatka, the Aleutians, Sitka, and Kodiak Is.
RANGE: Disjunct sites in ne Eurasia, N Amer, and nw Greenland; grows on moist tundra barrens, meadows, and alpine ridges to 6550 ft (2000 m).
ID: H 4–10 in (10–25 cm). LVS: Fern-like, green or reddish, lanceolate, pinnately lobed, in a basal tuft. One to several, smooth, leafy stems. FLS: Borne in a showy, loose, leafy spike at tip of stem. Bright pink, with a prominently arched helmet that has 2 minute teeth near the protruding pistil. A large landing petal attracts insect pollinators to the flower's nectary.

Lapland Lousewort
Pedicularis lapponica

ALSO: Laplands-Troldurt, Pédiculaire de Laponie, Lappland-Läusekraut, Мытник лапландский. SN means "Lapland lousewort." CN refers to the type locality.
RANGE: Circumpolar, on dry tundra and in alpine meadows to 3300 ft (1000 m).

ID: H 4–8 in (10–20 cm). Dwarf perennial. Stems simple or branched, smooth or downy, purplish brown, leafy. LVS: Fern-like, with halberd-like projections at the leaf base. FLS: Very fragrant, with pale yellow corollas. Borne in a few-flowered spike.

Sudetan Lousewort
Pedicularis sudetica

ALSO: Swedish Lousewort, Purple Rattle, Pédiculaire de Sudètes, Мытник судетский. SN means "Sudetan lousewort." CN refers to Czechoslovakia's Sudet Mtns, where the species was first described.

RANGE: Grows in Eurasia and n N Amer in wet calcareous soils on tundra, meadows, rocky slopes, and lakeshores.

ID: H 4–10 in (10–25 cm). Forms large, showy tufts. LVS: Fern-like, long-petioled, deeply lobed, in a basal cluster. One to several smooth, dark purple, nearly leafless stems. FLS: Jun–Jul. Reddish purple, with a paler lower lip; helmet has 2 prominent teeth near the apex. Inflorescence appears first in a dense white-woolly head, then ascends on an elongated stem.

USE: Flowering stems can be pickled and made into a type of sauerkraut. The rootstock is also edible and can be boiled for soup.

Whorled Lousewort
Pedicularis verticillata

ALSO: Quirlblättriges Läusekraut, Pédiculaire verticillée, Мытник мутовчатый.

SN means "whorled lousewort," referring to the whorl of flowers and leaves around the stem.

RANGE: Eurasia and nw N Amer, in meadows and on rocky slopes to 4250 ft (1300 m).

ID: H 6–12 in (15–30 cm). LVS: Fern-like, lanceolate, pinnately lobed, in a basal tuft. Stems erect, reddish; sessile stem leaves. FLS: Purple to magenta.

GENUS *BOSCHNIAKIA*
Northern Groundcone
Boschniakia rossica

ALSO: Poque, Бошнякия, Tulukkam nauligaafa. SN means "Boschniak's groundcone," after Russian botanist Alexander Boschniak (1786–1831).

RANGE: Amphi-Beringian, in alder woodland, on subalpine slopes, and on riverbanks.

ID: H 6–16 in (15–35 cm). Looks like an upright pinecone. Lacks chlorophyll and must siphon all food from the roots of host plants, mainly Green Alder (*Alnus viridis*). LVS: Fleshy, sessile scales. FLS: May–Jul. Dense spike of dark maroon flowers is partially hidden in the leaves.

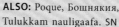
Leaves and flowers in whorls around the stem

Northern Groundcone
Boschniakia rossica
Amphi-Beringian
H 6–16 in (15–35 cm)

Whorled Lousewort
Pedicularis verticillata
Eurasia, nw N Amer
H 6–12 in (15–30 cm)

Sudetan Lousewort
Pedicularis sudetica
Eurasia, nw N Amer
H 4–10 in (10–25 cm)

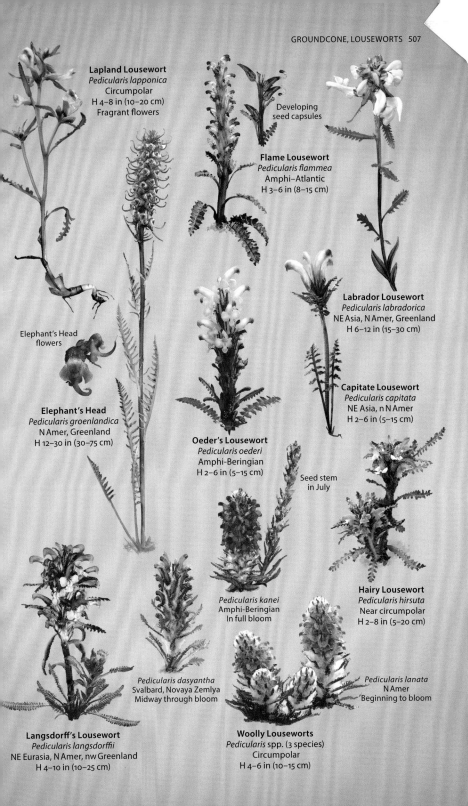

Lapland Lousewort
Pedicularis lapponica
Circumpolar
H 4–8 in (10–20 cm)
Fragrant flowers

Developing
seed capsules

Flame Lousewort
Pedicularis flammea
Amphi–Atlantic
H 3–6 in (8–15 cm)

Elephant's Head
flowers

Labrador Lousewort
Pedicularis labradorica
NE Asia, N Amer, Greenland
H 6–12 in (15–30 cm)

Elephant's Head
Pedicularis groenlandica
N Amer, Greenland
H 12–30 in (30–75 cm)

Capitate Lousewort
Pedicularis capitata
NE Asia, n N Amer
H 2–6 in (5–15 cm)

Oeder's Lousewort
Pedicularis oederi
Amphi-Beringian
H 2–6 in (5–15 cm)

Seed stem
in July

Hairy Lousewort
Pedicularis hirsuta
Near circumpolar
H 2–8 in (5–20 cm)

Pedicularis kanei
Amphi-Beringian
In full bloom

Pedicularis dasyantha
Svalbard, Novaya Zemlya
Midway through bloom

Pedicularis lanata
N Amer
Beginning to bloom

Langsdorff's Lousewort
Pedicularis langsdorffii
NE Eurasia, N Amer, nw Greenland
H 4–10 in (10–25 cm)

Woolly Louseworts
Pedicularis spp. (3 species)
Circumpolar
H 4–6 in (10–15 cm)

GENUS *CASTILLEJA*: This genus, which honors Spanish botanist Domingo Castillejo (1744–1793), contains the lovely Indian paintbrushes and painted-cups. These herbaceous plants are hemi-parasitic, taking some nutrients from the roots of grasses and herbs. Their minute snapdragon-like flowers are concealed by showy, brightly colored, modified leaves called *bracts*. The tiny flower petals are edible and sweet. However, the roots, stem, and leaves absorb selenium from the soil and store it in their tissues; these plant parts can be toxic if ingested in quantity.

Elegant Painted-cup

Castilleja elegans
ALSO: Кастиллея. SN means "elegant paintbrush."

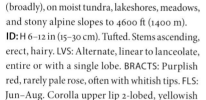

RANGE: Amphi-Beringian (broadly), on moist tundra, lakeshores, meadows, and stony alpine slopes to 4600 ft (1400 m).
ID: H 6–12 in (15–30 cm). Tufted. Stems ascending, erect, hairy. LVS: Alternate, linear to lanceolate, entire or with a single lobe. BRACTS: Purplish red, rarely pale rose, often with whitish tips. FLS: Jun–Aug. Corolla upper lip 2-lobed, yellowish green with purple margin; lower lip distinctly 3-lobed, purple, short; pistil green.

Port Clarence Indian Paintbrush

Castilleja caudata
ALSO: SN means "paintbrush with a tailed [leaf tip]."
RANGE: Amphi-Beringian. Grows on streambanks and in meadows to 3900 ft (1200 m).
ID: H 12–24 in (30–60 cm). Tufted. Stem single, dark red. LVS: Burgundy, alternate, lanceolate, 3-ribbed, entire. BRACTS/FLS: Greenish yellow; bracts sometimes reddish at the base.

Raup's Indian Paintbrush

Castilleja raupii
ALSO: Purple Painted-cup. SN means "Raup's paintbrush," honoring American botanist and ecologist Hugh Miller Raup (1901–1995).

RANGE: C Alaska and n Canada, on streambanks, lakeshores, sandy beaches, gravel ridges, disturbed open land, and roadsides.
ID: H 6–12 in (15–30 cm). Tufted. Stems slender, often purplish. LVS: Alternate, sessile, entire, linear, to 2 in (5 cm) long. BRACTS/FLS: Jun–Aug. Pink to dark purple; lower lip of corolla distinctly lobed.

Northern Indian Paintbrush

Castilleja hyperborea
ALSO: SN means "northern paintbrush."
RANGE: Amphi-Beringian, in disjunct locations, on

stony alpine slopes to 6550 ft (2000 m).
ID: H 6–10 in (15–25 cm). Low, tufted perennial. Stems and calyx hairy. LVS: Deeply cleft. BRACTS/FLS: Yellow; lower lip of corolla lobed.

Alaska Indian Paintbrush

Castilleja unalaschcensis
ALSO: SN means "Alaska paintbrush."
RANGE: Attu Is (Aleutians), s Alaska, and w Canada, in moist meadows.
ID: H 12–32 (30–80 cm). Tufted. LVS: Lanceolate to ovate-lanceolate, somewhat acute, hairy, entire. BRACTS: Yellow, with a bright green base. FLS: Green, with yellow edge on upper lip.

Labrador Indian Paintbrush

Castilleja septentrionalis
ALSO: Pale Paintbrush, Castilléjie septrionale. SN means "northern paintbrush." Freely hybridizing;

notorious for being what Nicholas Polunin of McGill University called "an atrocious *typus polymorphus*."
RANGE: Grows in n/e Canada in rock crevices, ledges, forest clearings, and sandy banks, often on conglomerate or basaltic bedrock.
ID: H 8–20 in (20–50 cm). Polymorphic. Stem erect, smooth. LVS: Linear to lanceolate, entire, sometimes tinged purple; variants sometimes lobed. BRACTS/FLS: Pale green, yellow, or pink.

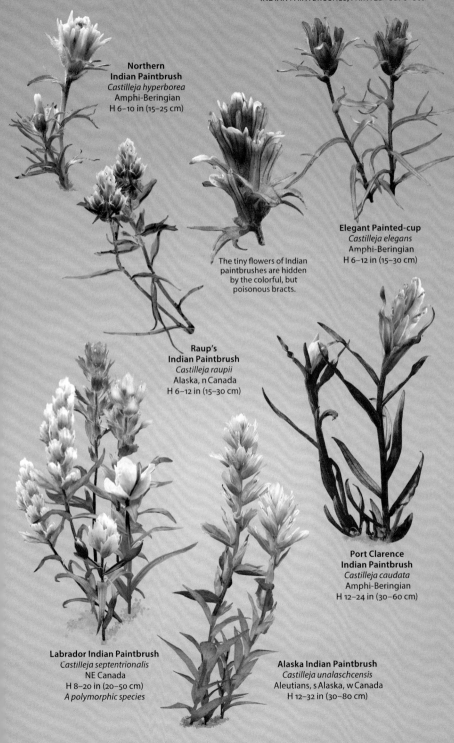

**Northern
Indian Paintbrush**
Castilleja hyperborea
Amphi-Beringian
H 6–10 in (15–25 cm)

Elegant Painted-cup
Castilleja elegans
Amphi-Beringian
H 6–12 in (15–30 cm)

The tiny flowers of Indian
paintbrushes are hidden
by the colorful, but
poisonous bracts.

**Raup's
Indian Paintbrush**
Castilleja raupii
Alaska, n Canada
H 6–12 in (15–30 cm)

**Port Clarence
Indian Paintbrush**
Castilleja caudata
Amphi-Beringian
H 12–24 in (30–60 cm)

Labrador Indian Paintbrush
Castilleja septentrionalis
NE Canada
H 8–20 in (20–50 cm)
A polymorphic species

Alaska Indian Paintbrush
Castilleja unalaschcensis
Aleutians, s Alaska, w Canada
H 12–32 in (30–80 cm)

GENUS *EUPHRASIA*
Eyebright

Euphrasia spp.
ALSO: Augentrost, Augetrøst, Euphraise, Очанка.
SN means "good cheer"; this and the CN "eyebright" refer to the plant's use as a remedy for eye infections.
RANGE: Near circumpolar (absent Siberia); grows around snowbeds, in alpine meadows, on grassy shorelines, and along roads, mainly in the subarctic zone.
ID: H 2–10 in (5–25 cm). Annual. Hemi-parasitic on grasses. LVS: Small, sessile, oval, with toothed margins. FLS: Jul–Aug. Lilac to white, usually with a yellow blotch on the lower petal, which attracts pollinating insects. Corolla short-tubed; upper lip 2-lobed; lower lip long, 3-lobed.

GENUS *BARTSIA*
Alpine Bartsia

Bartsia alpina
ALSO: Velvetbells, Europäischer Alpenhelm, Bartsie des Alpes, Svarttoppslekta, Бартсия альпийская. SN means "Bartsch's alpine [plant]," honoring German physician Johann Bartsch (1709–1738), who assisted Linnaeus in the publication of *Flora Lapponica*.
RANGE: Amphi-Atlantic; grows on moist turf on seacliffs, alpine slopes, and in pastures.
ID: H 2–8 in (5–20 cm). Tufted perennial. Hemi-parasitic on grasses and herbs. Stem erect or ascending, covered with sticky hairs. LVS: Opposite, sessile, oval, with crenate or serrate margins; upper leaves purple. FLS: Dark purple, to 1 in (2 cm) long, borne in the uppermost leaf axils. Calyx hairy, green to purple.

FAMILY PLANTAGINACEAE
PLANTAINS

This diverse, cosmopolitan family is found mostly in the N Hemisphere temperate zones. Many Plantaginaceae species contain the glucoside aucuboside, which has anti-inflammatory properties utilized in traditional medicine. The family's taxonomy has been revised to include some species formerly in Scrophulariaceae.

GENUS *LAGOTIS*
Weaselsnout

Lagotis minor
ALSO: Vanilla Grass, a Siberian reference to the plant's sweet scent. SN means "bluish gray hare's ear," referring to flower color and stem leaf shape.
RANGE: Widespread in Eurasia, the Aleutians, and Alaska on damp tundra, alpine meadows, and rocky slopes.
ID: H 6–12 in (15–30 cm). Decumbent perennial. LVS: Ovate-orbicular or broadly lanceolate; margins crenate to dentate. One to several basal leaves; sessile stem leaves emerge at flower bracts. FLS: Irregular, purple to blue, in an ovate or cylindrical terminal spike. FR: Two-seeded capsule appearing by mid-July.

GENUS *VERONICA*
Alpine Speedwell

Veronica alpina
ALSO: Hairy Speedwell, Wormskjold's Speedwell, Alpenehrenpreis, Véronique des Alpes, Fjellveronika. SN means "Veronica's plant of the mountains," referring to Saint Veronica, who wiped the face of Christ as he carried the cross to Calvary. CN comes from an old use of the word *speed*, meaning "to thrive," an allusion to the plant's use in treating edema, digestive discomfort, and skin disorders.
RANGE: Disjunct distribution in the Aleutians, N Amer, Greenland, Iceland, the UK, and n Europe, in moist alpine meadows, forest understory, streambanks, near snowbeds, gravelly riverbanks, and cliffs, to 6550 ft (2000 m).
ID: H 2–12 in (5–30 cm). Decumbent to erect perennial. Stems mostly unbranched, coated with long hairs. LVS: Opposite, sessile, ovate to lanceolate, with entire or shallowly toothed margins. FLS: Jul–Aug. Bluish purple, 4-parted; corolla wheel-shaped, with a short tube; sepals hairy, lance-shaped. Borne in a hairy, glandular, rounded, terminal raceme.
RELATED SPECIES: GYPSYWEED, *Veronica officinalis*, widespread in Eurasia; introduced into N Amer. LARGEFLOWERED SPEEDWELL, *V. grandiflora*, Kamchatka and the Aleutians.

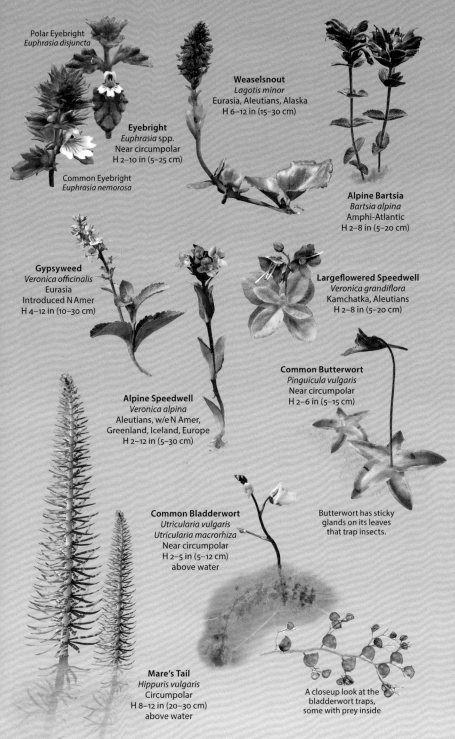

Polar Eyebright
Euphrasia disjuncta

Weaselsnout
Lagotis minor
Eurasia, Aleutians, Alaska
H 6–12 in (15–30 cm)

Eyebright
Euphrasia spp.
Near circumpolar
H 2–10 in (5–25 cm)

Common Eyebright
Euphrasia nemorosa

Alpine Bartsia
Bartsia alpina
Amphi-Atlantic
H 2–8 in (5–20 cm)

Gypsyweed
Veronica officinalis
Eurasia
Introduced N Amer
H 4–12 in (10–30 cm)

Largeflowered Speedwell
Veronica grandiflora
Kamchatka, Aleutians
H 2–8 in (5–20 cm)

Common Butterwort
Pinguicula vulgaris
Near circumpolar
H 2–6 in (5–15 cm)

Alpine Speedwell
Veronica alpina
Aleutians, w/e N Amer,
Greenland, Iceland, Europe
H 2–12 in (5–30 cm)

Common Bladderwort
Utricularia vulgaris
Utricularia macrorhiza
Near circumpolar
H 2–5 in (5–12 cm)
above water

Butterwort has sticky
glands on its leaves
that trap insects.

Mare's Tail
Hippuris vulgaris
Circumpolar
H 8–12 in (20–30 cm)
above water

A closeup look at the
bladderwort traps,
some with prey inside

GENUS *HIPPURIS*
Mare's Tail

Hippuris vulgaris
ALSO: Tannenwedel, Queue-de-cheval, Hesterump-eslekta, Хвостник обыкновенный. SN means "common horsetail."
RANGE: Circumpolar, in shallow ponds, streams, and small lakes.
ID: H 8–12 (20–30 cm) above water; submerged stems to 24 in (60 cm) long. Aquatic. LVS: Linear, sessile, entire, in whorls of 6–12; submerged leaves flaccid, thin, pale green, translucent. FLS: Concealed in leaf axils; not all plants produce flowers. Can be mistaken for Common Horsetail, *Equisetum arvense* (*see p. 439*).

FAMILY LENTIBULARIACEAE
BUTTERWORTS & BLADDERWORTS

This is a family of carnivorous plants that uses bladder-like traps or sticky, glandular leaves to trap and digest insects in order to supplement the poor mineral nutrition they obtain from the environment.

GENUS *PINGUICULA*
Common Butterwort

Pinguicula vulgaris
ALSO: Fettkräuter, Grassette, Blærerot, Жирянка. SN means "common fat-leaved butterwort."

The name *butterwort* comes from the Scandinavian practice of using these plants to make yogurt-like buttermilk (*tätmjölk* and *filmjölk*) from fresh milk. The process involves rubbing the inside of a container with butterwort leaves, adding lukewarm milk, and leaving the mixture to ferment for a few days. The butterwort's digestive enzymes degrade the proteins and thicken the milk.
RANGE: Near circumpolar (absent Siberia), on moist calcareous soil along brooks and ponds, and in damp meadows and fens.
ID: H 2–6 in (5–15 cm). LVS: Yellowish green, succulent, elliptical-spatulate, with entire, inrolled margins. Prostrate in star-shaped basal rosette. Glands on the upper leaf surface secrete a sticky mucus for trapping prey and digesting enzymes to dissolve their tissues, providing additional nutrition to that gained through photosynthesis. FLS: Jun–Jul. Solitary, irregular, to 0.5 in (1.5 cm) long. Borne at top of a leafless stem covered with glandular hairs. Corolla 2-lipped, bright violet, with a white blotch in the throat; lower lip terminates in a slightly curved, slender spur. Pollinated by bees; also propagates via bulb-like buds.

GENUS *UTRICULARIA*
Common Bladderwort

Utricularia vulgaris
Utricularia macrorhiza
ALSO: Wasserschläuche, Utriculaire, Storblærerot, Пузырчатка обыкновенная. SN means "common bladderwort" and "long-root bladderwort," respectively.

These carnivorous plants capture small pond organisms by means of bladder-shaped traps, thus the name "bladderwort." New bladders are greenish and transparent, older ones dark brown to black. The traps are extremely sophisticated. The primed bladder is under negative osmotic pressure. When a prey animal such as a water flea, nematode, fish fry, or mosquito larva brushes against the trigger hairs around the trapdoor, the door opens, sucking water and prey into the bladder. The bladder door abruptly snaps shut, trapping the prey inside, where it is dissolved by digestive secretions. The bladder walls later pump the water out, readying the membranous sac for its next capture.
RANGE: Near circumpolar; *U. vulgaris* is found in Eurasia, *U. macrorhiza* in N Amer and e Asia. Grows in ponds, ditches, and other still waters.
ID: H 2–5 in (5–12 cm) floats above water; most of the plant is submerged, including stems to 3 ft (1 m) long. LVS: Finely pinnately divided, to 3 in (8 cm) long, with attached flask-shaped traps that float just below the water surface. FLS: Jun–Aug. Yellow, snapdragon-like, 5-parted. Lower lip of corolla has a sickle-like, forward-facing spur. A short branched aerial stem holds a cluster of 2–10 flowers above the water surface.

Dipsacales: Honeysuckles, Valerian, Twinflower, and Allies

FAMILY CAPRIFOLIACEAE
HONEYSUCKLES

GENUS *VALERIANA*
Capitate Valerian
Valeriana capitata

ALSO: Mountain Heliotrope, Kopfiger Baldrian, Valériane, Валериана головчатая. SN means "valerian with a head-like inflorescence." *Valerian* derives from *valere*, the Latin word for strength, an allusion to the potency of these herbs as nerve and muscle relaxants. *Valerian* also refers to isovaleric acid, a rancid-smelling compound that is found in the roots of *Valeriana* species and also in human sweat.

RANGE: Occurs from e Europe across Siberia to the e Aleutians, Alaska, and nw Canada. Often found growing in thick but scattered patches on alpine meadows, hillsides, and in small forest clearings, to 5000 ft (1500 m).

ID: H 12–20 in (30–50 cm). Slim, tall, single-stemmed perennial. LVS: Basal leaves elliptical, long-petioled, entire. Stem leaves opposite, sessile, shallowly lobed, growing once or twice along the stem. FLS: May–Jul. Fragrant, white to rose or purple, funnel-form, in a capitate head at the top of the stem. Seedhead plumose when in fruit.

GENUS *LINNAEA*
Twinflower
Linnaea borealis

ALSO: Moosglöckchen, Linnée boréale, Linnea, Линнея. CN refers to the paired blossoms. SN means "northern twinflower." The genus name honors Carolus Linnaeus (1707–1778), the Swedish botanist and zoologist known as the father of binomial nomenclature and modern taxonomy. *Linnaea* was Linnaeus's favorite plant and the only one named for him. He took it as his personal emblem and used it on his coat of arms when he was raised to the Swedish nobility in 1757. He once wrote of this plant, "*Linnaea* … is a plant of Lapland, lowly, insignificant, disregarded, flowering but for a brief time. From Linnaeus, who resembles it."

RANGE: Circumpolar; grows in moist forests and heaths in the north, in mountains farther south. Foresters consider this plant an indicator species of ancient woodlands.

ID: H 4–6 in (10–15 cm). Prostrate, creeping perennial, with downy, somewhat woody young twigs. LVS: Leathery, opposite, oval to round. Slender, ascending stems, with 1–2 pairs of leaves. FLS: Fragrant, nodding, pale pink, each with a 5-lobed, bell-shaped corolla. Borne in a terminal inflorescence of paired blossoms.

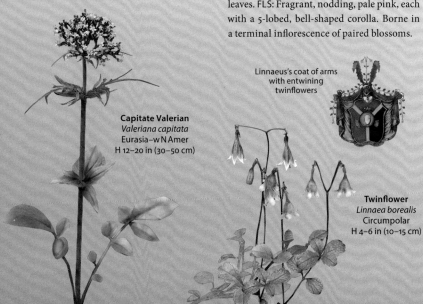

Linnaeus's coat of arms with entwining twinflowers

Capitate Valerian
Valeriana capitata
Eurasia–w N Amer
H 12–20 in (30–50 cm)

Twinflower
Linnaea borealis
Circumpolar
H 4–6 in (10–15 cm)

Asterales: Composites, Harebells, and Allies

Asterales is the second largest order of flowering plants after Orchidaceae. It comprises about 11 families, the largest of which are Asteraceae (sunflowers, daisies, asters, and allies), with about 25,000 species, and Campanulaceae (harebells), with about 2000 species.

FAMILY ASTERACEAE (COMPOSITAE)
COMPOSITES

Asteraceae derives from the Latin word *aster*, meaning "star." *Compositae*, meaning "composite," is the older, alternative family name. Both names refer to the structure of a typical daisy inflorescence—a *pseudanthium* (Greek for "false flower"), in which multiple flowers are grouped together to form a composite flower head, or *capitulum*. The capitulum has a whorl of bracts, or *involucrum*, below it.

A close look with a hand lens will reveal that the capitulum is composed of two different types of small *florets*. The *disc florets* in the flower head center are radially symmetrical, bisexual, fertile, and their minute petals are fused into a tube. The *ray florets* around the edge of the flower head are bilaterally symmetrical, female (pistillate), and fertile. Each ray floret is actually a single petal. Disc florets and ray florets both lack a true calyx. The calyx is so highly modified into hairs, bristles, or scales that it is given the alternative name *pappus*. The pappus is an adaptation for wind dispersal of the fruit, which is a small, nut-like *cypsela*.

GENUS *ARCTANTHEMUM*
Arctic Daisy

Arctanthemum arcticum

ALSO: Arctic Chrysanthemum, Chrysanthemen, Arktisk margerit, Хризантема. SN means "arctic chrysanthemum."

RANGE: A seaside species, found in disjunct sites in Eurasia and N Amer in moist saline meadows, on gravel beaches, and in rock crevices.

ID: H 2–16 in (5–40 cm). Stems smooth or woolly, sometimes branched, with a few small leaves. LVS: Basal, wedge-shaped, with 3 teeth and 3 lobes at the apex. FLS: Jul–Aug. Daisy-like, to 1 in (2.5 cm) across. Ray florets white; disc florets yellow.

GENUS *EURYBIA*
Siberian Aster

Eurybia sibirica

ALSO: Arctic Aster, Sibirisk aster, Aster de Sibérie, Sibirstjerne. SN means "Siberian aster with few [ray florets]."

RANGE: Amphi-Beringian (broadly), across Siberia to w N Amer; found in aspen and spruce forest clearings, riparian thickets, lakeshores, sandy streambanks, and moist alpine meadows, to 7200 ft (2200 m).

ID: H 2–20 in (5–50 cm). Stems 1–5, ascending to decumbent, often purplish, sometimes branched. LVS: Alternate, dark green above, paler below, stiff, with coarsely serrate margins. FLS: Jun–Aug. Ray florets 12–50, few, lanceolate, white to pale purple or blue. Disc florets 25–125, yellow, becoming purplish with age. FR: Hairy cypsela with downy seeds.

GENUS *HULTENIELLA*
Entireleaf Daisy

Hulteniella integrifolia

ALSO: Small Arctic Daisy, *Chrysanthemum integrifolium*. SN means "Hultén's daisy with entire-margined leaves," honoring Oskar Eric Gunnar Hultén (1894–1981), Swedish botanist and author of *Flora of Alaska*.

RANGE: Kamchatka, Chukotka, and n N Amer; grows in well-drained areas of stony calcareous barrens, gravelly tundra, tundra hummocks, dry meadows, and on margins of ponds, brooks, and streams.

ID: H 1–4 in (2–10 cm). Dwarf tufted perennial. Stems erect, short, densely haired near the inflorescence. LVS: Crowded, linear, alternate, with entire margins, existing for a single season or less. FLS: Jul–Sep. Large, solitary, daisy-like. Ray florets white, disc florets yellow.

GENUS *TRIPLEUROSPERMUM*
Seashore Chamomile

Tripleurospermum maritimum
ALSO: Sea Mayweed, Pineapple Weed, Strand-kamille, Matricaire de mer, Strandbalderbrå, Трёхрёберник приморский, *Matricaria maritima*. SN means "3-sided seed of seashore [chamomile]."
RANGE: Near circumpolar, mainly on seashores, sometimes on roadsides and inland grassy sites near human habitation.
ID: H 4–24 in (10–60 cm). One to several leafy stems often tinged with red at the base. LVS: Finely lobed, feathery, somewhat fleshy, with a scent like chamomile when crushed. Stem leaves alternate, with a very short stalk. FLS: Jun–Sep. Daisy-like, 1–2.5 in (3–6 cm) across, with long, white ray florets and a dome of yellow disc florets that swells as flower matures. FR: Dark brown, flat cypsela, with 2 red or yellow, aromatic oil glands.

GENUS *ARNICA*: Most arnicas contain a POISONOUS lactone, helenalin, which can induce severe gastroenteritis. Contact can cause skin irritation.

Narrowleaf Arnica

Arnica angustifolia
ALSO: Alpine Arnica, Arctic Leopardbane, Arnika, Arnica à feuilles éntroites, Smalsolblom, Арника, *A. alpina*. SN means "narrowleaf arnica"; *Arnica* derives from the Greek *arna*, meaning "lamb," referring to some species' soft, hairy leaves.
RANGE: Circumpolar, on dry gravelly or sandy slopes, often below bird cliffs.
ID: H 2–16 in (5–40 cm). LVS: Variable; linear to broadly lanceolate, with smooth or densely white-woolly, sticky surfaces. FLS: One to several flowers at stem tip. Ray and disc florets yellow.
SIMILAR SPECIES: NODDING ARNICA, *Arnica lessingii*, Amphi-Beringian, grows in alpine meadows. SNOW ARNICA, *A. frigida*, Amphi-Beringian, grows on alpine barrens and dry stony slopes.

GENUS *SENECIO*: Most of these widespread perennial herbs, as well as those in the genera *Tephroseris* and *Packera*, have woolly-haired stems and yellow, daisy-like flowers borne in branched clusters. Most species contain the alkaloid senecionine, which is toxic to livestock—a condition first noted by the Greek physician Dioscorides (AD 40–90).

Seabeach Senecio

Senecio pseudoarnica
ALSO: Seaside Ragwort, False Arnica, Greiskräut, Séneçon faux-arnica, Strandsvineblom, Крестовник, *Arnica maritima*. SN means "old man false arnica," alluding to the gray hairs of the pappus.
RANGE: Seacoasts of e Asia, the Aleutians, and w/e N Amer.
ID: H 8–24 in (20–60 cm). Grows in crowded masses on sandy beaches. Stems single, erect, stout, covered with white woolly hairs. LVS: Obovate to oblanceolate, to 6 in (15 cm) long, with tapered bases and serrate-dentate margins. Leaves often wither before flowering occurs. FLS: Jul–Aug. Yellow, 1–5, borne in corymbs. Ray florets long, usually numbering 21.

Black-tipped Groundsel

Senecio lugens
ALSO: Small Blacktip Ragwort. CN derives from the Old Anglo-Saxon *groundeswelge*, meaning "ground swallower," referring to the rapid way some species spread. Scottish naturalist Sir John Richardson (1787–1865) discovered this species at Bloody Fall on the Coppermine Rvr. He applied the SN *lugens*, which means "to mourn," as a memorial to the 1771 Bloody Fall massacre of a tribe of sleeping Inuit who were slaughtered by Chipewyan Indians serving as guides to explorer and fur trader Samuel Hearne (1745–1792).
RANGE: Alaska, nw Canada, and the Rocky Mtns; grows on moist herb mats, lakeshores, riverbanks, and willow thickets, to 6550 ft (2000 m).
ID: H 2–20 in (5–50 cm). Stems solitary or clustered, with white woolly hairs. LVS: Basal

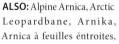

leaves obovate, tapering to a narrow petiole. Stem leaves lanceolate; leaf margins variable. FLS: Yellow. Conspicuous black tips on the involucral bracts. Borne in loose corymbs at stem tip.

GENUS *PACKERA*
Dwarf Arctic Groundsel

Packera cymbalaria
ALSO: Buek's Groundsel, Dwarf Arctic Ragwort, *P. heterophylla, Senecio resedifolius.* SN means "Packer's groundsel with cymbal-shaped [leaves]," honoring American botanist John G. Packer, former curator of the University of Alberta Herbarium in Canada.
RANGE: Alaska, w/e Canada, and in Eurasia from the Ural Mtns to Chukotka; found on tundra, moist meadows, and rocky slopes to 6250 ft (1900 m).
ID: H 2–10 in (5–25 cm). LVS: Petiolate, ovate to reniform, with serrated margins. Tall, slender flowering stem, with few sessile stem leaves. FLS: Jun–Aug. Yellow ray florets may be present (radiate) or absent (aradiate). Disc florets golden, numbering 60–75. Involucral bracts deep red or green with red tips.

GENUS *TEPHROSERIS*
Marsh Ragwort

Tephroseris palustris
ALSO: Mastodon Flower, Marsh Fleabane, Marsh Fleawort, Northern Swamp Groundsel, Moor-Aschenkraut, Sénecon des marais, Myrsvineblom, Пепельник болотный, *Cineraria congestus, Senecio congestus.* SN means "marsh [plant] with ashy gray silky hairs," referring to the translucent hairs covering the plant.
RANGE: Near circumpolar, in moist meadows, swamps, pond edges, ditches, burn sites, and around mining camps, to 3300 ft (1000 m).
ID: H 6–40 in (15–100 cm). Coarse and weedy. Erect, stout, hollow stem. Translucent hairs on the leaves, stem, and flower heads allow the sun to warm the tissues and prevent the heat from escaping. LVS: Alternate, sessile with clasping bases, oblong to spatulate, to 8 in (20 cm) long, with entire or irregularly toothed margins.

FLS: Jun–Aug. Yellow, 0.5 in (1.5 cm) across, in dense clusters, sometimes incompletely opened.
USE: Young leaves and flowering stems may be eaten raw, cooked, or pickled.

Arctic Groundsel

Tephroseris frigida
ALSO: *Senecio atropurpureus.* SN means "groundsel found in cold [places]."
RANGE: Amphi-Beringian; grows on peaty soil on heath tundra, wet meadows, marshes, and around the margins of ponds and streams, to 3300 ft (1000 m).
ID: H 2–8 in (5–20 cm). Creeping rootstock. LVS: Ovate, petiolate, to 1 in (2 cm) long, often withering before flowering occurs. Stem leaves 4–6, sessile, linear-lanceolate, with wavy, finely toothed, slightly inrolled margins. FLS: Jun–Aug. Solitary. Yellow. Long or short ray florets.

GENUS *SOLIDAGO*
Northern Goldenrod

Solidago multiradiata
ALSO: Goldrute, Verge d'or à rayons nombreux, Gullris, Золотарник. SN means "many-rayed healing [plant]," alluding to its use to counter kidney stones and infections.
RANGE: N Amer, with a similar species, *S. virgaurea* (*not illus.*), found in arctic-alpine Eurasia; grows in dry, stony sites on tundra, meadows, and alpine slopes to 12,150 ft (3700 m).
ID: H 4–20 in (10–50 cm). LVS: In a basal tuft, oblanceolate to elliptic, stalked, smooth, with crenate-serrate margins bearing soft, long hairs on the edge. Stem leaves linear, shorter, sessile. FLS: Jul–Sep. Small yellow heads crowded in a large, showy, dense corymb.

GENUS *ERIGERON*: These weedy, low herbs have white, pink, or lilac ray florets and yellow disc florets. Most species have a whorl, or *involucre*, of densely haired bracts, at the flower base. The calyx is modified into a ring of white hairs, the *pappus,* which aids in

Entireleaf Daisy
Hulteniella integrifolia
Kamchatka, Chukotka, n N Amer
H 1–4 in (2–10 cm)

Arctic Daisy
Arctanthemum arcticum
Disjunct sites along
coasts of Eurasia, N Amer
H 2–16 in (5–40 cm)

Short ray
florets

Long ray
florets

Arctic Groundsel
Tephroseris frigida
Amphi-Beringian
H 2–8 in (5–20 cm)

Dwarf Arctic Groundsel
Packera cymbalaria
Eurasia, nw/ne N Amer
H 2–10 in (5–25 cm)

Radiate
inflorescence

Aradiate
inflorescence

Seashore Chamomile
Tripleurospermum maritimum
Near circumpolar
H 4–24 in (10–60 cm)

Common Groundsel
Senecio vulgaris
Circumpolar
H 4–16 in (10–40 cm)

Black tips
on the
bracts

Black-tipped Groundsel
Senecio lugens
NW N Amer
H 2–20 in (5–50 cm)

Seabeach Senecio
Senecio pseudoarnica
Coasts of ne Asia,
Aleutians, w/e N Amer
H 8–24 in (20–60 cm)

Siberian Aster
Eurybia sibirica
Amphi-Beringian
H 2–20 in (5–50 cm)

Marsh Ragwort
Tephroseris palustris
Near circumpolar
H 6–40 in (15–100 cm)

Snow Arnica
Arnica frigida
Amphi-Beringian
H 2–10 in (5–25 cm)
Poisonous

Nodding Arnica
Arnica lessingii
Amphi-Beringian
H 2–16 in (5–40 cm)
Poisonous

Narrowleaf Arnica
Arnica angustifolia
Circumpolar
H 2–16 in (5–40 cm)
Poisonous

Northern Goldenrod
Solidago multiradiata
N Amer
H 4–20 in (10–50 cm)

wind dispersal of the seeds. The pappus opens into a plumose ball very soon after flowering, and its early appearance may be the source of the generic name *Erigeron*, Greek for "prematurely gray." The fruit is a nut-like *cypsela* formed from a double ovary, only one side of which produces a seed.

Bitter Fleabane

Erigeron acris
ALSO: Blue Fleabane, Scharfes Berufkraut, Vergerette âcre, Bakkestjerne, Мелколепестник острый. CN derives from the old belief that dried plants repelled fleas. SN means "bitter tasting fleabane."
RANGE: Eurasia and n N Amer, in dry meadows, gravel pits, rocky sites, and along roads.
ID: H 8–20 in (20–50 cm). Stem erect, reddish, hairy. LVS: Basal leaves stalked, oblanceolate, hairy, with entire margins; upper stem leaves sessile, narrowly elliptical. FLS: Jun–Aug. Borne in many small heads. Ray florets white or lilac, strap-shaped. Disc florets yellow, tubular, bisexual, with thread-like, female intermediate florets. Bracts green, often purple-tipped, hairy.

Cutleaf Fleabane

Erigeron compositus
ALSO: Dwarf or Trifid Mountain Fleabane, Cutleaf Daisy, Geteiltblättriges Berufkraut, Vergerette à feuilles segmentées, Мелколепестник сложноцветный. SN means "aster-flowered fleabane."
RANGE: Wrangel Is, n Chukotka, N Amer, and Greenland, on gravelly, alpine slopes.
ID: H 2–6 in (5–15 cm). Densely tufted. LVS: Basal, crowded, trifoliate, and again deeply dissected (the only arctic fleabane with divided leaves). FLS: In solitary heads. Disc florets yellow. Ray florets white or pale lilac.

Large-flower Fleabane

Erigeron grandiflorus
ALSO: SN means "large-flowered fleabane."
RANGE: Chukotka and

nw N Amer, on alpine slopes and dry tundra.
ID: H 4–6 in (10–15 cm). Gray, sticky hairs cover the plant parts. Stout erect flowering stems. LVS: Basal leaves erect or spreading, oblanceolate, to 2 in (5 cm) long. Stem leaves small, 2–4. FLS: Borne in solitary heads, to 1.5 in (3.5 cm) across. Ray florets lavender, later yellow. Disc florets yellow, with lavender tips.

Arctic Alpine Fleabane

Erigeron humilis
ALSO: Lowly Fleabane, Niedriges Berufkraut, Petit vergerette, Svartbakkestjerne, Nunaraqpait. SN means "humble fleabane."
RANGE: NE Asia, n N Amer, Greenland, Iceland, Svalbard, and n Europe, on dry tundra, gravel, glacial till, and near snowbeds.
ID: H 2–8 in (5–20 cm). Plant parts covered with purple to black, sticky, woolly hairs. Single, erect flowering stem. LVS: Spatulate to oblanceolate, in a basal tuft. FLS: In solitary heads. Disc florets yellow. Ray florets white, later bluish violet.

One-flower Fleabane

Erigeron uniflorus
ALSO: Vergerette à capitule laineux, Snøbakkestjerne, Einköpfiges Berufkraut. SN means "single-flowered fleabane."
RANGE: Near circumpolar, on alpine tundra, dry slopes, glacial till, and near snowbeds.
ID: H 2–8 in (5–20 cm). Plant parts covered with long, sticky, woolly hairs. Multiple, stout stems. LVS: Oblanceolate, entire, in a basal tuft. Stem leaves few, spirally arranged, sessile, narrowly elliptical. FLS: Jul–Aug. Borne in a large head. Ray florets white, later lilac. Disc florets yellow. Bracts slender, reddish or green, hairy.

GENUS *SAUSSUREA*
Narrowleaf Saw-wort

Saussurea angustifolia
ALSO: Fireworks Flower, Alpenscharten, Соссюре.
SN means "Saussure's narrowleaf," honoring Swiss physicist and alpinist Horace-Bénédict de Saussure (1740–1799).

Arctic Alpine Fleabane
Erigeron humilis
NE Asia, n N Amer, Greenland,
Iceland, Svalbard, n Europe
H 2–8 in (5–20 cm)

One-flower Fleabane
Erigeron uniflorus
Near circumpolar
H 2–8 in (5–20 cm)

Bitter Fleabane
Erigeron acris
Eurasia, N Amer
H 8–20 in (20–50 cm)

Cutleaf Fleabane
Erigeron compositus
Wrangel Is, Chukotka,
N Amer, Greenland
H 2–6 in (5–15 cm)

Large-flower Fleabane
Erigeron grandiflorus
Amphi-Beringian
H 4–6 in (10–15 cm)

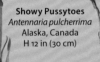

Showy Pussytoes
Antennaria pulcherrima
Alaska, Canada
H 12 in (30 cm)

**Narrowleaf Saw-wort
"Fireworks Flower"**
Saussurea angustifolia
E Asia, Alaska
H 4–12 in (10–30 cm)

Dwarf Hawksbeard
Crepis nana
E Asia, N Amer
H 0.5–3 in (1–8 cm)

Fries' Pussytoes
Antennaria friesiana
Amphi-Beringian
H 6 in (15 cm)

♀ flowerheads,
the "pussytoes"
Antennaria spp.

*Taraxacum
brachyceras*

♂ flowerheads
Antennaria spp.

*Taraxacum
hyparcticum*

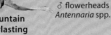
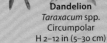

**Mountain
Everlasting**
Antennaria dioica
Eurasia, Aleutians
H 8 in (20 cm)

Dandelion
Taraxacum spp.
Circumpolar
H 2–12 in (5–30 cm)

RANGE: E Asia, Alaska, and nw Canada, on tundra, riverbanks, grassy slopes, willow thickets, and spruce forests, to 4250 ft (1300 m).
ID: H 4–12 in (10–30 cm). LVS: Linear to narrowly elliptical, to 5 in (12 cm) long, tapering to a narrow petiole; margin entire to sinuate. Stems dark purple, leafy. FLS: Jul–Aug. Purple. Dense, terminal, woolly flower heads with 3–5 thistle-like inflorescences.

GENUS *ANTENNARIA*
Pussytoes and Everlastings
Antennaria spp.

ALSO: Catsfoot, Katzen-pfötchen, Pieds de chat, Kattefot, Кошачья лапка. SN means "having antenna-like [projecting stamens]." CN *pussytoe* and *catsfoot* refer to the female seedheads, which resemble kittens' feet. *Everlasting* refers to the dried plants, which retain their freshness for several months.
RANGE: Circumpolar. MOUNTAIN EVERLASTING, *A. dioica*, grows in Eurasia and the Aleutians on dry heath or stony ground. FRIES' PUSSYTOES, *A. friesiana*, grows in Siberia and N Amer on tundra and dry alpine slopes. SHOWY PUSSYTOES, *A. pulcherrima*, grows in N Amer in meadows, river flats, and on alpine slopes.
ID: H 4–12 in (10–30 cm). LVS: Linear-oblong, in a basal tuft. Stems have a few sessile, strap-like leaves. FLS: Terminal corymb of 1–8 small, white, pink, or tan flower heads. Male and female flower heads on separate plants; female flowers narrow and thread-like; male flowers tubular.

GENUS *TARAXACUM*
Dandelion
Taraxacum spp.

ALSO: Löwenzahn, Dent de lion, Løvetann, Одуванчик. SN *Taraxacum* is Persian for bitter herb. The approximately 20 arctic species are closely related, wild variants of the Common Dandelion, *T. officinale*.
RANGE: Circumpolar. Widespread and common.
ID: H 2–12 in (5–30 cm). LVS: Linear-oblanceolate to oblanceolate, margins toothed to denticulate,

petioles slightly winged. Leaves are edible. FLS: Yellow, rarely white or pink. Terminal on smooth, erect, reddish stems. FR: Seedhead spherical, plumose, with fluffy white pappus "parachutes," each bearing a single seed.

GENUS *CREPIS*
Dwarf Hawksbeard
Crepis nana

ALSO: Pippau, Crépide, Haukeskjegg, Скерда. SN means "dwarf shoe."
RANGE: Arctic-alpine zones of e Asia and N Amer, on streambanks, gravel bars, and talus slopes to 13,125 ft (4000 m).
ID: H 0.5–3 in (1–8 cm). Branched, hairy stems. LVS: Basal, often purplish, rounded to spatulate, with entire or lobed margins. FLS: May–Sep. Ray florets 9–12, yellow above, purplish below. Heads grow among the leaves. FR: Elongated brown seeds on downy, white pappus.

GENUS *ACHILLEA*
Common Yarrow
Achillea millefolium

ALSO: Milfoil, Schaf-garbe, Achillée, Ryllik, Тысячелистник обыкновенный. SN means "Achilles's thousand-leaved yarrow," referring to the Greek warrior Achilles, who used yarrow to treat the wounds of his men.
RANGE: Near circumpolar, in meadows, woodland, and on disturbed ground.
ID: H 8–24 in (20–60 cm). Creeping, branching rootstock. LVS: Several times pinnately divided, frilly, hairy, somewhat aromatic. FLS: White, rarely yellow or pink, in large clusters at the top of the stem.

GENUS *ARTEMISIA*
Northern Wormwood
Artemisia borealis

ALSO: Boreal Sagewort, Boreal Sagebrush, Feldbeifuß, Armoise boréale, Markmalurt, Полынь северная, *A. campestris*. SN means "northern artemisia," after Artemis, Greek goddess of the hunt.
RANGE: Near circumpolar. Widely distributed

in meadows, on streambanks, sandy shores, and well-drained slopes to 11,500 ft (3500 m). **ID:** H 4–16 in (10–40 cm). Aromatic and bitter tasting. Stems ascending, simple or branched, downy or smooth, often purplish. **LVS:** Mostly basal, stalked; blade bi- or tri-pinnately lobed, feathery, withered by time of flowering. **FLS:** Aug–Sep. Borne in small, round, yellow orange, or deep red heads.

GENUS *PETASITES*
Arctic Sweet Coltsfoot
Petasites frigidus

ALSO: Arctic Butterbur, Pestwurz, Pétasite, Pestrot, Белокопытник, *Nardosmia angulosa* (Russia). SN means "hat from the cold," alluding to the use of leaves for decorating headgear. **RANGE:** Eurasia and nw N Amer, on wet tundra, along streams, and in standing water in marshes, bogs, and ditches, to 7500 ft (2300 m). **ID:** H 6–14 in (15–36 cm). Thick, creeping rhizome. **LVS:** Basal leaves rounded, with shallowly lobed, coarsely toothed margin, deeply cleft base; underside woolly-haired. Stem hairy, with a few large clasping leaves. **FLS:** Bloom before the leaves appear; 5–12 cream to pink heads, with dark red calyx. **FR:** Round, plumose seedheads. **USE:** Plants are edible when cooked.

FAMILY MENYANTHACEAE
BUCKBEANS AND ALLIES
GENUS *MENYANTHES*
Buckbean
Menyanthes trifoliata

ALSO: Bogbean, Marsh Trefoil, Scharbocks, Trèfle d'eau, Bukkeblad, Вахта. SN means "3-leaved moon flower," a name the ancient Greek Theophrastus applied to another plant. **RANGE:** Circumpolar, in bogs and ponds. **ID:** H 4–16 in (10–40 cm). Aquatic. Creeping black rootstock. Tall, smooth flowering stem. **LVS:** Three fleshy leaflets, to 2 in (5 cm) long. Old leaf bases persist from season to season. **FLS:** May–Jul. To 0.75 in (2 cm) across, 5-parted. Fused petals outwardly rose-colored and white, coarsely bearded within, with reddish stamens. Thick short spike of flowers opens sequentially from bottom to top over a period of a month. **FR:** A round capsule holds the seeds, or buckbeans.

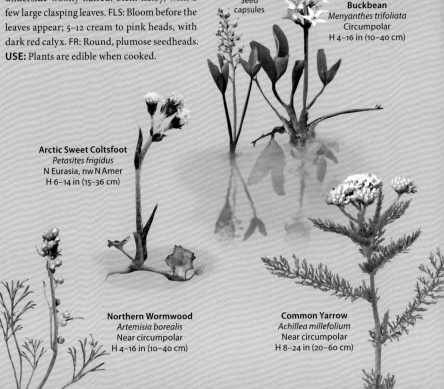

Seed capsules

Buckbean
Menyanthes trifoliata
Circumpolar
H 4–16 in (10–40 cm)

Arctic Sweet Coltsfoot
Petasites frigidus
N Eurasia, nw N Amer
H 6–14 in (15–36 cm)

Northern Wormwood
Artemisia borealis
Near circumpolar
H 4–16 in (10–40 cm)

Common Yarrow
Achillea millefolium
Near circumpolar
H 8–24 in (20–60 cm)

FAMILY CAMPANULACEAE
HAREBELLS AND BELLFLOWERS

Campanula is Latin for "little bell," referring to the bell-shaped flowers of most plants in this family. The stems and leaves exude a non-toxic, milky latex when injured or broken.

GENUS *CAMPANULA*
Common Harebell

Campanula rotundifolia

ALSO: Bluebell Bellflower, Rundblättrige Glocken-blume, Arktisk blåklokke, Campanule à feuilles rondes, Колокольчик круглолистный. SN means "harebell with rounded [basal] leaves." The folk song "Bluebells of Scotland" refers to this species: "O where and O where does your highland laddie dwell? He dwells in merry Scotland where the blue bells sweetly smell."

RANGE: Circumpolar, on tundra, in dry grasslands, heaths, edges of thickets, often on nutrient-poor, sandy or gravelly soils.

ID: H 4–20 in (10–50 cm). LVS: Basal leaves dark green, rounded, slightly toothed, with conspicuous pores that exude water. Leaves may wither early or persist all season. Stem leaves linear, almost thread-like; upper stem leaves sessile. FLS: Jun–Sep. Pale blue, sometimes white, pink, or violet; bell-shaped, to 1 in (2.5 cm) long, 5-parted, borne singly or in loose racemes on long thin stalks.

Mountain Harebell

Campanula lasiocarpa

ALSO: Alaska Bellflower. SN means "harebell with woolly fruit," referring to hairs on the enlarged flower receptacle.

RANGE: Amphi-Beringian; found in n Japan, Kamchatka, Aleutians, and Alaska, south to the Cascade Range of Washington State, on sandy tundra and alpine heath to 5250 ft (1600 m).

ID: H 2–6 in (5–15 cm). Dwarf perennial herb with creeping underground rootstock. LVS: Basal leaves petiolate, oblanceolate to elliptical, serrate, less than 1 in (2.5 cm) long. Stem leaves similar, alternate, few, reduced. FLS: Jul–Aug. Blue, bell-shaped; 1 or rarely 2 flowers borne at the stem tip. Calyx lobes narrow, with a few slender teeth. FR: Three-celled, cylindrical seed capsule, to 0.4 in (1 cm) long.

Alpine Bluebell

Campanula uniflora

ALSO: Arctic Dwarf Hare-bell, Einblütige Glocken-blume, Campanule uniflore, Høyfjellskolkke, Колокольчик одноцветковый. SN means "single-flowered harebell."

RANGE: N Amer, Greenland, Iceland, n Europe, and Svalbard; grows on gravelly ridges on the tundra, in rock crevices, and on alpine cliff ledges to 5000 ft (1500 m).

ID: H 2–12 in (5–30 cm). LVS: Basal, alternate, leathery, spatulate, dark green. Stout, ascending, unbranched, leafy stems. FLS: Jul. Solitary, deep blue, 5-parted, narrowly bell-shaped, nodding when young.

Alpine Bluebell
Campanula uniflora
N Amer, Greenland,
Iceland, n Europe, Svalbard
H 2–12 in (5–30 cm)

Common Harebell
Campanula rotundifolia
Circumpolar
H 4–20 in (10–50 cm)

Mountain Harebell
Campanula lasiocarpa
Amphi-Beringian
H 2–6 in (5–15 cm)

MONOCOTYLEDONS

This group of flowering plants includes the grasses, lilies, orchids, and irises. The seeds of these plants sprout with two seed leaves. Monocot stems lack a central pith and have fibrous vascular strands scattered throughout the stem. Leaves are usually parallel-veined and some have the lower portion of the leaf, the sheath, clasping the stem. Flower parts are normally in threes or multiples thereof, rarely in twos, fours, or sixes, and never in fives.

Poales: Grasses, Rushes, and Sedges

FAMILY POACEAE (GRAMINAE)
TRUE GRASSES

True grasses have jointed, hollow stems called *culms*, which are plugged with plant tissue at the *nodes*—the points along the culm where the leaves arise. The leaves are arranged alternately in two vertical rows (distichous) on opposite sides of the culm. Each leaf is composed of a *sheath*, *ligule*, and *blade*. The sheath hugs the culm at the leaf base. Rising from the top of the sheath is the ligule, a flat membrane that prevents water or insects from penetrating into the sheath and damaging this area where new growth occurs. The leaf blade is linear, parallel-veined, and has entire margins. Some species have leaf margins hardened with silicates, which discourage animals from browsing and killing the plant.

Flowers are arranged in *spikelets*. Two membranous bracts called the *glumes* surround the spikelet base (glumes are the husk of a cereal grain). Each spikelet has one or more *florets*, which are surrounded by two bracts; the external bract is called the *lemma*, the internal one the *palea*. Florets are typically bisexual and wind-pollinated. The fruit is a *caryopsis*—a dry, single seed, such as a grain of rice or wheat that fuses to the hard seed coat.

Grass species are notoriously difficult to identify, even for experts. A hand lens, a manual to the arctic graminae, and the deductive bent of Sherlock Holmes are essential for field study. The following accounts and illustrations of some of the common circumpolar species may provide a starting point for your investigation into these ubiquitous plants, which yield grains and cereal crops vital to human economies and provide some 20 percent of the earth's vegetative cover.

GENUS *ALOPECURUS*
Alpine Foxtail

Alopecurus alpinus
ALSO: Fuchsschwanzgräser, Vulpin, Kavlar, Лисохвост. SN means "mountain foxtail."
RANGE: Circumpolar; grows on wet tundra and sandy soils.
ID: H 6–12 in (15–30 cm). LVS: Flat, somewhat succulent leaves, with inflated sheaths. FLS: Spikelets woolly, single-flowered, in a dense, spike-like, purplish gray panicle.

GENUS *ARCTAGROSTIS*
Wideleaf Polar Grass

Arctagrostis latifolia
ALSO: Straußgräser, Russgräs, Арктагростис. SN means "broad-leaved bear grass."
RANGE: Circumpolar, on tundra and edges of brooks, ponds, and lakes.
ID: H 4–20 in (10–50 cm). Creeping stolons. LVS: Few, broad, coarse. FLS: Purplish terminal panicle of single-flowered spikelets; inflorescence dense in plants growing in cold habitats, diffuse and spreading at warmer sites.

GENUS *CALAMAGROSTIS*
Slimstem Reedgrass

Calamagrostis stricta
ALSO: Reed Bentgrass, Reitgräser, Smårørkvein, Røyrkvein, Вейник, *C. neglecta*. SN means "erect reed-like grass."
RANGE: Circumpolar in arctic-alpine zones, in moist meadows and along lakeshores.
ID: H 8–16 in (20–40 cm). LVS: Coarse, flat, linear, inrolled. FLS: Oblong, diffuse to dense, purplish, terminal panicles of single-flowered spikelets, with a distinct bristle on the lemma.

GENUS *DESCHAMPSIA*
Tufted Hairgrass
Deschampsia caespitosa

ALSO: Schmielen, Fjell-bunke, Tåtlar, Луговик. SN means "Deschamps's tufted grass," after French naturalist Louis Auguste Deschamps (1765–1842). **RANGE:** Circumpolar, on wet gravel and clay on tundra, meadows, and lakeshores. **ID:** H 8–20 in (20–50 cm). Densely tufted. LVS: Narrow, often inrolled. FLS: Open pyramidical or narrow panicles of feathery, somewhat shiny, purplish, twin-flowered spikelets.

GENUS *LEYMUS*
Sea Lyme Grass
Leymus arenarius
Leymus mollis

ALSO: Dunegrass, Sand Ryegrass, Quecken, Strandhafer, Elyme de sable, Kveke, Волоснец. SN means "millet-like grass." **RANGE:** Grows on sandy seacoasts. *L. arenarius* (pale green), on coasts of n Europe. *L. mollis* (dark green), on coasts of Asia, N Amer, Greenland. **ID:** H 10–35 in (25–100 cm). Large clumps spring from creeping underground stolons. LVS: Grayish green, smooth, flat, broadly lanceolate, with pointed tips. FLS: Terminal panicle of twin-flowered spikelets, to 6 in (15 cm) long, pale green, narrow, bristly. **USE:** Native people weave this grass into mats, tote bags, and baskets. The tough, sharply pointed leaves were once used as sewing needles. Often planted to stabilize the sand on exposed beaches.

GENUS *POA*
Arctic Bluegrass
Poa arctica

ALSO: Rispengräser, Pâturin artique, Jervrapp, Gröen, Мятлик. SN means " lawn grass of the Arctic." **RANGE:** Circumpolar. Widespread on tundra, meadows, and around human habitation. **ID:** H 6–10 in (15–25 cm). LVS: Narrow, folded or flat, with a flattened sheath and membranous ligule. FLS: Pyramidical panicle of 2–6 flowered spikelets. FR: Purplish blue seeds with a navy blue husk turn brown at maturity.

GENUS *FESTUCA*
Alpine Fescue
Festuca brachyphylla

ALSO: Iviit, Schwingel, Fétuque à feuilles courtes, Svingel, Овсяница. SN means "short-leaf grass." **RANGE:** Circumpolar, on beaches, sandy riverbanks, meadows, and near animal dens. **ID:** H 2–14 in (5–35 cm). Tufted or stoloniferous, turf-forming perennial. Smooth, wiry culms. LVS: Narrow, inrolled, stiff, and bristle-like. FLS: Panicle narrow or diffuse, spike-like.

GENUS *HIEROCHLOE*
Holy Grass
Hierochloe odorata

ALSO: Iviit, Sweetgrass, Buffalo or Vanilla Grass, Mariengras, Hiérochloé odorant, Myskgräs, Зубровка. SN means "sweet holy grass," referring to the plant's pleasant fragrance and use in Native American purification ceremonies. **RANGE:** Circumpolar; grows on lakeshores and in sandy meadows. **ID:** H 8–16 in (20–40 cm). Solitary culms rise from a thin, creeping rootstock. LVS: Mostly flat, lanceolate; basal leaves short and broad, sheaths tinged with purple. Fragrant when dried. FLS: Glossy, yellowish brown spikelets. **USE:** *Żubrówka*, the Polish buffalo-grass vodka, is distilled with rye grain and infused with extract of Holy Grass. **RELATED SPECIES:** *H. alpina* (pale green on map) grows on dry tundra and acidic rock; panicle is contracted and somewhat 1-sided. *H. pauciflora* (midgreen line) grows on wet tundra on the High Arctic coasts; low, delicate grass with a narrow, dark red, 1-sided panicle.

GENUS *PHIPPSIA*
Icegrass
Phippsia algida

ALSO: Snøgress, Snøgras, Фиппсия, *Phippsia concinna*. SN means "Phipps's cold [grass]," honoring British Royal Navy officer Constantine John Phipps (1744–1792), who led a naval expedition from Svalbard toward the North Pole.

RANGE: Circumpolar, on tundra hummocks, river terraces, wet ridges, seashores, bogs, disturbed ground, and around snow patches. **ID:** H 1–6 in (2–15 cm). Tufted, decumbent perennial. **LVS:** Flat, smooth, yellowish green leaves, with inrolled margins. Ascending stems, barely overtopping the leaves. **FLS:** Narrow panicle of very small, single-flowered spikelets.

GENUS *TRISETUM*
Spike Trisetum

Trisetum spicatum
ALSO: Ähren-Grannenhafer, Трищетинник колосистый, Trisè à épi. SN means "3-bristled spikelet awn." **RANGE:** Circumpolar; widespread in rocky and gravelly sites. **ID:** H 4–16 in (10–40 cm). **LVS:** Flat, downy. **FLS:** Spike-like, lanceolate-oblong, somewhat shiny panicle, with protruding, bent, twisted bristles (awns).

FAMILY JUNCACEAE
RUSHES

The leaves of rushes are arranged in 3 rows (*tristichous*) and each row is located one-third of the way around the stem from the previous leaf. The inflorescence of small florets is located at the top or side of the round stem. The outer rim of the flower (*perianth*) typically has reduced floral segments called *tepals*. These are usually arranged in 2 whorls, each containing 2 scale-like sepals and petals, 3 or 6 stamens, a single short style and 3 hairy stigmas. The fruit of a rush is a 3-sectioned dehiscent capsule.

GENUS *JUNCUS*
Chestnut Rush

Juncus castaneus
ALSO: Bog Rush, Binsen, Kastanjesiv, Jonc marron, Sev, Ситник. SN means "rush with chestnut-colored [seed capsule]"; *Juncus* is said to be the Latin name for rushes as applied by Roman playwright, Titus Macchius Plautus (254–184 BC). **RANGE:** Circumpolar, on wet soils on the tundra and in the mountains. **ID:** H 4–16 in (10–40 cm). **LVS:** Flat or cylindrical, mostly basal. Culm erect, stiff, coarse. **FLS:** Heads 1–3, with the lower involucral leaf extending beyond inflorescence. Sepals dark brown, linear, acute. **FR:** Shiny, chestnut to dark purple capsule.

Two-flowered Rush

Juncus biglumis
ALSO: Ivisuka, Jonc à deux glumes, Zweiblütige Binse, Tvillingsiv. SN means "rush with a twin-flowered spike." **RANGE:** Circumpolar; wet tundra or riverbanks. **ID:** H 2–8 in (5–20 cm). Small, compact tufts. Stiff, erect culms. **LVS:** Single leaf and bladeless sheaths at culm base. **FLS:** Two, one flower above the other, and supported by a dark brown, leafy bract, to 1 in (3 cm) long. **FR:** Dark brown capsule.

GENUS *LUZULA*
Northern Woodrush

Luzula confusa
ALSO: Hainsimsen, Luzule trompeuse, Frytle, Ожика. SN means "rush easily mistaken for another"; *Luzula* derives from the Latin *lux*, meaning "light," possibly referring to the leaf margin hairs, which look shiny when covered with dew. **RANGE:** Circumpolar, on dry tundra heath and rocky slopes to 6900 ft (2100 m). **ID:** H 4–14 in (10–36 cm). Tufted. Stiff culm, with lustrous purple basal sheaths. **LVS:** Narrow, channeled, acute. **FLS:** Crowded terminal spikes.

FAMILY CYPERACEAE
SEDGES

Sedges are found most often in wet places such as mires and bogs. The leaves are mostly basal and spiral around the stem. Unlike rushes, the culms of sedges are triangular and have prominent edges. To avoid confusing the two, examine the stem and heed the saying, "rushes are round and sedges have edges."

GENUS *CAREX*
Bigelow's Sedge

Carex bigelowii
ALSO: Stivstarr, Carex de Bigelow, Осока Бигелоу.

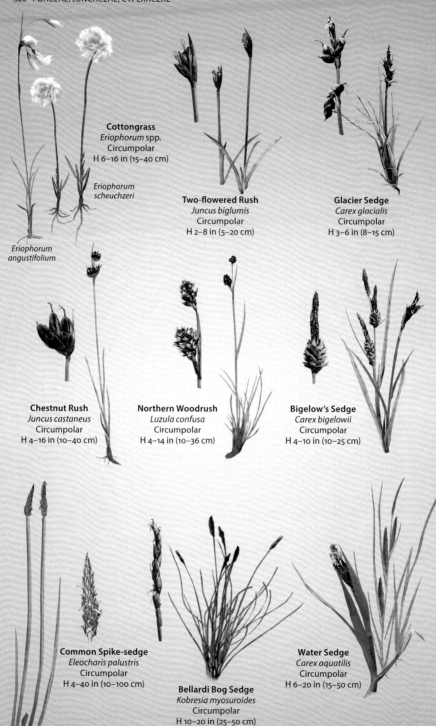

Cottongrass
Eriophorum spp.
Circumpolar
H 6–16 in (15–40 cm)

Eriophorum scheuchzeri

Eriophorum angustifolium

Two-flowered Rush
Juncus biglumis
Circumpolar
H 2–8 in (5–20 cm)

Glacier Sedge
Carex glacialis
Circumpolar
H 3–6 in (8–15 cm)

Chestnut Rush
Juncus castaneus
Circumpolar
H 4–16 in (10–40 cm)

Northern Woodrush
Luzula confusa
Circumpolar
H 4–14 in (10–36 cm)

Bigelow's Sedge
Carex bigelowii
Circumpolar
H 4–10 in (10–25 cm)

Common Spike-sedge
Eleocharis palustris
Circumpolar
H 4–40 in (10–100 cm)

Bellardi Bog Sedge
Kobresia myosuroides
Circumpolar
H 10–20 in (25–50 cm)

Water Sedge
Carex aquatilis
Circumpolar
H 6–20 in (15–50 cm)

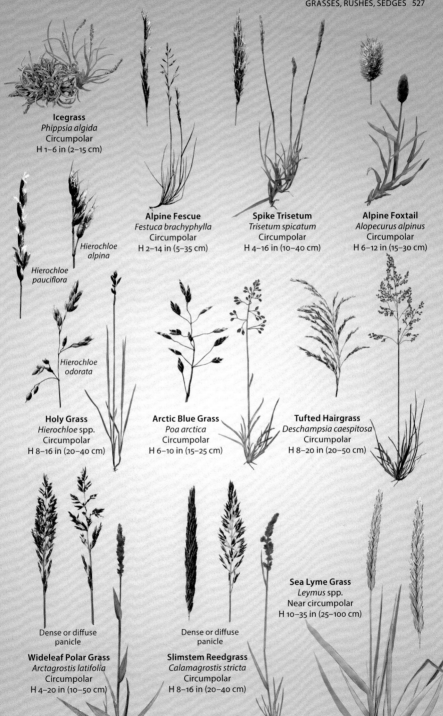

Icegrass
Phippsia algida
Circumpolar
H 1–6 in (2–15 cm)

Alpine Fescue
Festuca brachyphylla
Circumpolar
H 2–14 in (5–35 cm)

Spike Trisetum
Trisetum spicatum
Circumpolar
H 4–16 in (10–40 cm)

Alpine Foxtail
Alopecurus alpinus
Circumpolar
H 6–12 in (15–30 cm)

Hierochloe alpina

Hierochloe pauciflora

Hierochloe odorata

Holy Grass
Hierochloe spp.
Circumpolar
H 8–16 in (20–40 cm)

Arctic Blue Grass
Poa arctica
Circumpolar
H 6–10 in (15–25 cm)

Tufted Hairgrass
Deschampsia caespitosa
Circumpolar
H 8–20 in (20–50 cm)

Dense or diffuse panicle

Dense or diffuse panicle

Sea Lyme Grass
Leymus spp.
Near circumpolar
H 10–35 in (25–100 cm)

Wideleaf Polar Grass
Arctagrostis latifolia
Circumpolar
H 4–20 in (10–50 cm)

Slimstem Reedgrass
Calamagrostis stricta
Circumpolar
H 8–16 in (20–40 cm)

Broad leaves

Linear leaves

SN means "Bigelow's cutter," alluding to the sharp leaf margins and honoring Jacob Bigelow (1786–1879), professor of Materia Medica at Harvard and author of *American Medical Botany*. **RANGE:** Circumpolar. Grows in dry grassy turf, often in mountains.
ID: H 4–10 in (10–25 cm). Stout scaly stolons, with shiny, dark reddish brown sheaths. Culms stiff, smooth, sharply triangular, with withered leaves at base. **LVS:** Stiff, strongly ribbed, light green. **FLS:** Terminal, linear spikelet.

Glacier Sedge

Carex glacialis
ALSO: Ridge Sedge, Rabbestarr, Carex des glaces, Laîche des glaciers, Осока ледниковая. SN means "sedge of the glaciers."
RANGE: Circumpolar, on dry gravel ridges, cliffs, and alpine slopes.
ID: H 3–6 in (8–15 cm). Densely tufted. Culms smooth. **LVS:** Narrow, flat, somewhat curved. **FLS:** Terminal, erect, staminate spikelet.

Water Sedge

Carex aquatilis
ALSO: Seggen, Laîche, Starr, Осока водная, *C. stans*. SN means "water rush."
RANGE: Circumpolar, in bogs, mires, pond edges, lakeshores, sheltered marine beaches, and wet tundra turf, to 2000 ft (600 m).
ID: H 6–20 in (15–50 cm). **LVS:** Coarse, flat; basal and cauline, or sometimes all basal. **FLS:** Terminal, compound spikes; single-flowered spiklet, borne in the axil of a scale-like bract.

GENUS *ELEOCHARIS*
Common Spike-sedge

Eleocharis palustris
ALSO: Spikerush, Sumpf-binsen, Scirpe des marais, болотница болотная, *Scirpus palustris*. SN means "graceful marsh dweller."
RANGE: Circumboreal; grows in marshes, ditches, and shorelines.

ID: H 4–40 in (10–100 cm). Semi-aquatic. Culm erect, tall, stiff, triangular, often with blunt ridges when dry; culm is photosynthetic. **LVS:** Reduced to reddish basal sheaths. **FLS:** Solitary, pointed spikelet, covered with shaggy, brownish scales. **FR:** Golden brown to purplish, nutlet-like achene.

GENUS *KOBRESIA*
Bellardi Bog Sedge

Kobresia myosuroides
ALSO: Nackt-Schuppenried, Kobrésie fausse-queue-de-souris, Кобрезия. SN means "Cobres's false mousetail," honoring the German bibliophile Joseph Paul von Cobres (1747–1823). CN honors Italian botany professor Carlo Antonio Lodovico Bellardi (1741–1826).
RANGE: Circumpolar; grows on hummocks, gravel bars, and sparsely vegetated rocky slopes to 11,500 ft (3500 m).
ID: H 10–20 in (25–50 cm). Stiff culm with many bladeless, somewhat glossy, brown sheaths at base. **LVS:** Stiff, filiform, as long as culm. **FLS:** Spike is about 1 in (2 cm) long, narrow, with brown scales; each spikelet has 1 staminate and 1 pistillate flower.

GENUS *ERIOPHORUM*
Cottongrass

Eriophorum angustifolium
Eriophorum scheuchzeri
ALSO: Tall Cottongrass, White Cottongrass, Bog-cotton, Wollgräser, Linaigrette, Myrull, Пушица. SN means "bearing wool or cotton"; *angustifolium* means "narrow leaves"; *scheuchzeri* honors Swiss physician Johann Jakob Scheuchzer (1672–1733), author of a 3-volume work on the natural history of Switzerland.
RANGE: Circumpolar, in bogs, around shallow ponds, and on wet turf.
ID: H 6–16 in (15–40 cm). Erect culms. **LVS:** Dark green, linear, mostly basal. **FLS:** One spikelet (*scheuchzeri*) to several spikelets (*angustifolium*). When in flower, the long, silky, white bristles resemble cotton balls.

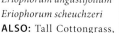

Liliales: Lilies and Allies

The order Liliales contains about 1300 species of herbaceous monocots that have food-storage organs such as bulbs or rhizomes. Some species contain poisonous alkaloids.

FAMILY LILIACEAE
GENUS *LLOYDIA*
Common Alp Lily
Lloydia serotina

ALSO: Snowdon Lily, Mountain Spiderwort, Späte Faltenlilie, Gagée, Gullstjerne, Лілійка пізня, *Gagea serotina*. SN means "Lloyd's late bloomer," honoring Welsh botanist Edward Lhuyd [Lloyd] (1660–1709), who discovered the plant on Mount Snowdon in Wales. The Welsh name, *Brwynddail y mynydd*, means "mountain rush-leaves."

RANGE: E Asia and nw N Amer, on tundra hummocks, rocky sites, and alpine meadows, to 5900 ft (1800 m).

ID: H 2–6 in (5–15 cm). Erect stems, with several brownish, withered bracts at stem base. LVS: Long, stiff, grass-like, to 4 in (10 cm) long. FLS: May. Solitary, white, with greenish to purplish veins.

FAMILY ALLIACEAE
GENUS *ALLIUM*
Wild Chives
Allium schoenoprasum

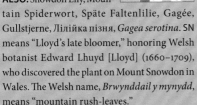

ALSO: Schnittlauch, Ciboulette, Graslaukur, Gressløk, Лук скорода, Paatitaak. SN means "rush-leaved onion."

RANGE: Eurasia and N Amer, on rocky or gravelly streambanks and lakeshores, and in wet alpine meadows, to 11,500 ft (3500 m). The only *Allium* native to both the Old and New World.

ID: H 8–20 in (20–50 cm). Erect stem. LVS: Usually 2, with hollow, rounded blade; lower leaves ensheathe half the stem; persistent. FLS: Jun–Aug. Umbel of 30–50 bell-shaped, pale purple to deep pink blossoms that dry to pink or white and become papery. Pollinated by bees, which are attracted by the plant's sulfur compounds.

FAMILY TOFIELDIACEAE
GENUS *TOFIELDIA*
False Asphodel
Tofieldia pusilla

ALSO: Scotch, Western, or Little False Asphodel, Kleine Simsenlilie, Tofieldie naine, Bjønnbrodd, Тофилдия маленькая. SN means "Tofield's tiny asphodel," honoring English botanist Thomas Tofield (1730–1779). CN derives from the Greek *asphodelos*, an everlasting flower said to grow in the Elysian Fields.

Mountain Death Camas
Anticlea elegans
W N Amer
H 8–24 in (20–60 cm)
Poisonous

False Asphodel
Tofieldia pusilla
Circumpolar
H 1–12 in (3–30 cm)

Common Alp Lily
Lloydia serotina
E Eurasia, nw N Amer
H 2–6 in (5–15 cm)

White False Hellebore
Veratrum album
Eurasia
H 20–70 in (50–175 cm)
Poisonous

**Northern
False Asphodel**
Tofieldia coccinea
Near circumpolar,
absent n Europe
H 1–8 in (3–20 cm)

Wild Chives
Allium schoenoprasum
Eurasia, N Amer
H 8–20 in (20–50 cm)

Flower of
Veratrum viride

RANGE: Circumpolar, in wet chalky soil on heaths, bogs, meadows, mossy streambanks, and alpine ridges, to 7550 ft (2300 m).
ID: H 1–12 in (3–30 cm). LVS: Flat, sword-shaped, to 3.25 in (8 cm) long. FLS: May–Jun. Petals white to yellow green, purple veined; whitish bracts deeply 3-lobed; 3–35 flowers borne in a spike.

Northern False Asphodel
Tofieldia coccinea
ALSO: Tofieldie écarlate, Тофилдия краснеющая. SN means "scarlet asphodel."

RANGE: Near circumpolar (absent n Europe); grows on heaths, tundra, stony open land, and meadows, to 4925 ft (1500 m).
ID: H 1–8 in (3–20 cm). LVS: Grass-like, to 3 in (8 cm) long, in a basal tuft. Stems purplish brown. FLS: Jun. Petals yellowish green, suffused with pink or crimson; 5–30 flowers borne in a raceme.

FAMILY MELANTHIACEAE
BUNCHFLOWERS AND ALLIES
GENUS *VERATRUM*
White False Hellebore
Veratrum album
ALSO: False Helleborine, European White Hellebore,

Weiße Germer, Vératre blanc, Чемерица. SN means "white hellebore." CN *Hellebore* comes from the Greek *elein*, meaning "to injure" and *bora*, meaning "food" alluding to the plant's poisonous nature. The root contains toxic alkaloids, which have a paralyzing effect on the nervous system and can cause cardiac failure if ingested.
RANGE: Eurasia, in moist alpine meadows and grassy places.
ID: H 20–70 in (50–175 cm). Vertical rhizome has onion-like odor and is covered with old leaf sheaths. Stout, solid, hairy, green stem. LVS: Spirally arranged, to 14 in (36 cm) long; elliptical to broad lanceolate, heavily ribbed, downy on the underside. FLS: Jun–Jul. Bell-shaped; borne in a large spike or branched inflorescence. Petals 6, cream to greenish, fringed. POISONOUS.
USE: Small doses were formerly used to treat cholera, gout, hypertension, and herpes lesions. Hellebores are no longer used medicinally.

Green False Hellebore
Veratrum viride
ALSO: Bear's Foot, Vérâtre vert, Tabac du diable. SN means "green hellebore."

RANGE: Disjunct distribution in subarctic e/w N Amer, in meadows, swamps, and marshes.
ID: H 20–70 in (50–175 cm). LVS: Oval to linear, conspicuously parallel-veined. Slender, erect, hairy stem, with clasping stem leaves. FLS: Green, in a branched inflorescence, often nodding at maturity. POISONOUS.

GENUS *ANTICLEA*
Mountain Death Camas
Anticlea elegans
ALSO: Alkali Grass, Poison Sego, Zigadène élégant,

Zigadenus elegans. SN means "Anticlea's elegant camas," after Anticlea, mother of Odysseus.
RANGE: W N Amer, in moist grasslands, forest bogs, and riverbanks, to 11,800 ft (3600 m).
ID: H 8–24 in (20–60 cm). Slender, erect stem. LVS: Mostly basal, alternate, grass-like, grayish green. FLS: Jun–Aug. Star-shaped. Petals 6, white, with greenish yellow glands on each petal; sepals cream to green; bracts often tinged with purple or pink. EXTREMELY POISONOUS TO HUMANS. Also toxic to livestock, especially sheep, which eat the plants in early spring, when no other forage is available.

Asparagales: Orchids, Irises, and Allies
Orchids, formerly in their own order, Orchidales, and the irises, formerly in the order Liliales, have recently been incorporated into the order Asparagales.

FAMILY ORCHIDACEAE
ORCHIDS
The word *orchid* derives from the Greek *orchis*, meaning "testicle," a reference to the shape of the twin tubers of some species. Theophrastus (371–286 BC), Greek successor to Aristotle and designated Father of Botany, first applied the word to these plants in his monumental botanical treatise *On the Natural History of Plants* (*De Historia Plantarum*).

Orchidaceae is the largest family of flowering plants, with some 880 genera and 22,000 accepted species, encompassing 6 to 11 percent of all seed plants. In addition, over 100,000 horticultural varieties of orchids have been created. The number of orchid species equals about four times the number of mammal species and more than twice the number of bird species.

Orchids are generally 3- or 6-parted, and their leaves have parallel veins. The flower has an outer whorl of sepals and an inner whorl of petals, which are collectively known as *tepals*. Orchids produce a myriad of dust-like seeds, but the seeds lack an endosperm, which in most plants provides food reserves needed for survival after the seed has dispersed. In the orchid, a fungus assumes this function. It attaches its filamentous mycelium to the seed and provides water and mineral nutrients so the seed can germinate. At first, this relationship favors only the orchid, but later, as it matures, the orchid provides the fungus with photosynthesized sugars in a mutually beneficial symbiosis.

SUBFAMILY CYPRIPEDIOIDEAE
LADY'S SLIPPER ORCHIDS

The flowers of these orchids have 3 sepals and 3 petals. The lower petal forms a slipper-shaped pouch adapted to attract insect pollinators such as bees. When bees land on the slippery surface of the lip, they slide into the sac-like pouch and are trapped there. Translucent "windows" on the lip illuminate the flower's narrow column and lure the bee forward. Once in the column, the bee inches past the male stigma, where a sticky mass of pollen falls onto its back. As the bee crawls past the female stamen, the pollen rubs off and fertilizes the flower. The bee exits the column and flies off carrying a bit of pollen to the next orchid, thus ensuring cross-pollination.

GENUS *CYPRIPEDIUM*
Spotted Lady's Slipper
Cypripedium guttatum
ALSO: Aphrodite's Slipper, Gesprenkelter Frauenschuh, Башмачок пятнистый. SN means "Aphrodite's slipper," from Cypria, surname of Aphrodite.

RANGE: Eurasia, Aleutians, and w N Amer, in open forest, tundra, meadows, and scree slopes, to 2600 ft (800 m).
ID: H 5–15 in (12–38 cm). LVS: Ovate, to 6 in (15 cm) long; 2–3 midway up stem. FLS: Jun–Jul. Solitary. Sepals and pouch exterior blotched with white, pink, and magenta; pouch lip creamy white.

Sparrow's Egg Lady's Slipper
Cypripedium passerinum
ALSO: Franklin's Lady's-slipper, Sperlingsei-Frauenschuh. SN means "sparrow's-egg slipper."

RANGE: N Amer, in moist coniferous forests and clearings, on tundra, gravel terraces, and streambanks, sea level to 7200 ft (0–2200 m).
ID: H 5–15 in (12–38 cm). LVS: Elliptical to ovate-lanceolate, 3–7, evenly placed along the stem. FLS: Jun–Jul. Ivory-colored egg-shaped pouch; greenish tepals; white, pink-spotted lip.

Yellow Lady's Slipper
Cypripedium calceolus
ALSO: Gelbe Frauenschuh, Cypripède soulier, Sabot de Vénus, Marisko, Башмачок настоящий, *C. parviflorum*. SN means "Aphrodite's small shoe."

RANGE: Eurasia and N Amer, in damp forest, woodland, and meadows, to 9500 ft (2900 m).
ID: H 8–30 in (20–75 cm). LVS: Broadly ovate, 3–5, to 8 in (20 cm) long, clasping the stem. FLS: May–Jul. One to 3, in axis of bracts. Faint rose fragrance. Pouch yellow, often with purple veins; sepals greenish yellow to purplish brown, commonly spotted or striped, usually twisted.

SUBFAMILY ORCHIDOIDEAE
MONANDROUS ORCHIDS

These orchids have a single fertile anther.

GENUS *COELOGLOSSUM*
Frog Orchid
Coeloglossum viride
ALSO: Long-bracted Green Orchid, Grüne Hohlzunge, Orchis grenouille, Grønn-kurle, Пололепестник

зелёный, *Dactylorhiza viridis*. SN means "hollow-tongued green [orchid]," referring to the hollow nectar spur on the tongue-like lip.
RANGE: Near circumboreal (absent Greenland), in damp forests, wet tundra, prairies, meadows, thickets, heaths, and bogs, to 9200 ft (2800 m).
ID: H 4–22 in (10–55 cm). LVS: Alternate, 2–6, to 6 in (15 cm) long, obovate to elliptical at the plant base, lanceolate on the stem. FLS: May–Jun. Green, often deeply suffused with dull red, in a spike of 7–70 blossoms; dark green sepals and petals form a hood; flat split lip has a long nectar spur.

GENUS *CORALLORHIZA*
Northern Coral-root
Corallorhiza trifida

ALSO: Early Coral-root, Yellow Coral-root, Korallenwurz, Corallorhize trifide, Korallrot. SN means "3-parted coral-root." Despite the name, this orchid lacks true roots. Instead it has a hard, knobby rhizome containing fungal mycelia that feed the plant.
RANGE: Circumboreal, in spruce swamps and wet woodlands, to 10,150 ft (3100 m).
ID: H 4–10 in (10–25 cm). LVS: Scale-like or absent. FLS: Jun–Jul. Petals pale yellow green, often spotted with purple; sepals 6, yellowish to green, strongly recurved; lip white, often purple-spotted, with 2 small lateral lobes or teeth. Spike of 3–18, small, irregular blossoms.

GENUS *GOODYERA*
Dwarf Rattlesnake Plaintain
Goodyera repens

ALSO: Creeping Ladies' Tresses, Kriechendes Netzblatt, Goodyérie rampante, Knerot, Гудайера ползучая. SN means "Goodyer's creeper," referring to the green underground runner and honoring English botanist John Goodyer (1592–1664).
RANGE: Near circumboreal (absent Greenland), in old-growth forests and woods, sometimes in bogs or cedar swamps, to 9500 ft (2900 m).
ID: H 2–8 in (5–20 cm) LVS: In a basal rosette, short-stalked, ovate, with entire margins; blade uniformly green or with green lateral veins

edged with white. FLS: Jul–Aug. White, irregular, somewhat bell shaped, hairy; fragrant, 1-sided, in a spiraling spike of 7–36 blossoms.

GENUS *PLATANTHERA*
Northern Green Orchid
Platanthera hyperborea

ALSO: Tall Leafy Green Orchis, Isländische Waldhyazinthe, Habénaire hyperboréale, Friggjargras, *Habenaria hyperborea*. SN means "northern [orchid with] thick anthers."
RANGE: N Amer, Greenland, and Iceland, on wet lowland tundra and peat bogs.
ID: H 3–12 in (7–30 cm). LVS: Oblong-lanceolate, 3–4. FLS: Jun–Jul. Small, green, pale greenish white, or yellowish green, in a raceme of 10–60.

Northern Bog Orchid
Platanthera obtusata

ALSO: Bluntleaf Orchid, Wenigblütige Waldhyazinthe, Platanthère à grandes feuilles, Любка. SN means "[orchid with] thick anthers and blunt [leaves]."
RANGE: N Amer and isolated sites in Eurasia, in damp coniferous forest, sphagnum bogs, streambanks, moist tundra, and roadsides, sea level to 11,500 ft (0–3500 m).
ID: H 2–10 in (5–25 cm). Grows in clusters. LVS: One, rarely 2, basal, spreading to ascending, elliptical or broadly obovate. FLS: Jun–Aug. Small, greenish white to yellowish green, borne in a loose, slender cluster of 4–18, at stem tip.

GENUS *NEOTTIA*
Heartleaf Twayblade
Neottia cordata

ALSO: Zweiblatt, Listère cordée, Småtveblad, Тайник сердцевидный, *Listera cordata*. SN means "heart-leaved bird-nest [orchid]." CN means "2 cordate leaves," referring to the pair of opposite leaves at the base of the flowering stem.
RANGE: Circumboreal, in moist, mossy places in woods and meadows.
ID: H 2–13 in (5–33 cm). LVS: Heart-shaped, to 1.5 in (3.8 cm) across, in opposite pairs at

Northern Coral-root
Corallorhiza trifida
Circumboreal
H 4–10 in (10–25 cm)

**Heartleaf
Twayblade**
Neottia cordata
Circumboreal
H 2–13 in (5–33 cm)

Northern Bog Orchid
Platanthera obtusata
Eurasia, N Amer
H 2–10 in (5–25 cm)

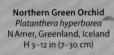

Northern Green Orchid
Platanthera hyperborea
N Amer, Greenland, Iceland
H 3–12 in (7–30 cm)

Irish Ladies' Tresses
Spiranthes romanzoffiana
N Amer, UK, Ireland
H 3–22 in (8–55 cm)

Variable
leaves

**Dwarf Rattlesnake
Plaintain**
Goodyera repens
Near circumboreal,
absent Greenland
H 2–8 in (5–20 cm)

Frog Orchid
Coeloglossum viride
Near circumboreal,
absent Greenland
H 4–22 in (10–55 cm)

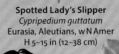

Spotted Lady's Slipper
Cypripedium guttatum
Eurasia, Aleutians, w N Amer
H 5–15 in (12–38 cm)

Variable colored,
twisted sepals
Pouch yellow

Yellow Lady's Slipper
Cypripedium calceolus
Eurasia, N Amer
H 8–30 in (20–75 cm)

**Sparrow's Egg
Lady's Slipper**
Cypripedium passerinum
N Amer
H 5–15 in (12–38 cm)

Arctic Iris
Iris setosa
Amphi-Beringian
H 12–24 in (30–60 cm)

mid-stem. Stems green to reddish purple, slightly 4-angled, succulent, smooth below the leaves, hairy above. FLS: Jun–Jul. Yellow green, green, or reddish purple; sepals and petals reflexed; twin-lobed lower lip is coated with nectar to attract insects. Borne in racemes of 5–25 blossoms.

GENUS *SPIRANTHES*
Irish Ladies' Tresses

Spiranthes romanzoffiana
ALSO: Hooded Lady's Tresses, Romanzoffs Drehwurz, Скрученник. CN refers to the spiral florets that resemble locks of braided hair. SN means "Romanzoff's spiral [of flowers]," honoring Nikolai Romanzoff (1754–1826), who sponsored a Russian scientific expedition to the Americas.
RANGE: N Amer, UK, and Ireland, on tundra, moist meadows, marshes, prairies, streambanks, coastal bluffs, and dunes, to 11,150 ft (3400 m).
ID: H 3–22 in (8–55 cm). LVS: Mostly basal, elliptical-lanceolate, to 10 in (25 cm) long; stem leaves reduced in size. FLS: Jun–Sep. White to ivory, hooded, with abruptly reflexed lips. Arranged in a tight spiral, with 3 flowers per cycle of spiral.

FAMILY IRIDACEAE
IRISES

Linnaeus named this family after Iris, the Greek goddess who carried messages from Olympus to earth along a rainbow.

GENUS *IRIS*
Arctic Iris

Iris setosa
ALSO: Wild Flag, Beachhead Iris, Borsten-Schwertlilie, Ирис; called Beachhead Iris in Canada because it is tolerant of salt air and maritime conditions, and is often encountered in rocky ground above shorelines. SN means "bristly iris."
RANGE: Amphi-Beringian, in boggy meadows, shores, and sand dunes.
ID: H 12–24 in (30–60 cm). Grows in clumps from branched rhizomes covered with old leaf remnants. Rhizomes contain irisin, which can cause skin irritation and abdominal pain, if ingested. LVS: Basal, green tinged with purple at base, ribbed, sword-shaped, with sharp edges and a pointed tip. FLS: Jul–Aug. Dark bluish violet to reddish purple; sheathing bracts (spathes) green, often flushed with purple.

Dwarf Fireweed, Devon Is, Canada

SELECTED BIBLIOGRAPHY

Arutyunov, S. A., I. I. Krupnik, and M. A. Chlenov. 1982. "Kitovaya alleya." *Drevnosti ostrovov proliva Senyavina* ("Whalebone alley." Antiquities of the islands in Proliv Senyavina.) Izd. Akad. Nauk SSR, Inst. Ethnogr. N.S. Miklukho-Maklai.

Bailey, L. H. 1938. *Manual of Cultivated Plants*. New York: The Macmillan Company.

Blamey, Marjorie, Richard Fitter, and Alistair Fitter. 1996. *Wildflowers of Britain and Northern Europe*. 5th ed. London: HarperCollins.

Bliss, L. C. 1997. "Arctic Ecosystems of North America," in F. E. Wielgolaski (ed.), *Polar and Alpine Tundra*, pp. 551–683. Amsterdam: Elsevier.

Brodo, Irwin M., Sylvia Duran Sharnoff, and Stephen Sharnoff. 2001. *Lichens of North America*. New Haven, CT, and London: Yale Univ. Press.

Brown, Roland Wilbur. 1956. *Composition of Scientific Words*. Washington, DC: Smithsonian Books.

Burt, Page. 1991. *Barrenland Beauties*. Yellowknife: Outcrop Ltd.

CAVM Team. 2003. *Circumpolar Arctic Vegetation Map*. Scale 1:7,500,000. Conservation of Arctic Flora and Fauna (CAFF), Map No. 1. U.S. Fish and Wildlife Service, Anchorage, Alaska.

Chernov, Yu. I., and N. V. Matveyeva. 1997. "Arctic Ecosystems in Russia," in F. E. Wielgolaski (ed.), *Polar and Alpine Tundra*, pp. 361–507. Amsterdam: Elsevier.

Chernov, Yu. I., and A. G. Tatarinov. 2006. "Butterflies (Lepidoptera, Rhopalocera) in the Arctic fauna." *Entomological Review*, vol. 86, number 7, 760–786.

Collins, Henry B., et al. 1945. *The Aleutian Islands: Their People and Natural History*. Washington, DC: Smithsonian Institution Press.

Cronquist, Arthur. 1981. *An Integrated System of Classification of Flowering Plants*. New York: Columbia Univ. Press.

Davis, T. Neil. 1989. *Alaska Science Nuggets*. Fairbanks: Univ. of Alaska Press.

Elphick, Jonathan (ed.). 2007. *Atlas of Bird Migration: Tracing the Great Journeys of the World's Birds*. Buffalo: Firefly Books Ltd.

Evans, James , and J. L. Berggren. 2007. *Geminos's Introduction to the Phenomena: A Translation and Study of a Hellenistic Survey of Astronomy*. Princeton, NJ: Princeton Univ. Press.

Fitzhugh, William W., and Aron Crowell. 1988. *Crossroads of the Continents: Cultures of Siberia and Alaska*. Washington, DC: Smithsonian Institution Press.

Flint, V. E., et al. 1984. *A Field Guide to the Birds of the USSR*. Princeton, NJ: Princeton Univ. Press.

Forbes, Bruce, and Steve Young. 2014. *Introduction to the Circumpolar World*. Saskatoon, Saskatchewan: University of the Arctic.

Forsyth, Adrian. 1999. *Mammals of North America: The Temperate and Arctic Regions*. Buffalo: Firefly Books.

Gaston, Anthony J. 2004. *Seabirds: A Natural History*. New Haven, CT: Yale Univ. Press.

Gledhill, D. 1985. *The Names of Plants*. Cambridge, UK: Cambridge Univ. Press.

Godfrey, W. Earl. 1979. *The Birds of Canada*. Ottawa: National Museums of Canada.

Graves, Jonquil, and Ed Hall. 1988. *Arctic Animals*. Yellowknife: Dept. of Renewable Resources, Government of the Northwest Territories.

Hultén, Eric. 1968. *Flora of Alaska and Neighboring Territories*. Stanford, CA: Stanford Univ. Press.

Jobling, James A. 1991. *A Dictionary of Scientific Bird Names*. Oxford, UK: Oxford Univ. Press.

Johnsgard, Paul A. 1978. *Ducks, Geese, and Swans of the World*. Lincoln: Univ of Nebraska Press.

Johnson, Karen L. 1987. *Wildflowers of Churchill and the Hudson Bay Region*. Winnipeg: Manitoba Museum of Man and Nature.

Johnson, Terry, and Kurt Byers (eds.). 2003. *The Bering Sea and Aleutian Islands: Region of Wonders*. Fairbanks: Alaska Sea Grant College Program.

Knystautas, Algirdas. 1987. *The Natural History of the USSR*. New York: McGraw-Hill.

Lavigne, David M., and Kit M. Kovacs. 1988. *Harps and Hoods: Ice-breeding Seals of the Northwest Atlantic*. Waterloo, Ontario: Univ. of Waterloo Press.

Layberry, Ross, P. Hall, and J. D. Lafontaine. 1998. *The Butterflies of Canada*. Toronto: Univ. of Toronto Press.

Lopez, Barry. 1986. *Arctic Dreams: Imagination and Desire in a Northern Landscape*. New York: Charles Scribner's Sons.

Mabberley, D. J. 2008. *Mabberley's Plant-Book*. 3rd ed. Cambridge, UK: Cambridge Univ. Press.

Macdonald, David W., and Priscilla Barrett. 1993. *Mammals of Europe*. Princeton, NJ: Princeton Univ. Press.

Nybakken, Oscar E. 1959. *Greek and Latin in Scientific Terminology*. Ames: Iowa State Univ. Press.

Pielou, E. C. 1994. *A Naturalist's Guide to the Arctic*. Chicago: Univ. of Chicago Press.

Porsild, A. E. 1973. *Illustrated Flora of the Canadian Arctic Archipelago (1957)*. Bulletin No. 146. Ottawa: National Museum of Canada.

Prater, A. J., et al. 1977. *Guide to the Identification and Aging of Holarctic Waders*. Tring: British Trust for Ornithology.

Sage, Bryan. 1986. *The Arctic and Its Wildlife*. New York: Facts on File Publications.

Sale, Richard. 2006. *A Complete Guide to Arctic Wildlife*. Richmond Hill, ON, Canada: Firefly Books Ltd.

Sekretareva, Nadezhda. 1999. *The Vascular Plants of the Russian Arctic and Adjacent Territories*. Sofia and Moscow: Pensoft Publishers.

Sibley, Charles G., and Burt L. Monroe. 1991. *Distribution and Taxonomy of Birds of the World*. New Haven, CT, and London: Yale Univ. Press.

Sibley, David A. 2000. *The Sibley Guide to Bird Life and Behavior*. New York: Alfred A. Knopf.

Sibley, David A., et al. 2001. National Audubon Society: *The Sibley Guide to Birds*. New York: Alfred A. Knopf.

Randall R. Reeves, Brent S. Stewart, Phillip J. Clapham, James A. Powell, and Peter Folkens. 2002. *National Audubon Society Guide to Marine Mammals of the World*. New York: Knopf.

Stonehouse, Bernard. 1989. *Polar Ecology*. New York: Chapman and Hall.

Svensson, Lars, Peter Grant, et al. 1999. *Birds of Europe*. Princeton, NJ: Princeton Univ. Press.

Tolman, Tom, and Richard Lewington. 2008. *Collins Butterfly Guide*. London: HarperCollins.

Webster, Donald H., and Wilfried Zibell. 1970. *Iñupiat Eskimo Dictionary*. Fairbanks: Summer Institute of Linguistics, Inc.

White, Helen A. (ed.). 1974. *The Alaska-Yukon Wild Flowers Guide*. Anchorage: Alaska Northwest Publishing.

Young, Steven B. 1989. *To the Arctic: An Introduction to the Far Northern World*. New York: John Wiley.

WEB SITES

Alaska Department of Fish and Game. http://www.adfg.alaska.gov

Alaska Wildflowers. http://www.alaskawildflowers.us

Athropolis: Cold, Icy, and Arctic. http://www.athropolis.com/index-b.htm

Avibase: The World Bird Database. http://avibase.bsc-eoc.org/avibase.jsp?lang=EN

Birds/Mammals of Svalbard: Norwegian Polar Institute. http://www.npolar.no/en/species/the-arctic.html

Birds of North America Online: Cornell Laboratory of Ornithology. http://bna.birds.cornell.edu/bna

Butterflies of Alaska. http://welovebutterflies.com/butterflies-of-alaska/

California Botanical Names. http://www.calflora.net/botanicalnames/

Canada's Polar Life. http://www.arctic.uoguelph.ca

Canadian Butterflies. http://www.cbif.gc.ca/spp_pages/butterflies/taxonomy_e.php

Caribou and Reindeer: Univ of Alaska Fairbanks. http://www.lars.uaf.edu/sponsor/caribou

Fauna of British Columbia. http://www.efauna.bc.ca

FishBase. http://www.fishbase.org/home.htm

Flora of the Canadian Arctic Archipelago. http://nature.ca/aaflora/data/index.htm

Flora/Fauna of Iceland: Icelandic Institute of Natural History. http://en.ni.is/

Flora of Kamchatka. http://www.vulkaner.no/t/kamchat/flora.html

Flora of North America. http://www.efloras.org/index.aspx

Flora of Svalbard. http://svalbardflora.no/

Flora/Fauna of the World: Funet Finland. http://www.funet.fi/pub/sci/bio/life/index.html

Internet Bird Collection. http://ibc.lynxeds.com

ITIS: Integrated Taxonomic Information System. http://www.itis.gov/

IUCN Red List of Threatened Species. http://www.iucnredlist.org/

Lepidoptera of Siberia and Central Asia. http://pisum.bionet.nsc.ru/kosterin/lepido.htm

Lichens of North America. http://www.lichen.com/index.html

Online Guide to North American Birds. http://www.audubon.org

NatureGate Finland. http://www.luontoportti.com/suomi/en/

NOAA's Arctic Report Card on climate change. http://http://www.arctic.noaa.gov/reportcard/

University of Alberta Entomology Collection. http://www.entomology.ualberta.ca

University of Michigan Animal Diversity Web. http://animaldiversity.ummz.umich.edu

USDA: Plants of North America. http://plants.usda.gov/index.html

Wikipedia. https://en.wikipedia.org/wiki/Main_Page

Xeno-canto: Sharing bird sounds from around the world. http://www.xeno-canto.org/

COMMON NAMES

Accentor
  Black-throated 343
  Hedge 342
  Siberian 343
Albatross
  Black-footed 168
  Laysan 168
  Short-tailed 169
Alder
  Gray 448
  Green 448
Anemone
  Narcissus 458
  Northern White 458
  Richardson's 458
Arktos 10
Arnica 515
  Frigid 515
  Narrowleaf 515
  Nodding 515
Aspen
  Quaking 454
  Trembling 453
Asphodel
  False 529
  Northern False 530
Aster, Siberian 514
Auklet
  Cassin's 186
  Crested 186
  Least 185
  Parakeet 184
  Rhinoceros 188
  Whiskered 185
Avens
  Alpine 482
  Glacier 482
  Largeleaf 484
  Mountain 484
Azalea, Alpine 477

Bartsia, Alpine 510
Bear
  American Black 92
  Brown 91
  Grizzly 91
  Kodiak 91
  Polar 25, 90
Bearberry
  Alpine Black 476
  Red 476
Beaver
  American 38
  Eurasian 39
Bedstraw, Northern 502
Bees 403
Bilberry, Bog 475
Birch
  Arctic Dwarf 446
  Downy 447
  Dwarf Resin 447
  Paper 447
  Silver 447
Bistort
  Alpine 466
  Meadow 466
Bittercress, Alpine 468
Blackbird
  Eurasian 320
  Red-winged 371
  Rusty 371

Bladderpod, Arctic 470
Bladderwort 512
Blueberry, Alpine 475
Bluebell
  Alpine 522
  Sea 503
  Tall 503
Bluethroat 313
Brambling 364
Brookfoam 494
Buckbean 521
Buffaloberry 488
Bullfinch, Eurasian 366
Bunting
  Little 355
  McKay's 354
  Pallas's Reed 355
  Pine 356
  Reed 355
  Rustic 355
  Snow 352
  Yellow-breasted 356
Burbot 392
Burnet
  Canadian 488
  Great 486
Buttercup
  Birdfoot 457
  Creeping Spearwort 457
  High Northern 457
  Lapland 456
  Pallas's 457
  Pygmy 457
  Snow 456
  Water Crowfoot 457
Butterfish 394
Butterfly
  Alpine 414
  Apollo 407
  Arctic 418
  Blue 420
  Copper 420
  Fritillary 412
  Geranium Argus 501
  Grayling, Norse 416
  Green Hairstreak 420
  Hoary Comma 419
  Mourning Cloak 418
  Parnassius 406, 489
  Ringlet, Lapland 413
  Skipper 422
  Sulphur 410
  Swallowtail 406, 449
  Tortoiseshell 418
  White 408
Butterwort 512
Buzzard, Common 276

Campion
  Arctic 464
  Moss 464
  Purple Bladder- 464
Capelin 386
Capercaillie
  Black billed 264
  Western 264
Caribou 58
Chaffinch 364
Chamomile 515
Char, Arctic 381
Chickadee
  Black-capped 327
  Boreal 326

Chickweed 463
Chiffchaff
  Common 333
  Siberian 333
Chipmunk, Siberian 32
Chives, Wild 529
Cinquefoil
  Alpine 486
  Arctic 484
  Marsh 486
  Norwegian 485
  Pretty 485
  Red-stemmed 485
  Seaside 486
  Shrubby 486
  Snow 485
  Vahl's 485
Cisco
  Arctic 382
  Least 384
Cloudberry 481
Clubmoss
  Fir 438
  Stiff 438
Cod
  Arctic 390
  Atlantic 390
  Greenland 390
  Pacific 390
  Polar 390
  Saffron 390
Coltsfoot, Arctic 521
Cormorant
  Double-crested 164
  European Shag 164
  Great 164
  Pelagic 166
  Red-faced 166
Cottongrass 528
Coyote, Northern 73, 79
Crane
  Eurasian 262
  Sandhill 262
  Siberian White 262
Cranesbill, Wood 500
Crossbill
  Parrot 371
  Red 370
  White-winged 371
Crow
  American 302
  Carrion 302
  Hooded 302
Crowberry, Black 474
Cuckoo
  Common 289
  Oriental 289
Cuckoo Flower 468
Curlew
  Bristle-thighed 202
  Eskimo 202
  Eurasian 203
  Far Eastern 203
  Little 203
Daisy
  Arctic 514
  Entireleaf 514
Dandelion 520
Death Camas 530
Dipper
  American 324
  White-throated 324
Dock, Arctic 466

Dog
  Alaskan Malamute 75
  Canadian Inuit 75
  Greenland 75
  Samoyed 75
  Siberian Husky 76
Dolly Varden 381
Dolphin
  Atlantic White-sided 116
  Pacific White-sided 115
  White-beaked 116
Dotterel, Eurasian 196
Dovekie 176
Dowitcher
  Long-billed 212
  Short-billed 212
Draba 470
  Alpine 470
  Golden 471
  Milky 472
  Snowbed 471
Dryad
  Arctic 484
  Eight-petal 484
Duck
  Bufflehead 151
  Canvasback 144
  Eider, Common 147
  Eider, King 148
  Eider, Spectacled 148
  Eider, Steller's 150
  Goldeneye, Barrow's 151
  Goldeneye, Common 152
  Harlequin 152
  Long-tailed 156
  Mallard 142
  Merganser 158
  Pintail, Northern 144
  Scaup, Greater 146
  Scaup, Lesser 147
  Scoter, Black 154
  Scoter, Common 154
  Scoter, Siberian 155
  Scoter, Surf 154
  Scoter, Velvet 155
  Scoter, White-wing 155
  Shoveler, Northern 143
  Smew 156
  Teal, Baikal 140
  Teal, Green-winged 142
  Tufted 146
  Wigeon, American 140
  Wigeon, Eurasian 140
Dunlin 222
Dunnock 342

Eagle
  Bald 272
  Golden 271
  Steller's Sea- 274
  White-tailed Sea- 272
Eelpout 394
Elk, Eurasian 64
Ermine 82
Everlasting 520
Eyebright 510

Falcon
  Gyrfalcon 279
  Peregrine 280
Fern
  Fragile Bladderfern 441
  Fragrant Shield 440